Recent Titles in the
Children's and Young Adult Literature Reference Series
Catherine Barr, Series Editor

Best Books for Middle School and Junior High Readers: Grades 6–9. Supplement to the First Edition
John T. Gillespie and Catherine Barr

Best Books for High School Readers: Grades 9–12. Supplement to the First Edition
John T. Gillespie and Catherine Barr

War and Peace: A Guide to Literature and New Media, Grades 4–8
Virginia A. Walter

Across Cultures: A Guide to Multicultural Literature for Children
Kathy East and Rebecca L. Thomas

Best Books for Children, Supplement to the 8th Edition: Preschool through Grade 6
Catherine Barr and John T. Gillespie

Best Books for Boys: A Resource for Educators
Matthew D. Zbaracki

Beyond Picture Books: Subject Access to Best Books for Beginning Readers
Barbara Barstow, Judith Riggle, and Leslie Molnar

A to Zoo: Subject Access to Children's Picture Books. Supplement to the 7th Edition
Carolyn W. Lima and Rebecca L. Thomas

Gentle Reads: Great Books to Warm Hearts and Lift Spirits, Grades 5–9
Deanna J. McDaniel

Best New Media, K–12: A Guide to Movies, Subscription Web Sites, and Educational Software and Games
Catherine Barr

Historical Fiction for Young Readers (Grades 4–8): An Introduction
John T. Gillespie

Twice Upon a Time: A Guide to Fractured, Altered, and Retold Folk and Fairy Tales
Catharine Bomhold and Terri E. Elder

POPULAR SERIES FICTION FOR K–6 READERS

A READING AND SELECTION GUIDE

2ND EDITION

Rebecca L. Thomas and Catherine Barr

Children's and Young Adult Literature Reference
Catherine Barr, Series Editor

A Member of the Greenwood Publishing Group

Westport, Connecticut • London

Library of Congress Cataloging-in-Publication Data

Thomas, Rebecca L.
  Popular series fiction for K–6 readers : a reading and selection guide /
Rebecca L. Thomas and Catherine Barr. — 2nd ed.
      p. cm. — (Children's and young adult literature reference)
  Includes bibliographical references and index.
  ISBN 978-1-59158-659-3 (alk. paper)
  1. Children's literature in series—Bibliography. 2. Children's stories—
Bibliography. 3. Children—Books and reading—Bibliography.
4. Children's libraries—Book selection. I. Barr, Catherine, 1951–
II. Title. III. Title: Popular series fiction for kindergarten–6th [grade]
readers.
  Z1037.T4654   2009
  011.62—dc22   2008038124

British Library Cataloguing in Publication Data is available.

Library of Congress Catalog Card Number: 2008038124
ISBN: 978-1-59158-659-3

First published in 2009

Libraries Unlimited, 88 Post Road West, Westport, CT 06881
A Member of the Greenwood Publishing Group, Inc.
www.lu.com

Printed in the United States of America

The paper used in this book complies with the
Permanent Paper Standard issued by the National
Information Standards Organization (Z39.48–1984).

10   9   8   7   6   5   4   3   2   1

CONTENTS

PREFACE

Wow! Series fiction has exploded in the last few years. In the first edition of *Popular Series Fiction* (2004), we had more than 1,500 series. Now there are nearly 2,200.

Librarians and teachers frequently call children's fiction series a mixed blessing. Series are wonderful in that they encourage children to read, but keeping up with the growing number of titles being published is an ongoing struggle. Librarians not only must keep tabs on new titles in existing series, but also must evaluate each new series (and each re-packaging and re-presentation of an old series) and decide whether to purchase it. Teachers work to find series books that meet the needs of the variety of readers in their classrooms. Librarians frequently hear questions such as "Do you know any mystery books like the Boxcar Children but for a less able reader?" and "What fantasy books do you recommend for middle-grade students?"

As we discussed these issues and more at conferences, in schools, and in libraries, *Reading in Series* was born; that book (Bowker, 1999) evolved into the current two volumes: *Popular Series Fiction for K–6 Readers: A Reading and Selection Guide* and *Popular Series Fiction for Middle School and Teen Readers: A Reading and Selection Guide*, now in their second editions.

RESEARCH AND SELECTION

We use a variety of sources to identify the children's series—current reviewing sources such as *Booklist* and *School Library Journal;* reference compilations including *A to Zoo, Best Books for Children*, and *Children's Catalog;* and online sources including publisher and author Web sites, bookselling sites such as amazon.com and barnesandnoble.com, series sites such as those at Mid-Continent Public Library (http://www.mcpl.lib. mo.us) and Monroe County Library (http://www.monroe.lib.in.us/childrens/serieslist.html), and other specialized library sites.

As we search libraries and bookstores for the books themselves, the following criteria are applied:

1. The series we select are content-based groupings of books with a consistent theme, setting, or group of characters. Series grouped by other criteria—for instance, grade level—are not included. Thus, Goosebumps—which includes monsters, creatures, and weird encounters—is here. The HarperCollins I Can Read series—which includes books by many different authors and featuring different characters—is not. Series such as Frog and Toad, Little Bear, and Mittens,

however, which are part of the I Can Read series but which feature several books with the same characters, are included.

2. A series generally needs three or more books. However, we have included some developing series that promise to become popular.

3. The grade range of the books in this volume is from kindergarten through grade 6. Board books, manipulative books, bathtime books, etc., are not included. Decisions about grade levels are based on knowledge of the audience, examination of the books, consultation of professional resources, and library experience. Thus, the Ghosts of Fear Street series, which has elements of horror and suspense for upper elementary readers, is included, but the Fear Street series, which includes more-graphic details suitable for an older audience, is not. (Fear Street is in *Popular Series Fiction for Middle School and Teen Readers*.)

4. As we annotate each series, we make every effort to examine several books, hoping to offer better insight to librarians making purchasing decisions or recommending these books to readers.

5. A priority is given to new series: the books that readers are asking about. We have scoured libraries, bookstores, publishers' catalogs, and Web sites looking for new series and the newest titles in existing series. Some "future titles" are included in an effort to be as current as possible. Titles for 2009 books may end up being changed, but their inclusion will alert librarians that additions to the series are forthcoming.

6. Older series are included, too, especially those considered "classics." The Chronicles of Narnia, the Oz books, Avonlea, and the Little House books had to be included, of course. But other well-known series, such as Betsy-Tacy, Eddie Wilson, Mrs. Piggle-Wiggle, and Miss Pickerell, are here too. However, many picture books from our own childhoods are not being read today. In selecting the "older" series to include, we relied on our judgment, on the judgment of our contributors, and on our ability to find copies of several titles in libraries and bookstores.

7. We focus on including series with some of the titles still in print. This is a problem, especially for many paperback series. Some very popular books that were published only a few years ago are no longer available, but we decided to include these series because they are still available in many libraries. Librarians and teachers who want to update their collections can use the Genre/Subject Index to find newer, similar books.

ANATOMY OF AN ENTRY

Each entry provides the following information:

Series title: Cross-referenced as needed.

Author: If individual books within a series have different authors, they are listed with the books.

Publisher: Many series have had several publishers over the years. The publisher shown is the most recent publisher. In some cases both hardback and paperback publishers are listed.

Grade level: This volume covers series for grades K–6 (grades 6–YA are covered in the companion volume of *Popular Series Fiction*). Toddler and board books are not included here although they may be mentioned in the annotations.

Genres: These are broad thematic areas that will help link similar series. The genres included are: Adventure, Animal Fantasy, Family Life, Fantasy, Historical, Horror, Humor, Mystery, Real Life, Recreation, Science Fiction, and Values.

Accelerated Reader: The notation A/R indicates that Accelerated Reader resources are available for some or all of the titles in the series.

Annotation: This descriptive examination of the series provides information about important characters, plots, themes, and issues in the series. Specific books are often described in detail. Related materials such as dolls, accessories, and toys may also be mentioned.

List of titles in the series: This list is compiled using the books themselves and the selection sources mentioned above, as well as Books in Print (R. R. Bowker) and the CLEVNET database (which serves a large number of member libraries in northeast Ohio including the Cleveland Public Library). These resources (along with the publisher catalogs and Web sites) often provide conflicting information about exact titles and copyright dates, so there may be some inconsistencies; however, every effort has been made to be as complete and accurate as possible. Book titles are shown in chronological order by year of publication. Numbered series are shown in number order, which is usually also chronological. Where series include prequels or alternative reading orders, this is mentioned in the annotation.

INDEXES AND APPENDIXES

Author and Title indexes will help the user who is searching for new series by a given author or who knows only one title in a series. The Genre/Subject Index gives access by genre and by more specific topics. Thus, the fan of horror can easily find more series in that genre; and young readers can quickly identify series about horses. The addition of grade levels after the series titles allows users to pinpoint grade-appropriate series quickly. To make access easier, real animals and fantasy animals (mice that wear clothes and go to school, for example) are listed together.

In addition, there are lists of series of special interest to boys, girls, reluctant readers, and students of English as a second language. These are not comprehensive lists; series were selected for their current appeal to readers. The books for boys often feature as the main characters a group of boys who are involved in mysteries, sports, school problems, friendship, and the supernatural. The books for girls often feature one or more girls involved in mysteries, sports (horseback riding and skating, in particular), school problems, friendship, and growing up. The books for reluctant readers were chosen for their popular appeal, and feature media tie-ins, monsters and creatures, and well-known characters such as Amber Brown, Arthur, and The Plant that Ate Dirty Socks. Some of the books for reluctant readers are included for their direct plots and simple text, and these have been marked with an asterisk (*) as being suitable for ESL students too.

There will be many ways for librarians and teachers to use *Popular Series Fiction*. The Genre/Subject Index will point the way to series on topics of interest. Do your students like the books about Ramona? Look at the genre Family Life to find similar books, including stories about Russell, Elisa, Julian and Huey, and Sam Krupnik. For readers who want legends of King Arthur and Merlin, consult the subject Arthurian Legends to find Jane Yolen's Young Merlin.

Popular Series Fiction is also a selection guide. Librarians may want to add new series or update titles in series that have already been purchased. If your students like mysteries, look at the new Bones books. For sports, there is Comeback Kids. For adventure, there is Adventures with the Parkers. Add the newer titles to existing series or fill in titles you may have missed. Reading the annotations, you can compare series and make decisions about which will best fit your needs.

Popular Series Fiction builds on the earlier *Reading in Series*. Compilation of that book involved the efforts of librarians and teachers who are well qualified in fiction for children:

Connie Parker	Cuyahoga County (Ohio) Public Library
Deanna McDaniel	Westerville (Ohio) City Schools
Jacqueline Albers	Cuyahoga County (Ohio) Public Library
Karen Breen	Program Officer, New Visions for Public Schools, New York, NY
Doris Gebel	Northport (NY) Public Library
Debbie Gold	Cuyahoga County (Ohio) Public Library

We would like to thank Barbara Ittner of Libraries Unlimited for her encouragement and support and Julie Miller, Christine Weisel McNaull, and Kris Aparacio for their work on the database, design and composition, editing, and research.

SERIES A–Z

A Is for Amber *see* Amber Brown: A Is for Amber

A to Z Mysteries

Roy, Ron

RANDOM HOUSE ◆ **GRADES K–3** ◆ **A/R**

MYSTERY

Dink, Josh, and Ruth Rose are friends in Green Lawn, an average American town. Together, they solve mysteries beginning with every letter of the alphabet. The mysteries are simple enough that readers can collect clues and solve them along with the characters.

1. The Absent Author ◆ 1997
2. The Bald Bandit ◆ 1997
3. The Canary Caper ◆ 1998
4. The Deadly Dungeon ◆ 1998
5. The Empty Envelope ◆ 1998
6. The Falcon's Feathers ◆ 1998
7. The Goose's Gold ◆ 1999
8. The Haunted Hotel ◆ 1999
9. The Invisible Island ◆ 1999
10. The Jaguar's Jewel ◆ 2000
11. The Kidnapped King ◆ 2000
12. The Lucky Lottery ◆ 2000
13. The Missing Mummy ◆ 2001
14. The Ninth Nugget ◆ 2001
15. The Orange Outlaw ◆ 2001
16. The Panda Puzzle ◆ 2002
17. The Quicksand Question ◆ 2002
18. The Runaway Racehorse ◆ 2002
19. The School Skeleton ◆ 2003
20. The Talking T. Rex ◆ 2003
21. The Unwilling Umpire ◆ 2004
22. The Vampire's Vacation ◆ 2004
23. The White Wolf ◆ 2004
24. The X-ed-Out X-Ray ◆ 2005
25. The Yellow Yacht ◆ 2005
26. The Zombie Zone ◆ 2005

SUPER EDITIONS

1. Detective Camp ◆ 2006
2. Mayflower Treasure Hunt ◆ 2007
3. White House White-Out ◆ 2008

ABBY HAYES: THE AMAZING DAYS OF ABBY HAYES

Mazer, Anne

SCHOLASTIC ◆ GRADES 4–6 ◆ A/R

FAMILY LIFE | HUMOR | REAL LIFE

Abby's family is full of overachievers. As Abby begins fifth grade she is determined to find a way to be successful. Her journal entries chronicle her attempts to find out what she does best.

1. Every Cloud Has a Silver Lining ◆ 2000
2. The Declaration of Independence ◆ 2000
3. Reach for the Stars ◆ 2000
4. Have Wheels, Will Travel ◆ 2001
5. Look Before You Leap ◆ 2001
6. The Pen Is Mightier Than the Sword ◆ 2001
7. Two Heads Are Better Than One ◆ 2002
8. The More, the Merrier ◆ 2002
9. Out of Sight, Out of Mind ◆ 2002
10. Everything New Under the Sun ◆ 2003
11. Too Close for Comfort ◆ 2003
12. Good Things Come in Small Packages ◆ 2003
13. Some Things Never Change ◆ 2004
14. It's Music to My Ears ◆ 2005
15. Now You See It, Now You Don't ◆ 2005
16. That's the Way the Cookie Crumbles ◆ 2005
17. Home Is Where The Heart Is ◆ 2006
18. What Goes Up Must Come Down ◆ 2008

THE AMAZING DAYS OF ABBY HAYES SUPER SPECIAL EDITIONS

1. The Best Is Yet to Come ◆ 2004
2. Knowledge Is Power ◆ 2004

ABBY'S SOUTH SEAS ADVENTURES

Walls, Pamela

TYNDALE HOUSE ◆ GRADES 5–8 ◆ A/R

ADVENTURE | VALUES

In Hawaii in the mid-1800s, Abby and her family face many challenges to their safety and to their values. One adventure features Abby and her friend Luke searching for an arsonist before there is another fire. Their faith and their willingness to love and forgive sustain them.

1. Lost at Sea ◆ 2000
2. Quest for Treasure ◆ 2000

3. California Gold ◆ 2001
4. Secret at Cutter Grove ◆ 2001
5. King's Ransom ◆ 2001
6. Into the Dragon's Den ◆ 2001
7. Trouble in Tahiti ◆ 2002
8. Maui Mystery ◆ 2002

ABRACADABRA

Becker, Eve

BANTAM ◆ GRADES 5–7

FANTASY

Dawn, 13, can make things happen simply by arching her left eyebrow. Despite her grandmother's warnings, she uses this talent to great effect, making herself popular and generally getting everything she wants . . . until her powers wane and she has to rely on her own resources, which she discovers are sufficient after all.

1. Thirteen Means Magic ◆ 1989
2. The Love Potion ◆ 1989
3. The Magic Mix-Up ◆ 1989
4. The Sneezing Spell ◆ 1989
5. The Popularity Potion ◆ 1990
6. Too Much Magic ◆ 1990

ACCIDENTAL MONSTERS

Lubar, David

SCHOLASTIC ◆ GRADES 4–6 ◆ A/R

FANTASY

Unsuspecting children become monsters, such as vampires and ghosts. They not only face such dangers as monsters, but they must also try to find a way to return to their normal selves.

1. The Vanishing Vampire ◆ 1997
2. The Unwilling Witch ◆ 1997
3. The Wavering Werewolf ◆ 1997
4. The Gloomy Ghost ◆ 1998

ACROSS THE STEEL RIVER

Stenhouse, Ted

KIDS CAN ◆ GRADES 5–8 ◆ A/R

HISTORICAL | MYSTERY

In 1950s Canada, Will and Arthur, a white boy and an Indian boy who are friends despite local prejudices, are determined to find out what happened to an Indian they found barely alive near the railroad tracks. They later discover secrets about town residents and investigate a World War I mystery, all the while learning about racism and friendship.

1. Across the Steel River ◆ 2001
2. A Dirty Deed ◆ 2003
3. Murder on the Ridge ◆ 2005

ADAM JOSHUA CAPERS

Smith, Janice Lee

HARPERCOLLINS ◆ GRADES 1–4 ◆ A/R

REAL LIFE

Elementary-schooler Adam Joshua and his classmates comically confront all kinds of everyday situations in this humorous series. Adam Joshua is fairly level-headed, while his best friend, Nelson, is always coming up with crazy ideas. Together, they enter a science fair, adopt "egg babies" for a class assignment, and celebrate holidays from Thanksgiving to Valentine's Day. This series has been reformatted in paperback with some renamed titles, different sequencing of stories, and attractive covers. The original hardbacks are still available, too. Both sets of books are listed here.

1. The Monster in the Third Dresser Drawer, and Other Stories About Adam Joshua ◆ 1981
2. The Kid Next Door, and Other Headaches: Stories About Adam Joshua ◆ 1984
3. The Show-and-Tell War, and Other Stories About Adam Joshua ◆ 1988
4. It's Not Easy Being George ◆ 1989
5. The Turkey's Side of It ◆ 1990
6. There's a Ghost in the Coatroom: Adam Joshua's Christmas ◆ 1991
7. Nelson in Love: An Adam Joshua Valentine's Day Story ◆ 1992
8. Serious Science: An Adam Joshua Story ◆ 1993
9. The Baby Blues: An Adam Joshua Story ◆ 1994

THE ADAM JOSHUA CAPERS PAPERBACK SERIES

1. The Monster in the Third Dresser Drawer ◆ 1995
2. The Kid Next Door ◆ 1995
3. Superkid! ◆ 1995
4. The Show-and-Tell War ◆ 1995
5. The Halloween Monster ◆ 1995
6. George Takes a Bow (-Wow): Stories About Adam Joshua (And His Dog) ◆ 1995
7. Turkey Trouble: Adam Joshua's Thanksgiving ◆ 1995

8. The Christmas Ghost: Adam Joshua's Christmas ◆ 1995
9. Nelson in Love ◆ 1996
10. Serious Science ◆ 1996
11. Baby Blues ◆ 1996

ADAM MOUSE BOOKS *see* Cucumbers Trilogy

ADAM SHARP

Stanley, George Edward
RANDOM HOUSE ◆ GRADES 2–4 ◆ A/R
MYSTERY

Adam Sharp, 8, is a spy who works on unusual cases, such as recovering DOGBARK, a secret computer program that understands the language of dogs. In one book, Adam and the other IM-8 agents go back to spy school and find that school secrets are being leaked.

1. Adam Sharp: The Spy Who Barked ◆ 2002
2. London Calling ◆ 2002
3. Adam Sharp: Swimming With Sharks ◆ 2003
4. Operation Spy School ◆ 2003
5. Moose Master ◆ 2004
6. Code Word Kangaroo ◆ 2004

ADDIE

Lawlor, Laurie
WHITMAN; POCKET BOOKS ◆ GRADES 4–6 ◆ A/R
HISTORICAL | REAL LIFE

Addie's father takes the family west from Sabula, Iowa, to the Dakota Territory to homestead 100 acres. Addie is unhappy about leaving her friends and slowly adjusts to the hard life of prairie homesteaders. She shows courage in the face of difficult situations of various kinds and learns to make new friends. Through the course of these stories, Addie comes of age, prepares to leave her family to attend high school, and meets a young man. *George on His Own* describes the efforts of Addie's brother to manage the family while Addie is away at school. *Addie's Forever Friend* is a prequel to *Addie Across the Prairie*.

1. Addie Across the Prairie ◆ 1986
2. Addie's Dakota Winter ◆ 1989
3. Addie's Long Summer ◆ 1992
4. George on His Own ◆ 1993
5. Addie's Forever Friend ◆ 1997

ADDIE

Robins, Joan

HARPERCOLLINS ◆ GRADES K–3 ◆ A/R

FAMILY LIFE | HUMOR | REAL LIFE

These are delightful beginning readers. Making friends, having bad days, and running away are all simple adventures that any child learning to read will enjoy and be able to master.

1. Addie Meets Max ◆ 1985
2. Addie Runs Away ◆ 1989
3. Addie's Bad Day ◆ 1993

ADDIE

Rock, Gail

KNOPF ◆ GRADES 3–5 ◆ A/R

FAMILY LIFE | HISTORICAL

First introduced as CBS TV specials, these four holiday stories set in the 1940s demonstrate something of the real meaning of the celebrations. Ten-year-old Addie can't understand why her father will not allow her to have a Christmas tree. Her kind and wise grandmother helps her come to understand why it is so difficult for her widowed father to provide this. Other holidays offer opportunities to learn about friendship.

1. The House Without a Christmas Tree ◆ 1974
2. The Thanksgiving Treasure ◆ 1974
3. A Dream for Addie ◆ 1975
4. Addie and the King of Hearts ◆ 1976

ADDY *see* American Girls: Addy

ADIRONDACK KIDS

VanRiper, Justin, and Gary VanRiper

ADIRONDACK KIDS PRESS ◆ GRADES 3–6

ADVENTURE

Family visits to the Adirondacks evolved into these environmental adventures written by a father (Gary) and son (Justin, who was 10 when the series started). Three friends—Justin Robert, Jackie Salsberry, and Nick Barnes—enjoy the beauty of the Adirondacks. In the first book, Justin Robert is determined to protect the loons that are on the lake. In another, the friends think that climbing Bald Mountain will help Nick's fear of heights.

1. The Adirondack Kids ◆ 2001
2. Rescue on Bald Mountain ◆ 2002
3. The Lost Lighthouse ◆ 2003
4. The Great Train Robbery ◆ 2004

ADVENTURES IN AMERICA

Various authors

SILVER MOON PRESS ◆ GRADES 4–6 ◆ A/R

HISTORICAL

Gold rush days in California, slaves escaping to freedom, and Mohawk skywalkers building the Empire State Building. These are some of the historical events featured in this series. Like the Dear America and My Name Is America books, these books conclude with nonfiction information about the era.

1. Empire Dreams (Wax, Wendy) ◆ 2000
2. First Heroes for Freedom (Bjerregaard, Marcia) ◆ 2000
3. Seasons of the Trail (Glaze, Lynn) ◆ 2000
4. Making Tracks (Wolfert, Adrienne) ◆ 2000
5. Thunder on the Sierra (Balmes, Kathy) ◆ 2001
6. Raid at Red Mill (McGahan, Mary) ◆ 2001
7. Ambush in the Wilderness (Hemphill, Kris) ◆ 2003
8. In the Hands of the Enemy (Sheely, Robert,) ◆ 2003
9. Night Journey to Vicksburg (Masters, Susan) ◆ 2003
10. Race to Kitty Hawk (Raffa, Edwina) ◆ 2003
11. Brothers of the Falls (Emery, Joanna) ◆ 2004

ADVENTURES OF A YOUNG SAILOR

Dowswell, Paul

BLOOMSBURY ◆ GRADES 5–8 ◆ A/R

ADVENTURE | HISTORICAL

At the beginning of the 19th century, 13-year-old Sam Witchall finds himself a powder monkey—supplying the gunpowder to the cannon crew—on the *HMS Miranda,* and his love of the sea is subdued by the conditions and the violent fighting of the Napoleonic Wars. In *Prison Ship,* Sam and his friend Richard have been falsely accused of cowardice. They are sent to Australia, where they face a wide variety of challenges. By the end of the third book, Sam is back in England, in the Navy, and preparing for the famous Battle of Trafalgar. These books are historically accurate and full of action.

1. Powder Monkey ◆ 2005
2. Prison Ship ◆ 2006
3. Battle Fleet ◆ 2008

THE ADVENTURES OF BEATRICE BAILEY

Forrester, Sandra

BARRON'S ◆ GRADES 5–8 ◆ A/R

FANTASY

In the first book, 11-year-old Beatrice is assigned a quest before receiving her final witch classification. She and her friends must rescue a famous sorcerer and his daughters, who have been seized by a rival wizard and are being guarded by monsters. In following books, she learns about her family as she frees the captives one by one, facing peril at every turn. This series has many elements of the Harry Potter stories.

1. The Everyday Witch ◆ 2002
2. The Witches of Friar's Lantern ◆ 2003
3. The Witches of Sea-Dragon Bay ◆ 2003
4. The Witches of Winged-Horse Mountain ◆ 2004
5. The Witches of Bailiwick ◆ 2005
6. The Witches of Widdershins Academy ◆ 2007

ADVENTURES OF BENNY AND WATCH *see*

Boxcar Children: Adventures of Benny and Watch

THE ADVENTURES OF COMMANDER ZACK PROTON *see* Zack Proton

ADVENTURES OF DANIEL BOOM AKA LOUD BOY

Steinberg, D. J.

GROSSET & DUNLAP ◆ GRADES 4–7 ◆ A/R

HUMOR

Daniel Boom has a problem . . . actually, several problems. First, he is new in town. Second, he is loud. Third, the Kid-Rid corporation has invented the Soundsucker LX—a machine that will silence the world. This sounds like a job for Loud Boy, Daniel's inner superhero. In the second book, Kid-Rid invades the school cafeteria and makes a mind controlling mac and cheese. The graphic novel format will be a winner with reluctant readers.

1. Sound Off! ◆ 2008
2. Mac Attack! ◆ 2008
3. Game On! ◆ 2009

ADVENTURES OF JENNA *see* Jenna V.

ADVENTURES OF MARY-KATE AND ASHLEY *see* Mary-Kate and Ashley: Adventures of Mary-Kate and Ashley

ADVENTURES OF OTTO *see* Otto

ADVENTURES OF SHIRLEY HOLMES

Various authors

BANTAM ◆ GRADES 4–6

MYSTERY

Shirley is the great-grandniece of Sherlock Holmes. Like him, she uses logic to solve mysteries. In one story, she investigates a horse race that seems to be fixed. There was a television program of the same series name and these books are novelizations—two episodes per book.

1. The Case of the Blazing Star and the Case of the King of Hearts (Angell, Judie) ◆ 1999
2. The Case of the Burning Building and the Case of the Ruby Ring (Angell, Judie) ◆ 1999
3. The Case of the Maestro's Ghost and the Case of the Second Sight (Whitman, John) ◆ 1999
4. The Case of the Missing Marbles and the Case of the Rising Moon (Whitman, John) ◆ 1999

THE ADVENTURES OF THE BAILEY SCHOOL KIDS *see* Bailey School: The Adventures of the Bailey School Kids

THE ADVENTURES OF UNCLE STINKY

Rumble, Chris

TRICYCLE PRESS ◆ GRADES 4–7 ◆ A/R

HUMOR

Hold your nose, here comes a smelly superhero—Uncle Stinky. In *Stink Trek,* Uncle Stinky outwits Theo Durzindapance at the 319th Annual Hootenhollerama and then is captured by intergalactic clowns. There is plenty of foolishness, as when Mayor Naise is beamed into the City Hall outhouse and the door is sealed with super glue, making it a "poo-poo prison." And there is an abundance of cartoon-style illustrations. At times, the text is totally replaced by action displayed in cartoon panels. Consider this for fans of Captain Underpants.

1. The Good, the Bad, and the Smelly ◆ 2004
2. Stink Trek ◆ 2004
3. Moby Stink ◆ 2005

ADVENTURES OF WISHBONE *see* Wishbone Adventures

ADVENTURES WITH THE PARKERS

Graf, Mike

FULCRUM ◆ GRADES 5–8 ◆ A/R

ADVENTURE

Ten-year-old twin brother and sister James and Morgan Parker learn about nature and ecology and have adventures as they explore the national parks with their parents. For example, in *Bryce and Zion,* the twins help to rescue an injured woman, encounter a rattlesnake, and play important roles when their father slips and falls in a rainstorm. Sketches and photographs bring the locations to life, and maps and diagrams add background material.

1. Bryce and Zion: Danger in the Narrows ◆ 2006
2. Grand Canyon: The Tail of the Scorpion ◆ 2006
3. Yosemite: Harrowing Ascent of Half Dome ◆ 2007
4. Yellowstone: Eye of the Grizzly ◆ 2007
5. Olympic National Park: Touch of the Tide Pool, Crack of the Glacier ◆ 2009
6. The Great Smoky Mountains: Ridge Runner Rescue ◆ 2009

AGAPANTHUS HUM

Cowley, Joy

PHILOMEL ◆ GRADES 1–3 ◆ A/R

FAMILY LIFE | REAL LIFE

Agapanthus Hum is an active girl. She has problems when she starts wearing glasses because they keep falling off. But she figures out a way to cope. In the second book, she gets a puppy. In the third, she loses a tooth. Readers will relate to the gentle humor and everyday issues in these beginning chapter books.

1. Agapanthus Hum and the Eyeglasses ◆ 1999
2. Agapanthus Hum and Major Bark ◆ 2001
3. Agapanthus Hum and the Angel Hoot ◆ 2003

AGE OF MAGIC TRILOGY

McGowen, Tom

LODESTAR/DUTTON ◆ **GRADES 5–9** ◆ **A/R**

FANTASY

The troll wizard Gwolchmig foresees an invasion from beyond the sky and the destruction of Earth. He puts aside lifelong animosities to unite the five races of Earth: trolls, humans, little people, Alfar (elves), and dragons. Twelve-year-old Lithim faces fierce opposition from the Atlan domain and devises a plan that will save the planet.

1. The Magical Fellowship ◆ 1991
2. The Trial of Magic ◆ 1992
3. The Question of Magic ◆ 1993

AGNES PARKER

O'Dell, Kathleen

DIAL ◆ **GRADES 4–6** ◆ **A/R**

REAL LIFE

Agnes feels she is ordinary. As she begins sixth grade she decides to make changes. She wants to be cool and confident. Maybe then the new boy will notice her. In *Agnes Parker . . . Keeping Cool in Middle School,* Agnes is starting middle school. Her best friend Prejean is coping with the separation of her parents. Agnes tries to be a supportive friend even though Prejean puts her in an awkward situation.

1. Agnes Parker . . . Girl in Progress ◆ 2003
2. Agnes Parker . . . Happy Camper? ◆ 2005
3. Agnes Parker . . . Keeping Cool in Middle School ◆ 2007

THE A.I. GANG

Coville, Bruce

NEW AMERICAN LIBRARY ◆ **GRADES 4–6** ◆ **A/R**

ADVENTURE

Five children are taken by their scientist parents to a deserted island where research is being done on artificial intelligence. The children have their own agenda—they want to outwit their parents—but first they must stop a threat to destroy the island. This series was originally published in the 1980s and has been reissued.

1. Operation Sherlock ◆ 1986
2. Robot Trouble ◆ 1986
3. Forever Begins Tomorrow ◆ 1986

AIRY FAIRY

Ryan, Margaret

BARRON'S ◆ GRADES 2–4

FANTASY | HUMOR

In this British import, life is never dull at Fairy Gropplethorpe's Academy for Good Fairies. Not with Airy Fairy around. She's cute, but she's a mess. Her spells often go awry—as when she conjurs up ten red goats instead of ten red coats. Her nemesis is Scary Fairy, who always seems to do everything right and who enjoys getting Airy Fairy in trouble. In *Magic Mischief!*, Airy Fairy will miss the Christmas party if she cannot straighten out her spells.

1. Magic Muddle! ◆ 2005
2. Magic Mess! ◆ 2005
3. Magic Mix-up! ◆ 2005
4. Magic Mischief! ◆ 2005

AKIKO

Crilley, Mark

DELACORTE ◆ GRADES 4–7 ◆ A/R

FANTASY

Akiko, 10, is in fourth grade on Earth when she is asked to help rescue a kidnapped prince. Assisted by aliens, she goes on an intergalactic mission searching for the kidnapper, Alia Rellapor.

1. Akiko on the Planet Smoo ◆ 2000
2. Akiko in the Sprubly Islands ◆ 2000
3. Akiko and the Great Wall of Trudd ◆ 2001
4. Akiko in the Castle of Alia Rellapor ◆ 2001
5. Akiko and the Intergalactic Zoo ◆ 2002
6. Akiko and the Alpha Centauri 5000 ◆ 2003

7. Akiko and the Journey to Toog ◆ 2003
8. Akiko: The Training Master ◆ 2005
9. Akiko: Pieces of Gax ◆ 2006
10. Akiko and the Missing Misp ◆ 2008

AKIKO GRAPHIC NOVELS

Crilley, Mark

SIRIUS ENTERTAINMENT ◆ GRADES 4–7

FANTASY

In the opening trilogy, Akiko is on summer vacation when she is sent to the Planet Smoo to the castle of Alia Rellapor. She battles a dragon but then she and her colleagues are captured by Loza Throck. They escape . . . only to be confronted by Alia Rellapor herself. How will they rescue the prince? The adventures of Akiko were originally released as a monthly series and are gathered into this collection.

1. Menace of Alia Rellapor, Part 1 ◆ 2001
2. Menace of Alia Rellapor, Part 2 ◆ 2001
3. Menace of Alia Rellapor, Part 3 ◆ 2001
4. The Story Tree ◆ 2001
5. Bornstone's Elixir ◆ 2001
6. Stranded in Komura/Moonshopping ◆ 2003
7. The Battle of Boach's Keep ◆ 2004

AKIMBO

McCall Smith, Alexander

BLOOMSBURY ◆ GRADES 2–4 ◆ A/R

ADVENTURE | REAL LIFE

Akimbo lives on a game preserve in Africa. His father is a ranger on the preserve. In *Akimbo and the Elephants,* Akimbo devises a plan to catch a gang of poachers who have been killing elephants for their tusks. In *Akimbo and the Crocodile Man,* a zoologist studying crocodiles is injured and Akimbo must travel alone to get help. Each book in this series is an exciting adventure that features the bravery and ingenuity of Akimbo, a young African boy who appears to be around 8 or 9 years old.

1. Akimbo and the Elephants ◆ 2005
2. Akimbo and the Lions ◆ 2005
3. Akimbo and the Crocodile Man ◆ 2006
4. Akimbo and the Snakes ◆ 2006

AL (ALEXANDRA)

Greene, Constance C.

VIKING; PUFFIN ◆ GRADES 5–8 ◆ A/R

FAMILY LIFE | REAL LIFE

Al is the new kid, "a little on the fat side," with glasses and pigtails, and a self-proclaimed nonconformist. She becomes the best friend of the unnamed seventh-grade narrator. Their friendship grows and helps them deal with the problems they face. Al's mother, divorced for several years, begins to date; her father visits for the first time in years; and Al sacrifices a summer visit at her father's farm to take care of her sick mother. Together, the friends face life's ups and downs with humor.

1. A Girl Called Al ◆ 1969
2. I Know You, Al ◆ 1975
3. Your Old Pal, Al ◆ 1979
4. Alexandra the Great ◆ 1982
5. Just Plain Al ◆ 1986
6. Al's Blind Date ◆ 1989

ALBERT (THE DUCK)

Tryon, Leslie

ATHENEUM ◆ GRADES K–2 ◆ A/R

ANIMAL FANTASY

Albert is the most industrious duck in Pleasant Valley. He creates an unusual playground for the schoolchildren (with everything in alphabetical order). He patiently assists the P.T.A. president in preparing a Thanksgiving feast. In the spring, he organizes a baseball team. One of the newer books features Albert as a detective who solves a mystery involving pumpkins that are missing from Miss Patsy Pig's pumpkin patch. There is minimal text in these books. The detailed illustrations advance the story and provide enjoyment for readers, who often know more of what is going on than the characters do.

1. Albert's Alphabet ◆ 1991
2. Albert's Play ◆ 1992
3. Albert's Field Trip ◆ 1993
4. Albert's Thanksgiving ◆ 1994
5. Albert's Ballgame ◆ 1995
6. Albert's Christmas ◆ 1996
7. Albert's Halloween: The Case of the Stolen Pumpkins ◆ 1998
8. Albert's Birthday ◆ 1999

ALDEN ALL STARS

Hallowell, Tommy, and David Halecroft

PENGUIN ◆ GRADES 4–8 ◆ A/R

REAL LIFE | RECREATION

Soccer, baseball, basketball, and football are all featured in this sports series. Three seventh- and eighth-grade boys star in separate books. Nick is the wise guy; Dennis is the leader and captain of the basketball team. Justin's sport is soccer, but Alden Junior High doesn't have a team, so he goes to a camp and stands out there. All of the books in the series are loaded with sports details, but there are also some points made about relationships and the importance of studying. Fans of Matt Christopher's books will enjoy this series.

1. Duel on the Diamond ◆ 1990
2. Jester in the Back Cover ◆ 1990
3. Shot from Midfield ◆ 1990
4. Last Chance Quarterback ◆ 1990
5. Blindside Blitz ◆ 1991
6. Breaking Loose ◆ 1991
7. Championship Summer ◆ 1991
8. Hotshot on Ice ◆ 1991
9. Power Play ◆ 1991
10. Setting the Pace ◆ 1991
11. Wild Pitch ◆ 1991
12. Benched! ◆ 1991

ALDO SOSSI

Hurwitz, Johanna

MORROW ◆ GRADES 3–5 ◆ A/R

FAMILY LIFE | HUMOR | REAL LIFE

Eight-year-old Aldo is interested in everything, especially animals. The first book, set in New York City, introduces the Sossi family, including his older sisters, Karen, age 11, and Elaine, age 13. Aldo's love of animals creates a conflict for him when a class project introduces chameleons to the cricket tank. Aldo becomes a vegetarian, and we get a glimpse of the strength of his loving, supportive parents. As he graduates into fourth grade, his family moves from city to suburbs, and Aldo deals with the difficulties of moving and making new friends. He tries an ice-cream-making business, but finds more success helping his mother do volunteer work for senior citizens. Companion volumes include *Tough Luck Karen* (1982) and *Hurricane Elaine* (1986).

1. Much Ado About Aldo ◆ 1978
2. Aldo Applesauce ◆ 1979

3. Aldo Ice Cream ◆ 1981
4. Aldo Peanut Butter ◆ 1990

ALEX

Levene, Nancy Simpson
CHARIOT BOOKS ◆ GRADES 2–4
FAMILY LIFE | REAL LIFE | VALUES

Alex Brackenbury faces a variety of problems in this series, including a clumsy friend who struggles to participate in soccer, stuck-up girls who won't be her friends, and a neighborhood bully. Mother reminds her of the importance of being kind and asking for God's guidance. Dad helps her to accept the weaknesses of others and honor God. Each book in this series focuses on a specific value. For example, *Cherry Cola Champions* deals with compassion, and *Peanut Butter and Jelly Secrets* is about obedience. Each book cover states "Readers will learn from Alex's mistakes and understand that they have the same sources of help that she turns to: A God who loves them and parents who understand." The books are listed here in the sequence given by the publisher.

1. Shoelaces and Brussels Sprouts ◆ 1987
2. French Fry Forgiveness ◆ 1987
3. Hot Chocolate Friendship ◆ 1987
4. Peanut Butter and Jelly Secrets ◆ 1987
5. Mint Cookie Miracles ◆ 1988
6. Cherry Cola Champions ◆ 1988
7. Peach Pit Popularity ◆ 1989
8. The Salty Scarecrow Solution ◆ 1989
9. T-Bone Trouble ◆ 1990
10. Grapefruit Basket Upset ◆ 1991
11. Apple Turnover Treasure ◆ 1992
12. Crocodile Meatloaf ◆ 1993
13. Chocolate Chips and Trumpet Tricks ◆ 1994
14. Alex's Triple Treat ◆ 1996

ALEX MACK *see* Secret World of Alex Mack

ALEXANDER

Viorst, Judith
ATHENEUM; SCHOLASTIC ◆ GRADES K–3 ◆ A/R
FAMILY LIFE | HUMOR

Judith Viorst does a wonderful job of exploring the everyday frustrations of children through the eyes of a little boy named Alexander. He tries to save money, has bad days, and struggles with his two older brothers and his mother. Ray Cruz's illustrations are delightful. These are books meant to be shared and enjoyed together.

1. I'll Fix Anthony ◆ 1969
2. Alexander and the Terrible, Horrible, No Good, Very Bad Day ◆ 1972
3. Alexander, Who Used to be Rich Last Sunday ◆ 1978
4. Alexander, Who's Not (Do You Hear Me? I Mean It!) Going to Move ◆ 1995
5. Absolutely Positively Alexander: The Complete Stories ◆ 1997

ALFIE ROSE

Hughes, Shirley

LOTHROP, LEE & SHEPARD; CANDLEWICK ◆ GRADES K–2

FAMILY LIFE | REAL LIFE

Alfie accidentally locks his mother and baby sister Annie Rose outside and can't reach the latch to let them in. Readers are introduced to the whole neighborhood as they get involved in the rescue. Double-page spreads illustrate both sides of the door. Delightful vignettes portray daily life for the children and their loving family. Companion volumes include *The Big Alfie and Annie Rose Story Book* and *The Big Alfie Out of Doors Story Book*. Four of the stories about Alfie have been gathered into a collection titled *All About Alfie*.

1. Alfie Gets in First ◆ 1982
2. Alfie's Feet ◆ 1983
3. Alfie Gives a Hand ◆ 1984
4. An Evening at Alfie's ◆ 1984
5. Rhymes for Annie Rose ◆ 1995
6. Alfie and the Birthday Surprise ◆ 1998
7. Alfie's ABC ◆ 1998
8. Alfie's 1 2 3 ◆ 2000

ALI BABA BERNSTEIN

Hurwitz, Johanna

MORROW ◆ GRADES 2–4 ◆ A/R

HUMOR | REAL LIFE

David, age 8, is tired of being one of four Davids in his class and is determined to set himself apart with his new name, Ali Baba. He celebrates an exciting ninth birthday when he invites all the David Bernsteins in the phone book to his party. Ali Baba, always intrigued by mysteries, thinks about becoming a detective and getting a dog.

1. The Adventures of Ali Baba Bernstein ◆ 1985
2. Hurray for Ali Baba Bernstein ◆ 1989
3. Ali Baba Bernstein, Lost and Found ◆ 1992

ALICE

Naylor, Phyllis Reynolds

ATHENEUM; DELL ◆ GRADES 5–8 ◆ A/R

FAMILY LIFE | HUMOR

Affectionate and humorous, these stories feature Alice getting into all kinds of funny scrapes, mostly because of her good intentions. Putting up with the boys at school, getting her first boyfriend, making and keeping friends, and dealing with her father and older brother Lester are all part of the fun. As Alice matures (from 6th grade in the first book to eleventh grade in *Almost Alice*), the books deal with more mature topics, such as her questions about sexuality and intimacy. The prequels follow Alice from third grade, when she has just moved to Takoma Park and faces many changes, to fifth grade, a time of discovery.

1. The Agony of Alice ◆ 1985
2. Alice in Rapture, Sort of ◆ 1989
3. Reluctantly Alice ◆ 1991
4. All But Alice ◆ 1992
5. Alice in April ◆ 1993
6. Alice In-Between ◆ 1994
7. Alice the Brave ◆ 1995
8. Alice in Lace ◆ 1996
9. Outrageously Alice ◆ 1997
10. Achingly Alice ◆ 1998
11. Alice on the Outside ◆ 2000
12. The Grooming of Alice ◆ 2000
13. Alice Alone ◆ 2001
14. Simply Alice ◆ 2002
15. Patiently Alice ◆ 2003
16. Including Alice ◆ 2004
17. Alice on Her Way ◆ 2005
18. Alice in the Know ◆ 2006
19. Dangerously Alice ◆ 2007
20. Almost Alice ◆ 2008

ALICE PREQUELS

1. Starting with Alice ◆ 2002
2. Alice in Blunderland ◆ 2003
3. Lovingly Alice ◆ 2005

ALIEN ADVENTURES

Coville, Bruce

POCKET BOOKS ◆ GRADES 4–7 ◆ A/R

HUMOR | SCIENCE FICTION

Rod Allbright's science project has just been invaded! Tiny aliens have landed there and they want Rod's help. First they need to capture an interstellar criminal, then Rod is taken to another dimension. Rod's troubles continue when he and the aliens go through space to the home of the Mental Masters. But the worst is yet to come; Rod's body is stolen by a fiend and his personality must share space with Seymour, a blue alien. Like Coville's My Teacher books, this series combines science fiction and humor as Rod and the aliens stumble their way through intergalactic adventures.

1. Aliens Ate My Homework ◆ 1993
2. I Left My Sneakers in Dimension X ◆ 1994
3. The Search for Snout ◆ 1995
4. Aliens Stole My Body ◆ 1998

ALIEN CLONES FROM OUTER SPACE

Homzie, H. B.

ALADDIN ◆ GRADES 2–4 ◆ A/R

FANTASY | HUMOR

Barton and Nancy are twins. Aliens arrive and clone the two children, creating many silly situations. Like Amelia Bedelia, Beta, Barton's clone, gets words and their meanings confused—Is a living room really alive? At first, the twins want to keep the clones from ruining their lives. Later, they use the clones as replacements with funny results.

1. Two Heads Are Better Than One ◆ 2002
2. Who Let the Dogs Out? ◆ 2002
3. The Baby-Sitters Wore Diapers ◆ 2003
4. Food Fight! ◆ 2003

ALIENS

Various authors

RANDOM HOUSE ◆ GRADES 2–4 ◆ A/R

HUMOR | SCIENCE FICTION

Aric is a space creature from Planet Ganoob who ends up on Earth in the home of Richard Bickerstaff. (Richard's mother opened a free sample of cereal that contained Aric.) Aric is on a mission to stop aliens from taking over Earth. In one book, an alien is disguised as a member of Richard's class. In another, aliens are planning to steal all of the desserts on Earth, and in the third, the aliens are bringing their toxic waste to Earth. Aric is a fast-talking extraterrestrial who makes wisecracks to Richard and his friend Henry Ball while he involves them in these funny adventures.

1. Aliens for Breakfast (Etra, Jonathan, and Stephanie Spinner) ◆ 1988
2. Aliens for Lunch (Etra, Jonathan, and Stephanie Spinner) ◆ 1991
3. Aliens for Dinner (Spinner, Stephanie) ◆ 1994

ALISTAIR

Sadler, Marilyn

SIMON & SCHUSTER ◆ **GRADES K–2**

FANTASY | HUMOR

Alistair is an unusual boy in more ways than one. He is always polite and wears neatly pressed clothes. Every day he thanks his teacher for giving him homework. Also, he builds a spaceship and keeps an elephant for a pet, all without missing any school. In search of more pond life for his collection, he builds a small submarine, discovers some frog people, and saves them from a sea monster, all in time for supper. When captured by aliens, his main concern is some library books that are due; and when more aliens invade Earth, he is delighted when they present him with an unusual plant that he can use for a school project. Illustrations show the neatly dressed and unflappable Alistair in each bizarre situation.

1. Alistair's Elephant ◆ 1983
2. Alistair in Outer Space ◆ 1984
3. Alistair's Time Machine ◆ 1986
4. Alistair Underwater ◆ 1990
5. Alistair and the Alien Invasion ◆ 1994

ALL-AMERICAN PUPPIES

Saunders, Susan

AVON ◆ **GRADES 2–4** ◆ **A/R**

HUMOR

These pups have personality! Jake is a 3-month-old mutt that has been adopted from the animal shelter. He meets the neighborhood dogs and they join together to be helpful. For example, Rosie is a pooch that has been abandoned. Jake and the gang come to her rescue. In *Puppysaurus,* Jake finds a BIG bone. Could it be . . . ? Dog lovers will love these books.

1. New Pup on the Block ◆ 2001
2. On the Scent of Trouble ◆ 2001

3. Camp Barkalot ◆ 2001
4. Uptown Poodle, Downtown Pups ◆ 2001
5. Puppysaurus ◆ 2001
6. The Bake-Off Burglar ◆ 2001

ALL-OF-A-KIND FAMILY

Taylor, Sydney

BANTAM DOUBLEDAY DELL ◆ GRADES 4–6 ◆ A/R

FAMILY LIFE | HISTORICAL

Five little girls live with their parents in a four-room flat on New York's Lower East Side before and during World War I. They don't have much money, but they have lots of companionship, books, outings, games, and friends. Frightening things happen to the family too: Sarah and Ella come down with scarlet fever, and Henny gets lost at Coney Island. A new brother doesn't change the closeness of this all-of-a-kind family. Summers at Rockaway Beach, the celebration of Jewish holidays, and the victory parade at the end of the war are some of the events chronicled in these warm stories of family life.

1. All-of-a-Kind Family ◆ 1951
2. More All-of-a-Kind Family ◆ 1954
3. All-of-a-Kind Family Uptown ◆ 1958
4. All-of-a-Kind Family Downtown ◆ 1972
5. Ella of All-of-a Kind Family ◆ 1978

ALLIE NICHOLS *see* Ghost

AL'S WORLD

Leonard, Elise

ALADDIN ◆ GRADES 4–8 ◆ A/R

HUMOR

Al is an ordinary kid who likes to pal around with his friend Keith. One Monday morning he becomes involved in a CIA chase when an agent bumps into Al and slides a flash drive into Al's pocket. The preposterous situations and Al's regular-guy goofiness should appeal to middle school readers, even reluctant ones.

1. Monday Morning Blitz ◆ 2007
2. Killer Lunch Lady ◆ 2007
3. Scared Stiff ◆ 2007
4. Monkey Business ◆ 2008

ALTERNAMORPHS *see* Animorphs: Alternamorphs

ALWAYS FRIENDS

Meyers, Susan
TROLL ◆ GRADES 2–4
REAL LIFE

Meg, Cricket, Amy, and Brittany become the Always Friends Club as they enjoy parties, class activities, and neighborhood fun. Each girl is featured in two books in this series, which focuses on ordinary experiences like sleepovers and pets but also includes special events such as auditioning for a TV show and a haunted house contest. In *Meg and the Secret Scrapbook,* Meg and Cricket discover a scrapbook in the attic and find out that their mothers were best friends and even had a special club.

1. Amy's Haunted House ◆ 1995
2. Beautiful Brittany ◆ 1995
3. Cricket Goes to the Dogs ◆ 1995
4. Hello, Jenny ◆ 1995
5. Meg and the Secret Scrapbook ◆ 1995
6. Amy Onstage ◆ 1997
7. Brittany's New Friend ◆ 1997
8. Cricket's Pet Project ◆ 1997

ALWAYS TROUBLE SOMEWHERE *see* Rachel Yoder—Always Trouble Somewhere

AMAZING GRACE *see* Grace

AMBER BROWN

Danziger, Paula
PUTNAM ◆ GRADES 2–4 ◆ A/R
FAMILY LIFE | HUMOR

Amber Brown begins this series in third grade. Through the series, Amber faces with humor the trials of growing up, her parents' divorce, and her mother's marriage to Max. These short novels, written in the first person with plenty of witty dialog, have a ring of authenticity.

1. Amber Brown Is Not a Crayon ◆ 1995
2. You Can't Eat Your Chicken Pox, Amber Brown ◆ 1996
3. Amber Brown Goes Fourth ◆ 1996

4. Amber Brown Wants Extra Credit ◆ 1997
5. Forever Amber Brown ◆ 1997
6. Amber Brown Sees Red ◆ 1998
7. Amber Brown Is Feeling Blue ◆ 1998
8. I Amber Brown ◆ 1999
9. Amber Brown Is Green with Envy ◆ 2003

AMBER BROWN: A IS FOR AMBER

Danziger, Paula

PUTNAM ◆ GRADES K–2 ◆ A/R

HUMOR | REAL LIFE

Popular series character Amber Brown is now found in books for beginning readers. She's younger but just as feisty. In one book, she hopes for a watch for her birthday. In another, she wonders if the new second-grade teacher will like her. Fans of Young Cam Jansen will like these books.

1. What a Trip, Amber Brown ◆ 2001
2. It's Justin Time, Amber Brown ◆ 2001
3. It's a Fair Day, Amber Brown ◆ 2002
4. Get Ready for Second Grade, Amber Brown ◆ 2002
5. Second Grade Rules, Amber Brown ◆ 2004
6. Orange You Glad It's Halloween, Amber Brown? ◆ 2005

AMELIA

Moss, Marissa

TRICYCLE PRESS; PLEASANT CO.; SIMON & SCHUSTER ◆ GRADES 4–8 ◆ A/R

REAL LIFE

Amelia's notebooks (the covers of these books look like actual composition books) are actually top-secret journals chronicling the ups and downs of this young girl's life. Amelia is 9 at the beginning of the series; as she grows older and enters middle school, the books deal with issues of that age group. The scrapbook-like design is a large part of the appeal of these books. *My Notebook (With Help from Amelia)* invites kids to begin their own journal keeping. Related titles are *Amelia's School Survival Guide* (2002) and *Amelia's Card Game: The Game of Silly Sentences* (2001). There are Amelia guide books on such topics as babysitting, bullies, resolutions, and gossip.

1. Amelia's Notebook ◆ 1995
2. Amelia Writes Again ◆ 1996
3. Amelia Hits the Road ◆ 1997
4. Amelia Takes Command ◆ 1998

5. Dr. Amelia's Boredom Survival Guide ◆ 1999
6. The All-New Amelia ◆ 1999
7. Luv, Amelia Luv, Nadia ◆ 1999
8. Amelia's Family Ties ◆ 2000
9. Amelia's Easy-As-Pie Drawing Guide ◆ 2000
10. Amelia Works it Out ◆ 2000
11. Oh Boy, Amelia ◆ 2001
12. Madame Amelia Tells All ◆ 2001
13. Amelia Lends a Hand ◆ 2002
14. Amelia's Best Year Ever ◆ 2003
15. Amelia's 6th-Grade Notebook ◆ 2005
16. Amelia's Most Unforgettable Embarrassing Moments ◆ 2005
17. Amelia's Book of Notes and Note Passing ◆ 2006
18. Amelia's Longest, Biggest, Most-Fights-Ever Family Reunion ◆ 2006
19. Amelia's 5th-Grade Notebook ◆ 2006
20. Amelia's Are-We-There-Yet Longest Ever Car Trip ◆ 2006
21. Amelia's Bully Survival Guide ◆ 2006
22. The All-New Amelia ◆ 2007
23. Amelia's 7th-Grade Notebook ◆ 2007
24. Vote 4 Amelia ◆ 2007
25. Amelia's Itchy-Twitchy, Lovey-Dovey Summer at Camp Mosquito ◆ 2008

AMELIA BEDELIA

Parish, Peggy, and Herman Parish

HARPERCOLLINS; GREENWILLOW ◆ GRADES K–2 ◆ A/R

HUMOR

Amelia Bedelia's literalness causes problems when she tries to follow Mrs. Rogers's instructions for household chores. She changes towels, dresses the chicken, dusts potato bugs, and sews seeds. She always does exactly as she is told, but the results are never what is expected! Laugh-out-loud funny, these books will surely entertain. Herman Parish took over writing the series following the death of his aunt in 1988. New illustrations for some of the older books give them a fresh look. *Amelia Bedelia and the Christmas List; Be My Valentine, Amelia Bedelia;* and *Amelia Bedelia Goes Back to School* are related lift-the-flap books.

1. Amelia Bedelia ◆ 1963
2. Thank You, Amelia Bedelia ◆ 1964
3. Amelia Bedelia and the Surprise Shower ◆ 1966
4. Come Back, Amelia Bedelia ◆ 1971
5. Play Ball, Amelia Bedelia ◆ 1972
6. Good Work, Amelia Bedelia ◆ 1976
7. Teach Us, Amelia Bedelia ◆ 1977
8. Amelia Bedelia Helps Out ◆ 1979
9. Amelia Bedelia and the Baby ◆ 1981

10. Amelia Bedelia Goes Camping ◆ 1985
11. Merry Christmas, Amelia Bedelia ◆ 1986
12. Amelia Bedelia's Family Album ◆ 1988
13. Good Driving, Amelia Bedelia ◆ 1995
14. Bravo, Amelia Bedelia! ◆ 1997
15. Amelia Bedelia 4 Mayor ◆ 1999
16. Calling Dr. Amelia Bedelia ◆ 2002
17. Amelia Bedelia, Bookworm ◆ 2003
18. Happy Haunting, Amelia Bedelia ◆ 2004
19. Amelia Bedelia, Rocket Scientist? ◆ 2005
20. Amelia Bedelia Under Construction ◆ 2006
21. Amelia Bedelia's Masterpiece ◆ 2007
22. Amelia Bedelia and the Cat ◆ 2008
23. Amelia Bedelia Talks Turkey ◆ 2008

AMELIA RULES!

Gownley, Jimmy
RENAISSANCE PRESS ◆ GRADES 3–5
REAL LIFE

After her parents' divorce, Amelia, grade four, is living with her mom (who is still recovering from her failed marriage) and her cool Aunt Tanner. She is in a new school and hoping to make friends, which she does. She joins a group that calls itself G.A.S.P. (Gathering of Awesome Superpals) that attempts to solve neighborhood and personal problems. This series is a collection of comic books (usually four in each book), not a true graphic novel. Still, it is a great choice to introduce elementary grade readers to this format. Babymouse is another sassy character for this younger crowd. *Amelia Rules Funny Stories* (2008) is a collection of the funniest comics from the other books (and earlier comic books). There is an ameliarules.com Web site.

1. The Whole World's Crazy ◆ 2006
2. What Makes You Happy ◆ 2006
3. Superheroes ◆ 2006
4. When the Past Is a Present ◆ 2007

AMERICAN ADVENTURE

Roddy, Lee
BETHANY HOUSE ◆ GRADES 5–8 ◆ A/R
HISTORICAL | VALUES

Hildy Corrigan faces many challenges during the Great Depression as she and her family move, hoping for a better life. The different locations of this series put Hildy in situations that test her faith. Searching for a thief, adjusting to a new home, helping a girl whose father is a thief, and being accused of stealing a watch give Hildy opportunities to realize God's strength, love, and power of forgiveness. Readers looking for books in which characters struggle to be true to their values will want to read this series and other books by Lee Roddy.

1. The Overland Escape ◆ 1989
2. The Desperate Search ◆ 1989
3. Danger on Thunder Mountain ◆ 1989
4. The Secret of the Howling Cave ◆ 1990
5. The Flaming Trap ◆ 1990
6. Terror in the Sky ◆ 1991
7. Mystery of the Phantom Gold ◆ 1991
8. The Gold Train Bandits ◆ 1992
9. High Country Ambush ◆ 1992

THE AMERICAN ADVENTURE

Various authors

BARBOUR PUBLISHING; CHELSEA HOUSE ◆ GRADES 3–6 ◆ A/R

ADVENTURE | HISTORICAL | VALUES

The Smythe family travels to the New World aboard the *Mayflower* to escape religious persecution in Holland. Their adventures in reaching America and surviving the harsh first winter in Plymouth Colony are told from the point of view of 12-year-old John Smythe in *The Mayflower Adventure* and *Plymouth Pioneers*. More than 40 additional books tell the story of the Smythe family's devout Christian relatives, descendants, and friends living through episodes in American history, all the way through World War II. There are books on the American Revolution, the World's Fair in Chicago, Irish immigration, women's suffrage, and the Ku Klux Klan. The theme of God's hand at work in American history is present throughout the series.

1. The Mayflower Adventure (Reece, Colleen L.) ◆ 1997
2. Plymouth Pioneers (Reece, Colleen L.) ◆ 1997
3. Dream Seekers (Lough, Loree) ◆ 1997
4. Fire by Night (Lough, Loree) ◆ 1997
5. Queen Anne's War (Grote, JoAnn) ◆ 1997
6. Danger in the Harbor (Grote, JoAnn) ◆ 1997
7. Smallpox Strikes! (Lutz, Norma Jean) ◆ 1997
8. Maggie's Choice (Lutz, Norma Jean) ◆ 1997
9. Boston Revolts! (Miller, Susan Martins) ◆ 1997
10. The Boston Massacre (Miller, Susan Martins) ◆ 1997
11. The American Revolution (Grote, JoAnn) ◆ 1997
12. The American Victory (Grote, JoAnn) ◆ 1997
13. Adventure in the Wilderness (Jones, Veda Boyd) ◆ 1997
14. Earthquake in Cincinnati (Hinman, Bonnie) ◆ 1997
15. Trouble on the Ohio River (Lutz, Norma Jean) ◆ 1997

16. Escape to Freedom (Lutz, Norma Jean) ◆ 1997
17. Cincinnati Epidemic (Jones, Veda Boyd) ◆ 1997
18. Riot in the Night (Hinman, Bonnie) ◆ 1997
19. Fight for Freedom (Lutz, Norma Jean) ◆ 1997
20. Enemy or Friend (Lutz, Norma Jean) ◆ 1997
21. Danger on the Railroad (Miller, Susan Martins) ◆ 1998
22. Time for Battle (Miller, Susan Martins) ◆ 1998
23. The Rebel Spy (Lutz, Norma Jean) ◆ 1998
24. War's End (Lutz, Norma Jean) ◆ 1998
25. Centennial Celebration (Grote, JoAnn) ◆ 1998
26. The Great Mill Explosion (Grote, JoAnn) ◆ 1998
27. Lights for Minneapolis (Miller, Susan Martins) ◆ 1998
28. Streetcar Riots (Miller, Susan Martins) ◆ 1998
29. Chicago World's Fair (Grote, JoAnn) ◆ 1998
30. A Better Bicycle (Grote, JoAnn) ◆ 1998
31. The New Citizen (Jones, Veda Boyd) ◆ 1998
32. The San Francisco Earthquake (Hinman, Bonnie) ◆ 1998
33. Marching with Sousa (Lutz, Norma Jean) ◆ 1998
34. Clash with the Newsboys (Lutz, Norma Jean) ◆ 1998
35. Prelude to War (Lutz, Norma Jean) ◆ 1998
36. The Great War (Lutz, Norma Jean) ◆ 1998
37. The Flu Epidemic (Grote, JoAnn) ◆ 1998
38. Women Win the Vote (Grote, JoAnn) ◆ 1998
39. Battling the Klan (Lutz, Norma Jean) ◆ 1998
40. The Bootlegger Menace (Hinman, Bonnie) ◆ 1998
41. Black Tuesday (Grote, JoAnn) ◆ 1998
42. The Great Depression (Grote, JoAnn) ◆ 1998
43. Starting Over (Miller, Susan Martins) ◆ 1998
44. Changing Times (Miller, Susan Martins) ◆ 1998
45. Rumblings of War (Lutz, Norma Jean) ◆ 1999
46. War Strikes (Lutz, Norma Jean) ◆ 1999
47. The Home Front (Hinman, Bonnie) ◆ 1999
48. Coming Home (Jones, Veda Boyd) ◆ 1999

AMERICAN ADVENTURES

Pryor, Bonnie
HARPERCOLLINS ◆ GRADES 4–6 ◆ A/R
ADVENTURE | HISTORICAL | REAL LIFE

This series follows the adventures of three boys during different eras in American history. Thomas, 10, cares for his mother and family while his father is fighting in the Revolutionary War. Luke, 11, lives on the prairie in 1849. He longs for an opportunity to develop his artistic talent. In 1861, Joseph lives in Kentucky where the community is divided over the issues of the Civil War. There is a pair of books about each boy.

1. Thomas: 1778, Patriots on the Run ◆ 1999

2. Thomas in Danger ◆ 1999
3. Luke: 1849, On the Golden Trail ◆ 1999
4. Luke on the High Seas ◆ 2000
5. Joseph: 1861, A Rumble of War ◆ 1999
6. Joseph's Choice: 1861 ◆ 2000

AMERICAN CHILLERS

Rand, Johnathan

AUDIOCRAFT PUBLISHING ◆ GRADES 4–6 ◆ A/R

HORROR | MYSTERY

Each book in this series is a mystery/horror story set in a different state. In the first book, Rick Owens goes to Camp Willow in Michigan. On his first night there, he has a nightmare that glowing red eyes are looking through the window. Is this really just a bad dream?

1. The Michigan Mega-Monsters ◆ 2001
2. Ogres of Ohio ◆ 2002
3. Florida Fog Phantoms ◆ 2002
4. New York Ninjas ◆ 2002
5. Terrible Tractors of Texas ◆ 2002
6. Invisible Iguanas of Illinois ◆ 2002
7. Wisconsin Werewolves ◆ 2002
8. Minnesota Mall Mannequins ◆ 2003
9. Iron Insects Invade Indiana ◆ 2003
10. Missouri Madhouse ◆ 2003
11. Poisonous Pythons Paralyze Pennsylvania ◆ 2003
12. Dangerous Dolls of Delaware ◆ 2003
13. Virtual Vampires of Vermont ◆ 2004
14. Creepy Condors of California ◆ 2004
15. Nebraska Nightcrawlers ◆ 2004
16. Alien Androids Assault Arizona ◆ 2004
17. South Carolina Sea Creatures ◆ 2005
18. Washington Wax Museum ◆ 2006
19. North Dakota Night Dragons ◆ 2006
20. Mutant Mammoths of Montana ◆ 2007
21. Terrifying Toys of Tennessee ◆ 2007
22. Nuclear Jellyfish of New Jersey ◆ 2007
23. Wicked Velociraptors of West Virginia ◆ 2008
24. Haunting in New Hampshire ◆ 2008

AMERICAN DIARIES

Duey, Kathleen

ALADDIN ◆ GRADES 4–6

HISTORICAL | REAL LIFE

Each book in this series features the adventures of a girl during an era of American history. After opening with a diary entry, the text describes the time and circumstances of the main character. A diary entry then closes the book. The eras and characters are diverse, providing readers with glimpses of different ways of life. Sarah Anne Hartford lives in Massachusetts in 1651 and must accept responsibility for violating Puritan standards of behavior. In Missouri in 1857, Evie Peach and her father have been emancipated by their owner and are now hoping to buy Mama's freedom. Celou Sudden Shout is the daughter of a French fur trapper and a Shoshone living in Idaho in 1826. Dramatic historical events are woven into these stories, which feature spirited female main characters.

1. Sarah Anne Hartford, Massachusetts, 1651 ◆ 1996
2. Emma Eileen Grove, Mississippi, 1865 ◆ 1996
3. Anisett Lundberg, California, 1851 ◆ 1996
4. Mary Alice Peale, Philadelphia, 1777 ◆ 1996
5. Willow Chase, Kansas Territory,1847 ◆ 1997
6. Ellen Elizabeth Hawkins, Mobeetie, Texas 1886 ◆ 1997
7. Alexia Ellery Finsdale, San Francisco, 1905 ◆ 1997
8. Evie Peach, St. Louis, 1857 ◆ 1997
9. Celou Sudden Shout, Idaho, 1826 ◆ 1998
10. Summer MacCleary, Virginia, 1749 ◆ 1998
11. Agnes May Gleason, Walsenburg, Colorado, 1932 ◆ 1998
12. Amelina Carrett, Bayou Grand Coeur, Louisiana, 1863 ◆ 1999
13. Josie Poe, Paulouse, Washington, 1943 ◆ 1999
14. Rosa Moreno, Hollywood, California, 1928 ◆ 1999
15. Maddie Retta Lauren, Sandersville, Georgia, C.S.A., 1864 ◆ 2000
16. Nell Dunne, Ellis Island, 1904 ◆ 2000
17. Francesca Vigilucci, Washington, D.C., 1913 ◆ 2000
18. Janey G. Blue, Pearl Harbor, 1941 ◆ 2001
19. Zellie Blake, Lowell, Massachusetts, 1834 ◆ 2002

AMERICAN GIRL TODAY *see* American Girls: Girl of the Year

AMERICAN GIRLS

GRADES 2–5
HISTORICAL | REAL LIFE

The American Girls stories have a big following among intermediate readers. They portray strong young girls and women growing up in the United States during different time periods. Not only does the series do a good job of describing what life was like then, it also portrays typical family life and friendships: growing up, struggles and successes, secrets, and adventures.

AMERICAN GIRLS: ADDY

Porter, Connie

PLEASANT COMPANY ◆ GRADES 2–5 ◆ A/R

HISTORICAL | REAL LIFE

Addy and her family are slaves in North Carolina. When Poppa and her brother Sam are sold, Addy and her mother leave Baby Esther on the plantation and escape to Philadelphia. Addy attends school there and learns to read and write. At a church festival, she and her friends earn money to help family members search for loved ones separated by slavery and the Civil War. Poppa and Sam find Addy and Mother, and they all try to find Baby Esther. Historical details are presented within the context of Addy's everyday activities, giving readers a glimpse of life during this era. As part of the American Girls Collection, many related items are available, including an Addy doll with clothes, furniture, and artifacts.

1. Meet Addy: An American Girl ◆ 1993
2. Addy Learns a Lesson: A School Story ◆ 1993
3. Addy's Surprise: A Christmas Story ◆ 1993
4. Happy Birthday, Addy: A Springtime Story ◆ 1994
5. Addy Saves the Day: A Summer Story ◆ 1994
6. Changes for Addy: A Winter Story ◆ 1994

AMERICAN GIRLS: AMERICAN GIRL MYSTERIES

Various authors

AMERICAN GIRL ◆ GRADES 2–6 ◆ A/R

MYSTERY | HISTORICAL

Fans of the American Girl books will enjoy reading about their favorite characters in these mysteries. In *The Stolen Sapphire,* Samantha and her adopted sister Nellie are sailing to Europe on an ocean liner. A famous archaeologist is also on board, taking a Blue Star sapphire to a museum in London. The mystery begins when the sapphire goes missing. In *Danger at the Zoo,* Kit is writing a story about a friend who is volunteering at the zoo. The "mystery" involves missing monkeys and stolen food. Kit solves the mystery and clears her friend. As with other American Girl books, factual information relevant to the story is appended.

1. The Curse of Ravenscourt: A Samantha Mystery (Buckey, Sarah Masters) ◆ 2005
2. Danger at the Zoo: A Kit Mystery (Ernst, Kathleen) ◆ 2005
3. The Silent Stranger: A Kaya Mystery (Shaw, Janet Beeler) ◆ 2005
4. A Spy on the Home Front: A Molly Mystery (Hart, Alison) ◆ 2005
5. Peril at King's Creek: A Felicity Mystery (Jones, Elizabeth McDavid) ◆ 2006

6. Secrets in the Hills: A Josefina Mystery (Ernst, Kathleen) ◆ 2006
7. The Stolen Sapphire: A Samantha Mystery (Buckey, Sarah Masters) ◆ 2006
8. The Light in the Cellar: A Molly Mystery (Buckey, Sarah Masters) ◆ 2007
9. Midnight at Lonesome Hollow: A Kit Mystery (Ernst, Kathleen) ◆ 2007
10. Shadows on Society Hill: An Addy Mystery (Coleman, Evelyn) ◆ 2007
11. The Runaway Friend: A Kirsten Mystery (Ernst, Kathleen) ◆ 2008
12. A Thief in the Theater: A Kit Mystery (Buckey, Sarah Masters) ◆ 2008
13. Traitor in Williamsburg: A Felicity Mystery (Jones, Elizabeth McDavid) ◆ 2008
14. The Tangled Web: A Julie Mystery (Reiss, Kathryn) ◆ 2009

AMERICAN GIRLS: FELICITY

Tripp, Valerie

PLEASANT COMPANY ◆ GRADES 2–5 ◆ A/R

HISTORICAL | REAL LIFE

Felicity lives in Williamsburg in the 1770s. Her father owns one of the town's largest shops, and he has one apprentice, Ben, a patriot and friend of Felicity. In the first book, she and Ben befriend a beautiful horse that has fallen into the hands of a cruel man. They let the horse go, and Felicity hopes she will find her again some day. In subsequent books, she takes lessons in how to be a lady and meets Elizabeth, who becomes her best friend. At Christmastime, she and Ben quarrel because she wants a new dress for a ball. Her mother becomes ill, and Felicity is reunited with the horse. Notes at the end of each book offer information about the history of the period. Beautiful full-color paintings illustrate the books. Many related items are available, including dolls, furniture, and artifacts.

1. Meet Felicity: An American Girl ◆ 1991
2. Felicity Learns a Lesson: A School Story ◆ 1991
3. Felicity's Surprise: A Christmas Story ◆ 1991
4. Happy Birthday, Felicity! A Springtime Story ◆ 1992
5. Felicity Saves the Day: A Summer Story ◆ 1992
6. Changes for Felicity: A Winter Story ◆ 1992

AMERICAN GIRLS: GIRL OF THE YEAR

Various authors

PLEASANT COMPANY ◆ GRADES 3–6

REAL LIFE

These are stories about contemporary girls from diverse backgrounds and facing a variety of situations. Ten-year-old Nicki spends much of her summer helping to train a service dog and realizes how much fun she has had to forgo. Lindsey, 10, always means well but her interference in other people's affairs often causes trouble. Kailey takes on wealthy developers whose plans will endanger wildlife.

1. Lindsey (Atkinson, Chryssa) ◆ 2001
2. Kailey (Koss, Amy Goldman) ◆ 2003
3. Marisol (Soto, Gary) ◆ 2004
4. Jess (Casanova, Mary) ◆ 2006
5. Nicki (Creel, Ann Howard) ◆ 2006
6. Thanks to Nicki (Creel, Ann Howard) ◆ 2007
7. Mia (Yep, Laurence) ◆ 2008
8. Bravo, Mia! (Yep, Laurence) ◆ 2008

AMERICAN GIRLS: GIRLS OF MANY LANDS

Various authors

PLEASANT COMPANY ◆ GRADES 4–8 ◆ A/R

HISTORICAL | REAL LIFE

This historical series features 12-year-old girls during times of change. Cecile is a servant in the French court of Louis XIV. What begins as an opportunity becomes a challenge. Neela lives in India during the independence movement (1939). In 1846, Saba is kidnapped from her home in Ethiopia and taken to the court of the emperor. Girls who like books about female characters facing challenges will enjoy this series. As with other books from this publisher, historical facts follow each story.

1. Cecile: Gates of Gold, 1711 (Casanova, Mary) ◆ 2002
2. Isabel: Taking Wing, 1592 (Dalton, Annie) ◆ 2002
3. Minuk: Ashes in the Pathway, 1890 (Hill, Kirkpatrick) ◆ 2002
4. Neela: Victory Song, 1939 (Divakaruni, Chitra Banerjee) ◆ 2002
5. Spring Pearl: The Last Flower, 1857 (Yep, Laurence) ◆ 2002
6. Saba: Under the Hyena's Foot, 1846 (Kurtz, Jane) ◆ 2003
7. Kathleen: The Celtic Knot, 1937 (Parkinson, Siobhan) ◆ 2003
8. Leyla: The Black Tulip, 1720 (Croutier, Alev Lytle) ◆ 2003

AMERICAN GIRLS: HISTORY MYSTERIES

Various authors

PLEASANT COMPANY ◆ GRADES 4–7 ◆ A/R

HISTORICAL | MYSTERY

Louisiana during the War of 1812; the Pony Express trail in 1860 Nebraska; San Francisco after the 1906 earthquake. These are just some of the places and times presented in this series. In each book, a girl who is around 12 years old becomes involved in a mysterious situation. There are concerns about spies, pirates, the Ku Klux Klan, and kidnappers. The intrepid behavior of the main characters saves the day. Historical information follows each novel. This is a good choice for girls who enjoy action.

1. The Smuggler's Treasure (Buckey, Sarah Masters) ◆ 1999
2. Hoofbeats of Danger (Hughes, Holly) ◆ 1999
3. The Night Fliers (Jones, Elizabeth McDavid) ◆ 1999
4. Voices at Whisper Bend (Ayres, Katherine) ◆ 1999
5. Secrets on 26th Street (Jones, Elizabeth McDavid) ◆ 1999
6. Mystery of the Dark Tower (Coleman, Evelyn) ◆ 2000
7. Trouble at Fort La Pointe (Ernst, Kathleen) ◆ 2000
8. Under Copp's Hill (Ayres, Katherine) ◆ 2000
9. Watcher in the Piney Woods (Jones, Elizabeth McDavid) ◆ 2000
10. Shadows in the Glasshouse (McDonald, Megan) ◆ 2000
11. The Minstrel's Melody (Tate, Eleanora E.) ◆ 2001
12. Riddle of the Prairie Bride (Reiss, Kathryn) ◆ 2001
13. Enemy in the Fort (Buckey, Sarah Masters) ◆ 2001
14. Circle of Fire (Coleman, Evelyn) ◆ 2001
15. Mystery on Skull Island (Jones, Elizabeth McDavid) ◆ 2001
16. Whistler in the Dark (Ernst, Kathleen) ◆ 2002
17. Mystery at Chilkoot Pass (Steiner, Barbara) ◆ 2002
18. The Strange Case of Baby H (Reiss, Kathryn) ◆ 2002
19. Danger at the Wild West Show (Hart, Alison) ◆ 2003
20. Gangsters at the Grand Atlantic (Buckey, Sarah Masters) ◆ 2003
21. Ghost Light on Graveyard Shoal (Jones, Elizabeth McDavid) ◆ 2003
22. Betrayal at Cross Creek (Ernst, Kathleen) ◆ 2004

AMERICAN GIRLS: JOSEFINA

Tripp, Valerie

PLEASANT COMPANY ◆ GRADES 2–5 ◆ A/R

HISTORICAL | REAL LIFE

Josefina Montoya is a Hispanic girl living in New Mexico in 1824. Her mother is dead, but Josefina is supported by her sisters and her extended family. Learning to read, celebrating her birthday and Christmas, and weaving traditional designs are some of her activities. Besides the Josefina doll, other related items include a small weaving loom and an adobe oven.

1. Meet Josefina: An American Girl ◆ 1997
2. Josefina Learns a Lesson: A School Story ◆ 1997
3. Josefina's Surprise: A Christmas Story ◆ 1997
4. Happy Birthday, Josefina! A Springtime Story ◆ 1998
5. Josefina Saves the Day: A Summer Story ◆ 1998
6. Changes for Josefina: A Winter Story ◆ 1998

AMERICAN GIRLS: JULIE

McDonald, Megan
AMERICAN GIRLS ◆ GRADES 2–5 ◆ A/R
REAL LIFE | HISTORICAL

Julie Allbright lives in San Francisco in 1974. Now that her parents are divorced, Julie has moved from Chinatown to an apartment a few miles away. She misses her best friend, her pet rabbit, and her dad and she is challenged by the rules at her new school. For example, the coach won't allow girls to play on the basketball team. The 1970s were a time of social change, especially for women and girls. This series of books explores issues of that era including the women's movement and the increasing divorce rate. Each book has additional information appended. *Good Luck, Ivy* (2007) is a companion book about Julie's best friend Ivy.

1. Meet Julie ◆ 2007
2. Julie Tells Her Story ◆ 2007
3. Happy New Year, Julie ◆ 2007
4. Julie and the Eagles ◆ 2007
5. Julie's Journey ◆ 2007
6. Changes for Julie ◆ 2007

AMERICAN GIRLS: KAYA

Shaw, Janet B.
PLEASANT COMPANY ◆ GRADES 2–5 ◆ A/R
HISTORICAL | REAL LIFE

Like the other American Girl books, these offer readers a fascinating story while describing another era and way of life. Kaya is a member of the Nez Perce tribe. In *Meet Kaya,* she rides her horse, Steps High, even though her father disapproves. In subsequent books, Kaya and her sister are captured by enemy invaders. Kaya escapes but Speaking Rain, who is blind, remains captive for a longer time. Although fictional, these books provide everyday details about life in the 1760s. Historical information follows each novel. *Kaya and the River Girl* (2003) is a collection of short stories and *Welcome to Kaya's World, 1764: Growing up in a Native American Homeland* (2003) is a nonfiction companion to the series. Related products include dolls, artifacts, and teacher materials.

1. Meet Kaya: An American Girl ◆ 2002
2. Kaya's Escape: A Survival Story ◆ 2002
3. Kaya's Hero: A Story of Giving ◆ 2002
4. Kaya and Lone Dog: A Friendship Story ◆ 2002
5. Kaya Shows the Way: A Sister Story ◆ 2002
6. Changes for Kaya: A Story of Courage ◆ 2002

AMERICAN GIRLS: KIRSTEN

Shaw, Janet B.

PLEASANT COMPANY ◆ **GRADES 2–5** ◆ **A/R**

HISTORICAL | **REAL LIFE**

Kirsten makes a long and dangerous journey from Sweden to a new home on a Minnesota farm during pioneer times. At first she finds school difficult but she makes a friend and enjoys both Swedish traditions and her new life. Many related items are available, including dolls, clothes, furniture, and artifacts.

1. Meet Kirsten: An American Girl ◆ 1986
2. Kirsten Learns a Lesson: A School Story ◆ 1986
3. Kirsten's Surprise: A Christmas Story ◆ 1986
4. Happy Birthday, Kirsten: A Springtime Story ◆ 1987
5. Kirsten Saves the Day: A Summer Story ◆ 1988
6. Changes for Kirsten: A Winter Story ◆ 1988

AMERICAN GIRLS: KIT

Tripp, Valerie

PLEASANT COMPANY ◆ **GRADES 2–5** ◆ **A/R**

HISTORICAL | **REAL LIFE**

These books set during the Great Depression join the other American Girls novels that tell vivid stories in a historical context. Kit's father has been forced to close his business. The family takes in boarders and Kit even sees her father visit the local soup kitchen. Each book is followed by historical information. *Kit's Railway Adventure* by Harriet Brown is a photo-journal of Kit's trip with her aunt. There are many other related materials including dolls, artifacts, and teacher resources.

1. Meet Kit: An American Girl ◆ 2000
2. Kit Learns a Lesson: A School Story ◆ 2000
3. Kit's Surprise: A Christmas Story ◆ 2000
4. Happy Birthday, Kit! A Springtime Story ◆ 2001
5. Kit Saves the Day! A Summer Story ◆ 2001
6. Changes for Kit: A Winter Story ◆ 2001

AMERICAN GIRLS: MOLLY

Tripp, Valerie

PLEASANT COMPANY ◆ **GRADES 2–5** ◆ **A/R**

HISTORICAL | **REAL LIFE**

During World War II, Molly's dad is overseas working at a hospital. In *Meet Molly,* we learn about life on the home front. Victory gardens, patriotism, and waiting for the boys to come home are part of everyday life. An English refugee comes to live with Molly's family in the birthday story and, after some misunderstandings, the girls have a wonderful party together. In the school story, Molly's class has a contest to see whether the boys or the girls can do the most for the war effort. Molly's rival says they should knit socks, which Molly and her friends Linda and Susan don't think is such a good idea. Molly and her family are excited when they learn Father is coming home. Many related items are available, including dolls, clothes, furniture, and artifacts.

1. Meet Molly: An American Girl ◆ 1986
2. Molly Learns a Lesson: A School Story ◆ 1986
3. Molly's Surprise: A Christmas Story ◆ 1986
4. Happy Birthday, Molly! A Springtime Story ◆ 1987
5. Molly Saves the Day: A Summer Story ◆ 1988
6. Changes for Molly: A Winter Story ◆ 1988

AMERICAN GIRLS: SAMANTHA

Tripp, Valerie

PLEASANT COMPANY ◆ GRADES 2–5 ◆ A/R

HISTORICAL | REAL LIFE

Samantha Parkington is a young girl being raised by her grandmother in the early 1900s. The changes she experiences in her life mirror the changes the United States experienced at the time—social and economic upheavals brought about by the Industrial Revolution. In each of the six books, Samantha learns a lesson—about friendship, human nature, and generosity. These books are accompanied by a Samantha doll and accessories, as well as books of paper dolls, crafts, and recipes.

1. Meet Samantha: An American Girl ◆ 1986
2. Samantha Learns a Lesson: A School Story ◆ 1986
3. Samantha's Surprise: A Christmas Story ◆ 1986
4. Happy Birthday, Samantha! A Springtime Story ◆ 1987
5. Samantha Saves the Day: A Summer Story ◆ 1988
6. Changes for Samantha: A Winter Story ◆ 1989

AMERICAN GOLD GYMNASTS

Charbonnet, Gabrielle

BANTAM ◆ GRADES 4–7

RECREATION

Kelly Reynolds, 12, loves gymnastics. After her mother remarries, Kelly has a stepsister her own age who is also a gymnast—from Russia. At first the girls are wary of each other, but they become supportive friends. They even work together to deal with a difficult coach.

1. Competition Fever ◆ 1996
2. Balancing Act ◆ 1996
3. Split Decision ◆ 1996
4. The Bully Coach ◆ 1996

AMERICAN GOLD SWIMMERS

Wyeth, Sharon Dennis

BANTAM ◆ GRADES 4–7

RECREATION

The focus here is on swimming—practice, training, and competition. In one book, Kristy's interest in video games may keep her away from her swimming event. In another book, Kristy is older and is embarrassed about her appearance. She avoids swimming until she is needed for an important competition.

1. Winning Stroke ◆ 1996
2. The Human Shark ◆ 1996
3. Splash Party ◆ 1996
4. In Deep Water ◆ 1996

AMERICAN QUILTS

Kirby, Susan E.

ALADDIN ◆ GRADES 4–6 ◆ A/R

HISTORICAL

Lacey's great-grandmother Tandy tells stories that connect with the quilts she keeps in an old trunk. *Hattie's Story* features a family of abolitionists in Illinois. Their home is a stop on the Underground Railroad and they face danger and discovery. In *Ida Lou's Story,* the family deals with the tensions of World War I. These books describe family struggles during various periods in history.

1. Hattie's Story ◆ 2000
2. Ellen's Story ◆ 2000
3. Daniel's Story ◆ 2001
4. Ida Lou's Story ◆ 2001

AMERICAN SISTERS

Lawlor, Laurie
MINSTREL ◆ GRADES 4–6 ◆ A/R
HISTORICAL | REAL LIFE

These books feature intrepid female characters in dramatic historical situations. In 1852, Harriet Scott and her family journey to Oregon Territory. Harriet, nicknamed Duck, has seven sisters and three brothers. With so many siblings, Harriet really wants her father's attention and approval. In *Voyage to a Free Land,* the date is 1630. Abigail and Hannah Garrett travel across the Atlantic to escape religious persecution in England. This series should appeal to the fans of the Dear America books.

1. West Along the Wagon Road, 1852 ◆ 2000
2. A Titanic Journey Across the Sea, 1912 ◆ 2000
3. Voyage to a Free Land, 1630 ◆ 2001
4. Adventure on the Wilderness Road, 1775 ◆ 2001
5. Crossing the Colorado Rockies, 1864 ◆ 2001
6. Down the Rio Grande, 1829 ◆ 2001
7. Horseback on the Boston Post Road, 1704 ◆ 2002
8. Exploring the Chicago World's Fair, 1893 ◆ 2002
9. Pacific Odyssey to California, 1905 ◆ 2002

AMONG THE . . . *see* Shadow Children

AMY

Hoban, Julia
HARPERCOLLINS ◆ GRADES K–2
FAMILY LIFE | REAL LIFE

In the four books in this series, Amy enjoys her everyday activities in each season. In spring, Amy and Mommy go out in the rain to pick up Daddy. When summer comes, Amy enjoys warm-weather activities. In the fall, Amy watches the wind tug at balloons and blow leaves off the trees. When it snows, Amy makes a snowman, with the help of Daddy and Mommy.

1. Amy Loves the Sun ◆ 1988
2. Amy Loves the Wind ◆ 1988
3. Amy Loves the Rain ◆ 1989
4. Amy Loves the Snow ◆ 1989

AMY AND LAURA

Sachs, Marilyn

DOUBLEDAY ◆ GRADES 4–6

FAMILY LIFE | REAL LIFE

Amy and her older sister Laura struggle to adjust to their new neighborhood in the Bronx community of New York during the 1930s. The girls deal with more difficulties when their mother is seriously injured in an automobile accident and must be hospitalized for months. Aunt Minnie comes to live with the family and take care of the girls. It is the strength of the family that pulls the girls through these trials and all the awkward times of early adolescence in these touching stories. The books were reissued in 2001.

1. Amy Moves In ◆ 1964
2. Laura's Luck ◆ 1965
3. Amy and Laura ◆ 1966

AMY HODGEPODGE

Wayans, Kim, and Kevin Knotts

GROSSET & DUNLAP ◆ GRADES 4–6 ◆ A/R

REAL LIFE

Amy is apprehensive about attending public school. For one thing, she has been home schooled and she is worried about making friends and fitting in. Also, she is from a racially mixed family—part Asian, part Caucasian, part African American. At her new school, she is included in the talent show and earns an affectionate nickname—Amy Hodgepodge.

1. All Mixed Up! ◆ 2008
2. Happy Birthday to Me ◆ 2008
3. Lost and Found ◆ 2008
4. Playing Games ◆ 2008
5. The Secret's Out ◆ 2009
6. Digging Up Trouble ◆ 2009

ANASTASIA KRUPNIK

Lowry, Lois

HOUGHTON MIFFLIN ◆ GRADES 4–6 ◆ A/R

FAMILY LIFE | HUMOR

This series chronicles the life of Anastasia Krupnik beginning at age 10. Each episodic chapter relates an amusing incident in the life of this young girl as she deals with the ups and downs of growing up. Her father, an English professor, and her mother, an artist, are always supportive as she adjusts to a new brother in the first book and to a move from the city to the Boston suburbs in the second. Anastasia takes on a challenging first job in *Anastasia at Your Service;* a science fair project goes awry in *Anastasia, Ask Your Analyst;* and her parents go away in *Anastasia on Her Own.* This is a humorous series that portrays a warm and loving family. There is a related series about Anastasia's brother, Sam.

1. Anastasia Krupnik ◆ 1979
2. Anastasia Again! ◆ 1981
3. Anastasia at Your Service ◆ 1982
4. Anastasia, Ask Your Analyst ◆ 1984
5. Anastasia on Her Own ◆ 1985
6. Anastasia Has the Answers ◆ 1986
7. Anastasia's Chosen Career ◆ 1987
8. Anastasia at This Address ◆ 1991
9. Anastasia, Absolutely ◆ 1996

ANATOLE

Titus, Eve

MCGRAW-HILL ◆ **GRADES K–2** ◆ **A/R**

ANIMAL FANTASY

In all of France, there is no braver mouse than Anatole, whose deeds are recounted in these ten adventures. Tired of hunting in people's homes for food, Anatole devises a plan. He travels in secret each night to the cheese factory of M'sieu Duval and begins the work of improving his cheeses. Not only do Duval's cheeses become the finest in France, but Anatole, who prefers to remain unknown, acquires a reputation as a cheese connoisseur. He befriends a cat named Gaston, travels to Italy, and develops his musical talents. Without a doubt, he is a mouse *magnifique*!

1. Anatole ◆ 1956
2. Anatole and the Cat ◆ 1957
3. Anatole and the Robot ◆ 1960
4. Anatole over Paris ◆ 1961
5. Anatole and the Poodle ◆ 1965
6. Anatole and the Piano ◆ 1966
7. Anatole and the Thirty Thieves ◆ 1969
8. Anatole and the Toyshop ◆ 1970
9. Anatole in Italy ◆ 1973
10. Anatole and the Pied Piper ◆ 1979

ANDREW LOST

Greenburg, J. C.

RANDOM HOUSE ◆ **GRADES 2–4** ◆ **A/R**

FANTASY | **HUMOR**

Andrew thinks his new invention is amazing until he and his cousin Judy are shrunk down to microscopic size. Landing on the dog, they are taken to ordinary places that are now extraordinary. They end up in the garden, in the kitchen, and even in the bathroom. They finally get unshrunk only to activate another wacky invention.

1. Andrew Lost on the Dog ◆ 2002
2. Andrew Lost in the Bathroom ◆ 2002
3. Andrew Lost in the Kitchen ◆ 2002
4. Andrew Lost in the Garden ◆ 2003
5. Andrew Lost Under Water ◆ 2003
6. Andrew Lost in the Whale ◆ 2003
7. Andrew Lost on the Reef ◆ 2004
8. Andrew Lost in the Deep ◆ 2004
9. Andrew Lost in Time ◆ 2004
10. Andrew Lost on Earth ◆ 2005
11. Andrew Lost With the Dinosaurs ◆ 2005
12. Andrew Lost in the Ice Age ◆ 2005
13. Andrew Lost in the Garbage ◆ 2006
14. Andrew Lost With the Bats ◆ 2006
15. Andrew Lost in the Jungle ◆ 2007
16. Andrew Lost in Uncle Al ◆ 2007
17. Andrew Lost in the Desert ◆ 2008
18. Andrew Lost With the Frogs ◆ 2008

ANDY RUSSELL

Adler, David A.

HARCOURT ◆ **GRADES 2–5** ◆ **A/R**

FAMILY LIFE | **REAL LIFE**

Andy Russell is in fourth grade and he deals with many everyday problems. He struggles with fractions. He adjusts to the idea that there will be a new baby in his family. He helps a friend in need. Andy is a caring, realistic character. When his friend Tamika needs a new foster home placement, Andy convinces his family to accept her. Readers will relate to the humor and compassion in these books. Fans of Jake Drake will enjoy this series.

1. The Many Troubles of Andy Russell ◆ 1998
2. Andy and Tamika ◆ 1999
3. School Trouble for Andy Russell ◆ 1999

4. Parachuting Hamsters and Andy Russell ◆ 2000
5. Andy Russell, NOT Wanted by the Police ◆ 2001
6. It's a Baby, Andy Russell ◆ 2005

ANDY SHANE

Jacobson, Jennifer Richard

CANDLEWICK ◆ GRADES 1–3 ◆ A/R

REAL LIFE

As this series begins, Andy Shane dislikes school. Dolores Starbuckle is there to interrupt him, tattle on him, and generally be a pest. Andy's Granny Webb helps him deal with Dolores. In subsequent books, Andy and Dolores have a better relationship—but she is still a pest!

1. Andy Shane and the Very Bossy Dolores Starbuckle ◆ 2005
2. Andy Shane and the Pumpkin Trick ◆ 2006
3. Andy Shane and the Queen of Egypt ◆ 2008
4. Andy Shane is NOT in Love ◆ 2008

ANGEL

Delton, Judy

HOUGHTON MIFFLIN ◆ GRADES 3–5 ◆ A/R

FAMILY LIFE | HUMOR

Ever since their father left them, Angel O'Leary has been responsible for keeping her little brother Rags safe. It is a responsibility that weighs heavily on her, and it's not until a classmate invites Angel to the town pool that Mrs. O'Leary realizes that Angel needs to get out of the backyard and have some friends of her own. The next books introduce her mother's boyfriend, a professional clown she met on vacation, and the ensuing wedding is followed by a happy addition to the family.

1. Back Yard Angel ◆ 1983
2. Angel in Charge ◆ 1985
3. Angel's Mother's Boyfriend ◆ 1986
4. Angel's Mother's Wedding ◆ 1987
5. Angel's Mother's Baby ◆ 1989
6. Angel Spreads Her Wings ◆ 1999
7. Angel Bites the Bullet ◆ 2000

ANGEL PARK ALL-STARS

Hughes, Dean

KNOPF ◆ GRADES 4–6 ◆ A/R

REAL LIFE | RECREATION

Early books in this series follow the efforts of three rookie players: Jacob Scott, Kenny Sandoval, and Harlan Sloan. In these books, the boys struggle with developing their playing skills, being accepted by their teammates, and dealing with such problems as slumps and bad grades (which keep Jacob from playing for a while.) In *Championship Game,* the Angel Park Dodgers win the league title. The next book, *Superstar Team,* begins with the team feeling the pressure of being the defending champions. Coach Wilkens provides advice and playing strategies that are incorporated into the narrative. The Dodgers are a coed, multicultural team, and these fast-paced books with lots of baseball plays and action will appeal to sports enthusiasts.

1. Making the Team ◆ 1990
2. Big Base Hit ◆ 1990
3. Winning Streak ◆ 1990
4. What a Catch! ◆ 1990
5. Rookie Star ◆ 1990
6. Pressure Play ◆ 1990
7. Line Drive ◆ 1990
8. Championship Game ◆ 1990
9. Superstar Team ◆ 1991
10. Stroke of Luck ◆ 1991
11. Safe at First ◆ 1991
12. Up to Bat ◆ 1991
13. Play-Off ◆ 1991
14. All Together Now ◆ 1991

ANGEL PARK HOOP STARS

Hughes, Dean

KNOPF ◆ GRADES 4–6 ◆ A/R

REAL LIFE | RECREATION

In *Go to the Hoop!,* Harlan Sloan is the weakest player on the Angel Park Lakers. Coach Donaldson tries to encourage him, but Harlan still can't pull his game together. When he thinks about quitting the team, his friends Kenny and Miles help him realize that before he can play well he must relax and believe in himself. *Nothing but Net* features the arrival of Miles "Tip" Harris, a great player with a bad attitude. Kenny Sandoval helps him adjust to being a team player on the Lakers. Basketball statistics and plays are displayed following the story. Other books feature the concerns of different teammates as they try to play well and cope with insecurities and other problems.

1. Nothing but Net ◆ 1992
2. Point Guard ◆ 1992
3. Go to the Hoop! ◆ 1993
4. On the Line ◆ 1993

ANGEL PARK SOCCER STARS

Hughes, Dean

KNOPF ◆ GRADES 4–6 ◆ A/R

REAL LIFE | RECREATION

Heidi Wells is one of the best players on the coed Angel Park Pride soccer team, where she has to compete with and against boys. She is featured in several of the books in this series, making it attractive to girls as well as to boys. Other books feature other players, including Jacob Scott, who is trying to adjust to playing soccer after being successful at playing baseball; Nate Matheson, who must learn to control his temper in order to play well; and Clayton Lindsay, who has to learn to play as part of a team. Coach Toscano keeps this diverse group working together and succeeding. There is a glossary of soccer terms and some statistics and diagrams of plays at the end of each book.

1. Kickoff Time ◆ 1991
2. Defense! ◆ 1991
3. Victory Goal ◆ 1992
4. Psyched! ◆ 1992
5. Backup Goalie ◆ 1992
6. Total Soccer ◆ 1992
7. Shake Up ◆ 1993
8. Quick Moves ◆ 1993

ANGELA

Robinson, Nancy K.

SCHOLASTIC ◆ GRADES 3–5 ◆ A/R

FAMILY LIFE | HUMOR

Six-year-old Angela is looking forward to Christmas. But all the talk about adopting an orphan is confusing and upsetting. *Oh Honestly, Angela!* is all anyone ever says to her, especially her big sister Tina. Robinson portrays the Steele family children in a believable, honest, and often funny manner.

1. Oh Honestly, Angela! ◆ 1985
2. Angela, Private Citizen ◆ 1989
3. Angela and the Broken Heart ◆ 1991

ANGELA ANACONDA CHAPTER BOOKS

Various authors

SIMON & SCHUSTER ◆ GRADES 2–4 ◆ A/R

HUMOR | REAL LIFE

In Tapwater Springs, Angela Anaconda has two best friends—Gina Lash and Johnny Abatti—and a dog named King. She also has a nemesis/rival/non-friend—Nanette Manoir. Many books in this series describe humorous confrontations between Angela and Nanette. There is even a parallel diary with their conflicting thoughts on events. Related items include a joke book and a newspaper guide. The books are adapted from the TV program scripts.

1. Be Nice, Nanette? (Willson, Sarah) ◆ 2001
2. The Best Dad (McCreary, Laura) ◆ 2001
3. Friends and Foes (Calamari, Barbara) ◆ 2001
4. The Trouble with Teachers (Calamari, Barbara) ◆ 2001
5. The Bidding War (Redeker, Kent) ◆ 2001
6. The Fright Before Christmas (Calamari, Barbara) ◆ 2001
7. Angela Anaconda, C'est Moi (Redeker, Kent) ◆ 2001
8. Dueling Diaries (Redeker, Kent) ◆ 2001
9. Nanette Manoir's Guide to Being Perfect (Ferrone, Joane) ◆ 2001
10. Angela Anaconda, My Notebook (Redeker, Kent) ◆ 2001
11. Green with Envy (Calamari, Barbara) ◆ 2002

ANGELINA BALLERINA

Holabird, Katharine

PLEASANT COMPANY ◆ GRADES K–2 ◆ A/R

ANIMAL FANTASY

Angelina the mouse wants nothing more than to be a ballerina. She practices every day until she finally becomes a famous dancer. When she is not dancing, she has many other adventures. She dreams about going to the fair, but must take along her little cousin Henry. When a new mouse baby joins the family, Angelina finds it's not easy being a big sister. Nevertheless, she and her friends always find ways to have fun—celebrating holidays and putting on special shows, for instance. Companion books include *Angelina's Birthday and Address Book* (1986) and *Angelina's Book and Doll Package* (1989). There are also counting and alphabet books; many of the later books are tied into the TV series.

1. Angelina Ballerina ◆ 1983
2. Angelina and the Princess ◆ 1984
3. Angelina at the Fair ◆ 1985
4. Angelina's Christmas ◆ 1985
5. Angelina on Stage ◆ 1986
6. Angelina and Alice ◆ 1987
7. Angelina's Birthday Surprise ◆ 1989
8. Angelina's Baby Sister ◆ 1991
9. Angelina Ice Skates ◆ 1993
10. Angelina and the Princess ◆ 2000
11. Angelina's Ballet Class ◆ 2001
12. Angelina's Halloween ◆ 2002

13. Angelina and the Rag Doll ◆ 2002
14. Angelina and Henry ◆ 2002
15. Angelina and the Butterfly ◆ 2002
16. Angelina at the Fair ◆ 2002
17. Angelina in the Wings ◆ 2002
18. Angelina Loves ◆ 2002
19. Angelina's Birthday ◆ 2002
20. Christmas in Mouseland ◆ 2003
21. Angelina Ballerina's Invitation to the Ballet ◆ 2003
22. Angelina's Lucky Penny ◆ 2003
23. Angelina, Star of the Show ◆ 2004
24. Angelina and the Rag Doll ◆ 2004
25. Angelina's Dance of Friendship ◆ 2004
26. Angelina's Purse ◆ 2004
27. Angelina's Silver Locket ◆ 2004

ANGELINA BALLERINA: ANGELINA'S DIARY

Holabird, Katharine

GROSSET & DUNLAP ◆ GRADES 1–3 ◆ A/R

ANIMAL FANTASY

This chapter book series is just right for readers who enjoyed the Angelina Ballerina picture books. Angelina enjoys many fun experiences such as going to her first sleepover and going to a birthday party for Princess Sophie. The diary format will add to the appeal.

1. The Best Sleepover Ever! ◆ 2006
2. A Party for the Princess ◆ 2006
3. A Very Special Secret ◆ 2006
4. The Bridesmaid Ballet ◆ 2006

ANGELS UNLIMITED

Dalton, Annie

HARPERCOLLINS ◆ GRADES 4–7 ◆ A/R

FANTASY

Mel Beeby is 13 when she dies and enters the Angel Academy. Mel and her schoolmates, including Orlando and Lola, travel to Earth to help with problems, arriving in different regions and centuries. These kids still party and gossip even as they face dangers from the Opposition. These books first appeared in the early 2000s and were then repackaged under the name Mel Beeby: Agent Angel.

1. Winging It ◆ 2001

2. Losing the Plot ◆ 2001
3. Flying High ◆ 2001
4. Calling the Shots ◆ 2002
5. Fighting Fit ◆ 2003
6. Fogging Over ◆ 2003
7. Making Waves ◆ 2003
8. Budding Star ◆ 2004
9. Keeping It Real ◆ 2005

ANGELWINGS

Napoli, Donna Jo

SIMON & SCHUSTER; ALADDIN ◆ GRADES 3–5 ◆ A/R

FANTASY | VALUES

To earn their wings, young angels are sent out to help others. In the first book, the Little Angel of Friendship helps Patricia, a deaf girl, to adjust to her new home in the city. Other books feature Little Angels of Empathy, Persistence, and Happiness. These books might be useful in a character education program.

1. Friends Everywhere ◆ 1999
2. Little Creatures ◆ 1999
3. On Her Own ◆ 1999
4. One Leap Forward ◆ 1999
5. Give and Take ◆ 2000
6. No Fair! ◆ 2000
7. April Flowers ◆ 2000
8. Playing Games ◆ 2000
9. Lies and Lemons ◆ 2000
10. Running Away ◆ 2000
11. Know-It-All ◆ 2000
12. New Voices ◆ 2000
13. Left Out ◆ 2000
14. Happy Holidays ◆ 2000
15. Partners ◆ 2001
16. Hang in There ◆ 2001

ANIKA SCOTT

Rispin, Karen

TYNDALE HOUSE ◆ GRADES 5–8

ADVENTURE | REAL LIFE | VALUES

When Anika Scott, 12, and her mother, father, and sister Sandy are involved in an adventure, they look to their Christian faith to guide them. On a trip to Africa, Anika finds that the elephants are in danger from poachers. Anika disobeys her parents when she leaves the camp and goes out into the Amboseli Game Preserve on her own. The strength of Anika's beliefs is tested as she faces danger and deals with the recent appearance of her half-brother Rick.

1. The Impossible Lisa Barnes ◆ 1992
2. Tianna the Terrible ◆ 1992
3. Anika's Mountain ◆ 1994
4. Ambush at Amboseli ◆ 1994
5. Sabrina the Schemer ◆ 1994

ANIMAL ARK

Baglio, Ben M.

SCHOLASTIC ◆ GRADES 3–5 ◆ A/R

REAL LIFE

Mandy's parents are veterinarians, and she sometimes helps out at their Animal Ark Veterinary Hospital. Her interest in animals makes her useful around the neighborhood, too. Along with her friend James, Mandy tries to find homes for stray kittens and puppies, protects a show pony, and even rescues an injured mother hedgehog and her babies. Readers who enjoy animal stories will like the additional information about veterinary practices contained in these books. They will also like reading about a character who is actively involved in helping others.

1. Kittens in the Kitchen ◆ 1994
2. Pony on the Porch ◆ 1994
3. Puppies in the Pantry ◆ 1994
4. Goat in the Garden ◆ 1994
5. Hedgehogs in the Hall ◆ 1994
6. Badger in the Basement ◆ 1994
7. Sheepdog in the Snow ◆ 1994
8. Cub in the Cupboard ◆ 1994
9. Piglet in a Playpen ◆ 1994
10. Ponies at the Point ◆ 1994
11. Owl in the Office ◆ 1995
12. Lamb in the Laundry ◆ 1995
13. Kitten in the Cold ◆ 1996
14. Goose on the Loose ◆ 1996
15. Bunnies in the Bathroom ◆ 1996
16. Hamster in a Handbasket ◆ 1996
17. Squirrels in the School ◆ 1996
18. Fox in the Frost ◆ 1996
19. Guinea Pig in the Garage ◆ 1996
20. Shetland in the Shed ◆ 1997
21. Raccoons on the Roof ◆ 1997
22. Dolphin in the Deep ◆ 1997

23. Bears in the Barn ◆ 1997
24. Foals in the Field ◆ 1997
25. Dog at the Door ◆ 1997
26. Horse in the House ◆ 1998
27. Pony in a Package ◆ 1999
28. Puppy in a Puddle ◆ 1999
29. Tabby in the Tub ◆ 1999
30. Pup at the Palace ◆ 2000
31. Mare in the Meadow ◆ 2000
32. Cats at the Campground ◆ 2001
33. Hound at the Hospital ◆ 2001
34. Terrier in the Tinsel ◆ 2003
35. Hamster in the Holly ◆ 2003
36. Husky in a Hut ◆ 2003
37. Polar Bears on the Path ◆ 2005
38. Labrador on the Lawn ◆ 2005
39. Siamese in the Sun ◆ 2005
40. Racehorse in the Rain ◆ 2005
41. Kitten in the Candy Corn ◆ 2005
42. Colt on Christmas Eve ◆ 2005
43. Collie with a Card ◆ 2005
44. Bunny in a Basket ◆ 2005
45. Beagle in a Backpack ◆ 2005
46. Leopard at the Lodge ◆ 2007
47. Husky with a Heart ◆ 2007
48. Spaniel in a Stocking ◆ 2007
49. Mustang in the Mist ◆ 2007

ANIMAL ARK HAUNTINGS

Baglio, Ben M.
SCHOLASTIC ◆ GRADES 3–5 ◆ A/R
MYSTERY | REAL LIFE

Mandy and her best friend James confront unusual, mysterious situations. For example, the jockeys at Folan's Racing Stables believe the stables are haunted by a ghostly stallion.

1. Stallion in the Storm ◆ 2001
2. Cat in the Crypt ◆ 2002
3. Dog in the Dungeon ◆ 2002
4. Colt in the Cave ◆ 2002
5. Foal in the Fog ◆ 2003
6. Hound on the Heath ◆ 2003
7. Wolf at the Window ◆ 2003
8. Cats in the Castle ◆ 2003
9. Deer in the Darkness ◆ 2003

ANIMAL ARK PETS

Baglio, Ben M.

SCHOLASTIC ◆ GRADES 3–5

REAL LIFE

Mandy and James continue their adventures with animals.

1. Puppy Puzzle ◆ 1999
2. Kitten Crowd ◆ 1999
3. Rabbit Race ◆ 1999
4. Hamster Hotel ◆ 1999
5. Mouse Magic ◆ 1999
6. Chick Challenge ◆ 1999
7. Pony Parade ◆ 1999
8. Guinea Pig Gang ◆ 1999
9. Gerbil Genius ◆ 2000
10. Duckling Diary ◆ 2000
11. Lamb Lessons ◆ 2000
12. Doggy Dare ◆ 2000
13. Cat Crazy ◆ 2000
14. Ferret Fun ◆ 2000
15. Bunny Bonanza ◆ 2001
16. Frog Friends ◆ 2001
17. Pets' Party ◆ 2001

ANIMAL EMERGENCY

Costello, Emily

AVON/CAMELOT ◆ GRADES 2–4 ◆ A/R

REAL LIFE

Stella Sullivan, 9, helps her veterinarian aunt to care for many needy animals. A wounded mountain lion, a missing kitten, and an abused bear cub are among the animals they help. In one book, there is a forest fire near their Montana home and Stella's puppy may be in danger.

1. Abandoned Puppy ◆ 1999
2. Ducks in Danger ◆ 1999
3. Bad Luck Lion ◆ 1999
4. Runaway Wolf Pups ◆ 1999
5. Rabbit Rescue ◆ 2000
6. Lost Kitten ◆ 2000
7. Hit-and-Run Retriever ◆ 2000
8. Frightened Fawn ◆ 2000
9. Pony in Trouble ◆ 2000
10. Lonely Lamb ◆ 2000

ANIMAL INN

Vail, Virginia

SCHOLASTIC ◆ GRADES 3–6

REAL LIFE

Val Taylor is in eighth grade. She wants to be a veterinarian and she helps her dad at his clinic, Animal Inn. In the first book, a horse that is going blind is to be put to sleep. Val intervenes and saves the horse. In a later book, she tries to earn money for an operation for the horse. Each book deals with injured animals or issues such as animal abuse.

1. Pets Are for Keeps ◆ 1986
2. A Kid's Best Friend ◆ 1986
3. Monkey Business ◆ 1987
4. Scaredy Cat ◆ 1987
5. Adopt-a-Pet ◆ 1987
6. All the Way Home ◆ 1987
7. The Pet Makeover ◆ 1990
8. Petnapped! ◆ 1990
9. One Dog Too Many ◆ 1990
10. Parrot Fever ◆ 1990
11. Oh, Deer! ◆ 1990
12. Gift Horse ◆ 1991

ANIMORPHS

Applegate, K. A.

SCHOLASTIC ◆ GRADES 4–8 ◆ A/R

ADVENTURE | SCIENCE FICTION

This fast-paced series involves the Yeerk—who have infected the brains of humans to control them—and the Animorphs, who have been given special powers by a dying Andalite. A special group of five friends find satisfaction in fighting the evil Yeerk. The Animorphs are able to "thought speak" and morph (for a period of two hours) into any animal they touch. A detailed discussion of the change process will hook readers as will the eye-catching covers. Short sentences plus continuous drama will keep readers involved. An *Animorph* television series and videos helped make this popular.

1. The Invasion ◆ 1996
2. The Visitor ◆ 1996
3. The Encounter ◆ 1996
4. The Message ◆ 1996
5. The Predator ◆ 1996
6. The Capture ◆ 1997
7. The Stranger ◆ 1997

8. The Alien ◆ 1997
9. The Secret ◆ 1997
10. The Android ◆ 1997
11. The Forgotten ◆ 1997
12. The Reaction ◆ 1997
13. The Change ◆ 1997
14. The Unknown ◆ 1998
15. The Escape ◆ 1998
16. The Warning ◆ 1998
17. The Underground ◆ 1998
18. The Decision ◆ 1998
19. The Departure ◆ 1998
20. The Discovery ◆ 1998
21. The Threat ◆ 1998
22. The Solution ◆ 1998
23. The Pretender ◆ 1998
24. The Suspicion ◆ 1998
25. The Extreme ◆ 1999
26. The Attack ◆ 1999
27. The Exposed ◆ 1999
28. The Experiment ◆ 1999
29. The Sickness ◆ 1999
30. The Reunion ◆ 1999
31. The Conspiracy ◆ 1999
32. The Separation ◆ 1999
33. The Illusion ◆ 1999
34. The Prophecy ◆ 1999
35. The Proposal ◆ 1999
36. The Mutation ◆ 1999
37. The Weakness ◆ 2000
38. The Arrival ◆ 2000
39. The Hidden ◆ 2000
40. The Other ◆ 2000
41. The Familiar ◆ 2000
42. The Journey ◆ 2000
43. The Test ◆ 2000
44. The Unexpected ◆ 2000
45. The Revelation ◆ 2000
46. The Deception ◆ 2000
47. The Resistance ◆ 2000
48. The Return ◆ 2000
49. The Diversion ◆ 2001
50. The Ultimate ◆ 2001
51. The Absolute ◆ 2001
52. The Sacrifice ◆ 2001
53. The Answer ◆ 2001
54. The Beginning ◆ 2001

ANIMORPHS: ALTERNAMORPHS

Applegate, K. A.

SCHOLASTIC ◆ GRADES 4–8 ◆ A/R

ADVENTURE | SCIENCE FICTION

Choose your own adventure in these related Animorphs books.

1. The First Journey ◆ 1999
2. The Next Passage ◆ 2000

ANIMORPHS: ANIMORPH CHRONICLES

Applegate, K. A.

SCHOLASTIC ◆ GRADES 4–8 ◆ A/R

ADVENTURE | SCIENCE FICTION

This is a prequel series to the Animorphs. It describes how Elfangor, an Andalite war-prince, gave five young humans the ability to morph into any animal they touch. Readers learn about other adventures of the Andalites.

1. The Andalite Chronicles ◆ 1997
2. The Hork-Bajir Chronicles ◆ 1998
3. Visser ◆ 1999
4. The Ellimist Chronicles ◆ 2000

ANIMORPHS: MEGAMORPHS

Applegate, K. A.

SCHOLASTIC ◆ GRADES 5–8 ◆ A/R

ADVENTURE | SCIENCE FICTION

Animorphs can morph into any animal, present-day or extinct, which can be a challenge if you choose to be a dinosaur. In these books, the Animorphs battle the Yeerk. In the fourth book, a decision is made to undo the creation of the Animorphs by traveling back in time and changing the original decision.

1. The Andalite's Gift ◆ 1997
2. In the Time of Dinosaurs ◆ 1998
3. Elfangor's Secret ◆ 1999
4. Back to Before ◆ 2000

ANNA

Kerr, Judith

BANTAM DOUBLEDAY DELL ◆ GRADES 4–8 ◆ A/R

HISTORICAL

Anna, aged 9, flees Berlin with her family when Hitler is elected. Anna must leave behind most of her possessions, including her beloved pink rabbit. The family travels through Switzerland and France eventually to reach England. These stories of a Jewish refugee family trying to stay together with dignity and pride in the face of anti-Semitism and depression are based on the author's own childhood.

1. When Hitler Stole Pink Rabbit ◆ 1971
2. The Other Way Round ◆ 1975
3. A Small Person Far Away ◆ 1978

ANNABEL ANDREWS

Rogers, Mary

HARPERCOLLINS ◆ GRADES 5–7 ◆ A/R

FANTASY | HUMOR

Annabel wakes up one morning to find she has turned into her mother. Annabel and her mother reverse roles for a day, and each gains a more sympathetic understanding of the other's life. Annabel blunders her way through the day and comes to appreciate her mother's daily trials, while her mother experiences life from her 13-year-old daughter's perspective. In the sequel, *A Billion for Boris,* Annabel and her 15-year-old boyfriend Boris discover a TV set that broadcasts tomorrow's news. And in *Summer Switch* it is brother Ben's turn to switch bodies with his father.

1. Freaky Friday ◆ 1972
2. A Billion for Boris ◆ 1974
3. Summer Switch ◆ 1982

ANNABEL THE ACTRESS

Conford, Ellen

SIMON & SCHUSTER ◆ GRADES 2–4 ◆ A/R

HUMOR | REAL LIFE

Annabel wants to be a star. Until then, she will accept smaller parts like playing a gorilla at a child's birthday party. When she gets a part in a real play, her costar is a drooling dog. Later, she enjoys being in a drama camp production and appearing as an extra in a movie. Annabel faces each situation with panache.

1. Annabel the Actress Starring in Gorilla My Dreams ◆ 1999
2. Annabel the Actress Starring in Just a Little Extra ◆ 2000
3. Annabel the Actress Starring in the Hound of the Barkervilles ◆ 2002
4. Annabel the Actress Starring in Camping It Up ◆ 2004

ANNE SHIRLEY *see* Avonlea

ANNIE AND SNOWBALL

Rylant, Cynthia

SIMON & SCHUSTER ◆ GRADES K–2 ◆ A/R

REAL LIFE

Many readers will be familiar with Annie from her appearances with her cousin Henry in the Henry and Mudge books. Now she has her own series—along with her pet rabbit, Snowball. Annie is still as particular as ever. In the first book, Annie wants everyone at her birthday party to "dress up," meaning party clothes. Henry and his family arrive in costumes. In the second book, Annie and Henry visit the attic at Henry's house to find items to decorate Annie's home, which is next door.

1. Annie and Snowball and the Dress-Up Birthday ◆ 2007
2. Annie and Snowball and the Prettiest House ◆ 2007
3. Annie and Snowball and the Teacup Club ◆ 2008
4. Annie and Snowball and the Pink Surprise ◆ 2008

ANNIE BANANIE

Komaiko, Leah

HARPERCOLLINS ◆ GRADES 2–4 ◆ A/R

REAL LIFE

Libby lives on a boring street with boring friends. She lives with her parents; her grandmother, who is deaf when she wants to be; and her brother Carl, who plays the piano. Her life changes completely when Annie Bananie moves to her street. Annie Bananie has a dog named Boris and wants to be friends with everyone in the neighborhood, including Bonnie, who wants to be a cat, and Nina, who thinks she's a horse. They form a club, and Libby is elected president; but then she's not sure exactly what the club is supposed to do. Annie comes to her rescue, not for the last time. Libby returns the favor when Annie gets in trouble with their eccentric neighbors and they take her to court. The first book about Annie Bananie is a picture book with a rhyming text. Subsequent books are easy chapter books for independent readers.

1. Annie Bananie ◆ 1989

2. Annie Bananie Moves to Barry Avenue ◆ 1996
3. Annie Bananie: Best Friends to the End ◆ 1997
4. Annie Bananie and the People's Court ◆ 1997
5. Annie Bananie and the Pain Sisters ◆ 1998

ANNIE PITTS

DeGroat, Diane

SEASTAR ◆ GRADES 2–4 ◆ A/R

REAL LIFE

Annie wants to be an actress. Being an artichoke in the school play is not what she had in mind. She thinks she should be in a grocery store commercial, but her expectations are not fulfilled. Later, she wants to be a swamp monster in a video project and she auditions to be on a poster for a fast-food restaurant. The short chapters in these books make them a quick read for middle-elementary readers.

1. Annie Pitts, Artichoke ◆ 1992
2. Annie Pitts, Swamp Monster ◆ 1994
3. Annie Pitts, Burger Kid ◆ 2000

ANTHONY ANT

Philpot, Lorna, and Graham Philpot

RANDOM HOUSE ◆ GRADES K–2

ANIMAL FANTASY

An amusing set of interactive picture books. Readers lift the flaps and look for clues as Anthony Ant and his creepy-crawly friends have various adventures.

1. Amazing Anthony Ant ◆ 1994
2. Anthony Ant's Creepy Crawly Party ◆ 1995
3. Hide and Seek with Anthony Ant ◆ 1995
4. Out and About with Anthony Ant ◆ 1995
5. Who's at Home with Anthony Ant? ◆ 1995
6. Anthony Ant's Treasure Hunt ◆ 1996

ANTHONY MONDAY

Bellairs, John

DIAL ◆ GRADES 5–7 ◆ A/R

ADVENTURE | MYSTERY

Fourteen-year-old Anthony and his friend, librarian Miss Eells, search for a treasure rumored to have been hidden by wealthy eccentric Alpheus Winterborn. Anthony follows the clues to the Winterborn mansion and then back to the public library, where he outwits the efforts of another person who is seeking the treasure. In *The Lamp from the Warlock's Tomb,* Miss Eells buys an antique lamp and mysterious events begin to occur. There are strange voices, odd behavior, and an encounter with a ghost. These are suspenseful stories featuring supernatural events and puzzling mysteries.

1. The Treasure of Alpheus Winterborn ◆ 1978
2. The Dark Secret of Weatherend ◆ 1984
3. The Lamp from the Warlock's Tomb ◆ 1988
4. The Mansion in the Mist ◆ 1992

THE ANYBODIES

Bode, N. E.

HARPERCOLLINS ◆ GRADES 5–8 ◆ A/R

FANTASY

Fern Drudger has been growing up with the wrong family. A mistake at the hospital sent her home with the dull, boring Drudgers instead of her magical shape-shifting family. She is reunited with her widowed father and begins an adventure to restore his lost powers. As the series progresses, Fern and her grandmother defeat the evil Blue Queen and Fern discovers she is a Royal Anybody (shape shifter). As in the Series of Unfortunate Events books, there are fast-paced cliffhanging moments along with comments from the author to the reader throughout.

1. The Anybodies ◆ 2004
2. The Nobodies ◆ 2005
3. The Somebodies ◆ 2006

ARABEL AND MORTIMER

Aiken, Joan

HARPERCOLLINS ◆ GRADES 4–6 ◆ A/R

HUMOR

From the moment Arabel's father brings Mortimer, an injured raven, into their home, life for the Jones family becomes one chaotic episode after another. The irrepressible raven does as he pleases, shouting just one word, "Nevermore!" Each episode is more outrageous than the last. Fast-paced wit and humor are complemented by delightful illustrations.

1. Arabel's Raven ◆ 1974
2. Arabel and Mortimer ◆ 1981
3. Mortimer's Cross ◆ 1982
4. Mortimer Says Nothing, and Other Stories ◆ 1985

ARABUS FAMILY SAGA

Collier, James Lincoln, and Christopher Collier
DELL; DELACORTE ◆ GRADES 5–8 ◆ A/R
HISTORICAL

Daniel Arabus struggles to be free during the uncertain times of the Revolutionary War. Daniel's late father was granted freedom for his service to the Continental Army, but unscrupulous men want to deny that freedom to Daniel and his mother. Two related books feature young African American women—Willy Freeman and Carrie—who are involved in the conflicts of the war and their desire for personal freedom. The lives of Daniel and his family intersect with each young woman. Entertaining reading that aptly describes the plight of African Americans during this period.

1. Jump Ship to Freedom ◆ 1981
2. War Comes to Willy Freeman ◆ 1983
3. Who Is Carrie? ◆ 1984

ARAMINTA SPOOKIE

Sage, Angie
HARPERCOLLINS ◆ GRADES 2–4 ◆ A/R
FANTASY

Upset by her Aunt Tabby's plans to sell their Victorian house, Araminta seeks help from Uncle Drac and a couple of ghosts. They succeed in driving away real estate agents but have less luck with the Wizzard family. All turns out well when the Wizzards accept Aunt Tabby's invitation to move in. In subsequent books, Araminta and her friend Wanda Wizzard investigate various unexpected and mildly spooky happenings.

1. My Haunted House ◆ 2006
2. The Sword in the Grotto ◆ 2006
3. Frognapped ◆ 2007
4. Vampire Brat ◆ 2007
5. Ghostsitters ◆ 2008

THE ARCHIVES OF ANTHROPOS

White, John

INTERVARSITY ◆ GRADES 4–8 ◆ A/R

FANTASY

The strange land of Anthropos is the setting for much of the action of these stories. Cousins Mary, Wesley, Lisa, and Kurt magically travel to Anthropos—a land of kings, sorcerers, and magic—to assist in the High Emperor's fight against evil. This series is modeled after the Chronicles of Narnia series and will appeal to children who enjoy allegorical fantasy stories.

1. The Tower of Geburah ◆ 1978
2. The Iron Sceptre ◆ 1981
3. The Sword Bearer ◆ 1986
4. Gaal the Conqueror ◆ 1989
5. Quest for the King ◆ 1995
6. The Dark Lord's Demise ◆ 2001

ARE YOU AFRAID OF THE DARK?

Various authors

MINSTREL/POCKET BOOKS ◆ GRADES 5–8

HORROR

Based on the Nickelodeon television series, these books are similar to Goosebumps and other books in the scary-stories genre. In one book, Duncan Evans is given three wishes and finds that the adage "be careful what you wish for" is very true. Another book features Glynis Barrons, who makes a rash statement that she lives to regret. There are sinister statues, ghost riders, secret mirrors, and a virtual nightmare. This is sure to be a hit with fans of horror books.

1. The Tale of the Sinister Statues (Peel, John) ◆ 1995
2. The Tale of Cutter's Treasure (Seidman, David L.) ◆ 1995
3. The Tale of the Restless House (Peel, John) ◆ 1995
4. The Tale of the Nightly Neighbors (MacHale, D. J., and Kathleen Derby) ◆ 1995
5. The Tale of the Secret Mirror (Strickland, Brad) ◆ 1995
6. The Tale of the Phantom School Bus (Strickland, Brad) ◆ 1996
7. The Tale of the Ghost Riders (Vornholt, John) ◆ 1996
8. The Tale of the Deadly Diary (Strickland, Brad) ◆ 1996
9. The Tale of the Virtual Nightmare (Pedersen, Ted) ◆ 1996
10. The Tale of the Curious Cat (Gallagher, Diana G.) ◆ 1996

11. The Tale of the Zero Hour (Peel, John) ◆ 1997
12. The Tale of the Shimmering Shell (Weiss, David Cody, and Bobbi J. G. Weiss) ◆ 1997
13. The Tale of the Three Wishes (Peel, John) ◆ 1997
14. The Tale of the Campfire Vampires (Emery, Clayton) ◆ 1997
15. The Tale of the Bad-Tempered Ghost (Mitchell, V. E.) ◆ 1997
16. The Tale of the Souvenir Shop (Cohen, Alice E.) ◆ 1997
17. The Tale of the Ghost Cruise (Weiss, David Cody, and Bobbi J. G. Weiss) ◆ 1998
18. The Tale of the Pulsating Gate (Gallagher, Diana G.) ◆ 1998
19. The Tale of the Stalking Shadow (Weiss, Bobbi J. G., and David Cody Weiss) ◆ 1998
20. The Tale of the Egyptian Mummies (Mitchell, Mark) ◆ 1998
21. The Tale of the Terrible Toys (Byers, Richard Lee) ◆ 1998
22. The Tale of the Mogul Monster (Weiss, David Cody, and Bobbi J. G. Weiss) ◆ 1998
23. The Tale of the Horrifying Hockey Team (Rodriguez, K. S.) ◆ 1999

ARNIE

Carlson, Nancy L.
VIKING ◆ GRADES K–2
ANIMAL FANTASY

Arnie is a little cat who has his fears and problems. He interacts with his friends, other cats, and some dogs and rabbits and learns to get along while still being his own "person." When he becomes part of a skateboarding gang, the "cool" kid skates down a steep hill and dares the others to do it. Arnie makes the sensible choice, and the rest of the kids go along with him. Away at summer camp, Arnie is miserable at first because he doesn't know anyone and a kid in his cabin likes to play tricks. When they go on a hike, he holds a snake and decides nature is fun. Together, he and the other kids play a trick on their counselor. These are easy picture books with plenty of encouragement for solving peer problems.

1. Arnie and the Stolen Markers ◆ 1987
2. Arnie Goes to Camp ◆ 1988
3. Arnie and the New Kid ◆ 1990
4. Arnie and the Skateboard Gang ◆ 1995

ARNOLD *see* Hey Arnold!

AROUND THE WORLD IN 80 MYSTERIES
see Carole Marsh Mysteries: Around the World in 80 Mysteries

ARTEMIS FOWL

Colfer, Eoin
MIRAMAX/HYPERION ◆ GRADES 5–8 ◆ A/R
FANTASY

Artemis Fowl, 12, comes from a criminal family, so his larcenous talents are not surprising. He captures an elf and demands a ransom only to be confronted by the fairy police force. Later, Artemis takes action to find his father but he needs help from the fairies. Once his father is home, Artemis commits to a life without crime . . . after one more caper. A graphic novel version of the first book was published in 2007.

1. Artemis Fowl ◆ 2001
2. The Arctic Incident ◆ 2002
3. The Eternity Code ◆ 2003
4. The Opal Deception ◆ 2005
5. The Lost Colony ◆ 2006
6. The Time Paradox ◆ 2008

ARTHUR

Brown, Marc
LITTLE, BROWN ◆ GRADES K–3 ◆ A/R
ANIMAL FANTASY | FAMILY LIFE

Marc Brown's Arthur series is well known, complete with a TV series, videotapes, interactive stories on computer CDs, a fan club, a Web site, and, of course books! Arthur is an aardvark who puts up with his sister, D.W. (who has her own series), deals with his parents, and has fun with his friends at home and at school. Readers will identify with Arthur's everyday trials and tribulations. A 25th-anniversary edition of *Arthur's Nose* was published in 2001.

1. Arthur's Nose ◆ 1976
2. Arthur's Eyes ◆ 1979
3. Arthur's Valentine ◆ 1980
4. Arthur Goes to Camp ◆ 1982
5. Arthur's Halloween ◆ 1982
6. Arthur's April Fool ◆ 1983
7. Arthur's Thanksgiving ◆ 1983
8. Arthur's Christmas ◆ 1984
9. Arthur's Tooth ◆ 1985
10. Arthur's Teacher Trouble ◆ 1986
11. Arthur's Baby ◆ 1987
12. Arthur's Birthday ◆ 1989
13. Arthur's Pet Business ◆ 1990
14. Arthur Meets the President ◆ 1991

15. Arthur Babysits ◆ 1992
16. Arthur's New Puppy ◆ 1993
17. Arthur's Chicken Pox ◆ 1994
18. Arthur's First Sleepover ◆ 1994
19. Arthur's TV Trouble ◆ 1995
20. Arthur's Family Vacation ◆ 1995
21. Arthur and the True Francine ◆ 1996
22. Arthur Writes a Story ◆ 1996
23. Arthur's Computer Disaster ◆ 1997
24. Arthur Lost and Found ◆ 1998
25. Arthur's Underwear ◆ 1999
26. Arthur's Teacher Moves In ◆ 2000
27. Arthur's Perfect Christmas ◆ 2000
28. Arthur, It's Only Rock 'n' Roll ◆ 2002

ARTHUR READERS (RANDOM HOUSE)

1. Arthur's Reading Race ◆ 1995
2. Arthur Tricks the Tooth Fairy ◆ 1997
3. Arthur in a Pickle ◆ 1999
4. Arthur, Clean Your Room ◆ 1999
5. Arthur's Fire Drill ◆ 2000
6. Arthur's First Kiss ◆ 2001
7. Arthur's Hiccups ◆ 2001
8. Arthur's Lost Puppy ◆ 2001
9. Arthur's Back to School Surprise ◆ 2002
10. Arthur and the School Pet ◆ 2003
11. Arthur's Science Fair Trouble ◆ 2003
12. Arthur and the New Kid ◆ 2004

ARTHUR'S ADVENTURES (L,B KIDS)

1. Arthur's Heart Mix-Up ◆ 2004
2. Arthur's Jelly Beans ◆ 2004
3. Arthur's Birthday Surprise ◆ 2004
4. Arthur's Homework ◆ 2004
5. Arthur's Off to School ◆ 2004
6. Arthur's Mystery Babysitter ◆ 2004
7. Arthur Tells a Story ◆ 2005
8. Arthur Helps Out ◆ 2005
9. Arthur and the Big Snow ◆ 2005
10. Arthur and the Dog Show ◆ 2006
11. Arthur to the Rescue ◆ 2006
12. Arthur Jumps Into Fall ◆ 2006
13. Arthur's Tree House ◆ 2007

ARTHUR: POSTCARDS FROM BUSTER *see*
Postcards from Buster

ARTHUR CHAPTER BOOKS

Krensky, Stephen

LITTLE, BROWN ◆ GRADES 3–6 ◆ A/R

ANIMAL FANTASY | FAMILY LIFE

Marc Brown's Arthur books have continued with this series for the intermediate chapter book reader. Each book has some kind of dilemma or mystery. These books, based on teleplays from the TV program, have a text by Stephen Krensky but feature all the popular Arthur characters, including Arthur, his sister D.W., his friends Buster and Francine, and his teacher, Mr. Ratburn.

1. Arthur's Mystery Envelope ◆ 1998
2. Arthur and the Scare-Your-Pants-Off Club ◆ 1998
3. Arthur Makes the Team ◆ 1998
4. Arthur and the Crunch Cereal Contest ◆ 1998
5. Arthur Accused! ◆ 1998
6. Locked in the Library ◆ 1998
7. Buster's Dino Dilemma ◆ 1998
8. The Mystery of the Stolen Bike ◆ 1998
9. Arthur and the Lost Diary ◆ 1998
10. Who's in Love with Arthur? ◆ 1998
11. Arthur Rocks with BINKY ◆ 1998
12. Arthur and the Popularity Test ◆ 1998
13. King Arthur ◆ 1998
14. Francine, Believe It or Not ◆ 1999
15. Arthur and the Cootie-Catcher ◆ 1999
16. Buster Makes the Grade ◆ 1999
17. Muffy's Secret Admirer ◆ 1999
18. Arthur and the Poetry Contest ◆ 1999
19. Buster Baxter, Cat Saver ◆ 2000
20. Arthur and the Big Blow-Up ◆ 2000
21. Arthur and the Perfect Brother ◆ 2000
22. Francine the Superstar ◆ 2000
23. Buster's New Friend ◆ 2000
24. Binky Rules ◆ 2000
25. Arthur and the Double Dare ◆ 2002
26. Arthur and the No-Brainer ◆ 2002
27. Arthur and the Comet Crisis ◆ 2002
28. Arthur and the 1,001 Dads ◆ 2003
29. Arthur Plays the Blues ◆ 2003
30. Arthur and the Bad-Luck Brain ◆ 2003
31. Arthur Loses His Marbles ◆ 2004
32. Arthur and the Nerves of Steal ◆ 2004
33. Arthur and the World Record ◆ 2005

ARTHUR CHAPTER BOOKS: GOOD SPORTS

Krensky, Stephen

LITTLE, BROWN ◆ GRADES 3–6 ◆ A/R

ANIMAL FANTASY | FAMILY LIFE | RECREATION

Arthur and the gang participate in sports including baseball, football, running, and basketball. In the sixth book, Arthur has been writing to his penpal about his basketball talent. When the penpal comes to visit, Arthur is on the spot. These stories connect to the popular TV programs on PBS.

1. Arthur and the Race to Read ◆ 2001
2. Arthur and the Seventh-Inning Stretcher ◆ 2001
3. Arthur and the Recess Rookie ◆ 2001
4. Arthur and the Best Coach Ever ◆ 2001
5. Arthur and the Goalie Ghost ◆ 2001
6. Arthur and the Pen-Pal Playoff ◆ 2001

ARTHUR THE CHIMPANZEE

Hoban, Lillian

HARPERCOLLINS ◆ GRADES K–2 ◆ A/R

ANIMAL FANTASY

Arthur the chimpanzee lives with his parents and his younger sister Violet. In this series of easy-to-read books, he has many experiences that will be familiar to young readers. He goes camping, celebrates holidays (Christmas, Halloween, Valentine's Day) and loses a tooth. In one book, he learns about school bus safety and gets a surprise in his lunch box. Large print and lots of white space make this a good choice for beginning readers.

1. Arthur's Christmas Cookies ◆ 1972
2. Arthur's Honey Bear ◆ 1974
3. Arthur's Pen Pal ◆ 1976
4. Arthur's Prize Reader ◆ 1978
5. Arthur's Funny Money ◆ 1981
6. Arthur's Halloween Costume ◆ 1984
7. Arthur's Loose Tooth ◆ 1985
8. Arthur's Great Big Valentine ◆ 1989
9. Arthur's Camp Out ◆ 1993
10. Arthur's Back to School Days ◆ 1996
11. Arthur's Birthday Party ◆ 1999

ARTHUR THE KID

Coren, Alan

LITTLE, BROWN; ROBSON BOOKS ◆ GRADES 3–5

HISTORICAL | HUMOR

Ten-year-old Arthur parodies the adventures—or misadventures—of such personages as the Lone Ranger, Custer, Sherlock, Billy the Kid, Buffalo Bill, and a Klondike gold miner in these funny historical novels.

1. Arthur the Kid ◆ 1977
2. Arthur's Last Stand ◆ 1977
3. Railroad Arthur ◆ 1977
4. Buffalo Arthur ◆ 1978
5. Lone Arthur ◆ 1978
6. Klondike Arthur ◆ 1979
7. Arthur and the Great Detective ◆ 1980
8. Arthur and the Purple Panic ◆ 1981
9. Arthur Versus the Rest ◆ 1985
10. Arthur and the Bellybutton Diamond ◆ 2003

ASTROKIDS

Elmer, Robert

BETHANY HOUSE ◆ GRADES 3–5 ◆ A/R

SCIENCE FICTION | VALUES

CLEO-7 is a space station orbiting the moon. The AstroKids live there and enjoy space travel and adventures. They rely on their faith to deal with problems, like the arrival of a famous star who wants DeeBee to be in her show . . . but not the other kids.

1. The Great Galaxy Goof ◆ 2000
2. The Zero-G Headache ◆ 2000
3. Wired Wonder Woof ◆ 2001
4. Miko's Muzzy Mess ◆ 2001
5. About-Face Space Race ◆ 2001
6. The Cosmic Camp Caper ◆ 2001
7. The Super-Duper Blooper ◆ 2002
8. AstroBall Free-4-All ◆ 2002
9. Mid-Air Zillionaire ◆ 2002
10. Tow-Away Stowaway ◆ 2002

ASTROSAURS

Cole, Steve

ALADDIN ◆ GRADES 3–5 ◆ A/R

FANTASY

Dinosaurs are not extinct. They survived and travel through space fighting evil. In *Riddle of the Raptors,* Teggs and the crew of the DSS Sauropod are bringing fellow plant-eating athletes to the Great Dinosaur Games. Meat-eating raptors (who hope to win at the games) capture two athletes and the race is on. The action-filled plot and numerous illustrations will attract reluctant readers.

1. Riddle of the Raptors ◆ 2006
2. The Hatching Horror ◆ 2006
3. The Seas of Doom ◆ 2006
4. The Mind-Swap Menace ◆ 2007

ATOMIC BETTY

Various authors

GROSSET & DUNLAP ◆ GRADES 4–6

SCIENCE FICTION

Betty is a Galactic Guardian working for peace across the galaxy. Her main enemy is the Supreme Overlord Maximus I.Q. Betty's intergalactic crew includes her pilot, Sparky, and a robot, X-5. In the second book, Maximus I.Q. wants to improve villainy by opening a School for Super Villains.

1. Supreme Overlord Penelope (West, Tracey) ◆ 2005
2. Maximus's School for Villains (West, Tracey) ◆ 2006
3. Halloween Invasion (Bryant, Megan E.) ◆ 2007

ATTOLIA

Turner, Megan Whelan

HARPERCOLLINS ◆ GRADES 5–10

FANTASY

In an ancient time a talented thief named Gen (Eugenides) is asked to steal a legendary jewel from the queen of Attolia. In exchange Gen will get his freedom. As the series progresses, Gen's right hand is cut off for his theft but he nonetheless falls in love with the queen, and in the third book they are married but Gen must cope with resentment and political intrigue. The first of these well-written and intricately plotted volumes was a Newbery Honor book in 1997.

1. The Thief ◆ 1996
2. The Queen of Attolia ◆ 2000
3. The King of Attolia ◆ 2006

AUNT EATER

Cushman, Doug

HARPERCOLLINS ◆ GRADES K–2 ◆ A/R

ANIMAL FANTASY | MYSTERY

In this series of books for beginning readers, Aunt Eater is an anteater who loves to read and solve mysteries. Each book includes four different mysteries for Aunt Eater to solve, such as the case of the switched bag on the train and the mysterious torn note left in her mailbox. Aunt Eater's adventures involve various friends and neighbors in her community and on her vacations at the Hotel Bathwater.

1. Aunt Eater Loves a Mystery ◆ 1987
2. Aunt Eater's Mystery Vacation ◆ 1992
3. Aunt Eater's Mystery Christmas ◆ 1995
4. Aunt Eater's Mystery Halloween ◆ 1998

AUNT NINA

Brandenberg, Franz

GREENWILLOW ◆ GRADES K–2

FAMILY LIFE | HUMOR

Aunt Nina is young and pretty and lives in a big house with no children of her own. She is visited by her six nieces and nephews, three boys and three girls ranging in age from a toddler to a boy of about ten. At Aunt Nina's house they have a birthday party for Fluffy the cat. When the cat disappears they search for it all over the house, finding treasures and having fun in each room. When they finally find Fluffy, they discover that she has had kittens: six, of course. On another visit, they go through the classic stalling devices to avoid going to sleep and all end up in Aunt Nina's bed. Detailed full-color pictures capture the fun.

1. Aunt Nina and Her Nephews and Nieces ◆ 1984
2. Aunt Nina's Visit ◆ 1984
3. Aunt Nina, Good Night! ◆ 1989

AUSTIN FAMILY *see* Vicky Austin

AUSTRALIAN CHILDREN

Lester, Alison

HOUGHTON MIFFLIN ◆ **GRADES K–2**

REAL LIFE

Clive, Tessa, Rosie, Frank, Ernie, Nicky, and Celeste are friends, but each has his or her way of doing things. These books celebrate their individuality. For example, they all laugh, but at different things. They earn money doing different jobs. Their differences make them unique and interesting. These books provide an entertaining way for groups of children to share information about themselves.

1. Clive Eats Alligators ◆ 1986
2. Rosie Sips Spiders ◆ 1989
3. Tessa Snaps Snakes ◆ 1991
4. When Frank Was Four ◆ 1994
5. Celeste Sails to Spain ◆ 1999
6. Ernie Dances to the Didgeridoo ◆ 2001

AVALON 1: WEB OF MAGIC

Roberts, Rachel

SCHOLASTIC; TOR/SEVEN SEAS ◆ **GRADES 4–7** ◆ **A/R**

FANTASY

Three girls—Emily, Kara, and Adriane—explore deep into the woods. There they find a passage to another world. While some who travel through the passage come in peace, others have sinister plans. The girls face trials by earth, water, air, and fire as they confront the evil. The entire series was reissued by Tor/Seven Seas in trade paperback in late 2008 with new manga-style covers and interior illustrations. The first volume was initially published under the authorship of Shelly Roberts.

1. Circles in the Stream ◆ 2001
2. All that Glitters ◆ 2001
3. Cry of the Wolf ◆ 2001
4. Secret of the Unicorn ◆ 2002
5. Spellsinger ◆ 2002
6. Trial by Fire ◆ 2002

AVALON 2: QUEST FOR MAGIC

Roberts, Rachel

CDS BOOKS ◆ **GRADES 4–7** ◆ **A/R**

FANTASY

The adventures continue for the three girls who have found Ravenswood—Emily, Kara, and Adriane. In one book, Adriane faces the Spider Witch that is threatening the woods. In another, Kara finds a mysterious portal. Fans of the Avalon: Web of Magic series may want to continue with these books. The entire series was being reissued by Macmillan in trade paperback in late 2008 with new manga-style covers and interior illustrations.

1. Song of the Unicorns ◆ 2003
2. All's Fairy in Love and War ◆ 2003
3. Ghost Wolf ◆ 2004
4. Heart of Avalon ◆ 2004
5. The Dark Mage ◆ 2004

AVATAR: THE EARTH KINGDOM CHRONICLES

Teitelbaum, Michael

SIMON SPOTLIGHT ◆ GRADES 4–7

FANTASY

Meet the main characters of the popular Nickelodeon cartoon series *Avatar,* including Aang, his earthbending teacher Toph, and Azula and Zuko of the Fire Nation. Each book features a different character, providing readers with plenty of background information about their skills and destiny.

1. The Tale of Aang ◆ 2007
2. The Tale of Azula ◆ 2007
3. The Tale of Toph ◆ 2007
4. The Tale of Sokka ◆ 2007
5. The Tale of Zuko ◆ 2008
6. The Tale of Katara ◆ 2008

AVATAR: THE LAST AIRBENDER

Various authors

SIMON SPOTLIGHT ◆ GRADES 4–7 ◆ A/R

FANTASY

Each of the "scrolls" presented here describes one of the four nations: Water Tribes, Earth Kingdom, Air Nomads, and Fire Nation. Aang is reluctant to accept his role as an airbender, one who can bend all four elements. As he begins his travels, he encounters challenges that lead him to his destiny. Fans of the Nickelodeon cartoon series will enjoy these books that feature Aang and his friends Katara and Sokka as they save the world from war with the Fire Nation.

1. The Lost Scrolls: Water (Teitelbaum, Michael) ◆ 2006
2. The Lost Scrolls: Fire (Mason, Tom, and Danko, Dan) ◆ 2006
3. The Lost Scrolls: Air (Mason, Tom, and Danko, Dan) ◆ 2007
4. The Lost Scrolls: Earth (Teitelbaum, Michael) ◆ 2007

AVATAR GRAPHIC NOVELS

DiMartino, Michael Dante

TOKYOPOP ◆ GRADES 4–7

FANTASY

Vivid illustrations by Bryan Konietzko are a highlight in this cine-manga adaptation of the cartoon series seen on Nickelodeon. Aang and his companions Sokka, Katara, and Toph face threats from the Fire Nation. In Volume 4, the group flies to the island of Kyoshi. While Aang is distracted by the adulation of the people on the island, the Fire Nation attacks.

1. Vol. 1-3: Boxed Set ◆ 2006
2. Vol. 4 ◆ 2007
3. Vol. 5 ◆ 2007
4. Vol. 6 ◆ 2007
5. Vol. 7 ◆ 2008
6. Vol. 8 ◆ 2008

AVATAR (READY TO READ)

Various authors

SIMON SPOTLIGHT ◆ GRADES 2–4

FANTASY

In *Sokka, the Sword Master,* Sokka trains with Piandao, a swordmaster from the Fire Nation. When Piandao discovers that Sokka is from the Water Tribe, he challenges Sokka to a duel. These books feature characters from the popular Nickelodeon cartoon series, including Aang the Avatar, Toph the Earthbender, and Katara the Waterbender, who is Sokka's sister. Younger fans of the cartoons will enjoy these easier readers.

1. Sokka, the Sword Master (Gerstein, Sherry) ◆ 2008
2. Aang's School Days (Teitelbaum, Michael) ◆ 2008
3. Love Potion #8 (Reisner, Molly) ◆ 2008

AVONLEA

Montgomery, Lucy Maud

RANDOM HOUSE ◆ GRADES 5–8 ◆ A/R

FAMILY LIFE │ HISTORICAL │ REAL LIFE

Red-haired, imaginative Anne Shirley is mistakenly sent from an orphanage to live with the Cuthberts, who requested a boy to help on their farm. This series details the results. Montgomery tells Anne's life story from age 11 until well into her married years. Readers watch Anne blossom from an impetuous child into a mature woman, gaining not only physical beauty but a sense of self. Though the setting of these books is small-town Canada in the early 20th century, the themes of maturity, community, and friendship will surely resonate with today's readers. Girls who enjoy imagination and creativity will become fast friends with Anne.

1. Anne of Green Gables ◆ 1908
2. Anne of Avonlea ◆ 1909
3. Chronicles of Avonlea ◆ 1912
4. Anne of the Island ◆ 1915
5. Anne's House of Dreams ◆ 1917
6. Rainbow Valley ◆ 1919
7. Further Chronicles of Avonlea ◆ 1920
8. Rilla of Ingleside ◆ 1921
9. Anne of Windy Poplars ◆ 1936
10. Anne of Ingleside ◆ 1939

BABAR

de Brunhoff, Jean, and Laurent de Brunhoff
HARRY ABRAMS ◆ GRADES K–3 ◆ A/R
ANIMAL FANTASY

An elephant is born in a great forest. When his mother is killed by hunters, he runs away to the big city, where he is befriended by a rich Old Lady who loves elephants. One day, his two little cousins, Arthur and Celeste, run away to the city, and Babar decides to return to the forest with them. Babar has learned so much in the city that he becomes the King of the Elephants, and he and Celeste are married. The rest of the series is about various adventures, both in the forest and on travels. The original books were by Jean de Brunhoff. Laurent de Brunhoff continued the series, beginning with *Babar's Cousin, That Rascal Arthur* in 1948. A related book is *Babar's Yoga for Elephants* (2002).

1. The Story of Babar the Little Elephant ◆ 1933
2. The Travels of Babar ◆ 1934
3. Babar the King ◆ 1934
4. Babar and Zephir ◆ 1937
5. Babar and His Children ◆ 1938
6. Babar and Father Christmas ◆ 1940
7. Babar's Cousin, That Rascal Arthur ◆ 1948
8. Babar's Picnic ◆ 1949
9. Babar's Fair Will Be Opened Next Sunday ◆ 1954
10. Babar and the Professor ◆ 1957
11. Babar's Castle ◆ 1962
12. Babar's French Lessons ◆ 1963

13. Babar Comes to America ◆ 1965
14. Babar's Spanish Lessons ◆ 1965
15. Babar Loses His Crown ◆ 1967
16. Babar's Birthday Surprise ◆ 1970
17. Meet Babar and His Family ◆ 1973
18. Babar and the Wully-Wully ◆ 1975
19. Babar Saves the Day ◆ 1976
20. Babar Learns to Cook ◆ 1978
21. Babar's Mystery ◆ 1978
22. Babar and the Ghost ◆ 1981
23. Babar's ABC ◆ 1983
24. Babar's Book of Color ◆ 1984
25. Babar's Little Girl ◆ 1987
26. Babar's Little Circus Star ◆ 1988
27. Babar's Battle ◆ 1992
28. The Rescue of Babar ◆ 1993
29. Babar and the Succotash Bird ◆ 2000
30. Babar's Counting Book ◆ 2003
31. Babar's Museum of Art ◆ 2003
32. Babar's World Tour ◆ 2005

BABES

Dhami, Narinder
DELACORTE ◆ GRADES 5–7
REAL LIFE

Amber, Jazz, and Gina Dhillon are sisters who live with their father in England. They miss their mother, who died recently. The girls enjoy a lot of freedom and are indulged by their father even though he is distant and busy. They are surprised and a bit put out when their father's sister comes from India to stay with them. Their plan is to find a way to get rid of Auntie—perhaps by marrying her off. In the second book, the sisters become involved with a fading Bollywood movie star. And in the third book, they are looking forward to Auntie's marriage to the head of their school. The Indian heritage of the family adds to the flavor of the books.

1. Bindi Babes ◆ 2004
2. Bollywood Babes ◆ 2005
3. Bhangra Babes ◆ 2006
4. Superstar Babes ◆ 2008

BABY DUCK

Hest, Amy
CANDLEWICK ◆ GRADES K–1 ◆ A/R
ANIMAL FANTASY | FAMILY LIFE

Baby Duck does not like some of the things around her, including the rain, her new eyeglasses, and the new baby. In each gentle story, Grampa helps Baby Duck accept change and inconvenience. He gives her the special attention that youngsters need.

1. In the Rain with Baby Duck ◆ 1995
2. Baby Duck and the Bad Eyeglasses ◆ 1996
3. You're the Boss, Baby Duck ◆ 1997
4. Off to School, Baby Duck! ◆ 1999
5. Baby Duck and the Cozy Blanket ◆ 2002
6. Make the Team, Baby Duck! ◆ 2002
7. Guess Who, Baby Duck! ◆ 2004
8. You Can Swim, Baby Duck ◆ 2005

BABY-SITTERS CLUB

Martin, Ann M.

SCHOLASTIC ◆ GRADES 4–7 ◆ A/R

REAL LIFE

The Baby-Sitters Club of Stoneybrook, Connecticut, is a group of five eighth-grade girls who are best friends and meet three times a week to take calls from parents who need sitters. Hardworking Kristy formed the club and tries to keep everyone in line. Quiet, sensitive Mary Anne is the secretary and sets up appointments. Stacey is the sophisticated one and has a great sense of style because she comes from New York City. The club's meetings are held at Claudia's house because she has a private phone in her room. She is the artistic member of the group and a junk-food addict. Each book in the series focuses on a different girl, and as the series goes on, Dawn moves to California, divorced parents remarry (two of the girls become stepsisters), and the girls deal with problems. Stacey is diabetic, Mary Anne's father won't let her grow up, and they all occasionally have difficulty getting along with the children they babysit or the parents they work for. In every story, they work together to resolve problems with good will and humor.

1. Kristy's Great Idea ◆ 1986
2. Claudia and the Phantom Phone Calls ◆ 1986
3. The Truth About Stacey ◆ 1986
4. Mary Anne Saves the Day ◆ 1987
5. Dawn and the Impossible Three ◆ 1987
6. Kristy's Big Day ◆ 1987
7. Claudia and Mean Janine ◆ 1987
8. Boy-Crazy Stacey ◆ 1987
9. The Ghost at Dawn's House ◆ 1988
10. Logan Likes Mary Anne! ◆ 1988
11. Kristy and the Snobs ◆ 1988
12. Claudia and the New Girl ◆ 1988
13. Good-bye Stacey, Good-bye ◆ 1988

14. Hello, Mallory ◆ 1988
15. Little Miss Stoneybrook . . . and Dawn ◆ 1988
16. Jessi's Secret Language ◆ 1988
17. Mary Anne's Bad Luck Mystery ◆ 1988
18. Stacey's Mistake ◆ 1988
19. Claudia and the Bad Joke ◆ 1988
20. Kristy and the Walking Disaster ◆ 1989
21. Mallory and the Trouble with the Twins ◆ 1989
22. Jessi Ramsey, Pet-Sitter ◆ 1989
23. Dawn on the Coast ◆ 1989
24. Kristy and the Mother's Day Surprise ◆ 1989
25. Mary Anne and the Search for Tigger ◆ 1989
26. Claudia and the Sad Good-bye ◆ 1989
27. Jessi and the Superbrat ◆ 1989
28. Welcome Back, Stacey! ◆ 1989
29. Mallory and the Secret Diary ◆ 1989
30. Mary Anne and the Great Romance ◆ 1990
31. Dawn's Wicked Stepsister ◆ 1990
32. Kristy and the Secret of Susan ◆ 1990
33. Claudia and the Great Search ◆ 1990
34. Mary Anne and Too Many Boys ◆ 1990
35. Stacey and the Mystery of Stoneybrook ◆ 1990
36. Jessi's Baby-Sitter ◆ 1990
37. Dawn and the Older Boy ◆ 1990
38. Kristy's Mystery Admirer ◆ 1990
39. Poor Mallory! ◆ 1990
40. Claudia and the Middle School Mystery ◆ 1991
41. Mary Anne vs. Logan ◆ 1991
42. Jessi and the Dance School Phantom ◆ 1991
43. Stacey's Emergency ◆ 1991
44. Dawn and the Big Sleepover ◆ 1991
45. Kristy and the Baby Parade ◆ 1991
46. Mary Anne Misses Logan ◆ 1991
47. Mallory on Strike ◆ 1991
48. Jessi's Wish ◆ 1991
49. Claudia and the Genius of Elm Street ◆ 1991
50. Dawn's Big Date ◆ 1992
51. Stacey's Ex-Best Friend ◆ 1992
52. Mary Anne + 2 Many Babies ◆ 1992
53. Kristy for President ◆ 1992
54. Mallory and the Dream Horse ◆ 1992
55. Jessi's Gold Medal ◆ 1992
56. Keep Out, Claudia! ◆ 1992
57. Dawn Saves the Planet ◆ 1992
58. Stacey's Choice ◆ 1992
59. Mallory Hates Boys (and Gym) ◆ 1992
60. Mary Anne's Makeover ◆ 1993
61. Jessi and the Awful Secret ◆ 1993
62. Kristy and the Worst Kid Ever ◆ 1993

63. Claudia's—Freind—Friend ◆ 1993
64. Dawn's Family Feud ◆ 1993
65. Stacey's Big Crush ◆ 1993
66. Maid Mary Anne ◆ 1993
67. Dawn's Big Move ◆ 1993
68. Jessi and the Bad Baby-Sitter ◆ 1993
69. Get Well Soon, Mallory! ◆ 1993
70. Stacey and the Cheerleaders ◆ 1993
71. Claudia and the Perfect Boy ◆ 1994
72. Dawn and the We Love Kids Club ◆ 1994
73. Mary Anne and Miss Priss ◆ 1994
74. Kristy and the Copycat ◆ 1994
75. Jessi's Horrible Prank ◆ 1994
76. Stacey's Lie ◆ 1994
77. Dawn and Whitney, Friends Forever ◆ 1994
78. Claudia and Crazy Peaches ◆ 1994
79. Mary Anne Breaks the Rules ◆ 1994
80. Mallory Pike, #1 Fan ◆ 1994
81. Kristy and Mr. Mom ◆ 1995
82. Jessi and the Troublemaker ◆ 1995
83. Stacey vs. the BSC ◆ 1995
84. Dawn and the School Spirit War ◆ 1995
85. Claudia Kishi, Live from WSTO! ◆ 1995
86. Mary Anne and Camp BSC ◆ 1995
87. Stacey and the Bad Girl ◆ 1995
88. Farewell, Dawn ◆ 1995
89. Kristy and the Dirty Diapers ◆ 1995
90. Welcome to BSC, Abby ◆ 1995
91. Claudia and the First Thanksgiving ◆ 1995
92. Mallory's Christmas Wish ◆ 1995
93. Mary Anne and the Memory Garden ◆ 1996
94. Stacey McGill, Super Sitter ◆ 1996
95. Kristy + Bart = ? ◆ 1996
96. Abby's Lucky Thirteen ◆ 1996
97. Claudia and the World's Cutest Baby ◆ 1996
98. Dawn and Too Many Baby-Sitters ◆ 1996
99. Stacey's Broken Heart ◆ 1996
100. Kristy's Worst Idea ◆ 1996
101. Claudia Kishi, Middle School Dropout ◆ 1996
102. Mary Anne and the Little Princess ◆ 1996
103. Happy Holidays, Jessi ◆ 1996
104. Abby's Twin ◆ 1997
105. Stacey the Math Whiz ◆ 1997
106. Claudia, Queen of the Seventh Grade ◆ 1997
107. Mind Your Own Business, Kristy! ◆ 1997
108. Don't Give Up, Mallory ◆ 1997
109. Mary Anne to the Rescue ◆ 1997
110. Abby the Bad Sport ◆ 1997
111. Stacey's Secret Friend ◆ 1997

112. Kristy and the Sister War ◆ 1997
113. Claudia Makes Up Her Mind ◆ 1997
114. The Secret Life of Mary Anne Spier ◆ 1998
115. Jessi's Big Break ◆ 1998
116. Abby and the Best Kid Ever ◆ 1998
117. Claudia and the Terrible Truth ◆ 1998
118. Kristy Thomas, Dog Trainer ◆ 1998
119. Stacey's Ex-Boyfriend ◆ 1998
120. Mary Anne and the Playground Fight ◆ 1998
121. Abby in Wonderland ◆ 1998
122. Kristy in Charge ◆ 1998
123. Claudia's Big Party ◆ 1998
124. Stacey McGill . . . Matchmaker? ◆ 1998
125. Mary Anne in the Middle ◆ 1998
126. The All-New Mallory Pike ◆ 1999
127. Abby's Un-Valentine ◆ 1999
128. Claudia and the Little Liar ◆ 1999
129. Kristy at Bat ◆ 1999
130. Stacey's Movie ◆ 1999
131. The Fire at Mary Anne's House ◆ 1999

BABY-SITTERS CLUB FRIENDS FOREVER

Martin, Ann M.
SCHOLASTIC ◆ GRADES 4–7 ◆ A/R
REAL LIFE

The girls have more babysitting adventures.

1. Kristy's Big News ◆ 1999
2. Stacey vs. Claudia ◆ 1999
3. Mary Anne's Big Breakup ◆ 1999
4. Claudia and the Friendship Feud ◆ 1999
5. Kristy Power! ◆ 2000
6. Stacey and the Boyfriend Trap ◆ 2000
7. Claudia Gets Her Guy ◆ 2000
8. Mary Anne's Revenge ◆ 2000
9. Kristy and the Kidnapper ◆ 2000
10. Stacey's Problem ◆ 2000
11. Welcome Home, Mary Anne ◆ 2000
12. Claudia and the Disaster Date ◆ 2000

BABY-SITTERS CLUB FRIENDS FOREVER SPECIAL EDITIONS

1. Everything Changes ◆ 1999
2. Graduation Day ◆ 2000

BABY-SITTERS CLUB GRAPHIC NOVELS

Martin, Ann M.

SCHOLASTIC/GRAPHIX ◆ GRADES 4–7 ◆ A/R

REAL LIFE

Adapted from some of the very first Baby-sitters Club books, these graphic novels are a great way to capitalize on the popular series and discuss the graphic novel format. In the first book, Kristy has the idea for the club. Raina Telgemeier illustrated these books and adapted the story.

1. Kristy's Great Idea ◆ 2006
2. The Truth About Stacey ◆ 2006
3. Mary Anne Saves the Day ◆ 2007

BABY-SITTERS CLUB MYSTERIES

Martin, Ann M.

SCHOLASTIC ◆ GRADES 4–7 ◆ A/R

MYSTERY | REAL LIFE

The five girls from Stoneybrook, Connecticut, who formed the Baby-Sitters Club have their own mystery series. Kristy, founder and president of the group, Dawn the Californian, sophisticated Stacey, shy Mary Anne, and artistic Claudia run into mysteries involving empty houses that aren't really empty, missing rings, counterfeit money, and more—mysteries that they try to solve Nancy Drew style.

1. Stacey and the Missing Ring ◆ 1991
2. Beware Dawn! ◆ 1991
3. Mallory and the Ghost Cat ◆ 1992
4. Kristy and the Missing Child ◆ 1992
5. Mary Anne and the Secret in the Attic ◆ 1992
6. The Mystery at Claudia's House ◆ 1992
7. Dawn and the Disappearing Dogs ◆ 1993
8. Jessi and the Jewel Thieves ◆ 1993
9. Kristy and the Haunted Mansion ◆ 1993
10. Stacey and the Mystery Money ◆ 1993
11. Claudia and the Mystery at the Museum ◆ 1993
12. Dawn and the Surfer Ghost ◆ 1993
13. Mary Anne and the Library Mystery ◆ 1994
14. Stacey and the Mystery at the Mall ◆ 1994
15. Kristy and the Vampires ◆ 1994
16. Claudia and the Clue in the Photograph ◆ 1994
17. Dawn and the Halloween Mystery ◆ 1994
18. Stacey and the Mystery at the Empty House ◆ 1994
19. Kristy and the Missing Fortune ◆ 1995
20. Mary Anne and the Zoo Mystery ◆ 1995

21. Claudia and the Recipe for Danger ◆ 1995
22. Stacey and the Haunted Masquerade ◆ 1995
23. Abby and the Secret Society ◆ 1996
24. Mary Anne and the Silent Witness ◆ 1996
25. Kristy and the Middle School Vandal ◆ 1996
26. Dawn Schafer, Undercover Babysitter ◆ 1996
27. Claudia and the Lighthouse Ghost ◆ 1996
28. Abby and the Mystery Baby ◆ 1997
29. Stacey and the Fashion Victim ◆ 1997
30. Kristy and the Mystery Train ◆ 1997
31. Mary Anne and the Music Box Secret ◆ 1997
32. Claudia and the Mystery in the Painting ◆ 1997
33. Stacey and the Stolen Hearts ◆ 1998
34. Mary Anne and the Haunted Bookstore ◆ 1998
35. Abby and the Notorious Neighbor ◆ 1998
36. Kristy and the Cat Burglar ◆ 1998

SUPER MYSTERIES

1. Baby-Sitters' Haunted House ◆ 1995
2. Baby-Sitters Beware ◆ 1995
3. Baby-Sitters' Fright Night ◆ 1996
4. Baby-Sitters' Christmas Chiller ◆ 1997

BABY-SITTERS CLUB PORTRAIT COLLECTION

Martin, Ann M.
SCHOLASTIC ◆ GRADES 4–7 ◆ A/R

REAL LIFE

Vignettes from other books provide insight into the personality and behavior of each girl.

1. Stacey's Book ◆ 1994
2. Claudia's Book ◆ 1995
3. Dawn's Book ◆ 1995
4. Kristy's Book ◆ 1996
5. Mary Anne's Book ◆ 1996
6. Abby's Book ◆ 1997

BABY-SITTERS CLUB SUPER SPECIALS

Martin, Ann M.
SCHOLASTIC ◆ GRADES 4–7 ◆ A/R

REAL LIFE

The Super Specials are about twice as long as the regular Baby-Sitters Club books and deal with events such as weddings or a group visit to see Dawn when she moves to California. The books are narrated by all five girls, taking different chapters in turn. There are also special Super Chillers books.

1. Baby-Sitters on Board! ◆ 1988
2. Baby-Sitters' Summer Vacation ◆ 1989
3. Baby-Sitters' Winter Vacation ◆ 1989
4. Baby-Sitters' Island Adventure ◆ 1990
5. California Girls! ◆ 1990
6. New York, New York! ◆ 1991
7. Snowbound ◆ 1991
8. Baby-Sitters at Shadow Lake ◆ 1992
9. Starring the Baby-Sitters Club ◆ 1992
10. Sea City, Here We Come! ◆ 1993
11. The Baby-Sitters Remember ◆ 1994
12. Here Come the Bridesmaids ◆ 1994
13. Aloha, Baby-Sitters! ◆ 1996
14. BSC in the USA ◆ 1997
15. Baby-Sitters' European Vacation ◆ 1998

BABY-SITTERS LITTLE SISTER

Martin, Ann M.
SCHOLASTIC ◆ GRADES 2–3 ◆ A/R
REAL LIFE

Kristy, of the famous Baby-Sitters Club series, has a little stepsister called Karen who lives with her at weekends. The series is about Karen's life, which occasionally involves Kristy and the other baby-sitters. In a typical book, Karen falls in love with her handsome baby-sitter and thinks he has asked her out on a date, when he really has a date with Kristy. There are holiday stories involving Santa and leprechauns. Karen quarrels and makes up with her brother Andrew and with Kristy and learns to get along with her stepparents.

1. Karen's Witch ◆ 1988
2. Karen's Roller Skates ◆ 1988
3. Karen's Worst Day ◆ 1989
4. Karen's Kittycat Club ◆ 1989
5. Karen's School Picture ◆ 1989
6. Karen's Little Sister ◆ 1989
7. Karen's Birthday ◆ 1990
8. Karen's Haircut ◆ 1990
9. Karen's Sleepover ◆ 1990
10. Karen's Grandmothers ◆ 1990
11. Karen's Prize ◆ 1990
12. Karen's Ghost ◆ 1990

13. Karen's Surprise ◆ 1990
14. Karen's New Year ◆ 1991
15. Karen's in Love ◆ 1991
16. Karen's Goldfish ◆ 1991
17. Karen's Brothers ◆ 1991
18. Karen's Home Run ◆ 1991
19. Karen's Good-bye ◆ 1991
20. Karen's Carnival ◆ 1991
21. Karen's New Teacher ◆ 1991
22. Karen's Little Witch ◆ 1991
23. Karen's Doll ◆ 1991
24. Karen's School Trip ◆ 1992
25. Karen's Pen Pal ◆ 1992
26. Karen's Ducklings ◆ 1992
27. Karen's Big Joke ◆ 1992
28. Karen's Tea Party ◆ 1992
29. Karen's Cartwheel ◆ 1992
30. Karen's Kittens ◆ 1992
31. Karen's Bully ◆ 1992
32. Karen's Pumpkin Patch ◆ 1992
33. Karen's Secret ◆ 1992
34. Karen's Snow Day ◆ 1993
35. Karen's Doll Hospital ◆ 1993
36. Karen's New Friend ◆ 1993
37. Karen's Tuba ◆ 1993
38. Karen's Big Lie ◆ 1993
39. Karen's Wedding ◆ 1993
40. Karen's Newspaper ◆ 1993
41. Karen's School ◆ 1993
42. Karen's Pizza Party ◆ 1993
43. Karen's Toothache ◆ 1993
44. Karen's Big Weekend ◆ 1993
45. Karen's Twin ◆ 1994
46. Karen's Baby-Sitter ◆ 1994
47. Karen's Kite ◆ 1994
48. Karen's Two Families ◆ 1994
49. Karen's Stepmother ◆ 1994
50. Karen's Lucky Penny ◆ 1994
51. Karen's Big Top ◆ 1994
52. Karen's Mermaid ◆ 1994
53. Karen's School Bus ◆ 1994
54. Karen's Candy ◆ 1994
55. Karen's Magician ◆ 1994
56. Karen's Ice Skates ◆ 1994
57. Karen's School Mystery ◆ 1995
58. Karen's Ski Trip ◆ 1995
59. Karen's Leprechaun ◆ 1995
60. Karen's Pony ◆ 1995
61. Karen's Tattletale ◆ 1995

62. Karen's New Bike ◆ 1995
63. Karen's Movie ◆ 1995
64. Karen's Lemonade Stand ◆ 1995
65. Karen's Toys ◆ 1995
66. Karen's Monsters ◆ 1995
67. Karen's Turkey Day ◆ 1995
68. Karen's Angel ◆ 1995
69. Karen's Big Sister ◆ 1996
70. Karen's Granddad ◆ 1996
71. Karen's Island Adventure ◆ 1996
72. Karen's New Puppy ◆ 1996
73. Karen's Dinosaur ◆ 1996
74. Karen's Softball Mystery ◆ 1996
75. Karen's Country Fair ◆ 1996
76. Karen's Magic Garden ◆ 1996
77. Karen's School Surprise ◆ 1996
78. Karen's Half Birthday ◆ 1996
79. Karen's Big Fight ◆ 1996
80. Karen's Christmas Tree ◆ 1996
81. Karen's Accident ◆ 1997
82. Karen's Secret Valentine ◆ 1997
83. Karen's Bunny ◆ 1997
84. Karen's Big Job ◆ 1997
85. Karen's Treasure ◆ 1997
86. Karen's Telephone Trouble ◆ 1997
87. Karen's Pony Camp ◆ 1997
88. Karen's Puppet Show ◆ 1997
89. Karen's Unicorn ◆ 1997
90. Karen's Haunted House ◆ 1997
91. Karen's Pilgrim ◆ 1997
92. Karen's Sleigh Ride ◆ 1997
93. Karen's Cooking Contest ◆ 1998
94. Karen's Snow Princess ◆ 1998
95. Karen's Promise ◆ 1998
96. Karen's Big Move ◆ 1998
97. Karen's Paper Route ◆ 1998
98. Karen's Fishing Trip ◆ 1998
99. Karen's Big City Mystery ◆ 1998
100. Karen's Book ◆ 1998
101. Karen's Chain Letter ◆ 1998
102. Karen's Black Cat ◆ 1998
103. Karen's Movie Star ◆ 1998
104. Karen's Christmas Carol ◆ 1998
105. Karen's Nanny ◆ 1998
106. Karen's President ◆ 1999
107. Karen's Copycat ◆ 1999
108. Karen's Field Day ◆ 1999
109. Karen's Show and Share ◆ 1999
110. Karen's Swim Meet ◆ 1999

111. Karen's Spy Mystery ◆ 1999
112. Karen's New Holiday ◆ 1999
113. Karen's Hurricane ◆ 1999
114. Karen's Chicken-Pox ◆ 1999
115. Karen's Runaway Turkey ◆ 1999
116. Karen's Reindeer ◆ 1999
117. Karen's Mistake ◆ 2000
118. Karen's Figure Eight ◆ 2000
119. Karen's Yo-Yo ◆ 2000
120. Karen's Easter Parade ◆ 2000
121. Karen's Gift ◆ 2000
122. Karen's Cowboy ◆ 2000

BABY-SITTERS LITTLE SISTER SUPER SPECIALS

Martin, Ann M.

SCHOLASTIC ◆ GRADES 2–4 ◆ A/R

REAL LIFE

Karen Brewer is the little stepsister of Kristy of the Baby-Sitters Club. Karen and her brother Andrew are the children of Kristy's stepfather. Karen lives with Kristy's family on the weekends and with her mother, who has also remarried, during the week. In these Super Specials, something extra is offered. Karen flies on a plane to visit her grandmother, and there are games, activities, and recipes included at the end of each book. Karen and her three friends spend a busy summer together, and each of the girls tells part of the story.

1. Karen's Wish ◆ 1990
2. Karen's Plane Trip ◆ 1991
3. Karen's Mystery ◆ 1991
4. Karen, Hannie, and Nancy: The Three Musketeers ◆ 1992
5. Karen's Baby ◆ 1992
6. Karen's Campout ◆ 1993

BABYMOUSE

Holm, Jennifer L., and Matthew Holm

RANDOM HOUSE ◆ GRADES 3–6 ◆ A/R

HUMOR | ANIMAL FANTASY

Babymouse is slick and sassy. She always has a comeback no matter the situation. In *Puppy Love,* Babymouse buries five pet goldfish. She does not want another pet fish! Her mom keeps saying "No" to a dog, so Babymouse tries a hamster, a turtle, a ferret, a salamander, and more. She even daydreams about a horse. When she finally gets a dog, "Buddy" is not what she expected.

1. Babymouse: Queen of the World! ◆ 2005
2. Babymouse: Our Hero ◆ 2005
3. Babymouse: Beach Babe ◆ 2006
4. Babymouse: Rock Star ◆ 2006
5. Babymouse: Heartbreaker ◆ 2006
6. Camp Babymouse ◆ 2007
7. Babymouse: Skater Girl ◆ 2007
8. Babymouse: Puppy Love ◆ 2007
9. Babymouse: Monster Mash! ◆ 2008

BAD DOG

Chatterton, Martin

SCHOLASTIC ◆ GRADES 3–5 ◆ A/R

ANIMAL FANTASY | HUMOR

At the beginning of each book, Bad Dog is in the pound with three days left to live. Then, an improbable event occurs. A Hollywood agent picks him to be in a movie. The president needs him. He is chosen to go to Mars. Readers will enjoy the preposterous situations.

1. Bad Dog and That Hollywood Hoohah ◆ 2004
2. Bad Dog and Those Crazy Martians ◆ 2004
3. Bad Dog and the Curse of the President's Knee ◆ 2004
4. Bad Dog Goes Barktastic ◆ 2004

BAGTHORPE SAGA

Cresswell, Helen

MACMILLAN ◆ GRADES 5–6 ◆ A/R

FAMILY LIFE | HUMOR

Because every member of the Bagthorpe family is creative and talented, Jack devises a plan to become more than an "ordinary" member of this unusual household. *Ordinary Jack* begins the humorous saga of an eccentric, lovable family whose life is never dull. The cast of characters includes the colorful, but not as brilliant, Parker family—Uncle Parker, Aunt Celia, and Daisy. Continuous drama portrays family values with comical mishaps, mix-ups, and much human interaction.

1. Ordinary Jack ◆ 1977
2. Absolute Zero ◆ 1978
3. Bagthorpes Unlimited ◆ 1978
4. Bagthorpes vs. the World ◆ 1979
5. Bagthorpes Abroad ◆ 1984

6. Bagthorpes Haunted ◆ 1985
7. Bagthorpes Liberated ◆ 1985

BAILEY CITY MONSTERS

Jones, Marcia Thornton, and Debbie Dadey

SCHOLASTIC ◆ GRADES 2–4 ◆ A/R

FANTASY | HUMOR

There is something strange about the new family next door. Ben and
Annie have never seen such strange parents as Boris and Hilda Hauntly.
Their son Kilmer is in Ben's fourth-grade class, and he is weird too. With
their friend Jane, Ben and Annie try to find out more about the owners
of the Hauntly Manor Inn, until they see the guests! This series, by the
authors of the Adventures of the Bailey School Kids series, combines
weird creatures with spooky situations and lots of humor. This is a good
choice for readers looking for a mild dose of monsters.

1. The Monsters Next Door ◆ 1997
2. Howling at the Hauntlys' ◆ 1998
3. Vampire Trouble ◆ 1998
4. Kilmer's Pet Monster ◆ 1999
5. Double Trouble Monsters ◆ 1999
6. Spooky Spells ◆ 1999
7. Vampire Baby ◆ 1999
8. Snow Monster Mystery ◆ 1999
9. Happy Boo Day ◆ 2000

BAILEY CITY MONSTERS SUPER SPECIALS

1. Hauntlys' Hairy Surprise ◆ 1999

BAILEY SCHOOL: THE ADVENTURES OF THE BAILEY SCHOOL KIDS

Dadey, Debbie, and Marcia Thornton Jones

SCHOLASTIC ◆ GRADES 2–4 ◆ A/R

FANTASY | HUMOR

Bailey City is a weird place. The students in Mrs. Jeeper's third-grade
class find mysterious adventures around every corner. There are even
strange things happening at the library, where King Arthur's wizard,
Merlin, has brought his magic! And there may be a dragon cooking the
pizzas. Each book has unusual characters—vampires, genies, aliens, zombies, Martians, angels, and skeletons. There is lots of action, with plot
twists that leave the reader guessing. The length of the books and the
fast-paced plots will appeal to many readers.

1. Vampires Don't Wear Polka Dots ◆ 1990
2. Werewolves Don't Go to Summer Camp ◆ 1991
3. Santa Claus Doesn't Mop Floors ◆ 1991
4. Leprechauns Don't Play Basketball ◆ 1992
5. Ghosts Don't Eat Potato Chips ◆ 1992
6. Frankenstein Doesn't Plant Petunias ◆ 1993
7. Aliens Don't Wear Braces ◆ 1993
8. Genies Don't Ride Bicycles ◆ 1994
9. Pirates Don't Wear Pink Sunglasses ◆ 1994
10. Witches Don't Do Backflips ◆ 1994
11. Skeletons Don't Play Tubas ◆ 1994
12. Cupid Doesn't Flip Hamburgers ◆ 1995
13. Gremlins Don't Chew Bubble Gum ◆ 1995
14. Monsters Don't Scuba Dive ◆ 1995
15. Zombies Don't Play Soccer ◆ 1995
16. Dracula Doesn't Drink Lemonade ◆ 1995
17. Elves Don't Wear Hard Hats ◆ 1995
18. Martians Don't Take Temperatures ◆ 1996
19. Gargoyles Don't Drive School Buses ◆ 1996
20. Wizards Don't Need Computers ◆ 1996
21. Mummies Don't Coach Softball ◆ 1996
22. Cyclops Doesn't Roller Skate ◆ 1996
23. Angels Don't Know Karate ◆ 1996
24. Dragons Don't Cook Pizza ◆ 1997
25. Bigfoot Doesn't Square Dance ◆ 1997
26. Mermaids Don't Run Track ◆ 1997
27. Bogeymen Don't Play Football ◆ 1997
28. Unicorns Don't Give Sleigh Rides ◆ 1997
29. Knights Don't Teach Piano ◆ 1998
30. Hercules Doesn't Pull Teeth ◆ 1998
31. Ghouls Don't Scoop Ice Cream ◆ 1998
32. Phantoms Don't Drive Sports Cars ◆ 1998
33. Giants Don't Go Snowboarding ◆ 1998
34. Frankenstein Doesn't Slam Hockey Pucks ◆ 1998
35. Trolls Don't Ride Roller Coasters ◆ 1999
36. Wolfmen Don't Hula Dance ◆ 1999
37. Goblins Don't Play Video Games ◆ 1999
38. Ninjas Don't Bake Pumpkin Pies ◆ 1999
39. Dracula Doesn't Rock and Roll ◆ 1999
40. Sea Monsters Don't Ride Motorcycles ◆ 2000
41. The Bride of Frankenstein Doesn't Bake Cookies ◆ 2000
42. Robots Don't Catch Chicken Pox ◆ 2001
43. Vikings Don't Wear Wrestling Belts ◆ 2001
44. Ghosts Don't Ride Wild Horses ◆ 2001
45. Wizards Don't Wear Graduation Gowns ◆ 2002
46. Sea Serpents Don't Juggle Water Balloons ◆ 2002
47. Frankenstein Doesn't Start Food Fights ◆ 2003
48. Dracula Doesn't Play Kickball ◆ 2004
49. Werewolves Don't Run for President ◆ 2004

50. The Abominable Snowman Doesn't Roast Marshmallows ◆ 2005
51. Dragons Don't Throw Snowballs ◆ 2006

THE ADVENTURES OF THE BAILEY SCHOOL KIDS SUPER SPECIALS

1. Mrs. Jeepers Is Missing! ◆ 1996
2. Mrs. Jeeper's Batty Vacation ◆ 1997
3. Mrs. Jeepers' Secret Cave ◆ 1998
4. Mrs. Jeepers in Outer Space ◆ 1999
5. Mrs. Jeepers' Monster Class Trip ◆ 2000
6. Mrs. Jeepers on Vampire Island ◆ 2001

THE ADVENTURES OF THE BAILEY SCHOOL KIDS HOLIDAY SPECIALS

1. Swamp Monsters Don't Chase Wild Turkeys ◆ 2001
2. Aliens Don't Carve Jack-o'-Lanterns ◆ 2002
3. Mrs. Claus Doesn't Climb Telephone Poles ◆ 2002
4. Leprechauns Don't Play Fetch ◆ 2003
5. Ogres Don't Hunt Easter Eggs ◆ 2004
6. Mrs. Jeepers' Scariest Halloween Ever ◆ 2005

BAKER STREET IRREGULARS

Dicks, Terrance

DUTTON ◆ GRADES 4–7

MYSTERY

Four London youngsters recover a lost painting and become known as "The Baker Street Irregulars" after Sherlock Holmes's gang of street kids. The youngest, Mickey, welcomes all the attention and publicity and wants to solve another crime. Dan, the leader of the group, and Jeff, the one with the most common sense, are reluctant to get involved again. When a crime wave hits their neighborhood, Dan, Jeff, and Mickey, along with their friend Liz, find themselves drawn in almost in spite of themselves. Dan is capable of drawing conclusions by intuitive leaps, Jeff sometimes plays the Dr. Watson role, and Liz and Mickey are fearless in dangerous situations. Don, a young police detective, comes to rely on their expertise as the young quartet takes on more cases. Lots of action and fairly complex clues for young mystery fans.

1. The Case of the Missing Masterpiece ◆ 1978
2. The Case of the Fagin File ◆ 1978
3. The Case of the Blackmail Boys ◆ 1979
4. The Case of the Cinema Swindle ◆ 1980
5. The Case of the Ghost Grabbers ◆ 1981
6. The Case of the Cop Catchers ◆ 1981
7. The Case of the Disappearing Diplomat ◆ 1986
8. The Case of the Comic Crooks ◆ 1986

9. The Case of the Haunted Holiday ◆ 1987
10. The Case of the Criminal Computer ◆ 1987

BAKER'S DOZEN

Various authors

TARGUM PRESS ◆ GRADES 4–6

FAMILY LIFE | REAL LIFE

There are 14 people in the Baker family—Mr. and Mrs. Baker and their 12 children. Asher is the oldest at 16 and he is living at a yeshivah. At 13, Bracha is the oldest girl and, while Asher is away, she is the oldest one at home. Then there are the quintuplets—Rivka, Zahava, Dina, Tikva, and Yocheved—who receive lots of attention not only for being quints but also for being in such a large family. Moishy, Chezky, Donny, Saraleh, and Rachel round out this large, lively family. The activities in this house revolve around Jewish holidays and traditions, like attending a pre-Purim concert celebration or planning a bas mitzvah. Readers will enjoy the everyday problems faced by the different personalities in the Baker family.

1. On Our Own (Lazewnik, Libby) ◆ 1991
2. Ghosthunters! (Siegel, Malky) ◆ 1992
3. And the Winner Is . . . (Stein, Aidel) ◆ 1992
4. Stars in Their Eyes (Stein, Aidel) ◆ 1992
5. The Inside Story (Lazewnik, Libby) ◆ 1992
6. Trapped! (Lazewnik, Libby, et al.) ◆ 1992
7. Ima Come Home (Stein, Aidel) ◆ 1993
8. Hey Waiter! (Zitter, Emmy) ◆ 1993
9. Through Thick and Thin (Garfunkel, Debby) ◆ 1993
10. Do Not Disturb (Stein, Aidel) ◆ 1994
11. The Do-Gooders (Stein, Aidel) ◆ 1994
12. The Baker Family Circus (Rose, Miriam) ◆ 1994
13. Something's Fishy (Stein, Aidel) ◆ 1994
14. Summer Jobs (Stein, Aidel) ◆ 1995
15. Sorry About That (Steinberg, Rugh) ◆ 1995
16. Baker's Best (Lazewnik, Libby) ◆ 1996

BALLERINA DREAMS

Bryant, Ann

USBORNE ◆ GRADES 2–5

REAL LIFE

Imported from England, this series features girls attending ballet classes. Poppy and Jasmine are best friends. Then Rose joins their class. At first there are problems but the three become friends. Show these books to girls who read Royal Ballet School and Ballet Friends.

1. Poppy's Secret Wish ◆ 2006
2. Jasmine's Lucky Star ◆ 2006
3. Rose's Big Decision ◆ 2006
4. Dancing Princess ◆ 2006
5. Dancing with the Stars ◆ 2006
6. Dancing Forever ◆ 2006
7. The Christmas Nutcracker ◆ 2006

BALLET FRIENDS

Michaels, Kitty
BOOKSURGE PUBLISHING ◆ GRADES 4–7
REAL LIFE

Jessie Garrett, 12, is a tomboy turned ballerina. Because of her competitive nature she pushes herself to be the best. Bianca has been taking ballet for years and she is used to being on top. Instead of confronting each other, Bianca helps Jessie and the two girls become best friends. Performances, a trip to Lincoln Center, injuries, and a fire at the dance studio are among the events that Jessie, Bianca, and their friends face. Royal Ballet School would be another series for readers who like these books.

1. Toe-tally Fabulous ◆ 2008
2. Barred from Ballet ◆ 2008
3. Birthday at the Ballet ◆ 2008
4. Nowhere to Turn ◆ 2008
5. Waiting in the Wings ◆ 2008

BALLET SLIPPERS

Giff, Patricia Reilly
VIKING ◆ GRADES 2–4 ◆ A/R
REAL LIFE

Rosie wants to be a ballerina. In the first book of the series, *Dance with Rosie,* she begins a class with Miss Deidre and learns how challenging ballet is. In another book, she takes her brother Andrew to see *The Sleeping Beauty* only to have him cause a problem. Later, her ballet class performs the same ballet. In still another book, Rosie worries that her Grandpa's trip will upset her plans—and that she will miss him. The ballet activities are woven into the everyday lives of Rosie and her friends.

1. Dance with Rosie ◆ 1996
2. Rosie's Nutcracker Dreams ◆ 1996
3. Starring Rosie ◆ 1997
4. Not-So-Perfect Rosie ◆ 1997

5. Glass Slipper for Rosie ◆ 1997
6. Rosie's Big City Ballet ◆ 1998

BARBIE MYSTERY FILES

Aber, Linda Williams

SCHOLASTIC ◆ GRADES 3–5 ◆ A/R

MYSTERY

While working for the Willow *Daily News,* Barbie becomes involved in mysteries. Strange things are happening at Mr. Willow's mansion. Is it haunted? In another book, Barbie investigates who is causing problems at the Battle of the Bands.

1. The Haunted Mansion Mystery ◆ 2002
2. The Mystery of the Jeweled Mask ◆ 2002
3. Mystery Unplugged ◆ 2003
4. The Mystery of the Missing Stallion ◆ 2003
5. The Mystery of the Lost Valentine ◆ 2003

BARBIE (STEP INTO READING)

Various authors

RANDOM HOUSE ◆ GRADES K–3

FANTASY

Barbie fans will love seeing their favorite doll in these beginning-to-read books. From a favorite fairy tale—"The Twelve Dancing Princesses"—to butterflies, castles, fairies, and unicorns, this series is sure to attract young girls.

1. One Pink Shoe (Orr, Sally) ◆ 1998
2. Kitty's Surprise (Richards, Barbara) ◆ 1999
3. Two Princesses (Gordh, Bill) ◆ 2000
4. Ballet Buddies (Richards, Barbara) ◆ 2000
5. Lost and Found (Pugliano-Martin, Carol) ◆ 2002
6. A Day at the Fair (Pugliano-Martin, Carol) ◆ 2003
7. A Dress-Up Day (Parker, Jessie) ◆ 2003
8. On the Road (Capozzi, Suzy, and Karen Wolcott) ◆ 2004
9. School Days (Jordan, Apple, and Karen Wolcott) ◆ 2004
10. On Your Toes (Jordan, Apple, and Karen Wolcott) ◆ 2005
11. Barbie and the Magic of Pegasus (Random House Editors) ◆ 2005
12. Barbie Fairytopia (Landolf, Diane Wright) ◆ 2006
13. Barbie in the Twelve Dancing Princesses (Redbank, Tennant) ◆ 2006
14. The Island Princess (Alberto, Daisy) ◆ 2007
15. Love Is in the Air (Jordan, Apple, and Karen Wolcott) ◆ 2007
16. Mariposa (Webster, Christy) ◆ 2008
17. Barby and the Diamond Castle (Depken, Kristen L.) ◆ 2008

THE BARKERS

dePaola, Tomie

PUTNAM ◆ GRADES K–2 ◆ A/R

ANIMAL FANTASY

Morgan and Moffat are twins looking forward to starting school. They make friends, earn gold stars, and deal with a bully. The family adopts Marcos, 3, who only speaks Spanish. The Barkers are depicted as dogs and were inspired by dePaola's own terriers. There are board books on colors and counting. Newer books have been packaged as Tomie dePaola's The Barker Twins and have been written by various authors with illustrations in the style of Tomie dePaola.

1. Meet the Barkers: Morgan and Moffat Go to School ◆ 2001
2. Boss for a Day ◆ 2001
3. Hide-and-Seek All Week ◆ 2001
4. New Barker in the House ◆ 2002
5. Trouble in the Barkers' Class ◆ 2003

THE BARKERS: TOMIE DEPAOLA'S THE BARKER TWINS

1. Triple Checkup (Poploff, Michelle) ◆ 2004
2. T-Ball Trouble (Herman, Gail) ◆ 2004
3. Morgie's Surprise (Frith, Margaret) ◆ 2004
4. Go Away, Girls! (Hackney, Ann) ◆ 2004
5. The Big Sleepover (Herman, Gail) ◆ 2004

BARKHAM STREET

Stolz, Mary

HARPERCOLLINS ◆ GRADES 4–6 ◆ A/R

FAMILY LIFE | REAL LIFE

In *The Explorer of Barkham Street,* Martin Hastings is 13 and he dreams of being a hero. His everyday life is filled with problems, some involving his father, but his biggest concern is finding a way to get back his dog, Rufus. A successful baby-sitting job gives Martin a reason to feel good about himself. Earlier books show how Martin got (and lost) his dog and how he bullied Edward Frost. Martin experiences emotional growth as he deals with his anger and disappointments and begins to accept responsibility for his actions.

1. A Dog on Barkham Street ◆ 1960
2. The Bully of Barkham Street ◆ 1963
3. The Explorer of Barkham Street ◆ 1985

BARKLEY'S SCHOOL FOR DOGS

Jones, Marcia Thornton, and Debbie Dadey

VOLO/HYPERION ◆ **GRADES 2–4** ◆ **A/R**

ANIMAL FANTASY | **HUMOR**

Jack the Wonder Dog attends Barkley's School for Dogs. There, he confronts a bullying Doberman and tries out for an appearance in a television commercial. The dogs have lively personalities. Middle-elementary readers will enjoy their humorous antics.

1. Playground Bully ◆ 2001
2. Puppy Trouble ◆ 2001
3. Top Dog ◆ 2001
4. Ghost Dog ◆ 2001
5. Snow Day ◆ 2001
6. Sticks and Stones and Doggie Bones ◆ 2002
7. Buried Treasure ◆ 2002
8. Blue-Ribbon Blues ◆ 2002
9. Santa Dog ◆ 2002
10. Tattle Tails ◆ 2002
11. Puppy Love ◆ 2002
12. Puppies on Parade ◆ 2003

BARNSTORMERS

Long, Loren

SIMON & SCHUSTER ◆ **GRADES 3–6**

HISTORICAL | **RECREATION** | **FANTASY**

In 1899, a traveling baseball team "barnstorms" across America playing games with other teams. Three children, Griffith, Ruby, and Graham, and their mother go along with the Travelin' Nine. Their father, who recently died, used to play for the team and their mother (disguised as a man) has taken his place. The children have been give a baseball that was their father's. When all of them touch the baseball, mysterious events occur.

1. Game 1: Porkopolis ◆ 2007
2. Game 2: The River City ◆ 2007
3. Game 3: The Windy City ◆ 2008
4. Game 4: Water, Water Everywhere ◆ 2009

THE BARTIMAEUS TRILOGY

Stroud, Jonathan

HYPERION/MIRAMAX KIDS ◆ GRADES 5–9 ◆ A/R

FANTASY

Bartimaeus is a djinn (genie) called forth by a 10-year-old magician, Nathaniel. Nathaniel orders Bartimaeus to steal the Amulet of Samarkand from Simon Lovelace. In the second book, Nathaniel is 14 and is responsible for capturing members of the Resistance. Readers will be intrigued by this magical fantasy series.

1. The Amulet of Samarkand ◆ 2003
2. The Golem's Eye ◆ 2004
3. Ptolemy's Gate ◆ 2006

BASEBALL CARD ADVENTURES

Gutman, Dan

HARPERCOLLINS ◆ GRADES 4–8 ◆ A/R

FANTASY | RECREATION

Joe Stoshack, 12, travels back through time to meet star baseball players of the past. The first adventure happens when Joe finds a valuable Honus Wagner card. That night, Honus Wagner appears in Joe's bedroom and they time-travel to the 1909 World Series. In the Babe Ruth story, Joe's dad comes too. They plan to have Babe Ruth autograph items to take back to the present and sell, but their plans hit a snag.

1. Honus and Me ◆ 1997
2. Jackie and Me ◆ 1999
3. Babe and Me ◆ 2000
4. Shoeless Joe and Me ◆ 2002
5. Mickey and Me ◆ 2003
6. Abner and Me ◆ 2005
7. Satch and Me ◆ 2005
8. Jim and Me ◆ 2008
9. Ray and Me ◆ 2009

BASIL OF BAKER STREET

Titus, Eve

SIMON & SCHUSTER ◆ GRADES 2–5 ◆ A/R

ANIMAL FANTASY | MYSTERY

Mouse detectives Basil of Baker Street and his faithful companion Dr. David Q. Dawson live in the basement of Sherlock Holmes's house and sneak into the great detective's living room to learn from the master. When the young twins of their neighbors are mousenapped, the detective duo goes into action. They find clues about the mouse who delivered the ransom note, demanding that Basil and all his neighbors give the criminals their cozy homes in the Baker Street basement. The case is solved, and the twins are returned to their parents, but of course this is just the beginning of many adventures. The two mouse detectives travel to the United States and Mexico as their fame spreads and their help is requested by mice all over.

1. Basil of Baker Street ◆ 1958
2. Basil and the Lost Colony ◆ 1964
3. Basil and the Pygmy Cats ◆ 1971
4. Basil in Mexico ◆ 1976
5. Basil in the Wild West ◆ 1982

BATMAN (SCHOLASTIC READER)

Various authors

SCHOLASTIC ◆ GRADES 1–4 ◆ A/R

FANTASY

These comic-book-style readers will be attractive to reluctant readers and to readers who love superheroes. Batman and other characters from the popular comics/TV shows/movies are involved in many adventures. In the fifth book, The Joker escapes from captivity and crashes a fancy birthday party. Will Batman stop his nemesis?

1. The Copycat Crime (Grayson, Devin) ◆ 2003
2. Time Thaw (McCann, Jesse Leon) ◆ 2003
3. The Mad Hatter (Augustyn, Brian) ◆ 2004
4. The Purr-fect Crime (Hernandez-Rosenblatt, Jason) ◆ 2004
5. The Birthday Bash (Muntz, Percival) ◆ 2004

BEANY

Wojciechowski, Susan

CANDLEWICK ◆ GRADES 2–5 ◆ A/R

HUMOR | REAL LIFE

In this humorous series, Beany, whose real name is Bernice, worries about so many things she is almost overwhelmed. Her friend, Carol Ann, always seems to have a suggestion for Beany. But Beany must learn to stand up for herself. Middle-elementary readers who like Amber Brown and Ramona Quimby books will enjoy this series.

1. Don't Call Me Beanhead! ◆ 1994
2. Beany (Not Beanhead) and the Magic Crystal ◆ 1997

3. Beany and the Dreaded Wedding ◆ 2000
4. Beany Goes to Camp ◆ 2002
5. Beany and the Meany ◆ 2005

BEAR

Asch, Frank

PARENTS MAGAZINE PRESS ◆ GRADES K–2 ◆ A/R

ANIMAL FANTASY | FAMILY LIFE

This series of books features a young bear, usually with his parents. In *Popcorn,* Bear is left home while his parents go to a Halloween party. He has his own party, but must clean up a mess of popcorn. For a surprise, his parents bring him more popcorn. These stories have a gentle humor that appeals to young children. Frank Asch also features bears in his Moonbear series.

1. Sandcake ◆ 1978
2. Popcorn ◆ 1979
3. Bread and Honey ◆ 1981
4. Milk and Cookies ◆ 1982

BEAR

Winthrop, Elizabeth

HOLIDAY HOUSE ◆ GRADES K–1

ANIMAL FANTASY | HUMOR

Young children will relate to the feeling of anxiety that Bear (a teddy bear who acts like a child) feels when Nora leaves him with a baby-sitter, Mrs. Duck. While Nora is away, Bear plans to be difficult, but Mrs. Duck—who is a duck—proves to be a very wise baby-sitter. At Christmas, Mrs. Duck returns while Nora goes shopping, and Bear learns a lesson about peeking into presents. In another book, Nora brings home a new bear who is to be Bear's sister. It takes Bear a while to accept this big new panda bear into his heart, but he does. Like Amy Hest's books about Baby Duck, this series is right on target with the fears and simple concerns of young children. Charming illustrations add to the warmth of this picture book series.

1. Bear and Mrs. Duck ◆ 1988
2. Bear's Christmas Surprise ◆ 1991
3. Bear and Roly-Poly ◆ 1996

BEAR

Wilson, Karma

SIMON & SCHUSTER ◆ GRADES K–2 ◆ A/R

ANIMAL FANTASY

Bear's friends support him through a variety of trials and tribulations in this gently humorous series. In the first book, Bear continues to hibernate while a collection of animals enjoy the warmth of his cave; luckily he wakes up in time to share their food. *Bear Wants More* tells how his friends help him satisfy his appetite and then deal with the consequences of his growing girth. In *Bear Feels Scared,* Bear is lost in the woods and frightened by the noises around him. Jane Chapman's illustrations effectively reveal the little bear's experiences. There are board book versions of the first two titles.

1. Bear Snores On ◆ 2002
2. Bear Wants More ◆ 2003
3. Bear Stays Up for Christmas ◆ 2004
4. Bear's New Friend ◆ 2006
5. Bear Feels Sick ◆ 2007
6. Bear Feels Scared ◆ 2008

BEAST QUEST

Blade, Adam

SCHOLASTIC ◆ GRADES 3–5 ◆ A/R

FANTASY

There is trouble throughout the kingdom. Crops are dying; rivers are drying up. Tom begins a quest to save his village only to realize that he must save the kingdom. In the first book, the king gives Tom a silver key to release Ferno the Fire Dragon from the Dark Wizard Malvel. In subsequent books, Tom is joined by Elenna as he faces other beasts.

1. Ferno the Fire Dragon ◆ 2007
2. Sepron the Sea Serpent ◆ 2007
3. Cypher the Mountain Giant ◆ 2007
4. Tagus the Night Horse ◆ 2007
5. Tartok the Ice Beast ◆ 2007
6. Epos the Winged Flame ◆ 2008
7. Zepha the Monster Squid ◆ 2008
8. Claw the Giant Ape ◆ 2008

BEATRICE BAILEY *see* The Adventures of Beatrice Bailey

BEEZUS AND RAMONA *see* Ramona Quimby

BEEZY

McDonald, Megan
ORCHARD BOOKS ◆ GRADES 1–2 ◆ A/R
FAMILY LIFE | HUMOR

Beezy enjoys many of the everyday activities that will be familiar to readers. She plays with her dog, Funnybone; enjoys Gran's baking and stories; and plays softball with her friend Sarafina. Picking blackberries, waiting out a big storm, and enjoying the company of her friend Merlin are also described. Short chapters, each a complete story, make this an accessible book for younger readers. The humor and realistic situations will also be appealing.

1. Beezy ◆ 1997
2. Beezy Magic ◆ 1998
3. Beezy at Bat ◆ 1998
4. Beezy and Funnybone ◆ 2000

BELINDA

Young, Amy
VIKING ◆ GRADES K–3 ◆ A/R
REAL LIFE

Belinda is a ballerina with a difference—extremely large feet. Her development as a dancer has been challenging. When she was young (*Belinda Begins Ballet,* a prequel), she was told to be a clown for the talent show. During the show she began to dance and the audience was enchanted. A ballerina was born. Still, there are other challenges to come—such as lost ballet shoes on a trip to Paris and a performance as Cinderella that mirrors the real story when Belinda is locked in a closet during the performance and rescued by the fairy godmother dancer. This series is about self-image and following your dream as well as about ballet.

1. Belinda, the Ballerina ◆ 2002
2. Belinda in Paris ◆ 2005
3. Belinda and the Glass Slipper ◆ 2006
4. Belinda Begins Ballet ◆ 2008

BELLA BAXTER

Mason, Jane B., and Sarah Hines Stephens

ALADDIN ◆ GRADES 2–4 ◆ A/R

REAL LIFE

Meet 7-year-old Bella Baxter. Her family has moved to a seaside town with plans to renovate an old house and open an inn. Well, the house is a mess. There is even a skunk in the basement. Bella goes to the library and meets Trudy, who is not only helpful as a librarian. She also comes to the house and provides hands-on help with the remodeling. This is a fun choice for middle-grade chapter book readers. Bella has the spunk of Gooney Bird Greene and Judy Moody.

1. Bella Baxter Inn Trouble ◆ 2005
2. Bella Baxter and the Itchy Disaster ◆ 2005
3. Bella Baxter and the Lighthouse Mystery ◆ 2006

BERENSTAIN BEARS

Berenstain, Stan, and Jan Berenstain

RANDOM HOUSE; HARPERCOLLINS ◆ GRADES K–2 ◆ A/R

ANIMAL FANTASY | HUMOR

Papa and Mama Bear live with their children, Brother and Sister Bear, in a tree house in Bear Country. They have a happy family life and get along well together. Most of the books in the series teach a lesson in healthy, safe, and sensible living. In a story about eating well, the young bears and their father have been eating too much junk food. The mother tries to get them on a better diet and insists that they go to see the doctor. The doctor tells them all about their bodies and why a proper diet is important. Similar books discuss TV, talking to strangers, and peer pressure. There are different formats featuring the Berenstain Bears. There are lift-the-flap, activity, and sticker books for very young children. There are board books, workbooks, "Do-It" books, and mini-books for toddlers. The longer chapter books and Bear Scouts books are listed separately. Listed below are other groupings of these popular books. All books since 2005 are published by HarperCollins.

BRIGHT AND EARLY BOOKS

Very few words; designed for beginning readers.

1. Inside Outside Upside Down ◆ 1968
2. Bears on Wheels ◆ 1969
3. The Bears' Christmas ◆ 1970
4. Old Hat, New Hat ◆ 1970
5. Bears in the Night ◆ 1971

6. The Berenstains' B Book ◆ 1971
7. He Bear, She Bear ◆ 1974
8. The Berenstain Bears and the Spooky Old Tree ◆ 1978
9. The Berenstain Bears on the Moon ◆ 1985
10. The Berenstains' C Book ◆ 1997

BEGINNER BOOKS

Few words; designed for beginning readers.

1. The Big Honey Hunt ◆ 1962
2. The Bike Lesson ◆ 1964
3. The Bears' Picnic ◆ 1966
4. The Bear Scouts ◆ 1967
5. The Bears' Vacation ◆ 1968
6. The Bear Detectives ◆ 1975
7. The Berenstain Bears and the Missing Dinosaur Bones ◆ 1980

BERENSTAIN BEARS FIRST TIME BOOKS

Longer story; picture-book format.

1. The Berenstain Bears' New Baby ◆ 1974
2. The Berenstain Bears Go to School ◆ 1978
3. The Berenstain Bears and the Homework Hassle ◆ 1979
4. The Berenstain Bears and the Sitter ◆ 1981
5. The Berenstain Bears Go to the Doctor ◆ 1981
6. The Berenstain Bears' Moving Day ◆ 1981
7. The Berenstain Bears Visit the Dentist ◆ 1981
8. The Berenstain Bears Get in a Fight ◆ 1982
9. The Berenstain Bears Go to Camp ◆ 1982
10. The Berenstain Bears in the Dark ◆ 1982
11. The Berenstain Bears and the Messy Room ◆ 1983
12. The Berenstain Bears and the Truth ◆ 1983
13. The Berenstain Bears' Trouble with Money ◆ 1983
14. The Berenstain Bears and Mama's New Job ◆ 1984
15. The Berenstain Bears and Too Much TV ◆ 1984
16. The Berenstain Bears Meet Santa Bear ◆ 1984
17. The Berenstain Bears and Too Much Junk Food ◆ 1985
18. The Berenstain Bears Forget Their Manners ◆ 1985
19. The Berenstain Bears Learn about Strangers ◆ 1985
20. The Berenstain Bears and the Bad Habit ◆ 1986
21. The Berenstain Bears and the Trouble with Friends ◆ 1986
22. The Berenstain Bears and the Week at Grandma's ◆ 1986
23. The Berenstain Bears and Too Much Birthday ◆ 1986
24. The Berenstain Bears Get Stage Fright ◆ 1986
25. The Berenstain Bears Go Out for the Team ◆ 1986
26. The Berenstain Bears: No Girls Allowed ◆ 1986
27. The Berenstain Bears' Trouble at School ◆ 1986
28. The Berenstain Bears and the Bad Dream ◆ 1988
29. The Berenstain Bears and the Double Dare ◆ 1988

30. The Berenstain Bears Get the Gimmies ◆ 1988
31. The Berenstain Bears and the In-Crowd ◆ 1989
32. The Berenstain Bears and Too Much Vacation ◆ 1989
33. The Berenstain Bears Trick or Treat ◆ 1989
34. The Berenstain Bears and the Prize Pumpkin ◆ 1990
35. The Berenstain Bears and the Slumber Party ◆ 1990
36. The Berenstain Bears' Trouble with Pets ◆ 1990
37. The Berenstain Bears Don't Pollute (Anymore) ◆ 1991
38. The Berenstain Bears and the Trouble with Grownups ◆ 1992
39. The Berentain Bears and Too Much Pressure ◆ 1992
40. The Berenstain Bears and the Bully ◆ 1993
41. The Berenstain Bears and the Green-Eyed Monster ◆ 1994
42. The Berenstain Bears' New Neighbors ◆ 1994
43. The Berenstain Bears and Too Much Teasing ◆ 1995
44. The Berenstain Bears Count Their Blessings ◆ 1995
45. The Berenstain Bears and the Blame Game ◆ 1997
46. The Berenstain Bears Fly It ◆ 1997
47. The Berenstain Bears Get the Grouchies ◆ 1997
48. The Berenstain Bears Thanksgiving ◆ 1997
49. The Berenstain Bears Get Their Kicks ◆ 1998
50. The Berenstain Bears Lend a Helping Hand ◆ 1998
51. The Berenstain Bears' Comic Valentine ◆ 1998
52. The Berenstain Bears Easter Surprise ◆ 1998
53. The Berenstain Bears Get the Don't Haftas ◆ 1998
54. The Berenstain Bears Get the Screamies ◆ 1998
55. The Berenstain Bears Go Platinum ◆ 1998
56. The Berenstain Bears Play Ball ◆ 1998
57. The Berenstain Bears and the Big Question ◆ 1999
58. The Berenstain Bears Get the Noisies ◆ 1999
59. The Berenstain Bears Get the Scaredies ◆ 1999
60. The Berenstain Bears Go Hollywood ◆ 1999
61. The Berenstain Bears Mad, Mad, Toy Craze ◆ 1999
62. The Berenstain Bears Think of Those in Need ◆ 1999
63. The Birds, The Bees, and the Berenstain Bears ◆ 1999
64. The Berenstain Bears and Baby Makes Five ◆ 2000
65. The Berenstain Bears and the Big Blooper ◆ 2000
66. The Berenstain Bears and the Excuse Note ◆ 2001
67. The Berenstain Bears' Dollars and Sense ◆ 2001
68. The Berenstain Bears and the Real Easter Eggs ◆ 2002
69. The Berenstain Bears' Report Card Trouble ◆ 2002
70. The Berenstain Bears and the Papa's Day Surprise ◆ 2003
71. The Berenstain Bears' Funny Valentine ◆ 2003
72. The Berenstain Bears and the Mama's Day Surprise ◆ 2004
73. The Berenstain Bears' Bedtime Battle ◆ 2005
74. The Berenstain Bears Go on a Ghost Walk ◆ 2005
75. The Berenstain Bears and the Trouble with Chores ◆ 2005
76. The Berenstain Bears and the Wishing Star ◆ 2005
77. The Berenstain Bears' New Puppy ◆ 2005
78. The Berenstain Bears and Too Much Car Trip ◆ 2006

79. The Berenstain Bears Go on Vacation ◆ 2006
80. The Berenstain Bears Hug and Make Up ◆ 2006
81. The Berenstain Bears and the Big Spelling Bee ◆ 2007
82. The Berenstain Bears and the Trouble with Commercials ◆ 2007
83. The Berenstain Bears Trim the Tree ◆ 2007
84. The Berenstain Bears Lose a Friend ◆ 2007
85. The Berenstain Bears' Baby Easter Bunny ◆ 2008
86. The Berenstain Bears and the Bad Influence ◆ 2008
87. The Berenstain Bears' Really Big Pet Show ◆ 2008

BERENSTAIN BEARS FIRST TIME READERS

Similar to picture books but a little easier for children to read.

1. The Berenstain Bears and the Big Road Race ◆ 1987
2. The Berenstain Bears and the Missing Honey ◆ 1987
3. The Berenstain Bears Blaze a Trail ◆ 1987
4. The Berenstain Bears on the Job ◆ 1987
5. The Day of the Dinosaur ◆ 1987
6. After the Dinosaurs ◆ 1988
7. The Berenstain Bears and the Ghost of the Forest ◆ 1988
8. The Berenstain Bears Ready, Get Set, Go! ◆ 1988

STEP INTO READING BOOKS

Simple text with different levels for begining readers.

1. The Berenstain Bears' Big Bear, Small Bear ◆ 1998
2. The Berenstain Bears Ride the Thunderbolt ◆ 1998
3. The Berenstain Bears by the Sea ◆ 1998
4. The Berenstain Bears Go Up and Down ◆ 1998
5. The Berenstain Bears Catch the Bus ◆ 1999
6. The Berenstain Bears in the House of Mirrors ◆ 1999
7. The Berenstain Bears and the Escape of the Bogg Brothers ◆ 2000
8. The Berenstain Bears and the Tic-Tac-Toe Mystery ◆ 2000
9. The Berenstain Bears Go In and Out ◆ 2000
10. The Berenstain Bears and the Missing Watermelon ◆ 2001

HARPERCOLLINS I CAN READ BOOKS

Simple text for beginning readers.

1. The Berenstain Bears Clean House ◆ 2005
2. The Berenstain Bears Play T-Ball ◆ 2005
3. The Berenstain Bears' New Pup ◆ 2005
4. The Berenstain Bears and the Baby Chipmunk ◆ 2005
5. The Berenstain Bears and the Wishing Star ◆ 2005
6. The Berenstain Bears' Seashore Treasure ◆ 2005
7. The Berenstain Bears Down on the Farm ◆ 2006
8. The Berenstain Bears Out West ◆ 2006
9. The Berenstain Bears' New Kitten ◆ 2006

STEPPING STONE BOOKS

1. The Goofy, Goony Guy ◆ 2001
2. The Runamuck Dog Show ◆ 2001
3. The Wrong Crowd ◆ 2001
4. Ride like the Wind ◆ 2002
5. Too Small for the Team ◆ 2003

BERENSTAIN BEARS: BEAR SCOUTS

Berenstain, Stan, and Jan Berenstain

LITTLE APPLE / SCHOLASTIC ◆ GRADES 1–3 ◆ A/R

ANIMAL FANTASY | HUMOR

The Bear Scouts work as a team, but each has individual skills. Scout Lizzy has an affinity for animals; Scout Fred is smart; Scout Sister is high-spirited and full of energy; and Scout Brother is the sensible, thoughtful leader. As in the picture books and easy readers about the Bear family, Papa Q. Bear is a bit of a buffoon whose decisions often cause problems. In *The Berenstain Bear Scouts and the Humongous Pumpkin,* Papa is duped by Ralph Ripoff and Weasel McGreed, who also cause problems in other books in the series. Good triumphs, however, as the Bear Scouts outwit the smarmy bad guys. The slapstick humor in these somewhat predictable early chapter books will meet the expectations of fans of the books for younger readers.

1. The Berenstain Bear Scouts and the Humongous Pumpkin ◆ 1995
2. The Berenstain Bear Scouts in the Giant Bat Cave ◆ 1995
3. The Berenstain Bear Scouts Meet Bigpaw ◆ 1995
4. The Berenstain Bear Scouts and the Coughing Catfish ◆ 1996
5. The Berenstain Bear Scouts and the Sci-Fi Pizza ◆ 1996
6. The Berenstain Bear Scouts and the Terrible Talking Termite ◆ 1996
7. The Berenstain Bear Scouts Ghost Versus Ghost ◆ 1996
8. The Berenstain Bear Scouts Save That Backscratcher ◆ 1996
9. The Berenstain Bear Scouts and the Ice Monster ◆ 1997
10. The Berenstain Bear Scouts and the Magic Crystal Caper ◆ 1997
11. The Berenstain Bear Scouts and the Run-Amuck Robot ◆ 1997
12. The Berenstain Bear Scouts and the Sinister Smoke Ring ◆ 1997
13. The Berenstain Bear Scouts and the Missing Merit Badge ◆ 1998
14. The Berenstain Bear Scouts and the Really Big Disaster ◆ 1998
15. The Berenstain Bears Scouts and the Search for Naughty Ned ◆ 1998
16. The Berenstain Bear Scouts Scream Their Heads Off ◆ 1998
17. The Berenstain Bear Scouts and the Evil Eye ◆ 1998
18. The Berenstain Bear Scouts and the Ripoff Queen ◆ 1998
19. The Berenstain Bear Scouts and the Stinky Milk Mystery ◆ 1999
20. The Berenstain Bear Scouts and the Whitewater Mystery ◆ 1999

BERENSTAIN BEARS: BIG CHAPTER BOOKS

Berenstain, Stan, and Jan Berenstain

RANDOM HOUSE ◆ GRADES 1–3 ◆ A/R

ANIMAL FANTASY | HUMOR

These books feature the Bear Country cubs in a variety of entertaining situations. Some of the stories take place at Bear Country School. For example, Queenie McBear gets a crush on the new art teacher, Mr. Smock, making Too-Tall Grizzly jealous. Other stories take place in locations in the area, such as a Halloween Festival at Farmer Ben's farm and a visit to the Freaky Funhouse. Brother and Sister often have ideas that involve their friends Queenie McBear, Barry Bruin, and Too-Tall Grizzly. Readers who loved the picture books about the Bears will want to read these Big Chapter Books, which also connect with the Berenstain Bear Scouts series.

1. The Berenstain Bears and the Drug Free Zone ◆ 1993
2. The Berenstain Bears and the New Girl in Town ◆ 1993
3. The Berenstain Bears Gotta Dance! ◆ 1993
4. The Berenstain Bears and the Nerdy Nephew ◆ 1993
5. The Berenstain Bears Accept No Substitutes ◆ 1993
6. The Berenstain Bears and the Female Fullback ◆ 1994
7. The Berenstain Bears and the Red-Handed Thief ◆ 1994
8. The Berenstain Bears and the Wheelchair Commando ◆ 1994
9. The Berenstain Bears and the School Scandal Sheet ◆ 1994
10. The Berenstain Bears and the Galloping Ghost ◆ 1994
11. The Berenstain Bears at Camp Crush ◆ 1994
12. The Berenstain Bears and the Giddy Grandma ◆ 1994
13. The Berenstain Bears and the Dress Code ◆ 1995
14. The Berenstain Bears' Media Madness ◆ 1995
15. The Berenstain Bears in the Freaky Funhouse ◆ 1995
16. The Berenstain Bears and the Showdown at Chainsaw Gap ◆ 1995
17. The Berenstain Bears at the Teen Rock Café ◆ 1996
18. The Berenstain Bears in Maniac Mansion ◆ 1996
19. The Berenstain Bears and the Bermuda Triangle ◆ 1997
20. The Berenstain Bears and the Ghost of the Auto Graveyard ◆ 1997
21. The Berenstain Bears and the Haunted Hayride ◆ 1997
22. The Berenstain Bears and Queenie's Crazy Crush ◆ 1997
23. The Berenstain Bears and the Big Date ◆ 1998
24. The Berenstain Bears and the Love Match ◆ 1998
25. The Berenstain Bears and the Perfect Crime (Almost) ◆ 1998
26. The Berenstain Bears Go Platinum ◆ 1998
27. The Berenstain Bears and the G-Rex Bones ◆ 1999
28. The Berenstain Bears in the Wax Museum ◆ 1999
29. The Berenstain Bears Lost in Cyberspace ◆ 1999
30. The Berenstain Bears and the Great Ant Attack ◆ 2000

31. The Berenstain Bears and the No Guns Allowed ◆ 2000
32. The Berenstain Bears Phenom in the Family ◆ 2001

BERNIE MAGRUDER *see* Bessledorf Hotel

BERYL E. BEAN

Stern, Ricki

HARPERCOLLINS ◆ GRADES 3–6 ◆ A/R

REAL LIFE

Beryl E. Bean cannot play soccer because her arm is broken. To fill her time, her stepfather suggests that she become a Mighty Adventurer of the Planet (MAPster). Her investigation takes her to the Natural History Museum where she helps the paleontologists with a discovery. Other books find her at camp with her ex-best friend and later trying to bring her friends together.

1. Mighty Adventurer of the Planet ◆ 2002
2. Expedition Sleepaway Camp ◆ 2002
3. Adventure: Lonely Leader ◆ 2003
4. Mission: Impossible Friendship ◆ 2004

BESSLEDORF HOTEL

Naylor, Phyllis Reynolds

SIMON & SCHUSTER ◆ GRADES 5–7 ◆ A/R

FAMILY LIFE | HUMOR | MYSTERY

The Magruder family lives in an apartment at the Bessledorf Hotel. The father, Theodore, manages the hotel. Alma helps out, but she dreams of writing romance novels. Son Joseph goes to veterinary college, and daughter Delores works at a parachute factory. Bernie likes to solve mysteries, and the old hotel provides plenty of them to solve. A ghost appears to Bernie in one book and he must figure out what it wants so that it will rest in peace. The Magruder family's exploits have also been repackaged and reissued in the Bernie Magruder series.

1. The Mad Gasser of Bessledorf Street ◆ 1983
2. The Bodies in the Bessledorf Hotel ◆ 1986
3. Bernie and the Bessledorf Ghost ◆ 1990
4. The Face in the Bessledorf Funeral Parlor ◆ 1993
5. The Bomb in the Bessledorf Bus Depot ◆ 1996
6. The Treasure of Bessledorf Hill ◆ 1997
7. Peril in the Bessledorf Parachute Factory ◆ 1999

BERNIE MAGRUDER

1. Bernie Magruder and the Haunted Hotel ◆ 2001
2. Bernie Magruder and the Case of the Big Stink ◆ 2001
3. Bernie Magruder and the Disappearing Bodies ◆ 2001
4. Bernie Magruder and the Bus Station Blow Up ◆ 2001
5. Bernie Magruder and the Pirate's Treasure ◆ 2001
6. Bernie Magruder and the Parachute Peril ◆ 2001
7. Bernie Magruder and the Drive-Thru Funeral Parlor ◆ 2003
8. Bernie Magruder and the Bats in the Belfry ◆ 2003

BEST ENEMIES

Leverich, Kathleen
GREENWILLOW ◆ GRADES 2–3
HUMOR | REAL LIFE

With an easily read format of four short chapters in each title, this series focuses on school rivalry. In *Best Enemies*, Priscilla Robin begins primary school with all new classmates. Her hope to make new friends fades when she meets Felicity Doll, described by her sister Eve as "a snake." Felicity is the bully and braggart whose obnoxious tricks make Priscilla's life miserable. Patient and long-suffering, Priscilla finally uses her wits to outsmart her archenemy and continues to successfully turn the tables in each new title. The behavior of the main characters might provide worthwhile discussions for classroom teachers and parents.

1. Best Enemies ◆ 1989
2. Best Enemies Again ◆ 1991
3. Best Enemies Forever ◆ 1995

BEST FRIENDS

Stahl, Hilda
CROSSWAY BOOKS ◆ GRADES 4–6
REAL LIFE | VALUES

Four middle-school girls live in a comfortable suburb and have formed the "Best Friends" club. They meet regularly to study the Bible and pray together. They encourage each other and work through problems together. Hannah is Native American, and the problem of racism is addressed in several books. The girls have problems with boys and families that are resolved using scriptural guidelines.

1. Chelsea and the Outrageous Phone Bill ◆ 1992
2. Big Trouble for Roxie ◆ 1992
3. Kathy and the Babysitting Hassle ◆ 1992
4. Hannah and the Special Fourth of July ◆ 1992

5. Roxie and Red Rose Mystery ◆ 1992
6. Kathy's New Brother ◆ 1992
7. A Made-Over Chelsea ◆ 1992
8. No Friends for Hannah ◆ 1992
9. Tough Choices for Roxie ◆ 1993
10. Chelsea's Special Touch ◆ 1993
11. Mystery at Bellwood Estate ◆ 1993
12. Hannah and the Daring Escape ◆ 1993
13. Hannah and the Snowy Hideaway ◆ 1993
14. Chelsea and the Alien Invasion ◆ 1993
15. Roxie's Mall Madness ◆ 1993
16. The Secret Tunnel Mystery ◆ 1994

BEST FRIENDS

Dale, Jenny
MACMILLAN ◆ GRADES 1–3 ◆ A/R

ANIMAL FANTASY

In the first book, Sparkle is a kitten who acts like a dog. Snowflake is a puppy who likes to cat nap. When Sparkle needs him, Snowflake is ready to go. Another book features Monty, a sheepdog who is afraid of sheep, and Minty, a lamb who becomes his friend. Animal lovers will love this series, which was originally published in England.

1. Amber and Alfie ◆ 2002
2. Blossom and Beany ◆ 2002
3. Bramble and Berry ◆ 2002
4. Carrot and Clover ◆ 2002
5. Lottie and Ludo ◆ 2002
6. Minty and Monty ◆ 2002
7. Pogo and Pip ◆ 2002
8. Skipper and Sky ◆ 2002
9. Snowflake and Sparkle ◆ 2002

BEST FRIENDS

Smith, Susan
POCKET BOOKS ◆ GRADES 4–7

REAL LIFE

Sonya moves back to California after living with her father in New York for two years. She renews her friendship with Terri, Angela, and Dawn, her best friends from fourth grade. Celia, a pretty and popular girl, takes an interest in her, and Sonya starts seeing faults in her old friends. Sonya decides to stick with them, though, after Celia asks her to cheat on a test. The rest of the series sees the friends through their middle-school years.

Celia remains the "enemy," and she and her friends are a rival crowd. A fifth girl, Linda, becomes one of the Best Friends. There are boyfriends and school activities as the girls pursue their various interests.

1. Sonya Begonia and the Eleventh Birthday Blues ◆ 1988
2. Angela and the King-Size Crusade ◆ 1988
3. Dawn Selby, Super Sleuth ◆ 1988
4. Terri the Great ◆ 1989
5. Sonya and the Chain Letter Gang ◆ 1989
6. Angela and the Greatest Guy in the World ◆ 1989
7. One Hundred Thousand Dollar Dawn ◆ 1990
8. The Terrible Terri Rumors ◆ 1990
9. Linda and the Little White Lies ◆ 1990
10. Sonya and the Haunting of Room 16A ◆ 1990
11. Angela and the Great Book Battle ◆ 1990
12. Dynamite Dawn vs. Terrific Terri ◆ 1991
13. Who's Out to Get Linda ◆ 1991
14. Terri and the Shopping Mall Disaster ◆ 1991
15. The Sonya and Howard Wars ◆ 1991
16. Angela and the Accidental-on-Purpose Romance ◆ 1991

BETSY

Haywood, Carolyn
MORROW ◆ GRADES 1–3 ◆ A/R
FAMILY LIFE | HUMOR

Betsy lives with her mother and father and little sister Star in the United States of the 1950s. The series centers around Betsy and her neighborhood friends as they play in the summerhouse that Betsy's father builds for them, find stray cats that they want to keep, and put on shows for the neighbors, sometimes with funny results. In the winter, Father turns the basement into a "winterhouse" for the children. When they build a dollhouse by themselves, they forget to add a door and Billy is trapped inside. Occasional black-and-white drawings decorate the series.

1. B Is for Betsy ◆ 1939
2. Betsy and Billy ◆ 1941
3. Back to School with Betsy ◆ 1943
4. Betsy and the Boys ◆ 1945
5. Betsy's Little Star ◆ 1950
6. Betsy and the Circus ◆ 1954
7. Betsy's Busy Summer ◆ 1956
8. Betsy's Winterhouse ◆ 1958
9. Snowbound with Betsy ◆ 1962
10. Betsy and Mr. Kilpatrick ◆ 1967
11. Merry Christmas from Betsy ◆ 1970
12. Betsy's Play School ◆ 1977

BETSY-TACY

Lovelace, Maud Hart

HARPERCOLLINS ◆ GRADES 2–5 ◆ A/R

HISTORICAL | REAL LIFE

Little Betsy lives with her family in a pleasant house in a Minnesota town in the early part of the 20th century. She is the only girl on her street, so she is glad when a new family moves in with a daughter, Tacy. Betsy and Tacy become such good friends that people refer to them in the same breath, as Betsy-Tacy. Tib, a blond-haired girl from a German family, comes along in the second book, and from then on the three girls are inseparable. They grow up together, go to high school, are part of a good "crowd," decide about careers, have beaus and eventually get married. Lois Lenski's illustrations and the girls' adventures give a good sense of the flavor of the times.

1. Betsy-Tacy ◆ 1940
2. Betsy-Tacy and Tib ◆ 1941
3. Betsy and Tacy Go Over the Big Hill ◆ 1942
4. Betsy and Tacy Go Down Town ◆ 1943
5. Heaven to Betsy ◆ 1945
6. Betsy in Spite of Herself ◆ 1946
7. Betsy Was a Junior ◆ 1947
8. Betsy and Joe ◆ 1948
9. Betsy and the Great World ◆ 1952
10. Betsy's Wedding ◆ 1955

BEVERLY BILLINGSLY

Stadler, Alexander

HARCOURT ◆ GRADES K–2

HUMOR

Beverly Billingsly has her own library card and is raring to go. Unfortunately, she keeps the book past the due date. After hearing about dreadful consequences and having nightmares, she returns the book. The librarian just reminds her to be more careful. Beverly is a lively character (the illustrations show her as a light-gray animal). She has problems children relate to—such as failing to get the best part in the play.

1. Beverly Billingsly Borrows a Book ◆ 2002
2. Beverly Billingsly Takes a Bow ◆ 2003
3. Beverly Billingsly Can't Catch ◆ 2004
4. Beverly Billingsly Takes the Cake ◆ 2005

BEWARE

Haas, Jessie

GREENWILLOW ◆ GRADES 3–5 ◆ A/R

REAL LIFE

Lily has outgrown her pony, and her grandfather, a livestock dealer, buys her a mare named Beware. Despite Beware's ominous name, Lily discovers that she just likes to have her belly scratched, and she will bump up against her owners when she wants them to do it. In the second book of this series Lily competes on Beware against her best friend, Mandy. They both win some ribbons and stay friends, even though they are rivals. In another book, Beware becomes sick and Lily, her Mom, and Gramp try to save her. Even Gran, who doesn't like horses, is concerned.

1. Beware the Mare ◆ 1993
2. A Blue for Beware ◆ 1995
3. Be Well, Beware ◆ 1996
4. Beware and Stogie ◆ 1998

BEYOND THE SPIDERWICK CHRONICLES

see Spiderwick: Beyond the Spiderwick Chronicles

BIG ANTHONY AND STREGA NONA *see*

Strega Nona and Big Anthony

BIG APPLE BARN

Earhart, Kristin

SCHOLASTIC ◆ GRADES 3–5 ◆ A/R

REAL LIFE

Big Apple Barn is a riding school and Happy Go Lucky is one of the horses. Happy learns what it takes to be a school pony, including adjusting to the arrival of a new pony, Sassafras Surprise—nicknamed Sassy. This series is a fun choice for younger readers who enjoy horses especially because it gives the horse's point of view.

1. Happy Go Lucky ◆ 2007
2. Happy's Big Plan ◆ 2007
3. A Sassy Surprise ◆ 2007
4. Saddle Up, Happy! ◆ 2007
5. Happy's Holiday ◆ 2007
6. Roscoe and the Pony Parade ◆ 2008

BIG BOB

Pinkwater, Daniel (Manus)

SCHOLASTIC ◆ GRADES 1–3 ◆ A/R

HUMOR

Big Bob is in the second grade. His nickname is appropriate because he is big for his age. Luckily, he is friends with another large kid in his class, Big Gloria. In the Thanksgiving story, the two friends make potato decorations for the holiday because they are vegetarians and they LOVE potatoes. Big Gloria even replaces pumpkins with potatoes at Halloween. This series is full of Pinkwater's signature off-the-wall humor.

1. Big Bob and the Thanksgiving Potatoes ◆ 2000
2. Big Bob and the Magic Valentine's Day Potato ◆ 2000
3. Big Bob and the Winter Holiday Potato ◆ 2001
4. Big Bob and the Halloween Potatoes ◆ 2002

BIG RED *see* Red

BILL AND PETE

dePaola, Tomie

PUTNAM ◆ GRADES K–2

ANIMAL FANTASY

Bill is a crocodile whose full name is William Everett Crocodile. Pete is his toothbrush bird and buddy. In these picture books, the two friends have adventures around the world. Along the way, they outwit the Bad Guy from Cairo and his Big Bad Brother and rescue little Jane Alison Crocodile. The colorful illustrations show dePaola's skill at creating humorous personalities.

1. Bill and Pete ◆ 1978
2. Bill and Pete Go Down the Nile ◆ 1987
3. Bill and Pete to the Rescue ◆ 1998

BILLY AND BLAZE *see* Blaze

BILLY HOOTEN, OWLBOY

Sniegoski, Tom

YEARLING ◆ GRADES 3–6 ◆ A/R

FANTASY

Billy Hooten, 12, loves comic books—especially ones with superheroes. Imagine his surprise when he meets Archebold, a goblin who tells Billy that he is Owlboy, a superhero charged with defending Monstros City. With his Owlmobile and Roost (hideout), Billy confronts Monkey Demons and other monsters. Fast-paced and fun, this series is a good choice for reluctant readers.

1. Billy Hooten, Owlboy ◆ 2007
2. The Girl With the Destructo Touch ◆ 2007
3. Tremble at the Terror of Zis-Boom-Bah ◆ 2008
4. The Flock of Fury ◆ 2008

BINGO BROWN

Byars, Betsy

VIKING ◆ GRADES 4–7 ◆ A/R

HUMOR | REAL LIFE

Bingo Brown is in sixth grade at the beginning of this series and is just discovering "mixed-sex conversations." He falls in and out of love many times but ends up being in love with Melissa. He is devastated when she moves to Oklahoma. That summer, he racks up a huge phone bill calling her and is pursued by her best friend. His parents go through a crisis of their own when his mother discovers she is pregnant. As Bingo enters seventh grade, he has a new baby brother, and is an acknowledged authority on romance among his friends.

1. The Burning Questions of Bingo Brown ◆ 1988
2. Bingo Brown and the Language of Love ◆ 1989
3. Bingo Brown, Gypsy Lover ◆ 1990
4. Bingo Brown's Guide to Romance ◆ 1992

BIONICLE ADVENTURES

Farshtey, Greg

SCHOLASTIC ◆ GRADES 4–7 ◆ A/R

FANTASY

Six Toa guard the city of Metru Nui. These warriors protect the Matoran. When the city is attacked, the Toa face unexpected dangers. There are related items including a sticker book, an *Official Guide to Bionicles,* and comic books. These stories are based on LEGO action figures.

1. Mystery of Metru Nui ◆ 2004
2. Trial by Fire ◆ 2004
3. Darkness Below ◆ 2004

4. Legends of Metru Nui ◆ 2004
5. Voyage of Fear ◆ 2004
6. Maze of Shadows ◆ 2004

BIONICLE CHRONICLES

Various authors

SCHOLASTIC ◆ GRADES 4–7 ◆ A/R

FANTASY

Mata Nui is an ancient land that has been peaceful until Makuta brings fear and darkness. Who will face the darkness? Six Toa, mighty warriors, are destined to rescue the land of Mata Nui. The Bionicle Chronicles describe the arrival of the Toa and their battles. Related items include a sticker book, an *Official Guide to Bionicles,* and comic books. These stories are based on LEGO action figures.

1. Tale of the Toa (Hapka, C. A.) ◆ 2003
2. Beware the Bohrok (Hapka, C. A.) ◆ 2003
3. Makuta's Revenge (Hapka, C. A.) ◆ 2003
4. Tales of the Masks (Farshtey, Greg) ◆ 2003

BIONICLE LEGENDS

Farshtey, Greg

SCHOLASTIC ◆ GRADES 4–7 ◆ A/R

FANTASY

This series features legends of the Toa's exploits. Facing the evil Piraka, retrieving the Mask of Life, and awakening the Great Spirit of Mata Nui are among the stories featured in these books.

1. Island of Doom ◆ 2006
2. Dark Destiny ◆ 2006
3. Power Play ◆ 2006
4. Legacy of Evil ◆ 2006
5. Inferno ◆ 2006
6. City of the Lost ◆ 2007
7. Prisoners of the Pit ◆ 2007
8. Downfall ◆ 2008
9. Shadows in the Sky ◆ 2008

THE BIRCHBARK HOUSE *see* Omakayas

BISCUIT READERS

Capucilli, Alyssa Satin

HARPERCOLLINS ◆ GRADES K–1 ◆ A/R

REAL LIFE

This series is just right for beginning readers. The words are simple and the print is large enough for young children who are just learning to focus on the text and decode it. Young readers will be delighted by the antics of Biscuit the puppy—avoiding his bedtime, finding a duckling, and going on a picnic. There are also picture books for preschoolers, along with board books, lift-the-flap, and scratch-and-sniff books about Biscuit.

1. Biscuit ◆ 1996
2. Biscuit Finds a Friend ◆ 1997
3. Biscuit's Picnic ◆ 1998
4. Hello, Biscuit! ◆ 1998
5. Bathtime for Biscuit ◆ 1998
6. Biscuit's New Trick ◆ 2001
7. Biscuit Goes to School ◆ 2002
8. Biscuit Visits the Farm ◆ 2002
9. Biscuit Wants to Play ◆ 2002
10. Biscuit's Big Friend ◆ 2003
11. Biscuit Wins a Prize ◆ 2003
12. Biscuit and the Baby ◆ 2005
13. Biscuit Visits the Big City ◆ 2006
14. Biscuit's Day at the Farm ◆ 2007
15. Biscuit and the Little Pup ◆ 2008

BIZZY BONES

Martin, Jacqueline Briggs

LOTHROP, LEE & SHEPARD ◆ GRADES K–2

ANIMAL FANTASY | FAMILY LIFE

Two mice, Bizzy Bones and Uncle Ezra, live together in an old shoe house near the edge of Piney Woods. Uncle Ezra tries very hard to remember how it was to be a very young mouse and reacts with kindness to all of young Bizzy's fears. Fierce winds, losing a beloved blanket, and staying with Uncle's friend, Mouse Mouse, are plots explored in this series. The softly detailed illustrations add to the gentle charm and depict Bizzy's fears and Uncle Ezra's wisdom.

1. Bizzy Bones and Uncle Ezra ◆ 1984
2. Bizzy Bones and Mouse Mouse ◆ 1986
3. Bizzy Bones and the Lost Quilt ◆ 1988

BLACK BELT CLUB

Barnes, Dawn
SCHOLASTIC ◆ GRADES 3–6 ◆ A/R
FANTASY

Max, Antonio, Maia, and Jamie are all members of the top-secret Black Belt Club. They use their martial arts skills to confront evil. In *Night on the Mountain of Fear,* they face Hate Master Heyoka. Despite their best efforts, the kids struggle until they realize it is not anger and aggression that will defeat the Hate Master, it is the strength of their feelings of friendship. The books are a combination of text and comic panel illustrations by Bernard Chang. The message in the stories encourages readers to use their inner strength to overcome obstacles.

1. Seven Wheels of Power ◆ 2005
2. Night on the Mountain of Fear ◆ 2006
3. Beware of the Haunted Eye ◆ 2007

BLACK CAT CLUB

Saunders, Susan
HARPERCOLLINS ◆ GRADES 2–4
HUMOR

In Maplewood, things are pretty quiet—until Robert, Belinda, Andrew, and Sam decide to form the Black Cat Club and investigate supernatural events. They end up adding a new member to their club—Alice, who is a ghost! These mild horror books are more humorous than frightening. For example, when the friends want to change the food in the cafeteria, they find that the new food is even worse—eyeballs and worms! Another book takes place in a haunted movie theater. Still another involves a creepy camping trip. Ghosts, phantoms, mummies, and other creatures add to the appeal of this series.

1. The Ghost Who Ate Chocolate ◆ 1996
2. The Haunted Skateboard ◆ 1996
3. The Curse of the Cat Mummy ◆ 1997
4. The Ghost of Spirit Lake ◆ 1997
5. The Revenge of the Pirate Ghost ◆ 1997
6. The Phantom Pen Pal ◆ 1997
7. The Case of the Eyeball Surprise ◆ 1997
8. The Chilling Tale of Crescent Pond ◆ 1998
9. The Creature Double Feature ◆ 1998
10. The Creepy Camp-Out ◆ 1998

BLACK LAGOON

Thaler, Mike

SCHOLASTIC ◆ GRADES K–4 ◆ A/R

HUMOR

A small boy relates the horrific stories he has heard about school, the teachers, the principal, and other school officials. The stories are all illustrated with cartoonlike exaggeration on each page. Teachers are portrayed as monsters of one sort or another, and the children are cut in half, put in freezers, or reduced to piles of ashes. On the last few pages, the boy meets the real adults, who turn out to be kind and helpful. For instance, the school nurse cures the blue spots on his hand by wiping off the ink, and his teacher is young, pretty, and loving. The Black Lagoon Adventures are early readers.

1. The Teacher from the Black Lagoon ◆ 1989
2. The Principal from the Black Lagoon ◆ 1993
3. The Gym Teacher from the Black Lagoon ◆ 1994
4. The School Nurse from the Black Lagoon ◆ 1995
5. The Librarian from the Black Lagoon ◆ 1997
6. The Cafeteria Lady from the Black Lagoon ◆ 1998
7. The School Bus Driver from the Black Lagoon ◆ 1999
8. The Music Teacher from the Black Lagoon ◆ 2000
9. The Custodian from the Black Lagoon ◆ 2001
10. The Class from the Black Lagoon ◆ 2002
11. The Art Teacher from the Black Lagoon ◆ 2003
12. The New Kid from the Black Lagoon ◆ 2004
13. The School Secretary from the Black Lagoon ◆ 2006
14. The Class Pet from the Black Lagoon ◆ 2008
15. The Dentist from the Black Lagoon ◆ 2008
16. The Bully from the Black Lagoon ◆ 2008
17. The Substitute Teacher from the Black Lagoon ◆ 2009

BLACK LAGOON ADVENTURES

1. The Class Trip from the Black Lagoon ◆ 2004
2. The Talent Show from the Black Lagoon ◆ 2004
3. The Class Election from the Black Lagoon ◆ 2004
4. The Science Fair from the Black Lagoon ◆ 2005
5. The Halloween Party from the Black Lagoon ◆ 2004
6. The School Carnival from the Black Lagoon ◆ 2005
7. Valentine's Day from the Black Lagoon ◆ 2006
8. The Field Day from the Black Lagoon ◆ 2008

BLACK STALLION

Farley, Walter

RANDOM HOUSE ◆ GRADES 5–8 ◆ A/R

ADVENTURE

On his way home from visiting his missionary uncle, Alec is shipwrecked along with a wild black stallion. They are rescued, and Alec takes the horse back to New York and boards him at a nearby farm to be trained by Henry Dailey. Because there are no official papers on "the Black," Alec cannot enter him in races. However, in a special race for the fastest horse in the country, Alec and "the Black" earn the respect they deserve. In another book, Alec travels to Arabia to research the claim of a man who is trying to take away his horse. The series continues as the stallion sires foals that Alec and Henry train and race. Walter Farley wrote the early books in the series. Walter and Steven Farley wrote *The Young Black Stallion,* and Steven Farley is continuing the series. The Island Stallion series features another young man and a horse; the Young Black Stallion series by Steven Farley also features Alec Ramsay.

1. The Black Stallion ◆ 1941
2. The Black Stallion Returns ◆ 1945
3. Son of the Black Stallion ◆ 1947
4. The Black Stallion and Satan ◆ 1949
5. The Blood Bay Colt (retitled The Black Stallion's Blood Bay Colt) ◆ 1950
6. The Black Stallion's Filly ◆ 1952
7. The Black Stallion Revolts ◆ 1953
8. The Black Stallion's Sulky Colt ◆ 1954
9. The Black Stallion's Courage ◆ 1956
10. The Black Stallion Mystery ◆ 1957
11. The Black Stallion and Flame ◆ 1960
12. The Black Stallion Challenged ◆ 1964
13. The Black Stallion's Ghost ◆ 1969
14. The Black Stallion and the Girl ◆ 1971
15. The Black Stallion Legend ◆ 1983
16. The Young Black Stallion (Farley, Walter, and Steven Farley) ◆ 1989
17. The Black Stallion's Shadow (Farley, Steven) ◆ 1996

BLACK STALLION: YOUNG BLACK STALLION

Farley, Steven

RANDOM HOUSE ◆ GRADES 5–8 ◆ A/R

REAL LIFE

Danielle Connor, 13, is upset that Alec Ramsay has turned her family's farm into a Thoroughbred training center. Her own horse, Redman, has been sold and Danielle now works in the stables that her family owned.

1. The Promise ◆ 1998
2. A Horse Called Raven ◆ 1998
3. The Homecoming ◆ 1999
4. Wild Spirit ◆ 1999
5. The Yearling ◆ 1999
6. Hard Lessons ◆ 1999

BLACKBOARD BEAR

Alexander, Martha

DIAL ◆ GRADES K–1 ◆ A/R

ANIMAL FANTASY

"Take your bear and go home," the older boys tell the small hero, and so he does. Then he decides to toss the bear out the window and draw a better one on the blackboard. This bear is huge and wears a red collar. He comes to life, and the two have many adventures.

1. Blackboard Bear ◆ 1969
2. And My Mean Old Mother Will Be Sorry, Blackboard Bear ◆ 1972
3. I Sure Am Glad to See You, Blackboard Bear ◆ 1976
4. We're in Big Trouble, Blackboard Bear ◆ 1980
5. You're a Genius, Blackboard Bear ◆ 1995
6. I'll Never Share You, Blackboard Bear ◆ 2003

BLAST TO THE PAST

Deutsch, Stacy, and Rhody Cohon

ALADDIN ◆ GRADES 2–4 ◆ A/R

FANTASY

The kids in Mr. Caruthers's class love Mondays because Mr. Caruthers starts each week with a question about history and a time-traveling adventure begins. Abigail, Jacob, Zack, and Bo meet important figures in American history at pivotal moments in their lives. In *King's Courage,* Dr. King is questioning his ability to continue the struggle for civil rights. In *Washington's War,* George Washington is ready to give up the fight at Valley Forge. In each book, the kids convince the "hero" to persevere. The mix of history and fantasy will attract readers of the Magic Tree House series and the Time Warp Trio books.

1. Lincoln's Legacy ◆ 2005
2. Disney's Dream ◆ 2005
3. Bell's Breakthrough ◆ 2005

4. King's Courage ◆ 2005
5. Sacagawea's Strength ◆ 2006
6. Ben Franklin's Fame ◆ 2006
7. Washington's War ◆ 2007
8. Betsy Ross's Star ◆ 2007

BLAZE

Anderson, C. W.

SIMON & SCHUSTER ◆ GRADES K–2

REAL LIFE

Billy loves horses. For his birthday, Billy's parents give him a pony that he names Blaze. Billy takes very good care of Blaze, while learning to ride him and to jump. When they enter a horse show, they win the silver cup, jumping over all the fences without a fault. Even Billy's dog, Rex, jumps with them. Each book features a new adventure: Billy and Blaze dramatically ride across fields, streams, and fences to warn about a brush fire and they rescue a lost calf from a mountain lion, for example.

1. Billy and Blaze: A Boy and His Pony ◆ 1936
2. Blaze and the Gypsies ◆ 1937
3. Blaze and the Forest Fire ◆ 1938
4. Blaze Finds the Trail ◆ 1950
5. Blaze and Thunderbolt ◆ 1955
6. Blaze and the Mountain Lion ◆ 1959
7. Blaze and the Indian Cave ◆ 1964
8. Blaze and the Lost Quarry ◆ 1966
9. Blaze and the Gray Spotted Pony ◆ 1968
10. Blaze Shows the Way ◆ 1969
11. Blaze Finds Forgotten Roads ◆ 1970

BLOODHOUNDS, INC.

Myers, Bill

BETHANY HOUSE ◆ GRADES 4–6 ◆ A/R

MYSTERY | VALUES

Two young detectives, Sean Hunter and his sister Melissa, along with their dog called Slobs solve problems that occur in Midvale. Robberies, vampires, an invisible knight, ghosts, and hidden treasure are among the things they investigate. Bible teachings and their faith in God guide them.

1. The Ghost of Krzy ◆ 1997
2. The Mystery of the Invisible Knight ◆ 1997
3. Phantom of the Haunted Church ◆ 1998

4. Invasion of the UFOs ◆ 1998
5. Fangs for the Memories ◆ 1999
6. The Case of the Missing Minds ◆ 1999
7. The Secret of the Ghostly Hot Rod ◆ 2000
8. I Want My Mummy ◆ 2000
9. The Curse of the Horrible Hair Day ◆ 2001
10. The Scam of the Screwball Wizards ◆ 2001
11. Mystery of the Melodies from Mars ◆ 2002
12. Room with a Boo ◆ 2002

BLOODWATER MYSTERIES

Hautman, Pete, and Mary Logue
PUTNAM ◆ GRADES 5–9 ◆ A/R

MYSTERY

Roni Delicata is the crime reporter for the high school newspaper. Brian Bain, 13, is a freshman with a specialty in science. Together they investigate mysteries in the town of Bloodwater. In *Doppelganger,* Roni sees a picture of a missing child that has been age-progressed. It looks a lot like Brian, who was born in Korea and adopted. As they look into Brian's past, they encounter other mysterious activities. There are kidnappings, schemes, and dangerous attacks that keep the reader involved. A good choice for reluctant readers.

1. Snatched ◆ 2006
2. Skullduggery ◆ 2007
3. Doppelganger ◆ 2008

BLOSSOM CULP

Peck, Richard
DELL ◆ GRADES 5–7 ◆ A/R

FANTASY | MYSTERY

Blossom Culp lives on the wrong side of the tracks in a small midwestern town at the turn of the century. Her mother is a fortune teller, who is jealous when it seems that Blossom has "the gift." Alexander, the son of a wealthy and prominent family, lives right across the tracks, and his barn is right in Blossom's back yard. The barn is inhabited by a ghost that Blossom can see. Alexander is reluctantly drawn into this adventure, only the first of many inspired by Blossom's gift. Blossom's contacts with the dead bring her fame and a certain social standing in the town. She moves into her high school years and has more encounters with the beyond, including an Egyptian princess and time travel 70 years into the future.

1. The Ghost Belonged to Me ◆ 1975

2. Ghosts I Have Been ◆ 1977
3. The Dreadful Future of Blossom Culp ◆ 1983
4. Blossom Culp and the Sleep of Death ◆ 1986

THE BLOSSOM FAMILY

Byars, Betsy
DELL ◆ GRADES 4–7 ◆ A/R
FAMILY LIFE | HUMOR

Maggie, Junior, and Vern Blossom live with their mother, Vicki, and their grandfather, Pap. Their father, Cotton, was killed riding a bull in the rodeo when the children were small. Vicki is a trick rider and goes out on the rodeo circuit, leaving the children behind with Pap in a rural section of the eastern United States. They make friends with a lady who lives a hermit's life in a cave. One of the boys almost drowns making a raft to float on the river. Two of the children break into prison when Pap is arrested, and Maggie makes her debut in trick riding. In each book, the stories of all the family members intersect.

1. The Not-Just-Anybody Family ◆ 1986
2. The Blossoms Meet the Vulture Lady ◆ 1986
3. The Blossoms and the Green Phantom ◆ 1987
4. A Blossom Promise ◆ 1987
5. Wanted—Mud Blossom ◆ 1991

BOBBSEY TWINS

Hope, Laura Lee
PUTNAM ◆ GRADES 3–5 ◆ A/R
FAMILY LIFE

The Stratemeyer Syndicate's first series, the Bobbsey Twins, was first published in 1904. The books feature two sets of twins. Flossie and Freddie Bobbsey, the younger twins, are blond, blue-eyed 4-year-olds. Then there are the 8-year-old twins, Nan and Bert, who are dark-haired, dark-eyed, and responsible. The twins' father owns a lumber company, and Mrs. Bobbsey is a housewife, involved in social and charitable activities. The Bobbseys are always doing exciting things, such as acquiring an actual miniature railroad. By the 1960s, the Bobbseys had aged slightly—Nan and Bert are 12 and Flossie and Freddie are 6—and they have become amateur detectives. Continuing to keep up with the times, by the 1980s the twins occasionally play in a rock band.

1. Bobbsey Twins ◆ 1904
2. Bobbsey Twins in the Country ◆ 1904
3. Bobbsey Twins at the Seashore ◆ 1907

4. Bobbsey Twins at School ◆ 1913
5. Bobbsey Twins at Snow Lodge ◆ 1913
6. Bobbsey Twins on a Houseboat ◆ 1915
7. Bobbsey Twins at Meadow Brook ◆ 1915
8. Bobbsey Twins at Home ◆ 1916
9. Bobbsey Twins in a Great City ◆ 1917
10. Bobbsey Twins on Blueberry Island ◆ 1917
11. Bobbsey Twins on the Deep Blue Sea ◆ 1918
12. Bobbsey Twins in Washington ◆ 1919
13. Bobbsey Twins in the Great West ◆ 1920
14. Bobbsey Twins at Cedar Camp ◆ 1921
15. Bobbsey Twins at the Country Fair ◆ 1922
16. Bobbsey Twins Camping Out ◆ 1923
17. Bobbsey Twins and Baby May ◆ 1924
18. Bobbsey Twins Keeping House ◆ 1925
19. Bobbsey Twins at Cloverbank ◆ 1926
20. Bobbsey Twins at Cherry Corners ◆ 1927
21. Bobbsey Twins and Their Schoolmates ◆ 1928
22. Bobbsey Twins Treasure Hunting ◆ 1929
23. Bobbsey Twins at Spruce Lake ◆ 1930
24. Bobbsey Twins' Wonderful Secret ◆ 1931
25. Bobbsey Twins at the Circus ◆ 1932
26. Bobbsey Twins on an Airplane Trip ◆ 1933
27. Bobbsey Twins Solve a Mystery ◆ 1934
28. Bobbsey Twins on a Ranch ◆ 1935
29. Bobbsey Twins in Eskimo Land ◆ 1936
30. Bobbsey Twins in a Radio Play ◆ 1937
31. Bobbsey Twins at Windmill Cottage ◆ 1938
32. Bobbsey Twins at Lighthouse Point ◆ 1939
33. Bobbsey Twins at Indian Hollow ◆ 1940
34. Bobbsey Twins at the Ice Carnival ◆ 1941
35. Bobbsey Twins in the Land of Cotton ◆ 1942
36. Bobbsey Twins in Echo Valley ◆ 1943
37. Bobbsey Twins on the Pony Trail ◆ 1944
38. Bobbsey Twins at Mystery Mansion ◆ 1945
39. Bobbsey Twins at Sugar Maple Hill ◆ 1946
40. Bobbsey Twins in Mexico ◆ 1947
41. Bobbsey Twins' Toy Shop ◆ 1948
42. Bobbsey Twins in Tulip Land ◆ 1949
43. Bobbsey Twins in Rainbow Valley ◆ 1950
44. Bobbsey Twins' Own Little Railroad ◆ 1951
45. Bobbsey Twins at Whitesail Harbor ◆ 1952
46. Bobbsey Twins and the Horseshoe Riddle ◆ 1953
47. Bobbsey Twins at Big Bear Pond ◆ 1954
48. Bobbsey Twins on a Bicycle Trip ◆ 1955
49. Bobbsey Twins' Own Little Ferryboat ◆ 1956
50. Bobbsey Twins at Pilgrim Rock ◆ 1957
51. Bobbsey Twins' Forest Adventure ◆ 1958
52. Bobbsey Twins at London Tower ◆ 1959

53. Bobbsey Twins in the Mystery Cave ◆ 1960
54. Bobbsey Twins in Volcano Land ◆ 1961
55. Bobbsey Twins and the Goldfish Mystery ◆ 1962
56. Bobbsey Twins and the Big River Mystery ◆ 1963
57. Bobbsey Twins and the Greek Hat Mystery ◆ 1963
58. Bobbsey Twins' Search for the Green Rooster ◆ 1965
59. Bobbsey Twins and Their Camel Adventure ◆ 1966
60. Bobbsey Twins and the Mystery of the King's Puppet ◆ 1967
61. Bobbsey Twins and the Secret of Candy Castle ◆ 1968
62. Bobbsey Twins and the Doodlebug Mystery ◆ 1969
63. Bobbsey Twins and the Talking Fox Mystery ◆ 1970
64. Bobbsey Twins and the Blue Mystery ◆ 1971
65. Bobbsey Twins and Doctor Funnybone's Secret ◆ 1972
66. Bobbsey Twins and the Tagalong Giraffe ◆ 1973
67. Bobbsey Twins and the Flying Clown ◆ 1974
68. Bobbsey Twins and the Sun-Moon Cruise ◆ 1975
69. Bobbsey Twins and the Freedom Bell Mystery ◆ 1976
70. Bobbsey Twins and the Smoky Mountain Mystery ◆ 1977
71. Bobbsey Twins in a TV Mystery Show ◆ 1978
72. Bobbsey Twins and the Coral Turtle Mystery ◆ 1979
73. Bobbsey Twins and the Blue Poodle Mystery ◆ 1980
74. Bobbsey Twins and the Secret in the Pirate's Cave ◆ 1980
75. Bobbsey Twins and the Dune Buggy Mystery ◆ 1980
76. Bobbsey Twins and the Missing Pony Mystery ◆ 1981
77. Bobbsey Twins and the Rose Parade Mystery ◆ 1981
78. Bobbsey Twins and the Camp Fire Mystery ◆ 1981
79. Bobbsey Twins and Double Trouble ◆ 1982
80. Bobbsey Twins and the Mystery of the Laughing Dinosaur ◆ 1983
81. Bobbsey Twins and the Music Box Mystery ◆ 1983
82. Bobbsey Twins and the Ghost in the Computer ◆ 1984
83. Bobbsey Twins and the Scarecrow Mystery ◆ 1984
84. Bobbsey Twins and the Haunted House Mystery ◆ 1985
85. Bobbsey Twins and the Mystery of the Hindu Temple ◆ 1985
86. Bobbsey Twins and the Grinning Gargoyle Mystery ◆ 1986

BOBBSEY TWINS: THE NEW BOBBSEY TWINS

Hope, Laura Lee
POCKET BOOKS ◆ GRADES 3–5
FAMILY LIFE | MYSTERY

Nan and Bert, the older twins, and Freddie and Flossie, the younger twins, continue sleuthing in the New Bobbsey Twins series. This intuitive foursome solves big and small mysteries, from burglaries in their town to missing documents. The Bobbseys sometimes make mistakes when several people seem suspicious. However, by cooperating with each other and using thinking skills, these siblings always discover the culprit.

1. The Secret of Jungle Park ◆ 1987
2. The Case of the Runaway Money ◆ 1987
3. The Clue that Flew Away ◆ 1987
4. The Secret of the Sand Castle ◆ 1988
5. The Case of the Close Encounter ◆ 1988
6. Mystery on the Mississippi ◆ 1988
7. Trouble in Toyland ◆ 1988
8. The Secret of the Stolen Puppies ◆ 1988
9. The Clue in the Classroom ◆ 1988
10. The Chocolate-Covered Clue ◆ 1989
11. The Case of the Crooked Contest ◆ 1989
12. The Secret of the Sunken Treasure ◆ 1989
13. The Case of the Crying Clown ◆ 1989
14. The Mystery of the Missing Mummy ◆ 1989
15. Secret of the Stolen Clue ◆ 1989
16. The Case of the Missing Dinosaur ◆ 1990
17. The Case at Creepy Castle ◆ 1990
18. The Secret at Sleepaway Camp ◆ 1990
19. Show and Tell Mystery ◆ 1990
20. The Weird Science Mystery ◆ 1990
21. The Great Skate Mystery ◆ 1990
22. The Super-Duper Cookie Caper ◆ 1991
23. The Monster Mouse Mystery ◆ 1991
24. The Case of the Goofy Game Show ◆ 1991
25. The Case of the Crazy Collections ◆ 1991
26. The Clue at Casper Creek ◆ 1991
27. The Big Pig Puzzle ◆ 1991
28. The Case of the Vanishing Video ◆ 1992
29. The Case of the Tricky Trickster ◆ 1992
30. Mystery of the Mixed-Up Mail ◆ 1992

BONE CHILLERS

Haynes, Betsy

HARPERCOLLINS ◆ GRADES 5–8 ◆ A/R

HORROR | HUMOR

The covers of these books make statements like "Bone Chillers: They'll make your skin crawl!" and "Bone Chillers: They'll scare the words right out of your mouth!" With spooky situations and creepy creatures, this series is similar to others in the horror genre. The books feature different characters. Azie Appleton always tells lies until one day her claim about giant termites comes true. Isabella Richmond thinks that gargoyles are kidnapping neighborhood kids. Some books are not just spooky but gross: Jeremy Wilson sneezes and his mucus becomes a slimy green glob. Readers who want horror and humor will devour this series.

1. Beware the Shopping Mall! ◆ 1994

2. Little Pet Shop of Horrors ◆ 1994
3. Back to School ◆ 1994
4. Frankenturkey ◆ 1994
5. Strange Brew ◆ 1995
6. Teacher Creature ◆ 1995
7. Welcome to Alien Inn ◆ 1995
8. Attack of the Killer Ants ◆ 1996
9. Slime Time ◆ 1996
10. Toilet Terror ◆ 1996
11. Night of the Living Clay ◆ 1996
12. The Thing Under the Bed ◆ 1997
13. A Terminal Case of the Uglies ◆ 1997
14. Tiki Doll of Doom ◆ 1997
15. The Queen of the Gargoyles ◆ 1997
16. Why I Quit the Baby-Sitter's Club ◆ 1997
17. blowtorch@psycho.com ◆ 1997
18. The Night Squawker ◆ 1997
19. Scare Bear ◆ 1997
20. The Dog Ate My Homework ◆ 1997
21. Killer Clown of Kings County ◆ 1998
22. Romeo and Ghouliette ◆ 1998

BONES

Adler, David A.

VIKING ◆ GRADES K–2

MYSTERY

Young Jeffrey Bones is a detective who has a detective bag of tools for solving mysteries. In the first book, Jeffrey takes notes and uses reasoning to find a missing school bus. In the second book, he looks for his dog, Curly. Fans of Young Cam Jansen will like these books.

1. Bones and the Big Yellow Mystery ◆ 2004
2. Bones and the Dog Gone Mystery ◆ 2004
3. Bones and the Cupcake Mystery ◆ 2005
4. Bones and the Dinosaur Mystery ◆ 2005
5. Bones and the Birthday Mystery ◆ 2007
6. Bones and the Math Test Mystery ◆ 2008
7. Bones and the Roller Coaster Mystery ◆ 2009

BONES AND THE DUCHESS MYSTERY

Eden, Alexandra

ALLEN A. KNOLL ◆ GRADES 4–6

MYSTERY

"Bones" Fatzinger is an ex-police officer turned private investigator. His unlikely partner is Verity Buscador, a 12-year-old girl with Asperger's syndrome. In the first book, they investigate the disappearance of two friends. In the second book, the case involves a mysterious fire at a church.

1. To Oz and Back ◆ 2002
2. Holy Smoke ◆ 2004
3. The Duchess to the Rescue ◆ 2006

BONNETS AND BUGLES

Morris, Gilbert
MOODY PRESS ◆ GRADES 5–7 ◆ A/R
HISTORICAL | VALUES

The Civil War splits neighbors and friends and provides opportunities for spiritual growth for five young people and their families. Tom and Jeff and their parents decide to move to Virginia and fight for the Confederacy, leaving Leah and Sarah and their parents in Kentucky as Union sympathizers. Mrs. Majors dies giving birth to Esther, and, with all the men off to war, there is no one to care for the baby. They turn to the Carters, who take her in to raise as their own. Throughout the course of the war, Jeff is a drummer boy and the other two boys are soldiers seeing action in major battles. They manage to get back to the girls often as Jeff courts Leah and Tom and Sarah become engaged. Tom loses his leg in Gettysburg and comes close to losing his faith in God, but the others help him back to spiritual health.

1. Drummer Boy at Bull Run ◆ 1995
2. Yankee Belles in Dixie ◆ 1995
3. The Secret of Richmond Manor ◆ 1995
4. The Soldier Boy's Discovery ◆ 1996
5. Blockade Runner ◆ 1996
6. The Gallant Boys of Gettysburg ◆ 1996
7. The Battle of Lookout Mountain ◆ 1996
8. Encounter at Cold Harbor ◆ 1997
9. Fire over Atlanta ◆ 1997
10. Bring the Boys Home ◆ 1997

BOOKSTORE CAT

Maitland, Barbara
DUTTON ◆ GRADES K–2 ◆ A/R
HUMOR | MYSTERY

The "ghosts" in this series are really cute mice that cooperate with Cobweb the cat to help Mr. Brown at the Black Cat Bookstore. The bookstore only sells scary stories, so patrons are fascinated when it seems the bookstore is haunted. The clever cat and mice scare a thief and play matchmaker for Mr. Brown. This beginning chapter book series is just right for primary-grade readers.

1. The Bookstore Ghost ◆ 1998
2. The Bookstore Burglar ◆ 2001
3. The Bookstore Valentine ◆ 2004

BORROWERS

Norton, Mary

HARCOURT ◆ GRADES 3–6 ◆ A/R

FANTASY

Under the floor of an old house, the little Borrowers live by borrowing from the family. They are the reason, Kate realizes, why there is never a needle when you need one. Pod, Homily, and their daughter, little Arrietty, live a quiet life by themselves, but once there were many other Borrowers in the old house. Arrietty is "seen" by a boy who comes to live in the house, and he tells her that her family may be the last Borrowers left. He begins to bring them things from a dollhouse, and that leads to the little family being discovered by the adults and harassed out of the house. As the series continues, the Borrowers find a little creature named Spiller who helps them find their relatives, who are living in a cottage. They stay with them until the cottage is sold. The rest of the series is about their attempts to find a new place to live as they travel by raft and hot-air balloon.

1. The Borrowers ◆ 1952
2. The Borrowers Afield ◆ 1955
3. The Borrowers Afloat ◆ 1959
4. The Borrowers Aloft ◆ 1961
5. Poor Stainless ◆ 1966
6. The Borrowers Avenged ◆ 1982

BOXCAR CHILDREN

Warner, Gertrude Chandler

WHITMAN ◆ GRADES 2–5 ◆ A/R

FAMILY LIFE | MYSTERY

Four children run away because their parents have died and they are being sent to their grandfather, who they think doesn't like them. They find an abandoned boxcar in the woods and fix it up to live in. Henry, the oldest, goes into a nearby town to find work; and Jessie, the oldest girl, tries to keep house with help from Violet and little Benny. When Violet becomes ill, Henry and Jessie seek help from the elderly gentleman for whom Henry has been working. The gentleman turns out to be their grandfather. In the rest of the series, the children live happily with their wealthy grandfather and get involved in a number of mysteries. The Special Edition books include pages with games and activities.

1. The Boxcar Children ◆ 1924
2. Surprise Island ◆ 1949
3. The Yellow House Mystery ◆ 1953
4. Mystery Ranch ◆ 1958
5. Mike's Mystery ◆ 1960
6. Blue Bay Mystery ◆ 1961
7. The Woodshed Mystery ◆ 1962
8. The Lighthouse Mystery ◆ 1963
9. Mountain Top Mystery ◆ 1964
10. Schoolhouse Mystery ◆ 1965
11. Caboose Mystery ◆ 1966
12. Houseboat Mystery ◆ 1967
13. Snowbound Mystery ◆ 1968
14. Tree House Mystery ◆ 1969
15. Bicycle Mystery ◆ 1970
16. Mystery in the Sand ◆ 1971
17. Mystery Behind the Wall ◆ 1973
18. The Bus Station Mystery ◆ 1974
19. Benny Uncovers a Mystery ◆ 1976
20. The Haunted Cabin Mystery ◆ 1991
21. The Deserted Library Mystery ◆ 1991
22. The Animal Shelter Mystery ◆ 1991
23. The Old Motel Mystery ◆ 1991
24. The Mystery of the Hidden Painting ◆ 1992
25. The Amusement Park Mystery ◆ 1992
26. The Mystery of the Mixed-Up Zoo ◆ 1992
27. The Camp-Out Mystery ◆ 1992
28. The Mystery Girl ◆ 1992
29. The Mystery Cruise ◆ 1992
30. The Disappearing Friend Mystery ◆ 1992
31. The Mystery of the Singing Ghost ◆ 1992
32. The Mystery in the Snow ◆ 1992
33. The Pizza Mystery ◆ 1993
34. The Mystery Horse ◆ 1993
35. The Mystery at the Dog Pound ◆ 1993
36. The Castle Mystery ◆ 1993
37. The Mystery of the Lost Village ◆ 1993
38. The Mystery of the Purple Pool ◆ 1994
39. The Ghost Ship Mystery ◆ 1994
40. The Canoe Trip Mystery ◆ 1994
41. The Mystery of the Hidden Beach ◆ 1994
42. The Mystery of the Missing Cat ◆ 1994

92. The Tattletale Mystery ◆ 2002
93. The Comic Book Mystery ◆ 2003
94. The Ice Cream Mystery ◆ 2003
95. The Midnight Mystery ◆ 2003
96. The Mystery in the Fortune Cookie ◆ 2003
97. The Radio Mystery ◆ 2003
98. The Mystery of the Runaway Ghost ◆ 2004
99. The Finders Keepers Mystery ◆ 2004
100. The Mystery of the Haunted Boxcar ◆ 2004
101. The Clue in the Corn Maze ◆ 2004
102. The Ghost of the Chattering Bones ◆ 2005
103. The Sword of the Silver Knight ◆ 2005
104. The Game Store Mystery ◆ 2005
105. The Mystery of the Orphan Train ◆ 2005
106. The Vanishing Passenger ◆ 2006
107. The Giant Yo-Yo Mystery ◆ 2006
108. The Creature in Ogopogo Lake ◆ 2006
109. The Rock 'n' Roll Mystery ◆ 2006
110. The Secret of the Mask ◆ 2007
111. The Seattle Puzzle ◆ 2007
112. The Ghost in the First Row ◆ 2007
113. The Box That Watch Found ◆ 2007
114. A Horse Named Dragon ◆ 2008
115. The Great Detective Race ◆ 2008
116. The Ghost at the Drive-In Movie ◆ 2008
117. The Mystery of the Traveling Tomatoes ◆ 2008

BOXCAR CHILDREN SPECIALS

1. The Mystery on the Ice ◆ 1994
2. The Mystery in Washington, D.C. ◆ 1994
3. The Mystery at Snowflake Inn ◆ 1995
4. The Mystery at the Ballpark ◆ 1995
5. The Pilgrim Village Mystery ◆ 1995
6. The Mystery at the Fair ◆ 1996
7. The Pet Shop Mystery ◆ 1996
8. The Niagara Falls Mystery ◆ 1997
9. The Mystery in the Old Attic ◆ 1997
10. The Windy City Mystery ◆ 1998
11. The Mystery of the Queen's Jewels ◆ 1998
12. The Mystery of the Black Raven ◆ 1999
13. The Mystery in New York ◆ 1999
14. The Home Run Mystery ◆ 2000
15. The Honeybee Mystery ◆ 2000
16. The Mystery of the Screech Owl ◆ 2001
17. The Mystery of the Tiger's Eye ◆ 2001
18. The Candy Factory Mystery ◆ 2002
19. The Mystery of Alligator Swamp ◆ 2002

20. The Great Shark Mystery ◆ 2003
21. The Black Widow Spider Mystery ◆ 2003

BOXCAR CHILDREN: ADVENTURES OF BENNY AND WATCH

Warner, Gertrude Chandler
WHITMAN ◆ GRADES 1–3 ◆ A/R
FAMILY LIFE

The Boxcar Children books by Gertrude Chandler Warner have been popular for many years. This new series, based on the books she created, is designed for younger readers. The text is not as long as in the original mysteries and there are more illustrations to provide support for beginning readers. Benny Alden, the youngest of the Boxcar Children, is featured in these books, which include stories of family, friendship, and simple mysteries. Watch, the family dog, plays a prominent role in these stories.

1. Meet the Boxcar Children ◆ 1998
2. A Present for Grandfather ◆ 1998
3. Benny's New Friend ◆ 1998
4. The Magic Show Mystery ◆ 1998
5. Benny Goes into Business ◆ 1999
6. Watch Runs Away ◆ 1999
7. The Secret Under the Tree ◆ 2001
8. Benny's Saturday Surprise ◆ 2001
9. Sam Makes Trouble ◆ 2002
10. Watch, the Superdog! ◆ 2002
11. Keys and Clues for Benny ◆ 2004
12. Benny's Boxcar Sleepover ◆ 2004

BOYDS WILL BE BOYDS

Weeks, Sarah
SCHOLASTIC ◆ GRADES 4–6 ◆ A/R
HUMOR

Nat Boyd and Boyd Fink share the same name and the same sense of humor. As best friends, they stick together no matter what the trouble. In the first book, Fink uses his cleverness to help his unlucky friend Nat face up to a bully named Mad Dog. In other books, the boys look forward to going to camp and don't look forward to a dance at school.

1. Beware of Mad Dog! ◆ 2006
2. Get Well Soon or Else! ◆ 2006
3. Danger! Boys Dancing! ◆ 2006
4. Fink's Funk! ◆ 2006

BRADY BRADY

Shaw, Mary

STODDART KIDS; FITZHENRY & WHITESIDE ◆ **GRADES 1–3** ◆ **A/R**

RECREATION

Brady is wild about hockey. He is so wrapped up in the sport that his family has to call him twice to get his attention. Now he is known as "Brady Brady." The cartoon art will attract many readers—especially those interested in sports.

1. Brady Brady and the Great Rink ◆ 2002
2. Brady Brady and the Runaway Goalie ◆ 2002
3. Brady Brady and the Great Exchange ◆ 2003
4. Brady Brady and the Singing Tree ◆ 2003
5. Brady Brady and the Twirlin' Torpedo ◆ 2003
6. Brady Brady and the Big Mistake ◆ 2003
7. Brady Brady and the Most Important Game ◆ 2004
8. Brady Brady and the MVP ◆ 2004
9. Brady Brady and the B Team ◆ 2006

BRAMBLY HEDGE

Barklem, Jill

PUTNAM ◆ **GRADES 3–5** ◆ **A/R**

ANIMAL FANTASY

A colony of mice live a sort of 19th-century idyllic life in a hedge, illustrated in great detail. They have a dairy, a mill, and a storehouse where everyone can help themselves to what they need. Lord and Lady Woodmouse live in a palace with their daughter Primrose and take care of everyone. The first four stories follow the mice through the seasons. The series continues with more stories about the mouse community. A companion book, *The Four Seasons of Brambly Hedge,* collects the seasonal stories.

1. Winter Story ◆ 1980
2. Autumn Story ◆ 1980
3. Spring Story ◆ 1980
4. Summer Story ◆ 1980
5. The Secret Staircase ◆ 1983
6. The High Hills ◆ 1986
7. The Sea Story ◆ 1991
8. Poppy's Babies ◆ 1995

BRATZ

Various authors

GROSSET & DUNLAP ◆ GRADES 4–7 ◆ A/R

HUMOR | REAL LIFE

Tweens will enjoy the activities of Yasmin, Cloe, Jade and Sasha. The girls love fashion, dancing, parties, and fun. Sometimes, they even focus on school. In one book, the Homecoming Dance is coming and the girls are trapped in the mall. In another book, Cloe's artistic talent brings her some special attention. There are related materials with stickers and activities, like a guide to slumber party ideas. These are breezy books with lots of attitude.

1. Keepin' It Real: Bratz, the Video (O'Connor, Charles) ◆ 2004
2. Model Friendship (Krulik, Nancy) ◆ 2004
3. All-Night Mall Party! (O'Connor, Charles) ◆ 2004
4. Will Work for Fashion (Krulik, Nancy) ◆ 2004

BRATZ: CLUED IN!

Various authors

GROSSET & DUNLAP ◆ GRADES 4–7 ◆ A/R

HUMOR | REAL LIFE

The Bratz girls solve mysteries in these books. In *Behind-the-Scenes Secrets*, the girls are in a fashion show but first they have to find out who is causing the backstage problems that may ruin the show. Bratz fans will rush to read these.

1. Behind-the-Scenes Secrets (Goldman, Leslie) ◆ 2005
2. Seeing Double (Roberts, Christine N.) ◆ 2005
3. Breaking News (Burns, Laura J.) ◆ 2006
4. Accessory to the Crime (Fishman, Zoe) ◆ 2006

BRATZ: LIL' BRATZ

GROSSET & DUNLAP ◆ GRADES 4–7

HUMOR | REAL LIFE

Meet the Lil' Bratz: Nazalia, Zada, Ailani, and Talia. Like the older Bratz, these girls love fashion and fun. In *Hangin' with the Lil' Bratz,* you can read diary entries for each girl. In *Catwalk Cuties,* the girls plan a fashion show to raise money for an animal shelter. There are coloring books and other novelties that go with this series. Tween girls will love the nail polish and emery board that come with *Sweet Lil' Nails!*

1. Friends 4-Ever! ◆ 2004
2. Hangin' with the Lil' Bratz! ◆ 2004
3. Makin' It Up! ◆ 2004
4. School Time Style ◆ 2004
5. Dancin' Divas ◆ 2004
6. Beauty Sleepover Bash! ◆ 2005
7. Sweet Lil' Nails! ◆ 2005
8. Fashion Funk ◆ 2005
9. The Fabulous Style Swap ◆ 2005
10. Lights, Camera, Star! ◆ 2005
11. Funkhouse Adventure ◆ 2006
12. Around the World with the Lil' Bratz ◆ 2006
13. Catwalk Cuties ◆ 2006
14. Stylin' in the Sun ◆ 2007

BRAVE KIDS

Goodman, Susan E.

SIMON & SCHUSTER ◆ GRADES 2–3 ◆ A/R

HISTORICAL

These books are based on actual events. Cora Frear, 10, survives a prairie fire in 19th-century Iowa. Robert Henry Hendershot, 12, is a drummer boy in the Civil War. In 1918, Hazelle Boxberg rides on an orphan train to Texas. Like the Dear America and American Girl books, these will appeal to readers who enjoy historical fiction.

1. Cora Frear ◆ 2002
2. Robert Henry Hendershot ◆ 2003
3. Hazelle Boxberg ◆ 2004

BRIAN ROBESON

Paulsen, Gary

DELACORTE ◆ GRADES 4–8 ◆ A/R

ADVENTURE | REAL LIFE

In *Hatchet,* 13-year-old Brian Robeson is stranded in the Canadian wilderness after a plane crash. He struggles to survive before being rescued just as winter approaches. *The River* features Brian returning to the site of his adventure with a psychologist, Derek Holtzer, who plans to observe and record the experience. Their trip turns into another struggle to survive. *Brian's Winter* is a continuation of *Hatchet,* but with the premise that Brian is not rescued before winter arrives and must struggle to survive even harsher circumstances. Fast-paced action—told in short, direct sentences—could appeal to reluctant readers. A related book is *Guts: The True Stories Behind Hatchet and the Brian Books* (2001).

1. Hatchet ◆ 1987
2. Brian's Return ◆ 1989
3. The River ◆ 1991
4. Brian's Winter ◆ 1996
5. Brian's Hunt ◆ 2004

BRIGID THRUSH BOOKS

Leverich, Kathleen

RANDOM HOUSE ◆ GRADES 2–3

FANTASY

Brigid Thrush is an average 9-year-old who wishes for a fairy godmother. She gets one, but not exactly what she was expecting: her fairy godmother is another 9-year-old who also turns into a large cat and appears at the most unexpected moments. In one story, she magically helps Brigid overcome her fear of the new high dive at the local pool. An entertaining series for young chapter book readers.

1. Brigid Bewitched ◆ 1994
2. Brigid Beware ◆ 1995
3. Brigid the Bad ◆ 1995

THE BROADWAY BALLPLAYERS

Holohan, Maureen

ALADDIN ◆ GRADES 4–7 ◆ A/R

RECREATION

Five girls who live on Broadway Avenue participate in a variety of sports. As in the Matt Christopher books, there are many dramatic moments involving injuries, family issues, jealousy, and "making the team." Each book features a different girl—Molly, Penny, Rosie, Wil, and Angel. In one book, Angel's feet are hurting but she won't tell anyone because she does not want to be left out of the big race. Sports fans will enjoy the action.

1. Friday Nights, by Molly ◆ 1998
2. Everybody's Favorite, by Penny ◆ 1998
3. Left Out, by Rosie ◆ 1998
4. Sideline Blues, by Wil ◆ 1998
5. Don't Stop, by Angel ◆ 1998
6. Ice Cold, by Molly ◆ 1999
7. Catch Shorty, by Rosie ◆ 1999

BROWNIE GIRL SCOUT BOOKS *see* Here
Come the Brownies

BUBBA AND BEAU

Appelt, Kathi

HARCOURT ◆ GRADES K–2 ◆ A/R

REAL LIFE

Bubba, a baby, and Beau, a bloodhound puppy, are inseparable. They play in the mud and endure a visit from the relatives. These simple chapter books are a good choice for beginning readers.

1. Bubba and Beau, Best Friends ◆ 2002
2. Bubba and Beau Go Night-Night ◆ 2003
3. Bubba and Beau Meet the Relatives ◆ 2004

BUDGIE

The Duchess of York

ALADDIN ◆ GRADES K–1

FANTASY

Budgie is a small helicopter with a big heart. He is always ready to help. In an adventure at sea, he delivers the mail and helps in a rescue. During a blizzard, Budgie brings a young couple to a medical facility just in time for the arrival of their new baby. Budgie and his friend Pippa the Piper Warrior leave the air show to rescue two boys at Bendick's Point. Budgie is an endearing character, and these simple stories will attract readers who want mild adventure and predictable, satisfying conclusions.

1. Budgie at Bendick's Point ◆ 1989
2. Budgie the Little Helicopter ◆ 1989
3. Budgie and the Blizzard ◆ 1991
4. Budgie Goes to Sea ◆ 1991

BUNNICULA

Howe, James, and Deborah Howe

ATHENUM: MORROW ◆ GRADES 3–5 ◆ A/R

ANIMAL FANTASY | HUMOR | MYSTERY

Harold the dog and Chester the cat are living happily with their family until the day their boy, Toby, brings home a rabbit. Chester, who can read and knows things about the world, decides that the bunny is a vampire when they find vegetables drained dry and an empty cage at night. Harold makes friends with the little rabbit and decides that he is harmless, but Chester tries to starve him. In the end, Chester decides that Bunnicula is a vampire all right, but a modern one who wants only vegetable juice. The three animals become friends, and later in the series a puppy, Howie, is added to the household. They all go on to have adventures together. The first Bunnicula book was written by Deborah and James Howe; the remaining books are by James Howe. This series includes both picture books and chapter books for older readers.

CHAPTER BOOKS (ATHENEUM)

1. Bunnicula: A Rabbit-Tale of Mystery ◆ 1979
2. Howliday Inn ◆ 1982
3. The Celery Stalks at Midnight ◆ 1983
4. Nighty-Nightmare ◆ 1987
5. Return to Howliday Inn ◆ 1992
6. Bunnicula Strikes Again ◆ 1999
7. Bunnicula Meets Edgar Allan Crow ◆ 2006

PICTURE BOOKS (MORROW)

1. Harold and Chester in the Fright Before Christmas ◆ 1989
2. Harold and Chester in Scared Silly: A Halloween Treat ◆ 1989
3. Harold and Chester in Hot Fudge ◆ 1990
4. Harold and Chester in Creepy-Crawly Birthday ◆ 1991
5. Harold and Chester in Rabbit-Cadabra ◆ 1993

BUNNICULA: TALES FROM THE HOUSE OF BUNNICULA

Howe, James

ATHENEUM ◆ GRADES 2–5 ◆ A/R

ANIMAL FANTASY | HUMOR | MYSTERY

Howie the dachshund wants to be an "author" like his Uncle Harold, who "wrote" the Bunnicula books. This new series is a lot of fun, often playing with the traditional elements of crime stories. In one book, Howie sees himself as a tough private investigator. In another, Howie creates a crime-fighting super hero, Stinky Dog.

1. It Came from Beneath the Bed! ◆ 2002
2. Invasion of the Mind Sweepers from Asteroid 6! ◆ 2002
3. Howie Monroe and the Doghouse of Doom ◆ 2002
4. Screaming Mummies of the Pharoah's Tomb II ◆ 2003
5. Bud Barkin, Private Eye ◆ 2003
6. The Amazing Odorous Adventures of Stinky Dog ◆ 2003

BUNNICULA AND FRIENDS

Howe, James

ATHENEUM ◆ GRADES K–2 ◆ A/R

ANIMAL FANTASY | HUMOR | MYSTERY

The original Bunnicula books have been adapted for beginning readers. The large print, easy vocabulary, and short chapters make the classic stories accessible to a younger audience.

1. The Vampire Bunny ◆ 2004
2. Hot Fudge ◆ 2004
3. Scared Silly ◆ 2005
4. Rabbit Cadabra! ◆ 2006
5. The Fright Before Christmas ◆ 2006
6. Creepy-Crawly Birthday ◆ 2007

BUNNY TROUBLE

Wilhelm, Hans

SCHOLASTIC ◆ GRADES K–2

ANIMAL FANTASY | HUMOR | RECREATION

Ralph is a rabbit who is supposed to work with other rabbits decorating eggs for the Easter Bunny. Unfortunately, Ralph likes playing soccer more than doing his job. Luckily, Ralph's soccer skills do come in handy. In one book, Ralph uses his soccer kicking ability to stop some foxes from turning bunnies into rabbit stew. This is an entertaining series of books that should attract readers who like sports and cute bunnies.

1. Bunny Trouble ◆ 1980
2. More Bunny Trouble ◆ 1990
3. Bad, Bad Bunny Trouble ◆ 1995

BUTT-UGLY MARTIANS CHAPTER BOOKS

Various authors

SCHOLASTIC ◆ GRADES 2–5

FANTASY

Three Martians—Do-Wah Diddy, 2-T-Fru-T, and B. Bop-A-Luna—have been sent to conquer Earth. Of course, they love it here. They make friends with some Earth kids and try to stay here while keeping their superiors happy. Quiz books, coloring books, drawing books, and activity books are also available.

1. The Big Bang Theory (Bailey, Gerry) ◆ 2001
2. Meet Gorgon (Bailey, Gerry) ◆ 2001
3. That's No Puddle—That's Angela (Bailey, Gerry) ◆ 2001
4. Teenage Spaceland (Mason, Tom) ◆ 2002

BUTT-UGLY MARTIANS STORYBOOKS (GRADES K–1)

1. The Martians Have Landed (Bailey, Gerry) ◆ 2001
2. Do-Wah Rocks (Bailey, Gerry) ◆ 2002
3. 2-T's Spoof Video (Bailey, Gerry) ◆ 2002
4. B-Bop's Brainwave (Bailey, Gerry) ◆ 2002

BUTT WARS

Griffiths, Andy
SCHOLASTIC ◆ GRADES 5–8 ◆ A/R
HUMOR

Twelve-year-old Zack Freeman's butt takes off for its own adventures. Yes, his butt runs away! There are battles with other butts, numerous butt wordplays, and lots of gross humor. Head butts, butt kicking, cluster butts, alien butts, even Great White Butts—you get the picture. This Australian import (which has been Americanized with butt for bum) is sure to be a hit with fans of Captain Underpants and the Riot Brothers.

1. The Day My Butt Went Psycho! Based on a True Story ◆ 2003
2. Zombie Butts from Uranus! ◆ 2004
3. Butt Wars! The Final Conflict ◆ 2005

BUTTERFIELD SQUARE *see* Miss Know It All

BUZZ BEAKER BRAINSTORM

Nickel, Scott
STONE ARCH ◆ GRADES 2–5 ◆ A/R
SCIENCE FICTION

Buzz Beaker is a boy who loves science. In *Billions of Bats,* Buzz saves the day when a classmate's science project of a cosmic copier goes haywire producing thousands of copies of a pet bat. In another book, Buzz battles a berserk robot. The graphics by Andy J. Smith should attract many readers, including reluctant readers.

1. Backyard Bug Battle: A Buzz Beaker Brainstorm ◆ 2006
2. Robot Rampage: A Buzz Beaker Brainstorm ◆ 2006
3. Billions of Bats: A Buzz Beaker Brainstorm ◆ 2007

4. Attack of the Mutant Lunch Lady: A Buzz Beaker Brainstorm ◆ 2008
5. Wind Power Whiz Kid: A Buzz Beaker Brainstorm ◆ 2008

B.Y. TIMES

Klein, Leah

TARGUM/FELDHEIM ◆ GRADES 4–8

REAL LIFE

A group of girls attend the same middle school, Bais Yaakov, and work on their school newspaper, the *B.Y. Times*. The staff of the paper changes as students leave the school. In an early book, Shani Baum is the editor-in-chief; in a later book, Chani Kaufman has that job. There are references to school events and to Jewish events and holidays. An issue of the *B.Y. Times* is printed at the end of each book.

1. Shani's Scoop ◆ 1991
2. Batya's Search ◆ 1991
3. Twins in Trouble ◆ 1991
4. War! ◆ 1991
5. Spring Fever ◆ 1992
6. Party Time ◆ 1992
7. Changing Times ◆ 1992
8. Summer Daze ◆ 1992
9. Here We Go Again ◆ 1992
10. The New Kids ◆ 1992
11. Dollars and Sense ◆ 1993
12. Talking It Over ◆ 1993
13. Flying High ◆ 1993
14. Nechama on Strike ◆ 1993
15. Secrets! ◆ 1993
16. Babysitting Blues ◆ 1994
17. Jen Starts Over ◆ 1994
18. Who's Who ◆ 1994

B.Y. TIMES KID SISTERS

Various authors

TARGUM/FELDHEIM ◆ GRADES 2–6

REAL LIFE

Sarah Chin, Naomi Kaufman, Melissa Farber, and Rivky Segal are the younger sisters of the girls who work on the Bais Yaakov middle school paper, the *B.Y. Times*. Like their older sisters, these elementary school girls enjoy friendship, school, and neighborhood adventures. There is a greater emphasis on everyday activities as the girls deal with a popular new girl, work to save a tree (and their tree house), and endure problems between best friends. Jewish events receive much less emphasis than in the series featuring the older sisters.

1. The I-Can't-Cope Club (Harkohav-Kamins, Tamar) ◆ 1992
2. The Treehouse Kids (Harkohav-Kamins, Tamar) ◆ 1992
3. Rivky's Great Idea (Harkohav-Kamins, Tamar) ◆ 1993
4. Sarah's Room (Klein, Leah) ◆ 1993
5. Running Away (Prenzlau, Sheryl) ◆ 1993
6. Teacher's Pet (Prenzlau, Sheryl) ◆ 1993
7. Growing Up (Sutton, Esther) ◆ 1994
8. Changing Places (Prenzlau, Sheryl) ◆ 1994
9. Missing! (Prenzlau, Sheryl) ◆ 1994
10. Giant Steps (Prenzlau, Sheryl) ◆ 1995
11. The Wrong Way (Prenzlau, Sheryl) ◆ 1995
12. Ups and Downs (Prenzlau, Sheryl) ◆ 1995

CABIN CREEK MYSTERIES

Gregory, Kristiana

SCHOLASTIC ◆ GRADES 4–6 ◆ A/R

MYSTERY

Cabin Creek is a small town but there are many mysteries for brothers Jeff and David and their cousin Claire. In *The Secret of Robber's Cave* the kids explore Lost Island, looking for clues to a rumored treasure. On the island, Robber's Cave is a good place to start and the kids are surprised to find a skeleton! There are many clues for readers to examine and the plot is exciting and full of action, making this a good choice for reluctant readers.

1. The Clue at the Bottom of the Lake ◆ 2008
2. The Secret of Robber's Cave ◆ 2008
3. The Legend of Skull Cliff ◆ 2008
4. The Haunting of Hillside School ◆ 2008
5. The Blizzard of Blue Mountain ◆ 2009

CALDER AND PETRA *see* Petra and Calder

CALICO CAT

Charles, Donald

CHILDREN'S PRESS ◆ GRADES K–1

HUMOR

The Calico Cat books often feature concepts that would be appropriate for preschool and primary-grade children. Seasons, colors, telling time, and animals are among the topics presented. Most of the books have a brief text with some rhyming elements, which make them more accessible to struggling readers. The colorful illustrations add to their appeal.

1. Count on Calico Cat ◆ 1974
2. Letters from Calico Cat ◆ 1974
3. Calico Cat Looks Around ◆ 1975
4. Calico Cat's Rainbow ◆ 1975
5. Fat, Fat Calico Cat ◆ 1977
6. Calico Cat Meets Bookworm ◆ 1978
7. Time to Rhyme with Calico Cat ◆ 1978
8. Calico Cat at School ◆ 1981
9. Calico Cat at the Zoo ◆ 1981
10. Calico Cat's Exercise Book ◆ 1982
11. Calico Cat's Year ◆ 1984
12. Calico Cat's Sunny Smile ◆ 1990

THE CALLAHAN COUSINS

Carey, Elizabeth Doyle

LITTLE, BROWN ◆ GRADES 3–6 ◆ A/R

FAMILY LIFE

Four cousins, all 12-year-old girls, spend the summer with their grandmother on Gull Island. Each book features one of the cousins. In *Summer Begins,* Hillary is dealing with the divorce of her parents; on the island, she helps resolve a longstanding feud.

1. Summer Begins ◆ 2005
2. Home Sweet Home ◆ 2005
3. Keeping Cool ◆ 2006
4. Together Again ◆ 2006

CAM JANSEN

Adler, David A.

VIKING ◆ GRADES 2–4 ◆ A/R

MYSTERY

When Cam Jansen closes her eyes and says "click," her friends know she is using her photographic memory to solve crimes. Her friend Eric offers help and support to the elementary-school sleuth. In one story, they are at the mall when they learn that someone is stealing shopping bags. Cam takes a mental picture of the people who were around at the time of the crime and leads police to the culprit. Standing in line to buy tickets to a rock concert, Eric and Cam see a person dressed as a ghost who is scaring people. Cam's skills help them identify this person, who is trying to sabotage the band. Short, easy-reading chapters and black-and-white illustrations are suitable for beginning readers. Super Special editions include three mysteries.

1. Cam Jansen and the Mystery of the Stolen Diamonds ◆ 1980
2. Cam Jansen and the Mystery of the UFO ◆ 1980
3. Cam Jansen and the Mystery of the Dinosaur Bones ◆ 1981
4. Cam Jansen and the Mystery of the Television Dog ◆ 1981
5. Cam Jansen and the Mystery of the Gold Coins ◆ 1982
6. Cam Jansen and the Mystery of the Babe Ruth Baseball ◆ 1982
7. Cam Jansen and the Mystery of the Circus Clown ◆ 1983
8. Cam Jansen and the Mystery of the Monster Movie ◆ 1984
9. Cam Jansen and the Mystery of the Carnival Prize ◆ 1984
10. Cam Jansen and the Mystery at the Monkey House ◆ 1985
11. Cam Jansen and the Mystery of the Stolen Corn Popper ◆ 1986
12. Cam Jansen and the Mystery of Flight 54 ◆ 1989
13. Cam Jansen and the Mystery at the Haunted House ◆ 1992
14. Cam Jansen and the Chocolate Fudge Mystery ◆ 1993
15. Cam Jansen and the Triceratops Pops Mystery ◆ 1995
16. Cam Jansen and the Ghostly Mystery ◆ 1996
17. Cam Jansen and the Scary Snake Mystery ◆ 1997
18. Cam Jansen and the Catnapping Mystery ◆ 1998
19. Cam Jansen and the Barking Treasure Mystery ◆ 2001
20. Cam Jansen and the Birthday Mystery ◆ 2002
21. Cam Jansen and the School Play Mystery ◆ 2002
22. Cam Jansen and the First Day of School Mystery ◆ 2002
23. Cam Jansen and the Tennis Trophy Mystery ◆ 2003
24. Cam Jansen and the Snowy Day Mystery ◆ 2004
25. Cam Jansen and the Valentine Baby Mystery ◆ 2005
26. Cam Jansen and the Secret Service Mystery ◆ 2006
27. Cam Jansen and the Mystery Writer Mystery ◆ 2007
28. Cam Jansen and the Green School Mystery ◆ 2008

SUPER SPECIAL

1. The Summer Camp Mysteries ◆ 2007

CAM JANSEN: YOUNG CAM JANSEN

Adler, David A.
VIKING ◆ GRADES 1–3 ◆ A/R
MYSTERY

Cam Jansen, the star of a mystery series for older readers, is in second grade in this series, and already sleuthing. Her friend Eric tells everyone about her amazing photographic memory, and she says "click" when she wants to remember something. When their friend is missing a cookie out of his lunch box, Cam remembers seeing crumbs and rightly concludes that it was his dog who stole the cookie. Young Cam Jansen is part of the

Viking Easy to Read series featuring short sentences and easy vocabulary but not much word repetition. After reading these books, many children will go on to the Cam Jansen series.

1. Young Cam Jansen and the Dinosaur Game ◆ 1996
2. Young Cam Jansen and the Missing Cookie ◆ 1996
3. Young Cam Jansen and the Lost Tooth ◆ 1997
4. Young Cam Jansen and the Ice Skate Mystery ◆ 1998
5. Young Cam Jansen and the Baseball Mystery ◆ 1999
6. Young Cam Jansen and the Pizza Shop Mystery ◆ 2000
7. Young Cam Jansen and the Library Mystery ◆ 2001
8. Young Cam Jansen and the Double Beach Mystery ◆ 2002
9. Young Cam Jansen and the Zoo Note Mystery ◆ 2003
10. Young Cam Jansen and the New Girl Mystery ◆ 2004
11. Young Cam Jansen and the Substitute Mystery ◆ 2005
12. Young Cam Jansen and the Spotted Cat Mystery ◆ 2006
13. Young Cam Jansen and the Lions' Lunch Mystery ◆ 2007
14. Young Cam Jansen and the Molly Shoe Mystery ◆ 2008

CAMP CONFIDENTIAL

Morgan, Melissa
GROSSET & DUNLAP ◆ GRADES 4–7 ◆ A/R
REAL LIFE

When the series begins, the girls featured in each book are 11 and they are worried about being new at camp and making friends. For example, in *Jenna's Dilemma* Jenna is trying to cope with her parents' separation. Then, in *A Fair to Remember,* Jenna is 13 and upset that her twin brother has invited her old boyfriend to a family activity. At first, there is a core group of friends. They visit each other during the year after camp (when they are in sixth grade) and return to the camp the next summer. As the series continues, different girls are featured and their concerns reflect their growing maturity. In *Suddenly Last Summer,* Camp Lakeview is closed.

1. Natalie's Secret ◆ 2006
2. Jenna's Dilemma ◆ 2006
3. Grace's Twist ◆ 2006
4. Alex's Challenge ◆ 2006
5. TTYL ◆ 2006
6. RSVP ◆ 2006
7. Second Time's the Charm ◆ 2006
8. Wish You Weren't Here ◆ 2006
9. Best (Boy)friend Forever ◆ 2006
10. Over & Out ◆ 2006
11. Falling In Like ◆ 2006
12. Winter Games ◆ 2006

13. A Fair to Remember ◆ 2007
14. Hide and Shriek ◆ 2007
15. Reality Bites ◆ 2007
16. Golden Girls ◆ 2007
17. Freaky Tuesday ◆ 2007
18. And the Winner Is . . . ◆ 2007
19. Charmed Forces ◆ 2008
20. Suddenly Last Summer ◆ 2008

CAMP SUNNYSIDE

Kaye, Marilyn

AVON ◆ GRADES 4–7

REAL LIFE

Five girls from different parts of the country and with very different personalities meet every summer at Camp Sunnyside. Katie is a born leader and always has a scheme up her sleeve. Trina is more mature and thoughtful, while Erin is the sophisticated one of the group. Rounding out the complement of characters are Sarah, the intellectual, and Megan, the daydreamer. In *No Boys Allowed,* a neighboring boys camp has been destroyed by fire, and plans are made for the campers to stay at Camp Sunnyside temporarily. Katie, who has obnoxious older brothers, is vehemently opposed to the idea, and plans to let the boys know they are not welcome. She recruits the other girls to join her, but one by one they meet boys they like who share their interests. Eventually even Katie succumbs to a boy's advance. The series continues for several summers until the girls are in junior high.

1. No Boys Allowed ◆ 1989
2. Cabin Six Plays Cupid ◆ 1989
3. Color War! ◆ 1989
4. New Girl in Cabin Six ◆ 1989
5. Looking for Trouble ◆ 1990
6. Katie Steals the Show ◆ 1990
7. A Witch in Cabin Six ◆ 1990
8. Too Many Counselors ◆ 1990
9. The New and Improved Sarah ◆ 1990
10. Erin and the Movie Star ◆ 1991
11. The Problem with Parents ◆ 1991
12. The Tennis Trap ◆ 1991
13. Big Sister Blues ◆ 1991
14. Megan's Ghost ◆ 1991
15. Christmas Break ◆ 1991
16. Happily Ever After ◆ 1992
17. Camp Spaghetti ◆ 1992
18. Balancing Act ◆ 1992

CAMP ZOMBIE

Stine, Megan, and H. William Stine
RANDOM HOUSE ◆ GRADES 5–7
HORROR

Five people once drowned in the lake at Camp Harvest Moon in Maine. Years later, the camp reopens and Corey and his sister Amanda are among the first new campers. But something very strange is going on. Amanda, an excellent swimmer, is almost drowned, and she is sure something grabbed her. Corey and Amanda and some other campers confront the five zombies from the lake and a new zombie—a dead camp counselor. The next summer, their cousin Griffen is sent to the same camp! And the next summer, on a trip with their grandparents, the cousins meet the zombies again. There are plot twists and dramatic moments when the zombies are just inches away that will provide readers with moments of spine-tingling suspense.

1. Camp Zombie ◆ 1994
2. Camp Zombie: The Second Summer ◆ 1995
3. Camp Zombie: The Lake's Revenge ◆ 1996

CANDY APPLE

Various authors
SCHOLASTIC ◆ GRADES 4–6 ◆ A/R
REAL LIFE

Tween girls will love this series featuring a group of middle school girls. In the first book, Kylie, who is lively and outgoing, decides to sign up for cheerleading tryouts and lists Sophie, her shy friend, as her partner. Sophie's talent as a gymnast helps her get chosen for the squad while Kylie ends up as the mascot—a mule. The girls' friendship is strained as Sophie hangs with the cheerleaders and even dates a popular boy. Additional books feature other girls in everyday situations—like Kaitlyn and Nola who compete for the best babysitting jobs and Annabelle who gets a Valentine surprise from the wrong boy.

1. The Accidental Cheerleader (McCoy, Mimi) ◆ 2007
2. The Boy Next Door (Dower, Laura) ◆ 2007
3. Miss Popularity (Sedita, Francesco) ◆ 2007
4. How to be a Girly Girl In Just Ten Days (Papademetriou, Lisa) ◆ 2007
5. Drama Queen (Bergen, Lara) ◆ 2007
6. The Babysitting Wars (McCoy, Mimi) ◆ 2007
7. Totally Crushed (Willard, Eliza) ◆ 2008
8. I've Got a Secret (Bergen, Lara) ◆ 2008
9. Callie for President (Wasserman, Robin) ◆ 2008

10. Making Waves (Reisfeld, Randi, and H. B. Gilmour) ◆ 2008
11. Sister Switch (Mason, J., and S. Stephens) ◆ 2008
12. Accidentally Fabulous (Papademetriou, Lisa) ◆ 2008
13. Confessions of a Bitter Secret Santa (Bergen, Lara) ◆ 2008

THE CAPED 6TH GRADER

Quinn, Zoe
YEARLING ◆ GRADES 4–6 ◆ A/R
FANTASY | MYSTERY

Until she turned 12, Zoe Richards thought she was an ordinary kid. Then her grandfather told her she was a superhero. Now instead of just going to Sweetbriar Middle School and hanging with her friends, Zoe must begin training to improve her superpowers. Along the way she solves some easy mysteries. In *Cabin Fever,* Zoe attends a camp with other kids who have unusual abilities.

1. Happy Birthday, Hero! ◆ 2006
2. Totally Toxic ◆ 2006
3. Lightning Strikes! ◆ 2006
4. Cabin Fever ◆ 2006

CAPITAL MYSTERIES

Roy, Ron
RANDOM HOUSE ◆ GRADES 2–4 ◆ A/R
MYSTERY

KC Corcoran and her friend Marshall are observant youngsters who become involved in strange happenings in Washington, D.C. They discover that the president has been cloned, and they foil an attempt to take the treasures of the Smithsonian. They also find out who has been telling White House secrets—including that KC's mom is going to marry the president. Ron Roy's A to Z Mysteries have been a big hit with middle-elementary readers and this series should appeal also.

1. Who Cloned the President? ◆ 2001
2. Kidnapped at the Capital ◆ 2002
3. The Skeleton in the Smithsonian ◆ 2003
4. A Spy in the White House ◆ 2004
5. Who Broke Lincoln's Thumb? ◆ 2005
6. Fireworks at the FBI ◆ 2006
7. Trouble at the Treasury ◆ 2006
8. Mystery at the Washington Monument ◆ 2007
9. A Thief at the National Zoo ◆ 2007

10. The Election-Day Disaster ◆ 2008
11. The Secret at Jefferson's Mansion ◆ 2009

CAPTAIN UNDERPANTS

Pilkey, Dav

SCHOLASTIC ◆ GRADES 3–8 ◆ A/R

HUMOR

Kids love these irreverent comic-book-style stories. They are gross, rude, and hilarious. George and Harold are the troublemakers. Adults are the dupes—the "butt" of the jokes. Just look at some of their names—Professor Poopypants and Stinky Jingleberry. Spanish editions and two activity books are also available. The Riot Brothers (Amato) and Butt Wars (Griffiths) are equally irreverent series.

1. The Adventures of Captain Underpants ◆ 1997
2. Captain Underpants and the Attack of the Talking Toilets ◆ 1999
3. Captain Underpants and the Invasion of the Incredibly Naughty Cafeteria Ladies from Outer Space ◆ 1999
4. Captain Underpants and the Perilous Plot of Professor Poopypants ◆ 2000
5. Captain Underpants and the Wrath of the Wicked Wedgie Woman ◆ 2001
6. Captain Underpants and the Big, Bad Battle of the Bionic Booger Boy, Part 1: The Night of the Nasty Nostril Nuggets ◆ 2003
7. Captain Underpants and the Big, Bad Battle of the Bionic Booger Boy, Part 2: The Revenge of the Ridiculous Robo-Boogers ◆ 2003
8. Captain Underpants and the Preposterous Plight of the Purple Potty People ◆ 2006

CAPTAIN UNDERPANTS: SUPER DIAPER BABY

Pilkey, Dav

SCHOLASTIC ◆ GRADES 3–6 ◆ A/R

HUMOR

Harold and George (from Captain Underpants) have created a new hero—Super Diaper Baby. With lots of illustrations, this graphic novel describes how Deputy Dangerous is turned into "poop" and renamed Deputy Doo-Doo. There are silly jokes and a sophomoric focus on bodily functions that kids love. Fans of Captain Underpants will line up for these.

1. The Adventures of Super Diaper Baby ◆ 2002
2. Super Diaper Baby 2: The Invasion of the Potty Snatchers ◆ 2005

CARDCAPTOR SAKURA

Ohkawa, Ageha, team leader

TOKYOPOP ◆ GRADES 4–6

ADVENTURE | FANTASY

This series of books is based on an animated television series. Sakura begins the adventure by releasing some mysterious cards. The guardian, Kero, and her friends, Madison and Li, help with her efforts to recover the cards. This series has been one of the most popular with Japanese girls.

1. Volume 1 ◆ 2002
2. Volume 2 ◆ 2002
3. Volume 3 ◆ 2002
4. Volume 4 ◆ 2002
5. Volume 5 ◆ 2002
6. Volume 6 ◆ 2002
7. Volume 7 ◆ 2002
8. Volume 8 ◆ 2002
9. Volume 9 ◆ 2002
10. Volume 10 ◆ 2002

CARL

Day, Alexandra

FARRAR, STRAUS & GIROUX ◆ GRADES K–1

ANIMAL FANTASY | HUMOR

In these almost wordless picture books, Carl, a huge Rottweiler, takes care of a baby in unique ways. In a typical book, the mother takes them shopping and tells Carl on the first page to "take good care of the baby" while she goes upstairs. The baby promptly climbs on the dog's back and away they go, wreaking havoc in the toy department, reading *Rottweilers I Have Known* in the book department, and watching themselves on camera in the electronics department. Chaos continues as they let all the animals out of their cages in the pet shop. The baby's mother never suspects the mischief these two get into. In other books, Carl watches the baby at home, where they dress up and feast in the kitchen, and at daycare, where Carl again takes charge.

1. Good Dog, Carl ◆ 1987
2. Carl Goes Shopping ◆ 1989
3. Carl's Christmas ◆ 1990
4. Carl's Afternoon in the Park ◆ 1991
5. Carl's Masquerade ◆ 1992
6. Carl Goes to Daycare ◆ 1993
7. Carl Makes a Scrap-Book ◆ 1994
8. Carl's Birthday ◆ 1995
9. Follow Carl! ◆ 1998
10. Carl's Sleepy Afternoon ◆ 2005
11. Carl's Summer Vacation ◆ 2008

CARMEN BROWNE

Moore, Stephanie Perry

LIFT EVERY VOICE ◆ GRADES 4–6

REAL LIFE | VALUES

Carmen Browne, 10, is entering fifth grade in a new school and trying to make new friends. Adding to her concerns is the family's decision to tell her brother Clay that he is adopted. Carmen relies on her faith to help her through challenging situations. By the fifth book, Carmen is in sixth grade. She deals with issues of self-esteem and maturation while accepting God's guidance.

1. True Friends ◆ 2005
2. Sweet Honesty ◆ 2005
3. Golden Spirit ◆ 2006
4. Perfect Joy ◆ 2006
5. Happy Princess ◆ 2007

CARMEN SANDIEGO MYSTERIES

Various authors

HARPERCOLLINS ◆ GRADES 4–6 ◆ A/R

MYSTERY

Maya's aunt is the head of a world-famous crime-fighting organization called ACME. Maya and Ben are her youngest and best secret agents and they travel the world mostly in pursuit of one master criminal—Carmen Sandiego. Carmen is a former ACME agent who now commits outrageous crimes just for the fun of pitting her wits against theirs. She dresses in red and flies in a red jet, and she often leaves a calling card at the scene of the crime. Maya and Ben use his computer knowledge and her athletic skill to solve the crimes, but they never quite catch Carmen.

1. Hasta la Vista, Blarney (Peterson, Melissa) ◆ 1997
2. Color Me Criminal (Weiss, Ellen, and Mel Friedman) ◆ 1997
3. The Cocoa Commotion (Peterson, Melissa) ◆ 1997
4. One T. Rex Over Easy (Bader, Bonnie, and Tracey West) ◆ 1997
5. Take the Mummy and Run (Weiss, Ellen, and Mel Friedman) ◆ 1997
6. Highway Robbery (Bader, Bonnie, and Tracey West) ◆ 1997

CAROLE MARSH MYSTERIES: AROUND THE WORLD IN 80 MYSTERIES

Marsh, Carole

GALLOPADE ◆ GRADES 3–4 ◆ A/R

MYSTERY

Part travelogue, part mystery, this series follows the adventures of Mimi, Papa, Grant, and Christina as they travel around the world.

1. The Mystery of Big Ben ◆ 2005
2. The Mystery at the Eiffel Tower ◆ 2005
3. The Mystery at the Roman Colosseum ◆ 2005
4. The Mystery at the Ancient Pyramids ◆ 2006
5. The Mystery on the Great Wall of China ◆ 2006
6. The Mystery on the Great Barrier Reef ◆ 2006
7. The Mystery at Mount Fuji ◆ 2008
8. The Mystery in the Amazon Rainforest ◆ 2007
9. The Mystery at Dracula's Castle ◆ 2008
10. The Curse of the Ancient Acropolis ◆ 2008

CAROLE MARSH MYSTERIES: REAL KIDS, REAL PLACES

Marsh, Carole

GALLOPADE ◆ GRADES 3–4 ◆ A/R

MYSTERY

Mixing information about geography and travel, this series features Mimi, Papa, Grant and Christina in well-known locations.

1. The Mystery of Biltmore House ◆ 1998
2. The Mystery on the Freedom Trail ◆ 2003
3. The Mystery of Blackbeard The Pirate ◆ 2003
4. The Mystery of the Alamo Ghost ◆ 2003
5. The Mystery of the California Mission Trail ◆ 2003
6. The Mystery of the Missing Dinosaurs ◆ 2003
7. The White House Christmas Mystery ◆ 2003
8. The Mystery of the Iditarod Trail ◆ 2003
9. The Mystery at Kill Devil Hills ◆ 2003
10. The Mystery in New York City ◆ 2003
11. The Mystery at Disney World ◆ 2003
12. The Mystery on the Underground Railroad ◆ 2003
13. The Mystery in the Rocky Mountains ◆ 2004
14. The Mystery on the Mighty Mississippi ◆ 2004
15. The Mystery at the Kentucky Derby ◆ 2004
16. The Mystery of the Grand Canyon ◆ 2004
17. The Mystery at Jamestown ◆ 2006
18. The Mystery in Chocolate Town . . . Hershey, Pennsylvania ◆ 2007
19. The Gosh Awful Gold Rush Mystery ◆ 2007
20. The Counterfeit Constitution Mystery ◆ 2008

THE CAROLINE YEARS *see* Little House: The Caroline Years

CASCADE MOUNTAIN RAILROAD MYSTERIES

Capeci, Anne

PEACHTREE ◆ **GRADES 4–6** ◆ **A/R**

ADVENTURE | MYSTERY

In a small town in 1926, a crate of dynamite is missing. Billy, a fourth-grader, and his friends try to figure out what happened. The events in these books take place in Scenic, Washington, at the time when the Cascade Tunnel was being built for the railroad. One book focuses on Prohibition and illegal transport of liquor. The adventures move quickly and may appeal to reluctant readers.

1. Danger: Dynamite! ◆ 2003
2. Daredevils ◆ 2004
3. Ghost Train ◆ 2004
4. Missing! ◆ 2005

CASE OF THE . . .

Bonsall, Crosby

HARPERCOLLINS ◆ **GRADES K–3** ◆ **A/R**

MYSTERY

In this beginning-to-read series, Wizard has decided to become a private eye and his friends Skinny and Tubby are a part of the business. Snitch, Wizard's little brother, is always around as they solve various cases: who stole Snitch's cat, who took Mrs. Meech's pie, and so on. Readers will want to continue reading to see the outcome of each mystery.

1. The Case of the Hungry Stranger ◆ 1963
2. The Case of the Cat's Meow ◆ 1965
3. The Case of the Dumb Bells ◆ 1966
4. The Case of the Scaredy Cats ◆ 1971
5. The Case of the Double Cross ◆ 1980

CASEBUSTERS

Nixon, Joan Lowery

DISNEY PRESS ◆ **GRADES 2–4**

MYSTERY

Brian and his younger brother Sean are the sons of a private detective, and they help with his cases and sometimes work on cases of their own. In *Beware the Pirate Ghost,* they help their father find a spoiled young boy who fakes his own kidnapping and then finds himself in real danger.

On their own in *The Internet Escapade,* they find out who has been sabotaging the school computers and shifting the blame to Sean. The boys have friends who are intrigued by their detective work and want to help, and their parents and other adults in town are supportive. Their frequent use of computers makes their stories up to date. Boys who are too young for The Hardy Boys will enjoy this series.

1. The Statue Walks at Night ◆ 1995
2. The Legend of the Deadman's Mine ◆ 1995
3. Backstage with a Ghost ◆ 1995
4. Check in to Danger ◆ 1995
5. The House Has Eyes ◆ 1996
6. The Secret of the Time Capsule ◆ 1996
7. Beware the Pirate Ghost ◆ 1996
8. Catch a Crooked Clown ◆ 1996
9. Fear Stalks Grizzly Hill ◆ 1996
10. Sabotage on the Set ◆ 1996
11. The Internet Escapade ◆ 1997
12. Bait for a Burglar ◆ 1997

CASEY, JENNY, AND KATE

Hest, Amy

MORROW ◆ GRADES 2–4

REAL LIFE

The emphasis in this series is on friendship and fun. The books are narrated by Casey, who provides insights and side comments throughout. Sometimes, because there are three friends, problems develop, as at the three-girl pajama party at which Kate gets homesick and Jenny and Casey try not to think she is a baby. Or when the girls watch Baby Daisy and don't always agree on what to do. In each book, the girls experience familiar activities, including ice skating and a birthday party. Many readers will relate to and enjoy their lives.

1. Pajama Party ◆ 1992
2. Nannies for Hire ◆ 1994
3. Party on Ice ◆ 1995

CASEY, TRACEY AND COMPANY

Giff, Patricia Reilly

DELACORTE; DELL YEARLING ◆ GRADES 3–6 ◆ A/R

REAL LIFE

Casey and her friends have various difficulties to overcome in each of these books, and manage to do so in adventurous and humorous ways.

Raising worms to sell and trying to outdo a cousin, experiencing divorce and dealing with being called names, even putting a cast on an arm to get out of playing a game—all these experiences are related with tenderness and humor.

1. Fourth Grade Celebrity ◆ 1979
2. Left-Handed Shortstop ◆ 1980
3. The Winter Worm Business ◆ 1981
4. The Girl Who Knew It All ◆ 1984
5. Rat Teeth ◆ 1984
6. Love, from the Fifth-Grade Celebrity ◆ 1986
7. Poopsie Pomerantz, Pick Up Your Feet ◆ 1989

CASSIE PERKINS

Hunt, Angela Elwell

TYNDALE HOUSE ◆ GRADES 4–7

REAL LIFE | VALUES

Cassie Perkins thinks she has the perfect life until her father walks out on her family. Later, her parents tell Cassie and her beloved little brother Max that he is going to live with their father. Cassie lands the lead in her school's production of *Oklahoma*. This makes her friend Andrea envious because she has a crush on Chip, the male lead. He becomes a good friend to Cassie, and leads her to faith in Christ. Her music teacher recommends her to a performing arts high school, but her mother doesn't think they can afford it. Cassie learns to trust in God for this and everything else.

1. No More Broken Promises ◆ 1991
2. A Forever Friend ◆ 1991
3. A Basket of Roses ◆ 1991
4. A Dream to Cherish ◆ 1992
5. The Much-Adored Sandy Shore ◆ 1992
6. Love Burning Bright ◆ 1992
7. Star Light, Star Bright ◆ 1993
8. The Chance of a Lifetime ◆ 1993
9. The Glory of Love ◆ 1993

CASTAWAYS OF THE FLYING DUTCHMAN

Jacques, Brian

PHILOMEL ◆ GRADES 5–8 ◆ A/R

FANTASY

Neb and his dog Ned stowed away on the *Flying Dutchman*. After falling into the sea during a storm, they were rescued by an angel and granted immortality. Now they roam the earth bringing aid to those in need. In the first book, it is 1896 and Neb—who is now called Ben—saves a village from being overrun by a shady businessman's plans for industrial development.

1. Castaways of the Flying Dutchman ◆ 2001
2. The Angel's Command ◆ 2003
3. Voyage of Slaves ◆ 2006

CASTLE COURT KIDS

Snyder, Zilpha Keatley

DELL YEARLING ◆ GRADES 3–5 ◆ A/R

REAL LIFE

The kids who live on the cul-de-sac at the end of Castle Court are friends who have banded together to do neighborhood projects. In one book, Carlos Garcia helps them get organized to build a baseball diamond, but two of the friends, Kate Nicely and Aurora Pappas, don't want a special grove of trees cut down for the field. In another book, Carlos and his friends Eddy Wong and Bucky Brockhurst have found a buried treasure, but when they look for it again, it is gone! Although the group often works together as friends, they have their differences—for instance when the boys surprise the girls who are ghost hunting. This is an easy-to-read series for middle-elementary children who enjoy books featuring familiar neighborhood activities.

1. The Diamond War ◆ 1995
2. The Box and the Bone ◆ 1995
3. Ghost Invasion ◆ 1995
4. Secret Weapons ◆ 1995

CAT

Schade, Susan, and Jon Buller

RANDOM HOUSE ◆ GRADES K–2 ◆ A/R

ANIMAL FANTASY | RECREATION

These beginning readers feature Cat, who loves athletics. Each book features a different sport and Cat is right in the middle of it. She does gymnastics, plays baseball, and even tries ice skating with an unlikely friend, Rat.

1. Cat on the Mat ◆ 1998
2. Cat at Bat ◆ 2000
3. Cat on Ice ◆ 2001

THE CAT PACK *see* Club of Mysteries

CATDOG (CHAPTER BOOKS)

Various authors

SIMON SPOTLIGHT/NICKELODEON ◆ GRADES 2–5

FANTASY

CatDog is just that—part cat and part dog. Of course, this causes a lot of problems—when the two parts bicker about what to cook on a live cooking show. Or when they have to work as a team to save Christmas. In addition to these chapter books, there are two books of CatDog tales and two books in a beginning reader format. There are also joke books, cartoon books, and activity books. Fans of the Nickelodeon cartoon program will like these.

1. Romancing the Shriek (Auerbach, Annie, Greg Crosby, and Lisa Ann Marsoli) ◆ 1999
2. Cat's Big Night/Dog Behind Bars (Krulik, Nancy E.) ◆ 1999
3. The Perfect Bone (Collins, Terry) ◆ 1999
4. Way Off Broadway (Crosby, Greg) ◆ 1999
5. CatDog's Vacation (Banks, Steven) ◆ 2000
6. CatDog Undercover (Banks, Steven) ◆ 2000
7. Cookin' With CatDog (Auerbach, Annie) ◆ 2000
8. The Most World Records (Auerbach, Annie) ◆ 2000
9. A Rancid Little Christmas (Collins, Terry) ◆ 2000

CATHERINE MARSHALL'S CHRISTY *see* Christy

CATKID

James, Brian

SCHOLASTIC ◆ GRADES 3–5

HUMOR

CatKid is both a kid and a cat. She is curious and confident. While she lives like a kid—going to school and on field trips, she has the interests of a cat. On the class field trip to the aquarium, CatKid is *really* interested in the fish. The juxtaposition of a feline girl with everyday concerns about friends, the school play, and a haunted house makes for fun reading.

1. The Fishy Field Trip ◆ 2007
2. I'm No Fraidy Cat ◆ 2007
3. A Purrfect Princess ◆ 2007
4. Three's a Crowd ◆ 2008

CAT'S EYE CORNER

Griggs, Terry

RAINCOAST BOOKS ◆ GRADES 4–7 ◆ A/R

FANTASY

Oliver is invited to visit his eccentric grandfather for the summer. Grandfather's third wife, Sylvia de Whosit of Whatsit, seems quite eccentric; however, she starts Oliver off on a scavenger hunt that becomes a fantastic adventure. Oliver is befriended by a fountain pen and a dragonfly. They, along with other items Oliver finds, help him succeed on a dangerous mission. Lots of wordplay and creative situations will remind readers of Juster's *The Phantom Tollbooth*.

1. Cat's Eye Corner ◆ 2003
2. The Silver Door ◆ 2004
3. Invisible Ink ◆ 2006

CATWINGS

LeGuin, Ursula K.

FRANKLIN WATTS ◆ GRADES 3–6 ◆ A/R

ANIMAL FANTASY

In a rough city neighborhood, four kittens are born with wings. Their mother does not know why until she realizes that the wings will enable her children to leave the city and find a better life elsewhere. The kittens—Roger, Thelma, Harriet, and James—say good-bye to their mother and fly to the country, where they must adjust to a new life with new risks, including the Owl. Eventually, they meet two children, Susan and Hank Brown, who convince the kittens to live in an abandoned barn. The series continues with the "Catwings" returning to visit their mother in the city and helping a normal kitten, Alexander Furby, who is lost in the woods.

1. Catwings ◆ 1988
2. Catwings Return ◆ 1989
3. Wonderful Alexander and the Catwings ◆ 1994
4. Jane on Her Own ◆ 1999

¡CHANA!

Ramirez, Michael Rose

AVON ◆ GRADES 3–5

FAMILY LIFE | REAL LIFE

Chana and her family have moved to California. There are so many adjustments—new home, new friends, new school. Chana misses her old friends in the Puerto Rican neighborhood in New York City. This series describes how she learns to fit in. Many readers will appreciate the Spanish words and phrases that are incorporated into these stories.

1. Hola, California! ◆ 1997
2. Hoppin' Halloween ◆ 1997
3. Gingerbread Sleepover ◆ 1997
4. Live from Cedar Hills! ◆ 1998

CHARLIE AND LOLA

Child, Lauren

CANDLEWICK; DIAL; GROSSET & DUNLAP ◆ GRADES K–2

FAMILY LIFE

Charlie, 7, describes his role as 4-year-old Lola's big brother. She is a fussy eater, so feeding her is a problem. She does not want to go to school, and bedtime is a disaster. Readers enjoy these fun books about two likable siblings. An animated television series has been very popular too, and there are many related items including board books, coloring books, puzzle books, and sticker books. The original picture books were published by Candlewick with both Dial and Grosset and Dunlap publishing book versions of television episodes.

1. I Will Never Not Ever Eat a Tomato ◆ 2000
2. I Am Not Sleepy and I Will Not Go to Bed ◆ 2001
3. I Am Too Absolutely Small for School ◆ 2004

CHARLIE AND LOLA (DIAL)

1. But, Excuse Me, That Is My Book ◆ 2005
2. Snow Is My Favorite and My Best ◆ 2006
3. Say Cheese! ◆ 2007
4. I Completely Know About Guinea Pigs ◆ 2008

CHARLIE AND LOLA (GROSSET & DUNLAP)

1. My Wobbly Tooth Must Not Ever Never Fall Out ◆ 2006
2. We Honestly Can Look After Your Dog ◆ 2006
3. Whoops! But It Wasn't Me ◆ 2006
4. Boo! Made You Jump! ◆ 2007
5. I'm Really Ever So Not Well ◆ 2007
6. But I Am an Alligator ◆ 2008
7. I Am Really, Really Concentrating ◆ 2008
8. I Can Do Anything That's Everything All on My Own ◆ 2008
9. I Want to Be Much More Bigger Like You ◆ 2008
10. I've Won, No I've Won, No I've Won ◆ 2008
11. Sizzles Is Completely Not Here ◆ 2008

12. This Is Actually My Party ◆ 2008
13. You Can Be My Friend ◆ 2008

CHARLIE BONE *see* Children of the Red King

CHARLIE SMALL

Small, Charlie

RANDOM HOUSE ◆ GRADES 3–5 ◆ A/R

HUMOR

Who is Charlie Small? There are only his journals to describe his adventures. Did this 8-year-old really ride a rhino, defeat a crocodile, and lead the gorillas? Could he hobnob with pirates? This is an imaginative series that kids will love.

1. Gorilla City ◆ 2008
2. The Perfumed Pirates of Perfidy ◆ 2008
3. The Puppet Master ◆ 2009

THE CHARLOTTE YEARS *see* Little House: The Charlotte Years

CHESTER CRICKET

Seldon, George

FARRAR, STRAUS & GIROUX ◆ GRADES 3–6 ◆ A/R

ANIMAL FANTASY | HUMOR

Chester Cricket travels unwillingly in a picnic basket from the country to New York City. There he meets Mario Bellini and his family, who run a newsstand in Times Square. His musical talent is discovered, and he plays wonderful concerts that bring large crowds to the Bellinis' newsstand. Eventually he tires of city life and wants to go back to his home in the country, so Harry Kitten and Tucker Mouse put him on a train for Connecticut. The rest of the series includes some picture books and some novel-length books, all about the further adventures of one or all of the animals. *Harry Kitten and Tucker Mouse* is a prequel to *The Cricket in Times Square*.

1. The Cricket in Times Square ◆ 1960
2. Tucker's Countryside ◆ 1969
3. Harry Cat's Pet Puppy ◆ 1974
4. Chester Cricket's Pigeon Ride ◆ 1981
5. Chester Cricket's New Home ◆ 1983

6. Harry Kitten and Tucker Mouse ◆ 1986
7. The Old Meadow ◆ 1987

CHESTNUT HILL

Brooke, Lauren
SCHOLASTIC ◆ GRADES 4–7 ◆ A/R
REAL LIFE

This series focuses on five girls at Chestnut Hill, a boarding school in Virginia that features classes, horses, and competition. Dylan, Malory, Lani, Honey, and Razina are given individual stories. In *All or Nothing*, for example, Malory wonders about making the summer riding team, and in *Playing for Keeps* Lani must convince her parents to allow her to stay at Chestnut Hill. The Heartland series, also by Lauren Brooke, would be another choice for girls who like horses as would the Thoroughbred books and the Saddle Club series.

1. New Class ◆ 2005
2. Making Strides ◆ 2005
3. Heart of Gold ◆ 2006
4. Playing for Keeps ◆ 2006
5. Scheme Team ◆ 2006
6. All or Nothing ◆ 2007

CHET GECKO MYSTERIES

Hale, Bruce
HARCOURT ◆ GRADES 4–7 ◆ A/R
ANIMAL FANTASY | MYSTERY

Chet Gecko, fourth-grade lizard detective, and his partner, Natalie Attired, solve mysteries. The first case involves finding Sally Chameleon's missing brother. In *Give My Regrets . . . ,* Chet searches for an actor missing from a school musical. There are nasty mice, tough hamsters, and bad bats in this wise-cracking series. All the books are subtitled *From the Tattered Casebook of Chet Gecko, Private Eye. Chet Gecko's Detective Handbook (and Cookbook): Tips for Private Eyes and Snack Food Lovers* (2005) is a spiral-bound companion to the series.

1. The Chameleon Wore Chartreuse ◆ 2000
2. The Mystery of Mr. Nice ◆ 2000
3. Farewell, My Lunchbag! ◆ 2001
4. The Big Nap ◆ 2001
5. The Hamster of the Baskervilles ◆ 2002
6. This Gum for Hire ◆ 2002

7. The Malted Falcoln ◆ 2003
8. Trouble Is My Beeswax ◆ 2003
9. Give My Regrets to Broadway ◆ 2004
10. Murder, My Tweet ◆ 2004
11. The Possum Always Rings Twice ◆ 2006
12. Key Lardo ◆ 2006
13. Hiss Me Deadly ◆ 2007

CHICAGO AND THE CAT

Koontz, Robin Michal

DUTTON ◆ GRADES K–2 ◆ A/R

ANIMAL FANTASY

One day, Chicago the rabbit finds that a cat is living in her house. Chicago wonders how soon the cat will leave. Then, she eats the carrot pancakes that the cat has made for her. Delicious! The cat does not like being outdoors at night. She does not like getting wet when she goes rafting with Chicago. *The Family Reunion* describes how the cat deals with the crowd of rabbits when Chicago's family comes to visit. With simple chapters and controlled vocabulary, this is a great choice for beginning readers.

1. Chicago and the Cat ◆ 1993
2. Chicago and the Cat: The Camping Trip ◆ 1994
3. Chicago and the Cat: The Halloween Party ◆ 1994
4. Chicago and the Cat: The Family Reunion ◆ 1996
5. Chicago and the Cat at the Country Fair ◆ 1998

CHILDREN OF AMERICA

Armstrong, Jennifer

RANDOM HOUSE ◆ GRADES 2–4 ◆ A/R

HISTORICAL

Each book in this series focuses on the immigration experiences of different children. Patrick Doyle is growing up in the Hell's Kitchen area of New York, enjoying his new life, new friends, and a new sport—baseball. *Foolish Gretel* describes the life of a 10-year-old German American girl in Texas. And, although Lili Alesund loves Norway, she must travel on a huge ship when her parents decide to go to Minnesota. The characters are high-spirited as they face their new lives in America.

1. Patrick Doyle Is Full of Blarney ◆ 1996
2. Lili the Brave ◆ 1997
3. Foolish Gretel ◆ 1997

CHILDREN OF THE LAMP

Kerr, P. B.

ORCHARD ◆ GRADES 5–8 ◆ A/R

FANTASY

Having their wisdom teeth removed starts the adventure for 12-year-old twins John and Philippa Gaunt. They begin to have strange experiences and when they visit their Uncle Nimrod in London, they learn of their djinn (genie) heritage. They receive training in Egypt where they search for the lost tomb of Akhenaten. In subsequent books they travel around the world confronting evil djinns, curses, and cults.

1. The Akhenaten Adventure ◆ 2004
2. The Blue Djinn of Babylon ◆ 2006
3. The Cobra King of Kathmandu ◆ 2007
4. The Day of the Djinn Warriors ◆ 2008

CHILDREN OF THE RED KING

Nimmo, Jenny

SCHOLASTIC ◆ GRADES 4–7 ◆ A/R

FANTASY

Charlie Bone, 10, is from a seemingly ordinary family. When he begins to hear the people in photographs speaking to him, he is identified as having the Yewbeam gift. He is sent to Bloor's Academy to develop and to meet other gifted children. In the second book, Charlie encounters Henry Yewbeam, a young ancestor who disappeared in 1916. By the fifth book, Charlie has turned 12 is searching for his father while facing an ancient threat. These books are popular with Harry Potter fans.

1. Midnight for Charlie Bone ◆ 2003
2. Charlie Bone and the Time Twister ◆ 2003
3. Charlie Bone and the Invisible Boy ◆ 2004
4. Charlie Bone and the Castle of Mirrors ◆ 2005
5. Charlie Bone and the Hidden King ◆ 2006
6. Charlie Bone and the Beast ◆ 2007
7. Charlie Bone and the Shadow ◆ 2008

CHINA TATE

Johnson, Lissa Halls

FOCUS ON THE FAMILY ◆ GRADES 5–8

REAL LIFE | VALUES

At Camp Crazy Bear, China Tate and her best friend Deedee Kiersey have adventures involving bear cubs, a lost dog, and the beginning of romance. China is the daughter of missionaries and many of her actions are guided by her faith in God. In one book, China befriends a charismatic young man and her interest in him makes her question the importance of her beliefs. In another book, China and Deedee learn a lesson about disobedience after they feed some wild bear cubs. Values and Christian beliefs are incorporated into each story.

1. Sliced Heather on Toast ◆ 1994
2. The Secret in the Kitchen ◆ 1994
3. Project Black Bear ◆ 1994
4. Wishing Upon a Star ◆ 1995
5. Comedy of Errors ◆ 1995
6. The Ice Queen ◆ 1996
7. The Never-Ending Day ◆ 1997

CHINATOWN MYSTERY

Yep, Laurence

HARPERCOLLINS ◆ GRADES 5–8 ◆ A/R

MYSTERY

Lily Lew's great aunt is a former movie star who appeared as "Tiger Lil." On the set of a television show, the two work as a team to help an actor under suspicion of using real bullets in a prop gun. In an earlier book, they team up to find out who is trying to sabotage a new restaurant. Details about their Chinese heritage are incorporated into these books.

1. The Case of the Goblin Pearls ◆ 1997
2. The Case of the Lion Dance ◆ 1998
3. The Case of the Firecrackers ◆ 1999

CHINCOTEAGUE

Henry, Marguerite

SIMON & SCHUSTER ◆ GRADES 3–6 ◆ A/R

REAL LIFE

Beginning with the shipwreck that marooned wild horses on an island just off the coast of Virginia, these books trace the story of Misty, who began her life on Assateague Island and was captured and brought to Chincoteague, and of her descendants. In each, there is the drama of real life: a tidal wave, the need to sell Misty to raise money, and the hard work of training and caring for horses.

1. Misty of Chincoteague ◆ 1947
2. Sea Star, Orphan of Chincoteague ◆ 1949

3. Stormy, Misty's Foal ◆ 1963
4. Misty's Twilight ◆ 1992

CHIP HILTON SPORTS SERIES

Bee, Coach Clair

BOARDMAN & HOLMAN ◆ GRADES 5–8 ◆ A/R

RECREATION

This series, which began in the 1940s, has been updated and reissued. A new title, *Fiery Fullback,* has also been released. Cynthia Bee Farley, the author's daughter, writes that the values and honesty of these books have connected with generations of readers. Like the Matt Christopher books, these cover a variety of sports and feature athletes in conflicts both on and off the field.

1. Touchdown Pass ◆ 1998
2. Championship Ball ◆ 1998
3. Strike Three! ◆ 1998
4. Clutch Hitter! ◆ 1998
5. A Pass and a Prayer ◆ 1999
6. Hoop Crazy ◆ 1999
7. Pitchers' Duel ◆ 1999
8. Dugout Jinx ◆ 1999
9. Freshman Quarterback ◆ 1999
10. Backboard Fever ◆ 1999
11. Fence Busters ◆ 1999
12. Ten Seconds to Play! ◆ 1999
13. Fourth Down Showdown ◆ 2000
14. Tournament Crisis ◆ 2000
15. Hardcourt Upset ◆ 2000
16. Pay-Off Pitch ◆ 2000
17. No-Hitter ◆ 2001
18. Triple-Threat Trouble ◆ 2001
19. Backcourt Ace ◆ 2001
20. Buzzer Basket ◆ 2001
21. Comeback Cagers ◆ 2001
22. Home Run Feud ◆ 2002
23. Hungry Hurler ◆ 2002
24. Fiery Fullback ◆ 2002

CHOOSE YOUR OWN ADVENTURE

Various authors

BANTAM ◆ GRADES 4–8

ADVENTURE | MYSTERY

With nearly 200 titles, this series has attracted a large audience. The format allows readers to make choices at key moments in the plot. Should you go left? Go right? Should you turn around? Each choice leads to a different page, more choices, and your own story. Then you can go back to an earlier choice, make different selections, and create a different story. Newer adventures feature ninjas, computers, aliens, cyberhacking, and mutant spider ants. This is a popular series with a fairly accessible reading level. See also the Choose Your Own Nightmare series.

1. Journey Under the Sea (Mountain, Robert) ◆ 1977
2. Deadwood City (Packard, Edward) ◆ 1978
3. The Cave of Time (Packard, Edward) ◆ 1979
4. By Balloon to the Sahara (Terman, Douglas) ◆ 1979
5. Your Code Name Is Jonah (Packard, Edward) ◆ 1979
6. Third Planet from Altair (Packard, Edward) ◆ 1979
7. Space and Beyond (Montgomery, Raymond) ◆ 1980
8. Mystery of Chimney Rock (Packard, Edward) ◆ 1980
9. Who Killed Harlowe Thrombey? (Packard, Edward) ◆ 1981
10. Lost Jewels of Nabooti (Montgomery, Raymond) ◆ 1981
11. Mystery of the Maya (Montgomery, Raymond) ◆ 1981
12. Inside UFO 54-40 (Packard, Edward) ◆ 1982
13. Abominable Snowman (Montgomery, Raymond) ◆ 1982
14. Forbidden Castle (Packard, Edward) ◆ 1982
15. House of Danger (Montgomery, Raymond) ◆ 1982
16. Survival at Sea (Packard, Edward) ◆ 1983
17. Race Forever (Montgomery, Raymond) ◆ 1983
18. Underground Kingdom (Packard, Edward) ◆ 1983
19. Secret of the Pyramids (Brightfield, Richard) ◆ 1983
20. Escape (Montgomery, Raymond) ◆ 1983
21. Hyperspace (Packard, Edward) ◆ 1983
22. Space Patrol (Goodman, Julius) ◆ 1983
23. Lost Tribe (Foley, Louise Munro) ◆ 1983
24. Lost on the Amazon (Montgomery, Raymond) ◆ 1983
25. Prisoner of the Ant People (Montgomery, Raymond) ◆ 1983
26. Phantom Submarine (Brightfield, Richard) ◆ 1983
27. Horror of High Ridge (Goodman, Julius) ◆ 1983
28. Mountain Survival (Packard, Edward) ◆ 1984
29. Trouble on Planet Earth (Montgomery, Raymond) ◆ 1984
30. Curse of Batterslea Hall (Brightfield, Richard) ◆ 1984
31. Vampire Express (Koltz, Tony) ◆ 1984
32. Treasure Diver (Goodman, Julius) ◆ 1984
33. Dragons' Den (Brightfield, Richard) ◆ 1984
34. Mystery of the Highland Crest (Foley, Louise Munro) ◆ 1984
35. Journey to Stonehenge (Graver, Fred) ◆ 1984
36. Secret Treasure of Tibet (Brightfield, Richard) ◆ 1984
37. War with the Evil Power Master (Montgomery, Raymond) ◆ 1984
38. Sabotage (Liebold, Jay) ◆ 1984
39. Supercomputer (Packard, Edward) ◆ 1984
40. Throne of Zeus (Goodman, Deborah Lerne) ◆ 1985
41. Search for the Mountain Gorillas (Wallace, Jim) ◆ 1985

42. Mystery of Echo Lodge (Foley, Louise Munro) ◆ 1985
43. Grand Canyon Odyssey (Liebold, Jay) ◆ 1985
44. Mystery of Ura Senke (Gilligan, Shannon) ◆ 1985
45. You Are a Shark (Packard, Edward) ◆ 1985
46. Deadly Shadow (Brightfield, Richard) ◆ 1985
47. Outlaws of Sherwood Forest (Kushner, Ellen) ◆ 1985
48. Spy for George Washington (Liebold, Jay) ◆ 1985
49. Danger at Anchor Mine (Foley, Louise Munro) ◆ 1985
50. Return to the Cave of Time (Packard, Edward) ◆ 1985
51. Magic of the Unicorn (Goodman, Deborah Lerne) ◆ 1985
52. Ghost Hunter (Packard, Edward) ◆ 1986
53. The Case of the Silk King (Gilligan, Shannon) ◆ 1986
54. Forest of Fear (Foley, Louise Munro) ◆ 1986
55. Trumpet of Terror (Goodman, Deborah Lerne) ◆ 1986
56. Enchanted Kingdom (Kushner, Ellen) ◆ 1986
57. Antimatter Formula (Liebold, Jay) ◆ 1986
58. Statue of Liberty Adventure (Kushner, Ellen) ◆ 1986
59. Terror Island (Koltz, Tony) ◆ 1986
60. Vanished! (Goodman, Deborah Lerne) ◆ 1986
61. Beyond Escape! (Montgomery, Raymond) ◆ 1986
62. Sugarcane Island (Packard, Edward) ◆ 1986
63. Mystery of the Secret Room (Kushner, Ellen) ◆ 1986
64. Volcano! (Siegman, Meryl) ◆ 1987
65. Mardi Gras Mystery (Foley, Louise Munro) ◆ 1987
66. Secret of the Ninja (Liebold, Jay) ◆ 1987
67. Seaside Mystery (Hodgman, Ann) ◆ 1987
68. Secret of the Sun God (Packard, Andrea) ◆ 1987
69. Rock and Roll Mystery (Wallace, Jim) ◆ 1987
70. Invaders of Planet Earth (Brightfield, Richard) ◆ 1987
71. Space Vampire (Packard, Edward) ◆ 1987
72. Brilliant Doctor Wogan (Montgomery, Raymond) ◆ 1987
73. Beyond the Great Wall (Liebold, Jay) ◆ 1987
74. Longhorn Territory (Newman, Marc) ◆ 1987
75. Planet of the Dragons (Brightfield, Richard) ◆ 1988
76. Mona Lisa Is Missing (Montgomery, Raymond) ◆ 1988
77. First Olympics (Baglio, Ben M.) ◆ 1988
78. Return to Atlantis (Montgomery, Raymond) ◆ 1988
79. Mystery of the Sacred Stones (Foley, Louise Munro) ◆ 1988
80. Perfect Planet (Packard, Edward) ◆ 1988
81. Terror in Australia (Gilligan, Shannon) ◆ 1988
82. Hurricane! (Brightfield, Richard) ◆ 1988
83. Track of the Bear (Montgomery, Raymond) ◆ 1988
84. You Are a Monster (Packard, Edward) ◆ 1988
85. Inca Gold (Beckett, Jim) ◆ 1988
86. Knights of the Round Table (Kushner, Ellen) ◆ 1988
87. Exiled to Earth (Montgomery, Richard) ◆ 1989
88. Master of Kung Fu (Brightfield, Richard) ◆ 1989

89. South Pole Sabotage (Johnson, Seddon) ◆ 1989
90. Mutiny in Space (Packard, Edward) ◆ 1989
91. You Are a Superstar (Packard, Edward) ◆ 1989
92. Return of the Ninja (Liebold, Jay) ◆ 1989
93. Captive! (Hampton, Bill) ◆ 1989
94. Blood on the Handle (Montgomery, Raymond) ◆ 1989
95. You Are a Genius (Packard, Edward) ◆ 1989
96. Stock Car Champion (Montgomery, Raymond) ◆ 1989
97. Through the Black Hole (Packard, Edward) ◆ 1990
98. You Are a Millionaire (Liebold, Jay) ◆ 1990
99. Revenge of the Russian Ghost (Liebold, Jay) ◆ 1990
100. Worst Day of Your Life (Packard, Edward) ◆ 1990
101. Alien, Go Home! (Johnson, Seddon) ◆ 1990
102. Master of Tae Kwon Do (Brightfield, Richard) ◆ 1990
103. Grave Robbers (Montgomery, Raymond) ◆ 1990
104. Cobra Connection (Foley, Louise Munro) ◆ 1990
105. Treasure of the Onyx Dragon (Gilligan, Alison) ◆ 1990
106. Hijacked! (Brightfield, Richard) ◆ 1990
107. Fight for Freedom (Liebold, Jay) ◆ 1990
108. Master of Karate (Brightfield, Richard) ◆ 1990
109. Chinese Dragons (Montgomery, Raymond) ◆ 1991
110. Invaders from Within (Packard, Edward) ◆ 1991
111. Smoke Jumper (Montgomery, Raymond) ◆ 1991
112. Skateboard Champion (Packard, Edward) ◆ 1991
113. Lost Ninja (Liebold, Jay) ◆ 1991
114. Daredevil Park (Compton, Sara) ◆ 1991
115. Island of Time (Montgomery, Raymond) ◆ 1991
116. Kidnapped! (Packard, Edward) ◆ 1991
117. Search for Aladdin's Lamp (Liebold, Jay) ◆ 1991
118. Vampire Invaders (Packard, Edward) ◆ 1991
119. Terrorist Trap (Gilligan, Shannon) ◆ 1991
120. Ghost Train (Foley, Louise Munro) ◆ 1992
121. Behind the Wheel (Montgomery, R. A.) ◆ 1992
122. Magic Master (Packard, Edward) ◆ 1992
123. Silver Wings (Montgomery, Raymond) ◆ 1992
124. Superbike (Packard, Edward) ◆ 1992
125. Outlaw Gulch (Montgomery, Ramsey) ◆ 1992
126. Master of Martial Arts (Brightfield, Richard) ◆ 1992
127. Showdown (Brightfield, Richard) ◆ 1992
128. Viking Raiders (Packard, Edward) ◆ 1992
129. Earthquake! (Gilligan, Alison) ◆ 1992
130. You Are Microscopic (Packard, Edward) ◆ 1992
131. Surf Monkeys (Liebold, Jay) ◆ 1993
132. Luckiest Day of Your Life (Packard, Edward) ◆ 1993
133. The Forgotten Planet (Wilhelm, Doug) ◆ 1993
134. Secret of the Dolphins (Packard, Edward) ◆ 1993
135. Playoff Champion (Von Moschzisker, Felix) ◆ 1993

136. Roller Star (Packard, Edward) ◆ 1993
137. Scene of the Crime (Wilhelm, Doug) ◆ 1993
138. Dinosaur Island (Packard, Edward) ◆ 1993
139. Motocross Mania (Montgomery, R. A.) ◆ 1993
140. Horror House (Packard, Edward) ◆ 1993
141. The Secret of Mystery Hill (Wilhelm, Doug) ◆ 1993
142. The Reality Machine (Packard, Edward) ◆ 1993
143. Project UFO (Montgomery, R. A.) ◆ 1994
144. Comet Crash (Packard, Edward) ◆ 1994
145. Everest Adventure (Montgomery, Anson) ◆ 1994
146. Soccer Star (Packard, Edward) ◆ 1994
147. The Antimatter Universe (Mueller, Kate) ◆ 1994
148. Master of Judo (Brightfield, Richard) ◆ 1994
149. Search the Amazon! (Wilhelm, Doug) ◆ 1994
150. Who Are You? (Packard, Edward) ◆ 1994
151. Gunfire at Gettysburg (Wilhelm, Doug) ◆ 1994
152. War with the Mutant Spider Ants (Packard, Edward) ◆ 1994
153. Last Run (Montgomery, R. A.) ◆ 1994
154. Cyberspace Warrior (Packard, Edward) ◆ 1994
155. Ninja Cyborg (Liebold, Jay) ◆ 1995
156. You Are an Alien (Packard, Edward) ◆ 1995
157. U.N. Adventure (Brightfield, Richard) ◆ 1995
158. Sky-jam! (Packard, Edward) ◆ 1995
159. Tattoo of Death (Montgomery, R. A.) ◆ 1995
160. The Computer Takeover (Packard, Edward) ◆ 1995
161. Possessed! (Montgomery, R. A.) ◆ 1995
162. Typhoon! (Packard, Edward) ◆ 1995
163. Shadow of the Swastika (Wilhelm, Doug) ◆ 1995
164. Fright Night (Packard, Edward) ◆ 1995
165. Snowboard Racer (Montgomery, Anson) ◆ 1995
166. Master of Aikido (Brightfield, Richard) ◆ 1995
167. Moon Quest (Montgomery, Anson) ◆ 1996
168. Hostage! (Packard, Edward) ◆ 1996
169. Terror on the Titanic (Brightfield, Richard) ◆ 1996
170. Greed, Guns, and Gold (Packard, Edward) ◆ 1996
171. Death in the Dorm (Montgomery, R. A.) ◆ 1996
172. Mountain Biker (Packard, Edward) ◆ 1996
173. The Gold Medal Secret (Wilhelm, Doug) ◆ 1996
174. The Power Dome (Packard, Edward) ◆ 1996
175. The Underground Railroad (Wilhelm, Doug) ◆ 1996
176. Master of Kendo (Brightfield, Richard) ◆ 1997
177. Killer Virus (Montgomery, Raymond) ◆ 1997
178. River of No Return (Lahey, Vince) ◆ 1997
179. Ninja Avenger (Liebold, Jay) ◆ 1997
180. Stampede! (Hill, Laban C.) ◆ 1997
181. Fire on Ice (Packard, Edward) ◆ 1998
182. Fugitive (Packard, Edward) ◆ 1998
183. CyberHacker (Montgomery, Anson) ◆ 1998
184. Mayday! (Packard, Edward, and Andrea Packard) ◆ 1998

CHOOSE YOUR OWN NIGHTMARE

Various authors

BANTAM ◆ GRADES 4–8

ADVENTURE | HORROR

A spin-off of the Choose Your Own Adventure series, these books capitalize on the popularity of horror fiction. From *Night of the Werewolf* on, they are filled with venomous snakes, killer insects, mummies, and haunted babies. With twists and turns, doom and demons, they are sure to appeal to the scary-story crowd.

1. Night of the Werewolf (Packard, Edward) ◆ 1995
2. Beware the Snake's Venom (McMurtry, Ken) ◆ 1995
3. Island of Doom (Brightfield, Richard) ◆ 1995
4. Castle of Darkness (Montgomery, R. A.) ◆ 1995
5. The Halloween Party (Jakab, E. A. M.) ◆ 1995
6. Risk Your Life Arcade (McMurtry, Ken) ◆ 1995
7. Biting for Blood (Packard, Edward) ◆ 1996
8. Bugged Out! (Hill, Laban C.) ◆ 1996
9. The Mummy Who Wouldn't Die (Jakab, E. A. M.) ◆ 1996
10. It Happened at Camp Pine Tree (Montgomery, R. A., and Janet Hubbard-Brown) ◆ 1996
11. Watch Out for Room 13 (Hill, Laban C.) ◆ 1996
12. Something's in the Woods (Brightfield, Richard) ◆ 1996
13. The Haunted Baby (Packard, Edward) ◆ 1997
14. The Evil Pen Pal (Hill, Laban C.) ◆ 1997
15. How I Became a Freak (Brightfield, Richard) ◆ 1997
16. Welcome to Horror Hospital (Hill, Laban C.) ◆ 1997
17. Attack of the Living Mask (Hirschfeld, Robert) ◆ 1997
18. The Toy Shop of Terror (Hill, Laban C.) ◆ 1997

CHOOSE YOUR OWN STAR WARS ADVENTURES

Golden, Christopher

BANTAM ◆ GRADES 4–8

ADVENTURE | SCIENCE FICTION

This series links two popular items: the *Star Wars* movies, plots, and characters and the Choose Your Own Adventure format. The familiar characters—Luke Skywalker, Princess Leia, Han Solo, and Darth Vader—are embroiled in more intergalactic intrigues, and the reader gets to make choices about which direction the plot will take. Will there be rebellion or destruction? Will you be loyal to the Jedi or embrace the dark side? The 3-D hologram on the cover of each book will attract many readers. This is sure to be a great choice for fans of movies and participatory fiction.

1. Star Wars: A New Hope ◆ 1998
2. Star Wars: The Empire Strikes Back ◆ 1998
3. Star Wars: Return of the Jedi ◆ 1998

CHOSEN GIRLS

Crouch, Cheryl

ZONDERKIDZ ◆ GRADES 4–6

VALUES

A new girl, Trinity, convinces Melody and Harmony to form a band. A neighborhood boy/computer geek puts their songs out on the Internet and they find themselves in demand. Calling their band Chosen Girls is a reference to their belief that God is guiding them in their lives. Although they are tested, their faith helps them make the right choices.

1. Backstage Pass ◆ 2007
2. Double-Booked ◆ 2007
3. Unplugged ◆ 2007
4. Solo Act ◆ 2007
5. Big Break ◆ 2007
6. Sold Out ◆ 2007
7. Overload ◆ 2007
8. Realty Tour ◆ 2007

CHRISTIE & COMPANY

Page, Katherine Hall

AVON ◆ GRADES 5–7

MYSTERY

Three girls—Christie, Maggie, and Vicky—meet at the boarding school where they begin eighth grade. They are from different backgrounds but they share an in interest in mysteries. Christie Montgomery is the main character and she directs the trio's activities, solving thefts at school, finding those responsible for the sabotage of an inn owned by Maggie's parents, and helping a family being threatened by a Chinese gang. While seeking solutions to these mysteries, the girls continue to grow and mature. There is lots of dialogue, making this fairly accessible. Children who enjoy mystery and adventure books featuring girls will like this series.

1. Christie & Company ◆ 1996
2. Christie & Company Down East ◆ 1997
3. Christie & Company in the Year of the Dragon ◆ 1998
4. Bon Voyage, Christie & Company ◆ 1999

CHRISTINA KATERINA

Gauch, Patricia Lee
PUTNAM ◆ GRADES K–3
FAMILY LIFE | REAL LIFE

In this picture book series, Christina Katerina quarrels and makes up with her family, loves her bears, and has a neighborhood war. When her parents come home with a baby sister, she gets her bears together for a journey. Caught in a seedy neighborhood in the rain, she is glad to see her father coming to get her. The best part of a journey, she tells the bears, is going home, especially if you have a baby sister waiting. When she is a little older, she has a falling out with her best friend, the rest of the neighborhood takes sides, and war is declared. Christina is a feisty and determined heroine in a loving family.

1. Christina Katerina and the Box ◆ 1971
2. Christina Katerina and the First Annual Grand Ballet ◆ 1973
3. Christina Katerina and the Time She Quit the Family ◆ 1987
4. Christina Katerina and the Great Bear Train ◆ 1990
5. Christina Katerina and Fats and the Great Neighborhood War ◆ 1997

CHRISTOPHER

Carrick, Carol
HOUGHTON MIFFLIN ◆ GRADES K–2
FAMILY LIFE | REAL LIFE

This series of books chronicles the everyday experiences of Christopher and his family. Several books focus on Christopher and his dog, Bodger, with *The Accident* describing Christopher's sense of loss when Bodger is hit by a truck and killed. Finding a stray puppy and accepting him is presented in *The Foundling*. One book shows how Christopher overcomes his fear of swimming in the pond; another describes a sleep-out; still another shows an encounter between Christopher's new dog, Ben, and a porcupine. The stories in this series convey a strong sense of family togetherness and respect for the beauty of nature.

1. Sleep Out ◆ 1973
2. Lost in the Storm ◆ 1974
3. The Accident ◆ 1976
4. The Foundling ◆ 1977
5. The Washout ◆ 1978
6. Ben and the Porcupine ◆ 1981
7. Dark and Full of Secrets ◆ 1984
8. Left Behind ◆ 1988

CHRISTY

Marshall, Catherine

TOMMY NELSON WORDKIDS ◆ GRADES 5–8

HISTORICAL | REAL LIFE | VALUES

Christy Huddleston, 19, goes to teach in the Great Smoky Mountains, where she finds hardships, heartache, and hope. Christy's idealism and energy often put her in conflict with people in the community, but she has the ongoing support of Dr. Neil MacNeill and the admiration of David Grantland. Christy meets Miss Alice, a veteran missionary who understands the mountain people and helps her adjust to their ways. The stories have an element of romance and are filled with Christy's commitment to her religion and her values. The series follows the format of the popular television series. Catherine Marshall based these stories on the real life of her mother around the turn of the century.

1. The Bridge to Cutter Gap ◆ 1995
2. Silent Superstitions ◆ 1995
3. The Angry Intruder ◆ 1995
4. Midnight Rescue ◆ 1995
5. The Proposal ◆ 1995
6. Christy's Choice ◆ 1996
7. The Princess Club ◆ 1996
8. Family Secrets ◆ 1996
9. Mountain Madness ◆ 1997
10. Stage Fright ◆ 1997
11. Goodbye, Sweet Prince ◆ 1997
12. Brotherly Love ◆ 1997

CHRONICLES OF ANCIENT DARKNESS

Paver, Michelle

HARPERCOLLINS ◆ GRADES 5–9 ◆ A/R

FANTASY | HISTORICAL | ADVENTURE

This series first published in Britain combines fantasy and adventure with a faithful re-creation of the culture of New Stone Age people in northern Europe. It features a 12-year-old Stone Age boy named Torak, part of the Wolf Clan; a girl named Renn who comes from the Raven Clan; and a wolf cub that Torak adopts and names Wolf. In *Wolf Brother,* Torak, Renn, and Wolf travel to the World of the Mountain Spirit in an effort to rid the clans of a dangerous, demon-possessed bear. Wolf disappears at the end of the book. In the second book, Torak is living with the Raven Clan but feels alone without Wolf. When a mysterious illness hits the clan, Torak sets off on a dangerous quest to find a cure. In *Soul Eater,* Wolf is kidnapped by the Soul Eaters and Torak and Renn must travel to the Arctic to rescue him. The books are thoroughly researched and present lots of details on Stone Age life—food, tools, housing, clothing, religious rites, and so forth. There is a site for fans at www.torak.info.

1. Wolf Brother ◆ 2005
2. Spirit Walker ◆ 2006
3. Soul Eater ◆ 2007
4. Outcast ◆ 2008
5. Oathbreaker ◆ 2008
6. Ghost Hunter ◆ 2009

CHRONICLES OF NARNIA

Lewis, C. S.

MACMILLAN ◆ GRADES 4–8 ◆ A/R

FANTASY

Lucy, Peter, Susan, and Edmund are British schoolchildren during World War II in this series of fantasy adventures. Entering a mirrored wardrobe, they find a magical world called Narnia peopled by fauns, witches, nymphs, dwarves, and talking animals. The children fight many battles against evil and eventually become rulers of the land. Quirks in the chronicles include the facts that Narnia's inhabitants have always supposed humans to be mythical creatures and that the adventures that seem to last forever in Narnia only fill a split second at home. There is debate about the best order in which to read these books. Many prefer the order in which they were published, but boxed sets now present the books in chronological sequence: *The Magician's Nephew; The Lion, the Witch, and the Wardrobe; The Horse and His Boy; Prince Caspian, The Voyage of the Dawn Treader; The Silver Chair; and The Last Battle.*

1. The Lion, the Witch, and the Wardrobe ◆ 1950
2. Prince Caspian ◆ 1951
3. The Voyage of the Dawn Treader ◆ 1952
4. The Silver Chair ◆ 1953
5. The Horse and His Boy ◆ 1954
6. The Magician's Nephew ◆ 1955
7. The Last Battle ◆ 1956

CIRCLE OF MAGIC

Doyle, Debra, and James D. Macdonald

TROLL ◆ GRADES 4–6 ◆ A/R

FANTASY

Randal, 12, enters the School of Wizardry, where he encounters magic and treachery. As he becomes more skilled, he is given tasks including protecting a statue with mysterious powers and coming to the aid of a prince. There was an earlier version of this series in the 1990s.

1. School of Wizardry ◆ 2000
2. Secret of the Tower ◆ 2000
3. The Wizard's Statue ◆ 2000
4. Danger in the Palace ◆ 2000
5. The Wizard's Castle ◆ 2001
6. The High King's Daughter ◆ 2001

CLAMP SCHOOL DETECTIVES

Ohkawa, Ageha, team leader

TOKYOPOP ◆ GRADES 4–8

FANTASY

CLAMP School is a school for geniuses. Three teens at the school create an investigative agency to protect their fellow students, especially the girls. Nokoru, a sixth-grader, founded the group and is joined by his friends Akira and Suoh. They look into unusual situations including a ghost in the art department.

1. Volume 1 ◆ 2004   3. Volume 3 ◆ 2004
2. Volume 2 ◆ 2004

CLARICE BEAN

Child, Lauren

CANDLEWICK ◆ GRADES 2–5 ◆ A/R

REAL LIFE

Flip, sassy Clarice Bean describes her life in this creatively designed series. Busy collage art is accompanied by changing text fonts and childlike drawings. The result is a perfect match for Clarice Bean's conversational comments about her brother, the missing guinea pig, a family protest, and school. The first few books are picture books; later books are novels for middle- and upper-elementary readers.

1. Clarice Bean, That's Me ◆ 1999
2. My Uncle Is a Hunkle, Says Clarice Bean ◆ 2000
3. Clarice Bean, Guess Who's Babysitting ◆ 2001
4. What Planet Are You From, Clarice Bean? ◆ 2002
5. Utterly Me, Clarice Bean ◆ 2003
6. Clarice Bean Spells Trouble ◆ 2005
7. Clarice Bean, Don't Look Now ◆ 2007

CLASS PETS

Asch, Frank

SIMON & SCHUSTER ◆ GRADES 2–4 ◆ A/R

ANIMAL FANTASY

Molly and Jake are mice siblings who make their home in an elementary school. Molly gets inside the school first and meets a hamster ghost, two birds, and a rabbit. Outside the school, Jake is threatened by an owl and a cat. Their adventures continue as they interact with other school activities.

1. The Ghost of P.S. 42 ◆ 2002
2. Battle in a Bottle ◆ 2003
3. Survival School ◆ 2004

CLEMENCY POGUE

Petty, J. T.

SIMON & SCHUSTER ◆ GRADES 4–6

FANTASY

After she is attacked by a fairy, Clemency Pogue utters a phrase that results in the death of seven fairies. Accompanied by her friend, the hobgoblin Chaphesmeeso, she begins a journey to learn the true name of each fairiy. As the series continues, Clemency struggles to cope with problems in her family while she is called upon to save Make Believe.

1. The Fairy Killer ◆ 2005
2. The Hobgoblin Proxy ◆ 2006
3. The Scrivener Bees ◆ 2007

CLEMENTINE

Pennypacker, Sara

HYPERION ◆ GRADES 2–5 ◆ A/R

REAL LIFE | HUMOR

Clementine is in third grade and, like Beverly Cleary's Ramona, she sometimes stumbles into trouble. There are mishaps at school and at home with her neighbor Margaret. Add this to the list of books about feisty female main characters such as Ramona, Ruby Lu, Judy Moody, and Junie B. Jones.

1. Clementine ◆ 2006
2. The Talented Clementine ◆ 2007
3. Clementine's Letter ◆ 2008

CLIFFORD

Bridwell, Norman

SCHOLASTIC ◆ GRADES K–2 ◆ A/R

ANIMAL FANTASY | HUMOR

Everyone loves Clifford. The big red dog and his little girl, Emily Elizabeth, have enchanted children for more than 30 years. There are many books about Clifford, including ones celebrating holidays and seasons and others building on the humor of a huge dog (bigger than a house) in awkward situations. Related books include board books, scratch-and-sniff books, even a barking book. There are cookie cutters, cassettes, a puppet, and a stuffed animal.

1. Clifford, the Big Red Dog ◆ 1962
2. Clifford Gets a Job ◆ 1965
3. Clifford Takes a Trip ◆ 1966
4. Clifford's Halloween ◆ 1967
5. Clifford's Tricks ◆ 1969
6. Clifford, the Small Red Puppy ◆ 1972
7. Clifford's Riddles ◆ 1974
8. Clifford's Good Deeds ◆ 1975
9. Clifford at the Circus ◆ 1977
10. Clifford Goes to Hollywood ◆ 1980
11. Clifford's ABC ◆ 1983
12. Clifford and the Grouchy Neighbors ◆ 1984
13. Clifford's Christmas ◆ 1984
14. Clifford's Family ◆ 1984
15. Clifford's Kitten ◆ 1984
16. Clifford's Pals ◆ 1985
17. Clifford's Manners ◆ 1985
18. Count on Clifford ◆ 1985
19. Clifford's Birthday Party ◆ 1987
20. Clifford's Puppy Days ◆ 1989
21. Clifford's Word Book ◆ 1990
22. Clifford, We Love You ◆ 1991
23. Clifford's Noisy Day ◆ 1992
24. Clifford's Thanksgiving Visit ◆ 1993
25. Clifford the Fire House Dog ◆ 1994
26. Clifford's First Christmas ◆ 1994
27. Clifford's Happy Easter ◆ 1994
28. Clifford and the Big Storm ◆ 1995
29. Clifford's First Halloween ◆ 1995
30. Clifford's Sports Day ◆ 1996
31. Clifford's First Autumn ◆ 1997
32. Clifford's First Valentine's Day ◆ 1997
33. Clifford's Spring Clean-Up ◆ 1997
34. Clifford and the Big Parade ◆ 1998

35. Clifford Makes a Friend ◆ 1998
36. Clifford's First Snow Day ◆ 1998
37. Clifford Keeps Cool ◆ 1998
38. Clifford's First School Day ◆ 1999
39. Clifford Grows Up ◆ 1999
40. Oops, Clifford ◆ 1999
41. Clifford to the Rescue ◆ 2000
42. Clifford Visits the Hospital ◆ 2001
43. Teacher's Pets ◆ 2001
44. Clifford's Hiccups ◆ 2001
45. Clifford's Happy Mother's Day ◆ 2001
46. The Missing Beach Ball ◆ 2002
47. Clifford's Busy Week ◆ 2002
48. Clifford Goes to Dog School ◆ 2002
49. Clifford's Class Trip ◆ 2002
50. Clifford's Day With Dad ◆ 2002
51. Clifford's Big Red Easter ◆ 2003
52. Clifford's First Sleepover ◆ 2004
53. Clifford Goes to Washington ◆ 2005
54. Clifford's First Halloween ◆ 2006
55. Clifford and His Friends ◆ 2007
56. Clifford's Funny Adventures ◆ 2007

CLIFFORD READERS

1. Clifford and the Halloween Parade ◆ 1999
2. The Big Leaf Pile ◆ 2000
3. Tummy Trouble ◆ 2000
4. Clifford's Big Red Reader ◆ 2001
5. Clifford's Valentines ◆ 2001
6. The Dog Who Cried 'Woof!'" ◆ 2001
7. The Stormy Day Rescue ◆ 2001
8. Show-and-Tell Surprise ◆ 2001
9. The Runaway Rabbit ◆ 2001
10. T-Bone Tells the Truth ◆ 2002
11. Cleo Cooperates ◆ 2002
12. Clifford's Loose Tooth ◆ 2002
13. The Big White Ghost ◆ 2003
14. The Big Itch ◆ 2003
15. The Snow Dog ◆ 2004
16. The Star of the Show ◆ 2004
17. The Biggest Easter Egg ◆ 2006

BIG RED CHAPTER BOOKS

1. Clifford Saves the Whales ◆ 2002
2. The Big Red Detective ◆ 2003
3. Cookie Crazy! ◆ 2003
4. Clifford Finds a Clue ◆ 2004

CLUB OF MYSTERIES

Naylor, Phyllis Reynolds
MACMILLAN ◆ GRADES 4–7 ◆ A/R
ANIMAL FANTASY | MYSTERY

House cats Marco and Polo are ready for mystery and adventure. They make a *Grand Escape* and soon come across the leader of a cat Club of Mysteries. They must pass a test in order to join this group. In the second book, they must convince the others that they are suitable to succeed their longtime leader.

1. The Grand Escape ◆ 1993
2. The Healing of Texas Jake ◆ 1997
3. Carlotta's Kittens and the Club of Mysteries ◆ 2000
4. Polo's Mother ◆ 2005

CLUBHOUSE

San Souci, Daniel
TRICYCLE ◆ GRADES 1–4 ◆ A/R
ADVENTURE

Author/illustrator San Souci relives some of the adventures of his youth in these gently nostalgic books about young Danny and his friends (including brother Bobby) in the Dangerous Snake and Reptile Club. A ghost is suspected in *The Amazing Ghost Detectives* when the gang returns to find that someone has been in the clubhouse but the door is still locked. In *Space Station Mars,* they are convinced they have found a meteor and decide to make contact with Martians. San Souci's illustrations extend the humor.

1. The Dangerous Snake and Reptile Club ◆ 2004
2. Space Station Mars ◆ 2005
3. The Amazing Ghost Detectives ◆ 2006
4. The Mighty Pigeon Club ◆ 2007

CLUE

Various authors
SCHOLASTIC ◆ GRADES 3–6
MYSTERY

The characters from the popular Parker Brothers board game are suspects in short mysteries, ten in each book. The solution for each one appears upside down at the end. The stories are filled with insults and puns. The characters maintain their distinct personalities. In each of the stories, they are the guests of Reginald Boddy, except Mrs. White, who is his maid. Typically, he shows them a certain treasure or engages them in a get-rich-quick scheme, and then one of them steals something. Readers are asked which one did it, in what room, and with what weapon, as in the game. A facsimile of the game's worksheet is shown to keep track of developments. The mysteries are challenging enough for older children, and the dialog is amusing.

1. Who Killed Mr. Boddy? (Weiner, Eric) ◆ 1992
2. The *Secret* Secret Passage (Weiner, Eric) ◆ 1992
3. The Case of the Invisible Cat (Weiner, Eric) ◆ 1992
4. Mystery at the Masked Ball (Weiner, Eric) ◆ 1993
5. Midnight Phone Calls (Weiner, Eric) ◆ 1994
6. Booby-Trapped! (Weiner, Eric) ◆ 1994
7. The Picture-Perfect Crime (Malcolm, Jahnna N.) ◆ 1994
8. The Clue in the Shadow (Malcolm, Jahnna N.) ◆ 1995
9. Mystery in the Moonlight (Jacks, Marie) ◆ 1995
10. The Screaming Skeleton (Jacks, Marie) ◆ 1995
11. Death by Candlelight (Jacks, Marie) ◆ 1995
12. The Haunted Gargoyle (Jacks, Marie) ◆ 1996
13. Revenge of the Mummy (Jacks, Marie) ◆ 1996
14. The Dangerous Diamond (Jacks, Marie) ◆ 1996
15. The Vanishing Vampire Clue (Jacks, Marie) ◆ 1997
16. Danger After Dark (Smith, Dona) ◆ 1997
17. The Clue in the Crystal Ball (Smith, Dona) ◆ 1997
18. Footprints in the Fog (Smith, Dona) ◆ 1997

CLUE JR.

Various authors

SCHOLASTIC ◆ GRADES 2–4

MYSTERY

Four fourth-graders form a Clue Club to talk about mysteries and to solve their own. The mysteries are all easy to work out using a little logic. Each two- or three-page chapter contains a separate case, and the solution is given upside down at the end. Peter, Samantha, Greta, and Mortimer are the "good guys" and use their skills to catch others in their class misbehaving. This series is for much younger children than the Clue series. The characters are not the ones from the popular Parker Brothers game and the crimes are much more easily solved.

1. The Case of the Secret Message (Teitelbaum, Michael, and Steve Morganstern) ◆ 1994
2. The Case of the Stolen Jewel (Teitelbaum, Michael, and Steve Morganstern) ◆ 1995
3. The Case of the Chocolate Fingerprints (Rowland, Della) ◆ 1995
4. The Case of the Missing Movie (Rowland, Della) ◆ 1995
5. The Case of the Zoo Clue (Rowland, Della) ◆ 1996

6. The Case of the Runaway Turtle (Rowland, Della) ◆ 1996
7. The Case of the Mystery Ghost (Rowland, Della) ◆ 1996
8. The Case of the Clubhouse Thief (Rowland, Della) ◆ 1997
9. The Case of the Karate Chop (Rowland, Della) ◆ 1997
10. The Case of the Secret Password (Rowland, Della) ◆ 1997
11. The Case of the Barking Dog (Rowland, Della) ◆ 1997
12. The Case of the Winning Skateboard (Rowland, Della) ◆ 1998
13. The Case of the Soccer Camp Mystery (Rowland, Della) ◆ 1998

COBBLE STREET COUSINS

Rylant, Cynthia

SIMON & SCHUSTER ◆ GRADES 1–4 ◆ A/R

REAL LIFE

Lily, Tess, and Rosie are 9 years old. Their respective parents are on a tour with the ballet so the cousins are staying with Aunt Lucy. This series is cozy and warm as the girls find activities to do together. Baking cookies, making crafts, and creating a newspaper are among their projects.

1. In Aunt Lucy's Kitchen ◆ 1998
2. A Little Shopping ◆ 1998
3. Special Gifts ◆ 1999
4. Some Good News ◆ 1999
5. Summer Party ◆ 2001
6. Wedding Flowers ◆ 2002

COBTOWN

Van Nutt, Julia

DOUBLEDAY ◆ GRADES 3–4 ◆ A/R

HISTORICAL

Using the diaries of her great-grandmother, the author describes the events in a small town in the 19th century. The design of the books conveys a sense of nostalgia. One book features a mysterious noise that turns out to be a piglet stuck in the gorge. In another book, the piglet, Oinkey, is stolen by inept scientists.

1. A Cobtown Christmas: A Cobtown Story: From the Diaries of Lucky Hart ◆ 1998
2. The Mystery of Mineral Gorge: A Cobtown Story: From the Diaries of Lucky Hart ◆ 1999
3. Pumpkins from the Sky: A Cobtown Story: From the Diaries of Lucky Hart ◆ 1999
4. The Monster in the Shadows: A Cobtown Story: From the Diaries of Lucky Hart ◆ 2000

5. Pignapped! A Cobtown Story: From the Diaries of Lucky Hart ◆ 2000
6. Skyrockets and Snickerdoodles: A Cobtown Story: From the Diaries of Lucky Hart ◆ 2001

CODY

Duffey, Betsy

VIKING ◆ GRADES 2–4 ◆ A/R

FAMILY LIFE | REAL LIFE

Cody Michaels, the new kid at school, invents outrageous stories about his family, calling himself Super Cody to impress the class. In *Virtual Cody,* he tries to discover the origin of his name for a class project. In *Spotlight on Cody,* all of the third-graders seem to have an ability to display for the talent show—except Cody. Cody's friends, Chip and Holly, are supportive and realistic. The easy chapters, funny and perceptive characters, and realistic dialogue make this a good choice for middle-grade readers.

1. Hey, New Kid! ◆ 1996
2. Virtual Cody ◆ 1997
3. Cody's Secret Admirer ◆ 1998
4. Spotlight on Cody ◆ 1998
5. Cody Unplugged ◆ 1999

COLLETTE MURPHY *see* Murphy Family

COLONIAL WILLIAMSBURG *see* Young Americans: Colonial Williamsburg

COMEBACK KIDS

Lupica, Mike

PHILOMEL ◆ GRADES 4–6 ◆ A/R

REAL LIFE | RECREATION

In *Hot Hand,* Billy, 10, is coping with his parents' separation. His father is also his basketball coach and his intense attitude is adding to Billy's struggle. In *Safe at Home,* twelve-year-old Nick faces the pressure of being the first seventh grader on the varsity baseball team. As a sportswriter and ESPN personality, Mike Lupica knows sports and the sports action in these books is great.

1. Hot Hand ◆ 2007
2. Two-Minute Drill ◆ 2007

   3. Safe at Home ◆ 2008
   4. Long Shot ◆ 2008

COMMANDER TOAD

Yolen, Jane

PUTNAM ◆ **GRADES K–3** ◆ **A/R**

ANIMAL FANTASY | HUMOR | SCIENCE FICTION

The "brave and bright" Commander Toad sails through the galaxy with his faithful crew in a parody of *Star Trek* and *Star Wars*. Mr. Hop looks solemn and thinks a lot, Doc Peeper is crotchety, and the eager Jake Skyjumper reads a lot of comics. Puns abound as they go from one adventure to another, especially wordplay relating to frogs and toads. They bravely save aliens from disasters, and in one episode they go after intergalactic spy 007 1/2. He is Commander Toad's cousin, and they are both "toadally handsome." Lieutenant Lily puts the ship in "high wart speed" and they take off. Adults and older children will enjoy the satire, while younger children will enjoy the adventures.

   1. Commander Toad in Space ◆ 1980
   2. Commander Toad and the Planet of the Grapes ◆ 1982
   3. Commander Toad and the Big Black Hole ◆ 1983
   4. Commander Toad and the Dis-asteroid ◆ 1985
   5. Commander Toad and the Intergalactic Spy ◆ 1986
   6. Commander Toad and the Space Pirates ◆ 1987
   7. Commander Toad and the Voyage Home ◆ 1998

THE COMPANIONS QUARTET

Golding, Julia

MARSHALL CAVENDISH ◆ **GRADES 5–8**

FANTASY

Connie Lionheart, 11, has always been different. Besides having mismatched eyes, she is often in the middle of unusual events involving animals. While visiting her aunt in England, Connie discovers she can communicate with all creatures. Aunt Evelyn is a member of a secret group dedicated to protecting mythical creatures and she needs Connie's skills when the sirens are threatened by a evil spirit. As in the Percy Jackson books, mythology and folklore are important elements in this series.

   1. Secret of the Sirens ◆ 2007
   2. The Gorgon's Gaze ◆ 2007
   3. Mines of the Minotaur ◆ 2008
   4. The Chimera's Curse ◆ 2008

THE COMPLICATED LIFE OF CLAUDIA CRISTINA CORTEZ

Gallagher , Diana G.
STONE ARCH ◆ GRADES 5–7

REAL LIFE

Claudia, 13, and her girlfriends hang out together as the "Whatever" club. When another good friend, Adam, wants to join them, they have to decide whether or not to let him. In *Dance,* Claudia is on the committee for the seventh-grade dance and she wants it to be casual and fun, but Anna, a popular girl, wants it to be more formal. These books are designed with different fonts and drawings that will attract many readers, including fans of Amelia (Moss).

1. Camp Can't ◆ 2007
2. Dance Trap ◆ 2007
3. Guilty! ◆ 2007
4. Whatever! ◆ 2007
5. Beach Blues ◆ 2008
6. Friends Forever? ◆ 2008
7. Party! ◆ 2008
8. Vote! ◆ 2008

COOPER KIDS

Peretti, Frank
TOMMY NELSON WORDKIDS ◆ GRADES 5–7 ◆ A/R

ADVENTURE | VALUES

Dr. Cooper, a biblical archeologist, travels all over the world with his two children, getting in and out of all sorts of danger and solving mysteries. Smart and competent, Jay and Lila help him out. Lila, traveling back to the United States from an assignment in Japan, is trapped at the bottom of the ocean. Her rescue is hampered by a conflict with Communist guerrillas in the Philippines. A hint of the supernatural is introduced in an episode involving a space-time warp, where the children are trapped in an old Western town and solve a century-old murder mystery. The eighth volume has been reissued with the title *Mayday at Two Thousand Five Hundred.* This series features lots of excitement and Christian characters, for whom prayer and trust in God is a part of life.

1. The Door in the Dragon's Throat ◆ 1985
2. Escape from the Island of Aquarius ◆ 1986
3. The Tombs of Anak ◆ 1987
4. Trapped at the Bottom of the Sea ◆ 1988
5. The Secret of the Desert Stone ◆ 1996
6. The Deadly Curse of Toco-Rey ◆ 1996

7. The Legend of Annie Murphy ◆ 1997
8. Flying Blind ◆ 1997

CORDUROY

Freeman, Don, and Barbara G. Hennessy
VIKING ◆ GRADES K–1 ◆ A/R
FANTASY

The two original books about Corduroy—*Corduroy* and *A Pocket for Corduroy*—feature a toy bear and his owner-friend Lisa. When he is left on his own, Corduroy can move around and has adventures in a department store and a laundromat. These books by Freeman have been extended by celebration stories (birthday and holiday) by Hennessy. There are also board books and lift-the-flap books featuring Corduroy. The new Viking easy-reading books are written by Alison Inches.

1. Corduroy (Freeman, Don) ◆ 1968
2. A Pocket for Corduroy (Freeman, Don) ◆ 1978
3. Corduroy's Christmas (Hennessy, Barbara G.) ◆ 1992
4. Corduroy's Halloween (Hennessy, Barbara G.) ◆ 1995
5. Corduroy's Birthday (Hennessy, Barbara G.) ◆ 1997
6. Corduroy Lost and Found (Hennessy, Barbara G.) ◆ 2006

VIKING EASY-TO-READ STORIES

1. Corduroy Makes a Cake ◆ 2001
2. Corduroy's Hike ◆ 2001
3. Corduroy's Garden ◆ 2002
4. Corduroy Writes a Letter ◆ 2002

COREY *see* My America: Corey

CORK AND FUZZ

Chaconas, Dori
VIKING ◆ GRADES K–2 ◆ A/R
ANIMAL FANTASY

Cork, a muskrat, and Fuzz, a possum, are friends who enjoy doing many things together. Sometimes their differences are a problem, like when Cork, who is short, tries to change his tall friend—maybe Fuzz could walk on his knees. In another book, Fuzz wins all their games and is a bit of a show-off, causing Cork to feel angry. This easy-reader series will appeal to children who like stories about animal friends—such as the Frog and Toad books.

1. Cork and Fuzz ◆ 2005
2. Cork and Fuzz: Short and Tall ◆ 2006
3. Cork and Fuzz: The Collectors ◆ 2007
4. Cork and Fuzz: Good Sports ◆ 2008
5. Cork and Fuzz: Finders Keepers ◆ 2009

COUSINS QUARTET

Mahy, Margaret
DELACORTE ◆ GRADES 4–6 ◆ A/R
FAMILY LIFE

Pete Fortune and his family (mother, father, brother Simon, and baby sister Bombshell) leave Australia and return to the home of the father's family in Fairfield, New Zealand. There, Pete meets his cousins and must try to fit in with the Good Fortunes Gang. Each book of the quartet features a different cousin and the struggle to both belong and be independent. There are meetings in a tree house, a visit to a graveyard, concerns about parents with problems, and a wedding. These are lively books with lots of entertaining dialogue and adventures.

1. The Good Fortunes Gang ◆ 1993
2. A Fortunate Name ◆ 1993
3. A Fortune Branches Out ◆ 1994
4. Tangled Fortunes ◆ 1994

COVEN TREE

Brittain, Bill
HARPERCOLLINS ◆ GRADES 3–6
FANTASY

Adventures both amusing and amazing await the readers of this series. When the Wish Giver comes to Coven Tree, four people find out that wishes aren't always what they expect. Professor Popkin promises an equally amazing product, and Dr. Dredd brings much more than the services of Bufu the Rainmaker.

1. The Wish Giver: Three Tales of Coven Tree ◆ 1983
2. Dr. Dredd's Wagon of Wonders ◆ 1987
3. Professor Popkin's Prodigious Polish: A Tale of Coven Tree ◆ 1990

COWGIRL KATE AND COCOA

Silverman, Erica

HARCOURT ◆ GRADES K–2 ◆ A/R

HUMOR | REAL LIFE

This series for beginning readers features a feisty cowgirl, Kate, and her sometimes difficult horse, Cocoa. In the first book, Cocoa tries to avoid herding cattle but Kate is able to change his mind. In another book, Kate goes to school and Cocoa misses her. The short chapters will appeal to young readers. The friendship between these two is reminiscent of the books about Henry and Mudge.

1. Cowgirl Kate and Cocoa ◆ 2005
2. Cowgirl Kate and Cocoa: Partners ◆ 2006
3. Cowgirl Kate and Cocoa: School Days ◆ 2007
4. Cowgirl Kate and Cocoa: Rain or Shine ◆ 2008

CRANBERRYPORT

Devlin, Wende, and Harry Devlin

MACMILLAN ◆ GRADES 1–3 ◆ A/R

FAMILY LIFE | MYSTERY

The residents of the small town of Cranberryport certainly keep busy solving mysteries, raising funds for good causes, and celebrating special holidays. Grandma is a prominent citizen, as is her granddaughter Maggie. Along with Mr. Whiskers, an old sea captain, Maggie solves minor mysteries. With full-page, comical illustrations, simple problems, and quick solutions, this series is fun for reading aloud or alone. Cranberry recipes are included in each title. The Tales from Cranberryport describe everyday life.

1. Cranberry Thanksgiving ◆ 1971
2. Cranberry Christmas ◆ 1976
3. Cranberry Mystery ◆ 1978
4. Cranberry Halloween ◆ 1982
5. Cranberry Valentine ◆ 1986
6. Cranberry Birthday ◆ 1988
7. Cranberry Easter ◆ 1990
8. Cranberry Summer ◆ 1992
9. Cranberry Autumn ◆ 1993

TALES FROM CRANBERRYPORT

1. Cranberry Moving Day ◆ 1994
2. Cranberry Trip to the Dentist ◆ 1994
3. A New Baby in Cranberryport ◆ 1994

4. Maggie Has a Nightmare ◆ 1994
5. Cranberry First Day of School ◆ 1995
6. Cranberry Lost at the Fair ◆ 1995

CRICKET KAUFMAN *see* Edison-Armstrong School

CRIME THROUGH TIME

Doyle, Bill

LITTLE, BROWN ◆ GRADES 4–8 ◆ A/R

MYSTERY

Generations of a family of famous detectives solve mysteries set during notable historical eras (and one future setting). Cyanide poisoning on a train, bootleggers and kidnapping, and a stolen Egyptian necklace are among the mysteries for the young sleuths. Sidebars, clues, maps, sketches, and more involve the reader in the action.

1. Swindled! The 1906 Journal of Fitz Morgan ◆ 2006
2. Nabbed! The 1925 Journal of G. Codd Fitzmorgan ◆ 2006
3. Silenced! The 1969 Journal of Malcolm Moorie ◆ 2006
4. Betrayed! The 1977 Journal of Zeke Moorie ◆ 2006
5. Iced! The 2007 Journal of Nick Fitzmorgan ◆ 2006
6. Trapped! The 2031 Journal of Otis Fitzmorgan ◆ 2006

CRITTERS OF THE NIGHT *see* Mercer Mayer's
Critters of the Night

THE CRONUS CHRONICLES

Ursu, Anne

ATHENEUM ◆ GRADES 5–9 ◆ A/R

FANTASY

There are plans to take over the Underworld and overthrow Hades. Philonecron, Poseidon's grandson, plans to steal the shadows of children and use them to restore life to the dead. Two cousins, Charlotte and Zee (a boy with a mysterious heritage), become involved the fight against Philonecron. This is a natural series to pair with Percy Jackson and the Olympians.

1. The Shadow Thieves ◆ 2006
2. The Siren Song ◆ 2007
3. The Promethian Flame ◆ 2009

CRYSTAL DOORS

Moesta, Rebecca, and Kevin J. Anderson

LITTLE, BROWN ◆ GRADES 5–8

FANTASY

Gwen and Vic, 14, are cousins whose family background is filled with strange occurrences. Both of their mothers just "appeared" in the jungle where their fathers were working on an archeological dig. Now, with the mysterious death of Gwen's parents and the disappearance of Vic's mother, the cousins begin a dangerous journey. They enter a room filled with crystals and are transported to Elantya, an island kingdom being threatened by merlons (sea monsters).

1. Crystal Doors: Island Realm ◆ 2006
2. Crystal Doors: Ocean Realm ◆ 2007
3. Crystal Doors: Sky Realm ◆ 2008

CUCUMBERS TRILOGY

Moore, Lilian

ATHENEUM ◆ GRADES 2–4 ◆ A/R

ADVENTURE | ANIMAL FANTASY

Adam Mouse is an introspective young mouse who observes the world around him and creates poetry from his reflections. His friend Junius is more lively and risk-taking. In *I'll Meet You at the Cucumbers,* Adam and Junius leave the security of their rural home and travel to the city, where they meet Adam's pen friend, Amanda. The second book describes Amanda's adventures when she visits the country. The third book is a collection of Adam's poems, which capture his feelings about nature, his home, his friends, and his hopes.

1. I'll Meet You at the Cucumbers ◆ 1988
2. Don't Be Afraid, Amanda ◆ 1992
3. Adam Mouse's Book of Poems ◆ 1992

CUL-DE-SAC KIDS

Lewis, Beverly

BETHANY HOUSE ◆ GRADES 3–6 ◆ A/R

REAL LIFE | VALUES

A group of children who live in the same neighborhood have a lot of stories to tell. Jason, Stacy, Abby, Dunkum, and more have problems to solve. Dunkum searches for his cousin's missing seeing-eye dog. Jason wants a new mountain bike. Carly loses the class guinea pig. These children rely on their values to help guide them.

1. The Double Dabble Surprise ◆ 1993
2. The Chicken Pox Panic ◆ 1993
3. The Crazy Christmas Angel Mystery ◆ 1994
4. No Grown-Ups Allowed ◆ 1995
5. Frog Power ◆ 1995
6. The Mystery of Case D. Luc ◆ 1995
7. The Stinky Sneakers Mystery ◆ 1996
8. Pickle Pizza ◆ 1996
9. Mailbox Mania ◆ 1996
10. The Mudhole Mystery ◆ 1996
11. Fiddlesticks ◆ 1996
12. The Crabby Cat Caper ◆ 1996
13. Tarantula Toes ◆ 1997
14. Green Gravy ◆ 1997
15. Backyard Bandit Mystery ◆ 1997
16. Tree House Trouble ◆ 1997
17. The Creepy Sleep-Over ◆ 1997
18. The Great TV Turn-Off ◆ 1997
19. Piggy Party ◆ 1999
20. The Granny Game ◆ 1999
21. Mystery Mutt ◆ 2000
22. Big Bad Beans ◆ 2000
23. The Upside-Down Day ◆ 2001
24. The Midnight Mystery ◆ 2001

CULPEPPER ADVENTURES

Paulsen, Gary
YEARLING ◆ GRADES 3–5 ◆ A/R
ADVENTURE | MYSTERY

Amos Binder and Duncan "Dunc" Culpepper are best friends who stumble into mysteries and adventures. In one book, the friends are in a haunted castle in Scotland; in another, they are in Santa Fe to find out who is rustling Uncle Woody's prize cattle. *Dunc and Amos Go to the Dogs* finds them investigating a dognapping scheme. Melissa Hansen is in some of the books, causing problems for Amos, who finds her very special (see *Amos Gets Married*). These books offer fast-paced adventure with zippy dialogue. They are a good choice for middle elementary grades and reluctant readers.

1. The Case of the Dirty Bird ◆ 1992
2. Dunc's Doll ◆ 1992
3. Culpepper's Cannon ◆ 1992
4. Dunc Gets Tweaked ◆ 1992
5. Dunc's Halloween ◆ 1992

   6. Dunc Breaks the Record ◆ 1992

   7. Dunc and the Flaming Ghost ◆ 1992

   8. Amos Gets Famous ◆ 1993

   9. Dunc and Amos Hit the Big Top ◆ 1993

  10. Dunc's Dump ◆ 1993

  11. Amos's Last Stand ◆ 1993

  12. Dunc and Amos and the Red Tattoos ◆ 1993

  13. Dunc's Undercover Christmas ◆ 1993

  14. The Wild Culpepper Cruise ◆ 1993

  15. Dunc and the Haunted Castle ◆ 1993

  16. Cowpokes and Desperadoes ◆ 1994

  17. Prince Amos ◆ 1994

  18. Coach Amos ◆ 1994

  19. Amos and the Alien ◆ 1994

  20. Dunc and Amos Meet the Slasher ◆ 1994

  21. Dunc and the Greased Sticks of Doom ◆ 1994

  22. Amos's Killer Concert Caper ◆ 1995

  23. Amos Gets Married ◆ 1995

  24. Amos Goes Bananas ◆ 1996

  25. Dunc and Amos Go to the Dogs ◆ 1996

  26. Amos and the Vampire ◆ 1996

  27. Amos and the Chameleon Caper ◆ 1996

  28. Amos Binder, Secret Agent ◆ 1997

  29. Dunc and Amos on Thin Ice ◆ 1997

  30. Super Amos ◆ 1997

CURIOUS GEORGE

Rey, Hans Augusto, and Margret Rey

HOUGHTON MIFFLIN ◆ GRADES K–2 ◆ A/R

ANIMAL FANTASY | HUMOR

The Man in the Yellow Hat brings George, a little monkey, home from the jungle to live with him. George is very curious and is always getting into trouble, but he always ends up making people laugh or solving a problem. When he goes to a friend's house to help bake a cake, he gets into everything and makes a terrible mess; but when the cake is done, his hostess finds her lost necklace inside. He takes a job delivering papers, but ends up making paper boats out of them. In one of the longest books, a scientist wants him to go up in a space capsule and parachute back down, which he does successfully, earning himself a medal. This series is all in picture-book format, but varies quite a bit in length. There are three groups of Curious George Books. The original Curious George books were by H. A. Rey (assisted by Margret Rey on *Curious George Flies a Kite* and *Curious George Goes to the Hospital*). Margret Rey and Allan Shalleck produced a series of books that correlated with the release of movies about Curious George. Houghton Mifflin has released a new series of books that feature Margret and H. A. Rey's Curious George. There are some board books, big books, and CD-ROM tie-ins, as well.

ORIGINAL CURIOUS GEORGE BOOKS

1. Curious George ◆ 1941
2. Curious George Takes a Job ◆ 1947
3. Curious George Rides a Bike ◆ 1952
4. Curious George Gets a Medal ◆ 1957
5. Curious George Flies a Kite ◆ 1958
6. Curious George Learns the Alphabet ◆ 1963
7. Curious George Goes to the Hospital ◆ 1966

CURIOUS GEORGE MOVIE BOOKS

1. Curious George and the Dump Truck ◆ 1984
2. Curious George Goes Sledding ◆ 1984
3. Curious George Goes to the Aquarium ◆ 1984
4. Curious George Goes to the Circus ◆ 1984
5. Curious George and the Pizza ◆ 1988
6. Curious George Goes Hiking ◆ 1985
7. Curious George Visits the Zoo ◆ 1988
8. Curious George at the Ballet ◆ 1985
9. Curious George Goes to a Costume Party ◆ 1986
10. Curious George Plays Baseball ◆ 1986
11. Curious George Walks the Pets ◆ 1986
12. Curious George at the Airport ◆ 1987
13. Curious George at the Laundromat ◆ 1987
14. Curious George Goes Fishing ◆ 1987
15. Curious George Visits the Police Station ◆ 1987
16. Curious George at the Beach ◆ 1988
17. Curious George at the Railroad Station ◆ 1988
18. Curious George Goes to a Restaurant ◆ 1988
19. Curious George Visits an Amusement Park ◆ 1988
20. Curious George and the Dinosaur ◆ 1989
21. Curious George Goes to an Ice Cream Shop ◆ 1989
22. Curious George Goes to School ◆ 1989
23. Curious George Goes to the Dentist ◆ 1989
24. Curious George Bakes a Cake ◆ 1990
25. Curious George Goes Camping ◆ 1990
26. Curious George Goes to a Toy Store ◆ 1990
27. Curious George Goes to an Air Show ◆ 1990

MARGRET AND H. A. REY'S CURIOUS GEORGE BOOKS

1. Curious George and the Hot Air Balloon ◆ 1998
2. Curious George and the Puppies ◆ 1998
3. Curious George Feeds the Animals ◆ 1998
4. Curious George Goes to the Chocolate Factory ◆ 1998
5. Curious George Goes to a Movie ◆ 1998
6. Curious George in the Snow ◆ 1998

7. Curious George Makes Pancakes ◆ 1998
8. Curious George's Dream ◆ 1998
9. Curious George and the Dump Truck ◆ 1999
10. Curious George at the Parade ◆ 1999
11. Curious George Goes Camping ◆ 1999
12. Curious George Goes to the Beach ◆ 1999
13. Curious George Goes Fishing ◆ 2001
14. Curious George Goes to a Costume Party ◆ 2001
15. Curious George in the Big City ◆ 2001
16. Curious George Takes a Train ◆ 2002
17. Curious George Visits a Toy Store ◆ 2002
18. Curious George and the Birthday Surprise ◆ 2003
19. Curious George Visits the Library ◆ 2003
20. Curious George and the Firefighters ◆ 2004
21. Curious George's First Day of School ◆ 2005
22. Curious George at the Baseball Game ◆ 2006
23. Curious George's Dinosaur Discovery ◆ 2006
24. Merry Christmas, Curious George ◆ 2006
25. Curious George at the Aquarium ◆ 2007

CURIOUS GEORGE PBS KIDS

1. Curious George Builds a House (Perez, Monica, adapter) ◆ 2006
2. Curious George: The Dog Show (Perez, Monica, adapter) ◆ 2006
3. Curious George: The Donut Delivery (Perez, Monica, adapter) ◆ 2006
4. Curious George: The Kite (Perez, Monica, adapter) ◆ 2006
5. Curious George Cleans Up (Krensky, Stephen, adapter) ◆ 2007
6. Curious George Plants a Seed (Zappy, Erica, adapter) ◆ 2007
7. Curious George Roller Coaster (Perez, Monica, adapter) ◆ 2007
8. Curious George Snowy Day (Moscovich, Rotem, adapter) ◆ 2007
9. Curious George Tadpole Trouble (Williams, Mark London, adapter) ◆ 2007
10. Curious George Takes a Trip (Moscovich, Rotem, adapter) ◆ 2007
11. Curious George Lost and Found (Zappy, Erica, adapter) ◆ 2008
12. Curious George Plays Mini Golf (Goldberg, Mary, adapter) ◆ 2008
13. Curious George: The Surprise Gift (Zappy, Erica, adapter) ◆ 2008

THE CUT-UPS

Marshall, James

PENGUIN ◆ GRADES K–3 ◆ A/R

HUMOR

Spud Jenkins and Joe Turner are a couple of "cut-ups" who terrorize their mothers and the neighborhood. Sitting in the movie theater, one says out loud to the other, "I thought you had the snake." They snorkel in the flooded bathroom and hook Spud's little brother to a kite. But they meet their match in Mary Frances, who catapults them into the yard of the kid-hating Lamar Spurgle. Full-color cartoony illustrations on every page add to the zany humor.

1. The Cut-Ups ◆ 1984
2. The Cut-Ups Cut Loose ◆ 1987
3. The Cut-Ups at Camp Custer ◆ 1989
4. The Cut-Ups Carry On ◆ 1990
5. The Cut-Ups Crack Up ◆ 1992

CYBER.KDZ

Balan, Bruce

AVON ◆ GRADES 4–6

ADVENTURE | MYSTERY

Seven friends—Josh, Tereza, Sanjeev, Deedee, Becky, Loren, and Paul—use their Cyber.kdz chat line to solve high-tech mysteries. In one book, Tereza and Josh vacation in the Amazon rainforest and are at risk from poachers. Using their computer skills, they contact friends who hack into a government computer network. In another book, the Cyber.kdz have added video cameras to their systems, which allows them to find out who is changing Becky's grades on the school's database. In addition to the text, there are e-mail messages and data transfers that add to the action. With each kid living in a different location, there are many opportunities to link up with events around the world.

1. In Search of Scum ◆ 1997
2. A Picture's Worth ◆ 1997
3. The Great NASA Flu ◆ 1997
4. Blackout in the Amazon ◆ 1997
5. In Pursuit of Picasso ◆ 1998
6. When the Chips Are Down ◆ 1998

CYBERQUEST

Brouwer, Sigmund

THOMAS NELSON ◆ GRADES 5–8

FANTASY

Set in the future, this series depicts Earth as a dangerous place. The Technocrats are in control, Christianity has been outlawed, and the Welfaros of Old Newyork are facing destruction. A leader is needed. Mok is chosen by the Committee to face virtual reality trials through history. His final trial is in ancient Jerusalem at the time of the crucifixion.

1. Pharaoh's Tomb ◆ 1997
2. Knight's Honor ◆ 1997
3. Pirate's Cross ◆ 1997

4. Outlaw's Gold ◆ 1997
5. Soldier's Aim ◆ 1997
6. Galilee Man ◆ 1997

DANA GIRLS

Keene, Carolyn

GROSSET & DUNLAP ◆ **GRADES 3–5**

MYSTERY

Published from 1934 to 1979 by the Stratemeyer Syndicate under the pseudonym of Carolyn Keene, this mystery series features two sisters: 17-year-old Louise, who is dark-haired and serious, and 16-year-old Jean, who is fair-haired and more impetuous. They are orphans who live with their Uncle Ned, a ship's captain, and his sister, Aunt Harriet. Because the Danas attend a boarding school, most of the mysteries take place in a school setting.

1. By the Light of the Study Lamp ◆ 1934
2. The Secret at Lone Tree Cottage ◆ 1934
3. In the Shadow of the Tower ◆ 1934
4. A Three-Cornered Mystery ◆ 1935
5. The Secret at the Hermitage ◆ 1936
6. The Circle of Footprints ◆ 1937
7. The Mystery of the Locked Room ◆ 1938
8. The Clue in the Cobweb ◆ 1939
9. The Secret at the Gatehouse ◆ 1940
10. The Mysterious Fireplace ◆ 1941
11. The Clue of the Rusty Key ◆ 1942
12. The Portrait in the Sand ◆ 1943
13. The Secret in the Old Well ◆ 1944
14. The Clue in the Ivy ◆ 1952
15. The Secret of the Jade Ring ◆ 1953
16. The Mystery at the Crossroads ◆ 1954
17. The Ghost in the Gallery ◆ 1955
18. The Clue of the Black Flower ◆ 1956
19. The Winking Ruby Mystery ◆ 1957
20. The Secret of the Swiss Chalet ◆ 1958
21. The Haunted Lagoon ◆ 1959
22. The Mystery of the Bamboo Bird ◆ 1960
23. The Sierra Gold Mystery ◆ 1961
24. The Secret of Lost Lake ◆ 1963
25. The Mystery of the Stone Tiger ◆ 1963
26. The Riddle of the Frozen Mountain ◆ 1964
27. The Secret of the Silver Dolphin ◆ 1965
28. The Mystery of the Wax Queen ◆ 1966
29. The Secret of the Minstrel's Guitar ◆ 1967
30. The Phantom Surfer ◆ 1968

31. The Curious Coronation ◆ 1976
32. The Hundred-Year Mystery ◆ 1977
33. The Mountain-Peak Mystery ◆ 1978
34. The Witch's Omen ◆ 1979

DANGER GUYS

Abbott, Tony

HARPERCOLLINS ◆ GRADES 3–5 ◆ A/R

ADVENTURE | MYSTERY

Noodle Newton and Zeek Pilinsky are best friends who attend the grand opening of Danger Guy, an adventure store. They buy Danger Guy equipment including jackets and backpacks and they are ready for action. Far-fetched plots and exotic locations such as Central America and Hollywood add to the drama. The boys face thieves, smugglers, prehistoric ice men, man-eating plants, and even a cyborg. Snappy dialogue and lots of action will attract some reluctant readers. The fact that Noodle is white and Zeek is African American may broaden the appeal.

1. Danger Guys ◆ 1994
2. Danger Guys: Hollywood Halloween ◆ 1994
3. Danger Guys Blast Off ◆ 1994
4. Danger Guys Hit the Beach ◆ 1995
5. Danger Guys on Ice ◆ 1995
6. Danger Guys and the Golden Lizard ◆ 1996

DANGER JOE SHOW

Schade, Susan

SCHOLASTIC ◆ GRADES 2–4 ◆ A/R

HUMOR

Joe's dad is a zoologist with his own wildlife television program—Danger Joe's Wild World. When Joe goes along for some of the episodes, trouble follows. Talk about lions and tigers and bears! Joe meets up with a grizzly, baboons, a hawk, and an angry alligator.

1. Growling Grizzly ◆ 2002
2. Bungee Baboon Rescue ◆ 2002
3. Hawk Talk ◆ 2002
4. Back to the Bayou ◆ 2003

DANIEL BOOM *see* Adventures of Daniel Boom aka Loud Boy

DANITRA BROWN

Grimes, Nikki

LOTHROP; HARPERCOLLINS ◆ GRADES 2–5 ◆ A/R

REAL LIFE

Danitra Brown and Zuri Jackson are best friends. In the first book, they enjoy riding bikes, jumping rope, and spending time together. In the second book, Danitra spends the summer at her aunt's house while Zuri remains in the city. In *Danitra Brown, Class Clown,* Zuri is nervous about the start of school and Danitra is there to support her. The poems in these books describe the ups and downs of their friendship.

1. Meet Danitra Brown ◆ 1994
2. Danitra Brown Leaves Town ◆ 2002
3. Danitra Brown, Class Clown ◆ 2005

DANNY AND THE DINOSAUR

Hoff, Syd

HARPERCOLLINS ◆ GRADES K–3 ◆ A/R

ANIMAL FANTASY

This series is an all-time favorite with beginning readers. Danny goes to the museum one day and finds the dinosaur area. He is wishing that they were alive when one of the dinosaurs speaks to him! They play together and have many amusing adventures throughout the series.

1. Danny and the Dinosaur ◆ 1958
2. Danny and the Dinosaur Go to Camp ◆ 1958
3. Happy Birthday, Danny and the Dinosaur! ◆ 1995

DANNY DUNN

Williams, Jay, and Raymond Abrashkin

MCGRAW-HILL ◆ GRADES 3–6

ADVENTURE | SCIENCE FICTION

Young readers who enjoy science will be especially interested in the Danny Dunn series. Danny is a boy who wants to become a scientist, and he has all kinds of adventures as a result of his curiosity. He is joined by local scientist Euclid Bullfinch, Dr. Grimes (another scientist), and friend Joe Pearson. This series has the potential to spark scientific interest by showing readers that science is exciting and entertaining.

1. Danny Dunn and the Anti-Gravity Paint ◆ 1956
2. Danny Dunn on a Desert Island ◆ 1957
3. Danny Dunn and the Homework Machine ◆ 1958
4. Danny Dunn and the Weather Machine ◆ 1959
5. Danny Dunn on the Ocean Floor ◆ 1960
6. Danny Dunn and the Fossil Cave ◆ 1961
7. Danny Dunn and the Heat Ray ◆ 1962
8. Danny Dunn, Time Traveller ◆ 1963
9. Danny Dunn and the Automatic House ◆ 1967
10. Danny Dunn and the Voice from Space ◆ 1967
11. Danny Dunn and the Smallifying Machine ◆ 1969
12. Danny Dunn and the Swamp Monster ◆ 1971
13. Danny Dunn, Invisible Boy ◆ 1974
14. Danny Dunn, Scientific Detective ◆ 1975
15. Danny Dunn and the Universal Glue ◆ 1977

DARCY J. DOYLE, DARING DETECTIVE

Mayfair, Linda Lee

ZONDERVAN ◆ GRADES 1–3 ◆ A/R

MYSTERY

Darcy J. Doyle, who also goes by D.J., likes to consider herself a "Daring Detective." Her dog Max is supposed to be her helper, but his efforts are not always fruitful. For example, when Darcy is on the trail of a Halloween prankster and orders Max to chase the costumed culprit, Max runs in the other direction and Darcy must chase the suspect herself. The problems that Darcy tackles are fairly simple—finding missing homework and solving neighborhood problems. Darcy's brother Willie is sometimes involved, as are her friends and classmates. Young readers who want longer chapter books will enjoy these easy mysteries.

1. The Case of the Mixed-Up Monster ◆ 1993
2. The Case of the Choosey Cheater ◆ 1993
3. The Case of the Giggling Ghost ◆ 1993
4. The Case of the Pampered Poodle ◆ 1993
5. The Case of the Creepy Campout ◆ 1994
6. The Case of the Bashful Bully ◆ 1994
7. The Case of the Angry Actress ◆ 1994
8. The Case of the Missing Max ◆ 1994
9. The Case of the Troublesome Treasure ◆ 1996
10. The Case of the Sweet-Toothed Shoplifter ◆ 1996
11. The Case of the Bashed-Up Bicycle ◆ 1996
12. The Case of the Near-Sighted Neighbor ◆ 1996

DARK IS RISING

Cooper, Susan

COLLIER ◆ GRADES 4–8 ◆ A/R

ADVENTURE | FANTASY

This is a classic fantasy series. Two of the five books are Newbery Medal winners. The story starts out with the three Drew children: Simon, Jane, and Barney. While on holiday, they discover an ancient manuscript that will reveal the true story of King Arthur. In the second book, Will Stanton, age 11, discovers that he is the last of the Old Ones who are able to triumph over the evil forces of the Dark. In *Greenwitch,* Jane and her brothers help the Old Ones uncover the grail. As the quest continues, Will and his companions must uncover the items necessary to vanquish the rising forces of the Dark. Fantasy lovers will be absorbed by this series and will also enjoy C. S. Lewis's Chronicles of Narnia and Tolkien's Lord of the Rings trilogy, which plunge readers into mysterious fantasy worlds.

1. Over Sea, Under Stone ◆ 1965
2. The Dark Is Rising ◆ 1973
3. Greenwitch ◆ 1974
4. The Grey King ◆ 1975
5. Silver on the Tree ◆ 1977

DARK REFLECTIONS TRILOGY

Meyer, Kai

SIMON & SCHUSTER ◆ GRADES 5–8 ◆ A/R

FANTASY

Merle, 14, and Junipa, 13, are orphans serving as apprentices to the magic mirror maker. The Egyptian army has besieged the city (an alternate Venice) for years but the Flowing Queen has protected Venice from destruction. Now the spirit of the Queen has been captured in a glass vial. To save the city, Merle drinks the water in the vial and becomes filled with the spirit of the Flowing Queen. Merle, Junipa, and Vermithrax the flying stone lion meet with the lord of Hell while Serafin, Merle's friend, stays to battle the Egyptians. In *The Glass Word,* the characters come together in Egypt to thwart Seth, the highest of the Horus priests, who is seeking revenge on the pharoah. Translated from German, this series will interest readers of Mary Hoffman's Stravaganza.

1. The Water Mirror ◆ 2005
2. The Stone Light ◆ 2006
3. The Glass Word ◆ 2008

THE DARKEST AGE

Lake, A. J.

BLOOMSBURY ◆ **GRADES 5–8** ◆ **A/R**

FANTASY

Edmund and Elspeth, both 11, are the only two survivors of a shipwreck. The son of a king, Edmund has kept his identity secret. Elspeth, the shipmaster's daughter, used her knowledge of the sea to help them survive. As they struggle to reach their home, they find that evil forces have taken over. Edmund and Elspeth realize their destiny as they become involved in the struggle to overcome the darkness. In the third book, they face Loki, the mythical trickster.

1. The Coming of Dragons ◆ 2006
2. The Book of the Sword ◆ 2007
3. The Circle of Stone ◆ 2008

DAUGHTERS OF LIBERTY

Massie, Elizabeth

POCKET BOOKS ◆ **GRADES 3–6** ◆ **A/R**

HISTORICAL

Patsy Black and Barbara Layman, two young girls living in Philadelphia at the time of the Revolution, form a club called Daughters of Liberty. They never dream that they will actually be involved in the fight for freedom. Each book finds the girls in the middle of a different adventure. British spies, runaway slaves, and secret notes make for entertaining reading as the girls become accidentally involved in the Revolution.

1. Barbara's Escape ◆ 1997
2. Patsy's Discovery ◆ 1997
3. Patsy and the Declaration ◆ 1997

DAVID

Shannon, David

SCHOLASTIC ◆ **GRADES K–2** ◆ **A/R**

HUMOR

The antics of a young boy are featured in these humorous books. David can't help creating chaos. The illustrations depict his energy and spirit. *No, David!* was a Caldecott Honor book.

1. No, David! ◆ 1998
2. David Goes to School ◆ 1999
3. David Gets in Trouble ◆ 2002

DAVID AND GOLIATH

Dicks, Terrance

SCHOLASTIC ◆ GRADES 1–3

REAL LIFE

Pet-loving David rescues Goliath from his lonely existence as the only mongrel dog in the pet store when Goliath is just a puppy. Soon Goliath grows big enough to live up to his name. Though David's parents are not initially as enthusiastic about Goliath's presence in the house, they do grow to love him. David, who is an only child and small for his age, enjoys the companionship and confidence that Goliath gives him. This series will appeal to all children who have experienced a special bond with a pet.

1. Goliath and the Dognappers ◆ 1985
2. Goliath in the Snow ◆ 1986
3. Goliath and the Burglar ◆ 1987
4. Goliath and the Buried Treasure ◆ 1987
5. Goliath at the Dog Show ◆ 1987
6. Goliath on Vacation ◆ 1987
7. Goliath's Christmas ◆ 1987
8. Goliath at Sports Day ◆ 1988
9. Goliath's Easter Parade ◆ 1988
10. Goliath at the Seaside ◆ 1989
11. Goliath Goes to Summer School ◆ 1989
12. Goliath and the Cub Scouts ◆ 1990
13. Big Match ◆ 1991
14. Goliath Gets a Job ◆ 1991
15. Goliath's Birthday ◆ 1992
16. Teacher's Pet ◆ 1992
17. David and Goliath on Their Own ◆ 1993
18. Goliath and the School Bully ◆ 1993

DAVY

Weninger, Brigitte

NORTH-SOUTH BOOKS ◆ GRADES K–2 ◆ A/R

ANIMAL FANTASY

Davy the rabbit seems to find trouble wherever he goes, although he always means well. He gives his family's Christmas dinner to hungry animals, loses his favorite stuffed rabbit, and reluctantly helps out by looking after the baby. Davy and his huge lop ears (he has a special red hood to cover them up) are charmingly painted in watercolors. A series of board books introduce Davy to younger children.

1. What Have You Done, Davy? ◆ 1996
2. Where Have You Gone, Davy? ◆ 1996
3. Will You Mind the Baby, Davy? ◆ 1997
4. What's the Matter, Davy? ◆ 1998
5. Merry Christmas, Davy! ◆ 1998
6. Why Are You Fighting, Davy? ◆ 1999
7. Happy Birthday, Davy! ◆ 2000
8. Happy Easter, Davy! ◆ 2001
9. Davy, Help! It's a Ghost ◆ 2002
10. Davy in the Middle ◆ 2004
11. Stay in Bed, Davy! ◆ 2006
12. Davy, Soccer Star! ◆ 2008

DEADTIME STORIES

Cascone, A. G.

TROLL ◆ GRADES 4–7

HORROR

What would you do if you encountered a man-eating spider? Has a ghost ever communicated with you through your cell phone? Have you ever wondered if your toys are planning a coup? These are some of the circumstances that occur in this series of books. Like others in the horror genre, this series features different characters in bizarre situations, often with spooky creatures. Applehead dolls that take the place of parents, magic tricks that can't be undone, and mutant sea creatures should capture the interest of horror fans.

1. Terror in Tiny Town ◆ 1996
2. Invasion of the Appleheads ◆ 1996
3. Along Came a Spider ◆ 1996
4. Ghost Knight ◆ 1996
5. Revenge of the Goblins ◆ 1996
6. Little Magic Shop of Horrors ◆ 1996
7. It Came from the Deep ◆ 1997
8. Grave Secrets ◆ 1997
9. Mirror Mirror ◆ 1997
10. Grandpa's Monster Movies ◆ 1997
11. Nightmare on Planet X ◆ 1997
12. Welcome to the Terror-Go-Round ◆ 1997
13. The Beast of Baskerville ◆ 1997
14. Trapped in Tiny Town ◆ 1997
15. Cyber Scare ◆ 1997
16. Night of the Pet Zombies ◆ 1997
17. Faerie Tale ◆ 1997

DEAF CHILD CROSSING

Matlin, Marlee

SIMON & SCHUSTER ◆ GRADES 4–6 ◆ A/R

REAL LIFE

Cindy, 9, moves into a new neighborhood and meets Megan, also 9, who is deaf. The two girls become friends and Cindy, who is a hearing child, learns about deaf culture and studies sign language. Megan, who wears hearing aids and lip reads, is very self-sufficient and the girls' friendship is tested when Cindy's attempts at helpfulness upset Megan.

1. Deaf Child Crossing ◆ 2002
2. Nobody's Perfect ◆ 2006
3. Leading Ladies ◆ 2007

DEAR AMERICA

Various authors

SCHOLASTIC ◆ GRADES 4–6 ◆ A/R

HISTORICAL | REAL LIFE

Well-known authors—including Kathryn Lasky, Joyce Hansen, Patricia McKissack, and Jim Murphy—create fictional characters to present historical information. Using a diary format, each author describes people, places, and events through the eyes of a young girl. On the Oregon Trail, Hattie Campbell describes the hardships and dangers of American pioneers. Another diary features the reflections of a freed slave girl, Patsy, while another diary gives the insights of a Jewish girl whose family is emigrating from Russia to the United States. A companion series featuring boys, My Name Is America, is also available. Readers who enjoy this series will also enjoy the Once Upon America books.

1. When Will This Cruel War Be Over? The Civil War Diary of Emma Simpson (Denenberg, Barry) ◆ 1996
2. The Winter of Red Snow: The Revolutionary War Diary of Abigail Jane Stewart (Gregory, Kristiana) ◆ 1996
3. Across the Wide and Lonesome Prairie: The Oregon Trail Diary of Hattie Campbell (Gregory, Kristiana) ◆ 1997
4. I Thought My Soul Would Rise and Fly: The Diary of Patsy, a Freed Girl (Hansen, Joyce) ◆ 1997
5. A Journey to the New World: The Diary of Remember Patience Whipple (Lasky, Kathryn) ◆ 1997
6. A Picture of Freedom: The Diary of Clotee, a Slave Girl (McKissack, Patricia C.) ◆ 1997
7. So Far from Home: The Diary of Mary Driscoll, a Mill Girl (Denenberg, Barry) ◆ 1997

8. Dreams in the Golden Country: The Diary of Zipporah Feldman, a Jewish Immigrant Girl (Lasky, Kathryn) ◆ 1998

9. A Line in the Sand: The Alamo Diary of Lucinda Lawrence (Garland, Sherry) ◆ 1998

10. Standing in the Light: The Captive Diary of Catherine Casey Logan (Osborne, Mary Pope) ◆ 1998

11. Voyage on the Great Titanic: The Diary of Margaret Ann Brady (White, Ellen Emerson) ◆ 1998

12. West to a Land of Plenty: The Diary of Teresa Angelino Viscardi (Murphy, Jim) ◆ 1998

13. A Light in the Storm: The Civil War Diary of Amelia Martin, Fenwick Island, Delaware (Hesse, Karen) ◆ 1999

14. Girl Who Chased Away Sorrow: The Diary of Sarah Nita, a Navajo Girl, New Mexico (Turner, Ann Warren) ◆ 1999

15. The Great Railroad Race: The Diary of Libby West, Utah Territory (Gregory, Kristiana) ◆ 1999

16. My Heart Is on the Ground: The Diary of Nannie Little Rose, a Sioux Girl, Carlisle Indian School, PA (Rinaldi, Ann) ◆ 1999

17. A Coal Miner's Bride: The Diary of Anetka Kaminska, Lattimer, Pennsylvania (Bartoletti, Susan Campbell) ◆ 2000

18. One Eye Laughing, the Other Weeping: The Diary of Julie Weiss, Vienna, Austria to New York (Denenberg, Barry) ◆ 2000

19. Color Me Dark: The Diary of Nellie Lee Love, the Great Migration North, Chicago, Illinois (McKissack, Patricia C.) ◆ 2000

20. My Secret War: The World War II Diary of Madeline Beck, Long Island, New York (Osborne, Mary Pope) ◆ 2000

21. Seeds of Hope: The Gold Rush Diary of Susanna Fairchild, California Territory (Gregory, Kristiana) ◆ 2001

22. Valley of the Moon: The Diary of Maria Rosalia de Milagros, Sonoma Valley, Alta California (Garland, Sherry) ◆ 2001

23. My Face to the Wind: The Diary of Sarah Jane Price, a Prairie Teacher, Broken Bow, Nebraska (Murphy, Jim) ◆ 2001

24. Christmas After All: The Great Depression Diary of Minnie Swift, Indianapolis, Indiana (Lasky, Kathryn) ◆ 2001

25. Early Sunday Morning: The Pearl Harbor Diary of Amber Billows, Hawaii (Denenberg, Barry) ◆ 2001

26. A Time for Courage: The Suffragette Diary of Kathleen Bowen, Washington, D.C. (Lasky, Kathryn) ◆ 2002

27. When Christmas Comes Again: The World War I Diary of Simone Spencer, New York City to the Western Front (Levine, Beth Seidel) ◆ 2002

28. Mirror, Mirror on the Wall: The Diary of Bess Brennan, the Perkins School of the Blind (Denenberg, Barry) ◆ 2002

29. Survival in the Storm: The Dust Bowl Diary of Grace Edwards, Dalhart, Texas (Janke, Katelan) ◆ 2002

30. Where Have All the Flowers Gone? The Diary of Molly MacKenzie Flaherty, Boston Massachusetts (White, Ellen Emerson) ◆ 2002

31. Love Thy Neighbor: The Tory Diary of Prudence Emerson, Greenmarsh, Massachusetts (Turner, Ann Warren) ◆ 2003

32. All the Stars in the Sky: The Santa Fe Trail Diary of Florrie Mack Ryder (McDonald, Megan) ◆ 2003
33. Land of the Buffalo Bones: The Diary of Mary Elizabeth Rodgers, an English Girl in Minnesota (Bauer, Marion Dane) ◆ 2003
34. I Walk in Dread: The Diary of Deliverance Trembley, Witness to the Salem Witch Trials (Fraustino, Lisa Rowe) ◆ 2004
35. Hear My Sorrow: The Diary of Angela Denoto, a Shirtwaist Worker, New York City (Hopkinson, Deborah) ◆ 2004
36. Look to the Hills: The Diary of Lozette Moreau, a French Slave Girl, New York Colony (McKissack, Patricia C.) ◆ 2004

DEAR DRAGON

Hillert, Margaret

MODERN CURRICULUM PRESS; STARFALL PUBLICATIONS; NORWOOD HOUSE PRESS ◆ GRADES K–3 ◆ A/R

FANTASY

A little boy and his dragon have various adventures as they go to the circus, celebrate holidays, and take care of each other. At the end of each book is a list of all the words contained in the story. Norwood House Press issued a new series of Beginning-to-Read books in 2008. Beginning readers will have much success with these books.

1. Happy Birthday, Dear Dragon ◆ 1977
2. Happy Easter, Dear Dragon ◆ 1981
3. Help for Dear Dragon ◆ 1981
4. I Love You, Dear Dragon ◆ 1981
5. It's Halloween Time, Dear Dragon ◆ 1981
6. Let's Go, Dear Dragon ◆ 1981
7. Merry Christmas, Dear Dragon ◆ 1981
8. Come to School, Dear Dragon ◆ 1985
9. A Friend for Dear Dragon ◆ 1985
10. Go to Sleep, Dear Dragon ◆ 1985
11. I Need You, Dear Dragon ◆ 1985
12. It's Circus Time, Dear Dragon ◆ 1985
13. Dear Dragon Goes to the Library ◆ 2008
14. Dear Dragon's A is for Apple ◆ 2008
15. Dear Dragon's Day with Father ◆ 2008
16. Happy Hanukkah, Dear Dragon ◆ 2008
17. It's St. Patrick's Day, Dear Dragon ◆ 2008

DEAR DUMB DIARY

Benton, Jim

SCHOLASTIC ◆ GRADES 5–8 ◆ A/R

REAL LIFE | HUMOR

In a diary format, Jamie Kelly of Mackeral Middle School describes her everyday experiences. Her comments about her life are supplemented by numerous cartoon-style illustrations. In the third book (*Am I the Princess or the Frog?*), Jamie describes the awful meat loaf served on Meat Loaf Day. Her comments are overheard by the lunch monitor, Miss Bruntford, who decides to teach Jamie a lesson. Jamie's best friend is Isabella and her nemesis is Angeline (aka Princess Turd of Turdsylvania). Fans of Captain Underpants will enjoy this series.

1. Let's Pretend This Never Happened ◆ 2004
2. My Pants Are Haunted ◆ 2004
3. Am I the Princess or the Frog? ◆ 2005
4. Never Do Anything, Ever ◆ 2005
5. Can Adults Become Human? ◆ 2006
6. The Problem with Here Is That It's Where I'm From ◆ 2007
7. Never Underestimate Your Dumbness ◆ 2008

DEAR MR. PRESIDENT

Various authors

WINSLOW PRESS ◆ GRADES 5–7 ◆ A/R

HISTORICAL

These books use historical documents—maps, timelines, archival sources—to illuminate a fictional correspondence between a young person and a famous historical figure. Through the letters, the reader learns about the events of the era: FDR and the Great Depression, Lincoln and slavery/the Civil War, and so forth. Readers who enjoy historical fiction books with a diary format, like the Dear America books, will connect with this series.

1. Thomas Jefferson: Letters from a Philadelphia Bookworm (Armstrong, Jennifer) ◆ 2000
2. Theodore Roosevelt: Letters from a Young Coal Miner (Armstrong, Jennifer) ◆ 2001
3. John Quincy Adams: Letters from a Southern Planter's Son (Kroll, Steven) ◆ 2001
4. Franklin Delano Roosevelt: Letters from a Mill Town Girl (Winthrop, Elizabeth) ◆ 2001
5. Abraham Lincoln: Letters from a Slave Girl (Pinkney, Andrea Davis) ◆ 2001
6. Dwight D. Eisenhower: Letters from a New Jersey Schoolgirl (Karr, Kathleen) ◆ 2003

DEEP SPACE NINE *see* Star Trek: Deep Space Nine

DELTORA: DELTORA QUEST

Rodda, Emily

SCHOLASTIC ◆ GRADES 4–7 ◆ A/R

FANTASY

Deltora is being threatened by the evil Shadow Lord. The magic belt of Deltora could overcome the evil but only if all seven stones are in the belt. Lief, 16, Barda, and Jasmine seek the stones.

1. The Forests of Silence ◆ 2000
2. The Lake of Tears ◆ 2000
3. City of the Rats ◆ 2000
4. The Shifting Sands ◆ 2001
5. Dread Mountain ◆ 2001
6. The Maze of the Beast ◆ 2001
7. The Valley of the Lost ◆ 2001
8. Return to Del ◆ 2001

DELTORA: DELTORA SHADOWLANDS

Rodda, Emily

SCHOLASTIC ◆ GRADES 4–7 ◆ A/R

FANTASY

Even though the Shadow Lord has been defeated, his evil still reigns over Deltora captives in the Shadowlands. In this new quest, Lief, Barda, and Jasmine seek the Pirran Pipe. This trilogy follows the adventures in the Deltora Quest series.

1. Cavern of the Fear ◆ 2002
2. The Isle of Illusion ◆ 2002
3. The Shadowlands ◆ 2002

DELTORA: DRAGONS OF DELTORA

Rodda, Emily

SCHOLASTIC ◆ GRADES 4–7 ◆ A/R

FANTASY

Another series set in Deltora and again featuring Lief, Jasmine, and Barda. Now they must get help from seven dragons to save Deltora from the seeds of death that are controlled by the Four Sisters. If they fail, the Shadow Lord will return. Companion books to the Deltora series, also illustrated by Marc McBride, are *The Deltora Book of Monsters* (2002),

How to Draw Deltora Monsters (2005), *Tales of Deltora* (2006)—a beautifully presented collection of Deltora stories about castles and dragons, magic and monsters.

1. Dragon's Nest ◆ 2004
2. Shadowgate ◆ 2004
3. Isle of the Dead ◆ 2004
4. Sister of the South ◆ 2005

DEPTFORD HISTORIES

Jarvis, Robin

SEASTAR/CHRONICLE ◆ GRADES 5–8 ◆ A/R

ANIMAL FANTASY

This series provides background information about the events in the Deptford Mice trilogy. How did Jupiter the cat gain his power over the sewer rats? What caused the wars between the bats and the squirrels?

1. The Alchemist's Cat ◆ 2003
2. The Oaken Throne ◆ 2005
3. Thomas ◆ 2006

DEPTFORD MICE

Jarvis, Robin

SEASTAR ◆ GRADES 5–8 ◆ A/R

ANIMAL FANTASY

Fans of the Redwall books by Brian Jacques will connect with this British import about the mice of the London borough of Deptford. They are a quiet group of mice who enjoy a simple life. But when Audrey Brown's father goes missing, the young mouse searches for him in the dangerous sewers. She is followed by her brother and some other brave young mice. In the sewers, the evil cat Jupiter controls the rats with a mysterious power. In the second book, the mice move to the country but the evil follows them. There is a series of prequels called the Deptford Histories.

1. The Dark Portal ◆ 2000
2. The Crystal Prison ◆ 2001
3. The Final Reckoning ◆ 2002

DEPTFORD MICE HISTORIES *see* Deptford Histories

DESDEMONA

Keller, Beverly

SIMON & SCHUSTER ◆ GRADES 4–6

FAMILY LIFE | HUMOR

Desdemona Blank must cope with great changes in her life when her mother leaves the family to "find herself" (*No Beasts! No Children!*). After ten months without a mother, the Blank family begins to adjust by moving to the only place that will accept three children and three dogs. They get a housekeeper to help with the 5-year-old twins, Aida and Anthony, and life begins to get better. Desdemona worries about animal rights issues, new friends, and Dad beginning to date. The plot development and humor are similar to Lowry's Anastasia series, providing light reading on issues that are still relevant today.

1. No Beasts! No Children! ◆ 1983
2. Desdemona: Twelve Going on Desperate ◆ 1986
3. Fowl Play, Desdemona ◆ 1989
4. Desdemona Moves On ◆ 1992

DETECTIVE MOLE

Quackenbush, Robert

LOTHROP, LEE & SHEPARD ◆ GRADES 1–3

ANIMAL FANTASY | MYSTERY

Armed with a diploma from detective school, a how-to manual, a magnifying glass, and his wits, Detective Maynard Mole begins his career solving puzzling crimes for the animals in his neighborhood. The reading level becomes more difficult as the series progresses. Colorful illustrations add to the interest.

1. Detective Mole ◆ 1976
2. Detective Mole and the Secret Clues ◆ 1977
3. Detective Mole and the Tip-Top Mystery ◆ 1978
4. Detective Mole and the Seashore Mystery ◆ 1979
5. Detective Mole and the Circus Mystery ◆ 1980
6. Detective Mole and the Halloween Mystery ◆ 1981
7. Detective Mole and the Haunted Castle Mystery ◆ 1985

DEXTER'S LABORATORY CHAPTER BOOKS

Various authors

SCHOLASTIC ◆ GRADES 2–5

FANTASY

Dexter invents all kinds of things in his laboratory, including a pen that hypnotizes his family and a potion that splits his personality in two. His rival, Mandark, uses both his science and his sneaky skills to foil Dexter. Dee Dee, Dexter's silly sister, is often the only person who can save him. There are related materials including a joke book, a calendar, coloring books, and books for very young children.

1. Dexter's Ink (Dewin, Howard) ◆ 2002
2. The Dex-Terminator (Weiss, Bobbi J. G.) ◆ 2002
3. Dr. Dee Dee and Dexter Hyde (Pollack, Pam) ◆ 2002
4. I Dream of Dexter (Pollack, Pam) ◆ 2003
5. The Incredible Shrinking Dexter (Pollack, Pam) ◆ 2003
6. Dexter's Big Switch (Pollack, Pam) ◆ 2003

THE DIAMOND BROTHERS

Horowitz, Anthony

PHILOMEL ◆ GRADES 5–8 ◆ A/R

HUMOR | MYSTERY

Tim and Nick are the Diamond Brothers. Tim is the older brother and he is not a very good detective. Nick, 13, manages to keep them both one step ahead of trouble and to solve the mystery too. In *The Falcon's Malteser,* Tim has been framed and is in jail for murder. Nick tries to deal with a mysterious package and find the real killer. These books have humorous moments that reflect on the genre of detective fiction.

1. The Falcon's Malteser ◆ 2004
2. Public Enemy, Number Two ◆ 2004
3. Three of Diamonds: Three Diamond Brothers Mysteries ◆ 2005
4. South by Southeast ◆ 2005
5. The Greek Who Stole Christmas ◆ 2008

DIARY OF A WIMPY KID

Kinney, Jeff

AMULET ◆ GRADES 5–8

HUMOR | REAL LIFE

Greg Heffley is just starting middle school. As a sixth-grader, he feels small and insignificant among the older students. He and his friend Rowley just try to survive in their new situation. Greg's story is told in diary entries that are enhanced by numerous illustrations. While this is not a true graphic novel, the illustrated format will attract many graphic novel readers. *The Diary of a Wimpy Kid Do-It-Yourself Book* is a journal with writing prompts and illustrations. This series began on the Web at www.funbrain.com.

1. Diary of a Wimpy Kid: Greg Heffley's Journal ◆ 2007
2. Diary of a Wimpy Kid: Rodrick Rules ◆ 2008
3. Diary of a Wimpy Kid: The Last Straw ◆ 2009

DIGBY AND KATE

Baker, Barbara

DUTTON ◆ GRADES 1–2 ◆ A/R

ANIMAL FANTASY

Digby the dog and Kate the cat are friends. In these brief chapter books for beginning readers, they share simple activities. When Digby wants to paint his walls, Kate asks to help, only to cover them with drawings of animals. Digby finds a way to finish his painting without hurting Kate's feelings. In another story, the two friends rake leaves together but end up jumping into them. Digby and Kate enjoy many familiar activities, such as playing checkers and walking in the rain. These are pleasant, easy-to-read books with simple chapters that are just right for beginning readers.

1. Digby and Kate ◆ 1988
2. Digby and Kate Again ◆ 1989
3. Digby and Kate and the Beautiful Day ◆ 1998
4. Digby and Kate, 1, 2, 3 ◆ 2004

DIGIMON DIGITAL MONSTERS

Various authors

HARPERCOLLINS ◆ GRADES 2–5

FANTASY

The adventures begin when seven children arrive at File Island, a digital world inhabited by digital monsters known as Digimons. Some of the Digimons befriend and protect the children. Others, like the evil Devimon, seek to destroy them. As the series evolves, the youngsters discover they are the DigiDestined, who have been sent to save the DigiWorld. There are many related items including calendars and a book on drawing Digimons.

1. Adventures on File Island (Whitman, John) ◆ 2000
2. The Invasion of the Black Gears (Nerz, Ryan) ◆ 2000
3. Andromon's Attack (Bright, J. E.) ◆ 2000
4. Leomon's Challenge (Whitman, John) ◆ 2000
5. Legend of the DigiDestined (Whitman, John) ◆ 2001
6. The Quest for Crests (Bright, J. E.) ◆ 2001
7. Mimi's Crest of Sincerity (Pollack, Pam) ◆ 2001
8. Piximon's Training Ground ◆ 2001

DIGIMON DIGITAL MONSTERS—SECOND SEASON

The second season of the Digimon cartoons features a new generation of DigiDestined with new Digimon friends and new adventures.

1. DigiArmor Energize! (Papademetriou, Lisa) ◆ 2000
2. The New DigiDestined (Sullivan, Michael) ◆ 2001
3. The Secret of the Digimon Emperor ◆ 2001

DIMWOOD FOREST

Avi

ORCHARD ◆ GRADES 4–6 ◆ A/R

ANIMAL FANTASY

Poppy, a deer mouse who initially surprises herself with her courage, tackles threats to family and friends in her woodland environment. Her friend Ragweed is killed by an owl in the first book. *Ragweed: A Tale from Dimwood Forest* is a prequel telling the story of Ragweed's adventures in the city, where he meets a band of fearless musical mice.

1. Poppy ◆ 1995
2. Poppy and Rye ◆ 1998
3. Ragweed ◆ 1999
4. Ereth's Birthday ◆ 2000
5. Poppy's Return ◆ 2005

DINAH

Mills, Claudia

MACMILLAN ◆ GRADES 3–6 ◆ A/R

HUMOR

So far in this series, Dinah has gone from being an irrepressible 10-year-old to her eighth-grade year. Nothing but fun, these stories of school (and especially the trials and tribulations of middle school) will delight readers. Class elections, the school play, confusing substitute teachers, eating 14 cups of ice cream at lunch—all these make for entertaining reading.

1. Dynamite Dinah ◆ 1990
2. Dinah for President ◆ 1992
3. Dinah in Love ◆ 1993
4. Dinah Forever ◆ 1995

DINOSAURS

Donnelly, Liza
SCHOLASTIC ◆ GRADES K–2
ANIMAL FANTASY

A small boy has adventures with dinosaur friends in a very simple picture book series. On Halloween, the boy goes out dressed as a dinosaur and is joined by another trick-or-treater in a strikingly realistic dino costume. When some bullies attack and demand their candy, the little dinosaur's friends rush to the rescue. At Christmas, he and his dog go sledding, right over a friendly Plateosaurus. Santa's helpers are trying to make dinosaurs, he explains, and they're making them all wrong. The boy straightens everything out, but then Santa's reindeer get the flu. Dinosaurs to the rescue again. Each book has dinosaur information at the end.

1. Dinosaur Day ◆ 1987
2. Dinosaurs' Halloween ◆ 1987
3. Dinosaur Beach ◆ 1989
4. Dinosaur Garden ◆ 1990
5. Dinosaurs' Christmas ◆ 1991
6. Dinosaur Valentine ◆ 1994
7. Dinosaurs' Thanksgiving ◆ 1995

DINOSAURS *see* How Do Dinosaurs . . .

DISH

Muldrow, Diane
GROSSET & DUNLAP ◆ GRADES 4–7 ◆ A/R
REAL LIFE

Amanda and Molly are 11-year-old twins who show an interest in cooking and are given cooking lessons. Later, they form a cooking club with friends. The club becomes a business, DISH, and the children have to deal with problems—too many customers, trying to balance school and work, and so forth. The girls represent diverse backgrounds; for example, Peichi helps with her family's celebration of Chinese New Year.

1. Stirring It Up ◆ 2002
2. Turning Up the Heat ◆ 2002
3. Boiling Point ◆ 2002
4. Into the Mix ◆ 2002
5. Truth Without the Trimmings ◆ 2002
6. On the Back Burner ◆ 2003
7. A Recipe for Trouble ◆ 2003
8. Lights, Camera, Cook ◆ 2003

9. Sweet-and-Sour Summer ◆ 2003
10. A Measure of Thanks ◆ 2003
11. Winner Takes the Cake ◆ 2003
12. Deep Freeze ◆ 2004
13. Working Lunch ◆ 2004

DISNEY FAIRIES

Levine, Gail Carson

DISNEY PRESS ◆ GRADES 1–3 ◆ A/R

FANTASY

While the Disney Fairies Chapter Books focus on the activities of individual fairies, Levine has written about all of the fairies and their home in Never Land. In the first book, Prilla, a new fairy in Never Land, does not know her talent. She is one of the fairies chosen to go on a quest to aid Mother Dove. In the second book, the fairies must rescue Fairy Haven from a mermaid's threat. David Christiana's lush illustrations add to the fantasy of the fairy world.

1. Fairy Dust and the Quest for the Egg ◆ 2005
2. Fairy Haven and the Quest for the Wand ◆ 2007

DISNEY FAIRIES (CHAPTER BOOKS)

Various authors

RANDOM HOUSE ◆ GRADES 1–4 ◆ A/R

FANTASY

The fairies in these books have special talents and personalities. Tinker Bell fixes things. In *The Trouble With Tink,* when she loses her hammer, she loses her talent. Rani is a water-talent fairy who has made sacrifices for others. Vidia is often selfish, while Lily is a garden-talent fairy. There are related book/merchandising items including books with a charm or necklace, sticker books, a calendar, and pop-up/fold-out books.

1. The Trouble With Tink (Thorpe, Kiki) ◆ 2006
2. Vidia and the Fairy Crown (Driscoll, Laura) ◆ 2006
3. Lily's Pesky Plant (Larsen, Kirsten) ◆ 2006
4. Beck and the Great Berry Battle (Driscoll, Laura) ◆ 2006
5. Rani in the Mermaid Lagoon (Papademetriou, Lisa) ◆ 2006
6. Fira and the Full Moon (Herman, Gail) ◆ 2006
7. A Masterpiece for Bess (Bergen, Lara) ◆ 2006
8. Prilla and the Butterfly Lie (Richards, Kitty) ◆ 2007
9. Tink, North of Neverland (Thorpe, Kiki) ◆ 2007
10. Beck Beyond the Sea (Morris, Kimberly) ◆ 2007

11. Dulcie's Taste of Magic (Herman, Gail) ◆ 2008
12. Silvermist and the Ladybug Curse (Herman, Gail) ◆ 2008

DISNEY GIRLS

Charbonnet, Gabrielle

DISNEY PRESS ◆ **GRADES 3–5**

REAL LIFE

Each girl in this series has a special affinity for a favorite Disney character. Isabelle relates to Belle in *Beauty in the Beast*; Ella to Cinderella; Ariel to The Little Mermaid; Jasmine to the princess in *Aladdin*; Yukiko to Snow White; and Paula to Pocahontas. The stories sometimes mirror the experiences of their favorite characters. Isabelle's neighbor, Kenny, acts like a beast and Ella makes gingerbread castles and needs the help of her stepfamily. The Disney Girls even dress up as their favorite characters and participate in the Magic Kingdom Princess Parade. Fans of the Disney films, videos, and TV programs will also enjoy these stories of friendship.

1. One of Us ◆ 1998
2. Attack of the Beast ◆ 1998
3. And Sleepy Makes Seven ◆ 1998
4. A Fish Out of Water ◆ 1998
5. Cinderella's Castle ◆ 1998
6. One Pet Too Many ◆ 1999
7. Adventure at Walt Disney World ◆ 1999
8. Beauty's Revenge ◆ 1999
9. Good-bye, Jasmine? ◆ 1999
10. Princess of Power ◆ 1999
11. The Gum Race ◆ 1999
12. The Divine Miss Ariel ◆ 1999

DISNEY HIGH SCHOOL MUSICAL STORIES FROM EAST HIGH *see* High School Musical Stories from East High

DISNEY PRINCESS

Marsoli, Lisa Ann

RANDOM HOUSE/DISNEY ◆ **GRADES 1–3**

FANTASY

Favorite princesses from Disney films and videos are featured in these easy books. In *My Best Friend Is Belle* a girl wishes she were as talented as Belle only to realize that she has her own special talents. In another book, Jasmine helps Jenna and her brother escape life on the streets of Agrabah. These books focus on solving problems and valuing your own abilities.

1. My Best Friend Is Ariel ◆ 2006
2. My Best Friend Is Belle ◆ 2006
3. My Best Friend Is Cinderella ◆ 2006
4. My Best Friend Is Jasmine ◆ 2006

DISNEY PRINCESS SECRETS

Various authors

RANDOM HOUSE/DISNEY ◆ GRADES 1–3

FANTASY

In *Ariel's Secret,* Ariel's father discovers her secret grotto and then Ariel tells another secret. *Belle's Secret* is that she has a hidden journal. The glittering covers and familiar Disney Princesses will draw young readers to these books.

1. Ariel's Secret (Lagonegro, Melissa) ◆ 2005
2. Belle's Secret (Posner-Sanchez, Andrea) ◆ 2005
3. Cinderella's Secret (Barad, Alexis) ◆ 2005
4. Snow White's Secret (Lagonegro, Melissa) ◆ 2005

DISNEY PRINCESSES: MY SIDE OF THE STORY

Various authors

DISNEY PRESS ◆ GRADES 1–3

FANTASY

Favorite princesses from Disney films are paired with the character who antagonized them. Each tells her side of the story, for example, Lady Tremaine explains that she did not ruin Cinderella's first ballgown, it already looked ragged since it had been made by birds. Princess fans will love this series.

1. Cinderella/Lady Tremaine (Skinner, Daphne) ◆ 2004
2. Snow White/The Queen (Skinner, Daphne) ◆ 2004
3. The Little Mermaid/Ursula (Skinner, Daphne) ◆ 2004
4. Sleeping Beauty/Maleficent (Thorpe, Kiki) ◆ 2004

DISNEY VILLAINS: MY SIDE OF THE STORY

Various authors

DISNEY PRESS ◆ GRADES 1–3

FANTASY

Disney fans will enjoy reading two sides of the same events told by favorite characters and their adversaries. Peter Pan and Captain Hook are matched along with 101 Dalmatians and Cruella de Vil. This is a companion series to the Disney Princesses: My Side of the Story.

1. Peter Pan/Captain Hook (Thorpe, Kiki) ◆ 2005
2. 101 Dalmatians/Cruella de Vil (Skinner, Daphne) ◆ 2005

THE DIVIDE TRILOGY

Kay, Elizabeth

CHICKEN HOUSE ◆ GRADES 5–9 ◆ A/R

FANTASY

While on vacation on the Continental Divide in Costa Rica, Felix, 13, is transported to a magical world whose creatures consider humans to be mythical. Felix convinces Betony, an elf, that he is really a human and the two begin a quest for a magical cure for Felix's heart defect. Their search is disrupted by Snakeweed, an evil pixie. At the close of the first book, Felix is cured and returns home, but Snakeweed finds his way to our world too.

1. The Divide ◆ 2003
2. Back to the Divide ◆ 2004
3. Jinx on the Divide ◆ 2005

DIXON TWINS

Markham, Marion M.

HOUGHTON MIFFLIN ◆ GRADES 1–3 ◆ A/R

MYSTERY

Mickey is interested in being a detective. Kate is interested in science. Together, the twins solve mysteries in their neighborhood. Their cases often occur at holidays or special occasions. For April Fool's Day, the twins look for a practical joker. Easy-to-read, this series will be enjoyed by children who like Nate the Great books.

1. The Halloween Candy Mystery ◆ 1982
2. The Christmas Present Mystery ◆ 1984

3. The Thanksgiving Day Parade Mystery ◆ 1986
4. The Birthday Party Mystery ◆ 1989
5. The April Fool's Day Mystery ◆ 1991
6. The Valentine's Day Mystery ◆ 1992
7. The St. Patrick's Day Shamrock Mystery ◆ 1995

D.J. DILLON ADVENTURES

Roddy, Lee

VICTOR BOOKS ◆ GRADES 4–6

ADVENTURE | VALUES

D.J. Dillon, 13, balances his Christian values with an adventurous life in the Sierra Nevada mountains. He searches for an arsonist, investigates the dumping of hazardous waste materials, goes on a bear hunt, and helps cope with a mudslide. One crisis of faith occurs when D.J. wants to seek revenge against the dog that attacked D.J.'s dog. D.J. is a loyal friend who overcomes efforts to undermine his devotion to God. The second book has also been released as *The Bear Cub Disaster* and the ninth book as *The Secret of Mud River*.

1. The Hair-Pulling Bear Dog ◆ 1985
2. The City Bear's Adventure ◆ 1985
3. Dooger, the Grasshopper Hound ◆ 1985
4. The Ghost Dog of Stoney Ridge ◆ 1985
5. Mad Dog of Lobo Mountain ◆ 1986
6. The Legend of the White Raccoon ◆ 1986
7. The Mystery of the Black Hole Mine ◆ 1987
8. Ghost of the Moaning Mansion ◆ 1987
9. The Hermit of Mad River ◆ 1988
10. Escape Down the Raging Rapids ◆ 1989

DOCTOR DOLITTLE

Lofting, Hugh

DELACORTE ◆ GRADES 4–6 ◆ A/R

ANIMAL FANTASY

Doctor Dolittle is an extraordinarily gifted man who can communicate with any animal. As one would imagine, this talent leads to an eccentric reputation and some amazing adventures. The doctor takes expert care of sick and wounded animals and, along with his animals, travels to exotic places, including the moon. Companion volumes include *Doctor Dolittle, a Treasury* (1967) and *Gub-Gub's Book, an Encyclopaedia of Food* (1932). This classic series will delight avid readers who are animal lovers. In one reissue of *The Story of Doctor Dolittle* (Morrow, 1997), Patricia C. McKissack and Fredrick L. McKissack discuss the controversy surrounding the stereotypical elements in the original book and the rationale for the revisions they made.

1. The Story of Doctor Dolittle (Doctor Dolittle) ◆ 1920
2. The Voyages of Doctor Dolittle (Doctor Dolittle and the Pirates) ◆ 1922
3. Doctor Dolittle's Post Office ◆ 1923
4. Doctor Dolittle's Circus ◆ 1924
5. Doctor Dolittle's Zoo ◆ 1925
6. Doctor Dolittle's Caravan ◆ 1926
7. Doctor Dolittle's Garden ◆ 1927
8. Doctor Dolittle in the Moon ◆ 1928
9. Doctor Dolittle's Return ◆ 1933
10. Doctor Dolittle and the Secret Lake ◆ 1948
11. Doctor Dolittle and the Green Canary ◆ 1950
12. Doctor Dolittle's Puddleby Adventures ◆ 1952

DOG WATCH

Casanova, Mary
ALADDIN ◆ GRADES 3–5 ◆ A/R

ADVENTURE | REAL LIFE

In the first book, only the dogs seem to notice that something is not right in their small Minnesota town. Kito, Chester, and the other dogs band together as "Dog Watch" and discover the source of the town's problems. In *The Turtle-Hatching Mystery,* three of the dogs are on vacation in Mexico where they use their skills to save the giant sea turtles.

1. Trouble in Pembrook ◆ 2006
2. Dog-Napped! ◆ 2006
3. Danger at Snow Hill ◆ 2006
4. To Catch a Burglar ◆ 2007
5. Extreme Stunt Dogs ◆ 2007
6. The Turtle-Hatching Mystery ◆ 2008

DOLL HOSPITAL

Holub, Joan
SCHOLASTIC ◆ GRADES 2–4 ◆ A/R

HISTORICAL

Two girls, Rose and Lila, visit their grandmother and learn about history as she describes the experiences of the dolls in her doll hospital. Tatiana traveled to Ellis Island from Russia. Glory followed the Underground Railroad. This series will appeal to girls who love dolls and who like imaginative re-creations of history.

1. Tatiana Comes to America: An Ellis Island Story ◆ 2002
2. Goldie's Fortune: A Story of the Great Depression ◆ 2002
3. Glory's Freedom: A Story of the Underground Railroad ◆ 2002
4. Saving Marissa: The Story of a Shaker Village ◆ 2003
5. Danielle's Dollhouse Wish ◆ 2003
6. Charlotte's Choice ◆ 2003

THE DOLL PEOPLE

Martin, Ann M.

HYPERION ◆ GRADES 3–6 ◆ A/R

FANTASY

These popular books describe the adventures of the Doll family of antique porcelain dolls and the upstart, plastic dolls in the Funcraft family. After some misunderstandings, Annabelle Doll and Tiffany Funcraft become friends and, in *The Meanest Doll in the World,* they confront the selfish and disagreeable Princess Mimi. Brian Selznick's illustrations imbue each doll with personality.

1. The Doll People ◆ 2000
2. The Meanest Doll in the World ◆ 2003
3. The Runaway Dolls ◆ 2008

DOLPHIN DIARIES

Baglio, Ben M.

SCHOLASTIC ◆ GRADES 3–6 ◆ A/R

REAL LIFE

Jody McGrath is living her dream. She and her family are researching dolphins as they sail around the world on the *Dolphin Dreamer.* Exotic places including the Caribbean, the Canary Islands, and Australia are the settings for Jody's encounters with dolphins. There is an ecological message in the books—Jody helps a dolphin that is caught in a net, rescues dolphins that are being mistreated in a show for tourists, and stops some poachers. Animal lovers will love these books.

1. Into the Blue ◆ 2000
2. Touching the Waves ◆ 2000
3. Riding the Storm ◆ 2000
4. Under the Stars ◆ 2000
5. Chasing the Dream ◆ 2001
6. Racing the Wind ◆ 2002
7. Following the Rainbow ◆ 2003
8. Dancing the Seas ◆ 2003

9. Leaving the Shallows ◆ 2004
10. Beyond the Sunrise ◆ 2004

DON'T TOUCH THAT REMOTE!

Abbott, Tony

MINSTREL ◆ GRADES 5–7 ◆ A/R

REAL LIFE

Slapstick situations are commonplace when the middle school becomes the site for a sitcom. Spencer Babbitt and his friends must come up with enough action to keep the cameras rolling. They succeed with immature, even gross, antics that should appeal to tween readers.

1. Sitcom School ◆ 1999
2. The Fake Teacher ◆ 1999
3. Stinky Business ◆ 1999
4. Freak Week ◆ 1999

DORK IN DISGUISE

Gorman, Carol

HARPERCOLLINS ◆ GRADES 4–6 ◆ A/R

REAL LIFE

As he is in a new school, Jerry (aka Dork), a sixth-grader, figures he can remake his image. He discovers that the cool crowd is not as interesting as the "dorky" kids. As the series progresses, Jerry is bullied, runs for class president (and wins), and helps with an Elizabethan Festival.

1. Dork in Disguise ◆ 1999
2. Dork on the Run ◆ 2002
3. A Midsummer Night's Dork ◆ 2004

DORRIE

Coombs, Patricia

HOUGHTON MIFFLIN ◆ GRADES K–3 ◆ A/R

FANTASY

Young readers can follow the adventures of a witch in training in this amusing series. Dorrie, a young witch, is earnest in her desire to learn, but sometimes she gets carried away. In a typical plot, Dorrie tries to use her powers to stop the rain, but bungles the spell and succeeds in creating a more severe storm. Dorrie's mother is understanding but firm in her reaction. Younger children fascinated by magic will enjoy this series.

1. Dorrie's Magic ◆ 1962
2. Dorrie and the Blue Witch ◆ 1964
3. Dorrie's Play ◆ 1965
4. Dorrie and the Weather Box ◆ 1966
5. Dorrie and the Witch Doctor ◆ 1967
6. Dorrie and the Wizard's Spell ◆ 1968
7. Dorrie and the Haunted House ◆ 1970
8. Dorrie and the Birthday Eggs ◆ 1971
9. Dorrie and the Goblin ◆ 1972
10. Dorrie and the Fortune Teller ◆ 1973
11. Dorrie and the Amazing Magic Elixir ◆ 1974
12. Dorrie and the Witch's Imp ◆ 1975
13. Dorrie and the Hallowe'en Plot ◆ 1976
14. Dorrie and the Dreamyard Monsters ◆ 1977
15. Dorrie and the Screebit Ghost ◆ 1979
16. Dorrie and the Witchville Fair ◆ 1980
17. Dorrie and the Witch's Camp ◆ 1983
18. Dorrie and the Museum Case ◆ 1986
19. Dorrie and the Pin Witch ◆ 1989
20. Dorrie and the Haunted Schoolhouse ◆ 1992

DOT AND JABBER

Walsh, Ellen Stoll

HARCOURT ◆ GRADES K–2 ◆ A/R

REAL LIFE

The mystery: How did an oak tree come to be growing in this particular spot? Two mice, Dot and Jabber, try to figure it out. A squirrel burying an acorn gives them the information that they need. In another book, the "missing" bugs in the meadow are really using camouflage.

1. Dot and Jabber and the Great Acorn Mystery ◆ 2001
2. Dot and Jabber and the Mystery of the Missing Steam ◆ 2002
3. Dot and Jabber and the Big Bug Mystery ◆ 2003

THE DOUBLE DUTCH CLUB

Singletary, Mabel Elizabeth

LIFT EVERY VOICE ◆ GRADES 5–7

REAL LIFE | VALUES

In *Just Jump!,* Nancy Adjei watches the group of sixth-grade girls from Mrs. Richards's class jump rope on the playground. She wants to join them but she is the "new girl" whose family has just moved to the United States from Sierra Leone. When Rachel Carter asks Nancy to turn the ropes, Nancy is excited and scared, and her fear gets the best of her. She starts to turn the ropes but drops them and runs back into the school. As the book progresses, readers meet other members of this multicultural group including Tanya Gordon, who must learn to control her temper; Ming Li, whose family emigrated from China; and Carla Rodriquez. The books are filled with the importance of faith in the power of God.

1. Just Jump! ◆ 2007
2. Something to Jump About ◆ 2008
3. A Promise and a Rainbow ◆ 2008

DOUG CHRONICLES

Various authors

DISNEY PRESS ◆ GRADES 2–4 ◆ A/R

HUMOR

Kids love their Saturday morning cartoons, and Doug and his friends attract many viewers. This series capitalizes on the interest in the television programs and related materials including home videos and Disney.com. The books feature everyday experiences of the familiar characters—Doug serving on the safety patrol and giving Patti a detention and Roger's investments falling after he follows Doug's advice. The humor is balanced by messages about friendship and fairness. There is also a picture book series featuring Doug and his pals. It includes *Doug's Big Shoe Disaster, Doug's Secret Christmas, Doug Counts Down,* and *Doug's Twelve Days of Christmas.*

1. Lost in Space (Grundmann, Tim) ◆ 1998
2. Porkchop to the Rescue (Rubin, Jim) ◆ 1998
3. A Picture for Patti (Garvey, Linda K.) ◆ 1998
4. A Day with Dirtbike (Goldman, Lisa) ◆ 1998
5. Power Trip (Nodelman, Jeffrey) ◆ 1998
6. The Funnie Haunted House (Grundmann, Tim) ◆ 1998
7. Poor Roger (Gross, Bill) ◆ 1998
8. Winter Games (Grundmann, Tim) ◆ 1998
9. Doug Rules (Krulik, Nancy E.) ◆ 1999
10. Funnie Family Vacation (Ryan, Pam Munoz) ◆ 1999
11. Itchy Situation (Nodelman, Jeffrey) ◆ 1999
12. Doug and the End of the World (Garvey, Dennis) ◆ 1999
13. Doug Cheats (Garvey, Linda K.) ◆ 1999
14. Skeeter Loves Patti? (Campbell, Danny) ◆ 1999

DOUG (DISNEY CHAPTER BOOKS)

Various authors

DISNEY PRESS ◆ GRADES 2–4 ◆ A/R

HUMOR

The popular character from Disney cartoons is featured in these easy chapter books. Reluctant readers may be attracted to the familiar character.

1. Doug's Big Comeback (Krulik, Nancy E.) ◆ 1997
2. Doug's Vampire Caper (Krulik, Nancy E.) ◆ 1997
3. Doug's Hoop Nightmare (Kassirer, Sue) ◆ 1997

DOYLE AND FOSSEY, SCIENCE DETECTIVES *see* Science Detectives

DR. MERLIN

Corbett, Scott

LITTLE, BROWN ◆ GRADES 1–3
FANTASY | HUMOR

On a very foggy day, while walking his dog Bert, Nick sees a new store—Dr. Merlin's Magic Shop. Although it is closed, Bert finds a way in and Nick follows. There he meets Dr. Merlin, who wreaks havoc with his magic. Using his wits, Nick is able to rescue Bert and they escape. Outside, the fog has cleared and Dr. Merlin's shop has disappeared. On other foggy days, Nick and Bert find Dr. Merlin in a bakery and they travel to Dinosaur Land. The books in this series combine zany magic and humorous situations with a text that is accessible to younger readers.

1. Dr. Merlin's Magic Shop ◆ 1973
2. The Great Custard Pie Panic ◆ 1974
3. The Foolish Dinosaur Fiasco ◆ 1978

DRAGON

Gannett, Ruth Stiles

KNOPF ◆ GRADES 1–3 ◆ A/R
ADVENTURE | FANTASY

This series is recommended for younger readers who enjoy adventure stories. It concerns the exploits of a curious, fearless young boy and a baby dragon. The dragon has a human personality, and he and the boy, Elmer, become good friends. They travel to far-off lands and arrive home with some very special souvenirs. The series is light and humorous, and the illustrations are lively and fun. There is even a map at the back of each book so that readers can see where the adventures take place.

1. My Father's Dragon ◆ 1948
2. Elmer and the Dragon ◆ 1950
3. The Dragons of Blueland ◆ 1951

DRAGON

Pilkey, Dav

ORCHARD ◆ GRADES 1–2 ◆ A/R

FANTASY | HUMOR

Dragon's silliness and his blue appearance will appeal to beginning readers, who will enjoy the creative solutions to problem situations such as finding a friend. Dragon's selection of an apple to be his friend will seem absurd to kids. In the holiday titles, Dragon shows kindness and caring when he does things like share his Christmas presents with the animals. Comical, bold illustrations add to the humor.

1. A Friend for Dragon ◆ 1991
2. Dragon Gets By ◆ 1991
3. Dragon's Merry Christmas ◆ 1991
4. Dragon's Fat Cat ◆ 1992
5. Dragon's Halloween ◆ 1993

DRAGON KEEPER TRILOGY

Wilkinson, Carole

HYPERION ◆ GRADES 5–8 ◆ A/R

FANTASY

Ping is an orphan who is a slave serving the Emperor's Dragon Keeper, who neglects the two dragons in his care. One of the dragons dies and Ping escapes with remaining dragon Danzi and they begin a journey to the sea. Danzi, who is an aged dragon, is protecting a mysterious purple stone, which hatches into a baby purple dragon, Kai. Danzi dies, leaving Ping to protect Kai, the last of the Imperial dragons, and keep him safe from his enemies.

1. Dragon Keeper ◆ 2005
2. Garden of the Purple Dragon ◆ 2007
3. Dragon Moon ◆ 2008

DRAGON SLAYERS' ACADEMY

McMullan, Kate

GROSSET & DUNLAP ◆ GRADES 3–5 ◆ A/R

FANTASY

There are lots of humorous moments as Wiglaf attends a special school to help him become a dragon slayer. Often, Wiglaf succeeds through silly circumstances rather than through talent. There are slimy, gross moments and many slapstick situations that should appeal to fans of Captain Underpants as well as to fans of dragon/wizard fantasies.

1. The New Kid at School ◆ 1997
2. Revenge of the Dragon Lady ◆ 1997
3. Class Trip to the Cave of Doom ◆ 1998
4. A Wedding for Wiglaf? ◆ 2003
5. Knight for a Day ◆ 2003
6. Sir Lancelot, Where Are You? ◆ 2003
7. Wheel of Misfortune ◆ 2003
8. Countdown to the Year 1000 ◆ 2003
9. 97 Ways to Train a Dragon ◆ 2003
10. Help! It's Parents Day at DSA ◆ 2004
11. Danger! Wizard at Work ◆ 2004
12. The Ghost of Sir Herbert Dungeonstone ◆ 2004
13. Beware! It's Friday The 13th! ◆ 2005
14. Pig Latin—Not Just for Pigs! ◆ 2005
15. Double Dragon Trouble ◆ 2005
16. World's Oldest Living Dragon ◆ 2006
17. Hail! Hail! Camp Dragononka! ◆ 2006
18. Never Trust a Troll! ◆ 2006
19. Little Giant—Big Trouble ◆ 2007

DRAGONLING

Koller, Jackie French
LITTLE, BROWN ◆ GRADES 2–4 ◆ A/R
ADVENTURE | FANTASY

After Darek rescues and raises a dragonling, he faces many problems. Dragons are feared in Darek's village and Zantor (the dragonling) is in danger. Darek must convince the townspeople, especially his family, that dragons can be trusted. Further adventures take Darek and his friends Rowena and Pol to Krad where they risk their lives to save Darek's father. With a quick-moving plot and lots of action, these books appeal to many readers, including reluctant readers.

1. The Dragonling ◆ 1990
2. A Dragon in the Family ◆ 1993
3. Dragon Quest ◆ 1997
4. Dragons of Krad ◆ 1997
5. Dragon Trouble ◆ 1997
6. Dragons and Kings ◆ 1998

DRAGONS OF DELTORA *see* Deltora: Dragons of Deltora

DUCK

Cronin, Doreen

SIMON & SCHUSTER ◆ GRADES K–2 ◆ A/R

ANIMAL FANTASY

It all starts with the cows typing requests to Farmer Brown. When he refuses to meet their needs, the cows go on strike. Eventually, there is an agreement with the cows and Duck ends up with the typewriter. In the second book, Duck tricks Farmer Brown's brother into providing many special treats. In the third book, Duck wins an election against Farmer Brown but realizes that running the farm is too difficult. So he runs for governor and then president. The first book received a Caldecott Honor medal. There are counting and alphabet books for younger children.

1. Click, Clack, Moo: Cows that Type ◆ 2000
2. Giggle, Giggle, Quack ◆ 2002
3. Duck for President ◆ 2004
4. Dooby Dooby Moo ◆ 2006
5. Thump, Quack, Moo: A Whacky Adventure ◆ 2008

DUEL MASTERS

Scholastic staff

SCHOLASTIC ◆ GRADES 3–5 ◆ A/R

FANTASY

These chapter books feature Shobu, a character from the Duel Masters television show. In the first book, he loses a tournament to Kaijudo Master and begins to question his own abilities. In the second book, he is challenged to a dangerous duel. Readers who look for adventure and animation will enjoy these chapter books.

1. Own the Zone ◆ 2004
2. Lost in Darkness ◆ 2004
3. Psych Out ◆ 2005
4. Winning Streak ◆ 2005

DUNCAN AND DOLORES

Samuels, Barbara

MACMILLAN; ORCHARD BOOKS ◆ GRADES K–3

FAMILY LIFE │ HUMOR

Faye and Dolores are sisters with different personalities. Faye is sensible while Dolores is boisterous. When Dolores decides she wants Duncan the cat to be her pet, she wants him to like her right away. Dolores must develop patience before Duncan will show he likes her. These are entertaining stories about sisters and a pet with personality.

1. Faye and Dolores ◆ 1985
2. Duncan and Dolores ◆ 1986
3. Happy Birthday, Dolores ◆ 1989

DUNGEONS AND DRAGONS: KNIGHTS OF THE SILVER DRAGON

Various authors

WIZARDS OF THE COAST ◆ GRADES 5–8 ◆ A/R

FANTASY

Set in the world of Greyhawk, a fantasy world of Dungeons and Dragons, three kids solve mysteries and face magical forces and creatures. Kellach, 14, is an apprentice wizard who is smart but self-centered. His younger brother, Driskoll, 12, is always ready to stand up for what he believes is right. Moyra, 13, is a thief whose live has been a struggle and, as a result, she is resilient and brave. The three are unlikely partners protecting the city of Curston.

1. Secret of the Spiritkeeper (Forbek, Matt) ◆ 2004
2. Riddle in Stone (Soesbee, Ree) ◆ 2004
3. Sign of the Shapeshifter (Donovan, Dale, and Linda Johns) ◆ 2004
4. Eye of Fortune (Graham, Denise R.) ◆ 2004
5. Figure in the Frost (Perez, Lana) ◆ 2005
6. Dagger of Doom (Roberts, Kerry Daniel) ◆ 2005
7. Hidden Dragon (Trumbauer, Lisa Trutkoff) ◆ 2005
8. The Silver Spell (Banerjee, Anjali) ◆ 2005
9. Key to the Griffon's Lair (Ransom, Candice) ◆ 2005
10. Curse of the Lost Grove (Graham, Denise R.) ◆ 2005
11. Mystery of the Wizard's Tomb (Plummer, Rachel) ◆ 2006
12. Mark of the Yuan-Ti (Roberts, Kerry Daniel) ◆ 2006
13. Revelations, Part 1: Prophecy of the Dragons (Forbek, Matt) ◆ 2006
14. Revelations, Part 2: The Dragons Revealed (Forbek, Matt) ◆ 2006

DUZ SHEDD STORIES *see* Genghis Khan

D.W.

Brown, Marc

LITTLE, BROWN ◆ GRADES K–2 ◆ A/R

ANIMAL FANTASY | FAMILY LIFE | HUMOR

Meet adventurous D.W., who is always in trouble with her older brother Arthur and the rest of her family. With determination and much confidence, D.W. never hesitates to tackle new situations, from trying new foods to riding a two-wheeler. No matter how difficult the challenge, D.W. plows her way through and lands on her feet. Laced with humor, these situations are very familiar to youngsters. They will laugh out loud at D.W.'s hilarious antics. *Glasses for D.W.* (1996) is part of the Random House Step into Reading series.

1. D.W. Flips! ◆ 1987
2. D.W. All Wet ◆ 1988
3. D.W. Rides Again ◆ 1993
4. D.W. Thinks Big ◆ 1993
5. D.W. the Picky Eater ◆ 1995
6. D.W.'s Lost Blankie ◆ 1997
7. D.W., Go to Your Room ◆ 1999
8. D.W.'s Library Card ◆ 2001
9. D.W.'s Guide to Preschool ◆ 2003
10. D.W.'s Guide to Perfect Manners ◆ 2006

D.W. 8x8 PAPERBACKS

1. Good Night, D.W. ◆ 2004
2. D.W.'s Perfect Present ◆ 2004
3. D.W.'s the Big Boss ◆ 2005

EAGLE-EYE ERNIE

Pearson, Susan

SIMON & SCHUSTER ◆ GRADES 1–3

MYSTERY

Moving from Virginia to Minnesota was hard enough for Ernestine Jones, whose nickname is Ernie, but getting blamed for stealing lunches on her first day of school is an outrage. Ernie uses her expert deductive powers and a good eye for detail to solve the lunch box thefts and is able to make friends and win the admiration of the whole school. The series continues with simple school situations that require the detective work of Ernie and her friends Rachel (R.T.), Michael, and William.

1. The Bogeyman Caper ◆ 1990
2. The Campfire Ghosts ◆ 1990
3. Eagle-Eye Ernie Comes to Town ◆ 1990
4. The Tap Dance Mystery ◆ 1990
5. The Green Magician Puzzle ◆ 1991
6. The 123 Zoo Mystery ◆ 1991
7. The Spooky Sleepover ◆ 1991
8. The Spy Code Caper ◆ 1991

EAGLESMOUNT TRILOGY

Baldry, Cherith

MONDO PUBLISHING ◆ **GRADES 4–6**

ANIMAL FANTASY

Lord Owl plans to usurp the Emerald Throne from the eagle kings. Vair, a brave pine marten, leads an army of small animals against Lord Owl and his followers. Vair is brave and a skillful swordsman; he is also the rightful High King. Readers who are not ready for the Redwall books will find this a more accessible series.

1. The Silver Horn ◆ 2002
2. The Emerald Throne ◆ 2003
3. The Lake of Darkness ◆ 2004

ECO KIDS

Makris, Kathryn

AVON CAMELOT ◆ **GRADES 3–5**

REAL LIFE

Three friends decide that they want to do things to help their community. Sienna, Jess, and Cary become involved in recycling by cleaning up their schoolyard. They start a group to help homeless pets find good homes, and they work to stop a developer from building on a wetlands area. These girls are spunky and their desire to become involved could serve as a model for readers.

1. The Five Cat Club ◆ 1994
2. The Clean-Up Crew ◆ 1994
3. The Green Team ◆ 1994

EDDIE DICKENS TRILOGY

Ardagh, Philip

SCHOLASTIC ◆ **GRADES 4–6** ◆ **A/R**

HUMOR

Like the children in Lemony Snicket's A Series of Unfortunate Events, Eddie Dickens seems destined for a difficult life. What else can you expect of a boy whose parents turn yellow, who must live with Mad Uncle Jack and Even Madder Aunt Maud, and who meets characters like the Great Zucchini? These books take dire situations and make them funny with odd people and improbable events.

1. A House Called Awful End: Book One ◆ 2003

2. Dreadful Acts: Book Two ◆ 2003
3. Terrible Times: Book Three ◆ 2003

EDDIE WILSON

Haywood, Carolyn

MORROW ◆ GRADES 1–3

REAL LIFE

Eddie Wilson and Boodles Carey are best friends in this series that chronicles their lives in a typical American town. Author Carolyn Haywood, also known for the Betsy series, has a knack for creating timeless characters, so the age of some of this material will not affect its impact on readers. Readers will recognize the adventures of Eddie and Boodles and will appreciate the crazy schemes that are the characters' trademarks.

1. Little Eddie ◆ 1947
2. Eddie and the Fire Engine ◆ 1949
3. Eddie and Gardenia ◆ 1951
4. Eddie's Pay Dirt ◆ 1953
5. Eddie and His Big Deals ◆ 1955
6. Eddie Makes Music ◆ 1957
7. Eddie and Louella ◆ 1959
8. Annie Pat and Eddie ◆ 1960
9. Eddie's Green Thumb ◆ 1964
10. Eddie the Dog Holder ◆ 1966
11. Ever-ready Eddie ◆ 1968
12. Eddie's Happenings ◆ 1971
13. Eddie's Valuable Property ◆ 1975
14. Eddie's Menagerie ◆ 1978
15. Merry Christmas from Eddie ◆ 1986
16. Eddie's Friend Boodles ◆ 1991

EDGAR AND ELLEN

Ogden, Charles

TRICYCLE PRESS ◆ GRADES 4–7 ◆ A/R

HUMOR

Edgar and Ellen are 12-year-old twins. They live in a dilapidated mansion and enjoy creating chaos. For example, they decorate the neighbor's pets and try to sell them as exotic animals. The *Edgar and Ellen Mischief Manual* (2007) is a guide to planning and perpetrating pranks. This series might be a choice for the fans of Lemony Snicket.

1. Rare Beasts ◆ 2003
2. Tourist Trap ◆ 2004

3. Under Town ◆ 2004
4. Pet's Revenge ◆ 2005
5. High Wire ◆ 2006
6. Nod's Limbs ◆ 2007
7. Frost Bites ◆ 2008
8. Split Ends ◆ 2009

EDGAR FONT'S HUNT FOR A HOUSE TO HAUNT

Doyle, Patrick

ARMADILLO BOOKS ◆ GRADES 4–7

FANTASY

Eccentric, elderly Edgar Font is looking for just the right place to haunt. In the first book, joined by his grandchildren, Audrey and Garrett, he explores an abandoned lighthouse that is already being haunted by a spirit that wants to be free.

1. The Castle Tower Lighthouse ◆ 2006
2. The Fakersville Power Station ◆ 2007
3. The Flint Island Treehouse ◆ 2008

EDGE CHRONICLES

Stewart, Paul, and Chris Riddell

DAVID FICKLING ◆ GRADES 5–9 ◆ A/R

FANTASY

The first three books in the Edge Chronicles feature Twig, 13, whose mother, a wood troll, reveals that she found him when he was a baby. So begins Twig's quest for his true identity, eventually leading him to his father, Cloud Wolf, a captain of the sky pirates. Twig assists his father in the search for stormphrax, a substance necessary to keep the floating city of Sanctaphrax from drifting away. The fourth book, *The Curse of the Gloamglozer,* is a prequel and describes the early lives of Twig's parents. The fifth book, *The Last of the Sky Pirates,* begins the Rook Barkwater sequence, featuring a knight librarian who challenges Vox Verlix plans to take over Edgeworld. Books 8 and 9 return to the early exploits of Twig's father. This British import has all the elements of a classic fantasy: a clearly defined setting—the Edge with the Deepwoods and a floating city, Sanctaphrax; a character on a quest—Twig searching for his identity and his destiny; and encounters with unusual creatures—sky pirates, spindlebugs, and gloamglozers. This should appeal to fans of Tolkein and other intricate fantasies.

1. Beyond the Deepwoods ◆ 2004

2. Stormchaser ◆ 2004
3. Midnight Over Sanctaphrax ◆ 2004
4. The Curse of the Gloamglozer ◆ 2005
5. The Last of the Sky Pirates ◆ 2005
6. Vox ◆ 2005
7. Freeglader ◆ 2006
8. The Winter Knights ◆ 2007
9. Clash of the Sky Galleons ◆ 2007

EDISON-ARMSTRONG SCHOOL

Hurwitz, Johanna
MORROW ◆ GRADES 3–5 ◆ A/R

REAL LIFE

The students at Edison-Armstrong school are introduced in *Class Clown.* Lucas Cott is very smart, but he is sometimes too smart for his own good. Other books feature Cricket Kaufman, who is used to being the teacher's favorite until Zoe Mitchell moves into town. Julio Sanchez tries to help Lucas be elected *Class President,* but his classmates choose him instead. In newer books, the friends are on summer vacation and then work together to keep their school from closing. The series expands with *Starting School,* in which Lucas's twin brothers, Marius and Marcus, enter the school's kindergarten. As with Hurwitz's books about Aldo and those featuring Ali Baba Bernstein, these are lots of fun and very popular.

1. Class Clown ◆ 1987
2. Teacher's Pet ◆ 1988
3. Class President ◆ 1990
4. School's Out ◆ 1991
5. School Spirit ◆ 1994
6. Starting School ◆ 1998

EDWARD THE UNREADY

Wells, Rosemary
DIAL ◆ GRADES K–1

ANIMAL FANTASY | FAMILY LIFE | HUMOR

Edward is a little bear who takes his time getting ready for familiar activities—going to school, learning to swim, and staying overnight with a friend. Refreshingly, his parents allow him to reject the activity until he's really ready. Droll pictures show a wide-eyed, sometimes mystified little bear who could be any child who's "not quite ready."

1. Edward Unready for School ◆ 1995

2. Edward in Deep Water ◆ 1995
3. Edward's Overwhelming Overnight ◆ 1995

EERIE INDIANA

Various authors

AVON CAMELOT ◆ GRADES 5–8

HORROR | MYSTERY

Marshall Teller and his family have left the crowded, noisy, crime-filled streets of a New Jersey city to live the bucolic small-town life in Eerie, Indiana. What a mistake! This town is not normal. Weird things happen here, like the release of characters from a cryogenic store—including Jesse James. Then, there is a dollhouse that looks like a real house and a doll that looks like a real girl and Marshall seems to be getting smaller. This series mixes the horror genre with bizarre situations that many readers will find amusing.

1. Return to Foreverware (Ford, Mike) ◆ 1997
2. Bureau of Lost (Peel, John) ◆ 1997
3. The Eerie Triangle (Ford, Mike) ◆ 1997
4. Simon and Marshall's Excellent Adventure (Peel, John) ◆ 1997
5. Have Yourself an Eerie Little Christmas (Ford, Mike) ◆ 1997
6. Fountain of Weird (Shahan, Sherry) ◆ 1998
7. Attack of the Two-Ton Tomatoes (Ford, Mike) ◆ 1998
8. Who Framed Alice Prophet? (Ford, Mike) ◆ 1998
9. Bring Me a Dream (James, Robert) ◆ 1998
10. Finger-Lickin' Strange (Roberts, Jeremy) ◆ 1998
11. The Dollhouse that Time Forgot (Ford, Mike) ◆ 1998
12. They Say (Ford, Mike) ◆ 1998
13. Switching Channels (Ford, Mike) ◆ 1998
14. The Incredible Shrinking Stanley (James, Robert) ◆ 1998
15. Halloweird (Ford, Mike) ◆ 1998
16. Eerie in the Mirror (James, Robert) ◆ 1998
17. We Wish You an Eerie Christmas (James, Robert) ◆ 1998

EINSTEIN ANDERSON

Simon, Seymour

VIKING; MORROW ◆ GRADES 3–6 ◆ A/R

MYSTERY

Fans of the Encyclopedia Brown series may also enjoy this humorous series about a boy genius who solves mysteries. Einstein uses his precocious knowledge of science to baffle even his teachers and his mother. Though Einstein loves science, children will also identify with his interest in sports. Readers have the opportunity to solve the several mysteries in each book along with Einstein. The Einstein Anderson, Science Sleuth books have been reformatted into the Einstein Anderson, Science Detective series (with some updated information, too). Both series are listed below.

EINSTEIN ANDERSON, SCIENCE SLEUTH (VIKING)

1. Einstein Anderson, Science Sleuth ◆ 1980
2. Einstein Anderson Shocks His Friends ◆ 1980
3. Einstein Anderson Makes Up for Lost Time ◆ 1981
4. Einstein Anderson Tells a Comet's Tale ◆ 1981
5. Einstein Anderson Goes to Bat ◆ 1982
6. Einstein Anderson Lights Up the Sky ◆ 1982
7. Einstein Anderson Sees Through the Invisible Man ◆ 1983

EINSTEIN ANDERSON, SCIENCE DETECTIVE (MORROW)

1. The Howling Dog and Other Cases ◆ 1997
2. The Halloween Horror and Other Cases ◆ 1997
3. The Gigantic Ants and Other Cases ◆ 1997
4. The Time Machine and Other Cases ◆ 1997
5. The On-Line Spaceman and Other Cases ◆ 1997
6. Wings of Darkness and Other Cases ◆ 1998
7. The Invisible Man and Other Cases ◆ 1998
8. The Mysterious Lights and Other Cases ◆ 1998

ELEPHANT AND PIGGIE

Willems, Mo

HYPERION ◆ GRADES K–2

HUMOR

This series of easy-readers is full of fun. Like Frog and Toad, Elephant and Piggie are good friends. Gerald the Elephant is dismayed that there is a bird on his head. Then, there are two birds on his head. Piggie tries to help and ends up with the birds on her head. Generally, Piggie is outgoing while Gerald is more reserved, even pessimistic. The cartoon-style illustrations and the use of speech bubbles will appeal to beginning readers. *There Is a Bird on Your Head!* won the Theodor Seuss Geisel Award.

1. My Friend Is Sad ◆ 2007
2. Today I Will Fly! ◆ 2007
3. I Am Invited to a Party! ◆ 2007
4. There Is a Bird on Your Head! ◆ 2007
5. I Love My New Toy! ◆ 2008
6. I Will Surprise My Friend! ◆ 2008
7. Watch me Throw the Ball! ◆ 2009
8. Are You Ready to Play Outside? ◆ 2009

ELISA *see* Riverside Kids: Elisa

ELIZABETH *see* My America: Elizabeth

ELIZABETI

Stuve-Bodeen, Stephanie
LEE & LOW BOOKS ◆ **GRADES K–2** ◆ **A/R**
REAL LIFE

Based on the author's experiences as a Peace Corps volunteer in Tanzania, these books introduce young readers to a child with similar emotions and hopes. In the first book, Elizabeti wants a special toy. In the newest book, she celebrates her first day of school. These are wonderful books to celebrate diversity.

1. Elizabeti's Doll ◆ 1998
2. Mama Elizabeti ◆ 2000
3. Elizabeti's School ◆ 2002

ELLA, THE ELEGANT ELEPHANT

D'Amico, Carmela, and Steven D'Amico
SCHOLASTIC ◆ **GRADES K–2** ◆ **A/R**
ANIMAL FANTASY

Ella is eager to start school. On the first day, she wears an elegant hat only to be mocked by the other students, especially Belinda. But when Belinda falls off a wall, it is Ella's hat that helps save the day. In other books, Ella shows that she is responsible when she delivers a cake for her mother, she demonstrates that her true talent is being a good friend, and she gets swept away in a small sailboat. Primary-grade children will appreciate Ella's kindness and spunk.

1. Ella, the Elegant Elephant ◆ 2004
2. Ella Takes the Cake ◆ 2005
3. Ella Sets the Stage ◆ 2006
4. Ella Sets Sail ◆ 2008

ELLEN FREMEDON

Givner, Joan
GROUNDWOOD ◆ **GRADES 5–7**
REAL LIFE

Ellen, 11, expects to spend a quiet summer in Partridge Cove writing a novel but things heat up when her family protests a new housing development and threats are made against Ellen and her twin brothers. In the second book, Ellen uncovers some shocking stories when she starts a newspaper with her best friend Jenny. These are thoughtful books, with the first-person narrative revealing Ellen's emotions and growing maturity as the series progresses.

1. Ellen Fremedon ◆ 2004
2. Ellen Fremedon, Journalist ◆ 2005
3. Ellen Fremedon, Volunteer ◆ 2007

ELLEN GRAE

Cleaver, Vera, and Bill Cleaver

J. B. LIPPINCOTT ◆ GRADES 3–6

REAL LIFE

Ellen Grae Derryberry is a girl who loves to tell strange, funny stories. She is irreverent and real. This series follows her adventures when her divorced parents send her to live with Mrs. McGruder. She struggles with authority figures and attempts to decipher such issues as the meaning of honesty and telling right from wrong. Told in the first person, this series should appeal especially to imaginative girls. Ellen Grae has the rare combination of being both humorous and thought-provoking.

1. Ellen Grae ◆ 1967
2. Lady Ellen Grae ◆ 1968
3. Grover ◆ 1970

ELLIOT'S PARK

Carman, Patrick

ORCHARD BOOKS ◆ GRADES 3–5

ANIMAL FANTASY

Elliot and his squirrel friends hang out in the park. Elliot is the smart one, Chip is clumsy, Crash is a flying squirrel from England, and Twitch is energetic—and she is Elliot's sister. In the first book, the group works to rescue a stuffed squirrel, Mr. Nibbles, who is also their friend.

1. Saving Mister Nibbles! ◆ 2008
2. Haunted Hike ◆ 2008
3. The Walnut Cup ◆ 2009

ELMER

McKee, David

LOTHROP, LEE & SHEPARD ◆ GRADES K–2 ◆ A/R

ANIMAL FANTASY | HUMOR

Elmer does not look like the other elephants. His colorful patchwork skin is a perfect match for his bright, creative personality. Elmer can always find a way to enliven the lives of the other elephants. In one book, Elmer's friend Harold pretends he is Elmer. In another, Elmer's cousin Wilbur (who is covered in black-and-white patchwork) comes to visit. *Hide-and-Seek Elmer* is a lift-the-flap book. There are companion board books for younger children that focus on friends, colors, days, and the weather. The series has been translated into languages including Spanish, Chinese, and Bengali.

1. Elmer ◆ 1989
2. Elmer Again ◆ 1992
3. Elmer in the Snow ◆ 1995
4. Elmer and Wilbur ◆ 1996
5. Elmer Takes Off ◆ 1998
6. Hide-and-Seek Elmer ◆ 1998
7. Elmer and the Lost Teddy ◆ 1999
8. Elmer and the Kangaroo ◆ 2000

ELOISE

Thompson, Kay

SIMON & SCHUSTER ◆ GRADES K–2 ◆ A/R

HUMOR

Eloise, 6, lives in the posh Plaza Hotel in New York City. She is a lively little girl with a mind of her own. This series takes her to Paris and to Moscow. Related items include a calendar, sticker book, lift-the-flap books, and *Eloise's Guide to Life* (2000) and *Eloise's What I Absolutely Love Love Love* (2004). *The Absolutely Essential Eloise* (1999, reissued in an anniversary edition in 2005) includes the original story and illustrations plus sketches of the illustrations as works-in-progress and photographs of the author when she was young.

1. Eloise ◆ 1969
2. Eloise at Christmastime ◆ 1999
3. Eloise in Paris ◆ 1999
4. Eloise in Moscow ◆ 2000
5. Eloise Takes a Bawth ◆ 2002

READY TO READ BOOKS (IN THE STYLE OF KAY THOMPSON AND HILARY KNIGHT)

1. Eloise Has a Lesson ◆ 2005
2. Eloise Breaks Some Eggs ◆ 2005
3. Eloise Dresses Up ◆ 2005
4. Eloise at the Wedding ◆ 2006
5. Eloise and the Very Secret Room ◆ 2006
6. Eloise and the Snowman ◆ 2006
7. Eloise and the Dinosaurs ◆ 2007
8. Eloise's New Bonnet ◆ 2007
9. Eloise Takes a Trip ◆ 2007
10. Eloise Goes to the Beach ◆ 2007
11. Eloise and the Big Parade ◆ 2007
12. Eloise's Summer Vacation ◆ 2007
13. Eloise's Pirate Adventure ◆ 2007
14. Eloise Decorates for Christmas ◆ 2007
15. Eloise at the Ball Game ◆ 2008
16. Eloise Throws a Party ◆ 2008
17. Eloise Skates ◆ 2008
18. Eloise's Mother's Day Surprise ◆ 2009
19. Eloise Visits the Zoo ◆ 2009

ELSIE EDWARDS

DeClements, Barthe

VIKING ◆ GRADES 4–8 ◆ A/R

REAL LIFE

Elsie Edwards and Jenny Sawyer become friends in fifth grade. This series chronicles their progress through the awkward middle school years. Elsie grows from an overweight fifth-grader to a slim ninth-grader, gaining self-confidence along the way. The girls in this series have typical concerns—school, family, and "fitting in"—and the books reinforce the importance of self-esteem and the value of friendship. Elsie and Jenny make cameo appearances in *Sixth Grade Can Really Kill You* (1985), which may attract readers to that book, too.

1. Nothing's Fair in Fifth Grade ◆ 1981
2. How Do You Lose Those Ninth Grade Blues? ◆ 1983
3. Seventeen and In-Between ◆ 1984

EMILY AND ALICE

Champion, Joyce

HARCOURT ◆ GRADES K–2 ◆ A/R

REAL LIFE

Friendship stories are always welcomed by young readers. This series features two girls whose love of peanut butter cookies sparks a friendship. Of course, there are ups and downs, as when they babysit a bulldog. The first two books were first presented as picture books, but were reissued in a reader format in paperback in 2001. The third book has a reader format.

1. Emily and Alice (paperback title: Emily and Alice: Best Friends) ◆ 1993
2. Emily and Alice Again (paperback title: Emily and Alice Stick Together) ◆ 1995
3. Emily and Alice Baby-Sit Burton ◆ 2001

EMILY EYEFINGER

Ball, Duncan
SIMON & SCHUSTER ◆ GRADES 2–4
ADVENTURE | FANTASY | HUMOR

Emily was born with an extra eye, right on the end of her finger. Despite the nuisance of getting dirt in it and keeping soap out of it, Emily enjoys being able to help others find things by seeing around corners or into difficult places. In the first volume, several chapters are devoted to establishing how Emily handles this oddity. Subsequent stories involve her in problem-solving adventures, including finding a lost treasure.

1. Emily Eyefinger ◆ 1992
2. Emily Eyefinger, Secret Agent ◆ 1993
3. Emily Eyefinger and the Lost Treasure ◆ 1994

EMILY WINDSNAP

Kessler, Liz
CANDLEWICK ◆ GRADES 4–7
FANTASY

When 12-year-old Emily Windsnap's mother finally lets her take swimming lessons, Emily realizes she is half mermaid and longs to meet her father. In the second book, Liz, reunited with her father and now living on an island where humans and mer-people coexist, endangers the community by waking a sleeping monster. Details of life underwater and the appealing illustrations will draw readers in.

1. The Tail of Emily Windsnap ◆ 2004
2. Emily Windsnap and the Monster from the Deep ◆ 2006
3. Emily Windsnap and the Castle in the Mist ◆ 2007

EMMA

Little, Jean

HARPERCOLLINS ◆ GRADES 1–3 ◆ A/R

REAL LIFE

Emma is shy. She worries about making friends with her new neighbor, Sally. The two girls pretend that their boots are magic, which ends up helping Emma overcome her shyness at school. Emma and her brother are featured in subsequent books. Beginning readers will like these simple stories.

1. Emma's Magic Winter ◆ 1998
2. Emma's Yucky Brother ◆ 2002
3. Emma's Strange Pet ◆ 2003

EMMA

McPhail, David

DUTTON ◆ GRADES K–3 ◆ A/R

ANIMAL FANTASY | HUMOR

Emma, a young bear, often sets her parents straight. When they go on vacation, it is Emma who shows her parents how to have fun. When Emma begins looking for a new pet, there is a surprise ending for all. Young children will enjoy these warm stories.

1. Fix It! ◆ 1984
2. Emma's Pet ◆ 1985
3. Emma's Vacation ◆ 1987

EMMA

Stevenson, James

GREENWILLOW ◆ GRADES K–3

FANTASY | HUMOR

Dolores and Lavinia, two witches, are constantly thinking of ways to torment Emma, a young and amiable witch. Throughout the series, Emma manages to outwit them with the help of her friends Roland the owl and Botsford the cat.

1. Yuck! ◆ 1984
2. Emma ◆ 1985

3. Fried Feathers for Thanksgiving ◆ 1986
4. Happy Valentine's Day, Emma! ◆ 1987
5. Un-happy New Year, Emma! ◆ 1989
6. Emma at the Beach ◆ 1990

EMMA

Warner, Sally

VIKING ◆ GRADES 2–4

REAL LIFE

Emma, 8, is an only child who has been attending a private school. When her mother loses her job, they have to move and Emma begins in a new school. Emma makes new friends, adjusts to her third-grade classroom, and deals with familiar everyday issues in ways that will resonate with middle-grade readers. Her "friendship" with Cynthia is very realistic as the two girls often compete for attention. Fans of Judy Moody, Clementine, and Amber Brown will be interested in these books too.

1. Only Emma ◆ 2005
2. Not-So-Weird Emma ◆ 2005
3. Super Emma ◆ 2006
4. Best Friend Emma ◆ 2007
5. Excellent Emma ◆ 2009

EMMA DILEMMA

Hermes, Patricia

MARSHALL CAVENDISH ◆ GRADES 3–5 ◆ A/R

FAMILY LIFE

Emma O'Fallon is a lively character in the tradition of Ramona Quimby and Junie B. Jones. Her good intentions often land her in challenging situations—dilemmas that she must resolve. In *Emma Dilemma and the Two Nannies,* Emma takes a book home (without permission) and her pet ferret ruins it. Will she take responsibility for what has happened? The family's nanny, Annie, is supportive of Emma and helps her make the right decisions. Middle-grade readers will enjoy these books and might also like to read the Clementine books by Sara Pennypacker and the Grace books by Charise Harper.

1. Emma Dilemma and the New Nanny ◆ 2006
2. Emma Dilemma and the Two Nannies ◆ 2007
3. Emma Dilemma and the Soccer Nanny ◆ 2008

ENCHANTED FOREST CHRONICLES

Wrede, Patricia C.

HARCOURT; SCHOLASTIC ◆ GRADES 4–7 ◆ A/R

FANTASY

Sensing the boredom that awaits her if she marries Prince Therandil as her parents require, reluctant princess Cimorene escapes to the Enchanted Forest to meet Kazul, King of the Dragons. With the dragons, Cimorene finally experiences the adventure she craves. Throughout the series, Cimorene and Kazul confront wicked wizards to save the forest.

1. Dealing with Dragons ◆ 1990
2. Searching for Dragons ◆ 1991
3. Calling on Dragons ◆ 1993
4. Talking to Dragons ◆ 1993

ENCYCLOPEDIA BROWN

Sobol, Donald J.

BANTAM ◆ GRADES 2–6 ◆ A/R

MYSTERY | REAL LIFE

Encyclopedia Brown earned his nickname for his vast knowledge of just about everything, which is even more impressive when one considers that Encyclopedia is only 10 years old. He uses his knowledge to fight crime in his hometown of Idaville, where his father is the police chief. Encyclopedia often confronts arch rival Bugs Meany and is always able to outsmart him, especially with the help of his assistant, Sally Kimball. The series allows readers to figure out the cases for themselves before Encyclopedia's answer is revealed, so it may make children want to do detective work of their own.

1. Encyclopedia Brown, Boy Detective ◆ 1963
2. Encyclopedia Brown and the Case of the Secret Pitch ◆ 1965
3. Encyclopedia Brown Finds the Clues ◆ 1966
4. Encyclopedia Brown Gets His Man ◆ 1967
5. Encyclopedia Brown Solves Them All ◆ 1968
6. Encyclopedia Brown Keeps Peace ◆ 1969
7. Encyclopedia Brown Saves the Day ◆ 1970
8. Encyclopedia Brown Tracks Them Down ◆ 1971
9. Encyclopedia Brown Shows the Way ◆ 1972
10. Encyclopedia Brown Takes the Case ◆ 1973
11. Encyclopedia Brown Lends a Hand ◆ 1974
12. Encyclopedia Brown and the Case of the Dead Eagles ◆ 1975
13. Encyclopedia Brown and the Case of the Midnight Visitor ◆ 1977
14. Encyclopedia Brown Carries On ◆ 1980
15. Encyclopedia Brown Sets the Pace ◆ 1981

16. Encyclopedia Brown Takes the Cake! ◆ 1983
17. Encyclopedia Brown and the Case of the Mysterious Handprints ◆ 1985
18. Encyclopedia Brown and the Case of the Treasure Hunt ◆ 1988
19. Encyclopedia Brown and the Case of the Disgusting Sneakers ◆ 1990
20. Encyclopedia Brown and the Case of the Two Spies ◆ 1994
21. Encyclopedia Brown and the Case of Pablo's Nose ◆ 1996
22. Encyclopedia Brown and the Case of the Sleeping Dog ◆ 1998
23. Encyclopedia Brown and the Case of the Slippery Salamander ◆ 1999
24. Encyclopedia Brown and the Case of the Jumping Frogs ◆ 2000

THE ENGLISH ROSES (CHAPTER BOOKS)

Madonna

PUFFIN ◆ GRADES 2–4

REAL LIFE

Meet Grace, Amy, Charlotte, Nicole, and Binah, a group of friends who call themselves The English Roses. Sometimes the girls squabble, as when a new boy enrolls in their school. Most of the time, however, they support each other. The girls deal with problems and learn lessons about friendship. The first two books in this series were presented as picture books: *The English Roses* and *The English Roses: Too Good to Be True*.

1. Friends for Life! ◆ 2007
2. Good-Bye Grace? ◆ 2007
3. The New Girl ◆ 2007
4. A Rose by Any Other Name ◆ 2007
5. Big-Sister Blues ◆ 2008
6. Being Binah ◆ 2008
7. Hooray for the Holidays ◆ 2008
8. A Perfect Pair ◆ 2008

ENOLA HOLMES

Springer, Nancy

PHILOMEL ◆ GRADES 5–8 ◆ A/R

MYSTERY | HISTORICAL

Meet Enola Holmes, 14, is the much younger sister of Sherlock and Mycroft Holmes. When Enola's mother disappears, her brothers arrive at the estate determined to solve the mystery. Enola thwarts their plan to send her to boarding school and sets off for London. Life in Victorian England is difficult for women and Enola faces many challenges and another mystery—the disappearance of a young marquess. Readers will relate to Enola's independent spirit and will enjoy solving the clues throughout the books.

1. The Case of the Missing Marquess: An Enola Holmes Mystery ◆ 2006
2. The Case of the Left-handed Lady: An Enola Holmes Mystery ◆ 2007
3. The Case of the Bizarre Bouquets: An Enola Holmes Mystery ◆ 2008
4. The Case of the Peculiar Pink Fan: An Enola Holmes Mystery ◆ 2008

EOIN COLFER'S LEGEND OF . . .

Colfer, Eoin
MIRAMAX ◆ **GRADES 3–5**
HUMOR

Brothers Will, 9, and Marty, 10, are sent to spend their summer afternoons reading in the library. Mrs. Murphy is the librarian. Her nickname is "Spud" because, legend has it, she uses a potato gun on troublemaking kids. After some funny confrontations, the boys end up enjoying reading. In the second book, the brothers meet up with a bloodthirsty pirate.

1. Eoin Colfer's Legend of Spud Murphy ◆ 2004
2. Eoin Colfer's Legend of Captain Crow's Teeth ◆ 2005
3. Eoin Colfer's Legend of the Worst Boy in the World ◆ 2008

ERIC STERLING, SECRET AGENT

Herndon, Ernest
ZONDERVAN ◆ **GRADES 4–6**
ADVENTURE

Eric Sterling and his friends Ax and Sharon work for Wildlife Special Investigations, a branch of the CIA. Eric is an unlikely hero: He is easily scared and doesn't like to take chances. Ax and Sharon are both more daring and athletic. Eric is recruited into the organization by mistake but he proves his worth on a mission to prevent genetic engineering of gigantic lizards. Their adventures take them to 'gator country to catch whoever has been butchering the alligators and to Central America and Alaska, with Eric and his friends falling in and out of trouble and facing villains of all kinds. Eric can't even escape danger on vacation: When his family goes to Hawaii, he runs into a girl desperate to protect her family farm, which is now on public land.

1. The Secret of Lizard Island ◆ 1994
2. Double-Crossed in Gator Country ◆ 1994
3. Night of the Jungle Cat ◆ 1994
4. Smugglers on Grizzly Mountain ◆ 1994
5. Sisters of the Wolf ◆ 1996
6. Trouble at Bamboo Bay ◆ 1996

7. Deathbird of Paradise ◆ 1997
8. Little People of the Lost Coast ◆ 1997

ERNEST AND CELESTINE

Vincent, Gabrielle

GREENWILLOW ◆ GRADES K–3

ANIMAL FANTASY

Ernest the bear and Celestine, the young mouse that he looks after, have a warm and wonderful relationship. When Celestine gets lost in the museum, Ernest finds her and comforts her. When Ernest is sick, Celestine does her best to take care of him. Young children will identify with Celestine and the lovable, caring Ernest.

1. Ernest and Celestine ◆ 1982
2. Bravo, Ernest and Celestine! ◆ 1982
3. Ernest and Celestine's Picnic ◆ 1982
4. Smile, Ernest and Celestine ◆ 1982
5. Merry Christmas, Ernest and Celestine! ◆ 1984
6. Ernest and Celestine's Patchwork Quilt ◆ 1985
7. Breakfast Time, Ernest and Celestine ◆ 1985
8. Where Are You, Ernest and Celestine? ◆ 1986
9. Feel Better, Ernest! ◆ 1988
10. Ernest and Celestine at the Circus ◆ 1988

ERNESTINE AND AMANDA

Belton, Sandra

SIMON & SCHUSTER ◆ GRADES 4–5 ◆ A/R

REAL LIFE

When Ernestine Harris and Amanda Clay are fifth-graders, they are more antagonistic than friendly at school, dance class, and neighborhood functions. These books follow the girls into sixth grade, describing their growth as their families change. Both girls are talented—Ernestine as a pianist and Amanda as a dancer. They are often rivals and sometimes friends willing to engage in girlish gossip and rumors. By the last title of the series, they are beginning to mature and accept more responsibilities. These books take place in the 1950s, and segregation is an issue for these two African American girls.

1. Ernestine and Amanda ◆ 1996
2. Ernestine and Amanda: Summer Camp, Ready or Not! ◆ 1997
3. Ernestine and Amanda, Members of the Club ◆ 1997
4. Ernestine and Amanda, Mysteries on Monroe Street ◆ 1998

ESCAPADE JOHNSON

Sullivan, Michael

BIG GUY BOOKS ◆ GRADES 4–6

FANTASY | HUMOR

You would think with a name like Escapade Johnson your life would be filled with adventure. Unfortunately, Escapade is boringly normal. Then, on a class field trip to Mount Moosilauke, Escapade finally lives up to his name. In the second book, he deals with zombies and in the third, witches.

1. Escapade Johnson and Mayhem at Mount Moosilauke ◆ 2007
2. Escapade Johnson and the Coffee Shop of the Living Dead ◆ 2008
3. Escapade Johnson and the Witches of Belknap County ◆ 2008

ETHAN

Hurwitz, Johanna

CANDLEWICK ◆ GRADES K–1 ◆ A/R

REAL LIFE

Part of the Brand New Readers series, these books feature the everyday life of an African American boy. Bedtime, cleaning the house, feeding the birds, and riding bikes are among Ethan's activities.

1. Ethan Out and About ◆ 2001
2. Ethan's Birds ◆ 2002
3. Ethan's Cat ◆ 2002
4. Ethan's Lunch ◆ 2002
5. Ethan At Home ◆ 2003

EVERETT ANDERSON

Clifton, Lucille

HOLT ◆ GRADES K–2 ◆ A/R

FAMILY LIFE | REAL LIFE

Many of the books about Everett Anderson incorporate such concepts as counting and numbers, days of the week, and months of the year. *Everett Anderson's Goodbye* describes his grief at the death of his father; *Everett Anderson's Nine Month Long* tells of his mother's remarriage to Mr. Perry and the excitement of waiting for a new baby. Friendship, holidays, and seasons are topics in other books. The rhyming text captures the joys, humor, worries, and fears of a young African American boy. *Everett Anderson's Christmas Coming* was updated in 1991 with new illustrations.

1. Some of the Days of Everett Anderson ◆ 1970

2. Everett Anderson's Christmas Coming ◆ 1971
3. Everett Anderson's Year ◆ 1974
4. Everett Anderson's Friend ◆ 1976
5. Everett Anderson's 1-2-3 ◆ 1977
6. Everett Anderson's Nine Month Long ◆ 1978
7. Everett Anderson's Goodbye ◆ 1983
8. One of the Problems of Everett Anderson ◆ 2001

EVERYBODY HATES CHRIS

Various authors
SIMON SPOTLIGHT ◆ GRADES 4–6 ◆ A/R

REAL LIFE | HUMOR

Chris can't stay out of trouble. In *Everybody Hates School Dances,* Chris tells everyone that he is taking a really cute girl to the dance . . . in a limo! And, he claims to be a super breakdancer. Will Chris be able to come through on his claims or will he face ridicule and bullying? This is based on the popular television series inspired by the life of comedian Chris Rock.

1. Everybody Hates School Dances (James, Brian) ◆ 2007
2. Everybody Hates Romeo and Juliet (Herman, Gail) ◆ 2007
3. Everybody Hates First Girlfriends (Pride, Felicia) ◆ 2007
4. Everybody Hates Best Friends (James, Brian) ◆ 2007
5. Everybody Hates School Presentations (Thornhill, Samantha) ◆ 2008
6. Everybody Hates School Politics (Pride, Felicia) ◆ 2008

EXILES

McKay, Hilary
SIMON & SCHUSTER ◆ GRADES 4–6 ◆ A/R

FAMILY LIFE | HUMOR

The author's own family could have been the model for this humorous series about four sisters. The Conroy sisters range in age from 6 to 13 and have very different personalities. A larger-than-life character is Big Grandma, as rough and strict as a drill sergeant. In *The Exiles,* the girls are sent to Big Grandma's for the summers and she attempts to change her book-loving, lazy granddaughters into industrious and productive girls. The sisters grow older with each new book, and in *The Exiles in Love* a French boy is introduced and a romantic dilemma occurs. The series is similar to Helen Cresswell's Bagthorpes family saga.

1. The Exiles ◆ 1992
2. The Exiles at Home ◆ 1994
3. The Exiles in Love ◆ 1998

THE EXTRAORDINARY ADVENTURES OF ORDINARY BOY

Boniface, William

HARPERCOLLINS ◆ GRADES 4–7 ◆ A/R

FANTASY | HUMOR

In a town of superheros, Ordinary Boy is ordinary. His friends in the fifth grade at Watson Elementary have superpowers, although they are a bit problematic; for example, whenever Stench uses his super strength, he creates a super stink. In the first book, super villain and evil genius Professor Brain Drain has a scheme involving collectible cards featuring the Amazing Indestructo. As Ordinary Boy investigates, he realizes that the professor is not really behind the scheme. The Amazing Indestructo, who has his own television show, is building on his endorsements and creating a shortage of his merchandise. In the second book, Ordinary Boy looks into the disappearance of Meteor Boy. Numerous cartoon illustrations by Stephen Gilpin add to the appeal.

1. The Hero Revealed ◆ 2006
2. The Return of Meteor Boy? ◆ 2008
3. The Great Powers Outage ◆ 2008

EXTREME TEAM

Christopher, Matt

LITTLE, BROWN ◆ GRADES 4–7 ◆ A/R

RECREATION

Mark Goldstein and his friends enjoy skateboarding and doing kickflips and ollies. But Mark is embarrassed because he is not as coordinated as the others. Taking kung fu classes helps improve his control and gives him insights into his feelings. In all the books, there is a nice mix of sports and character interaction.

1. One Smooth Move ◆ 2004
2. Day of the Dragon ◆ 2004
3. Roller Hockey Rumble ◆ 2004
4. On Thin Ice ◆ 2004
5. Rock On ◆ 2004
6. Into the Danger Zone ◆ 2004
7. Wild Ride ◆ 2005
8. Head to Head ◆ 2005

FABLEHAVEN

Mull, Brandon

SHADOW MOUNTAIN/ALADDIN ◆ GRADES 5–8 ◆ A/R

FANTASY | ADVENTURE

As the series begins, Kendra, 13, and Seth, 11, visit their grandparents and discover that Grandfather Sorenson is the caretaker of Fablehaven, a sanctuary for magical creatures. Fablehaven is being threatened by the evil Society of the Evening Star. Kendra and Seth must rely on their own skills and powers to face this evil and protect Fablehaven.

1. Fablehaven ◆ 2006
2. Rise of the Evening Star ◆ 2007
3. Grip of the Shadow Plague ◆ 2008

FAIRLY ODDPARENTS

Various authors

SIMON & SCHUSTER ◆ GRADES 1–5 ◆ A/R

FANTASY

Timmy Turner, 10, is "blessed" with fairy godparents Cosmo and Wanda. But their mixed-up magic creates havoc for Timmy. They are his "Fairly OddParents." This series is extended from the Nickelodeon cartoon program and there are several formats including picture books and beginning readers and cine-manga from TokyoPop. There are also related materials including a school survival guide, activity book, and joke book.

1. Lovestruck! (Lewman, David) ◆ 2004
2. Blast from the Past (Beechen, Adam) ◆ 2004
3. Timmy Turner's Top Secret Notebook (Pass, Erica) ◆ 2004
4. Wish upon a Mom (Beechen, Adam) ◆ 2004
5. The Long Hot Recess (Pass, Erica) ◆ 2004
6. Scary OddParents (Collins, Terry) ◆ 2004
7. Sleepover and Over (Pass, Erica) ◆ 2004
8. Ask Me Anything! (Ostrow, Kim) ◆ 2004
9. Timmy's Eggs-Ray Vision (Samuel, Catherine) ◆ 2005
10. Big Superhero Wish! (Pass, Erica, and Barry Goldberg) ◆ 2005

FAIRLY ODDPARENTS (FIRST READERS)

1. Up All Night (Ostrow, Kim) ◆ 2004
2. Lemonade with a Twist (Banks, Steven) ◆ 2004

3. A Mighty Big Wish (Ostrow, Kim) ◆ 2004
4. Too Many Turners (Wax, Wendy) ◆ 2004
5. In a Tizzy Over Turkey (Beechen, Adam) ◆ 2004
6. The Timmy Touch (Chipponeri, Kelli) ◆ 2005
7. For Love or Money (Wax, Wendy) ◆ 2005

FAIRLY ODDPARENTS (TOKYOPOP)

Hartman, Butch

TOKYOPOP ◆ **GRADES 3–6**

FANTASY

Timmy Turner is 10 and he has an unusual life. His babysitter, Vicky, is evil. And he has secret Fairy Godparents, Cosmo and Wanda, but their magical skills are very questionable, making them more like Fairly Odd-Parents.

1. Heroes and Monsters ◆ 2004
2. Beware the Babysitter ◆ 2004
3. Father Knows Less ◆ 2004
4. Let the Games Begin ◆ 2004

FAIRY CHRONICLES

Sweet, J. H.

SOURCEBOOK JABBERWOCKY ◆ **GRADES 3–5**

FANTASY

Beth, 9, is not looking forward to spending two weeks of her summer vacation with Aunt Evelyn, who has always seemed unusual. Aunt Evelyn has a surprise for Beth—they are both fairies. Aunt Evelyn helps Beth develop her magical powers. Then Beth, who is a marigold fairy, joins other young fairies, including Thistle and Dragonfly, to recover the Feather of Hope. Each book in the series features another young fairy. Fans of the Fairy Realm and the Disney Fairies books will like this series.

1. Marigold and the Feather of Hope: The Journey Begins ◆ 2007
2. Dragonfly and the Web of Dreams ◆ 2007
3. Thistle and the Shell of Laughter ◆ 2007
4. Firefly and the Quest of the Black Squirrel ◆ 2007
5. Periwinkle and the Cave of Courage ◆ 2007
6. Spiderwort and the Princess of Haiku ◆ 2007
7. Cinnabar and the Island of Shadows ◆ 2007
8. Mimosa and the River of Wisdom ◆ 2007
9. Luna and the Well of Secrets ◆ 2008
10. Primrose and the Magic Snowglobe ◆ 2008

FAIRY HOUSES

Kane, Tracy I.

LIGHT BEAMS ◆ **GRADES K–3** ◆ **A/R**

FANTASY

On vacation in Maine, Kristen sees something special. Using natural materials (shells, driftwood, and so forth), people have created houses for the fairies. Kristen makes a little house and is rewarded when the fairies appear.

1. Fairy Houses ◆ 2001
2. Fairy Boat ◆ 2002
3. Fairy Flight ◆ 2003

THE FAIRY LAIR

LeMieux, A. C.

ALADDIN ◆ **GRADES 4–6** ◆ **A/R**

FANTASY

Sylvia learns of the fairy world and discovers that the angry Gnome King has caused the drought in her community. Sylvia reluctantly works with Dana, who has been a bully, to try to appease the Gnome King.

1. A Special Place ◆ 1997
2. A Hidden Place ◆ 1998
3. A Magic Place ◆ 1998

FAIRY REALM

Rodda, Emily

HARPERCOLLINS ◆ **GRADES 2–4** ◆ **A/R**

FANTASY

Jessie travels to the Fairy Realm and recovers her grandmother's charm bracelet from Valda, a fairy who wants to be anointed as Queen. Jessie discovers that her grandmother left the Realm and her royal destiny to live in the mortal world. The Realm is a world of magic, unicorns, a mermaid kingdom, rainbow fairies, and more. *Enter the Realm* (2007) is a collection of three short stories.

1. The Charm Bracelet ◆ 2003
2. The Flower Fairies ◆ 2003
3. The Third Wish ◆ 2003
4. The Last Fairy-Apple Tree ◆ 2003
5. The Magic Key ◆ 2004

6. The Unicorn ◆ 2004
7. The Star Cloak ◆ 2005
8. The Water Sprites ◆ 2005
9. The Peskie Spell ◆ 2006
10. The Rainbow Wand ◆ 2006

FAIRY SCHOOL

Herman, Gail

SKYLARK ◆ GRADES 2–4 ◆ A/R

FANTASY

In the first book, Belinda is just starting fairy school. She dreams of being a tooth fairy but does poorly in her class. When a rival fairy teases her, Belinda tries to prove herself. Other books feature young fairies trying to succeed at their fairy school assignments.

1. Tooth Fairy Travels ◆ 1999
2. Fairy Cloud Parade ◆ 1999
3. Mixed-Up Magic ◆ 1999
4. The Best Book Ever! ◆ 1999
5. Look Out, Earth-Below! ◆ 2000
6. Little Star ◆ 2000
7. When Wishes Come True ◆ 2000
8. Hide and Peep ◆ 2000
9. A Fairy Merry Christmas ◆ 2000
10. The Icicle Forest ◆ 2000

FAITHGIRLZ: BOARDING SCHOOL MYSTERIES

Holl, Kristi

ZONDERKIDZ ◆ GRADES 4–6 ◆ A/R

MYSTERY | VALUES

Landmark School for Girls is a boarding school and Jeri McKane, 12, is the new girl. Jeri misses her home and wants to give up her scholarship. In these books, Jeri becomes involved in mysterious events that test her courage, honor, and faith. The www.faithgirlz.com Web site has activities and discussion suggestions.

1. Fading Tracks ◆ 2008
2. Secrets for Sale ◆ 2008
3. Smoke Screen ◆ 2008
4. Pick Your Poison ◆ 2008

FAITHGIRLZ: GIRLS OF 622 HARBOR VIEW

Carlson, Melody

ZONDERKIDZ ◆ GRADES 5–7 ◆ A/R

REAL LIFE | VALUES

Four girls live in a trailer park in Oregon. Their friendship is strengthened by their commitment to being good neighbors, helping others, and loving God. There is information for discussion at faithgirlz.com.

1. Project: Girl Power ◆ 2007
2. Project: Mystery Bus ◆ 2007
3. Project: Rescue Chelsea ◆ 2007
4. Project: Take Charge ◆ 2007
5. Project: Raising Faith ◆ 2008
6. Project: Runaway ◆ 2008
7. Project: Ski Trip ◆ 2008
8. Project: Secret Admirer ◆ 2008

FAITHGIRLZ: SOPHIE

Rue, Nancy N.

ZONDERKIDZ ◆ GRADES 4–6 ◆ A/R

REAL LIFE | VALUES

Sophie, 11, has a great imagination. She and her friends at Great Marsh Middle School are known as the "Flakes." They help each other and let their faith guide them. Another group, the "Pops," are the cool, popular girls. Although the two groups have differences, this series emphasizes the importance of accepting yourself and seeing God's love in everyone and everything. The faithgirlz.com Web site provides activities and questions for discussion.

1. Sophie's World ◆ 2004
2. Sophie's Secret ◆ 2004
3. Sophie and the Scoundrels ◆ 2005
4. Sophie's Irish Showdown ◆ 2005
5. Sophie's First Dance? ◆ 2005
6. Sophie's Stormy Summer ◆ 2005
7. Sophie Breaks the Code ◆ 2005
8. Sophie Tracks a Thief ◆ 2005
9. Sophie Flakes Out ◆ 2006
10. Sophie Loves Jimmy ◆ 2006
11. Sophie Loses the Lead ◆ 2006
12. Sophie's Encore ◆ 2006

FALCON

Gray, Luli

HOUGHTON MIFFLIN ◆ GRADES 4–7 ◆ A/R

FANTASY

Falcon, 11, finds an unusual red egg in Central Park and takes it home to hatch. Since her parents' divorce, Falcon has felt alienated. Her mother is focused on her own career while her father is often traveling. As she waits for the egg to hatch, Falcon reaches out to her neighbor Ardene, her great-great-aunt Emily, and an ornithologist. This group, called Friends of Egg, also provide Falcon with support and friendship. When the egg hatches, it is a dragon that they name Egg, who eventually leaves to find other dragons. In subsequent books, Falcon is reunited with Egg.

1. Falcon's Egg ◆ 1993
2. Falcon and the Charles Street Witch ◆ 2002
3. Falcon and the Carousel of Time ◆ 2005

FANCY NANCY

O'Connor, Jane

HARPERCOLLINS ◆ GRADES K–2 ◆ A/R

HUMOR

Fancy Nancy loves being fancy. She is sparkling and stylish from her tiara to her carefully chosen accessories. In *Fancy Nancy and the Posh Puppy,* she is convinced that she wants a papillon puppy. After watching a neighbor's dog, she realizes that she will make any puppy fashionable. The illustrations by Robin Preiss Glasser add to the fun, showing Nancy in all her fabulous finery. There is an alphabet book of fashionable terminology.

1. Fancy Nancy ◆ 2006
2. Fancy Nancy and the Posh Puppy ◆ 2007
3. Fancy Nancy Bonjour Butterfly ◆ 2008
4. Fancy Nancy's Collection of Fancy Words: From Accessories to Zany ◆ 2008

FANCY NANCY READERS

O'Connor, Jane

HARPERCOLLINS ◆ GRADES K–2 ◆ A/R

HUMOR

Kids who enjoyed the Fancy Nancy picture books will want to try these easy reading books. The illustrations by Ted Enik are in the style of those in the picture books.

1. Fancy Nancy and the Boy from Paris ◆ 2008
2. Fancy Nancy at the Museum ◆ 2008
3. Fancy Nancy Sees Stars ◆ 2009

FAR-FLUNG ADVENTURES

Stewart, Paul, and Chris Riddell

RANDOM HOUSE ◆ GRADES 3–5 ◆ A/R

ADVENTURE

Each character in this series experiences a "Far-Flung Adventure." Fergus Crane, 8, attends school aboard a clipper ship with teachers who resemble pirates. Corby Flood, 8, finds herself in a Greek fishing town while her family sails away. Hugo Pepper, 10, discovers he is the son of explorers and begins a search to learn more about his identity. Detailed illustrations by Chris Riddell add to the appeal.

1. Fergus Crane ◆ 2006
2. Corby Flood ◆ 2006
3. Hugo Pepper ◆ 2007

FAT GLENDA

Perl, Lila

CLARION ◆ GRADES 4–8

REAL LIFE

Overweight Glenda struggles with her weight over the course of the series. She loses pounds and finds a boyfriend, only to gain the weight back when he doesn't call. Later, she meets an even more obese teen who interests her in plus-size modeling. Throughout, her mother makes things more difficult for her by denying that she has a problem.

1. Me and Fat Glenda ◆ 1972
2. Hey, Remember Fat Glenda? ◆ 1981
3. Fat Glenda's Summer Romance ◆ 1986
4. Fat Glenda Turns Fourteen ◆ 1991

FEAR STREET: GHOSTS OF FEAR STREET

Stine, R. L.

POCKET BOOKS ◆ GRADES 4–8 ◆ A/R

HORROR

Shadow people, ooze, the bugman, the werecat, ghouls, ghosts, and other creatures populate these horror books. The unsuspecting characters experience nightmares; they encounter body switchers and screaming jokers; they have frightening Christmas celebrations and are attacked by aqua apes. There are many cliff-hangers—chapters ending with a scream or with fingers grabbing the character's neck—so readers enjoy lots of scary moments.

1. Hide and Shriek ◆ 1995
2. Who's Been Sleeping in My Grave? ◆ 1995
3. The Attack of the Aqua Apes ◆ 1995
4. Nightmare in 3-D ◆ 1996
5. Stay Away from the Treehouse ◆ 1996
6. The Eye of the Fortuneteller ◆ 1996
7. Fright Knight ◆ 1996
8. The Ooze ◆ 1996
9. The Revenge of the Shadow People ◆ 1996
10. The Bugman Lives! ◆ 1996
11. The Boy Who Ate Fear Street ◆ 1996
12. Night of the Werecat ◆ 1996
13. How to Be a Vampire ◆ 1996
14. Body Switchers from Outer Space ◆ 1996
15. Fright Christmas ◆ 1996
16. Don't Ever Get Sick at Granny's ◆ 1997
17. House of a Thousand Screams ◆ 1997
18. Camp Fear Ghouls ◆ 1997
19. Three Evil Wishes ◆ 1997
20. Spell of the Screaming Jokers ◆ 1997
21. The Creature from Club Lagoona ◆ 1997
22. Field of Screams ◆ 1997
23. Why I'm Not Afraid of Ghosts ◆ 1997
24. Monster Dog ◆ 1997
25. Halloween Bugs Me! ◆ 1997
26. Go to Your Tomb—Right Now! ◆ 1997
27. Parents from the 13th Dimension ◆ 1997
28. Hide and Shriek II ◆ 1998
29. The Tale of the Blue Monkey ◆ 1998
30. I Was a Sixth-Grade Zombie ◆ 1998
31. Escape of the He-Beast ◆ 1998
32. Caution: Aliens at Work ◆ 1998
33. Attack of the Vampire Worms ◆ 1998
34. Horror Hotel: The Vampire Checks In ◆ 1998
35. Horror Hotel: Ghost in the Guest Room ◆ 1998
36. Funhouse of Dr. Freek ◆ 1998

GHOSTS OF FEAR STREET CREEPY COLLECTION

1. Happy Hauntings ◆ 1998

2. Beastly Tales ◆ 1998
3. The Scream Tea ◆ 1998
4. Big Bad Bugs ◆ 1998
5. Ghoul Friends ◆ 1998
6. Weird Science ◆ 1998

FEATHER AND BONE: THE CROW CHRONICLES

Martini, Clem

KIDS CAN PRESS ◆ GRADES 5–8 ◆ A/R

ANIMAL FANTASY

In *The Mob,* the birds of the Crow clans have convened at the Gathering Tree. One crow, Kyp, endangers the flock and is banished. He returns to rescue the Family. Each book uses the device of an elder telling the stories of plagues, dangerous encounters with humans, and the search for a safe home.

1. The Mob ◆ 2004
2. The Plague ◆ 2005
3. The Judgment ◆ 2006

FELICITY *see* American Girls: Felicity

FIENDLY CORNERS

Leroe, Ellen W.

HYPERION ◆ GRADES 5–8

HORROR

In this small town, strange things happen. Like when the pizza parlor sends out toy robots with each pizza. The robots turn the residents into *Pizza Zombies* and Bryan Hartley must try to undo the damage and save the town. Another book features Jamie, who receives the contact lenses of a dead magician and is haunted by his ghost. A werewolf and an evil snowman cause problems in other books. Action, suspense, horror, and creatures make these a choice for the Goosebumps and Fear Street fans.

1. Monster Vision ◆ 1996
2. Pizza Zombies ◆ 1996
3. Revenge of the Hairy Horror ◆ 1996
4. Nasty the Snowman ◆ 1996

THE FIRE THIEF TRILOGY

Deary, Terry

KINGFISHER ◆ GRADES 4–6 ◆ A/R

FANTASY

Using the myth of Prometheus as a starting point, the Fire Thief books add action and humor. In the first book, after escaping punishment for stealing fire, Prometheus time-travels to the fictional Eden City in 1848 to begin his search for a human hero. Narrated by one of the characters, a young thief named Jim, these books include side remarks and contrivances that bring humor to the action. In subsequent books, Prometheus continues his time travels and his search.

1. The Fire Thief ◆ 2005
2. Flight of the Fire Thief ◆ 2006
3. The Fire Thief Fights Back ◆ 2007

FIREBALL

Christopher, John

DUTTON ◆ GRADES 5–7

FANTASY

Two cousins encounter a "fireball," which proves to be an entry into a parallel, "what-if" world in which the Roman Empire has endured and European society has been static for two thousand years. In our hemisphere, without interference from the white man, the Aztecs have conquered the Incas and taken over North and South America. Brad and Simon travel all over this world having one adventure after another. They provoke a revolution against the Empire in Britain, but then are victims of persecution by the new regime. They flee to the New World and become the heroes of an Aztec game. Then they run into a Chinese civilization that has also remained static. In all their adventures, they use their superior technical knowledge to come out on top. In the end, given the opportunity to go home, they decide to explore other possible worlds.

1. Fireball ◆ 1981
2. New Found Land ◆ 1983
3. Dragon Dance ◆ 1986

FIRST GRADE

Cohen, Miriam

GREENWILLOW ◆ GRADES K–2 ◆ A/R

REAL LIFE

In *Will I Have a Friend?* Jim is worried about the first day of school. By the end of the day, he has made a friend, Paul. Their adventure continues in *Best Friends*. The children in this class have many experiences that young readers will relate to—taking a test, getting lost, enjoying holidays, and performing in a play.

1. Will I Have a Friend? ◆ 1967
2. Best Friends ◆ 1971
3. The New Teacher ◆ 1972
4. Tough Jim ◆ 1974
5. When Will I Read? ◆ 1977
6. "Bee My Valentine" ◆ 1978
7. Lost in the Museum ◆ 1979
8. No Good in Art ◆ 1980
9. First Grade Takes a Test ◆ 1980
10. Jim Meets the Thing ◆ 1981
11. So What? ◆ 1982
12. See You Tomorrow, Charles ◆ 1983
13. Jim's Dog Muffins ◆ 1984
14. Starring First Grade ◆ 1985
15. Liar, Liar, Pants on Fire! ◆ 1985
16. Don't Eat Too Much Turkey! ◆ 1987
17. It's George! ◆ 1988
18. See You in Second Grade! ◆ 1989
19. The Real-Skin Rubber Monster Mask ◆ 1990

FIRST-GRADE FRIENDS

Maccarone, Grace
SCHOLASTIC ◆ GRADES 1–3
REAL LIFE

This series for beginning readers has a simple, rhyming text. The focus is on a group of first-graders—Sam, Pam, Dan, Jan, Kim, and Max. They are a diverse group: males and females; multicultural; one girl in a wheelchair. Sam is the one who seems to struggle with learning but then succeeds. These are amusing books about everyday experiences at school. *Fun with First-Grade Friends* (1996) includes the second and fourth books.

1. The Classroom Pet ◆ 1995
2. The Lunch Box Surprise ◆ 1995
3. The Gym Day Winner ◆ 1996
4. Recess Mess ◆ 1996
5. Sharing Time Troubles ◆ 1996
6. The Class Trip ◆ 1999
7. Softball Practice ◆ 2002
8. The Sleep Over ◆ 2003
9. Graduation Day Is Here ◆ 2006

FIRST GRADERS FROM MARS

Corey, Shana

SCHOLASTIC ◆ GRADES K–2 ◆ A/R

FANTASY

Horus is excited about first grade. He knows it will be different from "martiangarten." Maybe too different. Children will love the weird-looking creatures illustrated by Mark Teague. Other books feature classmates Pelly, Nergal, and Tera, who has a problem with being bossy.

1. Horus's Horrible Day ◆ 2001
2. The Problem with Pelly ◆ 2002
3. Nergal and the Great Space Race ◆ 2002
4. Tera, Star Student ◆ 2003

FITCH AND CHIP

Wheeler, Lisa

SIMON & SCHUSTER ◆ GRADES K–2 ◆ A/R

ANIMAL FANTASY

These beginning readers feature a pair of unlikely friends. Chip is a pig who is new to the neighborhood. When Chip goes to his new school, he sees a wolf. Fitch is the only wolf in the class and he is often on his own. The two become friends and enjoy helping each other. On Hero Day, they both pick meaningful heroes. Chip is apprehensive about having dinner with Fitch and his Granny. Will he end up being dinner? Designed for beginning readers, these books focus on themes such as tolerance and accepting differences. Frank Ansley's illustrations capture the fun and the friendship in these stories.

1. When Pigs Fly ◆ 2003
2. New Pig in Town ◆ 2003
3. Who's Afraid of Granny ◆ 2004
4. Invasion of the Pig Sisters ◆ 2005

FIVE LITTLE MONKEYS

Christelow, Eileen

CLARION ◆ GRADES K–3 ◆ A/R

ANIMAL FANTASY | HUMOR

The popular rhyme and fingerplay is expanded in these stories featuring a lively group of monkeys. They jump on a bed, tease an alligator, and narrowly miss being eaten. They even celebrate Mama's birthday. The hijinks and hilarity will delight young readers. There are also board books for younger readers.

1. Five Little Monkeys Jumping on the Bed ◆ 1989
2. Five Little Monkeys Sitting in a Tree ◆ 1991
3. Don't Wake Up Mama! Another Five Little Monkeys Story ◆ 1992
4. Five Little Monkeys with Nothing to Do ◆ 1996
5. Five Little Monkeys Wash the Car ◆ 2000
6. Five Little Monkeys Play Hide-and-Seek ◆ 2004

FLATFOOT FOX

Clifford, Eth

HOUGHTON MIFFLIN ◆ GRADES 2–4 ◆ A/R

ANIMAL FANTASY | HUMOR | MYSTERY

Flatfoot Fox is the smartest and greatest detective in the world, by his own admission and that of his faithful friend and companion, Secretary Bird. Principal Porcupine seeks Flatfoot's help in finding a missing schoolhouse. Flatfoot decides that he knows who stole it and just needs to find out how. Secretary Bird is shocked and thinks he should go about things in the usual way by finding clues and interviewing suspects. In the end, they find that Wackey Weasel caused the schoolhouse to be lost by moving the sign that pointed the way to it. In another case, Bashful Beaver and other animals are missing things that have been replaced with other things. This turns out to be the work of Rat a Tat Rat, who doesn't see anything wrong in "trading."

1. Flatfoot Fox and the Case of the Missing Eye ◆ 1990
2. Flatfoot Fox and the Case of the Nosy Otter ◆ 1992
3. Flatfoot Fox and the Case of the Missing Whooo ◆ 1993
4. Flatfoot Fox and the Case of the Bashful Beaver ◆ 1995
5. Flatfoot Fox and the Case of the Missing Schoolhouse ◆ 1997

FLETCHER MYSTERIES

Levy, Elizabeth

SIMON & SCHUSTER ◆ GRADES 2–5 ◆ A/R

ANIMAL FANTASY | MYSTERY

Fletcher, a basset hound aided by his personal flea, Jasper, solves mysteries with humor and panache.

1. A Hare-Raising Tail ◆ 2002
2. The Principal's on the Roof ◆ 2002
3. The Mixed-Up Mask Mystery ◆ 2003
4. The Mystery of the Too Many Elvises ◆ 2003
5. The Cool Ghoul Mystery ◆ 2004

FLICKA

O'Hara, Mary

HARPERCOLLINS ◆ GRADES 5–8 ◆ A/R

REAL LIFE

A dreamy young boy living on a ranch in Wyoming has trouble getting along with his practical father. His mother persuades his father to let him have a colt, hoping this will change things for him. Ken becomes devoted to the horse and is devastated when Flicka becomes seriously ill. His father is ready to shoot the ailing horse rather than see it suffer, but Ken persuades him to let her live. Kens wins his father's admiration in the end. The sequel, *Thunderhead,* is about Flicka's colt. Ken dreams of Thunderhead being a racehorse. The 1940s setting provides historical interest, and the relationships between the family members are complex and emotional.

1. My Friend Flicka ◆ 1941
2. Thunderhead ◆ 1943
3. Green Grass of Wyoming ◆ 1946

THE FLOODS

Thompson, Colin

HARPERCOLLINS ◆ GRADES 5–7 ◆ A/R

FANTASY | HUMOR

The Floods are not your ordinary family. They are a family of witches and wizards. There are seven kids, each stranger than the one before— except for Betty who looks normal but isn't. Having remodeled their house, the Floods are dismayed when the rude, noisy Dent family moves in next door. Well, they will just have to disappear. Creepy events, like when one of the Dents is devoured by a creature buried in the Floods' yard, will appeal to many readers.

1. Good Neighbors ◆ 2008
2. School Plot ◆ 2008
3. Witch Friend ◆ 2008

FLOWER GIRLS

Leverich, Kathleen

HARPERCOLLINS ◆ GRADES 2–4

REAL LIFE

Four girls with flower names all want to be flower girls, and each gets her chance, sometimes in a surprising way. Shy Violet ends up in a "punk" wedding, and Rose does the honors for her single mom. Each of the girls grows in an important way in "her" book.

1. Violet ◆ 1997
2. Daisy ◆ 1997
3. Heather ◆ 1997
4. Rose ◆ 1997

FLUFFY

McMullan, Kate

SCHOLASTIC ◆ GRADES K–2 ◆ A/R

ANIMAL FANTASY

Fluffy is a guinea pig in Ms. Day's class. His adventures connect with holidays and with seasons. One book describes how Fluffy goes to Emma's house for spring vacation. Readers will relate to Fluffy's experiences, which include learning to swim, taking a trip, and picking apples.

1. Fluffy Goes to School ◆ 1997
2. Fluffy's Thanksgiving ◆ 1997
3. Fluffy's Valentine's Day ◆ 1997
4. Fluffy Saves Christmas ◆ 1998
5. Fluffy's Happy Halloween ◆ 1998
6. Fluffy's Silly Summer ◆ 1998
7. Fluffy's Spring Vacation ◆ 1998
8. Fluffy Meets the Dinosaurs ◆ 1999
9. Fluffy's 100th Day at School ◆ 1999
10. Fluffy and the Firefighters ◆ 1999
11. Fluffy's School Bus Adventure ◆ 2000
12. Fluffy Meets the Tooth Fairy ◆ 2000
13. Fluffy's Funny Field Trip ◆ 2001
14. Fluffy Goes Apple Picking ◆ 2001
15. Fluffy Grows a Garden ◆ 2001
16. Fluffy Meets the Groundhog ◆ 2001
17. Fluffy's Lucky Day ◆ 2002
18. Fluffy Learns to Swim ◆ 2002
19. Fluffy, the Secret Santa ◆ 2002
20. Fluffy's Trick-or-Treat ◆ 2002
21. Fluffy Goes to Washington ◆ 2002
22. Fluffy and the Snow Pig ◆ 2003
23. Fluffy Plants a Jelly Bean ◆ 2004

FLY GUY

Arnold, Tedd

SCHOLASTIC ◆ GRADES K–2 ◆ A/R

HUMOR

The very simple text in these easy-readers is filled with fun. Fly Guy is a fly who meets a boy looking for a pet. In a surprise twist, Fly Guy says the boy's name—Buzz. Amazing! Kids love the fast-paced humor of this series.

1. Hi! Fly Guy ◆ 2005
2. Super Fly Guy ◆ 2006
3. Shoo, Fly Guy! ◆ 2006
4. There Was an Old Lady Who Swallowed Fly Guy ◆ 2007
5. Fly High, Fly Guy! ◆ 2008
6. Hooray for Fly Guy! ◆ 2008

FOG MOUND

Schade, Susan

SIMON & SCHUSTER ◆ GRADES 4–7 ◆ A/R

ANIMAL FANTASY

For Thelonious, a chipmunk, the existence of humans is a mysterious legend. After Thelonious is swept away from his home he arrives in the City of Ruins, a place of lawlessness filled with dangerous animals. He becomes friends with a bear, a porcupine, and a lizard. As they begin their journey to Fog Mound, they find clues about what happened to the humans. The chapters alternate between text and comic panels (illustrated by Jon Buller), which will appeal to fans of graphic novels.

1. Travels of Thelonious ◆ 2006
2. Faradawn ◆ 2007
3. Simon's Dream ◆ 2008

FOREVER ANGELS

Weyn, Suzanne

TROLL ◆ GRADES 4–7 ◆ A/R

FANTASY

Molly, Katie, Ashley, and Christina all have guardian angels. The books in this series generally feature one of the girls. In *An Angel for Molly*, for example, Molly finds her angel on a trip to Ireland. *Katie's Angel* describes Katie's loneliness after the death of her parents and how she finds and accepts her guardian angel. This is a series that will appeal to readers who like magic and who are reassured by the idea that someone is watching over them.

1. Ashley's Lost Angel ◆ 1995
2. The Baby Angel ◆ 1995
3. Christina's Dancing Angel ◆ 1995
4. Katie's Angel ◆ 1995
5. An Angel for Molly ◆ 1996
6. Ashley's Love Angel ◆ 1996
7. The Blossom Angel ◆ 1996
8. The Forgotten Angel ◆ 1996
9. The Golden Angel ◆ 1997
10. The Snow Angel ◆ 1997
11. The Movie Star Angel ◆ 1998

FORTUNE TELLERS CLUB

Enderle, Dotti

LLEWELLYN ◆ GRADES 4–6 ◆ A/R

FANTASY

Three girls—Gena, Anne, and Juniper, all 12—use their psychic powers to solve mysteries. In the first book, Juniper sees a vision of a missing child and the girls join together to find her. In *Mirror, Mirror,* Gena looks in the mirror and sees someone else. Ouija boards, Tarot cards, visions, magic crystals, ghosts, and more add to the spookiness of this series.

1. The Lost Girl ◆ 2003
2. Playing with Fire ◆ 2003
3. The Magic Shades ◆ 2003
4. Secret of Lost Arrow ◆ 2004
5. Hand of Fate ◆ 2004
6. Mirror, Mirror ◆ 2004
7. The Burning Pendulum ◆ 2005
8. The Ghost of Shady Lane ◆ 2005

THE FOURTEEN FOREST MICE

Iwamura, Kazuo

GARETH STEVENS ◆ GRADES K–3 ◆ A/R

ANIMAL FANTASY | FAMILY LIFE

The fourteen members of the Forest Mice family work and play together in the outdoors. There are four books in this series, one for each season. In the winter, the mice go sledding; in the spring, they picnic in the meadow; summer finds them doing their laundry in a stream; they admire the harvest moon in the fall. Readers will enjoy finding their favorite mice in each of these books about family togetherness and nature's beauty.

1. The Fourteen Forest Mice and the Harvest Moon Watch ◆ 1991
2. The Fourteen Forest Mice and the Spring Meadow Picnic ◆ 1991
3. The Fourteen Forest Mice and the Summer Laundry Day ◆ 1991
4. The Fourteen Forest Mice and the Winter Sledding Day ◆ 1991

FOURTH FLOOR TWINS

Adler, David A.

VIKING ◆ GRADES 1–4 ◆ A/R

MYSTERY

Two sets of twins who live on the fourth floor of an apartment building solve neighborhood mysteries by carefully observing and drawing conclusions. Their sleuthing leads them into many funny situations in these easy chapter books.

1. The Fourth Floor Twins and the Fish Snitch Mystery ◆ 1985
2. The Fourth Floor Twins and the Fortune Cookie Chase ◆ 1985
3. The Fourth Floor Twins and the Disappearing Parrot Trick ◆ 1986
4. The Fourth Floor Twins and the Silver Ghost Express ◆ 1986
5. The Fourth Floor Twins and the Skyscraper Parade ◆ 1987
6. The Fourth Floor Twins and the Sand Castle Contest ◆ 1988

FOX

Marshall, James

DIAL ◆ GRADES K–3 ◆ A/R

ANIMAL FANTASY | HUMOR

This series offers the hilarious adventures of a lovable, egotistical Fox and his friends Carmen the alligator and Dexter the pig. Fox's sister Louise, cool and collected, is the perfect foil to the dramatic Fox. During the series, Fox falls in love with the lovely Raisin, makes a video of himself, and learns how to twirl a baton, among other adventures.

1. Fox and His Friends ◆ 1982
2. Fox in Love ◆ 1982
3. Fox on Wheels ◆ 1983
4. Fox at School ◆ 1983
5. Fox All Week ◆ 1984
6. Fox on the Job ◆ 1988
7. Fox Be Nimble ◆ 1990
8. Fox Outfoxed ◆ 1992
9. Fox on Stage ◆ 1993

FRANCES

Hoban, Russell

HARPERCOLLINS ◆ GRADES K–3 ◆ A/R

ANIMAL FANTASY | FAMILY LIFE | HUMOR

Frances is a little badger who lives with her mother and father and younger sister Gloria. She quarrels and makes up with her friend Albert, adjusts to having a little sister, hides underneath the dining room table, and has a little song to sing for every occasion.

1. Bedtime for Frances ◆ 1960
2. A Baby Sister for Frances ◆ 1964
3. Bread and Jam for Frances ◆ 1964
4. A Birthday for Frances ◆ 1968
5. Best Friends for Frances ◆ 1969
6. A Bargain for Frances ◆ 1970
7. Eggs, Thoughts, and Other Frances Songs ◆ 1972

FRANCES IN THE FOURTH GRADE

Cooper, Ilene

KNOPF ◆ GRADES 3–5

FAMILY LIFE | REAL LIFE

Frances lives in a small town in Wisconsin, leading the ordinary life of an American schoolgirl. She likes to read and take ballet lessons, and although she has two friends, Lena and Polly, they are not part of the "popular" crowd. Her family—Mom, Dad and older siblings Elizabeth and Mike   are loving and supportive. During the series, she becomes less shy, makes new friends, and discovers new interests.

1. Frances Takes a Chance ◆ 1991
2. Frances Dances ◆ 1991
3. Frances Four-Eyes ◆ 1991
4. Frances and Friends ◆ 1991

FRANK AND ERNEST

Day, Alexandra

SCHOLASTIC ◆ GRADES 2–5

ANIMAL FANTASY | HUMOR

Frank, a bear, and his friend Ernest, an elephant, dress in normal human clothes and take a variety of temporary jobs. They take over a diner and a truck route and become managers of a baseball team. As they take on each new endeavor, they diligently learn the colorful slang of the trade.

When they work at the diner, they learn, among other things, that apple pie is "Eve with a lid" and milk is "cow juice." In subsequent books, the new words they learn are featured in boxes and are also listed at the end.

1. Frank and Ernest ◆ 1988
2. Frank and Ernest Play Ball ◆ 1990
3. Frank and Ernest on the Road ◆ 1994

FRANK AND JOE HARDY—THE CLUES BROTHERS *see* Hardy Boys: Frank and Joe Hardy: The Clues Brothers

FRANKLIN

Bourgeois, Paulette

SCHOLASTIC ◆ GRADES K–3 ◆ A/R

ANIMAL FANTASY

Franklin is a young turtle who goes through the trials and tribulations of childhood: making new friends, having sleepovers, being afraid of the dark. Franklin always finds a way out of his problems and has fun along the way. This has been a very popular series and related items include Franklin puppets.

1. Franklin in the Dark ◆ 1987
2. Hurry Up, Franklin ◆ 1991
3. Franklin Fibs ◆ 1992
4. Franklin Is Lost ◆ 1993
5. Franklin Is Bossy ◆ 1994
6. Franklin and Me ◆ 1995
7. Franklin Goes to School ◆ 1995
8. Franklin Is Messy ◆ 1995
9. Franklin Plays the Game ◆ 1995
10. Franklin Wants a Pet ◆ 1995
11. Franklin and the Tooth Fairy ◆ 1996
12. Franklin Has a Sleepover ◆ 1996
13. Franklin's Halloween ◆ 1996
14. Franklin's School Play ◆ 1996
15. Franklin Rides a Bike ◆ 1997
16. Franklin's Bad Day ◆ 1997
17. Franklin's Blanket ◆ 1997
18. Franklin's New Friend ◆ 1997
19. Finders Keepers for Franklin ◆ 1998
20. Franklin and the Thunderstorm ◆ 1998
21. Franklin Goes to Day Camp ◆ 1998
22. Franklin's Christmas Gift ◆ 1998
23. Franklin's Secret Club ◆ 1998

24. Franklin's Valentines ◆ 1998
25. Franklin's Class Trip ◆ 1999
26. Franklin's Neighborhood ◆ 1999
27. Franklin's Baby Sister ◆ 2000
28. Franklin Goes to the Hospital ◆ 2000
29. Franklin and Harriet ◆ 2001
30. Franklin's Thanksgiving ◆ 2001
31. Franklin Says I Love You ◆ 2002

FRANKLIN TV TIE-INS

1. Franklin and the Baby ◆ 1999
2. Franklin Says Sorry ◆ 1999
3. Franklin and the Hero ◆ 2000
4. Franklin Forgets ◆ 2000
5. Franklin Helps Out ◆ 2000
6. Franklin's Bicycle Helmet ◆ 2000
7. Franklin and the Babysitter ◆ 2001
8. Franklin Plants a Tree ◆ 2001
9. Franklin Runs Away ◆ 2001
10. Franklin's Birthday Party ◆ 2001
11. Franklin and Otter's Visit ◆ 2002
12. Franklin and the Big Kid ◆ 2002
13. Franklin Plays Hockey ◆ 2002
14. Franklin's Canoe Trip ◆ 2002
15. Franklin and His Friend ◆ 2002
16. Franklin and the Computer ◆ 2003
17. Franklin Makes a Deal ◆ 2003
18. Franklin Snoops ◆ 2003
19. Franklin Wants a Badge ◆ 2003
20. Franklin Forgives ◆ 2004
21. Franklin's Nickname ◆ 2004
22. Franklin and the New Teacher ◆ 2004
23. Franklin Celebrates ◆ 2005

FRANKLIN KIDS CAN READ

1. Franklin's Music Lessons ◆ 2002
2. Franklin and the Magic Show ◆ 2002
3. Franklin Stays Up ◆ 2003
4. Franklin's Trading Cards ◆ 2003
5. Franklin's Reading Club ◆ 2003
6. Franklin and the Contest ◆ 2004
7. Franklin and the Scooter ◆ 2004
8. Franklin's Surprise ◆ 2003
9. Franklin the Detective ◆ 2004
10. Franklin's Pumpkin ◆ 2004
11. Franklin and the Cookies ◆ 2005
12. Franklin's Pond Phantom ◆ 2005
13. Franklin's Library Book ◆ 2005

14. Franklin and the Tin Flute ◆ 2005
15. Franklin and the Bubble Gum ◆ 2006
16. Franklin's Soapbox Derby ◆ 2006

FRANNY K. STEIN, MAD SCIENTIST

Benton, Jim

SIMON & SCHUSTER ◆ GRADES 2–5 ◆ A/R

FANTASY

Franny is smart and she loves science. She creates an invention for Valentine's Day, but her new lab assistant, Igor (a dog, part labrador retriever), accidentally uses it to release a giant Cupid. How will Franny and Igor capture the Cupid? With many cartoon-style illustrations by the author, this will appeal to readers who like Ricky Ricotta and Johnny Mutton. Companion books encourage readers to be creative.

1. Lunch Walks Among Us ◆ 2003
2. Attack of the 50-Foot Cupid ◆ 2004
3. The Invisible Fran ◆ 2004
4. The Fran that Time Forgot ◆ 2005
5. Frantastic Voyage ◆ 2005
6. The Fran with Four Brains ◆ 2007
7. The Frandidate ◆ 2008

FRASER BROTHERS

Cutler, Jane

FARRAR ◆ GRADES 3–5 ◆ A/R

REAL LIFE

In *No Dogs Allowed,* Edward Fraser, 5, and his brother Jason, 8, have familiar experiences that middle-elementary readers will relate to. Because of their allergies, they cannot have a dog. So Edward pretends to be a dog. In each additional book, the boys are a little older. Readers can follow their growth and changes. For example, in *'Gator Aid,* Edward is a second-grader and Jason is a fifth-grader.

1. No Dogs Allowed ◆ 1992
2. Rats! ◆ 1996
3. 'Gator Aid ◆ 1999
4. Leap Frog ◆ 2002

THE FREAKY JOE CLUB

McMahon, P. J.

ALADDIN ◆ **GRADES 3–5** ◆ **A/R**

FANTASY

Conor, Timmy, and Jack have a mission. They want to solve mysteries in their hometown of Ship's Cove, Texas. They form the Freaky Joe Club with a list of rules that are revealed as needed. In one book, the boys investigate missing hockey equipment. With short chapters and lots of action, this series will appeal to reluctant readers.

1. The Mystery of the Swimming Gorilla: Secret File #1 ◆ 2004
2. The Case of the Smiling Shark: Secret File #2 ◆ 2004
3. The Mystery of the Morphing Hockey Stick: Secret File #3 ◆ 2004
4. The Case of the Psychic Hamster: Secret File #4 ◆ 2005
5. The Mystery of the Disappearing Dinosaurs: Secret File #5 ◆ 2005
6. The Case of the Singing SeaDragons: Secret File #6 ◆ 2005

FRED AND ANTHONY

Primavera, Elise

HYPERION ◆ **GRADES 3–4** ◆ **A/R**

HUMOR | HORROR

Humor and horror join forces in this series for middle-grade readers. In *Fred and Anthony Escape from the Netherworld,* the boys find a portal to a world of ghosts and monsters . . . all because they were trying to escape from doing their school assignment. With slapstick humor and numerous illustrations, this should attract reluctant readers.

1. Fred and Anthony Escape from the Netherworld ◆ 2007
2. Fred and Anthony Meet the Demented Super-de-Germ-O Zombie ◆ 2007
3. Fred and Anthony Meet the Heinie Goblins from the Black Lagoon ◆ 2008
4. Fred and Anthony's Horrible, Hideous Back-to-School Thriller ◆ 2008

FRED BEAR

Hayes, Sarah

LITTLE, BROWN ◆ **GRADES K–1** ◆ **A/R**

FANTASY | HUMOR

Fred is a toy bear who has several exciting adventures. He is lost in the dump, and left in the park overnight. His owner's dog tries to spoil Fred's picnic and a naughty little girl tries to steal Fred. Through it all, Fred is unflappable and children are delighted.

1. This Is the Bear ◆ 1986
2. This Is the Bear and the Picnic Lunch ◆ 1988
3. This Is the Bear and the Scary Night ◆ 1992
4. This Is the Bear and the Bad Little Girl ◆ 1995

FREDDY

Brooks, Walter R.
KNOPF ◆ GRADES 3–5 ◆ A/R

ANIMAL FANTASY

Freddy is a truly remarkable pig. He is by turns a cowboy, a detective, and a balloon rider. He has all these adventures at the Bean farm with his friends Jinx the cat, Mrs. Wiggins the cow, Charles the rooster, and the ducks Alice and Emma. Their relationships and humanlike qualities lead to some very funny situations.

1. To and Again (later renamed Freddy Goes to Florida) ◆ 1927
2. More To and Again (later renamed Freddy Goes to the North Pole) ◆ 1930
3. Freddy the Detective ◆ 1932
4. The Story of Freginald ◆ 1936
5. The Clockwork Twin ◆ 1937
6. Wiggins for President (later renamed Freddy the Politician) ◆ 1939
7. Freddy's Cousin Weedly ◆ 1940
8. Freddy and the Ignormus ◆ 1941
9. Freddy and the Perilous Adventure ◆ 1942
10. Freddy and the Bean Home News ◆ 1943
11. Freddy and Mr. Camphor ◆ 1944
12. Freddy and the Popinjay ◆ 1945
13. Freddy the Pied Piper ◆ 1946
14. Freddy the Magician ◆ 1947
15. Freddy Goes Camping ◆ 1948
16. Freddy Plays Football ◆ 1949
17. Freddy the Cowboy ◆ 1950
18. Freddy Rides Again ◆ 1951
19. Freddy the Pilot ◆ 1952
20. Freddy and the Space Ship ◆ 1953
21. Freddy and the Men from Mars ◆ 1954
22. Freddy and the Baseball Team from Mars ◆ 1955
23. Freddy and Simon the Dictator ◆ 1956
24. Freddy and the Flying Saucer Plans ◆ 1957
25. Freddy and the Dragon ◆ 1958

FREDDY AURATUS *see* The Golden Hamster Saga

FREDDY (KLEIN) *see* Ready, Freddy!

FRIENDS AND AMIGOS

Giff, Patricia Reilly
BANTAM DOUBLEDAY DELL ◆ GRADES 2–4 ◆ A/R
REAL LIFE

Sarah and Anna are best friends who are often bothered by a pesky class-mate, Benjamin. In one book, Sarah tries to learn Spanish while Anna is at camp. In another, the girls organize a program for Columbus Day and plan for a visit from Anna's cousin from Colombia. Their librarian, Mrs. Munoz, helps them with many of their projects. Anna and her family are bilingual (speaking English and Spanish) and the series incorporates simple Spanish words, phrases, and lessons into the text.

1. Adios, Anna ◆ 1995
2. Say Hola, Sarah ◆ 1995
3. Ho, Ho Benjamin, Feliz Navidád ◆ 1995
4. Happy Birthday Anna, Sorpresa! ◆ 1996
5. Good Dog, Bonita ◆ 1996
6. It's a Fiesta, Ben ◆ 1996

FRIENDS FOR A SEASON

Byrd, Sandra
BETHANY HOUSE ◆ GRADES 5–8 ◆ A/R
REAL LIFE | VALUES

Faith plays a role in each of these stories about young teen girls facing new situations. In *Island Girl*, 13-year-old Meg—on vacation at her grandparents' farm in Oregon—makes friends with Tia, whose Hispanic father oversees the farm, and tries to decide whether to live with her father or with her mother and her new husband. In *Chopstick*, 13-year-olds Paige and Kate are competing in a worship-music contest, each so sure of winning that she has already promised the $500 prize to charity.

1. Island Girl ◆ 2005
2. Chopstick ◆ 2005
3. Red Velvet ◆ 2005
4. Daisy Chains ◆ 2006

FRIGHTMARES

Kehret, Peg

MINSTREL/POCKET BOOKS ◆ GRADES 2–6 ◆ A/R

ADVENTURE | MYSTERY

Rosie and Kayo have a Care Club to look after animals, which keeps getting them into dangerous situations that give their parents "frightmares." An elderly neighbor has to find a new home for her cat because her nephew is allergic to it. Naturally, the girls try to help her, and in the process they discover that someone is trying to poison the old woman. As the plot unfolds, the girls get into ever deeper trouble, and even the police can't help. A similar situation occurs when the girls go camping with Rosie's parents. Everything always ends happily, but readers are in for some scares.

1. Cat Burglar on the Prowl ◆ 1995
2. Bone Breath and the Vandals ◆ 1995
3. Don't Go Near Mrs. Tallie ◆ 1995
4. Desert Danger ◆ 1995
5. The Ghost Followed Us Home ◆ 1996
6. Race to Disaster ◆ 1996
7. Screaming Eagles ◆ 1996
8. Backstage Fright ◆ 1996

FROG

Mayer, Mercer

DIAL ◆ GRADES K–1

ANIMAL FANTASY | HUMOR

A boy and his dog go out to catch a frog. They give up in disgust, but the frog has been having fun and decides to go home with them. When the frog stows away in the boy's pocket for a family visit to a fancy restaurant, the words "fancy restaurant" are there on the sign. The boy, the dog, and the frog acquire a turtle, who joins their adventures. One day, the frog runs away, and the boy and dog have several mishaps looking for him. These books are wordless except for occasional signposts in the illustrations.

1. A Boy, a Dog, and a Frog ◆ 1967
2. Frog, Where Are You? ◆ 1969
3. A Boy, a Dog, a Frog, and a Friend ◆ 1971
4. Frog on His Own ◆ 1973
5. Frog Goes to Dinner ◆ 1974
6. One Frog Too Many ◆ 1975

FROG

Velthuijs, Max

MORROW ◆ GRADES K–2

ANIMAL FANTASY | VALUES

Four animal friends deal with life issues in these gentle stories. Hare is the one who is wise and mentors the other three. When Frog feels very strange, "hot and cold and something going thump thump inside," Hare decides he must be in love with the white duck. Pig says they can't be in love because "you're green and she's white." Frog doesn't let that bother him, and they fall in love. When a stranger moves into their neighborhood, Pig says he is just a dirty rat, but Hare pleads for tolerance. Rat proves to be hard-working, helpful, and clever. In another book, when a blackbird dies, the four friends find comfort in the continuance of everyday life.

1. Frog in Love ◆ 1989
2. Frog and the Birdsong ◆ 1991
3. Frog in Winter ◆ 1993
4. Frog and the Stranger ◆ 1994
5. Frog Is Frightened ◆ 1995
6. Frog Is a Hero ◆ 1996
7. Frog Is Frog ◆ 2000
8. Frog and the Wide World ◆ 2000
9. Frog Is Sad ◆ 2003

FROG AND TOAD

Lobel, Arnold

HARPERCOLLINS ◆ GRADES K–3 ◆ A/R

ANIMAL FANTASY | HUMOR

Frog and Toad live in little houses in the forest, and they like to visit each other, take walks, and enjoy the seasons together. Frog is the more sensible of the two and gently helps out as Toad worries about how his bathing suit looks or doing things on his list. In each of the five little stories that make up these easy readers, they express their friendship with humor and affection. Companion volumes include *The Frog and Toad Coloring Book* and *The Frog and Toad Pop-up Book*.

1. Frog and Toad Are Friends ◆ 1970
2. Frog and Toad Together ◆ 1972
3. Frog and Toad All Year ◆ 1976
4. Days with Frog and Toad ◆ 1979

FROGGY

London, Jonathan

VIKING ◆ GRADES K–3 ◆ A/R

ANIMAL FANTASY | HUMOR

Froggy and his parents go through the simple routines of living and learning, with amusing takes on the parent-child relationship. Froggy doesn't want to learn to swim; when he finally does learn, he doesn't want to stop. He has a terrible dream the night before his first day of school—he goes to school in his underwear. All ends happily when he wakes up and leapfrogs with his parents out to the bus stop.

1. Froggy Gets Dressed ◆ 1992
2. Let's Go, Froggy! ◆ 1994
3. Froggy Learns to Swim ◆ 1995
4. Froggy Goes to School ◆ 1996
5. Froggy's First Kiss ◆ 1998
6. Froggy Plays Soccer ◆ 1999
7. Froggy's Halloween ◆ 1999
8. Froggy Bakes a Cake ◆ 2000
9. Froggy Goes to Bed ◆ 2000
10. Froggy's Best Christmas ◆ 2000
11. Froggy Eats Out ◆ 2001
12. Froggy Goes to the Doctor ◆ 2002
13. Froggy Plays in the Band ◆ 2002
14. Froggy's Baby Sister ◆ 2003
15. Froggy's Day with Dad ◆ 2004
16. Froggy's Sleepover ◆ 2005
17. Froggy Rides a Bike ◆ 2006
18. Froggy Plays T-Ball ◆ 2007
19. Froggy Goes to Camp ◆ 2008

FROM THE HIGHLY SCIENTIFIC NOTEBOOKS OF PHINEAS L. MACGUIRE

see Phineas L. MacGuire

FUDGE

Blume, Judy

BANTAM ◆ GRADES 3–5 ◆ A/R

HUMOR | REAL LIFE

Peter Hatcher is a fairly ordinary middle school kid with an extraordinary nuisance of a little brother known as Fudge. (Besides saying embarrassing things in public and ruining Peter's school projects, Fudge swallows

Peter's pet turtle whole.) The Hatchers spend a summer sharing a rented house in Maine with Sheila Tubman's family. Peter hates Sheila when the summer begins, but after some shared adventures babysitting Fudge, they begin to get along. Sheila is featured in a related book, *Otherwise Known as Sheila the Great* (1972).

1. Tales of a Fourth Grade Nothing ◆ 1972
2. Superfudge ◆ 1980
3. Fudge-a-mania ◆ 1990
4. Double Fudge ◆ 2002

FULL HOUSE: CLUB STEPHANIE

Various authors

POCKET BOOKS ◆ GRADES 4–6 ◆ A/R

REAL LIFE

In the other Full House series books, the focus is on the activities of the Tanner family. In this group, the focus is on Stephanie and her friends Darcy, Anna, Kayla, and Allie and their interests: friendship, boys, projects, boys, summertime, and boys. Stephanie and her friends are often bothered by a group of snobby, popular girls called the Flamingoes. Readers who enjoy the television show will like seeing Stephanie in her own adventures. They will also like the breezy style of writing and the light, entertaining plots.

1. Fun, Sun, and Flamingoes (Quin-Harkin, Janet) ◆ 1997
2. Fireworks and Flamingoes (Ecco, Emily) ◆ 1997
3. Flamingo Revenge (Quin-Harkin, Janet) ◆ 1997
4. Too Many Flamingoes (Eisenberg, Lisa) ◆ 1998
5. Friend or Flamingo? (Haley, Wendy) ◆ 1998
6. Flamingoes Overboard! (Alexander, Brandon) ◆ 1998
7. Five Flamingo Summer (Clark, Kathy) ◆ 1999
8. Forget It, Flamingoes! (Clark, Kathy) ◆ 1999
9. Flamingoes Forever? (Clark, Kathy) ◆ 1999
10. Truth or Dare (Clark, Kathy) ◆ 2001
11. Summertime Secrets (Clark, Kathy) ◆ 2001
12. The Real Thing (Clark, Kathy) ◆ 2001
13. Rumor Has It (Clark, Kathy) ◆ 2001
14. Three's a Crowd (Clark, Kathy) ◆ 2001
15. He's the One! (Clark, Kathy) ◆ 2001

FULL HOUSE: DEAR MICHELLE

Various authors

HARPERCOLLINS ◆ GRADES 2–5 ◆ A/R

REAL LIFE

The success of Full House—now in reruns on cable—and of the Olsen twins who played Michelle—has generated another series. Michelle is responsible for the advice column in the class newspaper and receives questions about topics ranging from Christmas to pet rabbits. You can imagine the mishaps that result from her suggestions.

1. Help! There's a Ghost in My Room! (Katschke, Judy) ◆ 2003
2. How Will Santa Find Me? (Katschke, Judy) ◆ 2003
3. Who Will Be My Valentine? (Waricha, Jean) ◆ 2003
4. I've Got Bunny Business (Noll, Katherine) ◆ 2004

FULL HOUSE: MICHELLE

Various authors

POCKET BOOKS ◆ GRADES 2–4 ◆ A/R

FAMILY LIFE | REAL LIFE

As the youngest child in the main family in the *Full House* TV series, Michelle is cute and sassy. The books in this series put her in situations involving her older sisters, D.J. and Stephanie, and her dad, Danny. Other regulars include Joey Gladstone and Uncle Jesse. Michelle is seen participating in sleepovers, ballet, science fair projects, efforts to be cool, and other familiar activities.

1. The Great Pet Project (Carrol, Jacqueline) ◆ 1995
2. The Super-Duper Sleepover Party (Stine, Megan) ◆ 1995
3. My Two Best Friends (Dubowski, Cathy East) ◆ 1995
4. Lucky, Lucky Day (O'Neil, Laura) ◆ 1995
5. The Ghost in My Closet (Dubowski, Cathy East) ◆ 1995
6. Ballet Surprise (Waricha, Jean) ◆ 1996
7. Major League Trouble (O'Neil, Laura) ◆ 1996
8. My Fourth-Grade Mess (Dubowski, Cathy East) ◆ 1996
9. Bunk 3, Teddy and Me (Dubowski, Cathy East) ◆ 1996
10. My Best Friend Is a Movie Star! (Dubowski, Cathy East) ◆ 1996
11. The Big Turkey Escape (Waricha, Jean) ◆ 1996
12. The Substitute Teacher (Dubowski, Cathy East) ◆ 1997
13. Calling All Planets (Verney, Sarah) ◆ 1997
14. I've Got a Secret (Dubowski, Cathy East) ◆ 1997
15. How to Be Cool (Weyn, Suzanne) ◆ 1997
16. The Not-So-Great Outdoors (Waricha, Jean) ◆ 1997
17. My Ho-Ho Horrible Christmas (Preiss, Pauline) ◆ 1997
18. My Almost Perfect Plan (Verney, Sarah) ◆ 1998
19. April Fools! (Alexander, Nina) ◆ 1998
20. My Life Is a Three-Ring Circus (Dubowski, Cathy East) ◆ 1998
21. Welcome to My Zoo (Waricha, Jean) ◆ 1998
22. The Problem with Pen Pals (McMahon, Maggie) ◆ 1998

23. Merry Christmas, World! (Davis, Gibbs) ◆ 1998
24. Tap Dance Trouble (Dubowski, Cathy East) ◆ 1999
25. The Fastest Turtle in the West (Dubowski, Cathy East) ◆ 1999
26. The Baby-Sitting Boss (Dubowski, Cathy East) ◆ 1999
27. The Wish I Wish I Never Wished (Dubowski, Cathy East) ◆ 1999
28. Pigs, Pies and Plenty of Problems (Dubowski, Cathy East) ◆ 1999
29. If I Were President (Katschke, Judy) ◆ 1999
30. How to Meet a Superstar (Carrol, Jacqueline) ◆ 2000
31. Unlucky in Lunch (Dubowski, Cathy East) ◆ 2000
32. There's Gold in My Backyard! (Katschke, Judy) ◆ 2000
33. Field Day Foul-Up (Dubowski, Cathy East) ◆ 2000
34. Smile and Say "Woof!" (Katschke, Judy) ◆ 2001
35. The Penguin Skates! (Katschke, Judy) ◆ 2001
36. For the Birds (Carrol, Jacqueline) ◆ 2001
37. Is This Funny, or What? (Krohn, Katherine) ◆ 2001
38. Camp Hide-a-Pet (West, Cathy) ◆ 2001
39. Hip, Hip, Parade! (Katschke, Judy) ◆ 2001
40. Too Many Teddies (Reymes, Ellen) ◆ 2001

FULL HOUSE: SISTERS

Various authors

SIMON & SCHUSTER ◆ GRADES 3–5 ◆ A/R

FAMILY LIFE | REAL LIFE

Stephanie and Michelle have the usual sibling interactions. Sometimes they are in conflict—as when Stephanie is Michelle's camp counselor. At other times, they help each other . . . sort of. When Michelle tries to be a matchmaker between Stephanie and a neighbor boy, there is a big mix-up. The ongoing popularity of this series (in reruns on cable) and of the Olsen twins (who played Michelle) stimulates demand for these books.

1. Two on the Town (Speregen, Devra Newberger) ◆ 1998
2. One Boss Too Many (Speregen, Devra Newberger) ◆ 1998
3. And the Winner Is (Alexander, Nina) ◆ 1999
4. How to Hide a Horse (Winfrey, Elizabeth) ◆ 1999
5. Problems in Paradise (Perlberg, Deborah) ◆ 1999
6. Will You Be My Valentine? (Burke, Diana G.) ◆ 2000
7. Let's Put on a Show (Winfrey, Elizabeth) ◆ 2000
8. Baby-Sitters & Company (Alexander, Nina) ◆ 2000
9. Substitute Sister (Burke, Diana G.) ◆ 2000
10. Ask Miss Know-It-All (Weyn, Suzanne) ◆ 2000
11. Matchmakers (Gallagher, Diana G.) ◆ 2000
12. No-Rules Weekend! (Strickland, Brad) ◆ 2001
13. A Dog's Life (Gallagher, Diana G.) ◆ 2001
14. Once Upon a Mix-Up (Ellis, Carol) ◆ 2001

FULL HOUSE: STEPHANIE

Various authors

POCKET BOOKS ◆ GRADES 4–6 ◆ A/R

FAMILY LIFE | REAL LIFE

Fans of the TV comedy *Full House* will enjoy reading these books about Stephanie. As the middle daughter (D.J. is older; Michelle is younger), Stephanie sometimes struggles to get attention and cope with problems. After the death of Stephanie's mom, her dad—Danny—struggles to raise three daughters. His friend Joey Gladstone and the girls' Uncle Jesse help him. Plots include Stephanie wanting to be on her school's TV show and what happens when she takes riding lessons. Girlfriends and the beginning of relationships with boys are also featured. These are lighthearted problems that are neatly wrapped up at the end of each book.

1. Phone Call from a Flamingo (Speregen, Devra Newberger) ◆ 1993
2. The Boy-Oh-Boy Next Door (Miami, Rita) ◆ 1993
3. Twin Troubles (Wright, Mary) ◆ 1994
4. Hip Hop Till You Drop (Speregen, Devra Newberger) ◆ 1994
5. Here Comes the Brand-New Me (Carroll, Jacqueline) ◆ 1994
6. The Secret's Out (Kimball, Katie) ◆ 1994
7. Daddy's Not-So-Little Girl (Thomas, Lucinda) ◆ 1995
8. P.S. Friends Forever (Speregen, Devra Newberger) ◆ 1995
9. Getting Even With The Flamingoes (Umansky, Diane) ◆ 1995
10. The Dude of My Dreams (Bentley, Karen) ◆ 1995
11. Back-to-School Cool (Speregen, Devra Newberger) ◆ 1995
12. Picture Me Famous (Simon, Lisa) ◆ 1995
13. Two-For-One Christmas Fun (Landesman, Peter) ◆ 1996
14. The Big Fix-up Mix-up (Speregen, Devra Newberger) ◆ 1996
15. Ten Ways to Wreck a Date (Landesman, Peter) ◆ 1996
16. Wish Upon a VCR (Speregen, Devra Newberger) ◆ 1996
17. Doubles or Nothing (West, Eliza) ◆ 1996
18. Sugar and Spice Advice (Speregen, Devra Newberger) ◆ 1996
19. Never Trust a Flamingo (Speregen, Devra Newberger) ◆ 1996
20. The Truth About Boys (Costello, Emily) ◆ 1997
21. Crazy About the Future (Speregen, Devra Newberger) ◆ 1997
22. My Secret Secret Admirer (Umansky, Diane) ◆ 1997
23. Blue Ribbon Christmas (Costello, Emily) ◆ 1997
24. The Story on Older Boys (Weyn, Suzanne) ◆ 1998
25. My Three Weeks as a Spy (Steiber, Ellen) ◆ 1998
26. No Business Like Show Business (Herman, Gail) ◆ 1998
27. Mail-Order Brother (O'Neil, Laura) ◆ 1998
28. To Cheat or Not to Cheat (Speregen, Devra Newberger) ◆ 1998
29. Winning Is Everything (Dokey, Cameron) ◆ 1999
30. Hello Birthday, Good-Bye Friend (O'Neil, Laura) ◆ 1999
31. The Art of Keeping Secrets (Verney, Sarah) ◆ 1999

32. What Can You Grow on a Family Tree? (Speregen, Devra Newberger)
♦ 1999
33. Girl Power! (Steiber, Ellen) ♦ 1999

FUN DAY FAIRIES *see* Rainbow Magic: Fun Day Fairies

FUNNY BOY

Gutman, Dan
HYPERION ♦ GRADES 3–5
FANTASY | HUMOR

Meet the world's newest superhero—Funny Boy. He uses wit and humor to solve problems. He stops the alien barbers from giving everyone a bad hair day. This is part of the L.A.F. series from Hyperion that will appeal to fans of Dav Pilkey.

1. Funny Boy Meets the Airsick Alien from Andromeda ♦ 1999
2. Funny Boy Versus the Bubble-Brained Barbers from the Big Bang ♦ 2000
3. Funny Boy Takes On the Chit-Chatting Cheeses from Chattanooga ♦ 2001

FUNNY FIRSTS

Thaler, Mike
TROLL ♦ GRADES K–1
HUMOR

How did you cope with your first trip to the dentist? Or with the first time you went to camp? Snarvey Gooper faces these first-time events and finds the humor in them. Taking his pet to the vet, moving to a new neighborhood, even trick-or-treating for the first time are anxious moments for Snarvey. Readers will be assured by how he worries and frets before finding a way to overcome his fears.

1. Camp Rotten Time ♦ 1993
2. Fang the Dentist ♦ 1993
3. My Cat Is Going to the Dogs ♦ 1993
4. The Schmo Must Go On ♦ 1994
5. Love Stinks ♦ 1996
6. Moving to Mars ♦ 1996
7. I'm Dracula, Who Are You? ♦ 1997

FUNNYBONES

Ahlberg, Allan

GREENWILLOW; MULBERRY ◆ GRADES K–3

FANTASY | HUMOR

Colorful cartoon-style illustrations show big skeleton, little skeleton, and their dog skeleton. In one book, they go for a late night walk, hoping to frighten someone. No one is out, so they play in the park and visit the skeleton animals in the zoo. In another book, they solve some mini-mysteries as they drive around town. There is lots of fun with these not-so-scary skeletons.

1. Funnybones ◆ 1980
2. The Black Cat ◆ 1990
3. The Pet Shop ◆ 1990
4. Dinosaur Dreams ◆ 1991
5. Mystery Tour ◆ 1991
6. Skeleton Crew ◆ 1991
7. Bumps in the Night ◆ 1991
8. Give the Dog a Bone ◆ 1991
9. Ghost Train ◆ 1992

FURTHER TALES

Catanese, P. W.

ALADDIN ◆ GRADES 4–6 ◆ A/R

FANTASY

Expanded fairy tales are very popular and this series will add to that genre. In *The Brave Apprentice,* Patch, a tailor's apprentice, is called upon to destroy the giant trolls that are threatening the kingdom. Like the Brave Little Tailor before him, Patch uses his cleverness to defeat the trolls. Of course, *The Thief and the Beanstalk* reworks Jack and the Beanstalk. A young ruffian, Nick, meets Jack, who gives him magical beans that take him to the land of giants and a treasure but instead of stealing the treasure, Nick decides to free the giant's wife.

1. The Brave Apprentice: A Further Tales Adventure ◆ 2005
2. The Eye of the Warlock: A Further Tales Adventure ◆ 2005
3. The Thief and the Beanstalk: A Further Tales Adventure ◆ 2006
4. The Mirror's Tale: A Further Tales Adventure ◆ 2006
5. The Riddle of the Gnome: A Further Tales Adventure ◆ 2007

GALAXY OF FEAR *see* Star Wars Galaxy of Fear

GARY PAULSEN'S WORLD OF ADVENTURE *see* World of Adventure

THE GASKITTS

Ahlberg, Allan

CANDLEWICK ◆ GRADES 2–4 ◆ A/R

FANTASY

In *The Man Who Wore All His Clothes,* brief, easy-reading chapters tell the action-packed, entertaining story of how the Gaskitt family—Santa Claus-playing father, taxi-driver mother, and twins Gus and Gloria—contribute to the capture of a bank robber. In *The Woman Who Won Things,* Mrs. Gaskitt has a streak of good luck and the twins must cope with a substitute teacher with an unfortunate habit.

1. The Man Who Wore All His Clothes ◆ 2001
2. The Woman Who Won Things ◆ 2002
3. The Cat Who Got Carried Away ◆ 2003
4. The Children Who Smelled a Rat ◆ 2005

THE GATEKEEPERS

Horowitz, Anthony

SCHOLASTIC ◆ GRADES 5–9 ◆ A/R

ADVENTURE | FANTASY

Five teens are destined to save the world from the evil of the Old Ones. In *Raven's Gate,* Matt, 14, is sent to live in a village in Yorkshire with Mrs. Deverill, who turns out to be a witch. Raven's Gate, an ancient portal to the world of evil, is opening and it is up to Matt to stop it. In *Evil Star,* Matt travels to South America and meets Pedro, a Peruvian teen who joins in the efforts to fight evil. In *Nightrise,* two more teens join the struggle—Scott and Jamie, Native American twins with telepathic skills. Readers of Horowitz's Alex Rider books will enjoy the fast-paced, almost breathless action of this series.

1. Raven's Gate ◆ 2006
2. Evil Star ◆ 2006
3. Nightrise ◆ 2007

GATOR GIRLS

Calmenson, Stephanie, and Joanna Cole

MORROW ◆ GRADES 1–3 ◆ A/R

ANIMAL FANTASY | HUMOR

Easy-to-read, humorous stories feature likable friends Amy and Allie Gator and a pest, Marvin Gator. The short, fast-paced chapters involve childlike problems with predictable endings that leave the characters and the readers happy. Camp Wogga-Bog almost ruins the summer for the Gator girls, especially when Allie gets accepted at the last minute—without her friend Amy. Quick thinking averts that near disaster. Lots of action and laughter along with strong friendship models will entertain early readers.

1. The Gator Girls ◆ 1995
2. Rockin' Reptiles ◆ 1997
3. Get Well, Gators! ◆ 1998
4. Gator Halloween ◆ 1999

GENGHIS KHAN

Sharmat, Marjorie Weinman

RANDOM HOUSE ◆ GRADES 2–3

HUMOR

The Shedd family's life changes dramatically when young Fred brings home a stray dog, Duz. The dog only *looks* mean and scary, resembling Dracula with fanglike teeth. Duz wins a look-alike contest and is chosen to replace a famous movie star dog. The family moves to Hollywood for more adventures with Duz, alias Genghis Khan. Short sentences, quick action, and easy chapters will make this series attractive to early readers.

1. The Great Genghis Khan Look-Alike Contest ◆ 1993
2. Genghis Khan: A Dog Star Is Born ◆ 1994
3. Genghis Khan: A Dog-Gone Hollywood ◆ 1995
4. Dirty Tricks ◆ 2000

GEORGE AND HIS DRAGON

Robertson, M. P.

PUTNAM; DIAL ◆ GRADES K–2 ◆ A/R

FANTASY

George finds a special egg and cares for it until it hatches into a baby dragon who looks to George as his mother. George accepts the responsibility and teaches the dragon basic behaviors like breathing fire and flying until the dragon is able to leave George to find his own family. In the second book, the dragon returns and, with George's help, rescues a baby dragon from a witch.

1. The Egg ◆ 2001
2. The Great Dragon Rescue ◆ 2004
3. The Dragon Snatcher ◆ 2004

GEORGE AND MARTHA

Marshall, James

HOUGHTON MIFFLIN ◆ GRADES K–2 ◆ A/R

ANIMAL FANTASY | HUMOR

Two hippos are best friends in this series. They have many little quarrels caused by miscommunication, but all comes out happily in the end. In one story, Martha doesn't want to use suntan lotion and gets sunburned. George doesn't say "I told you so" because "that's not what friends do." Most of the stories end with this kind of twist. In one, George has a secret club, and Martha is furious until she finds out it's her fan club. Each book has several self-contained stories, with full-color cartoon-like illustrations on every other page.

1. George and Martha ◆ 1972
2. George and Martha Encore ◆ 1973
3. George and Martha Rise and Shine ◆ 1976
4. George and Martha One Fine Day ◆ 1978
5. George and Martha, Tons of Fun ◆ 1980
6. George and Martha Back in Town ◆ 1984
7. George and Martha Round and Round ◆ 1988

GEORGE AND MARTHA EARLY READERS

1. George and Martha ◆ 2007
2. George and Martha: Two Great Friends ◆ 2007
3. George and Martha Round and Round ◆ 2008
4. George and Martha: The Best of Friends ◆ 2008

GEORGE AND MATILDA MOUSE

Buchanan, Heather S.

SIMON & SCHUSTER ◆ GRADES K–3 ◆ A/R

ANIMAL FANTASY

George and Matilda are lovable and adventurous mice who live in an old dollhouse with their family. Readers are able to look at the world through the eyes of small mice and watch their escapades.

1. George Mouse's First Summer ◆ 1985

2. Emily Mouse's First Adventure ◆ 1985
3. George Mouse Learns to Fly ◆ 1985
4. Emily Mouse Saves the Day ◆ 1985
5. Matilda Mouse's Garden ◆ 1986
6. George Mouse's Covered Wagon ◆ 1987
7. George Mouse's Riverboat Band ◆ 1987
8. Emily Mouse's Beach House ◆ 1987
9. Emily Mouse's Garden ◆ 1987
10. George and Matilda Mouse and the Doll's House ◆ 1988
11. George and Matilda Mouse and the Floating School ◆ 1990
12. George and Matilda Mouse and the Moon Rocket ◆ 1992
13. The Christmas Journey of George and Matilda Mouse ◆ 1993

GEORGIE

Bright, Robert

DOUBLEDAY ◆ GRADES 1–3

FANTASY | HUMOR

Georgie is a polite, kind little ghost who lives in the Whittakers' attic. With his friends Herman the cat and Miss Oliver the owl, he does what he can to help out the Whittakers and their friends. When they go out west, he catches a gang of horse thieves and recovers a stolen pony. In the Christmas book, he plays Santa Claus to the town Scrooge.

1. Georgie ◆ 1944
2. Georgie to the Rescue ◆ 1956
3. Georgie's Halloween ◆ 1958
4. Georgie and the Robbers ◆ 1963
5. Georgie and the Magician ◆ 1966
6. Georgie and the Noisy Ghost ◆ 1971
7. Georgie Goes West ◆ 1973
8. Georgie's Christmas Carol ◆ 1975
9. Georgie and the Buried Treasure ◆ 1979
10. Georgie and the Ball of Yarn ◆ 1983
11. Georgie and the Baby Birds ◆ 1983
12. Georgie and the Little Dog ◆ 1983
13. Georgie and the Runaway Balloon ◆ 1983

GERALDINE

Keller, Holly

GREENWILLOW ◆ GRADES K–2 ◆ A/R

ANIMAL FANTASY | FAMILY LIFE | HUMOR

Geraldine is a young pig who has the same concerns as many children. Why does she have to give up her blanket? When will the snow come so she can use her new sled? Why is her new baby brother, Willie, such a nuisance? Each simple story has a reassuring ending as Mama and Papa understand Geraldine's frustrations and help her solve her problems. Additional books deal with being an older sister and celebrating Christmas.

1. Geraldine's Blanket ◆ 1984
2. Geraldine's Big Snow ◆ 1988
3. Geraldine's Baby Brother ◆ 1994
4. Geraldine First ◆ 1996
5. Merry Christmas, Geraldine ◆ 1997
6. Geraldine and Mrs. Duffy ◆ 2000

GERMY

Jones, Rebecca C.

DUTTON ◆ GRADES 3–6 ◆ A/R

HUMOR | REAL LIFE

Jeremy Bluett, called "Germy Blew It" by everyone except adults and new kids, wants to be on TV. He organizes a strike at school when field trips are canceled, but no one else participates. When he finds out that TV cameras came to school while he was gone, he tries one scheme after another to be famous. Finally, with the help of his friend Squirrel, he organizes a bubble-gum blowing contest at his house. He gets his wish to be on TV, but ends up owing the school money. In subsequent books, he tries a variety of get-rich-quick schemes to pay back the school, starts a school newspaper, and is elected to student council.

1. Germy Blew It ◆ 1987
2. Germy Blew It—Again ◆ 1988
3. Germy Blew the Bugle ◆ 1990
4. Germy in Charge ◆ 1993

GERONIMO STILTON

Stilton, Geronimo

SCHOLASTIC ◆ GRADES 3–5 ◆ A/R

ANIMAL FANTASY

Geronimo Stilton is an unwilling mouse adventurer who travels around the world facing dangerous situations. He hunts ghosts in New Mouse City trying to outwit Sally Ratmousen. With his sister Thea and his cousin Trap, he travels to the jungle. He even searches for the Ruby of Fire in a temple filled with booby traps. Geronimo is a timid mouse who would prefer the quiet life on Mouse Island. His action-packed adventures will appeal to many readers, who will also be attracted to the full-color illustrations. The Special Editions include extra features such as recipes, jokes, and games.

1. Lost Treasure of the Emerald Eye ◆ 2004
2. The Curse of the Cheese Pyramid ◆ 2004
3. Cat and Mouse in a Haunted House ◆ 2004
4. I'm Too Fond of My Fur! ◆ 2004
5. Four Mice Deep in the Jungle ◆ 2004
6. Paws Off, Cheddarface ◆ 2004
7. Red Pizzas for a Blue Count ◆ 2004
8. Attack of the Bandit Cats ◆ 2004
9. A Fabumouse Vacation for Geronimo ◆ 2004
10. All Because of a Cup of Coffee ◆ 2004
11. It's Halloween, You 'Fraidy Mouse ◆ 2004
12. Merry Christmas, Geronimo! ◆ 2004
13. The Phantom of the Subway ◆ 2004
14. The Temple of the Ruby of Fire ◆ 2004
15. The Mona Mousa Affair ◆ 2005
16. A Cheese-Colored Camper ◆ 2005
17. Watch Your Whiskers, Stilton! ◆ 2005
18. Shipwreck on the Pirate Islands ◆ 2005
19. My Name is Stilton, Geronimo Stilton ◆ 2005
20. Surf's Up, Geronimo! ◆ 2005
21. The Wild, Wild West ◆ 2005
22. The Secret of Cacklefur Castle ◆ 2005
23. Valentine's Day Disaster ◆ 2005
24. Field Trip to Niagara Falls ◆ 2006
25. The Search for Sunken Treasure ◆ 2006
26. The Mummy with No Name ◆ 2006
27. The Christmas Toy Factory ◆ 2006
28. Wedding Crasher ◆ 2007
29. Down and Out Down Under ◆ 2007
30. The Mouse Island Marathon ◆ 2007
31. The Mysterious Cheese Thief ◆ 2007
32. Valley of the Giant Skeletons ◆ 2008
33. Geronimo and the Gold Medal Mystery ◆ 2008
34. Geronimo Stilton, Secret Agent ◆ 2008
35. A Very Merry Christmas ◆ 2008

SPECIAL EDITIONS

1. A Christmas Tale ◆ 2005
2. Christmas Catastrophe ◆ 2007

GET READY FOR GABI

Montes, Marisa
SCHOLASTIC ◆ GRADES 2–5 ◆ A/R
FAMILY LIFE

Third-grader Gabi, a Puerto Rican American, speaks Spanish at home and English at school and sometimes gets confused under stress. In the first book this stress arrives in the form of a science project with her nemesis Johnny Wiley. In the third book, Gabi tries to keep to English but this causes problems at home. Readers will recognize many familiar situations and those who don't speak Spanish will learn lots of useful vocabulary, while those who do will feel right at home.

1. A Crazy Mixed-Up Spanglish Day ◆ 2003
2. Who's That Girl? ◆ 2003
3. No More Spanish! ◆ 2004
4. Please Don't Go! ◆ 2004

GET REAL

Ellerbee, Linda
AVON/HARPERCOLLINS ◆ GRADES 4–6
REAL LIFE

Casey Smith, 11, wants to be a journalist. Her middle school has not had a school newspaper for years. Casey wants to revive it but so does Megan. The two girls compete for the leadership of the paper and its contents. Casey wants to focus on serious news and issues; Megan wants to feature advice and fashion.

1. Girl Reporter Blows Lid Off Town! ◆ 1999
2. Girl Reporter Sinks School! ◆ 2000
3. Girl Reporter Stuck in Jam! ◆ 2000
4. Girl Reporter Snags Crush! ◆ 2000
5. Girl Reporter Digs Up Zombies! ◆ 2000
6. Girl Reporter Rocks Polls! ◆ 2001
7. Girl Reporter Gets the Skinny! ◆ 2001
8. Girl Reporter Bytes Back ◆ 2001

GHOST

DeFelice, Cynthia
FARRAR, STRAUS & GIROUX ◆ GRADES 4–6 ◆ A/R
FANTASY

Allie Nichols, 11, is a ghost magnet. She discovered her skill when she was at Fossil Glen. Several years ago, a girl called Lucy disappeared. Allie finds a grave marker and becomes involved in the mystery. She is guided by voices that only she hears and by the feeling that there is a presence near her. After solving Lucy's mystery, Allie encounters the ghost of John Walker. The ghost in the third book is a dog that was abused.

1. The Ghost of Fossil Glen ◆ 1998

2. The Ghost and Mrs. Hobbs ◆ 2001
3. The Ghost of Cutler Creek ◆ 2004

GHOST SQUAD

Hildick, E. W.

DUTTON ◆ GRADES 5–8

FANTASY | MYSTERY

Joe, Danny, Karen, and Carlos are ghosts who have learned how to communicate with living people using a computer. They make contact with Carlos and Danny's best friends, Buzz and Wacko, and together the four ghosts and two boys form the Ghost Squad to solve crimes. Joe, the group's leader, was murdered and wants to find out who did it and assure his wife that it was not a suicide. Karen and Danny also want to help their families, but Carlos's family has adjusted to his death. His concern is with computers, and he figures out how to use a ghost's "micro-micro energy" to operate a word processor. The Ghost Squad battles both living enemies and Malevs (ghosts who try to harm living people) in their adventures, which include plenty of action.

1. The Ghost Squad Breaks Through ◆ 1984
2. The Ghost Squad and the Halloween Conspiracy ◆ 1985
3. The Ghost Squad Flies Concorde ◆ 1985
4. The Ghost Squad and the Ghoul of Grunberg ◆ 1986
5. The Ghost Squad and the Prowling Hermits ◆ 1987
6. The Ghost Squad and the Menace of the Malevs ◆ 1988

GHOST STORIES

Coville, Bruce

BANTAM ◆ GRADES 5–6 ◆ A/R

MYSTERY

The active involvement of a ghost in each of these titles creates special mysteries for sixth-grade friends Nina and Chris. The girls meet during an audition in a theater said to be haunted by an actress who was murdered on stage fifty years before. Of course, only the girls can see the ghostly apparitions and it becomes their responsibility to unravel the strange adventures.

1. The Ghost in the Third Row ◆ 1987
2. The Ghost Wore Gray ◆ 1988
3. The Ghost in the Big Brass Bed ◆ 1991

GHOSTHUNTERS

Funke, Cornelia

SCHOLASTIC ◆ GRADES 3–5 ◆ A/R

FANTASY

An IRG (Incredibly Revolting Ghost) is causing problems for an ASG (Averagely Spooky Ghost) at Tom's house. Tom's grandmother calls in her friend Hetty Hyssop, who is a renowned ghosthunter. Tom, 9, helps Hetty rid the home of the IRG. In the fourth book, Tom, who is now 11, prepares to take the test to receive his Ghosthunting Diploma. There is a lot of humor and not much horror in this series.

1. Ghosthunters and the Incredibly Revolting Ghost! ◆ 2006
2. Ghosthunters and the Gruesome Invincible Lightning Ghost! ◆ 2006
3. Ghosthunters and the Totally Moldy Baroness! ◆ 2007
4. Ghosthunters and the Muddy Monster of Doom! ◆ 2007

GHOSTS OF FEAR STREET *see* Fear Street: Ghosts of Fear Street

GHOSTVILLE ELEMENTARY

Jones, Marcia Thornton, and Debbie Dadey

SCHOLASTIC ◆ GRADES 3–5 ◆ A/R

FANTASY

Welcome to Sleepy Hollow. It's a quiet town with a problem. The basement of the elementary school is haunted. Jeff, Cassidy, and Nina are among the students whose classroom is in the basement. They are haunted by sinister dolls, play a basketball game with some ghosts, and have other supernatural encounters.

1. Ghost Class ◆ 2002
2. Ghost Game ◆ 2003
3. New Ghoul in School ◆ 2003
4. Happy Haunting ◆ 2004
5. Stage Fright ◆ 2004
6. Happy Boo-Day to You ◆ 2004
7. Hide-and-Spook ◆ 2004
8. Ghosts Be Gone ◆ 2005
9. Beware of the Blabbermouth ◆ 2005
10. Class Trip to the Haunted House ◆ 2005
11. The Treasure Haunt ◆ 2005
12. Frights, Camera, Action! ◆ 2006

GHOSTWRITER

Various authors

BANTAM ◆ GRADES 4–6

MYSTERY | SCIENCE FICTION | FANTASY

Four children living in the inner city make contact with a ghost who communicates by rearranging letters into messages that only the children can see. The children and the ghost form a crime-fighting team, using the ghost's unique skills and the children's expertise with codes and secret writing. Over the course of the series, new members are added to the team and the adventures become more fantastic. The series is a companion to the PBS series of the same name, which stresses the importance of literacy. *The Ghostwriter Detective Guide* provides information on criminal investigation and the use of various techniques.

1. A Match of Wills (Weiner, Eric) ◆ 1992
2. Courting Danger and Other Stories (Anastasio, Dina) ◆ 1992
3. Dress Code Mess (St. Antoine, Sara) ◆ 1992
4. Steer Clear of Haunted Hill (Weiner, Eric) ◆ 1993
5. Amazement Park Adventure (Chevat, Richie) ◆ 1994
6. Alias Diamond Jones (Salat, Cristina) ◆ 1993
7. Blackout! (Weiner, Eric) ◆ 1993
8. A Blast with the Past (Wilsdon, Christine) ◆ 1994
9. Digging for Clues (Keyishian, Amy) ◆ 1994
10. Disappearing Act (Blundell, Judy) ◆ 1994
11. The Book Chase (Woodson, Jacqueline) ◆ 1994
12. Clinton Street Crime Wave (Hill, Laban C.) ◆ 1994
13. Ghost Story (Kleinbaum, N. H.) ◆ 1995
14. The Big Stink & Five Other Mysteries (Chevat, Richie) ◆ 1995
15. The Chocolate Bar Bust (Barry, Miranda) ◆ 1995
16. Daycamp Nightmare: Camp at Your Own Risk #1 (Butcher, Nancy) ◆ 1995
17. Disaster on Wheels: Camp at Your Own Risk #2 (Butcher, Nancy) ◆ 1995
18. Creepy Sleepaway: Camp at Your Own Risk #3 (Butcher, Nancy) ◆ 1995
19. Night of the Living Cavemen (Weiner, Eric) ◆ 1995
20. A Crime of Two Cities (Leeden, Ivy D., and Kermit Frazier) ◆ 1995
21. Just in Time (Hyman, Fracaswell) ◆ 1996
22. Deadline (Weiner, Eric) ◆ 1996
23. Attack of the Slime Monster (Baker, Cari Greenberg) ◆ 1996
24. The Man Who Vanished (Keyishian, Amy) ◆ 1996
25. Alien Alert (Korman, Susan) ◆ 1996
26. Caught in the Net (Butcher, Nancy) ◆ 1997
27. Hector's Haunted House (Korman, Susan) ◆ 1997

GIDEON THE CUTPURSE

Buckley-Archer, Linda

SIMON & SCHUSTER ◆ GRADES 5–8 ◆ A/R

FANTASY

In England, Peter and Kate, 12, are transported from the 21st century to 1763. Kate's father has been working on an anti-gravity machine but it has been stolen by the Tar Man. The children are befriended by a thief, Gideon, who helps them adjust to the era and in their search for a way home. In *The Time Thief,* Kate has returned to the 21st century, but so has the Tar Man. Peter is stranded in the past. When Kate and her father return for Peter, they enter the wrong time and Peter is in his forties. Peter keeps his identity hidden, hoping that Kate and her father will find a way to the right time. The title of the first book was changed to *The Time Travelers* for the paperback edition.

1. Gideon the Cutpurse ◆ 2006
2. The Time Thief ◆ 2007
3. The Splintering of Time ◆ 2009

GILBERT

deGroat, Diane

HARPERCOLLINS; CHRONICLE ◆ GRADES K–2 ◆ A/R

ANIMAL FANTASY

Expressive illustrations and stories full of familiar situations make this series about a young opossum a hit with children. Will Gilbert get a prize at the end of the year (*No More Pencils . . .*)? Is there really a ghost at their campsite (*Good Night, Sleep Tight*)? Gilbert's little sister Lola appears in many of the stories, and there are books about her for younger readers.

1. Roses Are Pink, Your Feet Really Stink ◆ 1996
2. Trick or Treat, Smell My Feet ◆ 1998
3. Happy Birthday to You, You Belong in a Zoo ◆ 1999
4. Jingle Bells, Homework Smells ◆ 2000
5. We Gather Together . . . Now Please Get Lost! ◆ 2001
6. Good Night, Sleep Tight, Don't Let the Bedbugs Bite! ◆ 2002
7. Liar, Liar, Pants on Fire ◆ 2002
8. Brand-New Pencils, Brand-New Books ◆ 2005
9. No More Pencils, No More Books, No More Teacher's Dirty Looks! ◆ 2006
10. Last One In Is a Rotten Egg! ◆ 2007
11. Mother, You're the Best! (But Sister, You're a Pest!) ◆ 2008
12. April Fool! Watch Out at School! ◆ 2009
13. Gilbert, the Surfer Dude ◆ 2009

GIRLHOOD JOURNEYS: JULIET

Kirwan, Anna

SIMON & SCHUSTER ◆ GRADES 4–6 ◆ A/R

FAMILY LIFE | HISTORICAL

Juliet lives in England in the 14th century. Her father, a freeman, works for Sir Pepin D'Arsy, and her best friend is Sir Pepin's daughter Marguerite. There is intrigue involving mysterious guests, Marguerite's betrothal, and a lost falcon. Juliet is an energetic character who solves problems on her own, even given the restrictions of her era. For example, when her little brother Alban accidentally releases the falcon, Juliet searches for it, finds it, and returns it. There is an afterword describing daily life in the Middle Ages.

1. A Dream Takes Flight, England, 1339 ◆ 1996
2. Rescue at Marlehead Manor ◆ 1997
3. Midsummer at Greenchapel ◆ 1997

GIRLHOOD JOURNEYS: KAI

Various authors

SIMON & SCHUSTER ◆ GRADES 4–6 ◆ A/R

FAMILY LIFE | HISTORICAL

It is 1440, and Kai lives in a Yoruba village in Africa (in the area that is now Nigeria). Each book portrays Kai as a strong-willed, resourceful young woman. In one book, she and her sister Jamila help their people during a time of famine. In another book, Kai, Jamila, and their friend Aisha travel to Oyo, where Kai works with the master sculptor Akibu. Her efforts to fulfill her artistic dreams take her away from her home, and she must develop self-reliance and confidence. There is a glossary of terms as well as a section of information about the Yoruba in history and today.

1. A Mission for Her Village, Africa, 1440 (Thomas, Dawn C. Gill) ◆ 1996
2. A Big Decision (Gayle, Sharon Shavers) ◆ 1997
3. The Lost Statue (Welch, Leona Nicholas) ◆ 1997

GIRLHOOD JOURNEYS: MARIE

Various authors

SIMON & SCHUSTER ◆ GRADES 4–6 ◆ A/R

FAMILY LIFE | HISTORICAL

Marie La Marche and her family live in Paris in the years just before the French Revolution. Marie's interest in ballet seems destined to be unfulfilled until she receives some attention and support. The first two books focus on Marie's interest in the world of dance and on the behaviors and intrigues of 18th-century Paris. These adventures involve her friend Joelle. The third book follows the family to the country for the summer, where Marie makes friends with her cousin Jeannette. When Jeannette must leave the family to find work, Marie's resourcefulness helps her use her talents to earn money and stay at home. This is a lively series with an emphasis on relationships. A glossary of French words opens the book and helps with the reading; an afterword focuses on French life in this era.

1. An Invitation to Dance, Paris, 1775 (Kudlinski, Kathleen V.) ◆ 1996
2. Mystery at the Paris Ballet (Greene, Jacqueline D.) ◆ 1997
3. Summer in the Country (Greene, Jacqueline D.) ◆ 1997

GIRLHOOD JOURNEYS: SHANNON

Kudlinski, Kathleen V.

SIMON & SCHUSTER ◆ GRADES 4–6 ◆ A/R

FAMILY LIFE | HISTORICAL

Arriving in San Francisco from Ireland, Shannon O'Brien and her family must adjust to new customs in this lively new home. It is 1880, and Shannon meets a Chinese immigrant, Mi Ling, who involves her in several mysteries. Shannon finds out about prejudice toward Mi Ling as well as narrow attitudes about her Irish heritage when she attends school. These stories involve adventure and are fast-paced. There is an afterword describing California in the late 19th century.

1. A Chinatown Adventure, San Francisco, 1880 ◆ 1996
2. Lost and Found ◆ 1997
3. The Schoolmarm Mysteries ◆ 1997

GIRLS OF AVENUE Z

Pielichaty, Helena

ALADDIN ◆ GRADES 5–7 ◆ A/R

REAL LIFE

Originally published in England as the "After School Club" series, these books feature girls who are left on their own after school. They could become involved in problem situations. Instead, they attend the Avenue Z Club. Each book features a different girl and her problems. In *Starring Jolene,* Jolene has run away and goes with her aunt to the club. There, she notices a young boy with bruises and she decides to get involved.

1. Starring Sammie ◆ 2006

2. Starring Brody ◆ 2006
3. Starring Alex ◆ 2006
4. Starring Jolene ◆ 2007

THE GIRLS OF LIGHTHOUSE LANE

Kinkade, Thomas

HARPERCOLLINS ◆ GRADES 4–6 ◆ A/R

HISTORICAL | REAL LIFE

In early 20th-century New England, four girls with different backgrounds and aspirations find they can be friends; these novels by the popular painter are similar to his works for adults.

1. Katherine's Story ◆ 2004
2. Rose's Story ◆ 2004
3. Lizabeth's Story ◆ 2004
4. Amanda's Story ◆ 2004

GIRLS OF MANY LANDS *see* American Girls: Girls of Many Lands

GIRLS ONLY (GO!)

Lewis, Beverly

BETHANY HOUSE ◆ GRADES 4–6 ◆ A/R

RECREATION | VALUES

Several girls form a "Girls Only" club to provide support for each other as they pursue their dreams. Jenna Song is a champion gymnast dreaming of the Olympics. In *Only the Best,* she is focused on going to the Olympic Training Center in Colorado Springs. Her parents are excited about adopting a baby from Korea to expand their Korean American family. Jenna seeks guidance from God as she deals with her conflicted emotions. In another book, Heather and Kevin Bock have been ice dancing partners for years. Now, Heather wants to try figure skating. She needs help from her friends and her faith to make the right decision.

1. Dreams on Ice ◆ 1998
2. Only the Best ◆ 1998
3. A Perfect Match ◆ 1999
4. Reach for the Stars ◆ 1999
5. Follow the Dream ◆ 2000
6. Better Than Best ◆ 2000
7. Photo Perfect ◆ 2001
8. Star Status ◆ 2002

GO GIRL

Various authors

FEIWEL & FRIENDS ◆ GRADES 3–5

REAL LIFE

Each book in this series features a different girl and her problem. Tamsin is a new girl who is worried that she will not make friends, especially when she learns that there is a secret club and she may not be asked to join it. Gemma wants to be a gymnast. Cassie is having problems with her older sister. Olivia is worried about her first sleepover. Imported from Australia, these books feature likable characters with believable, everyday concerns.

1. The Secret Club (Perry, Chrissie) ◆ 2007
2. The Worst Gymnast (Kalkipsakis, Thalia) ◆ 2007
3. Sister Spirit (Kalkipsakis, Thalia) ◆ 2007
4. Lunchtime Rules (Steggall, Vicki) ◆ 2007
5. Sleepover (McAuley, Rowan) ◆ 2008
6. Surf's Up! (Perry, Chrissie) ◆ 2008
7. Dancing Queen (Kalkipsakis, Thalia) ◆ 2008
8. Catch Me If You Can (Kalkipsakis, Thalia) ◆ 2008
9. The New Girl (McAuley, Rowan) ◆ 2008
10. Basketball Blues (Kalkipsakis, Thalia) ◆ 2008
11. Camp Chaos (Badger, Meredith) ◆ 2008
12. Back to School (Badger, Meredith) ◆ 2008

THE GOLDEN HAMSTER SAGA

Reiche, Dietlof

SCHOLASTIC ◆ GRADES 3–6 ◆ A/R

ANIMAL FANTASY

Freddy Auratus, an unusually smart and savvy hamster, chooses to let Sophie buy him. At Sophie's house, Freddy learns to read, but he is forced to leave because of Sophie's mother's allergies. His next home is with Mr. John, who has two guinea pigs and a cat. Using Mr. John's computer, Freddy learns to write, and in *Freddy in Peril,* Professor Fleischkopf wants to capture and dissect Freddy and study his brain. This series has lively plots and numerous illustrations (by Joe Cepeda) that will attract readers.

1. I, Freddy ◆ 2003
2. Freddy in Peril ◆ 2004
3. Freddy to the Rescue ◆ 2005
4. The Haunting of Freddy ◆ 2006
5. Freddy's Final Quest ◆ 2007

GOLDSTONE TRILOGY

Lawson, Julie
STODDART ◆ GRADES 5–7 ◆ A/R
FANTASY | REAL LIFE

In early 20th-century British Columbia, 12-year-old Karin, a girl of Swedish descent, inherits a goldstone pendant when her mother is killed in an avalanche. This necklace allows Karin to dream of the future. In the first book, she foresees a second avalanche. In *Turns on a Dime,* set in the 1950s, lonely and uncertain 11-year-old Jo inherits the pendant and finds it gives her strength and self-confidence. In the final volume, Jo passes the pendant on to her niece Ashley, who is challenged by a ghost seeking to return the goldstone to its original home.

1. Goldstone ◆ 1998
2. Turns on a Dime ◆ 1999
3. The Ghost of Avalanche Mountain ◆ 2000

GOLIATH *see* David and Goliath

GOLLY SISTERS

Byars, Betsy
HARPERCOLLINS ◆ GRADES K–2 ◆ A/R
HISTORICAL | HUMOR

Rose and May-May Golly have a traveling road show that takes them across the western frontier. Their show is funny and so are the predicaments that they experience. In one story, they put on a show for an audience of dogs; in another, May-May decides to use pigs in her magic act instead of rabbits ("Everyone uses rabbits"); in still another, the sisters visit a talking rock. The appealing illustrations, brief chapters, and simple text make this a good choice for beginning readers, and the humor will attract reluctant readers.

1. The Golly Sisters Go West ◆ 1985
2. Hooray for the Golly Sisters! ◆ 1990
3. The Golly Sisters Ride Again ◆ 1994

GONERS

Simons, Jamie, and E. W. Scollon
AVON CAMELOT ◆ GRADES 4–6
ADVENTURE | SCIENCE FICTION

The books in this series link the creatures on a planetoid in the future with past events on Earth. Dr. Autonomou has identified some Goners— interplanetary diplomats who were sent to various times and places on Earth but were lost when the transport system was destroyed. The doctor is now experimenting with ways to bring them back, including sending other creatures from Planetoid Roma to Planet RU1:2 (a.k.a. Earth). After undergoing "biological osmosis" to look like earthlings, Rubidoux, Xela, Gogol, and Arms Akimbo experience adventures with Thomas Jefferson, Christopher Columbus, and Edward VI.

1. RU1:2 ◆ 1998
2. The Hunt Is On ◆ 1998
3. All Hands on Deck ◆ 1998
4. Spitting Image ◆ 1998
5. Rabid Transit ◆ 1998
6. Under Loch and Key ◆ 1998
7. Spell Bound ◆ 1999
8. Space Race ◆ 1999
9. Double Trouble ◆ 1999
10. Disorderly Conduct ◆ 1999

GOOD KNIGHT

Thomas, Shelley Moore
PENGUIN ◆ GRADES K–2 ◆ A/R
ANIMAL FANTASY

A good knight comes across three little dragons and is kind enough to look after their demands (a drink of water, a story, a song, a kiss). In the second book, the little dragons have colds and the knight must find a remedy. *Take Care, Good Knight* (2006) and *A Cold Winter's Good Knight* (2008) are picture books for younger readers

1. Good Night, Good Knight ◆ 2000
2. Get Well, Good Knight ◆ 2002
3. Happy Birthday, Good Knight ◆ 2006

GOONEY BIRD GREENE

Lowry, Lois
HOUGHTON MIFFLIN ◆ GRADES 1–3 ◆ A/R
REAL LIFE

When Gooney Bird Greene enters the second grade at Watertower Elementary School she causes a commotion. Her clothing is unusual (pajamas and cowboy boots) and her stories are fantastic. As the new student, she is allowed to introduce herself and, eventually, readers learn the origins of her unusual name. While Gooney Bird tells her stories she incorporates details about telling (and writing) stories—like including interesting characters and dramatic vocabulary. This is a great transitional chapter book series.

1. Gooney Bird Greene ◆ 2002
2. Gooney Bird and the Room Mother ◆ 2005
3. Gooney, the Fabulous ◆ 2007

GOOSEBUMPS

Stine, R. L.

SCHOLASTIC ◆ GRADES 4–8 ◆ A/R

HORROR

According to the publisher, more than 200 million copies of Goosebumps have been sold. There are spin-off series, television tie-ins, and a Web site (http://www.scholastic.com/goosebumps). The books are filled with creatures and gore, with implausible situations and frightening circumstances. The characters are often unsuspecting innocents—just like your neighbors and friends, or even yourself—caught in the clutches of gnomes, werewolves, monsters, vampires, and other creatures. The locations include a mummy's tomb, Camp Nightmare, Horrorland, and the Haunted School. This popular series brings the horror genre to a younger audience, giving them dripping blood, shrunken heads, and monsters awaiting their next victim.

1. Welcome to Dead House ◆ 1992
2. Stay Out of the Basement ◆ 1992
3. Monster Blood ◆ 1992
4. Say Cheese and Die! ◆ 1992
5. Curse of the Mummy's Tomb ◆ 1993
6. Let's Get Invisible! ◆ 1993
7. Night of the Living Dummy ◆ 1993
8. The Girl Who Cried Monster ◆ 1993
9. Welcome to Camp Nightmare ◆ 1993
10. The Ghost Next Door ◆ 1993
11. The Haunted Mask ◆ 1993
12. Be Careful What You Wish For ◆ 1993
13. Piano Lessons Can Be Murder ◆ 1993
14. The Werewolf of Fever Swamp ◆ 1993
15. You Can't Scare Me! ◆ 1994
16. One Day at Horrorland ◆ 1994
17. Why I'm Afraid of Bees ◆ 1994
18. Monster Blood II ◆ 1994
19. Deep Trouble ◆ 1994
20. The Scarecrow Walks at Midnight ◆ 1994
21. Go Eat Worms! ◆ 1994
22. Ghost Beach ◆ 1994

23. Return of the Mummy ◆ 1994
24. Phantom of the Auditorium ◆ 1994
25. Attack of the Mutant ◆ 1994
26. My Hairiest Adventure ◆ 1994
27. A Night in Terror Tower ◆ 1995
28. The Cuckoo Clock of Doom ◆ 1995
29. Monster Blood III ◆ 1995
30. It Came from Beneath the Sink! ◆ 1995
31. Night of the Living Dummy II ◆ 1995
32. The Barking Ghost ◆ 1995
33. The Horror at Camp Jellyjam ◆ 1995
34. Revenge of the Lawn Gnomes ◆ 1995
35. A Shocker on Shock Street ◆ 1995
36. The Haunted Mask II ◆ 1995
37. The Headless Ghost ◆ 1995
38. The Abominable Snowman of Pasadena ◆ 1995
39. How I Got My Shrunken Head ◆ 1996
40. Night of the Living Dummy III ◆ 1996
41. Bad Hare Day ◆ 1996
42. Egg Monsters from Mars ◆ 1996
43. The Beast from the East ◆ 1996
44. Say Cheese and Die—Again! ◆ 1996
45. Ghost Camp ◆ 1996
46. How to Kill a Monster ◆ 1996
47. Legend of the Lost Legend ◆ 1996
48. Attack of the Jack-O'-Lanterns ◆ 1996
49. Vampire Breath ◆ 1996
50. Calling All Creeps! ◆ 1996
51. Beware, the Snowman ◆ 1997
52. How I Learned to Fly ◆ 1997
53. Chicken Chicken ◆ 1997
54. Don't Go to Sleep! ◆ 1997
55. The Blob That Ate Everyone ◆ 1997
56. The Curse of Camp Cold Lake ◆ 1997
57. My Best Friend Is Invisible ◆ 1997
58. Deep Trouble II ◆ 1997
59. The Haunted School ◆ 1997
60. Werewolf Skin ◆ 1997
61. I Live in Your Basement! ◆ 1997
62. Monster Blood IV ◆ 1998

GOOSEBUMPS: GIVE YOURSELF GOOSEBUMPS

Stine, R. L.

SCHOLASTIC ◆ GRADES 4–8

HORROR | ADVENTURE

What do you get when you cross the incredibly popular horror stories of Goosebumps with the popular format of Choose Your Own Adventure? You get Give Yourself Goosebumps. The cover of each book announces "Choose from over 20 different scary endings," giving readers many different ways to direct the adventures. Like the basic Goosebumps books, these are scary stories where characters try to escape from weird creatures or are attacked by monsters or lost in a swamp. You meet werewolves, vampires, and terrible toys. You visit such places as the Carnival of Horrors and the Dead-End Hotel. Depending on the choices, the reader can triumph over the evil creatures, just barely escape, or be swallowed by a sea monster. The two popular genres represented in this series are sure to capture the interest of even the most reluctant readers.

1. Escape from the Carnival of Horrors ◆ 1995
2. Tick Tock, You're Dead! ◆ 1995
3. Trapped in Bat Wing Hall ◆ 1995
4. The Deadly Experiments of Dr. Eek ◆ 1996
5. Night in Werewolf Woods ◆ 1996
6. Beware of the Purple Peanut Butter ◆ 1996
7. Under the Magician's Spell ◆ 1996
8. The Curse of the Creeping Coffin ◆ 1996
9. The Knight in Screaming Armor ◆ 1996
10. Diary of a Mad Mummy ◆ 1996
11. Deep in the Jungle of Doom ◆ 1996
12. Welcome to the Wicked Wax Museum ◆ 1996
13. Scream of the Evil Genie ◆ 1997
14. The Creepy Creations of Professor Shock ◆ 1997
15. Please Don't Feed the Vampire! ◆ 1997
16. Secret Agent Grandma ◆ 1997
17. Little Comic Shop of Horrors ◆ 1997
18. Attack of the Beastly Baby-Sitter ◆ 1997
19. Escape from Camp Run-for-Your-Life ◆ 1997
20. Toy Terror: Batteries Included ◆ 1997
21. The Twisted Tale of Tiki Island ◆ 1997
22. Return to the Carnival of Horrors ◆ 1997
23. Zapped in Space ◆ 1997
24. Lost in Stinkeye Swamp ◆ 1997
25. Shop 'Til You Drop . . . Dead ◆ 1998
26. Alone in Snakebite Canyon ◆ 1998
27. Checkout Time at the Dead-End Hotel ◆ 1998
28. Night of a Thousand Claws ◆ 1998
29. Invaders from the Big Screen ◆ 1998
30. You're Plant Food! ◆ 1998
31. The Werewolf of Twisted Tree Lodge ◆ 1998
32. It's Only a Nightmare ◆ 1998
33. It Came from the Internet ◆ 1999
34. Elevator to Nowhere ◆ 1999
35. Hocus-Pocus Horror ◆ 1999
36. Ship of Ghouls ◆ 1999
37. Escape from Horror House ◆ 1999

38. Into the Twister of Terror ◆ 1999
39. Scary Birthday to You! ◆ 1999
40. Zombie School ◆ 2000
41. Danger Time ◆ 2000
42. All-Day Nightmare ◆ 2000

GIVE YOURSELF GOOSEBUMPS SPECIAL EDITIONS

1. Into the Jaws of Doom ◆ 1998
2. Return to Terror Tower: The Nightmare Continues ◆ 1998
3. Power Play: Trapped in the Circus of Fear ◆ 1998
4. The Ultimate Challenge: One Night in Payne House ◆ 1998
5. The Curse of the Cave Creatures ◆ 1999
6. Revenge of the Body Squeezers ◆ 1999
7. Trick or . . . Trapped ◆ 1999
8. Weekend at Poison Lake ◆ 1999

GOOSEBUMPS GRAPHIX

Stine, R. L.

GRAPHIX ◆ GRADES 4–8 ◆ A/R

HORROR

Familiar Goosebumps stories have been reformatted as graphic novels. As in the original stories, there are twists and turns that leave the reader breathless. Goosebumps books have always been popular; adding the graphic novel illustrations and format will reach many new fans, including reluctant readers.

1. Creepy Creatures ◆ 2006
2. Terror Trips ◆ 2007
3. Scary Summer ◆ 2007

GOOSEBUMPS HORRORLAND

Stine, R. L.

SCHOLASTIC ◆ GRADES 4–8 ◆ A/R

HORROR

Welcome to Horrorland! An amusement park that will thrill you . . . to death! In the first book, Britney, 12, has a frightening encounter with a ventriloquist's dummy. Then, on a trip to Horrorland, Britney discovers that the terror is just beginning. In *Creep from the Deep,* Billy and his sister Sheena are on an underwater ride of doom. Goosebumps fans will delight in this new series of books.

1. Revenge of the Living Dummy ◆ 2008
2. Creep from the Deep ◆ 2008

3. Monster Blood for Breakfast! ◆ 2008
4. The Scream of the Haunted Mask ◆ 2008
5. Dr. Maniac vs. Robby Schwartz ◆ 2008
6. Who's Your Mummy? ◆ 2009
7. My Friends Call Me Monster ◆ 2009

GOOSEBUMPS PRESENTS

Stine, R. L.

SCHOLASTIC ◆ GRADES 3–6 ◆ A/R

HORROR

This TV tie-in series features adaptations of plots that were shown as part of the *Goosebumps* program. The plots include encounters with a headless ghost, mutants, and avenging lawn gnomes. In the middle of the books, there are color photographs from the television show. Some of these books are much shorter adaptations of books in the original Goosebumps series, but the addition of photographs from the show will attract many readers.

1. The Girl Who Cried Monster ◆ 1996
2. The Cuckoo Clock of Doom ◆ 1996
3. Welcome to Camp Nightmare ◆ 1996
4. Return of the Mummy ◆ 1996
5. Night of the Living Dummy II ◆ 1996
6. My Hairiest Adventure ◆ 1996
7. The Headless Ghost ◆ 1996
8. Be Careful What You Wish For ◆ 1997
9. Go Eat Worms! ◆ 1997
10. Bad Hare Day ◆ 1997
11. Let's Get Invisible ◆ 1997
12. Attack of the Mutant ◆ 1997
13. Ghost Beach ◆ 1997
14. You Can't Scare Me! ◆ 1997
15. Monster Blood ◆ 1997
16. Attack of the Jack-O'-Lanterns ◆ 1997
17. Calling All Creeps ◆ 1997
18. Revenge of the Lawn Gnomes ◆ 1998

GOOSEBUMPS SERIES 2000

Stine, R. L.

SCHOLASTIC ◆ GRADES 4–8 ◆ A/R

HORROR

Advertised as having a "scarier edge," Goosebumps 2000 capitalizes on the popularity of the horror genre and the familiar name of Goosebumps.

The danger in these books is a bit more intense and could appeal to an older audience and provide a transition to YA horror titles. As with the related series, there are weird creatures and slime, ghosts, and gore.

1. Cry of the Cat ◆ 1998
2. Bride of the Living Dummy ◆ 1998
3. Creature Teacher ◆ 1998
4. Invasion of the Body Squeezers, Part 1 ◆ 1998
5. Invasion of the Body Squeezers, Part 2 ◆ 1998
6. I Am Your Evil Twin ◆ 1998
7. Revenge R Us ◆ 1998
8. Fright Camp ◆ 1998
9. Are You Terrified Yet? ◆ 1998
10. Headless Halloween ◆ 1998
11. Attack of the Graveyard Ghouls ◆ 1998
12. Brain Juice ◆ 1998
13. Return to Horrorland ◆ 1999
14. Jekyll and Heidi ◆ 1999
15. Scream School ◆ 1999
16. The Mummy Walks ◆ 1999
17. The Werewolf in the Living Room ◆ 1999
18. Horrors of the Black Ring ◆ 1999
19. Return to Ghost Camp ◆ 1999
20. Be Afraid—Be Very Afraid! ◆ 1999
21. The Haunted Car ◆ 1999
22. Full Moon Fever ◆ 1999
23. Slappy's Nightmare ◆ 1999
24. Earth Geeks Must Go! ◆ 1999
25. Ghost in the Mirror ◆ 2000

GORDIE BARR *see* Third Grade

GORDY SMITH

Hahn, Mary Downing
CLARION ◆ GRADES 5–7 ◆ A/R
FAMILY LIFE | HISTORICAL

This series begins during World War II when best friends Elizabeth and Margaret spy on their sixth-grade classmate—a bully named Gordy Smith. They discover that he is hiding his brother Stu, who is an Army deserter. This is a grave moral dilemma for these patriotic friends. The sequels focus on Gordy as he is separated from his abusive family and sent to live with a grandmother in North Carolina. On her sudden death, Gordy returns to his hometown and the lingering perceptions that he is a bully from a "trashy" family. These are thoughtfully written books with realistic insights into the era and the characters.

1. Stepping on the Cracks ◆ 1991
2. Following My Own Footsteps ◆ 1996
3. As Ever, Gordy ◆ 1998

GRACE

Hoffman, Mary

DIAL ◆ GRADES 1–4 ◆ A/R

REAL LIFE

The first two picture books introduced Grace—a spunky character with independent ideas. A strong black character with African roots, Grace chooses West African kente robes as her princess costume in the third picture book. The chapter books follow Grace and her friends as they put on plays and interact with peers at school. The setting is not specified but seems to be London. Still, the story and characters are universal.

PICTURE BOOKS

1. Amazing Grace ◆ 1991
2. Boundless Grace ◆ 1995
3. Princess Grace ◆ 2008

CHAPTER BOOKS

1. Starring Grace ◆ 2000
2. Encore, Grace ◆ 2003
3. Bravo, Grace! ◆ 2005

GRACE (HARPER) *see* Just Grace

GRADUATION SUMMER *see* Mary-Kate and Ashley: Graduation Summer

GRAIL QUEST

Gilman, Laura Anne

HARPERCOLLINS ◆ GRADES 5–8

FANTASY

On the eve of King Arthur's quest for the Holy Grail, three young teens of different backgrounds—Gerard, Newt, and Ailias—must reverse a spell crippling all adults. This trilogy is suspenseful, with characters readers will recognize as well as fantastic creatures.

1. The Camelot Spell ◆ 2006
2. Morgain's Revenge ◆ 2006
3. The Shadow Companion ◆ 2006

GRANDADDY

Griffith, Helen V.

GREENWILLOW ◆ GRADES 2–4
FAMILY LIFE | REAL LIFE

Janetta's Grandaddy lives in rural Georgia and Janetta and her Mom live in Baltimore. When Janetta is about six, her Mom decides it is time they meet, so they take the train down to the farm. At first, Janetta is uncertain about Grandaddy and his animals, and she is sure they don't like her. She is especially afraid of his mule. Sitting on the porch that night, Grandaddy tells a story about a star that fell to Earth and wanted to go back to the sky. The mule jumped up with the star on its back. The story is the beginning of friendship between Janetta, Grandaddy, and his animals. As the series of picture books continues, they share more stories and love.

1. Georgia Music ◆ 1986
2. Grandaddy's Place ◆ 1987
3. Grandaddy and Janetta ◆ 1993
4. Grandaddy's Stars ◆ 1995

GRANDMAS

McCully, Emily Arnold

HARPERCOLLINS ◆ GRADES K–3 ◆ A/R
FAMILY LIFE

A delightful beginning-to-read series that illustrates how very different people can learn to compromise. Pip's two grandmas are exactly opposite: one is very strict, one is too lenient. His parents are exactly right: in between both extremes. Pip, sometimes with his friend Ski, tries to set the grandmas straight on what is really acceptable for children his age. Young readers will enjoy the way Pip tackles his grandmothers in this humorous and gentle book.

1. The Grandma Mix-Up ◆ 1988
2. Grandmas at the Lake ◆ 1990
3. Grandmas at Bat ◆ 1993
4. Grandmas Trick or Treat ◆ 2001

GRANDMA'S ATTIC

Richardson, Arleta

DAVID C. COOK ◆ GRADES 3–6

FAMILY LIFE | VALUES

A little girl visits her grandmother and hears stories about her childhood, prompted by found items in the attic or around the house. The grandmother was a girl in the late 1800s, and all the stories are nostalgic and idealistic portrayals of that time. The family is Christian, and Christian values permeate the stories. The format is the same throughout the series: short anecdotes tied together by the child's questions. The grandmother sometimes comments on the moral. The fifth, sixth, and seventh books have been reissued as *Away from Home, A School of Her Own,* and *Wedding Bells Ahead.* Companion books include *The Grandma's Attic Cookbook* (1995).

1. In Grandma's Attic ◆ 1974
2. More Stories from Grandma's Attic ◆ 1979
3. Still More Stories from Grandma's Attic ◆ 1980
4. Treasures from Grandma ◆ 1984
5. Sixteen and Away from Home ◆ 1985
6. Eighteen and on Her Own ◆ 1986
7. Nineteen and Wedding Bells Ahead ◆ 1987
8. At Home in North Branch ◆ 1988
9. New Faces, New Friends ◆ 1989
10. Stories from the Growing Years ◆ 1991
11. Christmas Stories from Grandma's Attic ◆ 1993

GRANDPA

Stevenson, James

GREENWILLOW ◆ GRADES 1–4 ◆ A/R

FAMILY LIFE | HUMOR

When Mary Ann and Louie visit their Grandpa, they try to tell him interesting things. He responds with exaggerated, slapstick stories of similar situations from his own childhood. If Mary Ann and Louie look forward to their Easter egg hunt, then Grandpa tells them about his trip to the Frammistan Mountains to hunt for an enormous Easter egg. And, of course, when Mary Ann and Louie are bored, Grandpa describes an even more boring time (sort of). Some of Grandpa's stories involve his brother Wainwright (Wainey). Children love these wild stories and great illustrations.

1. Could Be Worse! ◆ 1977
2. That Terrible Halloween Night ◆ 1980
3. What's Under My Bed? ◆ 1983
4. Grandpa's Great City Tour ◆ 1983

5. The Great Big Especially Beautiful Easter Egg ◆ 1983
6. Worse than Willie! ◆ 1984
7. That Dreadful Day ◆ 1985
8. No Friends ◆ 1986
9. There's Nothing to Do! ◆ 1986
10. Will You Please Feed Our Cat? ◆ 1987
11. We Hate Rain! ◆ 1988
12. Grandpa's Too-Good Garden ◆ 1989
13. Brrr! ◆ 1991
14. That's Exactly the Way It Wasn't ◆ 1991

GRANDPA SPANIELSON'S CHICKEN POX STORIES

Cazet, Denys

HARPERCOLLINS ◆ GRADES K–2 ◆ A/R

HUMOR

Barney, a puppy, has chicken pox and his grandfather tries to distracting with "anti-itch" tall tales from his adventurous youth—about a huge battle he had with an angry octopus, how he saved Mrs. Piggerman's life when he was fire chief, and an encounter with a tribe of head-shrinkers. Cartoon-style illustrations add to the fun.

1. The Octopus ◆ 2005
2. A Snout for Chocolate ◆ 2006
3. The Shrunken Head ◆ 2007

GRAVEYARD SCHOOL

Stone, Tom B.

BANTAM ◆ GRADES 4–7 ◆ A/R

HORROR | MYSTERY

Grove School is right next to a graveyard. So naturally the kids call it Graveyard School. Park, who considers himself a detective, and his friend Staccy solve mysteries and get into some terrifying situations. At the beginning of their sixth-grade year, the principal, Dr. Morehouse, introduces a new lunch room supervisor who promises tasty meals at low cost. Soon after, pets start disappearing all over town. The series continues as the friends solve more scary mysteries at the school.

1. Don't Eat the Mystery Meat ◆ 1994
2. The Skeleton on the Skateboard ◆ 1994
3. The Headless Bicycle Rider ◆ 1994
4. Little Pet Werewolf ◆ 1995
5. Revenge of the Dinosaurs ◆ 1995

6. Camp Dracula ◆ 1995
7. Slime Lake ◆ 1995
8. Let's Scare the Teacher to Death ◆ 1995
9. The Abominable Snow Monster ◆ 1995
10. There's a Ghost in the Boy's Bathroom ◆ 1996
11. April Ghoul's Day ◆ 1996
12. Scream, Team! ◆ 1996
13. Tales Too Scary to Tell at Camp ◆ 1996
14. The Tragic School Bus ◆ 1996
15. The Fright Before Christmas ◆ 1996
16. Don't Tell Mummy ◆ 1997
17. Jack and the Beanstalker ◆ 1997
18. The Dead Sox ◆ 1997
19. The Gator Ate Her ◆ 1997
20. Creature Teacher ◆ 1997
21. The Skeleton's Revenge ◆ 1997
22. Boo Year's Eve ◆ 1998
23. The Easter Egg Haunt ◆ 1998
24. Scream Around the Campfire ◆ 1998
25. Escape from Vampire Park ◆ 1998
26. Little School of Horrors ◆ 1998
27. Here Comes Santa Claws ◆ 1998
28. The Spider Beside Her ◆ 1998

THE GREAT BRAIN

Fitzgerald, John D.
DIAL ◆ GRADES 5–7 ◆ A/R
HISTORICAL | HUMOR | REAL LIFE

Tom, Sweyn, and J.D. are three brothers growing up in a small Utah town in the late 1800s. Tom has a great brain and an insatiable love for money, a combination that leads him to concoct endless schemes for swindling his friends and family. One of his first enterprises is to charge the neighborhood kids to see his family's toilet, the first in town. Occasionally, he has fits of conscience and promises to reform, most notably when the neighborhood kids decide to stop speaking to him. Sweyn, the oldest brother, is amused by Tom's schemes, but J.D., the youngest brother and narrator, always seems to be taken in.

1. The Great Brain ◆ 1967
2. More Adventures of the Great Brain ◆ 1969
3. Me and My Little Brain ◆ 1971
4. The Great Brain at the Academy ◆ 1972
5. The Great Brain Reforms ◆ 1973
6. The Return of the Great Brain ◆ 1974

7. The Great Brain Does It Again ◆ 1975
8. The Great Brain Is Back ◆ 1995

THE GREAT GOOD THING *see* Sylvie Cycle

THE GREAT MCGONIGGLE

Corbett, Scott
LITTLE, BROWN ◆ GRADES 2–3
ADVENTURE | MYSTERY

Mac McGoniggle and his friend Ken Wetzel manage to solve crimes more quickly than the police. They foil a jewel thief, retrieve a valuable prize, and outsmart a player on their ball team in this fast-paced mystery series. Two of the books deal with sports, which will attract reluctant readers. Cartoonlike line drawings will appeal to this audience, too.

1. The Great McGoniggle's Gray Ghost ◆ 1975
2. The Great McGoniggle's Key Play ◆ 1976
3. The Great McGoniggle Rides Shotgun ◆ 1978
4. The Great McGoniggle Switches Pitches ◆ 1980

THE GREAT SKINNER

Tolan, Stephanie S.
MACMILLAN ◆ GRADES 4–7
FAMILY LIFE | HUMOR

Jennifer Skinner narrates the hilarious adventures of the not-quite-normal Skinner family. The slide from normalcy begins when her mother decides to go on strike to get her family to do more of the housework. The strike gains national attention, much to the disgust of Jennifer and her siblings. The strike is finally settled when everyone in the family agrees to do more around the house. But Mr. Skinner has been irrevocably changed by the whole business. He decides to quit his job and start a family business, which turns out to be too successful. Just as the family is hoping to settle down again, he buys a motor home and they start off on a trip across the country.

1. The Great Skinner Strike ◆ 1983
2. The Great Skinner Enterprise ◆ 1986
3. The Great Skinner Getaway ◆ 1987
4. The Great Skinner Homestead ◆ 1988

GREEN KNOWE

Boston, L. M.

HARCOURT ◆ GRADES 4–8 ◆ A/R

FANTASY

An ancient house in Great Britain is rich with history and stories of the children who have lived there over the centuries. Lonely young Tolly goes to live there with his Great-Grandmother Oldknow in the early 1930s. Tolly soon discovers that his great-grandmother's stories about the children who used to live there literally come to life. We are not sure at first whether he is time-traveling or seeing the children's ghosts, but it soon becomes clear that all time blends together in this house. The series continues with more stories of children from different eras and with mysteries about the house itself, including hidden treasure.

1. The Children of Green Knowe ◆ 1954
2. The Treasure of Green Knowe ◆ 1958
3. The River at Green Knowe ◆ 1959
4. A Stranger at Green Knowe ◆ 1961
5. An Enemy at Green Knowe ◆ 1964
6. The Stones of Green Knowe ◆ 1976

GREY GRIFFINS

Benz, Derek, and J. S. Lewis

SCHOLASTIC ◆ GRADES 5–8 ◆ A/R

FANTASY

Max, Harley, Natalia, and Ernie enjoy playing a fantasy role playing game called Round Table. Using cards and dice, the game features witches, faeries, goblins, and other magical creatures. Mr. Iverson, the elderly owner of an antique shop, plays with them. When Max inadvertently releases one of the game card characters, other characters begin to leave the game and enter reality. Max and his friends, who call themselves the Grey Griffins, need to find a way to return the creatures to the game. They begin to realize that there is more to the game than they expected as Max is revealed to be a descendant of King Arthur and the Knights Templar.

1. The Revenge of the Shadow King ◆ 2006
2. The Rise of the Black Wolf ◆ 2007
3. The Fall of the Templar ◆ 2008

GRK

Doder, Joshua

RANDOM HOUSE; ANDERSEN PRESS ◆ GRADES 5–7 ◆ A/R

ADVENTURE

Tim Malt, a plucky British 12-year-old, discovers a dog that belongs to the Stanislavian ambassador's family. Only trouble is, the family is no longer in London. Tim sets off to Stanislavia with Grk in tow and plunges into an adventure full of fast-paced action. In the second book, Tim, Grk, and the Stanislavian children are off to Brazil on the trail of bank robbers.

1. A Dog Called Grk ◆ 2007
2. Grk: Operation Tortoise ◆ 2007
3. Grk and the Pelotti Gang ◆ 2007
4. Grk Smells a Rat ◆ 2008
5. Grk and the Hot Dog Trail ◆ 2008

THE GROSSE ADVENTURES

Auerbach, Annie

TOKYOPOP ◆ GRADES 4–7 ◆ A/R

HUMOR

Stinky and Stan Grosse are twin brothers with a smelly skill—passing gas. Their odor-producing ability is helpful when they encounter aliens. The brothers are always on the lookout for adventure. The stories are presented with graphic novel sections along with more traditional text. Show these to fans of the Riot Brothers and Captain Underpants.

1. The Good, the Bad & the Gassy ◆ 2006
2. Stinky & Stan Blast Off! ◆ 2007
3. Trouble at Twilight Cave ◆ 2007

GRUMPY BUNNY

Korman, Justine

TROLL ◆ GRADES K–1

ANIMAL FANTASY | HUMOR

Hopper is a grumpy bunny, even on holidays and other special occasions. At Easter, he is grumpy because he must give away so many Easter treats. On Valentine's Day, he does not like all that mushy stuff. On the first day of school, he dreads his kinderbunny class. Cute illustrations add to the appeal of these stories.

1. The Grumpy Bunny Goes to School ◆ 1997
2. The Grumpy Easter Bunny ◆ 1995
3. I Love You, Grumpy Bunny ◆ 1997
4. The Grumpy Bunny Goes West ◆ 1997
5. The Grumpy Bunny's Snowy Day ◆ 1997
6. The Grumpy Bunny Joins the Team ◆ 1998
7. The Grumpy Bunny's Field Trip ◆ 1998
8. Merry Christmas, Grumpy Bunny ◆ 1999

9. The Grumpy Bunny's Spooky Night ◆ 2000
10. The Grumpy Bunny's Too Many Bunnybabies ◆ 2002

GUARDIANS OF GA'HOOLE

Lasky, Kathryn

SCHOLASTIC ◆ GRADES 4–8 ◆ A/R

FANTASY

The Academy for Orphaned Owls is not a kind place. Soren, a barn owl, discovers this when he arrives and is given a number to replace his name. All the young owls are made to follow the very strict rules. With the help of an old owl, Soren and his friends subvert the rules. They learn to fly and to confront the evil that surrounds them. Fans of Avi's books about Poppy and Brian Jacques's Redwall should try this series.

1. The Capture ◆ 2003
2. The Journey ◆ 2003
3. The Rescue ◆ 2003
4. The Siege ◆ 2004
5. The Shattering ◆ 2004
6. The Burning ◆ 2004
7. The Hatchling ◆ 2005
8. The Outcast ◆ 2005
9. The First Collier ◆ 2006
10. The Coming of Hoole ◆ 2006
11. To Be a King ◆ 2006
12. The Golden Tree ◆ 2007
13. The River of Wind ◆ 2007
14. Exile ◆ 2008
15. The War of the Ember ◆ 2008

GUS AND GRANDPA

Mills, Claudia

FARRAR, STRAUS & GIROUX ◆ GRADES K–2 ◆ A/R

FAMILY LIFE | REAL LIFE

This is a charming series highlighting the special, loving relationship between Gus, who is almost 7, and his grandfather, who is almost 70. They love spending time together, playing with Grandpa's dog, Skipper, celebrating their birthdays, and baking Christmas cookies. Because Gus is young and Grandpa is old, they sometimes forget things, but they help each other cope. They both love trains, and one book features a special ride on a steam engine. Another book describes how Gus visits and helps Grandpa in the hospital after a heart attack. Beginning readers will find the larger print and simple sentences very accessible.

1. Gus and Grandpa ◆ 1996
2. Gus and Grandpa Ride the Train ◆ 1997
3. Gus and Grandpa and the Christmas Cookies ◆ 1997
4. Gus and Grandpa at the Hospital ◆ 1998
5. Gus and Grandpa and the Two-Wheeled Bike ◆ 1999
6. Gus and Grandpa and Show-and-Tell ◆ 2000
7. Gus and Grandpa at Basketball ◆ 2001
8. Gus and Grandpa and the Halloween Costume ◆ 2002
9. Gus and Grandpa Go Fishing ◆ 2003
10. Gus and Grandpa and the Piano Lesson ◆ 2004

GUS THE HEDGEHOG

Williams, Jacklyn

PICTURE WINDOW BOOKS ◆ GRADES K–2 ◆ A/R

ANIMAL FANTASY

Gus the hedgehog enjoys everyday activities and holidays. With many classrooms choosing hedgehogs as pets, this series of easy readers will be a fun choice.

1. Happy Easter, Gus! ◆ 2004
2. Happy Halloween, Gus! ◆ 2004
3. Happy Valentine's Day, Gus! ◆ 2004
4. Merry Christmas, Gus! ◆ 2004
5. Happy Birthday, Gus! ◆ 2005
6. Happy Thanksgiving, Gus! ◆ 2005
7. Let's Go Fishing, Gus! ◆ 2006
8. Welcome to Third Grade, Gus! ◆ 2006
9. Make a New Friend, Gus! ◆ 2006
10. Pick a Pet, Gus! ◆ 2006

GUY STRANG

Weeks, Sarah

HARPERCOLLINS ◆ GRADES 5–8 ◆ A/R

REAL LIFE

Guy Strang, 12, wonders if he's in the right family. His parents are eccentric, often even embarrassing. For example, his father sucks oysters up his nose. When Guy and his friend Buzz find a classmate with the same birthday as Guy, they become convinced that Guy was switched at birth. In the second book, Guy's parents separate and Guy adjusts to his changing feelings about girls.

1. Regular Guy ◆ 1999
2. Guy Time ◆ 2000

3. My Guy ◆ 2001
4. Guy Wire ◆ 2003

GWYN GRIFFITHS TRILOGY

Nimmo, Jenny

SCHOLASTIC ◆ GRADES 4–7 ◆ A/R

FANTASY

Gwyn's sister has disappeared in the Welsh mountains. Gwyn's grand-mother gives him five magic gifts to help him solve this mystery. In the second book, Gwyn and a girl called Nia save Gwyn's cousin Emlyn from the creatures that snatched Gwyn's sister. The series concludes as Gwyn uses his magical powers to capture an evil spirit. This series was reissued in 2006–2007 as the Magician Trilogy. The middle volume, *Orchard of the Crescent Moon,* was renamed *Emlyn's Moon.*

1. The Snow Spider ◆ 1987
2. Orchard of the Crescent Moon ◆ 1989
3. The Chestnut Soldier ◆ 1991

GYM SHORTS

Hicks, Betty

ROARING BROOK PRESS ◆ GRADES 2–5 ◆ A/R

HUMOR | RECREATION

Henry, Goose, Rocky, Rita, and Jazz are friends who enjoy participating in sports together. In *Basketball Bats,* Henry organizes a basketball game but then hogs the ball. In *Goof-Off Goalie,* Goose works hard to improve at soccer. Sports fans will be attracted to these books which also include situations for discussion and character development.

1. Basketball Bats ◆ 2008
2. Goof-Off Goalie ◆ 2008
3. Swimming with Sharks ◆ 2008
4. Scaredy-Cat Catcher ◆ 2009

GYMNASTS

Levy, Elizabeth

SCHOLASTIC ◆ GRADES 4–6

REAL LIFE | RECREATION

Six girls—Cindi, Darlene, Lauren, Jodi, Ti An, and Ashley—are on a gymnastics team called the Pinecones. They aren't the best team, but they stick together and learn from each other and their coach, Patrick. There's a lot of information about gymnastics woven in, but the girls also deal with situations in their families and with boys and friends.

1. The Beginners ◆ 1988
2. First Meet ◆ 1988
3. Nobody's Perfect ◆ 1988
4. Winner ◆ 1989
5. Trouble in the Gym ◆ 1989
6. Bad Break ◆ 1989
7. Tumbling Ghosts ◆ 1989
8. The Captain of the Team ◆ 1989
9. Crush on the Coach ◆ 1990
10. Boys in the Gym ◆ 1990
11. Mystery at the Meet ◆ 1990
12. Out of Control ◆ 1990
13. First Date ◆ 1990
14. World Class Gymnast ◆ 1990
15. Nasty Competition ◆ 1991
16. Fear of Falling ◆ 1991
17. Gymnast Commandos ◆ 1991
18. The New Coach ◆ 1991
19. Tough at the Top ◆ 1991
20. The Gymnasts' Gift ◆ 1991
21. Team Trouble ◆ 1992
22. Go for the Gold ◆ 1992

THE HALL FAMILY

Langton, Jane

HARPERCOLLINS ◆ GRADES 4–6 ◆ A/R

FANTASY

The Hall family is different. In their house in Concord, Massachusetts, Eddy and Eleanor Hall discover family secrets—including a magical attic that leads them into a mysterious dream world. Subsequent books are equally magical, including the Newbery Honor-winning *The Fledgling*, in which Georgie Hall believes she can fly.

1. The Diamond in the Window ◆ 1962
2. The Swing in the Summerhouse ◆ 1967
3. The Astonishing Stereoscope ◆ 1971
4. The Fledgling ◆ 1980
5. The Fragile Flag ◆ 1984
6. The Time Bike ◆ 2000
7. The Mysterious Circus ◆ 2005
8. The Dragon Tree ◆ 2008

HAMLET CHRONICLES

Maguire, Gregory
CLARION ◆ GRADES 4–7 ◆ A/R
FANTASY

In Hamlet, Vermont, problems arise when seven frozen prehistoric Siberian snow spiders thaw. Each imprints on a different girl in the Tattletale Club. Things are fine while the spiders are small. But when they begin to grow, they become mean and have plans for the boys in the Copycat Club and their teacher, Miss Earth. The same students return in other books as the Tattletales and Copycats continue their rivalry.

1. Seven Spiders Spinning ◆ 1994
2. Six Haunted Hairdos ◆ 1997
3. Five Alien Elves ◆ 1998
4. Four Stupid Cupids ◆ 2000
5. Three Rotten Eggs ◆ 2002
6. A Couple of April Fools ◆ 2004
7. One Final Firecracker ◆ 2005

HANK THE COWDOG

Erickson, John R.
MAVERICK ◆ GRADES 4–6 ◆ A/R
ANIMAL FANTASY | HUMOR

Hank is the "Head of Ranch Security" at Sally May and Loper's place. He bosses around his fellow guard dog, Drover, and quarrels with Pete the cat. In the first book, Hank is falsely accused of killing a chicken. He runs away and decides to become an outlaw. After outwitting a pack of coyotes, he returns to the ranch and tracks a "badger" that turns out to be a skunk. In subsequent books, Hank gets involved in other mysteries around the ranch. The humor comes from Hank's buffoonery as he swaggers and boasts but actually does very little guarding.

1. Hank the Cowdog ◆ 1983
2. Further Adventures of Hank the Cowdog ◆ 1983
3. It's a Dog's Life ◆ 1984
4. Murder in the Middle Pasture ◆ 1984
5. Faded Love ◆ 1985
6. Let Sleeping Dogs Lie ◆ 1986
7. The Curse of the Incredible Priceless Corncob ◆ 1989
8. The Case of the One-Eyed Killer Stud Horse ◆ 1989
9. The Case of the Halloween Ghost ◆ 1989
10. Every Dog Has His Day ◆ 1989
11. Lost in the Dark Unchanted Forest ◆ 1989
12. The Case of the Fiddle-Playing Fox ◆ 1989

13. The Wounded Buzzard on Christmas Eve ◆ 1989
14. Hank the Cowdog and Monkey Business ◆ 1990
15. The Case of the Missing Cat ◆ 1990
16. Lost in the Blinded Blizzard ◆ 1991
17. The Case of the Car-Barkaholic Dog ◆ 1991
18. The Case of the Hooking Bull ◆ 1992
19. The Case of the Midnight Rustler ◆ 1992
20. The Phantom in the Mirror ◆ 1993
21. The Case of the Vampire Cat ◆ 1993
22. The Case of the Double Bumblebee Sting ◆ 1994
23. Moonlight Madness ◆ 1994
24. The Case of the Black-Hooded Hangman ◆ 1995
25. The Case of the Swirling Killer Tornado ◆ 1995
26. The Case of the Kidnapped Collie ◆ 1996
27. The Case of the Night Stalking Bone Monster ◆ 1996
28. The Mopwater Files ◆ 1997
29. The Case of the Vampire Vacuum Sweeper ◆ 1997
30. The Case of the Haystack Kitties ◆ 1998
31. The Case of the Vanishing Fishhook ◆ 1998
32. The Garbage Monster from Outer Space ◆ 1999
33. The Case of the Measled Cowboy ◆ 1999
34. Slim's Goodbye ◆ 2000
35. The Case of the Saddle House Robbery ◆ 2000
36. The Case of the Raging Rottweiler ◆ 2000
37. The Case of the Deadly Ha-Ha Game ◆ 2001
38. The Fling ◆ 2001
39. The Secret Laundry Monster Files ◆ 2002
40. The Case of the Missing Bird Dog ◆ 2002
41. The Case of the Shipwrecked Tree ◆ 2003
42. The Case of the Burrowing Robot ◆ 2003
43. The Case of the Twisted Kitty ◆ 2004
44. The Dungeon of Doom ◆ 2004
45. The Case of the Falling Sky ◆ 2005
46. The Case of the Tricky Trap ◆ 2005
47. The Case of the Tender Cheeping Chickies ◆ 2006
48. The Case of the Monkey Burglar ◆ 2006
49. The Case of the Booby-Trapped Pickup ◆ 2007
50. The Case of the Most Ancient Bone ◆ 2007
51. The Case of the Blazing Sky ◆ 2008
52. The Quest for the Great White Quail ◆ 2008

HANK ZIPZER

Winkler, Henry, and Lin Oliver

GROSSET & DUNLAP ◆ GRADES 3–5 ◆ A/R

REAL LIFE

Hank is in fourth grade and struggles with his schoolwork. In the first book, he decides to make a model of Niagara Falls instead of writing a summer vacation report. It turns out to be a classroom mess! Hank's music teacher arranges for him to be tested for disabilities and Hank gets help with his learning problems. Like the Joey Pigza books, this series gives a sympathetic portrayal of a student with learning difficulties.

1. Niagara Falls or Does It? ◆ 2003
2. I Got a "D" in Salami ◆ 2003
3. Day of the Iguana ◆ 2003
4. The Zippity Zinger ◆ 2003
5. The Night I Flunked My Field Trip ◆ 2004
6. Holy Enchilada! ◆ 2004
7. Help! Somebody Get Me Out of Fourth Grade ◆ 2004
8. Summer School! What Genius Thought Up That? ◆ 2005
9. My Secret Life as a Ping-Pong Wizard ◆ 2005
10. My Dog's a Scaredy-Cat: A Halloween Tail ◆ 2006
11. The Curtain Went Up, My Pants Fell Down ◆ 2007
12. Barfing in the Backseat: How I Survived My Family Road Trip ◆ 2007
13. Who Ordered This Baby? Definitely Not Me! ◆ 2007
14. The Life of Me: Enter at Your Own Risk ◆ 2008

HANNAH AND THE ANGELS

Keep, Linda Lowery

RANDOM HOUSE ◆ GRADES 3–5 ◆ A/R

ADVENTURE | FANTASY

Hannah is an intrepid girl who is aided by angels as she confronts problems around the world. She faces poachers in Australia, disease in Africa, thieves in Mexico, and a kidnapping in the Appalachian Mountains. Throughout, the angels guide her adventures and provide her with help.

1. Mission Down Under ◆ 1998
2. Searching for Lulu ◆ 1998
3. Mexican Treasure Hunt ◆ 1998
4. Notes from Blue Mountain ◆ 1998
5. Saving Uncle Sean ◆ 1999
6. Mardi Gras Mix-Up ◆ 1999
7. Trouble on Ice ◆ 1999
8. Last Chance in France ◆ 2000
9. Missing Piece in Greece ◆ 2000

HANNAH MONTANA

Various authors

DISNEY PRESS ◆ GRADES 3–6 ◆ A/R

REAL LIFE

Tween-age girls cannot get enough of Miley Cyrus/Hannah Montana. This series is based on episodes from the mega-popular Disney Channel television program. Miley plays Miley Stewart, a girl with a double life. She seems like an ordinary girl; however, with make-up, a wig, and colorful costumes she becomes pop sensation Hannah Montana. Of course, her secret life often puts her in crazy situations. There are many related items including puzzle and sticker books, calendars, posters, DVDs, and more.

1. Keeping Secrets (Beechwood, Beth) ◆ 2006
2. Face-Off (Alfonsi, Alice) ◆ 2006
3. Super Sneak (McElroy, Laurie) ◆ 2006
4. Truth or Dare (King, M. C.) ◆ 2007
5. Hold on Tight (McElroy, Laurie) ◆ 2007
6. Crush-Tastic! (Beechwood, Beth) ◆ 2007
7. Nightmare on Hannah Street (McElroy, Laurie) ◆ 2007
8. Seeing Green (King, M. C.) ◆ 2007
9. Face the Music (Beechwood, Beth) ◆ 2007
10. Don't Bet on It (Lloyd, Ann) ◆ 2008
11. Sweet Revenge (King, M. C.) ◆ 2008
12. Win or Lose (Alexander, Heather) ◆ 2008
13. True Blue (McElroy, Laurie) ◆ 2008
14. On the Road (Richards, Kitty) ◆ 2008
15. Game of Hearts (King, M. C.) ◆ 2008
16. Wishful Thinking (McElroy, Laurie) ◆ 2009
17. One of a Kind (McElroy, Laurie) ◆ 2009

HANNAH MONTANA (TOKYOPOP)

Taylor, Julie, editor

TOKYOPOP ◆ GRADES 3–6

REAL LIFE

Two episodes from the Hannah Montana television series are featured in each book. In the first book, Miley and Lily sneak out to attend a movie premiere hoping to meet Ashton Kutcher. The second episode presents a dilemma for Miley when Lily asks her to go to a Hannah Montana concert. Remember, Miley is Hannah and Lily does not know her secret. This cine-manga uses pictures from the Disney television program.

1. Secrets and Super Sneaks ◆ 2007
2. Crushes and Camping ◆ 2007
3. Boys and Beauty Blunders ◆ 2007
4. Cars and Superstars ◆ 2007
5. School Blues and Family Feuds ◆ 2008
6. Awards and Rewards ◆ 2008

HANNAH OF FAIRFIELD *see* Pioneer Daughters

HANNAH WEST

Johns, Linda

PUFFIN ◆ GRADES 4–6 ◆ A/R

MYSTERY

Set in Seattle, this series features light mysteries and an intrepid sleuth. Hannah West, 12, and her mom move into a fancy apartment building only to become involved in an art theft. Other mysteries include dognapping, missing antiques, and an environmental problem.

1. Hannah West in the Belltown Towers ◆ 2006
2. Hannah West in Deep Water ◆ 2006
3. Hannah West in the Center of the Universe ◆ 2007
4. Hannah West on Millionaire's Row ◆ 2007

HAPPY AND HONEY

Godwin, Laura

MARGARET K. MCELDERRY ◆ GRADES K–1 ◆ A/R

REAL LIFE

Honey is a lively little kitten that wants to play. Happy is a dog that wants to sleep. Honey keeps trying to get Happy to play. Finally, he wakes up and joins in her fun. This is a very simple reader for children who are just beginning to read. When readers have finished these books, suggest Biscuit and Puppy Mudge.

1. Happy and Honey ◆ 2000
2. Honey Helps ◆ 2000
3. The Best Fall of All ◆ 2002
4. Happy Christmas, Honey! ◆ 2002

HARDY BOYS

Dixon, Franklin W.

SIMON & SCHUSTER ◆ GRADES 5–7 ◆ A/R

MYSTERY

Frank and Joe Hardy, the sons of famous detective Fenton Hardy, have become well-known detectives in their own right, even though they are still in their teens. In each book, the two boys are pursuing their various interests when they are confronted with a crime or mystery. After much action and adventure, the mystery is solved, the criminal caught, and all is well again in Bayport. Frank is cast as the serious and thoughtful one, while Joe is more athletic and impulsive. They are aided occasionally by their friend Chet and their father's sister Gertrude.

1. The Tower Treasure ◆ 1927
2. The House on the Cliff ◆ 1927
3. The Secret of the Old Mill ◆ 1927
4. The Missing Chums ◆ 1928
5. Hunting for Hidden Gold ◆ 1928
6. The Shore Road Mystery ◆ 1928
7. Secret of the Caves ◆ 1929
8. Mystery of Cabin Island ◆ 1929
9. Great Airport Mystery ◆ 1930
10. What Happened at Midnight? ◆ 1931
11. While the Clock Ticked ◆ 1932
12. Footprints Under the Window ◆ 1933
13. The Mark on the Door ◆ 1934
14. The Hidden Harbor Mystery ◆ 1935
15. Sinister Signpost ◆ 1936
16. Figure in Hiding ◆ 1937
17. Secret Warning ◆ 1938
18. The Twisted Claw ◆ 1939
19. The Disappearing Floor ◆ 1940
20. Mystery of the Flying Express ◆ 1941
21. The Clue of the Broken Blade ◆ 1942
22. The Flickering Torch Mystery ◆ 1943
23. The Melted Coins ◆ 1944
24. Short-Wave Mystery ◆ 1945
25. The Secret Panel ◆ 1946
26. The Phantom Freighter ◆ 1947
27. The Secret of Skull Mountain ◆ 1948
28. The Sign of the Crooked Arrow ◆ 1949
29. The Secret of the Lost Tunnel ◆ 1950
30. The Wailing Siren Mystery ◆ 1951
31. The Secret of Wildcat Swamp ◆ 1952
32. The Yellow Feather Mystery ◆ 1953
33. The Crisscross Shadow ◆ 1953
34. The Hooded Hawk Mystery ◆ 1954
35. The Clue in the Embers ◆ 1955
36. The Secret of Pirates' Hill ◆ 1957
37. The Ghost at Skeleton Rock ◆ 1957
38. Mystery at Devil's Paw ◆ 1959
39. Mystery of the Chinese Junk ◆ 1960
40. Mystery of the Desert Giant ◆ 1961
41. Clue of the Screeching Owl ◆ 1962
42. The Viking Symbol Mystery ◆ 1963
43. Mystery of the Aztec Warrior ◆ 1964
44. The Haunted Fort ◆ 1965
45. Mystery of the Spiral Bridge ◆ 1966
46. Secret Agent on Flight 101 ◆ 1967
47. Mystery of the Whale Tattoo ◆ 1968
48. The Arctic Patrol Mystery ◆ 1969
49. Bombay Boomerang ◆ 1970

50. Danger on Vampire Trail ◆ 1971
51. The Masked Monkey ◆ 1972
52. The Shattered Helmet ◆ 1973
53. The Clue of the Hissing Serpent ◆ 1974
54. The Mysterious Caravan ◆ 1975
55. The Witchmaster's Key ◆ 1976
56. The Jungle Pyramid ◆ 1977
57. Firebird Rocket ◆ 1978
58. The Sting of the Scorpion ◆ 1979
59. Night of the Werewolf ◆ 1979
60. The Mystery of the Samurai Sword ◆ 1979
61. The Pentagon Spy ◆ 1980
62. The Apeman's Secret ◆ 1980
63. The Mummy Case ◆ 1980
64. Mystery of Smuggler's Cove ◆ 1980
65. The Stone Idol ◆ 1981
66. The Vanishing Thieves ◆ 1981
67. The Outlaw's Silver ◆ 1981
68. Deadly Chase ◆ 1981
69. The Four-Headed Dragon ◆ 1981
70. The Infinity Clue ◆ 1981
71. The Track of the Zombie ◆ 1982
72. The Voodoo Plot ◆ 1982
73. The Billion Dollar Ransom ◆ 1982
74. Tic-Tac Terror ◆ 1982
75. Trapped at Sea ◆ 1982
76. Game Plan for Disaster ◆ 1982
77. The Crimson Flame ◆ 1983
78. Cave-In! ◆ 1983
79. Sky Sabotage ◆ 1983
80. The Roaring River Mystery ◆ 1984
81. The Demon's Den ◆ 1984
82. The Blackwing Puzzle ◆ 1984
83. The Swamp Monster ◆ 1985
84. Revenge of the Desert Phantom ◆ 1985
85. The Skyfire Puzzle ◆ 1985
86. The Mystery of the Silver Star ◆ 1987
87. Program for Destruction ◆ 1987
88. Tricky Business ◆ 1988
89. Sky Blue Frame ◆ 1988
90. Danger on the Diamond ◆ 1988
91. Shield of Fear ◆ 1988
92. The Shadow Killers ◆ 1988
93. The Serpent's Tooth Mystery ◆ 1988
94. Breakdown in Axeblade ◆ 1989
95. Danger on the Air ◆ 1989
96. Wipeout ◆ 1989

97. Cast of Criminals ◆ 1989
98. Spark of Suspicion ◆ 1989
99. Dungeon of Doom ◆ 1989
100. The Secret of the Island Treasure ◆ 1990
101. The Money Hunt ◆ 1990
102. Terminal Shock ◆ 1990
103. The Million-Dollar Nightmare ◆ 1990
104. Tricks of the Trade ◆ 1990
105. The Smoke Screen Mystery ◆ 1990
106. Attack of the Video Villains ◆ 1991
107. Panic on Gull Island ◆ 1991
108. Fear on Wheels ◆ 1991
109. The Prime-Time Crime ◆ 1991
110. The Secret of Sigma Seven ◆ 1991
111. Three-Ring Terror ◆ 1991
112. The Demolition Mission ◆ 1992
113. Radical Moves ◆ 1992
114. The Case of the Counterfeit Criminals ◆ 1992
115. Sabotage at Sports City ◆ 1992
116. Rock 'n' Roll Renegades ◆ 1992
117. The Baseball Card Conspiracy ◆ 1992
118. Danger in the Fourth Dimension ◆ 1993
119. Trouble at Coyote Canyon ◆ 1993
120. The Case of the Cosmic Kidnapping ◆ 1993
121. The Mystery in the Old Mine ◆ 1993
122. Carnival of Crime ◆ 1993
123. The Robot's Revenge ◆ 1993
124. Mystery with a Dangerous Beat ◆ 1993
125. Mystery on Makatunk Island ◆ 1994
126. Racing with Disaster ◆ 1994
127. Reel Thrills ◆ 1994
128. Day of the Dinosaur ◆ 1994
129. The Treasure at Dolphin Bay ◆ 1994
130. Sidetracked to Danger ◆ 1995
131. Crusade of the Flaming Sword ◆ 1995
132. Maximum Challenge ◆ 1995
133. Crime in the Kennel ◆ 1995
134. Cross-Country Crime ◆ 1995
135. The Hypersonic Secret ◆ 1995
136. The Cold Cash Caper ◆ 1996
137. High-Speed Showdown ◆ 1996
138. The Alaskan Adventure ◆ 1996
139. The Search for the Snow Leopard ◆ 1996
140. Slam Dunk Sabotage ◆ 1996
141. The Desert Thieves ◆ 1996
142. Lost in the Gator Swamp ◆ 1997
143. The Giant Rat of Sumatra ◆ 1997

144. The Secret of Skeleton Reef ◆ 1997
145. Terror at High Tide ◆ 1997
146. The Mark of the Blue Tattoo ◆ 1997
147. Trial and Terror ◆ 1998
148. The Ice-Cold Case ◆ 1998
149. The Chase for the Mystery Twister ◆ 1998
150. The Crisscross Crime ◆ 1998
151. The Rocky Road to Revenge ◆ 1998
152. Danger in the Extreme ◆ 1998
153. Eye on Crime ◆ 1998
154. The Caribbean Cruise Caper ◆ 1999
155. The Hunt for the Four Brothers ◆ 1999
156. A Will to Survive ◆ 1999
157. The Lure of the Italian Treasure ◆ 1999
158. The London Deception ◆ 1999
159. Daredevils ◆ 1999
160. A Game Called Chaos ◆ 2000
161. Training for Trouble ◆ 2000
162. The End of the Trail ◆ 2000
163. The Spy that Never Lies ◆ 2000
164. Skin and Bones ◆ 2000
165. Crime in the Cards ◆ 2001
166. Past and Present Danger ◆ 2001
167. Trouble Times Two ◆ 2001
168. The Castle Conundrum ◆ 2001
169. Ghost of a Chance ◆ 2001
170. Kickoff to Danger ◆ 2001
171. The Test Case ◆ 2002
172. Trouble in Warp Space ◆ 2002
173. Speed Times Five ◆ 2002
174. Hide and Sneak ◆ 2002
175. Trick-or-Trouble ◆ 2002
176. In Plane Sight ◆ 2002
177. The Case of the Psychic's Vision ◆ 2003
178. The Mystery of the Black Rhino ◆ 2003
179. Passport to Danger ◆ 2003
180. Typhoon Island ◆ 2003
181. Double Jeopardy ◆ 2003
182. The Secret of the Soldier's Gold ◆ 2003
183. Warehouse Rumble ◆ 2004
184. The Dangerous Transmission ◆ 2004
185. Wreck and Roll ◆ 2004
186. Hidden Mountain ◆ 2004
187. No Way Out ◆ 2004
188. Farming Fear ◆ 2004
189. One False Step ◆ 2005
190. Motocross Madness ◆ 2005

HARDY BOYS: FRANK AND JOE HARDY: THE CLUES BROTHERS

Dixon, Franklin W.

POCKET BOOKS ◆ GRADES 2–3 ◆ A/R

MYSTERY

Younger versions of the popular Hardy Boys characters are presented in this series. Nine-year-old Frank and his 8-year-old brother Joe move from New York City to the suburb of Bayport when their father resigns from his position as police detective to take an office job. Along with their friends Chet and Mike, the brothers solve all kind of mysteries. Joe loves ghost stories and always looks for paranormal explanations for their cases. While sleuthing, the boys confront bullies and adapt to their new town.

1. The Gross Ghost Mystery ◆ 1997
2. The Karate Clue ◆ 1997
3. First Day, Worst Day ◆ 1997
4. Jump Shot Detectives ◆ 1998
5. Dinosaur Disaster ◆ 1998
6. Who Took the Book? ◆ 1998
7. The Abracadabra Case ◆ 1998
8. The Doggone Detectives ◆ 1998
9. The Pumped Up Pizza Problem ◆ 1998
10. The Walking Snowman ◆ 1999
11. The Monster in the Lake ◆ 1999
12. King for a Day ◆ 1999
13. Pirates Ahoy! ◆ 1999
14. All Eyes on First Prize ◆ 1999
15. Slip, Slide, and Slap Shot ◆ 1999
16. The Fish-Faced Mask of Mystery ◆ 2000
17. The Bike Race Ruckus ◆ 2000

HARDY BOYS, UNDERCOVER BROTHERS

Dixon, Franklin W.

ALADDIN ◆ GRADES 5–9 ◆ A/R

MYSTERY

In this updated Hardy Boys series, the brothers now work undercover for A.T.A.C.—American Teens Against Crime. They still overcome the odds to catch criminals. In the first book, extreme athletes are gathering in Philadelphia for the Big Air Games. It's up to Frank and Joe to prevent anything from disrupting the games. Short sentences and lots of action will attract reluctant readers.

1. Extreme Danger ◆ 2005
2. Running on Fumes ◆ 2005
3. Boardwalk Bust ◆ 2005
4. Thrill Ride ◆ 2005
5. Rocky Road ◆ 2005
6. Burned ◆ 2005
7. Operation: Survival ◆ 2005
8. Top Ten Ways to Die ◆ 2006
9. Martial Law ◆ 2006
10. Blown Away ◆ 2006
11. Hurricane Joe ◆ 2006
12. Trouble in Paradise ◆ 2006
13. The Mummy's Curse ◆ 2006
14. Hazed ◆ 2007
15. Death and Diamonds ◆ 2007
16. Bayport Buccaneers ◆ 2007
17. Murder at the Mall ◆ 2007
18. Pushed ◆ 2007
19. Foul Play ◆ 2007
20. Feeding Frenzy ◆ 2008
21. Comic Con Artist ◆ 2008
22. House Arrest ◆ 2008

HARDY BOYS, UNDERCOVER BROTHERS MURDER HOUSE TRILOGY

1. Deprivation House: Book One in the Murder House Trilogy ◆ 2008
2. House Arrest: Book Two in the Murder House Trilogy ◆ 2008
3. Murder House: Book Three in the Murder House Trilogy ◆ 2008

HARDY BOYS, UNDERCOVER BROTHERS SUPER MYSTERIES

1. Wanted ◆ 2006
2. Kidnapped at the Casino ◆ 2007
3. Haunted ◆ 2008

HARDY BOYS, UNDERCOVER BROTHERS: GRAPHIC NOVELS

Lobdell, Scott

PAPERCUTZ ◆ GRADES 5–9

MYSTERY

Mystery, action, suspense—all of the expected elements of a Hardy Boys book plus the added attraction of the graphic novel format. Various illustrators use bold lines and sharp angles to give these books a manga-inspired look. This could appeal to middle school/junior high reluctant readers.

1. The Ocean of Osyria ◆ 2005
2. Identity Theft ◆ 2005
3. Mad House ◆ 2005
4. Malled ◆ 2006
5. Sea You, Sea Me! ◆ 2006
6. Hyde and Shriek ◆ 2006
7. The Opposite Numbers . . . ◆ 2006
8. Board to Death ◆ 2007
9. To Die or Not to Die? ◆ 2007
10. A Hardy Day's Night ◆ 2007
11. Abracadeath ◆ 2008
12. Dude Ranch O'Death ◆ 2008
13. The Deadliest Stunt ◆ 2008
14. Haley Danelle's Top Eight ◆ 2008
15. Live Free, Die Hardy! ◆ 2008
16. Shhhhh! ◆ 2008

HAROLD AND CHESTER *see* Bunnicula

HAROLD AND THE PURPLE CRAYON

Johnson, Crockett

HARPERCOLLINS ◆ GRADES K–2 ◆ A/R

FANTASY

Whatever Harold draws with his purple crayon becomes real. He draws a highway and then a forest. When a dragon that he draws to guard the apple tree in the forest scares him, his hand shakes and makes the ocean. To solve this problem, he just draws a boat. One night, he gets up from bed and draws a castle with a garden. A garden fairy he adds gives him a wish, and with that and the magic carpet he creates, he makes it home in time for a story.

1. Harold and the Purple Crayon ◆ 1955
2. Harold's Fairy Tale: Further Adventures with the Purple Crayon ◆ 1956
3. Harold's Trip to the Sky ◆ 1957
4. Harold at the North Pole: A Christmas Journey with the Purple Crayon ◆ 1958
5. Harold's Circus: An Astounding, Colossal Purple Crayon Event ◆ 1959
6. A Picture for Harold's Room: A Purple Crayon Adventure ◆ 1960
7. Harold's ABC ◆ 1963

HARRIET

Carlson, Nancy L.

CAROLRHODA ◆ GRADES K–2 ◆ A/R

ANIMAL FANTASY | REAL LIFE

Harriet is a dog who faces everyday frustrations and dilemmas, such as watching out for her little brother, Walt, when she really wants to play, or being honest about spoiling a neighbor's prize flower. There is a gentle lesson in each book as Harriet solves simple problems.

1. Harriet's Recital ◆ 1982
2. Harriet's Halloween Candy ◆ 1982
3. Harriet and the Roller Coaster ◆ 1982
4. Harriet and Walt ◆ 1983
5. Harriet and the Garden ◆ 1982
6. Harriet and George's Christmas Treat ◆ 2001

HARRIET

Maestro, Betsy, and Giulio Maestro

CROWN ◆ GRADES K–1

ANIMAL FANTASY

A perky young elephant demonstrates important concepts to very young children. One simple line of text on each page is accompanied by a brightly colored illustration featuring a posterlike Harriet. Concepts illustrated include time, ordinal numbers, reading signs, and prepositions.

1. Harriet Goes to the Circus ◆ 1977
2. Harriet Reads Signs and More Signs ◆ 1981
3. Around the Clock with Harriet ◆ 1984
4. Harriet at Play ◆ 1984
5. Harriet at School ◆ 1984
6. Harriet at Home ◆ 1984
7. Harriet at Work ◆ 1984
8. Through the Year with Harriet ◆ 1985
9. Dollars and Cents for Harriet ◆ 1988

HARRIET BEAN

McCall Smith, Alexander

BLOOMSBURY ◆ GRADES 2–4 ◆ A/R

HUMOR

Harriet Bean's father is truly absent minded—he forgot that he has five sisters. Harriet, 9, goes searching for her aunts and along the way she has entertaining adventures which develop into mysteries in the second and third books. In *Harriet Bean and the League of Cheats,* Harriet solves a mystery at the race track. In *The Cowgirl Aunt of Harriet Bean,* she travels to America to help Aunt Formica deal with cattle rustlers.

1. The Five Lost Aunts of Harriet Bean ◆ 2006
2. Harriet Bean and the League of Cheats ◆ 2006
3. The Cowgirl Aunt of Harriet Bean ◆ 2006

HARRIET M. WELSCH

Various authors

HARPERCOLLINS; DELACORTE ◆ GRADES 4–6 ◆ A/R

REAL LIFE

The award-winning first book in this trilogy introduces us to Harriet M. Welsch, a student at a private school in New York in the 1960s. She fancies herself a spy and keeps a notebook in which she records her impressions of her friends. When the notebook is found and read, she learns some valuable lessons about herself and others. The second book focuses on her friend Beth Ellen. They are spending the summer in a small town in upstate New York. Harriet is still keeping her notebook, trying to find out who is leaving strange notes all over town. The third book is about one of Harriet's friends, Sport, a boy who takes care of his absentminded father. The first three books were written by Louise Fitzhugh; the later two retain the charm of the original character.

1. Harriet the Spy (Fitzhugh, Louise) ◆ 1964
2. The Long Secret (Fitzhugh, Louise) ◆ 1965
3. Sport (Fitzhugh, Louise) ◆ 1979
4. Harriet Spies Again (Ericson, Helen) ◆ 2002
5. Harriet the Spy, Double Agent (Gold, Maya) ◆ 2005

HARRIET THE SPY *see* Harriet M. Welsch

HARRY

Porte, Barbara Ann

HARPERCOLLINS ◆ GRADES 1–3

HUMOR | REAL LIFE

Harry lives with his widowed father. This fully illustrated easy-reader series is about everyday events in their lives. Harry's Aunt Rose gets married in one book, and in another Harry wins a pony. Harry is surrounded by wise and loving grown-ups and good friends.

1. Harry's Visit ◆ 1983

2. Harry's Dog ◆ 1984
3. Harry's Mom ◆ 1985
4. Harry in Trouble ◆ 1989
5. Harry Gets an Uncle ◆ 1991
6. Harry's Birthday ◆ 1994
7. Harry's Pony ◆ 1997

HARRY AND CHICKEN

Sheldon, Dyan
CANDLEWICK ◆ GRADES 3–5
FAMILY LIFE | FANTASY | HUMOR

Harry is a talking cat—actually, he's an alien being from the planet Arcana who has taken on the form of a cat. In the first book, we watch Chicken—a girl—try to keep her new friend Harry secret until he insinuates himself into her family: a mother who doesn't like cats, a sister who is allergic to them, and a brother who has two birds. In the following two books, Harry uses a little space magic to transport them to a small boat in the middle of a strange lake (*Harry the Explorer*) and takes his revenge on Chicken's bullying siblings (*Harry on Vacation*).

1. Harry and Chicken ◆ 1992
2. Harry the Explorer ◆ 1992
3. Harry on Vacation ◆ 1993

HARRY AND EMILY

Ruelle, Karen Gray
HOLIDAY HOUSE ◆ GRADES K–2 ◆ A/R
ANIMAL FANTASY

Harry and Emily are cat siblings dealing with everyday events. Harry camps outside and gets scared. Harry and Emily make apple pies with their grandparents. And they find a perfect Valentine's Day present. Transitional readers want simple chapter books and these are just right.

1. The Thanksgiving Beast Feast ◆ 1999
2. The Monster in Harry's Backyard ◆ 1999
3. Snow Valentines ◆ 2000
4. Spookier Than a Ghost ◆ 2001
5. Easy as Apple Pie ◆ 2002
6. April Fool ◆ 2002
7. Mother's Day Mess ◆ 2003
8. The Crunchy, Munchy Christmas Tree ◆ 2003
9. Easter Egg Disaster ◆ 2004
10. Just in Time for New Year's ◆ 2004

11. Great Groundhogs! ◆ 2006
12. Dear Tooth Fairy ◆ 2006

HARRY POTTER

Rowling, J. K.

SCHOLASTIC ◆ GRADES 3–9 ◆ A/R

FANTASY

Harry Potter's adventures at Hogwarts, a school for wizards and witches, are chronicled in this series. From his initial discovery of his magical past to his developing skills at spells and Quidditch to his realization that there are dark forces at work around him, these books have attracted the attention of readers around the world. Many younger children (in grades three and four) read the earlier books, especially after seeing the movies. They also have the books read to them or listen to them on audio. With each book, as Harry matures, the description of creatures, spells, and violence becomes more graphic and detailed. The optimum audience for the complete series is grades five and up. The books are available in many languages and the movies have been wildly successful. There are many related items including toys, games, books about Quidditch and Beasts, puzzles, computer programs, and more.

1. Harry Potter and the Sorcerer's Stone ◆ 1998
2. Harry Potter and the Chamber of Secrets ◆ 1999
3. Harry Potter and the Prisoner of Azkaban ◆ 1999
4. Harry Potter and the Goblet of Fire ◆ 2000
5. Harry Potter and the Order of the Phoenix ◆ 2003
6. Harry Potter and the Half-Blood Prince ◆ 2005
7. Harry Potter and the Deathly Hallows ◆ 2007

HARRY THE DIRTY DOG

Zion, Gene

HARPERCOLLINS ◆ GRADES K–3

HUMOR

Harry is a white dog with black spots who gets into one funny scrape after another. At the beach, he becomes entangled in seaweed so that everyone thinks he is a sea monster. A relative sends him an ugly sweater that he can't get rid of. At the end of every misadventure, Harry is reunited with his loving family.

1. Harry the Dirty Dog ◆ 1956
2. No Roses for Harry ◆ 1958
3. Harry and the Lady Next Door ◆ 1960
4. Harry by the Sea ◆ 1965

HARRY THE HIPPO

Colorado, Nani, and Jesús Gaban

GARETH STEVENS ◆ GRADES K–2 ◆ A/R

ANIMAL FANTASY

Harry is a bright pink hippo who can count on the help of Mama and Papa when he tries to do big things like dress himself, feed himself, and take a bath. Very young children will enjoy reading or hearing about Harry's adventures.

1. Harry the Hippo ◆ 1992
2. Harry's Mealtime Mess ◆ 1992
3. Harry Dresses Himself ◆ 1992
4. Tub Time for Harry ◆ 1992
5. Harry's Sandbox Surprise ◆ 1992

HARRY THE HIPPO

Ziefert, Harriet

VIKING ◆ GRADES K–2 ◆ A/R

ANIMAL FANTASY

Harry is a hippo who enjoys many ordinary activities. He visits an amusement park, goes to school, and takes a bath. These are very easy reader books that will be useful for children who are developing their skills.

1. Harry Takes a Bath ◆ 1987
2. Harry Goes to Fun Land ◆ 1989
3. Harry Goes to Day Camp ◆ 1990
4. Harry Gets Ready for School ◆ 1991

HARVEY

Clifford, Eth

HOUGHTON MIFFLIN ◆ GRADES 3–5 ◆ A/R

HUMOR | MYSTERY

Whenever Harvey's cousin Nora comes for a visit, Harvey knows he's in for a wacky adventure, probably involving a strange mystery. When Nora visits Harvey for spring break, they catch a prowler and a raccoon. The raccoon leads them to counterfeiters and the cousins become heroes. Nora is flamboyant and loves animals. Harvey is more low-key, which adds to the humor of their adventures.

1. Harvey's Horrible Snake Disaster ◆ 1984

2. Harvey's Marvelous Monkey Mystery ◆ 1987
3. Harvey's Wacky Parrot Adventure ◆ 1990
4. Harvey's Mystifying Raccoon Mix-Up ◆ 1994

HARVEY ANGELL TRILOGY

Hendry, Diana
POCKET/MINSTREL ◆ GRADES 4–7 ◆ A/R
FANTASY | MYSTERY

Henry, an orphan living in a depressing boarding house with his miserly Aunt Agatha, is cheered by the arrival of new resident Harvey Angell, who brings music and a kit full of magical gadgets. Henry calls for Harvey's help with mysteries in subsequent books. In the third, Henry discovers an abandoned baby that has antennae. These entertaining stories were first published in Britain.

1. Harvey Angell ◆ 2001
2. Harvey Angell and the Ghost Child ◆ 2002
3. Harvey Angell Beats Time ◆ 2002

HATCHET *see* Brian Robeson

HATFORD BOYS

Naylor, Phyllis Reynolds
DELACORTE ◆ GRADES 3–5 ◆ A/R
HUMOR | REAL LIFE

The Hatford boys and the Malloy girls just can't seem to get along. The boys think they are smarter and try to prove it by tricking the girls. Will the girls fall for their schemes? Disgusting gifts (neatly wrapped), trading places, and creating a creature are some of the antics in these funny books.

1. The Boys Start the War ◆ 1993
2. The Girls Get Even ◆ 1993
3. Boys Against Girls ◆ 1994
4. The Girls' Revenge ◆ 1998
5. A Traitor Among the Boys ◆ 1999
6. A Spy Among the Girls ◆ 2000
7. The Boys Return ◆ 2001
8. The Girls Take Over ◆ 2002
9. Boys in Control ◆ 2003
10. Girls Rule! ◆ 2004
11. Boys Rock! ◆ 2005
12. Who Won the War? ◆ 2006

HATTIE RABBIT

Gackenbach, Dick

HARPERCOLLINS ◆ GRADES K–2 ◆ A/R

ANIMAL FANTASY | HUMOR

Little Hattie Rabbit spars with the adults and friends in her life and sometimes comes out on top in this easy-reader series. In one story, she wishes her Mom had a neck like a giraffe, feet like a chicken, and a nose like an elephant—until she realizes how silly this would look. In another, when she has to go to bed in the summer light, she persuades her Mom to paint a night scene on her window shade.

1. Hattie Rabbit ◆ 1976
2. Hattie Be Quiet, Hattie Be Good ◆ 1977
3. Mother Rabbit's Son Tom ◆ 1977
4. Hattie, Tom, and the Chicken Witch: A Play and a Story ◆ 1980
5. Hurray for Hattie Rabbit ◆ 1986

HAUNTING WITH LOUISA

Cates, Emily

BANTAM ◆ GRADES 5–8

MYSTERY

Dee Forest comes to Misty Island to live with her Aunt Winnifred after her mother dies and her father cannot cope with his grief. There she meets Louisa, a young ghost who must help four of her living relatives before she can go on to the next life. With Dee's help, and after many adventures, Louisa finds three of them. In the last book, they discover that Dee herself is Louisa's distant cousin, and Louisa saves her life. Meanwhile, Louisa is concerned that Dee doesn't have any living friends and urges her to make some. At the same time, Dee's father finds a new romance, which Dee comes to accept.

1. The Ghost in the Attic ◆ 1990
2. The Mystery of Misty Island Inn ◆ 1991
3. The Ghost Ferry ◆ 1991

HAZEL GREEN

Hirsch, Odo

BLOOMSBURY ◆ GRADES 3–5 ◆ A/R

REAL LIFE

The annual Frogg Day parade does not allow kids to participate. Hazel Green wants to be in the parade. She convinces the parade leaders to allow her and her friends to have a float in the parade. There are problems—such as making the float—but Hazel is a spunky character who overcomes obstacles. In the third book, Hazel deals with a situation involving prejudice as one of the tenants in her building speaks disparagingly about the building's custodian. Hazel's plan to confront this prejudice is not a success at first, but she perseveres and is able to bring attention to the problem.

1. Hazel Green ◆ 2003
2. Something's Fishy, Hazel Green ◆ 2005
3. Have Courage Hazel Green ◆ 2006

HEARTLAND

Brooke, Lauren

SCHOLASTIC ◆ GRADES 4–7 ◆ A/R

REAL LIFE

Heartland is a farm in Virginia that specializes in caring for horses that have been mistreated. Amy, 14, is developing her skills as a horse whisperer. Throughout the series as Amy works with horses, she also deals with different people and their problems. By the end of the series, Amy has finished high school and has a boyfriend, Ty. The Special Editions follow her progress at college, where she is in a pre-vet program.

1. Coming Home ◆ 2000
2. After the Storm ◆ 2000
3. Breaking Free ◆ 2000
4. Taking Chances ◆ 2001
5. Come What May ◆ 2001
6. One Day You'll Know ◆ 2001
7. Out of the Darkness ◆ 2002
8. Thicker than Water ◆ 2002
9. Every New Day ◆ 2002
10. Tomorrow's Promise ◆ 2002
11. True Enough ◆ 2003
12. Sooner or Later ◆ 2003
13. Darkest Hour ◆ 2003
14. Everything Changes ◆ 2003
15. Love Is a Gift ◆ 2004
16. Holding Fast ◆ 2004
17. A Season of Hope ◆ 2004
18. New Beginnings ◆ 2005
19. From This Day On ◆ 2005
20. Always There ◆ 2005

SPECIAL EDITIONS

1. A Holiday Memory ◆ 2004

2. A Winter's Gift ◆ 2007
3. Beyond the Horizon ◆ 2007
4. A Summer to Remember ◆ 2008

HEARTLAND

Lawlor, Laurie

MINSTREL/POCKET BOOKS ◆ GRADES 3–6

FAMILY LIFE | HISTORICAL

In Luck, Wisconsin, in the early 1900s, Madeline "Moe" McDonohugh longs for adventure. Her life seems so restricted. There are the expectations of her parents and grandparents. There are the social conventions of her era. Moe is high-spirited, which sometimes lands her in trouble. Her adventures include encounters with gypsies, a visit from her cousins, finding a tarantula, and taking a trip to her grandparents' farm to view Halley's Comet. This series will appeal to girls who like historical fiction and who enjoy energetic female protagonists.

1. Come Away with Me ◆ 1996
2. Take to the Sky ◆ 1996
3. Luck Follows Me ◆ 1996

HELP! I'M TRAPPED

Strasser, Todd

SCHOLASTIC ◆ GRADES 5–8 ◆ A/R

FANTASY | HUMOR

Jake Sherman seems like an ordinary middle school student, but he has a secret. He can body switch. He has been trapped in his teacher's body, his sister's body, the President's body, and his gym teacher's body. He has even been trapped in a dog's body. In some of the books, he is trapped in repeating events. For example, he has to live through the first day of school until he makes the right choices that break the cycle. Readers will like the implausible situations and the ensuing confusion. These are entertaining books with lots of clever dialogue, albeit at the humor level of a junior high school audience.

1. Help! I'm Trapped in My Teacher's Body ◆ 1993
2. Help! I'm Trapped in the First Day of School ◆ 1994
3. Help! I'm Trapped in Obedience School ◆ 1995
4. Help! I'm Trapped in My Gym Teacher's Body ◆ 1996
5. Help! I'm Trapped in the President's Body ◆ 1996
6. Help! I'm Trapped in Obedience School Again ◆ 1997
7. Help! I'm Trapped in Santa's Body ◆ 1997
8. Help! I'm Trapped in My Sister's Body ◆ 1997

9. Help! I'm Trapped in the First Day of Summer Camp ◆ 1997
10. Help! I'm Trapped in an Alien's Body ◆ 1998
11. Help! I'm Trapped in a Movie Star's Body ◆ 1998
12. Help! I'm Trapped in My Principal's Body ◆ 1998
13. Help! I'm Trapped in My Lunch Lady's Body ◆ 1999
14. Help! I'm Trapped in a Professional Wrestler's Body ◆ 2000
15. Help! I'm Trapped in a Vampire's Body ◆ 2000
16. Help! I'm Trapped in a Supermodel's Body ◆ 2001

HENRIETTA

Hoff, Syd

GARRARD ◆ GRADES K–2

ANIMAL FANTASY

Henrietta the hen is dissatisfied with her life, so she runs away from the farm. In the city, she is able to organize a special egg hunt for the children. Henrietta goes on to have adventures at the circus and on holidays. The simple text of these books is designed for beginning readers.

1. Henrietta Lays Some Eggs ◆ 1977
2. Henrietta, the Early Bird ◆ 1978
3. Henrietta, Circus Star ◆ 1978
4. Henrietta Goes to the Fair ◆ 1979
5. Henrietta's Halloween ◆ 1980
6. Merry Christmas, Henrietta ◆ 1980
7. Henrietta's Fourth of July ◆ 1981
8. Happy Birthday, Henrietta ◆ 1983

HENRY

Carlson, Nancy L.

PENGUIN ◆ GRADES K–2 ◆ A/R

ANIMAL FANTASY

These gentle stories about Henry the mouse will reassure children coping with their first day at school, learning to read, and other rites of passage. In *Henry's Amazing Imagination,* he finds his imagination running away with him in show-and-tell.

1. Look Out Kindergarten, Here I Come! ◆ 1999
2. Henry's Show and Tell ◆ 2004
3. Henry's 100 Days of Kindergarten ◆ 2005
4. First Grade, Here I Come! ◆ 2006
5. I Don't Like to Read! ◆ 2007
6. Henry's Amazing Imagination ◆ 2008
7. Henry and the Valentine Surprise ◆ 2008

HENRY AND MUDGE

Rylant, Cynthia

SIMON & SCHUSTER ◆ GRADES K–3 ◆ A/R

HUMOR | REAL LIFE

Mudge is a huge dog owned by Henry. The series takes them through the seasons, with special times for each one. Stories continue with their encounters with a fussy cousin named Annie, a straggly stray cat, and even all the relatives at a family reunion. Henry's mother and father are kind and understanding when owning a big dog like Mudge causes problems for Henry. Dealing with real-life fun and worries, these beginning readers are just right for students in early elementary grades. There is a Henry and Mudge fan club for more fun. Annie and Snowball is a related series.

1. Henry and Mudge ◆ 1987
2. Henry and Mudge in Puddle Trouble ◆ 1987
3. Henry and Mudge in the Green Time ◆ 1987
4. Henry and Mudge Under the Yellow Moon ◆ 1987
5. Henry and Mudge in the Sparkle Days ◆ 1988
6. Henry and Mudge and the Forever Sea ◆ 1989
7. Henry and Mudge Get the Cold Shivers ◆ 1989
8. Henry and Mudge and the Happy Cat ◆ 1990
9. Henry and Mudge and the Bedtime Thumps ◆ 1991
10. Henry and Mudge Take the Big Test ◆ 1991
11. Henry and Mudge and the Long Weekend ◆ 1992
12. Henry and Mudge and the Wild Wind ◆ 1993
13. Henry and Mudge and the Careful Cousin ◆ 1994
14. Henry and Mudge and the Best Day of All ◆ 1995
15. Henry and Mudge in the Family Trees ◆ 1997
16. Henry and Mudge and the Sneaky Crackers ◆ 1998
17. Henry and Mudge and the Starry Night ◆ 1998
18. Henry and Mudge and Annie's Good Move ◆ 1998
19. Henry and Mudge and the Snowman Plan ◆ 1999
20. Henry and Mudge and Annie's Perfect Pet ◆ 1999
21. Henry and Mudge and the Tall Tree House ◆ 2000
22. Henry and Mudge and Mrs. Hopper's House ◆ 2003
23. Henry and Mudge and the Wild Goose Chase ◆ 2003
24. Henry and Mudge and the Funny Lunch ◆ 2004
25. Henry and Mudge and a Very Merry Christmas ◆ 2004
26. Henry and Mudge and the Great Grandpas ◆ 2005
27. Henry and Mudge and the Tumbling Trip ◆ 2005
28. Henry and Mudge and the Big Sleepover ◆ 2006

HENRY AND MUDGE: PUPPY MUDGE

Rylant, Cynthia
SIMON & SCHUSTER ◆ GRADES K–2 ◆ A/R
HUMOR | REAL LIFE

Henry's big dog Mudge was once a puppy. He enjoyed puppy fun like taking a bath that gets water everywhere! These are easier than the Henry and Mudge books. After reading these, try the Biscuit series.

1. Puppy Mudge Takes a Bath ◆ 2002
2. Puppy Mudge Has a Snack ◆ 2003
3. Puppy Mudge Loves His Blanket ◆ 2004
4. Puppy Mudge Finds a Friend ◆ 2004
5. Puppy Mudge Wants to Play ◆ 2005

HENRY HUGGINS

Cleary, Beverly
MORROW ◆ GRADES 1–4 ◆ A/R
HUMOR | REAL LIFE

Henry Huggins lives with his Mom and Dad and dog Ribsy on Klickitat Street, near Beezus and Ramona. His adventures parallel the Ramona books but are more typical of a boy's activities in the 1950s. Ribsy and Henry often get in and out of scrapes, such as when Ribsy steals a roast from a neighbor's barbecue. Henry's overwhelming desire is for a bike, and he engages in many money-making schemes to obtain one.

1. Henry Huggins ◆ 1950
2. Henry and Beezus ◆ 1952
3. Henry and Ribsy ◆ 1954
4. Henry and the Paper Route ◆ 1957
5. Henry and the Clubhouse ◆ 1962
6. Ribsy ◆ 1964

HENRY REED

Robertson, Keith
VIKING ◆ GRADES 4–6 ◆ A/R
HUMOR | REAL LIFE

Henry Reed is a very mature 15-year-old who has traveled all over the world with his diplomat father. Henry spends his summers with his aunt and uncle in Grover's Corners near Princeton, New Jersey. The time is the 1950s and the series is in the form of a journal that Henry keeps. In the first book, he and his friend and neighbor Midge start a research service, getting into many funny situations. The series continues with a trip across the country by car and Henry's second summer with Midge, when they start a baby-sitting service.

1. Henry Reed, Inc. ◆ 1958
2. Henry Reed's Journey ◆ 1963
3. Henry Reed's Baby-Sitting Service ◆ 1966
4. Henry Reed's Big Show ◆ 1970
5. Henry Reed's Think Tank ◆ 1986

HENRY THE CAT

Calhoun, Mary

MORROW ◆ GRADES K–2 ◆ A/R

ADVENTURE | ANIMAL FANTASY

Henry is most unusual. He is a very clever Siamese cat who likes to walk on his hind legs and has exciting adventures wherever he happens to land. Henry shows up in unusual situations—a sailing excursion, skiing in the mountains, and a ballooning trip—all by chance. He gets upset when a new puppy steals the attention in *High-Wire Henry*. Short sentences and lots of action will hold the attention of readers. The illustrations add to the suspense and the humor, capturing Henry and his family's sense of adventure.

1. Cross-Country Cat ◆ 1979
2. Hot-Air Henry ◆ 1981
3. High-Wire Henry ◆ 1991
4. Henry the Sailor Cat ◆ 1994
5. Blue-Ribbon Henry ◆ 1999
6. Henry the Christmas Cat ◆ 2004

HENRY THE EXPLORER

Taylor, Mark

ATHENEUM ◆ GRADES K–3

ADVENTURE | HUMOR

Henry and his dog, Laird Angus McAngus, read about exciting places and then set out to explore the countryside around their home, always sure to take flags with them to mark the way. They capture a tiger, save a forest from fire, and get lost in a snowstorm.

1. Henry the Explorer ◆ 1966
2. Henry Explores the Jungle ◆ 1968
3. Henry the Castaway ◆ 1970
4. Henry Explores the Mountains ◆ 1975

HERBIE JONES

Kline, Suzy

PUTNAM ◆ GRADES 1–4 ◆ A/R

REAL LIFE

In Miss Pinkham's third-grade class, Herbie Jones and Raymond Martin are in the lowest reading group. Not only do they dislike being in this group, they dislike the group's name, the Apples. When Herbie starts to do well in spelling, he is moved out of the Apples, leaving his best friend behind. Although he can't get Raymond out of the low reading group, Herbie can help him get the group's name changed—to the Spiders! The stories about Herbie and his friends feature events that will be familiar to many students: birthday parties, baseball games, spelling tests, and finding a stray dog. The friendships are realistic, even Herbie's friendship with the smartest girl in the class, Annabelle Louisa Hodgekiss. Humor is mixed in with the everyday concerns. *Herbie Jones Readers' Theater* (1992) is a companion book of excerpts arranged for student performance. There are now books about Herbie when he is in second grade. These books are a bit easier than the original Herbie Jones books.

FOR GRADES 2–4

1. Herbie Jones ◆ 1985
2. What's the Matter with Herbie Jones? ◆ 1986
3. Herbie Jones and the Class Gift ◆ 1987
4. Herbie Jones and the Monster Ball ◆ 1988
5. Herbie Jones and Hamburger Head ◆ 1989
6. Herbie Jones and the Dark Attic ◆ 1992
7. Herbie Jones and the Birthday Showdown ◆ 1993
8. Herbie Jones Moves On ◆ 2003

FOR GRADES 1–3

1. Herbie Jones Sails into Second Grade ◆ 2006
2. Herbie Jones and the Second Grade Slippers ◆ 2006

HERCULEAH JONES

Byars, Betsy

PENGUIN ◆ GRADES 5–7 ◆ A/R

HUMOR | MYSTERY

Herculeah Jones is the daughter of a divorced police detective and a private investigator, so mystery solving comes naturally to her. Her friend Meat appreciates being allowed to help out, and occasionally works on his own. In *Dead Letter,* Herculeah buys a coat at a thrift store and finds a note in its hem. A woman is trapped and someone is going to kill her.

Meat and Herculeah trace the note to a wealthy older woman being cared for by her nephew. In and out of danger the whole time, they are eventually responsible for the culprit's arrest. Herculeah is proud of being strong, and her hair always stands on end when there is danger. Girls will appreciate tough, smart Herculeah, and the relationship between her and Meat provides some humor.

1. The Dark Stairs ◆ 1994
2. Tarot Says Beware ◆ 1995
3. Dead Letter ◆ 1996
4. Death's Door ◆ 1997
5. Disappearing Acts ◆ 1998
6. King of Murder ◆ 2006
7. The Black Tower ◆ 2006

THE HERDMAN KIDS

Robinson, Barbara

HARPERCOLLINS ◆ GRADES 4–6 ◆ A/R

HUMOR

The Best Christmas Pageant Ever introduces the Herdman kids: six incorrigible children who terrorize their town. Beginning with the Nativity program at the church, the kids then direct their antics at their teachers and classmates at Woodrow Wilson Elementary School. Finally, they take on Halloween. Even when the mayor cancels trick-or-treating and the stores hide their candy, the Herdman kids still succeed in creating chaos.

1. The Best Christmas Pageant Ever ◆ 1972
2. The Best School Year Ever ◆ 1994
3. The Best Halloween Ever ◆ 2004

HERE COME THE BROWNIES

Various authors

PUTNAM ◆ GRADES 1–3

REAL LIFE

The girls in 2-B are all in the same Brownie Girl Scout group. Each book describes a simple problem that is solved through the camaraderie and caring of the group. After she moves to town, Corrie joins the group and makes many new friends. Sarah learns to speak up and share her good ideas with her friends. Krissy S. finds a way to earn some money for a special event. At the end of each book, there is a section called Girl Scout Ways that suggests projects and activities—making a friendship bracelet or designing a card to share with friends in a home for the elderly.

1. Corrie's Secret Pal (O'Connor, Jane) ◆ 1993
2. Sarah's Incredible Idea (O'Connor, Jane) ◆ 1993
3. Make Up Your Mind, Marsha! (O'Connor, Jane) ◆ 1993
4. Amy's (Not So) Great Camp-Out (O'Connor, Jane) ◆ 1993
5. Think, Corrie, Think! (O'Connor, Jane) ◆ 1994
6. Lauren and the New Baby (O'Connor, Jane) ◆ 1994
7. Take a Bow, Krissy! (Leonard, Marcia) ◆ 1994
8. Is That Really You, Amy? (Leonard, Marcia) ◆ 1994
9. Lights Out, Sarah! (Leonard, Marcia) ◆ 1995
10. Marsha's Unbearable Day (Leonard, Marcia) ◆ 1995
11. JoAnn and the Surprise Party (Leonard, Marcia) ◆ 1996
12. Krissy and the Big Show (Leonard, Marcia) ◆ 1996

HERMUX TANTAMOQ ADVENTURES

Hoeye, Michael

PUTNAM ◆ GRADES 5–8 ◆ A/R

ANIMAL FANTASY | MYSTERY

Hermux Tantamoq, a mouse, is a watchmaker who enjoys a quiet and orderly life . . . until the intrepid aviatrix Linka Perflinger appears, dragging him into adventure and mystery in *Time Stops for No Mouse*. In the sequels, he continues to show courage while investigating such mysteries as the early relationship between mice and cats.

1. Time Stops for No Mouse ◆ 2002
2. The Sands of Time ◆ 2003
3. No Time Like Show Time ◆ 2004

HEROES A2Z

Anthony, David, and Charles David

SIGIL PUBLISHING ◆ GRADES 3–5

FANTASY | HUMOR

Three superheroes—twins Abigail and Andrew and Baby Zoe—fight aliens, a blob made of fudge, and chocolate bunnies that bite back. Set in Traverse City, Michigan, the wacky humor and improbable situations should attract readers.

1. Alien Ice Cream ◆ 2007
2. Bowling Over Halloween ◆ 2007
3. Cherry Bomb Squad ◆ 2007
4. Digging for Dinos ◆ 2008
5. Easter Egg Haunt ◆ 2008
6. Fowl Mouthwash ◆ 2008

HEROIC MISADVENTURES OF HICCUP HORRENDOUS HADDOCK III

Cowell, Cressida

LITTLE, BROWN ◆ **GRADES 3–5** ◆ **A/R**

HUMOR

In the first book, Hiccup Horrendous Haddock III is in training to join his Viking clan, the Tribe of the Hairy Hooligans. His first test is to catch and train a dragon. Hiccup is mocked for choosing a small, toothless dragon. However, when the Vikings are attacked, Hiccup and his dragon come to the rescue. These books are written as if Hiccup is the author and there are many humorous side remarks and character names. This is a fun series for middle-grade readers.

1. How to Train Your Dragon ◆ 2004
2. How to Be a Pirate ◆ 2005
3. How to Speak Dragonese ◆ 2006
4. How to Cheat a Dragon's Curse ◆ 2007
5. How to Twist a Dragon's Tale ◆ 2008

HEY ARNOLD!

Bartlett, Craig, and Maggie Groening

SIMON & SCHUSTER ◆ **GRADES 3–6** ◆ **A/R**

REAL LIFE

Arnold is the featured character in the popular Nickelodeon cartoon series. In one book, Arnold and Helga run for president of their fourth-grade class. Another book revolves around an e-mail bulletin board at school. Helga, who secretly loves Arnold, may finally declare her love, so long as she is hidden by her e-mail identity. There is also a book called *Hey Arnold: The Movie Novelization* and there are many related products.

1. Arnold for President ◆ 2000
2. Return of the Sewer King ◆ 2000
3. Arnold's Valentine ◆ 2001
4. Parents Day ◆ 2001
5. Summer Love ◆ 2001
6. The Mystery of the Bermuda Triangle ◆ 2001
7. Arnold's Christmas ◆ 2001
8. Arnold's E-Files ◆ 2001

HEY L'IL D!

Lanier, Bob, and Heather Goodyear

SCHOLASTIC ◆ GRADES 2–4

RECREATION

Bob Lanier is in the NBA Hall of Fame. These books use vignettes from his childhood to focus on friendship, teamwork, training, and problem solving. Lanier's father was a popular basketball player whose nickname was Dobber, so Bob became L'il Dobber or L'il D. The kids in L'il D's fourth-grade group are depicted as from diverse backgrounds. In one book, Sam (Samantha) is showing a greater interest in clothes and girlfriends than in basketball.

1. It's All in the Name ◆ 2003
2. Take the Court ◆ 2003
3. Stuck in the Middle ◆ 2003
4. Out of Bounds ◆ 2003

HICCUP HORRENDOUS HADDOCK III *see*
Heroic Misadventures of Hiccup Horrendous Haddock III

HIGH HURDLES

Snelling, Lauraine

BETHANY HOUSE ◆ GRADES 4–7 ◆ A/R

FAMILY LIFE | REAL LIFE | VALUES

DJ Randall, 13 at the start of the series, loves horses. She lives with her mother and has never met her father. As the series progresses, her biological father makes contact for the first time in 14 years. Her mother remarries and DJ must adjust to a stepfather and stepsiblings. DJ spends a lot of time at the riding academy. Like many teens, she is busy with friends, family, and activities. She seeks God's guidance to help her with problems. As the series closes, DJ helps save the horses from a fire and is seriously burned. Her faith helps her face the challenges of her recovery.

1. Olympic Dreams ◆ 1995
2. DJ's Challenge ◆ 1995
3. Setting the Pace ◆ 1996
4. Out of the Blue ◆ 1996
5. Storm Clouds ◆ 1997
6. Close Quarters ◆ 1998
7. Moving Up ◆ 1998

8. Letting Go ◆ 1999
9. Raising the Bar ◆ 1999
10. Class Act ◆ 2000

HIGH-RISE PRIVATE EYES

Rylant, Cynthia
GREENWILLOW ◆ GRADES K–2 ◆ A/R
ANIMAL FANTASY | MYSTERY

Bunny Brown, a rabbit, and Jack Jones, a raccoon, solve mysteries. They find out who is taking Mr. Paris's balloons. They discover what happened to Melvin's lucky fluffy dice. The reader can try to solve the mystery as the clues are revealed. G. Brian Karas's illustrations add to these entertaining stories for beginning readers.

1. The Case of the Missing Monkey ◆ 2000
2. The Case of the Climbing Cat ◆ 2000
3. The Case of the Puzzling Possum ◆ 2001
4. The Case of the Troublesome Turtle ◆ 2001
5. The Case of the Sleepy Sloth ◆ 2002
6. The Case of the Fidgety Fox ◆ 2003
7. The Case of the Baffled Bear ◆ 2004
8. The Case of the Desperate Duck ◆ 2005

HIGH SCHOOL MUSICAL STORIES FROM EAST HIGH

Various authors
DISNEY PRESS ◆ GRADES 4–8 ◆ A/R
REAL LIFE

Tween fans of the Disney High School Musical movies will be thrilled with these books. All of their favorite characters are featured, including Troy, Sharpay, Ryan, Chad, Taylor, and Gabriella. There are performances as well as familiar school activities such as pep rallies, sports, and Spirit Week. Numerous other spin-off items are available from trivia books and calendars to a Super Special book, *Under the Stars* (2008).

1. Battle of the Bands (Grace, N. B) ◆ 2007
2. Wildcat Spirit (Hapka, Catherine) ◆ 2007
3. Poetry in Motion (Alfonsi, Alice) ◆ 2007
4. Crunch Time (Grace, N. B.) ◆ 2007
5. Broadway Dreams (Grace, N. B.) ◆ 2007
6. Heart to Heart (Perelman, Helen) ◆ 2007
7. Friends 4Ever (Hapka, Catherine) ◆ 2008
8. Get Your Vote On! (Grace, N. B., and Beth Beechwood) ◆ 2008

9. Ringin' It In (Grace, N. B.) ◆ 2008
10. Turn Up the Heat (Perelman, Helen) ◆ 2008
11. In the Spotlight (Hapka, Catherine) ◆ 2008
12. Bonjour, Wildcats (Grace, N. B.) ◆ 2008

HISTORY MYSTERIES *see* American Girls: History Mysteries

THE HIT AND RUN GANG

Kroll, Steven
AVON ◆ GRADES 2–4
REAL LIFE | RECREATION

Each book features a different member of this small-town baseball team, the Raymondtown Rockets. Luke is in a hitting slump, Jenny muffs an easy fly ball, Brian's hitting streak comes to an end, Justin does not want to change his pitching style, and Adam is benched. Andy plays hooky from a game, and Vicky loses her confidence. Baseball action mixes with believable friendships. Many of the books teach readers about being good sports and accepting victory and defeat.

1. New Kid in Town ◆ 1992
2. Playing Favorites ◆ 1992
3. The Slump ◆ 1992
4. The Streak ◆ 1992
5. Pitching Trouble ◆ 1994
6. You're Out! ◆ 1994
7. Second Chance ◆ 1994
8. Pride of the Rockets ◆ 1994

HITTY'S TRAVELS

Weiss, Ellen
ALADDIN ◆ GRADES 2–4 ◆ A/R
HISTORICAL

Rachel Field won the 1930 Newbery Medal for her book *Hitty, Her First Hundred Years*. In this series of books, Hitty, a doll, travels to various eras in history. Readers learn about immigration, the Civil War, the gold rush, and the days of suffragettes.

1. Civil War Days ◆ 2001
2. Gold Rush Days ◆ 2001
3. Voting Rights Days ◆ 2002
4. Ellis Island Days ◆ 2002

HOBIE HANSON

Gilson, Jamie

LOTHROP, LEE & SHEPARD ◆ GRADES 4–6 ◆ A/R

HUMOR | REAL LIFE

Realistic dialogue and lots of action keep fans of Hobie Hanson coming back for more of this popular series. In *Thirteen Ways to Sink a Sub*, Hobie organizes his classmates to make their substitute teacher cry. Other escapades feature Hobie and his friends on a camping trip, playing soccer, and attending school in a vacant store at the mall while the regular school is being repaired following a flood. Humorous situations with a good sense of fair play and a variety of interesting characters make this series a winner.

1. Thirteen Ways to Sink a Sub ◆ 1982
2. 4B Goes Wild ◆ 1983
3. Hobie Hanson, You're Weird ◆ 1987
4. Double Dog Dare ◆ 1988
5. Hobie Hanson, Greatest Hero of the Mall ◆ 1989
6. Sticks and Stones and Skeleton Bones ◆ 1991
7. Soccer Circus ◆ 1993

HOLIDAY FIVE

Cooper, Ilene

VIKING ◆ GRADES 3–5 ◆ A/R

REAL LIFE

Five girls (Lia, Maddy, Jill, Erin, and Kathy) who meet at summer camp plan visits on holidays throughout the year and call themselves the Holiday Five. The stories focus on everyday concerns—being popular, getting along with your family, and developing a positive self-image. In one book, *Stupid Cupid,* Lia and Maddy become rivals for the attention of a boy; another focuses on a visit the five girls make to New York City. These books have realistic dialogue and events that many girls will find familiar.

1. Trick or Trouble? ◆ 1994
2. The Worst Noel ◆ 1994
3. Stupid Cupid ◆ 1995
4. No-Thanks Thanksgiving ◆ 1996
5. Star Spangled Summer ◆ 1996

HOLIDAY FRIENDS

Hermes, Patricia

SCHOLASTIC ◆ GRADES 3–5

REAL LIFE

Many girls will identify with Katie Potts. Despite her best intentions, she seems to cause problems. At Christmas, she and her best friend Amelia have a fight. At Thanksgiving, Katie wants the lead in the play but perfect Tiffany already has the perfect costume. Other books feature Katie and her friends at other holidays. This series is entertaining reading for middle-elementary girls.

1. Turkey Trouble ◆ 1996
2. Christmas Magic ◆ 1996
3. My Secret Valentine ◆ 1996
4. Something Scary ◆ 1996
5. Hoppy Easter ◆ 1998

HOLIDAY MICE

Roberts, Bethany

CLARION ◆ GRADES K–2 ◆ A/R

ANIMAL FANTASY

Holidays and mice are both very popular with primary-grade children. Put them together and you have this series. Rhyming verses follow the antics of a group of mice as they enjoy Thanksgiving, Christmas, Easter, the Fourth of July, and more.

1. Halloween Mice! ◆ 1995
2. Valentine Mice! ◆ 1997
3. Christmas Mice! ◆ 2000
4. Thanksgiving Mice! ◆ 2001
5. Birthday Mice! ◆ 2002
6. Easter Mice! ◆ 2003
7. Fourth of July Mice! ◆ 2003

HOLLYWOOD SISTERS

Wilcox, Mary

DELACORTE ◆ GRADES 5–8 ◆ A/R

MYSTERY | REAL LIFE

Jessica, 13, is shy while her older sister, Eva, is an outgoing actress who has a role in a television sitcom. As Jessica adjusts to their new home and her new school, she also solves a few light mysteries, such as who is planting stories about Eva in the tabloids and who is causing the pranks on the set. The Hollywood setting adds to the appeal of this series.

1. Backstage Pass ◆ 2006
2. On Location ◆ 2007
3. Caught on Tape ◆ 2007
4. Star Quality ◆ 2008
5. Truth or Dare ◆ 2009

THE HOME SCHOOL DETECTIVES

Bibee, John

INTERVARSITY PRESS ◆ GRADES 4–6

MYSTERY | VALUES

Featuring a multiracial group of kids, these books describe their mystery adventures within the context of their home-schooling experiences. In cooperation with their church, the families support Christian values in their educational efforts. Beyond this context, the stories are filled with adventure as the characters stumble onto a mysterious cave, solve a series of thefts, and deal with a stolen treasure. Siblings Josh and Emily are tall, blond, and athletic. Becky and Billy are twins of African American heritage. Julie has a Mexican brother, Carlos, who was adopted by her father, Pastor Brown.

1. The Mystery of the Homeless Treasure ◆ 1994
2. The Mystery of the Missing Microchips ◆ 1995
3. The Mystery of the Mexican Graveyard ◆ 1995
4. The Mystery of the Campus Crook ◆ 1996
5. The Mystery of the Vanishing Cave ◆ 1996
6. The Mystery at the Broken Bridge ◆ 1997
7. The Mystery in Lost Canyon ◆ 1997
8. The Mystery of the Widow's Watch ◆ 1998

HOOFBEATS

Duey, Kathleen

DUTTON ◆ GRADES 3–5 ◆ A/R

HISTORICAL | REAL LIFE

Katie Rose, 9, an orphan in an unhappy situation, befriends a mustang and the two, accompanied by Hiram, a farm hand, make a difficult trip across America in the 1840s. The second quartet follows 9-year-old Lara, whose life in turbulent medieval Ireland is tied to that of a beautiful foal; she eventually finds peace for herself and her horse in an abbey. The most recent books also feature independent girls whose affection for their horses helps them meet challenges.

KATIE AND THE MUSTANG

1. Katie and the Mustang: Book 1 ◆ 2004
2. Katie and the Mustang: Book 2 ◆ 2004
3. Katie and the Mustang: Book 3 ◆ 2004
4. Katie and the Mustang: Book 4 ◆ 2004

LARA AND THE SILVER MARE

1. Lara and the Gray Mare: Book 1 ◆ 2005

2. Lara and the Moon-Colored Filly: Book 2 ◆ 2005
3. Lara at Athenry Castle: Book 3 ◆ 2005
4. Lara and the Silent Place: Book 4 ◆ 2005

INDIVIDUAL TITLES

1. Silence and Lily: 1773 ◆ 2007
2. Margret and Flynn: 1875 ◆ 2008

HOPE *see* My America: Hope

HOPPER

Pfister, Marcus

NORTH-SOUTH BOOKS ◆ GRADES K–2 ◆ A/R

ANIMAL FANTASY

These are gentle stories about a rabbit and his Mama. Hopper looks for spring and makes friends with a squirrel who teaches him to climb a tree and with a stag who helps him down. His mother teaches him to avoid enemies and to find food, even in winter.

1. Hopper ◆ 1991
2. Hopper Hunts for Spring ◆ 1992
3. Hopper's Easter Surprise ◆ 1992
4. Hang On, Hopper! ◆ 1995
5. Hopper's Treetop Adventure ◆ 1997

HOPSCOTCH HILL SCHOOL

Tripp, Valerie

PLEASANT COMPANY ◆ GRADES 1–2 ◆ A/R

REAL LIFE

Young readers will enjoy the upbeat atmosphere at Hopscotch Hill School. The children are caring and supportive. The teacher focuses empathetically on individual problems. Hallie struggles with handwriting; Skylar needs to control her impulsiveness; Logan worries about having a cold. This multicultural class will be appreciated by beginning readers.

1. Bright, Shiny Skylar ◆ 2003
2. Hallie's Horrible Handwriting ◆ 2003
3. Thank You, Logan ◆ 2003
4. Good Sport, Gwen ◆ 2004
5. Teasing Trouble ◆ 2004
6. The Fair-Share Pair ◆ 2004

7. Lindy's Happy Ending ◆ 2004
8. The One and Only Delaney ◆ 2005

HORACE SPLATTLY: THE CUPCAKED CRUSADER

David, Lawrence

DUTTON ◆ **GRADES 2–5** ◆ **A/R**

HUMOR

After his sister's cupcakes give him superpowers, Horace, 10, confronts the silly problems in Blootinville. There are hypnotized second graders, an overload of pink dodo birds, and a forest full of monstrous Clownosauruses. Like Dav Pilkey's Captain Underpants, these books are irreverent and funny.

1. Horace Splattly: The Cupcaked Crusader ◆ 2002
2. When Second Graders Attack ◆ 2002
3. The Terror of the Pink Dodo Birds ◆ 2003
4. To Catch a Clownosaurus ◆ 2003
5. The Invasion of the Shag Carpet Creature ◆ 2004
6. The Most Evil, Friendly Villain Ever ◆ 2004

HORRIBLE HARRY

Kline, Suzy

VIKING ◆ **GRADES 2–4** ◆ **A/R**

REAL LIFE

Horrible Harry and the kids in Miss Mackle's Room 2B have many experiences that will be familiar to readers. Harry continually has horrible ideas that turn out well. They put on a play, celebrate Christmas, care for an ant farm, fall "in love," and share secrets. Many of Harry's adventures involve Song Lee, a Korean girl, and Doug, Harry's friend. A sister series to Song Lee.

1. Horrible Harry in Room 2B ◆ 1988
2. Horrible Harry and the Green Slime ◆ 1989
3. Horrible Harry and the Ant Invasion ◆ 1989
4. Horrible Harry's Secret ◆ 1990
5. Horrible Harry and the Christmas Surprise ◆ 1991
6. Horrible Harry and the Kickball Wedding ◆ 1992
7. Horrible Harry and the Dungeon ◆ 1996
8. Horrible Harry and the Purple People ◆ 1997
9. Horrible Harry and the Drop of Doom ◆ 1998
10. Horrible Harry Moves Up to Third Grade ◆ 1998
11. Horrible Harry Goes to the Moon ◆ 2000

12. Horrible Harry at Halloween ◆ 2000
13. Horrible Harry Goes to Sea ◆ 2001
14. Horrible Harry and the Dragon War ◆ 2002
15. Horrible Harry and the Mud Gremlins ◆ 2003
16. Horrible Harry and the Holidaze ◆ 2003
17. Horrible Harry and the Locked Closet ◆ 2004
18. Horrible Harry and the Goog ◆ 2005
19. Horrible Harry Takes the Cake ◆ 2006
20. Horrible Harry and the Triple Revenge ◆ 2006
21. Horrible Harry Cracks the Code ◆ 2007
22. Horrible Harry Bugs the Three Bears ◆ 2008
23. Horrible Harry and the Dead Letters ◆ 2008

HORRID HENRY

Simon, Francesca

HYPERION ◆ GRADES 3–5 ◆ A/R

HUMOR

Henry is horrid! He bothers his brother, Perfect Peter, even trying to sell him in a garage sale. He is a problem for his parents and torments his teachers. This is part of the L.A.F. series from Hyperion that will appeal to fans of Dav Pilkey. The books were originally published in Great Britain and more titles are available from the British publisher.

1. Horrid Henry ◆ 1999
2. Horrid Henry Strikes It Rich ◆ 2000
3. Horrid Henry's Head Lice ◆ 2000

HORSELAND

Various authors

HARPERENTERTAINMENT ◆ GRADES 3–6

REAL LIFE

Four girls—Sarah, Molly, Chloe, and Zoey—are featured in this series about horses and friendship. When Sarah arrives at the Horseland Ranch in a limousine, everyone expects her to be spoiled, but she proves her dedication to the ranch and her friends. After a fall, Molly is afraid to ride again. And, Chloe and Zoey want to take fashion and music gear on the trail ride. These books are based on episodes from a television series.

1. Welcome to Horseland (Auerbach, Annie) ◆ 2007
2. Back in the Saddle Again (Auerbach, Annie) ◆ 2007
3. Trail Ride Terror (Auerbach, Annie) ◆ 2007
4. Rein or Shine (Chesterfield, Sadie) ◆ 2007
5. Western Riding Winner (Auerbach, Annie) ◆ 2008

6. If the Horseshoe Fits (Auerbach, Annie) ◆ 2008
7. It's Just a Horse (Auerbach, Annie) ◆ 2008

HORSESHOE TRILOGIES

Daniels, Lucy
HYPERION/VOLO ◆ GRADES 4–6 ◆ A/R
REAL LIFE

This "trilogy" features three horses—Faith, Hope, and Charity. In the
first book, Josie Grace, 12, and her family are facing financial problems
and have to close their stables. They must find new homes for their horses. Faith goes to a family whose daughter has been injured. Hope goes to
a facility that works with special needs children. Charity goes to another
farm nearby. Girls who like horses will like this series.

1. Keeping Faith ◆ 1999
2. Last Hope ◆ 1999
3. Sweet Charity ◆ 1999
4. In Good Faith ◆ 2003
5. Where There's Hope ◆ 2003
6. Charity at Home ◆ 2003
7. Leap of Faith ◆ 2004
8. Where There's Hope ◆ 2004
9. Charity's Gift ◆ 2004

HORSESHOES

Leitch, Patricia
HARPERCOLLINS ◆ GRADES 5–7
REAL LIFE | RECREATION

Living in a manor in Scotland gives Sally Lorimer what she has always
wanted: the chance to own a horse. After finding the right horse, Sally
and her friend Thalia take riding lessons, participate in horse shows, and
make the Pony Club team. In one book, Thalia is injured in a riding
accident and Sally helps Thalia deal with her father's decision to take
away her horse. Girls who enjoy the many horse and riding series set in
America will enjoy the Scottish setting and riding details in these books.

1. The Perfect Horse ◆ 1992
2. Jumping Lessons ◆ 1992
3. Cross-Country Gallop ◆ 1996
4. Pony Club Rider ◆ 1996
5. Show Jumper Wanted ◆ 1997
6. Mystery Horse ◆ 1997

HOT DOG AND BOB

Rovetch, L. Bob

CHRONICLE ◆ **GRADES 3–6** ◆ **A/R**

HUMOR

Move over Captain Underpants, there is a talking hot dog in town. In the first book, Miss Lamphead (the fifth-grade teacher) turns into an evil alien pizza. Hot Dog uses everything—including mustard, ketchup, and relish—to restore her. Gross events (she vomits out the students she ate) and names (Barfalot) should appeal to reluctant readers. Ample illustrations also add to the appeal.

1. Hot Dog and Bob and the Seriously Scary Attack of the Evil Alien Pizza Person ◆ 2006
2. Hot Dog and Bob and the Particularly Pesky Attack of the Pencil People ◆ 2006
3. Hot Dog and Bob and the Dangerously Dizzy Attack of the Hypno Hamsters ◆ 2007
4. Hot Dog and Bob and the Exceptionally Eggy Attack of the Game Gators ◆ 2007
5. Hot Dog and Bob and the Surprisingly Slobbery Attack of the Dog-Wash Doggies ◆ 2007

HOUDINI CLUB MAGIC MYSTERY

Adler, David A.

RANDOM HOUSE ◆ **GRADES 1–3** ◆ **A/R**

MYSTERY

Herman Foster has a nickname: Houdini. He has formed the Houdini Club so that he can perform magic tricks for his friends and teach them the techniques. In these amusing mystery stories, Houdini and his cousin Janet Perry solve simple mysteries such as the disappearance and reappearance of the classroom hamster, a missing coat at the library, and a theft at the mall. At the end of each book, readers are shown how to do a magic trick. See how to make a torn dollar bill whole again or predict the star that will be randomly selected. Readers will enjoy the simple mysteries and the opportunity to learn magic.

1. Onion Sundaes ◆ 1994
2. Wacky Jacks ◆ 1994
3. Lucky Stars ◆ 1996
4. Magic Money ◆ 1997

HOUNDSLEY AND CATINA

Howe, James

CANDLEWICK ◆ GRADES K–2 ◆ A/R

ANIMAL FANTASY

Like Frog and Toad, Houndsley, a dog, and Catina, a cat, are best friends. In the first book, Catina wants to be a famous writer but she does not enjoy writing. Houndsley enjoys cooking but he becomes flustered when he is in a cooking contest. The two friends encourage each other to do their best at whatever they enjoy. The easy-reader format is just right for beginners.

1. Houndsley and Catina ◆ 2006
2. Houndsley and Catina and the Birthday Surprise ◆ 2006
3. Houndsley and Catina and the Quiet Time ◆ 2008

"HOUR" BOOKS

Williams, Maiya

AMULET ◆ GRADES 5–8 ◆ A/R

FANTASY

After the death of their mother, 13-year-old Rowan and 11-year-old Nina Popplewell are sent to spend the summer with their great-aunts in Maine. They meet Xanthe and Xavier, 14-year-old African American twins, and begin to explore an abandoned resort. The resort offers a time-travel portal at "the golden hour" (right before sunset). In the first book, Nina disappears and the others follow her to Paris in 1789. Other adventures take place in ancient Egypt and in the Old West at the time of the gold rush. In addition to the historical and fantasy elements, the characters in this series deal with realistic present-day problems, such as the death of Rowan and Nina's mother in an accident involving a drunk driver. The stories have a lot to offer including action, history, and time travel, which make them a good choice for reluctant readers.

1. The Golden Hour ◆ 2004
2. The Hour of the Cobra ◆ 2006
3. The Hour of the Outlaw ◆ 2007

HOUSE OF HORRORS

Various authors

HARPERCOLLINS ◆ GRADES 5–7

HORROR

What would you do if a ghost were stalking your brother? And then, what if your Aunt Wendy came to visit and took off her head? How about if your dog turned into an angry beast and brought home a gross claw that wasn't quite dead? These are just some of the problems faced by Sara and Michael Buckner in the House of Horrors series. There are oozing eggs and a scheming gargoyle. Readers who enjoy being scared and disgusted will want to read these creepy adventures.

1. My Brother, the Ghost (Weyn, Suzanne) ◆ 1994
2. Rest in Pieces (Weyn, Suzanne) ◆ 1994
3. Jeepers Creepers (Weyn, Suzanne) ◆ 1995
4. Aunt Weird (Lloyd, Alan) ◆ 1995
5. Knock, Knock . . . You're Dead (Stine, Megan) ◆ 1995
6. Night of the Gargoyle (Lloyd, Alan) ◆ 1995
7. Evil on Board (Moore, Leslie) ◆ 1995

HOUSE ON CHERRY STREET

Philbrick, W. Rodman

SCHOLASTIC ◆ GRADES 5–8 ◆ A/R

FANTASY

Ghosts haunt the vacation cabin of Jason, 12, and his younger sister, Sally. These are not friendly, Casper-like ghosts. These are demons that victimize the children and their babysitter. They may even have caused the death of a former vacationer.

1. The Haunting ◆ 1995
2. The Horror ◆ 1995
3. The Final Nightmare ◆ 1995

HOW DO DINOSAURS . . .

Yolen, Jane

SCHOLASTIC ◆ GRADES K–2

ANIMAL FANTASY

The rhyming text in these books describes how dinosaurs perform everyday human activities. Young readers will laugh as the oversized dinosaurs fill each page and add to the mayhem around them. The human parents and the cozy setting create more fun. Mark Teague's illustrations make the situation seem believable. *How Do Dinosaurs Learn Their Colors?*, *How Do Dinosaurs Count to Ten? How Do Dinosaurs Clean Their Rooms?*, and *How Do Dinosaurs Play With Their Friends?* are board books.

1. How Do Dinosaurs Say Good Night? ◆ 2000
2. How Do Dinosaurs Get Well Soon? ◆ 2003

3. How Do Dinosaurs Eat Their Food? ◆ 2005
4. How Do Dinosaurs Go to School? ◆ 2007

HOW I SURVIVED MIDDLE SCHOOL

Krulik, Nancy E.

SCHOLASTIC ◆ GRADES 4–7 ◆ A/R

REAL LIFE

Middle school is not easy and Jenny McAfee faces typical problems—making and keeping friends, quelching rumors, and suspecting others of cheating. Jenny and her friends do everything they can to stop the popular Pops from running the joint; Jenny even runs for class president!

1. Can You Get an F in Lunch? ◆ 2007
2. Madame President ◆ 2007
3. I Heard a Rumor ◆ 2007
4. The New Girl ◆ 2007
5. Cheat Sheet ◆ 2007
6. P.S. I Really Like You ◆ 2008
7. Who's Got Spirit? ◆ 2008
8. It's All Downhill from Here ◆ 2009

HOWIE

Henderson, Sara

ZONDERKIDZ ◆ GRADES K–2

VALUES

Howie is a cute, energetic puppy. In *Howie's Tea Party,* Emma wants Howie to be a quiet party guest, but Howie is too lively and rambunctious. Emma learns that God makes all creatures with their own strengths and weaknesses. These books for beginning readers teach lessons about God's role in the lives of young children.

1. Howie Finds a Hug ◆ 2008
2. Howie Goes Shopping ◆ 2008
3. Howie Wants to Play ◆ 2008
4. Howie's Tea Party ◆ 2008

HUMBUG

Balian, Lorna

ABINGDON PRESS ◆ GRADES K–1 ◆ A/R

HUMOR

This whimsical series teases the reader into believing in the existence of Santa, witches, and the Easter Bunny. There are no connecting characters in the books, although the illustrations provide some continuity with familiar-looking characters. *Bah! Humbug?* and *Humbug Rabbit* try to create doubt about the identity of Santa Claus and the Easter Bunny, while *Humbug Witch* is a gentle reminder that dressing up as a witch does not guarantee your magic will work. The subtle humor will appeal to early readers and as a read-aloud.

1. Humbug Witch ◆ 1965
2. Humbug Rabbit ◆ 1974
3. Bah! Humbug? ◆ 1977
4. Humbug Potion ◆ 1984

HUMPHREY

Birney, Betty G.
PUTNAM ◆ GRADES 2–4 ◆ A/R
ANIMAL FANTASY

Humphrey is a hamster who narrates these books about his life as a classroom pet. Brought into the classroom by a substitute teacher, Humphrey connects with the students and their families (on weekend visits). The problem comes when Ms. Brisbane, the regular classroom teacher, returns. Humphrey's visit to Ms. Brisbane's home changes her opinion. Humphrey helps the kids in the class deal with everyday issues of loneliness, kindness, and shyness.

1. The World According to Humphrey ◆ 2004
2. Friendship According to Humphrey ◆ 2005
3. Trouble According to Humphrey ◆ 2007
4. Surprises According to Humphrey ◆ 2008

I AM AMERICAN

Various authors
NATIONAL GEOGRAPHIC ◆ GRADES 4–7
HISTORICAL

A series of historical novels that blend fiction and fact, using a combination of fictional journals, letters, and narrative with background details and photographs. *Cowboys on the Western Trail* portrays the excitement of a cattle drive in 1887, using an appealing magazine format. In *Servant to Abigail Adams,* a teenage servant accompanies First Lady Abigail Adams to the Executive Mansion in Philadephia and later to the new presidential residence in Washington, D.C.

1. Yankee Blue or Rebel Grey? The Civil War Adventures of Sam Shaw (Connell, Kate) ◆ 2003
2. The Eve of Revolution: The Colonial Adventures of Benjamin Wilcox (Burt, Barbara) ◆ 2003
3. Servant to Abigail Adams: The Early American Adventures of Hannah Cooper (Connell, Kate) ◆ 2003
4. We Came Through Ellis Island: The Immigrant Adventures of Emma Markowitz (Thompson, Gare) ◆ 2003
5. Our Journey West: The Oregon Trail Adventures of Sarah Marshall (Thompson, Gare) ◆ 2003
6. When the Mission Padre Came to the Rancho: The Early California Adventures of Rosalinda and Simon Delgado (Thompson, Gare) ◆ 2004
7. Cowboys on the Western Trail: The Cattle Drive Adventures of Josh McNabb and Davy Bartlett (Oatman, Eric) ◆ 2004
8. Escape to Freedom: The Underground Railroad Adventures of Callie and William (Simon, Barbara Brooks) ◆ 2004
9. Hoping for Rain: The Dust Bowl Adventures of Patty and Earl Buckler (Connell, Kate) ◆ 2004

I WAS A SIXTH GRADE ALIEN

Coville, Bruce

MINSTREL/POCKET BOOKS ◆ GRADES 3–6 ◆ A/R

FANTASY

An alien embassy in Syracuse, New York? Yes! And Pleskit Meenom, son of the alien ambassador, is enrolled in sixth grade. He teams up with Tim Tompkins and together they face ongoing threats to Earth. The fast-paced action and humorous situations will appeal to reluctant readers.

1. I Was a Sixth Grade Alien ◆ 1999
2. The Attack of the Two-Inch Teacher ◆ 1999
3. I Lost My Grandfather's Brain ◆ 1999
4. Peanut Butter Lover Boy ◆ 2000
5. Zombies of the Science Fair ◆ 2000
6. Don't Fry My Veeblax! ◆ 2000
7. Too Many Aliens ◆ 2000
8. Snatched from Earth ◆ 2000
9. There's an Alien in My Backpack ◆ 2000
10. The Revolt of the Miniature Mutants ◆ 2001
11. There's an Alien in My Underwear ◆ 2001
12. Farewell to Earth ◆ 2001

IF YOU GIVE A . . .

Numeroff, Laura

HARPERCOLLINS ◆ **GRADES K–2** ◆ **A/R**

HUMOR | ANIMAL FANTASY

As everyone knows, if you give a mouse a cookie this will just set off a chain of demands (milk, a straw, and so forth). Similarly, a pig with a pancake will probably want syrup and then a bath to get the syrup off and then . . . .

1. If You Give a Mouse a Cookie ◆ 1985
2. If You Give a Moose a Muffin ◆ 1991
3. If You Give a Pig a Pancake ◆ 1998
4. If You Take a Mouse to the Movies ◆ 2000
5. If You Take a Mouse to School ◆ 2002
6. If You Give a Pig a Party ◆ 2005
7. If You Give a Cat a Cupcake ◆ 2008

IKE AND MAMA

Snyder, Carol

JEWISH PUBLICATION SOCIETY ◆ **GRADES 3–5**

FAMILY LIFE | HISTORICAL

Ike is a Jewish boy living in New York City during the 1920s. His father has tuberculosis and is in the hospital for much of this easy-chapter series. The stories center on Ike, his mother, and their close-knit neighborhood. Ike's mother is a woman of extraordinary wisdom and strength. In one book, she organizes the neighborhood to plan a wedding for a family that can't afford one. With humor and sympathy, Jewish ways and the sense of this time and place are woven into the stories.

1. Ike and Mama and the Once-a-Year Suit ◆ 1978
2. Ike and Mama and the Block Wedding ◆ 1979
3. Ike and Mama and the Once-in-a-Lifetime Movie ◆ 1981
4. Ike and Mama and the Trouble at School ◆ 1983
5. Ike and Mama and the Seven Surprises ◆ 1985

IKE AND MEM

Jennings, Patrick

HOLIDAY HOUSE ◆ **GRADES 1–5**

FAMILY LIFE

Ike and his little sister Mem end up making a new friend when they dare to investigate a spooky old house in the first book. In *The Tornado Watches,* Ike worries about missing a tornado alert and stays awake all night for a couple of nights; when there is an alert he's so tired he sleeps right through it. Early readers will enjoy these stories.

1. The Bird Shadow: An Ike and Mem Story ◆ 2001
2. The Tornado Watches: An Ike and Mem Story ◆ 2002
3. The Weeping Willow: An Ike and Mem Story ◆ 2002
4. The Lightning Bugs: An Ike and Mem Story ◆ 2003
5. The Ears of Corn: An Ike and Mem Story ◆ 2003
6. The Pup Tent: An Ike and Mem Story ◆ 2005

THE ILLMOOR CHRONICLES

Stone, David Lee

HYPERION ◆ GRADES 5–9 ◆ A/R

FANTASY | HUMOR

As in the Pied Piper of Hamlin, rats have overtaken the city of Dullitch and the Duke offers a reward to be rid of them. Diek Westapha, who possesses evil magic, accomplishes the task but is not given the reward. Again, as in the Pied Piper, he leads the children out of town. A motley collection of citizens (including an ex-wizard, a barbarian, a dwarf, and a thief) band together to try to rescue the children. In the second book, a new threat looms as the evil Yowler plans to change the people of Dullitch into rocks. A vampire, thief/gravedigger, and the Duke are among those who confront the Yowler. Puns and jokes throughout the text will keep readers interested.

1. The Ratastrophe Catastrophe ◆ 2004
2. The Yowler Foul-Up ◆ 2006
3. The Shadewell Shenanigans ◆ 2006

IN THE CARDS

Fredericks, Mariah

ATHENEUM ◆ GRADES 5–8 ◆ A/R

REAL LIFE

Tarot cards, fortune-telling, and predictions are the twist in this series about eighth-grade girls. In *Love,* Anna's elderly neighbor dies leaving her a set of tarot cards. Anna and her friends Eve and Syd consult the cards about dating, school success, and the future. Anna's reading leads her to begin dating Declan Kelso. Eventually she realizes that her fantasy about

Declan was not realistic. In *Fame,* Eve wants to be a musical star while *Life* focuses on Syd's family and fears.

1. Love ◆ 2007
2. Fame ◆ 2008
3. Life ◆ 2008

INCOGNITO MOSQUITO

Hass, E. A.

RANDOM HOUSE ◆ GRADES 4–6 ◆ A/R

HUMOR | MYSTERY

Incognito Mosquito is an insect detective who describes his best cases in corny puns and silly twists on names. The first volume sets up his persona as he recounts five cases to a reporter whose job it is to interview the "famous" detective. Subsequent books offer other reasons for him to describe his exploits, including appearing on the TV talk show *Late Flight with David Litterbug.* Each case includes clues to help the reader guess how Incognito Mosquito figures out "who dunnit."

1. Incognito Mosquito, Private Insective ◆ 1982
2. Incognito Mosquito Flies Again ◆ 1985
3. Incognito Mosquito Takes to the Air ◆ 1986
4. Incognito Mosquito Makes History ◆ 1987

THE INDIAN IN THE CUPBOARD

Banks, Lynne Reid

DOUBLEDAY; AVON ◆ GRADES 4–6 ◆ A/R

ADVENTURE | FANTASY

This series, also known as the Omri series, begins with *The Indian in the Cupboard.* Omri discovers that, with the turn of a special key, he can bring plastic figures to life. An Indian, Little Bear, is the first figure. When Omri's best friend, Patrick, finds out, he brings Boone, his plastic cowboy, to life. The boys soon learn the consequences of using this magic to bring people across time and space. Each book continues the adventures. A very brief retelling of previous events is included in the subsequent novels, which aides in comprehension. A movie version of *The Indian in the Cupboard* expanded the popularity of the books.

1. The Indian in the Cupboard ◆ 1981
2. The Return of the Indian ◆ 1986
3. The Secret of the Indian ◆ 1989
4. The Mystery of the Cupboard ◆ 1993
5. The Key to the Indian ◆ 1998

INDIE KIDD

McCombie, Karen
YEARLING ◆ GRADES 3–5 ◆ A/R

REAL LIFE

Indie Kidd is 10 and hoping to celebrate her birthday, except she is not done with her school assignment. Her friends, Sophie and Fee, try to help her finish. In the second book, Indie spends so much time helping her stepbrother make friends that she almost loses her own friends. Originally published in England, there are additional titles that are not yet available in the United States.

1. How to Be Good (ish) ◆ 2007
2. Oops, I Lost My Best (est) Friends ◆ 2007
3. Being Grown-Up is Cool (Not!) ◆ 2007
4. Are We Having Fun Yet (Hmmm?) ◆ 2008

INHERITANCE

Paolini, Christopher
KNOPF ◆ GRADES 5–12 ◆ A/R

FANTASY

Eragon, 15, finds a dragon egg that hatches. Out comes a female dragon he names Saphira. The two of them have a strange psychic connection that comes to their aid as they face challenges. Eragon discovers his destiny as a Dragon Rider, a new generation of warriors who are rising against King Galbatorix. Filled with magic and epic battles, this series will attract fans of the Lord of the Rings (Tolkien) and McCaffrey's Pern/Dragonrider books. *Eragon* was made into a popular movie.

1. Eragon ◆ 2003
2. Eldest ◆ 2005
3. Brisingr ◆ 2008

THE INK DRINKER

Sanvoisin, Eric
DELACORTE ◆ GRADES 4–7 ◆ A/R

FANTASY

Draculink, an ink-drinking vampire bites Odilon, a boy who hates reading. Now Odilon sips the words out of the books in his father's bookstore, leaving them filled with empty pages. A new classmate, Camilla, is also an ink drinker and the two enjoy sharing books—until they are drawn into a Little Red Riding Hood story.

1. The Ink Drinker ◆ 1998
2. A Straw for Two ◆ 1999
3. The City of Ink Drinkers ◆ 2002
4. Little Red Ink Drinker ◆ 2003

INKHEART

Funke, Cornelia

SCHOLASTIC ◆ GRADES 5–12 ◆ A/R

FANTASY | ADVENTURE

As the series begins, Meggie, 12, discovers that her father, Mo, can bring book characters to life when he reads aloud. After reading a book called *Inkheart,* Mo has released some dangerous characters and Meggie must help her father escape from them. In the second book, Meggie enters Inkworld and with Farid, an apprentice, faces war and the possible execution of her father.

1. Inkheart ◆ 2003
2. Inkspell ◆ 2005
3. Inkdeath ◆ 2008

INTERNET DETECTIVES

Coleman, Michael

BANTAM ◆ GRADES 4–6

ADVENTURE | MYSTERY

Using electronic mail and the Internet, three friends—Tamsyn Smith, Josh Allan, and Rob Zanelli—solve crimes around the world. Rob lives in Manor House in Portsmouth, England. After being paralyzed in a traffic accident, Rob is tutored at home and spends a lot of his time surfing the Net. Tamsyn and Josh attend Abbey School in Portsmouth. When Rob is in danger, his computer links to Tamsyn and Josh bring help. In later adventures, Rob attends Abbey School with his friends. The format of the series incorporates computer screens and messages into the narrative. The characters connect with others around the world to gather information and solve mysteries involving art theft, blackmail, and kidnapping as well as a computer hacking and cyber-codes.

1. Net Bandits ◆ 1997
2. Escape Key ◆ 1997
3. Speed Surf ◆ 1997
4. Cyber Feud ◆ 1998
5. System Crash ◆ 1998

INVESTIGATORS OF THE UNKNOWN

Lisle, Janet Taylor

ORCHARD ◆ GRADES 3–5 ◆ A/R

FAMILY LIFE | FANTASY

The Investigators of the Unknown form their group while trying to make contact with an invisible spirit who leaves letters filled with gold dust for Angela Harrell. Angela's friend Poco talks to animals, and her friend Georgina is as down-to-earth and practical as the other two are fanciful. Their investigations are always tinged with magical happenings that turn out to be grounded in reality, although a touch of magic or the unexplainable remains. In the second and third volumes, Angela is living with her father and brother in Mexico, and a fourth character—Walter, an orphan—is introduced. His story is featured in book three when he begins to get ghostly messages from his dead mother. By the fourth book, Angela has returned from Mexico and is acting strangely and reporting having been abducted by aliens.

1. The Gold Dust Letters ◆ 1994
2. Looking for Juliette ◆ 1994
3. A Message from the Match Girl ◆ 1995
4. Angela's Aliens ◆ 1996

INVISIBLE

Jocelyn, Marthe

DUTTON ◆ GRADES 3–6 ◆ A/R

FANTASY

In New York City, Billie Stoner, 10, feels stifled by her mother's rules and restrictions. On a trip to Central Park, Billie finds a make-up bag. When she tries one of the powders, she becomes invisible. Now that she has freedom, she realizes there are challenges that come with it. In the second book, Billie turns a puppy invisible so she can have a pet.

1. The Invisible Day ◆ 1997
2. The Invisible Harry ◆ 1998
3. The Invisible Enemy ◆ 2002

INVISIBLE DETECTIVES

Richards, Justin

DUTTON/SLEUTH ◆ GRADES 5–9 ◆ A/R

MYSTERY | FANTASY

Who is the Invisible Detective? In London in 1936, four young people work as a team to help solve crimes. They keep their involvement and identities a secret, working as one. Art, 14, is part of the team helping Scotland Yard (where Art's father works) solve strange crimes. The crimes are not just robberies and kidnappings; they involve murderous puppets, an underground monster, and a zombie army. One arc of this series is the inclusion of a present-day teen, Arthur Drake, who reads about the crimes in a journal that seems to be written by him.

1. Double Life ◆ 2005
2. Shadow Beast ◆ 2005
3. Ghost Soldiers ◆ 2006

INVISIBLE INC.

Levy, Elizabeth

SCHOLASTIC ◆ GRADES 1–3 ◆ A/R

HUMOR | MYSTERY

Each member of Invisible Inc. contributes something special: Chip is invisible; Justin has learned to read lips because of a hearing loss; and Charlene is both very strong-willed and very brave. The simple mysteries in these books revolve around the three friends, their school, and their neighborhood. In one book, someone is stealing the snacks in the classroom; in another, Justin's karate belt is stolen. With no element of real danger and a very accessible format, these books are just right for younger elementary school students. There are also many humorous moments, which often stem from Chip being invisible.

1. The Schoolyard Mystery ◆ 1994
2. The Mystery of the Missing Dog ◆ 1995
3. The Snack Attack Mystery ◆ 1996
4. The Creepy Computer Mystery ◆ 1996
5. The Karate Class Mystery ◆ 1996
6. Parents' Night Fright ◆ 1998

IRIS AND WALTER

Guest, Elissa Haden

HARCOURT ◆ GRADES K–2 ◆ A/R

REAL LIFE

Iris used to live in the city. She is trying to adjust to life in the country, but she misses her familiar city routine. A friendly boy, Walter, helps her see the wonderful things around them, including his horse Rain. As the series progresses, Baby Rose joins Iris's family and she faces another adjustment. The events in these books, including sleepovers and school, will be familiar to young readers.

1. Iris and Walter ◆ 2000
2. True Friends ◆ 2001
3. Iris and Walter and Baby Rose ◆ 2002
4. The Sleepover ◆ 2002
5. The School Play ◆ 2003
6. Iris and Walter and Cousin Howie ◆ 2003
7. Lost and Found ◆ 2004
8. Iris and Walter and the Substitute Teacher ◆ 2004
9. Iris and Walter and the Field Trip ◆ 2005
10. Iris and Walter and the Birthday Party ◆ 2006

IRVING AND MUKTUK

Pinkwater, Daniel (Manus)

HOUGHTON MIFFLIN ◆ GRADES K–3 ◆ A/R

HUMOR

Irving and Muktuk are two naughty polar bears with a great appetite for muffins. The first book sees them being shipped off to a zoo in Bayonne, New Jersey, after disrupting the Yellowtooth Blueberry Muffin Festival. In *Bad Bears in the Big City,* they have trouble adjusting to life at the zoo, and in *Bad Bear Detectives,* they are falsely accused of stealing muffins and set out to identify the real culprits. Jill Pinkwater's illustrations add to the humor.

1. Irving and Muktuk: Two Bad Bears ◆ 2003
2. Bad Bears in the Big City ◆ 2003
3. Bad Bears and a Bunny ◆ 2005
4. Bad Bear Detectives ◆ 2006
5. Bad Bears Go Visiting ◆ 2007

ISABELLE

Greene, Constance C.

VIKING ◆ GRADES 3–6

HUMOR | REAL LIFE

Isabelle is a feisty 10-year-old who is well known for her ability to get in trouble. Throughout the series, she tries to recruit other people to learn the art of itchiness—i.e., troublemaking—often with surprising results. Entertaining reading.

1. Isabelle the Itch ◆ 1973
2. Isabelle Shows Her Stuff ◆ 1984
3. Isabelle and Little Orphan Frannie ◆ 1988

ISLAND STALLION

Farley, Walter

RANDOM HOUSE ◆ GRADES 4–6 ◆ A/R

ADVENTURE

Steve Duncan finds a wild red stallion on Azul Island in the Caribbean Sea. Naming the stallion Flame, Steve wants to train and race it, but first he must gain its trust. On the island, Flame battles with other stallions. With Steve, Flame competes against the best horses in the world. Horse-loving readers will appreciate the action-packed races and the many insights into horses and riding. Like Farley's Black Stallion series, this will appeal to readers who enjoy animal stories and adventure.

1. The Island Stallion ◆ 1948
2. The Island Stallion's Fury ◆ 1951
3. The Island Stallion Races ◆ 1955

IVY AND BEAN

Barrows, Annie

CHRONICLE ◆ GRADES 1–4 ◆ A/R

REAL LIFE

In the first book, Bean, 7, meets her new neighbor Ivy. Ivy is quiet and enjoys reading; Bean is boisterous and free-spirited. At first, Bean does not see Ivy as a possible friend. When Ivy helps Bean out of trouble and reveals that she (Ivy) is practicing to be a witch, Bean changes her mind and their friendship begins.

1. Ivy and Bean ◆ 2006
2. Ivy and Bean and the Ghost That Had to Go ◆ 2006
3. Ivy and Bean Break the Fossil Record ◆ 2007
4. Ivy and Bean Take Care of the Babysitter ◆ 2008

JACK HENRY

Gantos, Jack

FARRAR, STRAUS & GIROUX ◆ GRADES 5–8 ◆ A/R

HUMOR

It's the late 1960s. Jack's family moves a lot—he's lived in nine houses and he's only in the sixth grade. Jack feels confused and disoriented yet he strives to find his own identity. In the second book, the family has moved again. This time they are in Barbados and Jack keeps a journal of his year there. The books follow a sequence that is different from their chronological release dates: *Jack Adrift, Jack on the Tracks, Heads or Tails, Jack's New Power,* and *Jack's Black Book.*

1. Heads or Tails: Stories from the Sixth Grade ◆ 1994
2. Jack's New Power: Stories from a Caribbean Year ◆ 1995
3. Jack's Black Book ◆ 1997
4. Jack on the Tracks: Four Seasons of Fifth Grade ◆ 1999
5. Jack Adrift: Fourth Grade Without a Clue ◆ 2003

JACK JAMESON AND DANNY ONE

Slote, Alfred

HarperCollins ◆ Grades 2–4 ◆ A/R

Adventure | Science fiction

Jack Jameson gets a special present for his 10th birthday: a robot twin. Named Danny One, the robot will keep Jack company, play with him, and participate in many outer-space adventures. In *C.O.L.A.R.,* which stands for Community of Lost Atkins Robots, Jack and Danny One find a community of lost robots that were made by Dr. Atkins, who also made Danny. In another story, Jack travels alone to Alpha I and finds that his Aunt Katherine is behaving strangely and he must find out why. Each book is fast-paced and imaginative, involving futuristic scenarios and creative characters.

1. My Robot Buddy ◆ 1975
2. My Trip to Alpha I ◆ 1978
3. C.O.L.A.R. ◆ 1981
4. Omega Station ◆ 1983
5. The Trouble on Janus ◆ 1985

JACK RUSSELL: DOG DETECTIVE

Odgers, Darrel, and Sally Odgers

Scholastic; Kane Miller ◆ Grades 3–5 ◆ A/R

Mystery

In the town of Doggeroo lives Jack, a dog who will put up with some things (a lost boot, perhaps) but rebels when things go too far (a stolen blanket and ball). He investigates all kinds of infractions with his sidekick Foxie and his not-so-bright friend Lord "Red" Setter, with lots of doggy wordplay in the process.

1. Dog Den Mystery ◆ 2006
2. The Phantom Mudder ◆ 2006
3. The Mugged Pug ◆ 2007
4. The Lying Postman ◆ 2007
5. The Awful Pawful ◆ 2007

6. The Sausage Situation ◆ 2007
7. The Buried Biscuits ◆ 2008
8. The Kitnapped Creature ◆ 2008

JACK SPARROW

Kidd, Rob

DISNEY PRESS ◆ GRADES 4–6 ◆ A/R

FANTASY

Building on the popularity of the Pirates of the Caribbean movies, this series features Jack Sparrow as a teenager. In *The Coming Storm,* young Jack steals a sack from a pirate in a tavern in Tortuga. A tavern maid, Arabella, helps him escape and the first adventure begins. With a ragtag crew—and with Arabella as his first mate—Jack starts out on a quest for treasure beginning with the Sword of Cortes.

1. The Coming Storm ◆ 2006
2. The Siren Song ◆ 2006
3. The Pirate Chase ◆ 2006
4. The Sword of Cortes ◆ 2006
5. The Age of Bronze ◆ 2006
6. Silver ◆ 2007
7. City of Gold ◆ 2007
8. The Timekeeper ◆ 2007
9. Dance of the Hours ◆ 2007
10. Sins of the Fathers ◆ 2007
11. Poseidon's Peak ◆ 2008
12. Bold New Horizons ◆ 2008

JACKIE CHAN ADVENTURES

Various authors

GROSSET & DUNLAP ◆ GRADES 4–8

ADVENTURE | FANTASY

When Jackie's talisman breaks in half, he becomes two people—Jackie Light and Jackie Dark. The two must team up to rescue Jackie's niece, Jade, from the dangers of the group called the Dark Hand. The Super Special book, *Day of the Dragon,* includes puzzles and a secret message from Jackie.

1. The Dark Hand (Willard, Eliza) ◆ 2001
2. Jade's Secret Power (West, Cathy) ◆ 2002
3. Sign of the Ox (Stine, Megan) ◆ 2002
4. Enter . . . the Viper (Carroll, Jacqueline) ◆ 2002
5. Shendu Escapes! (Slack, David) ◆ 2002

6. A New Enemy (Ashby, R. S.) ◆ 2002
7. Revenge of the Dark Hand (Willard, Eliza) ◆ 2002
8. The Power of the Rat (Stine, Megan) ◆ 2002
9. Stronger than Stone (Ashby, R. S.) ◆ 2002
10. Uncle's Big Surprise (Carroll, Jacqueline) ◆ 2002
11. The Jade Monkey (Katschke, Judy) ◆ 2002
12. The Strongest Evil (Carroll, Jacqueline) ◆ 2002
13. Day of the Dragon: Super Special (Willard, Eliza) ◆ 2003

JACKIE CHAN ADVENTURES (TOKYOPOP)

1. Enter the Dark Hand ◆ 2003
2. Legend of the Zodiac ◆ 2004
3. Jackie and Jade Save the Day ◆ 2004

JACKSON FRIENDS

Edwards, Michelle

HARCOURT ◆ GRADES 2–4 ◆ A/R

REAL LIFE

Calliope, Howie (Howardina), and Pa Lia are best friends. They help each other deal with problems. When it is grandparents day at school and Calliope has *Zero Grandparents,* Calliope comes up with a creative solution to her dilemma. The three girls are from diverse backgrounds. Pa Lia's family is from Laos, Calliope is white, and Howie is African American. Black-and-white illustrations add to the story.

1. Pa Lia's First Day ◆ 1999
2. Zero Grandparents ◆ 2001
3. The Talent Show ◆ 2002
4. Stinky Stern Forever ◆ 2005

JACKSON JONES

Quattlebaum, Mary

DELACORTE ◆ GRADES 3–6

REAL LIFE

Inner-city African American boy Jackson wants a basketball for his tenth birthday but instead gets a garden plot and money for seeds and equipment. Swallowing his disappointment, he sets out to grow flowers for cash but meets many obstacles along the way. In the second book, despite a surfeit of zucchini, Jackson defends his garden vigorously against plans to develop the site.

1. Jackson Jones and the Puddle of Thorns ◆ 1994
2. Jackson Jones and Mission Greentop ◆ 2004
3. Jackson Jones and the Curse of the Outlaw Rose ◆ 2006

JAFTA

Lewin, Hugh
CAROLRHODA ◆ GRADES K–3 ◆ A/R
FAMILY LIFE

Jafta lives with his mother and father in South Africa. His father works in the city, but Jafta receives plenty of love and attention from his mother and other adults in the village. One book shows preparation for a village wedding, and one is about Jafta waiting for his father's return from the city. All of the adults in Jafta's life, but especially his parents, are treated with the utmost respect and affection. Each page in this picture-book series is illustrated in brown and black watercolors. Very simple text and large print make this accessible to beginning readers. Occasional Zulu words are explained in a note at the end.

1. Jafta ◆ 1981
2. Jafta's Father ◆ 1983
3. Jafta's Mother ◆ 1983
4. Jafta and the Wedding ◆ 1983
5. Jafta: The Journey ◆ 1984
6. Jafta: The Town ◆ 1984
7. Jafta: The Homecoming ◆ 1994

JAKE DRAKE

Clements, Andrew
SIMON & SCHUSTER/ALADDIN ◆ GRADES 2–5 ◆ A/R
REAL LIFE

Many children will relate to Jake Drake. He is not the most popular student or the smartest or the best athlete. He is a regular fourth-grader with lots of ordinary problems. When he does a few helpful things at school and his teachers all gush, making him seem to be a "teacher's pet," Jake has to figure out a way to go back to being a regular guy.

1. Jake Drake, Bully Buster ◆ 2001
2. Jake Drake, Know-It-All ◆ 2001
3. Jake Drake, Teacher's Pet ◆ 2001
4. Jake Drake, Class Clown ◆ 2002

JAMAICA

Havill, Juanita

HOUGHTON MIFFLIN ◆ GRADES K–2 ◆ A/R

FAMILY LIFE | REAL LIFE

Jamaica is an African American child living in a loving middle-class family with her mother, father, and older brother. The series is about Jamaica's relationships with family and friends, and each book contains a very gentle lesson about getting along. In one, a small boy wants to play with her. She rebuffs him at first, but after considering how she felt when her brother wouldn't let her play, she builds a sandcastle with him. It turns out so well that her brother wants to help. All the stories have this kind of wholesome, intelligent approach to getting along.

1. Jamaica's Find ◆ 1986
2. Jamaica Tag-Along ◆ 1989
3. Jamaica and Brianna ◆ 1993
4. Jamaica's Blue Marker ◆ 1996
5. Jamaica and the Substitute Teacher ◆ 1999
6. Brianna, Jamaica, and the Dance of Spring ◆ 2002

JAMELA

Daly, Niki

FARRAR, STRAUS & GIROUX ◆ GRADES K–2 ◆ A/R

REAL LIFE | FAMILY LIFE

Jamela lives in South Africa with her Mama. In *What's Cooking, Jamela?*, Mama is planning to cook their red chicken for Christmas dinner. Jamela has become attached to the bird and is distressed to think that it will become their dinner. Mama decides to give Jamela the chicken (alive) for her Christmas gift. Young readers will relate to Jamela and get a glimpse into life in South Africa.

1. Jamela's Dress ◆ 1999
2. What's Cooking, Jamela? ◆ 2002
3. Where's Jamela? ◆ 2004
4. Happy Birthday, Jamela! ◆ 2006

JAMES STEVENSON'S AUTOBIOGRAPHICAL STORIES

Stevenson, James

GREENWILLOW ◆ GRADES 1–3

REAL LIFE

With this series of autobiographical memoirs, James Stevenson gives readers a sense of family relationships. He creates intimacy and nostalgia with fond memories of his childhood summers on the beach with grandparents in *July* and simple pleasures like burning leaves in *Fun/No Fun*. As his young daughter experiences events, Stevenson recalls them in *I Meant to Tell You*. Stevenson's watercolor illustrations are brief and faceless, allowing the reader to fill in their own thoughts and memories. This is pleasurable reading for young and old.

1. When I Was Nine ◆ 1986
2. Higher on the Door ◆ 1987
3. July ◆ 1990
4. Don't You Know There's a War On? ◆ 1992
5. Fun/No Fun ◆ 1994
6. I Had a Lot of Wishes ◆ 1995
7. I Meant to Tell You ◆ 1996

JAMESTOWN'S AMERICAN PORTRAITS

Various authors

GLENCOE/MCGRAW-HILL ◆ GRADES 5–8 ◆ A/R

HISTORICAL

An indentured servant in Virginia, an immigrant girl working in a New York City sweatshop, and a teen pilot in the Women's Airforce Service Pilots are among the characters featured in this series. In *All for Texas*, Thomas Jefferson "Jeff" Byrd, 13, moves to Texas with his family in the 1830s. Jeff faces hardships and loss as both his father and a young friend are killed in battles with Mexican soldiers. Show these books to readers who enjoyed the Survival series by Kathleen Duey and Karen A. Bale.

1. All For Texas: A Story of Texas Liberation (Wisler, G. Clifton) ◆ 2001
2. Corn Raid: A Story of the Jamestown Settlement (Collier, James Lincoln) ◆ 2001
3. Eye for an Eye: A Story of the Revolutionary War (Roop, Peter) ◆ 2001
4. Revenge of the Aztecs: A Story of 1920s Hollywood (Pfeffer, Susan Beth) ◆ 2001
5. The Road to Freedom: A Story of the Reconstruction (Asim, Jabari) ◆ 2001
6. Sweet America: An Immigrant's Story (Kroll, Steven) ◆ 2001
7. This Generation of Americans: A Story of the Civil Rights Movement (McKissack, Fredrick L.) ◆ 2001
8. To Touch the Stars: A Story of World War II (Zeinert, Karen) ◆ 2001
9. When I Dream of Heaven: Angelina's Story (Kroll, Steven) ◆ 2001
10. Wind on the River: A Story of the Civil War (Lawlor, Laurie) ◆ 2001
11. The Worst of Times: A Story of the Great Depression (Collier, James Lincoln) ◆ 2001

JEFFREY'S GHOST

Adler, David A.

HOLT ◆ GRADES 4–6 ◆ A/R

HUMOR | MYSTERY

Bradford was a boy of 10 when he was killed by a horse in a barn. His ghost lived on in the barn, and when the barn when was torn down, the ghost went to live in a nearby house. When Jeffrey moves into the house, he meets Bradford; and together with Jeffrey's friend Laura they begin to solve problems. He helps a baseball team made up of kids that no other team wants and finds out who is cheating in the games at a fair. Bradford also causes problems for Jeffrey and Laura, being both invisible and mischievous, and this leads to some humorous situations.

1. Jeffrey's Ghost and the Leftover Baseball Team ◆ 1984
2. Jeffrey's Ghost and the Fifth-Grade Dragon ◆ 1985
3. Jeffrey's Ghost and the Ziffel Fair Mystery ◆ 1987

JENNA V.

Hoehne, Marcia

CROSSWAY BOOKS ◆ GRADES 4–6

FAMILY LIFE | VALUES

This series begins when Jenna is 10 years old. As part of an active family, she sometimes struggles to find her place. When a foster child arrives, Jenna's feelings of isolation intensify. Her faith in God helps her realize the importance of giving love to others. In subsequent books, Jenna is still seeking to establish her identity, but she learns to value her own talents and reach out to others, including a young woman who is dying. Values like trust, honesty, and belief in God are an integral part of this series.

1. A Place of My Own ◆ 1993
2. A Pocket in My Heart ◆ 1994
3. The Fairy-Tale Friend ◆ 1994
4. Sunflower Girl ◆ 1995

JENNY AND THE CAT CLUB

Averill, Esther

HARPERCOLLINS ◆ GRADES 3–6

ANIMAL FANTASY

Jenny is a shy little cat with a red scarf who lives with her friend Captain Tinker in New York City. She wants to join the Cat Club and spy on their meetings. Mr. President calls them to order, and each cat does something special. One cat plays a flute, and another dances. Jenny runs away because she can't do anything. Then the Captain makes four silver ice skates for her, and she learns to cut figure eights and flowers. Jenny becomes a member of the Cat Club, and the rest of the series is about her and all the other cats in the neighborhood. Some are tough, with no homes at all, while others live pampered lives and have to sneak away from overprotective owners. Delicate black-and-white drawings with occasional red or yellow splashes of color are on nearly every page.

1. The Cat Club; or, The Life and Times of Jenny Linsky ◆ 1944
2. The Adventures of Jack Ninepins ◆ 1944
3. The School for Cats ◆ 1947
4. Jenny's First Party ◆ 1948
5. Jenny's Moonlight Adventure ◆ 1949
6. When Jenny Lost Her Scarf ◆ 1951
7. Jenny's Adopted Brothers ◆ 1952
8. How the Brothers Joined the Cat Club ◆ 1953
9. Jenny's Birthday Book ◆ 1954
10. Jenny Goes to Sea ◆ 1957
11. Jenny's Bedside Book ◆ 1959
12. The Fire Cat ◆ 1961
13. The Hotel Cat ◆ 1969
14. Captains of the City Streets: A Story of the Cat Club ◆ 1972
15. Jenny and the Cat Club: A Collection of Favorite Stories About Jenny Linsky ◆ 1973

JENNY ARCHER

Conford, Ellen

LITTLE, BROWN ◆ GRADES 2–4 ◆ A/R

HUMOR | REAL LIFE

Jenny Archer lives with her parents in a comfortable middle-class neighborhood. This easy chapter book series is about her experiences as she enthusiastically throws herself into life. In one book, she is offered the chance to make a TV commercial. Her enthusiasm dims when she discovers that the commercial is for gerbil food. In other books, she writes her autobiography with some embellishments and learns first aid. Her parents and her friends Wilson and Beth provide unfailing understanding and support in all her endeavors.

1. A Job for Jenny Archer ◆ 1988
2. A Case for Jenny Archer ◆ 1988
3. Jenny Archer, Author ◆ 1989
4. What's Cooking, Jenny Archer? ◆ 1989
5. Jenny Archer to the Rescue ◆ 1990
6. Can Do, Jenny Archer ◆ 1991
7. Nibble, Nibble, Jenny Archer ◆ 1993
8. Get the Picture, Jenny Archer? ◆ 1994

JENNY LINSKY *see* Jenny and the Cat Club

THE JERSEY

Various authors

DISNEY PRESS ◆ GRADES 4–7 ◆ A/R

FANTASY

A group of friends have a jersey with magical powers. When they use it, they connect with a well-known sports star. In *Fight for Your Right,* Morgan boxes with Laila Ali. Other famous sports figures who appear in these stories include skateboarder Tony Hawk, BMX star Dave Mirra, and track star Michael Johnson. Gordon Korman created the series for television and these books are adapted from several episodes.

1. It's Magic (Sinclair, Jay) ◆ 2000
2. No Girly Girls Allowed (Sinclair, Jay) ◆ 2000
3. Nick's a Chick (Selman, Matty) ◆ 2000
4. This Rocks! (Selman, Matty) ◆ 2000
5. Team Player (Mantell, Paul) ◆ 2001
6. Head over Heels (Mantell, Paul) ◆ 2001
7. Fight for Your Right (Mantell, Paul) ◆ 2001
8. Need for Speed (Rees, Elizabeth M.) ◆ 2001

JESSE BEAR

Carlstrom, Nancy White

SIMON & SCHUSTER ◆ GRADES K–1 ◆ A/R

ANIMAL FANTASY

This picture-book series stars a happy little bear named Jesse and his parents. They live in a cozy little house that is illustrated—by Bruce Degen—in great detail in full color. Each book has a rhyming text that illustrates a concept. One shows counting, with a rhyme for bubbles, stars, Band-Aids, and other things that Jesse and his parents count. Birthdays, clothes, and getting wet are some of the other themes that are given this treatment. There are related and board books for younger children.

1. Jesse Bear, What Will You Wear? ◆ 1986
2. Better Not Get Wet, Jesse Bear ◆ 1988
3. It's About Time, Jesse Bear and Other Rhymes ◆ 1990
4. How Do You Say It Today, Jesse Bear? ◆ 1992
5. Happy Birthday, Jesse Bear ◆ 1994
6. Let's Count It Out, Jesse Bear ◆ 1996
7. Guess Who's Coming, Jesse Bear ◆ 1998
8. What a Scare, Jesse Bear! ◆ 1999

9. Where Is Christmas, Jesse Bear? ◆ 2000
10. Climb the Family Tree, Jesse Bear ◆ 2004

JEWEL FAIRIES *see* Rainbow Magic: Jewel Fairies

JEWEL KINGDOM

Malcolm, Jahnna N.
SCHOLASTIC ◆ GRADES 3–4
FANTASY

The Jewel Kingdom consists of White Winterland, Rushing River, Greenwood, Mysterious Forest, Blue Lake, Red Mountains, and Jewel Palace. The Jewel Princesses rule these lands and contend with wizards, dragons, and fantastic events. The plots are simple and the reading level is accessible to middle-grade readers. A jewel necklace is included with each book, which should attract many girls.

1. The Ruby Princess Runs Away ◆ 1997
2. The Sapphire Princess Meets the Monster ◆ 1997
3. The Emerald Princess Plays a Trick ◆ 1997
4. The Diamond Princess Saves the Day ◆ 1997
5. The Ruby Princess Sees a Ghost ◆ 1997
6. The Sapphire Princess Hunts for Treasure ◆ 1998
7. The Jewel Princesses and the Missing Crown ◆ 1998
8. The Emerald Princess Finds a Fairy ◆ 1998
9. The Diamond Princess and the Magic Ball ◆ 1998
10. The Ruby Princess and the Baby Dragon ◆ 1998
11. The Emerald Princess Follows a Unicorn ◆ 1999
12. The Diamond Princess Steps Through the Mirror ◆ 1999
13. The Sapphire Princess Helps a Mermaid ◆ 1999

JIGGY MCCUE

Lawrence, Michael
DUTTON ◆ GRADES 4–7 ◆ A/R
FANTASY | HUMOR

In the first of these entertaining adventures imported from Britain, Jiggy and his friends investigate what is haunting his new house and suspect it's the ghost of a goose. In the second, Jiggy and his friend Angie end up switching bodies after playing a beta version of a computer game, causing much confusion.

1. The Poltergoose ◆ 2002
2. The Killer Underpants ◆ 2002

3. The Toilet of Doom ◆ 2002
4. The Snottle ◆ 2003
5. Maggot Pie ◆ 2004
6. Nudie Dudie ◆ 2004
7. Neville the Devil ◆ 2005
8. Ryan's Brain ◆ 2006
9. The Iron, the Switch and the Broom Cupboard ◆ 2007

JIGSAW JONES MYSTERY

Preller, James

SCHOLASTIC ◆ GRADES K–2 ◆ A/R

MYSTERY

Jigsaw (real name Theodore) Jones, detective, is in second grade. A fan of puzzles, he and his partner Mila Yeh tackle all sorts of mysteries with the help of Jigsaw's top secret detective journal. *Jigsaw Jones's Detective Tips* (2006) is a companion book that reveals all sorts of strategies for successful detecting.

1. The Case of Hermie the Missing Hamster ◆ 1998
2. The Case of the Christmas Snowman ◆ 1998
3. The Case of the Secret Valentine ◆ 1999
4. The Case of the Spooky Sleepover ◆ 1999
5. The Case of the Stolen Baseball Cards ◆ 1999
6. The Case of the Mummy Mystery ◆ 1999
7. The Case of the Runaway Dog ◆ 1999
8. The Case of the Great Sled Race ◆ 1999
9. The Case of the Stinky Science Project ◆ 2000
10. The Case of the Ghostwriter ◆ 2000
11. The Case of the Marshmallow Monster ◆ 2001
12. The Case of the Class Clown ◆ 2000
13. The Case of the Detective in Disguise ◆ 2001
14. The Case of the Bicycle Bandit ◆ 2001
15. The Case of the Haunted Scarecrow ◆ 2001
16. The Case of the Sneaker Sneak ◆ 2001
17. The Case of the Disappearing Dinosaur ◆ 2002
18. The Case of the Bear Scare ◆ 2002
19. The Case of the Golden Key ◆ 2002
20. The Case of the Race Against Time ◆ 2003
21. The Case of the Rainy Day Mystery ◆ 2003
22. The Case of the Best Pet Ever ◆ 2003
23. The Case of the Perfect Prank ◆ 2004
24. The Case of the Glow-in-the-Dark Ghost ◆ 2004
25. The Case of the Vanishing Painting ◆ 2004
26. The Case of the Double Trouble Detectives ◆ 2005
27. The Case of the Frog-Jumping Contest ◆ 2005

28. The Case of the Food Fight ◆ 2005
29. The Case of the Snowboarding Superstar ◆ 2005
30. The Case of the Kidnapped Candy ◆ 2007
31. The Case of the Spoiled Rotten Spy ◆ 2007
32. The Case of the Groaning Ghost ◆ 2007

JIGSAW JONES MYSTERY SUPER SPECIALS

1. The Case of the Buried Treasure ◆ 2001
2. The Case of the Million-Dollar Mystery ◆ 2002
3. The Case of the Missing Falcon ◆ 2004
4. The Case of the Santa Claus Mystery ◆ 2006

JIMMY AND JANET

Cleary, Beverly

MORROW ◆ GRADES K–2 ◆ A/R

FAMILY LIFE | HUMOR

These charming, old-fashioned family stories could have been taken from the author's own experiences with her twin children. Throughout the series, twins Jimmy and Janet remain 4 years old and become involved in simple plots in an ideal family setting. For example, in *The Growing-Up Feet,* the twins' feet are not quite ready for new shoes, so shiny red boots are substituted. Janet and Jimmy then wait impatiently for rain puddles until Dad provides a solution. Other titles deal with sibling rivalry, growing into big beds, and sharing. Full-color illustrations have updated these books, which were originally published in the 1960s.

1. The Real Hole ◆ 1960
2. Two Dog Biscuits ◆ 1961
3. Janet's Thingamajigs ◆ 1987
4. The Growing-Up Feet ◆ 1987

JIMMY SNIFFLES

Various authors

STONE ARCH ◆ GRADES 2–5 ◆ A/R

SCIENCE FICTION

Jimmy Sniffles has a super-powered nose that helps him "sniff out" evil doings. His arch enemy is Dr. Von Snotenstein, who will stop at nothing to wreak havoc. In *Double Trouble,* Dr. Von Snotenstein creates an evil twin Jimmy. In *The Super-Powered Sneeze,* Jimmy has a cold and the evil doctor tries to take over the city. Bright, colorful cartoon illustrations by Steve Harpster will attract reluctant readers.

1. A Nose for Danger (Temple, Bob) ◆ 2006
2. Dognapped! (Nickel, Scott) ◆ 2006
3. Double Trouble (Nickel, Scott) ◆ 2007
4. The Super-Powered Sneeze (Nickel, Scott) ◆ 2007
5. Up the President's Nose (Nickel, Scott) ◆ 2008

JIMMY'S BOA

Noble, Trinka Hakes

DIAL ◆ GRADES K–2

HUMOR

What would happen if a student took his pet boa constrictor on a class field trip to a farm? Or to a birthday party at SeaLand? Jimmy takes his large, friendly boa to very inappropriate events and the results are chaotic. Adding to the humor is the way the stories are presented, as Maggie describes the events to her mother bit by bit. Steven Kellogg's illustrations are detailed and full of fun, capturing the frenzied activities of Jimmy and his boa.

1. The Day Jimmy's Boa Ate the Wash ◆ 1980
2. Jimmy's Boa Bounces Back ◆ 1984
3. Jimmy's Boa and the Big Splash Birthday Bash ◆ 1989
4. Jimmy's Boa and the Bungee Jump Slam Dunk ◆ 2003

JOE SHERLOCK, KID DETECTIVE

Keane, Dave

HARPERCOLLINS ◆ GRADES 3–6 ◆ A/R

HUMOR | MYSTERY

When unusual items, including a glass eyeball, are stolen from his neighbor, Joe Sherlock is on the case. He is the only kid detective in Baskerville and he investigates mysteries that range from a stolen picture to how doggy messes can be left in a fenced-in yard. Reader who enjoy gross elements—poop, farts, snot—along with silly mysteries will like this series. Try the Riot Brothers, too. With many cartoon-style illustrations, reluctant readers should find these accessible.

1. The Haunted Toolshed ◆ 2006
2. The Neighborhood Stink ◆ 2006
3. The Missing Monkey-Eye Diamond ◆ 2006
4. The Headless Mummy ◆ 2007
5. The Art Teacher's Vanishing Masterpiece ◆ 2007

JOEY PIGZA

Gantos, Jack

FARRAR, STRAUS & GIROUX ◆ GRADES 5–9 ◆ A/R

REAL LIFE

Joey Pigza is out of control. His hyperactivity causes him trouble at school. He can't pay attention; he can't sit still. His medication works for a while, but it wears off. He finally gets his meds balanced only to visit his father who wants him to try going without them. This series provides a revealing look at a special education student. The second book received a Newbery Honor award.

1. Joey Pigza Swallowed the Key ◆ 1998
2. Joey Pigza Loses Control ◆ 2000
3. What Would Joey Do? ◆ 2002
4. I Am Not Joey Pigza ◆ 2007

JOHNNY DIXON

Bellairs, John, and Brad Strickland

DIAL ◆ GRADES 5–8 ◆ A/R

FANTASY | MYSTERY

Johnny Dixon's mother is dead and his dad is fighting in the Korean War. He lives with his grandparents across the street from the eccentric but kindly Professor Childermass. The two strike up a strange friendship, and together with Johnny's friend Fergie they solve mysteries involving ghosts, demon possession, and even time travel. Johnny is a small, almost timid boy who seems an unlikely candidate for such adventures. The professor is knowledgeable in many areas and sometimes unwillingly draws the boys into things. Fergie is a bit of a smart aleck and adds humor to the situations. Edward Gorey's black-and-white drawings add to the air of mystery. *The Drum, the Doll, and the Zombie* was completed by Strickland after Bellairs's death. The last three books are by Strickland.

1. The Curse of the Blue Figurine ◆ 1983
2. The Mummy, the Will, and the Crypt ◆ 1983
3. The Spell of the Sorcerer's Skull ◆ 1984
4. The Revenge of the Wizard's Ghost ◆ 1985
5. The Eyes of the Killer Robot ◆ 1986
6. The Trolley to Yesterday ◆ 1989
7. The Chessmen of Doom ◆ 1989
8. The Secret of the Underground Room ◆ 1990
9. The Drum, the Doll, and the Zombie ◆ 1994
10. The Hand of the Necromancer ◆ 1996

11. The Bell, the Book, and the Spellbinder ◆ 1997
12. The Wrath of the Grinning Ghost ◆ 1999

JOHNNY LION

Hurd, Edith Thacher

HARPERCOLLINS ◆ **GRADES K–1**

ANIMAL FANTASY | HUMOR

A little lion lives with his understanding mother and father in this first-reader series. He catches a bad cold and has to take medicine, which he thinks is making him have bad dreams. He learns to read, and his mother buys him a book about another lion, which he reads when his parents go out. Then he pretends that he is the lion in the book and jokingly tells his parents that he did the same things that Oliver P. Lion did.

1. Johnny Lion's Book ◆ 1965
2. Johnny Lion's Bad Day ◆ 1970
3. Johnny Lion's Rubber Boots ◆ 1972

JOHNNY MAXWELL

Pratchett, Terry

HARPERCOLLINS ◆ **GRADES 5–8** ◆ **A/R**

HUMOR | FANTASY | SCIENCE FICTION

Johnny Maxwell is already facing enough problems—his parents' unhappy marriage and constant scenes of fighting in the 1991 Gulf War—when his new computer game, Only You Can Save Mankind, throws out a new challenge. In the second volume in this funny trilogy, ghosts of "post-senior citizens" seek Johnny's help when their cemetery is under threat. The final volume involves time travel as Johnny and friends seek to save his English village from a bomb that will fall on it in World War II. These books were first published in Britain in the 1990s.

1. Only You Can Save Mankind: If Not You, Who Else? ◆ 2005
2. Johnny and the Dead ◆ 2006
3. Johnny and the Bomb ◆ 2007

JOHNNY MAY

Branscum, Robbie

HARPERCOLLINS ◆ **GRADES 4–6**

FAMILY LIFE | HISTORICAL | MYSTERY

Johnny May is an orphan who lives with and takes care of her grandparents in a poverty-stricken area of the Arkansas hills. This resourceful 11-year-old wonders in one book how she can provide a Christmas for herself and her grandparents. As the book opens, she comes upon a man shooting another man. As she and her friend Aron try to solve this mystery, Johnny deals with her feelings about violence in general, even as it relates to hunting animals. Other books in the series deal with her sort-of-romance with Aron and a mix-up with another neighbor they think is a killer.

1. Johnny May ◆ 1975
2. The Adventures of Johnny May ◆ 1984
3. Johnny May Grows Up ◆ 1987

JOHNNY MUTTON

Proimos, James

HARCOURT ◆ **GRADES 3–5** ◆ **A/R**

FANTASY | HUMOR

Momma Mutton (a human) has found a baby on her doorstep. Momma has bad eyesight and she does not notice that the baby is a sheep. She takes him in and raises him as a little boy. So begins this silly series. Johnny grows up and seems to fit right in. He has an idea for the science fair, he plans a birthday party for a friend, and he runs a cooking contest. The colorful graphic novel/comic format is perfect for these irreverent antics.

1. The Many Adventures of Johnny Mutton ◆ 2001
2. Johnny Mutton, He's So Him! ◆ 2003
3. Mutton Soup: More Adventures of Johnny Mutton ◆ 2004

JONATHAN RAND'S AMERICAN CHILLERS *see* American Chillers

JOSEFINA *see* American Girls: Josefina

JOSHUA *see* My America: Joshua

JOSHUA T. BATES

Shreve, Susan Richards

KNOPF ◆ **GRADES 3–6** ◆ **A/R**

REAL LIFE

Just as school is going to begin, Joshua T. Bates finds out that he will be repeating third grade. Even though everyone explains the situation very carefully and with sensitivity, he is dismayed to be "flunking." He works very hard and is promoted to fourth grade in the middle of the school year. Once he is moved up, he worries about fitting in and must deal with a school bully. These situations will be familiar to many students, who will admire Joshua's efforts to solve his problems.

1. The Flunking of Joshua T. Bates ◆ 1984
2. Joshua T. Bates Takes Charge ◆ 1993
3. Joshua T. Bates in Trouble Again ◆ 1997

JOURNAL OF A CARDBOARD GENIUS

Asch, Frank

KIDS CAN PRESS ◆ GRADES 3–5 ◆ A/R

SCIENCE FICTION

Alex's little brother Jonathan is "the biggest pain in the butt this side of Alpha Centauri." Alex's solution: build a spaceship (out of cardboard, duct tape, and other household items) and star jump across the universe and away from Jonathan. Alex's scientific abilities are phenomenal and his inventions are quite creative. Numerous black-and-white drawings add to the appeal.

1. Star Jumper: Journal of a Cardboard Genius ◆ 2006
2. Gravity Buster: Journal #2 of a Cardboard Genius ◆ 2007
3. Time Twister: Journal #3 of a Cardboard Genius ◆ 2008

JOURNEY OF ALLEN STRANGE

Various authors

ALADDIN ◆ GRADES 4–7

SCIENCE FICTION

Allen Strange is an alien from Xela. He was left behind by his spaceship and he has adopted the appearance of an African American human boy. He needs Robbie Stevenson's help but Robbie does not believe he is an alien until Allen appears as he really looks. Allen and Robbie help prevent several alien invasions, including the arrival of the insect-like Arubii. This is fun for fans of science fiction.

1. The Arrival (Weiss, Bobbi J. G., and David Cody Weiss) ◆ 1999
2. Invasion (Gallagher, Diana G.) ◆ 1999
3. Split Image (Dubowski, Cathy East) ◆ 1999
4. Legacy (Odom, Mel) ◆ 1999
5. Depth Charge (Weiss, Bobbi J. G., and David Cody Weiss) ◆ 1999
6. Alien Vacation (Weiss, Bobbi J. G., and David Cody Weiss) ◆ 1999

7. Election Connection (Ponti, James) ◆ 1999
8. Changeling Diapers (Weiss, Bobbi J. G., and David Cody Weiss) ◆ 2000
9. Joyride (Vornholt, John) ◆ 2000

JUDGE AND JURY

Banks, Jacqueline Turner

HOUGHTON MIFFLIN ◆ GRADES 4–6 ◆ A/R

FAMILY LIFE | REAL LIFE

Judge and Jury Jenkins are twin brothers with very different personalities. Judge's dyslexia makes it difficult for him to do well at school. As sixth-graders at Plank Elementary School, the brothers and their friends work to help a student who needs a motorized wheelchair. Judge needs Jury's help to participate in the egg-drop contest for their science class. There are realistic events and dialogue in these novels, which feature African Americans as the main characters and deal with issues of diversity, including prejudice. The fourth book is narrated by Japanese American Tommy, who enlists his friends' help in building a speed bump while worrying about his mother's activism.

1. Project Wheels ◆ 1993
2. The New One ◆ 1994
3. Egg-Drop Blues ◆ 1995
4. A Day for Vincent Chin and Me ◆ 2001

JUDGE BENJAMIN

McInerney, Judith Whitelock

HOLIDAY HOUSE; POCKET BOOKS ◆ GRADES 4–6 ◆ A/R

ANIMAL FANTASY | HUMOR

The narrator of this series is a huge St. Bernard who loves and protects his family through thick and thin—whether they appreciate him or not. Seth, Kathleen, and Ann Elizabeth look forward to staying with their grandmother while their parents are away, but Judge Benjamin feels that his territory is being invaded when the grandmother's dog comes along. With the children's parents away, the dogs form an uneasy partnership to solve problems. In other books in the series, Judge Benjamin stows away in the family's camper, finds a mate, and solves a mystery while snow-bound in a cabin with his family.

1. Judge Benjamin: Superdog ◆ 1982
2. Judge Benjamin: The Superdog Secret ◆ 1983
3. Judge Benjamin: The Superdog Rescue ◆ 1984

4. Judge Benjamin: The Superdog Surprise ◆ 1985
5. Judge Benjamin: The Superdog Gift ◆ 1986

JUDY MOODY

McDonald, Megan

CANDLEWICK PRESS ◆ GRADES 3–5 ◆ A/R

REAL LIFE

The series begins with Judy Moody in a back-to-school bad mood. She is entering third grade and her teacher is Mr. Todd. She is not looking forward to the first assignment until she finds out it is a "Me-Collage." Now she can really express herself. Judy Moody's moods change depending on whether she is with her little brother, Stink; her best friend, Rocky; or a friend who pesters her, Frank Pearl. Middle-elementary readers will enjoy Judy's antics. There is a series about Stink, too.

1. Judy Moody ◆ 2000
2. Judy Moody Gets Famous! ◆ 2001
3. Judy Moody Saves the World! ◆ 2002
4. Judy Moody Predicts the Future ◆ 2003
5. Judy Moody, M.D.: The Doctor Is In! ◆ 2004
6. Judy Moody Declares Independence ◆ 2005
7. Judy Moody: Around the World in 8 1/2 Days ◆ 2006
8. Judy Moody and Stink: The Holly Joliday ◆ 2007
9. Judy Moody Goes to College ◆ 2008

JULEP O'TOOLE

Trueit, Trudi

PENGUIN ◆ GRADES 4–7 ◆ A/R

FAMILY LIFE

In the first book, poor Julep, 11, is a middle child, stuck (and generally ignored) between a perfect older sister and an asthmatic and demanding younger brother. By the second book, the focus is more on her needs and her wish to be more independent, to choose her own clothes. Julep's diary entries, interspersed throughout the text, reveal her point of view.

1. Julep O'Toole: Confessions of a Middle Child ◆ 2005
2. Julep O'Toole: Miss Independent ◆ 2006
3. Julep O'Toole: What I Really Want To Do Is Direct ◆ 2007

JULI SCOTT SUPER SLEUTH

Reece, Colleen L.

BARBOUR PUBLISHING ◆ GRADES 5–8

MYSTERY | VALUES

Juli Scott imagines that she will be an author of Nancy Drew-style stories. Meanwhile, she solves some of her own mysteries, including the mysterious "death" of her own father. In *Mysterious Monday,* Juli's father, Gary, who is a policeman, loses his memory after an explosion. Trying to trick some drug dealers, the local police tell Juli and her mother, Anne, that Gary is dead. In other books, Juli tries to rescue her friend Shannon Riley from the influence of a spiritualist, and Juli and her boyfriend, Dave Gilmore, are in danger as witnesses to a robbery. Juli and her family incorporate Christian values into their daily lives and activities. Juli often writes in her journal, struggling with her conscience, beliefs, and spiritual questions.

1. Mysterious Monday ◆ 1997
2. Trouble on Tuesday ◆ 1997
3. Wednesday Witness ◆ 1998
4. Thursday Trials ◆ 1998
5. Friday Flight ◆ 1998
6. Saturday Scare ◆ 1998

JULIA REDFERN

Cameron, Eleanor

DUTTON ◆ GRADES 4–6

FAMILY LIFE | HUMOR | REAL LIFE

Julia is a girl who loves to write, just like her father. He goes off to fight in World War I, where he is killed. But Julia has a dream just as he is dying, in which he asks her to tell her mother to be sure to go through his papers. There she finds a story that he wrote just before he went away, which eventually is accepted for publication. Starting when Julia is about four, the series follows her through high school as she writes about the people around her. First love, writing, and the love and support of her adored Uncle Hugh are the themes of the rest of the series.

1. A Room Made of Windows ◆ 1971
2. Julia and the Hand of God ◆ 1977
3. That Julia Redfern ◆ 1982
4. Julia's Magic ◆ 1984
5. The Private Worlds of Julia Redfern ◆ 1988

JULIAN AND HUEY

Cameron, Ann

FARRAR, STRAUS & GIROUX ◆ **GRADES 2–4** ◆ **A/R**

FAMILY LIFE

Julian is full of creative ideas for activities and projects, many of which involve his younger brother, Huey, and their friend Gloria. One time, the friends form the Crimebusters and notice many mysterious circumstances. Another time, Julian tries to find out what his father is dreaming so that he can get his father the best birthday gift. Julian sometimes takes advantage of Huey's gullibility, but throughout the stories there is a strong sense of family support and love. Huey and Gloria each have books that highlight their own preoccupations.

1. The Stories Julian Tells ◆ 1981
2. More Stories Julian Tells ◆ 1986
3. Julian's Glorious Summer ◆ 1987
4. Julian, Secret Agent ◆ 1988
5. Julian, Dream Doctor ◆ 1990
6. The Stories Huey Tells ◆ 1995
7. More Stories Huey Tells ◆ 1997
8. Gloria's Way ◆ 2000
9. Gloria Rising ◆ 2002

JULIE *see* American Girls: Julie

JULIE OF THE WOLVES

George, Jean Craighead

HARPERCOLLINS ◆ **GRADES 5–8** ◆ **A/R**

ADVENTURE

Beginning with the Newbery-winning *Julie of the Wolves,* George explores the experiences of people and animals in the Alaskan tundra. Julie's story follows her quest for her identity through her return to her father's home. *Julie's Wolf Pack* describes the hardships faced by Kapu, first seen as a pup in the first book. The wolves face famine, disease, rivalries, and other dangers. These are exciting, realistic adventure novels. Readers will also relate to George's series about Sam Gribley and the falcon called Frightful.

1. Julie of the Wolves ◆ 1972
2. Julie ◆ 1996
3. Julie's Wolf Pack ◆ 1997

JULIET *see* Girlhood Journeys: Juliet

JUNEBUG

Mead, Alice

FARRAR, STRAUS & GIROUX ◆ GRADES 4–7 ◆ A/R

REAL LIFE

These realistic novels begin when Reeve McClain, Jr., "Junebug," is 10 years old. His family lives in the projects, facing all the threats of urban life—drugs, gangs, and loneliness. In the second book, they have moved to a safer neighborhood where Junebug's mother is the supervisor of a home for the elderly. Junebug helps her and interacts with Reverend Ashford. The third book finds Junebug meeting up with his friend Robert, who still lives in the projects. Junebug faces his family problems (his father has been in jail) and makes choices about his future.

1. Junebug ◆ 1995
2. Junebug and the Reverend ◆ 1998
3. Junebug in Trouble ◆ 2003

JUNIE B. JONES

Park, Barbara

RANDOM HOUSE ◆ GRADES 1–2 ◆ A/R

HUMOR | REAL LIFE

Junie B. Jones is a very strong-willed kindergarten student. She hides in the school building so she won't have to ride the bus, she learns about right and wrong when she loses her special new mittens, and she doesn't like her school picture. Throughout her adventures, Junie B. is helped by her teacher (whom she calls "Mrs."), her parents, and her grandparents. She speaks up for herself and for her friends, Grace and Lucille.

1. Junie B. Jones and the Stupid Smelly Bus ◆ 1992
2. Junie B. Jones and a Little Monkey Business ◆ 1993
3. Junie B. Jones and Her Big Fat Mouth ◆ 1993
4. Junie B. Jones and Some Sneaky Peeky Spying ◆ 1994
5. Junie B. Jones and the Yucky Blucky Fruitcake ◆ 1995
6. Junie B. Jones and That Meanie Jim's Birthday ◆ 1996
7. Junie B. Jones Loves Handsome Warren ◆ 1996
8. Junie B. Jones Has a Monster Under Her Bus ◆ 1997
9. Junie B. Jones Is Not a Crook ◆ 1997
10. Junie B. Jones Is a Party Animal ◆ 1997
11. Junie B. Jones Is a Beauty Shop Guy ◆ 1998

12. Junie B. Jones Smells Something Fishy ◆ 1998
13. Junie B. Jones Is (Almost) a Flower Girl ◆ 1999
14. Junie B. Jones and the Mushy Gushy Valentine ◆ 1999
15. Junie B. Jones Has a Peep in Her Pocket ◆ 2000
16. Junie B. Jones Is Captain Field Day ◆ 2001
17. Junie B. Jones Is a Graduation Girl ◆ 2001
18. Junie B., First Grader (at last!) ◆ 2001
19. Junie B., First Grader: Boss of Lunch ◆ 2002
20. Junie B., First Grader: Toothless Wonder ◆ 2002
21. Junie B., First Grader: Cheater Pants ◆ 2003
22. Junie B., First Grader: One-Man Band ◆ 2003
23. Junie B., First Grader: Shipwrecked ◆ 2004
24. Junie B., Boo . . . and I Mean It! ◆ 2004
25. Junie B., First Grader: Jingle Bells, Batman Smells! (P.S. So Does May) ◆ 2005
26. Junie B., First Grader: Aloha-ha-ha! ◆ 2006
27. Junie B., First Grader: Dumb Bunny ◆ 2007

JUNIOR GYMNASTS

Slater, Teddy

SCHOLASTIC ◆ GRADES 3–5

REAL LIFE | RECREATION

A group of girls are on a local gymnastics team. Their goal is to be in the Olympics. When a new girl, Amanda Calloway, joins the team, there is some friction and jealousy. Dana Lewis had been looking forward to her first competition, thinking she was the best member of the team. But Amanda is a great gymnast, too. This series emphasizes the training, effort, dedication, and energy that go into competitive gymnastics. There are also issues of competition and supporting teammates. An introduction by Olympic Gymnast Dominique Dawes stresses the importance of doing your best to fulfill your dreams.

1. Dana's Competition ◆ 1996
2. Katie's Big Move ◆ 1996
3. Amanda's Perfect Ten ◆ 1996
4. Dana's Best Friend ◆ 1996
5. Katie's Gold Medal ◆ 1996
6. Amanda's Unlucky Day ◆ 1997

JUNIOR JEDI KNIGHTS *see* Star Wars Junior Jedi Knights

JURASSIC PARK ADVENTURES

Ciencin, Scott

RANDOM HOUSE ◆ GRADES 4–7

FANTASY

Here are three stories set in Jurassic Park. In the first book, Eric is 13 and he goes para-sailing with Ben (his mother's boyfriend) to observe the dinosaurs from a safe distance above. There is an accident and Ben is killed. Eric is trapped on the island of Jurassic Park. Fans of the **movie** will enjoy this series.

1. Survivor ◆ 2001
2. Prey ◆ 2001
3. Flyers ◆ 2001

JUST . . .

Griffiths, Andy

SCHOLASTIC ◆ GRADES 5–8

HUMOR

Barf, poop, flesh-eating zombies, and other outrageous topics are just right for many middle school readers. The humorous stories in these books are sure to attract fans of Griffiths's Butt Wars books.

1. Just Annoying! ◆ 2003
2. Just Joking! ◆ 2003
3. Just Wacky! ◆ 2004
4. Just Stupid! ◆ 2004
5. Just Disgusting! ◆ 2004
6. Just Shocking! ◆ 2008

JUST GRACE

Harper, Charise Mericle

HOUGHTON MIFFLIN ◆ GRADES 2–4 ◆ A/R

REAL LIFE

Because there are three other girls named Grace in her third-grade classroom, Grace Stewart is called "Just Grace." At school, Just Grace enjoys most of her classmates—except for Sammy Stringer. In *Still Just Grace*, Grace leaves for summer vacation. When she returns, her best friend Mimi has teamed up with a new neighbor, Max, and has even made friends with Sammy! The Ivy and Bean books (Barrows) and Jacobson's Clementine stories offer similar stories of friendship.

1. Just Grace ◆ 2007
2. Still Just Grace ◆ 2007
3. Just Grace Walks the Dog ◆ 2008

JUST ME AND MY DAD

Gauthier, Bertrand

GARETH STEVENS ◆ GRADES 1–3 ◆ A/R

FAMILY LIFE | REAL LIFE

Zachary and his dad, a single parent, are on their own. They have a lot of fun together in these simple, short tales for young readers. They go shopping, ice skating, and camping together. Zachary and his dad don't always get along; sometimes Zachary gets angry (but not for long). He even gets lost in one book. These are comforting stories that "only children" and children in single-parent households will relate to.

1. Zachary in I'm Zachary ◆ 1993
2. Zachary in the Championship ◆ 1993
3. Zachary in the Winter ◆ 1993
4. Zachary in the Present ◆ 1993
5. Zachary in the Wawabongbong ◆ 1993
6. Zachary in Camping Out ◆ 1993

JUSTICE TRILOGY

Hamilton, Virginia

GREENWILLOW ◆ GRADES 5–8 ◆ A/R

FANTASY | SCIENCE FICTION

Justice and her two brothers discover that they are the first of a new race with extraordinary powers. Together with their friend Dorian, they form a unit that is able to travel into the distant future. Among the beings they find there is Duster, the leader of a group of young people. He is hindered, as is all of this world, by the evil Mal. When the Mal is defeated, all the friends they have made are free to be themselves. When Justice and her brothers return to their own time, they find that they have lost some of their powers but have gained maturity.

1. Justice and Her Brothers ◆ 1978
2. Dustland ◆ 1980
3. The Gathering ◆ 1981

KAI *see* Girlhood Journeys: Kai

KANE FAMILY

Caseley, Judith

GREENWILLOW ◆ GRADES 3–4

FAMILY LIFE | REAL LIFE

This series explores such childhood experiences as starting school, feeling lonely, getting lost, confronting a school bully, and family relationships. Each title focuses on one of the Kane children, with lots of interaction within the family. In *Dorothy's Darkest Days,* Dorothy must confront her feelings about a classmate who has died, particularly the fact that Dorothy did not like her. Harry is a busy, charming preschooler in *Hurricane Harry.* In *Harry and Arney,* he must relinquish his role as the youngest child and accept a new baby in the family. Affectionate humor and an accessible reading level make this a good choice for middle-elementary school.

1. Hurricane Harry ◆ 1991
2. Starring Dorothy Kane ◆ 1992
3. Chloe in the Know ◆ 1993
4. Harry and Arney ◆ 1994
5. Dorothy's Darkest Days ◆ 1997

THE KARMIDEE

Haptie, Charlotte

HOLIDAY HOUSE ◆ GRADES 4–7 ◆ A/R

FANTASY

The City of Trees is an isolated place surrounded by mountains and magic. The Normals are in power and they make rules to control those with magical powers, the Karmidee. Otto believes he is a Normal and is surprised to learn that his father, a librarian, is actually the King of the Karmidee. Otto's life is totally upended and he faces dangers as he tries to protect the Karmidee from the prejudice of the Normals. In the third book, Otto and a young girl named Rhiannon who opposes magic find themselves thrown together in a quest to save Otto's people.

1. Otto and the Flying Twins: The First Book of the Karmidee ◆ 2004
2. Otto and the Bird Charmers: The Second Book of the Karmidee ◆ 2005
3. Otto in the Time of the Warrior ◆ 2006

KATE

Brisson, Pat

SIMON & SCHUSTER ◆ GRADES 2–4

REAL LIFE

Kate, a young girl from New Jersey, travels across the country, writing letters to her best friend back home. At every stop she describes interesting things she sees, and the trials and tribulations of dealing with Brian, her pesky younger brother. In Baltimore, they go to the aquarium and he says they should have brought Kate's pet goldfish, because the sharks look hungry. In Washington, they visit the National Air and Space Museum, where Brian tells Kate she should be an astronaut, because she looks like something from outer space. The family makes a circle of the eastern states and comes back to New Jersey. In sequels, Kate visits the Southwest and tours the West Coast. Full-color illustrations on every page make this an entertaining way for younger students to study the states.

1. Your Best Friend, Kate ◆ 1989
2. Kate Heads West ◆ 1990
3. Kate on the Coast ◆ 1992

KATIE

McDaniel, Becky Bring

CHILDREN'S PRESS ◆ GRADES K–1 ◆ A/R

REAL LIFE

In a beginning-reader format with a controlled vocabulary, this series focuses on Katie, the youngest and smallest child in her family. Katie struggles to do things that her older siblings, Jenny and Kris, can already do. She is pleased with her accomplishments, such as teaching the dog a trick and giving her mother flowers. Sometimes her siblings are supportive, but other times they take advantage of her being the youngest. Young readers will empathize with the predicament of being little and wanting to do more. The simple text will provide a satisfying reading experience for beginners. *Katie Did It* is also available in a Spanish version *Kathy lo hizo* (2003).

1. Katie Did It ◆ 1983
2. Katie Couldn't ◆ 1985
3. Katie Can ◆ 1987

KATIE JOHN

Calhoun, Mary

HARPERCOLLINS ◆ **GRADES 4–8** ◆ **A/R**

FAMILY LIFE | **REAL LIFE**

Katie John's story begins when her parents inherit a huge, decrepit house in a small town. They decide to move there for the summer, but Katie is not happy about leaving her friends. Over the summer, she makes new friends and begins to appreciate the house and its family history. In the end, she convinces her parents to stay and make a living by renting out rooms. She agrees to help with all the work involved in such an endeavor. In subsequent books, she starts a "boy haters" club but later she becomes a romantic after reading *Wuthering Heights* and begins to look for her Heathcliff.

1. Katie John ◆ 1960
2. Depend on Katie John ◆ 1961
3. Honestly, Katie John! ◆ 1963
4. Katie John and Heathcliff ◆ 1980

KATIE KAZOO, SWITCHEROO

Krulik, Nancy E.

PUFFIN; GROSSET & DUNLAP ◆ **GRADES 2–4** ◆ **A/R**

FANTASY

Katie Carew, a third-grader, can wish to be someone else and a magic wind makes it happen. She turns into a hamster, a field trip guide, a child actress, the school principal, and more. In her "switcheroo" role, she tries to solve problems. She advances to fourth grade during the series.

1. Anyone but Me ◆ 2002
2. Out to Lunch ◆ 2002
3. Oh, Baby! ◆ 2002
4. Girls Don't Have Cooties ◆ 2002
5. I Hate Rules ◆ 2003
6. Get Lost! ◆ 2003
7. Drat! You Copycat! ◆ 2003
8. Doggone It! ◆ 2003
9. Any Way You Slice It ◆ 2003
10. Quiet on the Set! ◆ 2003
11. No Messin' with My Lesson ◆ 2004
12. No Bones About It ◆ 2004
13. On Your Mark, Get Set, Laugh! ◆ 2004
14. Friends for Never ◆ 2004

15. Love Stinks! ◆ 2004
16. Bad Rap ◆ 2005
17. Write On! ◆ 2005
18. Karate Katie ◆ 2006
19. Gotcha! Gotcha Back! ◆ 2006
20. Be Nice to Mice! ◆ 2006
21. I'm Game! ◆ 2006
22. It's Snow Joke! ◆ 2006
23. Open Wide ◆ 2007
24. No Biz Like Show Biz ◆ 2007
25. My Pops Is Tops! ◆ 2007
26. Something's Fishy ◆ 2007
27. Flower Power ◆ 2007
28. Free the Worms! ◆ 2008
29. Major League Mess-up ◆ 2008
30. Vote for Katie Suzanne ◆ 2008

SUPER SPECIALS

1. Who's Afraid of Fourth Grade? (Super Special) ◆ 2004
2. A Whirlwind Vacation ◆ 2005
3. A Katie Kazoo Christmas ◆ 2005
4. Witch Switch ◆ 2006
5. Camp Rules! ◆ 2007
6. On Thin Ice ◆ 2007

KATIE LYNN COOKIE COMPANY

Stanley, George Edward

RANDOM HOUSE ◆ GRADES 2–4 ◆ A/R

REAL LIFE

Katie Lynn uses Grandma's recipe and secret ingredient in her cookies. The cookies are so good that a local restaurant buys them. Katie and her friend Tina bake all summer and earn enough money to bring Grandma to visit. Grandma decides to stay and, in the fourth book, she gets married.

1. The Secret Ingredient ◆ 1999
2. Frogs' Legs for Dinner? ◆ 2000
3. The Battle of the Bakers ◆ 2000
4. Wedding Cookies ◆ 2001

KATIE MORAG

Hedderwick, Mairi

LITTLE, BROWN ◆ GRADES 1–2

FAMILY LIFE

A new baby, a visit from mischievous cousins, and rivalry between Grannie Island and Grannie Mainland are some of the plots presented in this light-hearted series. Katie Morag lives in a tiny fishing village off the coast of Scotland. Whimsical details of the setting are captured in the humorous illustrations. Katie Morag is a young girl who gives early readers a glimpse of growing up in another country. *The Big Katie Morag Storybook* (1996) features three stories and a collection of verses; there are also activity books.

1. Katie Morag Delivers the Mail ◆ 1984
2. Katie Morag and the Two Grandmothers ◆ 1985
3. Katie Morag and the Tiresome Ted ◆ 1986
4. Katie Morag and the Big Boy Cousins ◆ 1987
5. Katie Morag and the Grand Concert ◆ 1988
6. Katie Morag and the New Pier ◆ 1994
7. Katie Morag and the Wedding ◆ 1996

KATIE POTTS *see* Holiday Friends

KAYA *see* American Girls: Kaya

KEEKER *see* Sneaky Pony

THE KEEPERS

Koller, Jackie French

ALADDIN ◆ GRADES 4–6 ◆ A/R

FANTASY

In Eldearth, people and magical beings live together. A search is being conducted for a new Imperial Wizard and Princess Arenelle (Nell) dreams of being chosen even though girls should be witches. Nell embarks on the quest anyway and succeeds. Just as she is to become the wizard's apprentice, her father, King Einar, intervenes. Nell is a strong character who will appeal to fans who want a female Harry Potter.

1. A Wizard Named Nell ◆ 2003
2. The Wizard's Apprentice ◆ 2003
3. The Wizard's Scepter ◆ 2004

KENAN AND KEL

Various authors

ALADDIN; SIMON SPOTLIGHT ◆ GRADES 4–6

REAL LIFE

In the Nickelodeon television program, Kenan Thompson and Kel Mitchell are best friends. These books follow some of their adventures. In one book, they are transported to the Old West and end up as Sheriff Kenan and Deputy Kel. In another book, Kel comes along on vacation with Kenan and his family. The two friends fall asleep and wake up in the wrong car. Kenan and Kel are African Americans, so this would be a good selection to expand multicultural collections.

1. Aw, Here It Goes! (Freeman, Steve) ◆ 1998
2. Family and Food and Orange Soda (Freeman, Steve) ◆ 1998
3. aLIEns (Holland, Steve) ◆ 1999
4. Summer Vacation (Holland, Steve) ◆ 1999
5. Kel Got Game (Holland, Steve) ◆ 1999
6. FranKELstein (Holland, Steve) ◆ 1999
7. Westward, Whoa! (Holland, Steve) ◆ 1999
8. A-Campin' We Will Go (Holland, Steve) ◆ 1999

KERBY MAXWELL BOOKS *see* Trick Books

KEYS TO THE KINGDOM

Nix, Garth

SCHOLASTIC ◆ GRADES 5–8 ◆ A/R

FANTASY

Mister Monday wants to recover a mysterious key from Arthur Penhaligon. It turns out that Arthur is the heir to "the Will" and there are seven keys that he must acquire. The Second Key brings him into contact with Grim Tuesday. Arthur battles to save not only the Earth but also the magical worlds that have been revealed to him.

1. Mister Monday ◆ 2003
2. Grim Tuesday ◆ 2004
3. Drowned Wednesday ◆ 2005
4. Sir Thursday ◆ 2006
5. Lady Friday ◆ 2007
6. Superior Saturday ◆ 2008

KEYSTONE STABLES

Hubler, Marsha

ZONDERKIDZ ◆ GRADES 5–8 ◆ A/R

REAL LIFE

After being in foster homes, Skye, 13, is difficult and belligerent. The juvenile court is ready to send her to a detention center until Mr. and Mrs. Chambers agree to become her new foster family. The Chambers own Keystone Stables and as Skye begins to connect with the horses, she begins to trust the people around her, too. Guided by her new family, Skye finds faith in God's love.

1. The Trouble with Skye ◆ 2004
2. A True Test for Skye ◆ 2004
3. Trouble Times Two ◆ 2005
4. Teamwork at Camp Tioga ◆ 2005
5. The Winning Summer ◆ 2005
6. Skye's Final Test ◆ 2005

KIDNAPPED

Korman, Gordon

SCHOLASTIC ◆ GRADES 5–8 ◆ A/R

ADVENTURE

Meg, 11, and Aiden, 15, have been fugitives from the FBI (see the On the Run series). Just as their lives begin to settle down, Meg is kidnapped. Although he still distrusts them, Aiden must cooperate with the FBI to find his sister. Meanwhile, Meg is trying to escape from her captors. This is an action-packed series with cliff-hanging moments and plot twists that leave the reader breathless.

1. Abduction ◆ 2006
2. Search ◆ 2006
3. Rescue ◆ 2006

KIDS FROM KENNEDY MIDDLE SCHOOL

Cooper, Ilene

MORROW ◆ GRADES 5–7 ◆ A/R

REAL LIFE

Friends and foes at a middle school are the focus of this series. Robin and Veronica are friends but when Veronica creates an exclusive club, Robin is uneasy. If she speaks up, she'll be left out. Jon Rossi is a sixth-grader who plays basketball but dislikes his coach's negative approach. If he leaves the team, he'll disappoint his father. Gretchen, 12, loses weight, but she still remembers the way she was treated.

1. Queen of the Sixth Grade ◆ 1988
2. Choosing Sides ◆ 1990
3. Mean Streak ◆ 1991
4. The New, Improved Gretchen Hubbard ◆ 1992

KIDS IN MS. COLEMAN'S CLASS

Martin, Ann M.

SCHOLASTIC ◆ GRADES 1–3

REAL LIFE

There are sixteen students in Ms. Coleman's second-grade class—six boys and ten girls. Each book involves these students in common classroom situations. In *Science Fair,* Bobby and his group are studying a mouse named Harriet. When Harriet goes missing, is the science project ruined? In *Snow War,* Ian Johnson loves to read. He even reads while his friends are building snow forts and throwing snowballs. But he stops reading when he realizes that his friends have started to get mean in their snow fights. Other books deal with being afraid of animals, enjoying a favorite author, being on summer vacation, and celebrating holidays. There is diversity in the class and a common theme is that the boys often feel out-numbered, which should appeal to many readers.

1. Teacher's Pet ◆ 1995
2. Author Day ◆ 1996
3. Class Play ◆ 1996
4. Second Grade Baby ◆ 1996
5. Snow War ◆ 1997
6. Twin Trouble ◆ 1997
7. Science Fair ◆ 1997
8. Summer School ◆ 1997
9. Halloween Parade ◆ 1997
10. Holiday Time ◆ 1997
11. Spelling Bee ◆ 1998
12. Baby Animal Zoo ◆ 1998

KIDS OF THE POLK STREET SCHOOL *see*
Polk Street School: Kids of the Polk Street School

KIDS ON BUS 5

Leonard, Marcia

MINSTREL/POCKET BOOKS ◆ **GRADES 1–3**

REAL LIFE

Natalie Adams and James Perry are in third grade at Maple Street School. They are good friends and they enjoy school, except for riding the bus to get there. The bus driver, Mr. Balter, tries to keep control of things, but he yells so much the kids call him "Old Yeller." Natalie, James, and Natalie's little brother Cody must deal with bullies on the bus, a breakdown, and wondering if someone on their route is a thief. When Mr. Balter is sick for a while, the kids find out that his substitutes bring different problems. Readers who ride the bus will recognize many of these situations and will be reassured by the satisfying solutions.

1. The Bad News Bully ◆ 1996
2. Wild Man at the Wheel ◆ 1996
3. Finders Keepers ◆ 1997
4. I Survived on Bus Five ◆ 1997

KIM POSSIBLE (CHAPTER BOOKS)

Various authors

HYPERION; DISNEY PRESS ◆ **GRADES 4–7**

FANTASY

Kim Possible will save the world. She faces the evil Drakken. She finds a kidnapped scientist. She stops DNAmy from creating a stuffed-animal army. All the while, she manages to stay involved with cheerleading, ski trips, and watching television. There are related items to this series including a puzzle book, *Code Word: Kim*.

1. Bueno Nacho (Thorpe, Kiki) ◆ 2003
2. The New Ron (Thorpe, Kiki) ◆ 2003
3. Showdown at Camp Wannaweep (Thorpe, Kiki) ◆ 2003
4. Downhill (Jones, Jasmine) ◆ 2003
5. Killigan's Island (Pascoe, Jim) ◆ 2004
6. Monkey Business (Cerasini, Marc) ◆ 2004
7. Attack of the Killer Bebes (Pascoe, Jim) ◆ 2004
8. Royal Pain (Jones, Jasmine) ◆ 2004
9. Extreme (unknown) ◆ 2004
10. Tweeb Trouble (unknown) ◆ 2004
11. Grudge Match (unknown) ◆ 2005
12. Cloned (Cling, Jacqueline) ◆ 2006

KIM POSSIBLE: PICK A VILLAIN

Various authors

DISNEY PRESS ◆ GRADES 4–7

FANTASY

Here's a Kim Possible series with a "Choose Your Own Adventure" format. You pick the villain and then you decide what Kim will do to save the world.

1. Game On! (Ciencin, Scott, and Mark McCorkle) ◆ 2005
2. Badical Battles (Schooley, Bob, and Mark McCorkle) ◆ 2005
3. Masters of Mayhem (Ciencin, Scott) ◆ 2005
4. So Not the Drama! (Schooley, Bob, and Mark McCorkle) ◆ 2005

KIM POSSIBLE (TOKYOPOP)

Schooley, Bob, and Mark McCorkle

TOKYOPOP ◆ GRADES 4–7

FANTASY

Kim Possible is a typical high school girl who saves the world from evil villains in her spare time.

1. Bueno Nacho and Tick Tick Tick ◆ 2003
2. Monkey Fist Strikes and Attack of the Killer Bebes ◆ 2003
3. The New Ron and Mind Games ◆ 2003
4. Royal Pain and Twin Factor ◆ 2003
5. Animal Attraction and All the News ◆ 2004
6. Sink or Swim and Number One ◆ 2004
7. Monkey Ninjas in Space and Crush ◆ 2004

KIM POSSIBLE CINE-MANGA

1. Vol. 1 ◆ 2003
2. Vol. 2 ◆ 2003
3. Vol. 3 ◆ 2004
4. Vol. 4 ◆ 2004
5. Vol. 5 ◆ 2004
6. Vol. 6 ◆ 2004
7. Vol. 7 ◆ 2004

KING ARTHUR

Talbot, Hudson, reteller

MORROW ◆ GRADES 3–5

FANTASY

This adaptation of the original Arthur story has the appeal of simpler language and vivid illustrations. The series is filled with the pageantry of medieval times. The tale begins in *The Sword in the Stone* when 16-year-old Arthur discovers he has been chosen to be king of Britain. Sir Ector, his adoptive father, fully understands the truth when Arthur pulls the fabled sword from its stone and becomes the rightful king. Merlin, the ancient magician, becomes Arthur's guide in uniting the country. In other books, Arthur's feat becomes legendary, he establishes the model for chivalry, and creates Camelot. The illustrations bring the adventures to life, especially for younger readers.

1. King Arthur: The Sword in the Stone ◆ 1991
2. King Arthur and the Round Table ◆ 1995
3. Excalibur ◆ 1996
4. Lancelot ◆ 1999

KIPPER

Inkpen, Mick
RED WAGON BOOKS ◆ GRADES K–2 ◆ A/R
ANIMAL FANTASY

Kipper is a puppy who enjoys everyday activities. After he straightens his basket, he misses his familiar things. In another book, Kipper cannot find one of his toys. There are numerous related items including DVDs (from the Nickelodeon television program), stuffed animals, and board books.

1. Kipper's Snowy Day ◆ 1999
2. Kipper ◆ 1999
3. Kipper's Birthday ◆ 2000
4. Kipper's Christmas Eve ◆ 2000
5. Kipper's A to Z: An Alphabet Adventure ◆ 2001
6. Kipper's Monster ◆ 2002
7. Kipper's Toybox ◆ 2002
8. Kipper and Roly ◆ 2003

KIPPER: LITTLE KIPPERS

Inkpen, Mick
RED WAGON BOOKS ◆ GRADES K–2 ◆ A/R
ANIMAL FANTASY

More adventures with Kipper and his friends. Many young readers will know these characters from the Nick Jr. television program and the available DVDs and toys.

1. Arnold ◆ 1999
2. Honk! ◆ 1999
3. Sandcastle ◆ 1999
4. Splosh! ◆ 1999
5. Butterfly ◆ 2000

6. Hissss! ◆ 2000
7. Meow! ◆ 2000
8. Swing ◆ 2000
9. Picnic ◆ 2001
10. Rocket ◆ 2001
11. Skates ◆ 2001
12. Thing ◆ 2001

KIRSTEN *see* American Girls: Kirsten

KIT *see* American Girls: Kit

KITTEN FRIENDS

Dale, Jenny
ALADDIN ◆ GRADES K–2 ◆ A/R
REAL LIFE

Kids and kittens, what could be better? Michael wants a kitten but his mom says no. Then, he finds Star. Lucy is a kitten who loves her owner but is still lonely. Young readers will love these easy books.

1. Felix the Fluffy Kitten ◆ 2000
2. Bob the Bouncy Kitten ◆ 2000
3. Star the Snowy Kitten ◆ 2001
4. Nell the Naughty Kitten ◆ 2001
5. Leo the Lucky Kitten ◆ 2001
6. Patch the Perfect Kitten ◆ 2001
7. Lucy the Lonely Kitten ◆ 2001

KITTY

Delton, Judy
HOUGHTON MIFFLIN ◆ GRADES 3–6 ◆ A/R
HISTORICAL | REAL LIFE

Set in the 1930s, the first book in this series finds third-grader Kitty changing from one Catholic school to another. At her new school, she meets Margaret Mary, an A student, the oldest of many children, a great help to her mother, and a devout Catholic. She also meets Eileen, a wealthy only child who is bored with school and indifferent to the Church. The three girls form an unlikely friendship and for the rest of the series, Kitty feels herself pulled between the other two. In fourth grade, they experience first love and explore an old house together. The series follows them up to high school, where Margaret Mary's behavior takes a surprising turn and they all discover boys. *Kitty from the Start* is a prequel to the earlier books.

1. Kitty in the Middle ◆ 1979
2. Kitty in the Summer ◆ 1980
3. Kitty in High School ◆ 1984
4. Kitty from the Start ◆ 1987

KLONDIKE KID

Hopkinson, Deborah
ALADDIN ◆ GRADES 3–5 ◆ A/R
HISTORICAL

Davey Hill, 11, is an orphan living in Seattle in the late 1800s. He is trying to earn enough money to travel to Alaska hoping to find his Uncle Walt. When gold is discovered in the Klondike, there is a rush to go there. Davy's money is stolen and he becomes a stowaway on a ship bound for Alaska. His search for his uncle takes him into the wilderness providing readers with an exciting adventure.

1. Sailing for Gold ◆ 2004
2. The Long Trail ◆ 2004
3. Adventure in Gold Town ◆ 2004

KLOOZ

Banscherus, J.
STONE ARCH BOOKS ◆ GRADES 4–7 ◆ A/R
MYSTERY

Klooz is a young detective who investigates mysteries like a haunted school and sabotage at the carnival. He even checks on an attack by flying cows. Reluctant readers will find the format—spacious text layout and numerous illustrations—accessible.

1. After School Ghost Hunter ◆ 2007
2. Clues in the Car Wash ◆ 2007
3. Detective's Duel ◆ 2007
4. The Great Snake Swindle ◆ 2007
5. The Mysterious Mask ◆ 2007
6. Trouble Under the Big Top ◆ 2007
7. The Night of the Blue Heads ◆ 2008
8. The Puzzle of the Power Drain ◆ 2008
9. The Secret of the Flying Cows ◆ 2008
10. The Snarling Suspect ◆ 2008

KNIGHTS OF THE SILVER DRAGON *see*

Dungeons and Dragons: Knights of the Silver Dragon

A KNIGHT'S STORY

Stewart, Paul, and Chris Riddell

ATHENEUM ◆ **GRADES 4–8** ◆ **A/R**

ADVENTURE

As an unbonded knight, "Free Lance" participates in a variety of adventures. In the first book, Lord Big Nose challenges him to recover a crown from the Lake of Skulls. Jousts, treachery, and damsels in distress contribute to the medieval setting. Battles and action along with exciting illustrations by Chris Riddell should attract readers.

1. Lake of Skulls ◆ 2004
2. Joust of Honor ◆ 2005
3. Dragon's Hoard ◆ 2005

KOBIE ROBERTS

Ransom, Candice F.

SCHOLASTIC ◆ **GRADES 4–7**

REAL LIFE

Kobie lives with her parents in the country. We first meet Kobie persuading her best friend, Gretchen, to help her build a roller coaster ride. She is 10 at the time, and the series follows her until she is 15. The series deals in some depth with her maturing process as she learns to get along better with her mother, with Gretchen, and with the other children in her class. A good artist, but a poor student, she learns to make the most of her abilities and to see things from others' points of view.

1. Thirteen ◆ 1986
2. Fourteen and Holding ◆ 1987
3. Fifteen at Last ◆ 1987
4. Going on Twelve ◆ 1988
5. Almost Ten and a Half ◆ 1990

KYLA MAY MISS. BEHAVES

May, Kyla

PRICE STERN SLOAN ◆ **GRADES 4–7** ◆ **A/R**

REAL LIFE | HUMOR

"Hi, my name is Kyla May!! I am 11 years old & i live in Australia . . . and i have a very, very active *imagination*." This is the opening of the first Kyla May book but add in a lot of decorations—like a heart around "Hi," and a cloud around "May," and many different fonts, drawings, and colors (red, pink, purple, and black). Kyla can't help day-dreaming—especially when she is at school. Music class makes her think about being a pop-star! Kyla May has earned her nickname: Miss. Behaves. Fans of Marissa Moss's Amelia books will want to check these out.

1. Introducing Kyla May Miss. Behaves ◆ 2005
2. Kyla May Miss. Behaves Around the World ◆ 2005
3. Kyla May Miss. Behaves Live on Stage ◆ 2005
4. Kyla May Miss. Behaves as an International Superspy ◆ 2006

LAB COAT GIRL

Palatini, Margie

HYPERION ◆ GRADES 3–5

FANTASY | HUMOR

Trudie (a.k.a. Lab Coat Girl) and Benjamin are working on a class project when they discover that food can have strange effects on Ben. For example, eating carrots gives him "super vision." Trudie experiments with different foods to examine the results. This is part of the L.A.F. imprint from Hyperion that will appeal to fans of Dav Pilkey.

1. Lab Coat Girl and the Amazing Benjamin Bone ◆ 1999
2. Lab Coat Girl in Cool Fuel ◆ 2000
3. Lab Coat Girl in My Triple-Decker Hero ◆ 2000

LADD FAMILY

Roddy, Lee

FOCUS ON THE FAMILY ◆ GRADES 4–6 ◆ A/R

ADVENTURE | FAMILY LIFE | VALUES

This series features exotic locations as the Ladd family spends time in Hawaii and Alaska and goes on a cruise to Mexico. Josh Ladd, 12, and his friend Tank are featured in most of the stories, which include dealing with poachers, surviving a hurricane, adapting to the wilderness, recovering a stolen surfboard, and searching for treasure in shark-infested waters. Occasionally, there is an element of mystery in these books, but the main emphasis is on values such as friendship, honesty, trust, and obedience.

1. The Secret of the Shark Pit ◆ 1988
2. The Legend of Fire ◆ 1988
3. The Mystery of the Island Jungle ◆ 1989
4. The Secret of the Sunken Sub ◆ 1990

5. The Dangerous Canoe Race ◆ 1990
6. The Mystery of the Wild Surfer ◆ 1990
7. Peril at Pirate's Point ◆ 1992
8. Terror at Forbidden Falls ◆ 1993
9. Case of the Dangerous Cruise ◆ 1994
10. The Eye of the Hurricane ◆ 1994
11. The Night of the Vanishing Lights ◆ 1994
12. Panic in the Wild Waters ◆ 1995
13. Hunted in the Alaskan Wilderness ◆ 1996
14. Stranded on Terror Island ◆ 1997
15. Tracked by the Wolf Pack ◆ 1997

LAND OF ELYON

Carman, Patrick

SCHOLASTIC ◆ GRADES 4–6 ◆ A/R

FANTASY

After the death of Thomas Warvold, the founder of a walled community, 12-year-old Alexa secretly journeys outside the walls. There she uses her magical ability to speak with animals and learns of the hardships caused by the walls. Alexa and the animals join together to bring down the walls. Originally planned as a trilogy, the series has grown. The fourth book is a prequel focusing on the early adventures of Thomas Warvold and his brother. The fifth book returns to Alexa and her adventures.

1. The Dark Hills Divide ◆ 2005
2. Beyond the Valley of Thorns ◆ 2005
3. The Tenth City ◆ 2006
4. Into the Mist ◆ 2007
5. Stargazer ◆ 2008

LANDON SNOW

Mortenson, R. K.

BARBOUR ◆ GRADES 5–8 ◆ A/R

FANTASY | VALUES

Landon Snow, 11, is an ordinary boy searching for meaning in life, a search which requires him to find extraordinary courage. In the first book, he enters the Book of meaning and finds a fantasy world. There he is challenged to solve riddles that eventually help him rescue his sister who has been under an enchantment. As the series continues, Landon travels to the Island of Arcanum to free the animals of Wonderwood. Christian values guide and support Landon on his journeys.

1. Landon Snow and the Auctor's Riddle ◆ 2005
2. Landon Snow and the Shadows of Malus Quidam ◆ 2006
3. Landon Snow and the Island of Arcanum ◆ 2006
4. Landon Snow and the Volucer Dragon ◆ 2007
5. Landon Snow and the Auctor's Kingdom ◆ 2007

LARRY THE POLAR BEAR

Pinkwater, Daniel (Manus)

MARSHALL CAVENDISH ◆ GRADES K–3 ◆ A/R

HUMOR

Larry the polar bear had a great childhood in Baffin Bay eating the tourists' muffins. Sent out into the world by his mother, he falls asleep on an ice floe and winds up in New Jersey, where he gets a job as a lifeguard and finds a home in a hotel. In the second book he is reunited with his brother Roy, who lives at the zoo. In other books, he enjoys playing the bongo drums, becomes an ice cream spokesman, and forms a dance company. Illustrations by Jill Pinkwater add to the fun.

1. Young Larry ◆ 1997
2. At the Hotel Larry ◆ 1997
3. Bongo Larry ◆ 1998
4. Ice Cream Larry ◆ 1999
5. Dancing Larry ◆ 2006
6. Sleepover Larry ◆ 2007

LARUE

Teague, Mark

SCHOLASTIC ◆ GRADES K–2 ◆ A/R

HUMOR

In the first book, Ike is a dog who has misbehaved and been sent to obedience school. He writes his owner, Gertrude LaRue, describing the horrible conditions at the school. In reality, the obedience school is more like a spa and Ike exaggerates in the hopes that his owner will bring him home. In the second book, Ike writes letters to try to explain why he has been accused in the disappearance of two cats. Mark Teague shows Ike's version of each story in black and white while the reality is depicted in color.

1. Dear Mrs. LaRue: Letters from Obedience School ◆ 2002
2. Detective LaRue: Letters from the Investigation ◆ 2004
3. LaRue for Mayor: Letters from the Campaign Trail ◆ 2008

LASSIE

Bray, Marian F., adapter

CHARIOT BOOKS ◆ GRADES 4–8

REAL LIFE | VALUES

These books feature the familiar characters of Lassie and the Harmon family. Jimmy and Lassie are more than owner and pet; they are best friends. In one book, Lassie is lost and Jimmy is devastated. His father, Reverend Harmon, reminds Jimmy of his faith in God and helps him accept the circumstances and trust God's judgment. When Lassie returns, Jimmy and his family are thankful, knowing that their prayers have been answered. Lessons about honesty, hope, courage, and faith pervade these books, supporting the Christian values of the publishers, a division of Cook Communications Ministries.

1. Under the Big Top ◆ 1995
2. Treasure at Eagle Mountain ◆ 1995
3. To the Rescue ◆ 1995
4. Hayloft Hideout ◆ 1996
5. Danger at Echo Cliffs ◆ 1996

LAST APPRENTICE

Delaney, Joseph

GREENWILLOW ◆ GRADES 5–8 ◆ A/R

HORROR

Old Gregory is the Spook who has protected the village from demons, creatures, and beasts. As he approaches the end of his life, he searches for an apprentice. Many have tried to serve as his apprentice, but all have failed. The only one left is Thomas Ward, 12, the seventh son of a seventh son. Thomas begins his apprenticeship with a huge challenge. While the Spook is away, Mother Malkin, an evil witch, escapes and it is up to Thomas to stop her attacks. As Thomas's apprenticeship continues, his challenges increase in danger and difficulty.

1. Revenge of the Witch ◆ 2005
2. Curse of the Bane ◆ 2006
3. Night of the Soul Stealer ◆ 2007
4. Attack of the Fiend ◆ 2008
5. Wrath of the Bloodeye ◆ 2008

THE LAURA YEARS *see* Little House

LazyTown (8 x 8 Books)

Various authors

SIMON SPOTLIGHT/NICK JR. ◆ GRADES K–1

HUMOR

Fans of the Nick Jr. television series will enjoy reading about their favorite characters in these picture books that have been adapted from the series. Robbie Rotten is always trying to get the kids of LazyTown to misbehave, and our hero, Sportacus, is always there to save the day. Readers learn lessons in each book, such as the importance of brushing your teeth (and not eating too much candy). Related items include board books, lift-the-flap books, and a paint box book.

1. Sleepless in LazyTown (Scheving, Magnus) ◆ 2006
2. It's Sports Day! (Scheving, Magnus) ◆ 2006
3. Teacher Trouble (Spelvin, Justin) ◆ 2006
4. A LazyTown Christmas (Teitelbaum, Michael) ◆ 2006
5. It's My Party! (Spelvin, Justin) ◆ 2006
6. Happy Brush Day! (Spelvin, Justin) ◆ 2007

LazyTown (Ready to Read)

Various authors

SIMON SPOTLIGHT/NICK JR. ◆ GRADES K–1

HUMOR

Robbie Rotten, Sportacus, and the gang from LazyTown enjoy a treasure hunt, deal with a soccer-playing robot gone wild, and search for a missing cake. These books are adapted from the Nick Jr. television series.

1. Picnic Day (Wax, Wendy) ◆ 2006
2. Who Took the Cake? (Zucker, Zoey) ◆ 2006
3. The Soccer Game (Parent, Nancy) ◆ 2006
4. Pirates! (Gerver, Jane E.) ◆ 2007

Lechow Family

Benary-Isbert, Margot

HARCOURT ◆ GRADES 5–8

FAMILY LIFE | HISTORICAL

Set in postwar Germany, *The Ark* begins the trilogy of the Lechow family. Mrs. Lechow is trying to keep her family alive while her husband is in a Russian prison camp. The family fortunately finds its way to Rowan

Farm and makes a home in the Ark, an old railroad car. The author was born in Germany, lived under Nazi rule, and arrived in the United States in 1957. The stories, translated from German, are based on the author's childhood.

1. The Ark ◆ 1948
2. Rowan Farm ◆ 1949
3. Castle on the Border ◆ 1956

Lenny and Mel

Kraft, Erik P.

Simon & Schuster ◆ **Grades 2–5** ◆ **A/R**

Humor

In the first book, twin brothers Lenny and Mel celebrate holidays in unusual ways, like putting the Thanksgiving turkey leftovers under Mel's pillow so the Leftover Fairy will bring them cash. In the second book, the boys plan to just hang out all summer but their parents have other ideas. Show these to readers who have finished Captain Underpants (Pilkey) and the Riot Brothers (Amato).

1. Lenny and Mel ◆ 2002
2. Lenny and Mel's Summer Vacation ◆ 2003
3. Lenny and Mel: After-School Confidential ◆ 2004

Leo and Emily

Brandenberg, Franz

Greenwillow ◆ **Grades K–3**

Humor | Real life

This is a charming series of beginning chapter books. Leo and Emily are best friends. They go on a hike and search for dragons, make their babysitter earn his money, and generally have a good time.

1. Leo and Emily ◆ 1981
2. Leo and Emily's Big Ideas ◆ 1982
3. Leo and Emily and the Dragon ◆ 1984
4. Leo and Emily's Zoo ◆ 1988

Leven Thumps

Skye, Obert

Shadow Mountain ◆ **Grades 5–8** ◆ **A/R**

Fantasy

As this fantasy series begins there are two worlds—Reality and Foo, which is the land of dreams and hope. In Foo, the evil ruler Sabine is looking for a way to enter Reality and in so doing destroy both worlds. The fate of these worlds is in the hands of Leven Thumps, 14, from Burnt Culvert, Oklahoma. Lev discovers a gateway to Foo and with the help of three companions discovers his special powers and confronts the dangers that threaten the two worlds. These books are filled with humor; for example, Geth has been transformed into a toothpick. In the second book, Leven and his compatriots strive to free Geth, the rightful heir of Foo.

1. Leven Thumps and the Gateway to Foo ◆ 2005
2. Leven Thumps and the Whispered Secret ◆ 2006
3. Leven Thumps and the Eyes of the Want ◆ 2007
4. Leven Thumps and the Wrath of Ezra ◆ 2008

LEWIS BARNAVELT

Bellairs, John, and Brad Strickland

DIAL ◆ GRADES 5–8 ◆ A/R

FANTASY

Lewis is a 10-year-old orphan who goes to live with his Uncle Jonathan in the small town of New Zebedee. His uncle is a kind old man who practices "white magic," and his neighbor and best friend is Mrs. Zimmerman, who is a good witch. Jonathan lives in a big old house that was previously owned by an evil man who practiced black magic. Lewis makes a new friend toward the end of the first book in the series: Rose Rita, who loves baseball and lives in a nearby mansion. Some of the books in the series feature Rose Rita and Mrs. Zimmerman as they fight black magic together. The first three books were written by Bellairs; the fourth and fifth were completed by Strickland after Bellairs's death; and the remaining books were written by Strickland and are based on the characters of Bellairs.

1. The House with a Clock in its Walls ◆ 1973
2. The Figure in the Shadows ◆ 1975
3. The Letter, the Witch, and the Ring ◆ 1976
4. The Ghost in the Mirror ◆ 1993
5. The Vengeance of the Witch-Finder ◆ 1993
6. The Doom of the Haunted Opera ◆ 1995
7. The Specter from the Magician's Museum ◆ 1998
8. The Beast under the Wizard's Bridge ◆ 2000
9. The Tower at the End of the World ◆ 2001
10. The Whistle, the Grave and the Ghost ◆ 2003
11. The House Where Nobody Lived ◆ 2006

THE LIFE AND TIMES

Denenberg, Barry

SCHOLASTIC ◆ GRADES 4–7 ◆ A/R

ADVENTURE | HISTORICAL

This series begins with two adventures. One features the life of a slave in a wealthy home in the Roman Republic. Although his master is kind, Atticus becomes caught up in the intrigues and plots. The second book tells the story of a young girl, Pandora, who is dreading her 14th birthday. On that day, she will be old enough to marry. Her father has already arranged an engagement for her. Pandora chafes under the restrictions of life in ancient Athens.

1. Atticus of Rome, 30 B.C. ◆ 2004
2. Pandora of Athens, 399 B.C. ◆ 2004
3. Maia of Thebes, 1463 B.C. ◆ 2005

LIGHTHOUSE FAMILY

Rylant, Cynthia

SIMON & SCHUSTER ◆ GRADES 2–4 ◆ A/R

ANIMAL FANTASY

Pandora is a cat who runs a lighthouse. She gives aid and comfort to those lost at sea. When Seabold the dog is washed ashore, she helps him recover. He decides to stay with her. Their family is complete when they rescue three young mice—Whistler, Lila, and their baby sister Tiny. These animals live together in peace. When Whistler and Lila are lost in the woods, they are rescued by a gentle eagle.

1. The Storm ◆ 2002
2. The Whale ◆ 2003
3. The Eagle ◆ 2004
4. The Turtle ◆ 2005

LILI

Isadora, Rachel

PUTNAM ◆ GRADES K–2

RECREATION

When Lili attends her ballet class, the reader learns some of the terminology and expectations. Later, Lili appears in "The Nutcracker." She even goes behind the scenes of a performance of "Sleeping Beauty." These books are beautifully illustrated by the author, and young dance enthusiasts will be enchanted by Lili.

1. Lili at Ballet ◆ 1993
2. Lili on Stage ◆ 1995
3. Lili Backstage ◆ 1997

LILLY

Henkes, Kevin

GREENWILLOW ◆ GRADES K–2 ◆ A/R

ANIMAL FANTASY | HUMOR

Best friends Chester and Wilson are dismayed when the flamboyant Lilly moves into their neighborhood. However, Lilly comes to their rescue and the three mice become friends. In another story, Lilly looks forward to the arrival of her baby brother—until he actually gets there. Then she is not amused. At first, she is not a very good big sister; but when her cousin is disdainful of baby Julius, Lilly rises to his defense. The third book shows Lilly at school. She loves her teacher, Mr. Slinger. After he takes away her special treasures (including her new purple plastic purse), her temper gets the better of her. This is an amusing group of books with lively language and situations. There are related board and activity books.

1. Chester's Way ◆ 1988
2. Julius, the Baby of the World ◆ 1990
3. Lilly's Purple Plastic Purse ◆ 1998
4. Lilly's Big Day ◆ 2006

LILO AND STITCH: THE SERIES

TOKYOPOP ◆ GRADES 2–4 ◆ A/R

ADVENTURE | FANTASY

The Disney Channel television series is the basis for this cine-manga series. Lilo and Stitch, with the help of their friends, search Hawaii for the experiments from Dr. Jacques von Hamsterviel.

1. The Search Begins ◆ 2004
2. Sparring and Charring ◆ 2004
3. Contents Under Pressure ◆ 2005

LILY

Warner, Sally

KNOPF ◆ GRADES 2–4 ◆ A/R

REAL LIFE | FAMILY LIFE

Narrated by 6-year-old Lily, these books focus on the everyday concerns of a young child. Lily's mother has recently moved Lily and her often bothersome older brother into a small apartment and Lily wants to find a place where she can have some privacy. Surprisingly, her brother helps her mother find a space for Lily. Lily copes with issues such as making new friends, bedwetting, and her father's incarceration, which could make this series a good choice for discussions.

1. Private Lily ◆ 1998
2. Sweet and Sour Lily ◆ 1998
3. Accidental Lily ◆ 1999
4. Leftover Lily ◆ 1999

LILY B.

Kimmel, Elizabeth Cody

HARPERCOLLINS ◆ GRADES 5–8 ◆ A/R

REAL LIFE

With her best friend at summer camp, Lily Blennerhassett, 13, feels her summer is doomed. She enjoys writing in her journal but the details of her life are so boring! Then, at her cousin's wedding, she meets the super cool LeBlanc family. She is drawn into their activities, even defying her parents, only to discover they are taking advantage of her good nature. Readers will enjoy reading Lily B.'s insights in her diary.

1. Lily B. on the Brink of Cool ◆ 2003
2. Lily B. on the Brink of Love ◆ 2005
3. Lily B. on the Brink of Paris ◆ 2006

LILY QUENCH

Prior, Natalie Jane

PUFFIN ◆ GRADES 4–7 ◆ A/R

FANTASY

Dragons, quests, magic, and a battle with dangers from the past are all part of this fantasy series. Lily Quench has been paired with the Queen Dragon to try to protect Ashby from Gordon, the Black Count, and his army. One of their adventures helps them learn the secrets of the Eyes of Time.

1. Lily Quench and the Dragon of Ashby ◆ 2004
2. Lily Quench and the Black Mountains ◆ 2004
3. Lily Quench and the Treasure of Mote Ely ◆ 2004
4. Lily Quench and the Lighthouse of Skellig Mor ◆ 2004
5. Lily Quench and the Magician's Pyramid ◆ 2004
6. Lily Quench and the Hand of Manuelo ◆ 2004
7. Lily Quench and the Search for King Dragon ◆ 2005

LINCOLN LIONS BAND

Giff, Patricia Reilly

DELL ◆ GRADES 2–4

HUMOR

Chrissie, Willie, Kenny, and Michelle are a part of a new "junior" band at school. Each experiences the trials and tribulations of elementary school life, such as a little fibbing, inability to keep a clean desk, a parent who isn't home enough, and the capacity to get into scrapes with one another. Each book features a different problem and resolves it realistically and with gentle humor. After the first book, the remaining volumes involve a season or a holiday.

1. Meet the Lincoln Lions Band ◆ 1992
2. Yankee Doodle Drumsticks ◆ 1992
3. The Jingle Bell Jam ◆ 1992
4. The Rootin' Tootin' Bugle Boy ◆ 1992
5. The Red, White, and Blue Valentine ◆ 1993
6. The Great Shamrock Disaster ◆ 1993

LIONBOY TRILOGY

Corder, Zizou

DIAL ◆ GRADES 4–8 ◆ A/R

FANTASY

Charlie Ashanti's parents have been kidnapped. With his special power to communicate with cats, Charlie begins his search for them. His journey takes him (and his lion friends) from London to various sites around the world. This series is written by a mother and her young daughter using a pseudonym.

1. Lionboy ◆ 2003
2. Lionboy: The Chase ◆ 2004
3. Lionboy: The Truth ◆ 2005

LIONEL

Krensky, Stephen

DIAL ◆ GRADES 1–2 ◆ A/R

REAL LIFE

This is a series of short, episodic tales about young Lionel and his family and friends. Lionel has a new teacher, goes trick-or-treating, gets a shot from the doctor, and goes to his first sleepover. Gently comic illustrations enhance the good-natured text. Suitable both for reading aloud and reading alone. Lionel's older sister Louise has her own series.

1. Lionel at Large ◆ 1986
2. Lionel in the Fall ◆ 1987
3. Lionel in the Spring ◆ 1990
4. Lionel and Louise ◆ 1992
5. Lionel in the Winter ◆ 1994
6. Lionel and His Friends ◆ 1996
7. Lionel in the Summer ◆ 1998
8. Lionel at School ◆ 2002
9. Lionel's Birthday ◆ 2003

LITTLE BEAR

Minarik, Else Holmelund
HARPERCOLLINS ◆ GRADES K–2 ◆ A/R
ANIMAL FANTASY | FAMILY LIFE

Each book in this series contains four vignettes about Little Bear, who acts much like a preschool child. In *Little Bear,* he persuades his mother to make him a winter outfit, makes himself some birthday soup, takes an imaginary trip to the moon, and goes happily to sleep when his mother tells him a story about Little Bear. In *Father Bear Comes Home,* Little Bear has the hiccups, looks for a mermaid, goes fishing, and welcomes Father home from the sea. Little Bear becomes friends with a little girl named Emily in *Little Bear's Friend.* This series was the first in the I Can Read series, published at a time when there was a lack of good easy-to-read children's books.

ORIGINAL LITTLE BEAR BOOKS

1. Little Bear ◆ 1957
2. Father Bear Comes Home ◆ 1959
3. Little Bear's Friend ◆ 1960
4. Little Bear's Visit ◆ 1961
5. A Kiss for Little Bear ◆ 1968

LITTLE BEAR

Waddell, Martin
CANDLEWICK ◆ GRADES K–1 ◆ A/R
ANIMAL FANTASY | VALUES

These are picture book stories featuring Big Bear and Little Bear. In the first, Little Bear is afraid of the darkness inside and outside their cave, so Big Bear shows him the light he's missing. In the second, Little Bear is afraid of the noises he hears while on a walk. Once again, Big Bear reassures him. The third book is more about shared activities and learning to spend time alone. In each, the interaction between the two bears highlights a tender, caring relationship between a very young "child" and a patient, understanding "adult."

1. Can't You Sleep, Little Bear? ◆ 1988
2. Let's Go Home, Little Bear ◆ 1991
3. You and Me, Little Bear ◆ 1996
4. Good Job, Little Bear ◆ 1999

LITTLE BEAR: MAURICE SENDAK'S LITTLE BEAR

Minarik, Else Holmelund

HarperFestival ◆ Grades K–2 ◆ A/R

Animal Fantasy | Family Life

Else Holmelund Minarik's classic Little Bear has been adapted into an animated television series. Young children enjoy seeing Little Bear celebrate holidays, go on a picnic, and enjoy family and friends.

1. Father's Flying Flapjacks ◆ 2002
2. Little Bear's New Friend ◆ 2002
3. A Present for Mother Bear ◆ 2002
4. The Search for Spring ◆ 2002
5. To Grandmother's House ◆ 2002
6. Little Bear and the Missing Pie ◆ 2002
7. Little Bear Makes a Scarecrow ◆ 2002
8. Little Bear's Loose Tooth ◆ 2002
9. Little Bear's Scary Night ◆ 2002
10. April Fools! ◆ 2002
11. I Miss You, Father Bear ◆ 2002
12. Little Bear's Valentine ◆ 2002
13. Get Well Soon, Little Bear! ◆ 2002
14. The Snowball Fight ◆ 2002
15. Father Bear's Special Day ◆ 2003
16. Little Bear's Egg ◆ 2003
17. Mother Bear's Picnic ◆ 2003
18. Spring Cleaning ◆ 2003
19. Little Bear Makes a Mask ◆ 2003
20. Little Bear's Picture ◆ 2003
21. The Cricket Who Came to Dinner ◆ 2003
22. Little Bear's Bad Day ◆ 2003
23. The Butterfly Garden ◆ 2004
24. Lost in Little Bear's Room ◆ 2004
25. Lucky Little Bear ◆ 2004
26. The Toys' Wedding ◆ 2004
27. Asleep under the Stars ◆ 2004
28. Emily's Birthday ◆ 2004

LITTLE BILL

Cosby, Bill

SCHOLASTIC ◆ GRADES K–2 ◆ A/R

REAL LIFE | VALUES

Comedian Bill Cosby has developed a series of fully illustrated easy readers that gently teach values to children and parents. Little Bill and his friends encounter a bully who makes a game of insults. Little Bill is advised to simply say "So?" and the strategy works by making the situation funny. When Little Bill develops a crush on a girl, he makes her a special valentine but then is afraid to give it to her. His friends try to make it easier for him, and he conquers his fear. The same friends learn that it is more fun to have imaginative play than to watch TV all the time. Each of the books begins with a note from psychiatrist Alvin F. Poussaint explaining the lesson to parents.

1. The Best Way to Play ◆ 1997
2. The Meanest Thing to Say ◆ 1997
3. The Treasure Hunt ◆ 1997
4. Super-Fine Valentine ◆ 1997
5. Money Troubles ◆ 1998
6. Shipwreck Saturday ◆ 1998
7. The Day I Was Rich ◆ 1999
8. Hooray for the Dandelion Warriors ◆ 1999
9. My Big Lie ◆ 1999
10. One Dark and Scary Night ◆ 1999
11. The Worst Day of My Life ◆ 1999
12. The Day I Saw My Father Cry ◆ 2000

LITTLE BILL (NICKELODEON)

Various authors

SIMON SPOTLIGHT ◆ GRADES K–2 ◆ A/R

REAL LIFE | VALUES

In *Elephant on the Loose*, Elephant is the name of Little Bill's hamster. When Elephant escapes, the family helps search for him. These stories deal with everyday issues and offer opportunities for discussions. The problems are solved creatively and the characters show compassion for each other. Little Bill is a popular TV character created by Bill Cosby.

1. An Adventure with Captain Brainstorm! (Hyman, Fracaswell) ◆ 2001
2. Elephant on the Loose (Watson, Kim) ◆ 2001
3. Just Like Dad (Watson, Kim) ◆ 2001
4. Presents for Everyone (Bergen, Lara Rice) ◆ 2001
5. A Trip to the Hospital (Watson, Kim) ◆ 2001
6. The Big Storm (Reid, Robin) ◆ 2002

7. The Halloween Costume Hunt (Watson, Kim) ◆ 2002
8. Happy Valentine's Day (Scull, Robert) ◆ 2002
9. Super Detective Little Bill (Lukas, Catherine)◆ 2002
10. A Visit to the Dentist (Fremont, Eleanor) ◆ 2002
11. The Big Day at School (Fremont, Eleanor) ◆ 2003
12. Happy Easter , Everyone (Morton, Hopi) ◆ 2003
13. Hello, Santa! (Lukas, Catherine) ◆ 2003
14. Hooray for Mother's Day (Lukas, Catherine) ◆ 2003
15. Little Bill's Birthday Party (Lukas, Catherine) ◆ 2003
16. Thank You, Dr. King (Reid, Robin) ◆ 2003
17. Is It My Turn Now? (Lukas, Catherine) ◆ 2004
18. A Visit to the Farm (Bergen, Lara Rice) ◆ 2004

LITTLE BROWN BEAR

Lebrun, Claude
CHILDREN'S PRESS ◆ GRADES K–1
ANIMAL FANTASY | FAMILY LIFE

This series, originally published in France, offers glimpses into everyday activities with which very young children will identify. Each story presents typical situations and problems. Small-format pages of brief text face full-color illustrations.

1. Little Brown Bear Gets Dressed ◆ 1979
2. Little Brown Bear Says No ◆ 1979
3. Little Brown Bear Takes a Bath ◆ 1979
4. Little Brown Bear Is Ill ◆ 1979
5. Little Brown Bear Wakes Up ◆ 1982
6. Little Brown Bear Wants a Kiss ◆ 1982
7. Little Brown Bear's Cold ◆ 1982
8. Little Brown Bear Is Cross ◆ 1982
9. Little Brown Bear's Story ◆ 1982
10. Little Brown Bear's Tricycle ◆ 1982
11. Little Brown Bear's Walk ◆ 1982
12. Little Brown Bear Won't Eat! ◆ 1982
13. Little Brown Bear's Bad Days ◆ 1983
14. Little Brown Bear's Breakfast Egg ◆ 1983
15. Little Brown Bear Can Cook! ◆ 1983
16. Little Brown Bear Is Big! ◆ 1983
17. Little Brown Bear's Playtime ◆ 1983
18. Little Brown Bear's Snowball ◆ 1983
19. Little Brown Bear Plays With His Doll ◆ 1986
20. Little Brown Bear Says "No" to Everything ◆ 1995
21. Little Brown Bear Is Afraid of the Dark ◆ 1995
22. Little Brown Bear Is Sick ◆ 1995
23. Little Brown Bear Wants to Go to School ◆ 1995
24. Little Brown Bear Does Not Want to Eat ◆ 1995

25. Little Brown Bear Is Growing Up ◆ 1995
26. Little Brown Bear Wants to Be Read To ◆ 1996
27. Little Brown Bear Learns to Share ◆ 1995
28. Little Brown Bear Dresses Himself ◆ 1996
29. Little Brown Bear Goes on a Trip ◆ 1996
30. Little Brown Bear Helps His Mama ◆ 1996
31. Little Brown Bear Takes a Bath ◆ 1996
32. Little Brown Bear Goes Exploring ◆ 1996
33. Good Morning, Little Brown Bear! ◆ 1997
34. Little Brown Bear Has Fun at the Park ◆ 1997
35. Little Brown Bear Plays with Shoes ◆ 1997
36. Little Brown Bear Plays in the Snow ◆ 1997

LITTLE CHICK

Kwitz, Mary DeBall

HARPERCOLLINS ◆ GRADES K–2

ANIMAL FANTASY

This is a delightful beginning-to-read series about life on a farm. Little Chick runs away from Broody Hen when she doesn't want to take a nap, and discovers the animals in a pond. As Little Chick waits for breakfast, she finds out what all the other animals eat. This series could be useful both as practice for beginning readers and as part of a discovery unit about life on a farm.

1. Little Chick's Story ◆ 1978
2. Little Chick's Big Day ◆ 1981
3. Little Chick's Breakfast ◆ 1983
4. Little Chick's Friend, Duckling ◆ 1992

LITTLE FUR

Carmody, Isobelle

RANDOM HOUSE ◆ GRADES 3–6

ANIMAL FANTASY

Little Fur is half elf and half troll and lives in a magical forest. In *The Legend Begins,* Little Fur is responsible for protecting seven ancient trees from the humans who plan to burn them. With her animal friends, Little Fur goes on a quest to save the trees by connecting with the power hidden deep in the earth. In subsequent books, she faces the evil of the Troll King and continues her efforts to protect the earth and its creatures.

1. Little Fur: The Legend Begins ◆ 2006
2. Little Fur: A Fox Called Sorrow ◆ 2007
3. Little Fur: A Mystery of Wolves ◆ 2008

LITTLE GENIE

Jones, Miranda

DELACORTE ◆ GRADES 2–4 ◆ A/R

FANTASY

Ali, 9, discovers a genie and learns that magical wishes can lead to big problems. Especially since she finds that she cannot unwish her wishes. In *Make a Wish,* she wishes for a tiger. In *Double Trouble,* she tries to make a better wish but still causes chaos.

1. Make a Wish ◆ 2004
2. Double Trouble ◆ 2004
3. A Puff of Pink ◆ 2004
4. Castle Magic ◆ 2004
5. Home on the Range ◆ 2008
6. Meanie Genie ◆ 2008

LITTLE HOUSE

Wilder, Laura Ingalls

HARPERCOLLINS ◆ GRADES 3–6 ◆ A/R

FAMILY LIFE | HISTORICAL

These are the original Little House books, now also known as the Laura Years. Nine stories narrate the life of the author and her family during the 1870s and 1880s. From Laura's childhood home in Wisconsin, the family moves west to Kansas, lives for a while in a dugout in Minnesota, and then moves to the Dakota Territory, where Laura lives until her marriage to Almanzo Wilder. The stories, narrated by Laura, are filled with humor and tenderness as this closely knit pioneer family overcomes adversity and hardship. This series has been extended and repackaged into other series (see following entries). In addition to the related series, there are toddler board books, pioneer activity books, cookbooks, craft books, and other novelty books and items.

1. Little House in the Big Woods ◆ 1932
2. Farmer Boy ◆ 1933
3. Little House on the Prairie ◆ 1935
4. On the Banks of Plum Creek ◆ 1937
5. By the Shores of Silver Lake ◆ 1939
6. The Long Winter ◆ 1940
7. Little Town on the Prairie ◆ 1941
8. These Happy Golden Years ◆ 1943
9. The First Four Years ◆ 1971

LITTLE HOUSE: MY FIRST LITTLE HOUSE BOOKS

Wilder, Laura Ingalls

HARPERCOLLINS ◆ GRADES K–2 ◆ A/R

FAMILY LIFE │ HISTORICAL

The original Little House books are classics in children's literature. These picture books are adaptations of the original books and make some of the stories more accessible to younger readers. All of the familiar characters are here—Pa, Ma, Mary, Laura, and Carrie—and there is even a book that features Laura's future husband, Almanzo Wilder. Warm illustrations portray the loving family moments of these well-known stories.

1. Dance at Grandpa's ◆ 1994
2. Winter Days in the Big Woods ◆ 1994
3. Christmas in the Big Woods ◆ 1995
4. The Deer in the Wood ◆ 1995
5. Going to Town ◆ 1995
6. Bedtime for Laura ◆ 1996
7. Going West ◆ 1996
8. Summertime in the Big Woods ◆ 1996
9. Winter on the Farm ◆ 1996
10. Country Fair ◆ 1997
11. Prairie Day ◆ 1997
12. A Little House Birthday ◆ 1997
13. My Little House 123 ◆ 1997
14. My Little House ABC ◆ 1997
15. A Farmer Boy Birthday ◆ 1998
16. A Little Prairie House ◆ 1998
17. My Little House Book of Animals ◆ 1998
18. My Little House Book of Family ◆ 1998
19. Sugar Snow ◆ 1998

LITTLE HOUSE: THE CAROLINE YEARS

Various authors

HARPERCOLLINS ◆ GRADES 3–6 ◆ A/R

FAMILY LIFE │ HISTORICAL

This series features the early years of Caroline Quiner, who would grow up to marry Charles Ingalls and become the mother of Laura and her sisters. The family moved to towns and settlements in Wisconsin, experiencing life on frontier outposts. *Little House in Brookfield* introduces us to Caroline and her family of five brothers and sisters. Her father was lost at sea the year before the book begins, and resourceful Caroline is busy helping her family cope with the loss. *Little Town at the Crossroads* tells more of Caroline's life in the growing town of Brookfield. This series provides background information about the years prior to the Little House Books. It has also been called the Brookfield Years.

1. Little House in Brookfield (Wilkes, Maria D.) ◆ 1996
2. Little Town at the Crossroads (Wilkes, Maria D.) ◆ 1997
3. Little Clearing in the Woods (Wilkes, Maria D.) ◆ 1998
4. On Top of Concord Hill (Wilkes, Maria D.) ◆ 2000
5. Across the Rolling River (Wilkins, Celia) ◆ 2001

LITTLE HOUSE: THE CHARLOTTE YEARS

Wiley, Mclissa
HARPERCOLLINS ◆ **GRADES 3–6** ◆ **A/R**
FAMILY LIFE | **HISTORICAL**

Continuing the Little House books, this series describes the childhood of Charlotte Tucker, who would grow up to be the grandmother of Laura Ingalls Wilder.

1. Little House by Boston Bay ◆ 1999
2. On Tide Mill Lane ◆ 2001
3. The Road from Roxbury ◆ 2002
4. Across the Puddingstone Dam ◆ 2004

LITTLE HOUSE: THE MARTHA YEARS

Wiley, Melissa
HARPERCOLLINS ◆ **GRADES 3–6** ◆ **A/R**
FAMILY LIFE | **HISTORICAL**

Set in the Scottish countryside, this series follows the childhood of Martha Morse, the great-grandmother of Laura Ingalls Wilder.

1. Little House in the Highlands ◆ 1999
2. The Far Side of the Loch ◆ 2000
3. Down to the Bonny Glen ◆ 2001
4. Beyond the Heather Hills ◆ 2003

LITTLE HOUSE: THE ROSE YEARS

MacBride, Roger Lea
HARPERCOLLINS ◆ **GRADES 3–6** ◆ **A/R**
FAMILY LIFE | **HISTORICAL**

This continuation of the popular Little House series follows the childhood of Rose, the daughter of Laura and Almanzo Wilder. Written by Rose Wilder's adopted grandson, this series maintains the warmth and charm of the Little House series, reflecting a place and time that appeals to many young readers. This series has also been called the Rocky Ridge Years.

1. Little House on Rocky Ridge ◆ 1993
2. Little Farm in the Ozarks ◆ 1994
3. In the Land of the Big Red Apple ◆ 1995
4. On the Other Side of the Hill ◆ 1995
5. Little Town in the Ozarks ◆ 1996
6. New Dawn on Rocky Ridge ◆ 1997
7. On the Banks of the Bayou ◆ 1998
8. Bachelor Girl ◆ 1999

LITTLE HOUSE CHAPTER BOOKS: CAROLINE

Wilkes, Maria D.
HARPERCOLLINS ◆ GRADES K–2 ◆ A/R
FAMILY LIFE | HISTORICAL

These books are adapted from the series Little House: The Caroline Years. Caroline Quiner would grow up to marry Charles Ingalls and become the mother of Laura and her sisters. These chapter books have fewer than 100 pages and are more accessible to younger readers.

1. Brookfield Days ◆ 1997
2. Caroline and Her Sister ◆ 2000
3. Frontier Family ◆ 2000
4. Brookfield Friends ◆ 2000
5. A New Little Cabin ◆ 2001

LITTLE HOUSE CHAPTER BOOKS: LAURA

Wilder, Laura Ingalls
HARPERCOLLINS ◆ GRADES K–2 ◆ A/R
FAMILY LIFE | HISTORICAL

The books for this series are adapted from the original Little House books. They feature some of the more exciting and entertaining moments, including Laura's escapades with her dog, Jack, and the family's struggles after a prairie fire and a blizzard. The shorter chapters will be more accessible to younger readers who enjoy these high-spirited stories of pioneer life.

1. The Adventures of Laura and Jack ◆ 1997
2. Pioneer Sisters ◆ 1997
3. Animal Adventures ◆ 1997
4. School Days ◆ 1997
5. Farmer Boy Days ◆ 1998
6. Hard Times on the Prairie ◆ 1998
7. Laura and Nellie ◆ 1998
8. Little House Farm Days ◆ 1998
9. Little House Friends ◆ 1998
10. Christmas Stories ◆ 1998
11. Laura's Ma ◆ 1999
12. Laura's Pa ◆ 1999
13. Little House Parties ◆ 1999
14. Laura and Mr. Edwards ◆ 1999

LITTLE HOUSE CHAPTER BOOKS: ROSE

MacBride, Roger Lea

HARPERCOLLINS ◆ GRADES K–2 ◆ A/R

FAMILY LIFE | HISTORICAL

These books are adapted from the series Little House: The Rose Years. Rose was the daughter of Laura and Almanzo Wilder. These chapter books have fewer than 100 pages and are more accessible to younger readers.

1. Missouri Bound ◆ 1999
2. Rose at Rocky Ridge ◆ 2000
3. Rose and Alva ◆ 2000
4. The Adventures of Rose and Swiney ◆ 2000
5. Missouri School Days ◆ 2001

LITTLE KIPPERS *see* Kipper: Little Kippers

LITTLE MOUSE

Kraus, Robert

GREENWILLOW ◆ GRADES K–1 ◆ A/R

ANIMAL FANTASY

Little Mouse is lonely because he thinks he is nobody's mouse in the first book of the series, *Whose Mouse Are You?* In the other stories, Little Mouse accepts a cat's invitation to come out and play, and runs away from home to find a family who will pay more attention to him. Kraus's simple text and Jose Aruego and Ariane Dewey's bright, inventive illustrations combine to make this a winning series.

   1. Whose Mouse Are You? ◆ 1970
   2. Where Are You Going, Little Mouse? ◆ 1986
   3. Come Out and Play, Little Mouse ◆ 1987

LITTLE POLAR BEAR

de Beer, Hans

NORTH-SOUTH BOOKS ◆ GRADES K–3 ◆ A/R

ANIMAL FANTASY

Lars the Little Polar Bear lives at the North Pole, where he finds plenty to do. He is often alone, but sometimes encounters animal playmates, or the scientists at the nearby polar research station. Charming illustrations of Lars against white snow and a pink and blue sky make these engrossing books for beginning readers. There are related pop-up and specialty books.

   1. Little Polar Bear ◆ 1987
   2. Ahoy There, Little Polar Bear ◆ 1988
   3. Little Polar Bear Finds a Friend ◆ 1990
   4. Little Polar Bear and the Brave Little Hare ◆ 1992
   5. Little Polar Bear, Take Me Home! ◆ 1996
   6. Little Polar Bear and the Husky Pup ◆ 1999
   7. Little Polar Bear and the Big Balloon ◆ 2002

LITTLE SOUP *see* Soup: Little Soup

LITTLE TOOT

Gramatky, Hardie

PUTNAM ◆ GRADES K–1 ◆ A/R

ADVENTURE | FANTASY | VALUES

In the first book, Little Toot is a small tugboat who doesn't really want to do anything but play. Best of all, he loves to make huge figure eights, which get in the way of other tugboats. When he finally decides to get serious, the other boats don't believe him. Eventually, he saves an ocean liner and proves his worth. Subsequent stories find him in different exotic locales, with descriptions of famous landmarks. In each story, his resourcefulness is tested and he comes through to save the situation, often with the use of a figure eight. Little messages about the important things in life are woven through his thoughts. After the author's death, the last book was completed from unfinished sketches and drawings.

   1. Little Toot ◆ 1939
   2. Little Toot on the Thames ◆ 1964

3. Little Toot on the Grand Canal ◆ 1968
4. Little Toot on the Mississippi ◆ 1973
5. Little Toot Through the Golden Gate ◆ 1975
6. Little Toot and the Loch Ness Monster ◆ 1989

LITTLE WHISTLE

Rylant, Cynthia

HARCOURT ◆ GRADES K–2 ◆ A/R

ANIMAL FANTASY

Little Whistle is a guinea pig who lives in a Toytown toy store. When the store is closed, Little Whistle gets out of his cage and looks for adventure. In one book, he helps a toy soldier who has bumped his head. Lovely illustrations by Tim Bowers extend these sweet stories.

1. Little Whistle ◆ 2001
2. Little Whistle's Dinner Party ◆ 2001
3. Little Whistle's Medicine ◆ 2002
4. Little Whistle's Christmas ◆ 2003

LITTLE WITCH

Hautzig, Deborah

RANDOM HOUSE ◆ GRADES K 2 ◆ A/R

FANTASY

Little Witch acts like any other little girl except she is a witch. She worries about her birthday party. She tries to fit in at school by giving the other children rides on her broomstick. She has to stay home on Halloween as punishment for being too good. These books are fun for beginning readers. There are also some Little Witch books for preschoolers.

1. Happy Birthday, Little Witch ◆ 1985
2. Little Witch Goes to School ◆ 1998
3. Little Witch's Bad Dream ◆ 2000
4. Little Witch Learns to Read ◆ 2003
5. Little Witch's Big Night ◆ 2003
6. Little Witch Loves to Write ◆ 2004

LITTLE WOLF

Whybrow, Ian

CAROLRHODA ◆ GRADES 3–5 ◆ A/R

ANIMAL FANTASY | HUMOR

Little Wolf is sent to school to learn to be bad. At Cunning College, he takes lessons from Uncle Bigbad. Later, he has lots of adventures—he opens his own school, he tries running a detective agency, he becomes an advice columnist, and more. His stories are told through his letters, complete with scratchouts and misspellings. The poetry book was published by First Avenue Editions.

1. Little Wolf's Book of Badness ◆ 2000
2. Little Wolf's Diary of Daring Deeds ◆ 2000
3. Little Wolf's Haunted Hall for Small Horrors ◆ 2000
4. Little Wolf, Forest Detective ◆ 2001
5. Dear Little Wolf ◆ 2002
6. Little Wolf's Handy Book of Poems ◆ 2002
7. Little Wolf, Pack Leader ◆ 2002
8. Little Wolf, Terror of the Silvery Sea ◆ 2004

LITTLE WOMEN JOURNALS

Emerson, Charlotte

AVON ◆ GRADES 4–6

FAMILY LIFE | HISTORICAL

These books, published in association with a series of dolls, extend the stories of Louisa May Alcott's *Little Women*. Each book features one of the March sisters. Amy faces a dilemma in an art contest; Beth tries to rescue a pony; Jo is tense about the publication of her first story; Meg is embarrassed when she is asked to the home of a wealthy family and is expected to help out with chores. Girls who have been reading the American Girls series may enjoy this similar series.

1. Amy's True Prize ◆ 1998
2. Beth's Snow Dancer ◆ 1998
3. Jo's Troubled Heart ◆ 1998
4. Meg's Dearest Wish ◆ 1998

THE LITTLES

Peterson, John

SCHOLASTIC ◆ GRADES 2–4 ◆ A/R

FANTASY

The Little family lives in the walls of the home of Mr. and Mrs. George Bigg and their son, Henry. Mr. William T. Little, the father, is tall (for a Little) at 6 inches; and, like all Littles, he looks just like a small person with a tail. The Little family has adventures involving their size and the secrecy of their existence. The first book, *The Littles*, describes what happens when the Bigg family goes on a three-month vacation and rents their home in the country to a couple from the city. Because the New-combs are messy, mice come into the home and create a problem for the Littles. Later, they encounter a dangerous cat and must find a way to get rid of it. Lucy Little's bravery saves her father, brother Tom, and Uncle Pete. Other adventures include Uncle Nick, Cousin Dinky, and Mr. Speck. The humor and escapades will attract many readers. A series of Littles First Readers, by Teddy Slater, adapts many of the original books for a younger audience.

1. The Littles ◆ 1967
2. The Littles Take a Trip ◆ 1968
3. The Littles to the Rescue ◆ 1968
4. The Littles Have a Wedding ◆ 1971
5. The Littles Give a Party ◆ 1972
6. Tom Little's Great Halloween Scare ◆ 1975
7. The Littles and the Trash Tinies ◆ 1977
8. The Littles Go Exploring ◆ 1978
9. The Littles and the Big Storm ◆ 1979
10. The Littles and Their Friends ◆ 1981
11. The Littles Go to School ◆ 1983
12. The Littles and the Lost Children ◆ 1991
13. The Littles and the Terrible Tiny Kid ◆ 1993
14. The Littles and Their Amazing New Friend ◆ 1999

THE LITTLES FIRST READERS

1. The Littles Go Around the World ◆ 2000
2. The Littles Make a Friend ◆ 2000
3. The Littles and the Scary Halloween ◆ 2001
4. The Littles and the Big Blizzard ◆ 2001
5. The Littles Get Trapped! ◆ 2001
6. The Littles and the Secret Letter ◆ 2001
7. The Littles and the Summer Storm ◆ 2002
8. The Littles Do Their Homework ◆ 2002
9. The Littles Have a Merry Christmas ◆ 2002
10. The Littles Go on a Hike ◆ 2002
11. The Littles Have a Happy Valentine's Day ◆ 2003

LIZA, BILL AND JED

Parish, Peggy
MACMILLAN ◆ GRADES 2–5 ◆ A/R
ADVENTURE | MYSTERY

This mystery-adventure series features siblings Liza, Bill, and Jed Roberts, who always seem to find a mystery when visiting their grandparents. The three young sleuths go on treasure hunts and solve puzzles involving ghosts and lost treasure. Peggy Parish is also the author of the ever-popular Amelia Bedelia books.

1. Key to the Treasure ◆ 1966
2. Clues in the Woods ◆ 1968
3. Haunted House ◆ 1971
4. Pirate Island Adventure ◆ 1975
5. Hermit Dan ◆ 1977
6. The Ghosts of Cougar Island ◆ 1986

LIZZIE LOGAN

Spinelli, Eileen
SIMON & SCHUSTER ◆ GRADES 2–4
FAMILY LIFE

Heather's first encounter in her new neighborhood is with bold, bossy Lizzie Logan. Lizzie scares Heather with gruesome stories and demands to be her friend. Lizzie and Heather do become friends, and together they battle school bullies, celebrate family events, and cope with growing up. In *Lizzie Logan Gets Married,* Lizzie's mom remarries, making Lizzie's wish for a real father come true. *Lizzie Logan, Second Banana* shows Lizzie's insecurity as she is about to become a big sister. Both Lizzie and Heather are sincere, likeable, and funny in these real-life situations.

1. Lizzie Logan Wears Purple Sunglasses ◆ 1995
2. Lizzie Logan Gets Married ◆ 1997
3. Lizzie Logan, Second Banana ◆ 1998

LIZZIE MCGUIRE

Various authors
DISNEY PRESS ◆ GRADES 4–7 ◆ A/R
FAMILY LIFE | REAL LIFE

Lizzie McGuire was a popular character in a Disney television series. She was a live-action character with a cartoon alter ego. She would hang out with her friends at school talking about boys, family, and projects. In the first book, she is eager to go on a camping trip but is chagrined to discover her mom is a chaperone. In another book, she models in a fashion show. There is a lot of Lizzie McGuire merchandise for preteens.

1. When Moms Attack! (Ostrow, Kim) ◆ 2002
2. Totally Crushed! (Thorpe, Kiki) ◆ 2002
3. Lizzie Goes Wild (Larsen, Kirsten) ◆ 2002
4. The Rise and Fall of the Kate Empire (Larsen, Kirsten) ◆ 2002
5. Picture This (Jones, Jasmine) ◆ 2003
6. New Kid in School (Jones, Jasmine) ◆ 2003
7. Broken Hearts (Thorpe, Kiki) ◆ 2003

8. A Very Lizzie Christmas (Jones, Jasmine) ◆ 2003
9. Just like Lizzie (Jones, Jasmine) ◆ 2003
10. Lizzie Loves Ethan (Jones, Jasmine) ◆ 2003
11. On the Job (Goldman, Leslie) ◆ 2004
12. Head over Heels (Jones, Jasmine) ◆ 2004
13. Best Dressed (Jones, Jasmine) ◆ 2004
14. Mirror, Mirror (Jones, Jasmine) ◆ 2004
15. Freaked Out (Alfonsi, Alice) ◆ 2004
16. Lizzie for President (Alfonsi, Alice) ◆ 2004
17. Oh, Brother! (Jones, Jasmine) ◆ 2005
18. The Importance of Being Gordo (Jones, Jasmine) ◆ 2005
19. All Over It (Jones, Jasmine) ◆ 2005
20. The 'Rents (Alfonsi, Alice) ◆ 2005
21. High Five! (Alfonsi, Alice) ◆ 2006

LIZZIE MCGUIRE MYSTERIES

Banim, Lisa
DISNEY PRESS ◆ **GRADES 4–7** ◆ **A/R**
MYSTERY | REAL LIFE

Lizzie and her friends are back in these light mysteries. In the first book, Lizzie sets out to prove she is not responsible for the creepy notes kids have been getting. In the third book, Lizzie has hurt Audrey's feelings and now Audrey is missing. Gordo and Miranda go with Lizzie to a science fiction convention looking for Audrey and find some really strange characters.

1. Get a Clue! ◆ 2004
2. Case at Camp Get-Me-Outie ◆ 2004
3. Case of the Missing She-Geek ◆ 2004
4. Hands Off My Crush-Boy! ◆ 2004
5. In the Doghouse ◆ 2005
6. Case of the Kate Haters ◆ 2005
7. Spring It On! ◆ 2006

LIZZIE MCGUIRE (TOKYOPOP)

Minsky, Terri
TOKYOPOP ◆ **GRADES 4–7**
REAL LIFE

Lizzie McGuire is in junior high and her life revolves around school. No! Her life revolves around boys and her friends! Lizzie is a live-action character with a cartoon alter ego. This cine-manga captures all the flair of this popular character.

1. Pool Party and Picture Day ◆ 2003
2. Rumors and I've Got Rhythmic ◆ 2003
3. When Moms Attack and Misadventures in Babysitting ◆ 2003
4. I Do, I Don't and Come Fly with Me ◆ 2003
5. Lizzie's Nightmare and Sibling Bonding ◆ 2004
6. Mom's Best Friend and Movin' On Up ◆ 2004
7. Over the Hill and Just Friends ◆ 2004
8. Gordo and the Girl and You're a Good Man Lizzie McGuire ◆ 2004
9. Magic Train and Grubby Longjohn's Olde Tyme Revue ◆ 2004
10. Inner Beauty and Best Dressed for Less ◆ 2005
11. In Miranda, Lizzie Does Not Trust and The Longest Yard ◆ 2005

LOG CABIN

Howard, Ellen

HOLIDAY HOUSE ◆ GRADES K–3

HISTORICAL

After Elvirey's mother dies, the family moves from Carolina to Michigan, where they build a log cabin. Elvirey is lonely and has trouble adapting; it is not until winter comes and she is chinking the holes in the walls with her grandmother's quilting scraps that her mother is mentioned and she feels really at home. The hardships of frontier life are clear, but Elvirey manages to make a warm, comforting Christmas nonetheless.

1. The Log Cabin Quilt ◆ 1996
2. The Log Cabin Christmas ◆ 2000
3. The Log Cabin Church ◆ 2002
4. The Log Cabin Wedding ◆ 2006

LOGAN FAMILY

Taylor, Mildred D.

DIAL ◆ GRADES 4–7 ◆ A/R

HISTORICAL | REAL LIFE

Cassie tells the story of the African American Logan family, living in Mississippi during the Great Depression. High taxes and the mortgage on their house have forced her father to take a job away from home on the railroad. Mrs. Logan works as a schoolteacher. Although poor, the Logans are economically self-sufficient, which makes them more fortunate than their neighbors, who are all in debt to the local store. When Mrs. Logan is fired for teaching black history and Mr. Logan loses his job when he is injured by some angry white men, the family lives in fear that they will lose their land. *Roll of Thunder, Hear My Cry* is a Newbery Medal winner. *Song of the Trees* is written for younger readers. *The Land* is a prequel to *Roll of Thunder, Hear My Cry*. Members of the Logan family also appear in other books by this author.

1. Song of the Trees ◆ 1975
2. Roll of Thunder, Hear My Cry ◆ 1976
3. Let the Circle Be Unbroken ◆ 1981
4. The Road to Memphis ◆ 1990
5. The Well: David's Story ◆ 1995
6. The Land ◆ 2001

THE LONELY DOLL

Wright, Dare

HOUGHTON MIFFLIN ◆ GRADES K–2 ◆ A/R

FANTASY

From the first Lonely Doll book (published in 1957 and since reissued) through the many sequels, readers have been enchanted. Illustrated with black-and-white photographs of Edith, a doll, in adventurous settings, the books blend fantasy and reality. Edith is lonely until she makes friends with the teddy bears who join in her outings. They meet horses and a duckling and go on a holiday. These books still have a loyal following.

1. The Lonely Doll ◆ 1957
2. Holiday for Edith and the Bears ◆ 1958
3. The Lonely Doll Learns a Lesson ◆ 1961
4. Edith and Mr. Bear ◆ 1964
5. A Gift from the Lonely Doll ◆ 1966
6. Edith and Little Bear Lend a Hand ◆ 1972
7. Edith and Midnight ◆ 1978
8. Edith and the Duckling ◆ 1981

LONG POND

George, William T., and Lindsay Barrett George
GREENWILLOW ◆ GRADES K–2 ◆ A/R

REAL LIFE

The main character in this series is really Long Pond, shown throughout the cycle of the seasons. Readers observe a wealth of animal residents and a few appreciative humans who fish and enjoy the landscape. Cutting a tree for Christmas becomes a nature trek for an observant father and son in *Christmas at Long Pond*. *Fishing at Long Pond* is a memorable experience for Grandpa and Katie. The extremely detailed, almost photographic illustrations, coupled with a brief text, draw the reader into this celebration of nature. The first book, *Beaver at Long Pond,* was written by both William T. George and Lindsay Barrett George. The remaining books are written by William T. George. All the books are illustrated by Lindsay Barrett George.

1. Beaver at Long Pond ◆ 1988
2. Box Turtle at Long Pond ◆ 1989
3. Fishing at Long Pond ◆ 1991
4. Christmas at Long Pond ◆ 1992

LORD OF THE RINGS

Tolkien, J. R. R.

HOUGHTON MIFFLIN ◆ GRADES 5–12 ◆ A/R

FANTASY

When Hobbit Bilbo Baggins is visited by Gandalf the wizard, he finds himself tricked into being part of a dangerous quest. Together, they seek to recover a stolen treasure hidden in Lonely Mountain, guarded by Smaug the Dragon. *The Hobbit* (1937) is the introduction to Middle Earth and the Lord of the Rings trilogy, in which Bilbo names his cousin, Frodo Baggins, his heir. Frodo embarks on a journey to destroy the Ring of Power, a ring that would enable evil Sauron to destroy all that is good in Middle Earth. It is up to Frodo and his servant, Sam, to carry the Ring to the one place it can be destroyed. Author Tolkien was an eminent philologist and an authority on myths and sagas. *The Silmarillion* (1977) tells the story of the First Age, an ancient drama to which characters in the main trilogy look back. These books have been made into a popular series of movies.

1. The Fellowship of the Ring ◆ 1954
2. The Two Towers ◆ 1954
3. The Return of the King ◆ 1955

LOSERS, INC.

Mills, Claudia

FARRAR, STRAUS & GIROUX ◆ GRADES 4–7 ◆ A/R

REAL LIFE

Ethan and Julius are both in sixth grade. They feel so left out that they form their own club—Losers, Inc. Ethan wants to be more like his smart, athletic older brother. Julius's mom tries to help him develop more confidence. Lizzie and Alex also feel like losers. These stories should give readers insights into kids on the outside.

1. Losers, Inc ◆ 1997
2. You're a Brave Man, Julius Zimmerman ◆ 1999
3. Lizzie at Last ◆ 2000

4. Alex Ryan, Stop That ◆ 2003
5. Makeovers by Marcia ◆ 2005

LOST IN SPACE, THE NEW JOURNEYS

Various authors
SCHOLASTIC ◆ GRADES 3–5
SCIENCE FICTION

Lost in Space was a campy television show created in the 1960s. The movie version in the 1990s revived interest in the Robinson family. This series describes some new adventures. In one book, their robot is kidnapped by a giant brain. In another, Will becomes involved in a strange boy's dangerous quest.

1. Robotworld (Gardner, J. J., and Jordan Horowitz) ◆ 1998
2. The Passengers (Krulik, Nancy E.) ◆ 1998
3. Perils of Quadrant X (Krulik, Nancy E.) ◆ 1998
4. Journey to the Planet of the Blawps (Krulik, Nancy E.) ◆ 1998
5. Warriors (Gardner, J. J.) ◆ 1999
6. The Virus (Krulik, Nancy E.) ◆ 1999

LOTTERY LUCK

Delton, Judy
HYPERION ◆ GRADES 4–6
FAMILY LIFE

Daisy Green thinks her family is unusual. Her mother spends a lot of time gardening on the rooftop of their condo building while her father makes copper animals to decorate lawns (the copper alligators are the best sellers). Her brother, Delphie, is named after her mother's prize delphiniums. Money is often a problem until Daisy and her friend Lois find a way to buy some lottery tickets—and the Greens win! One book describes their efforts to cash in the tickets while other books have moments of risk as thieves seem to be after their winnings. Finally, the Greens move to St. Paul and Daisy is sad to be leaving Lois. All ends well when Lois and her family move to Minneapolis. These stories feature friendship and adventure and are accessible to middle-grade readers.

1. Winning Ticket! ◆ 1995
2. Prize-Winning Private Eyes ◆ 1995
3. Ten's a Crowd! ◆ 1995
4. Moving Up ◆ 1995
5. Ship Ahoy ◆ 1995
6. Next Stop, The White House ◆ 1995
7. Royal Escapade ◆ 1995
8. Cabin Surprise ◆ 1995

LOUANNE PIG

Carlson, Nancy L.

CAROLRHODA ◆ GRADES K–2 ◆ A/R

ANIMAL FANTASY | FAMILY LIFE

There is warmth, love, and fun in these stories about Louanne Pig. She is envious of her friend George's large family until she finds out that she has the talent to make a good master of ceremonies. She also realizes that looks can be deceiving as she gets to know the "witch lady." Carlson creates charming animal characters in both the text and the illustrations.

1. Louanne Pig in the Perfect Family ◆ 1986
2. Louanne Pig in Making the Team ◆ 1986
3. Louanne Pig in Witch Lady ◆ 1986
4. Louanne Pig in the Talent Show ◆ 1986
5. Louanne Pig in the Mysterious Valentine ◆ 1986

LOUD BOY *see* Adventures of Daniel Boom AKA Loud Boy

LOUDMOUTH GEORGE

Carlson, Nancy L.

CAROLRHODA ◆ GRADES K–1 ◆ A/R

ANIMAL FANTASY | HUMOR

George is a rabbit whose outspoken attitudes and pushy nature have earned him the nickname "Loudmouth." (Actually, he is referred to as Loudmouth George in the titles, but in the text he is just George.) Younger readers will get the message in these mildly didactic books as George learns what it feels like to be picked on. When a family of pigs moves into the neighborhood, George must develop more tolerance for those who are different. In another book, George finds out that being a show-off can cause problems. In spite of his faults, George is a likable character who just needs to use more restraint and better judgment so he can get along with others. The situations will ring true to young children.

1. Loudmouth George and the Big Race ◆ 1983
2. Loudmouth George and the Cornet ◆ 1983
3. Loudmouth George and the Fishing Trip ◆ 1983
4. Loudmouth George and the New Neighbors ◆ 1983
5. Loudmouth George and the Sixth-Grade Bully ◆ 1985

LOUIE

Keats, Ezra Jack

GREENWILLOW/FOUR WINDS ◆ GRADES K–1 ◆ A/R

FAMILY LIFE | REAL LIFE

Louie is a shy, withdrawn boy whose first friend is a puppet. In other books in the series, Louie moves into a new neighborhood, where he creates a shoebox diorama and makes an imaginary flight back to see some friends; Louie longs for a father and finds one in a junkman named Barney; and Louie has an imaginary visit to outer space in a rocket made of junkyard castoffs. Keats's colorful collage illustrations depict inner-city life.

1. Louie ◆ 1975
2. The Trip ◆ 1978
3. Louie's Search ◆ 1980

LOUISE

Krensky, Stephen

DIAL ◆ GRADES 2–4 ◆ A/R

REAL LIFE

Louise has problems with the new girl, Trelawney. First, Trelawney chose the number seven for her soccer uniform. Louise wanted that number. Then, Trelawney gets to play the soccer position that Louise wanted. Will Louise find a way to like the new girl from England? Louise is Lionel's older sister and appears in some of the Lionel books, too.

1. Louise Takes Charge ◆ 1998
2. Louise Goes Wild ◆ 1999
3. Louise, Soccer Star? ◆ 2000

LOWTHAR'S BLADE

LaFevers, R. L.

DUTTON ◆ GRADES 5–8 ◆ A/R

FANTASY

Lord Mordig has been kidnapping blacksmiths and forcing them to work on a powerful sword, one that will make him invincible. Kenric's father, a blacksmith, is being held by Lord Mordig. Kenric defeats Lord Mordig and returns the true king to power. As the series continues, Lord Mordig escapes and Kenric must unite with the goblins, the Fey folk, and other creatures to save Lowthar.

1. The Forging of the Blade ◆ 2004
2. The Secrets of Grim Woods ◆ 2005
3. The True Blade of Power ◆ 2005

LU AND CLANCY

Various authors

KIDS CAN PRESS ◆ GRADES K–2 ◆ A/R

ANIMAL FANTASY │ MYSTERY

This series for beginning readers features two dog detectives—Lu and Clancy. In *The Drop of Doom,* they are at a carnival and discover a plot to rob the patrons of the Drop of Doom ride. In *Secret Spies,* they put on disguises and follow Aunt Izzy. Short sentences and colorful illustrations by Pat Cupples make this a good choice for young readers, especially those who have enjoyed Nate the Great. There were earlier Lu and Clancy books in a different format.

1. The Disappearing Magician (Dickson, Louise) ◆ 2007
2. The Drop of Doom (Mason, Adrienne) ◆ 2007
3. Lost and Found (Mason, Adrienne) ◆ 2008
4. Secret Spies (Mason, Adrienne) ◆ 2008

LUCKY

Duffey, Betsy

SIMON & SCHUSTER ◆ GRADES 2–4 ◆ A/R

FAMILY LIFE │ HUMOR

George has wanted a puppy for such a long time. Now he has Lucky, and he is finding out how hard it is to train and care for a dog. The first book, *A Boy in the Doghouse,* describes George's efforts to housebreak Lucky. Subsequent books focus on Lucky and baseball and Lucky being lost. Chapters alternate from George's point of view (e.g., "Why can't Lucky learn to come to me?") to Lucky's interpretation of the events ("What does the boy mean by 'Come?'") This shift in perspective gives readers insight into the puppy and adds to the humor and interest.

1. A Boy in the Doghouse ◆ 1991
2. Lucky in Left Field ◆ 1992
3. Lucky on the Loose ◆ 1993
4. Lucky Christmas ◆ 1994

LUCY ROSE

Kelly, Katy
DELACORTE ◆ GRADES 3–5 ◆ A/R

REAL LIFE

According to her family, Lucy Rose, 8, is a "smart cookie" with an "eventful" life. In the first book, Lucy's parents have separated. Lucy and her mother have moved to Washington, D.C., near Lucy's mother's parents. In her diary, Lucy records the "eventful" experiences in her new home, including being the new kid at school and losing the class pet.

1. Lucy Rose: The Beginning ◆ 2004
2. Lucy Rose: Big on Plans ◆ 2005
3. Lucy Rose: Busy Like You Can't Believe ◆ 2006
4. Lucy Rose: Working Myself to Pieces & Bits ◆ 2007

LUDELL

Wilkinson, Brenda
HARPERCOLLINS ◆ GRADES 5–8

FAMILY LIFE | HISTORICAL

Ludell Wilson is an African American girl growing up in the rural town of Waycross, Georgia, in the mid-1950s. She is being raised by her loving, protective, but strict grandmother because her mother is living in New York City. *Ludell* depicts three years in a segregated southern school, Ludell's friends and family, and the people who affect her life. In *Ludell and Willie,* Ludell and her boyfriend are seniors in high school, frustrated by the standards of their small town. In *Ludell's New York Time,* Ludell moves to Harlem to plan her wedding. A strong portrait of growing up in the South in the 1950s and 1960s.

1. Ludell ◆ 1975
2. Ludell and Willie ◆ 1977
3. Ludell's New York Time ◆ 1980

LULU BAKER

Dunbar, Fiona
ORCHARD ◆ GRADES 4–7 ◆ A/R

FANTASY

With her father's remarriage imminent, Lulu Baker, 13, finds a mysterious cookbook with a recipe for "truth" cookies. If her father's fiancée eats one, Lulu knows her father will realize the fiancée's duplicity. Readers will enjoy the combination of magic and cooking in these books.

1. The Truth Cookie ◆ 2005
2. Cupid Cakes ◆ 2005
3. Chocolate Wishes ◆ 2005

LUNCHROOM

Hodgman, Ann
SPLASH/BERKLEY ◆ GRADES 4–6
HUMOR

Hollis Elementary School may *seem* like any other school, but wait until you visit their new cafeteria. There are neon signs, an ornamental waterfall, vending machines, and a milkshake machine that will make 30 shakes at once. There is even a machine that makes 100 pizzas at once, although a programming error makes 1,000. The cafeteria serves pizza every day until the freezer is finally empty. There are problems with cookies, french fries, and stew. The events are implausible, the adults are dim-witted, and the kids are lively.

1. Night of a Thousand Pizzas ◆ 1990
2. Frog Punch ◆ 1990
3. The Cookie Caper ◆ 1990
4. The French Fry Aliens ◆ 1990
5. Rubberband Stew ◆ 1990
6. The Flying Popcorn Experiment ◆ 1990
7. Invasion of the Fast Food ◆ 1990
8. Space Food ◆ 1990
9. Day of the Monster Plant ◆ 1991
10. Mutant Garbage ◆ 1991

LYLE

Waber, Bernard
HOUGHTON MIFFLIN ◆ GRADES K–3 ◆ A/R
ANIMAL FANTASY | FAMILY LIFE

When the Primm family moves into the house on East 88th Street, they discover a performing crocodile, Lyle, in their bathtub. He had been left there by former resident Hector P. Valenti, star of stage and screen. It is not long before Lyle wins the hearts of the family, but Hector is always thinking of ways to lure Lyle away from the Primms. In other adventures, Lyle's mother, Felicity, becomes a permanent resident at the Primm household and nurse to their new baby.

1. The House on East Eighty Eighth Street ◆ 1962
2. Lyle, Lyle, Crocodile ◆ 1965
3. Lyle and the Birthday Party ◆ 1966

4. Lovable Lyle ◆ 1969
5. Lyle Finds His Mother ◆ 1974
6. Funny, Funny Lyle ◆ 1987
7. Lyle at the Office ◆ 1994
8. Lyle at Christmas ◆ 1998

M AND M

Ross, Pat
VIKING ◆ GRADES 1–3 ◆ A/R
HUMOR | MYSTERY

Mandy and Mimi are two little girls living in the same apartment building who have active imaginations that get them into adventures. In one
book, they sneak into a museum early to see a mummy exhibit; a haunted house provides a way to scare a friend in another story. At Halloween,
they see a shadow that appears to be a headless monster, but it turns out
to be a new boy in the building carrying his football helmet. "Drops of
blood" are really red paint, and at a party they find out that some of their
"creepy" neighbors are not so scary after all. Some of their escapades are
less frightening, as when they baby-sit for a neighbor and find a way to
make her badly behaved twins into perfect angels. In a story about learning to read, they take a list to the grocery store, with funny results. All of
the books have short, easy-to-read chapters.

1. Meet M and M ◆ 1980
2. M and M and the Haunted House Game ◆ 1980
3. M and M and the Big Bag ◆ 1981
4. M and M and the Bad News Babies ◆ 1983
5. M and M and the Mummy Mess ◆ 1985
6. M and M and the Santa Secrets ◆ 1985
7. M and M and the Superchild Afternoon ◆ 1987
8. M and M and the Halloween Monster ◆ 1991

M. T. ANDERSON'S THRILLING TALES

Anderson, M. T.
HARCOURT ◆ GRADES 4–7 ◆ A/R
HUMOR | MYSTERY

Lily's father works for a mad scientist named Larry who wants to take over
the world using mind-controlled whales with laser beam eyes. Lily and
her friends Kate and Jasper have to stop Larry and save the world. The
wacky humor and kids vs. adults premise will appeal to tween audiences.

1. Whales on Stilts ◆ 2005

2. The Clue of the Linoleum Lederhosen ◆ 2006
3. Jasper Dash and the Flame-Pits of Delaware ◆ 2009

McBROOM

Fleischman, Sid

LITTLE, BROWN; PRICE STERN SLOAN ◆ GRADES 3–5 ◆ A/R

FANTASY | HUMOR

McBroom and his wife live with their 11 children on the prairie, and McBroom tells stories of their life there, exaggerated to the point of being tall tales. In his story of the Big Wind, he tells of fitting out his children with iron shoes to keep them from blowing away. He also tells about mosquitoes that grew so large that they could use chicken wire for mosquito netting. But when he enters the World Champion Liar's Contest, he is disqualified for telling the truth. These are short, easy books, illustrated on every page. Some of the titles are available with new illustrations.

1. McBroom Tells the Truth ◆ 1966
2. McBroom and the Big Wind ◆ 1967
3. McBroom's Ear ◆ 1969
4. McBroom's Ghost ◆ 1971
5. McBroom's Zoo ◆ 1972
6. McBroom the Rainmaker ◆ 1973
7. McBroom Tells a Lie ◆ 1976
8. McBroom and the Beanstalk ◆ 1978
9. McBroom and the Great Race ◆ 1980
10. McBroom's Almanac ◆ 1984
11. McBroom's Wonderful One-Acre Farm ◆ 1992
12. Here Come McBroom ◆ 1998

McDUFF

Wells, Rosemary

HYPERION ◆ GRADES K–1 ◆ A/R

REAL LIFE

McDuff is a white West Highland Terrier who escapes from the dog catcher and finds his way to a sympathetic couple, Fred and Lucy, who decide to keep him. His life is filled with the typical adventures of a lucky little dog, including chasing a rabbit and getting lost, coming to grips with a new baby, and learning that he is still loved. McDuff's problems are closer to dog problems than child problems, even when he encounters Santa Claus. There are related lift-the-flap and other books and toys.

1. McDuff Moves In ◆ 1997
2. McDuff Comes Home ◆ 1997

3. McDuff and the Baby ◆ 1997
4. McDuff's New Friend ◆ 1998
5. McDuff Goes to School ◆ 2001
6. McDuff Saves the Day ◆ 2002
7. McDuff's Wild Romp ◆ 2005

McGee and Me!

Various authors

TYNDALE HOUSE ◆ GRADES 4–6 ◆ A/R

FAMILY LIFE | VALUES

Nicholas Martin and his best friend McGee—an animated character who talks to Nick—get involved in many familiar situations, including wanting to win the big baseball game and being a contestant on a TV game show. Throughout these books (from the Living Bible International), there are positive messages about family, values, and the importance of accepting God in everyday life. Concepts discussed include honesty, obedience, faith, jealousy, trusting God, and experiencing God's love. A McGee and Me video series is also available.

1. The Big Lie (Myers, Bill, and Ken Johnson) ◆ 1989
2. A Star in the Breaking (Myers, Bill, and Ken Johnson) ◆ 1989
3. The Not-So-Great Escape (Myers, Bill, and Ken Johnson) ◆ 1989
4. Skate Expectations (Myers, Bill, and Ken Johnson) ◆ 1989
5. Twister and Shout (Myers, Bill, and Ken Johnson) ◆ 1989
6. Back to the Drawing Board (Teske, Robert T.) ◆ 1990
7. Do the Bright Thing (Teske, Robert T.) ◆ 1990
8. Take Me Out of the Ball Game (Myers, Bill) ◆ 1990
9. 'Twas the Fight Before Christmas (Myers, Bill) ◆ 1990
10. In the Nick of Time (Myers, Bill, and Robert West) ◆ 1993
11. The Blunder Years (Myers, Bill, and Robert West) ◆ 1993
12. Beauty in the Least (Myers, Bill, and Robert West) ◆ 1993

MacGregor Family Adventure

Trout, Richard

PELICAN PUBLISHING COMPANY ◆ GRADES 5–8 ◆ A/R

ADVENTURE

The MacGregors are scientists who deal with environmental issues around the world. Dr. Jack MacGregor is a zoologist and his wife Mavis is a paleontologist. Their three teenaged children—Chris, Heather, and Ryan—are often in the middle of these adventures. In *Sign of the Dragon,* the family is in China, where the teens expose poachers and the illegal distribution of dinosaur bones.

1. Cayman Gold: Lost Treasure of Devils Grotto ◆ 2005
2. Elephant Tears: Mask of the Elephant ◆ 2006
3. Falcon of Abydos: Oracle of the Nile ◆ 2006
4. Czar of Alaska: The Cross of Charlemagne ◆ 2006
5. Sign of the Dragon ◆ 2007
6. Devil's Breath Volcano ◆ 2008

McGROWL

Balaban, Bob

SCHOLASTIC ◆ GRADES 3–6 ◆ A/R

FANTASY

Thomas Wiggins has wanted a dog forever, but his family has always refused. When Thomas and his friend Violet find a lost dog, it seems perfect. Thomas is allowed to keep the dog, named McGrowl, and his family adjusts. But then, McGrowl receives bionic powers including x-ray vision and super strength. He can even communicate with Thomas telepathically. Now Thomas and McGrowl make an amazing team as they face exciting adventures.

1. Beware of Dog ◆ 2002
2. It's a Dog's Life ◆ 2003
3. Every Dog Has His Day ◆ 2003
4. Good Dog! ◆ 2004
5. It's a Dog-Eat-Dog World ◆ 2004

McGURK

Hildick, E. W.

MACMILLAN ◆ GRADES 2–5

HUMOR | MYSTERY

Ten-year-old McGurk runs his detective organization with an iron fist, leading a team with different talents and abilities. The narrator, Joey, is good with words; scientific expertise is provided by "Brains." Willie has a good nose, and Wanda likes high places and danger. In a typical story, an old lady asks the group to baby-sit her nephew. They indignantly tell her that the McGurk organization does not baby-sit. She admits that there is a case she wants them to solve. There seems to be a gigantic frog making noise in her house. Clever investigating leads the group to discover that her lonely nephew has been secretly harboring a pet frog, a type that makes a very loud noise. The humor here comes from the pint-size tyrant's control over his "officers" and their mishaps on the way to solving cases. McGurk's adventures take a fantastic turn in some of the books, which combine time travel and solving mysteries.

1. The Nose Knows ◆ 1973
2. Dolls in Danger ◆ 1974
3. The Case of the Condemned Cat ◆ 1975
4. The Case of the Nervous Newsboy ◆ 1976
5. The Great Rabbit Robbery ◆ 1976
6. The Case of the Invisible Dog ◆ 1977
7. The Case of the Secret Scribbler ◆ 1978
8. The Case of the Phantom Frog ◆ 1979
9. The Case of the Treetop Treasure ◆ 1980
10. The Case of the Snowbound Spy ◆ 1980
11. The Case of the Bashful Bank Robber ◆ 1981
12. The Case of the Four Flying Fingers ◆ 1981
13. McGurk Gets Good and Mad ◆ 1982
14. The Case of the Felon's Fiddle ◆ 1982
15. The Case of the Slingshot Sniper ◆ 1983
16. The Case of the Vanishing Ventriloquist ◆ 1985
17. The Case of the Muttering Mummy ◆ 1986
18. The Case of the Wandering Weathervanes ◆ 1988
19. The Case of the Purloined Parrot ◆ 1990
20. The Case of the Dragon in Distress ◆ 1991
21. The Case of the Weeping Witch ◆ 1992
22. The Case of the Desperate Drummer ◆ 1993
23. The Case of the Fantastic Footprints ◆ 1994
24. The Case of the Absent Author ◆ 1995
25. The Case of the Wiggling Wig ◆ 1996

THE MACK FAMILY

Doyle, Roddy

SCHOLASTIC ◆ GRADES 2–5 ◆ A/R

HUMOR

Fans of Captain Underpants will enjoy the gross humor of these books. *The Giggler Treatment* introduces readers to Mr. Mack, who is about to step into "dog poo." The wild antics of the characters trying to stop him are hilarious. These books have plenty of slapstick action.

1. The Giggler Treatment ◆ 2000
2. Rover Saves Christmas ◆ 2001
3. The Meanwhile Adventures ◆ 2004

MAD SCIENCE

Various authors

SCHOLASTIC ◆ GRADES 3–5 ◆ A/R

HUMOR | REAL LIFE

Mr. Flask's science classes at Einstein Elementary are incredible. The kids, including Prescott, Luis, and Alberta, get involved in some wacky experiments. Meanwhile, Professor von Offel competes with Mr. Flask for scientific breakthroughs.

1. What a Blast: The Explosive Escapades of Ethan Flask and Professor von Offel (Burkett, Kathy) ◆ 2002
2. Now You See It! The Incredible Illusions of Ethan Flask and Professor von Offel (Capeci, Anne) ◆ 2002
3. Mucus Attack! The Icky Investigations of Ethan Flask and Professor von Offel (Burkett, Kathy) ◆ 2002
4. Watch Out! The Daring Disasters of Ethan Flask and Professor von Offel (Capeci, Anne) ◆ 2002
5. Clue Me In! The Detective Work of Ethan Flask and Professor von Offel (Burkett, Kathy) ◆ 2003
6. Feed Me! Funky Food Science from Ethan Flask and Professor von Offel (Capeci, Anne) ◆ 2003
7. Out of This World! Ethan Flask and Professor von Offel Take on Space Science (Burkett, Kathy) ◆ 2003
8. Foul Play! Ethan Flask and Professor von Offel Sports Science Match (Burkett, Kathy) ◆ 2003

MADELINE

Bemelmans, Ludwig
VIKING ◆ GRADES K–2 ◆ A/R
HUMOR

The classic picture book and its sequels tell of brave young Madeline, who lives in a boarding school in Paris with 11 other little girls and their teacher, Miss Clavel. Madeline is a brave little girl, and says "'pooh' to the tiger in the zoo." When she has her appendix out, she gets such nice presents and has such a great scar that all the other girls want to have theirs out too. Madeline, Miss Clavel, and the girls continue their adventures in many sequels. One tells of the Spanish ambassador's son, who is a "bad hat." In another, Madeline travels to London and has an adventure with a horse. The recent film version has sparked interest. *Madeline's Christmas* is the reprint of a *McCall's* magazine feature.

1. Madeline ◆ 1939
2. Madeline's Rescue ◆ 1953
3. Madeline and the Bad Hat ◆ 1956
4. Madeline and the Gypsies ◆ 1959
5. Madeline in London ◆ 1961
6. Madeline's Christmas ◆ 1985

MAGGIE MARMELSTEIN

Sharmat, Marjorie Weinman
HARPERCOLLINS ◆ **GRADES 4–6** ◆ **A/R**
HUMOR | **REAL LIFE**

Thad and Maggie are sometimes friends, sometimes rivals, sometimes enemies in typical and humorous upper-grade-school situations. In one book, Thad decides to run for class president. Maggie volunteers to be his campaign manager, but Thad refuses, infuriating Maggie to the point that she decides to run for president herself. She recruits Noah, the smartest boy in the class, to be her campaign manager, and it soon becomes apparent that he is much better qualified to be president than either Thad or Maggie. In another story, Maggie's mother talks Thad into helping her cook, and Maggie catches him in an apron. Each story involves the complicated relationships among Thad, Maggie, Noah, and Maggie's shy friend Ellen.

1. Getting Something on Maggie Marmelstein ◆ 1971
2. Maggie Marmelstein for President ◆ 1975
3. Mysteriously Yours, Maggie Marmelstein ◆ 1982

MAGGIE VALLEY

Madden, Kerry
VIKING ◆ **GRADES 5–8** ◆ **A/R**
FAMILY LIFE | **HISTORICAL**

Livy Two, 12, reads about the world but feels trapped in the struggles of her family in the hills of North Carolina in the 1960s. With eight siblings, including a little sister who is blind, Livy Two often shoulders adult responsibilities. A visit from Grandma seems a burden at first, but Grandma's strength helps sustain Livy Two through desperate circumstances.

1. Gentle's Holler ◆ 2005
2. Louisiana's Song ◆ 2007
3. Jessie's Mountain ◆ 2008

MAGIC ATTIC CLUB

Various authors
MAGIC ATTIC PRESS (MILLBROOK) ◆ **GRADES 2–4** ◆ **A/R**
ADVENTURE | **FANTASY**

The Magic Attic Club begins when Heather Hardin, Alison McCann, Keisha Vance, and Megan Ryder find a golden key that unlocks a neighbor's attic. There they find a trunk filled with beautiful clothes and a magic mirror that transports them to unusual places in the past. Some of the adventures feature the group, including Rose Hopkins, who joins them later. Others feature individual girls. The girls represent diverse backgrounds (Keisha is African American; Rose has ancestors who were Cheyenne). Their adventures are exotic, often including special interests such as ballet, dressage, gymnastics, cheerleading, and magic.

1. The Secret of the Attic (Sinykin, Sheri Cooper) ◆ 1995
2. Alison Goes for the Gold (Connor, Catherine) ◆ 1995
3. Alison on the Trail (Connor, Catherine) ◆ 1995
4. Cowgirl Megan (Magraw, Trisha) ◆ 1995
5. Heather at the Barre (Sinykin, Sheri Cooper) ◆ 1995
6. Heather, Belle of the Ball (Sinykin, Sheri Cooper) ◆ 1995
7. Keisha the Fairy Snow Queen (Reed, Teresa) ◆ 1995
8. Princess Megan (Magraw, Trisha) ◆ 1995
9. Three Cheers for Keisha (Reed, Teresa) ◆ 1995
10. Alison Saves the Wedding (Connor, Catherine) ◆ 1996
11. Alison Walks the Wire (Sinykin, Sheri Cooper) ◆ 1996
12. Downhill Megan (Magraw, Trisha) ◆ 1996
13. Heather Takes the Reins (Sinykin, Sheri Cooper) ◆ 1996
14. Keisha Leads the Way (Reed, Teresa) ◆ 1996
15. Keisha to the Rescue (Reed, Teresa) ◆ 1996
16. Megan's Masquerade (Magraw, Trisha) ◆ 1996
17. Viva Heather! (Sinykin, Sheri Cooper) ◆ 1996
18. Alison of Arabia (Alexander, Nina) ◆ 1997
19. Cheyenne Rose (Williams, Laura E.) ◆ 1997
20. Heather Goes to Hollywood (Sinykin, Sheri Cooper) ◆ 1997
21. Keisha's Maze Mystery (Benson, Lauren) ◆ 1997
22. Megan's Balancing Act (Korman, Susan) ◆ 1997
23. Rose Faces the Music (Alexander, Nina, and Laura E. Williams) ◆ 1997
24. Rose's Magic Touch (Alexander, Nina) ◆ 1997
25. Trapped Beyond the Magic Attic (Sinykin, Sheri Cooper) ◆ 1997
26. Alison Rides the Rapids (Alexander, Nina) ◆ 1998
27. Ghost of Camp Whispering Pines (Korman, Susan) ◆ 1998
28. Heather and the Pink Poodles (Engle, Marion) ◆ 1998
29. Island Rose (Williams, Laura E.) ◆ 1998
30. Keisha Discovers Harlem (Lewis, Zoe) ◆ 1998
31. Megan in Ancient Greece (Korman, Susan) ◆ 1998
32. Keisha to the Rescue (Reed, Teresa) ◆ 1998
33. A Tale of Two Alisons (Alexander, Nina) ◆ 1999
34. Champion Rose (Williams, Laura E.) ◆ 1999
35. Heather's Fashion World (Sinykin, Sheri Cooper) ◆ 1999
36. The Jewel of the Sea Cruise (Korman, Susan) ◆ 1999
37. Megan and the Borealis Butterfly (Alexander, Nina) ◆ 1999
38. The Mystery of the Pharaoh's Tomb (Korman, Susan) ◆ 1999

MAGIC MATT

Maccarone, Grace

SCHOLASTIC ◆ GRADES K–2

FANTASY

Matt has magical powers but they are not always completely under his control. For example, he wants to conjure a cat but gets a bat, a rat, a dog, and a lion. In another book, he conjures a dinosaur. This easy-to-read series will be a good start for beginners.

1. Magic Matt and the Cat ◆ 2003
2. Magic Matt and the Skunk in the Tub ◆ 2003
3. Magic Matt and the Jack O'Lantern ◆ 2003
4. Magic Matt and the Dinosaur ◆ 2004

MAGIC PICKLE GRAPHIC NOVELS

Morse, Scott

GRAPHIX ◆ GRADES 5–8 ◆ A/R

HUMOR

Born in a top secret U.S. Army lab, the Magic Pickle is a flying kosher dill superhero. His mission, to stop other remnants of the experiment from destroying the world. The rotten vegetables have formed an evil society, the Brotherhood of Evil Produce. After years in a cryogenic state, Magic Pickle is released and bursts through the floor of JoJo Wigman's bedroom. Together, they face the attacks of the Brotherhood. Share this with fans of humorous superheroes and graphic novels.

1. Magic Pickle ◆ 2008
2. Magic Pickle vs. the Egg Poacher ◆ 2008
3. Magic Pickle and the Planet of the Grapes ◆ 2008

MAGIC SCHOOL BUS

Cole, Joanna

SCHOLASTIC ◆ GRADES 1–4 ◆ A/R

ADVENTURE | FANTASY | HUMOR

Although these books are packed with information, the basic premise of the series is fantastic. Ms. Frizzle uses a magic school bus to take her class on incredible field trips. Arnold, Ralphie, Dorothy Ann, Phoebe, Carlos, Florrie, Shirley, Tim, and the other members of the class learn science on these wild rides. They go inside the body, out into space, into a beehive, and back to the time of dinosaurs. The journey is always educational, with information presented in the text and the illustrations. For example, student reports on lined notebook paper cover such topics as "Why Do Bees Sting?" and "How to Feed Baby Bees." There are many jokes and humorous remarks, and Bruce Degen's illustrations add both fun and information. Many of the books are tie-ins to the PBS television series. There are activity books and Explorations books that guide students and teachers through science experiments.

1. The Magic School Bus at the Waterworks ◆ 1986
2. The Magic School Bus Inside the Earth ◆ 1987
3. The Magic School Bus Inside the Human Body ◆ 1989
4. The Magic School Bus Lost in the Solar System ◆ 1990
5. The Magic School Bus on the Ocean Floor ◆ 1992
6. The Magic School Bus in the Time of the Dinosaurs ◆ 1994
7. The Magic School Bus Inside a Hurricane ◆ 1996
8. The Magic School Bus Inside a Beehive ◆ 1996
9. The Magic School Bus and the Electric Field Trip ◆ 1997
10. The Magic School Bus Explores the Senses ◆ 2001
11. The Magic School Bus and the Science Fair Expedition ◆ 2006

MAGIC SCHOOL BUS TV TIE-IN BOOKS

1. The Magic School Bus Gets Baked in a Cake: A Book About Kitchen Chemistry ◆ 1995
2. The Magic School Bus Hops Home: A Book About Animal Habitats ◆ 1995
3. The Magic School Bus in the Haunted Museum: A Book About Sound ◆ 1995
4. The Magic School Bus Inside Ralphie: A Book About Germs ◆ 1995
5. The Magic School Bus Meets the Rot Squad: A Book About Decomposition ◆ 1995
6. The Magic School Bus Plants Seeds: A Book About How Living Things Grow ◆ 1995
7. The Magic School Bus All Dried Up: A Book About Deserts ◆ 1996
8. The Magic School Bus Blows its Top: A Book About Volcanoes ◆ 1996
9. The Magic School Bus Butterfly and the Boy Beast: A Book About Butterfly Camouflage ◆ 1996
10. The Magic School Bus Gets Ants in Its Pants: A Book About Ants ◆ 1996
11. The Magic School Bus Gets Eaten: A Book About Food Chains ◆ 1996
12. The Magic School Bus Going Batty: A Book About Bats ◆ 1996
13. The Magic School Bus Out of This World: A Book About Space Rocks ◆ 1996
14. The Magic School Bus Wet All Over: A Book About the Water Cycle ◆ 1996
15. The Magic School Bus Gets Planted: A Book About Photosynthesis ◆ 1997
16. The Magic School Bus Goes Upstream: A Book About Salmon Migration ◆ 1997

17. The Magic School Bus Makes a Rainbow: A Book About Color ◆ 1997

18. The Magic School Bus Plays Ball: A Book About Forces ◆ 1997

19. The Magic School Bus Shows and Tells: A Book About Archaeology ◆ 1997

20. The Magic School Bus Takes Flight: A Book About Flight ◆ 1997

21. The Magic School Bus Ups and Downs: A Book About Floating and Sinking ◆ 1997

22. The Magic School Bus Gets Cold Feet: A Book About Warm- and Cold-Blooded Animals ◆ 1998

23. The Magic School Bus in a Pickle: A Book About Microbes ◆ 1998

24. The Magic School Bus in the Rainforest: A Book About Rainforest Ecology ◆ 1998

25. The Magic School Bus Spins a Web: A Book About Spiders ◆ 1998

26. The Magic School Bus in the Arctic: A Book About Heat ◆ 1998

27. The Magic School Bus Takes a Dive: A Book About Coral Reefs ◆ 1998

28. The Magic School Bus Answers Questions: A Book of Questions and Answers ◆ 1999

29. The Magic School Bus Gets a Bright Idea: A Book About Light ◆ 1999

30. The Magic School Bus Gets Programmed: A Book About Computers ◆ 1999

31. The Magic School Bus Sees Stars: A Book About Stars ◆ 1999

32. The Magic School Bus Kicks Up a Storm: A Book About Weather ◆ 2000

33. The Magic School Bus Explores the World of Animals ◆ 2000

34. The Magic School Bus Explores the World of Bugs ◆ 2002

MAGIC SCHOOL BUS SCHOLASTIC READERS

1. The Magic School Bus: The Wild Leaf Ride (Stamper, Judith) ◆ 2003

2. The Magic School Bus Sleeps for the Winter (Moore, Eva) ◆ 2003

3. The Magic School Bus Flies from the Nest (Cole, Joanna) ◆ 2004

4. The Magic School Bus Lost in the Snow (Cole, Joanna) ◆ 2004

5. The Magic School Bus Takes a Moonwalk (Cole, Joanna) ◆ 2004

6. The Magic School Bus Flies with the Dinosaurs (Schwabacher, Martin) ◆ 2005

7. The Magic School Bus Gets Crabby (Earhart, Kristin) ◆ 2005

8. The Magic School Bus Has a Heart (Capeci, Anne) ◆ 2005

9. The Magic School Bus Sleeps for the Winter (Moore, Eva) ◆ 2005

10. The Magic School Bus and the Missing Tooth (Lane, Jeanette) ◆ 2007

11. The Magic School Bus and the Shark Adventure (Smith, Elizabeth) ◆ 2007

12. The Magic School Bus Gets Caught in a Web (Lane, Jeanette) ◆ 2007

13. The Magic School Bus Gets Recycled (Capeci, Anne) ◆ 2007

14. The Magic School Bus Takes a Moonwalk (Cole, Joanna) ◆ 2007

MAGIC SCHOOL BUS: MS. FRIZZLE'S ADVENTURES

Cole, Joanna

SCHOLASTIC ◆ GRADES 1–4 ◆ A/R

ADVENTURE | FANTASY | HUMOR

Like the Magic School Bus picture books, this series combines facts and fantasy for a fun, informative presentation. Ms. Frizzle (without the bus) takes trips that lead her back in time to different eras. In *Ancient Egypt,* she parachutes into Ancient Egypt where she helps build a pyramid and learns about mummies. Bruce Degen's illustrations add to the fun. The combination of fact, fantasy, and humor make these a popular choice for many readers.

1. Ancient Egypt ◆ 2001
2. Medieval Castle ◆ 2003
3. Imperial China ◆ 2005

MAGIC SCHOOL BUS SCIENCE CHAPTER BOOKS

Various authors

SCHOLASTIC ◆ GRADES 2–5 ◆ A/R

ADVENTURE | FANTASY | HUMOR

Ms. Frizzle and the gang expand their science adventures in these chapter books for middle-elementary readers. Bats, whales, dinosaurs, insects, and volcanoes are among the topics they investigate.

1. The Truth About Bats (Moore, Eva) ◆ 1999
2. The Search for Missing Bones (Moore, Eva) ◆ 1999
3. The Wild Whale Watch (Moore, Eva) ◆ 2000
4. Space Explorers (Moore, Eva) ◆ 2000
5. Twister Trouble (Schreiber, Anne) ◆ 2000
6. The Giant Germ (Capeci, Anne) ◆ 2000
7. The Great Shark Escape (Johnston, Jennifer) ◆ 2001
8. Penguin Puzzle (Stamper, Judith Bauer) ◆ 2001
9. Dinosaur Detectives (Stamper, Judith Bauer) ◆ 2001
10. Expedition Down Under (Carmi, Rebecca) ◆ 2001
11. Insect Invaders (Capeci, Anne) ◆ 2001
12. Amazing Magnetism (Carmi, Rebecca) ◆ 2001
13. Polar Bear Patrol (Stamper, Judith Bauer) ◆ 2002
14. Electric Storm (Capeci, Anne) ◆ 2002
15. Voyage to the Volcano (Stamper, Judith Bauer) ◆ 2003
16. Butterfly Battle (White, Nancy) ◆ 2003
17. Food Chain Frenzy (Capeci, Anne) ◆ 2003
18. The Fishy Field Trip (Schwabacher, Martin) ◆ 2004

19. Color Day Relay (Herman, Gail) ◆ 2004
20. Rocky Road Trip (Stamper, Judith Bauer) ◆ 2004

MAGIC SHOP

Coville, Bruce

HARCOURT ◆ GRADES 3–6 ◆ A/R

FANTASY

Each of these stories centers on a new character in an entirely different setting. All of the central characters make a purchase at a magic shop that travels from town to town, owned by the mysterious Mr. Elives. Their encounters lead to adventures with talking toads, baby dragons, and ancient skulls. The stories generally teach a lesson, such as the importance of inner beauty over outer beauty.

1. The Monster's Ring ◆ 1982
2. Jeremy Thatcher, Dragon Hatcher ◆ 1991
3. Jennifer Murdley's Toad ◆ 1992
4. The Skull of Truth ◆ 1997
5. Juliet Dove, Queen of Love ◆ 2003

MAGIC TREE HOUSE

Osborne, Mary Pope

RANDOM HOUSE ◆ GRADES 2–4 ◆ A/R

FANTASY | MYSTERY

Jack and Annie discover a mysterious tree house in the woods near their home in Frog Creek, Pennsylvania. The tree house is filled with books that can trigger trips through time. In their first adventure, the two children accidentally travel to the time of the dinosaurs and must use their wits to return home. Later, they find out that the tree house belongs to Morgan le Fay, a librarian-magician from the time of King Arthur. She helps Jack and Annie become Master Librarians so that they can help her save stories from ancient libraries. The adventures take Jack and Annie to ancient Egypt, the Amazon River, the old West, the moon, a volcano, and ancient China. The fast-paced action and short sentences make this a good choice for reluctant readers as well as for students looking for beginning chapter books. Magic Tree House Research Guides are nonfiction companions and cover such topics as dolphins, the American Revolution, and ancient Greece.

1. Dinosaurs Before Dark ◆ 1992
2. The Knight at Dawn ◆ 1993
3. Mummies in the Morning ◆ 1993
4. Pirates Past Noon ◆ 1994

5. Night of the Ninjas ◆ 1995
6. Afternoon on the Amazon ◆ 1995
7. Sunset of the Sabertooth ◆ 1996
8. Midnight on the Moon ◆ 1996
9. Dolphins at Daybreak ◆ 1997
10. Ghost Town at Sundown ◆ 1997
11. Lions at Lunchtime ◆ 1997
12. Polar Bears Past Bedtime ◆ 1997
13. Vacation Under the Volcano ◆ 1998
14. Day of the Dragon King ◆ 1998
15. Viking Ships at Sunrise ◆ 1998
16. Hour of the Olympics ◆ 1998
17. Tonight on the Titanic ◆ 1999
18. Buffalo Before Breakfast ◆ 1999
19. Tigers at Twilight ◆ 1999
20. Dingoes at Dinnertime ◆ 2000
21. Civil War on Sunday ◆ 2000
22. Revolutionary War on Wednesday ◆ 2000
23. Twister on Tuesday ◆ 2001
24. Earthquake in the Early Morning ◆ 2001
25. Stage Fright on a Summer Night ◆ 2002
26. Good Morning, Gorillas ◆ 2002
27. Thanksgiving on Thursday ◆ 2002
28. High Tide in Hawaii ◆ 2003

MERLIN MISSIONS

29. Christmas in Camelot ◆ 2001
30. Haunted Castle on Hallow's Eve ◆ 2003
31. Summer of the Sea Serpent ◆ 2004
32. Winter of the Ice Wizard ◆ 2004
33. Carnival at Candlelight ◆ 2005
34. Season of the Sandstorms ◆ 2005
35. Night of the New Magicians ◆ 2006
36. Blizzard of the Blue Moon ◆ 2006
37. Dragon of the Red Dawn ◆ 2007
38. Monday With a Mad Genius ◆ 2007
39. Dark Day in the Deep Sea ◆ 2008
40. Eve of the Emperor Penguin ◆ 2008

MAGICAL MYSTERY

Stanton, Mary
BERKLEY ◆ GRADES 4–6
FANTASY | MYSTERY

In this series, Natalie Ross, 13, deals with the magical powers of her 6-year-old brother Denny. One adventure features an unusual, bad-tempered aunt, whom Denny turns into a griffin. Natalie must find a way to undo the spell. Another book follows Natalie's interest in equestrian events; she even lets Denny use his magic to help her, which sets off a series of problems. In *Next Door Witch,* Natalie encourages Denny to use his powers to help undo the spells of Zeuxippe Smith. The magical elements will appeal to many readers.

1. My Aunt, the Monster ◆ 1997
2. White Magic ◆ 1997
3. Next Door Witch ◆ 1997

THE MAGICAL STATES OF AMERICA

Peel, John

ALADDIN ◆ **GRADES 4–6** ◆ **A/R**

FANTASY

Chrissie Scott has a mirror twin, Chris. Chrissie lives in our world; Chris lives in a world of magic. Chris contacts Chrissie through the bathroom mirror. He needs her help in defeating Lori, an evil witch who plans to control all the magic in the world.

1. Suddenly Twins! ◆ 2001
2. Twice the Trouble! ◆ 2001
3. Double Disaster! ◆ 2002

MAGICIAN TRILOGY

McGowen, Tom

PENGUIN ◆ **GRADES 4–7** ◆ **A/R**

FANTASY | SCIENCE FICTION

Far in the future, civilization has been destroyed by war, and the people look back at our era as the Age of Magic and call our inventions "spells." People who seek wisdom are called Sages, and they attempt to make sense of the ruins and find out what ancient objects were used for. The head of these Sages, Armindor, takes as an apprentice a boy named Tigg, who had been a pickpocket. Together they travel to the Wild Lands and find a tape recorder with a tape that they believe will help them find the key to the ancient language. First, they must fight a terrible threat from intelligent ratlike creatures bent on taking over the human race. With Jilla, an orphan girl, and Reepah, a "grubber," they travel to the city of Ingarron and lead a successful attack.

1. The Magician's Apprentice ◆ 1987
2. The Magician's Company ◆ 1988
3. The Magician's Challenge ◆ 1989

MAGICIAN TRILOGY (Nimmo) *see* Gwyn Griffiths Trilogy

MAGICIAN'S HOUSE QUARTET

Corlett, William

POCKET BOOKS ◆ GRADES 5–8 ◆ A/R

FANTASY

William Constant, 13, and his younger sisters, Mary and Alice, are spending Christmas in Wales with their Uncle Jack. As they investigate Uncle Jack's home, they discover a secret room in the chimney. There they meet a magician who warns them of the tests they will soon face. In subsequent books, they return to Golden House for more magical adventures. This series was originally published in England in the early 1990s.

1. The Steps Up the Chimney ◆ 2000
2. The Door in the Tree ◆ 2000
3. The Tunnel Behind the Waterfall ◆ 2001
4. The Bridge in the Clouds ◆ 2001

MAIN STREET

Martin, Ann M.

SCHOLASTIC ◆ GRADES 4–6 ◆ A/R

REAL LIFE

Flora and her younger sister Ruby are still grieving over the death of their parents in a car accident. Now they have to move and live with their grandmother Min in Camden Falls, Massachusetts. As they adjust to their loss, the girls cope with new people and surroundings. Life in a small New England town is not what they are used to. Gradually, they find solace in their new home. Their grandmother is the co-owner of a sewing shop, "Needle and Thread." Flora finds that her interest in sewing helps her cope with all of the changes. As the series progresses, readers meet many diverse characters and enjoy the gentle pace of small-town life.

1. Welcome to Camden Falls ◆ 2007
2. Needle and Thread ◆ 2007
3. 'Tis the Season ◆ 2007
4. Best Friends ◆ 2008
5. The Secret Book Club ◆ 2008
6. September Surprises ◆ 2009

MAISY THE MOUSE

Cousins, Lucy

CANDLEWICK ◆ GRADES K–2

ANIMAL FANTASY

This is a series of lift-the-flap and pull-the-tab books. Children will enjoy playing with Maisy as they help her write a story, dance like a ballerina, paint pictures, and more. There are related board books.

1. Maisy Goes Swimming ◆ 1990
2. Maisy Goes to Bed ◆ 1990
3. Maisy Goes to School ◆ 1992
4. Maisy Goes to the Playground ◆ 1992
5. Maisy's ABC ◆ 1995
6. Maisy at the Farm ◆ 1998
7. Happy Birthday, Maisy ◆ 1998
8. Maisy's Bedtime ◆ 1999
9. Maisy Makes Gingerbread ◆ 1999
10. Maisy Dresses Up ◆ 1999
11. Maisy Takes a Bath ◆ 2000
12. Doctor Maisy ◆ 2001
13. Maisy at the Fair ◆ 2001
14. Maisy Goes Shopping ◆ 2001
15. Maisy's Morning on the Farm ◆ 2001
16. Maisy Cleans Up ◆ 2002
17. Maisy Makes Lemonade ◆ 2002
18. Maisy Goes to Work ◆ 2002
19. Maisy's Snowy Christmas Eve ◆ 2003
20. Maisy Goes Camping ◆ 2004
21. Maisy's Pirate Treasure Hunt ◆ 2004

MALCOLM IN THE MIDDLE

Various authors

SCHOLASTIC ◆ GRADES 4–6

FAMILY LIFE | HUMOR

The characters from the Fox television series are featured in these books, which parallel some of the episodes from the show. In one book, Malcolm and his older brother Reese are at a water park. Malcolm ends up at the top of the biggest, scariest water slide. In another book, Malcolm's younger brother Dewey invites two escaping crooks into their house. There are related books.

1. Life Is Unfair (Mason, Tom, and Dan Danko) ◆ 2000
2. Water Park (Mason, Tom, and Dan Danko) ◆ 2000

3. The Bad Luck Charm (Pollack, Pam, and Meg Belviso) ◆ 2001
4. The Exchange Student (Pollack, Pam, and Meg Belviso) ◆ 2001
5. Malcolm for President (Mason, Tom, and Dan Danko) ◆ 2001
6. The Hostage Crisis (Mason, Tom, and Dan Danko) ◆ 2001
7. The Krelboyne Parrot (Pollack, Pam, and Meg Belviso) ◆ 2001

MALLORY

Friedman, Laurie
CAROLRHODA ◆ GRADES 2–4 ◆ A/R
REAL LIFE

In the first book, Mallory is moving and is upset about leaving her friends. As she adjusts to her new home, she makes friends with her new neighbor, Joey. As the series progresses, Mallory has fun at school, deals with her brother and his new puppy, and goes to camp. Fans of Judy Moody and Amber Brown will enjoy the Mallory books.

1. Mallory on the Move ◆ 2004
2. Back to School, Mallory ◆ 2004
3. Mallory vs. Max ◆ 2005
4. Happy Birthday, Mallory! ◆ 2005
5. In Business With Mallory ◆ 2006
6. Heart-to-Heart With Mallory ◆ 2006
7. Mallory on Board ◆ 2007
8. Honestly, Mallory! ◆ 2007
9. Campfire Mallory ◆ 2008
10. Step Fourth, Mallory! ◆ 2008

MALLOY GIRLS *see* Hatford Boys

MAMA REX AND T

Vail, Rachel
SCHOLASTIC; ORCHARD ◆ GRADES 1–3 ◆ A/R
ANIMAL FANTASY

Mama Rex helps her young dinosaur, "T," with everyday experiences. They make a diorama for a school assignment. They stay up late. They spend time together when the electricity is off. These books have chapters, colorful illustrations, and more text per page than most easy readers. They are a good choice for children who are becoming more independent readers.

1. Homework Trouble ◆ 2001
2. The Horrible Play Date ◆ 2001

3. The (Almost) Perfect Mother's Day ◆ 2003
4. Halloween Knight ◆ 2003
5. The Reading Champion ◆ 2003
6. Stay Up Late ◆ 2003
7. Turn Off the TV ◆ 2003

MANDIE

Leppard, Lois Gladys
BETHANY HOUSE ◆ GRADES 4–6 ◆ A/R
ADVENTURE | HISTORICAL | MYSTERY

Mandie Shaw and her friends get involved in exciting adventures around the turn of the 20th century. In one book, they find a map that leads them to discover a hidden treasure and restore it to its rightful owner. In another book, Grandmother Taft takes Mandie to Washington, D.C., for the inauguration of President McKinley. Mandie's friends Sallie, Celia, and Joe often get entangled in the mysteries, and readers travel around the world following the intrepid young teens. Companion books include *Mandie Diary, Mandie Datebook, Mandie and Joe's Christmas Surprise*, and *Mandie's Cookbook*.

1. Mandie and the Secret Tunnel ◆ 1983
2. Mandie and the Cherokee Legend ◆ 1983
3. Mandie and the Ghost Bandits ◆ 1984
4. Mandie and the Forbidden Attic ◆ 1985
5. Mandie and the Trunk's Secret ◆ 1985
6. Mandie and the Medicine Man ◆ 1986
7. Mandie and the Charleston Phantom ◆ 1986
8. Mandie and the Abandoned Mine ◆ 1987
9. Mandie and the Hidden Treasure ◆ 1987
10. Mandie and the Mysterious Bells ◆ 1988
11. Mandie and the Holiday Surprise ◆ 1988
12. Mandie and the Washington Nightmare ◆ 1989
13. Mandie and the Midnight Journey ◆ 1989
14. Mandie and the Shipboard Mystery ◆ 1990
15. Mandie and the Foreign Spies ◆ 1990
16. Mandie and the Silent Catacombs ◆ 1990
17. Mandie and the Singing Chalet ◆ 1991
18. Mandie and the Jumping Juniper ◆ 1991
19. Mandie and the Mysterious Fisherman ◆ 1992
20. Mandie and the Windmill's Message ◆ 1992
21. Mandie and the Fiery Rescue ◆ 1993
22. Mandie and the Angel's Secret ◆ 1993
23. Mandie and the Dangerous Imposter ◆ 1994
24. Mandie and the Invisible Troublemaker ◆ 1994
25. Mandie and Her Missing Kin ◆ 1995
26. Mandie and the Schoolhouse Secret ◆ 1996

27. Mandie and the Courtroom Battle ◆ 1996
28. Mandie and Jonathan's Predicament ◆ 1997
29. Mandie and the Unwanted Gift ◆ 1997
30. Mandie and the Long Goodbye ◆ 1998
31. Mandie and the Buried Stranger ◆ 1999
32. Mandie and the Seaside Rendezvous ◆ 2000
33. Mandie and the Dark Alley ◆ 2000
34. Mandie and the Tornado! ◆ 2001
35. Mandie and the Quilt Mystery ◆ 2002
36. Mandie and the New York Secret ◆ 2003
37. Mandie and the Night Thief ◆ 2003
38. Mandie and the Hidden Past ◆ 2003

MARIE *see* Girlhood Journeys: Marie

MARS YEAR ONE

Strickland, Brad, and Thomas E. Fuller
SIMON & SCHUSTER ◆ GRADES 5–8 ◆ A/R
SCIENCE FICTION

It is 2085. Sean is leaving the turmoil on Earth to travel to Mars. There are only 20 teenagers in the colony and Sean must try to fit in and find a way to contribute.

1. Marooned! ◆ 2004
2. Missing! ◆ 2004
3. Marsquake! ◆ 2005

MARSHA

Bottner, Barbara
RANDOM HOUSE ◆ GRADES 1–3 ◆ A/R
FAMILY LIFE | REAL LIFE

Marsha, Lulu's little sister, often creates problems. When Marsha has the chicken pox, Lulu feels left out. Then, when Lulu is going to have a solo in her ballet recital, Marsha's feelings are hurt. Beginning readers will enjoy this easy-to-read series.

1. Marsha Is Only a Flower ◆ 2000
2. It's Not Marsha's Birthday ◆ 2001
3. Marsha Makes Me Sick ◆ 2003

MARTHA

Meddaugh, Susan

HOUGHTON MIFFLIN ◆ GRADES K–2 ◆ A/R

ANIMAL FANTASY | HUMOR

Martha the dog can speak! When her family feeds her alphabet soup, the letters go to Martha's brain and she talks. Now she can tell her family when she wants to go out or come in, or eat, or watch television. In fact, she talks so much her family can't stand it. However, when Martha calls the police to report a robbery at their home, her family realizes that having a talking dog can be very helpful. Other books feature Martha talking on the telephone and the manufacturer changing the recipe for alphabet soup. This is a humorous, imaginative series with delightful illustrations that will attract young readers.

1. Martha Speaks ◆ 1992
2. Martha Calling ◆ 1994
3. Martha Blah Blah ◆ 1996
4. Martha Walks the Dog ◆ 1998
5. Martha and Skits ◆ 2000
6. Perfectly Martha ◆ 2004

THE MARTHA YEARS *see* Little House: The Martha Years

MARTIN BRIDGE

Kerrin, Jessica Scott

KIDS CAN PRESS ◆ GRADES 2–4 ◆ A/R

REAL LIFE

These easy-reading chapter books feature a likable main character whose everyday activities will connect with many readers. Martin helps his friends, experiences problems at home, and loses his new bike. Martin's emotions ring true as he deals with family, friends, and enemies. In *Martin Bridge: Out of Orbit!*, Martin is disappointed when his classmate's astronaut costume is better than his.

1. Martin Bridge: Ready for Takeoff! ◆ 2005
2. Martin Bridge: On the Lookout! ◆ 2005
3. Martin Bridge: Blazing Ahead! ◆ 2006
4. Martin Bridge: Sound the Alarm! ◆ 2007

5. Martin Bridge: Out of Orbit! ◆ 2007
6. Martin Bridge: In High Gear! ◆ 2008
7. Martin Bridge: The Sky's the Limit ◆ 2008

MARVIN REDPOST

Sachar, Louis

RANDOM HOUSE ◆ GRADES 1–3

FAMILY LIFE | HUMOR

Marvin Redpost's active imagination often get this 9-year-old boy into difficult situations. In the first book, Marvin is convinced that he is really descended from royalty because he is the only member of his family with red hair and blue eyes. His friends believe him, but Mr. and Mrs. Redpost react differently to this news. Marvin's adventures with his best friends, Stuart and Nick, involve growing up and assuming responsibility. This easy chapter series offers readers lots of dialogue as well as appealing humor.

1. Marvin Redpost: Kidnapped at Birth? ◆ 1992
2. Marvin Redpost: Why Pick on Me? ◆ 1993
3. Marvin Redpost: Is He a Girl? ◆ 1993
4. Marvin Redpost: Alone in His Teacher's House ◆ 1994
5. Marvin Redpost: Class President ◆ 1999
6. Marvin Redpost: A Flying Birthday Cake? ◆ 1999
7. Marvin Redpost: Super Fast, Out of Control! ◆ 2000
8. Marvin Redpost: A Magic Crystal? ◆ 2000

MARVIN THE MAGNIFICENT

Van Leeuwen, Jean

DIAL ◆ GRADES 3–5

ANIMAL FANTASY

Merciless Marvin and his two fearless gang members, Raymond and Fats, are mice who live in a luxury dollhouse in Macy's toy department in New York City. In one adventure, Henry Simpson, a known mouse torturer, captures Fats, and Marvin and Raymond must rescue him. In another adventure, the mice are accidentally packaged and sent to a 10-year-old boy at a Vermont camp. These humorous, lively books are similar to Margery Sharp's Rescuers series.

1. The Great Cheese Conspiracy ◆ 1969
2. The Great Christmas Kidnapping Caper ◆ 1975
3. The Great Rescue Operation ◆ 1982
4. The Great Summer Camp Catastrophe ◆ 1992
5. The Great Googlestein Museum Mystery ◆ 2003

MARY-KATE AND ASHLEY: ADVENTURES OF MARY-KATE AND ASHLEY

Various authors

SCHOLASTIC ◆ GRADES 4–7 ◆ A/R
FAMILY LIFE | MYSTERY | REAL LIFE

The Olsen twins, Mary-Kate and Ashley, have achieved great popularity on television, video, and in movies. This series capitalizes on the popularity of these appealing twins.

1. The Case of the Christmas Caper (Waricha, Jean) ◆ 1996
2. The Case of the Mystery Cruise (Thompson, Carol) ◆ 1996
3. The Case of the Fun House Mystery (Scholastic staff) ◆ 1996
4. The Case of the U.S. Space Camp Mission (Scholastic staff and Bonnie Bader) ◆ 1996
5. The Case of the Sea World Adventure (Dubowski, Cathy East) ◆ 1996
6. The Case of the Shark Encounter (Krulik, Nancy E.) ◆ 1997
7. The Case of the Hotel Who-Done-It (O'Neil, Laura) ◆ 1997
8. The Case of the Volcano Mystery (Thompson, Carol) ◆ 1997
9. The Case of the U.S. Navy Adventure (Perlberg, Deborah) ◆ 1997
10. The Case of Thorn Mansion (Alexander, Nina) ◆ 1997

THE NEW ADVENTURES OF MARY-KATE AND ASHLEY

1. The Case of the 202 Clues (Alexander, Nina) ◆ 1998
2. The Case of the Ballet Bandit (O'Neil, Laura) ◆ 1998
3. The Case of the Blue-Ribbon Horse (Swobud, I. K) ◆ 1998
4. The Case of the Haunted Camp (Alexander, Nina) ◆ 1998
5. The Case of the Wild Wolf River (Katschke, Judy) ◆ 1998
6. The Case of the Rock and Roll Mystery (Eisenberg, Lisa) ◆ 1998
7. The Case of the Missing Mummy (Lantz, Francess) ◆ 1999
8. The Case of the Surprise Call (Metz, Mclinda) ◆ 1999
9. The Case of the Disappearing Princess (Eisenberg, Lisa) ◆ 1999
10. The Case of the Great Elephant Escape (Doolittle, June) ◆ 1999
11. The Case of the Summer Camp Caper (Katschke, Judy) ◆ 1999
12. The Case of the Surfing Secret (Dubowski, Cathy East) ◆ 1999
13. The Case of the Green Ghost (Ellis, Carol) ◆ 1999
14. The Case of the Big Scare Mountain Mystery (Ellis, Carol) ◆ 1999
15. The Case of the Slam Dunk Mystery (Dubowski, Cathy East) ◆ 2000
16. The Case of the Rock Star's Secret (Metz, Melinda) ◆ 2000
17. The Case of the Cheerleading Camp Mystery (Fiedler, Lisa) ◆ 2000
18. The Case of the Flying Phantom (Metz, Melinda) ◆ 2000
19. The Case of the Creepy Castle (Katschke, Judy) ◆ 2000
20. The Case of the Golden Slipper (Metz, Melinda) ◆ 2000
21. The Case of the Flapper 'Napper (Katschke, Judy) ◆ 2001
22. The Case of the High Seas Secret (Leonhardt, Alice) ◆ 2001
23. The Case of the Logical I Ranch (Preiss, Pauline) ◆ 2001

24. The Case of the Dog Camp Mystery (Katschke, Judy) ◆ 2001
25. The Case of the Screaming Scarecrow (Katschke, Judy) ◆ 2001
26. The Case of the Jingle Bell Jinx (Leonhardt, Alice) ◆ 2001
27. The Case of the Game Show Mystery (Thomas, Jim) ◆ 2002
28. The Case of the Mall Mystery (Leonhardt, Alice) ◆ 2002
29. The Case of the Weird Science Mystery (Katschke, Judy) ◆ 2002
30. The Case of Camp Crooked Lake (Ellis, Carol) ◆ 2002
31. The Case of the Giggling Ghost (Metz, Melinda) ◆ 2002
32. The Case of the Candy Cane Clue (Katschke, Judy) ◆ 2002
33. The Case of the Hollywood Who-Done-It (Metz, Melinda) ◆ 2003
34. The Case of the Sundae Surprise (Metz, Melinda) ◆ 2003
35. The Case of Clue's Circus Caper (Katschke, Judy) ◆ 2003
36. The Case of Camp Pom-Pom (Alexander, Heather) ◆ 2003
37. The Case of the Tattooed Cat (Alexander, Heather) ◆ 2003
38. The Case of the Nutcracker Ballet (Stine, Megan) ◆ 2003
39. The Case of the Clue at the Zoo (Katschke, Judy) ◆ 2004
40. The Case of the Easter Egg Race (Alexander, Heather) ◆ 2004
41. The Case of the Dog Show Mystery (author not available) ◆ 2004
42. The Case of the Cheerleading Tattletale (author not available) ◆ 2004
43. The Case of the Haunted Maze (author not available) ◆ 2004
44. The Case of the Hidden Holiday Riddle (author not available) ◆ 2004
45. The Case of the Icy Igloo Inn (author not available) ◆ 2005
46. The Case of the Unicorn Mystery (author not available) ◆ 2005

MARY-KATE AND ASHLEY: GRADUATION SUMMER

Various authors

HARPERENTERTAINMENT ◆ GRADES 4–7 ◆ A/R

REAL LIFE

It's the end of the senior year of high school for Mary-Kate and Ashley. They are savoring the fun parties and prom even as they anticipate the start of college. In the third book, the girls begin college, meeting their roommates, making new friends, and meeting lots of cute boys.

1. We Can't Wait! (Harrison, Emma) ◆ 2004
2. Never Say Good-bye (Butcher, Nancy) ◆ 2004
3. Everything I Want (Dokey, Cameron) ◆ 2004

MARY-KATE AND ASHLEY: SO LITTLE TIME

Olsen, Mary-Kate, and Ashley Olsen

HARPERCOLLINS ◆ GRADES 4–7 ◆ A/R

FAMILY LIFE | REAL LIFE

Based on the television series *So Little Time,* in which Mary-Kate and Ashley Olsen play Chloe and Riley Carlson. The girls enjoy being in high school, paying some attention to books and studying but spending most of their time on boys and dating.

1. How to Train a Boy ◆ 2002
2. Instant Boyfriend ◆ 2002
3. Too Good to Be True ◆ 2002
4. Just Between Us ◆ 2002
5. Tell Me About It ◆ 2002
6. Secret Crush ◆ 2002
7. Girl Talk ◆ 2002
8. The Love Factor ◆ 2003
9. Dating Game ◆ 2003
10. A Girl's Guide to Guys ◆ 2003
11. Boy Crazy ◆ 2003
12. Best Friends Forever ◆ 2003
13. Love Is in the Air ◆ 2003
14. Spring Breakup ◆ 2004
15. Get Real ◆ 2004
16. Surf Holiday ◆ 2004
17. The Makeover Experiment ◆ 2005

MARY-KATE AND ASHLEY: TWO OF A KIND

Various authors

HARPERCOLLINS ◆ GRADES 4–7 ◆ A/R

FAMILY LIFE | REAL LIFE

In this series, Mary-Kate and Ashley are older and they love shopping and hanging out with their friends. They also have hopes about boys and dating. Tween girls will enjoy these books.

1. It's a Twin Thing (Katschke, Judy) ◆ 1999
2. How to Flunk Your First Date (Stine, Megan) ◆ 1999
3. The Sleepover Secret (Katschke, Judy) ◆ 1999
4. One Twin Too Many (Stine, Megan) ◆ 1999
5. To Snoop or Not to Snoop (Katschke, Judy) ◆ 1999
6. My Sister the Supermodel (Stine, Megan) ◆ 1999
7. Two's a Crowd (Katschke, Judy) ◆ 1999
8. Let's Party (Katschke, Judy) ◆ 1999
9. Calling All Boys (Katschke, Judy) ◆ 2000
10. Winner Take All (Banim, Lisa) ◆ 2000
11. P.S. Wish You Were Here (Stine, Megan) ◆ 2000
12. The Cool Club (Katschke, Judy) ◆ 2000
13. War of the Wardrobes (Stine, Megan) ◆ 2000
14. Bye-Bye-Boy Friend (Katschke, Judy) ◆ 2000
15. It's Snow Problem (Butcher, Nancy) ◆ 2001

16. Likes Me, Likes Me Not (Stine, Megan) ◆ 2001
17. Shore Thing (Katschke, Judy) ◆ 2001
18. Two for the Road (Butcher, Nancy) ◆ 2001
19. Surprise, Surprise! (Stine, Megan) ◆ 2001
20. Sealed with a Kiss (Katschke, Judy) ◆ 2001
21. Now You See Him, Now You Don't (Stine, Megan) ◆ 2002
22. April Fools' Rules (Katschke, Judy) ◆ 2002
23. Island Girls (Butcher, Nancy) ◆ 2002
24. Surf, Sand, and Secrets (Butcher, Nancy) ◆ 2002
25. Closer than Ever (Katschke, Judy) ◆ 2002
26. The Perfect Gift (Stine, Megan) ◆ 2002
27. The Facts About Flirting (Katschke, Judy) ◆ 2003
28. The Dream Date Debate (Stine, Megan) ◆ 2003
29. Love-Set-Match (Dubowski, Cathy East) ◆ 2003
30. Making a Splash (Stine, Megan) ◆ 2003
31. Dare to Scare (Katschke, Judy) ◆ 2003
32. Santa Girls (Gallagher, Diana G.) ◆ 2003
33. Heart to Heart (Katschke, Judy) ◆ 2004
34. Prom Princess (Gallagher, Diana G.) ◆ 2004
35. Camp Rock 'n' Roll (Katschke, Judy) ◆ 2004
36. Twist and Shout (Katschke, Judy) ◆ 2004
37. Hocus-Pocus (Gikow, Louise) ◆ 2004
38. Holiday Magic (Gallagher, Diana G.) ◆ 2004
39. Candles, Cake, Celebrate! (Katschke, Judy) ◆ 2005
40. Wish on a Star (Gikow, Louise) ◆ 2005

Mary-Kate and Ashley in Action

Olsen, Mary-Kate, and Ashley Olsen
HarperCollins ◆ Grades 4–7 ◆ A/R
Family life | Mystery | Real life

There are mysteries to be solved. Mary-Kate and Ashley go undercover as secret agents Misty and Amber. They are on the spot when strange things happen and they investigate such mysteries as why a restaurant is too popular and why all the radio stations are playing the same song. There are lots of cartoon-style illustrations in these books, which add to the appeal.

1. Makeup Shake-Up ◆ 2002
2. The Dream Team ◆ 2002
3. Fubble Bubble Trouble ◆ 2002
4. Operation Evaporation ◆ 2003
5. Dog Gone Mess ◆ 2003
6. The Music Meltdown ◆ 2003
7. Password: Red Hot ◆ 2003
8. Fast Food Fight ◆ 2003

MARY-KATE AND ASHLEY STARRING IN

• • •

Various authors

HARPERCOLLINS ◆ **GRADES 4–7** ◆ **A/R**

FAMILY LIFE | **REAL LIFE**

These books feature the Olsen twins in stories from their video series. In one book, the girls play twins who switch places. Emma is popular but her father gives more attention to her sister, Sam. Sam is athletic but wants to attract a cute guy. Emma and Sam switch and develop an understanding for each other. In another book, the Olsens play twins whose family has moved to Australia to escape the wrath of a jewel thief they helped to catch. Of course, the thief ends up in Australia, too.

1. Switching Goals (Fiedler, Lisa) ◆ 2000
2. Our Lips Are Sealed (Willard, Eliza) ◆ 2001
3. Winning London (Kruger, Elizabeth) ◆ 2001
4. School Dance Party (Willard, Eliza) ◆ 2001
5. Holiday in the Sun (Willard, Eliza) ◆ 2001
6. When in Rome (Stine, Megan) ◆ 2002
7. The Challenge (author not available) ◆ 2003

MARY-KATE AND ASHLEY SWEET 16

Olsen, Mary-Kate, and Ashley Olsen

HARPERCOLLINS ◆ **GRADES 4–7** ◆ **A/R**

FAMILY LIFE | **REAL LIFE**

The Olsen twins turn 16! They can drive, go to parties, visit the mall, and enjoy their friends—including boyfriends.

1. Never Been Kissed ◆ 2002
2. Wishes and Dreams ◆ 2002
3. The Perfect Summer ◆ 2002
4. Getting There ◆ 2002
5. Starring You and Me ◆ 2002
6. My Best Friend's Boyfriend ◆ 2002
7. Playing Games ◆ 2003
8. Cross Our Hearts ◆ 2003
9. All That Glitters ◆ 2003
10. Keeping Secrets ◆ 2003
11. Little White Lies ◆ 2003
12. Dream Holiday ◆ 2003
13. Love and Kisses ◆ 2004
14. Spring into Style ◆ 2004
15. California Dreams ◆ 2004
16. Truth or Dare ◆ 2004

17. Forget Me Not ◆ 2005
18. I Want My Sister Back ◆ 2005

MARY MARGARET

MacLean, Christine Kole
DUTTON ◆ GRADES 3–5 ◆ A/R
REAL LIFE

In *Mary Margaret, Center Stage,* Mary Margaret, 9, loves the positive attention she gets from her teacher, Mr. Mooney. He appreciates her creativity and energy. Then Ellie joins their fourth-grade class and Mr. Mooney praises Ellie too. Guess who gets the part of Cinderella in the community play . . . Ellie. Guess who feels left out and angry . . . Mary Margaret. This series features realistic situations that will resonate with middle-grade readers. Fans of Judy Moody will enjoy these books.

1. Mary Margaret and the Perfect Pet Plan ◆ 2004
2. Mary Margaret, Center Stage ◆ 2007
3. Mary Margaret Meets Her Match ◆ 2007
4. Mary Margaret Mary Christmas ◆ 2008

MARY MARONY

Kline, Suzy
PUTNAM ◆ GRADES 2–4 ◆ A/R
REAL LIFE

Mary Marony is in second grade. She likes her teacher, Mrs. Bird, and she likes her friend Elizabeth Conway. She does not like the way Marvin Higgins teases her. Mary stutters, often on the letter "m," but also with other letters and even more so when she is nervous. Her parents and her teacher are understanding and helpful, but there are so many times when a student is called upon to speak. For example, Mary's favorite author is coming to school, and Mary is chosen to speak in front of the school. Another time, Mary's teacher organizes a surprise for her students by hiding something in the wrappers of five chocolate bars. Marvin tries to spoil the fun for Mary, but she ends up winning a prize and feeling good about herself.

1. Mary Marony and the Snake ◆ 1991
2. Mary Marony Hides Out ◆ 1993
3. Mary Marony, Mummy Girl ◆ 1994
4. Mary Marony and the Chocolate Surprise ◆ 1995

MARY POPPINS

Travers, P. L.

HARCOURT ◆ GRADES 4–6 ◆ A/R

FANTASY

A middle-class British family is having trouble finding a nanny for their difficult children, Jane and Michael. With a combination of magic, sternness, and real love for the children, Mary Poppins brings order to the household and delight into the children's lives. She leaves when the wind changes, but she returns twice, and other books in the series are to be imagined as happening during the times when she was there. In a typical story, a starling speaks to the newborn twins and asks if they remember everything from before they were born. They assure him that they do, and he moans that they will forget, just as all before them have—all, that is, except Mary Poppins.

1. Mary Poppins ◆ 1934
2. Mary Poppins Comes Back ◆ 1935
3. Mary Poppins Opens the Door ◆ 1943
4. Mary Poppins in the Park ◆ 1945
5. Mary Poppins from A to Z ◆ 1963
6. Mary Poppins in the Kitchen ◆ 1975
7. Mary Poppins in Cherry Tree Lane ◆ 1982
8. Mary Poppins and the House Next Door ◆ 1989

MARY ROSE

Clifford, Eth

HOUGHTON MIFFLIN ◆ GRADES 3–5 ◆ A/R

HUMOR | REAL LIFE

Mary Rose and Jo-Beth are sisters as different as night and day. Mary Rose, the older by three years, is practical, responsible, and dependable. Jo-Beth is a daydreamer who has a hard time with reality. Through a series of mishaps, they are stranded during a blizzard in an old house that has been turned into a library. They find an exhibit from the 1800s and dress up in the old-fashioned clothes to hide from burglars. They find the librarian, who has tripped and fallen, and think of a way to help her save the old house. When their cousin Jeff runs away to an island, they follow him and manage to stop a pair of robbers before they can get away with stolen money. The intermediate reading level—with lots of humor, mystery, and excitement—will appeal to real-life and adventure fans.

1. Help, I'm a Prisoner in the Library! ◆ 1979
2. The Dastardly Murder of Dirty Pete ◆ 1981
3. Just Tell Me When We're Dead ◆ 1983

4. Scared Silly ◆ 1988
5. Never Hit a Ghost with a Baseball Bat ◆ 1993

MATT CHRISTOPHER SPORTS STORIES

Various authors

LITTLE, BROWN ◆ GRADES 3–7 ◆ A/R

RECREATION

Generations of readers have enjoyed the action in these sports stories. Football, baseball, soccer, swimming, volleyball, snowboarding, swimming, and more are featured in this classic series. Many of the books have lessons about tolerance, teamwork, competition, and preparation. Matt Christopher died in 1997. Newer books are published under the "Matt Christopher" name, although they are written by various authors.

1. The Lucky Baseball Bat (Christopher, Matt) ◆ 1954
2. Baseball Pals (Christopher, Matt) ◆ 1956
3. Basketball Sparkplug (Christopher, Matt) ◆ 1957
4. Slide, Danny, Slide (Christopher, Matt) ◆ 1958
5. Two Strikes on Johnny (Christopher, Matt) ◆ 1958
6. Little Lefty (Christopher, Matt) ◆ 1959
7. Touchdown for Tommy (Christopher, Matt) ◆ 1959
8. Break for the Basket (Christopher, Matt) ◆ 1960
9. Long Stretch at First Base (Christopher, Matt) ◆ 1960
10. Tall Man in the Pivot (Christopher, Matt) ◆ 1961
11. Challenge at Second Base (Christopher, Matt) ◆ 1962
12. Crackerjack Halfback (Christopher, Matt) ◆ 1962
13. Baseball Flyhawk (Christopher, Matt) ◆ 1963
14. Shoot for the Hoop (Christopher, Matt) ◆ 1963
15. Sink It, Rusty (Christopher, Matt) ◆ 1963
16. Catcher With a Glass Arm (Christopher, Matt) ◆ 1964
17. Wingman on Ice (Christopher, Matt) ◆ 1964
18. The Counterfeit Tackle (Christopher, Matt) ◆ 1965
19. Too Hot to Handle (Christopher, Matt) ◆ 1965
20. Long Shot for Paul (Christopher, Matt) ◆ 1966
21. The Reluctant Pitcher (Christopher, Matt) ◆ 1966
22. Miracle at the Plate (Christopher, Matt) ◆ 1967
23. The Basket Counts (Christopher, Matt) ◆ 1968
24. The Year Mom Won the Pennant (Christopher, Matt) ◆ 1968
25. Catch That Pass! (Christopher, Matt) ◆ 1969
26. Hard Drive to Short (Christopher, Matt) ◆ 1969
27. Johnny Long Legs (Christopher, Matt) ◆ 1970
28. Shortstop from Tokyo (Christopher, Matt) ◆ 1970
29. Look Who's Playing First Base: 0 (Christopher, Matt) ◆ 1971
30. Tough to Tackle (Christopher, Matt) ◆ 1971
31. Face-Off (Christopher, Matt) ◆ 1972
32. The Kid Who Only Hit Homers (Christopher, Matt) ◆ 1972

82. Long-Arm Quarterback (Christopher, Matt) ◆ 1999
83. Snowboard Showdown (Christopher, Matt) ◆ 1999
84. Spike It! (Christopher, Matt) ◆ 1999
85. Tie Breaker (Christopher, Matt) ◆ 1999
86. Soccer Duel (Christopher, Matt) ◆ 2000
87. Tennis Ace (Christopher, Matt) ◆ 2000
88. Wheel Wizards (Christopher, Matt) ◆ 2000
89. Skateboard Renegades (Mantell, Paul) ◆ 2000
90. Cool as Ice (Mantell, Paul) ◆ 2001
91. Football Nightmare (Hirschfeld, Robert) ◆ 2001
92. Inline Skater (Hirschfeld, Robert) ◆ 2001
93. Dive Right In (Hirschfeld, Robert) ◆ 2002
94. Goalkeeper in Charge (Hirschfeld, Robert) ◆ 2002
95. Run for It (Hirschfeld, Robert) ◆ 2002
96. Windmill Windup (Mantell, Paul) ◆ 2002
97. Body Check (Hirschfeld, Robert) ◆ 2003
98. Fairway Phenom (Mantell, Paul) ◆ 2003
99. Nothin' But Net (Mantell, Paul) ◆ 2003
100. Slam Dunk (Hirschfeld, Robert) ◆ 2004
101. Snowboard Champ (Mantell, Paul) ◆ 2004
102. Stealing Home (Mantell, Paul) ◆ 2004
103. Comeback of the Home Run Kid (Peters, Stephanie True) ◆ 2006
104. Soccer Hero (Peters, Stephanie True) ◆ 2007
105. Football Double Threat (Peters, Stephanie True) ◆ 2008
106. Lacrosse Firestorm (Peters, Stephanie True) ◆ 2008

MATTHEW MARTIN

Danziger, Paula
DELACORTE ◆ GRADES 4–5 ◆ A/R
FAMILY LIFE | HUMOR

Matthew Martin is a sixth-grader who always seems to be in trouble both at home and at school. He is saddled with an older sister, Amanda, who can make his life miserable or rescue him from disaster. Matthew's escapades range from mummifying one of his friends for an Egyptian project to earning money for a computer program. Matthew and his loyal group of friends show some signs of maturity in *Not for a Billion Gazillion Dollars*. Written in a breezy style with puns and witty dialogue, this series will appeal to readers looking for humor and may be a good choice for boys who are reluctant readers.

1. Everyone Else's Parents Said Yes ◆ 1989
2. Make Like a Tree and Leave ◆ 1990
3. Earth to Matthew ◆ 1991
4. Not for a Billion Gazillion Dollars ◆ 1992

MAURICE SENDAK'S LITTLE BEAR *see*

Little Bear: Maurice Sendak's Little Bear

MAURICE SENDAK'S SEVEN LITTLE MONSTERS *see* Seven Little Monsters

MAX

Grindley, Sally

SIMON & SCHUSTER ◆ GRADES 3–5 ◆ A/R

REAL LIFE

Max, 9, is small for his age and is sometimes the target of bullies. He is also dealing with the recent death of his father. He begins a correspondence with his favorite author, D. J. Lucas, who responds to Max with encouragement and writing suggestions. They support each other—Max becomes the model for the author's next book and D. J. Lucas even shares her own problems with Max. Set in England and originally published there, the series includes some British phrases, but readers who connect with Max will meet a resilient, engaging character.

1. Dear Max ◆ 2006
2. Bravo, Max! ◆ 2007
3. Relax Max ◆ 2007

MAX-A-MILLION

Wiebe, Trina

LOBSTER PRESS ◆ GRADES 3–5 ◆ A/R

HUMOR

Max wants to be a millionaire but none of his schemes to get rich have worked. In the first book, Max decides he will use magic to make his millions. In subsequent books, he makes a movie and then tries saving lives to collect the rewards. With his friend Sid, Max is determined to succeed.

1. Max the Magnificent ◆ 2008
2. Max the Movie Director ◆ 2008
3. Max the Mighty Superhero ◆ 2008

MAX AND MO

Lakin, Patricia

ALADDIN ◆ GRADES K–1 ◆ A/R

HUMOR

In the first book, classroom hamsters Max and Mo have to teach a new group of students their names. Other books feature seasonal activities such as apple-picking, building a snowman, and making masks for Halloween. The easy reader series is just right for beginners.

1. Max and Mo's First Day at School ◆ 2007
2. Max and Mo Go Apple Picking ◆ 2007
3. Max and Mo Build a Snowman ◆ 2007
4. Max and Mo's Halloween Surprise ◆ 2008

MAX AND RUBY

Wells, Rosemary

DIAL; VIKING ◆ GRADES K–2 ◆ A/R

ANIMAL FANTASY | HUMOR

Ruby, the older of two little rabbits, thinks she knows everything, and is eager to instruct her little brother Max in the ways of the world. Max is just as sure that she is wrong, and he is mostly proved right in this picture book series. In a typical book, Ruby tells Max that whoever finds the most eggs on Easter morning gets the chocolate chicken. Max can't find any eggs, but he does find mud, acorns, ants, and a spoon, and makes ant and acorn pancakes. Then he steals and eats the chocolate chicken, much to Ruby's dismay. But all is not lost—the Easter Bunny leaves another one. When their grandmother's birthday comes around, Max makes an earthworm cake for her. In another book, they learn about money by buying presents for their grandmother. There are many Max board books for toddlers.

1. Max's Christmas ◆ 1986
2. Max's Chocolate Chicken ◆ 1989
3. Max's Dragon Shirt ◆ 1991
4. Max and Ruby's First Greek Myth ◆ 1993
5. Max and Ruby's Midas ◆ 1995
6. Bunny Cakes ◆ 1997
7. Bunny Money ◆ 1997
8. Max Cleans Up ◆ 2000
9. Bunny Party ◆ 2001
10. Ruby's Beauty Shop ◆ 2002
11. Bunny Mail ◆ 2004
12. Max's ABC ◆ 2006

13. Max Counts His Chickens ◆ 2007
14. Max's Bunny Business ◆ 2009

MAX MALONE

Herman, Charlotte

HOLT ◆ GRADES 2–5 ◆ A/R

HUMOR | REAL LIFE

Max Malone lives with his mother, father, and older sister Rosalie. His best friend Gordy lives close by; and the youngest kid in the neighborhood, Austin Healy, lives down the street. When we meet Max, he is annoyed at cereal companies because the things he sends for turn out to be junk. At the same time, he is planning to trade baseball cards with Austin and take advantage of his ignorance. By the end of the book, Max makes the connection and instead of taking advantage of Austin, he helps him make a wise purchase at a garage sale. In a subsequent book, Max decides to make a million dollars, but while he and Gordy fumble around, Austin actually starts some businesses that make money. Austin and Max continue their relationship when Max fails to get a part in a commercial and decides instead to become Austin's manager.

1. Max Malone and the Great Cereal Rip-Off ◆ 1990
2. Max Malone Makes a Million ◆ 1991
3. Max Malone, Superstar ◆ 1992
4. Max Malone the Magnificent ◆ 1993

MAX REMY *see* Spy Force

MAX THE DOG

Kalman, Maria

VIKING ◆ GRADES K–2

ANIMAL FANTASY

Max the dog is a poet. He wants to become famous and he wants to achieve his success in Paris. With help from his owners and a few friends, Max actually heads for France and this wacky fantasy series begins. Written and illustrated with a rhythm that bounces off the pages, these books will have great appeal for beginning readers.

1. Max Makes a Million ◆ 1990
2. Ooh La La: Max in Love ◆ 1991
3. Max in Hollywood, Baby ◆ 1992
4. Swami on Rye: Max in India ◆ 1995

MAXIMUM BOY

Greenburg, Dan

SCHOLASTIC ◆ GRADES 3–5 ◆ A/R

FANTASY | HUMOR

Max Silver, 11, is Maximum Boy, a superhero. After touching space rocks in a museum, Max develops special powers. Now he faces villains such as Tastemaker—who wants everything to taste like broccoli. Fans of Dav Pilkey books will enjoy the humor in these books, too, like the character Trevor Fartmeister, the school bully.

1. How I Became a Superhero ◆ 2001
2. The Day Everything Tasted Like Broccoli ◆ 2001
3. Superhero . . . or Super Thief? ◆ 2001
4. The Invasion from the Planet of the Cows ◆ 2001
5. Maximum Girl Unmasked ◆ 2002
6. The Attack of the Soggy Underwater People ◆ 2002
7. Meet Super Sid, Crime-Fighting Kid ◆ 2002
8. The Worst Bully in the Universe ◆ 2003

MAY BIRD

Anderson, Jodi Lynn

ATHENEUM ◆ GRADES 5–7 ◆ A/R

FANTASY

May Bird has lived in isolation with only her pet cat, Somber Kitty, for a companion. After she falls into the lake, she enters the world of Ever After and is transformed—she can see and communicate with ghosts. May Bird begins a quest in Ever After seeking her own destiny. In the third book, May Bird goes back home only to realize that she belongs in Ever After. She returns there only to find that everything has changed and it is up to her to restore this world.

1. May Bird and the Ever After ◆ 2005
2. May Bird Among the Stars ◆ 2006
3. May Bird, Warrior Princess ◆ 2007

MAYA'S WORLD

Angelou, Maya

RANDOM HOUSE ◆ GRADES K–2 ◆ A/R

REAL LIFE

Angelina worries that there will be no more pizza if the Leaning Tower of Pisa (Pizza) falls down. Mikale lives on the ocean but is afraid of the water until he is shown how welcoming it is. These picture books share stories about young people in different countries.

1. Angelina of Italy ◆ 2004
2. Izak of Lapland ◆ 2004
3. Mikale of Hawaii ◆ 2004
4. Renée Marie of France ◆ 2004

MEASLE

Ogilvy, Ian

HARPERCOLLINS ◆ GRADES 4–7 ◆ A/R

FANTASY

Ten-year-old Measle Stubbs is being raised by a mad guardian/wizard Basil Tramplebone. To punish Measle for playing with his miniature trains, Basil shrinks the boy and places him in the train set environment. Measle faces cockroaches and bats and must try to regain his proper size. As the series continues, Measle finds his parents and continues to battle magical dangers.

1. Measle and the Wrathmonk ◆ 2004
2. Measle and the Dragodon ◆ 2005
3. Measle and the Mallockee ◆ 2006

MEG *see* My America: Meg

MEG MACKINTOSH: A SOLVE-IT-YOURSELF MYSTERY

Landon, Lucinda

SECRET PASSAGE PRESS ◆ GRADES 1–3 ◆ A/R

MYSTERY

This series encourages the reader to work along with Meg Mackintosh to solve the mysteries she uncovers. In the first book, Meg finds her grandfather's autographed baseball, which has been missing for more than 50 years. In another book, Meg and her friends visit a medieval castle and Meg identifies the thief of a jeweled chalice. Many of the clues are linked to the illustrations. For example, in *Meg Mackintosh and the Mystery at the Medieval Castle,* studying the floor plan of the castle leads to solving the theft. The participation element and the brief chapters, simple sentences, and interrelationship between the text and illustrations make this a fine choice for reluctant readers and mystery fans.

1. Meg Mackintosh and the Case of the Missing Babe Ruth Baseball ◆ 1986
2. Meg Mackintosh and the Case of the Curious Whale Watch ◆ 1987
3. Meg Mackintosh and the Mystery at the Medieval Castle ◆ 1989
4. Meg Mackintosh and the Mystery at Camp Creepy ◆ 1990
5. Meg Mackintosh and the Mystery in the Locked Library ◆ 1993
6. Meg Mackintosh and the Mystery at the Soccer Match ◆ 1997

MEG MURRY *see* Time Fantasy Series

MEL BEEBY: AGENT ANGEL *see* Angels Unlimited

MELANIE MARTIN

Weston, Carol

KNOPF ◆ GRADES 4–6 ◆ A/R

FAMILY LIFE | REAL LIFE

In the third book, Melanie is in fifth grade and she accompanies her parents and her annoying younger brother on a trip to Spain. There, she meets Miguel and begins a sweet friendship. Girls will love the combination of diary entries and first-person narration. In previous books, Melanie traveled to Italy and Holland.

1. The Diary of Melanie Martin ◆ 2000
2. Melanie Martin Goes Dutch ◆ 2002
3. With Love from Spain, Melanie Martin ◆ 2004

MELENDY FAMILY

Enright, Elizabeth

VIKING ◆ GRADES 4–6 ◆ A/R

FAMILY LIFE | REAL LIFE

The Melendys are living in New York City just before the Second World War when they are introduced to the reader. Their mother is dead and their father is often away, so the children are looked after by Cuffy, their nurse-housekeeper-cook. They decide to pool their Saturday allowances and take turns having one terrific day out. In the next book, their father decides to move them all to the country and finds a remarkable house called the Four-Story Mistake. Here the children continue their adventures and pursue their different interests. Mona wants to be an actress and, after the children put on an informal show, a guest offers her a spot on a radio show. Rush is talented in music, and Oliver wants to study insects. Randy loves dancing and art, and all the children enjoy the outdoors. In *Then There Were Five,* the family adopts an orphan boy they have befriended.

1. The Saturdays ◆ 1941
2. The Four-Story Mistake ◆ 1942
3. Then There Were Five ◆ 1944
4. Spiderweb for Two ◆ 1951

MELVIN BEEDERMAN, SUPERHERO

Trine, Greg

HOLT ◆ GRADES 2–4 ◆ A/R

HUMOR

Melvin Beederman is a recent graduate from the Superhero Academy and has been assigned to Los Angeles to catch bad guys. He takes his red cape to the cleaners and when he picks it up, it's the wrong cape! Candace Brinkwater, who is playing Red Riding Hood in a play, has his superhero cape. Will Melvin be able to thwart the McNasty brothers or will they be able to block his powers with bologna?

1. The Curse of the Bologna Sandwich ◆ 2006
2. The Revenge of the McNasty Brothers ◆ 2006
3. The Grateful Fred ◆ 2006
4. Terror in Tights ◆ 2007
5. The Fake Cape Caper ◆ 2007
6. Attack of the Valley Girls ◆ 2008
7. The Brotherhood of the Traveling Underpants ◆ 2009

MENNYMS

Waugh, Sylvia

GREENWILLOW ◆ GRADES 5–8 ◆ A/R

FAMILY LIFE | FANTASY

This is a fantasy quintet set in England that older readers will enjoy. The Mennyms are a family of rag dolls that are able to pass quietly for human—that is to say, until various adventures happen to them. First there is the Australian owner of the house who comes to pay a visit. Then they discover that they are in the care of an antiques dealer, who, it seems, will shortly discover their secret. Readers will want to read all five books in the series.

1. The Mennyms ◆ 1994
2. Mennyms in the Wilderness ◆ 1995
3. Mennyms Under Siege ◆ 1996

4. Mennyms Alone ◆ 1996
5. Mennyms Alive ◆ 1997

MERCER MAYER'S CRITTERS OF THE NIGHT

Farber, Erica, and J. R. Sansevere
RANDOM HOUSE ◆ GRADES K–4 ◆ A/R
FANTASY | HUMOR

These books feature a variety of creepy characters in not very scary adventures. These are monsters, dragons, mummies, walking dead, vampires, werewolves, and zombies. Mercer Mayer's illustrations are colorful and add humor to the series, making it a good choice for younger audiences.

1. If You Dream a Dragon ◆ 1996
2. Kiss of the Mermaid ◆ 1996
3. No Howling in the House ◆ 1996
4. Pirate Soup ◆ 1996
5. Purple Pickle Juice ◆ 1996
6. The Goblin's Birthday Party ◆ 1996
7. The Headless Gargoyle ◆ 1996
8. The Vampire Brides ◆ 1996
9. Werewolves for Lunch ◆ 1996
10. Zombies Don't Do Windows ◆ 1996
11. To Catch a Little Fish ◆ 1996
12. Night of the Walking Dead, Part 1 ◆ 1997
13. Night of the Walking Dead, Part 2 ◆ 1997
14. Midnight Snack ◆ 1997
15. Chomp Chomp ◆ 1998
16. Ooey Gooey ◆ 1998
17. Roast and Toast ◆ 1998
18. Zoom on My Broom ◆ 1998

MERCY WATSON

DiCamillo, Kate
CANDLEWICK ◆ GRADES K–2 ◆ A/R
ANIMAL FANTASY | HUMOR

When Mercy Watson, a pig, crawls into bed with Mr. and Mrs. Watson, a human couple who have adopted her, the bed falls through a hole in the floor. Mercy is always on the lookout for hot buttered toast even when she is supposed to be helping the Watsons. In another book, Mercy goes for an automobile ride with Mr. Watson. Colorful illustrations by Chris Van Dusen add to the appeal of this series.

1. Mercy Watson to the Rescue ◆ 2005
2. Mercy Watson Goes for a Ride ◆ 2006
3. Mercy Watson Fights Crime ◆ 2006
4. Mercy Watson: Princess in Disguise ◆ 2007
5. Mercy Watson Thinks Like a Pig ◆ 2008

MERMAID S. O. S.

Shields, Gillian

BLOOMSBURY ◆ **GRADES 2–4**

FANTASY

In Coral Kingdom, the Mermaid Sisters of the Sea are facing challenges. They are looking for the six Magic Crystals that are the source of their powers. But Mantora, a wicked mermaid, has sent a storm to block them. Originally published in England, there are additional titles that are not yet available in the United States.

1. Misty to the Rescue ◆ 2008
2. Ellie and the Secret Potion ◆ 2008
3. Sophie Makes a Splash ◆ 2008
4. Holly Takes a Risk ◆ 2008
5. Scarlett's New Friend ◆ 2008
6. Lucy and the Magic Crystal ◆ 2008
7. Amber's First Task ◆ 2009
8. Katie and the Snow Babies ◆ 2009

MESSY BESSEY

McKissack, Patricia C., and Fredrick McKissack

CHILDREN'S PRESS ◆ **GRADES K–1** ◆ **A/R**

HUMOR | REAL LIFE

Messy Bessey introduces young readers to Bessey, a girl with a very messy room, which she cleans by pushing everything into the closet. Of course, when she opens the closet, everything falls out. So she decides to give away the things she does not need. In a later book, Bessey cares for her garden. These books have a rhyming, predictable text that can be helpful to beginning readers.

1. Messy Bessey ◆ 1987
2. Messy Bessey's Closet ◆ 1989
3. Messy Bessey's Garden ◆ 1991
4. Messy Bessey's School Desk ◆ 1998
5. Messy Bessey and the Birthday Overnight ◆ 1998
6. Messy Bessey's Holidays ◆ 1999
7. Messy Bessey's Family Reunion ◆ 2000

MIAMI

McKissack, Patricia C., and Fredrick McKissack

GOLDEN BOOKS ◆ GRADES 2–4 ◆ A/R

REAL LIFE

Michael Andrew "Miami" Jackson is involved with his friends. In one book, he and his friends attend a summer baseball camp. In another, he copes with a difficult fourth-grade teacher. Miami learns lessons about perseverance, choices, and values. Miami is an African American and his friends are from diverse backgrounds, which should expand the appeal of this series.

1. Miami Gets It Straight ◆ 2000
2. Miami Sees It Through ◆ 2002
3. Miami Makes the Play ◆ 2004

MICHELLE *see* Full House: Michelle

MICHELLE KWAN PRESENTS SKATING DREAMS *see* Skating Dreams

THE MIDNIGHT LIBRARY

Graves, Damien

SCHOLASTIC ◆ GRADES 5–8 ◆ A/R

HORROR

Each book in this series features three scary stories. In *Voices,* Kate hears voices telling her about her future. What she hears may scare her to death! In *End Game,* when the computer game is over, so is your life. The format of these books—three short stories—and the high-interest content should make them popular with reluctant readers.

1. Voices ◆ 2006
2. Blood and Sand ◆ 2006
3. End Game ◆ 2006
4. The Cat Lady ◆ 2007
5. Liar ◆ 2007
6. Shut Your Mouth ◆ 2007
7. I Can See You ◆ 2007
8. The Deadly Catch ◆ 2008

MIJOS

Gonzales, David
SCHOLASTIC ◆ GRADES 3–5 ◆ A/R
REAL LIFE

Mijo Park is the neighborhood gathering place for the kids in the barrio, including Mousy, Spooky, Lil Dre, Chico, Selena, and more. In *The Fiesta Face-Off,* the kids are looking forward to the annual fiesta. There will be food, fun, and a float contest and the friends are competing to produce the best float. In another book, developers are planning to buy Mijo Park and the kids try to stop them. Many reluctant readers will relate to the urban setting of these books.

1. The Fiesta Face-Off ◆ 2005
2. Save Mijo Park ◆ 2005
3. Spooky's Nightmare ◆ 2005
4. Field Trip Trouble ◆ 2005

MIKE AND HARRY

Christopher, Matt
LITTLE, BROWN ◆ GRADES 1–3 ◆ A/R
ANIMAL FANTASY | HUMOR

Harry is an Airedale who looks like any other dog. He is not! Harry can communicate with Mike telepathically. Together, they participate in sports activities, sometimes using their skill in unusual ways. In *The Dog That Stole Football Plays,* the two decide that they will not use Harry's ability to learn the other team's plays. Mike's team may win or lose, but they won't cheat. In *The Dog That Called the Pitch,* Harry helps out the umpire after his glasses are broken. This has been a popular series since the first book in 1980. It is easy to read and lots of fun—a good choice for reluctant readers.

1. The Dog That Stole Football Plays ◆ 1980
2. The Dog That Called the Signals ◆ 1982
3. The Dog That Pitched a No-Hitter ◆ 1988
4. The Dog That Stole Home ◆ 1993
5. The Dog That Called the Pitch ◆ 1998

MIKE LUPICA'S COMEBACK KIDS *see*
Comeback Kids

MILLION DOLLAR SERIES

Gutman, Dan

HYPERION ◆ GRADES 4–6 ◆ A/R

RECREATION

Want to win a million dollars? Just perform one of the sports feats in these books. Eddie, 11, must sink a foul shot at the NBA finals. Whisper, 13, tries to kick a goal against a local soccer star. The combination of sports action and the million-dollar dream-come-true makes this series a winner.

1. The Million Dollar Shot ◆ 1997
2. The Million Dollar Kick ◆ 2001
3. The Million Dollar Goal ◆ 2003
4. The Million Dollar Strike ◆ 2004

MIND OVER MATTER

Zach, Cheryl

AVON ◆ GRADES 4–8

ADVENTURE | MYSTERY

Quinn McMann lives with his cousin Jamie Anderson and her mother Maggie. Although they live in Los Angeles, Maggie's job as a television producer allows the group to travel for some of their adventures. The two 12-year-old cousins join forces to solve mysteries. Quinn has psychic powers, and Jamie is a genius and a computer whiz. These books combine supernatural elements with mysterious adventures. One book features a mummy that is stalking Quinn in his nightmares. When Quinn and Jamie get locked in a museum, they are able to find the hidden entrance to a vault filled with stolen treasures. In other books, they find out who is sabotaging a movie production and Quinn answers the call of an ancient skull.

1. The Mummy's Footsteps ◆ 1997
2. The Phantom of the Roxy ◆ 1997
3. The Curse of the Idol's Eye ◆ 1997
4. The Gypsy's Warning ◆ 1997

MINERVA CLARK

Karbo, Karen

BLOOMSBURY ◆ GRADES 5–8 ◆ A/R

MYSTERY

Like many young teens, Minerva Clark, 13, is an insecure, self-conscious adolescent. Then she is zapped by lightning and her life and personality change. Minerva becomes confident and resourceful. She begins investigating local mysteries, like finding a missing red diamond and tracking a kidnapper. Fans of Sammy Keyes will enjoy these light mysteries.

1. Minerva Clark Gets a Clue ◆ 2005
2. Minerva Clark Goes to the Dogs ◆ 2006
3. Minerva Clark Gives Up the Ghost ◆ 2007

MINERVA LOUISE

Stoeke, Janet Morgan

DUTTON ◆ GRADES K–3 ◆ A/R

ANIMAL FANTASY | HUMOR

Minerva Louise is a lovable but silly chicken who lives on a farm. She is sure she has everything figured out: The playpen must be a rabbit hutch, the hose is a scarf that is way too big, and the bedspread is a meadow of flowers. Children will laugh as they read about her silly antics on and off the farm.

1. Minerva Louise ◆ 1988
2. A Hat for Minerva Louise ◆ 1994
3. Minerva Louise at School ◆ 1996
4. A Friend for Minerva Louise ◆ 1997
5. Minerva Louise at the Fair ◆ 2000
6. Minerva Louise and the Red Truck ◆ 2002
7. Minerva Louise and the Colorful Eggs ◆ 2006
8. Minerva Louise on Christmas Eve ◆ 2007

MINNIE AND MOO

Cazet, Denys

DK ◆ GRADES 1–3 ◆ A/R

ANIMAL FANTASY | HUMOR

Minnie and Moo are cows who live the high life. They enjoy spending hours in the farmer's hot tub—and scare away some aliens. They eat cream puffs and drink cocoa. They take a bus tour to exotic locations.

1. Minnie and Moo Go Dancing ◆ 1998
2. Minnie and Moo Go to the Moon ◆ 1998
3. Minnie and Moo Go to Paris ◆ 1999
4. Minnie and Moo Save the Earth ◆ 1999
5. Minnie and Moo and the Musk of Zorro ◆ 2000
6. Minnie and Moo and the Thanksgiving Tree ◆ 2000

MINNIE AND MOO CHAPTER BOOKS (HARPERCOLLINS)

In one book, Minnie and Moo find out what is frightening the animals in the barn. In another, they help an alien named Spud complete his space mission. These easy chapter books will be right for beginning readers.

1. Minnie and Moo Meet Frankenswine ◆ 2001
2. Minnie and Moo and the Potato from Planet X ◆ 2002
3. Minnie and Moo: The Night Before Christmas ◆ 2002
4. Minnie and Moo: Will You Be My Valentine? ◆ 2003
5. Minnie and Moo: The Night of the Living Bed ◆ 2003
6. Minnie and Moo: The Attack of the Easter Bunnies ◆ 2004
7. Minnie and Moo: The Case of the Missing Jelly Donut ◆ 2005
8. Minnie and Moo: Wanted Dead or Alive ◆ 2006

MINNIE AND MOO (ATHENEUM)

A longer chapter book that is more appropriate for middle-elementary readers.

1. Minnie and Moo and the Seven Wonders of the World ◆ 2003

MIRETTE

McCully, Emily Arnold
PUTNAM ◆ GRADES K-2 ◆ A/R
ADVENTURE

In the first book, which received the Caldecott Medal, circus performer Bellini helps young Mirette learn to walk on the high wire. While helping her learn, he overcomes his own fears. In the second book, Mirette and Bellini are on a tour of European cities. In St. Petersburg, Bellini is imprisoned for encouraging the crowds to seek freedom. Mirette walks on a wire across a river in the dark to help him escape. Set in the 1800s, these are exciting stories with an intrepid female main character.

1. Mirette on the High Wire ◆ 1992
2. Starring Mirette and Bellini ◆ 1997
3. Mirette and Bellini Cross Niagara Falls ◆ 2000

MISFITS, INC.

Delaney, Mark
PEACHTREE ◆ GRADES 5-9 ◆ A/R
MYSTERY

Four high school students who are outsiders band together to solve mysteries. Jake, Peter, Byte, and Mattie have individual skills that help with each mystery. In the first book, they clear a security guard and find the real thief of a powerful computer chip.

1. The Vanishing Chip ◆ 1998
2. Of Heroes and Villains ◆ 1999
3. Growler's Horn ◆ 2000
4. The Kingfisher's Tale ◆ 2000
5. The Protester's Song ◆ 2001
6. Hit and Run ◆ 2002

MISHMASH

Cone, Molly

POCKET BOOKS ◆ GRADES 3–4 ◆ A/R

FAMILY LIFE | HUMOR

Pete's parents have finally granted his wish for a dog. Mishmash is more than a large friendly mutt—he thinks he is a human. This leads to several wacky adventures solving mysteries, confronting a grocery store robot, and dealing with tests and substitute teachers. In *Mishmash and the Big Fat Problem,* Mishmash must lose extra doggy pounds with help from Pete and Wanda. This series offers plenty of humor and lively action along with positive family and school situations.

1. Mishmash ◆ 1962
2. Mishmash and the Substitute Teacher ◆ 1963
3. Mishmash and the Sauerkraut Mystery ◆ 1965
4. Mishmash and Uncle Looey ◆ 1968
5. Mishmash and the Venus Flytrap ◆ 1976
6. Mishmash and the Robot ◆ 1981
7. Mishmash and the Big Fat Problem ◆ 1982

MISS BINDERGARTEN

Slate, Joseph

DUTTON ◆ GRADES K–2 ◆ A/R

ANIMAL FANTASY | HUMOR

Miss Bindergarten has a class of 26 students with names from Adam to Zach. Each student is an animal that alphabetically matches its first name. Adam is an alligator; Brenda is a beaver; and so on to Zach the Zebra. In the first book, Miss Bindergarten prepares her room for the first day of school. Other books deal with a field trip, the circus, and the 100th day of school. Ashley Wolff's colorful illustrations add to the appeal.

1. Miss Bindergarten Gets Ready for Kindergarten ◆ 1996
2. Miss Bindergarten Celebrates the 100th Day of Kindergarten ◆ 1998

3. Miss Bindergarten Stays Home from Kindergarten ◆ 2000
4. Miss Bindergarten Takes a Field Trip with Kindergarten ◆ 2001
5. Miss Bindergarten Plans a Circus with Kindergarten ◆ 2002
6. Miss Bindergarten Has a Wild Day in Kindergarten ◆ 2005
7. Miss Bindergarten Celebrates the Last Day of Kindergarten ◆ 2005

MISS FLORA MCFLIMSEY

Mariana

LOTHROP, LEE & SHEPARD ◆ GRADES K–2

FANTASY

Miss Flora McFlimsey is a whimsical doll who lives with Diana and her sister Toto, but remembers a time long before when she was owned by a little girl with "red-topped shoes." The Christmas story recalls the time when she was forgotten and neglected in the attic and was restored by an angel and placed under the tree so Diana and Toto would find her. Some of the other holiday stories are about Flora's life with the long-ago girl, the conceited PooKoo Cat, and other woodland friends. Easter finds her with Diana, recalling the time when she won a prize for the bonnet that was given to her by Peterkins Rabbit. There is a book for most holidays, and all are illustrated throughout with nostalgic pastels.

1. Miss Flora McFlimsey's Christmas Eve ◆ 1949
2. Miss Flora McFlimsey's Easter Bonnet ◆ 1951
3. Miss Flora McFlimsey and the Baby New Year ◆ 1951
4. Mc Flora McFlimsey's Birthday ◆ 1952
5. Miss Flora McFlimsey and Little Laughing Water ◆ 1954
6. Miss Flora McFlimsey and the Little Red School House ◆ 1957
7. Miss Flora McFlimsey's Valentine ◆ 1962
8. Miss Flora McFlimsey's May Day ◆ 1969
9. Miss Flora McFlimsey's Halloween ◆ 1972

MISS KNOW IT ALL

York, Carol Beach

BANTAM ◆ GRADES 2–4

FANTASY

The Good-Day Orphanage on Butterfield Square has 28 girls and a very good friend in Miss Know It All, a magical lady who does seem to know everything. Miss Plum and Miss Lavender try to run the orphanage with kindness and love, but it is Miss Know It All who steps in with her unique gifts when the girls have a problem. She sends tickets for everyone in the orphanage, even the cook, to go to the circus, and helps out when the girls want to have their own circus. Her magic delights all the girls, especially her always-full box of chocolates.

1. Miss Know It All ◆ 1966
2. The Christmas Dolls ◆ 1967
3. The Good Day Mice ◆ 1968
4. Good Charlotte ◆ 1969
5. The Ten O'Clock Club ◆ 1970
6. Miss Know It All Returns ◆ 1972
7. Kate Be Late ◆ 1987
8. Miss Know It All and the Wishing Lamp ◆ 1987
9. Miss Know It All and the Three-Ring Circus ◆ 1988
10. Miss Know It All and the Secret House ◆ 1988
11. Miss Know It All and the Magic House ◆ 1988

MISS MALARKEY

Finchler, Judy, and Kevin O'Malley

WALKER & CO. ◆ GRADES K–3 ◆ A/R

REAL LIFE | HUMOR

Miss Malarkey deals with many common misconceptions and frustrations of teaching. From the humorous idea that the teachers live at school to more serious issues such as standardized testing, these books feature a teacher who is committed to the success of her students. Kevin O'Malley's illustrations add to the humor.

1. Miss Malarkey Doesn't Live in Room 10 ◆ 1995
2. Miss Malarkey Won't Be In Today ◆ 1998
3. Testing Miss Malarkey ◆ 2000
4. You're a Good Sport, Miss Malarkey ◆ 2002
5. Miss Malarkey's Field Trip ◆ 2004
6. Miss Malarkey Leaves No Reader Behind ◆ 2006

MISS MALLARD

Quackenbush, Robert

PRENTICE-HALL ◆ GRADES 2–4

ANIMAL FANTASY | HUMOR | MYSTERY

Miss Mallard, the globe-trotting "ducktective," recovers stolen art in Venice, rescues an abducted scientist in Rio, and uncovers a crooked archaeologist's plans in Central America. On that particular trip, some of the travelers are afraid of a headless monster. Through clever reasoning, she proves that the monster is a sham created by an archaeologist who is a rival of the expedition's leader.

1. Express Train to Trouble ◆ 1981
2. Cable Car to Catastrophe ◆ 1982
3. Dig to Disaster ◆ 1982

4. Gondola to Danger ◆ 1983
5. Stairway to Doom ◆ 1983
6. Rickshaw to Horror ◆ 1984
7. Taxi to Intrigue ◆ 1984
8. Stage Door to Terror ◆ 1985
9. Bicycle to Treachery ◆ 1985
10. Surfboard to Peril ◆ 1986
11. Texas Trail to Calamity ◆ 1986
12. Dog Sled to Dread ◆ 1987
13. Danger in Tibet ◆ 1989
14. Lost in the Amazon ◆ 1990
15. Evil Under the Sea ◆ 1992
16. Flamenco to Mischief ◆ 2000
17. Miss Mallard's Case Book ◆ 2000
18. Mishap in Kaiserslautern ◆ 2001

MISS NELSON

Marshall, James

HOUGHTON MIFFLIN ◆ GRADES K–3 ◆ A/R

HUMOR

When the kids in Miss Nelson's class begin to take advantage of her sweet nature, she decides to take action. She becomes Miss Viola Swamp, the meanest substitute teacher in the world. A little dose of Miss Swamp is all it takes for the kids to appreciate Miss Nelson again and to behave. The class impersonates Miss Nelson while she impersonates Miss Swamp in one book; in the third, Miss Swamp is brought in to whip the football team into shape. The illustrations are colorful and cartoony and the humor is satirical in this picture book series.

1. Miss Nelson Is Missing! ◆ 1977
2. Miss Nelson Is Back ◆ 1982
3. Miss Nelson Has a Field Day ◆ 1985

MISS PICKERELL

MacGregor, Ellen, and Dora Pantell

McGRAW-HILL ◆ GRADES 4–5

ADVENTURE

Miss Pickerell will take up a good cause in a flash, using all her wits and energy to cope with a strange earthquake, oil spills, or even to take an exciting voyage to a new place. Her adventures always include her very bright nephew, Euphus, who is very useful. The original stories, written by MacGregor in the 1950s, ceased with her death in 1954. The series continued ten years later written by Dora Pantell, who sent Miss Pickerell on to further action.

1. Miss Pickerell Goes to Mars ◆ 1951
2. Miss Pickerell and the Geiger Counter ◆ 1953
3. Miss Pickerell Goes Undersea ◆ 1953
4. Miss Pickerell Goes to the Arctic ◆ 1954
5. Miss Pickerell on the Moon ◆ 1965
6. Miss Pickerell Goes on a Dig ◆ 1966
7. Miss Pickerell Harvests the Sea ◆ 1968
8. Miss Pickerell and the Weather Satellite ◆ 1971
9. Miss Pickerell Meets Mr. H. U. M. ◆ 1974
10. Miss Pickerell Takes the Bull By the Horns ◆ 1976
11. Miss Pickerell to the Earthquake Rescue ◆ 1977
12. Miss Pickerell and the Supertanker ◆ 1978
13. Miss Pickerell Tackles the Energy Crisis ◆ 1980
14. Miss Pickerell on the Trail ◆ 1982
15. Miss Pickerell and the Blue Whales ◆ 1983
16. Miss Pickerell and the War of the Computers ◆ 1984
17. Miss Pickerell and the Lost World ◆ 1986

MISS SPIDER

Kirk, David
SCHOLASTIC ◆ GRADES K–2 ◆ A/R

ANIMAL FANTASY

Miss Spider is 1 lonely spider who wants to invite other bugs to tea; but from 2 beetles (Ike and May) to 9 moths, they say no. Finally, holding 10 cups of tea, Miss Spider aids a wet moth, who tells the others of her kindness. In other stories, Miss Spider marries Holley and they go looking for the perfect car. The rhyming text and lush paintings capture the personalities of the many characters. A miniature hardcover series for younger children features Miss Spider's childhood and is called Little Miss Spider.

1. Miss Spider's Tea Party ◆ 1994
2. Miss Spider's Wedding ◆ 1995
3. Miss Spider's New Car ◆ 1997
4. Miss Spider's ABC ◆ 1998
5. Miss Spider's Sunny Patch Kids ◆ 2004

MISTMANTLE CHRONICLES

McAllister, Margaret I.
MIRAMAX ◆ GRADES 4–7 ◆ A/R

ANIMAL FANTASY

On the island of Mistmantle, Urchin, an orphaned squirrel, has been raised by Crispin, another squirrel who serves King Brushen, a hedgehog. When the King's son is killed, Crispin is accused and banished. Urchin remains on Mistmantle, working for Padma the otter and determined to clear Crispin's name. As the series progresses, Crispin becomes King of Mistmantle while Urchin serves him as a captain. These books should appeal to fans of the Dimwood Forest books by Avi as well as the Redwall books by Brian Jacques.

1. Urchin of the Riding Stars ◆ 2005
2. Urchin and the Heartstone ◆ 2006
3. The Heir of Mistmantle ◆ 2007
4. Urchin and the Raven War ◆ 2008

MISTY SERIES *see* Chincoteague

MITT AND MINN

Wargin, Kathy-jo
MITTEN PRESS ◆ GRADES 2–4
ANIMAL FANTASY

Mitt is a white-footed mouse from Michigan. His home is a red mitten, which is a cozy place until a young boy takes the mitten. As Mitt searches for his home, he is joined by Minn, another white-footed mouse. Their adventures take them through midwestern states. Information about the states is incorporated into the stories.

1. Mitt, the Michigan Mouse ◆ 2006
2. Minn from Minnesota ◆ 2006
3. Mitt and Minn at the Wisconsin Cheese Jamboree ◆ 2007
4. Mitt and Minn's Illinois Adventure ◆ 2007

MITTENS

Schaefer, Lola M.
HARPERCOLLINS ◆ GRADES K–1 ◆ A/R
REAL LIFE

Young children will love Mittens. He is an adorable kitten adjusting to his new home. Everywhere he goes is not right for him. Finally, he hides under the bed, where his new owner, Nick, finds him. Nick gently coaxes Mittens into his arms and the two begin their relationship. The illustrations by Susan Kathleen Hartung depict a darling little kitty. Like the books about Biscuit, these are great choices for beginning readers.

1. Mittens ◆ 2007

2. Follow Me, Mittens ◆ 2008
3. What's That, Mittens? ◆ 2008

THE MOFFATS

Estes, Eleanor

HARCOURT ◆ GRADES 3–6 ◆ A/R

FAMILY LIFE

The Moffats are a warm, fun-loving family in New England who just manage to make ends meet. The books take place approximately 50 years ago in a small town and provide a good feel for that time period. Readers will find many humorous moments.

1. The Moffats ◆ 1941
2. The Middle Moffat ◆ 1943
3. Rufus M. ◆ 1943
4. The Moffat Museum ◆ 1983

MOLE AND SHREW

Koller, Jackie French

RANDOM HOUSE; SIMON & SCHUSTER ◆ GRADES 2–4 ◆ A/R

ANIMAL FANTASY

Mole and Shrew are friends who deal with simple problems. When Buzzard plans to have the Rabbits for dinner, Mole and Shrew figure out what is really happening. He has invited the Rabbits to eat with him. Mole and Shrew celebrate holidays and describe what makes them friends.

1. Mole and Shrew Step Out ◆ 1992
2. Mole and Shrew All Year Through ◆ 1997
3. Mole and Shrew Are Two ◆ 2000
4. Mole and Shrew Have Jobs to Do ◆ 2001
5. Mole and Shrew Find a Clue ◆ 2001

MOLE AND TROLL

Johnston, Tony

BANTAM DOUBLEDAY DELL ◆ GRADES K–3 ◆ A/R

ANIMAL FANTASY

Mole and Troll are very good friends. As good friends do, they share their fears, have their quarrels, and generally enjoy themselves.

1. The Adventures of Mole and Troll ◆ 1989

2. Mole and Troll Trim the Tree ◆ 1989
3. Night Noises: And Other Mole and Troll Stories ◆ 1989
4. Happy Birthday, Mole and Troll ◆ 1989

MOLE SISTERS

Schwartz, Roslyn

ANNICK PRESS ◆ GRADES K–1 ◆ A/R

ANIMAL FANTASY

The happy life of the Mole Sisters is filled with simple pleasures. A rainy day becomes an opportunity to splash in a puddle/pool. On a winter day, they get lost. Instead of being upset, they enjoy the adventure. The positive attitude of the Mole Sisters could lead to a discussion on facing problems.

1. The Mole Sisters and the Piece of Moss ◆ 1999
2. The Mole Sisters and the Rainy Day ◆ 1999
3. The Mole Sisters and the Busy Bees ◆ 2000
4. The Mole Sisters and the Wavy Wheat ◆ 2000
5. The Mole Sisters and the Blue Egg ◆ 2001
6. The Mole Sisters and the Moonlit Night ◆ 2001
7. The Mole Sisters and the Cool Breeze ◆ 2002
8. The Mole Sisters and the Question ◆ 2002
9. The Mole Sisters and the Fairy Ring ◆ 2003
10. The Mole Sisters and the Way Home ◆ 2003

MOLESONS

Bos, Burny

NORTH-SOUTH BOOKS ◆ GRADES K–2 ◆ A/R

ANIMAL FANTASY | FAMILY LIFE

Dug and Dusty Moleson are twin moles from a close, working-class, mole family. Their parents, Molly and Morris (called Mud), are lots of fun and unpredictable. When Dug and Dusty decide to do the dishes in the backyard, their parents join in instead of getting angry. Their mother even joins the twins in applying fake chicken pox so they can stay in bed all day. Grandma takes them for rides on her electric wheelchair. Often, the stories are about family projects or outings that go wrong, usually thanks to Mud's miscalculations.

1. Meet the Molesons ◆ 1994
2. More from the Molesons ◆ 1995
3. Leave It to the Molesons! ◆ 1995
4. Good Times with the Molesons ◆ 2001
5. Fun with the Molesons ◆ 2002

MOLLY

Chaikin, Miriam

HARPERCOLLINS ◆ GRADES 4–7 ◆ A/R

FAMILY LIFE | HISTORICAL | REAL LIFE

A Jewish immigrant family living in Brooklyn during World War II struggles with staying true to its roots while at the same time becoming more American. Molly has an older brother, Joey; a younger sister, Rebecca; and Yaaki, the beautiful baby brother whom everyone adores. Molly's best friend is Tsippi, but she has other friends at school with whom she quarrels and makes up in typical schoolgirl fashion. One of them asks her to go to a restaurant that is not kosher, and she sneaks out and goes, only to get sick. As she talks to God about this (from a special window she reserves for this purpose), she realizes she was wrong. The series follows her to her upper elementary years, when many of her friends get their periods, causing her to feel left behind. Details of Jewish life are woven into all the books.

1. I Should Worry, I Should Care ◆ 1979
2. Finders Weepers ◆ 1980
3. Getting Even ◆ 1982
4. Lower! Higher! You're a Liar! ◆ 1984
5. Friends Forever ◆ 1988

MOLLY *see* American Girls: Molly

MOLLY MOON

Byng, Georgia

HARPERCOLLINS ◆ GRADES 4–6 ◆ A/R

FANTASY

Molly Moon is a lonely orphan who is ostracized by the children and staff at the orphanage. After reading a book on hypnotism, she is able to influence everyone and she leaves the orphanage and becomes a child star. Of course, an evil professor wants to steal the book and thwart her plans. In the second book, Molly tries to stop the efforts of another hypnotist. Fans of Lemony Snicket may turn to these books.

1. Molly Moon's Incredible Book of Hypnotism ◆ 2003
2. Molly Moon Stops the World ◆ 2003
3. Molly Moon's Hypnotic Time Travel Adventure ◆ 2005

MONSTER FAMILY *see* Very Worst Monster

MONSTER MANOR

Martin, Paul, and Manu Boisteau

VOLO/HYPERION BOOKS FOR CHILDREN ◆ GRADES 3–5 ◆ A/R

FANTASY | HUMOR

Vampires, specters, zombies, and other monsters inhabit monster manor. Eye-Gore and Steve are zombie brothers and Steve is missing. Has he been kidnapped . . . make that zombie-napped? Only Eye-Gore seems worried. This series will appeal to the fans of the Bailey School stories.

1. Von Skalpel's Experiment ◆ 2003
2. Frankie Rocks the House ◆ 2003
3. Beatrice's Spells ◆ 2003
4. Wolf Man Stu Bites Back ◆ 2004
5. Horror Gets Slimed ◆ 2004
6. Count Snobula Vamps It Up ◆ 2004
7. Sally Gets Silly ◆ 2004
8. Runaway Zombie ◆ 2004

MONSTER OF THE MONTH CLUB

Regan, Dian Curtis

HOLT ◆ GRADES 4–6

FANTASY

Rilla's attic is the home for her stuffed animals, including the monsters that she receives each month. The monsters come to life and help her with her problems, including finding the father she has not seen for years.

1. Monster of the Month Club ◆ 1994
2. Monsters in the Attic ◆ 1995
3. Monsters in Cyberspace ◆ 1997
4. Monsters and My One True Love ◆ 1998

MONSTER UNDER THE BED

Arnold, Tedd

SCHOLASTIC ◆ GRADES K–2 ◆ A/R

FANTASY | HUMOR

Huggly is the "Monster Under the Bed." He is cute and friendly and, like many young children, he makes mistakes when he tries new things. In the bath, he scrubs between his toes with the toothbrushes. At school, Huggly and his friends Booter and Grubble really have some fun.

1. Huggly and the Toy Monster ◆ 1999
2. Huggly Gets Dressed ◆ 1999
3. Huggly Takes a Bath ◆ 1999
4. Huggly Goes to School ◆ 2000
5. Huggly's Pizza ◆ 2000
6. Huggly's Christmas ◆ 2001

MOOMINTROLL

Jansson, Tove

FARRAR, STRAUS & GIROUX ◆ GRADES 4–6

FANTASY

From Scandinavia comes the story of beasties who inhabit the Moomin-valley. The black-and-white drawings show them as little hippo-like creatures, but they have very human qualities. They are supposed to sleep all winter and wake to adventures in the spring, but in one of the books Moomintroll wakes up in January and finds all of his summer haunts gone. The stories are full of human-like foibles, slightly surreal happenings, and gentle satire. They were written in the 1950s and 1960s; the dates listed here are American publications.

1. Finn Family Moomintroll ◆ 1989
2. Comet in Moominland ◆ 1990
3. Moominsummer Madness ◆ 1991
4. Moominland Midwinter ◆ 1992
5. Moominpappa at Sea ◆ 1993
6. Moominpappa's Memoirs ◆ 1994
7. Tales from Moominvalley ◆ 1995
8. Moominvalley in November ◆ 2003

MOONBEAR

Asch, Frank

SIMON & SCHUSTER; SCHOLASTIC ◆ GRADES K–2 ◆ A/R

ANIMAL FANTASY | FAMILY LIFE

Many of these books feature Bear's interest in the moon, while others include Bear's friend, Little Bird. Bear wants to dance with the moon. He searches for gold at the end of the rainbow and finds honey. He discovers a pet fish only to realize it is a pollywog (that becomes a frog). Like Asch's Bear stories, these are filled with gentle humor.

1. Moon Bear ◆ 1978
2. Happy Birthday, Moon ◆ 1982
3. Mooncake ◆ 1983
4. Moongame ◆ 1984

5. Skyfire ◆ 1984
6. Bear Shadow ◆ 1985
7. Bear's Bargain ◆ 1985
8. Goodbye House ◆ 1986
9. Moonbear's Pet ◆ 1987
10. Moondance ◆ 1993
11. Moonbear's Dream ◆ 1999

MOONGOBBLE

Coville, Bruce

SIMON & SCHUSTER ◆ **GRADES 3–5** ◆ **A/R**

FANTASY | **HUMOR**

Nothing ever happens in Pigbone and Edward is bored. Then Moongobble the Magician and Urk, his toad, move there. Edward becomes Moongobble's helper—and he needs help. Moongobble's spells are often mixed-up or missing important parts. The result is humorous and lighthearted. Short chapters make this accessible to middle-elementary readers.

1. The Dragon of Doom ◆ 2003
2. The Evil Elves ◆ 2004
3. The Weeping Werewolf ◆ 2004

MOOSE AND HILDY

Greene, Stephanie

MARSHALL CAVENDISH ◆ **GRADES K–2** ◆ **A/R**

ANIMAL FANTASY | **HUMOR**

Moose and Hildy (a pig) are good friends who each enjoy a fair degree of self-importance. In *Moose Crossing*, Moose assumes a signpost has been erected for the benefit of his fans and is surprised to find that celebrity isn't fun. Hildy finds a way to set the situation right. In the third book, Hildy assumes a pig pickin' is a beauty contest and Moose must rescue her from a horrible fate. These easy chapter books are full of wordplay and lighthearted pencil and gray-wash drawings. *Not Just Another Moose* (2000) features Moose and Hildy but is not usually considered part of this series.

1. Moose's Big Idea ◆ 2005
2. Moose Crossing ◆ 2005
3. Pig Pickin' ◆ 2006
4. The Show-Off ◆ 2007

MORRIS AND BORIS

Wiseman, Bernard
PUTNAM ◆ GRADES K–2 ◆ A/R

ANIMAL FANTASY | HUMOR

Each book in this series builds on the literal-mindedness of Morris the Moose and the practical nature of Boris the Bear. At the circus, Morris rides "bear" back on Boris. When Morris has a cold, Boris wants to make him some tea, but Morris wonders about the other letters—*a, b, c,* etc. There is a lot of fun in the situations and in the misunderstandings.

1. Morris the Moose ◆ 1959
2. Morris Is a Cowboy, a Policeman, and a Baby Sitter ◆ 1960
3. Morris Goes to School ◆ 1970
4. Morris and Boris ◆ 1974
5. Halloween with Morris and Boris ◆ 1975
6. Morris Has a Cold ◆ 1978
7. Morris Tells Boris Mother Goose Stories and Rhymes ◆ 1979
8. Christmas with Morris and Boris ◆ 1983
9. Morris Has a Birthday Party ◆ 1983
10. Morris and Boris at the Circus ◆ 1988

MOSES

Millman, Isaac
FARRAR, STRAUS & GIROUX ◆ GRADES K–2 ◆ A/R

REAL LIFE

Moses, a deaf child, participates in a variety of ordinary experiences. Alongside the stories, sidebar boxes show American Sign Language interpretations. Moses attends a special school for hearing impaired children and his classmates have diverse backgrounds and abilities. This series will be helpful when exploring and discussing the special needs of children.

1. Moses Goes to a Concert ◆ 1998
2. Moses Goes to School ◆ 2000
3. Moses Goes to the Circus ◆ 2003
4. Moses Sees a Play ◆ 2004

MOSTLY GHOSTLY

Stine, R. L.
DELACORTE ◆ GRADES 3–5 ◆ A/R

FANTASY

Max, 11, wants to be a magician. He is surprised one day when he meets Nicky and Tara. They are ghosts! They were former residents of the house where Max lives and they want to find their parents. Their efforts are complicated by an evil ghost named Phears. Fans of Stine's other supernatural thrillers will want to try this series.

1. Who Let the Ghosts Out? ◆ 2004
2. Have You Met My Ghoulfriend? ◆ 2004
3. Little Camp of Horrors ◆ 2005
4. One Night in Doom House ◆ 2005

MOUSE AND MOLE

Cushman, Doug

SCIENTIFIC AMERICAN ◆ GRADES K–3

ANIMAL FANTASY

This series shows two lovable creatures, Mouse and Mole, enjoying the outdoors. At the bottom of each page are simple scientific explanations of elements of the story: firefly light, seaweed, short winter nights, frost, and so on. Young scientists will enjoy the stories along with the information.

1. Mouse and Mole and the Year-Round Garden ◆ 1994
2. Mouse and Mole and the Christmas Walk ◆ 1994
3. Mouse and Mole and the All-Weather Train Ride ◆ 1995

MOUSE AND MOLE

Yee, Wong Herbert

HOUGHTON MIFFLIN ◆ GRADES K–2 ◆ A/R

ANIMAL FANTASY

In the tradition of Frog and Toad, this series is about Mouse and Mole. At first, their differences may keep them from being friends. Mouse lives right above Mole and in the evening when she sweeps her home, the dirt falls into Mole's house. Mole is frustrated because he cleans his house every morning. They discuss the problem and find a simple solution— they will work together to sweep their houses—first upstairs Mouse, then downstairs Mole. Beginning readers will enjoy the short chapters and colorful illustrations (by the author).

1. Upstairs Mouse, Downstairs Mole ◆ 2005
2. Abracadabra! Magic with Mouse and Mole ◆ 2007
3. A Brand-New Day with Mouse and Mole ◆ 2008

MOUSEKIN

Miller, Edna

PRENTICE-HALL ◆ GRADES K–2

REAL LIFE

Mousekin is a gentle white-footed mouse who lives in a lovely forest portrayed in watercolors on every page. People living on the edge of the forest sometimes touch the mouse's life, as when they leave a jack-o'-lantern into which Mousekin crawls. In the Christmas story, he is attracted to a house by its bright lights. Another book deals with dangers from predators, as Mousekin is pursued by an owl. Other animals in the forest hibernate, but Mousekin does not. One book portrays his winter adventures, while another tells of his mate and children. Accurate nature information combines with narrative in a unique way in this picture book series.

1. Mousekin's Golden House ◆ 1964
2. Mousekin's Christmas Eve ◆ 1965
3. Mousekin Finds a Friend ◆ 1967
4. Mousekin's Family ◆ 1969
5. Mousekin's Woodland Sleepers ◆ 1970
6. Mousekin's ABC ◆ 1972
7. Mousekin's Woodland Birthday ◆ 1974
8. Mousekin Takes a Trip ◆ 1976
9. Mousekin's Close Call ◆ 1978
10. Mousekin's Fables ◆ 1982
11. Mousekin's Mystery ◆ 1983
12. Mousekin's Thanksgiving ◆ 1985
13. Mousekin's Easter Basket ◆ 1987
14. Mousekin's Frosty Friend ◆ 1990
15. Mousekin's Lost Woodland ◆ 1992

MR. AND MRS. GREEN

Baker, Keith

HARCOURT ◆ GRADES K–2 ◆ A/R

ANIMAL FANTASY

Mr. and Mrs. Green are fun-loving alligators. There are three stories in each book. In the first book, the Greens go camping, deal with overeating, and enjoy going to the fair. In the second book, they go fishing, do some painting, and spend time in the park. These stories are charming and very accessible to young readers.

1. Meet Mr. and Mrs. Green ◆ 2002
2. More Mr. and Mrs. Green ◆ 2004
3. Lucky Days with Mr. and Mrs. Green ◆ 2005
4. On the Go with Mr. and Mrs. Green ◆ 2006

MR. AND MRS. PIG

Rayner, Mary

ATHENEUM; MACMILLAN ◆ GRADES K–3

ANIMAL FANTASY | FAMILY LIFE | HUMOR

The first book of this series, *Mr. and Mrs. Pig's Evening Out,* shows readers how quickly the ten piglets use their wits to unmask the true identity of their baby-sitter. Clever Mrs. Wolf tries to steal the piglets in subsequent titles, but she is always foiled by the quick-thinking pigs. Mrs. Pig is also very good at being clever, particularly when the piglets want only ketchup—even for dessert. Full watercolor illustrations, satisfying solutions, and gentle humor in familiar family situations will engage young readers.

1. Mr. and Mrs. Pig's Evening Out ◆ 1976
2. Garth Pig and the Ice Cream Lady ◆ 1978
3. Mrs. Pig's Bulk Buy ◆ 1981
4. Mrs. Pig Gets Cross and Other Stories ◆ 1987
5. Garth Pig Steals the Show ◆ 1993

MR. PIN

Monsell, Mary Elise

MACMILLAN; POCKET ◆ GRADES 2–4 ◆ A/R

ANIMAL FANTASY | HUMOR | MYSTERY

A chocolate-loving penguin named Mr. Pin investigates mysteries from his base in a Chicago diner.

1. The Mysterious Cases of Mr. Pin ◆ 1989
2. Mr. Pin: The Chocolate Files ◆ 1990
3. The Spy Who Came North from the Pole ◆ 1993
4. A Fish Named Yum ◆ 1994

MR. PUTTER AND TABBY

Rylant, Cynthia

HARCOURT ◆ GRADES K–3 ◆ A/R

HUMOR | REAL LIFE

In the first book, Mr. Putter is lonely and decides to get a cat. He goes to the pet store, but they have only kittens, so he goes to the shelter and finds an old cat. After a while, neither can remember what life was like without the other. Now Mr. Putter has someone with whom he can share his English muffins, tea, and stories. Tabby likes to roll in his tulips, and each knows what the other is going to do. In subsequent books, they take care of the neighbor's dog and have other gentle adventures. Each book in this easy-reader series is divided into short chapters and illustrated in full color.

1. Mr. Putter and Tabby Pour the Tea ◆ 1994
2. Mr. Putter and Tabby Walk the Dog ◆ 1994
3. Mr. Putter and Tabby Bake the Cake ◆ 1994
4. Mr. Putter and Tabby Pick the Pears ◆ 1995
5. Mr. Putter and Tabby Row the Boat ◆ 1997
6. Mr. Putter and Tabby Fly the Plane ◆ 1997
7. Mr. Putter and Tabby Toot the Horn ◆ 1998
8. Mr. Putter and Tabby Take the Train ◆ 1998
9. Mr. Putter and Tabby Paint the Porch ◆ 2000
10. Mr. Putter and Tabby Feed the Fish ◆ 2001
11. Mr. Putter and Tabby Catch the Cold ◆ 2002
12. Mr. Putter and Tabby Stir the Soup ◆ 2003
13. Mr. Putter and Tabby Write the Book ◆ 2004
14. Mr. Putter and Tabby Make a Wish ◆ 2005
15. Mr. Putter and Tabby Spin the Yarn ◆ 2006

MR. ROSE'S CLASS

Ziefert, Harriet

LITTLE, BROWN ◆ GRADES K–3

REAL LIFE

In a simple and humorous way, Mr. Rose challenges his students to make scientific deductions with the materials he gives them. For example, in *Egg-Drop Day,* each student is challenged to discover a material that will protect eggs from breaking when they are dropped. Everybody joins in the fun! In *Worm Day,* the students find out everything they can about worms. At the end of each book, there is an assignment from Mr. Rose that the reader can do at home.

1. Mystery Day ◆ 1988
2. Pet Day ◆ 1988
3. Trip Day ◆ 1988
4. Worm Day ◆ 1988
5. Egg-Drop Day ◆ 1988

MR. YOWDER

Rounds, Glen

HOLIDAY HOUSE ◆ GRADES 3–5

HISTORICAL | HUMOR

Mr. Yowder is a wandering sign painter in the old West. His adventures are of the tall-tale variety, told in laconic style and illustrated with humorous black-and-white drawings. In one book, he befriends a body-building bull snake. The snake becomes so big that Mr. Yowder rides him like a horse. Together, they hunt buffalo and put Buffalo Bill out of a job. In another story, he obtains an old lion who is worthless except for his roar. So Mr. Yowder decides to put his roar into capsules and sell it. Disaster strikes when a rainstorm releases all the roars too early. Another story tells how Mr. Yowder rigged up sails on prairie schooners, with predictable results.

1. Mr. Yowder and the Lion Roar Capsules ◆ 1976
2. Mr. Yowder and the Steamboat ◆ 1977
3. Mr. Yowder and the Giant Bull Snake ◆ 1978
4. Mr. Yowder, the Peripatetic Sign Painter ◆ 1980
5. Mr. Yowder and the Train Robbers ◆ 1981
6. Mr. Yowder and the Windwagon ◆ 1983

MRS. COVERLET

Nash, Mary

LITTLE, BROWN ◆ GRADES 3–5 ◆ A/R

FAMILY LIFE | HUMOR

Usually, the three Persever children—Malcolm, Molly, and Toad (a nickname for Theobald)—are very well-behaved. Their housekeeper, Mrs. Coverlet, sees to that. But when their father goes to New Zealand and Mrs. Coverlet leaves to care for her grandchildren, the Persever household is topsy-turvy. This well-known, old-fashioned series is still a choice for readers. Like Mary Poppins, these books feature intrepid children inexplicably left on their own. Their humorous antics make for entertaining reading.

1. While Mrs. Coverlet Was Away ◆ 1958
2. Mrs. Coverlet's Magicians ◆ 1961
3. Mrs. Coverlet's Detectives ◆ 1965

MRS. FRISBY see Rats of NIMH

MRS. GADDY

Gage, Wilson

GREENWILLOW ◆ GRADES K–3

HUMOR

A wonderful humorous series for beginning chapter readers. Whether it's outwitting a ghost, a fast-growing vine, or a greedy crow, Mrs. Gaddy always has a silly way of solving her problems so that everybody is happy. *My Stars, It's Mrs. Gaddy* (1991) combines all three stories in one volume.

1. Mrs. Gaddy and the Ghost ◆ 1979
2. The Crow and Mrs. Gaddy ◆ 1984
3. Mrs. Gaddy and the Fast-Growing Vine ◆ 1985

MRS. PEPPERPOT

Proysen, Alf

FARRAR, STRAUS & GIROUX ◆ GRADES 2–5

FANTASY | HUMOR

Mr. and Mrs. Pepperpot live an ordinary, quiet life on a farm, except that every once in a while, with no warning and for no reason, Mrs. Pepperpot shrinks to the size of a pepperpot. When they go for an outing in their new car, Mr. Pepperpot unwittingly drops an ice cream cone on her. All is well when a little kitten licks her clean. In another story, she scares a bothersome moose while she is small and he never troubles her again. Some of the books in this series are quite a bit longer than the others.

1. Little Old Mrs. Pepperpot, and Other Stories ◆ 1959
2. Mrs. Pepperpot Again, and Other Stories ◆ 1960
3. Mrs. Pepperpot to the Rescue, and Other Stories ◆ 1963
4. Mrs. Pepperpot's Busy Day ◆ 1967
5. Mrs. Pepperpot in the Magic Wood, and Other Stories ◆ 1968
6. Mrs. Pepperpot's Year ◆ 1970
7. Mrs. Pepperpot's Outing, and Other Stories ◆ 1971
8. Mrs. Pepperpot Goes Berry Picking ◆ 1990
9. Mrs. Pepperpot and the Moose ◆ 1991

MRS. PIGGLE-WIGGLE

MacDonald, Betty

HARPERCOLLINS ◆ GRADES 3–6 ◆ A/R

FANTASY | HUMOR

Generations of children have loved the Mrs. Piggle-Wiggle stories. She is a grandmotherly person whom every child wishes they knew. She lives in an upside-down house and was once married to a pirate, who left buried treasure in the yard. Parents love her for her magical (and very humorous) cures: for tattletales, for selfishness, and so on. Not only just good chapter book choices, these also make fun read-alouds. Picture book adaptations for younger readers include *Mrs. Piggle-Wiggle's Won't-Take-a-Bath Cure* and *Mrs. Piggle-Wiggle's Won't-Pick-up-Toys Cure* (both 1997).

1. Mrs. Piggle-Wiggle ◆ 1947
2. Mrs. Piggle-Wiggle's Magic ◆ 1949
3. Mrs. Piggle-Wiggle's Farm ◆ 1954
4. Hello, Mrs. Piggle-Wiggle ◆ 1957

MRS. TOGGLE

Pulver, Robin

FOUR WINDS ◆ GRADES K–3 ◆ A/R

HUMOR

Mrs. Toggle is a perfectly lovable teacher who enlists the help of her class whenever she has a problem. From being stuck inside her coat when the zipper won't work to losing her blue shoe during a game of kickball, her class is always able to help her out.

1. Mrs. Toggle's Zipper ◆ 1990
2. Mrs. Toggle and the Dinosaur ◆ 1991
3. Mrs. Toggle's Beautiful Blue Shoe ◆ 1994
4. Mrs. Toggle's Class Picture Day ◆ 2000

MRS. ZOOKEY'S SECOND GRADE *see* Table Two

MS. FRIZZLE'S ADVENTURES *see* Magic School Bus: Ms. Frizzle's Adventures

MUD FLAT

Stevenson, James

GREENWILLOW ◆ GRADES K–2 ◆ A/R

ANIMAL FANTASY | HUMOR

The community of Mud Flat is filled with many animals who enjoy activities such as playing April Fool's Day jokes and organizing an

Olympics. Different animals are featured in different books. In *Mud Flat April Fool,* Alice the mole teases Mr. Goodhue the bear. George the fox gets Lila the dog with his squirting rose and she pays him back later. In *The Mud Flat Olympics,* Harold the owl judges the Deepest Hole Contest (entered by three moles), and old Mr. Tokay wins the Smelliest Skunk Contest. These are funny books with a simple text and delightful illustrations. Most young readers will appreciate the sly humor and will find the short chapters very accessible.

1. The Mud Flat Olympics ◆ 1994
2. Yard Sale ◆ 1996
3. Heat Wave at Mud Flat ◆ 1997
4. The Mud Flat Mystery ◆ 1997
5. Mud Flat April Fool ◆ 1998
6. Mud Flat Spring ◆ 1999
7. Christmas at Mud Flat ◆ 2000
8. Flying Feet at Mud Flat ◆ 2004

MUMMY CHRONICLES

Wolverton, Dave
SKYLARK ◆ GRADES 4–7 ◆ A/R

FANTASY

Alex O'Connell, 12, wants to be a Medjai—one who works against the forces of darkness. It is 1937 and Alex is in Egypt. He discovers that his amulet gives him special powers. Alex battles mummies and faces a special test. In the spirit of Young Indiana Jones, Alex rescues the world from evil powers.

1. Revenge of the Scorpion King ◆ 2001
2. Heart of the Pharaoh ◆ 2001
3. The Curse of the Nile ◆ 2001
4. Flight of the Phoenix ◆ 2001

MURPHY FAMILY

McKenna, Colleen O'Shaughnessy
SCHOLASTIC ◆ GRADES 4–6 ◆ A/R

FAMILY LIFE | HUMOR

This series begins when Collette is in third grade. She is the oldest of four children, and although she loves her younger brothers and sister, it bothers her that her mother is too busy tending to the other children to do things with her alone. Collette wishes she were an only child and is surprised when her wish comes true. In other books, she goes to summer camp, she and her friends run a camp for kids in the neighborhood, her mother is expecting another child and has to stay off of her feet, and Collette starts sixth grade in a new school on an island.

1. Too Many Murphys ◆ 1988
2. Fourth Grade Is a Jinx ◆ 1989
3. Fifth Grade, Here Comes Trouble ◆ 1989
4. Eenie, Meenie, Murphy, No! ◆ 1990
5. Murphy's Island ◆ 1990
6. The Truth About Sixth Grade ◆ 1991
7. Mother Murphy ◆ 1992
8. Camp Murphy ◆ 1993

MUSTANG MOUNTAIN

Siamon, Sharon

WALRUS BOOKS ◆ GRADES 5–8 ◆ A/R

REAL LIFE | ADVENTURE

Three girls, Meg, Alison, and Becky, face adventure and danger in the Rocky Mountains at Mustang Mountain Ranch. In *Sky Horse,* Meg and Alison come to visit the ranch and they are met by Becky and Jesse, the driver. On their trip from the airport to the ranch, they are caught in a snowstorm. Meg and Becky take the horses from the trailer they have been towing and search for help. Instead, they find a plane that has crashed. In *Night Horse,* the girls spend the night in the Rockies protecting a stallion from bounty hunters. Fans of horse books like Saddle Club and Thoroughbred will enjoy these books.

1. Sky Horse ◆ 2001
2. Fire Horse ◆ 2002
3. Night Horse ◆ 2002
4. Wild Horse ◆ 2003
5. Rodeo Horse ◆ 2003
6. Brave Horse ◆ 2004
7. Free Horse ◆ 2004
8. Swift Horse ◆ 2005
9. Dark Horse ◆ 2005
10. Stone Horse ◆ 2006

MY AMERICA: COREY

Wyeth, Sharon Dennis

SCHOLASTIC ◆ GRADES 2–5 ◆ A/R

HISTORICAL | REAL LIFE

It is 1857 and Corey, 9, is a slave with a secret. He can read. He escapes from slavery by following an Underground Railroad route. For a while, he lives in Canada. Later, he returns to Ohio and becomes a conductor on the Underground Railroad. This series blends historical facts with a dramatic story. The books are in a diary format that appeals to many readers.

1. Freedom's Wings: Corey's Diary, Kentucky to Ohio, 1857 ◆ 2001
2. Flying Free: Corey's Underground Railroad Diary, Book 2 ◆ 2002
3. Message in the Sky: Corey's Underground Railroad Diary, Book 3 ◆ 2003

MY AMERICA: ELIZABETH

Hermes, Patricia

SCHOLASTIC ◆ GRADES 2–5 ◆ A/R

HISTORICAL | REAL LIFE

Elizabeth and her family have left England and settled in Jamestown, Virginia. It is 1609 and there are many hardships—long hours of hard work, poor living conditions, scarce food, and more. Elizabeth records her observations in her journal. This series blends historical facts with a dramatic story. The books are in a diary format that appeals to many readers.

1. Our Strange New Land: Elizabeth's Diary, Jamestown, Virginia, 1609 ◆ 2000
2. The Starving Time: Elizabeth's Jamestown Colony Diary, Book 2 ◆ 2001
3. Season of Promise: Elizabeth's Jamestown Colony Diary, Book 3 ◆ 2002

MY AMERICA: HOPE

Gregory, Kristiana

SCHOLASTIC ◆ GRADES 2–5 ◆ A/R

HISTORICAL | REAL LIFE

In 1776 Philadelphia, 10-year-old Hope describes her experiences during the Revolutionary War. The British capture the city. Hope and her family cope with the hardships of war and the danger of being supporters of the Continental Army. This series blends historical facts with a dramatic story. The books are in a diary format that appeals to many readers.

1. Five Smooth Stones: Hope's Diary, Philadelphia, Pennsylvania, 1776 ◆ 2002
2. We Are Patriots: Hope's Revolutionary War Diary, Book 2 ◆ 2002
3. When Freedom Comes: Hope's Revolutionary War Diary, Book 3 ◆ 2004

MY AMERICA: JOSHUA

Hermes, Patricia

SCHOLASTIC ◆ GRADES 2–5 ◆ A/R

HISTORICAL | REAL LIFE

Joshua and his family follow the Oregon Trail where they face adventures and hardships. They finally settle in the Willamette Valley and work on creating a home and community. This series blends historical facts with a dramatic story. The books are in a diary format that appeals to many readers.

1. Westward to Home: Joshua's Diary, The Oregon Trail, 1848 ◆ 2001
2. A Perfect Place: Joshua's Oregon Trail Diary, Book 2 ◆ 2002
3. The Wild Year: Joshua's Oregon Trail Diary, Book 3 ◆ 2003

MY AMERICA: MEG

McMullan, Kate

SCHOLASTIC ◆ GRADES 2–5 ◆ A/R

HISTORICAL | REAL LIFE

Because of the cholera epidemic in St. Louis, Meg and her younger brother have been sent to live in the Kansas Territory. Later, the rest of the family joins them on the prairie. Historical issues of the mid-1850s— slavery, women's rights, and conflicts about the settlements—are woven into this series, which blends facts with a dramatic story. The books are in a diary format that appeals to many readers.

1. As Far As I Can See: Meg's Diary, St. Louis to the Kansas Territory, 1856 ◆ 2002
2. For This Land: Meg's Prairie Diary, Book 2 ◆ 2003
3. A Fine Start: Meg's Prairie Diary, Book 3 ◆ 2003

MY AMERICA: SOFIA

Lasky, Kathryn

SCHOLASTIC ◆ GRADES 2–5 ◆ A/R

HISTORICAL | REAL LIFE

Sofia, 9, describes her family's journey from Italy to America. At Ellis Island, Sofia is quarantined and deals with harsh conditions until she is reunited with her family. Once they are settled in Boston, Sofia meets people—including a teacher and a doctor—who help change her life. This series blends historical facts with a dramatic story. The books are in a diary format that appeals to many readers.

1. Hope in My Heart: Sofia's Ellis Island Diary, 1903 ◆ 2003
2. Home at Last: Sofia's Immigrant Diary, Book Two ◆ 2004
3. An American Spring: Sofia's Immigrant Diary, Book Three ◆ 2003

MY AMERICA: VIRGINIA

Osborne, Mary Pope

SCHOLASTIC ◆ GRADES 2–5 ◆ A/R

HISTORICAL | REAL LIFE

Virginia Dickens is 9 years old. Her family's farm is right in the middle of the conflicts of the Civil War. As the war ends, her family settles in Washington, D.C. They later move to New York City hoping to find work. This series blends historical facts with a dramatic story. The books are in a diary format that appeals to many readers.

1. My Brother's Keeper: Virginia's Diary, Gettysburg, Pennsylvania, 1863 ◆ 2000
2. After the Rain: Virginia's Civil War Diary, Book 2 ◆ 2002
3. A Time to Dance: Virginia's Civil War Diary, Book 3 ◆ 2003

MY BABYSITTER

Hodgman, Ann

MINSTREL/POCKET BOOKS ◆ GRADES 4–6

HORROR

When this series begins, Meg Swain is 11 and she resents having to be left with a babysitter. Her resentment turns to dismay when she begins to suspect that her weird babysitter, Vincent Graver, is really a vampire. Meg and her brother Trevor outwit the vampire and escape, only to encounter him again . . . and again . . . and again. In one book, Meg and her friend Kelly Pitts are old enough to be babysitters themselves, but the baby they are watching seems very strange—he likes bats and hides from the sunshine. And what about Vodar, the exchange student in *My Babysitter Flies by Night,* with his pale skin and pointed teeth? This series could meet the needs of readers who have read Goosebumps and other eerie series.

1. My Babysitter Is a Vampire ◆ 1991
2. My Babysitter Has Fangs ◆ 1992
3. My Babysitter Bites Again ◆ 1993
4. My Babysitter Flies by Night ◆ 1994
5. My Babysitter Goes Bats ◆ 1994
6. My Babysitter Is a Movie Monster ◆ 1995

MY DOG

Adler, David A.

HOLIDAY HOUSE ◆ GRADES 1–2

MYSTERY

Humorous, easy mysteries are solved with Jennie's observant eye and her big shaggy pet, simply called My Dog. In *My Dog and the Birthday Mystery*, Jennie's friends trick her into solving a mystery that is really a surprise birthday party. My Dog helps to solve the Green Sock and Knock-Knock mysteries with simple animal instincts. Easy sentence structure and humorous color illustrations make this series appealing to first readers.

1. My Dog and the Key Mystery ◆ 1982
2. My Dog and the Knock Knock Mystery ◆ 1985
3. My Dog and the Green Sock Mystery ◆ 1986
4. My Dog and the Birthday Mystery ◆ 1987

MY FATHER'S DRAGON *see* Dragon

MY FIRST LITTLE HOUSE books *see* Little House: My First Little House Books

MY MOM

Delton, Judy

WHITMAN; DELACORTE; RANDOM HOUSE ◆ GRADES 1–3

FAMILY LIFE

Archie is miserable about going to camp but he ends up having a great time. The same is true when he goes to school—and when he takes piano lessons, especially once he realizes he could be a star!

1. My Mom Hates Me in January ◆ 1977
2. My Mom Made Me Go to Camp ◆ 1990
3. My Mom Made Me Go to School ◆ 1991
4. My Mom Made Me Take Piano Lessons ◆ 1994

MY NAME IS AMERICA

Various authors

SCHOLASTIC ◆ GRADES 4–6 ◆ A/R

HISTORICAL

This series is similar in format to the Dear America series, except that the fictional journal entries are written by boys. Written by different authors, including Jim Murphy, who has received a Newbery Honor award, this series merges historical facts with personal reflections. One book examines the experiences of an orphan who becomes a spy for the colonists during the Revolutionary War. The Civil War is the setting for another book that describes the brutality and courage of people in this conflict. Lots of action, as well as personal insights, make this a choice for upper elementary school readers.

1. The Journal of William Thomas Emerson: A Revolutionary War Patriot, Boston, Massachusetts, 1774 (Denenberg, Barry) ◆ 1998
2. The Journal of James Edmond Pease: A Civil War Union Soldier, Virginia, 1863 (Murphy, Jim) ◆ 1998
3. The Journal of Joshua Loper: A Black Cowboy, the Chisholm Trail, 1871 (Myers, Walter Dean) ◆ 1999
4. The Journal of Sean Sullivan: A Transcontinental Railroad Worker, Nebraska and and Points West, 1867 (Durbin, William) ◆ 1999
5. The Journal of Ben Uchida: Citizen 13559, Mirror Lake Internment Camp, California, 1942 (Denenberg, Barry) ◆ 1999
6. The Journal of Scott Pendleton Collins: A World War II Soldier, Normandy, France, 1944 (Myers, Walter Dean) ◆ 1999
7. The Journal of Wong Ming-Chung: A Chinese Miner, California, 1852 (Yep, Laurence) ◆ 2000
8. The Journal of Jasper Jonathan Pierce: A Pilgrim Boy, Plymouth, 1620 (Rinaldi, Ann) ◆ 2000
9. The Journal of Otto Peltonen: A Finnish Immigrant, Hibbing, Minnesota, 1905 (Durbin, William) ◆ 2000
10. The Journal of Augustus Pelletier: The Lewis and Clark Expedition, 1804 (Lasky, Kathryn) ◆ 2000
11. The Journal of Biddy Owens: The Negro Leagues, Birmingham, Alabama, 1948 (Myers, Walter Dean) ◆ 2001
12. The Journal of Jesse Smoke: A Cherokee Boy, the Trail of Tears, 1838 (Bruchac, Joseph) ◆ 2001
13. The Journal of Douglas Allen Deeds: The Donner Party Expedition, 1846 (Philbrick, W. Rodman) ◆ 2001
14. The Journal of Jedediah Barstow: An Emigrant on the Oregon Trail, 1845 (Levine, Ellen) ◆ 2001
15. The Journal of C. J. Jackson: A Dust Bowl Migrant, Oklahoma to California, 1935 (Durbin, William) ◆ 2002
16. The Journal of Patrick Seamus Flaherty: A United States Marine Corps, Khe Sanh, Vietnam, 1968 (White, Ellen Emerson) ◆ 2002
17. The Journal of Finn Reardon: A Newsie, New York City, 1899 (Bartoletti, Susan Campbell) ◆ 2003
18. The Journal of Rufus Rowe: A Witness to the Battle of Fredericksburg, Bowling Green, Virginia, 1862 (Hite, Sid) ◆ 2003
19. The Journal of Brian Doyle: A Greenhorn on an Alaskan Whaling Ship, the Florence, 1874 (Murphy, Jim) ◆ 2003

MY PONY JACK

Meister, Cari
VIKING ◆ GRADES K–2 ◆ A/R
REAL LIFE

Here's an easy-reader for horse-crazy kids. Lacy rides and cares for her pony Jack. Simple horse-related terms (groom, curry, halter) are included in the rhyming couplets and then listed in a brief glossary. Colorful illustrations by Amy Young add to the appeal.

1. My Pony Jack ◆ 2005
2. My Pony Jack at Riding Lessons ◆ 2005
3. My Pony Jack at the Horse Show ◆ 2006

MY ROBOT BUDDY *see* Jack Jameson and Danny One

MY SIDE OF THE MOUNTAIN

George, Jean Craighead
DUTTON ◆ GRADES 4–8 ◆ A/R
REAL LIFE

Sam Gribley leaves his home in the city to spend a year in the Catskill Mountains. He survives and develops a relationship with a falcon he names Frightful. The third book is presented from Frightful's point of view. The fourth book is a picture book that focuses on Oksi, Frightful's daughter, as she grows from a hatchling to a young falcon. *My Side of the Mountain* was a Newbery Honor book.

1. My Side of the Mountain ◆ 1959
2. On the Far Side of the Mountain ◆ 1990
3. Frightful's Mountain ◆ 1999
4. Frightful's Daughter ◆ 2002

MY SIDE OF THE STORY

Various authors
KINGFISHER ◆ GRADES 4–8 ◆ A/R
HISTORICAL

Two perspectives of the same event are presented in this historical fiction series. In *The Brothers' War,* a family's loyalties are divided as Melody's family supports the Union while her cousin's family is siding with the Confederacy. In another book, Lizzy works in the mill where conditions are deplorable. Her childhood friendship with Josh, the mill owner's son, is threatened when she joins with fellow workers in a protest.

1. The Brothers' War (Hermes, Patricia) ◆ 2005
2. Escape from War (Riordan, James) ◆ 2005
3. Journey to Jamestown (Ruby, Lois) ◆ 2005
4. Trouble at the Mill (Wooderson, Philip) ◆ 2005
5. The Plague (Wooderson, Philip) ◆ 2006
6. Salem Witch (Hermes, Patricia) ◆ 2006

MY SIDE OF THE STORY (DISNEY PRINCESSES) *see* Disney Princesses: My Side of the Story

MY SIDE OF THE STORY (DISNEY VILLIANS) *see* Disney Villains: My Side of the Story

MY SISTER, THE GHOST

Singleton, Linda Joy
HARPERCOLLINS ◆ GRADES 4–6
FANTASY

Miranda Mitchell's twin sister, Melody, drowned when they were 2 years old. Now Melody has returned as a ghost to help Miranda stop their mother from marrying the wrong man. Their adventures continue and involve other ghosts and mysterious events.

1. Twin Again ◆ 1995
2. Escape from Ghostland ◆ 1995
3. Teacher Trouble ◆ 1996
4. Babysitter Beware ◆ 1996

MY SISTER THE VAMPIRE

Mercer, Sienna
HARPERCOLLINS ◆ GRADES 5–8 ◆ A/R
FANTASY

When Ivy and Olivia meet at Franklin Grove Middle School they discover they are twins who were separated at birth. They have very *very* different personalities—Olivia is an outgoing cheerleader while Ivy is a vampire. This series is not about blood lust and gore, instead it deals with tween concerns including friendship, identity, and dating.

1. Switched ◆ 2007
2. Fangtastic! ◆ 2007
3. Re-Vamped! ◆ 2007
4. Vampalicious! ◆ 2008

MY TEACHER IS AN ALIEN

Coville, Bruce

MINSTREL/POCKET BOOKS ◆ GRADES 4–6 ◆ A/R

ADVENTURE | SCIENCE FICTION

In the first book of this series, *My Teacher Is an Alien,* Peter Thompson and his friend Susan Simmons discover that aliens have invaded his sixth-grade class. It is Peter's mission to save the class. In succeeding adventures, the aliens attempt to attack and destroy Earth. There is enough suspense in each title to sustain interest in this fast-paced adventure series. A companion volume full of crosswords, quizzes, jokes, and puzzles is *Is Your Teacher an Alien?* (1997).

1. My Teacher Is an Alien ◆ 1989
2. My Teacher Fried My Brains ◆ 1991
3. My Teacher Glows in the Dark ◆ 1991
4. My Teacher Flunked the Planet ◆ 1992

MY WEIRD SCHOOL

Gutman, Dan

HARPERCOLLINS ◆ GRADES 2–5 ◆ A/R

HUMOR

This humorous series focuses on A.J., a second-grade student who hates school. Then he meets his teacher, Miss Daisy, and the fun begins. In one book, the principal, Mr. Klutz, does some pretty strange things including painting his bald head orange. Mrs. Roopy, the librarian, is weird too. As are the art teacher and the gym teacher and . . . .

1. Miss Daisy Is Crazy! ◆ 2004
2. Mr. Klutz Is Nuts! ◆ 2004
3. Mrs. Roopy Is Loopy! ◆ 2004
4. Ms. Hannah Is Bananas! ◆ 2004
5. Miss Small Is Off the Wall! ◆ 2005
6. Mr. Hynde Is Out of His Mind! ◆ 2005
7. Mrs. Cooney Is Loony! ◆ 2005
8. Ms. LaGrange Is Strange! ◆ 2005
9. Miss Lazar Is Bizarre! ◆ 2005
10. Mr. Docker Is Off His Rocker! ◆ 2006
11. Mrs. Kormel Is Not Normal! 2006

12. Ms. Todd Is Odd! ◆ 2006
13. Mrs. Patty Is Batty! ◆ 2006
14. Miss Holly Is Too Jolly! ◆ 2006
15. Mr. Macky Is Wacky! ◆ 2006
16. Ms. Coco Is Loco! ◆ 2007
17. Miss Suki Is Kooky! ◆ 2007
18. Mrs. Yonkers Is Bonkers! ◆ 2007
19. Dr. Carbles Is Losing His Marbles! ◆ 2007
20. Mr. Louie Is Screwy! ◆ 2007
21. Ms. Krup Cracks Me Up! ◆ 2008

MY WEIRD SCHOOL DAZE

Gutman, Dan

HARPERTROPHY ◆ GRADES 2–5 ◆ A/R

HUMOR

The gang from My Weird School is finished with second grade and moving up to third grade at Ella Mentry School. But first, summer vacation at the beach where there is a weird (of course) lifeguard, Mr. Sunny. Follow the antics of A.J. and his pals in Mr. Granite's classroom.

1. Mrs. Dole Is Out of Control! ◆ 2008
2. Mr. Sunny Is Funny! ◆ 2008
3. Mr. Granite Is from Another Planet! ◆ 2008
4. Coach Hyatt Is a Riot! ◆ 2008
5. Officer Spence Makes No Sense! ◆ 2009

MYSTERIES IN OUR NATIONAL PARKS

Skurzynski, Gloria, and Alane Ferguson

NATIONAL GEOGRAPHIC ◆ GRADES 5–8 ◆ A/R

ADVENTURE | MYSTERY

Jack, 12, and his younger sister, Ashley, travel with their parents to national parks. On these trips, they encounter mysteries that they try to solve. At Yellowstone, a pack of wolves may have killed a hunting dog. Jack and Ashley find out what is really happening. At Carlsbad Caverns National Park, Jack and Ashley search for a lost boy and become lost in the caverns. This series written by popular author Skurzynski and her daughter offers fast-paced adventure and brief information about each park.

1. Wolf Stalker: A Mystery in Yellowstone National Park ◆ 2001
2. Rage of Fire ◆ 2001
3. Cliff Hanger: A Mystery in Mesa Verde National Park ◆ 2001
4. Deadly Waters: A Mystery in Glacier National Park ◆ 2001

5. The Hunted: A Mystery in Virgin Islands National Park ◆ 2001
6. Ghost Horses: A Mystery in Zion National Park ◆ 2002
7. Over the Edge: A Mystery in Grand Canyon National Park ◆ 2002
8. Valley of Death: A Mystery in Death Valley National Park ◆ 2002
9. Escape from Fear: A Mystery in Virgin Islands National Park ◆ 2002
10. Out of the Deep: A Mystery in Acadia National Park ◆ 2002
11. Running Scared: A Mystery in Carlsbad Caverns National Park ◆ 2002
12. Buried Alive: A Mystery in Denali National Park ◆ 2003
13. Night of the Black Bear: A Mystery in Great Smoky Mountains National Park ◆ 2007

MYSTERY FILES OF SHELBY WOO

Various authors

ALADDIN ◆ GRADES 4–6

MYSTERY

Shelby Woo has always dreamed of being a detective because her grandfather solved crimes for the San Francisco Police Department. Now she lives with him in Florida and works as an intern for Detective Whit Hineline of the Cocoa Beach Police Department. As a budding sleuth, she likes to take neglected investigations into her own hands. She solves cases with her friends Cindy and Noah, even though the police want her to stay out of the way. In the early books, Shelby establishes her credentials as she works on such cases as a series of muggings at C.J.'s, a local eatery. In later books, Shelby has developed a more official role with the police department and works on cases like the disappearance of a comic book creator—right from her grandfather's bed-and-breakfast! Each book opens with a synopsis of the case file. Bold-faced text written in the first person provides Shelby's perspective. This series connects with the Nickelodeon TV programs.

1. A Slash in the Night (Goodman, Alan) ◆ 1997
2. Takeout Stakeout (Gallagher, Diana G.) ◆ 1997
3. Hot Rock (Peel, John) ◆ 1997
4. Rock 'n' Roll Robbery (Marano, Lydia C.) ◆ 1997
5. Cut and Run (Gallagher, Diana G.) ◆ 1998
6. House Arrest (Marano, Lydia C.) ◆ 1998
7. Comic Book Criminal (Dubowski, Cathy East, and Mark Dubowski) ◆ 1998
8. Frame-Up (Strickland, Brad, and Barbara Strickland) ◆ 1998
9. History Mystery (Ponti, James) ◆ 1998
10. High Wire (Dubowski, Cathy East) ◆ 1998
11. Fireproof (Collins, Suzanne) ◆ 1999
12. The Green Monster (Ponti, James) ◆ 1999
13. Man Overboard! (Strickland, Brad) ◆ 1999

14. Friends in Need (Ponti, James) ◆ 1999
15. Ski-Slope Sabotage (Erwin, Vicki Berger) ◆ 2000

MYSTIC KNIGHTS OF TIR NA NOG

Various authors

HARPERCOLLINS ◆ GRADES 5–8

FANTASY

Ivan, Rohan, Deirdre, and Angus confront many dangers, including dragons and other creatures. They battle the forces of the evil queen Maeve and hope to earn their armor. The stories include references to Celtic heroes and legends. A television program featured these characters.

1. The Legend of the Ancient Scroll (Teitelbaum, Michael) ◆ 1999
2. Fire Within, Air Above! (Simpson, Robert) ◆ 1999
3. Water Around, Earth Below! (Brightfield, Richard) ◆ 1999
4. The Taming of the Pyre (Whitman, John) ◆ 1999
5. Dragata Revealed! (Teitelbaum, Michael) ◆ 1999

MYSTIC LIGHTHOUSE MYSTERIES

Williams, Laura E.

SCHOLASTIC ◆ GRADES 2–4

FANTASY | MYSTERY

In Mystic, Maine, Jen and Zeke are twins who experience paranormal events. In one book, there is a haunted theater where the performance is interrupted with ghostly noises and apparitions. Is the town cursed?

1. The Mystery of the Dark Lighthouse ◆ 2002
2. The Mystery of Dead Man's Curve ◆ 2002
3. The Mystery of the Bad Luck Curse ◆ 2002
4. The Mystery of the Missing Tiger ◆ 2002
5. The Mystery of the Phantom Ship ◆ 2002
6. The Mystery of the Haunted Playhouse ◆ 2002

MYTH ADVENTURES

Asprin, Robert

ACE ◆ GRADES 5–8 ◆ A/R

FANTASY

Skeeve, a magician's apprentice, begins a series of adventures. He jumps to different dimensions and confronts characters such as the evil wizard Isstvan. Skeeve and his companions, Aahz and Tanada, have humorous, fast-paced encounters with many strange creatures. There have been a variety of editions and reissues of this series.

1. Another Fine Myth ◆ 1985
2. Myth Conceptions ◆ 1985
3. Myth Directions ◆ 1985
4. Hit or Myth ◆ 1985
5. Myth-ing Persons ◆ 1986
6. Little Myth Marker ◆ 1986
7. M.Y.T.H. Inc. Link ◆ 1986
8. Myth-Nomers and Im-Pervections ◆ 1990
9. M.Y.T.H. Inc. in Action ◆ 1990
10. Sweet Myth-tery of Life ◆ 2000
11. Something M.Y.T.H. Inc. ◆ 2002
12. Myth-ion Improbable ◆ 2002
13. Myth-told Tales ◆ 2003
14. Myth Alliances ◆ 2003
15. Myth-taken Identity ◆ 2004

MYTH-O-MANIA

McMullan, Kate

HYPERION/VOLO ◆ GRADES 4–7 ◆ A/R

FANTASY | HUMOR

Everyone thinks they know the real Greek myths, but they are wrong. Hades, King of the Underworld, tells his side of the stories here. Like the one about Hercules. Do you really think he did the "XII Labors" by himself? No way! This series takes a creative look at some of the best-known stories.

1. Have a Hot Time, Hades! ◆ 2002
2. Phone Home, Persephone! ◆ 2002
3. Say Cheese, Medusa! ◆ 2002
4. Nice Shot, Cupid ◆ 2002
5. Stop that Bull, Theseus! ◆ 2003
6. Keep a Lid on It, Pandora! ◆ 2003
7. Get to Work, Hercules! ◆ 2003
8. Go for the Gold, Atalanta! ◆ 2003

MYTHIC MISADVENTURES

Hennesy, Carolyn

BLOOMSBURY ◆ GRADES 5–8

FANTASY

Building on the story of "Pandora's Box," this series features Pandora as a 13-year-old girl. Pandy finds a box that is supposed to be filled with ancient evils, so she takes it to school for her school project. She is not planning to open the box; however, the box gets opened and the evils are released. Zeus and Hera are not pleased. Pandy is given a year to collect all the evils. Along with her BFFs Alcie and Iole, she begins the search.

1. Pandora Gets Jealous ◆ 2007
2. Pandora Gets Vain ◆ 2008
3. Pandora Gets Lazy ◆ 2009

MYTHQUEST

Various authors

BANTAM BOOKS ◆ GRADES 4–8

FANTASY

In *The Minotaur,* Alex and Cleo Bellows want to find their father, an archaeologist whose computer research into ancient times opened a portal into the world of ancient myths. Alex is transported to ancient Crete where he faces the Minotaur. As the series continues, the teens travel to other myths. These novelizations were based on a PBS series.

1. The Minotaur ◆ 2002
2. Hammer of the Gods ◆ 2003
3. Red Wolf's Daughter ◆ 2003
4. Minokichi ◆ 2003

NANCY DREW

Keene, Carolyn

SIMON & SCHUSTER ◆ GRADES 4–7 ◆ A/R

MYSTERY

Nancy Drew is a teenage detective who solves crimes while her friends George and Bess tag along. In one book, Bess is working for a wedding consultant based in an old mansion on the outskirts of River Heights. During a busy week in June, she asks George and Nancy to help out. As the first wedding begins, it seems that someone is trying to sabotage it. Nancy suspects a cousin of the bride; but when a second wedding is sabotaged, suspicion shifts to the sister of the wedding manager. The history of the old house eventually helps to solve the mystery. Throughout the series, Nancy is thorough, methodical, and undistracted. Bess and George provide contrast, Bess being a food-loving flirt and George serious and athletic.

1. The Secret of the Old Clock ◆ 1930
2. The Hidden Staircase ◆ 1930
3. The Bungalow Mystery ◆ 1930
4. The Mystery at Lilac Inn ◆ 1930

5. The Secret of Shadow Ranch ◆ 1930
6. The Secret of Red Gate Farm ◆ 1931
7. The Clue in the Diary ◆ 1932
8. Nancy's Mysterious Letter ◆ 1932
9. The Sign of the Twisted Candles ◆ 1933
10. The Password to Larkspur Lane ◆ 1933
11. The Clue of the Broken Locket ◆ 1934
12. The Message in the Hollow Oak ◆ 1935
13. The Mystery of the Ivory Charm ◆ 1936
14. The Whispering Statue ◆ 1937
15. The Haunted Bridge ◆ 1937
16. The Clue of the Tapping Heels ◆ 1939
17. The Mystery of the Brass-Bound Trunk ◆ 1940
18. The Mystery of the Moss-Covered Mansion ◆ 1941
19. The Quest of the Missing Map ◆ 1942
20. The Clue in the Jewel Box ◆ 1943
21. The Secret in the Old Attic ◆ 1944
22. The Clue in the Crumbling Wall ◆ 1945
23. The Mystery of the Tolling Bell ◆ 1946
24. The Clue in the Old Album ◆ 1947
25. The Ghost of Blackwood Hall ◆ 1948
26. The Clue of the Leaning Chimney ◆ 1949
27. The Secret of the Wooden Lady ◆ 1950
28. The Clue of the Black Keys ◆ 1951
29. The Mystery at the Ski Jump ◆ 1952
30. The Clue of the Velvet Mask ◆ 1953
31. The Ringmaster's Secret ◆ 1953
32. The Scarlet Slipper Mystery ◆ 1954
33. The Witch Tree Symbol ◆ 1955
34. The Hidden Window Mystery ◆ 1957
35. The Haunted Showboat ◆ 1957
36. The Secret of the Golden Pavilion ◆ 1959
37. The Clue in the Old Stagecoach ◆ 1960
38. The Mystery of the Fire Dragon ◆ 1961
39. The Clue of the Dancing Puppet ◆ 1962
40. The Moonstone Castle Mystery ◆ 1963
41. The Clue of the Whistling Bagpipes ◆ 1964
42. The Phantom of Pine Hill ◆ 1965
43. The Mystery of the 99 Steps ◆ 1966
44. The Clue in the Crossword Cypher ◆ 1967
45. The Spider Sapphire Mystery ◆ 1968
46. The Invisible Intruder ◆ 1969
47. The Mysterious Mannequin ◆ 1970
48. The Crooked Bannister ◆ 1971
49. The Secret of Mirror Bay ◆ 1972
50. The Double Jinx Mystery ◆ 1974
51. The Mystery of the Glowing Eye ◆ 1974
52. The Secret of the Forgotten City ◆ 1975
53. The Sky Phantom ◆ 1976

54. Strange Message in the Parchment ◆ 1977
55. Mystery of Crocodile Island ◆ 1978
56. The Thirteenth Pearl ◆ 1979
57. Triple Hoax ◆ 1979
58. The Flying Saucer Mystery ◆ 1980
59. The Secret in the Old Lace ◆ 1980
60. The Greek Symbol Mystery ◆ 1981
61. The Swami's Ring ◆ 1981
62. The Kachina Doll Mystery ◆ 1981
63. The Twin Dilemma ◆ 1981
64. Captive Witness ◆ 1981
65. Mystery of the Winged Lion ◆ 1982
66. Race Against Time ◆ 1982
67. The Sinister Omen ◆ 1982
68. The Elusive Heiress ◆ 1982
69. Clue in the Ancient Disguise ◆ 1982
70. The Broken Anchor ◆ 1983
71. The Silver Cobweb ◆ 1983
72. The Haunted Carousel ◆ 1983
73. Enemy Match ◆ 1984
74. The Mysterious Image ◆ 1984
75. The Emerald-Eyed Cat ◆ 1984
76. The Eskimo's Secret ◆ 1985
77. The Bluebeard Room ◆ 1985
78. The Phantom of Venice ◆ 1985
79. The Double Horror of Fenley Place ◆ 1987
80. The Case of the Disappearing Diamonds ◆ 1987
81. Mardi Gras Mystery ◆ 1988
82. The Clue in the Camera ◆ 1988
83. The Case of the Vanishing Veil ◆ 1988
84. The Joker's Revenge ◆ 1988
85. The Secret of Shady Glen ◆ 1988
86. The Mystery of Misty Canyon ◆ 1988
87. The Case of the Rising Stars ◆ 1988
88. The Search for Cindy Austin ◆ 1988
89. The Case of the Disappearing Deejay ◆ 1989
90. The Puzzle at Pineview School ◆ 1989
91. The Girl Who Couldn't Remember ◆ 1989
92. The Ghost of Craven Cove ◆ 1989
93. The Case of the Safecracker's Secret ◆ 1990
94. The Picture-Perfect Mystery ◆ 1990
95. The Silent Suspect ◆ 1990
96. The Case of the Photo Finish ◆ 1990
97. The Mystery at Magnolia Mansion ◆ 1990
98. The Haunting of Horse Island ◆ 1990
99. The Secret at Seven Rocks ◆ 1991
100. The Secret in Time: Nancy Drew's 100th Anniversary Edition ◆ 1991
101. The Mystery of the Missing Millionaires ◆ 1991
102. The Secret in the Dark ◆ 1991

103. The Stranger in the Shadows ◆ 1991
104. The Mystery of the Jade Tiger ◆ 1991
105. The Clue in the Antique Trunk ◆ 1992
106. The Case of the Artful Crime ◆ 1992
107. The Legend of Miner's Creek ◆ 1992
108. The Secret of the Tibetan Treasure ◆ 1992
109. The Mystery of the Masked Rider ◆ 1992
110. The Nutcracker Ballet Mystery ◆ 1992
111. The Secret at Solitaire ◆ 1993
112. Crime in the Queen's Court ◆ 1993
113. The Secret Lost at Sea ◆ 1993
114. The Search for the Silver Persian ◆ 1993
115. The Suspect in the Smoke ◆ 1993
116. The Case of the Twin Teddy Bears ◆ 1993
117. Mystery on the Menu ◆ 1993
118. Trouble at Lake Tahoe ◆ 1994
119. The Mystery of the Missing Mascot ◆ 1994
120. The Case of the Floating Crime ◆ 1994
121. The Fortune-Teller's Secret ◆ 1994
122. The Message in the Haunted Mansion ◆ 1994
123. The Clue on the Silver Screen ◆ 1995
124. The Secret of the Scarlet Hand ◆ 1995
125. The Teen Model Mystery ◆ 1995
126. The Riddle in the Rare Book ◆ 1995
127. The Case of the Dangerous Solution ◆ 1995
128. The Treasure in the Royal Tower ◆ 1995
129. The Baby-Sitter Burglaries ◆ 1996
130. The Sign of the Falcon ◆ 1996
131. The Hidden Inheritance ◆ 1996
132. The Fox Hunt Mystery ◆ 1996
133. The Mystery at the Crystal Palace ◆ 1996
134. The Secret of the Forgotten Cave ◆ 1996
135. The Riddle of the Ruby Gazelle ◆ 1997
136. The Wedding Day Mystery ◆ 1997
137. In Search of the Black Rose ◆ 1997
138. Legend of the Lost Gold ◆ 1997
139. The Secret of Candlelight Inn ◆ 1997
140. The Door-to-Door Deception ◆ 1997
141. The Wild Cat Crime ◆ 1997
142. The Case of Capital Intrigue ◆ 1998
143. Mystery on Maui ◆ 1998
144. The E-Mail Mystery ◆ 1998
145. The Missing Horse Mystery ◆ 1998
146. The Ghost of the Lantern Lady ◆ 1998
147. The Case of the Captured Queen ◆ 1998
148. On the Trail of Trouble ◆ 1999
149. The Clue of the Gold Doubloons ◆ 1999
150. Mystery at Moorsea Manor ◆ 1999
151. The Chocolate-Covered Contest ◆ 1999

152. The Key in the Satin Pocket ◆ 1999
153. Whispers in the Fog ◆ 2000
154. The Legend of the Emerald Lady ◆ 2000
155. The Mystery in Tornado Alley ◆ 2000
156. The Secret in the Stars ◆ 2000
157. The Music Festival Mystery ◆ 2000
158. The Curse of the Black Cat ◆ 2001
159. The Secret of the Fiery Chamber ◆ 2001
160. The Clue on the Crystal Dove ◆ 2001
161. Lost in the Everglades ◆ 2001
162. The Case of the Lost Song ◆ 2001
163. The Clues Challenge ◆ 2001
164. The Mystery of the Mother Wolf ◆ 2002
165. The Crime Lab Case ◆ 2002
166. The Case of the Creative Crime ◆ 2002
167. Mystery By Moonlight ◆ 2002
168. The Bike Tour Mystery ◆ 2002
169. The Mistletoe Mystery ◆ 2002
170. No Strings Attached ◆ 2002
171. Intrigue at the Grand Opera ◆ 2003
172. The Riding Club Crime ◆ 2003
173. Danger on the Great Lakes ◆ 2003
174. A Taste of Danger ◆ 2003
175. Werewolf in a Winter Wonderland ◆ 2003

NANCY DREW: GIRL DETECTIVE

Keene, Carolyn

SIMON & SCHUSTER ◆ GRADES 4–7 ◆ A/R

MYSTERY

This updated series puts Nancy into more contemporary situations. She finds the money that is missing from the Bucks for Charity race. She is chosen to appear in a film and then ends the sabotage that is plaguing the production.

1. Without a Trace ◆ 2004
2. A Race Against Time ◆ 2004
3. False Notes ◆ 2004
4. High Risk ◆ 2004
5. Lights, Camera . . . ◆ 2004
6. Action! ◆ 2004
7. The Stolen Relic ◆ 2004
8. The Scarlet Macaw Scandal ◆ 2004
9. Secret of the Spa ◆ 2005
10. Uncivil Acts ◆ 2005
11. Riverboat Ruse ◆ 2005
12. Stop the Clock ◆ 2005

13. Trade Wind Danger ◆ 2005
14. Bad Times, Big Crimes ◆ 2005
15. Framed ◆ 2005
16. Dangerous Plays ◆ 2006
17. En Garde ◆ 2006
18. Pit of Vipers ◆ 2006
19. The Orchid Thief ◆ 2006
20. Getting Burned ◆ 2006
21. Close Encounters ◆ 2006
22. Dressed to Steal ◆ 2007
23. Troubled Waters ◆ 2007
24. Murder on the Set ◆ 2007
25. Trails of Treachery ◆ 2007
26. Fishing for Clues ◆ 2007
27. Intruder ◆ 2007
28. Mardi Gras Masquerade ◆ 2008
29. The Stolen Bones ◆ 2008
30. Pageant Perfect Crime ◆ 2008
31. Perfect Cover ◆ 2008
32. Perfect Escape ◆ 2008
33. Secret Identity ◆ 2008

NANCY DREW: GIRL DETECTIVE SUPER MYSTERIES

1. Where's Nancy ◆ 2005
2. Once Upon a Crime ◆ 2006
3. Real Fake ◆ 2007

NANCY DREW AND THE CLUE CREW

Keene, Carolyn

ALADDIN ◆ GRADES 2–4 ◆ A/R

MYSTERY

In this permutation of the Nancy Drew mysteries, Nancy and her friends George and Bess are at River Heights Elementary. The mysteries include missing chicks from the school science project, stolen money from the mall, and disappearing Thanksgiving food. Younger readers will enjoy having their own Nancy Drew stories. Check out some other mystery series such as the A to Z Mysteries and the Cam Jansen Mysteries.

1. Sleepover Sleuths ◆ 2006
2. Scream for Ice Cream ◆ 2006
3. Pony Problems ◆ 2006
4. The Cinderella Ballet Mystery ◆ 2006
5. The Case of the Sneaky Snowman ◆ 2006
6. The Fashion Disaster ◆ 2007
7. The Circus Scare ◆ 2007
8. Lights, Camera . . . Cats! ◆ 2007

9. The Halloween Hoax ◆ 2007
10. Ticket Trouble ◆ 2007
11. Ski School Sneak ◆ 2007
12. Valentine's Day Secret ◆ 2007
13. Chick-napped! ◆ 2008
14. The Zoo Crew ◆ 2008
15. Mall Madness ◆ 2008
16. Thanksgiving Thief ◆ 2008
17. Wedding Day Disaster ◆ 2008

NANCY DREW GRAPHIC NOVELS

Petrucha, Stefan

PAPERCUTZ ◆ GRADES 4–8 ◆ A/R

MYSTERY

Nancy and her friends face all-new mysteries in this graphic novel series from Papercutz. Mysterious strangers, evil plots, kidnapping, theft, and more—all solved by our intrepid sleuth. The illustrations have a manga feel with bold lines, sharp angles, and emphasized eyes. Reluctant readers will be attracted to these books.

1. The Demon of River Heights ◆ 2005
2. Writ in Stone ◆ 2005
3. The Haunted Dollhouse ◆ 2005
4. The Girl Who Wasn't There ◆ 2006
5. The Fake Heir ◆ 2006
6. Mr. Cheeters Is Missing ◆ 2006
7. The Charmed Bracelet ◆ 2006
8. Global Warning ◆ 2007
9. Ghost in the Machinery ◆ 2007
10. The Disoriented Express ◆ 2007
11. Monkey-Wrench Blues ◆ 2007
12. Dress Reversal ◆ 2008
13. Doggone Town ◆ 2008
14. Sleight of Dan ◆ 2008
15. Tiger Counter ◆ 2008
16. What Goes Up . . . ◆ 2008

NANCY DREW NOTEBOOKS

Keene, Carolyn

SIMON & SCHUSTER ◆ GRADES 2–4 ◆ A/R

MYSTERY

In this Nancy Drew spin-off for younger readers, Nancy and her friends, the cousins George and Bess, are in third grade and already solving mysteries. In *The Funny Face Fight,* there is a class election coming up and Nancy and Bess end up on one girl's side while George is on another's. Someone starts to put mustaches on campaign posters, and accusations fly on both sides. Nancy writes down all the clues in her notebook and eventually finds the culprit. Broken friendships are mended and apologies are made. In other books, Nancy solves mysteries that come up as the girls are trick-or-treating, on a skiing trip, or having a slumber party.

1. The Slumber Party Secret ◆ 1994
2. The Lost Locket ◆ 1994
3. The Secret Santa ◆ 1994
4. The Bad Day for Ballet ◆ 1995
5. The Soccer Shoe Clue ◆ 1995
6. The Ice Cream Scoop ◆ 1995
7. Trouble at Camp Treehouse ◆ 1995
8. The Best Detective ◆ 1995
9. The Thanksgiving Surprise ◆ 1995
10. Not Nice on Ice ◆ 1996
11. The Pen Pal Puzzle ◆ 1996
12. The Puppy Problem ◆ 1996
13. The Wedding Gift Goof ◆ 1996
14. The Funny Face Fight ◆ 1996
15. The Crazy Key Clue ◆ 1996
16. The Ski Slope Mystery ◆ 1997
17. Whose Pet Is Best? ◆ 1997
18. The Stolen Unicorn ◆ 1997
19. The Lemonade Raid ◆ 1997
20. Hannah's Secret ◆ 1997
21. Princess on Parade ◆ 1997
22. The Clue in the Glue ◆ 1998
23. Alien in the Classroom ◆ 1998
24. The Hidden Treasures ◆ 1998
25. Dare at the Fair ◆ 1998
26. The Lucky Horseshoes ◆ 1998
27. Trouble Takes the Cake ◆ 1998
28. Thrill on the Hill ◆ 1999
29. Lights! Camera! Clues! ◆ 1999
30. It's No Joke! ◆ 1999
31. The Fine-Feathered Mystery ◆ 1999
32. The Black Velvet Mystery ◆ 1999
33. The Gumdrop Ghost ◆ 1999
34. Trash or Treasure? ◆ 2000
35. Third-Grade Reporter ◆ 2000
36. The Make-Believe Mystery ◆ 2000
37. Dude Ranch Detective ◆ 2000
38. Candy Is Dandy ◆ 2000
39. The Chinese New Year Mystery ◆ 2000
40. Dinosaur Alert! ◆ 2001
41. Flower Power ◆ 2001
42. Circus Act ◆ 2001

43. The Walkie-Talkie Mystery ◆ 2001
44. The Purple Fingerprint ◆ 2001
45. The Dashing Dog Mystery ◆ 2001
46. The Snow Queen's Surprise ◆ 2002
47. The Crook Who Took the Book ◆ 2002
48. Crazy Carnival Case ◆ 2002
49. Sand Castle Mystery ◆ 2002
50. The Scarytales Sleepover ◆ 2002
51. The Old-Fashioned Mystery ◆ 2002
52. Big Worry in Wonderland ◆ 2003
53. Recipe for Trouble ◆ 2003
54. The Stinky Cheese Surprise ◆ 2003
55. The Day Camp Disaster ◆ 2003
56. Turkey Trouble ◆ 2003
57. The Carousel Mystery ◆ 2004
58. The Dollhouse Mystery ◆ 2004
59. The Bike Race Mystery ◆ 2004
60. The Lighthouse Mystery ◆ 2004
61. Space Case ◆ 2004
62. The Secret in the Spooky Woods ◆ 2004
63. The Snowman Surprise ◆ 2004
64. The Bunny-Hop Hoax ◆ 2005
65. The Strike-Out Scare ◆ 2005
66. Zoo Clue ◆ 2005
67. The Singing Suspects ◆ 2005
68. The Apple Bandit ◆ 2005
69. The Kitten Caper ◆ 2005

NASCAR POLE POSITION ADVENTURES

Calhoun, T. B.

HARPERCOLLINS ◆ GRADES 5–8

REAL LIFE | RECREATION

This series should appeal to stock-car racing enthusiasts. Kin Travis is 15. Along with his sister Laura and his brother Laptop, Kin is involved in adventures involving cars, mysteries, and high-speed action. Throughout the books, there is information about stock cars and NASCAR racing events. The Travis kids are helped by their grandfather, Hotshoe Hunter, a famous stock-car racer. His knowledge about racing and his connections with other racers give Kin and his siblings an up-close look at these exciting events.

1. Rolling Thunder ◆ 1998
2. In the Groove ◆ 1998
3. Race Ready ◆ 1998
4. Speed Demon ◆ 1999

5. Spinout ◆ 1999
6. Hammer Down ◆ 1999

NASCAR RACERS

Various authors

HARPERCOLLINS ◆ GRADES 3–5

REAL LIFE | RECREATION

NASCAR racing is one of the most popular sports in America. In these books, Team Fastex is driving in the Unlimited Series, which features fast, high-tech cars. Unfortunately, Team Rexcor is determined to win no matter what the cost or the danger.

1. The Fast Lane (Bright, J. E.) ◆ 2000
2. Taking the Lead (Teitelbaum, Michael) ◆ 2000
3. Tundra 2000 (Whitman, John) ◆ 2000
4. Daredevil (Bright, J. E.) ◆ 2000
5. All or Nothing (Bright, J. E.) ◆ 2000
6. Chain Reaction (Gilden, Mel) ◆ 2001
7. Red Flag (Teitelbaum, Michael) ◆ 2001
8. High Stakes (Bright, J. E.) ◆ 2001

NATE THE GREAT

Sharmat, Marjorie Weinman

DELACORTE; BANTAM DOUBLEDAY DELL ◆ GRADES 1–3 ◆ A/R

HUMOR | MYSTERY

Nate the Great solves mysteries around the neighborhood with his loyal dog Sludge. An avid pancake eater and deep thinker, Nate leads the reader through each step in solving a mystery. Written in the first person, this series has an easy format with simple sentences for young readers. However, these simple sentences relate Nate's intricate thought processes and wry observations.

1. Nate the Great ◆ 1972
2. Nate the Great Goes Undercover ◆ 1974
3. Nate the Great and the Lost List ◆ 1975
4. Nate the Great and the Phony Clue ◆ 1977
5. Nate the Great and the Sticky Case ◆ 1978
6. Nate the Great and the Missing Key ◆ 1981
7. Nate the Great and the Snowy Trail ◆ 1982
8. Nate the Great and the Fishy Prize ◆ 1985
9. Nate the Great Stalks Stupidweed ◆ 1986
10. Nate the Great and the Boring Beach Bag ◆ 1987
11. Nate the Great Goes Down in the Dumps ◆ 1989

12. Nate the Great and the Halloween Hunt ◆ 1989
13. Nate the Great and the Musical Note ◆ 1990
14. Nate the Great and the Stolen Base ◆ 1992
15. Nate the Great and the Pillowcase ◆ 1993
16. Nate the Great and the Mushy Valentine ◆ 1994
17. Nate the Great and the Tardy Tortoise ◆ 1995
18. Nate the Great and the Crunchy Christmas ◆ 1996
19. Nate the Great Saves the King of Sweden ◆ 1997
20. Nate the Great and Me: The Case of the Fleeing Fang ◆ 1998
21. Nate the Great and the Monster Mess ◆ 2001
22. Nate the Great, San Francisco Detective ◆ 2000
23. Nate the Great and the Big Sniff ◆ 2001
24. Nate the Great on the Owl Express ◆ 2003
25. Nate the Great Talks Turkey ◆ 2006

NATIONAL PARKS MYSTERY *see* Mysteries in Our National Parks

NEPTUNE ADVENTURES

Saunders, Susan

AVON ◆ GRADES 4–7

ADVENTURE | REAL LIFE

Dana Chapin and her cousin Tyler participate in Project Neptune, a resource designed to protect sea life from environmental threats. They also deal with the behavior of people whose greed or lack of knowledge puts sea creatures at risk. The two cousins help clean up after an oil spill; they come to the aid of a school of pilot whales; they protect a dolphin that has been released into the ocean. This series will appeal to readers who like to see characters like themselves taking action to help others and change the world.

1. Danger on Crab Island ◆ 1998
2. Disaster at Parson's Point ◆ 1998
3. The Dolphin Trap ◆ 1998
4. Stranding on Cedar Point ◆ 1998
5. Hurricane Rescue ◆ 1998
6. Red Tide Alert ◆ 1998

NEVER LAND

Barry, Dave, and Ridley Pearson

DISNEY ◆ GRADES 4–7

FANTASY | ADVENTURE

Considerably shorter than the Peter and the Starcatchers books, the adventures in these books happen while Peter is away but involve his Lost Boys, Captain Hook, and other familiar characters. In the first book, Princess Little Scallop of the Mollusk tribe goes exploring in the sea with her mermaid friends, Aqua and Surf. When they are quite far from Mollusk Island, Surf is captured by a gang of greedy men. The Lost Boys join in the rescue.

1. Escape from the Carnivale: A Never Land Book ◆ 2006
2. Cave of the Dark Wind: A Never Land Book ◆ 2007
3. Blood Tide: A Never Land Book ◆ 2008

NEVER SINK NINE

Davis, Gibbs

BANTAM DOUBLEDAY DELL ◆ GRADES 3–4

REAL LIFE | RECREATION

The Never Sink Nine series is centered around a group of baseball-loving kids. After Walter fails to make the fourth-grade team, he decides to create his own team. Walter's grandfather, who used to play in the minors, is their coach. The children learn to cooperate and begin to understand each other as the team competes. For example, Walter realizes that Melissa's collection of plastic horses is as important to her as his special socks are to him. Each book in the series contains an entire game.

1. Walter's Lucky Socks ◆ 1991
2. Major-League Melissa ◆ 1991
3. Slugger Mike ◆ 1991
4. Pete the Magnificent ◆ 1991
5. Tony's Double Play ◆ 1992
6. Christy's Magic Glove ◆ 1992
7. Olympic Otis ◆ 1993
8. Katie Kicks Off ◆ 1994
9. Diamond Park Dinosaur ◆ 1994
10. Pinheads, Unite! ◆ 1994

THE NEW BOBBSEY TWINS *see* Bobbsey Twins: The New Bobbsey Twins

NEXT GENERATION: STARFLEET ACADEMY *see* Star Trek: The Next Generation: Starfleet Academy

NFL MONDAY NIGHT FOOTBALL CLUB

Korman, Gordon

HYPERION ◆ GRADES 4–7 ◆ A/R

FANTASY | RECREATION

When Nick, 11, puts on an old football jersey, he is transported into the body of John Elway—right in the middle of a Monday Night Football game! Then, when Elliot tries on the jersey, he becomes Barry Sanders. Even Nick's sister Hilary puts on the jersey and is transformed—into Junior Seau. Football fans will like the action and humor of this series.

1. Quarterback Exchange: I Was John Elway ◆ 1997
2. Running Back Conversion: I Was Barry Sanders ◆ 1997
3. Super Brown Switch: I Was Dan Marino ◆ 1997
4. Heavy Artillery: I Was Junior Seau ◆ 1997
5. Ultimate Scoring Machine: I Was Jerry Rice ◆ 1998

THE NIC-NACS AND THE NIC-NAC NEWS

Nixon, Joan Lowery

YEARLING ◆ GRADES 2–4

MYSTERY | REAL LIFE

Four friends decide to create a neighborhood newspaper. They call themselves the Nic-Nacs because of their names—Nicone (Nic), Nelson (N), Amy (A), and Carlos (C). As they do research for the newspaper, they solve simple mysteries.

1. The Mystery Box ◆ 1991
2. Watch Out for Dinosaurs! ◆ 1991
3. The Honeycutt Street Celebrities ◆ 1991
4. The Haunted House on Honeycutt Street ◆ 1991

NICKELODEON ARE YOU AFRAID OF THE DARK? *see* Are You Afraid of the Dark?

NICKI HOLLAND

Hunt, Angela Elwell

THOMAS NELSON ◆ GRADES 5–6 ◆ A/R

MYSTERY

Nicki Holland and her best friends—Laura, Kim, Christine, and Meredith—solve mysteries together in this series. Sometimes the setting is at school, as in *The Case of the Terrified Track Star,* and sometimes they must save themselves from danger, as in *The Case of the Counterfeit Cash.* Regardless of where the puzzle begins, Nicki's resourceful and courageous actions always aid in solving the mystery.

1. The Case of the Mystery Mark ◆ 1991
2. The Case of the Phantom Friend ◆ 1991
3. The Case of the Teenager Terminator ◆ 1991
4. The Case of the Terrified Track Star ◆ 1992
5. The Case of the Counterfeit Cash ◆ 1992
6. The Case of the Haunting of Lowell Lanes ◆ 1992
7. The Case of the Birthday Bracelet ◆ 1993
8. The Secret of Cravenhill Castle ◆ 1993
9. The Riddle of Baby Rosalind ◆ 1993

THE NIGHT BEFORE . . .

Wing, Natasha

PENGUIN ◆ GRADES K–2 ◆ A/R

HUMOR

The classic poem "The Night Before Christmas" serves as the model for these picture books featuring other "night before" experiences. Anticipating the start of first grade, going to summer camp, and the arrival of a new baby are among the fun events in these rhyming stories. Lively illustrations by different illustrators add to the fun.

1. The Night Before Easter ◆ 1999
2. The Night Before Halloween ◆ 1999
3. The Night Before Kindergarten ◆ 2001
4. The Night Before Thanksgiving ◆ 2001
5. The Night Before Valentine's Day ◆ 2001
6. The Night Before Summer Vacation ◆ 2002
7. The Night Before the New Baby ◆ 2002
8. The Night Before the Night Before Christmas ◆ 2002
9. The Night Before the Tooth Fairy ◆ 2003
10. The Night Before First Grade ◆ 2005
11. The Night Before the 100th Day of School ◆ 2005
12. The Night Before Summer Camp ◆ 2007

NIGHTMARE ROOM

Stine, R. L.

AVON ◆ GRADES 4–7 ◆ A/R

HORROR

These stories are somewhat scary, with elements of mystery, the supernatural, and aliens. In *Liar, Liar,* Ross Arthur goes to a party and sees his twin. One problem—he does not have a twin. In another book, Alex Smith's blank journal is being written in, but not by Alex. When Alex reads the journal, he realizes he is learning about the future. Fans of creepy stories will enjoy these.

1. Don't Forget Me! ◆ 2000
2. Locker 13 ◆ 2000
3. My Name Is Evil ◆ 2000
4. Liar, Liar ◆ 2000
5. Dear Diary, I'm Dead ◆ 2001
6. They Call Me Creature ◆ 2001
7. The Howler ◆ 2001
8. Shadow Girl ◆ 2001
9. Camp Nowhere ◆ 2001
10. Full Moon Halloween ◆ 2001
11. Scare School ◆ 2001
12. Visitors ◆ 2001

NIGHTMARE ROOM THRILLOGY

Stine, R. L.

AVON ◆ GRADES 4–7 ◆ A/R

HORROR

More chills and thrills in the Nightmare Room, where it is not safe to be alone.

1. Fear Games ◆ 2001
2. What Scares You the Most? ◆ 2001
3. No Survivors ◆ 2001

NIGHTMARES! HOW WILL YOURS END?

Wulffson, Don L.

PRICE STERN SLOAN ◆ GRADES 4–7

HORROR

Your father and brother are missing in the jungles of Malaysia—which way do you choose to go? Or, you are on Earth but it has been invaded by aliens—what will you do? Readers are given scary situations and make choices to create different endings.

1. Castle of Horror ◆ 1995
2. Cave of Fear ◆ 1995
3. Planet of Terror ◆ 1995
4. Valley of the Screaming Statues ◆ 1995

NOAH

Topek, Susan Remick

KAR-BEN ◆ GRADES K–1

FAMILY LIFE

Noah is a likable young boy. His concerns are common, such as not knowing what kind of costume to wear for a holiday and worrying about disliking a certain Passover food. His classmates and teacher help him to feel comfortable and decide what to do. This series is easy to read and has friendly, bright illustrations.

1. A Holiday for Noah ◆ 1990
2. A Turn for Noah ◆ 1992
3. A Taste for Noah ◆ 1993
4. A Costume for Noah ◆ 1995

NOMES *see* Bromeliad

NORA

Ichikawa, Satomi

PHILOMEL ◆ GRADES 1–3

ADVENTURE | FANTASY

Author/illustrator Ichikawa invites readers into Nora's whimsical world in this enchanting series. Nora—with her dog, stuffed bear, and doll as faithful companions—turns any day or situation into an adventure. For example, a day spent inside with a cold turns exciting when friendly rose people appear and entertain her.

1. Nora's Castle ◆ 1986
2. Nora's Stars ◆ 1989
3. Nora's Duck ◆ 1991
4. Nora's Roses ◆ 1993
5. Nora's Surprise ◆ 1994

NORA AND TEDDY *see* Riverside Kids: Nora and Teddy

NORBY

Asimov, Janet, and Isaac Asimov

WALKER & CO. ◆ GRADES 5–7 ◆ A/R

ADVENTURE | SCIENCE FICTION

Jeff Wells is a student at the Space Academy. He buys Norby as a teaching robot, but he soon discovers that Norby is unique. Norby has many useful abilities because he was fashioned from salvaged spaceship parts. In each novel, Jeff and Norby become involved in intergalactic intrigue. Often they must help Jeff's older, but not wiser, brother Fargo and save the galaxy. Science fiction, humor, and believable characters work well together in this entertaining series.

1. Norby, the Mixed-Up Robot ◆ 1983
2. Norby's Other Secret ◆ 1984
3. Norby and the Lost Princess ◆ 1985
4. Norby and the Invaders ◆ 1985
5. Norby and the Queen's Necklace ◆ 1986
6. Norby Finds a Villain ◆ 1987
7. Norby Down to Earth ◆ 1989
8. Norby and Yobo's Great Adventure ◆ 1989
9. Norby and the Oldest Dragon ◆ 1990
10. Norby and the Court Jester ◆ 1991
11. Norby and the Terrified Taxi ◆ 1997

NORTHERN FRIGHTS

Slade, Arthur G.

ORCA ◆ GRADES 5–8 ◆ A/R

FANTASY

Exciting adventures are interwoven with Norse mythology in this Canadian series. On Drang Island off the coast of British Columbia, Michael, 15, meets Fiona and together they encounter ghosts, spirits, and other dangers. This could be a good choice for R. L. Stine fans.

1. The Haunting of Drang Island ◆ 1998
2. Draugr ◆ 1998
3. The Loki Wolf ◆ 2000

NORY RYAN

Giff, Patricia Reilly

DELACORTE; RANDOM HOUSE ◆ GRADES 5–8 ◆ A/R

HISTORICAL

Strong, resourceful, heroic, determined, courageous. These are just a few of the words to describe Nory Ryan. As this series begins, Nory, 12, is coping with the impact of the failure of the potato crop in Ireland in 1845. With Da (her father) at sea trying to earn money, the family is hungry and facing eviction. Nory looks for ways to support them, showing resilience and ingenuity. In *Maggie's Door*, Nory is sailing to America to join her sister in Brooklyn. Details about the voyage—filthy conditions, inadequate food, abusive passengers—accurately portray the experiences of many immigrants. Nory's friend, Sean Red Mallon, helps her deal with the difficulties. The third book, *Water Street,* focuses on Bridget (Bird) Mallon, who is Nory and Sean's youngest daughter.

1. Nory Ryan's Song ◆ 2000
2. Maggie's Door ◆ 2003
3. Water Street ◆ 2006

NOSE PICKERS FROM OUTER SPACE

Korman, Gordon
HYPERION ◆ GRADES 3–5 ◆ A/R
FANTASY | HUMOR

Devin is eager to meet his new exchange student buddy. Too bad! Stan is not what he hoped for. Stan is nerdy and has some gross personal habits. And one more thing—Stan is an alien from Pan. This is part of the L.A.F. imprint from Hyperion that should appeal to fans of Dav Pilkey.

1. Nose Pickers from Outer Space ◆ 1999
2. Planet of the Nose Pickers ◆ 2000
3. Your Mummy Is a Nose Picker ◆ 2000
4. Invasion of the Nose Pickers ◆ 2001

NUTTY NUTSELL

Hughes, Dean
ATHENEUM ◆ GRADES 4–6 ◆ A/R
HUMOR | REAL LIFE

"Nutty" Nutsell is a typical suburban fifth-grade boy when he is introduced in the first book of this series. However, when he meets William Bilks, Boy Genius, his life changes. Everyday situations are transformed into adventures as William challenges Nutty to try new things and stretch his mind to accomplish more. Each book develops the strong bond of friendship between Nutty and William. Together they take on the challenges of their school and begin to understand life.

1. Nutty for President ◆ 1981
2. Nutty and the Case of the Mastermind Thief ◆ 1985
3. Nutty and the Case of the Ski-Slope Spy ◆ 1985
4. Nutty Can't Miss ◆ 1987
5. Nutty Knows All ◆ 1988
6. Nutty, the Movie Star ◆ 1989
7. Nutty's Ghost ◆ 1993
8. Re-elect Nutty! ◆ 1995

OBADIAH STARBUCK

Turkle, Brinton

VIKING ◆ GRADES K–3

FAMILY LIFE | HISTORICAL

Obadiah Starbuck is an energetic and irrepressible Quaker boy who lives in early 19th-century Nantucket. In one book, his parents admonish him for telling wildly exaggerated tales. In another, he decides that the wild life of a pirate is not what he wants. Whatever the situation, Obadiah and his family are likable, and the warm illustrations add to the cozy family atmosphere of this bygone time.

1. Obadiah the Bold ◆ 1965
2. Thy Friend, Obadiah ◆ 1969
3. Adventures of Obadiah ◆ 1972
4. Rachel and Obadiah ◆ 1978

OCTONAUTS

Meomi

IMMEDIUM ◆ GRADES K–1

FANTASY

There are eight Octonauts and they live under the water in their Octopod. They spend their time on adventures, searching for treasure, and having fun. There are underlying messages in the books about friendship, individuality, attitude, and imagination.

1. The Octonauts and the Only Lonely Monster ◆ 2006
2. The Octonauts and the Sea of Shade ◆ 2007
3. The Octonauts and the Frown Fish ◆ 2008

O'DWYER AND GRADY

Heyes, Eileen

ALADDIN ◆ GRADES 4–6 ◆ A/R

MYSTERY | HISTORICAL

Set in the 1930s, these mysteries feature Billy O'Dwyer, 11, and Virginia Grady, also 11. Both are child actors during the early years of the movie business. In the first book, they try to prove the innocence of Billy's friend Roscoe Muldoon, an actor who has been accused of the murder of an actress. In the second book, the two find a skeleton in an abandoned house. There are details about the era and about the experiences of child actors in movies.

1. O'Dwyer and Grady Starring in Acting Innocent ◆ 2002
2. O'Dwyer and Grady Starring in Tough Act to Follow ◆ 2003
3. O'Dwyer and Grady Starring in the Missing Reel ◆ 2004

OKOMI

Dorman, Helen

DAWN PUBLICATIONS ◆ **GRADES K–1** ◆ **A/R**

REAL LIFE

Jane Goodall's research on chimpanzees inspired these books. Okomi is a baby chimp exhibiting all the curiosity and playfulness of real chimps. He explores the world around him and learns new behaviors like climbing a tree and playing in the leaves. His mother, Mama Du, is usually nearby watching him learn and ready to help. Young children will find these books reassuring and instructive.

1. Okomi the New Baby ◆ 2003
2. Okomi and the Tickling Game ◆ 2003
3. Okomi Plays in the Leaves ◆ 2003
4. Okomi Climbs a Tree ◆ 2003
5. Okomi Enjoys His Outings ◆ 2004
6. Okomi Wakes Up Early ◆ 2004
7. Okomi Goes "Fishing" ◆ 2004
8. Okomi Wanders Too Far ◆ 2004

OLD BEAR STORIES

Hissey, Jane

PHILOMEL ◆ **GRADES K–2** ◆ **A/R**

FANTASY

Have you ever wondered what toys do when kids aren't around? In this series, they have adventures of their own. Teddy bears and other stuffed animals play games, have parties, and travel to the beach. The books are divided into individual stories, with poems interspersed. There are related board books.

1. Old Bear ◆ 1986
2. Old Bear Tales ◆ 1988
3. Little Bear Lost ◆ 1989
4. Little Bear's Trousers ◆ 1990

OLD TURTLE

Kessler, Leonard

GREENWILLOW ◆ **GRADES K–3**

ANIMAL FANTASY | **HUMOR**

These are lovable stories about Old Turtle and his various animal friends, for students just beginning to read alone. They learn good sportsmanship when they play soccer and other games, write riddle and joke books, and generally have a good time.

1. Old Turtle's Baseball Stories ◆ 1982
2. Old Turtle's Winter Games ◆ 1983
3. Old Turtle's Soccer Team ◆ 1988

OLD WITCH

DeLage, Ida

GARRARD ◆ **GRADES K–2**

FANTASY | **HUMOR**

Students just beginning to read alone will enjoy these humorous stories about the Old Witch and how she solves her problems by tricking people.

1. The Farmer and the Witch ◆ 1966
2. Weeny Witch ◆ 1968
3. The Old Witch Goes to the Ball ◆ 1969
4. The Old Witch and the Snores ◆ 1970
5. What Does a Witch Need? ◆ 1971
6. Beware! Beware! A Witch Won't Share ◆ 1972
7. The Old Witch and the Wizard ◆ 1974
8. The Old Witch's Party ◆ 1976
9. The Old Witch and the Ghost Parade ◆ 1978
10. The Old Witch and Her Magic Basket ◆ 1978
11. The Old Witch and the Dragon ◆ 1979
12. The Old Witch Finds a New House ◆ 1979
13. The Old Witch Gets a Surprise ◆ 1981
14. The Old Witch and the Crows ◆ 1983

OLGA DA POLGA

Bond, Michael

MACMILLAN ◆ **GRADES 3–5**

ANIMAL FANTASY | **HUMOR**

Olga da Polga is a resourceful and imaginative guinea pig who goes to live with kind and loving humans who build her a wonderful home and take good care of her. In this series full of exaggerated tales of her life, she finds an appreciative audience in Noel, the cat; Fangio, the hedgehog; and other animal friends. Various adventures include an escape into the neighborhood, a visit from Santa, and another more-ominous experience with the dreaded "Surrey Puma." Olga's tall tales often get her in trouble, but she is seldom abashed for long.

1. The Tales of Olga da Polga ◆ 1971
2. Olga Meets Her Match ◆ 1973
3. Olga Carries On ◆ 1977
4. Olga Takes Charge ◆ 1982

OLIVER AND AMANDA PIG

Van Leeuwen, Jean

DIAL; PUFFIN ◆ GRADES K–2 ◆ A/R

ANIMAL FANTASY | FAMILY LIFE

Oliver Pig and his little sister Amanda have experiences that many siblings will identify with in this easy-reading series. Though Oliver can be bossy and Amanda can be a pest, in the end they always learn to get along. Their adventures include celebrating holidays and going to school.

1. Tales of Oliver Pig ◆ 1979
2. More Tales of Oliver Pig ◆ 1981
3. Amanda Pig and Her Big Brother Oliver ◆ 1982
4. Tales of Amanda Pig ◆ 1983
5. More Tales of Amanda Pig ◆ 1985
6. Oliver, Amanda, and Grandmother Pig ◆ 1987
7. Oliver and Amanda's Christmas ◆ 1989
8. Oliver Pig at School ◆ 1990
9. Amanda Pig on Her Own ◆ 1991
10. Oliver and Amanda's Halloween ◆ 1992
11. Oliver and Amanda and the Big Snow ◆ 1995
12. Amanda Pig, School Girl ◆ 1997
13. Amanda Pig and Her Best Friend Lollipop ◆ 1998
14. Oliver and Albert, Friends Forever ◆ 2000
15. Oliver the Mighty Pig ◆ 2003
16. Amanda Pig and the Awful Scary Monster ◆ 2004
17. Amanda Pig and the Really Hot Day ◆ 2005
18. Oliver Pig and the Best Fort Ever ◆ 2006
19. Amanda Pig, First Grader ◆ 2007
20. Amanda Pig and the Wiggly Tooth ◆ 2007

OLIVIA

Falconer, Ian

ATHENEUM ◆ **GRADES K–2** ◆ **A/R**

ANIMAL FANTASY

Olivia is a creative, independent pig. These books detail her energetic spirit. When her toy is missing, she searches for it and discovers that the dog is chewing on it. She takes her toy, fixes it a bit, and goes to the bed with her toy . . . and the dog. Falconer's illustrations capture Olivia's many moods. The first book received a Caldecott Honor medal. There are lots of related materials including board books, stationery, and magnets.

1. Olivia ◆ 2001
2. Olivia Saves the Circus ◆ 2002
3. Olivia and the Missing Toy ◆ 2003
4. Olivia Forms a Band ◆ 2006
5. Olivia Helps with Christmas ◆ 2007

OLIVIA KIDNEY

Potter, Ellen

PHILOMEL ◆ **GRADES 3–6** ◆ **A/R**

FANTASY

Because her father keeps losing his job, Olivia Kidney, 12, is always the new kid. Her new home is an apartment building in New York City where her father is the superintendent. As she meets the unusual residents, including a ghost, Olivia's loneliness is assuaged. In the second book, Olivia starts out in another new home. In the fourth book, Olivia is adjusting to a new school. *Olivia Kidney and the Exit Academy* was reissued in 2006 as *Olivia Kidney Stops for No One*.

1. Olivia Kidney ◆ 2003
2. Olivia Kidney and the Exit Academy ◆ 2005
3. Olivia Kidney Hot on the Trail ◆ 2006
4. Olivia Kidney and the Secret Beneath the City ◆ 2007

OLIVIA SHARP, AGENT FOR SECRETS

Sharmat, Marjorie Weinman, and Mitchell Sharmat

DELACORTE ◆ **GRADES K–3** ◆ **A/R**

REAL LIFE

Olivia Sharp is a "poor" rich girl . . . poor because she spends so much time on her own while her rich parents travel and party. To pass the time, Olivia decides to help people with "secret" problems. Originally published in the 1990s, the books were reissued in Aladdin paperbacks in 2005 with a cover design indicating that Olivia is Nate the Great's cousin; however these books are not mysteries, they are realistic stories about kids and their everyday concerns.

1. The Pizza Monster ◆ 1989
2. The Princess of Fillmore Street School ◆ 1989
3. The Sly Spy ◆ 1990
4. The Green Toenails Gang ◆ 1991

OMAKAYAS

Erdrich, Louise

HYPERION; HARPERCOLLINS ◆ GRADES 5–8

HISTORICAL

In the late 1840s, a young Ojibwa girl named Omakayas is living a contented life on an island on Lake Superior. Then smallpox hits the village and Omakayas, who was exposed as a baby, is the only one able to nurse the others but she cannot save them all. In the second book, the Ojibwa face eviction from their homes by white men, and the third book finds them searching for a home, facing a freezing winter and near-starvation. The details of Ojibwa life will appeal to fans of Laura Ingalls Wilder's books.

1. The Birchbark House ◆ 1999
2. The Game of Silence ◆ 2005
3. The Porcupine Year ◆ 2008

ON THE RUN

Korman, Gordon

SCHOLASTIC ◆ GRADES 5–8 ◆ A/R

ADVENTURE

After Frank Lindenaur, a CIA agent, disappeared, Meg and Aiden Falconer's parents were investigated and convicted of treason. Meg and Aiden are placed in a juvenile detention center, but they escape and begin their search for evidence to prove their parents' innocence. There are close calls and narrow escapes; Meg and Aiden are betrayed at every turn. They face danger not only from the FBI but also from a mysterious man who seems intent on stopping their search at any cost. Their adventure continues in the Kidnapped series.

1. Chasing the Falconers ◆ 2005
2. The Fugitive Factor ◆ 2005

3. Now You See Them, Now You Don't ◆ 2005
4. The Stowaway Solution ◆ 2005
5. Public Enemies ◆ 2005
6. Hunting the Hunter ◆ 2006

ON TIME'S WING

Various authors

ROUSSAN ◆ GRADES 5–8 ◆ A/R

HISTORICAL

This series features well-researched historical novels. In *Living Freight,* Emma has been orphaned and is waiting to go to the workhouse. Instead, she boards a ship sailing from England to Canada. Once in Canada, she tries to sell her mother's ring to fund her journey to British Columbia, where she hopes to look for gold. The ring brings Emma to the father she believed was dead. Each book features intrepid young teens who overcome obstacles.

1. Home Child (Haworth-Attard, Barbara) ◆ 1991
2. Candles (Kositsky, Lynne) ◆ 1996
3. Dark of the Moon (Haworth-Attard, Barbara) ◆ 1996
4. Living Freight (Campbell, Gaetz Dayle) ◆ 1998
5. Love-Lies-Bleeding (Haworth-Attard, Barbara) ◆ 1999
6. Rebecca's Flame (Kositsky, Lynne) ◆ 1999
7. Run for Your Life (Alexander, Wilma E.) ◆ 1999
8. Sunflower Diary (Boraks-Nemetz, Lillian) ◆ 1999
9. Danger in Disguise (Downie, Mary Alice) ◆ 2001
10. In Search of Klondike Gold (Wilson, Lynda) ◆ 2001
11. The Lenski File (Boraks-Nemetz, Lillian) ◆ 2001
12. Virtual Zone: Titanic's Race to Disaster (Wilson, Lynda) ◆ 2001

ONCE UPON AMERICA

Various authors

VIKING; PUFFIN ◆ GRADES 3–6 ◆ A/R

HISTORICAL

This historical fiction series is written by several authors, including Zibby Oneal, Kathleen V. Kudlinski, and Barthe deClements. Each book uses fictional characters to relate dramatic events from American history. Events such as the bombing of Pearl Harbor, the Alaskan gold rush, the Johnstown Flood, and the polio epidemic are brought to life through the eyes of people who were touched by them. This series would be a good one to share with readers of the American Girl books, Girlhood Diaries, and Dear America series.

1. Hannah's Fancy Notions: A Story of Industrial New England (Ross, Pat) ◆ 1988
2. Hero Over Here: A Story of World War I (Kudlinski, Kathleen V.) ◆ 1990
3. A Long Way to Go: A Story of Women's Right to Vote (Oneal, Zibby) ◆ 1990
4. It's Only Goodbye: An Immigrant Story (Gross, Virginia T.) ◆ 1990
5. The Day It Rained Forever: A Story of the Johnstown Flood (Gross, Virginia T.) ◆ 1991
6. Pearl Harbor Is Burning! A Story of World War II (Kudlinski, Kathleen V.) ◆ 1991
7. The Bite of the Gold Bug: A Story of the Alaskan Gold Rush (DeClements, Barthe) ◆ 1992
8. Child Star: When Talkies Came to Hollywood (Weaver, Lydia) ◆ 1992
9. Fire! The Beginnings of the Labor Movement (Goldin, Barbara Diamond) ◆ 1992
10. Close to Home: A Story of the Polio Epidemic (Weaver, Lydia) ◆ 1993
11. Earthquake! A Story of Old San Francisco (Kudlinski, Kathleen V.) ◆ 1993
12. Hard Times: A Story of the Great Depression (Antle, Nancy) ◆ 1993
13. Night Bird: A Story of the Seminole Indians (Kudlinski, Kathleen V.) ◆ 1993
14. The President Is Dead: A Story of the Kennedy Assassination (Gross, Virginia T.) ◆ 1993
15. Tough Choices: A Story of the Vietnam War (Antle, Nancy) ◆ 1993
16. Facing West: A Story of the Oregon Trail (Kudlinski, Kathleen V.) ◆ 1994
17. Lone Star: A Story of the Texas Rangers (Kudlinski, Kathleen V.) ◆ 1994
18. Red Means Good Fortune: A Story of San Francisco's Chinatown (Goldin, Barbara Diamond) ◆ 1994
19. Beautiful Land: A Story of the Oklahoma Land Rush (Antle, Nancy) ◆ 1994

ORMINGAT

Waugh, Sylvia
DELACORTE ◆ GRADES 5–8 ◆ A/R
FANTASY

Aliens from Ormingat living in England are collecting information on Earthlings and their behaviors. Each book in this series features a young person from Ormingat. In *Earthborn*, Nesta Gwynn, 12, learns a secret about her parents. They are aliens who are planning to return to Ormingat, but Nesta does not want to go.

1. Space Race ◆ 2000
2. Earthborn ◆ 2002
3. Who Goes Home ◆ 2004

ORP

Kline, Suzy

PUTNAM ◆ GRADES 4–6 ◆ A/R

HUMOR | REAL LIFE

Orp (Orville Rudemeyer Pygenski, Jr.) and his best friend Derrick are inseparable. When Derrick asks Orp to try out for the basketball team with him, Orp agrees—although he's not sure that he'll make it. Orp is a likable character whose experiences are common to junior high kids. He is loyal to his friends and is annoyed by his younger sister Chloe. Whether he's forming the "I Hate My Name Club" or the F.B.I. (Famous Bathtub Investigators), Orp turns everyday happenings into events.

1. Orp ◆ 1989
2. Orp and the Chop Suey Burgers ◆ 1990
3. Orp Goes to the Hoop ◆ 1991
4. Who's Orp's Girlfriend? ◆ 1993
5. Orp and the FBI ◆ 1995

ORPHAN TRAIN ADVENTURES

Nixon, Joan Lowery

DELACORTE ◆ GRADES 5–8 ◆ A/R

FAMILY LIFE | HISTORICAL

Originally published as a quartet of books, this series has been extended to relate more adventures of the Kelly children. The first book, *A Family Apart,* sets the stage for the series, which takes place in the mid-1800s. When their mother can no longer support them, the six Kelly children are sent from New York City to Missouri on an orphan train. They are placed with different farm families across the Great Plains. The series describes their experiences from the oldest, Frances Mary Kelly, to the youngest, Peaty. In *Caught in the Act,* Michael Patrick Kelly faces cruelty and a harsh life on a Missouri farm; in a later book, he becomes a Union soldier. Though orphan trains did exist, the characters and plots in this series are fictional.

1. A Family Apart ◆ 1987
2. Caught in the Act ◆ 1988
3. In the Face of Danger ◆ 1988
4. A Place to Belong ◆ 1989

5. A Dangerous Promise ◆ 1994

6. Keeping Secrets ◆ 1995

7. Circle of Love ◆ 1997

ORPHAN TRAIN CHILDREN

Nixon, Joan Lowery

DELACORTE ◆ GRADES 3–5 ◆ A/R

HISTORICAL

In the Orphan Train Adventures, Joan Lowery Nixon focused on the six children in the Kelly family. In the Orphan Train Children series, each book describes the circumstances of an individual child. There is no connection among the children other than their participation on the orphan trains. In *Aggie's Home,* Agatha Mae Vaughn gets a fresh start with the Bradons but there are adjustments along with the opportunities. David Howard, 11, arrives on a farm in Missouri knowing nothing about rural life and is aided by Amos, an ex-slave, in *David's Search*. Historical information, including documents and maps, follow each story.

1. Lucy's Wish ◆ 1998

2. Will's Choice ◆ 1998

3. Aggie's Home ◆ 1998

4. David's Search ◆ 1998

ORPHELINES

Carlson, Natalie Savage

BANTAM DOUBLEDAY DELL ◆ GRADES 3–4 ◆ A/R

FAMILY LIFE

The Orphelines series takes its name from the French word for girl orphans. Josine is the youngest of the 20 girls; Brigitte is known as the happiest. Madame Flattot takes care of them all and calls them her family. The girls consider the boys from the orphanage their brothers. This large family has many exciting times together. In one book, Josine finds a foundling baby boy whom they all want to adopt. Another time, they search for a grandmother to make their family complete. Their high spirits and imaginations sometimes get them into trouble, but matters are always resolved in a loving manner.

1. The Happy Orpheline ◆ 1957

2. A Brother for the Orphelines ◆ 1959

3. A Pet for the Orphelines ◆ 1962

4. The Orphelines in the Enchanted Castle ◆ 1964

5. A Grandmother for the Orphelines ◆ 1980

OSCAR J. NOODLEMAN

Manes, Stephen

DUTTON ◆ GRADES 3–5 ◆ A/R

HUMOR | SCIENCE FICTION

Oscar J. Noodleman has some of the world's strangest adventures in this series. It's not clear whether his world is the present or the future—it's more like a parallel universe. In one book, he has his own television network; in another, he eats his way across the United States with a crazy second cousin. These silly books are sure to tempt reluctant readers.

1. That Game from Outer Space ◆ 1983
2. The Oscar J. Noodleman Television Network ◆ 1984
3. Chicken Trek ◆ 1987

OSWALD (READY-TO-READ)

Various authors

SIMON SPOTLIGHT ◆ GRADES K–1 ◆ A/R

FANTASY

Oswald is a popular character in an animated show on Nickelodeon. Created by Dan Yaccarino and geared toward young children, Oswald is a blue octopus who is friends with Weenie, a hotdog; Henry, a penguin; and Daisy, a flower. This series of Ready to Read books presents a familiar character in a very easy to read format. In the first book, Henry is raking leaves but Oswald and Weenie want to play. There are also Oswald picture books for preschoolers.

1. Hooray for Fall! (Willson, Sarah) ◆ 2003
2. Ah-Choo! (Thorpe, Kiki) ◆ 2003
3. Oswald's Garden (Feldman, Heather) ◆ 2004

OTTO

Pene du Bois, William

VIKING ◆ GRADES 1–3

FANTASY

Otto is a world-famous giant dog. He has performed many heroic deeds that have earned him medals, such as catching some very bad men in Texas. Although Otto seems to be simply acting as any dog would, he is always in the right place at the right time. Otto and his master Duke sometimes find it difficult to relax because they are recognized wherever they go. Nevertheless, they enjoy helping the people they meet.

1. Giant Otto ◆ 1936
2. Otto at Sea ◆ 1936
3. Otto in Texas ◆ 1959
4. Otto in Africa ◆ 1961
5. Otto and the Magic Potatoes ◆ 1970

OTTO

Milgrim, David

ATHENEUM ◆ **GRADES K–2** ◆ **A/R**

FANTASY

Otto is a robot looking for adventure. He falls out of his spaceship and lands on Earth. There he meets many creatures including Peanut the Elephant and Flip and Flop the monkeys. This Ready-to-Read series will interest younger children.

1. See Otto ◆ 2002
2. Ride Otto Ride ◆ 2002
3. See Pip Point ◆ 2003
4. Swing Otto Swing! ◆ 2004
5. See Santa Nap ◆ 2004

OUTCAST

Golden, Christopher, and Thomas E. Sniegoski

ALADDIN ◆ **GRADES 4–7** ◆ **A/R**

FANTASY

Timothy is the son of a powerful mage. His father, now deceased, has kept Timothy hidden. Now Timothy has been discovered by Leader, a former apprentice, and he is introduced to the world of magic.

1. The Un-Magician ◆ 2004
2. Dragon Secrets ◆ 2004
3. Ghostfire ◆ 2005
4. Wurm War ◆ 2005

OUTER BANKS TRILOGY

Taylor, Theodore

DOUBLEDAY; HARPERCOLLINS ◆ **GRADES 5–8** ◆ **A/R**

ADVENTURE | **HISTORICAL**

This adventure trilogy is by the author of *The Cay*. Teetoncey is a frail young girl whom Ben helps rescue from a shipwreck. Many mysteries surround her. Later, as Ben searches for his brother, he discovers that their fates are more closely entwined than he first thought. HarperCollins reissued these books in 1995 with the following titles: *Stranger from the Sea: Teetoncey*; *Box of Treasures: Teetoncey and Ben O'Neal*; *Into the Wind: The Odyssey of Ben O'Neal*.

1. Teetoncey ◆ 1974
2. Teetoncey and Ben O'Neal ◆ 1975
3. The Odyssey of Ben O'Neal ◆ 1977

OUTRIDERS

Decter, Ed

ALADDIN ◆ GRADES 5–7 ◆ A/R

ADVENTURE

The Outriders are a group of 12-year-old friends who crave adventure and excitement. In *Expedition to Blue Cave,* they uncover a mystery involving stolen antiques. Before they can expose the thieves, Shelby's little sister is kidnapped. In *Expedition to Willow Key,* the friends first find chemical dumping and then alligator poachers. These are fast-paced, somewhat implausible adventure stories.

1. Expedition to Blue Cave ◆ 2007
2. Expedition to Willow Key ◆ 2007
3. Expedition to Pine Hollow ◆ 2007

OWEN FOOTE

Greene, Stephanie

CLARION ◆ GRADES 2–4 ◆ A/R

REAL LIFE

When this series begins, Owen is in second grade and is teased about being small. He tries weightlifting to improve his physique. He also stands up for himself with the school nurse. Later, Owen enters third grade where he eagerly participates in the science fair. Middle-elementary readers will enjoy these chapter books.

1. Owen Foote, Second Grade Strongman ◆ 1996
2. Owen Foote, Soccer Star ◆ 1998
3. Owen Foote, Frontiersman ◆ 1999
4. Owen Foote, Money Man ◆ 2000
5. Owen Foote, Super Spy ◆ 2001
6. Owen Foote, Mighty Scientist ◆ 2004

OWLY GRAPHIC NOVELS

Runton, Andy

TOP SHELF ◆ GRADES 1–4

ANIMAL FANTASY

Owly is a compassionate young owl. In the first book, he rescues Wormy
and the two become friends. In *Flying Lessons,* the two want to be friends
with a flying squirrel. Unfortunately, the squirrel is afraid of owls. When
Wormy is injured, the squirrel observes Owly caring for him and decides
to trust Owly too. The Owly books are not just graphic novels, they are
nearly wordless, making them accessible to children who may be struggling with their reading skills.

1. The Way Home and the Bittersweet Summer ◆ 2004
2. Just a Little Blue ◆ 2005
3. Flying Lessons ◆ 2005
4. A Time to Be Brave ◆ 2007
5. Tiny Tales ◆ 2008

OZ

Baum, Lyman Frank

MORROW; GREENWILLOW ◆ GRADES 4–8 ◆ A/R

FANTASY

The popular *Wizard of Oz* was only the first of a great many adventures
about the land of Oz, which were continued by others after Baum's
death. Dorothy returns many times and fights villains; and other children, such as Peter and Betsy Bobbins, find their way to the magical
land. The Tin Man and Scarecrow are involved in various battles for control of Oz, but Ozma of Oz is the rightful ruler. All the books share a
rich and detailed fantasy laced with satire. The first 15 books were written by L. Frank Baum. Other authors have extended the series. Greenwillow has reissued many of these titles in its Books of Wonder series.

ORIGINAL OZ BOOKS

1. The Wonderful Wizard of Oz ◆ 1900
2. The New Wizard of Oz ◆ 1903
3. The Marvelous Land of Oz ◆ 1904
4. Ozma of Oz ◆ 1907
5. Dorothy and the Wizard of Oz ◆ 1908
6. The Road to Oz ◆ 1909
7. The Emerald City of Oz ◆ 1910
8. The Patchwork Girl of Oz ◆ 1913
9. Tik-Tok of Oz ◆ 1914
10. The Scarecrow of Oz ◆ 1915
11. Rinktink in Oz ◆ 1916

12. The Lost Princess of Oz ◆ 1917
13. The Tin Woodman of Oz ◆ 1918
14. The Magic of Oz ◆ 1919
15. Glinda of Oz ◆ 1920

OZ CONTINUED

1. The Royal Book of Oz (Thompson, Ruth Plumly) ◆ 1921
2. The Cowardly Lion of Oz (Thompson, Ruth Plumly) ◆ 1923
3. Grampa in Oz (Thompson, Ruth Plumly) ◆ 1924
4. The Lost King of Oz (Thompson, Ruth Plumly) ◆ 1925
5. The Hungry Tiger in Oz (Thompson, Ruth Plumly) ◆ 1926
6. The Gnome King of Oz (Thompson, Ruth Plumly) ◆ 1927
7. The Giant Horse of Oz (Thompson, Ruth Plumly) ◆ 1928
8. Jack Pumpkinhead of Oz (Thompson, Ruth Plumly) ◆ 1929
9. The Yellow Knight of Oz (Thompson, Ruth Plumly) ◆ 1930
10. The Pirates in Oz (Thompson, Ruth Plumly) ◆ 1931
11. Purple Prince of Oz (Thompson, Ruth Plumly) ◆ 1932
12. Ojo in Oz (Thompson, Ruth Plumly) ◆ 1933
13. Speedy in Oz (Thompson, Ruth Plumly) ◆ 1934
14. Wishing Horse of Oz (Thompson, Ruth Plumly) ◆ 1935
15. Captain Salt in Oz (Thompson, Ruth Plumly) ◆ 1936
16. Kabumpo in Oz (Thompson, Ruth Plumly) ◆ 1936
17. Handy Mandy in Oz (Thompson, Ruth Plumly) ◆ 1937
18. The Silver Princess in Oz (Thompson, Ruth Plumly) ◆ 1938
19. Ozoplaning with the Wizard of Oz (Thompson, Ruth Plumly) ◆ 1939
20. The Wonder City of Oz (Neill, John R.) ◆ 1940
21. The Scalawagons of Oz (Neill, John R.) ◆ 1941
22. Lucky Bucky in Oz (Neill, John R.) ◆ 1942
23. The Magical Mimics in Oz (Snow, Jack) ◆ 1946
24. The Shaggy Man of Oz (Snow, Jack) ◆ 1949
25. Hidden Valley of Oz (Cosgrove, Rachel) ◆ 1951
26. Merry Go Round in Oz (McGraw, Eloise Jervis) ◆ 1963
27. Yankee in Oz (Thompson, Ruth Plumly) ◆ 1972
28. Autocrats of Oz (Suter, Jon Michael) ◆ 1976
29. Enchanted Island of Oz (Thompson, Ruth Plumly) ◆ 1976
30. Orange Knight of Oz (Suter, Jon Michael) ◆ 1976
31. Forbidden Fountain of Oz (McGraw, Eloise Jervis) ◆ 1980
32. Barnstormer in Oz (Farmer, Philip José) ◆ 1982
33. Return to Oz (Vinge, Joan Dennison) ◆ 1982
34. Dorothy and the Magic Belt (Baum, Roger S.) ◆ 1985
35. Mister Tinker of Oz (Howe, James) ◆ 1985
36. Dorothy of Oz (Baum, Roger S.) ◆ 1989
37. Rewolf of Oz (Baum, Roger S.) ◆ 1990
38. How the Wizard Came to Oz (Abbott, Donald) ◆ 1991
39. SillyOzbuls of Oz (Baum, Roger S.) ◆ 1991
40. The Nome King's Shadow in Oz (Sprague, Gilbert M.) ◆ 1992
41. The SillyOzbul of Oz and the Magic Merry-Go-Round (Baum, Roger S.) ◆ 1992
42. The SillyOzbul of Oz & Toto (Baum, Roger S.) ◆ 1992

43. The Blue Witch of Oz (Shanower, Eric) ◆ 1993
44. The Enchanted Apples of Oz (Shanower, Eric) ◆ 1993
45. The Forgotten Forest of Oz (Shanower, Eric) ◆ 1993
46. The Giant Garden of Oz (Shanower, Eric) ◆ 1993
47. The Magic Chest of Oz (Abbott, Donald) ◆ 1993
48. The Patchwork Bride of Oz (Sprague, Gilbert M.) ◆ 1993
49. Queen Ann in Oz (Carlson, Karyl, and Eric Gjovaag) ◆ 1993
50. Father Goose in Oz (Abbott, Donald) ◆ 1994
51. Christmas in Oz (Hess, Robin) ◆ 1995
52. The Glass Cat of Oz (Hulan, David) ◆ 1995
53. The Magic Dishpan of Oz (Freedman, Jeff) ◆ 1995
54. Masquerade in Oz (Campbell, Bill, and Irwin Terry) ◆ 1995
55. The Runaway in Oz (Neill, John R.) ◆ 1995
56. The Speckled Rose of Oz (Abbott, Donald) ◆ 1995
57. How the Wizard Saved Oz (Abbott, Donald) ◆ 1996
58. The Lavender Bear of Oz (Campbell, Bill) ◆ 1998

PADDINGTON

Bond, Michael

HOUGHTON MIFFLIN ◆ GRADES 2–5 ◆ A/R

ANIMAL FANTASY | HUMOR

After Mr. and Mrs. Brown see Paddington at the train station with a note that states, "Please look after this bear. Thank you," their lives are never the same. The Brown children, Jonathan and Judy, are delighted when Paddington arrives. He nearly floods the house when he takes his first bath. When asked to usher at a wedding, he gets the ring stuck on his paw. Paddington, a gentle, well-meaning bear, unwittingly causes havoc wherever he goes. There are related groups of picture books and activity books for very young children.

1. A Bear Called Paddington ◆ 1958
2. More About Paddington ◆ 1959
3. Paddington Helps Out ◆ 1960
4. Paddington Abroad ◆ 1961
5. Paddington at Large ◆ 1962
6. Paddington Marches On ◆ 1964
7. Paddington at Work ◆ 1966
8. Paddington Goes to Town ◆ 1968
9. Paddington Takes the Air ◆ 1970
10. Paddington on Top ◆ 1974
11. Paddington on Stage ◆ 1977
12. Paddington Takes the Test ◆ 1979

PADDY PORK

Goodall, John Strickland

ATHENEUM ◆ GRADES K–3

ANIMAL FANTASY

Paddy is a sophisticated, helpful pig whose adventures are portrayed without words in detailed drawings. He goes to Monte Carlo, tries to rescue a young pig's lost kite, and ends up on top of a car headed for the Swiss Alps. Later, the dauntless pig pursues a robber over land and sea and finally gets his man. When he tries to do odd jobs, he finds himself in one disaster after another; but he finally locates a missing child, to the delight of all the animals in town. Turn-of-the-century, Old World costumes and scenery surround the courtly pig and provide entertainment for young and old.

1. The Adventures of Paddy Pork ◆ 1968
2. The Ballooning Adventures of Paddy Pork ◆ 1969
3. Paddy's Evening Out ◆ 1973
4. Paddy Pork's Holiday ◆ 1976
5. Paddy's New Hat ◆ 1980
6. Paddy Goes Traveling ◆ 1982
7. Paddy Pork, Odd Jobs ◆ 1983
8. Paddy Under Water ◆ 1984
9. Paddy to the Rescue ◆ 1986

THE PAIN AND THE GREAT ONE

Blume, Judy

DELACORTE ◆ GRADES 1–3 ◆ A/R

FAMILY LIFE

The Pain and the Great One (Bradbury, 1984) was a picture book about the relationship between a brother and sister. Now there are chapter books that are just right for kids making the transition from easy readers to longer books. Jake, 6, and his sister Abigail, 8, squabble about everyday issues but they support each other too. Riding a bike, getting a haircut, going to the beach, and dealing with a bully are among the situations that the siblings confront. Fans of Judy Moody and Stink will enjoy these.

1. The Pain and the Great One ◆ 1984
2. Soupy Saturdays with the Pain and the Great One ◆ 2007
3. Cool Zone with the Pain and the Great One ◆ 2008
4. Going, Going, Gone! with the Pain and the Great One ◆ 2008

PALEOJOE'S DINOSAUR DETECTIVE CLUB

Kchodl, Joseph J., and Wendy Caszatt-Allen

MACKINAC ISLAND PRESS ◆ GRADES 3–5

MYSTERY

PaleoJoe is a paleontologist who investigates crimes. In the first book, Sue the dinosaur is stolen from the Field Museum in Chicago. PaleoJoe and his 11-year-old junior paleontologist Shelly are on the case. Facts about dinosaurs and doing research are woven into the story. This series is a fun choice for middle elementary grade readers.

1. The Disappearance of Dinosaur Sue ◆ 2006
2. Stolen Stegosaurus ◆ 2006
3. Secret Sabertooth ◆ 2007
4. Raptors Revenge ◆ 2007
5. Mysterious Mammoths ◆ 2008

PANDORA *see* Mythic Misadventures

PANGUR BAN

Sampson, Fay

LION ◆ GRADES 5–8

FANTASY

In ancient Wales, Pangur, a small white cat fleeing from a group of witches and their evil spells, befriends a monk called Niall. In *Pangur Ban,* the cat struggles to rescue Niall and the Princess Finnglas when they encounter a storm at sea and their lives are imperiled by mermaids and monsters. The fight between good and evil continues in later books and in *Finnglas and the Stones of Choosing,* the princess must face seven trials before she can become queen. These books were first published in Britain in the 1980s. An additional volume, *The White Horse Is Running,* is available in Britain.

1. Shape-Shifter: The Naming of Pangur Ban ◆ 2003
2. Pangur Ban: The White Cat ◆ 2003
3. Finnglas of the Horses ◆ 2003
4. Finnglas and the Stones of Choosing ◆ 2003
5. The Serpent of Senargad ◆ 2003

PAPER PRINCESS

Kleven, Elisa

DUTTON ◆ GRADES K–2 ◆ A/R

FANTASY

A little girl cuts out a doll from paper and decorates her to be a beautiful princess. The wind takes the doll, carrying her off in an adventure. With the help of a blue jay, the doll returns to the little girl. In the second book, the little girl is growing up and no longer plays with her paper princess. The doll is lonely so the dog carries her outside and again she is carried off by the wind. Eventually she reaches the home of another little girl who wants to play with her.

1. The Paper Princess ◆ 1994
2. The Paper Princess Finds Her Way ◆ 2003
3. The Paper Princess Flies Again (With Her Dog) ◆ 2005

PAPERBOY

Jeremiah, Omari

MORTON BOOKS ◆ GRADES 4–6

ADVENTURE

Michael Wood, 11, is an ordinary boy attending P.S. 244. When his classmates are bullied by Shorty Scarface and his gang, Michael becomes a superhero—Paperboy, so named because he defeats his enemies using folded paper. Paperboy fights against the LOEP—League of Evil People—in this comic book-style volume. Bernie Rollins's illustrations are an integral part of the books, and Michael is depicted as an African American. Omari Jeremiah began these books when he was 12.

1. Paperboy ◆ 2003
2. Paperboy 2: Overwhelming Odds ◆ 2005
3. Paperboy 3: The School of Doom ◆ 2006
4. Paperboy 4: LOEP's Worst Nightmare ◆ 2007

PARK PALS ADVENTURE

Hurwitz, Johanna

SEASTAR ◆ GRADES 2–4 ◆ A/R

ANIMAL FANTASY

Pee Wee is a guinea pig who can read. Once a pet, he was released into New York's Central Park when he was no longer wanted. There he meets a squirrel named Lexington, "Lexi," and they become friends. Even though Pee Wee was betrayed by the humans who owned him, the two friends reach out to help a stranger in the park. When Plush (another guinea pig) arrives, Pee Wee and Lexi help her adjust.

1. Pee Wee's Tale ◆ 2000
2. Lexi's Tale ◆ 2001
3. Pee Wee and Plush ◆ 2002
4. Squirrel World ◆ 2007

PARTS

Arnold, Tedd

PENGUIN ◆ GRADES K–2 ◆ A/R

HUMOR

A young boy worries that he is falling apart as he watches strands of hair falling, skin flaking off, stuff coming out of his nose! In the second book, his anxiety extends to various scary expressions—"Give me a hand," "jumps out of his skin," "hold your tongue." Things are not much better when he heads off to school in the third book. How can you cope when you have "lost your head"?

1. Parts ◆ 1997
2. More Parts ◆ 2001
3. Even More Parts ◆ 2004

PATRICK'S DINOSAURS

Carrick, Carol

HOUGHTON MIFFLIN ◆ GRADES K–2 ◆ A/R

HUMOR

Young Patrick is much alarmed by the facts his brother supplies on dinosaurs during a trip to the zoo and starts to see dinosaurs everywhere. His interest in dinosaurs continues in the second book, in which he imagines how dinosaurs and humans got along until the dinosaurs became disillusioned and left Earth on a spaceship.

1. Patrick's Dinosaurs ◆ 1983
2. What Happened to Patrick's Dinosaurs? ◆ 1986
3. Patrick's Dinosaurs on the Internet ◆ 1999

PATRICK'S PALS

Armstrong, Robb
HARPERCOLLINS ◆ **GRADES 3–6**
RECREATION

This fiction series features three real NBA players—Patrick Ewing, Dikembe Mutombo, and Alonzo Mourning—in stories that portray them as school-aged friends who love basketball. There is lots of basketball action, but there are also themes about teamwork, fair play, and the importance of an education. In one book, the friends are in a Thanksgiving play, but their math grades are suffering. Their math teacher gives them an ultimatum: better grades or no play . . . and no basketball, either. Patrick's friend Ronnie Miller (a fictional character) devises a plan to cheat, forcing Patrick to make a choice. Many reluctant readers will be attracted by the high-profile NBA stars.

1. Runnin' with the Big Dawgs ◆ 1998
2. In Your Face! ◆ 1998
3. Got Game? ◆ 1998
4. Stuffin' It ◆ 1998
5. Schoolin' ◆ 1998
6. Trashmaster ◆ 1999
7. Large and in Charge! ◆ 1999

P.C. HAWKE MYSTERIES

Zindel, Paul
HYPERION/VOLO ◆ **GRADES 5–8** ◆ **A/R**
MYSTERY

P.C. Hawke and his friend Mackenzie Riggs solve mysteries. In one book, their friend is accused of the murder of a biologist at the Natural History Museum. The investigation involves a necklace, hypnosis, and a tarantula. In another book, P.C. and Mac travel to Monaco and investigate the murder of a guest at a conference.

1. The Scream Museum ◆ 2001
2. The Surfing Corpse ◆ 2001
3. The E-Mail Murders ◆ 2001
4. The Lethal Gorilla ◆ 2001
5. The Square Root of Murder ◆ 2002
6. Death on the Amazon ◆ 2002
7. The Gourmet Zombie ◆ 2002
8. The Phantom of 86th Street ◆ 2002

9. The Houdini Whodunit ◆ 2002
10. Death by CB ◆ 2003
11. The Petrified Parrot ◆ 2003

PEACH STREET MUDDERS

Christopher, Matt

LITTLE, BROWN ◆ GRADES 2–4 ◆ A/R

REAL LIFE | RECREATION

Readers who are a little young for Matt Christopher's longer sports stories will enjoy these stories. Nicky is going after a league record for RBIs and is very superstitious about it. He goes through pre-batting rituals and doesn't want anyone to mention the record. The holder of the record tries a little sabotage but the effort is thwarted. Turtleneck, after being hit by a ball, becomes afraid, until a blind neighbor helps him to overcome his fears. There is enough baseball action and lingo here to satisfy diehard fans and enough of a story to appeal to all.

1. The Hit-Away Kid ◆ 1988
2. The Spy on Third Base ◆ 1988
3. Centerfield Ballhawk ◆ 1992
4. Man Out at First ◆ 1993
5. Zero's Slider ◆ 1994
6. All-Star Fever ◆ 1995
7. Shadow Over Second ◆ 1996
8. Stranger in Right Field ◆ 1997
9. The Catcher's Mask ◆ 1998

PEANUT BUTTER AND JELLY

Haas, Dorothy

SCHOLASTIC ◆ GRADES 2–4

REAL LIFE

After the death of her father, Polly Butterman and her family move to a new town. While living with Grandpa in Evanston, Illinois, Polly gets a new puppy, but struggles to adjust to being the new kid. Nicknamed Peanut, lively Polly meets Jillian "Jilly" Matthews. The two girls become friends and enjoy working on school projects and solving neighborhood problems. Many readers will relate to the common concerns, like the time that Peanut's best friend from Minneapolis—Regan—comes to visit. How can you have two best friends? The books in this series have been especially popular with middle-elementary girls.

1. New Friends ◆ 1988
2. Peanut and Jilly Forever ◆ 1988

3. The Haunted School ◆ 1988
4. Trouble at Alcott School ◆ 1989
5. Not Starring Jilly! ◆ 1989
6. Peanut in Charge ◆ 1989
7. The Friendship Test ◆ 1990
8. Two Friends Too Many ◆ 1990
9. Alcott Library Is Falling Down ◆ 1991

PEANUTS

Schulz, Charles M.

SIMON & SCHUSTER ◆ GRADES 1–3 ◆ A/R

HUMOR

These books for beginning readers (part of the Ready-to-Read series) are based on the popular characters from Charles Schulz's comic strip.

1. Forever Friends, Snoopy ◆ 2001
2. Kick the Football, Charlie Brown ◆ 2001
3. It's a Home Run, Charlie Brown! ◆ 2002
4. It's Time for School, Charlie Brown ◆ 2002
5. Snoopy, Flying Ace to the Rescue ◆ 2002
6. Take a Hike, Snoopy! ◆ 2002
7. Lose the Blanket, Linus ◆ 2003
8. Lucy's Advice ◆ 2003
9. Make a Trade, Charlie Brown! ◆ 2004

PEE WEE SCOUTS

Delton, Judy

BANTAM ◆ GRADES 2–4 ◆ A/R

REAL LIFE

The Pee Wee Scouts meet in Mrs. Peter's basement after school, and they love getting badges. They are a group of normal kids, including rude boys and the girls they annoy. Molly is the point-of-view character, but there are 13 scouts altogether. Each book in the series is about another badge that the scouts earn and their different reactions to it. A hobby badge is announced, and Molly can't think of anything to do, while most of the others have good ideas. Getting library cards doesn't sound like fun at first, but they all learn to enjoy reading more. Molly helps Tim, who is having trouble reading. The Pee Wee song and a Pee Wee badge to cut out are included in each title.

1. Cookies and Crutches ◆ 1988
2. Camp Ghost-Away ◆ 1988
3. Lucky Dog Days ◆ 1988

4. Blue Skies, French Fries ◆ 1988
5. Grumpy Pumkins ◆ 1988
6. Peanut-Butter Pilgrims ◆ 1988
7. A Pee Wee Christmas ◆ 1988
8. That Mushy Stuff ◆ 1989
9. Spring Sprouts ◆ 1989
10. The Pooped Troop ◆ 1989
11. The Pee Wee Jubilee ◆ 1989
12. Bad, Bad Bunnies ◆ 1990
13. Rosy Noses, Freezing Toes ◆ 1990
14. Sonny's Secret ◆ 1991
15. Sky Babies ◆ 1991
16. Trash Bash ◆ 1992
17. Pee Wees on Parade ◆ 1992
18. Lights, Action, Land-ho! ◆ 1992
19. Piles of Pets ◆ 1993
20. Fishy Wishes ◆ 1993
21. Pee Wees on Skis ◆ 1993
22. Greedy Groundhogs ◆ 1994
23. All Dads on Deck ◆ 1994
24. Tricks and Treats ◆ 1994
25. Pee Wees on First ◆ 1995
26. Super Duper Pee Wee! ◆ 1995
27. Teeny Weeny Zucchinis ◆ 1995
28. Eggs with Legs ◆ 1996
29. Pee Wee Pool Party ◆ 1996
30. Bookworm Buddies ◆ 1996
31. Moans and Groans and Dinosaur Bones ◆ 1997
32. Stage Frightened ◆ 1997
33. Halloween Helpers ◆ 1997
34. Planet Pee Wee ◆ 1998
35. Pedal Power ◆ 1998
36. Computer Clues ◆ 1998
37. Wild, Wild West ◆ 1999
38. Send in the Clowns ◆ 1999
39. Molly for Mayor ◆ 1999
40. A Big Box of Memories ◆ 2000

PEGGY THE PIG *see* Silly Thrillers with Peggy the Pig

PENDRAGON

MacHale, D. J.
ALADDIN ◆ GRADES 5–8 ◆ A/R
FANTASY

Bobby Pendragon, 14, seems normal, but he's not. He is going to save the world. First, by traveling to an alternate dimension, Denduron. Later, he continues his role as a Traveler and strives to save the land of Halla from the evil Saint Dane.

1. The Merchant of Death ◆ 2002
2. The Lost City of Faar ◆ 2003
3. The Never War ◆ 2003
4. The Reality Bug ◆ 2003
5. Black Water ◆ 2004
6. The Rivers of Zadaa ◆ 2005
7. The Quillan Games ◆ 2006
8. The Pilgrims of Rayne ◆ 2007
9. Raven Rise ◆ 2008

PENELOPE FRITTER, SUPER-SITTER

Wollman, Jessica

ALADDIN ◆ GRADES 2–4 ◆ A/R

FANTASY

Penelope Fritter is used to being ignored. Most people don't even notice her and those who do usually forget about her. But Penelope has a secret. When she eats something strawberry, she develops superpowers . . . and the fun begins.

1. The Chipster's Sister ◆ 2005
2. Meet the Phonees ◆ 2005
3. Bunches of Fun ◆ 2006

PENGUIN PETE

Pfister, Marcus

NORTH-SOUTH BOOKS ◆ GRADES K–2 ◆ A/R

ANIMAL FANTASY

Pete is a penguin who lives in an icy land. One adventure features Pete and his young son, Little Tim. Papa Pete shows Little Tim around the frozen landscape and when he is tired carries him home to Mother Pat. Another book finds Pete on an abandoned ship with a young mouse named Horatio. Pete finds it difficult to do the tasks on the ship, but he saves the day when his help is needed out at sea. This series features animal families and friends in sweet and humorous situations.

1. Penguin Pete ◆ 1987
2. Penguin Pete's New Friends ◆ 1988
3. Penguin Pete and Pat ◆ 1989

4. Penguin Pete, Ahoy! ◆ 1993
5. Penguin Pete and Little Tim ◆ 1994

PENROD

Christian, Mary Blount
MACMILLAN ◆ GRADES K–2 ◆ A/R
ANIMAL FANTASY

A little porcupine named Penrod always manages to hoodwink his best friend Griswold, a bear. Amusing, detailed, full-color illustrations accompany the short chapter stories. Griswold persuades Penrod that he needs glasses, but the only reason he can't see is that his hair is too long. Later, Penrod lets Griswold know that he is having a party but that Griswold is not invited. Griswold's reaction is "GRR" when he finds out the party is really a surprise for him.

1. Penrod's Pants ◆ 1986
2. Penrod Again ◆ 1987
3. Penrod's Party ◆ 1990
4. Penrod's Picture ◆ 1991

PERCY JACKSON AND THE OLYMPIANS

Riordan, Rick
MIRAMAX/HYPERION ◆ GRADES 5–9 ◆ A/R
FANTASY

Perseus Jackson, 12, has always been different, always in the middle of trouble. At school, his troubles are growing. One of his teachers turns into a monster—literally. And his best friend is revealed to be a satyr. Finally, Percy learns the secret. He is the son of Poseidon who had a liaison with a human—Percy's mother. As Poseidon's son, Percy is in danger. His mother appears to have been killed protecting him. Percy is sent to Camp Half-Blood to learn about his powers and prepare for the tasks that await him. In *The Battle of the Labyrinth,* Percy is in high school facing danger in Daedalus's Labyrinth. Many readers who loved the Harry Potter books have been drawn to this series.

1. The Lightning Thief ◆ 2005
2. The Sea of Monsters ◆ 2006
3. The Titan's Curse ◆ 2007
4. The Battle of the Labyrinth ◆ 2008
5. The Last Olympian ◆ 2009

PET FAIRIES *see* Rainbow Magic: Pet Fairies

PETE THE CAT

Kehret, Peg, and Pete the Cat

DUTTON ◆ GRADES 4–7 ◆ A/R

MYSTERY

Moving to a new neighborhood has been difficult for 12-year-old Alex. He is adjusting to his new school, but the kids there are not very friendly. And the boy who just moved in next door, Rocky, is downright rude. Then street signs are stolen and houses are set on fire. Alex wants to find out who is behind these destructive acts. Aiding Alex is his cat, Pete, who can fully understand humans although they cannot interpret his meows. Pete's perspective is presented in italics, which allows the reader to get inside his head. The mixture of mystery and Pete's "cat's-eye view" of the events is very enjoyable and could even attract reluctant readers. Pete is also given credit as a coauthor of these books.

1. The Stranger Next Door ◆ 2002
2. Spy Cat ◆ 2003
3. Trapped! ◆ 2008

PETER

Keats, Ezra Jack

VIKING ◆ GRADES K–2 ◆ A/R

FAMILY LIFE | REAL LIFE

In *The Snowy Day* (which won the Caldecott Medal), Peter is a young boy out on his own in the snow. Each succeeding book follows Peter on a new adventure as he grows older. In one book, he is apprehensive about the arrival of a new sibling. In another, he worries about what his friends will say when he invites a girl to his birthday party. Peter enjoys everyday activities such as learning to whistle for his dog Willie and playing with friends. When Peter is older, his young friend Archie becomes the focus of some stories—when the boys take part in a pet show and when they find a pair of goggles. This is a very popular series with African American characters and an urban setting.

1. The Snowy Day ◆ 1962
2. Whistle for Willie ◆ 1964
3. Peter's Chair ◆ 1967
4. A Letter to Amy ◆ 1968
5. Goggles ◆ 1969
6. Hi, Cat! ◆ 1970
7. Pet Show ◆ 1972

PETER AND THE STARCATCHERS

Barry, Dave, and Ridley Pearson

HYPERION ◆ GRADES 4–8 ◆ A/R

FANTASY | ADVENTURE

This series follows the adventures of a boy named Peter before he became Peter Pan. All of the familiar characters are there, including the pirate Black Stache (aka Captain Hook). In the first book, Peter and a gang of orphan boys have been sent to crew for the cruel pirate Black Stache on his ship *Never Land.* Also on the ship is Molly Aster, 14, who belongs to a secret society of Starcatchers. This group tries to find and protect "starstuff," a magical substance that falls from the heavens. When Peter, Molly, and Peter's gang find a missing trunk of "starstuff," the chase is on. This is an action-filled series with lots of adventure. Barry and Pearson also feature many of these characters in the Never Land series. Visit peterandthestarcatchers.com for more about the books.

1. Peter and the Starcatchers ◆ 2004
2. Peter and the Shadow Thieves ◆ 2006
3. Peter and the Secret of Rundoon ◆ 2007

PETER'S NEIGHBORHOOD

Suen, Anastasia

VIKING ◆ GRADES K–2 ◆ A/R

REAL LIFE

The characters from Ezra Jack Keats's Peter series now appear in these easy-to-read books. When the group wants to find a place to play, they clean up a neighborhood lot and make a clubhouse. Readers will enjoy following these stories of Peter, Archie, Louie, and their friends.

1. Hamster Chase ◆ 2001
2. Willie's Birthday ◆ 2001
3. The Clubhouse ◆ 2002
4. Loose Tooth ◆ 2002

PETRA AND CALDER

Balliet, Blue

SCHOLASTIC ◆ GRADES 5–8 ◆ A/R

MYSTERY

In the first book, a Vermeer painting has been stolen and Petra and Calder, both 11, become involved in the mystery. Throughout the book there are clues, codes, and cryptic letters that involve the reader in the solution. Reminiscent of *From the Mixed-Up Files of Mrs. Basil E. Frankweiler,* this series's characters use their creativity and problem-solving skills to expose the thieves. Recommend the Sammy Keyes mysteries to readers who have enjoyed these books.

1. Chasing Vermeer ◆ 2004
2. The Wright 3 ◆ 2006
3. The Calder Game ◆ 2008

PETS, INC.

Armstrong, Jennifer
SKYLARK ◆ GRADES 3–5
REAL LIFE

Two sisters, Carrie (grade four) and Jenny (grade five), love animals. They have two cats and a bird but when they have the opportunity to get a dog, their mother says no. The girls earn money to demonstrate responsibility and are rewarded. Girls who love animal stories will enjoy this series.

1. Puppy Project ◆ 1990
2. Too Many Pets ◆ 1990
3. Hilary to the Rescue ◆ 1990
4. That Champion Chimp ◆ 1990

PETS TO THE RESCUE

Clements, Andrew
SIMON & SCHUSTER ◆ GRADES K–2
REAL LIFE

These very easy readers feature animals that face danger to help others. In one book, Dolores the cat helps her owner escape a fire. In another, Norman, a dog that has gone blind, rescues a tired swimmer. These simple stories are exciting and dramatic.

1. Dolores and the Big Fire: A True Story ◆ 2000
2. Brave Norman: A True Story ◆ 2001
3. Ringo Saves the Day! A True Story ◆ 2001
4. Tara and Tiree, Fearless Friends! A True Story ◆ 2002

PETSITTERS CLUB

Krailing, Tessa

BARRON'S ◆ GRADES 2–4 ◆ A/R

REAL LIFE

Sam (Samantha) got the idea for the Petsitters Club while she was weeding Mrs. Bratby's garden. She and her friends Jovan, Matthew, and Katie were always looking for community service projects that would be acceptable to Mr. Grantham, the principal of their school. Watching a goat, worrying about a snake, even supervising a guess-the-weight contest for Scruncher the pig keep the friends busy. Originally published in Great Britain, the setting is not clearly defined. This a good choice for middle-elementary readers and pet enthusiasts.

1. Jilly the Kid ◆ 1998
2. The Cat Burglar ◆ 1998
3. Donkey Rescue ◆ 1998
4. Snake Alarm! ◆ 1998
5. Scruncher Goes Wandering ◆ 1998
6. Trixie and the Cyber Pet ◆ 1998
7. Oscar the Fancy Rat ◆ 1999
8. Where's Iggy? ◆ 1999
9. Pony Trouble ◆ 1999
10. The Rude Parrot ◆ 1999
11. Monkey Puzzle: Vacation Special ◆ 1999
12. The Christmas Kitten: Winter Special ◆ 1999

PETTICOAT PARTY

Karr, Kathleen

HARPERCOLLINS ◆ GRADES 5–8 ◆ A/R

HISTORICAL

Independence, Missouri, 1845. Twelve wagons head west for Oregon. In one wagon are Mr. and Mrs. Brown and their daughters Amelia and Phoebe. There is an accident and ten of the men are injured or killed. Now the women must take charge or the group will not survive. When the series begins, Phoebe is 12. After reaching Oregon when she is 15, she gets caught up in the gold rush and goes to California.

1. Go West, Young Women ◆ 1996
2. Phoebe's Folly ◆ 1996
3. Oregon, Sweet Oregon ◆ 1998
4. Gold-Rush Phoebe ◆ 1998

PETUNIA

Duvoisin, Roger

KNOPF ◆ GRADES K–2 ◆ A/R

ANIMAL FANTASY | HUMOR

Petunia, a silly goose, finds a book and remembers hearing the farmer say that books will make one wise. Thinking she can lose her reputation for silliness and become wise, she starts to carry the book around. Noisy the dog, Clover the cow, and the other animals begin to think she is wise and go along with her in all sorts of silly solutions to their problems. Other barnyard adventures include being wooed by an amorous raccoon and having a song written just for her by the farmer's wife. A funny, classic picture book series that makes a good family read-aloud.

1. Petunia ◆ 1950
2. Petunia and the Song ◆ 1951
3. Petunia's Christmas ◆ 1952
4. Petunia Takes a Trip ◆ 1953
5. Petunia, Beware! ◆ 1958
6. Our Veronica Goes to Petunia's Farm ◆ 1962
7. Petunia, I Love You ◆ 1965
8. Petunia's Treasure ◆ 1975

PHANTOM STALLION

Farley, Terri

AVON ◆ GRADES 4–6 ◆ A/R

REAL LIFE

Phantom, a silver mustang, rules a herd of wild horses. Samantha "Sam" Forster raised Phantom and worries about his herd and their safety. In *The Challenger,* a wildcat may be threatening the horses. And New Moon, a tall black horse and Phantom's son, may be ready to fight for leadership of the herd. Fans of horse stories will enjoy these exciting tales.

1. The Wild One ◆ 2002
2. Mustang Moon ◆ 2002
3. Dark Sunshine ◆ 2002
4. The Renegade ◆ 2002
5. Free Again ◆ 2003
6. The Challenger ◆ 2003
7. Desert Danger ◆ 2003
8. Golden Ghost ◆ 2003
9. Gift Horse ◆ 2003
10. Red Feather Filly ◆ 2004
11. Untamed ◆ 2004

12. Rain Dance ◆ 2004
13. Heartbreak Bronco ◆ 2004
14. Moonrise ◆ 2005
15. Kidnapped Colt ◆ 2005
16. The Wildest Heart ◆ 2005
17. Mountain Mare ◆ 2005
18. Firefly ◆ 2005
19. Secret Star ◆ 2006
20. Blue Wings ◆ 2006
21. Dawn Runner ◆ 2006
22. Wild Honey ◆ 2006
23. Gypsy Gold ◆ 2006
24. Run Away Home ◆ 2006

PHILIP HALL

Greene, Bette
DIAL; HARPERCOLLINS ◆ GRADES 4–7
REAL LIFE

Beth Lambert lives in a small town in Arkansas. She and her girlfriends are in a group called the Pretty Penny Club. But her best friend is a boy, Philip Hall. This series shows the experiences of African American children living in rural settings.

1. Philip Hall Likes Me, I Reckon Maybe ◆ 1974
2. Get On Out of Here, Philip Hall ◆ 1981
3. I've Already Forgotten Your Name, Philip Hall ◆ 2004

PHINEAS L. MACGUIRE

Dowell, Frances O'Roark
ATHENEUM ◆ GRADES 3–5 ◆ A/R
REAL LIFE

Phineas Listerman MacGuire, aka Mac, has a problem. His best friend has moved away and his teacher has assigned the new kid—Mac R.—to be his science fair partner. The new kid has been acting out and causing problems. As they work together, Mac discovers that the boy's name is really Ben and they create a successful science project and friendship. The science connection (including experiments in each book) adds to the series. Fans of Seymour Simon's Einstein Anderson books will enjoy this series.

1. Phineas L. MacGuire . . . Erupts! ◆ 2006
2. Phineas L. MacGuire . . . Gets Slimed! ◆ 2007
3. Phineas L. MacGuire . . . Blasts Off! ◆ 2008

PIG PIG

McPhail, David

DUTTON ◆ GRADES K–2 ◆ A/R

ANIMAL FANTASY | HUMOR

Pig Pig doesn't want to grow up. He insists on wearing his old baby clothes and riding in a too-small stroller. Then one day he is caught in an emergency with a real baby and decides to grow up fast. In *Pig Pig Rides,* he tells his mother at breakfast about all the adventures he is going to have on trains, planes, and motorcycles, and she wants to know if he'll be home for dinner. Adults will enjoy the absurd humor and full-color illustrations of this read-aloud series.

1. Pig Pig Grows Up ◆ 1980
2. Pig Pig Rides ◆ 1982
3. Pig Pig Goes to Camp ◆ 1983
4. Pig Pig and the Magic Photo Album ◆ 1986
5. Pig Pig Gets a Job ◆ 1990

PIGANEERS

Salmon, Michael

SIMON & SCHUSTER ◆ GRADES K–2

ANIMAL FANTASY | HUMOR

Climb aboard the *Hogwash* for fun and adventure. Captain Porker runs a shipshape ship—except when the crew plays a prank and hides his treasure. The crew is at it again when they have to let a woman on the ship—but no one will say no to Big Boar's mom! What do "piganeers" do when they are bored? How about putting on a talent show? The fourth book, *Peg Leg Pete and the Mermaid,* shows the piganeers at their best as they come to the aid of a mermaid. Cartoon-style illustrations add to the fun of this silly series.

1. Who Stole Captain Porker's Treasure? ◆ 1998
2. Big Boar's Mom Comes to Stay ◆ 1998
3. Talent Night Aboard the Hogwash ◆ 1998
4. Peg Leg Pete and the Mermaid ◆ 1998

PIGEON

Willems, Mo

HYPERION ◆ GRADES K–2 ◆ A/R

HUMOR

Like many young children, the pigeon wants what he wants. He flips out when he cannot drive the bus and he tries every excuse there is to avoid going to bed. Mo Willems won a Caldecott Honor for *Don't Let the Pigeon Drive the Bus!* There are also two board books: *The Pigeon Has Feelings, Too!* and *The Pigeon Loves Things That Go!*

1. Don't Let the Pigeon Drive the Bus! ◆ 2003
2. The Pigeon Finds a Hot Dog! ◆ 2004
3. Don't Let the Pigeon Stay Up Late! ◆ 2006
4. The Pigeon Wants a Puppy! ◆ 2008

PIGGINS

Yolen, Jane

HARCOURT ◆ GRADES K–3 ◆ A/R

ANIMAL FANTASY | MYSTERY

Piggins, the butler at the home of Mr. and Mrs. Reynard at 47 The Meadows, is a sophisticated and handsome pig. A veteran of the Boar Wars, he solves mysteries and is a favorite of the Reynard children, Rexy and Trixy. When they are in a royal wedding, Rexy is accused of stealing the wedding ring. Piggins is called in, concludes that the ring was a fake, and points the police to the real thief. On a picnic by the river, the children concoct their own mystery for him to solve—a birthday surprise. Detailed full-color illustrations portray a wealthy turn-of-the-century animal world.

1. Piggins ◆ 1988
2. Picnic with Piggins ◆ 1988
3. Piggins and the Royal Wedding ◆ 1989

PIGS

Dubanevich, Arlene

FRANKLIN WATTS ◆ GRADES K–2

ANIMAL FANTASY | FAMILY LIFE | HUMOR

Cartoonlike adventures of a large family of pig brothers and sisters feature zany action on every page. Pete is in charge when they go to the circus because their Mom gave him the money. Piggles, the baby, doesn't want to give up her hat at the hat check—and that's just the beginning of Pete's troubles with her. Chasing her balloon, she breaks up a team of pig acrobats and distracts a juggler who is trying to set the record for the most peanut butter sandwiches juggled. The whole circus joins in to rescue her when she chases the balloon up a tower. Other books find the pigs celebrating Christmas and playing hide-and-seek.

1. Pigs in Hiding ◆ 1983
2. Pig William ◆ 1985
3. Pigs at Christmas ◆ 1986
4. The Piggest Show on Earth ◆ 1988

PIGS

Geisert, Arthur

HOUGHTON MIFFLIN ◆ GRADES K–1

ANIMAL FANTASY

These adventures of a pig family use just one word: *oink*. Mama Pig shows her piglets around the farm until she goes to sleep, when they decide to go out on their own. In the next book, the piglets get into a field of corn and Mama comes roaring after them. They escape to the river and enjoy the corn. In *Pigs from 1 to 10,* the piglets are determined to find a "lost place with stone configurations." The configurations are the numbers 1 to 9, which also are hidden in each picture. Black-and-white drawings accompany the minimal text.

1. Pigs from A to Z ◆ 1986
2. Oink ◆ 1991
3. Pigs from 1 to 10 ◆ 1992
4. Oink Oink ◆ 1993

THE PINK PARROTS

Various authors

LITTLE, BROWN/SPORTS ILLUSTRATED FOR KIDS ◆ GRADES 3–5

RECREATION

Amy Hawk really wants to play baseball, not sit on the bench, so she forms her own all-girl team. It takes some time to get enough girls to play but the biggest problem is finding financial backing. The owner of the Pink Parrot beauty salon decides to sponsor the girls and become their coach, which leads to lots of fun on the field and off.

1. Girls Strike Back: The Making of the Pink Parrots (Probosz, Kathilyn Solomon) ◆ 1990
2. All That Jazz (Calhoun, B. B.) ◆ 1990
3. Mixed Signals (DiMeo, Crystal) ◆ 1991
4. Fielder's Choice (Calhoun, B. B.) ◆ 1991
5. Change-Up (Valentine, E. J.) ◆ 1991
6. No-Hitter (Jerome, Leah) ◆ 1991

PINKERTON

Kellogg, Steven

DIAL ◆ GRADES K–2 ◆ A/R

FAMILY LIFE | HUMOR

Pinkerton is a Great Dane whose size and enthusiasm create many predicaments for the little girl and her family who own him. In various books, Pinkerton is taken to obedience school, he and his family befriend a cat named Rose, he meets up with hunters searching for a fox, and he visits the Natural History Museum. Each situation offers a great opportunity for zany adventures. Kellogg's illustrations are great, filled with action and fun. Young readers will enjoy Pinkerton's antics.

1. Pinkerton, Behave! ◆ 1979
2. A Rose for Pinkerton ◆ 1981
3. Tallyho, Pinkerton ◆ 1983
4. Prehistoric Pinkerton ◆ 1987
5. A Penguin Pup for Pinkerton ◆ 2001

PINKY AND REX

Howe, James

SIMON & SCHUSTER ◆ GRADES 1–3 ◆ A/R

REAL LIFE

Pinky loves the color pink and stuffed animals. His friend Rex lives across the street, and she loves dinosaurs. They do everything together, including coping with Pinky's little sister Amanda. When they all go to a museum, they see a pink dinosaur in the gift shop but no one has enough money to buy it. They solve the problem by putting all their money together and sharing it. As the series continues, Pinky and Rex have a play wedding and compete in a school spelling bee.

1. Pinky and Rex ◆ 1990
2. Pinky and Rex Get Married ◆ 1990
3. Pinky and Rex and the Spelling Bee ◆ 1991
4. Pinky and Rex and the Mean Old Witch ◆ 1991
5. Pinky and Rex Go to Camp ◆ 1992
6. Pinky and Rex and the New Baby ◆ 1993
7. Pinky and Rex and the Double-Dad Weekend ◆ 1995
8. Pinky and Rex and the Bully ◆ 1996
9. Pinky and Rex and the New Neighbors ◆ 1997
10. Pinky and Rex and the Perfect Pumpkin ◆ 1998
11. Pinky and Rex and the School Play ◆ 1998
12. Pinky and Rex and the Just-Right Pet ◆ 2001

PINKY DINKY DOO

Jinkins, Jim

RANDOM HOUSE ◆ GRADES 1–3 ◆ A/R

HUMOR

Pinky Dinky Doo is a young girl with a big imagination. Whenever she faces a new or challenging situation she creates her own story. As she thinks about her story, her head grows in size and her solutions are creative and, sometimes, crazy. For example, she tells her little brother Tyler a story about shoes made of vegetables and other foods. Fans of the animated television series will enjoy these easy readers.

1. Polka Dot Pox ◆ 2004
2. Where Are My Shoes? ◆ 2004
3. Shrinky Pinky! ◆ 2005
4. Pinky Stinky Doo ◆ 2006
5. Think Pink! ◆ 2006
6. Back to School Is Cool! ◆ 2007

PIONEER DAUGHTERS

Van Leeuwen, Jean

DIAL ◆ GRADES 3–5 ◆ A/R

HISTORICAL

Hannah Perley, 9, lives with her family in Fairfield, Connecticut. Hannah helps around the house until her brother Ben leaves to join the colonial soldiers of the American Revolution. Hannah must then take over many of Ben's tasks on the farm and also worry about his safety.

1. Hannah of Fairfield ◆ 1999
2. Hannah's Helping Hands ◆ 1999
3. Hannah's Winter of Hope ◆ 2000

PIPPI LONGSTOCKING

Lindgren, Astrid

PENGUIN ◆ GRADES 3–5 ◆ A/R

HUMOR

Pippi (her full name is Pippilotta Delicatessa Windowshade Mackrelmint Efraim's Daughter Longstocking) lives alone in her house, Villa Villekulla, with only her horse and her monkey, Mr. Nilsson, for company. Not only that, she's "rich as a troll" (as she puts it) thanks to the suitcase of gold pieces her father left for her before he disappeared at sea. No wonder

Tommy and Annika—who live next door in an ordinary house with an ordinary father and mother—love to play with her! These stories are translated from the Swedish and have become popular all over the world.

1. Pippi Longstocking ◆ 1945
2. Pippi Goes on Board ◆ 1946
3. Pippi in the South Seas ◆ 1948
4. Pippi Longstocking's After-Christmas Party ◆ 1950

PIPPI LONGSTOCKING STORYBOOK SERIES

1. Do You Know Pippi Longstocking? ◆ 1999
2. Pippi Goes to School ◆ 1999
3. Pippi Goes to the Circus ◆ 2000
4. Pippi to the Rescue ◆ 2000
5. Pippi's Extraordinary Ordinary Day ◆ 2001
6. Pippi Longstocking in the Park ◆ 2001

PIPPO *see* Tom and Pippo

PIRATE HUNTER

Strickland, Brad, and Thomas E. Fuller
ALADDIN ◆ GRADES 5–8 ◆ A/R
ADVENTURE

Davy Shea, 12, joins his uncle Patch and Captain William Hunter on their ship, the *Aurora* as they search for the evil pirate Jack Steele. Although they appear to be pirates, too, they are really secret agents on a mission to break the control of the pirates in the Caribbean. With plenty of high seas action, this should appeal to fans of other pirate adventures, like the Jack Sparrow books.

1. Mutiny! ◆ 2002
2. The Guns of Tortuga ◆ 2003
3. Heart of Steele ◆ 2003

PIRATE PETE

Kennedy, Kim
ABRAMS ◆ GRADES K–2 ◆ A/R
ADVENTURE | HUMOR

Pirate Pete is devoted to treasure, especially gold. He and his parrot have many adventures but little luck. In the third book, they interview potential crewmembers, basing their choice on each candidate's ability to "talk pirate." They end up sailing off alone. Rhymes and repetition, plus the expressive illustrations, make these books appealing.

1. Pirate Pete ◆ 2002
2. Pirate Pete's Giant Adventure ◆ 2006
3. Pirate Pete's Talk Like a Pirate ◆ 2007

PIRATE PETE AND PIRATE JOE

Cannon, A. E.

PENGUIN ◆ GRADES K–2 ◆ A/R

ADVENTURE

Pirate Pete and Pirate Joe are two un-fierce pirates with a cat and a dog. In the course of the first book they acquire a parrot, but not a boat—they are afraid of water; instead they buy a mini-van called the "Jolly Roger." These books for beginning readers are full of fun, with rollicking text and vivid cartoon illustrations.

1. On the Go with Pirate Pete and Pirate Joe ◆ 2002
2. Let the Good Times Roll with Pirate Pete and Pirate Joe ◆ 2004
3. Way Out West with Pirate Pete and Pirate Joe ◆ 2006

PIRATE SCHOOL

James, Brian

GROSSET & DUNLAP ◆ GRADES 1–3 ◆ A/R

ADVENTURE

Pete, 10, and his friends are training to be pirates. On board the *Sea Rat,* the pirates—especially the first mate, Rotten Tooth—see the kids as a nuisance. In the first book, the kids hope to prove themselves by finding the treasure on Snake Island. In *Camp Buccaneer,* the kids compete against other pirate kids on an island that might be haunted by the White Skeleton Monkey.

1. The Curse of Snake Island ◆ 2007
2. Ahoy, Ghost Ship Ahead! ◆ 2007
3. Attack on the High Seas! ◆ 2007
4. Port of Spies ◆ 2007
5. Treasure Trouble ◆ 2008
6. Camp Buccaneer ◆ 2008
7. Yo-Ho-Ho! ◆ 2008
8. Shiver Me, Shipwreck! ◆ 2009

PIRATES OF THE CARIBBEAN *see* Jack Sparrow

PIXIE TRICKS

West, Tracey

SCHOLASTIC ◆ GRADES 2–4 ◆ A/R

FANTASY

A sprite needs help to trick some pixies, trolls, and goblins back to the fairy realm. He shares his secret with Violet Briggs and she agrees to help him.

1. Sprite's Secret ◆ 2000
2. The Greedy Gremlin ◆ 2000
3. The Pet-Store Sprite ◆ 2000
4. The Halloween Goblin ◆ 2000
5. The Angry Elf ◆ 2000
6. Sporty Sprite ◆ 2001
7. Double Trouble Dwarf ◆ 2001
8. The Wicked Wizard ◆ 2001

P.J. FUNNYBUNNY

Sadler, Marilyn

RANDOM HOUSE ◆ GRADES K–1 ◆ A/R

ANIMAL FANTASY | HUMOR

P.J. Funnybunny doesn't mean to be bad, but he is always getting into trouble with his family. When his cousin comes over to play, he is even worse than P.J. and all the Funnybunnys are glad to see him go. The whole family pitches in to help P.J. win the Great Turtle Creek Tricycle Race, even though he takes the first turn too fast and falls down. When he goes camping with his friends, he refuses to take his sister along. She and her friend come anyway, but ghosts scare them all home. Extra-large text and short sentences will appeal to beginning readers. There are skills books featuring P.J. Funnybunny.

1. It's Not Easy Being a Bunny ◆ 1983
2. P.J. the Spoiled Bunny ◆ 1986
3. P.J. Funnybunny in the Great Tricycle Race ◆ 1988
4. P.J. Funnybunny in the Perfect Hiding Place ◆ 1988
5. P.J. Funnybunny Camps Out ◆ 1994
6. P.J. Funnybunny and His Very Cool Birthday Party ◆ 1996
7. Honey Bunny Funnybunny ◆ 1997
8. P.J. Funnybunny's Bag of Tricks ◆ 2004

THE PLANT THAT ATE DIRTY SOCKS

McArthur, Nancy

AVON ◆ GRADES 4–6 ◆ A/R

HUMOR | SCIENCE FICTION

When the dirty socks in Michael and Norman's room start to disappear, the boys discover that they are being eaten by two strange plants in their room. The plants, grown from mysterious beans that arrived in the mail, develop distinct personalities; the brothers name them Stanley and Fluffy and they all become friends. Biological experts analyze the plants, the parents want to get rid of them, and the plants have children, some of which turn out not to be friendly at all. Other situations involve the boys' efforts to make sure the plants' unique qualities don't become public. The humor of the series comes from the relationship between the odd-couple brothers, with neat-freak Norman trying to keep Michael's mess on his side of the room.

1. The Plant That Ate Dirty Socks ◆ 1988
2. The Return of the Plant That Ate Dirty Socks ◆ 1990
3. The Escape of the Plant That Ate Dirty Socks ◆ 1992
4. The Secret of the Plant That Ate Dirty Socks ◆ 1993
5. More Adventures of the Plant That Ate Dirty Socks ◆ 1994
6. The Plant That Ate Dirty Socks Goes Up in Space ◆ 1995
7. The Mystery of the Plant That Ate Dirty Socks ◆ 1996
8. The Plant That Ate Dirty Socks Gets a Girlfriend ◆ 1997
9. The Plant That Ate Dirty Socks Goes Hollywood ◆ 1999

POLK STREET: NEW KIDS AT THE POLK STREET SCHOOL

Giff, Patricia Reilly

DELL ◆ GRADES 1–3 ◆ A/R

REAL LIFE

Stacy Arrow is Emily Arrow's little sister. Emily is one of the featured characters in Ms. Rooney's second-grade class at Polk Street School (from the Kids of the Polk Street School series). This New Kids series looks at the antics of younger children—Stacy and her friends—as they adjust to being in kindergarten with their teacher, Mrs. Zachary. Issues such as taking turns, saying kind things, being a good listener, and sharing are presented. In one book, the students make an About Me box; in another, Stacy cooperates to make stone soup. Although Stacy is the focus of the books, her friends Jiwon (a Korean American child) and Eddie are also featured. Readers looking for slightly longer chapter books with familiar situations will relate to these simple stories.

1. Watch Out! Man-Eating Snake ◆ 1988
2. Fancy Feet ◆ 1988
3. All About Stacy ◆ 1988
4. B-e-s-t Friends ◆ 1988
5. Spectacular Stone Soup ◆ 1988
6. Stacy Says Good-bye ◆ 1989

POLK STREET SCHOOL: KIDS OF THE POLK STREET SCHOOL

Giff, Patricia Reilly
DELL ◆ GRADES 1–3 ◆ A/R
HUMOR | REAL LIFE

A group of children learn to get along in the classroom in some very funny situations. The star of the series is Richard "Beast" Best, who is held back in the second grade, and keeps getting in trouble. In the first book, he becomes interested in reading. Emily has trouble with reading, and one of the books deals with her experiences with the library summer reading game. Matthew is Beast's best friend, and when he moves away, one of the books follows him. Short sentences and paragraphs characterize this easy chapter series. The Kids of the Polk Street School Specials include special sections with activities and projects. Some even have travel information as the kids become interested in different topics and places. See also the New Kids at the Polk Street School.

1. The Beast in Ms. Rooney's Room ◆ 1984
2. Fish Face ◆ 1984
3. The Candy Corn Contest ◆ 1984
4. December Secrets ◆ 1984
5. In the Dinosaur's Paw ◆ 1985
6. The Valentine Star ◆ 1985
7. Lazy Lions, Lucky Lambs ◆ 1985
8. Snaggle Doodles ◆ 1985
9. Purple Climbing Days ◆ 1985
10. Say "Cheese" ◆ 1985
11. Sunny-Side Up ◆ 1986
12. Pickle Puss ◆ 1986
13. Beast and the Halloween Horror ◆ 1990
14. Emily Arrow Promises to Do Better This Year ◆ 1990
15. Monster Rabbit Runs Amuck! ◆ 1991
16. Wake Up, Emily, It's Mother's Day ◆ 1991

KIDS OF THE POLK STREET SCHOOL SPECIALS

1. Write Up a Storm with the Polk Street School ◆ 1993

2. Count Your Money with the Polk Street School ◆ 1994
3. The Postcard Pest ◆ 1994
4. Turkey Trouble ◆ 1994
5. Look Out, Washington D.C.! ◆ 1995
6. Green Thumbs, Everyone ◆ 1996
7. Pet Parade ◆ 1996
8. Next Stop, New York City! ◆ 1997
9. Oh Boy, Boston! ◆ 1997
10. Let's Go, Philadelphia! ◆ 1998

POLKA DOT PRIVATE EYE

Giff, Patricia Reilly, and Blanche Sims

DELL ◆ GRADES 1–3 ◆ A/R

MYSTERY

Dawn Bosco, the Polka Dot Detective, is one of the Polk Street School kids. She has a detective box that includes a book called *The Polka Dot Private Eye,* a wig, and a big polka-dot detective hat. Her grandmother, Noni, takes Dawn and her friends Jill and Jason to the beach for the day and they encounter a teenage girl who has lost her necklace. Dawn takes the case and runs through several suspects before the necklace is found in her own box, where the girl dropped it accidentally. Jason is always glad to help Dawn on a case, but Jill is a terrible detective. Easy clues and Giff's characteristic short paragraphs make a nice introduction to mysteries.

1. The Mystery of the Blue Ring ◆ 1987
2. The Riddle of the Red Purse ◆ 1987
3. The Secret at the Polk Street School ◆ 1987
4. The Powder Puff Puzzle ◆ 1987
5. The Case of the Cool-Itch Kid ◆ 1989
6. Garbage Juice for Breakfast ◆ 1989
7. The Trail of the Screaming Teenager ◆ 1990
8. The Clue at the Zoo ◆ 1990

PONY-CRAZED PRINCESS

Kimpton, Diana

HYPERION ◆ GRADES 2–4 ◆ A/R

REAL LIFE

Princess Ellie loves ponies. With her best friend Kate, Ellie and her ponies enjoy adventures including solving mysteries, camping, and visiting Prince John's palace in the mountains where she becomes lost in a blizzard! A Super Special book was released in 2007: *Princess Ellie's Summer Vacation.*

1. Princess Ellie to the Rescue ◆ 2006
2. Princess Ellie's Secret ◆ 2006
3. Princess Ellie's Mystery ◆ 2006
4. Princess Ellie's Starlight Adventure ◆ 2006
5. Princess Ellie's Camping Trip ◆ 2006
6. A Surprise for Princess Ellie ◆ 2006
7. Princess Ellie Takes Charge ◆ 2007
8. Princess Ellie Solves a Mystery ◆ 2007
9. Princess Ellie's Snowy Ride ◆ 2007
10. Princess Ellie's Treasure Hunt ◆ 2008
11. Princess Ellie's Royal Jamboree ◆ 2008

PONY PALS

Betancourt, Jeanne
SCHOLASTIC ◆ GRADES 3–5 ◆ A/R
REAL LIFE │ RECREATION

Pam Crandal is one of the featured characters in the Pony Pals series. Her father is a veterinarian and her mother is a riding teacher, so Pam is used to being around animals. There is a trail behind her family's land that leads to Anna Harley's house, where Anna and her friend Lulu Sanders keep their horses. The three friends call themselves the Pony Pals, and these stories revolve around their problems with ponies and with friends. In one book, Pam's pony is sick and the girls try to find out why. In another, new neighbors block the Pony Pal Trail, and the girls worry about how they will get together. The cover art shows Pam as an African American girl, which may expand the appeal of this series. Pony Tails is a series similar to this one.

1. I Want a Pony ◆ 1994
2. A Pony for Keeps ◆ 1995
3. A Pony in Trouble ◆ 1995
4. Give Me Back My Pony ◆ 1995
5. Pony to the Rescue ◆ 1995
6. Too Many Ponies ◆ 1995
7. Runaway Pony ◆ 1995
8. Good-bye Pony ◆ 1996
9. The Wild Pony ◆ 1996
10. Don't Hurt My Pony ◆ 1996
11. Circus Pony ◆ 1996
12. Keep Out, Pony! ◆ 1996
13. The Girl Who Hated Ponies ◆ 1997
14. Pony-Sitters ◆ 1997
15. The Blind Pony ◆ 1997
16. The Missing Pony Pal ◆ 1997
17. Detective Pony ◆ 1998
18. The Saddest Pony ◆ 1998

19. Moving Pony ◆ 1999
20. Stolen Ponies ◆ 1999
21. The Winning Pony ◆ 1999
22. Western Pony ◆ 1999
23. The Pony and the Bear ◆ 1999
24. The Unlucky Pony ◆ 1999
25. The Lonely Pony ◆ 1999
26. Movie Star Pony ◆ 1999
27. The Pony and the Missing Dog ◆ 2000
28. The Newborn Pony ◆ 2000
29. Lost and Found ◆ 2001
30. Pony-4-Sale ◆ 2001
31. Ponies from the Past ◆ 2001
32. He's My Pony ◆ 2001
33. What's Wrong with My Pony? ◆ 2001
34. The Pony and the Lost Swan ◆ 2002
35. Magic Pony ◆ 2002
36. The Pony and the Haunted Barn ◆ 2002
37. No Ponies in the House! ◆ 2003
38. Ponies on Parade ◆ 2003

PONY PALS SUPER SPECIALS

1. The Baby Pony ◆ 1996
2. The Story of Our Ponies ◆ 1997
3. The Ghost Pony ◆ 1998
4. The Fourth Pony Pal ◆ 2001
5. Pony Problem ◆ 2003
6. The Last Pony Ride ◆ 2004

PONY TAILS

Bryant, Bonnie

BANTAM SKYLARK ◆ GRADES 3–5 ◆ A/R

REAL LIFE | RECREATION

Jasmine, Corey, and May are best friends who take riding lessons at the Pony Club. These books include details about riding that will appeal to younger horse enthusiasts. Girls will also relate to the problems among the three friends, such as when Corey is chosen to participate in the Starlight Ride and Jasmine is not. In *May's Runaway Ride,* May has such a difficult time that her friends think she has run away. Girls who read these books may also enjoy Jeanne Betancourt's Pony Pals series and then move on to Bonnie Bryant's series about older girls, The Saddle Club.

1. Pony Crazy ◆ 1995
2. May's Riding Lesson ◆ 1995
3. Corey's Pony Is Missing ◆ 1995
4. Jasmine's Christmas Ride ◆ 1995

5. May Takes the Lead ◆ 1996
6. Corey in the Saddle ◆ 1996
7. Jasmine Trots Ahead ◆ 1996
8. May Rides a New Pony ◆ 1996
9. Corey and the Spooky Pony ◆ 1996
10. Jasmine Helps a Foal ◆ 1996
11. May Goes to England ◆ 1997
12. Corey's Secret Friend ◆ 1997
13. Jasmine's First Horse Show ◆ 1997
14. May's Runaway Ride ◆ 1997
15. Corey's Christmas Wish ◆ 1997
16. Jasmine and the Jumping Pony ◆ 1998

POPPLETON

Rylant, Cynthia

SCHOLASTIC ◆ GRADES K–3 ◆ A/R

ANIMAL FANTASY | HUMOR

Poppleton the Pig and his friends Cherry Sue the Llama and Hudson the Mouse are good friends who help each other out and share good times together. When Poppleton and Cherry Sue first meet, she thinks she needs to invite him over every day, but he would rather be alone sometimes. Finally he gets frustrated and sprays her with a hose. She confesses that she likes to be alone sometimes too, and they become friends. When Poppleton and Hudson go to the beach together, the best part is when they tell Cherry Sue all about it.

1. Poppleton ◆ 1997
2. Poppleton and Friends ◆ 1997
3. Poppleton Everyday ◆ 1998
4. Poppleton Forever ◆ 1998
5. Poppleton in Spring ◆ 1999
6. Poppleton in Fall ◆ 1999
7. Poppleton Has Fun ◆ 2000
8. Poppleton in Winter ◆ 2001

POPPY *see* Dimwood Forest

PORTRAITS OF LITTLE WOMEN

Pfeffer, Susan Beth

BANTAM DOUBLEDAY DELL ◆ GRADES 4–6 ◆ A/R

FAMILY LIFE | HISTORICAL

Featuring the characters from Louisa May Alcott's *Little Women,* these are original stories. Each of the March sisters is true to her original personality: Jo is feisty, Beth is sensitive. The books give a sense of the era, including encounters with immigrants and details about life in the mid-1800s. There is a strong sense of family in these stories. Sometimes the loyalty of the girls is tested, as when Jo is invited to a picnic but Beth is not. The original *Little Women* is still very popular with girls, and this series will extend the interest and be accessible to a wider audience of readers.

1. Amy's Story ◆ 1997
2. Beth's Story ◆ 1997
3. Jo's Story ◆ 1997
4. Meg's Story ◆ 1997
5. Amy Makes a Friend ◆ 1998
6. Beth Makes a Friend ◆ 1998
7. Christmas Dreams: Four Stories ◆ 1998
8. Jo Makes a Friend ◆ 1998
9. Meg Makes a Friend ◆ 1998
10. A Gift for Amy ◆ 1999
11. A Gift for Beth ◆ 1999
12. A Gift for Jo ◆ 1999
13. A Gift for Meg ◆ 1999
14. Birthday Wishes ◆ 1999
15. Ghostly Tales ◆ 2000

POSTCARDS FROM BUSTER

Brown, Marc

LITTLE, BROWN ◆ GRADES K–3 ◆ A/R

ANIMAL FANTASY

Arthur's friend Buster Baxter travels and learns about various locations including Virginia Beach, Chinatown in San Francisco, San Antonio, and Chicago. He sends postcards describing each location to his friends. There is also *Buster's Activity Book* with projects and stickers. These beginning reader books are correlated with the PBS television series.

1. Buster on the Farm ◆ 2005
2. Buster Plays Along ◆ 2005
3. Buster and the Dance Contest ◆ 2005
4. Buster and the Giant Pumpkin ◆ 2005
5. Buster Hits the Trail ◆ 2005
6. Buster and the Great Swamp ◆ 2005
7. Buster Catches a Wave ◆ 2005
8. Buster Climbs the Walls ◆ 2005
9. Buster on the Town ◆ 2005
10. Buster Changes His Luck ◆ 2006
11. Buster Hunts for Dinosaurs ◆ 2006
12. Buster's Sugartime ◆ 2006

POWER RANGERS: NINJA STORM

TOKYOPOP ◆ GRADES 4–6

FANTASY

This cine-manga series connects with the cable television program about the Power Rangers. A ninja master must teach three students from the ninja academy to access the energies that will make them Power Rangers. Connor, Kira, and Ethan work together to stop Dino Thunder, who plans to send the world back to the age of the dinosaurs.

1. Dark Sky Overhead ◆ 2003
2. Lightning Strike ◆ 2003
3. Thunder Strangers ◆ 2004

POWERPUFF GIRLS CHAPTER BOOKS

Various authors

SCHOLASTIC ◆ GRADES 2–5 ◆ A/R

FANTASY

Blossom, Buttercup, and Bubbles are the Powerpuff Girls—three crime-fighting kindergarteners who must be done before bedtime. In one book, their archenemy, Mojo Jojo, makes a mini-clone of himself. In another book, there is a problem in the Pokey Oaks Kindergarten when Ms. Keane becomes Ms. Meane. Fans of the Cartoon Network series will enjoy these books. There are some picture books for younger children.

1. Powerpuff Professor (Rogers, Amy Keating) ◆ 2000
2. All Chalked Up (Rogers, Amy Keating) ◆ 2000
3. Cartoon Crazy (Mooney, E. S.) ◆ 2000
4. Blossoming Out (Mooney, E. S.) ◆ 2000
5. Teacher's Pest (Mooney, E. S.) ◆ 2001
6. Party Savers (Mooney, E. S.) ◆ 2001
7. Scary Princess (Mooney, E. S.) ◆ 2001
8. Sand Hassle (Dewin, Howard) ◆ 2001
9. Frighty Night (Mooney, E. S.) ◆ 2001
10. Smashing Lumpkins (Siefken, Paul) ◆ 2001
11. Mojo Mayhem (Mooney, E. S.) ◆ 2002
12. Ms. Meane (Mooney, E. S.) ◆ 2002
13. Little Miss Pokey Oaks (Dewin, Howard) ◆ 2002
14. Shrinky Jinx (Mooney, E. S.) ◆ 2002
15. Snow Fun (Mooney, E. S.) ◆ 2002
16. Mojo and Mini-Mo (Mooney, E. S.) ◆ 2003
17. The Fuzzy Lumpkins Show (Mooney, E. S.) ◆ 2003

PRAIRIE RIVER

Gregory, Kristiana

SCHOLASTIC ◆ GRADES 4–7 ◆ A/R

HISTORICAL | REAL LIFE

After Nessa Clemens, 14, runs away from the orphanage, she travels to Prairie River, Kansas. Against her wishes, she had been engaged to marry an older man. In Prairie River, she finds work as a schoolteacher and hopes to escape her past. In the third book, a man arrives who knows about her past and Nessa hopes the information will not cause the townspeople to turn against her. Albert, her best friend from the orphanage, arrives in the fourth book and Nessa finds the situation more awkward than she expected.

1. A Journey of Faith ◆ 2003
2. A Grateful Harvest ◆ 2003
3. Winter Tidings ◆ 2004
4. Hope Springs Eternal ◆ 2005

PRAIRIE SKIES

Hopkinson, Deborah

ALADDIN ◆ GRADES 2–4 ◆ A/R

HISTORICAL

In 1855, Charlie Keller, 8, travels with his family from Massachusetts to Kansas. The settlers hope to make Kansas a "free" state but prairie life is difficult. Charlie helps his mother when her baby is being born. He goes out into a blizzard to help the animals. Later, Charlie returns to Massachusetts to escape the violence in Kansas. Back home, he helps a runaway slave. Middle-elementary readers will find this series an accessible introduction to historical fiction.

1. Prairie Skies: Pioneer Summer ◆ 2002
2. Prairie Skies: Cabin in the Snow ◆ 2002
3. Prairie Skies: Our Kansas Home ◆ 2003

PRESTON

McNaughton, Colin

HARCOURT ◆ GRADES K–1 ◆ A/R

ANIMAL FANTASY | HUMOR

Preston, a young pig, blithely and unknowingly avoids the cunning and hungry big, bad wolf in this series. The wolf slips, trips, and crushes himself trying to get Preston. Each comical book has eye-catching illustrations that add to the humor. The large print aids in easy reading. There are also books for toddlers.

1. Suddenly! ◆ 1995
2. Boo! ◆ 1996
3. Oops! ◆ 1997
4. Preston's Goal! ◆ 1998
5. Yum! ◆ 1999
6. Oomph! ◆ 2001

PRETTY FREEKIN SCARY

Flesh, Chris P.

GROSSET & DUNLAP ◆ GRADES 5–8 ◆ A/R

HUMOR

Freekin is in love with Lilly but he has one big problem. He's dead . . . and decaying. (Yes, that's two problems.) Meanwhile, Pretty wants Freekin for herself, so once Freekin and Lilly are a couple, Pretty tries to break them up. Visit the Web site www.prettyfreekinscary.com for more creepy fun.

1. You Smell Dead ◆ 2007
2. Me So Pretty! ◆ 2007
3. The Mystery of the Mystery Meat ◆ 2008
4. Been There, Crossed Over ◆ 2008

PRINCE OF THE POND TRILOGY

Napoli, Donna Jo

DUTTON ◆ GRADES 3–6 ◆ A/R

FANTASY | HUMOR

These books merge a familiar folktale with laugh-out-loud humor. When the prince is turned into a frog, his biggest problem is communication. You try talking with a long, sticky tongue. In the second book, the prince's frog son is turned into a human boy, Jimmy, who deals with the attentions of Gracie.

1. The Prince of the Pond ◆ 1992
2. Jimmy, the Pickpocket of the Palace ◆ 1995
3. Gracie, the Pixie of the Puddle ◆ 2004

PRINCE TRILOGY *see* Sword of the Spirits

PRINCESS POWER

Williams, Suzanne

HARPERCOLLINS ◆ GRADES 3–5 ◆ A/R

FANTASY

Princess Lysandra wants adventure. Along with her three princess friends—Fatima, Elena, and Tansy—she faces challenging situations—as when the girls visit Tansy's kingdom and confront an ogre. Fans of the Fairy Realm and Little Genie books will enjoy this series.

1. The Perfectly Proper Prince ◆ 2006
2. The Charmingly Clever Cousin ◆ 2006
3. The Awfully Angry Ogre ◆ 2007
4. The Mysterious Mournful Maiden ◆ 2007
5. The Stubbornly Secretive Servant ◆ 2007
6. The Gigantic Genuine Genie ◆ 2007

THE PRINCESS SCHOOL

Mason, Jane B.

SCHOLASTIC ◆ GRADES 4–7 ◆ A/R

HUMOR

Familiar folktale females experience the difficulties of learning to be a princess. Elements from the classic stories about Ella, Rapunzel, Snow, and Rose are woven into these funny new versions. For example, Ella's fairy godmother is at a convention, so she'll have to make it on her own.

1. If the Shoe Fits ◆ 2004
2. Who's the Fairest? ◆ 2004
3. Let Down Your Hair ◆ 2004
4. Beauty Is a Beast ◆ 2005
5. Princess Charming ◆ 2005
6. Apple-y Ever After ◆ 2005
7. Thorn in Her Side ◆ 2006

THE PRINCESS TALES

Levine, Gail Carson

HARPERCOLLINS ◆ GRADES 3–6 ◆ A/R

FANTASY

Favorite folktales are expanded, revised, and enhanced in this series. "The Princess and the Pea" becomes *The Princess Test*, in which Prince Nicholas has already given his heart to Lorelei but will she pass muster?

"Cinderella" becomes "Cinderellis"—a boy who wants to win his Princess Charming.

1. The Fairy's Mistake ◆ 1999
2. Princess Sonora and the Long Sleep ◆ 1999
3. The Princess Test ◆ 1999
4. Cinderellis and the Glass Hill ◆ 2000
5. For Biddle's Sake ◆ 2002
6. The Fairy's Return ◆ 2002

PROFESSOR XARGLE

Willis, Jeanne

DUTTON ◆ GRADES K–3

HUMOR | SCIENCE FICTION

Professor Xargle, an alien, is constantly teaching his young alien students about Earth and the humans who inhabit it. With much tongue-in-cheek humor, he explores the silly things that humans do: in different kinds of weather, with their relatives, with their pets, and so on. Young readers will enjoy the silly stories and illustrations.

1. Earthlets, As Explained by Professor Xargle ◆ 1989
2. Earth Hounds, As Explained by Professor Xargle ◆ 1989
3. Earth Tigerlets, As Explained by Professor Xargle ◆ 1991
4. Earth Mobiles, As Explained by Professor Xargle ◆ 1991
5. Earth Weather, As Explained by Professor Xargle ◆ 1993
6. Relativity, As Explained by Professor Xargle ◆ 1993

PROTECTOR OF THE SMALL

Pierce, Tamora

RANDOM HOUSE ◆ GRADES 5–8 ◆ A/R

FANTASY

Keladry of Mindelan, 10, is training to be a page, an opportunity that has only been available to males. As a girl, she faces special challenges. She succeeds and wins the respect of the other pages. At age 18, Kel becomes a knight and is given an assignment to help save her homeland, Tortall.

1. First Test ◆ 1999
2. Page ◆ 2000
3. Squire ◆ 2001
4. Lady Knight ◆ 2002

PRYDAIN CHRONICLES

Alexander, Lloyd

DELL ◆ GRADES 5–8 ◆ A/R

FANTASY

Taran, a foundling who has no known parents, is Assistant Pig-Keeper for Hen Wen, an oracular pig who is kept in a safe, quiet place by Dallben the wizard. The country is Prydain, a fantasy land loosely based on Welsh legends. Taran dreams of adventure and longs to serve with Gwydion, a warrior of the House of Don. When Hen Wen runs away, Taran gives chase and runs into the warrior's life of which he dreamed. He meets a young enchantress named Eilonwy, and the two of them and many other friends fight against the Death Lord, who would enslave the whole land. They are finally victorious, and the House of Don decides to go to a perfect land. When Taran is invited to go with them, he decides instead to stay and take his rightful place as High King of Prydain. *The High King* won the Newbery Medal. A volume of short stories about Prydain, *The Foundling, and Other Tales of Prydain* was published in 1973.

1. The Book of Three ◆ 1964
2. The Black Cauldron ◆ 1965
3. The Castle of Llyr ◆ 1966
4. Taran Wanderer ◆ 1967
5. The High King ◆ 1968

PUP AND HOUND

Hood, Susan

KIDS CAN PRESS ◆ GRADES K–1 ◆ A/R

ANIMAL FANTASY

Pup and Hound are good friends and enjoy activities on the farm. Pup is energetic and full of mischief while Hound is levelheaded and responsible—he looks out for Pup. In *Pup and Hound Hatch an Egg*, Pup finds an egg but no barnyard bird will claim it. When the egg hatches, it is a turtle! When *Pup and Hound Play Copycats*, Hound gets tired of being followed by Pup. The rhyming text and colorful illustrations by Linda Hendry make this a good choice for beginning readers.

1. Pup and Hound ◆ 2004
2. Pup and Hound Move In ◆ 2004
3. Pup and Hound in Trouble ◆ 2005
4. Pup and Hound Stay Up Late ◆ 2005

5. Pup and Hound at Sea ◆ 2006
6. Pup and Hound Lost and Found ◆ 2006
7. Pup and Hound Catch a Thief ◆ 2007
8. Pup and Hound Hatch an Egg ◆ 2007
9. Pup and Hound Play Copycats ◆ 2007
10. Pup and Hound Scare a Ghost ◆ 2007

PUPPY FRIENDS

Dale, Jenny

ALADDIN ◆ GRADES 1–3 ◆ A/R

REAL LIFE

These are amusing stories about puppies. Gus loves to eat. He'll eat anything, including shoes. He wouldn't eat a diamond ring, would he? Billy's owner, Martin, reassures the scaredy-pup. Will Billy be brave enough to help Martin? Children who like animal stories will enjoy these books.

1. Gus the Greedy Puppy ◆ 2000
2. Lily the Lost Puppy ◆ 2000
3. Spot the Sporty Puppy ◆ 2000
4. Lenny the Lazy Puppy ◆ 2000
5. Max the Muddy Puppy ◆ 2000
6. Billy the Brave Puppy ◆ 2000
7. Nipper the Noisy Puppy ◆ 2000
8. Tilly the Tidy Puppy ◆ 2001
9. Spike the Special Puppy ◆ 2001

PUPPY MUDGE *see* Henry and Mudge: Puppy Mudge

PUPPY PATROL

Dale, Jenny

SCHOLASTIC ◆ GRADES 3–6 ◆ A/R

REAL LIFE

The Parker family owns the King Street Kennels. Dogs are groomed and boarded there and, occasionally, they are rescued from harmful circumstances. These books feature the children who live at the kennels and various dogs connected with them. In one book, Sarah rescues a lost puppy. In another book, Molly is the dog of a famous rock star. Molly's stay at the kennel attracts a lot of publicity and some problems, too. Readers who enjoy dog stories will want to know about this series. It was originally published in England and there are more titles available there. Listed here are the American editions from Scholastic. There is a related puzzle and game book.

1. Teacher's Pet ◆ 1999
2. Big Ben ◆ 1999
3. Abandoned! ◆ 2000
4. Double Trouble ◆ 2000
5. Star Paws ◆ 2000
6. Tug of Love ◆ 2000
7. Saving Skye ◆ 2001
8. Tuff's Luck ◆ 2001
9. Red Alert ◆ 2001
10. The Great Escape ◆ 2001
11. Perfect Puppy ◆ 2001
12. Sam and Delilah ◆ 2001
13. The Sea Dog ◆ 2001
14. Puppy School ◆ 2001
15. A Winter's Tale ◆ 2001
16. Puppy Love ◆ 2002
17. Best of Friends ◆ 2002
18. The King of the Castle ◆ 2003
19. Posh Pup ◆ 2003

THE PUPPY PLACE

Miles, Ellen

SCHOLASTIC ◆ GRADES 3–5 ◆ A/R

REAL LIFE

Charles and Lizzie Peterson want a puppy but their parents want them to develop responsibility. When the family takes in a golden retriever puppy named Goldie, the kids get their chance to show they can train and care for her. As the series progresses, the family serves as a foster family for abandoned and mistreated puppies, which are then given to new homes. In *Buddy*, Charles and Lizzie finally get a puppy to keep.

1. Goldie ◆ 2005
2. Snowball ◆ 2005
3. Shadow ◆ 2005
4. Rascal ◆ 2006
5. Buddy ◆ 2006
6. Flash ◆ 2006
7. Scout ◆ 2007
8. Patches ◆ 2007
9. Noodle ◆ 2008
10. Pugsley ◆ 2008
11. Princess ◆ 2008
12. Max and Maggie ◆ 2008

PURE DEAD MAGIC

Gliori, Debi

KNOPF ◆ **GRADES 5–8** ◆ **A/R**

FANTASY

In a Scottish castle, the Strega-Borgia children are in danger. Their father has been kidnapped and their new nanny is unusual. In the second book, their castle, StregaSchloss, is being repaired and Titus, 12, Pandora, 10, and baby Damp have to move. Like the Unfortunate Events books (Snicket) and Eddie Dickens (Ardagh), this series is dark and humorous.

1. Pure Dead Magic ◆ 2001
2. Pure Dead Wicked ◆ 2002
3. Pure Dead Brilliant ◆ 2003
4. Pure Dead Trouble ◆ 2005
5. Pure Dead Batty ◆ 2006
6. Pure Dead Frozen ◆ 2007

PYRATES

Archer, Chris

SCHOLASTIC ◆ **GRADES 5–7** ◆ **A/R**

FANTASY

George has always wondered about his family's heritage. Is he really descended from the famous pirate Captain Kidd? When George and his friends discover tunnels and an underground city, they face curses and creatures seeking to protect the buried treasure.

1. Secret City ◆ 2003
2. Eye of Eternity ◆ 2003
3. Dead Man's Chest ◆ 2003
4. Last Clue ◆ 2003

THE QUIGLEYS

Mason, Simon

D. FLICKLING BOOKS ◆ **GRADES 2–4** ◆ **A/R**

FAMILY LIFE | HUMOR

Meet Dad, Mum, Will, and Lucy—the Quigleys. Each family member is featured in one of the chapters. For example, Will wants a pet, Dad babysits, Lucy is a junior bridesmaid, and it's Mum's birthday. This is an entertaining British import.

1. The Quigleys ◆ 2002
2. The Quigleys at Large ◆ 2003
3. The Quigleys Not for Sale ◆ 2004
4. The Quigleys on the Go ◆ 2005
5. The Quigleys in a Spin ◆ 2006

RACHEL YODER—ALWAYS TROUBLE SOMEWHERE

Brunstetter, Wanda E.
BARBOUR ◆ GRADES 4–6
REAL LIFE

As this series begins, Rachel is 11 growing up in Lancaster County, Pennsylvania. Readers learn about the Amish way of life and traditions. Rachel is a spunky girl whose high spirits often create problems at home and school. In *New Beginnings,* Rachel's best friend moves away and a new girl seems to be causing trouble.

1. School's Out! ◆ 2007
2. Back to School ◆ 2007
3. Out of Control ◆ 2008
4. New Beginnings ◆ 2008
5. A Happy Heart ◆ 2008

RACING TO FREEDOM TRILOGY

Hart, Alison
PEACHTREE ◆ GRADES 5–8 ◆ A/R
HISTORICAL

During the Civil War, Gabriel, 12, is a slave on a Kentucky plantation caring for the Thoroughbred horses of his owner, Master Giles. There are renegade bands of soldiers attacking plantations for food, supplies, and horses. Gabriel saves Master Giles's Thoroughbreds and is rewarded with his freedom and a job as a jockey. As the trilogy continues, Gabriel develops his skills as a jockey and trainer. He joins his father, a free man in the Union Army, and experiences the horrors of battle. Issues of racism, freedom, slavery, conflict, and bravery are examined in this series, making it a good choice for discussions.

1. Gabriel's Horses ◆ 2007
2. Gabriel's Triumph ◆ 2007
3. Gabriel's Journey ◆ 2008

RAGGEDY ANN AND ANDY

Hall, Patricia

SIMON & SCHUSTER ◆ **GRADES 1–3**

FANTASY

These beloved dolls appear in these beginning readers. Other books are available including reissues of the classic Raggedy Ann and Andy stories and a series of board books for preschoolers.

1. Day at the Fair ◆ 2000
2. School Day Adventure ◆ 2000
3. Leaf Dance ◆ 2001
4. Going to Grandma's ◆ 2001
5. Hooray for Reading ◆ 2002
6. Old Friends, New Friends ◆ 2002

RAINBOW FAIRIES *see* Rainbow Magic: Rainbow Fairies

RAINBOW FISH

Pfister, Marcus

NORTH-SOUTH BOOKS ◆ **GRADES K–2** ◆ **A/R**

ANIMAL FANTASY

Rainbow Fish is the most beautiful fish in the ocean. He has silvery scales that make him different from all the other fish. When a little fish asks him for one, he refuses because he is selfish and vain. The other fish decide to have nothing to do with him and he becomes lonely until he talks to a wise octopus who advises him to give away his scales. Giving away just one to the little blue fish makes Rainbow Fish so happy that he decides to give away the others until he is left with just one. Two more stories in the series find Rainbow Fish helping everyone learn to get along.

1. The Rainbow Fish ◆ 1992
2. Rainbow Fish to the Rescue! ◆ 1995
3. Rainbow Fish and the Big Blue Whale ◆ 1998
4. Rainbow Fish and the Sea Monsters' Cave ◆ 2001
5. Rainbow Fish: The Dangerous Deep ◆ 2001
6. Rainbow Fish A,B,C ◆ 2002
7. Rainbow Fish 1,2,3 ◆ 2002
8. Rainbow Fish Finds His Way ◆ 2006

RAINBOW MAGIC: FUN DAY FAIRIES

Meadows, Daisy

SCHOLASTIC ◆ GRADES 1–3

FANTASY

The seven Fun Day Fairies bring joy and sparkle to each day of the week. Darn that Jack Frost . . . he has taken their special flags. Rachel and Kirsty must help the fairies find their flags. The reader helps, too, by finding the hidden flag in each book.

1. Sarah the Sunday Fairy ◆ 2008
2. Megan the Monday Fairy ◆ 2008
3. Tallulah the Tuesday Fairy ◆ 2008
4. Willow the Wednesday Fairy ◆ 2008
5. Thea the Thursday Fairy ◆ 2008
6. Freya the Friday Fairy ◆ 2008
7. Sienna the Saturday Fairy ◆ 2008

RAINBOW MAGIC: JEWEL FAIRIES

Meadows, Daisy

SCHOLASTIC ◆ GRADES 1–3 ◆ A/R

FANTASY

Seven jewels are missing from Queen Titania's crown and the fairies are losing their power. Once again, Jack Frost is to blame. Two girls, Rachel and Kirsty, help the fairies find the jewels and save Fairyland. There is a sparkly jewel in each book.

1. India the Moonstone Fairy ◆ 2007
2. Scarlett the Garnet Fairy ◆ 2007
3. Emily the Emerald Fairy ◆ 2007
4. Chloe the Topaz Fairy ◆ 2007
5. Amy the Amethyst Fairy ◆ 2007
6. Sophie the Sapphire Fairy ◆ 2007
7. Lucy the Diamond Fairy ◆ 2008

RAINBOW MAGIC: PET FAIRIES

Meadows, Daisy

SCHOLASTIC ◆ GRADES 1–3 ◆ A/R

FANTASY

There are seven pet fairies and each has a special pet. Jack Frost has stolen all of the pets. Without them, the fairies cannot do their job of matching pets to owners. Two girls, Rachel and Kirsty, help find the pets. This series was originally published in England.

1. Katie, the Kitten Fairy ◆ 2008
2. Bella, the Bunny Fairy ◆ 2008
3. Georgia, the Guinea Pig Fairy ◆ 2008
4. Lauren, the Puppy Fairy ◆ 2008
5. Harriet, the Hamster Fairy ◆ 2008
6. Molly, the Goldfish Fairy ◆ 2008
7. Penny, the Pony Fairy ◆ 2008

RAINBOW MAGIC: RAINBOW FAIRIES

Meadows, Daisy

SCHOLASTIC ◆ GRADES 1–3 ◆ A/R

FANTASY

The seven Rainbow Fairies work to keep Fairyland colorful and bright. But Fairyland is gray because Jack Frost has sent the seven sisters away. Rachel and Kirsty must find each fairy and save Fairyland.

1. Ruby the Red Fairy ◆ 2005
2. Amber the Orange Fairy ◆ 2005
3. Sunny the Yellow Fairy ◆ 2005
4. Fern the Green Fairy ◆ 2005
5. Sky the Blue Fairy ◆ 2005
6. Inky the Indigo Fairy ◆ 2006
7. Heather the Violet Fairy ◆ 2006

RAINBOW MAGIC: WEATHER FAIRIES

Meadows, Daisy

SCHOLASTIC ◆ GRADES 1–3 ◆ A/R

FANTASY

Jack Frost has stolen the magical feathers from Doodle the rooster and now the weather is a mess. The seven Weather Fairies must fix the weather. Each book in this series has a feather!

1. Crystal the Snow Fairy ◆ 2006
2. Abigail the Breeze Fairy ◆ 2006
3. Pearl the Cloud Fairy ◆ 2006
4. Goldie the Sunshine Fairy ◆ 2006
5. Evie the Mist Fairy ◆ 2006
6. Storm the Lightning Fairy ◆ 2007
7. Hayley the Rain Fairy ◆ 2007

RALPH S. MOUSE

Cleary, Beverly

MORROW ◆ GRADES 2–4 ◆ A/R

ANIMAL FANTASY | HUMOR

In the first book, *The Mouse and the Motorcycle,* a small brown mouse named Ralph discovers his motoring skills when he experiments with a toy motorcycle that belongs to a young guest staying in the hotel where Ralph lives. His daredevil antics get Ralph into many tricky situations and even take him on an adventure to a summer camp in *Runaway Ralph.* In *Ralph S. Mouse,* the inquisitive mouse must demonstrate how smart he is and ends up having some wild adventures at school. The great success of this series lies in Beverly Cleary's ability to view the harsh and humorous aspects of the human world from the perspective of a mouse.

1. The Mouse and the Motorcycle ◆ 1965
2. Runaway Ralph ◆ 1970
3. Ralph S. Mouse ◆ 1982

RAMONA QUIMBY

Cleary, Beverly

MORROW ◆ GRADES 2–4 ◆ A/R

FAMILY LIFE | HUMOR

First introduced as Beezus's pesky kid sister in the Henry Huggins series, Ramona inspired a successful series all her own and quickly became a favorite of young readers. The series follows Ramona from kindergarten through fourth grade as she encounters many of childhood's challenging situations—a strict teacher, a bossy big sister, a working mother, and a temporarily out-of-work father—and gets involved in some hilarious escapades. Young readers will relate to Ramona as she tries very hard to behave but sometimes just can't help acting up. Through it all, Ramona faces life with tenacity, spunk, and a wild imagination.

1. Beezus and Ramona ◆ 1955
2. Ramona the Pest ◆ 1968
3. Ramona the Brave ◆ 1975
4. Ramona and Her Father ◆ 1977
5. Ramona and Her Mother ◆ 1979
6. Ramona Quimby, Age 8 ◆ 1981
7. Ramona, Forever ◆ 1984
8. Ramona's World ◆ 1999

RANGER'S APPRENTICE

Flanagan, John

PHILOMEL ◆ GRADES 5–9 ◆ A/R

FANTASY

On Choosing Day, Will, 15, is disheartened when he is not selected for Battleschool. Instead, Will is to train as a Ranger and serve as an apprentice to Ranger Halt. As Will begins his training, the evil magical forces of Morgarath are planning an invasion. Will is included in a mission to stop the invaders. As the series progresses, Will and Evanlyn (a princess in disguise) are captured by the Skandians, raiders from the north country, and Ranger Halt leads a team to rescue them. Filled with invaders, magic, creatures, and battles, this series mirrors many other epic good versus evil series such as the Lord of the Rings.

1. The Ruins of Gorlan ◆ 2005
2. The Burning Bridge ◆ 2006
3. The Icebound Land ◆ 2007
4. The Battle for Skandia ◆ 2008
5. The Sorcerer of the North ◆ 2008

RATS OF NIMH

O'Brien, Robert C., and Jane Leslie Conly

ATHENEUM; HARPERCOLLINS ◆ GRADES 3–6 ◆ A/R

ANIMAL FANTASY │ SCIENCE FICTION

A delightful science fiction trilogy for intermediate readers. A group of rats build an intelligent community in Thorn Valley after escaping from a laboratory where they were test subjects. In the first book of the trilogy, Mrs. Frisby goes to these rats for advice because of their intelligence and wisdom. Many adventures ensue. In the second book, Mrs. Frisby's son Timothy meets up with Racso, and together they are able to save Thorn Valley from destruction. Finally, in the third book, the rat community helps two children who are lost and then depends on the children to protect the rats from discovery. *Mrs. Frisby and the Rats of NIMH* won the Newbery Medal. O'Brien's daughter, Jane Leslie Conly, continued the series after his death, writing the two sequels.

1. Mrs. Frisby and the Rats of NIMH ◆ 1971
2. Racso and the Rats of NIMH ◆ 1988
3. R-T, Margaret and the Rats of NIMH ◆ 1990

READY, FREDDY!

Klein, Abby

SCHOLASTIC ◆ GRADES K–2 ◆ A/R

REAL LIFE

Freddy is a first-grader with big ideas that often cause him problems. In *Homework Hassles,* he and his friend Robbie decide to go outside at night to find a nocturnal animal to study for their homework. Of course, this does not work out the way they planned. Young readers will identify with Freddy's concerns about home and school.

1. Tooth Trouble ◆ 2004
2. The King of Show and Tell ◆ 2004
3. Homework Hassles ◆ 2004
4. Don't Sit On My Lunch! ◆ 2005
5. Talent Show Scaredy-Pants ◆ 2005
6. Help! A Vampire's Coming! ◆ 2005
7. Yikes! Bikes! ◆ 2006
8. Halloween Fraidy-Cat ◆ 2006
9. Shark Tooth Tale ◆ 2006
10. Super-Secret Valentine ◆ 2007
11. The Pumpkin Elf Mystery ◆ 2007
12. Stop That Hamster! ◆ 2007
13. Camping Catastrophe! ◆ 2008
14. Thanksgiving Turkey Trouble ◆ 2008

REAL KIDS, REAL PLACES *see* Carole Marsh
Mysteries: Real Kids, Real Places

RED

Kjelgaard, Jim

HOLIDAY HOUSE ◆ GRADES 4–6 ◆ A/R

ADVENTURE

The adventures of a young boy and his lovable Irish setter form the basis for this series. Together they survive the rugged Wintupi wilderness. Other stories are about Big Red's offspring. This series will appeal to dog lovers and fans of *Old Yeller.*

1. Big Red ◆ 1945
2. Irish Red, Son of Big Red ◆ 1951
3. Outlaw Red, Son of Big Red ◆ 1953

RED ROCK MYSTERIES

Jenkins, Jerry B., and Chris Fabry

TYNDALE KIDS ◆ GRADES 5–8 ◆ A/R

MYSTERY

Sports, mysteries, and faith are the focus in this series featuring 13-year-old twins Ashley and Bryce Timberline. In *Double Fault*, the twins attend a tennis camp at the local country club and Bryce is accused of vandalism. While trying to clear his name, the twins also find out more about the plane crash that killed their father.

1. Haunted Waters ◆ 2005
2. Stolen Secrets ◆ 2005
3. Missing Pieces ◆ 2005
4. Wild Rescue ◆ 2005
5. Grave Shadows ◆ 2005
6. Phantom Writer ◆ 2005
7. Double Fault ◆ 2005
8. Canyon Echoes ◆ 2005
9. Instant Menace ◆ 2006
10. Escaping Darkness ◆ 2006
11. Windy City Danger ◆ 2006
12. Hollywood Hold Up ◆ 2006
13. Hidden Riches ◆ 2006
14. Wind Chill ◆ 2006
15. Dead End ◆ 2006

REDWALL

Jacques, Brian

PHILOMEL ◆ GRADES 4–8 ◆ A/R

ADVENTURE | ANIMAL FANTASY

Redwall Abbey is the focal point for the mice and other creatures who live in Mossflower Woods. In the first book, *Redwall*, an army of rats tries to conquer the abbey and the defending mice must find the lost sword of Martin the Warrior to save themselves and their beloved abbey. Subsequent titles introduce a changing cast of heroes, heroines, and evildoers who interact in an epic saga full of conspiracies, adventures and heroics. *The Great Redwall Feast* is a colorfully illustrated companion book directed toward a younger audience about the secret preparations by the Redwall creatures for a feast in honor of the Abbott. *A Redwall Winter's Tale* and *The Redwall Cookbook* are additional picture books directed at younger readers. And there is a *Redwall* graphic novel (2007). The books can also be read following events in chronological order: *Lord Brocktree, Martin The Warrior, Mossflower, The Legend of Luke, Outcast of*

Redwall, Mariel of Redwall, The Bellmaker, Salamandastron, Redwall, Mattimeo, The Pearls of Lutra, The Long Patrol, Marlfox, The Taggerung, Triss, Loamhedge, Rakkety Tam, High Rhulain, Eulalia!, and *Doomwyte.*

1. Redwall ◆ 1986
2. Mossflower ◆ 1988
3. Mattimeo ◆ 1989
4. Mariel of Redwall ◆ 1991
5. Salamandastron ◆ 1992
6. Martin the Warrior ◆ 1993
7. The Bellmaker ◆ 1994
8. Outcast of Redwall ◆ 1995
9. The Pearls of Lutra ◆ 1996
10. The Long Patrol ◆ 1997
11. Marlfox ◆ 1998
12. The Legend of Luke ◆ 1999
13. Lord Brocktree ◆ 2000
14. The Taggerung ◆ 2001
15. Triss ◆ 2002
16. Loamhedge ◆ 2003
17. Rakkety Tam ◆ 2004
18. High Rhulain ◆ 2005
19. Eulalia! ◆ 2007
20. Doomwyte ◆ 2008

REEL KIDS ADVENTURES

Gustaveson, Dave

YOUTH WITH A MISSION PUBLISHING ◆ GRADES 5–7

ADVENTURE | VALUES

Jeff Caldwell, 15, is interested in the Media Club at his new high school. The club has a mission—to spread a Christian message to other kids at home and around the world. In order to travel with the club, Jeff's parents insist that his 13-year-old sister Mindy be included. This causes some tension for Jeff as well as some scary moments that result from Mindy's impetuous actions. Quickly paced with lots of dialogue, this will appeal to readers who like action and discussions of values.

1. The Missing Video ◆ 1993
2. Mystery at Smokey Mountain ◆ 1994
3. The Stolen Necklace ◆ 1994
4. The Mysterious Case ◆ 1995
5. The Amazon Stranger ◆ 1995
6. The Dangerous Voyage ◆ 1995
7. The Lost Diary ◆ 1996
8. The Forbidden Road ◆ 1996
9. The Danger Zone ◆ 1997

REFLECTIONS OF A BLACK COWBOY

Miller, Robert H.

JUST US BOOKS ◆ GRADES 4–6

HISTORICAL

The four books in this series feature the Wild West/frontier adventures of African Americans. There are explorers, soldiers, cowboys, pioneers, hunters, trappers, and more. Readers will be intrigued by the contributions of these men and women.

1. Cowboys ◆ 2004
2. The Buffalo Soldiers ◆ 2004
3. Pioneers ◆ 2006
4. Mountain Men ◆ 2006

REGARDING THE . . .

Klise, Kate

HARCOURT ◆ GRADES 4–6

HUMOR

The principal of Dry Creek Middle School (later Geyser Creek Middle School) gets more than he bargains for when he decides that a new drinking fountain is needed. The whole town becomes involved in the ensuing, lively debate, much enhanced by the fifth grade's history project, which reveals all sorts of truths about key figures in the community. Letters, memos, newspaper articles, even police reports aid in the telling of these funny stories illustrated by M. Sarah Klise.

1. Regarding the Fountain: A Tale, in Letters, of Liars and Leaks ◆ 1998
2. Regarding the Sink: Where, Oh Where, Did Waters go? ◆ 2004
3. Regarding the Trees: A Splintered Saga Rooted in Secrets ◆ 2005
4. Regarding the Bathrooms: A Privy to the Past ◆ 2006
5. Regarding the Bee: A Lesson, in Letters, on Honey, Dating, and Other Sticky Subjects ◆ 2007

REMNANTS

Applegate, K. A.

SCHOLASTIC ◆ GRADES 5–9 ◆ A/R

SCIENCE FICTION

It is 2011. Earth will soon be gone, destroyed by a collision with an asteroid. A group of people are brought together and launched into space in a tube. They travel for five hundred years and awake in a strange world. There are complex adventures as the survivors face dangers from the new environment and from each other.

1. The Mayflower Project ◆ 2001
2. Destination Unknown ◆ 2001
3. Then ◆ 2001
4. Nowhere Land ◆ 2002
5. Mutation ◆ 2002
6. Breakdown ◆ 2002
7. Isolation ◆ 2002
8. Mother, May I? ◆ 2002
9. No Place like Home ◆ 2002
10. Lost and Found ◆ 2002
11. Dream Storm ◆ 2003
12. Aftermath ◆ 2003
13. Survival ◆ 2003
14. Begin Again ◆ 2003

THE RESCUERS

Sharp, Margery

LITTLE, BROWN ◆ GRADES 4–6 ◆ A/R

ADVENTURE | ANIMAL FANTASY

A lovely white mouse enjoys a special relationship with an ambassador's son, living in the embassy in great luxury. She is also Madam President of the Mouse Prisoners Aid Society, which was founded with the intent of cheering prisoners but ends up rescuing them. Miss Bianca is a well-brought-up mouse with exquisite manners, and Bernard is a brave but rough-around-the-edges companion. Together, with the help of the other mice in the society, they embark on one daring rescue after another. They travel to the Orient and the Antarctic and even to the Salt Mines. Their most frightening rescue, however, is one they perform right in their own embassy when the ambassador's niece is put under a spell by an evil doll.

1. The Rescuers ◆ 1959
2. Miss Bianca ◆ 1962
3. The Turret ◆ 1963
4. Miss Bianca in the Salt Mines ◆ 1966
5. Miss Bianca in the Orient ◆ 1970
6. Miss Bianca in the Antarctic ◆ 1971
7. Miss Bianca and the Bridesmaid ◆ 1972
8. Bernard the Brave ◆ 1977
9. Bernard into Battle ◆ 1978

REX AND LILLY

Brown, Laurie Krasny

LITTLE, BROWN ◆ GRADES K–2 ◆ A/R

ANIMAL FANTASY | FAMILY LIFE

Rex and Lilly are brother and sister dinosaurs. Each title has three stories about the siblings and their everyday experiences. Children can read about Rex and Lilly doing tricks in the pool, going to dance class, keeping themselves busy on rainy days, celebrating their mother's birthday, cleaning their house, and getting a new pet.

1. Rex and Lilly Family Time ◆ 1995
2. Rex and Lilly Play Time ◆ 1995
3. Rex and Lilly Schooltime ◆ 1997

THE RHIANNA CHRONICLES

Luckett, Dave

SCHOLASTIC ◆ GRADES 4–7 ◆ A/R

FANTASY

Rhianna Wildwood is the daughter of an ordinary blacksmith, but she has extraordinary powers. She has a spellcaster, which is connected to its twin at the Office of the Chancellor of Wizardly College in Avalon. In Book Three, Rhianna helps the Queen deal with Wild Magic at the Castle of Avalon. Originally published in Australia, this series features magical events and a spunky female main character who will be attractive to girls.

1. The Girl, the Dragon, and the Wild Magic: Book One of the Rhianna Chronicles ◆ 2003
2. The Girl, the Apprentice, and the Dogs of Iron: Book Two of the Rhianna Chronicles ◆ 2004
3. The Girl, the Queen, and the Castle: Book Three of the Rhianna Chronicles ◆ 2004

RICKY RICOTTA

Pilkey, Dav

BLUE SKY PRESS ◆ GRADES 2–5 ◆ A/R

ANIMAL FANTASY

Ricky Ricotta is a mouse who lives in Squeakville. Dr. Stinky McNasty sends a giant robot to destroy the town. When the robot refuses, Dr.

McNasty aims his retro-rocket at the robot. Ricky saves the robot and a partnership is formed. Kids love these heavily illustrated books, which are like graphic novels for the elementary grades. Pilkey includes instructions for drawing some of the characters. Some early editions were titled Ricky Ricotta's Giant Robot.

1. Ricky Ricotta's Mighty Robot ◆ 2000
2. Ricky Ricotta's Mighty Robot vs. the Mutant Mosquitoes from Mercury ◆ 2000
3. Ricky Ricotta's Mighty Robot vs. the Voodo Vultures from Venus ◆ 2001
4. Ricky Ricotta's Mighty Robot vs. the Mecha-Monkeys from Mars ◆ 2002
5. Ricky Ricotta's Mighty Robot vs. the Jurassic Jackrabbits from Jupiter ◆ 2002
6. Ricky Ricotta's Mighty Robot vs. the Stupid Stinkbugs from Saturn ◆ 2003
7. Ricky Ricotta's Mighty Robot vs. the Uranium Unicorns from Uranus ◆ 2005

RIDING ACADEMY

Hart, Alison

RANDOM HOUSE ◆ GRADES 4–6

REAL LIFE | RECREATION

Mary Beth, Andie, Jina, and Lauren are roommates at Foxhall Academy, a girls' prep school. Despite their different backgrounds and personalities, the four girls find a common bond in their love for horses. Luckily for them, the school offers an excellent riding program that helps the girls learn about competition, friendship, sharing, failure, and growing up. *Haunted Horseback Holiday* (1996) is a Riding Academy Super Special.

1. A Horse for Mary Beth ◆ 1994
2. Andie Out of Control ◆ 1994
3. Jina Rides to Win ◆ 1994
4. Lessons for Lauren ◆ 1994
5. Mary Beth's Haunted Ride ◆ 1994
6. Andie Shows Off ◆ 1994
7. Jina's Pain-in-the-Neck Pony ◆ 1995
8. The Craziest Horse Show Ever ◆ 1995
9. Andie's Risky Business ◆ 1995
10. Trouble at Foxhall ◆ 1995
11. Foxhunt ◆ 1995
12. Lauren Rides to the Rescue ◆ 1995
13. Rivals in the Ring ◆ 1996
14. Million-Dollar Mare ◆ 1998

RINALDO

Scheffler, Ursel

NORTH-SOUTH BOOKS ◆ GRADES 2–4 ◆ A/R

ANIMAL FANTASY | HUMOR

Rinaldo is a sly fox—in fact, he's a con man who spends most of his time avoiding the police and running from the poor souls (chickens, moles, cats, and other animals) he's swindled. Young readers (and listeners) will enjoy the stories of this wily adventurer, although the plot lines are sophisticated tales in the tradition of adult action-adventure novels.

1. Rinaldo, the Sly Fox ◆ 1992
2. The Return of Rinaldo, the Sly Fox ◆ 1993
3. Rinaldo on the Run ◆ 1995

RINKO

Uchida, Yoshiko

ATHENEUM ◆ GRADES 4–6 ◆ A/R

FAMILY LIFE | HISTORICAL

Rinko and her family live in California during the Great Depression. They maintain their connection to their relatives in Japan even as they try to adjust to life in the United States. Some of the events in the book revolve around visits from Japanese family and friends; others deal with the clash between the two cultures. Rinko is much more Americanized than her parents. These books provide information about the immigrant experience along with cultural details and historical information about the Depression.

1. A Jar of Dreams ◆ 1981
2. The Best Bad Thing ◆ 1983
3. The Happiest Ending ◆ 1985

RIOT BROTHERS

Amato, Mary

HOLIDAY HOUSE ◆ GRADES 4–7 ◆ A/R

HUMOR

Does putting underpants on your head make you laugh so hard the milk comes out your nose? If so, these are the books for you. In the first book, Wilbur, grade five, and Orville, grade three, have three adventures: they foil a bank robber, search for treasure, and build a catapult. There are numerous cartoon-style illustrations to support the antics. Fans of Captain Underpants will enjoy these books as will reluctant readers.

1. Snarf Attack, Underfoodle, and the Secret of Life: The Riot Brothers Tell All ◆ 2004
2. Drooling and Dangerous: The Riot Brothers Return! ◆ 2006
3. Stinky and Successful: The Riot Brothers Never Stop ◆ 2007
4. Take the Mummy and Run: The Riot Brothers Are on a Roll ◆ 2009

RIVERSIDE KIDS: ELISA

Hurwitz, Johanna

MORROW ◆ GRADES 1–3 ◆ A/R

FAMILY LIFE | HUMOR

Elisa Michaels is Russell's little sister. These books show her growing up: from a toddler to adjusting to a new baby brother to getting her own room to going to school. Elisa faces many situations that will be familiar to young readers. Children will also want to read the Russell books and the series about Elisa's friends, Nora and Teddy.

1. Russell and Elisa ◆ 1989
2. "E" Is for Elisa ◆ 1991
3. Make Room for Elisa ◆ 1993
4. Elisa in the Middle ◆ 1995
5. Ever-Clever Elisa ◆ 1997
6. Summer with Elisa ◆ 2000
7. Elisa Michaels, Bigger and Better ◆ 2003

RIVERSIDE KIDS: NORA AND TEDDY

Hurwitz, Johanna

PUFFIN ◆ GRADES 3–4 ◆ A/R

FAMILY LIFE

This character-based series focuses on Nora's observations and reactions to life and the people around her. Nora and Teddy find ample situations and people to observe in their apartment building. They discover that some people don't appreciate their insights. Curious, outgoing, and imaginative, Nora invites readers to share in her and Teddy's daily life. Each chapter is a new day for Nora and Teddy, which makes these books excellent for reading aloud. Nora and Teddy are friends with Russell and Elisa, who each have their own series of books.

1. Busybody Nora ◆ 1976
2. Nora and Mrs. Mind-Your-Own-Business ◆ 1977
3. New Neighbors for Nora ◆ 1979
4. Superduper Teddy ◆ 1980

RIVERSIDE KIDS: RUSSELL

Hurwitz, Johanna

MORROW ◆ GRADES 1–3 ◆ A/R

FAMILY LIFE | HUMOR

First introduced as a neighbor in the Nora and Teddy series by the same author, Russell inspired a series of his own. In the first stories, Russell is a rambunctious little boy who throws temper tantrums when things don't go his way. As he grows older, however, he learns to control his temper and even to appreciate his little sister, Elisa. Children will be able to relate to the emotional ups and downs Russell experiences in everyday life. Russell's sister Elisa has a spinoff series of her own. *Russell's Secret* (2001) is a picture book about Russell.

1. Rip-Roaring Russell ◆ 1983
2. Russell Rides Again ◆ 1985
3. Russell Sprouts ◆ 1987
4. Russell and Elisa ◆ 1989

ROBBIE PACKFORD

Sander, Heather

ORCA ◆ GRADES 4–6 ◆ A/R

SCIENCE FICTION

Robbie is a sixth-grader who is transformed by an alien into a big green monster. Jamie, the alien, is from the planet Kerbosky, which is being threatened by robots that eventually plan to take over the universe. Jamie needs Robbie's help to stop the robots.

1. Robbie Packford—Alien Monster ◆ 2004
2. Make Mine with Everything ◆ 2004
3. Whatever Happened to My Dog Cuddles? ◆ 2005

ROBERT

Seuling, Barbara

CRICKET BOOKS ◆ GRADES 2–4 ◆ A/R

REAL LIFE

In the first book, Robert Dorfman struggles to do well enough in school. In later books, he strives to get a dog, be on a game show, and learn about endangered animals. This series is a good choice for middle-elementary readers looking for chapter books.

1. Oh No, It's Robert ◆ 1999
2. Robert and the Great Pepperoni ◆ 2001
3. Robert and the Weird and Wacky Facts ◆ 2002
4. Robert and the Back-to-School Special ◆ 2002
5. Robert and the Lemming Problem ◆ 2003
6. Robert and the Great Escape ◆ 2003
7. Robert Takes a Stand ◆ 2004
8. Robert Finds a Way ◆ 2005
9. Robert and the Practical Jokes ◆ 2006
10. Robert and the Happy Endings ◆ 2007
11. Robert Goes to Camp ◆ 2007

ROBERTS FAMILY *see* Liza, Bill and Jed

ROBIN HILL SCHOOL

McNamara, Margaret
ALADDIN ◆ **GRADES K–2** ◆ **A/R**
REAL LIFE

The students in Mrs. Connor's first-grade class have many familiar experiences. They worry about teasing, being left out, and missing the 100th day of school celebration due to illness. In *The Playground Problem,* Emma is upset because the boys won't let her (or any girl) play soccer. This series has a simple vocabulary and short sentences that make it a good choice for beginning readers.

1. The Counting Race ◆ 2003
2. The Pumpkin Patch ◆ 2003
3. Too Many Valentines ◆ 2003
4. One Hundred Days (Plus One) ◆ 2003
5. Election Day ◆ 2004
6. The Playground Problem ◆ 2004
7. A Tooth Story ◆ 2004
8. First-Grade Bunny ◆ 2005
9. The First Day of School ◆ 2005
10. Happy Thanksgiving ◆ 2005
11. Groundhog Day ◆ 2005
12. Happy Graduation! ◆ 2006
13. Fall Leaf Project ◆ 2006
14. The Luck of the Irish ◆ 2007
15. Dad Goes to School ◆ 2007
16. Snow Day ◆ 2007
17. Martin Luther King Jr. Day ◆ 2007
18. Halloween Fun ◆ 2008

ROCKET POWER

Various authors

SIMON & SCHUSTER ◆ GRADES K–2 ◆ A/R

RECREATION

Extreme sports are featured in this series. Otto, Reggie, and the rest of the Rocket gang go climbing, skiing, and snowboarding. They go mountain boarding and try street luge (which turns out to be very dangerous). Many of the books feature competitions. There are colorful cartoon-style illustrations and lots of excitement for young readers.

ROCKET POWER READERS (K–2)

1. Watch Out, Otto! (Wax, Wendy) ◆ 2002
2. Wild River Adventure (Banks, Steven) ◆ 2002
3. The Big Sweep (Dubowski, Cathy East, and Mark Dubowski) ◆ 2003
4. Reggie's Secret Admirer (Wax, Wendy) ◆ 2004
5. A Time to Climb (Wax, Wendy) ◆ 2004

ROCKET POWER PICTURE BOOKS (K–2)

1. Avalanche Trail (Collins, Terry) ◆ 2002
2. Board Games (Beechen, Adam) ◆ 2002
3. Chasing Dad (Beechen, Adam) ◆ 2003
4. Hit the Streets (Collins, Terry) ◆ 2003

ROCKET POWER CHAPTER BOOKS (2–4)

1. Double Trouble (Banks, Steven) ◆ 2001
2. Surf's Up (Collins, Terry) ◆ 2001
3. The Cost of Cool (Beechen, Adam) ◆ 2002
4. Twister's Big Break (Beechen, Adam) ◆ 2002

THE ROCKY RIDGE YEARS *see* Little House: The Rose Years

ROLLER COASTER TYCOON

Various authors

GROSSET & DUNLAP ◆ GRADES 4–7

ADVENTURE

Based on a popular video game, these books use the "Choose Your Own Adventure" format to involve readers in decisions about characters in different amusement parks. In the first book, Marty and Megnolia inherit money and build their own park. Other books feature a haunted park and a park that may be controlled by aliens. Fans of the video game and fans of interactive reading will enjoy these books.

1. Sudden Turn (Breaux, Shane) ◆ 2002
2. Sabotage! (Breaux, Shane) ◆ 2002
3. The Great Coaster Contest (West, Tracey) ◆ 2003
4. Kidnapped! (Gorman, Larry Mike) ◆ 2003
5. Haunted Park (Noll, Katherine) ◆ 2003
6. Spaced Out! (Weiss, Bobbi J. G., and David M. Weiss) ◆ 2003

ROMAN MYSTERIES

Lawrence, Caroline

ROARING BROOK; PUFFIN ◆ GRADES 5–8 ◆ A/R

HISTORICAL | MYSTERY

Set in the Roman Empire of the first century A.D., this series features mysteries along with information about the social and political events of the era. Flavia Gemina solves mysteries along with her friends Lupus (a beggar), Jonathan and Miriam (her Christian neighbors), and Nubia (an African slave). In *The Charioteer of Delphi,* the friends search for a missing racehorse and try to discover who is working to sabotage the chariot races at the Circus Maximus. This series has had different publishers—the dates for books vary depending on the edition.

1. The Thieves of Ostia ◆ 2002
2. The Secrets of Vesuvius ◆ 2002
3. The Pirates of Pompeii ◆ 2004
4. The Assassins of Rome ◆ 2005
5. The Dolphins of Laurentum ◆ 2005
6. The Twelve Tasks of Flavia Gemina ◆ 2004
7. The Enemies of Jupiter ◆ 2005
8. The Gladiators from Capua ◆ 2006
9. The Colossus of Rhodes ◆ 2006
10. The Fugitive from Corinth ◆ 2006
11. The Sirens of Surrentum ◆ 2007
12. The Charioteer of Delphi ◆ 2007

RONALD MORGAN

Giff, Patricia Reilly

VIKING KESTREL ◆ GRADES K–3 ◆ A/R

HUMOR | REAL LIFE

Ronald Morgan is a second-grader who can't do anything right. However, with the support of his friends, Rosemary and Michael, and his teacher Miss Farley, Ronald keeps trying until he experiences success.

Young readers will recognize their own frustrations and relate to Ronald's feelings of pride when he achieves success.

1. Today Was a Terrible Day ◆ 1980
2. The Almost Awful Play ◆ 1984
3. Watch Out, Ronald Morgan! ◆ 1985
4. Happy Birthday, Ronald Morgan! ◆ 1986
5. Ronald Morgan Goes to Bat ◆ 1988
6. Ronald Morgan Goes to Camp ◆ 1995
7. Good Luck, Ronald Morgan ◆ 1996

ROOMMATES

Galbraith, Kathryn O.

SIMON & SCHUSTER ◆ GRADES 1–3

FAMILY LIFE

These early chapter books are warm and funny. Mimi and Beth are sisters. They first become roommates when their mom is going to have another baby. Even though they are very different people, they discover that being roommates can be lots of fun. As the series continues, they experience the arrival of a new baby in the house and go to camp together as roommates.

1. Roommates ◆ 1990
2. Roommates and Rachel ◆ 1991
3. Roommates Again ◆ 1994

ROSA TRILOGY

Williams, Vera B.

MULBERRY BOOKS ◆ GRADES K–3 ◆ A/R

FAMILY LIFE

A charming picture book trilogy about a small Hispanic family working together in the big city. The first title in the series, *A Chair for My Mother,* was a Caldecott Honor Book. Rosa's family has a big jar in which they put spare change, saving for special things: first a big chair for her mother after they lose everything in a fire; then an accordion for Rosa's birthday. The family pulls together once more in the last book when Rosa's grandmother is sick and Rosa and her friends play music to raise money.

1. A Chair for My Mother ◆ 1982
2. Something Special for Me ◆ 1983
3. Music, Music for Everyone ◆ 1984

ROSCOE RILEY RULES

Applegate, Katherine

HARPERCOLLINS ◆ GRADES 1–2

HUMOR | REAL LIFE

Move over Junie B. Jones, Roscoe Riley is here. Roscoe is in first grade and he is a normal kid who sometimes gets in trouble. In the first book, Roscoe finds some Super-Mega-Gonzo Glue in the junk drawer and tries it out. As the title of the first book states, Roscoe learns an important lesson—*Never Glue Your Friends to Chairs.* The short chapters (sometimes only one page) and numerous illustrations by Brian Biggs are just right for kids making the transition from "readers" to "chapter books."

1. Never Glue Your Friends to Chairs ◆ 2008
2. Never Swipe a Bully's Bear ◆ 2008
3. Don't Swap Your Sweater for a Dog ◆ 2008
4. Never Swim in Applesauce ◆ 2008
5. Don't Tap Dance on Your Teacher ◆ 2009

THE ROSE YEARS *see* Little House: The Rose Years

ROSIE

Matas, Carol

ALADDIN ◆ GRADES 4–6 ◆ A/R

HISTORICAL

After her mother becomes ill, Rosie, 11, secretly takes her mother's place working in the shirtwaist factory. The family is struggling and needs the money from this job to survive. In the factory, Rosie experiences the hardships of poor working conditions and unreasonable work expectations. She joins with striking employees only to be harassed and arrested. As the first book ends, the family moves to Chicago and then to Los Angeles, which are the locations for two more books.

1. Rosie in New York City: Gotcha! ◆ 2003
2. Rosie in Chicago: Play Ball! ◆ 2003
3. Rosie in Los Angeles: Action! ◆ 2004

ROSY COLE

Greenwald, Sheila

LITTLE, BROWN ◆ GRADES 3–5 ◆ A/R

FAMILY LIFE | HUMOR

Artistic Rosy Cole lives in Manhattan with her parents, her sisters, and her cat. This series chronicles her adventures with best friend Hermione Wong and other friends from her all-female private school. Over the course of the series, Rosy learns to accept herself and appreciate her talent for art. Rosy's observations about life and her efforts to succeed are often hilarious. Along with the funny stories is a fascinating look at life in New York.

1. Give Us a Great Big Smile, Rosy Cole ◆ 1981
2. Valentine Rosy ◆ 1984
3. Rosy Cole's Great American Guilt Club ◆ 1985
4. Write On, Rosy! ◆ 1988
5. Rosy's Romance ◆ 1989
6. Here's Hermione: A Rosy Cole Production ◆ 1991
7. Rosy Cole Discovers America! ◆ 1992
8. Rosy Cole: She Walks in Beauty ◆ 1994
9. Rosy Cole: She Grows and Graduates ◆ 1997
10. Rosy Cole's Worst Ever, Best Yet Tour of New York City ◆ 2003
11. Rosy Cole's Memoir Explosion: A Heartbreaking Story About Losing Friends, Annoying Family, and Ruining Romance ◆ 2006

ROTTEN RALPH

Gantos, Jack

HOUGHTON MIFFLIN ◆ GRADES K–1 ◆ A/R

ANIMAL FANTASY | HUMOR

Rotten Ralph is a cat who deserves his name because his behavior is awful. His owner, Sarah, hopes he will reform but he never does. He even misbehaves at his own birthday party. There are titles for Halloween, Valentine's Day, and Christmas and a book in which Ralph goes to school. Children enjoy Ralph's schemes and delight in his audacity.

1. Rotten Ralph ◆ 1976
2. Worse Than Rotten Ralph ◆ 1978
3. Rotten Ralph's Rotten Christmas ◆ 1984
4. Rotten Ralph's Rotten Romance ◆ 1984
5. Rotten Ralph's Trick or Treat ◆ 1986
6. Rotten Ralph's Show and Tell ◆ 1989
7. Happy Birthday, Rotten Ralph ◆ 1990
8. Not So Rotten Ralph ◆ 1994
9. Rotten Ralph's Rotten Romance ◆ 1997
10. Back to School for Rotten Ralph ◆ 1998
11. Rotten Ralph's Halloween Howl ◆ 1998
12. The Christmas Spirit Strikes Rotten Ralph ◆ 1998
13. Wedding Bells for Rotten Ralph ◆ 1999
14. Rotten Ralph's Thanksgiving Wish ◆ 1999
15. Wedding Bells for Rotten Ralph ◆ 1999

ROTTEN RALPH ROTTEN READERS

Gantos, Jack

FARRAR, STRAUS & GIROUX ◆ **GRADES 1–3**

ANIMAL FANTASY | HUMOR

A series of beginning readers featuring the ill-behaved cat and his long-suffering owner, Sarah.

1. Rotten Ralph Helps Out ◆ 2001
2. Practice Makes Perfect for Rotten Ralph ◆ 2002
3. Rotten Ralph Feels Rotten ◆ 2002
4. Best in Show for Rotten Ralph ◆ 2005

ROTTEN SCHOOL

Stine, R. L.

HARPERCOLLINS ◆ **GRADES 4–6** ◆ **A/R**

HUMOR

Founded by I. B. Rotten 100 years ago, Rotten School is a boarding school full of gross gags and silly, slimy situations. In *The Big Blueberry Barf-Off!*, the big question is "Who will barf first?" With an attention to bodily functions, armpits, and heinies and a Headmaster named Upchuck, this should be attractive to fans of Captain Underpants and the Riot Brothers.

1. The Big Blueberry Barf-Off! ◆ 2005
2. The Great Smelling Bee ◆ 2006
3. The Good, the Bad and the Very Slimy ◆ 2006
4. Lose, Team, Lose! ◆ 2006
5. Shake, Rattle, and Hurl! ◆ 2006
6. The Heinie Prize ◆ 2006
7. Dudes, the School is Haunted! ◆ 2006
8. The Teacher from Heck ◆ 2006
9. Party Poopers ◆ 2006
10. The Rottenest Angel ◆ 2006
11. Punk'd and Skunked ◆ 2007
12. Battle of the Dum Diddys ◆ 2007
13. Got Cake? ◆ 2007
14. Night of the Creepy Things ◆ 2007
15. Calling All Birdbrains ◆ 2007
16. Dumb Clucks ◆ 2008

ROWAN AND NINA *see* "Hour" books

ROWAN OF RIN

Rodda, Emily

GREENWILLOW ◆ GRADES 4–6

FANTASY

When the mountain stream slows to a trickle, the people of Rin send a group up the mountain where the legendary dragon lives. Rowan, a quiet village boy, is a surprise selection to be in the group. His actions help the group succeed. In a later book, Rin is threatened by a bitter winter and the frightening ice creepers that will eat any warm creatures. Again, Rowan faces the danger.

1. Rowan of Rin ◆ 2001
2. Rowan and the Travelers ◆ 2001
3. Rowan and the Keeper of the Crystal ◆ 2002
4. Rowan and the Zebak ◆ 2002
5. Rowan and the Ice Creepers ◆ 2003

ROYAL BALLET SCHOOL DIARIES

Moss, Alexandra

GROSSET & DUNLAP ◆ GRADES 4–7 ◆ A/R

REAL LIFE

Ellie Brown, 11, has loved ballet since she was four years old. Now she is in London, auditioning for the Royal Ballet School. Although she wants to be accepted at the school, she worries about her mother in America. Since the death of her father, there is no one to care for her mother, who is ill. Ellie must choose between going home or following her dream. As the series progresses, Ellie matures and, eventually, faces more dilemmas including *Boys or Ballet?*.

1. Ellie's Chance to Dance ◆ 2005
2. Lauren's Leap of Faith ◆ 2005
3. Isabelle's Perfect Performance ◆ 2005
4. Sophie's Flight of Fancy ◆ 2005
5. Kate's Special Secret ◆ 2005
6. Grace's Show of Strength ◆ 2006
7. New Girl ◆ 2006
8. Boys or Ballet? ◆ 2006

ROYAL DIARIES

Various authors

SCHOLASTIC ◆ GRADES 3–7 ◆ A/R

HISTORICAL

Readers are introduced to different eras in history through these fictional-ized diaries. Each book features events from the childhood or adolescence of a famous female. The books include historical notes, documents, maps, genealogy, and illustrations. Fans of Dear America would gain a new perspective on world history from these books.

1. Cleopatra VII: Daughter of the Nile, Egypt, 57 B.C. (Gregory, Kristiana) ◆ 1999
2. Elizabeth I: Red Rose of the House of Tudor, England, 1544 (Lasky, Kathryn) ◆ 1999
3. Marie Antoinette: Princess of Versailles, Austria-France, 1769 (Lasky, Kathryn) ◆ 2000
4. Isabel: Jewel of Castilla, Spain, 1466 (Meyer, Carolyn) ◆ 2000
5. Nzingha: Warrior Queen of Matamba, Angola, Africa, 1595 (McKissack, Patricia C.) ◆ 2000
6. Anastasia: The Last Grand Duchess, Russia, 1914 (Meyer, Carolyn) ◆ 2000
7. Kaiulani: The People's Princess, Hawaii, 1889 (White, Ellen Emerson) ◆ 2001
8. Lady of Ch'iao Kuo: Warrior of the South, Southern China, A.D. 531 (Yep, Laurence) ◆ 2001
9. Victoria: May Blossom of Britannia, England, 1829 (Kirwan, Anna) ◆ 2001
10. Mary: Queen of Scots, Queen Without a Country, France 1553 (Lasky, Kathryn) ◆ 2002
11. Sondok: Princess of the Moon and Stars, Korea, A.D. 595 (Holman, Sheri) ◆ 2002
12. Jahanara: Princess of Princesses, India, 1627 (Lasky, Kathryn) ◆ 2002
13. Eleanor: Crown Jewel of Aquitaine, France, 1136 (Lasky, Kathryn) ◆ 2002
14. Elisabeth of Austria: The Princess Bride, Austria-Hungary, 1853 (Denenberg, Barry) ◆ 2003
15. Kristina: The Girl King, Sweden, 1638 (Meyer, Carolyn) ◆ 2003
16. Weetamoo: Heart of the Pocassets, Massachusetts, 1653 (Smith, Patricia Clark) ◆ 2003
17. Lady of Palenque: Flower of Bacal, Mesoamerica, A.D. 749 (Kirwan, Anna) ◆ 2004
18. Kazunomiya: Prisoner of Heaven, Japan, 1858 (Lasky, Kathryn) ◆ 2004
19. Catherine: The Great Journey, Russia, 1743 (Gregory, Kristiana) ◆ 2005
20. Anacaona, Golden Flower: Haiti, 1490 (Danticat, Edwidge) ◆ 2005

RPM

Fabry, Chris
TYNDALE HOUSE ◆ GRADES 5–8 ◆ A/R
REAL LIFE | VALUES

Jamie Maxwell has grown up around auto racing. Her father is a successful NASCAR driver and Jamie dreams of being the first female to win the cup. Tim Carhardt is recovering from a harrowing crash. His confidence has been shaken and he is drifting. Both Jamie and Tim find that their faith is tested as they strive to reach their goals.

1. Blind Spot ◆ 2007
2. Over the Wall ◆ 2007
3. Overdrive ◆ 2008
4. Checkered Flag ◆ 2008

RUBY

Hill, Susan

HARPERCOLLINS ◆ GRADES K–2 ◆ A/R

ANIMAL FANTASY

Ruby is a raccoon who has lots of friends but is not afraid to spend time alone or to assert herself. In the first book, she seeks her friends' advice on baking a cake; in the second, she has to explain to disgruntled friends that she really has portrayed their best features in her picture—their smiles. The third book finds her enjoying a day by herself when everyone else is too busy to play. These well-illustrated books are just right for beginning readers.

1. Ruby Bakes a Cake ◆ 2004
2. Ruby Paints a Picture ◆ 2005
3. Ruby's Perfect Day ◆ 2006

RUGRATS (CHAPTER BOOKS)

Various authors

SIMON SPOTLIGHT ◆ GRADES 2–4 ◆ A/R

HUMOR

Tommy Pickles and his friend Chuckie, along with the twins Lil and Phil, have all kinds of fun. Tommy's cousin, Angelica, is older and tries to boss the babies around. In one book, Tommy's little brother Dil is chosen to appear on the jar for Rocket Pickles. Get it? Dil Pickles on the Pickle Jar! Angelica is jealous and tries to get in on some of the excitement. The Rugrats television program, videos, and movies are popular with children.

1. The Perfect Formula (Willson, Sarah) ◆ 1999
2. Tommy's Last Stand (Krulik, Nancy E.) ◆ 1999
3. Star-Spangled Babies (Richards, Kitty) ◆ 1999
4. Bonjour, Babies! (Luke, David) ◆ 1999
5. Chuckie's Big Wish (Dubowski, Cathy East) ◆ 1999

6. Just Wanna Have Fun (Willson, Sarah) ◆ 2000
7. Angelica the Grape (Krulik, Nancy E.) ◆ 2000
8. Book'em Tommy (Rosado, Maria) ◆ 2000
9. It Takes Two! (Dubowski, Cathy East) ◆ 2000
10. Dil in a Pickle (Ostrow, Kim) ◆ 2000
11. Stupid Cupid (Krulik, Nancy E.) ◆ 2001
12. Prince Chuckie (Willson, Sarah) ◆ 2001
13. Rugrats in the Ring (Willson, Sarah) ◆ 2002

RUGRATS FILES

Various authors

SIMON SPOTLIGHT ◆ **GRADES 2–5** ◆ **A/R**

FANTASY

Angelica and the babies travel through time in this series. They encounter pirates. They look for Leonardo da Vinci. They rescue the Knights of the Round Table. The Rugrats television program, videos, and movies are popular with children.

1. Case of the Missing Gold: A Time Travel Adventure (Lewman, David) ◆ 2000
2. Yo Ho Ho and a Bottle of Milk: A Time Travel Adventure (Richards, Kitty) ◆ 2000
3. The Quest for the Holey Pail: A Time Travel Adventure (Willson, Sarah) ◆ 2000
4. Tale of the Unfinished Masterpiece: A Time Travel Adventure (Rosado, Maria) ◆ 2001
5. In Search of Reptar: A Time Travel Adventure (Banks, Steven) ◆ 2002

RUMBLE'S CAVE HOTEL

Law, Felicia

PICTURE WINDOW BOOKS ◆ **GRADES K–2** ◆ **A/R**

FANTASY

A dragon named Rumble turns a cave into a hotel. Other animals, like Toad the plumber and a designing lizard named Lucas, help him create his hotel. Shelby the spider is always near, too. These books are a good choice for beginning readers.

1. Rumble the Dragon's Cave ◆ 2005
2. Rumble Meets Buddy Beaver ◆ 2005
3. Rumble Meets Keesha Kangaroo ◆ 2005
4. Rumble Meets Eli Elephant ◆ 2005
5. Rumble Meets Penny Panther ◆ 2005
6. Rumble Meets Shelby Spider ◆ 2005

7. Rumble Meets Sylvia and Sally Swan ◆ 2005
8. Rumble Meets Wally Warthog ◆ 2005
9. Joe's Day at Rumble's Cave Hotel ◆ 2006
10. Rumble Meets Chester the Chef ◆ 2006
11. Rumble Meets Harry Hippo ◆ 2006
12. Rumble Meets Lucas Lizard ◆ 2006
13. Rumble Meets Randy Rabbit ◆ 2006
14. Rumble Meets Todd Toad ◆ 2006
15. Rumble Meets Vikki Viper ◆ 2006
16. Rumble's Famous Granny ◆ 2006
17. Rumble Meets Milly the Maid ◆ 2006
18. Rumble Meets Wilson Wolf ◆ 2006

RUSSELL *see* Riverside Kids: Russell

RUSSELL THE SHEEP

Scotton, Rob

HARPERCOLLINS ◆ GRADES K–2 ◆ A/R

ANIMAL FANTASY

Russell the sheep just can't sleep. He tries various tricks—finding a comfortable spot, at the right temperature, counting stars. Nothing works until he starts counting sheep. In the second book, Russell thinks he has discovered a lot of junk until he realizes the joys of owning a camera, however old it is. The author's appealing illustrations add touches of humor. *Go to Sleep, Russell the Sheep* (2007) is an abridged version of the first book.

1. Russell the Sheep ◆ 2005
2. Russell and the Lost Treasure ◆ 2006
3. Russell's Christmas Magic ◆ 2007

SABRINA THE TEENAGE WITCH

Various authors

SIMON & SCHUSTER ◆ GRADES 4–6 ◆ A/R

FANTASY | HUMOR

This series features Sabrina, her aunts Hilda and Zelda, and her cat Salem. All of them have magical powers. The circumstances involve a lot of humor as the witches try to live in human society. This group of books is based on the popular television show. There is also a series of episode storybooks based on individual episodes and including photographs from the production.

1. Sabrina, the Teenage Witch (Weiss, David Cody, and Bobbi J. G. Weiss) ◆ 1997
2. Showdown at the Mall (Gallagher, Diana G.) ◆ 1997
3. Good Switch, Bad Switch (Weiss, David Cody, and Bobbi J. G. Weiss) ◆ 1997
4. Halloween Havoc (Gallagher, Diana G.) ◆ 1997
5. Santa's Little Helper (Dubowski, Cathy East) ◆ 1997
6. Ben There, Done That (Locke, Joseph) ◆ 1998
7. All You Need Is a Love Spell (Reisfeld, Randi) ◆ 1998
8. Salem on Trial (Weiss, David Cody, and Bobbi J. G. Weiss) ◆ 1998
9. A Dog's Life (Dubowski, Cathy East) ◆ 1998
10. Lotsa Luck (Gallagher, Diana G.) ◆ 1998
11. Prisoner of Cabin 13 (Vornholt, John) ◆ 1998
12. All That Glitters (Garton, Ray) ◆ 1998
13. Go Fetch! (Weiss, David Cody, and Bobbi J. G. Weiss) ◆ 1998
14. Spying Eyes (Holder, Nancy) ◆ 1998
15. Harvest Moon (Odom, Mel) ◆ 1998
16. Now You See Her, Now You Don't (Gallagher, Diana G.) ◆ 1998
17. Eight Spells a Week (Super Edition) ◆ 1999
18. I'll Zap Manhattan (Odom, Mel) ◆ 1999
19. Shamrock Shenanigans (Gallagher, Diana G.) ◆ 1999
20. The Age of Aquariums (Weiss, David Cody, and Bobbi J. G. Weiss) ◆ 1999
21. Prom Time (Weiss, David Cody, and Bobbi J. G. Weiss) ◆ 1999
22. Witchopoly (Vornholt, John) ◆ 1999
23. Bridal Bedlam (Gallagher, Diana G.) ◆ 1999
24. Scarabian Nights (Holder, Nancy) ◆ 1999
25. While the Cat's Away (Batrae, Margot) ◆ 1999
26. Fortune Cookie Fox (Dubowski, Cathy East) ◆ 1999
27. Haunts in the House (Vornholt, John) ◆ 1999
28. Up, Up and Away (Holder, Nancy) ◆ 1999
29. Millennium Madness ◆ 2000
30. Switcheroo (Batrae, Margot) ◆ 2000
31. Mummy Dearest (Odom, Mel) ◆ 2000
32. Reality Check (Gallagher, Diana G.) ◆ 2000
33. Knock on Wood (Vornholt, John) ◆ 2000
34. It's a Miserable Life! (Dubowski, Cathy East) ◆ 2000
35. Pirate Pandemonium (Odom, Mel) ◆ 2001
36. Wake-Up Call (Gallagher, Diana G.) ◆ 2001
37. Witch Way Did She Go? (Ruditis, Paul) ◆ 2001
38. Milady's Dragon (Dubowski, Cathy East) ◆ 2001
39. From the Horse's Mouth (Gallagher, Diana G.) ◆ 2001
40. Dream Boat (Odom, Mel) ◆ 2001
41. Tiger Tale (Odom, Mel) ◆ 2002
42. The Witch That Launched a Thousand Ships (Krulik, Nancy E.) ◆ 2002
43. Know-It-All (Fiedler, Lisa) ◆ 2002
44. Topsy-Turvy (Ruditis, Paul) ◆ 2002
45. Hounded by Baskervilles (Warriner, Mercer) ◆ 2002

46. Off to See the Wizard (Krulik, Nancy E.) ◆ 2002
47. Where in the World Is Sabrina Spellman? (Ruditis, Paul) ◆ 2003
48. Witch Glitch (Goldman, Leslie) ◆ 2003
49. The Truth Hurts (Goldman, Leslie) ◆ 2003
50. What a Doll! (Krulik, Nancy E.) ◆ 2003
51. Christmas Crisis (Krulik, Nancy E.) ◆ 2003
52. Ten Little Witches (Ruditis, Paul) ◆ 2003
53. Now and Again (Weiss, David Cody, and Bobbi J. G. Weiss) ◆ 2003

TV EPISODES

1. Becoming a Witch (Canning, Shelagh) ◆ 1998
2. Dream Date (Lundell, Margo) ◆ 1998
3. Cat Showdown (Dubowski, Cathy East) ◆ 1998
4. The Troll Bride (Locke, Joseph) ◆ 1998
5. Sabrina, the Teenage Boy (Herman, Gail) ◆ 1998
6. A Doll's Story (Dubowski, Cathy East) ◆ 1998

THE SADDLE CLUB

Bryant, Bonnie

BANTAM DOUBLEDAY DELL ◆ **GRADES 4–6** ◆ **A/R**

REAL LIFE | RECREATION

Stevie, Lisa, and Carole, young riders at the Pine Hollow stables, make up the Saddle Club. Competition and outsiders (occasionally boys) challenge their friendship, but the girls always manage to stay together. Carole is horse-crazy. The rest of her life is disorganized; but when she is around horses, she becomes focused. Stevie is a practical joker, always looking for fun and coming up with new schemes. Lisa is quiet and serious, a good student plagued by a pushy mother. The girls encounter snobby rich girls who don't want to take good care of horses and, at other times, excellent riders whom they admire. Their love for horses takes them to a dude ranch, to horse shows and competitions, and to riding camps and rodeos. More than 100 books will keep horse-lovers busy.

1. Horse Crazy ◆ 1988
2. Horse Shy ◆ 1988
3. Horse Sense ◆ 1989
4. Horse Power ◆ 1989
5. Trail Mates ◆ 1989
6. Dude Ranch ◆ 1989
7. Horse Play ◆ 1989
8. Horse Show ◆ 1989
9. Hoof Beat ◆ 1990
10. Riding Camp ◆ 1990
11. Horse Wise ◆ 1990
12. Rodeo Rider ◆ 1990
13. Starlight Christmas ◆ 1990

14. Sea Horse ◆ 1991
15. Team Play ◆ 1991
16. Horse Games ◆ 1991
17. Horsenapped ◆ 1991
18. Pack Trip ◆ 1991
19. Star Rider ◆ 1991
20. Snow Ride ◆ 1992
21. Racehorse ◆ 1992
22. Fox Hunt ◆ 1992
23. Horse Trouble ◆ 1992
24. Ghost Rider ◆ 1992
25. Show Horse ◆ 1992
26. Beach Ride ◆ 1993
27. Bridle Path ◆ 1993
28. Stable Manners ◆ 1993
29. Ranch Hands ◆ 1993
30. Autumn Trail ◆ 1993
31. Hayride ◆ 1993
32. Chocolate Horse ◆ 1994
33. High Horse ◆ 1994
34. Hay Fever ◆ 1994
35. Horse Tale ◆ 1994
36. Riding Lesson ◆ 1994
37. Stage Coach ◆ 1994
38. Horse Trade ◆ 1994
39. Purebred ◆ 1994
40. Gift Horse ◆ 1994
41. Stable Witch ◆ 1995
42. Saddlebags ◆ 1995
43. Photo Finish ◆ 1995
44. Horseshoe ◆ 1995
45. Stable Groom ◆ 1995
46. Flying Horse ◆ 1995
47. Horse Magic ◆ 1995
48. Mystery Ride ◆ 1995
49. Stable Farewell ◆ 1995
50. Yankee Swap ◆ 1996
51. Pleasure Horse ◆ 1996
52. Riding Class ◆ 1996
53. Horse-Sitters ◆ 1996
54. Gold Medal Rider ◆ 1996
55. Gold Medal Horse ◆ 1996
56. Cutting Horse ◆ 1996
57. Tight Rein ◆ 1996
58. Wild Horses ◆ 1996
59. Phantom Horse ◆ 1996
60. Hobbyhorse ◆ 1996
61. Broken Horse ◆ 1996
62. Horse Blues ◆ 1997

63. Stable Hearts ◆ 1997
64. Horse Capades ◆ 1997
65. Silver Stirrups ◆ 1997
66. Saddle Sore ◆ 1997
67. Summer Horse ◆ 1997
68. Summer Rider ◆ 1997
69. Endurance Ride ◆ 1997
70. Horse Race ◆ 1997
71. Horse Talk ◆ 1997
72. Holiday Horse ◆ 1997
73. Horse Guest ◆ 1998
74. Horse Whispers ◆ 1998
75. Painted Horse ◆ 1998
76. Horse Care ◆ 1998
77. Rocking Horse ◆ 1998
78. Horseflies ◆ 1998
79. English Horse ◆ 1998
80. English Rider ◆ 1998
81. Wagon Trail ◆ 1998
82. Quarter Horse ◆ 1998
83. Horse Thief ◆ 1998
84. Schooling Horse ◆ 1998
85. Horse Fever ◆ 1998
86. Secret Horse ◆ 1999
87. Show Jumper ◆ 1999
88. Sidesaddle ◆ 1999
89. Lucky Horse ◆ 1999
90. Driving Team ◆ 2000
91. Starting Gate ◆ 2000
92. Million-Dollar Horse ◆ 2000
93. Horse Love ◆ 2000
94. Horse Spy ◆ 2000
95. Show Judge ◆ 2000
96. New Rider ◆ 2001
97. Hard Hat ◆ 2001
98. Horse Feathers ◆ 2001
99. Trail Ride ◆ 2001
100. Stray Horse ◆ 2001
101. Best Friends ◆ 2001

SADDLE CLUB SUPER EDITIONS

1. A Summer Without Horses ◆ 1994
2. The Secret of the Stallion ◆ 1995
3. Western Star ◆ 1996
4. Dream Horse ◆ 1996

5. Before They Rode Horses ◆ 1997
6. Nightmare ◆ 1997
7. Christmas Treasure ◆ 1998
8. Horse Fever ◆ 1998

SADDLE CLUB: THE INSIDE STORY

1. Stevie: The Inside Story ◆ 1999
2. Lisa: The Inside Story ◆ 1999
3. Carole: The Inside Story ◆ 1999

SADDLE ISLAND

Siamon, Sharon

WALRUS BOOKS ◆ GRADES 5–8 ◆ A/R

REAL LIFE

Kelsie MacKay loves horses. On the eastern shore of Nova Scotia, Kelsie rescues a horse, Caspar, whose owner, Hank Harefield, plans to auction him off. Caspar is a difficult horse, but Kelsie plans to care for him and protect him. Along with her brother Andy she creates a sanctuary—Saddle Island—for unwanted, mistreated horses. Fans of the Mustang Mountain books will want to read these books, too.

1. Gallop to the Sea ◆ 2006
2. Secrets in the Sand ◆ 2006
3. Race to the Rescue ◆ 2007

SADDLES, STARS, AND STRIPES

Kent, Deborah

KINGFISHER ◆ GRADES 4–7 ◆ A/R

HISTORICAL

Horses, history and intrepid female main characters are the focus of this series. In one book, Lexie's brother was a rider for the Pony Express but he has been accused of theft. Lexie, 15, tries to clear his name. Other books take place during the gold rush, the Civil War, and the Revolutionary War. This would be a good choice for middle school reluctant readers.

1. Blackwater Creek ◆ 2005
2. Chance of a Lifetime ◆ 2005
3. Riding the Pony Express ◆ 2006
4. On the Edge of Revolution ◆ 2006

SAGWA, THE CHINESE SIAMESE CAT (READERS)

Daugherty, George

SCHOLASTIC ◆ GRADES K–2 ◆ A/R

ANIMAL FANTASY

The picture book by Amy Tan, *The Chinese Siamese Cat* (Simon & Schuster, 1994), became a popular television series that inspired this series of related easy-to-read books. There are also illustrated storybooks that allow readers to color some of the pages.

1. Acrobat Cats ◆ 2002
2. Princess Sheegwa ◆ 2002
3. New Year's Clean-Up ◆ 2004

SAILOR MOON NOVELS

Takeuchi, Naoko

TOKYOPOP ◆ GRADES 4–7

FANTASY

Serena meets a magical cat, Luna, and is given superpowers, becoming Sailor Moon. These novels connect to other TokyoPop manga about this popular character.

1. A Scout Is Born ◆ 1999
2. The Power of Love ◆ 1999
3. Mercury Rising ◆ 1999
4. Mars Attacks! ◆ 2000
5. Eternal Sleep ◆ 2000
6. Scouts on Film ◆ 2000
7. Cel Mates ◆ 2000
8. Diamonds Not Forever ◆ 2000

SALLY

Huneck, Stephen

ABRAMS; PENGUIN STUDIO ◆ GRADES K–2 ◆ A/R

REAL LIFE

In the first book, readers look inside the mind of a dog—Sally, a black lab. Readers will enjoy finding out about the "good dog" and "bad dog" hemispheres in her brain. In the rest of the series, Sally visits some familiar locations. Huneck's woodblock prints capture Sally's spirit.

1. My Dog's Brain ◆ 1997
2. Sally Goes to the Beach ◆ 2000
3. Sally Goes to the Mountains ◆ 2001
4. Sally Goes to the Farm ◆ 2002
5. Sally Goes to the Vet ◆ 2004
6. Sally's Snow Adventure ◆ 2006
7. Sally Gets a Job ◆ 2008

SALT AND PEPPER CHRONICLES

Poulsen, David A.

KEY PORTER ◆ GRADES 3–6 ◆ A/R

MYSTERY | FANTASY

Christine Bellamy, 12, is nicknamed "Salt" and her friend Patti McKenzie is "Pepper." In the first book, the girls are visiting England with Pepper's family. Salt's little brother, Hal, is also on the trip. When they arrive at the manor house where they will be staying, they see garlic everywhere! What's going on? Vampires! When a teenaged vampire asks for their help, the girls refuse and, as a result, Hal disappears. Now the girls must find Hal and face the vampires. In the second book, the mystery revolves around a movie production and a weird machine that may be hypnotizing everyone.

1. The Vampire's Visit ◆ 2006
2. The Hunk Machine ◆ 2007
3. No Time Like the Past ◆ 2007
4. The Book of Vampire ◆ 2007
5. The Prisoners and the Paintings ◆ 2008

SALTY

Rand, Gloria

HOLT ◆ GRADES K–2

ADVENTURE | REAL LIFE

Salty the dog and his master, Zack own a sailboat. They share many adventures, from actually building the sailboat to sailing to Alaska and Hawaii. The illustrations are not only attractive but do a nice job of illustrating the various parts of sailboats and the process of sailing.

1. Salty Dog ◆ 1989
2. Salty Sails North ◆ 1990
3. Salty Takes Off ◆ 1991
4. Aloha, Salty! ◆ 1996

SAM

Robberecht, Thierry

CLARION ◆ GRADES K–2 ◆ A/R

ANIMAL FANTASY

Sam is a dog whose experiences reflect the everyday concerns of children. In the first book, Sam seems fearless—until a spider lands on him and he cries. Will his friends think he is a scaredy-cat? In *Sam Is Not a Loser,* Sam hates to lose at soccer so he decides not to play. But then how can he win? Young readers will relate to Sam's situations.

1. Sam Is Never Scared ◆ 2006
2. Sam Tells Stories ◆ 2007
3. Sam's New Friend ◆ 2008
4. Sam Is Not a Loser ◆ 2008

SAM

Hest, Amy

CANDLEWICK ◆ GRADES K

ANIMAL FANTASY

These are gentle stories about a young bear and his mother. Sam can't sleep without a kiss, needs help swallowing his medicine, and is proud when he carries cakes to neighbors all by himself.

1. Kiss Good Night ◆ 2001
2. Don't You Feel Well, Sam? ◆ 2002
3. You Can Do It, Sam ◆ 2003

SAM AND ROBERT

Levy, Elizabeth

HARPERCOLLINS ◆ GRADES 2–4 ◆ A/R

HUMOR | MYSTERY

Sam and Robert live with their mother on the 19th floor of an apartment building. Both boys are fascinated with the supernatural and monsters, and Robert sleeps with a Dracula doll. In one of the books, an unpleasant man named Mr. Frank moves in, and the boys become convinced that he is the real Frankenstein. They begin investigating and find more similarities between the two. Other books in the series find the boys fascinated with Dracula and other monsters and wondering if people in their everyday lives are the real thing. Children who enjoy the Adventures of the Bailey School Kids will enjoy this series.

1. Frankenstein Moved In on the Fourth Floor ◆ 1979
2. Dracula Is a Pain in the Neck ◆ 1983
3. Gorgonzola Zombies in the Park ◆ 1993
4. Wolfman Sam ◆ 1996
5. Night of the Living Gerbil ◆ 2001
6. Vampire State Building ◆ 2002

SAM AND STEPHANIE

Oliver, Andrew

ADAMS-POMEROY ◆ GRADES 4–7 ◆ A/R

MYSTERY

Adventurous 12-year-olds Sam and Stephanie encounter danger when they investigate the disappearance of an elderly man in their small Wisconsin town in the first book in the series. Subsequent mysteries also require determination and courage from the young sleuths.

1. If Photos Could Talk ◆ 2005
2. Haunted Hill ◆ 2006
3. Scrambled ◆ 2007

SAM, DOG DETECTIVE

Labatt, Mary

KIDS CAN ◆ GRADES 3–5 ◆ A/R

ANIMAL FANTASY | MYSTERY

Sam the sheepdog, who considers herself a fine sleuth, can communicate telepathically with Jennie, the girl who lives next door. Together, the two find themselves investigating unscary mysteries in entertaining fashion.

1. The Ghost of Captain Briggs ◆ 1999
2. Spying on Dracula ◆ 1999
3. Strange Neighbors ◆ 2000
4. Aliens in Woodford ◆ 2000
5. A Weekend at the Grand Hotel ◆ 2001
6. The Secret of Sagawa Lake ◆ 2001
7. The Mummy Lives! ◆ 2002
8. One Terrible Halloween ◆ 2002

SAM GRIBLEY *see* My Side of the Mountain

SAM KRUPNIK

Lowry, Lois

HOUGHTON MIFFLIN ◆ GRADES 3–5

FAMILY LIFE | HUMOR

Anastasia Krupnik's little brother Sam has his own group of books. As a toddler, Sam is a handful. He flushes Anastasia's goldfish and adjusts to nursery school. He tries to find the very best birthday present for his mother. And he decides to run away. Sam is a lively, irrepressible little boy whose activities are filled with gentle humor.

1. All About Sam ◆ 1988
2. Attaboy, Sam! ◆ 1992
3. See You Around, Sam! ◆ 1996
4. Zooman Sam ◆ 1999

SAM (THE DOG)

Labatt, Mary

KIDS CAN PRESS ◆ GRADES K–2

REAL LIFE

These easy-to-read books feature a fluffy puppy named Sam. She enjoys playing in the backyard and making a new friend. She also has fun at Halloween and gets lost. This is a good choice for fans of Biscuit and Puppy Mudge.

1. Pizza for Sam ◆ 2003
2. Sam Finds a Monster ◆ 2003
3. A Friend for Sam ◆ 2003
4. Sam's First Halloween ◆ 2003
5. Sam Gets Lost ◆ 2004
6. Sam Goes to School ◆ 2004
7. A Parade for Sam ◆ 2005
8. Sam's Snowy Day ◆ 2005
9. Sam at the Seaside ◆ 2006
10. Sam Goes Next Door ◆ 2006

SAMANTHA *see* American Girls: Samantha

SAMMY KEYES

Van Draanen, Wendelin

KNOPF ◆ GRADES 5–8 ◆ A/R

MYSTERY

Sammy Keyes is in seventh grade. She lives with her grandmother in an apartment. While playing with some binoculars, she observes a thief at work. Unfortunately, the thief sees her, too. Now she has real problems. Other books have mysteries at Halloween and Christmas. In one book, she helps her actress mother when she is suspected of murdering a rival for an acting part.

1. Sammy Keyes and the Hotel Thief ◆ 1998
2. Sammy Keyes and the Skeleton Man ◆ 1998
3. Sammy Keyes and the Sisters of Mercy ◆ 1999
4. Sammy Keyes and the Runaway Elf ◆ 1999
5. Sammy Keyes and the Curse of Moustache Mary ◆ 2000
6. Sammy Keyes and the Hollywood Mummy ◆ 2001
7. Sammy Keyes and the Search for Snake Eyes ◆ 2002
8. Sammy Keyes and the Art of Deception ◆ 2003
9. Sammy Keyes and the Psycho Kitty Queen ◆ 2004
10. Sammy Keyes and the Dead Giveaway ◆ 2005
11. Sammy Keyes and the Wild Things ◆ 2007
12. Sammy Keyes and the Cold Hard Cash ◆ 2008

SAMURAI JACK CHAPTER BOOKS

Various authors

SCHOLASTIC ◆ GRADES 3–6

FANTASY

Samurai Jack is the popular main character of an animated series that appeared on Cartoon Network. Jack has fallen through a time portal and is searching for a way to return to his own time. As he goes on his quest, he faces danger from his nemesis, the evil shape-shifter Aku.

1. Mountain of Mayhem (West, Tracey) ◆ 2002
2. The Seven Labors of Jack (West, Tracey) ◆ 2003
3. Journey to the Impossible Islands (West, Tracey) ◆ 2003
4. Fighting Blind (Siefken, Paul) ◆ 2003
5. Jack and the Wanderers (West, Tracey) ◆ 2003

SANDY LANE STABLES

Various authors

EDC PUBLISHING ◆ GRADES 5–8 ◆ A/R

REAL LIFE

Horses and riding are featured in this series that includes show jumping, competitions, and horses being mistreated. The series was originally published in Britain.

1. A Horse for the Summer (Bates, Michelle) ◆ 1996
2. The Runaway Pony (Leigh, Susannah) ◆ 1996
3. Strangers at the Stables (Bates, Michelle) ◆ 1996
4. The Midnight Horse (Bates, Michelle) ◆ 1998
5. Dream Pony (Leigh, Susannah) ◆ 1998
6. Ride by Moonlight (Bates, Michelle) ◆ 1998
7. Horse in Danger (Bates, Michelle) ◆ 1998
8. The Perfect Pony (Bates, Michelle) ◆ 1999
9. Racing Vacation (Bates, Michelle) ◆ 2000

SANTA PAWS

Edwards, Nicholas

SCHOLASTIC ◆ GRADES 3–5 ◆ A/R

REAL LIFE

Gregory finds a stray puppy and names him Santa Paws. As the puppy grows, he performs acts of bravery. In one book, Santa Paws helps Gregory after a plane crash. In another book, Santa Paws foils the activities of burglars. Readers who like dogs and adventure will enjoy this series.

1. Santa Paws ◆ 1996
2. The Return of Santa Paws ◆ 2000
3. Santa Paws to the Rescue ◆ 2000
4. Santa Paws Comes Home ◆ 2000
5. Santa Paws, Our Hero ◆ 2002
6. Santa Paws and the New Puppy ◆ 2004

SARAH, PLAIN AND TALL

MacLachlan, Patricia

HARPERCOLLINS ◆ GRADES 3–5 ◆ A/R

HISTORICAL | REAL LIFE

In the Newbery Medal-winning first book, Sarah leaves Maine and travels to the prairie to work for (and perhaps marry) Jacob. The differences in their past experiences are a challenge, but their love for each other and for Jacob's children is triumphant. Subsequent books describe their life together. In the closing installment, Cassie, Sarah's fourth-grade daughter, mulls over her bonds with the rest of the family.

1. Sarah, Plain and Tall ◆ 1985
2. Skylark ◆ 1994
3. Caleb's Story ◆ 2001
4. More Perfect than the Moon ◆ 2004
5. Grandfather's Dance ◆ 2006

SARDINE IN OUTER SPACE

Guibert, Emmanuel, and Joan Sfar
ROARING BROOK ◆ GRADES 4–7
SCIENCE FICTION

A comic book space fantasy in which an independent-minded, redheaded young girl named Sardine enlists the help of her piratical Uncle Yellow Shoulder to foil the villainous plans of the slow-witted Supermuscleman. Originally published in France.

1. Sardine in Outer Space 1 ◆ 2006
2. Sardine in Outer Space 2 ◆ 2006
3. Sardine in Outer Space 3 ◆ 2007
4. Sardine in Outer Space 4 ◆ 2007
5. Sardine in Outer Space 5 ◆ 2008
6. Sardine in Outer Space 6 ◆ 2008

SCAREDY CATS

Stanley, George Edward
SIMON & SCHUSTER ◆ GRADES 1–3 ◆ A/R
HUMOR

Mrs. O'Dell's students find themselves in a horrifying situation that turns out to be humorous in *Mrs. O'Dell's Third-Grade Class Is Shrinking*. She does an experiment in shrinking plants and ends up shrinking the entire class. They don doll costumes and carry on with their day, which includes battling vicious squirrels. They are perfectly all right when their parents come to pick them up at three o'clock. Earlier books in this easy chapter-book series have different characters but the same blend of scariness, humor, and everyday life.

1. Bugs for Breakfast ◆ 1996
2. The Day the Ants Got Really Mad ◆ 1996
3. There's a Shark in the Swimming Pool ◆ 1996

4. Mrs. O'Dell's Third-Grade Class Is Shrinking ◆ 1996
5. Who Invited Aliens to My Slumber Party? ◆ 1997
6. The New Kid in School Is a Vampire Bat ◆ 1997
7. A Werewolf Followed Me Home ◆ 1997
8. The Vampire Kittens of Count Dracula ◆ 1997
9. Don't Look a Ghost Horse in the Mouth ◆ 1997

SCAREDY SQUIRREL

Watt, Melanie

KIDS CAN PRESS ◆ GRADES K–1 ◆ A/R

ANIMAL FANTASY

Scaredy Squirrel is afraid of everything. In the first book, he won't leave his tree and he has a kit ready for almost every emergency, including a shark attack. He always sticks to his schedule until one day something unexpected happens, changing his life forever. In subsequent books, Scaredy Squirrel tries new things, including making a friend and going to the beach. Young readers will feel superior to the silly fears of this squirrel.

1. Scaredy Squirrel ◆ 2006
2. Scaredy Squirrel Makes a Friend ◆ 2007
3. Scaredy Squirrel at the Beach ◆ 2008

SCARY GODMOTHER

Thompson, Jill

SIRIUS ENTERTAINMENT ◆ GRADES 3–5

FANTASY

When Hannah Marie goes trick-or-treating for the first time, her nasty cousin Jimmy locks her in a spooky basement. Hannah Marie is frightened until she meets Scary Godmother, who introduces Hannah Marie to the other monsters and creatures in the basement. Scary and her friends turn the tables on Jimmy and his friends, scaring them so much that they are afraid of Halloween. This is a fun graphic novel series for younger readers. There are DVDs available with additional stories.

1. Scary Godmother ◆ 1997
2. The Mystery Date ◆ 1999
3. The Boo Flu ◆ 2000
4. Wild About Harry ◆ 2001
5. Ghoul's Out for Summer ◆ 2002
6. Spooktacular Stories ◆ 2004

SCIENCE DETECTIVES

Torrey, Michelle

DUTTON ◆ GRADES 3–5 ◆ A/R

MYSTERY

Like Encyclopedia Brown and Einstein Anderson, Drake Doyle and Nell Fossey use scientific information to help them solve mysteries. In the first book, the two fifth-graders find out that discarded yeast and flour made the garbage can "burp." They also help with a stuck truck and with flattened frogs. There are science activities in each book.

1. The Case of the Gasping Garbage ◆ 2001
2. The Case of the Mossy Lake Monster ◆ 2002
3. The Case of the Graveyard Ghost ◆ 2002
4. The Case of the Barfy Birthday ◆ 2003

SCOOBY DOO MYSTERIES

Gelsey, James

SCHOLASTIC ◆ GRADES 3–5 ◆ A/R

MYSTERY

Shaggy, Velma, Fred, Daphne, and their dog Scooby-Doo go out for adventures in their vehicle, the Mystery Machine. In *Farmyard Fright*, the group is threatened by a mysterious scarecrow. In *Vicious Viking*, the plot is similar but the threat comes from an angry Viking at the Viking Village theme park. Although these are not graphic novels or cine-manga, there are numerous colorful cartoon pictures. Fans of the cartoon series will enjoy these books.

1. Scooby-Doo! and the Haunted Castle ◆ 1998
2. Scooby-Doo! and the Mummy's Curse ◆ 1998
3. Scooby-Doo! and the Snow Monster ◆ 1999
4. Scooby-Doo! and the Sunken Ship ◆ 1999
5. Scooby-Doo! and the Howling Wolfman ◆ 1999
6. Scooby-Doo! and the Vampire's Revenge ◆ 1999
7. Scooby-Doo! and the Carnival Creeper ◆ 1999
8. Scooby-Doo! and the Groovy Ghost ◆ 2000
9. Scooby-Doo! and the Zombie's Treasure ◆ 2000
10. Scooby-Doo! and the Spooky Strikeout ◆ 2000
11. Scooby-Doo! and the Fairground Phantom ◆ 2000
12. Scooby-Doo! and the Frankenstein Monster ◆ 2000
13. Scooby-Doo! and the Runaway Robot ◆ 2000
14. Scooby-Doo! and the Masked Magician ◆ 2001

15. Scooby-Doo! and the Phony Fortune-Teller ◆ 2001
16. Scooby-Doo! and the Toy Store Terror ◆ 2001
17. Scooby-Doo! and the Farmyard Fright ◆ 2001
18. Scooby-Doo! and the Caveman Caper ◆ 2001
19. Scooby-Doo! and the Rowdy Rodeo ◆ 2001
20. Scooby-Doo! and the Ghostly Gorilla ◆ 2002
21. Scooby-Doo! and the Vicious Viking ◆ 2002
22. Scooby-Doo! and the Seashore Slimer ◆ 2002
23. Scooby-Doo! and the Karate Caper ◆ 2002
24. Scooby-Doo! and the Bowling Boogeyman ◆ 2002
25. Scooby-Doo! and the Headless Horseman ◆ 2002
26. Scooby-Doo! and the Deep Sea Diver ◆ 2003
27. Scooby-Doo! and the Sinister Sorcerer ◆ 2003
28. Scooby-Doo! and the Witch Doctor ◆ 2003
29. Scooby-Doo! and the Gruesome Goblin ◆ 2004
30. Scooby-Doo! and the Virtual Villain ◆ 2004
31. Scooby-Doo! and the Hoopster Horror ◆ 2005
32. Scooby-Doo! and the Cactus Creature ◆ 2005
33. Scooby-Doo! and the Scary Skateboarder ◆ 2006

Scooby Doo Readers

Herman, Gail

Scholastic ◆ Grades 1–3 ◆ A/R

Humor | Mystery

The gang from the Scooby-Doo cartoons appear in these books. Their adventures include facing mummies, dealing with ghosts, and solving a dognapping. Younger readers will enjoy seeing these familiar characters—Velma, Shaggy, Daphne, Fred, and Scooby-Doo—in these easy-to-read books.

1. Scooby-Doo! and the Map in the Mystery Machine ◆ 2000
2. Scooby-Doo! and the Disappearing Donuts ◆ 2000
3. Scooby-Doo! and the Howling on the Playground ◆ 2000
4. Scooby-Doo! and the Ghost in the Garden ◆ 2001
5. Scooby-Doo! and the Shiny Spooky Knights ◆ 2001
6. Scooby-Doo! and the Mixed-Up Museum ◆ 2001
7. Scooby-Doo! and the Snack Snatcher ◆ 2001
8. Scooby-Doo! and the Race Car Monster ◆ 2001
9. Scooby-Doo! and the Haunted Ski Lodge ◆ 2001
10. Scooby-Doo! and the Valentine's Day Dognapping ◆ 2002
11. Scooby-Doo! and the Mummies at the Mall ◆ 2002
12. Scooby-Doo! and the Sea Monster Scare ◆ 2002
13. Scooby-Doo! and the Apple Thief ◆ 2002
14. Scooby-Doo! and the Football Fright ◆ 2002
15. Scooby-Doo! and the Secret Santa Mystery ◆ 2003

16. Title unavailable ◆ n.a.
17. Scooby-Doo! and the Thanksgiving Mystery ◆ 2005
18. Scooby-Doo! and the Camping Caper ◆ 2006
19. Scooby-Doo! and the School Play Surprise ◆ 2006
20. Scooby-Doo! and the Haunted Halloween Party ◆ 2006
21. Scooby-Doo! and the Big Bad Blizzard ◆ 2007
22. Scooby-Doo! and the Haunted Road Trip ◆ 2008

SCRAPPERS

Hughes, Dean
ATHENEUM ◆ GRADES 4–6 ◆ A/R

RECREATION

Robbie and Wilson put together a baseball team for the summer league. In one book, Gloria, the shortstop, berates her teammates for their errors. She is especially critical of Ollie, a pitcher who struggles to be confident. The team helps Ollie succeed and Gloria to be more tolerant. There is plenty of baseball action along with instances of teamwork and sportsmanship.

1. Play Ball! ◆ 1999
2. Home Run Hero ◆ 1999
3. Team Player ◆ 1999
4. Now We're Talking ◆ 1999
5. Bases Loaded ◆ 1999
6. No Easy Out ◆ 1999
7. Take Your Base ◆ 1999
8. No Fear ◆ 1999
9. Grand Slam ◆ 1999

SCRAPS OF TIME

McKissack, Patricia C.
VIKING ◆ GRADES 3–6 ◆ A/R

HISTORICAL

Gee tells stories to her grandchildren about pivotal moments in African American history. Focusing on family members, these stories connect with events like the civil rights movement, the Harlem Renaissance, and the settlement of the American West.

1. Abby Takes a Stand ◆ 2005
2. Away West ◆ 2006
3. A Song for Harlem ◆ 2007
4. The Homerun King ◆ 2008

SCREAM SHOP

West, Tracey
GROSSET & DUNLAP ◆ GRADES 3–5
FANTASY

Sebastian Cream's Shop is filled with unusual items just waiting for the right customer. Ben buys a Dr. Presto Magic Kit. The spells cause him problems and lead to an encounter with Dr. Presto. In another book, Tania buys a black marble that is really a gargoyle's eye. Readers decide how the stories develop in these "Pick Your Path" books.

1. Abracadanger ◆ 2003
2. Now You See Me, Now You Don't! ◆ 2003
3. Eye Spy Aliens ◆ 2003
4. Revenge of the Gargoyle ◆ 2003
5. Three Strikes and You're a Monster! ◆ 2004
6. The Day of the Dead ◆ 2004
7. Curse of Count Blood ◆ 2004
8. War of the Trolls ◆ 2004

SCREECH OWLS

MacGregor, Roy
MCCLELLAND & STEWART ◆ GRADES 4–7
MYSTERY | SPORTS

The Screech Owls are a Canadian high school hockey team. They frequently travel to competitions and often find themselves in the center of puzzling mysteries. Friendship, team rivalry, sportsmanship, and adventure are all part of these books, in addition to some great hockey.

1. Mystery at Lake Placid ◆ 1995
2. The Night They Stole the Stanley Cup ◆ 1995
3. The Screech Owls' Northern Adventure ◆ 1996
4. Murder at Hockey Camp ◆ 1997
5. Kidnapped in Sweden ◆ 1997
6. Terror in Florida ◆ 1997
7. The Quebec City Crisis ◆ 1998
8. The Screech Owls' Home Loss ◆ 1998
9. Nightmare in Nagano ◆ 1998
10. Danger in Dinosaur Valley ◆ 1999
11. The Ghost of the Stanley Cup ◆ 2000
12. The West Coast Murders ◆ 2000
13. Sudden Death in New York City ◆ 2000
14. Horror on River Road ◆ 2001
15. Death Down Under ◆ 2001

16. Power Play in Washington ◆ 2001
17. The Secret of the Deep Woods ◆ 2003
18. Murder at the Winter Games ◆ 2004
19. Attack on the Tower of London ◆ 2004
20. The Screech Owls' Reunion ◆ 2004

SEASONAL ADVENTURES

Hurwitz, Johanna
MORROW ◆ GRADES 4–6 ◆ A/R
HUMOR | REAL LIFE

In *The Hot and Cold Summer,* Rory and Derek are dismayed to learn that they are expected to entertain a girl named Bolivia over their much-awaited summer vacation. Although they initially put much effort into avoiding Bolivia, her personality eventually wins the boys over and the children learn to enjoy each other's company and work out the intricacies of a triangular friendship. Things work out so well that the threesome reunites for subsequent vacations.

1. The Hot and Cold Summer ◆ 1984
2. The Cold and Hot Winter ◆ 1988
3. The Up and Down Spring ◆ 1993
4. The Down and Up Fall ◆ 1996

SEBASTIAN BARTH

Howe, James
AVON ◆ GRADES 5–7 ◆ A/R
MYSTERY

Sebastian Barth lives in rural Connecticut, where he has a weekly radio show. He becomes involved in solving mysteries as he looks for scoops for the show. He is friends with Alex, the police chief, who helps him out. In *Dew Drop Dead,* he and his friends Corrie and David befriend a homeless man when Corrie's father, a minister, begins a ministry to the homeless. At the same time, the children find a body in an abandoned inn. Clues seem to point to the homeless man, but police work determines that the man died of exposure and the confused homeless man hid the body. Other mysteries are about poisoning in the school cafeteria, and a famous actress in danger.

1. What Eric Knew ◆ 1985
2. Stage Fright ◆ 1986
3. Eat Your Poison, Dear ◆ 1986
4. Dew Drop Dead ◆ 1990

SEBASTIAN (SUPER SLEUTH)

Christian, Mary Blount

MACMILLAN ◆ GRADES 3–5 ◆ A/R

ANIMAL FANTASY | MYSTERY

Sebastian is a lovable sheep dog who loves to dress up in human clothes and help his owner, Detective John Quincy Jones, solve puzzling crimes. Each title is devoted to a different mystery and illustrated with wonderfully detailed drawings.

1. Sebastian (Super Sleuth) ◆ 1974
2. Sebastian (Super Sleuth) and the Hair of the Dog Mystery ◆ 1983
3. Sebastian (Super Sleuth) and the Crummy Yummies Caper ◆ 1983
4. Sebastian (Super Sleuth) and the Bone to Pick Mystery ◆ 1983
5. Sebastian (Super Sleuth) and the Santa Claus Caper ◆ 1984
6. Sebastian (Super Sleuth) and the Secret of the Skewered Skier ◆ 1984
7. Sebastian (Super Sleuth) and the Clumsy Cowboy ◆ 1985
8. Sebastian (Super Sleuth) and the Purloined Sirloin ◆ 1986
9. Sebastian (Super Sleuth) and the Stars-in-his-Eyes Mystery ◆ 1987
10. Sebastian (Super Sleuth) and the Egyptian Connection ◆ 1988
11. Sebastian (Super Sleuth) and the Time Capsule Caper ◆ 1989
12. Sebastian (Super Sleuth) and the Baffling Bigfoot ◆ 1990
13. Sebastian (Super Sleuth) and the Mystery Patient ◆ 1991
14. Sebastian (Super Sleuth) and the Impossible Crime ◆ 1992
15. Sebastian (Super Sleuth) and the Copycat Crime ◆ 1993
16. Sebastian (Super Sleuth) and the Flying Elephant ◆ 1994

2ND-GRADE FRIENDS

Catalanotto, Peter, and Pamela Schembri

HOLT ◆ GRADES 1–3 ◆ A/R

REAL LIFE

Emily and Vinni are friends. They stick up for and support each other. And, of course, sometimes they have disagreements. When Vinni misses Emily's birthday party, Emily's feelings are hurt. She accepts Vinni's apology and their friendship continues. Like the Junie B. Jones books, this series provides a transition between easy-readers and longer chapter books.

1. The Secret Lunch Special ◆ 2006
2. No More Pumpkins ◆ 2007
3. The Veteran's Day Visitor ◆ 2008

SECRET AGENT DINGLEDORF AND HIS TRUSTY DOG SPLAT

Myers, Bill

TOMMY NELSON ◆ **GRADES 2–4** ◆ **A/R**

HUMOR | MYSTERY | VALUES

Bernie Dingledorf is 10 years old and in fourth grade. With his friend I.Q. and his dog Splat, Bernie tries to explain some unusual events. Why are all the teachers (and other responsible people) laughing? Could it be Dr. Chuckles? In another book, how will Bernie and company deal with B.A.D.D.—the Bungling Agents Dedicated to Destruction? Even with the slapstick humor, these books keep a focus on respect and faith when solving problems.

1. The Case of the Giggling Geeks ◆ 2002
2. The Case of the Chewable Worms ◆ 2002
3. The Case of the Flying Toenails ◆ 2002
4. The Case of the Drooling Dinosaurs ◆ 2003
5. The Case of the Hiccupping Ears ◆ 2003
6. The Case of the Yodeling Turtles ◆ 2004

SECRET AGENT JACK STALWART

Hunt, Elizabeth Singer

WEINSTEIN BOOKS ◆ **GRADES 1–4**

ADVENTURE

Nine-year-old Jack Stalwart is an agent with the Global Protection Force. He has a bagful of gadgets (neutralizing spray, goo tube, time-release vapors, and so forth), which he uses on missions around the world. In the first book, a dinosaur has been brought back to life and Jack must stop it before it destroys New York City. In *The Pursuit of the Ivory Poachers,* Jack is on the trail of criminals killing elephants for their tusks. These books provide plenty of background information that does not detract from the fast-paced adventure.

1. The Escape of the Deadly Dinosaur: USA ◆ 2007
2. The Search for the Sunken Treasure: Australia ◆ 2007
3. The Mystery of the Mona Lisa: France ◆ 2007
4. The Caper of the Crown Jewels: England ◆ 2007
5. The Secret of the Sacred Temple: Cambodia ◆ 2007
6. The Pursuit of the Ivory Poachers: Kenya ◆ 2008
7. The Puzzle of the Missing Panda: China ◆ 2008
8. Peril at the Grand Prix: Italy ◆ 2009

SECRET AGENT MJJ

Jefferies, Marc John, and Danny Hirsch

BIG SMILE ◆ GRADES 4–7

ADVENTURE

At the age of 13, African American Marc John Jefferies is already a Hollywood star when a call comes asking him to serve the cause of good against evil. His codename is Boogieman and his sidekick is Scooter Brosnan. In *The Volcano,* Boogieman has to leave a film set to tackle a volcano that is threatening disaster—is this a natural event?

1. The Missing Princess ◆ 2005
2. The Secret Portrait ◆ 2005
3. The Volcano ◆ 2005
4. The Fountain of Youth ◆ 2006
5. The Pirates of Marathon ◆ 2006
6. The Sun King ◆ 2006

SECRET WORLD OF ALEX MACK

Various authors

MINSTREL/POCKET BOOKS ◆ GRADES 5–8

ADVENTURE | FANTASY

Alex Mack was just an ordinary teenager until she was drenched with a strange chemical. Now she can move objects with her mind and change shapes by morphing into a liquid form. Alex and her friends—Ray Alvarado, Robyn Russo, Nicole Wilson, and boyfriend Hunter Reeves—get involved in adventures such as capturing a pet-napping ring. Alex also has to worry about keeping her special powers a secret; especially when she gets sick on a trip to New York and can't control her ability to become liquid. Readers who like the popular Nickelodeon television program will enjoy following the familiar characters in these adventures.

1. Alex, You're Glowing! (Gallagher, Diana G.) ◆ 1995
2. Bet You Can't! (Gallagher, Diana G.) ◆ 1995
3. Bad News Babysitting! (Lipman, Ken) ◆ 1995
4. Witch Hunt! (Gallagher, Diana G.) ◆ 1995
5. Mistaken Identity! (Gallagher, Diana G.) ◆ 1996
6. Cleanup Catastrophe! (Dubowski, Cathy East) ◆ 1996
7. Take a Hike! (Dubowski, Cathy East) ◆ 1996
8. Go for the Gold! (Gallagher, Diana G.) ◆ 1996
9. Poison in Paradise! (Gallagher, Diana G.) ◆ 1996
10. Zappy Holidays! (Super Edition) (Gallagher, Diana G.) ◆ 1996
11. Junkyard Jitters! (Barnes-Svarney, Patricia) ◆ 1997
12. Frozen Stiff! (Gallagher, Diana G.) ◆ 1997
13. I Spy! (Peel, John) ◆ 1997

14. High Flyer! (Barnes-Svarney, Patricia) ◆ 1997
15. Milady Alex! (Gallagher, Diana G.) ◆ 1997
16. Father-Daughter Disaster! (Emery, Clayton) ◆ 1997
17. Bonjour, Alex! (Dubowski, Cathy East) ◆ 1997
18. Close Encounters! (Weiss, David Cody, and Bobbi J. G. Weiss) ◆ 1997
19. Hocus Pocus! (Locke, Joseph) ◆ 1997
20. Halloween Invaders! (Vornholt, John) ◆ 1997
21. Truth Trap! (Dubowski, Cathy East) ◆ 1997
22. New Year's Revolution! (Gallagher, Diana G.) ◆ 1997
23. Lost in Vegas! (Peel, John) ◆ 1998
24. Computer Crunch! (Barnes-Svarney, Patricia) ◆ 1998
25. In Hot Pursuit! (Odom, Mel) ◆ 1998
26. Canine Caper! (Gallagher, Diana G.) ◆ 1998
27. Civil War in Paradise! (Stone, Bonnie D.) ◆ 1998
28. Pool Party Panic! (Mitchell, V. E.) ◆ 1998
29. Sink or Swim! (Dubowski, Cathy East) ◆ 1998
30. Gold Rush Fever! (Gallagher, Diana G.) ◆ 1998
31. New York Nightmare! (Pass, Erica) ◆ 1998
32. Haunted House Hijinks! (Vornholt, John) ◆ 1998
33. Lights Camera Action (Garton, Ray) ◆ 1998
34. Paradise Lost, Paradise Regained! (Gallagher, Diana G.) ◆ 1998

SECRETS OF DRIPPING FANG

Greenburg, Dan

HARCOURT ◆ GRADES 4–6 ◆ A/R

HUMOR | HORROR

Wally Shluffmuffin, 10, has really smelly feet. His twin, Cheyenne, has a slimy dripping nose. Residents of Jolly Days Orphanage, these two will never be adopted. Then two odd elderly sisters agree to take them home to Dripping Fang Forest. The two sisters warn the twins to keep out of the cellar, so of course Wally looks down there and realizes that the sisters are really giant ants. The boys escape back to the orphanage, where their adventures continue—including the return of the twins' father, who was killed in a strange Porta-Potty accident and is now a zombie. A cross between Captain Underpants and Lemony Snicket, this series is a choice for reluctant readers.

1. The Onts ◆ 2005
2. Treachery and Betrayal at Jolly Days ◆ 2006
3. The Vampire's Curse ◆ 2006
4. Fall of the House of Mandible ◆ 2006
5. The Shluffmuffin Boy Is History ◆ 2006
6. Attack of the Giant Octopus ◆ 2007
7. Please Don't Eat the Children ◆ 2007
8. When Bad Snakes Attack Good Children ◆ 2007

SECRETS OF DROON

Abbott, Tony

SCHOLASTIC ◆ GRADES 2–5 ◆ A/R

FANTASY

A magical doorway takes three friends to the world of Droon. Eric, Neal, and Julie meet Princess Keeah and become involved in adventures such as recovering a stolen jewel, finding a cure to change Neal back from being a giant bug, and facing an ancient snow beast. Fans of action and fantasies will enjoy this series.

1. The Hidden Stairs and the Magic Carpet ◆ 1999
2. Journey to the Volcano Palace ◆ 1999
3. The Mysterious Island ◆ 1999
4. City in the Clouds ◆ 1999
5. The Great Ice Battle ◆ 1999
6. The Sleeping Giant of Goll ◆ 2000
7. Into the Land of the Lost ◆ 2000
8. The Golden Wasp ◆ 2000
9. Tower of the Elf King: , ◆ 2000
10. Quest for the Queen: , ◆ 2000
11. The Hawk Bandits of Tarkoom ◆ 2001
12. Under the Serpent Sea ◆ 2001
13. The Mask of Maliban ◆ 2001
14. Voyage of the Jaffa Wind ◆ 2002
15. The Moon Scroll ◆ 2002
16. The Knights of Silversnow ◆ 2002
17. Dream Thief ◆ 2003
18. Search for the Dragon Ship ◆ 2003
19. The Coiled Viper ◆ 2003
20. In the Ice Caves of Krog ◆ 2003
21. Flight of the Genie ◆ 2004
22. The Isle of Mists ◆ 2004
23. The Fortress of the Treasure Queen ◆ 2004
24. The Race to Doobesh ◆ 2005
25. The Riddle of Zorfendorf Castle ◆ 2005
26. The Moon Dragon ◆ 2006
27. The Chariot of Queen Zara ◆ 2006
28. In the Shadow of Goll ◆ 2006
29. Pirates of the Purple Dawn ◆ 2007
30. Escape from Jabar-Loo ◆ 2007
31. Queen of Shadowthorn ◆ 2007
32. Treasure of the Orkins ◆ 2008
33. Flight of the Blue Serpent ◆ 2008

SECRETS OF DROON SPECIAL EDITIONS

1. The Magic Escapes ◆ 2002
2. Wizard or Witch? ◆ 2004

3. Voyagers of the Silver Sand ◆ 2005
4. Sorcerer ◆ 2006

SEPTIMUS HEAP

Sage, Angie

HARPERCOLLINS ◆ GRADES 5–8 ◆ A/R

FANTASY

Jenna has been raised by Silas Heap whose own son Septimus (the seventh son of a seventh son) was taken away at birth and is presumed to be dead. Jenna, 10, learns she is a princess and that she is in danger from the assassins of the Supreme Commander. Along with several companions, she escapes from the assassins only to be pursued by the agents of Necromancer DomDaniel. As the series progresses, Septimus Heap is revealed to be alive and serving as Apprentice to the ExtraOrdinary Wizard. Time travel, quests, ghosts, Darke Magyk and more are sure to appeal to fantasy fans.

1. Magyk ◆ 2005
2. Flyte ◆ 2006
3. Physik ◆ 2007
4. Queste ◆ 2008

A SERIES OF UNFORTUNATE EVENTS

Snicket, Lemony

HARPERCOLLINS ◆ GRADES 3–7 ◆ A/R

FANTASY

The lives of the Baudelaire children are full of woe. Their parents perished in a fire, leaving Violet, Klaus, and Sunny at the mercy of the villainous Count Olaf. Just when you think they may find happiness, it is snatched away. The books in this droll series include many side comments and dire predictions. Read them at your own peril. There are related items including boxed sets of books, posters, puzzles, postcards, calendars, and *Lemony Snicket: The Unauthorized Autobiography. The Beatrice Letters* (2006) is a (fictional) collection of letters between Lemony Snicket and the elusive Beatrice, offering insight into the author and his series.

1. The Bad Beginning: Book the First ◆ 1999
2. The Reptile Room: Book the Second ◆ 1999
3. The Wide Window: Book the Third ◆ 2000
4. The Miserable Mill: Book the Fourth ◆ 2000
5. The Austere Academy: Book the Fifth ◆ 2000
6. The Ersatz Elevator: Book the Sixth ◆ 2001

7. The Vile Village: Book the Seventh ◆ 2001
8. The Hostile Hospital: Book the Eighth ◆ 2001
9. The Carnivorous Carnival: Book the Ninth ◆ 2002
10. The Slippery Slope: Book the Tenth ◆ 2003
11. The Grim Grotto: Book the Eleventh ◆ 2004
12. The Penultimate Peril: Book the Twelfth ◆ 2005
13. The End—Too Dreadful to Picture: Book the Thirteenth ◆ 2006

SERIOUSLY SILLY STORIES

Anholt, Laurence

CAPSTONE ◆ GRADES 2—4 ◆ A/R

HUMOR

These are humorous fractured fairy tales with black-and-white cartoon illustrations. In *Little Red Riding Wolf,* a poor young wolf on his way to see his grandmother is terrorized by a Big Bad Girl. In other stories, the Aliens are Snow White's backup group and the three entrepreneurial pigs are horrible polluters under pressure from the wolf and his band of eco-logically minded supporters.

1. Billy Beast ◆ 2004
2. Eco-Wolf and the Three Pigs ◆ 2004
3. Foolish Jack and the Bean Stack ◆ 2004
4. Ghostyshocks and the Three Scares ◆ 2004
5. Little Red Riding Wolf ◆ 2004
6. Rumply Crumply Stinky Pin ◆ 2004
7. Shampoozel ◆ 2004
8. Snow White and the Seven Aliens ◆ 2004

SEVEN LITTLE MONSTERS

Yorinks, Arthur

HYPERION ◆ GRADES K—1

FANTASY

Maurice Sendak's Seven Little Monsters have been adapted into a series of television episodes (many of which are available on video/DVD). These books feature the monsters on a trip into space, finding a birthday gift for Mama, and telling time. The illustrations by Raymond Jafelice are in the style of Sendak's original book.

1. Monsters in Space ◆ 2003
2. We Love You, Mama! ◆ 2003
3. Bedtime Story ◆ 2004
4. What Time Is It? ◆ 2004

7TH HEAVEN

Various authors

RANDOM HOUSE ◆ GRADES 4–7

FAMILY LIFE | VALUES

The Camden family—characters from the popular television series—have further adventures in these books. Readers will enjoy more stories about Rev. and Mrs. Camden and their children and their friends. In one book, Ruthie wins a trip to Hollywood. In another, Lucy and Mary have a survival adventure in New York City. Family values and a commitment to faith infuse these novels. There are related items including a scrapbook and background information about the cast.

1. Nobody's Perfect (Christie, Amanda) ◆ 1999
2. Mary's Story (Christie, Amanda) ◆ 1999
3. Matt's Story (Christie, Amanda) ◆ 1999
4. Middle Sister (Clark, Catherine) ◆ 2000
5. Mr. Nice Guy (Christie, Amanda) ◆ 2000
6. Rivals (Cerasini, Marc) ◆ 2000
7. The Perfect Plan (Christie, Amanda) ◆ 2000
8. Secrets (Christie, Amanda) ◆ 2000
9. The New Me (Christie, Amanda) ◆ 2000
10. Sister Trouble (Christie, Amanda) ◆ 2001
11. Learning the Ropes (Thomas, Jim) ◆ 2001
12. Drive You Crazy (Cerasini, Marc) ◆ 2001
13. Camp Camden (Christie, Amanda) ◆ 2001
14. Lucy's Angel (Christie, Amanda) ◆ 2001
15. Winter Ball (Christie, Amanda) ◆ 2002
16. Dude Ranch (Christie, Amanda) ◆ 2002
17. Sisters Through the Seasons (Christie, Amanda, and Marc Cerasini) ◆ 2002
18. Mary's Rescue (Christie, Amanda) ◆ 2003
19. Wedding Memories (Christie, Amanda) ◆ 2004
20. The East-West Contest (Christie, Amanda) ◆ 2004

SHADOW CHILDREN

Haddix, Margaret Peterson

SIMON & SCHUSTER ◆ GRADES 5–8 ◆ A/R

FANTASY | SCIENCE FICTION

Luke, 12, is a third child in a future society that allows only two children. He must remain hidden. His family is victimized by "the Barons," the elite group of their society. Luke discovers a secret in the Baron house next door—another "shadow child." The series follows Luke and other third-born children as they struggle with being outcasts.

1. Among the Hidden ◆ 1998
2. Among the Imposters ◆ 2001
3. Among the Betrayed ◆ 2003
4. Among the Barons ◆ 2003
5. Among the Brave ◆ 2004
6. Among the Enemy ◆ 2005
7. Among the Free ◆ 2006

SHADOW ZONE

Black, J. R.

RANDOM HOUSE ◆ GRADES 4–6

FANTASY

In the first book, Toby is a sixth-grader being pestered by a ghost. Buddy (the ghost) died nearly 30 years ago and wants Toby to solve the mystery of his death. Other books feature aliens, Sasquatch, voodoo, and zombies.

1. The Ghost of Chicken Liver Hill ◆ 1993
2. Guess Who's Dating a Werewolf? ◆ 1993
3. The Witches Next Door ◆ 1993
4. Revenge of the Computer Phantoms ◆ 1993
5. The Undead Express ◆ 1994
6. Good Night, Mummy! ◆ 1994
7. One Slimy Summer ◆ 1994
8. Bite of the Living Dead ◆ 1994
9. Alien Under My Bed ◆ 1994
10. Scream Around the Campfire ◆ 1994
11. My Teacher Ate My Homework ◆ 1995
12. Skeleton in My Closet ◆ 1995
13. Attack of the Mutant Bugs ◆ 1995

THE SHAKESPEARE STEALER

Blackwood, Gary L.

DUTTON ◆ GRADES 5–8 ◆ A/R

HISTORICAL

In London in 1601, Widge is a 14-year-old orphan boy whose master sends him to steal an unpublished play—Hamlet. Instead of stealing the manuscript, Widge becomes an acting apprentice. He has many adventures with Shakespeare's company of actors.

1. The Shakespeare Stealer ◆ 1998
2. Shakespeare's Scribe ◆ 2000
3. Shakespeare's Spy ◆ 2003

SHANNA FIRST READERS

Marzollo, Jean

HYPERION/JUMP AT THE SUN ◆ GRADES K–1

REAL LIFE

This is a very easy reader series featuring an African American girl. The rhyming text adds to the fun as Shanna makes pizza, searches for her shoe, and asks easy riddles. There are "Shanna Show" books for pre-schoolers.

1. Animal Riddles ◆ 2004
2. Bear Hunt ◆ 2004
3. Hip, Hop, Hooray! ◆ 2004
4. Shanna's Pizza Party ◆ 2004
5. Shanna's Lost Shoe ◆ 2004
6. Shanna's Party Surprise ◆ 2004

SHANNON   *see* Girlhood Journeys: Shannon

SHEEP

Shaw, Nancy

HOUGHTON MIFFLIN ◆ GRADES K–3 ◆ A/R

ANIMAL FANTASY | HUMOR

A zany group of sheep have adventures that involve silly disasters that turn out all right in the end. On a ship, they "read a map" but "begin to nap," which results in a shipwreck. They make a raft and it drifts as the storm lifts. "Land Ho. Not far to go." When they go for a ride in a Jeep, they get stuck in the mud. Some friendly pigs pull them out, but then the driver sheep forgets to steer and they crash into a tree. The sentences all rhyme and are often just two words.

1. Sheep in a Jeep ◆ 1986
2. Sheep on a Ship ◆ 1989
3. Sheep in a Shop ◆ 1991
4. Sheep Out to Eat ◆ 1992
5. Sheep Take a Hike ◆ 1994
6. Sheep Trick or Treat ◆ 1997

SHELBY WOO   *see* Mystery Files of Shelby Woo

SHELTIE!

Clover, Peter

ALADDIN ◆ GRADES 2–4

REAL LIFE

Emma is really pleased with her new Shetland pony, Sheltie, and the clever pony loves Emma just as much. Together they solve mysteries and problems, help others, make friends. In *Sheltie in Danger,* Sheltie saves Emma when she falls through the ice, but puts his own life in jeopardy. Will Emma be able to keep Sheltie alive?

1. Sheltie the Shetland Pony ◆ 2000
2. Sheltie Saves the Day! ◆ 2000
3. Sheltie and the Runaway ◆ 2000
4. Sheltie Finds a Friend ◆ 2000
5. Sheltie to the Rescue ◆ 2001
6. Sheltie in Danger ◆ 2001
7. Sheltie Rides to Win ◆ 2001

SHILOH

Naylor, Phyllis Reynolds

SIMON & SCHUSTER ◆ GRADES 3–6 ◆ A/R

REAL LIFE

A touching dog story that deals with larger issues of prejudice and abuse. Marty makes friends with a beagle named Shiloh only to discover that the dog is being abused. Readers are faced with the problem of what Marty should do, because the dog is not his. As the trilogy proceeds, Marty is forced to deal with Judd, the man who abuses Shiloh and his other dogs, and finally must decide whether he believes that Judd can change. *Shiloh* won the Newbery Medal.

1. Shiloh ◆ 1991
2. Shiloh Season ◆ 1996
3. Saving Shiloh ◆ 1997

SHIMMER AND THORN

Yep, Laurence

HARPERCOLLINS ◆ GRADES 5–8 ◆ A/R

FANTASY

The Dragon Princess Shimmer is in exile. She teams up with a human boy, Thorn, to try to restore her Dragon Clan's home. Shimmer, Monkey, and other companions become prisoners of the Boneless King and Pomfret the dragon. They must escape and go into battle to save Thorn.

1. Dragon of the Lost Sea ◆ 1982
2. Dragon Steel ◆ 1985
3. Dragon Cauldron ◆ 1991
4. Dragon War ◆ 1992

SHIRLEY HOLMES *see* Adventures of Shirley Holmes

SHORT STIRRUP CLUB

Estes, Alison

POCKET BOOKS ◆ GRADES 4–6

REAL LIFE | RECREATION

Five friends share adventures at the Thistle Ridge Farm, a stable owned by Olympic rider Sharon Wyndham. Megan and Max Morrison are twins who enjoy riding and competing. Amanda Sloane's mother is interested in riding, and she is pushing Amanda into training. Amanda dislikes her lessons and horse shows, but she wants to please her well-to-do parents. Chloe Goodman must do chores at the farm in order to keep her horse there, while Keith Hill, whose parents are Mexican and Native American, enjoys riding as an extension of his heritage. The plots are related to horse shows for younger riders: Short Stirrup is a division for riders 12 and under. The characters overcome fears, deal with jealousy, and participate in competitions, which will appeal to the many horse aficionados.

1. Blue Ribbon Friends ◆ 1996
2. Ghost of Thistle Ridge ◆ 1996
3. The Great Gymkhana Gamble ◆ 1996
4. Winner's Circle ◆ 1996
5. Gold Medal Mystery ◆ 1996
6. Friends to the Finish ◆ 1996
7. Legend of the Zuni Stallion ◆ 1996
8. Victory Ride ◆ 1997
9. Playing for Keeps ◆ 1997
10. Pony Express ◆ 1997

SHREDDERMAN

Van Draanen, Wendelin

KNOPF ◆ GRADES 3–6 ◆ A/R

REAL LIFE

Nolan Byrd is in fifth grade. He is bothered by bullies so he creates a secret identity—Shredderman. With the help of his teacher, Mr. Green, Nolan uses his computer skills to expose the bad guys—including the school bully and some graffiti vandals.

1. Secret Identity ◆ 2004
2. Attack of the Tagger ◆ 2004
3. Meet the Gecko ◆ 2005
4. Shredderman: Enemy Spy ◆ 2006

SIDEKICKS

Danko, Dan, and Tom Mason

LITTLE, BROWN ◆ GRADES 5–8 ◆ A/R

HUMOR

Guy Martin is a normal 13-year-old . . . except when he is "Speedy," the world's fastest boy and member of a team of apprentice superheroes that helps to defend the world against evil. Sadly, Guy's work as sidekick to Pumpkin Pete (who has the powers of a pumpkin) is less than inspiring. In the third book, Speedy tries to save the beautiful Prudence from the Mole Master, hoping Pumpkin Pete will help rather than hinder for a change. With cartoon illustrations by Barry Gott, these books feature lots of young teen humor and should appeal to fans of Captain Underpants.

1. Sidekicks ◆ 2003
2. Operation Squish! ◆ 2003
3. Attack of the Mole Master ◆ 2004
4. The Candy Man Cometh ◆ 2004
5. The Brotherhood of Rotten Babysitters ◆ 2005
6. Invasion of the Evil Teachers from Planet Buttface ◆ 2005

SILLY THRILLERS WITH PEGGY THE PIG

Thiesing, Lisa

DUTTON ◆ GRADES K–2 ◆ A/R

HUMOR | ANIMAL FANTASY

Peggy the pig is featured in these scary, silly stories. In *The Viper*, Peggy is frightened by the phone calls she is getting from "the viper" only to discover that it is the window cleaner. Get it . . . wiper with an accent. "I vill come in one year." In another book, the aliens are coming, except that the aliens are a musical group. Beginning readers will be amused by these fun stories.

1. The Viper ◆ 2002
2. The Aliens Are Coming! ◆ 2004

3. A Dark and Noisy Night ◆ 2005
4. The Scarecrow's New Clothes ◆ 2006

SILLY TILLY

Hoban, Lillian

HARPERCOLLINS ◆ GRADES K–2 ◆ A/R

ANIMAL FANTASY

Silly Tilly the mole is forgetful and easily distracted, but she is lovable. Mr. Bunny and her animal friends are always getting her out of silly scrapes and end up having fun in the process. These I Can Read books will be fun for readers who are starting to have success reading by themselves. They are also enjoyable read-alouds for holiday groups of young children, who will have to listen closely to see what Silly Tilly is forgetting.

1. Silly Tilly and the Easter Bunny ◆ 1987
2. Silly Tilly's Thanksgiving Dinner ◆ 1990
3. Silly Tilly's Valentine ◆ 1997

SILVER BLADES

Lowell, Melissa

BANTAM ◆ GRADES 4–7 ◆ A/R

REAL LIFE | RECREATION

Four girls who dream of going to the Olympics practice and compete at an exclusive skating club, the Silver Blades. The series starts with Nikki's arrival in Seneca Hills. She meets Jill, Tori, and Danielle and begins to practice for her Silver Blades tryout. She also meets other girls from school, is invited to join in their activities, and becomes interested in a handsome hockey player. In the end, she realizes that skating is really what she wants to do most. Each of the four girls stars in subsequent books. Tori deals with her demanding mother, Jill moves to Colorado, and Danielle lands a starring role in an ice show. Lots of skating technicalities are a natural part of the stories. In the Olympic trilogy, Silver Blades Gold Medal Dreams, Tori overcomes the odds and gets the chance to compete in the Winter Games.

1. Breaking the Ice ◆ 1993
2. In the Spotlight ◆ 1993
3. The Competition ◆ 1994
4. Going for the Gold ◆ 1994
5. The Perfect Pair ◆ 1994
6. Skating Camp ◆ 1994
7. The Ice Princess ◆ 1995
8. Rumors at the Rink ◆ 1995

9. Spring Break ◆ 1995
10. Center Ice ◆ 1995
11. A Surprise Twist ◆ 1995
12. The Winning Spirit ◆ 1995
13. The Big Audition ◆ 1995
14. Nutcracker on Ice ◆ 1995
15. A New Move ◆ 1996
16. Ice Magic ◆ 1996
17. A Leap Ahead ◆ 1996
18. More Than Friends ◆ 1996
19. Natalia Comes to America ◆ 1997
20. The One Way to Win ◆ 1997
21. Rival Roomates ◆ 1997
22. Double Dare ◆ 1998
23. Wanted: One Perfect Boy ◆ 1998

SILVER BLADES GOLD MEDAL DREAMS

1. On the Edge ◆ 1997
2. Now or Never ◆ 1997
3. Chance of a Lifetime ◆ 1998

SILVER BLADES SUPER EDITIONS

1. Rinkside Romance ◆ 1996
2. Wedding Secrets ◆ 1996

SILVER BLADES FIGURE EIGHTS

Older, Effin

BANTAM ◆ GRADES 2–4 ◆ A/R
REAL LIFE | RECREATION

Randi Wong is the younger sister of Jill Wong of the Silver Blades figure-skating club. She goes to the rink with Jill every day, but she is not allowed to take lessons because her family has a rule that each child must have a different activity. Randi's activity is supposed to be the violin, but she wants to quit and take skating lessons instead. When she signs up for skating lessons without permission, Jill intercedes with her parents and they let her join the newly formed group—the Silver Blades Figure Eights—which includes her friends Woody and Anna. The rest of the series is about Randi and her friends and their adventures on and off the ice. Silver Blades Figure Eights Super Editions include *Double Birthday Trouble* (1996) and *Randi Goes for the Gold* (1998).

1. Ice Dreams ◆ 1996
2. Star for a Day ◆ 1996

3. The Best Ice Show Ever! ◆ 1996
4. Bossy Anna ◆ 1996
5. Special Delivery Mess ◆ 1997
6. Randi's Missing Skates ◆ 1997
7. My Worst Friend, Woody ◆ 1997
8. Randi's Pet Surprise ◆ 1997

SILVER SEQUENCE

McNish, Cliff
CAROLRHODA ◆ GRADES 5–9 ◆ A/R
SCIENCE FICTION | FANTASY

An evil force is threatening the world and six children are key to its survival. The six are mysteriously drawn to a refuse dump where they develop special skills and powers. Milo turns silver and becomes the protector. Thomas becomes a healer while Emily and Freda can move swiftly on all fours. Helen is a psychic and Walter grows to be a giant. As the series progresses, the six are joined by other children as they face an unknown creature called "The Roar." The plot is presented from the point of view of different characters. Readers who have enjoyed Madeleine L'Engle's Time Fantasy series will appreciate this complex story.

1. The Silver Child ◆ 2005
2. Silver City ◆ 2006
3. Silver World ◆ 2007

SILVERSKIN LEGACY

Whittemore, Jo
LLEWELLYN ◆ GRADES 5–8
FANTASY

Junior high students Ainsley and Megan are spying on their neighbor Mr. Niksrevlis when they find themselves transported to the land of Arylon. There they learn that Mr. Niksrevlis is a king of the Silverskin family and protector of a magical relic that can open portals to other worlds. In the second book, Ainsley and Megan are preparing to return to their own world when Ainsley falls ill. Can Megan find a cure in time? These books are full of magic and adventure.

1. Escape from Arylon ◆ 2006
2. Curse of Arastold ◆ 2006
3. Onaj's Horn ◆ 2007

SILVERWING

Oppel, Kenneth

EOS ◆ GRADES 5–8

ANIMAL FANTASY

A bat named Shade is the runt of the Silverwing colony, and he has strange ideas about sunlight. Shade becomes separated from the rest of the colony during its migration and, with the help of Marina, a bat cast out of her own community, tries to rejoin his flock and save them from evil cannibal bats. In the second book, Shade sets out to find his father and again must confront danger. Full of bat facts and lore, this series also provides plenty of action and a touch of romance. *Darkwing* is a stand-alone fantasy, set millions of years before this series, about the ancestors of bats.

1. Silverwing ◆ 1997
2. Sunwing ◆ 2000
3. Firewing ◆ 2003

SIMPLY SARAH

Naylor, Phyllis Reynolds

MARSHALL CAVENDISH ◆ GRADES 2–4 ◆ A/R

REAL LIFE

Eight-year-old Sarah lives in Chicago, has a multicultural group of friends, and is full of ideas for solving problems. In the first of these beginning chapter books, she succeeds in attracting customers to her friend's Chinese restaurant. In *Patches and Scratches,* Peter wants a pet but the animal must pass both his building's rules and his grandmother's prejudices. Sarah finds the perfect solution.

1. Anyone Can Eat Squid! ◆ 2005
2. Cuckoo Feathers ◆ 2006
3. Patches and Scratches ◆ 2007
4. Eating Enchiladas ◆ 2008

SINDBAD

Zeman, Ludmila

TUNDRA ◆ GRADES 2–5 ◆ A/R

FANTASY

The adventures of Sindbad are vividly portrayed in this picture-book trilogy. Lavish illustrations by the author capture the drama of meeting monsters and facing sea serpents. This series would be good to share along with the stories of the Arabian Nights.

1. Sindbad ◆ 1999
2. Sindbad in the Land of Giants ◆ 2001
3. Sindbad's Secret ◆ 2003

SIRIUS MYSTERIES

Wood, Beverley, and Chris Wood

POLESTAR ◆ GRADES 5–9 ◆ A/R

MYSTERY | FANTASY | ADVENTURE

Jeff is still mourning the loss of his dog Buddy when he goes on a cruise to Alaska with his parents. There he finds a statue of a dog and is transported back in time to the 1930s where he meets the bull terrier Patsy Ann and helps to solve a mystery at sea. In the second volume, Patsy Ann lures 14-year old Jack back to 1935 Juneau, where he identifies the real perpetrator of a crime. These books weave history and humor into the stories.

1. Dogstar ◆ 1997
2. Jack's Knife ◆ 2003
3. The Golden Boy ◆ 2006

SISTER MAGIC

Mazer, Anne

SCHOLASTIC ◆ GRADES 2–4

FANTASY

Eight-year-old Mabel is a very organized young lady. Her younger sister Violet has unexpected magical talents, but they are quite unreliable. Mabel never knows whether they will help or hinder her own plans. The combination of magic and sibling rivalry will appeal to beginning chapter book readers.

1. The Trouble with Violet ◆ 2007
2. Violet Makes a Splash ◆ 2007
3. Mabel Makes the Grade ◆ 2007
4. Violet Strikes a Chord ◆ 2008
5. Violet Takes the Cake ◆ 2008

SISTER SISTER

Quin-Harkin, Janet

POCKET BOOKS ◆ GRADES 4–6

FAMILY LIFE | REAL LIFE

Fans of the popular TV show *Sister Sister* will enjoy these light-hearted books about the adventures of twin sisters Tia and Tamera. Tia and her single mother, Lisa Landry, have moved in with Tamera and Tamera's father, Ray Campbell. (How the twins were split up and how they came to be living with Lisa and Ray is part of the story.) Their home situation causes some confusion, particularly in regard to decisions about child rearing. The adventures in this series primarily focus on the daily lives of the girls, including their interest in boys, projects at school, clubs, tests, and summer jobs. These are enjoyable books, and students will find it fun to read about familiar TV characters.

1. Cool in School ◆ 1996
2. You Read My Mind ◆ 1996
3. One Crazy Christmas ◆ 1996
4. Homegirl on the Range ◆ 1997
5. All Rapped Up ◆ 1997
6. Star Quality ◆ 1997
7. He's All That ◆ 1997
8. Summer Daze ◆ 1997

THE SISTERS GRIMM

Buckley, Michael

AMULET ◆ GRADES 4–6 ◆ A/R

FANTASY

Sent to live with their grandmother after their parents disappear, sisters Daphne and Sabrina Grimm find themselves in a magical town full of fairy tale characters called Everafters. Soon thereafter their grandmother goes missing. Will the girls, who now know they are descendants of Wilhelm, be able to find her? In later books they—with the help of a little magic and fairy tale characters—investigate mysteries and search for their parents.

1. The Fairy-Tale Detectives ◆ 2005
2. The Unusual Suspects ◆ 2005
3. The Problem Child ◆ 2006
4. Once Upon a Crime ◆ 2007
5. Magic and Other Misdemeanors ◆ 2007
6. Tales from the Hood ◆ 2008

THE SIXTH SENSE: SECRETS FROM BEYOND

Benjamin, David

SCHOLASTIC ◆ **GRADES 5–7**

FANTASY

Cole Sear has special powers. He sees and can communicate with the dead. There are secrets that the dead want Cole to share. These secrets will help solve mysteries surrounding their deaths. The popularity of the movie adds to the interest in these books.

1. Survivor ◆ 2000
2. Runaway ◆ 2001
3. Hangman ◆ 2001

SKATING DREAMS

Thacker, Nola

VOLO/HYPERION ◆ **GRADES 3–6** ◆ **A/R**

RECREATION

Skating enthusiasts will enjoy these stories of friendship and competition. In *The Winning Edge,* Lauren has been working with Coach Perry. She has enjoyed the one-to-one attention. Now, Courtney will be sharing coaching time with Lauren. Will the two girls get along? How will they deal with training together and then competing against each other? A special feature from Michelle Kwan is included in each book.

1. The Turning Point ◆ 2000
2. Staying Balanced ◆ 2000
3. Skating Backwards ◆ 2000
4. Champion's Luck ◆ 2000
5. The Winning Edge ◆ 2001
6. Coach's Choice ◆ 2001
7. Wishing for Gold ◆ 2001

SKINNER FAMILY *see* The Great Skinner

SKIPPYJON JONES

Schachner, Judy

DUTTON ◆ **GRADES K–3** ◆ **A/R**

HUMOR

Skippyjon Jones is a Siamese kitten with a great imagination. He pretends he is a chihuahua. In *Skippyjon Jones in Mummy Trouble,* he dreams of an adventure in ancient Egypt. Skippyjon Jones talks in a combination of Spanish words and an exaggerated Spanish accent (I heard a leetle birdito). There are board books as well as a flip/matching book.

1. Skippyjon Jones ◆ 2003
2. Skippyjon Jones in the Doghouse ◆ 2005
3. Skippyjon Jones in Mummy Trouble ◆ 2006
4. Skippyjon Jones and the Big Bones ◆ 2007

SLAM DUNK

Kindig, Tess Eileen
CONCORDIA PUBLISHING ◆ GRADES 4–6 ◆ A/R
RECREATION | VALUES

Mickey is in fourth grade. He plays for the Pinecrest Flying Eagles basketball team. Although he is not a starter, he is a key player, the "sixth man" who comes off the bench. In one book, Mickey's shot wins the game. In another book, his grades may keep him from being on the team. Mickey struggles to balance responsibilities at home and school with the demands of basketball. His faith sustains him through his problems.

1. Sixth Man Switch ◆ 1999
2. Spider McGhee and the Hoopla ◆ 1999
3. Zip, Zero, Zilch ◆ 2000
4. Muggsy Makes an Assist ◆ 2000
5. Gimme an "A" ◆ 2000
6. March Mania ◆ 2000
7. Double Whammy! ◆ 2001
8. Camp Bee-a-Champ ◆ 2001

SLAPSHOTS

Korman, Gordon
SCHOLASTIC ◆ GRADES 5–8 ◆ A/R
RECREATION

Hockey action is featured in this series. The Stars from Mars face a variety of opponents including the dreaded Oilers. Will the Stars win the trophy cup?

1. The Stars from Mars ◆ 1999
2. All-Mars All-Stars ◆ 1999
3. The Face-Off Phony ◆ 2000
4. Cup Crazy ◆ 2000

SLEEPOVER FRIENDS

Saunders, Susan

SCHOLASTIC ◆ GRADES 3–5

REAL LIFE

Kate Beekman and Lauren Hunter have been friends since they were very young, and they have enjoyed regular sleepover parties. In fourth grade, Stephanie Green moved to their neighborhood; and in fifth grade, Patti Jenkins joined the group. Now they spend a lot of time together, including Friday sleepovers. Their adventures involve fairly standard school and friendship activities: problems with boys, worries about arguing parents, and jealousy over performing in the school play and a rock video. Girls enjoy this series because of the familiar situations and enduring friendships.

1. Patti's Luck ◆ 1987
2. Starring Stephanie ◆ 1987
3. Kate's Surprise ◆ 1987
4. Patti's New Look ◆ 1988
5. Lauren's Big Mix-Up ◆ 1988
6. Kate's Camp-Out ◆ 1988
7. Stephanie Strikes Back ◆ 1988
8. Lauren's Treasure ◆ 1988
9. No More Sleepovers Patti? ◆ 1988
10. Lauren's Sleepover Exchange ◆ 1989
11. Stephanie's Family Secret ◆ 1989
12. Kate's Sleepover Disaster ◆ 1989
13. Patti's Secret Wish ◆ 1989
14. Lauren Takes Charge ◆ 1989
15. Stephanie's Big Story ◆ 1989
16. Kate's Crush ◆ 1989
17. Patti Gets Even ◆ 1989
18. Stephanie and the Magician ◆ 1989
19. The Great Kate ◆ 1990
20. Lauren in the Middle ◆ 1990
21. Starstruck Stephanie ◆ 1990
22. The Trouble with Patti ◆ 1990
23. Kate's Surprise Visitor ◆ 1990
24. Lauren's New Friend ◆ 1990
25. Stephanie and the Wedding ◆ 1990
26. The New Kate ◆ 1990
27. Where's Patti? ◆ 1990
28. Lauren's New Address ◆ 1990
29. Kate the Boss ◆ 1990
30. Big Sister Stephanie ◆ 1990
31. Lauren's Afterschool Job ◆ 1990
32. A Valentine for Patti ◆ 1991
33. Lauren's Double Disaster ◆ 1991
34. Kate the Winner! ◆ 1991

35. The New Stephanie ◆ 1991
36. Presenting Patti ◆ 1991
37. Lauren Saves the Day ◆ 1991
38. Patti's City Adventure ◆ 1991

SLEEPOVER FRIENDS SUPER EDITION

1. Super Beach Mystery ◆ 1991

SLEEPOVER SQUAD

Denton, P. J.

ALADDIN ◆ GRADES 1–3 ◆ A/R

REAL LIFE

Taylor, Emily, Jo, and Kara are just finishing second grade and planning their first sleepover party at Taylor's house. Emily is worried that her parents won't allow her to go. Things work out and the friends take turns hosting parties. When it is Emily's turn, the girls will sleep in a tent in her yard. Now Taylor is worried because she is afraid of bugs. These are sweet books about everyday kids. The illustrations depict a multicultural group.

1. Sleeping Over ◆ 2007
2. Camping Out ◆ 2007
3. The Trouble with Brothers ◆ 2007
4. Keeping Secrets ◆ 2008
5. Pony Party! ◆ 2008
6. The New Girl ◆ 2008

SLIMEBALLS

Gross, U. B.

RANDOM HOUSE ◆ GRADES 5–7

HUMOR

Two of the books in this series feature Gus, his friend Polly, and the class dullard Ray. Gus plans to win the science fair with his collection of unusual molds. The books are full of gross humor and weird characters. A wacko school nurse is fired and returns in another book as a crazed bus driver. The characters often behave in ways that will appeal to the middle school sense of humor—food fights, slime attacks, and rodents that take over a home.

1. Fun Gus and Polly Pus ◆ 1996
2. Fun Gus Slimes the Bus ◆ 1997
3. The Slithers Buy a Boa ◆ 1997

SLIPPERS

Clements, Andrew

DUTTON ◆ GRADES K–2 ◆ A/R

REAL LIFE

What a cute puppy! In *Slippers at School,* our puppy watches Laura get ready for the first day of school. He hides in her backpack and, after some misadventures, is discovered. Janie Bynum's illustrations are adorable. Fans of Biscuit will love Slippers.

1. Slippers at Home ◆ 2004
2. Naptime for Slippers ◆ 2005
3. Slippers at School ◆ 2005
4. Slippers Loves to Run ◆ 2006

SLY THE SLEUTH

Napoli, Donna Jo, and Robert Furrow

DIAL ◆ GRADES 2–4

MYSTERY

Sly (Sylvia) the detective may be young but she already has her own agency, Sleuth for Hire, and friends who help her investigate and provide added interest and an opportunity for wordplay. Each volume contains three separate, simple mysteries (Sly only takes on puzzles of interest to her cat, Taxi). They all involve snappy dialogue and some intuition.

1. Sly the Sleuth and the Pet Mysteries ◆ 2005
2. Sly the Sleuth and the Sports Mysteries ◆ 2006
3. Sly the Sleuth and the Food Mysteries ◆ 2007

SNARVEY GOOPER *see* Funny Firsts

SNEAKY PONY

Higginson, Hadley

CHRONICLE ◆ GRADES 1–3 ◆ A/R

REAL LIFE

Keeker is Catherine Corey Keegan Dana and she loves horses. In the first book, she gets a Shetland pony named Plum. Their adventures together are featured in this series. They participate in a horse show, go to a sleep-away camp, and go on a family vacation. This is a fun choice for younger horse fans.

1. Keeker and the Sneaky Pony ◆ 2006
2. Keeker and the Horse Show Show-Off ◆ 2006
3. Keeker and the Sugar Shack ◆ 2006
4. Keeker and the Springtime Surprise ◆ 2007
5. Keeker and the Pony Camp Catastrophe ◆ 2007
6. Keeker and the Not-So-Sleepy Hollow ◆ 2008
7. Keeker and the Crazy, Upside-Down Birthday ◆ 2008

SO LITTLE TIME *see* Mary-Kate and Ashley: So Little Time

SO WEIRD

Various authors

HYPERION ◆ GRADES 4–7

FANTASY

Fi experiences supernatural events. She helps the restless soul of a boy find peace. She uses her computer talents to find the sender of strange e-mails. Her friends Jack and Clu help her investigate these paranormal events.

1. Family Reunion (Dubowski, Cathy East) ◆ 2000
2. Shelter (Mantell, Paul) ◆ 2000
3. Escape (Rees, Elizabeth M.) ◆ 2000
4. Strangeling (Dubowski, Cathy East) ◆ 2000
5. Web Sight (Pollack, Pam) ◆ 2000

SOCCER 'CATS

Christopher, Matt

LITTLE, BROWN ◆ GRADES 2–4 ◆ A/R

RECREATION

This series has lots of soccer action. In *Kick It!*, Alan accidentally kicks one of the players from his own team. Edith "Eddie" Sweeny is taken away in an ambulance and Alan worries about her. Meanwhile, he is teased by teammates and becomes so distracted that he makes mistakes during a game. The team is co-ed, which should broaden the appeal.

1. The Captain Contest ◆ 1999
2. Operation Baby-Sitter ◆ 1999
3. Secret Weapon ◆ 2000

   4. Hat Trick ◆ 2000
   5. Master of Disaster ◆ 2001
   6. Heads Up ◆ 2001
   7. All Keyed Up ◆ 2002
   8. You Lucky Dog ◆ 2002
   9. Switch Play! ◆ 2003
  10. Kick It! ◆ 2003
  11. Making the Save ◆ 2004

SOCCER SHOCK

Napoli, Donna Jo
DUTTON ◆ GRADES 4–6 ◆ A/R
FANTASY

Have you ever heard of talking freckles? That's what happens to Adam when lightning strikes right next to him. His freckles give him advice that help him develop confidence. In one book, they try to solve Adam's problem with a girl.

   1. Soccer Shock ◆ 1991
   2. Shark Shock ◆ 1994
   3. Shelley Shock ◆ 2000

SOCCER STARS

Costello, Emily
BANTAM DOUBLEDAY DELL ◆ GRADES 3–6 ◆ A/R
REAL LIFE | RECREATION

Serious soccer players will enjoy this series packed full of game action. Off the field, the Soccer Stars (Rose, Jordan, Geena, Tess, Tameka, Lacey, Fiona, Yaz, and Nicole) are best friends; on the field, they're teammates and sometimes rivals. Endorsed by the American Youth Soccer Organization, with soccer tips at the back of each book, this is a series for girls who love this sport.

   1. Foul Play ◆ 1998
   2. On the Sidelines ◆ 1998
   3. Against the Rules ◆ 1998
   4. Best Friend Face-Off ◆ 1998
   5. Lottery Blues ◆ 1998
   6. Tournament Trouble ◆ 1998
   7. Calling the Shots ◆ 1999
   8. Teaming Up ◆ 1999

SOCK MONKEY

Bell, Cece

CANDLEWICK ◆ GRADES K–2 ◆ A/R

HUMOR

The popular stuffed toy is given his own adventures in these three books. Now a famous actor, Sock Monkey has been nominated for an award. Before he can go to the ceremony, he must take a bath—UGH! In the second book, Sock Monkey needs a dance partner but none of the other toys are the right choice so he makes another sock monkey—Sock Buddy.

1. Sock Monkey Goes to Hollywood: A Star is Bathed ◆ 2003
2. Sock Monkey Boogie-Woogie: A Friend Is Made ◆ 2004
3. Sock Monkey Rides Again ◆ 2006

SOFIA *see* My America: Sofia

SOLVE-IT-YOURSELF MYSTERY *see* Meg
Mackintosh: A Solve-It-Yourself Mystery

SOMETHING QUEER

Levy, Elizabeth

HYPERION ◆ GRADES 3–5 ◆ A/R

MYSTERY

Jill and Gwen are in a rock-and-roll band in *Something Queer in Rock 'n' Roll*. Gwen is fond of using disguises and always taps her braces and announces that she thinks "something queer" is going on. Their dog Fletcher is an important part of their act, howling along with them whenever they offer him pizza. The effect is so good that the band becomes a finalist in a contest, but their rivals capture Fletcher and force him to eat pizza until he is sick of it. All ends happily when Gwen discovers clues to solve the mystery and their rivals are disqualified. In another book, the girls have a lemonade stand that someone is trying to sabotage. All the books follow the same format, with easy-to-solve mysteries and plenty of humor.

1. Something Queer Is Going On ◆ 1973
2. Something Queer at the Ballpark ◆ 1975
3. Something Queer at the Library ◆ 1977
4. Something Queer on Vacation ◆ 1980
5. Something Queer at the Haunted School ◆ 1982

6. Something Queer at the Lemonade Stand ◆ 1982
7. Something Queer in Rock 'n' Roll ◆ 1987
8. Something Queer at the Birthday Party ◆ 1989
9. Something Queer in Outer Space ◆ 1993
10. Something Queer in the Cafeteria ◆ 1994
11. Something Queer at the Scary Movie ◆ 1995
12. Something Queer in the Wild West ◆ 1997

SONG LEE

Kline, Suzy

VIKING ◆ GRADES 2–4 ◆ A/R

HUMOR | REAL LIFE

Doug, the young narrator of this easy-reader series, relates the doings of his second-grade class. In *Song Lee and the Hamster Hunt,* Song brings her pet hamster to school and it escapes. The class makes posters to alert everyone in the school to watch for him. The janitor finally finds the hamster and brings him back. Another book finds the kids on a field trip and Song Lee makes friends with the class tattletale, Sidney. During the trip, due to Song's peacemaking efforts, Sidney learns not to tattle. The Horrible Harry series by the same author features the same characters and is also narrated by Doug, Harry's best friend.

1. Song Lee in Room 2B ◆ 1993
2. Song Lee and the Hamster Hunt ◆ 1994
3. Song Lee and the Leech Man ◆ 1995
4. Song Lee and the "I Hate You" Notes ◆ 1999

SONIC THE HEDGEHOG

Teitelbaum, Michael

TROLL ◆ GRADES 2–3

SCIENCE FICTION

Sonic is a blue hedgehog who travels the galaxy battling evil robots controlled by Dr. Robotnik. In one book, the robots want to do away with having fun; in another, Dr. Robotnik has the secret list that could lead to the destruction of the freedom fighters. These books are easy to read, with lots of action. Sonic behaves like a superhero as he faces dangers throughout the galaxy.

1. Sonic the Hedgehog ◆ 1993
2. Sonic the Hedgehog: Fortress of Fear ◆ 1994
3. Sonic the Hedgehog: Robotnik's Revenge ◆ 1994
4. Sonic the Hedgehog: Friend or Foe? ◆ 1995

SOOKAN BAK

Choi, Sook Nyul

HOUGHTON MIFFLIN ◆ **GRADES 5–8** ◆ **A/R**

FAMILY LIFE | **HISTORICAL**

In the first book of this trilogy, *Year of Impossible Goodbyes,* Sookan Bak is 10. It is the 1940s and she and her family are enduring the occupation of their homeland in northern Korea. When the country is divided at the end of the war, the family emigrates to the south, hoping for a better life. *Echoes of the White Giraffe* describes Sookan's life in Pusan and her growing friendship with Junho, a boy she knows from the church choir. In the final book, Sookan is in college in the United States, where she is challenged by a new language, a different culture, and the death of her mother.

1. Year of Impossible Goodbyes ◆ 1991
2. Echoes of the White Giraffe ◆ 1993
3. Gathering of Pearls ◆ 1994

SOPHIE

King-Smith, Dick

CANDLEWICK ◆ **GRADES 3–5** ◆ **A/R**

FAMILY LIFE | **HUMOR**

Sophie is a persistent little girl who is determined that one day she will be a farmer. Through all six books in this series, she saves her farm money and practices on everything from wood lice to cats. Her great-aunt Alice lives in Scotland and encourages Sophie's independence and zeal to become a farmer. Her twin brothers, Matthew and Mark, are fond of twirling a pointed finger at their heads to indicate what they think of Sophie, but readers will be charmed by her droll approach to life and friendships. Her growth is chronicled throughout the series, and eventually she and her family inherit Aunt Alice's farm and move to Scotland, where Sophie is given a pony called Lucky.

1. Sophie's Snail ◆ 1989
2. Sophie's Tom ◆ 1992
3. Sophie Hits Six ◆ 1993
4. Sophie in the Saddle ◆ 1994
5. Sophie Is Seven ◆ 1995
6. Sophie's Lucky ◆ 1996

SOUP

Peck, Robert Newton

KNOPF ◆ GRADES 3–5 ◆ A/R

ADVENTURE | HUMOR

Soup and Rob are always getting into mischievous trouble that usually ends up involving their entire community. Young readers will enjoy the hilarious escapades of these two pals living in rural Vermont where the author (*A Day No Pigs Would Die*) grew up. A couple of ABC Afterschool Specials were based on two of the series titles: *Soup and Me* and *Soup for President*. The Little Soup series features the boys when they are younger.

1. Soup ◆ 1974
2. Soup and Mc ◆ 1975
3. Soup for President ◆ 1978
4. Soup's Drum ◆ 1980
5. Soup on Wheels ◆ 1981
6. Soup in the Saddle ◆ 1983
7. Soup's Goat ◆ 1984
8. Soup on Ice ◆ 1985
9. Soup on Fire ◆ 1987
10. Soup's Uncle ◆ 1988
11. Soup's Hoop ◆ 1989
12. Soup in Love ◆ 1992
13. Soup Ahoy ◆ 1994
14. Soup 1776 ◆ 1995

SOUP: LITTLE SOUP

Peck, Robert Newton

DELL ◆ GRADES 2–3

HUMOR

In this series, Soup is much younger, but his antics with his friend Rob are just the same. The two manage to create problems at a Thanksgiving play and on a hayride. At Easter, they dye eggs—and a whole lot more. This is an easier series that sets the stage for the friendship between Soup and Rob that is more fully developed in the Soup series.

1. Little Soup's Hayride ◆ 1991
2. Little Soup's Birthday ◆ 1991
3. Little Soup's Turkey ◆ 1992
4. Little Soup's Bunny ◆ 1993

SPACE ABOVE AND BEYOND

Various authors

HARPERCOLLINS ◆ GRADES 5–8

SCIENCE FICTION

In 2063, an Earth space station has been destroyed by aliens and now Earth is in danger. Lieutenants Vansen, West, and Hawke are thrown together to accomplish a dangerous mission and face the Artificial Intelligence (AI) creatures. There are encounters on Mars, a mutiny in space, and an electromagnetic lightning storm. Fans of Star Trek and Deep Space Nine will enjoy these books.

1. The Aliens Approach (Royce, Easton) ◆ 1996
2. Dark Side of the Sun (Anastasio, Dina) ◆ 1996
3. Mutiny (Royce, Easton) ◆ 1996
4. The Enemy (Anastasio, Dina) ◆ 1996
5. Demolition Winter (Telep, Peter) ◆ 1997

SPACE BRAT

Coville, Bruce

POCKET BOOKS ◆ GRADES 3–5 ◆ A/R

HUMOR | SCIENCE FICTION

Blork the Space Brat throws the biggest tantrums on the planet Splat. Things began to go wrong for him when a piece of shell got stuck on his ear when he hatched and he was labeled a brat. When the Big Pest Squad starts to take away Lunk, his poodnoobie, he grabs one of their spaceships and goes to the land of the Things. The Things are huge, harmless creatures who are slaves to the evil tyrant Squat. Blork outwits Squat and sets the Things free, learning in the process how not to be a brat. He gains an evil twin and is kidnapped by Squat in the sequels, which are filled with the same zany humor.

1. Space Brat ◆ 1992
2. Blork's Evil Twin ◆ 1993
3. The Wrath of Squat ◆ 1994
4. The Planet of the Dips ◆ 1995
5. The Saber-Toothed Poodnoobie ◆ 1997

SPACE DOG

Standiford, Natalie

RANDOM HOUSE ◆ GRADES 1–3 ◆ A/R

HUMOR | SCIENCE FICTION

Space Dog is from the planet Queekrg. His spaceship crashes in Roy's backyard, which works out fine because Roy has been wanting a dog to protect him from a bully. Space Dog understands the problem because he volunteered to come to Earth to get away from a bully himself. He looks exactly like an Earth dog; and when he is with people he acts like one so that he can keep his mission secret. Only when he and Ray are alone does he read, write, talk, and walk on two legs. While he is stuck on Earth, he does a study of humans. Alice, Roy's friend, has a poodle named Blanche who likes Space Dog, but he thinks she is dumb, possibly because she's not allowed to go to school.

1. Space Dog and Roy ◆ 1990
2. Space Dog and the Pet Show ◆ 1990
3. Space Dog in Trouble ◆ 1991
4. Space Dog, the Hero ◆ 1991

SPACE SHIP UNDER THE APPLE TREE

Slobodkin, Louis

MACMILLAN ◆ GRADES 3–5

SCIENCE FICTION

Eddie Blow visits his grandmother on her farm during the summer months. One year, he meets a little man who is visiting from the planet Martinea. Marty, as he comes to be called, is short enough for Eddie's grandmother to think he is another boy, but he has powers of speed and levitation that depend on his planet's special tools. His mission is scientific: to learn about the United States. He and Eddie have many old-fashioned adventures together, with Eddie constantly having to bail Marty out of tight spots. In subsequent books, the two meet again, once in Central Park near Eddie's home. Their adventures take them to other planets as well, sometimes with Willie, a friend of Eddie's.

1. The Space Ship Under the Apple Tree ◆ 1952
2. The Space Ship Returns to the Apple Tree ◆ 1958
3. The Three-Seated Space Ship ◆ 1962
4. Round Trip Space Ship ◆ 1968
5. The Space Ship in the Park ◆ 1972

SPEED RACER

Wheeler, Chase

PENGUIN ◆ GRADES 4–8

ADVENTURE

Speed Racer is a talented young racing driver, son of an automobile engineer who has created a Mach 5 car with James Bond-style features. Speed hopes to become an international champion and often gets into dangerous situations. He remains close to his family and has a steady girlfriend, Trixie. *Go, Speed Racer, Go* (2008) is for younger readers and focuses on Speed's youth.

1. The Great Plan ◆ 2008
2. Challenge of the Masked Racer ◆ 2008
3. The Secret Engine ◆ 2008
4. Race Against the Mammoth Car ◆ 2008
5. The Most Dangerous Race ◆ 2008
6. Race for Revenge ◆ 2008

SPELL CASTERS

Warriner, Holly

ALADDIN ◆ GRADES 5–8 ◆ A/R

FANTASY

Lucinda is a witch who is conflicted about her powers. Her evil grandmother and her sinister cousin Rafe push her to fulfill her destiny. Lucinda's friendship with Sally and her everyday school activities provide a backdrop for spells, seances, and witchcraft.

1. Witch at the Door ◆ 1998
2. Full Moon Magic ◆ 1998
3. Witches' Brew ◆ 1998
4. Julian's Jinx ◆ 1998
5. Witches on Ice ◆ 1999
6. Phoebe's Fortune ◆ 1999

SPENCER'S ADVENTURES

Hogg, Gary

SCHOLASTIC ◆ GRADES 1–3

HUMOR

Wherever Spencer is, there is trouble, usually involving zany schemes and messy situations. Like Dennis the Menace, Spencer wreaks havoc throughout his neighborhood. Readers who laugh at humor involving garbage, toilet paper, and slime will find this great fun.

1. Stop That Eyeball! ◆ 1997
2. Garbage Snooper Surprise ◆ 1997
3. Hair in the Air ◆ 1997
4. The Great Toilet Paper Caper ◆ 1997

5. Don't Bake That Snake ◆ 1997
6. Let Go of That Toe! ◆ 1998

SPIDER

Kraus, Robert

SCHOLASTIC ◆ GRADES K–2

ANIMAL FANTASY

Lovable Spider and his good friends Fly and Ladybug have adventures as they save the day. The holiday connection appeals to many children.

1. The Trouble with Spider ◆ 1962
2. How Spider Saved Christmas ◆ 1970
3. How Spider Saved Halloween ◆ 1973
4. How Spider Saved Turkey ◆ 1981
5. How Spider Saved Valentine's Day ◆ 1985
6. Spider's First Day at School ◆ 1987
7. How Spider Saved Easter ◆ 1988
8. How Spider Saved the Baseball Game ◆ 1989
9. How Spider Saved Santa Bug ◆ 1989
10. Spider's Baby-Sitting Job ◆ 1990
11. How Spider Saved Thanksgiving ◆ 1991
12. How Spider Saved the Flea Circus ◆ 1991
13. How Spider Stopped the Litterbugs ◆ 1991
14. Dance, Spider, Dance! ◆ 1993

SPIDER RIDERS

Anasti, Tedd, and Patsy Cameron-Anasti

NEWMARKET PRESS ◆ GRADES 4–6 ◆ A/R

FANTASY

Hunter Steele, 13, falls down a hole to Arachnia, a world where humans and spiders live in peace. Arachnia is being attacked by mutant insects and Hunter joins the elite warriors to save Arachnia and, hopefully, return home. Before he can join the warriors, Hunter must overcome his arachnaphobia and learn to ride a giant battle spider called Shadow. Their mission is to recover the shards of a magical stone Oracle.

1. Shards of the Oracle ◆ 2004
2. Quest of the Earthen ◆ 2005
3. Reign of the Soul Eater ◆ 2006

SPIDERWICK: BEYOND THE SPIDERWICK CHRONICLES

DiTerlizzi, Tony, and Holly Black

SIMON & SCHUSTER ◆ **GRADES 4–6** ◆ **A/R**

FANTASY

In the first book of this spin-off series, Nick Vargas, 11, has moved to Florida with his newly remarried father. His stepsister, Laurie, is devoted to *Arthur Spiderwick's Field Guide to the Fantastical World* and is constantly on the lookout for faeries. Nick does not believe in faeries until he injures a nixie.

1. The Nixie's Song ◆ 2007
2. A Giant Problem ◆ 2008

THE SPIDERWICK CHRONICLES

DiTerlizzi, Tony, and Holly Black

SIMON & SCHUSTER ◆ **GRADES 4–6** ◆ **A/R**

FANTASY

Mallory Grace, 13, and her 9-year-old twin brothers Jared and Simon move into an old, rundown house. There they discover a guide to the faerie realm. They begin a series of adventures with boggarts, trolls, hobgoblins, and more. *Arthur Spiderwick's Field Guide to the Fantastical World Around You* (2006) is a large-format, illustrated guide to the inhabitants of the "Invisible World" featured in the series.

1. The Field Guide ◆ 2003
2. The Seeing Stone ◆ 2003
3. Lucinda's Secret ◆ 2003
4. The Ironwood Tree ◆ 2004
5. The Wrath of Mulgarath ◆ 2004

SPIRIT OF THE CIMARRON

Duey, Kathleen

DUTTON ◆ **GRADES 4–6** ◆ **A/R**

REAL LIFE

The DreamWorks film *Spirit, Stallion of the Cimarron* is the springboard for these books. Spirit is a wild horse that is captured but eventually returns to being free. The other stories describe adventures of other horses including Bonita and her foal Esperanza.

1. Bonita ◆ 2002

2. Sierra ◆ 2002
3. Esperanza ◆ 2002
4. Spirit ◆ 2002

SPIRIT OF THE GAME

Hafer, Todd

ZONDERKIDZ ◆ GRADES 5–8 ◆ A/R

VALUES | REAL LIFE | RECREATION

In each book of this series Cody Martin, 13, is involved in a sport and in different circumstances that test his faith and commitment to God. In *Goal-Line Stand,* Cody competes with his best friend for a position on the football team. In *Ultimate Challenge,* Cody, now 14, is adjusting to a new stepmother who is expecting a baby. Cody feels unsettled at home and then his best friend tells him he is moving. Cody prepares for the Ultimate Athlete competition while he copes with the changes in his life.

1. Goal-Line Stand ◆ 2004
2. Full-Court Press ◆ 2004
3. Second Wind ◆ 2004
4. Stealing Home ◆ 2004
5. Cody's Varsity Rush ◆ 2005
6. Three-Point Play ◆ 2005
7. Split Decision ◆ 2005
8. Ultimate Challenge ◆ 2005

SPONGEBOB SQUAREPANTS CHAPTER BOOKS

Various authors

SIMON & SCHUSTER ◆ GRADES 2–5 ◆ A/R

FANTASY

Join SpongeBob and the gang—Sandy Cheeks, Patrick Star, Squidward, and more—in these entertaining stories. In one book, a producer, Barry Cuda, promises to make SpongeBob a star. This chapter book series is just right for middle-elementary readers.

1. Tea at the Treedome (Collins, Terry) ◆ 2000
2. Naughty Nautical Neighbors (Auerbach, Annie) ◆ 2000
3. Hall Monitor (Auerbach, Annie) ◆ 2000
4. The World's Greatest Valentine (Collins, Terry) ◆ 2000
5. SpongeBob Superstar (Auerbach, Annie) ◆ 2001
6. Sandy's Rocket (Banks, Steven) ◆ 2001
7. SpongeBob NaturePants (Collins, Terry) ◆ 2001
8. SpongeBob Airpants: The Lost Episode (Richards, Kitty) ◆ 2003

9. New Student Starfish (Miglis, Jenny) ◆ 2003
10. Zoo Day Disaster (Lewman, David) ◆ 2005
11. Mother Knows Best (Willson, Sarah) ◆ 2006
12. For the Love of Bubbles (Banks, Steven) ◆ 2006
13. Where's Gary? (Lewman, David, and Barry Goldberg) ◆ 2007
14. Pirates of Bikini Bottom (Lewman, David) ◆ 2007

SPONGEBOB SQUAREPANTS (TOKYOPOP)

Hillenburg, Stephen

TOKYOPOP ◆ GRADES 3–5 ◆ A/R

FANTASY

In Bikini Bottom there lives a sea sponge named SpongeBob SquarePants. His positive attitude helps him in his job as a cook at the Krusty Krab. Still, SpongeBob seems to encounter problems frequently. But with his friends and his good nature, he finds a way to make things right. This cine-manga captures the antics of SpongeBob and his pals.

1. Krusty Krab Adventures ◆ 2003
2. Friends Forever ◆ 2003
3. Tales from Bikini Bottom ◆ 2004
4. Crime and Funishment ◆ 2004
5. Another Day, Another Sand Dollar ◆ 2004
6. Tales from Bikini Bottom ◆ 2004
7. Gone Jellyfishin' ◆ 2005
8. SpongeBob Saves the Day ◆ 2005
9. Gone Nutty ◆ 2005
10. Meow . . . Like a Snail?! ◆ 2005
11. The SpongeBob SquarePants Movie ◆ 2005
12. Who's Hungry? ◆ 2006
13. Mistaken Identity ◆ 2007

SPOOKSVILLE

Pike, Christopher

POCKET BOOKS ◆ GRADES 5–8 ◆ A/R

HORROR

Springville seems like an ordinary town, but a closer look reveals strange things going on. Cindy Mackey finds this out when her brother Neil is kidnapped by a ghost. Adam Freeman knows things are different. One of his best friends is Watch, a creature who has returned from the dead. Cindy, Adam, Watch, and their friends Sally Wilcox and Bryce Poole confront howling ghosts, aliens, witches, wicked cats, killer crabs, vampires, and other demons as they try to survive in a very strange town. This series will be a hit with readers who enjoy Goosebumps, Fear Street, and Buffy the Vampire Slayer.

1. The Secret Path ◆ 1995
2. The Howling Ghost ◆ 1995
3. The Haunted Cave ◆ 1995
4. Aliens in the Sky ◆ 1996
5. The Cold People ◆ 1996
6. The Witch's Revenge ◆ 1996
7. The Dark Corner ◆ 1996
8. The Little People ◆ 1996
9. The Wishing Stone ◆ 1996
10. The Wicked Cat ◆ 1996
11. The Deadly Past ◆ 1996
12. The Hidden Beast ◆ 1996
13. The Creature in the Teacher ◆ 1996
14. The Evil House ◆ 1997
15. Invasion of the No-Ones ◆ 1997
16. Time Terror ◆ 1997
17. The Thing in the Closet ◆ 1997
18. Attack of the Killer Crabs ◆ 1997
19. Night of the Vampire ◆ 1997
20. The Dangerous Quest ◆ 1998
21. The Living Dead ◆ 1998
22. The Creepy Creature ◆ 1998
23. Phone Fear ◆ 1998
24. The Witch's Gift ◆ 1999

SPOOKY THE CAT

Carlson, Natalie Savage

LOTHROP, LEE & SHEPHERD ◆ GRADES K–2

ANIMAL FANTASY

Spooky is a big black cat with big green eyes who used to belong to a witch down the road and now belongs to the Bascomb family. But the witch is never out of his life. In the first book, Spooky rescues Snowball, a ghost cat who lives with the witch but who comes to live with the Bascombs when she becomes real. In each of the following books, Spooky confronts and outwits the witch or her cohorts with the Bascombs none the wiser.

1. Spooky Night ◆ 1982
2. Spooky and the Ghost Cat ◆ 1985
3. Spooky and the Wizard's Bats ◆ 1986
4. Spooky and the Bad Luck Raven ◆ 1988
5. Spooky and the Witch's Goat ◆ 1989

SPOT

Hill, Eric

PUTNAM ◆ GRADES K–1

ANIMAL FANTASY

A little yellow dog with brown spots lives with his loving mother and father in this series for young readers. In *Where's Spot* his mother looks everywhere for him, but only finds various jungle animals until she looks in a little basket. In another book, Spot gets a little sister, and his friends come over to see her. The books were recently reissued and there are several different formats, including lift-the-flap and board books. There is also a popular video series.

1. Where's Spot? ◆ 1980
2. Spot's First Walk ◆ 1981
3. Spot's Birthday Party ◆ 1982
4. Spot's Busy Year ◆ 1983
5. Spot's First Christmas ◆ 1983
6. Spot Learns to Count ◆ 1983
7. Spot Tells the Time ◆ 1983
8. Spot's Alphabet ◆ 1983
9. Sweet Dreams, Spot ◆ 1984
10. Spot's Friends ◆ 1984
11. Spot's Toys ◆ 1984
12. Here's Spot ◆ 1984
13. Spot Goes Splash! ◆ 1984
14. Spot Goes to School ◆ 1984
15. Spot on the Farm ◆ 1985
16. Spot Goes to the Beach ◆ 1985
17. Spot at Play ◆ 1985
18. Spot at the Fair ◆ 1985
19. Spot Goes to the Circus ◆ 1986
20. Spot's First Words ◆ 1986
21. Spot's Doghouse ◆ 1986
22. Spot Looks at Colors ◆ 1986
23. Spot Looks at Shapes ◆ 1986
24. Spot Goes to the Farm ◆ 1987
25. Spot's First Picnic ◆ 1987
26. Spot Visits the Hospital ◆ 1987
27. Spot's Big Book of Words ◆ 1988
28. Spot's First Easter ◆ 1988
29. Spot Counts from One to Ten ◆ 1989
30. Spot Looks at Opposites ◆ 1989
31. Spot Looks at the Weather ◆ 1989
32. Spot's Baby Sister ◆ 1989
33. Spot Sleeps Over ◆ 1990
34. Spot Goes to the Park ◆ 1991
35. Spot in the Garden ◆ 1991

36. Spot's Toy Box ◆ 1991
37. Spot at Home ◆ 1991
38. Spot's Walk in the Woods ◆ 1992
39. Spot Goes to a Party ◆ 1993
40. Spot's Big Book of Colors, Shapes, and Numbers ◆ 1994
41. Spot Bakes a Cake ◆ 1994
42. Spot's Magical Christmas ◆ 1995
43. Spot Visits His Grandparents ◆ 1996
44. Spot and Friends Dress Up ◆ 1996
45. Spot and Friends Play ◆ 1996
46. Spot's Touch and Feel Day ◆ 1997
47. Spot's Favorite Words ◆ 1997
48. Spot's Favorite Numbers ◆ 1997
49. Spot's Favorite Colors ◆ 1997
50. Spot's Favorite Baby Animals ◆ 1997
51. Spot Joins the Parade ◆ 1998

SPY FORCE

Abela, Deborah
SIMON & SCHUSTER ◆ GRADES 4–7 ◆ A/R
ADVENTURE

Maxine Remy, 11, is bored and hostile, resenting everything about her life. While visiting her aunt and uncle in Pennsylvania, she discovers her uncle's Matter Transporter. Max convinces a friend, Linden, to join her in the transporter and they travel to London where they are kidnapped by a villain who wants the transporter. After they escape, they find out about a secret agency of spies. In the second book, Max and Linden are asked to join Spy Force. They join forces with another young spy, Ella. The trio goes undercover in a candy factory. Their mission—to stop the evil Mr. Blue from using food to control the minds of children.

1. Mission: in Search of the Time and Space Machine ◆ 2005
2. Mission: Spy Force Revealed ◆ 2005
3. Mission: The Nightmare Vortex ◆ 2005
4. Mission: Hollywood ◆ 2006

SPY GEAR

Barba, Rick
ALADDIN ◆ GRADES 4–6 ◆ A/R
ADVENTURE

In Stoneship Woods, Jake and Lucas Bixby and their friends Cyril and Lexi find an abandoned warehouse of spy equipment and high-tech gadgets. As they examine the cache, they attract the attention of enemy operatives. As the series progresses, the kids become part of Team Spy Gear and solve mysteries featuring hackers, mind-controlling computer programs, and dangerous links. This series is inspired by Wild Planet Toys Spy Gear. Fans of the Bionicle Adventures (another toy-related series) will enjoy these books.

1. The Secret of Stoneship Woods ◆ 2006
2. The Massively Multiplayer Mystery ◆ 2006
3. The Quantum Quandry ◆ 2006
4. The Doomsday Dust ◆ 2006
5. The Shrieking Shadow ◆ 2007
6. The Omega Operative ◆ 2007

SPY KIDS ADVENTURES

Lenhard, Elizabeth
MIRAMAX ◆ GRADES 4–6 ◆ A/R

FANTASY

After Carmen and her brother Juni Cortez learn that their parents are spies, they become part of the OSS spy organization. It seems that there are evil plots everywhere. The kids travel to Scotland and Spain; they rescue a famous pop star; they even stop a villain's plot to take over a mall! This series connects with the Spy Kids movies.

1. One Agent Too Many ◆ 2002
2. A New Kind of Super Spy ◆ 2003
3. Mucho Madness ◆ 2003
4. OSS Wilderness ◆ 2003
5. Mall of the Universe ◆ 2003
6. Spy TV ◆ 2003
7. Superstar Spies ◆ 2003
8. Freeze Frame ◆ 2004
9. Spring Fever ◆ 2004
10. Off Sides ◆ 2004

SPY MICE

Frederick, Heather Vogel
SIMON & SCHUSTER ◆ GRADES 4–6 ◆ A/R

FANTASY

Oz Levinson, grade five, is dealing with his family's move from Seattle to Washington, D.C. He has not made any friends and is being bothered by bullies. At the International Spy Museum, where his father works in the cafe, Oz meets Morning Glory Goldenleaf, a mouse working for the Spy Mouse Agency to stop the trouble-making rats. Details about the society of the mice and rats add to the fast-paced adventure. In the second book, the scene shifts to Manhattan; the third book takes place in London.

1. The Black Paw ◆ 2005
2. For Your Paws Only ◆ 2005
3. Goldwhiskers ◆ 2007

SPY X

Lerangis, Peter

SCHOLASTIC ◆ GRADES 4–6 ◆ A/R

REAL LIFE

On their 11th birthday, Andrew and Evie's mother disappeared. One year later, they receive a package from Spy X. It may help them find their mother. Andrew and Evie discover that a sinister company may be behind the mystery.

1. The Code ◆ 2004
2. Hide and Seek ◆ 2004
3. Proof Positive ◆ 2005
4. Tunnel Vision ◆ 2005

STANLEY

Brown, Jeff

HARPERCOLLINS ◆ GRADES K–3 ◆ A/R

FANTASY | HUMOR

Readers will giggle at the silly adventures that Stanley has as a result of all the strange things that happen to him. On the night after a bad storm, his family discovers he is still there but he has become invisible. Another time, the bulletin board falls on him and leaves him flat until his brother figures out how to blow him back up.

1. Flat Stanley ◆ 1964
2. Invisible Stanley ◆ 1996
3. Stanley and the Magic Lamp ◆ 1996
4. Stanley, Flat Again ◆ 2003
5. Stanley in Space ◆ 2003
6. Stanley's Christmas Adventure ◆ 2003

STAR SISTERZ

Various authors

WIZARDS OF THE COAST ◆ GRADES 4–7

REAL LIFE

For tween girls, this is a lighthearted series about a group of friends who receive mysterious messages that influence their actions. The series is connected to a game in which girls collect charms.

1. Nova Rocks! (Emesse, Tea) ◆ 2005
2. Carmen Dives In (Johns, Linda) ◆ 2005
3. Bright Lights for Bella (Perez, Lana) ◆ 2005
4. Rani and the Fashion Divas (Banerjee, Anjali) ◆ 2005
5. Nova and the Charmed Three (Emesse, Tea) ◆ 2006
6. Yumi Talks the Talk (Emesse, Tea) ◆ 2006
7. Carmen's Crystal Ball (Johns, Linda) ◆ 2006
8. Bella Goes Hollywood (Perez, Lana) ◆ 2006
9. Maya Made Over (Green, Debra) ◆ 2007
10. Rani and the Wedding Ghost (Banerjee, Anjali) ◆ 2008

STAR TREK: DEEP SPACE NINE

Various authors

POCKET BOOKS ◆ GRADES 4–8 ◆ A/R

ADVENTURE | SCIENCE FICTION

Fans of the television series *Deep Space Nine* will enjoy reading adventures featuring their favorite characters. Young Jake Sisko and his Ferengi friend Nog are involved in time travel, attending Starfleet Academy's summer space camp, and even a field trip through the Worm Hole. They meet unusual creatures and are often in situations that threaten the future of the world. Jake's father, Commander Benjamin Sisko, supervises the Deep Space Nine space station with the assistance of security officer Odo and first officer Major Kira Nerys. Other characters from the show, including Miles and Keiko O'Brien and the Ferengi businessman Quark, appear in the books. There is lots of action and imaginative situations that should attract science fiction fans.

1. The Star Ghost (Strickland, Brad) ◆ 1994
2. Stowaways (Strickland, Brad) ◆ 1994
3. Prisoners of Peace (Peel, John) ◆ 1994
4. The Pet (Gilden, Mel, and Ted Pedersen) ◆ 1994
5. Arcade (Gallagher, Diana G.) ◆ 1995
6. Field Trip (Peel, John) ◆ 1995
7. Gypsy World (Pedersen, Ted, and John Peel) ◆ 1996
8. Highest Score (Antilles, Kem) ◆ 1996
9. Cardassian Imps (Gilden, Mel) ◆ 1997

10. Space Camp (Pedersen, Ted, and John Peel) ◆ 1997
11. Day of Honor: Honor Bound (Gallagher, Diana G.) ◆ 1997
12. Trapped in Time (Pedersen, Ted) ◆ 1998

STAR TREK: ENTERPRISE

Various authors

POCKET BOOKS ◆ GRADES 5–10

ADVENTURE | SCIENCE FICTION

The television series *Star Trek: Enterprise* ran from 2001 to 2005. The adventures on this show preceded those of the original *Star Trek.* Jonathan Archer commands the *Enterprise,* Earth's first Warp 5 starship. On board is an intergalactic crew including T'Pol, a Vulcan, and Phlox, a Denobulan. The books issued through 2004 paralleled episodes of the television program. A relaunch of new titles began in 2006.

1. By the Book (Smith, Dean Wesley, and Kristine Kathryn Rusch) ◆ 2002
2. What Price Honor (Stern, Dave) ◆ 2002
3. Surak's Soul (Dillard, J. M.) ◆ 2003
4. The Expanse (Dillard, J. M., Rick Berman, and Brannon Braga) ◆ 2003
5. Daedalus: Part 1 of 2 (Stern, Dave) ◆ 2003
6. Daedalus's Children: Part 2 of 2 (Stern, Dave) ◆ 2004
7. Shockwave (Ruditis, Paul) ◆ 2004
8. Rosetta (Stern, Dave) ◆ 2006
9. Last Full Measure (Martin, Michael A., and Andy Mangels) ◆ 2006
10. The Good That Men Do (Martin, Michael A., and Andy Mangels) ◆ 2007
11. Broken Bow (Carey, Diane) ◆ 2007
12. Kobayashi Maru (Martin, Michael A., and Andy Mangels) ◆ 2008

STAR TREK: I. K. S. GORKON

DeCandido, Keith R. A.

POCKET BOOKS ◆ GRADES 5–10

ADVENTURE | SCIENCE FICTION

The books in this series follow the adventures of a Klingon Defense Force vessel *I. K. S. Gorkon.* Commanded by Captain Klag, its mission is to search for new civilizations and conquer them. Captain Klag does act with humanity and compassion and is, at times, operating outside the expectations of the Klingon Empire.

1. A Good Day to Die ◆ 2003

2. Honor Bound ◆ 2003
3. Enemy Territory ◆ 2005

STAR TREK: S. C. E.

Various authors

SIMON & SCHUSTER ◆ GRADES 5–10

ADVENTURE | SCIENCE FICTION

The original books about the Starfleet Corp of Engineers (S. C. E.) were issued between 2000 and 2006. The books in this new series are omnibus editions with each title presenting at least four books from the originals. For example, in *Have Tech Will Travel* there are four books from 2002: *The Belly of the Beast, Fatal Error, Hard Crash,* and *Interphase, Part 1*— each by a different author. The books describe the adventures of Captain David Gold, first officer Commander Sonya Gomez, and the crew of the *U.S.S. da Vinci* as they deal with alien attacks, ships trapped in interphase, subspace accelerators, and more. At Starfleet Headquarters they are supported by the S. C. E. under the direction of Captain Montgomery Scott.

1. Have Tech, Will Travel (DeCandido, Keith R. A., et al.) ◆ 2002
2. Miracle Workers (DeCandido, Keith R. A., et al.) ◆ 2002
3. Some Assembly Required (Brodeur, Gret, et al.) ◆ 2003
4. No Surrender (Collins, Mike, et al.) ◆ 2004
5. Foundations (Ward, Dayton, and Kevin Dilmore) ◆ 2005
6. Wildfire (DeCandido, Keith R. A., et al.) ◆ 2005
7. Breakdowns (DeCandido, Keith R. A., et al.) ◆ 2006
8. Aftermath (Bennett, Christopher L., et al.) ◆ 2006
9. Grand Designs (Ward, Dayton, et al.) ◆ 2007
10. Creative Couplings (Mack, David) ◆ 2007

STAR TREK: STARFLEET ACADEMY

Various authors

POCKET BOOKS ◆ GRADES 4–8 ◆ A/R

ADVENTURE | SCIENCE FICTION

Many fans of science fiction series want to know everything about the characters. These fans are often so enthralled with the series that publishers and media producers provide numerous spin-offs and related activities (computer games, Web sites, conventions, and so forth). *Star Trek* fans are among the most loyal and intense. The ongoing popularity of the television series, along with every related item, is a testament to that. This series examines the early lives and training of key characters: James T. Kirk, Spock, and Leonard McCoy. Their adventures at the Starfleet Academy include escaping from space pirates and saving earthquake victims on the planet Playamar. Fans will especially enjoy *Crisis on Vulcan,* in which Spock meets young Christopher Pike (who was the captain in the *Star Trek* pilot program).

1. Crisis on Vulcan (Strickland, Brad, and Barbara Strickland) ◆ 1996
2. Aftershock (Vornholt, John) ◆ 1996
3. Cadet Kirk (Carey, Diane L.) ◆ 1996

STAR TREK: THE NEXT GENERATION: STARFLEET ACADEMY

Various authors

POCKET BOOKS ◆ GRADES 4–8 ◆ A/R

ADVENTURE | SCIENCE FICTION

Focusing on the early years of the crew of the *U.S.S. Enterprise,* this series features the Starfleet Academy training experiences of familiar characters including Picard, Worf, Geordi, and Data. In *Deceptions,* Data participates in a research investigation of ancient ruins on the planet Arunu. When the communications system is sabotaged, Data must use his powers as an android to rescue his friends. In *Survival,* Worf and several Starfleet cadets work with a group of Klingon cadets to escape from the evil of an alien force. This series will interest fans of the television programs and movies as well as readers who like fast-paced adventures.

1. Worf's First Adventure (David, Peter) ◆ 1993
2. Line of Fire (David, Peter) ◆ 1993
3. Survival (David, Peter) ◆ 1993
4. Capture the Flag (Vornholt, John) ◆ 1994
5. Atlantis Station (Mitchell, V. E.) ◆ 1994
6. Mystery of the Missing Crew (Friedman, Michael J.) ◆ 1995
7. Secret of the Lizard People (Friedman, Michael J.) ◆ 1995
8. Starfall (Strickland, Brad, and Barbara Strickland) ◆ 1995
9. Nova Command (Strickland, Brad, and Barbara Strickland) ◆ 1995
10. Loyalties (Barnes-Svarney, Patricia) ◆ 1996
11. Crossfire (Vornholt, John) ◆ 1996
12. Breakaway (Weiss, Bobbi J. G., and David Cody Weiss) ◆ 1997
13. The Haunted Starship (Ferguson, Brad, and Kathi Ferguson) ◆ 1997
14. Deceptions (Weiss, Bobbi J. G., and David Cody Weiss) ◆ 1998

STAR TREK: VOYAGER: STARFLEET ACADEMY

Various authors

POCKET BOOKS ◆ GRADES 4–8 ◆ A/R

ADVENTURE | SCIENCE FICTION

The *Voyager* series (on television and in these books) revolves around Kathryn Janeway, daughter of Vice Admiral Edward Janeway. At the Starfleet Academy, Kathryn wants to step out from the shadow of her successful father and establish her own credentials. These adventures put her in situations involving alien animals and an outer-space quarantine that could prove deadly. There is lots of action in these books, which should be appealing to fans of the show and of science fiction. The creatures and outer-space setting may attract reluctant readers.

1. Lifeline (Weiss, Bobbi J. G., and David Cody Weiss) ◆ 1997
2. The Chance Factor (Gallagher, Diana G., and Martin R. Burke) ◆ 1997
3. Quarantine (Barnes-Svarney, Patricia) ◆ 1997

STAR WARS: A NEW HOPE—MANGA

Lucas, George

DARK HORSE ◆ GRADES 5–10

SCIENCE FICTION

The drawings for this series are by Hisao Tamaki. The events parallel Episode IV, which was the original *Star Wars* movie.

1. Manga #1 ◆ 1998
2. Manga #2 ◆ 1998
3. Manga #3 ◆ 1998
4. Manga #4 ◆ 1998

STAR WARS: BOBA FETT

Various authors

SCHOLASTIC ◆ GRADES 5–9 ◆ A/R

SCIENCE FICTION

Boba Fett learned to be a bounty hunter by accompanying his father Jango Fett on his bounty hunting missions. After Jango is killed, Boba is on his own. He is pursued by his father's enemies—especially Count Dooku, who cheated his father. Boba knows Count Dooku's secret—that he built the clone army. Working for Jabba the Hutt, Boba travels the galaxy as a young bounty hunter.

1. The Fight to Survive (Bisson, Terry) ◆ 2002
2. Crossfire (Bisson, Terry) ◆ 2002
3. Maze of Deception (Hand, Elizabeth) ◆ 2003
4. Hunted (Hand, Elizabeth) ◆ 2003
5. A New Threat (Hand, Elizabeth) ◆ 2004
6. Pursuit (Hand, Elizabeth) ◆ 2004

STAR WARS: EPISODE I THE PHANTOM MENACE—MANGA

Lucas, George

DARK HORSE ◆ GRADES 5–10

SCIENCE FICTION

The drawings for this series are by Kia Asamiya. The story parallels the *Phantom Menace* film.

1. Manga #1 ◆ 1999
2. Manga #2 ◆ 2000

STAR WARS: JEDI QUEST

Watson, Jude

SCHOLASTIC ◆ GRADES 5–9 ◆ A/R

SCIENCE FICTION

Obi-Wan Kenobi feels the power in young Anakin Skywalker. He also senses Anakin's restlessness. As Obi-Wan trains Anakin in the ways of the Jedi, the two travel the galaxy and confront evil—often trying to outwit the powerful Granta Omega. The events in this series take place between Episode I and Episode II.

1. The Way of the Apprentice ◆ 2002
2. The Trail of the Jedi ◆ 2002
3. The Dangerous Games ◆ 2002
4. The Master of Disguise ◆ 2002
5. The School of Fear ◆ 2003
6. The Shadow Trap ◆ 2003
7. The Moment of Truth ◆ 2003
8. The Changing of the Guard ◆ 2004
9. The False Peace ◆ 2004
10. The Final Showdown ◆ 2004

STAR WARS: THE EMPIRE STRIKES BACK—MANGA

Lucas, George

DARK HORSE ◆ GRADES 5–10

SCIENCE FICTION

The drawings for this series are by Toshiki Kudo. The action parallels the second *Star Wars* movie.

1. Manga #1 ◆ 1999
2. Manga #2 ◆ 1999
3. Manga #3 ◆ 1999
4. Manga #4 ◆ 1999

STAR WARS: THE LAST OF THE JEDI

Watson, Jude

SCHOLASTIC ◆ GRADES 5–9 ◆ A/R

SCIENCE FICTION

After the return of the Empire in Episode III, Obi-Wan Kenobi is on Tatooine protecting Luke Skywalker. Luke's father, Anakin, has embraced the dark side and become Darth Vader. With most of the Jedi destroyed, Obi-Wan gets word that his former apprentice, Ferus Olin, is still alive. Obi-Wan leaves Luke to find Ferus, who then begins a mission to find other Jedi and bring them together. To accomplish this, Ferus faces the Emperor and must choose between the Jedi and the dark side.

1. The Desperate Mission ◆ 2005
2. Dark Warning ◆ 2005
3. Underworld ◆ 2005
4. Death on Naboo ◆ 2006
5. Tangled Web ◆ 2006
6. Return of the Dark Side ◆ 2006
7. Secret Weapon ◆ 2007
8. Against the Empire ◆ 2007
9. Master of Deception ◆ 2007
10. Reckoning ◆ 2008

STAR WARS: THE RETURN OF THE JEDI—MANGA

Lucas, George

DARK HORSE ◆ GRADES 5–10

SCIENCE FICTION

The drawings for this series are by Shin-ichi Hiromoto. The action parallels the third *Star Wars* movie, in which Han Solo is encased in carbonite by Jabba the Hutt.

1. Manga #1 ◆ 1999
2. Manga #2 ◆ 1999
3. Manga #3 ◆ 1999
4. Manga #4 ◆ 1999

STAR WARS (DK READERS)

Various authors

DK ◆ GRADES 1–4 ◆ A/R

SCIENCE FICTION

Younger fans of Star Wars will enjoy these readers, which range in difficulty from Level 1—easier content and fewer words per page—to Level

4, which offers more advanced text. There are numerous pictures from the *Star Wars* films in each book, which will make them attractive to reluctant readers.

1. Galactic Crisis (Windham, Ryder) ◆ 2005
2. Star Pilot (Buller, Laura) ◆ 2005
3. Journey Through Space (Windham, Ryder) ◆ 2005
4. What Is a Wookiee? (Buller, Laura) ◆ 2005
5. Beware the Dark Side (Beecroft, Simon) ◆ 2007
6. I Want to Be a Jedi (Windham, Ryder) ◆ 2007
7. A Queen's Diary (Beecroft, Simon) ◆ 2007
8. Ready, Set, Podrace! (Beecroft, Simon) ◆ 2007
9. Epic Battles (Beecroft, Simon) ◆ 2008
10. The Clone Wars: Anakin in Action (Beecroft, Simon) ◆ 2008
11. The Clone Wars: Watch Out for Jabba the Hutt! (Beecroft, Simon) ◆ 2008

STAR WARS EPISODE 1: JOURNALS

Various authors

SCHOLASTIC ◆ GRADES 4–8 ◆ A/R

ADVENTURE | SCIENCE FICTION

First-person journal entries reveal entertaining insight into the youths of favorite characters, with discussion of early challenges and accomplishments.

1. Anakin Skywalker (Strasser, Todd) ◆ 1999
2. Queen Amidala (Watson, Jude) ◆ 1999
3. Darth Maul (Watson, Jude) ◆ 2000

STAR WARS GALAXY OF FEAR

Whitman, John

BANTAM ◆ GRADES 4–8 ◆ A/R

ADVENTURE | SCIENCE FICTION

Tash Arranda, 13, and her brother Zak, 12, travel through space encountering creatures and circumstances that threaten the security of space communities. In *Spore,* the two children and their Uncle Hoole visit a mining community that has released an ancient, evil force. *Clones* features a visit to a remote planet that is inhabited by familiar characters who turn out to be clones. Readers who enjoy *Star Wars* will like these adventures, many of which include appearances by characters from the movies, including Luke Skywalker and Darth Vader. These are exciting adventures with gruesome creatures that link the horror genre to science fiction.

1. Eaten Alive ◆ 1997

2. City of the Dead ◆ 1997
3. Planet Plague ◆ 1997
4. The Nightmare Machine ◆ 1997
5. Ghost of the Jedi ◆ 1997
6. Army of Terror ◆ 1997
7. The Brain Spiders ◆ 1997
8. The Swarm ◆ 1998
9. Spore ◆ 1998
10. The Doomsday Ship ◆ 1998
11. Clones ◆ 1998
12. The Hunger ◆ 1998

STAR WARS JUNIOR JEDI KNIGHTS

Various authors
BERKLEY ◆ GRADES 4–8 ◆ A/R
ADVENTURE | SCIENCE FICTION

Anakin Solo is the youngest son of Leia Organa Solo and Han Solo. In this series, Anakin attends Luke Skywalker's Jedi Academy, where he makes friends with a child of the Sand People named Tahiri. The friends go through a rigorous training program and become involved in many exciting adventures. In one book, they search the abandoned fortress of Darth Vader for Obi-Wan Kenobi's lightsaber. In another, they travel to the distant moon of Yavin 8 and try to break the curse of the Golden Globe. Readers who enjoy science fiction, especially those who like the *Star Wars* films, will be attracted to this series. The familiar characters and exciting situations should appeal to reluctant readers.

1. The Golden Globe (Richardson, Nancy) ◆ 1995
2. Lyric's World (Richardson, Nancy) ◆ 1996
3. Promises (Richardson, Nancy) ◆ 1996
4. Anakin's Quest (Moesta, Rebecca) ◆ 1997
5. Vader's Fortress (Moesta, Rebecca) ◆ 1997
6. Kenobi's Blade (Moesta, Rebecca) ◆ 1997

STAR WARS YOUNG JEDI KNIGHTS

Anderson, Kevin J., and Rebecca Moesta
BERKLEY ◆ GRADES 4–8 ◆ A/R
ADVENTURE | SCIENCE FICTION

Jacen and Jaina are the twin children of Han Solo and Princess Leia. They are the future of the New Republic and are being trained in the powers of the Force. In one book, the twins help Anja Gallandro, who had planned to destroy their family but has become their friend. In another, Lando Calrissian takes the twins and Anja on a vacation that turns deadly. Encounters with the Dark Side and adventures across the galaxy should attract fans of Star Wars and science fiction.

1. Heirs of the Force ◆ 1995
2. Shadow Academy ◆ 1995
3. The Lost Ones ◆ 1995
4. Lightsabers ◆ 1996
5. Darkest Knight ◆ 1996
6. Jedi Under Siege ◆ 1997
7. Shards of Alderaan ◆ 1997
8. Diversity Alliance ◆ 1997
9. Delusions of Grandeur ◆ 1997
10. Jedi Bounty ◆ 1997
11. The Emperor's Plague ◆ 1998
12. Return to Ord Mantell ◆ 1998
13. Trouble on Cloud City ◆ 1998
14. Crisis at Crystal Reef ◆ 1998

STARBUCK FAMILY *see* Starbucks Twins Mysteries

STARBUCKS TWINS MYSTERIES

Lasky, Kathryn
HARCOURT ◆ GRADES 4–6
MYSTERY

There are two sets of twins (12-year-olds Liberty and July and 5-year-olds Charly and Molly) in the Starbuck family, and they can both communicate telepathically. In the first book, they are in London investigating events that resemble Sherlock Holmes cases. In the second, their unique ability to communicate with dolphins helps to nab criminals dumping toxic waste off Florida. The series was reissued in 2008.

1. Double Trouble Squared ◆ 1991
2. Shadows in the Water ◆ 1992
3. A Voice in the Wind ◆ 1993

STARCATCHERS *see* Peter and the Starcatchers

STARFLEET ACADEMY *see* Star Trek: Starfleet Academy

STARLIGHT

Hill, Janet Muirhead

RAVEN ◆ GRADES 4–6

REAL LIFE

Staying on her grandparents' farm while her mother is looking for work, Miranda falls in love with a black stallion called Starlight. In the first book, Miranda resorts to lies to get her way and the story nearly ends in tragedy; however, she reforms and winds up winning the horse. In subsequent books, Miranda and Starlight have adventures together and Miranda matures and copes better with the challenges in her life.

1. Miranda and Starlight ◆ 2002
2. Starlight's Courage ◆ 2002
3. Starlight, Star Bright ◆ 2003
4. Starlight's Shooting Star ◆ 2003
5. Starlight Shines for Miranda ◆ 2004
6. Starlight Comes Home ◆ 2004

STARRING IN . . . *see* Mary-Kate and Ashley
Starring In . . .

STARSHINE!

Schwartz, Ellen

POLESTAR ◆ GRADES 4–6 ◆ A/R

FAMILY LIFE

Starshine Bliss Shapiro hates her name and loves spiders. She lives with her parents and little sister Peggy in Vancouver, British Columbia. Her parents are very relaxed and artistic and Star has a lot of freedom to be with her friends. In the first book, she organizes a play around the story of Arachne. The second book features her adventures at summer camp, including her discovery of a rare fanged vampire spider. In the third book, Star is selected to be in a commercial only to be upstaged by her little sister. Starshine is a believable character whose emotions will mirror those of many girls who will read this series.

1. Starshine! ◆ 1987
2. Starshine at Camp Crescent Moon ◆ 1994
3. Starshine on TV ◆ 1996
4. Starshine and the Fanged Vampire Spider ◆ 2000

STARVATION LAKE

Whelan, Gloria

RANDOM HOUSE; GOLDEN BOOKS ◆ GRADES 3–5 ◆ A/R

REAL LIFE

Being in the fourth grade at Starvation Lake Elementary School can be full of surprises. The class meets a rock star, raises money for a trip, and helps restore an old house. This is a good chapter book choice.

1. Welcome to Starvation Lake ◆ 2000
2. Rich and Famous in Starvation Lake ◆ 2001
3. Are There Bears in Starvation Lake? ◆ 2002
4. A Haunted House in Starvation Lake ◆ 2003

STEPHANIE *see* Full House: Stephanie and Full House: Club Stephanie

STEVIE DIAMOND MYSTERIES

Bailey, Linda

WHITMAN ◆ GRADES 4–6 ◆ A/R

MYSTERY

Stevie (formerly known as Stephanie) is a big fan of Nancy Drew, Hercule Poirot, and any other mystery books she can lay her hands on. So when mysterious things happen, she remembers how her detective heroes solve cases and uses their techniques to her advantage. She is aided in her sleuthing by a nerdy kid named Jesse, who lives in her building and who sometimes helps and sometimes hinders her investigations. Together they form the Diamond & Kulnicki Detective Agency . . . No Mystery Too Tough For Us. In each volume of the series, they solve real mysteries while trying unsuccessfully to stay out of trouble themselves.

1. How Come the Best Clues Are Always in the Garbage? ◆ 1992
2. How Can I Be a Detective If I Have to Baby Sit? ◆ 1993
3. Who's Got Gertie and How Can We Get Her Back? ◆ 1996
4. How Can a Frozen Detective Stay Hot on the Trail? ◆ 1996
5. What's a Daring Detective Like Me Doing in the Doghouse? ◆ 1997
6. How Can a Brilliant Detective Shine in the Dark? ◆ 1999
7. What's a Serious Detective Like Me Doing in Such a Silly Movie? ◆ 2003

STINK

McDonald, Megan
CANDLEWICK ◆ **GRADES 2–4** ◆ **A/R**

REAL LIFE | HUMOR

Fans of the Judy Moody books have already met her bother of a brother, Stink. Stink is convinced that he is unusually short for a second-grader. Of course, his sister agrees. At school, Stink chooses to do his President's Day report on James Madison, the shortest president. In *Stink and the World's Worst Super-Stinky Sneakers,* readers learn about how Stink got his name. These books are full of puns and funny situations guaranteed to make kids laugh out loud.

1. Stink: The Incredible Shrinking Kid ◆ 2005
2. Stink and the Incredible Super-Galactic Jawbreaker ◆ 2006
3. Stink and the World's Worst Super-Stinky Sneakers ◆ 2007
4. Stink and the Great Guinea Pig Express ◆ 2008

THE STINK FILES

Holm, Jennifer, and Jonathan Hamel
HARPERCOLLINS ◆ **GRADES 3–5**

MYSTERY

Not long after James Edward Bristlefur's master is murdered, the urbane British cat detective finds himself living in middle-class America and renamed Mr. Stink, much to his dismay. However, he adapts to his circumstances and takes time to help his new young master, Aaron, deal with a bully. In the third book, Mr. Stink wins a cat food competition and travels to France, where he is mistaken as a prince. In addition to finding the real royal, he uncovers secrets about his own past. Recommend this series to Geronimo Stilton fans.

1. Dossier 001: The Postman Always Brings Mice ◆ 2004
2. Dossier 002: To Scratch a Thief ◆ 2004
3. Dossier 003: You Only Have Nine Lives ◆ 2005

STINKY BOYS CLUB

Carse, Jodi, and Maria Gallagher
GROSSETT & DUNLAP ◆ **GRADES 3–6** ◆ **A/R**

REAL LIFE | HUMOR

Sam and his friends are tired of the antics of Sam's twin MJ and her friends, so Sam forms the Stinky Boys Club. Of course, the girls refuse to be excluded and the fun starts. There are competitions with the boys vs.

the girls and there are numerous pranks. The stories are presented in colorful cartoon panels.

1. Enough Is Enough! ◆ 2004
2. Winner Takes All! ◆ 2005
3. Gotta Have It! ◆ 2005
4. Catch That Kid! ◆ 2006

STONE BOOK QUARTET

Garner, Alan

DELL ◆ GRADES 3–5

FAMILY LIFE | HISTORICAL

This quartet is written in a rich prose combining modern English with the old northwest Mercian spoken pattern. The stories trace four generations of an English family of craftsmen from the Victorian era through World War II. Each book focuses on a different child—Mary, Joseph, Robert, and William—as he or she learns about a family craft and in doing so learns about the family ancestry and gains a deeper connection to both the past and to the present. Directed toward a young audience, the subject and fairly dark style of these books encourage readers to think about some very real issues, such as self-identity, courage, poverty, love, death, and the nature of the world around them.

1. The Stone Book ◆ 1976
2. Tom Fobble's Day ◆ 1977
3. Granny Reardun ◆ 1977
4. Aimer Gate ◆ 1978

THE STONEHEART TRILOGY

Fletcher, Charile

HYPERION ◆ GRADES 5–9 ◆ A/R

FANTASY

At the Natural History Museum in London, George, 12, damages a dragon statue and is transported to a parallel world where the statues have come to life and are at war. Because of his attack on the dragon statue, George is being pursued and searches for the stoneheart, the key to his release. He is befriended by Edie, a girl with secret powers, and by the Gunner, a statue of a World War I soldier. As the series progresses, the three face many enemies, including the Grid Man, the Minotaur, and the Walker. And George is being destroyed from within as three veins—marble, bronze, and stone—grow out of his hand toward his heart.

1. The Stoneheart ◆ 2007

2. The Ironhand ◆ 2008
3. Silvertongue ◆ 2009

STORIES FROM EAST HIGH *see* High School Musical Stories from East High

STORY GIRL

Montgomery, L. M., and Barbara Davoll, adapt.
ZONDERKIDZ ◆ GRADES 5–7
HISTORICAL | VALUES

Based on stories by L. M. Montgomery, these books set on Prince Edward Island at the turn of the 20th century feature Sara Stanley, a girl with a gift for telling stories with a Christian message. In the first book, two boys—the King cousins—visit relatives on Prince Edward Island and learn about church, raise funds for a school library, and hear a good story or two. In *Winter on the Island,* the cousins and their friends celebrate Christmas, make New Year's resolutions, start up a newspaper, and experience a blizzard.

1. The King Cousins ◆ 2004
2. Measles, Mischief, and Mishaps ◆ 2004
3. Summer Shenanigans ◆ 2004
4. Dreams, Schemes, and Mysteries ◆ 2004
5. Winter on the Island ◆ 2005
6. Wedding Wishes and Woes ◆ 2005
7. Midnight Madness and Mayhem ◆ 2005
8. Winds of Change ◆ 2005

STRANGE MATTER

Engle, Marty, and Johnny Ray Barnes, Jr.
GARETH STEVENS ◆ GRADES 4–6 ◆ A/R
HORROR

These scary tales are labeled "Brave Readers Only" to keep the faint-hearted at bay. Realistic stories of terror at school, at home, and at camp make entertaining reads. Danger usually arises when someone breaks a rule or takes a dare, but all the stories have safe resolutions.

1. No Substitutions ◆ 1995
2. The Midnight Game ◆ 1995
3. Driven to Death ◆ 1995
4. A Place to Hide ◆ 1995
5. The Last One In ◆ 1995

6. Bad Circuits ◆ 1995
7. Fly the Unfriendly Skies ◆ 1995
8. Frozen Dinners ◆ 1995
9. Deadly Delivery ◆ 1995
10. Knightmare ◆ 1996
11. Something Rotten ◆ 1996
12. Dead on Its Tracks ◆ 1996
13. Toy Trouble ◆ 1996
14. The Plant People ◆ 1996
15. Creature Features ◆ 1996
16. Weird, Weird West ◆ 1996
17. Tune into Terror ◆ 1996
18. The Fairfield Triangle ◆ 1996
19. Big Foot, Big Trouble ◆ 1996
20. Doorway to Doom ◆ 1996
21. Under Wraps ◆ 1996
22. Dangerous Waters ◆ 1996
23. Second Sighting ◆ 1996
24. Nightcrawlers ◆ 1997
25. Splitting Image ◆ 1997
26. Headless Rider of Carson Creek ◆ 1997
27. Primeval ◆ 1997
28. Off-Worlder ◆ 1997
29. Shadow Chaser ◆ 1997
30. Escape from Planet Earth ◆ 1997
31. Rilo Buro's Summer Vacation ◆ 1997
32. Probe ◆ 1997
33. Fathom ◆ 1997
34. From the Ashes ◆ 1997

STREGA NONA AND BIG ANTHONY

dePaola, Tomie

PUTNAM; SIMON & SCHUSTER ◆ GRADES K–3 ◆ A/R

FANTASY

These popular characters first appeared in the Caldecott Honor book *Strega Nona*. Big Anthony does not pay attention to what he is doing and Strega Nona must correct the results of his actions. When he uses her magic pasta pot, he nearly covers the town in spaghetti. Strega Nona knows the way to stop the pot and save the city.

1. Strega Nona ◆ 1975
2. Big Anthony and the Magic Ring ◆ 1979
3. Strega Nona's Magic Lessons ◆ 1982
4. Merry Christmas, Strega Nona ◆ 1986
5. Strega Nona Meets Her Match ◆ 1993
6. Strega Nona: Her Story ◆ 1996

7. Big Anthony: His Story ◆ 1998
8. Strega Nona Takes a Vacation ◆ 2000

THE STUPIDS

Allard, Harry

HOUGHTON MIFFLIN ◆ **GRADES K–2**

FAMILY LIFE | HUMOR

The Stupids are undoubtedly the stupidest family on Earth. This humorous series tells of the silly misadventures of Mr. Stanley Q. Stupid, his wife, and their two children, Buster and Petunia, whose backward approach to everything creates confusion in the family's everyday activities. Only their pets, Kitty the dog and Xylophone the cat, seem the least bit aware of the absurdity of it all. The hilarious antics described in the stories are accented by silly details in James Marshall's illustrations. A careful observer will notice that the Stupids keep jam and tuna on their bathroom shelf, their hanging picture of Lake Stupid shows a bucket of water, and Mr. Stupid brushes his teeth with anchovy toothpaste!

1. The Stupids Step Out ◆ 1974
2. The Stupids Have a Ball ◆ 1978
3. The Stupids Die ◆ 1981
4. The Stupids Take Off ◆ 1989

SUDDENLY SUPERNATURAL

Kimmel, Elizabeth Cody

LITTLE, BROWN ◆ **GRADES 5–8** ◆ **A/R**

FANTASY

Kat Roberts is starting a new school and she wants to fit in. That has been a challenge because Kat's mother is a medium—she sees the spirits of the dead. Now Kat realizes that she sees spirits, too. In fact, there is a spirit at her school that needs Kat's help.

1. School Spirit ◆ 2008
2. Scaredy Kat ◆ 2009
3. Unhappy Medium ◆ 2009

SUITE LIFE OF ZACK AND CODY

Various authors

DISNEY PRESS ◆ **GRADES 3–6**

HUMOR

Zack and Cody are 11-year-old identical twins who live with their mother in a posh Boston hotel called the Tipton. The boys get into all sorts of mischief, usually instigated by Zach. In *Check It Out,* they come up with a plan to get rid of the hotel inspector who is threatening to take over. The books are based on a Disney Channel series of the same name and include pages showing shots from the show.

1. Hotel Hangout (Richards, Kitty) ◆ 2006
2. Double Trouble (Grace, N. B.) ◆ 2006
3. Room of Doom (King, M. C.) ◆ 2006
4. Zack Attack (King, M. C.) ◆ 2006
5. Check It Out (Beechwood, Beth) ◆ 2007

THE SUMMER OF MAGIC QUARTET

Spalding, Andrea
ORCA ◆ GRADES 4–7
FANTASY

Canadians Chantel and Adam find a magic talisman soon after they arrive in England to visit their cousins. They become embroiled in a struggle between an ancient White Horse Wise One and an evil dragon. There is time travel and telepathic communication. The saga of the pending divorce of the children's parents adds a real-life element to this fantasy full of historical detail.

1. The White Horse Talisman ◆ 2002
2. Dance of the Stones ◆ 2003
3. Heart of the Hill ◆ 2005
4. Behind the Sorcerer's Cloak ◆ 2006

SUNKEN KINGDOM

Wilkins, Kim
RANDOM HOUSE ◆ GRADES 3–5 ◆ A/R
FANTASY

The evil Emperor Flood has destroyed the kingdom of the Star Lands. Asa and Rollo have escaped while their parents, the rulers of the Star Lands, seem to have been killed. The Emperor want to destroy these two royal children, too, so Asa and Rollo travel on the invisible ship *Northseeker,* hoping to discover the fate of their parents and free their kingdom from Emperor Flood and his minions, including ghosts and sea giants.

1. Ghost Ship ◆ 2006
2. Tide Stealers ◆ 2006
3. Sorcerer of the Waves ◆ 2008
4. The Star Queen ◆ 2008

SUPER GOOFBALLS

Hannan, Peter

HARPERCOLLINS ◆ **GRADES 4–8** ◆ **A/R**

HUMOR

To help pay the bills, the main character (Amazing Techno Dude) and his grandmother (Bodacious Backwards Woman) have taken in eight roommates, each extremely goofy and each a sort of superhero. Life at 1313 Thirteenth Street is crazier than ever. In *Goofballs in Paradise,* the gang goes on vacation and confronts the supervillain Mondo Grumpo. With short chapters and zany action, this may appeal to reluctant readers as well as to fans of Dav Pilkey books.

1. That Stinking Feeling ◆ 2007
2. Goofballs in Paradise ◆ 2007
3. Super Underwear . . . and Beyond ◆ 2007
4. Attack of the 50-Foot Alien Creep-oids ◆ 2007
5. Doomed in Dreamland ◆ 2008
6. Battle of the Brain-Sucking Robots ◆ 2008

SUPER HOOPS

Various authors

BANTAM ◆ **GRADES 4–6**

REAL LIFE | RECREATION

With lots of basketball action, this series is sure to appeal to sports fans. The Branford Bulls is a team of elementary school boys that includes Will Hopwood, Derek Roberts, Travis Barnes, and others. They are coached by two teenagers from the high school team: Nate Bowman and Will's brother, Jim. Having your brother for coach can be a problem, especially when you are the star center. Along with court activities, there are problems with ego, sportsmanship, and teamwork that are resolved. There is even a player named Michael Jordan, although he is not the NBA superstar. As the publisher notes, this is "A slammin', jammin', in-your-face action series!"

1. Crashing the Boards (Herman, Hank) ◆ 1996
2. In Your Face! (Herman, Hank) ◆ 1996
3. Trash Talk (Herman, Hank) ◆ 1996
4. Monster Jam (Herman, Hank) ◆ 1996
5. One on One (Herman, Hank) ◆ 1996
6. Show Time! (Weiss, Dan) ◆ 1996
7. Slam Dunk! (Herman, Hank) ◆ 1996
8. Ball Hog (Herman, Hank) ◆ 1996
9. Hang Time (Herman, Hank) ◆ 1997
10. Foul! (Herman, Hank) ◆ 1997

11. Above the Rim (Herman, Hank) ◆ 1997
12. In the Zone (Herman, Hank) ◆ 1997
13. Out of Bounds! (Herman, Hank) ◆ 1997
14. Who's the Man? (Herman, Hank) ◆ 1997
15. Rebound! (Herman, Hank) ◆ 1998

SUPERTWINS

James, B. J.
SCHOLASTIC ◆ GRADES K–3 ◆ A/R
FANTASY

Tabby and Timmy, twins with special powers, face alien poodles, the theft of teeth from under pillows, and evil robots. The format of this series makes it a good choice for beginning readers.

1. Supertwins Meet the Dangerous Dino-Robots ◆ 2003
2. Supertwins and Tooth Trouble ◆ 2003
3. Supertwins Meet Bad Dogs from Space ◆ 2003
4. Supertwins and the Sneaky, Slimy Book Worms ◆ 2004

SURVIVAL!

Duey, Kathleen, and Karen A. Bale
ALADDIN ◆ GRADES 5–8 ◆ A/R
ADVENTURE | HISTORICAL

The sinking of the *Titanic*, the San Francisco earthquake, the Colorado blizzard—imagine that you are there. The Survival! series places young characters in the middle of exciting, even dangerous situations. In 1850, twins Jess and Will find themselves stranded in Death Valley. In 1871, the Chicago Fire places Nate Cooper and Julie Flynn in great danger from the chaotic crowds and the spreading inferno. Dramatic events are woven into the historical context, which should attract readers who want stories with adventure and courageous characters.

1. Titanic: April 14, 1912 ◆ 1998
2. Earthquake: San Francisco, 1906 ◆ 1998
3. Blizzard: Estes Park, Colorado, 1886 ◆ 1998
4. Fire: Chicago, 1871 ◆ 1998
5. Flood: Mississippi, 1927 ◆ 1998
6. Stranded: Death Valley, Circa 1850 ◆ 1998
7. Cave-in: Pennsylvania, 1859 ◆ 1998
8. Train Wreck: Kansas, 1892 ◆ 1999
9. Hurricane: Open Seas, 1784 ◆ 1999
10. Forest Fire: Hinckley, Minnesota, 1894 ◆ 1999
11. Swamp: Bayou Teche, Louisiana, 1851 ◆ 1999

SWAT (SECRET WORLD ADVENTURE TEAM)

Thompson, Lisa
PICTURE WINDOW BOOKS ◆ GRADES 2–4
ADVENTURE

The Secret World Adventure Team recruits young people for missions abroad. Jason and Anita go to Tokyo, where they learn about Japanese culture while looking for a man they must help with a computer game. Will and Vika travel to England, where they enjoy London sights while searching for a valuable family heirloom. These are simple chapter books designed to extend reading skills.

1. Amazing Africa ◆ 2006
2. Incredible India ◆ 2006
3. Lookout London ◆ 2006
4. New York City ◆ 2006
5. Sent to Sydney ◆ 2006
6. Spectacular Spain ◆ 2006
7. Taste of Thailand ◆ 2006
8. Tokyo Techno ◆ 2006

SWEET 16 (MARY-KATE AND ASHLEY)

see Mary-Kate and Ashley Sweet 16

SWEET VALLEY: UNICORN CLUB

Pascal, Francine, creator
BANTAM ◆ GRADES 4–6 ◆ A/R
REAL LIFE

The Unicorn Club is a group of friends who attend Sweet Valley Middle School—Lila Fowler, Mandy Miller, Ellen Riteman, Kimberly Haver, and Jessica Wakefield are the main members. They worry about clothes, boys, school, and snacks. Their club is more an extension of their friendship than an official organization. As with any group of friends, there are disagreements. In *Mandy in the Middle,* the Unicorns are on the outs with a rival group called the Angels. Mandy is in the Unicorns but has friends in the Angels. She must decide if it is more important to follow the unfair demands of a group or to make her own choices. Other books feature the Unicorns participating in school events, worrying about boyfriends, and going on a Caribbean cruise. These are like the Sweet Valley High books but for a younger audience.

1. Save the Unicorns! ◆ 1994
2. Maria's Movie Comeback ◆ 1994

3. The Best Friend Game ◆ 1994
4. Lila's Little Sister ◆ 1994
5. Unicorns in Love ◆ 1995
6. The Unicorns at War ◆ 1995
7. Too Close for Comfort ◆ 1995
8. Kimberly Rides Again ◆ 1995
9. Ellen's Family Secret ◆ 1996
10. Mandy in the Middle ◆ 1996
11. Angels Keep Out ◆ 1996
12. Five Girls and a Baby ◆ 1996
13. Who Will Be Miss Unicorn Club? ◆ 1996
14. Lila on the Loose ◆ 1996
15. Too Cool for the Unicorns ◆ 1997
16. Bon Voyage, Unicorns! ◆ 1997
17. Boyfriends for Everyone ◆ 1997
18. Rachel's In, Lila's Out ◆ 1997
19. The Most Beautiful Girl in the World ◆ 1997
20. In Love with Mandy ◆ 1997
21. Snow Bunnies ◆ 1997
22. Jessica's Dream Date ◆ 1998
23. Trapped in the Mall ◆ 1998

SWEET VALLEY KIDS

Pascal, Francine, creator

BANTAM ◆ GRADES 3–5 ◆ A/R

REAL LIFE

Elizabeth and Jessica, the twins featured in the popular Sweet Valley Junior High and Sweet Valley High series, are 7 years old and in second grade at the start of this series of chapter books. Jessica already likes clothes and doesn't like school, whereas Elizabeth is just the opposite. The stories deal with family, friends, and school. In a typical book, one of their friends has a visiting cousin who tries to impress others by lying and causing trouble. All is forgiven when the girl says she was just trying to make friends, and the twins and their friends explain that lying is not the way to do it.

1. Surprise! Surprise! ◆ 1989
2. Runaway Hamster ◆ 1989
3. Twins' Mystery Teacher ◆ 1989
4. Elizabeth's Valentine ◆ 1989
5. Jessica's Cat Trick ◆ 1990
6. Lila's Secret ◆ 1990
7. Jessica's Big Mistake ◆ 1990
8. Jessica's Zoo Adventure ◆ 1990
9. Elizabeth's Super-Selling Lemonade ◆ 1990
10. Twins and the Wild West ◆ 1990

11. Crybaby Lois ◆ 1990
12. Sweet Valley Trick or Treat ◆ 1990
13. Starring Winston Egbert ◆ 1990
14. Jessica the Baby-Sitter ◆ 1990
15. Fearless Elizabeth ◆ 1991
16. Jessica the TV Star ◆ 1991
17. Caroline's Mystery Dolls ◆ 1991
18. Bossy Steven ◆ 1991
19. Jessica and the Jumbo Fish ◆ 1991
20. Twins Go to the Hospital ◆ 1991
21. Jessica and the Spelling-Bee Surprise ◆ 1991
22. Sweet Valley Slumber Party ◆ 1991
23. Lila's Haunted House Party ◆ 1991
24. Cousin Kelly's Family Secret ◆ 1991
25. Left-Out Elizabeth ◆ 1991
26. Jessica's Snobby Club ◆ 1991
27. Sweet Valley Cleanup Team ◆ 1992
28. Elizabeth Meets Her Hero ◆ 1992
29. Andy and the Alien ◆ 1992
30. Jessica's Unburied Treasure ◆ 1992
31. Elizabeth and Jessica Run Away ◆ 1992
32. Left Back ◆ 1992
33. Caroline's Halloween Spell ◆ 1992
34. Best Thanksgiving Ever ◆ 1992
35. Elizabeth's Broken Arm ◆ 1992
36. Elizabeth's Video Fever ◆ 1992
37. Big Race ◆ 1993
38. Good-bye, Eva? ◆ 1993
39. Ellen Is Home Alone ◆ 1993
40. Robin in the Middle ◆ 1993
41. Missing Tea Set ◆ 1993
42. Jessica's Monster Nightmare ◆ 1993
43. Jessica Gets Spooked ◆ 1993
44. Twin's Big Pow-Wow ◆ 1993
45. Elizabeth's Piano Lesson ◆ 1993
46. Get the Teacher! ◆ 1993
47. Elizabeth the Tattletale ◆ 1994
48. Lila's April Fool ◆ 1994
49. Jessica's Mermaid ◆ 1994
50. Steven's Twin ◆ 1994
51. Lois and the Sleepover ◆ 1994
52. Julie the Karate Kid ◆ 1994
53. The Magic Puppets ◆ 1994
54. Star of the Parade ◆ 1994
55. The Jessica and Elizabeth Show ◆ 1994
56. Jessica Plays Cupid ◆ 1994
57. No Girls Allowed ◆ 1995
58. Lila's Birthday Bash ◆ 1995
59. Jessica Plus Jessica Equals Trouble ◆ 1995
60. The Amazing Jessica ◆ 1995

61. Scaredy-Cat Elizabeth ◆ 1995
62. The Halloween War ◆ 1995
63. Lila's Christmas Angel ◆ 1995
64. Elizabeth's Horseback Adventure ◆ 1995
65. Steven's Big Crush ◆ 1995
66. And the Winner Is . . . Jessica Wakefield ◆ 1995
67. The Secret of Fantasy Forest ◆ 1996
68. The Roller Coaster for the Twins! ◆ 1996
69. Class Picture Day! ◆ 1997
70. Good-Bye, Mrs. Otis ◆ 1997
71. Jessica's Secret Friend ◆ 1997
72. The Macaroni Mess ◆ 1997
73. Witch in the Pumpkin Patch ◆ 1997
74. Sweet Valley Blizzard! ◆ 1998
75. Little Drummer Girls ◆ 1998
76. Danger: Twins at Work! ◆ 1998

SWEET VALLEY KIDS SUPER SNOOPER EDITIONS

1. The Case of the Secret Santa ◆ 1990
2. The Case of the Magic Christmas Bell ◆ 1991
3. The Case of the Haunted Camp ◆ 1992
4. The Case of the Christmas Thief ◆ 1992
5. The Case of the Hidden Treasure ◆ 1993
6. The Case of the Million-Dollar Diamonds ◆ 1993
7. The Case of the Alien Princess ◆ 1994

SWEET VALLEY KIDS SUPER SPECIAL EDITIONS

1. Trapped in Toyland ◆ 1994
2. Easter Bunny Battle ◆ 1995
3. Save the Turkey! ◆ 1995
4. Elizabeth Hatches an Egg ◆ 1996

SWORD OF THE SPIRITS

Christopher, John
ALADDIN ◆ GRADES 5–8
ADVENTURE | SCIENCE FICTION

Post-apocalyptic England is the setting of this trilogy. It is a world of warriors, dwarfs, mutants and seers. Luke Perry, the future ruler, is thrown into chaos as he finds out that his world is not as it seems. He must hide after his father is murdered and his half-brother takes the throne. Continuous action, drama, and intrigue create a satisfying read for fans of science fiction.

1. The Prince in Waiting ◆ 1970
2. Beyond the Burning Lands ◆ 1971
3. The Sword of the Spirits ◆ 1972

SYLVIE CYCLE

Townley, Roderick

ATHENEUM ◆ GRADES 5–9 ◆ A/R

FANTASY

Sylvie, 12, is a storybook princess who lives out her life in the pages of a fairy tale book. Her life has been dictated by her Readers. Now Sylvie has a goal—to accomplish one Great Good Thing. She transcends the text of her book and sets off on her own adventures, even saving the actual book she lives in. In the second book, Sylvie and the other characters are uploaded to the Internet for more adventures.

1. The Great Good Thing ◆ 2001
2. Into the Labyrinth ◆ 2002
3. The Constellation of Sylvie ◆ 2005

TABLE TWO

Gilson, Jamie

CLARION ◆ GRADES 2–3 ◆ A/R

REAL LIFE

As a second-grader, Richard often finds himself in embarrassing situations such as getting head lice or wearing bright purple pants that are too big. He and the other kids in Mrs. Zookey's class experience lots of familiar classroom activities, such as a science project on bats. As this series develops, more kids in the class became part of the action, including Patrick, the class pest. The newest book, *Chess! I Love It! I Love It! I Love It!,* is being called a "Table Two" adventure as the kids that are featured all sit at Table Two.

1. Itchy Richard ◆ 1991
2. It Goes Eeeeeeeeeeeee! ◆ 1994
3. Bug in a Rug ◆ 1998
4. Gotcha! ◆ 2006
5. Chess! I Love It! I Love It! I Love It! ◆ 2008

TACKY THE PENGUIN

Lester, Helen

HOUGHTON MIFFLIN ◆ GRADES K–2 ◆ A/R

ANIMAL FANTASY

Tacky the penguin is a lively, enthusiastic character whose unusual behavior often annoys his friends. *Three Cheers for Tacky* focuses on the Penguin Cheering Contest, which provides a perfect opportunity to showcase Tacky's individuality. Just when it looks as if Tacky will spoil everything, his energy and spirit bring success. In *Tacky in Trouble,* Tacky travels to a tropical island, an unusual spot for a penguin! Young readers will find it satisfying that Tacky is different but still accepted and appreciated.

1. Tacky the Penguin ◆ 1988
2. Three Cheers for Tacky ◆ 1994
3. Tacky in Trouble ◆ 1998
4. Tacky and the Emperor ◆ 2002
5. Tackylocks and the Three Bears ◆ 2002
6. Tacky and the Winter Games ◆ 2005

TAFFY SINCLAIR

Haynes, Betsy

BANTAM SKYLARK ◆ GRADES 4–6

REAL LIFE

Taffy Sinclair has various adventures in this series: getting a role in a real television soap opera, modeling, and, best of all, keeping ahead of the Fabulous Five, a club created by five girls specifically to get Taffy. The Fabulous Five has its own series.

1. The Against Taffy Sinclair Club ◆ 1976
2. Taffy Sinclair Strikes Again ◆ 1984
3. Taffy Sinclair, Queen of Soaps ◆ 1985
4. Taffy Sinclair and the Romance Machine Disaster ◆ 1987
5. Blackmailed by Taffy Sinclair ◆ 1987
6. Taffy Sinclair, Baby Ashley, and Me ◆ 1988
7. Taffy Sinclair and the Secret Admirer Epidemic ◆ 1988
8. The Truth About Taffy Sinclair ◆ 1988
9. Taffy Sinclair and the Melanie Makeover ◆ 1988
10. Taffy Sinclair Goes to Hollywood ◆ 1990
11. Nobody Likes Taffy Sinclair ◆ 1991

TALES FROM THE HOUSE OF BUNNICULA *see* Bunnicula: Tales from the House of Bunnicula

TALES FROM THE ODYSSEY

Osborne, Mary Pope

HYPERION ◆ GRADES 4–8 ◆ A/R

FANTASY

Homer's *Odyssey* is retold in this series. At the end of the Trojan War, Odysseus and his men begin the dangerous journey home. They encounter all the familiar mythical creatures including Cyclops, Circe, and Aeolus.

1. The One-Eyed Giant ◆ 2002
2. The Land of the Dead ◆ 2003
3. Sirens and Sea Monsters ◆ 2003
4. The Gray-Eyed Goddess ◆ 2003
5. Return to Ithaca ◆ 2004
6. The Final Battle ◆ 2004

TALES FROM THE SANDLOT

Gutman, Dan

SCHOLASTIC ◆ GRADES 4–6

FANTASY | HUMOR | RECREATION

Each book in this series features a different character who experiences a weird encounter. In one book, Jake Miller is able to read minds. His special ability, which appears after he is hit by a pitch, lets him know the strategies of the other teams—which puts him in danger. Lee Madigan, left fielder, doesn't think there are any monsters in Oregon, until he meets Bigfoot. And Rob Newton is a pitcher who has an out-of-body experience. Connecting sports with weird events will expand the appeal of this series.

1. The Shortstop Who Knew Too Much ◆ 1997
2. The Green Monster in Left Field ◆ 1997
3. The Catcher Who Shocked the World ◆ 1997
4. The Pitcher Who Went Out of His Mind ◆ 1997

TALES OF COVEN TREE *see* Coven Tree

TALES OF KING ARTHUR *see* King Arthur

TALES OF TERROR

Bradman, Tony

EGMONT ◆ GRADES 4–7

HORROR

Horror is the unifying theme in this series of British imports that take ordinary situations and give them scary twists. In *Final Cut,* Billy Gibson finds himself in a horror movie and must decide which side will win. In

Voodoo Child, Megan hopes a voodoo doll will get rid of her father's girlfriend. Bold illustrations add a sinister touch.

1. Deadly Game ◆ 2004
2. Final Cut ◆ 2004
3. Voodoo Child ◆ 2004

TALES OF THE DARK FOREST

Barlow, Steve, and Steve Skidmore

HARPERCOLLINS ◆ **GRADES 4–6**

FANTASY

In this fantasy series, each book features a different character. In *Goodknyght*, Will is a whipping boy for Symon, who takes pleasure in misbehaving so Will gets punished. Will's fate changes, however, when he begins a quest with the Runemaster.

1. Goodknyght ◆ 2003
2. Whizzard ◆ 2003
3. Trollogy ◆ 2003
4. Knyghtmare ◆ 2004

TALES OF THE FROG PRINCESS

Baker, E. D.

BLOOMSBURY ◆ **GRADES 4–7** ◆ **A/R**

FANTASY | HUMOR

Princess Emeralda, 14, kisses Eadric, a frog. In a twist on the usual tale, she turns into a frog. Emeralda and Eadric work together to try to undo the spell. Thus begins this series of twisted tales.

1. The Frog Princess ◆ 2002
2. Dragon's Breath ◆ 2003
3. Once Upon a Curse ◆ 2004
4. No Place for Magic ◆ 2006
5. The Salamander Spell ◆ 2007

TALES OF TROTTER STREET

Hughes, Shirley

LOTHROP, LEE & SHEPARD ◆ **GRADES K–2**

FAMILY LIFE

These are heartwarming tales of life in an urban neighborhood. *Wheels* has a little boy yearning for a bicycle that his mother cannot afford, but he is thrilled with the surprise birthday present of a go-cart made by his older brother. In *Angel Mae,* a little girl gets a new baby in her house for Christmas and appears in the Christmas play.

1. Angel Mae ◆ 1989
2. The Big Concrete Lorry ◆ 1990
3. The Snow Lady ◆ 1990
4. Wheels ◆ 1991

TANYA

Gauch, Patricia Lee

PUTNAM ◆ GRADES K–3 ◆ A/R

REAL LIFE

Tanya is a little girl who loves to dance. Her older sister has already been taking dance lessons, and Tanya wants nothing more than to dance like all the students in the class. However, her attempts are sometimes less than perfect. A gentle series about the delights of dancing.

1. Dance, Tanya ◆ 1989
2. Bravo, Tanya! ◆ 1992
3. Tanya and Emily in a Dance for Two ◆ 1994
4. Tanya Steps Out ◆ 1996
5. Tanya and the Magic Wardrobe ◆ 1997
6. Presenting Tanya, the Ugly Duckling ◆ 1999
7. Tanya and the Red Shoes ◆ 2002

TARTAN MAGIC TRILOGY

Yolen, Jane

HARCOURT ◆ GRADES 4–7 ◆ A/R

FANTASY

American twins Jennifer and Peter find Scotland to be a place full of magic in this series full of ghosts, local lore, adventure, and suspense. In the last book, they visit a graveyard and become embroiled in a 300-year-old feud between former lovers.

1. The Wizard's Map ◆ 1999
2. The Pictish Child ◆ 1999
3. The Bagpiper's Ghost ◆ 2002

TEDDY BEARS

Gretz, Susanna

FOUR WINDS ◆ GRADES K–3

FANTASY

The teddy bears, their dog Fred, and sometimes their Uncle Jerome share various adventures: They stay indoors and plan a trip to the moon; one of them gets a cold and the rest of the bears figure out how to make him better; on a train trip they discover that the white bears they are so afraid of are actually very friendly. Gretz's amusing illustrations contain lots for young readers to look at, and the stories are heartwarming.

1. Teddy Bears' Moving Day ◆ 1981
2. Teddy Bears Go Shopping ◆ 1982
3. Teddy Bears Cure a Cold ◆ 1984
4. Teddy Bears ABC ◆ 1986
5. Teddy Bears 1 to 10 ◆ 1986
6. Teddy Bears Stay Indoors ◆ 1987
7. Teddy Bears Take the Train ◆ 1987
8. Teddy Bears at the Seaside ◆ 1989

TEN COMMANDMENTS MYSTERIES

Murphy, Elspeth Campbell

CHARIOT BOOKS ◆ GRADES 3–5 ◆ A/R

MYSTERY | VALUES

Three cousins—Timothy, Titus, and Sarah-Jane—solve mysteries in this Christian series. Each mystery centers on one of the Ten Commandments and explores a Christian theme. For example, in *The Mystery of the Vanishing Present,* the story focuses on the commandment to remember the Sabbath by keeping it holy. The Christian theme is reverence. The T.C.D.C. (Three Cousins Detective Club) has to solve the mystery of a painting called *Sabbath Day*: who painted it, who left it for their grandfather, and who mysteriously took it. These entertaining mysteries, while centered on religious themes, are not too didactic. The cousins also appear in the Three Cousins Detective Club series.

1. The Mystery of the Vanishing Present ◆ 1988
2. The Mystery of the Laughing Cat ◆ 1988
3. The Mystery of the Messed-Up Wedding ◆ 1988
4. The Mystery of the Gravestone Riddle ◆ 1988
5. The Mystery of the Carousel Horse ◆ 1988
6. The Mystery of the Silver Dolphin ◆ 1988

7. The Mystery of the Tattletale Parrot ◆ 1988
8. The Mystery of the Second Map ◆ 1988
9. The Mystery of the Double Trouble ◆ 1988
10. The Mystery of the Silent Idol ◆ 1988

THIRD GRADE

Auch, Mary Jane
HOLIDAY HOUSE ◆ GRADES 2–4 ◆ A/R
FANTASY

While working on a science project, Brian hypnotizes his friend Josh instead of his dog Arful. Now Josh thinks he is a cat. Another friend, Dougie, saves the day. In later books, Arful can talk and he spies on Emily and guards a spunky chicken.

1. I Was a Third Grade Science Project ◆ 1998
2. I Was a Third Grade Spy ◆ 2001
3. I Was a Third Grade Bodyguard ◆ 2003

THIRD GRADE

McKenna, Colleen O'Shaughnessy
HOLIDAY HOUSE ◆ GRADES 2–4 ◆ A/R
REAL LIFE

At the start of third grade, Gordie Barr, 7, has a problem. He got the teacher he has wanted since kindergarten, Miss Tingle, but he has to share a locker with Lucy. Gordie comes up with a stinky plan to force Lucy out of his locker in *Third Grade Stinks!*. Other books in the series deal with Gordie being bullied about his Halloween costume, a class talent show, and rumors that his teacher is getting married and moving away. McKenna wrote an earlier book with "third grade" in the title, *Good Grief . . . Third Grade* (1993) that is not part of the Gordie Barr series.

1. Third Grade Stinks! ◆ 2001
2. Third Grade Ghouls! ◆ 2001
3. Doggone . . . Third Grade! ◆ 2002
4. Third Grade Wedding Bells? ◆ 2006

THIRD-GRADE DETECTIVES

Stanley, George Edward
SIMON & SCHUSTER/ALADDIN ◆ GRADES 2–4 ◆ A/R
MYSTERY

All the children are excited about Mr. Merlin, the new third-grade teacher. He says he used to be a spy and he teaches them logic and problem-solving techniques that help the students solve easy mysteries, such as establishing who wrote a mysterious letter or finding the driver who hit Misty's new bike.

1. The Clue of the Left-Handed Envelope ◆ 2000
2. The Puzzle of the Pretty Pink Handkerchief ◆ 2000
3. The Mystery of the Hairy Tomatoes ◆ 2001
4. The Cobweb Confession ◆ 2001
5. The Riddle of the Stolen Sand ◆ 2003
6. The Secret of the Green Skin ◆ 2003
7. The Case of the Dirty Clue ◆ 2003
8. The Secret of the Wooden Witness ◆ 2004
9. The Case of the Sweaty Bank Robber ◆ 2004
10. The Mystery of the Stolen Statue ◆ 2004

THE THIRTEEN MOONS

George, Jean Craighead
HARPERCOLLINS ◆ GRADES 3–6

REAL LIFE

This is a wonderful series, full of the amazing ways in which animals adapt to their surroundings. George, well known for her writing on the environment, has taken each of the 13 lunar months and highlighted one North American animal and how it adapts during that season in its native habitat. A wide variety of animals (alligators, wolves, mountain lions, etc.) and habitats (swamps, arctic tundras, deserts) are covered. Readers will enjoy the intricate illustrations and fascinating facts.

1. The Moon of the Owls ◆ 1967
2. The Moon of the Bears ◆ 1967
3. The Moon of the Salamanders ◆ 1967
4. The Moon of the Chickarees ◆ 1968
5. The Moon of the Monarch Butterflies ◆ 1968
6. The Moon of the Fox Pups ◆ 1968
7. The Moon of the Wild Pigs ◆ 1968
8. The Moon of the Mountain Lions ◆ 1968
9. The Moon of the Deer ◆ 1969
10. The Moon of the Alligators ◆ 1969
11. The Moon of the Gray Wolves ◆ 1969
12. The Moon of the Winter Bird ◆ 1969
13. The Moon of the Moles ◆ 1969

THOMAS AND GRANDFATHER

Stolz, Mary

HARPERCOLLINS ◆ GRADES 3–6 ◆ A/R

FAMILY LIFE

Thomas and his grandfather share many heartwarming moments in this series: fishing, having relatives come to visit, being brave during storms, and more. African heritage and bits of black history of the United States (such as the Negro Baseball League) are interwoven in these simple stories.

1. Storm in the Night ◆ 1988
2. Go Fish ◆ 1991
3. Stealing Home ◆ 1992
4. Coco Grimes ◆ 1994

THOROUGHBRED

Campbell, Joanna, creator

HARPERCOLLINS ◆ GRADES 4–7 ◆ A/R

REAL LIFE | RECREATION

Eighteen-year-old jockey Samantha McLean and her middle school-aged adopted sister live at Whitebrook, a Thoroughbred breeding and training farm in Kentucky. In addition to typical problems with school, friends, boyfriends, and parents, the girls handle the pressures of riding and racing. Girls who like horses will enjoy this series about what it's like to live on a horse farm.

1. A Horse Called Wonder ◆ 1991
2. Wonder's Promise ◆ 1991
3. Wonder's First Race ◆ 1991
4. Wonder's Victory ◆ 1991
5. Ashleigh's Dream ◆ 1993
6. Wonder's Yearling ◆ 1993
7. Samantha's Pride ◆ 1993
8. Sierra's Steeplechase ◆ 1993
9. Pride's Challenge ◆ 1994
10. Pride's Last Race ◆ 1994
11. Wonder's Sister ◆ 1994
12. Shining's Orphan ◆ 1994
13. Cindy's Runaway Colt ◆ 1995
14. Cindy's Glory ◆ 1995
15. Glory's Triumph ◆ 1995
16. Glory in Danger ◆ 1996
17. Ashleigh's Farewell ◆ 1996
18. Glory's Rival ◆ 1997
19. Cindy's Heartbreak ◆ 1997

20. Champion's Spirit ◆ 1997
21. Wonder's Champion ◆ 1997
22. Arabian Challenge ◆ 1997
23. Cindy's Honor ◆ 1997
24. The Horse of Her Dreams ◆ 1997
25. Melanie's Treasure ◆ 1998
26. Sterling's Second Chance ◆ 1998
27. Christina's Courage ◆ 1998
28. Camp Saddlebrook ◆ 1998
29. Melanie's Last Ride ◆ 1998
30. Dylan's Choice ◆ 1998
31. A Home for Melanie ◆ 1998
32. Cassidy's Secret ◆ 1999
33. Racing Parker ◆ 1999
34. On the Track ◆ 1999
35. Dead Heat ◆ 1999
36. Without Wonder ◆ 1999
37. Star in Danger ◆ 1999
38. Down to the Wire ◆ 1999
39. Living Legend ◆ 2000
40. Ultimate Risk ◆ 2000
41. Close Call ◆ 2000
42. Bad Luck Filly ◆ 2000
43. Fallen Star ◆ 2000
44. Perfect Image ◆ 2000
45. Star's Chance ◆ 2001
46. Racing Image ◆ 2001
47. Cindy's Desert Adventure ◆ 2001
48. Cindy's Bold Start ◆ 2001
49. Rising Star ◆ 2001
50. Team Player ◆ 2001
51. Distance Runner ◆ 2001
52. Perfect Challenge ◆ 2002
53. Derby Fever ◆ 2002
54. Cindy's Last Hope ◆ 2002
55. Great Expectations ◆ 2002
56. Hoofprints in the Snow ◆ 2002
57. Faith in a Long Shot ◆ 2003
58. Christina's Shining Star ◆ 2003
59. Star's Inspiration ◆ 2003
60. Taking the Reins ◆ 2003
61. Parker's Passion ◆ 2003
62. Unbridled Fury ◆ 2003
63. Starstruck ◆ 2004
64. The Price of Fame ◆ 2004
65. Bridal Dreams ◆ 2004
66. Samantha's Irish Luck ◆ 2004
67. Breaking the Fall ◆ 2004
68. Kaitlin's Wild Ride ◆ 2004

69. Melanie's Double Jinx ◆ 2004
70. Allie's Legacy ◆ 2005
71. Calamity Jinx ◆ 2005
72. Legacy's Gift ◆ 2005

THOROUGHBRED SUPER EDITIONS

1. Ashleigh's Christmas Miracle (Campbell, Joanna) ◆ 1994
2. Ashleigh's Diary (Campbell, Joanna) ◆ 1995
3. Ashleigh's Hope (Campbell, Joanna) ◆ 1996
4. Samantha's Journey (Campbell, Joanna, and Karen Bentley) ◆ 1997

THOROUGHBRED: ASHLEIGH

Campbell, Joanna
HARPERCOLLINS ◆ GRADES 4–7 ◆ A/R

REAL LIFE │ RECREATION

Before the Thoroughbred series, Ashleigh Griffen lived at her family's farm in Kentucky. This series begins when Ashleigh helps an abused horse, Lightning, back to health. When the humane society tells her that there is now a home for Lightning, Ashleigh is upset. She tries to find a way to keep Lightning. Girls who like horse stories will enjoy this series.

1. Lightning's Last Hope ◆ 1998
2. A Horse for Christmas ◆ 1998
3. Waiting for Stardust ◆ 1999
4. Goodbye, Midnight Wanderer ◆ 1999
5. The Forbidden Stallion ◆ 1999
6. A Dangerous Ride ◆ 1999
7. Derby Day ◆ 1999
8. The Lost Foal ◆ 2000
9. Holiday Homecoming ◆ 2000
10. Derby Dreams ◆ 2001
11. Ashleigh's Promise ◆ 2001
12. Winter Race Camp ◆ 2002
13. The Prize ◆ 2002
14. Ashleigh's Western Challenge ◆ 2002
15. Stardust's Foal ◆ 2003

THOROUGHBRED: ASHLEIGH'S COLLECTION

Campbell, Joanna
HARPERCOLLINS ◆ GRADES 4–7 ◆ A/R

REAL LIFE │ RECREATION

Here are three of Ashleigh's favorite stories. In the first book, Susan has fallen and worries about riding again. Then a mistreated horse, Evening Star, comes to the stable and begins to trust Susan. Can she overcome her fear and help Star? Fans of horse stories will enjoy this collection.

1. Star of Shadowbrook Farm ◆ 1998
2. The Forgotten Filly ◆ 1998
3. Battlecry Forever! ◆ 1998

THREE COUSINS DETECTIVE CLUB

Murphy, Elspeth Campbell
BETHANY HOUSE ◆ GRADES 2–4 ◆ A/R
MYSTERY | VALUES

Three cousins—Sarah-Jane, Timothy, and Titus—have formed the T.C.D.C. (Three Cousins Detective Club). In each of the books in this enjoyable series, they come across a different mystery to solve. In *The Mystery of the Haunted Lighthouse,* they discover who is trying to scare their uncle away from purchasing an old lighthouse. In *The Mystery of the Silent Nightingale,* they discover the mystery behind an old silver locket. In another book, the cousins search for a missing 4-year-old named Patience. When they find her, they must unravel her unusual story about dancing angels. Each book centers around a religious theme such as joy, self-control, or patience. The cousins also appear in the Ten Commandments Mysteries.

1. The Mystery of the White Elephant ◆ 1994
2. The Mystery of the Silent Nightingale ◆ 1994
3. The Mystery of the Wrong Dog ◆ 1994
4. The Mystery of the Dancing Angels ◆ 1995
5. The Mystery of the Hobo's Message ◆ 1995
6. The Mystery of the Magi's Treasure ◆ 1995
7. The Mystery of the Haunted Lighthouse ◆ 1995
8. The Mystery of the Dolphin Detective ◆ 1995
9. The Mystery of the Eagle Feather ◆ 1995
10. The Mystery of the Silly Goose ◆ 1996
11. The Mystery of the Copycat Clown ◆ 1996
12. The Mystery of the Honeybees' Secret ◆ 1996
13. The Mystery of the Gingerbread House ◆ 1997
14. The Mystery of the Zoo Camp ◆ 1997
15. The Mystery of the Goldfish Pond ◆ 1997
16. The Mystery of the Traveling Button ◆ 1997
17. The Mystery of the Birthday Party ◆ 1997
18. The Mystery of the Lost Island ◆ 1997
19. The Mystery of the Wedding Cake ◆ 1998
20. The Mystery of the Sand Castle ◆ 1998
21. The Mystery of the Sock Monkeys ◆ 1998
22. The Mystery of the African Gray ◆ 1998

23. The Mystery of the Butterfly Garden ◆ 1999
24. The Mystery of the Book Fair ◆ 1999
25. The Mystery of the Coon Cat ◆ 1999
26. The Mystery of the Runaway Scarecrow ◆ 1999
27. The Mystery of the Attic Lion ◆ 2000
28. The Mystery of the Backdoor Bundle ◆ 2000
29. The Mystery of the Painted Snake ◆ 2000
30. The Mystery of the Golden Reindeer ◆ 2000

THREE INVESTIGATORS

Various authors

RANDOM HOUSE ◆ GRADES 5–7 ◆ A/R

ADVENTURE | MYSTERY

Jupiter Jones and his friends Pete and Bob form the Three Investigators and operate out of a secret office in the junkyard owned by Jupiter's aunt and uncle. Jupiter is a young Sherlock Holmes, never missing anything and coming to conclusions that astonish his friends and nearly always turn out to be right. The mysteries are fairly complicated, and the solutions depend on historic or scientific knowledge. Jupiter, as the First Investigator, supplies the brains, and Pete, stronger and more athletic, is the Second Investigator. Bob is in charge of research and records. Boys who like the Hardy Boys will find more depth and realism in the Three Investigators.

1. The Secret of Terror Castle (Arthur, Robert) ◆ 1964
2. The Mystery of the Stuttering Parrot (Arthur, Robert) ◆ 1964
3. The Mystery of the Whispering Mummy (Arthur, Robert) ◆ 1965
4. The Mystery of the Green Ghost (Arthur, Robert) ◆ 1965
5. The Mystery of the Vanishing Treasure (Arthur, Robert) ◆ 1966
6. The Secret of Skeleton Island (Arthur, Robert) ◆ 1966
7. The Mystery of the Fiery Eye (Arthur, Robert) ◆ 1967
8. The Mystery of the Silver Spider (Arthur, Robert) ◆ 1967
9. The Mystery of the Screaming Clock (Arthur, Robert) ◆ 1968
10. The Mystery of the Moaning Cave (Arden, William) ◆ 1968
11. The Mystery of the Talking Skull (Arthur, Robert) ◆ 1969
12. The Mystery of the Laughing Shadow (Arden, William) ◆ 1969
13. The Secret of the Crooked Cat (Arden, William) ◆ 1970
14. The Mystery of the Coughing Dragon (West, Nick) ◆ 1970
15. The Mystery of the Flaming Footprints (Carey, M. V.) ◆ 1971
16. The Mystery of the Nervous Lion (West, Nick) ◆ 1971
17. The Mystery of the Singing Serpent (Carey, M. V.) ◆ 1972
18. The Mystery of the Shrinking House (Arden, William) ◆ 1972
19. The Secret of Phantom Lake (Arden, William) ◆ 1973
20. The Mystery of Monster Mountain (Carey, M. V.) ◆ 1973
21. The Secret of the Haunted Mirror (Carey, M. V.) ◆ 1974
22. The Mystery of the Dead Man's Riddle (Arden, William) ◆ 1974

23. The Mystery of the Invisible Dog (Carey, M. V.) ◆ 1975
24. The Mystery of Death Trap Mine (Carey, M. V.) ◆ 1976
25. The Mystery of the Dancing Devil (Arden, William) ◆ 1976
26. The Mystery of the Headless Horse (Arden, William) ◆ 1977
27. The Mystery of the Magic Circle (Carey, M. V.) ◆ 1978
28. The Mystery of the Deadly Double (Arden, William) ◆ 1978
29. The Mystery of the Sinister Scarecrow (Carey, M. V.) ◆ 1979
30. The Secret of Shark Reef (Arden, William) ◆ 1979
31. The Mystery of the Scar-Faced Beggar (Carey, M. V.) ◆ 1981
32. The Mystery of the Blazing Cliffs (Carey, M. V.) ◆ 1981
33. The Mystery of the Purple Pirate (Arden, William) ◆ 1982
34. The Mystery of the Wandering Caveman (Carey, M. V.) ◆ 1982
35. The Mystery of the Kidnapped Whale (Brandel, Marc) ◆ 1983
36. The Mystery of the Missing Mermaid (Carey, M. V.) ◆ 1983
37. The Mystery of the Two-Toed Pigeon (Brandel, Marc) ◆ 1984
38. The Mystery of the Smashing Glass (Arden, William) ◆ 1984
39. The Mystery of the Trail of Terror (Carey, M. V.) ◆ 1984
40. The Mystery of the Rogues' Reunion (Brandel, Marc) ◆ 1985
41. The Mystery of the Creep-Show Crooks (Carey, M. V.) ◆ 1985
42. The Mystery of Wrecker's Rock (Arden, William) ◆ 1986
43. The Mystery of the Cranky Collector (Carey, M. V.) ◆ 1986
44. The Case of the Savage Statue (Carey, M. V.) ◆ 1987

THREE INVESTIGATORS CRIMEBUSTERS

1. Hot Wheels (Arden, William) ◆ 1989
2. Murder to Go (Stine, Megan, and H. William Stine) ◆ 1989
3. Rough Stuff (Stone, G. H.) ◆ 1989
4. Funny Business (McCay, William) ◆ 1989
5. An Ear for Danger (Brandel, Marc) ◆ 1989
6. Thriller Diller (Stine, Megan, and H. William Stine) ◆ 1989
7. Reel Trouble (Stone, G. H.) ◆ 1989
8. Shoot the Works (McCay, William) ◆ 1990
9. Foul Play (Lerangis, Peter) ◆ 1990
10. Long Shot (Stine, Megan, and H. William Stine) ◆ 1990
11. Fatal Error (Stone, G. H.) ◆ 1990

TIARA CLUB

French, Vivian

HarperTrophy ◆ **Grades 1–4** ◆ **A/R**

Fantasy

Six princesses are sharing the Rose Room in a dormitory at the Royal Palace Academy for the Preparation of Perfect Princesses. They will be learning magic, dealing with dragons, going to balls, and meeting fairy godmothers. As they study, they earn points and when they have enough, they enter the Tiara Club and move to Silver Towers for more training.

There is a secret word in each book that can be used on the Tiara Club Web site (www.tiaraclubbooks.com) to print out a poster. There are games to play, too. This series was originally published in England and there is also a U.K. Web site.

1. Princess Charlotte and the Birthday Ball ◆ 2007
2. Princess Katie and the Silver Pony ◆ 2007
3. Princess Daisy and the Dazzling Dragon ◆ 2007
4. Princess Alice and the Magical Mirror ◆ 2007
5. Princess Sophia and the Sparkling Surprise ◆ 2007
6. Princess Emily and the Substitute Fairy ◆ 2007

TIARA CLUB: THE TIARA CLUB AT PEARL PALACE

French, Vivian

HARPERTROPHY ◆ GRADES 1–4

FANTASY

More princess adventures with games and activities on the Web site www.tiaraclubbooks.com. This series is being released in 2008–2009.

1. Princess Hannah and the Little Black Kitten ◆ 2008
2. Princess Isabella and the Snow-White Unicorn ◆ 2009
3. Princess Lucy and the Runaway Puppy ◆ 2009
4. Princess Grace and the Golden Nightingale ◆ 2009

TIARA CLUB: THE TIARA CLUB AT RUBY MANSION

French, Vivian

HARPERTROPHY ◆ GRADES 1–4 ◆ A/R

FANTASY

These princesses are in the Poppy Room at the Ruby Mansion. Princess Chloe wants to go to the Ruby Mansion Ball. Princess Jessica wants to make something special for her friends. Then, there is Princess Diamonde and Princess Gruella who try to spoil everything. Find the secret word and visit the Web site to get an activity.

1. Princess Chloe and the Primrose Petticoats ◆ 2007
2. Princess Jessica and the Best-Friend Bracelet ◆ 2008
3. Princess Georgia and the Shimmering Pearl ◆ 2008
4. Princess Olivia and the Velvet Cape ◆ 2008
5. Princess Lauren and the Diamond Necklace ◆ 2008
6. Princess Amy and the Forgetting Dust ◆ 2008

TIARA CLUB: THE TIARA CLUB AT SILVER TOWERS

French, Vivian

HARPERTROPHY ◆ **GRADES 1–4** ◆ **A/R**

FANTASY

These books continue the adventures of Charlotte, Katie, Daisy, Alice, Sophia, and Emily. They have left the Rose Room and are together again at Silver Towers. They are working to earn their silver sash and go to the Silver Ball. The www.tiaraclubbooks.com Web site cited leads to games and activities for these books, including the entry for the secret words and printable posters.

1. Princess Charlotte and the Enchanted Rose ◆ 2007
2. Princess Katie and the Mixed-Up Potion ◆ 2007
3. Princess Daisy and the Magical Merry-Go-Round ◆ 2007
4. Princess Alice and the Glass Slipper ◆ 2007
5. Princess Sophia and the Prince's Party ◆ 2007
6. Princess Emily and the Wishing Star ◆ 2007

TIGER MOTH

Reynolds, Aaron

STONE ARCH ◆ **GRADES 2–5** ◆ **A/R**

FANTASY | MYSTERY

Tiger Moth solves mysteries and fights crime. With his side kick, Kung Pow (a pillbug), Tiger investigates fortune cookie messages, missing dung beetles, and a stolen painting. Colorful art by Erik Lervold provides sequential action visuals for reluctant readers.

1. Tiger Moth and the Dragon Kite Contest ◆ 2006
2. The Dung Beetle Bandits ◆ 2007
3. Tiger Moth, Insect Ninja ◆ 2007
4. The Fortune Cookies of Weevil ◆ 2007
5. Kung Pow Chicken ◆ 2008

TILLERMAN CYCLE

Voigt, Cynthia

ATHENEUM ◆ **GRADES 5–8** ◆ **A/R**

FAMILY LIFE

Two of the books in this outstanding series have won awards: *Dicey's Song,* a Newbery, and *A Solitary Blue,* a Newbery Honor. In *Homecom-*

ing, the four Tillerman children are abandoned by their mother, and it is up to 13-year-old Dicey to get them safely to their grandmother's house, far away on Chesapeake Bay. *Dicey's Song* continues the story, with their adjustment to living with Gram. The rest of the titles are continuations of the story and companion titles about other people with whom the Tillermans come in contact.

1. Homecoming ◆ 1981
2. Dicey's Song ◆ 1982
3. A Solitary Blue ◆ 1983
4. The Runner ◆ 1985
5. Come a Stranger ◆ 1986
6. Sons from Afar ◆ 1987
7. Seventeen Against the Dealer ◆ 1989

TIME FANTASY SERIES

L'Engle, Madeleine

FARRAR, STRAUS & GIROUX; DELL ◆ GRADES 4–8 ◆ A/R

ADVENTURE | FANTASY

The four books in this fantasy series feature different members of the Murry family in the classic struggle between good and evil in the universe. *A Wrinkle in Time,* which won the Newbery Medal, chronicles Meg Murry's efforts to find her father, overcome the forces of darkness that are threatening the Earth, and recognize her own limitations and strengths. In doing these things, Meg, her brother Charles Wallace, and a friend, Calvin, travel through space and time to rescue Mr. Murry from the evil It. Later books focus on different members of the family as the struggle continues. Readers will be challenged by the intricate plot devices, including time travel and elements of classic literary tales. In all the books, there are complex issues of values, beliefs, and a connection with spiritual powers in the battle against cruelty, injustice, and intolerance.

1. A Wrinkle in Time ◆ 1962
2. A Wind in the Door ◆ 1973
3. A Swiftly Tilting Planet ◆ 1978
4. Many Waters ◆ 1986

TIME NAVIGATORS

Morris, Gilbert

BETHANY ◆ GRADES 4–6 ◆ A/R

FANTASY | VALUES

Fourteen-year-old twins Danny and Dixie Fortune travel through time having adventures. They appear on the *Mayflower,* meet George Washington during the French and Indian Wars, and visit Valley Forge during the Revolutionary War.

1. The Dangerous Voyage ◆ 1995
2. Vanishing Clues ◆ 1996
3. Race Against Time ◆ 1997

TIME SOLDIERS

Duey, Kathleen

BIG GUY BOOKS ◆ GRADES 3–5 ◆ A/R

FANTASY

Six friends become time soldiers traveling through a secret portal. Their adventures take them to encounters with dinosaurs, a pirate rescue, and the age of Camelot. Color photographs and digital illustrations extend the stories.

1. Rex ◆ 2002
2. Rex 2 ◆ 2002
3. Patch ◆ 2002
4. Arthur ◆ 2004
5. Mummy ◆ 2005
6. Samurai ◆ 2006
7. Pony Express ◆ 2008

TIME SPIES

Ransom, Candice

WIZARDS OF THE COAST ◆ GRADES 2–4 ◆ A/R

FANTASY | ADVENTURE

Like the Magic Tree House series, these books feature children who time-travel to events in history and literature. Alex and his sisters Mattie and Sophie touch a magic spyglass and are transported into adventures. They meet Houdini, see Seabiscuit race, and even visit a fairy-tale world.

1. Secret in the Tower ◆ 2006
2. Bones in the Badlands ◆ 2006
3. Giant in the Garden ◆ 2007
4. Magician in the Trunk ◆ 2007
5. Signals in the Sky ◆ 2007
6. Rider in the Night: A Tale of Sleepy Hollow ◆ 2007
7. Horses in the Wind: A Tale of Seabiscuit ◆ 2007
8. Gold in the Hills: A Tale of the Klondike Gold Rush ◆ 2008
9. Message in the Mountain ◆ 2008
10. Flames in the City: A Tale of the War of 1812 ◆ 2008

TIME SURFERS

Abbott, Tony

BANTAM DOUBLEDAY DELL ◆ GRADES 4–6 ◆ A/R

ADVENTURE | FANTASY

Since Ned Banks and his family moved to Lakewood, Ohio, strange things have been happening. Ned has become a Time Surfer, moving through time, making friends, and encountering strange creatures. In one book, Ned and his friend Ernie Somers must undo the work of Vorg, the evil master of time. In another book, Ned and Julie Tate must recover the stolen space shuttle and rescue Julie's father, Dr. Tate, a famous space scientist. There is plenty of action and enough weird creatures to interest fans of futuristic fantasies.

1. Space Bingo ◆ 1996
2. Orbit Wipeout! ◆ 1996
3. Mondo Meltdown ◆ 1996
4. Into the Zonk Zone! ◆ 1996
5. Splash Crash! ◆ 1997
6. Zero Hour ◆ 1997
7. Shock Wave ◆ 1997
8. Doom Star ◆ 1997

TIME TRAVEL MYSTERIES

Reiss, Kathryn

HARCOURT ◆ GRADES 5–9 ◆ A/R

MYSTERY

In *Dreadful Sorry* teenager Molly Teague is haunted by visions of a girl who disappeared more than 80 years ago. Molly hopes to escape the dreams by visiting her father and new stepmother in Maine. Instead, the dreams become even more vivid. What do they mean? Who is Clementine? And what does Molly's boyfriend have to do with the mystery? Other books in the series feature different characters in mysterious time travel situations.

1. Time Windows ◆ 1991
2. Dreadful Sorry ◆ 1993
3. Pale Phoenix ◆ 1994
4. PaperQuake ◆ 1998
5. Paint By Magic ◆ 2002

THE TIME TRAVELERS *see* Gideon the Cutpurse

TIME TRILOGY

Anderson, Margaret J.
KNOPF ◆ GRADES 5–8
FANTASY

In this science fantasy trilogy, Jennifer and Robert discover that they can slip through the Circle of Stones and travel through time to the year 2179. There they come upon a peaceful society trying to protect itself from a barbaric mechanized society. As the trilogy progresses, these people who refuse to meet violence with violence struggle to protect their community.

1. In the Keep of Time ◆ 1977
2. In the Circle of Time ◆ 1979
3. The Mists of Time ◆ 1984

TIME WARP TRIO

Scieszka, Jon
PENGUIN; HARPERCOLLINS ◆ GRADES 3–6 ◆ A/R
HUMOR | SCIENCE FICTION

Joe's uncle gives him a book for his birthday that is really a time machine. It envelops Joe and his friends Sam and Fred in a green fog, twists them out of shape, and lands them in any time they ask for. The book is always present somewhere in the time they are in, and they must find it before they can go home. Slapstick humor combines with historical information supplied by Sam, the brains of the group. Lane Smith's drawings capture the hapless trio's expressions of disgust at the situations they find themselves in as they travel to the Middle Ages, Ancient Egypt, and the American West. A highly entertaining series. The humor and length of the books are perfect for intermediate readers.

1. Knights of the Kitchen Table ◆ 1991
2. The Not-So-Jolly Roger ◆ 1991
3. The Good, the Bad and the Goofy ◆ 1992
4. Your Mother Was a Neanderthal ◆ 1993
5. 2095 ◆ 1995
6. Tut Tut ◆ 1996
7. Summer Reading Is Killing Me ◆ 1998
8. It's All Greek to Me ◆ 1999
9. See You Later, Gladiator ◆ 2000
10. Sam Samurai ◆ 2001
11. Hey Kid, Want to Buy a Bridge? ◆ 2002
12. Viking It and Liking It ◆ 2002
13. Me Oh Maya! ◆ 2003

14. Da Wild, Da Crazy, Da Vinci ◆ 2004
15. Oh Say, I Can't See ◆ 2005
16. Marco? Polo! ◆ 2006

I CAN READ BOOKS (HARPERCOLLINS; GRADES 1–3)

1. South Pole or Bust (an Egg) ◆ 2007
2. The High and the Flighty ◆ 2007

TIME WARP TRIO GRAPHIC NOVELS

Scieszka, Jon

HARPERTROPHY ◆ GRADES 3–6 ◆ A/R

HUMOR | SCIENCE FICTION

The popular Time Warp Trio books have become a television series. These graphic novels are adapted from episodes of the television shows. In the first book, the boys travel to 1816 where Frankenstein's monster is loose and he's looking for Mary Shelley, the author of the original book. In the second book, the boys are in Babylon facing the evil sun god. With numerous illustrations (from the television cartoons), this should appeal to reluctant readers.

1. Nightmare on Joe's Street ◆ 2006
2. The Seven Blunders of the World ◆ 2006
3. Plaid to the Bone ◆ 2007
4. Meet You at Waterloo ◆ 2007

TIME WARP TRIO (NOVELIZATIONS)

Scieszka, Jon

HARPERTROPHY ◆ GRADES 3–6 ◆ A/R

HUMOR | SCIENCE FICTION

Here's another permutation of the Time Warp Trio that evolved from the television show. Genghis Khan, Lewis and Clark, and a trip to ancient China are the focal elements of these books. Black-and-white illustrations (not by Lane Smith, as in most of the original TWT books) add to the presentation. There are numerous illustrations but this is not a graphic novel series.

1. You Can't, but Genghis Khan ◆ 2006
2. Lewis and Clark . . . and Jodie, Freddi, and Samantha ◆ 2006
3. Wushu Were Here ◆ 2007

TimeJumpers

Valentine, James

ALADDIN ◆ GRADES 5–8

FANTASY

Theo lives way in the future. When his TimeMaster JumpMan Pro mal-functions, he is stranded in the 21st century. Gen and Jules are in high school; Theo's appearance interrupts a tender moment between them. Theo has broken the first rule of TimeJumping by interfering with the past. Can these three teens find a way to return Theo to his own time? Originally published as Jumpman.

1. The Past Is Gone ◆ 2007
2. The Present Never Happens ◆ 2007
3. The Future Is Unknown ◆ 2007

Tiny

Meister, Cari

VIKING ◆ GRADES K–2 ◆ A/R

ANIMAL FANTASY | HUMOR

Tiny is a dog who once was small enough to fit in a shoe. But, like Clifford, he grew. These easy-readers describe some of his activities, such as getting a bath and playing in the snow. *Tiny on the Farm* (2008) is a picture book featuring the same character as these easy readers.

1. Tiny's Bath ◆ 1998
2. When Tiny Was Tiny ◆ 1999
3. Tiny Goes to the Library ◆ 2000
4. Tiny the Snow Dog ◆ 2001
5. Tiny Goes Camping ◆ 2004

Titch

Hutchins, Pat

GREENWILLOW ◆ GRADES K–2 ◆ A/R

FAMILY LIFE

Titch is the youngest in his family. This loving series chronicles the typical life of a youngest child: getting hand-me-down clothes, cleaning his room, feeling small, and playing with friends. The illustrations are delightful.

1. Titch ◆ 1972

2. You'll Soon Grow into Them, Titch ◆ 1983
3. Tidy Titch ◆ 1991
4. Titch and Daisy ◆ 1996

TJ BARNES

Hutchins, H. J.

ORCA ◆ GRADES 3–4 ◆ A/R

REAL LIFE

While his grandmother is on vacation, TJ Barnes agrees to watch her cats even though he does not like cats. When the cats create chaos, TJ decides to learn more about cats. His research leads him to develop an appreciation and even some affection for the animals. TJ is a likeable character. Middle-grade readers looking for easy chapter books like Ready, Freddy and Horrible Harry would enjoy this series.

1. TJ and the Cats ◆ 2002
2. TJ and the Haunted House ◆ 2003
3. TJ and the Rockets ◆ 2004
4. TJ and the Sports Fanatic ◆ 2006
5. TJ and the Quiz Kids ◆ 2007

TOAD RAGE

Gleitzman, Morris

RANDOM HOUSE ◆ GRADES 3–6 ◆ A/R

HUMOR

Humans hate cane toads and Limpy (a toad) wants to know why. Along with his cousin Goliath, Limpy begins a journey to the Olympics to change everyone's perception of toads. In the second book, Limpy looks for a place to be safe from humans. In *Toad Away,* he travels to the Amazon. Originally published in Australia, readers could be challenged by the Australian lingo but they should enjoy the slapstick humor of these books.

1. Toad Rage ◆ 2004
2. Toad Heaven ◆ 2005
3. Toad Away ◆ 2006

TOBY

Steig, William

HARPERCOLLINS ◆ GRADES K–2 ◆ A/R

ANIMAL FANTASY

In these imaginative picture books, Toby, a furry weasel-like creature, pretends to be a variety of objects. He is a clever creature who makes creative choices about who, what, and where. Children will enjoy guessing Toby's actions. Teryl Euvremer's soft illustrations are perfect for these books.

1. Toby, Where Are You? ◆ 2001
2. Toby, What Are You? ◆ 2001
3. Toby, Who Are You? ◆ 2004

TOM AND PIPPO

Oxenbury, Helen
CANDLEWICK ◆ GRADES K–1
FAMILY LIFE

A very small boy and his little monkey have small adventures that prove Tom's loyalty to his stuffed friend, Pippo. Pippo plays in the mud, gets dirty, and has to go in the washing machine. Tom hugs him because he's afraid he'll never see him again. Tom yearns to do everything that the older people do. When his father gets tired of reading books, Tom reads to Pippo. Tom and Pippo go to the beach with Tom's father, who insists that Tom wear a hat. Tom says that Pippo needs to wear a hat, too, and makes him one out of newspaper. The books in this series have minimal text with a black-and-white drawing on one side of a spread and a charming full-color illustration on the other.

1. Tom and Pippo Go Shopping ◆ 1988
2. Tom and Pippo's Day ◆ 1988
3. Tom and Pippo in the Garden ◆ 1988
4. Tom and Pippo Go for a Walk ◆ 1988
5. Tom and Pippo Make a Mess ◆ 1988
6. Tom and Pippo Read a Story ◆ 1988
7. Tom and Pippo See the Moon ◆ 1988
8. Tom and Pippo and the Washing Machine ◆ 1988
9. Pippo Gets Lost ◆ 1989
10. Tom and Pippo and the Dog ◆ 1989
11. Tom and Pippo in the Snow ◆ 1989
12. Tom and Pippo Make a Friend ◆ 1989
13. Tom and Pippo on the Beach ◆ 1993
14. Tom and Pippo and the Bicycle ◆ 1994

TOM SWIFT YOUNG INVENTOR

Appleton, Victor
ALADDIN ◆ GRADES 5–9 ◆ A/R
ADVENTURE | FANTASY

Updated scenarios and fast action will introduce new readers to the exploits of Tom Swift. In *Into the Abyss,* Tom's father is testing his underwater exploration vehicle but becomes lost during a storm. It is up to Tom to rescue him. In *The Robot Olympics,* an anti-science group threatens to disrupt a national science competition. Tom's sister, Sandy, figures in some of the adventures, including *The Space Hotel,* in which the two investigate a mysterious disappearance.

1. Into the Abyss ◆ 2006
2. The Robot Olympics ◆ 2006
3. The Space Hotel ◆ 2006
4. Rocket Racers ◆ 2007
5. On Top of the World ◆ 2007
6. Under the Radar ◆ 2007

TOOT AND PUDDLE

Hobbie, Holly

LITTLE, BROWN ◆ GRADES K–1 ◆ A/R

ANIMAL FANTASY

Toot and Puddle, both pigs, are best friends. In the first book, Toot goes on an adventurous trip around the world while Puddle is happy at home in Woodcock Pocket. In other books, everyday experiences are celebrated, like birthdays, visits, and holidays. These are sweet stories featuring two friends who really look out for each other. Other pig books like Poppleton or friendship stories like Mole and Mouse could be shared along with these books.

1. Toot & Puddle ◆ 1997
2. A Present for Toot ◆ 1998
3. You Are My Sunshine ◆ 1999
4. Puddle's ABC ◆ 2000
5. I'll Be Home for Christmas ◆ 2001
6. Top of the World ◆ 2002
7. Charming Opal ◆ 2003
8. The New Friend ◆ 2004
9. Wish You Were Here ◆ 2005
10. The One and Only ◆ 2006
11. Let It Snow ◆ 2007

TOPAZ

Bailey, Helen

HODDER ◆ GRADES 3–5

REAL LIFE

Topaz has been accepted at the Precious Gems Stage School. As she adjusts to the school, she makes new friends including Sapphire and Ruby. All of the girls have problems to overcome, for example, Ruby has stage fright while Sapphire wants attention from her movie-star mother. Topaz is insecure about her performances and she is reassured by her success at school. In *Topaz Takes a Break,* Topaz enters a talent contest while on vacation. Of course, her nemesis Octavia (who attends a rival theater school) is there and enters the contest, too.

1. Topaz Steals the Show ◆ 2007
2. Topaz Takes a Chance ◆ 2007
3. Topaz in the Limelight ◆ 2007
4. Topaz Takes a Break ◆ 2007
5. Topaz on Ice ◆ 2008
6. Topaz Takes the Stage ◆ 2008

TOTALLY SPIES!

Various authors

SIMON SPOTLIGHT ◆ GRADES 3–5 ◆ A/R

ADVENTURE

Fans of the Cartoon Network television series will enjoy reading the various book presentations of Totally Spies. Three teenaged girls—Sam, Alex, and Clover—live in Beverly Hills, California. They seem like ordinary teens but they are really spies for WHOOP (the World Organization of Human Protection). There are exotic locations and lots of action as the teens fight international crime.

1. Top-Secret Handbook (Wax, Wendy) ◆ 2005
2. Fashion Headquarters (Willson, Sarah) ◆ 2005
3. Mystery Messages (Willson, Sarah) ◆ 2006
4. The Code Caper (West, Tracey) ◆ 2006

TOKYOPOP CINE-MANGA (TOKYOPOP)

1. Spies in Disguise (Mayer, Ian) ◆ 2004
2. Spies vs. Spy (Lamoreaux, Michelle) ◆ 2005
3. Trouble in the Tropics (Stein, Erin) ◆ 2005
4. Time Spies When You're Having Fun (Stein, Erin) ◆ 2005
5. The Case of the Blob (Berry, Stephane) ◆ 2004

TOTALLY SPIES! CHAPTER BOOKS (SIMON SPOTLIGHT)

1. Getaway (Fulani, K. T.) ◆ 2005
2. The School of Mandy (Cerasini, Marc) ◆ 2005
3. Valentine Villains (Willson, Sarah) ◆ 2005
4. First Brat (Larsen, Kirsten) ◆ 2006
5. Scrambled Brains! (West, Tracey) ◆ 2006

TOTALLY SPIES! GRAPHIC NOVELS (PAPERCUTZ)

1. The O.P. ◆ 2006
2. I Hate the 80s ◆ 2006
3. Evil Jerry ◆ 2006
4. Spies in Space ◆ 2007
5. Mani-Maniac ◆ 2007

TOTALLY SPIES! READY TO READ (SIMON SPOTLIGHT)

1. Dolls of Danger (Bergen, Lara) ◆ 2005
2. The Christmas Bandit (Bergen, Lara) ◆ 2005
3. Makeup Mayhem (Ostrow, Kim) ◆ 2006
4. Space Case (Larsen, Kirsten) ◆ 2006

TRAILBLAZERS

Jackson, Dave, and Neta Jackson
BETHANY HOUSE ◆ GRADES 4–7 ◆ A/R
HISTORICAL | VALUES

Christian heroes from every era of American history are featured in stories based on their lives. Each book focuses on an ordinary child whose life has been changed. A young slave girl is helped to escape by Harriet Tubman after hearing stories about this Moses who helped her people by following the Northern Star. A young orphan boy meets Peter Cartwright, one of the circuit-riding preachers, and is helped to find his mother, who was taken away by Indians. Celeste Key is a turn-of-the-century child whose family is harassed by the Ku Klux Klan. They move to Florida, and Celeste enters a school started by Mary McLeod Bethune. Each story is followed by information about the historical figure featured.

1. Kidnapped by River Rats: William and Catherine Booth ◆ 1991
2. The Queen's Smuggler: William Tyndale ◆ 1991
3. Spy for the Night Riders: Martin Luther ◆ 1992
4. The Hidden Jewel: Amy Carmichael ◆ 1992
5. Escape from the Slave Traders: David Livingston ◆ 1992
6. The Chimney Sweep's Ransom: John Wesley ◆ 1992
7. Imprisoned in the Golden City: Adoniram and Ann Judson ◆ 1993
8. The Bandit of Ashley Downs: George Mueller ◆ 1993
9. Shanghaied to China: Hudson Taylor ◆ 1993
10. Listen for the Whippoorwill: Harriet Tubman ◆ 1993
11. Attack in the Rye Grass: Narcissa and Marcus Whitman ◆ 1994
12. Trial by Poison: Mary Slessor ◆ 1994
13. Flight of the Fugitives: Gladys Aylward ◆ 1994
14. The Betrayer's Fortune: Menno Simons ◆ 1994
15. Abandoned on the Wild Frontier: Peter Cartwright ◆ 1995
16. Danger on the Flying Trapeze: Dwight L. Moody ◆ 1995
17. The Runaway's Revenge: John Newton ◆ 1995

18. The Thieves of Tyburn Square: Elizabeth Fry ◆ 1995
19. Quest for the Lost Prince: Samuel Morris ◆ 1996
20. The Warrior's Challenge: David Zeisberger ◆ 1996
21. The Drummer Boy's Battle: Florence Nightingale ◆ 1996
22. Traitor in the Tower: John Bunyan ◆ 1996
23. Defeat of the Ghost Riders: Mary Bethune ◆ 1997
24. The Fate of the Yellow Woodbee: Nate Saint ◆ 1997
25. The Gold Miner's Rescue: Sheldon Jackson ◆ 1998
26. The Mayflower Secret: Governor William Bradford ◆ 1998
27. Assassins in the Cathedral: Festo Kivengere ◆ 1999
28. Mask of the Wolf Boy: Jonathan and Rosalind Goforth ◆ 1999
29. Race for the Record: Joy Ridderhof ◆ 1999
30. Ambushed in Jaguar Swamp: Barbrooke Grubb ◆ 1999
31. The Forty-Acre Swindle: George Washington Carver ◆ 2000
32. Hostage on the Nighthawk: William Penn ◆ 2000
33. Journey to the End of the Earth: William Seymour ◆ 2000
34. Drawn by a China Moon: Lottie Moon ◆ 2000
35. Sinking the Dayspring: John G. Paton ◆ 2001
36. Roundup of the Street Rovers: Charles Loring Brace ◆ 2001
37. Blinded by the Shining Path: Romulo Saune ◆ 2002
38. Risking the Forbidden Game: Maude Cary ◆ 2002
39. Exiled to the Red River: Chief Spokane Garry ◆ 2003
40. Caught in the Rebel Camp: Frederick Douglass ◆ 2003

TRANSFORMERS ARMADA (READERS)

Donkin, Andrew

DK ◆ GRADES 1–3 ◆ A/R

FANTASY

Fans of the Transformers will enjoy these adventures. The Autobots are confronted by the Decepticons. The Transformers are struggling to defeat Unicron and achieve a victory over Megatron. There are many related products, including toys.

1. The Awakening ◆ 2003
2. The Quest ◆ 2003
3. The Uprising ◆ 2004
4. The Unicron Battles ◆ 2004

TREASURE PLANET

Various authors

RANDOM HOUSE ◆ GRADES K–2

ADVENTURE | FANTASY | SCIENCE FICTION

Based on the film from Disney, these books describe the intergalactic adventures of Jim Hawkins and his friends. This futuristic *Treasure Island* has aliens, cyborgs, and robots. There are coloring books and books with tattoos.

1. Pirates Attack! (Shealy, Dennis R.) ◆ 2002
2. Jim's Journal (Vitamina, Eduardo) ◆ 2002
3. Space Case (Yaged, Kim) ◆ 2002
4. Treasure Planet (Shealy, Dennis R.) ◆ 2002
5. Disney's Treasure Planet: The Junior Novelization (Thorpe, Kiki) ◆ 2002
6. Disney's Treasure Planet: A Read Aloud Storybook (Hapka, Cathy) ◆ 2002

TREEHORN

Heide, Florence Parry

HOLIDAY HOUSE; DELL ◆ **GRADES 3–6**
FANTASY | HUMOR

Treehorn has all kinds of mysterious adventures while his parents remain completely oblivious. His mother is concerned only with luncheons and decorating, his father with work and the money his mother is spending. Meanwhile, young Treehorn is shrinking, finding a money tree, and meeting a genie. A black-and-white drawing facing each page of text emphasizes the bland reactions of Treehorn and his parents to the fantastic things that happen to the boy. Adults will appreciate the humor as much as children will, making this great for family read-alouds.

1. The Shrinking of Treehorn ◆ 1971
2. Treehorn's Treasure ◆ 1981
3. Treehorn's Wish ◆ 1984
4. Treehorn Times Three ◆ 1991

TRICK BOOKS

Corbett, Scott

LITTLE, BROWN ◆ **GRADES 3–6** ◆ **A/R**
HUMOR

Kerby Maxwell, his dog Waldo, and his friend Fenton are always getting mixed up in strange situations. A dangerous chemistry set, a trip around the haunted house on Hangman's Knob, and a disappearing dog are just a few of the amazing things readers will find out about in this entertaining and humorous series.

1. The Lemonade Trick ◆ 1960

2. The Mailbox Trick ◆ 1961
3. The Disappearing Dog Trick ◆ 1963
4. The Limerick Trick ◆ 1964
5. The Baseball Trick ◆ 1965
6. The Turnabout Trick ◆ 1967
7. The Hairy Horror Trick ◆ 1969
8. The Hateful Plateful Trick ◆ 1971
9. The Home Run Trick ◆ 1973
10. The Hockey Trick ◆ 1974
11. The Black Mask Trick ◆ 1976
12. The Hangman's Ghost Trick ◆ 1977

TRIPLET TROUBLE

Dadey, Debbie, and Marcia Thornton Jones

SCHOLASTIC ◆ GRADES K–3 ◆ A/R

REAL LIFE

Sam lives four doors down from the Tucker triplets. Alex is his best friend, and she is fun to be with, but sometimes her ideas get everyone in trouble. Ashley is quiet, and Adam is very smart. Sometimes they quarrel and Sam is caught in the middle. When their second-grade class is promised a pizza party for good behavior, everyone in the class blames Alex for spoiling it by being noisy. She wants to have a cookie-making contest and ends up making an awful mess. Short, easy chapters and everyday situations make this series accessible to young readers.

1. Triplet Trouble and the Talent Show Mess ◆ 1995
2. Triplet Trouble and the Runaway Reindeer ◆ 1995
3. Triplet Trouble and the Red Heart Race ◆ 1996
4. Triplet Trouble and the Field Day Disaster ◆ 1996
5. Triplet Trouble and the Cookie Contest ◆ 1996
6. Triplet Trouble and the Pizza Party ◆ 1996
7. Triplet Trouble and the Bicycle Race ◆ 1997
8. Triplet Trouble and the Class Trip ◆ 1997

TRIPODS

Christopher, John

MACMILLAN ◆ GRADES 5–8 ◆ A/R

SCIENCE FICTION

Aliens have taken over the Earth, and every Earth boy receives a cap at age 13 so the aliens can control his thoughts. The aliens take the form of huge metal tripods, and no one knows if that is their real form or if they are just machines that aliens use. Will, Henry, and Jean Paul escape to the White Mountains and find a colony of free men. Jean Paul, Will, and a German boy named Fritz are sent on a mission to the city of the aliens to learn their ways, and Will barely escapes with his life. The aliens are completely defeated as a result of what Fritz and Will are able to learn. *When the Tripods Came* is a prequel to the series, and readers may want to read it first.

1. The White Mountains ◆ 1967
2. The City of Gold and Lead ◆ 1967
3. The Pool of Fire ◆ 1968
4. When the Tripods Came ◆ 1988

TROLL KING

Vornholt, John

ALADDIN ◆ GRADES 4–7 ◆ A/R

FANTASY

The land of Bonespittle is ruled by the evil sorcerer Stygius Rex. The lowly trolls are oppressed—forced to work as laborers. One troll, Rollo, tries to change the plight of the trolls by leading them in a rebellion. Ogres, fairies, elves, gnomes, and other creatures add to the excitement in this fantasy series.

1. The Troll King ◆ 2002
2. The Troll Queen ◆ 2003
3. The Troll Treasure ◆ 2003

TROLL TRILOGY

Langrish, Katherine

EOS ◆ GRADES 5–8 ◆ A/R

FANTASY

After the death of his father, Peer Ulfsson is taken to live with his despicable twin uncles, who plan to give Peer to the Troll King to serve as a slave to the king's son. Aided by Hilde, a farm girl who lives nearby, Peer outwits his uncles, sending them to the Troll kingdom instead. In *Troll Blood,* Peer and Hilde, whose relationship is developing beyond friendship, voyage on a haunted Viking ship to Vinland. Nordic mythology is woven into this series.

1. Troll Fell ◆ 2004
2. Troll Mill ◆ 2006
3. Troll Blood ◆ 2008

TROLL TROUBLE

MacDonald, Alan

BLOOMSBURY ◆ GRADES 3–6 ◆ A/R

HUMOR

What would you do if the Troll family moved in next door? They are huge, loud, and may even eat humans! At first, the Priddle family is apprehensive. Eventually, after many humorous misadventures, the families accept their differences and develop a friendship. In *Trolls United*, Ulrik Troll tries out for the soccer team. This British import is full of slapstick fun.

1. Trolls, Go Home! ◆ 2007
2. Trolls United ◆ 2007
3. Goat Pie ◆ 2007
4. Trolls on Vacation ◆ 2008

TROUBLE WITH

Freeman, Martha

HOLIDAY HOUSE ◆ GRADES 3–5 ◆ A/R

REAL LIFE | FAMILY LIFE

There are many challenges facing Holly, a third grader. Holly and her mother have moved into the apartment of William, Holly's mother's new husband. Holly misses her house and her friends; she cannot stand her stepfather's cats. As she struggles to cope, Holly is helped by an understanding teacher and by the love of her mother and stepfather. In *The Trouble with Twins*, Holly has 2-year-old twin brothers. Holly's helpfulness at a birthday party for the twins and their friends is nearly a disaster.

1. The Trouble with Cats ◆ 2000
2. The Trouble with Babies ◆ 2002
3. The Trouble with Twins ◆ 2007

THE TUCKET ADVENTURES

Paulsen, Gary

DELACORTE ◆ GRADES 5–8 ◆ A/R

ADVENTURE | HISTORICAL

Francis Tucket is 14 when this series begins. While heading west on the Oregon Trail, Francis is separated from his family and captured by Pawnees. He is aided by Mr. Grimes, who teaches him survival skills but also gives him a look at the violent ways of a frontiersman. Francis leaves Mr. Grimes and searches for his family only to encounter more ruthless outlaws. This is a gritty series that does not romanticize the difficulties of life on the frontier. With lots of action, this should appeal to boys and perhaps to reluctant readers.

1. Mr. Tucket ◆ 1994
2. Call Me Francis Tucket ◆ 1995
3. Tucket's Ride ◆ 1997
4. Tucket's Gold ◆ 1999
5. Tucket's Home ◆ 2000

TURTLE AND SNAKE

Spohn, Kate

VIKING ◆ GRADES K–2 ◆ A/R

ANIMAL FANTASY

Turtle and Snake are best friends. They enjoy a pizza party, camping, and celebrating holidays. With large print, white space, and a simple vocabulary, this series is a good choice for beginning readers.

1. Turtle and Snake at Work ◆ 1999
2. Turtle and Snake and the Christmas Tree ◆ 2000
3. Turtle and Snake Go Camping ◆ 2000
4. Turtle and Snake Fix It ◆ 2002
5. Turtle and Snake's Spooky Halloween ◆ 2002
6. Turtle and Snake's Day at the Beach ◆ 2003
7. Turtle and Snake's Valentine's Day ◆ 2003

TWELVE CANDLES CLUB

Schulte, Elaine L.

BETHANY HOUSE ◆ GRADES 4–6 ◆ A/R

REAL LIFE | VALUES

Four friends—Jess McColl, Becky Hamilton, Cara Hernandez, and Tricia Bennett—have formed a club. All four girls are 12 years old, so they are the Twelve Candles Club. Their activities include doing chores, such as baby-sitting, light housekeeping, and helping at parties. They become involved in different situations, such as a drug-smuggling mystery and the theft of some art work; and some of the books feature exotic locations, like a trip to Israel and a Caribbean cruise. The girls also deal with everyday concerns such as the arrival of new girls (including an African American girl and a girl whose heritage is Chinese) and changing family situations. These books often place the girls in situations where their faith is tested and their Christian values influence their decisions.

1. Becky's Brainstorm ◆ 1992
2. Jess and the Fireplug Caper ◆ 1992

3. Cara's Beach Party Diaster ◆ 1993
4. Tricia's Got T-R-O-U-B-L-E! ◆ 1993
5. Melanie and the Modeling Mess ◆ 1994
6. Bridesmaid Blues for Becky ◆ 1994
7. Double Trouble for Jess McColl! ◆ 1995
8. Cara and the Terrible Teeners ◆ 1995
9. Tricia and the Money Mystery ◆ 1996
10. Melanie and the Cruise Caper ◆ 1996
11. Lily Vanessa and the Pet Panic ◆ 1996
12. Becky's Secret Surprise ◆ 1997

26 FAIRMOUNT AVENUE

DePaola, Tomie
PUTNAM ◆ GRADES 1–3 ◆ A/R
FAMILY LIFE | REAL LIFE

Tomie dePaola reflects on events from his childhood in this delightful series. Readers learn about Tomie's move to the house on 26 Fairmount Avenue. The books follow his experiences at school, including how he walked out of kindergarten and went home. Tomie's love of art, music, and dance add to the entertainment. The first book was a Newbery Honor book. The last three books, in a subset known as The War Years, see young Tomie coping with the blackout, rationing, and other hardships and sadnesses of World War II.

1. 26 Fairmount Avenue ◆ 1999
2. Here We All Are ◆ 2000
3. On My Way ◆ 2001
4. What a Year ◆ 2002
5. Things Will Never Be the Same ◆ 2003
6. I'm Still Scared: The War Years ◆ 2006
7. Why? The War Years ◆ 2007

TWISTED JOURNEYS

Various authors
LERNER ◆ GRADES 4–8
HORROR | ADVENTURE

Like the Choose-Your-Own-Adventure books, this graphic novel series lets readers create their own stories. Popular topics including pirates, time travel, and zombies add to the appeal and could also attract reluctant readers.

1. Captured by Pirates (Fontes, Justine) ◆ 2007
2. Escape from Pyramid X (Jolley, Dan) ◆ 2007

3. Terror in Ghost Mansion (Storrie, Paul D.) ◆ 2007
4. The Treasure of Mount Fate (Limke, Jeff) ◆ 2007
5. Nightmare on Zombie Island (Storrie, Paul D.) ◆ 2008
6. The Time Travel Trap (Jolley, Dan) ◆ 2008
7. Vampire Hunt (Jolley, Dan) ◆ 2008
8. Alien Incident on Planet J (Jolley, Dan) ◆ 2008

TWO OF A KIND *see* Mary-Kate and Ashley: Two of a Kind

2099

Peel, John

SCHOLASTIC ◆ GRADES 5–8 ◆ A/R

SCIENCE FICTION

It is 2099 and 14-year-old Tristan Connor has been working to stop the dangerous actions of Devon, only to discover that Devon is his clone. With the help of a policewoman and an Underworld crook, Tristan must stop the doomsday virus that Devon has released. With cliff-hanging endings, the books do not stand alone. The action comes to a dramatic conclusion in *Firestorm*. Fans of futuristic novels and computers will enjoy the cyber-action.

1. Doomsday ◆ 1999
2. Betrayal ◆ 1999
3. Traitor ◆ 2000
4. Revolution ◆ 2000
5. Meltdown ◆ 2000
6. Firestorm ◆ 2000

TYCO BASS

Cameron, Eleanor

LITTLE, BROWN ◆ GRADES 4–6 ◆ A/R

SCIENCE FICTION

David answers a mysterious ad for a boy to build a spaceship. The ad was placed by Tyco Bass, a kind and scholarly person from a small planet near Earth. He senses that his people are in some kind of trouble and that David and Chuck can somehow help out, so he tells them to ask their parents if they can go on a trip to the planet. The boys are amazed when their parents agree. They solve the problem of the gentle mushroom people with the help of a chicken that they bring along. More comings and goings between Earth and the mushroom people, as well as the efforts of the boys to keep the planet a secret, keep the series going.

1. The Wonderful Flight to the Mushroom Planet ◆ 1954
2. Stowaway to the Mushroom Planet ◆ 1956
3. Mr. Bass's Planetoid ◆ 1958
4. A Mystery for Mr. Bass ◆ 1960
5. Time and Mr. Bass ◆ 1967

ULYSSES MOORE

Baccalario, Pierdomenico

SCHOLASTIC ◆ GRADES 4–6 ◆ A/R

ADVENTURE | MYSTERY

Ostensibly written by Ulysses Moore, a mysterious adventurer and explorer, this series features twins Jason and Julie, 11, and their friend Rick. The twins have moved from London to a mansion in the country that is filled with artifacts from around the world. They explore the corridors and tunnels and find a mysterious locked door. That door becomes their portal to adventures. Throughout each book there are riddles, puzzles, and clues that will keep the reader involved in the story.

1. The Door to Time ◆ 2006
2. The Long-Lost Map ◆ 2006
3. The House of Mirrors ◆ 2007
4. The Isle of Masks ◆ 2008

UNCLE STINKY *see* The Adventures of Uncle Stinky

UNDERCOVER GIRL

Harris, Christine

SCHOLASTIC ◆ GRADES 5–7 ◆ A/R

MYSTERY

Jesse Sharp is a kid, an orphan, and a spy. Trained by C2, a secret spy organization, Jesse goes undercover to solve mysteries and expose the bad guys. In one book, she thwarts a kidnapping; in another, she must find a bomb before it explodes. Along with the mysteries there are questions about the actual purpose of C2. Is it a legitimate spy agency or does it have a hidden agenda?

1. Secrets ◆ 2005
2. Fugitive ◆ 2006
3. Nightmare ◆ 2006

4. Danger ◆ 2007
5. Twisted ◆ 2007

THE UNDERLAND CHRONICLES

Collins, Suzanne

SCHOLASTIC ◆ GRADES 4–8 ◆ A/R

FANTASY

Gregor, 11, and his sister Boots, 2, enter the Underland and encounter unusual humans along with giant cockroaches, spiders, rats, and bats. Gregor discovers that the humans are captives and that one of them is his father. The second book follows Gregor's return to the Underland to fulfill a prophecy, and Gregor later battles a terrible plague, defends the residents of the Underland, and must confront his own dark side.

1. Gregor the Overlander ◆ 2003
2. Gregor and the Prophecy of Bane ◆ 2004
3. Gregor and the Curse of the Warmbloods ◆ 2005
4. Gregor and the Marks of Secret ◆ 2006
5. Gregor and the Code of Claw ◆ 2007

UNDERWHERE

Hale, Bruce

HARPERCOLLINS ◆ GRADES 4–7 ◆ A/R

HUMOR

Zeke discovers that there is a world under ours . . . a world where the creatures wear underwear outside their clothes. Along with his twin sister Stephanie and their neighbor Hector, Zeke enters Underwhere and is proclaimed the prince. Zeke used to be an ordinary kid. Now he faces zombies, pirates, sea serpents, and more. The book shifts from text to extended pages in a graphic novel format, which should appeal to many kids.

1. Prince of Underwhere ◆ 2008
2. Pirates of Underwhere ◆ 2008
3. Flyboy of Underwhere ◆ 2008

UNICORN CHRONICLES

Coville, Bruce

SCHOLASTIC ◆ GRADES 5–8 ◆ A/R

FANTASY

A magic amulet allows Cara Hunter to enter the land of Luster. Cara's grandmother gave her the amulet and a message for the unicorn Queen. In Luster, Cara is accompanied on her journey by Lightfoot, an adolescent unicorn. Along the way they face danger from delvers, dragons, and a woman named Beloved, who hates unicorns and seeks to destroy them.

1. Into the Land of the Unicorns ◆ 1994
2. Song of the Wanderer ◆ 1999
3. Dark Whispers ◆ 2008

UNICORN CLUB *see* Sweet Valley: Unicorn Club

UNICORNS OF BALINOR

Stanton, Mary

SCHOLASTIC ◆ GRADES 4–6 ◆ A/R

FANTASY

Balinor is in danger from the evil of the Shifter. The King and Queen of Balinor and two Royal Princesses have all been kidnapped by the Shifter. Only Princess Arianna is still free. The Unicorns of Balinor, led by Atalanta, join with Arianna to save the kingdom.

1. The Road to Balinor ◆ 1999
2. Sunchaser's Quest ◆ 1999
3. Valley of Fear ◆ 1999
4. By Fire, By Moonlight ◆ 1999
5. Search for the Star ◆ 1999
6. Secrets of the Scepter ◆ 2000
7. Night of the Shifter's Moon ◆ 2000
8. Shadows over Balinor ◆ 2000

THE UNICORN'S SECRET

Duey, Kathleen

ALADDIN ◆ GRADES 2–4 ◆ A/R

FANTASY

Heart Avamir is a foundling with no memory of her past. She lives in a feudal village and is befriended by Ruth, a woman who helps with herbs and medicines. Heart connects with her past when she cares for a wounded horse (that is really a unicorn). Thus begins her quest to find a safe haven for the unicorns and to find the truth about her origins.

1. Moon Silver ◆ 2001
2. The Silver Thread ◆ 2001
3. The Silver Bracelet ◆ 2002

4. The Mountains of the Moon ◆ 2002
5. The Sunset Gates ◆ 2002
6. True Heart ◆ 2003
7. Castle Avamir ◆ 2003
8. The Journey Home ◆ 2003

UNLIKELY EXPLOITS

Ardagh, Philip

HOLT ◆ GRADES 4–6 ◆ A/R

FANTASY

Like Lemony Snicket's Series of Unfortunate Events, this series has dark humor, comments to the reader, and plot twists. In *The Fall of Fergal,* Fergal McNally falls 14 stories to his death. In the second book, Fergal's preserved brain is missing and his siblings search for it. Readers learn about his family and their creepy activities. This was originally published in England and the third book is available there.

1. The Fall of Fergal: The First Unlikely Exploit, or Not So Dingly in the Dell ◆ 2004
2. Heir of Mystery: The Second Unlikely Exploit ◆ 2004
3. The Rise of the House of McNally ◆ 2004

UPCHUCK AND THE ROTTEN WILLY

Wallace, Bill

MINSTREL/POCKET ◆ GRADES 3–6 ◆ A/R

ANIMAL FANTASY

A rottweiler called Willy takes pity on a cat called Chuck, who is stuck up a tree, starting a close but unusual friendship. This is challenged in *Running Wild* when two new cats in town disparage the relationship, but old loyalties prevail.

1. Upchuck and the Rotten Willy ◆ 1998
2. The Great Escape ◆ 1998
3. Running Wild ◆ 2000

USAGI YOJIMBO

Sakai, Stan

FANTAGRAPHICS BOOKS; DARK HORSE ◆ GRADES 5–8

FANTASY

Usagi Yojimbo is a ronin—a samurai without a master. He is also a rabbit. Usagi wanders across feudal Japan sometimes serving as a bodyguard. His adventures follow Japanese traditions and incorporate many Japanese legends. The first seven books were published by Fantagraphics Books; there have been many editions and the dates reflect the dates on amazon.com for currently available books. Beginning with the eighth book, the publisher is Dark Horse.

1. The Ronin ◆ 1987
2. Circles ◆ 1996
3. Gen's Story ◆ 1997
4. Shades of Death ◆ 1997
5. The Dragon Bellow Conspiracy ◆ 1998
6. Daisho ◆ 1998
7. The Brink of Life and Death ◆ 1998
8. Seasons ◆ 1999
9. Grasscutter ◆ 1999
10. Grey Shadows ◆ 2000
11. Demon Mask ◆ 2001
12. Lone Goat and Kid ◆ 2001
13. Grasscutter II: Journey to Atsuta Shrine ◆ 2002
14. Samurai ◆ 2002
15. The Wanderer's Road ◆ 2002
16. The Shrouded Moon ◆ 2003
17. Duel at Kitanoji ◆ 2003
18. Travels with Jotaro ◆ 2004
19. Fathers and Sons ◆ 2005
20. Glimpses of Death ◆ 2006
21. The Mother of Mountains ◆ 2007

VERA

Rosenberry, Vera
HOLT ◆ GRADES K–2 ◆ A/R
REAL LIFE

Vera is a spunky girl who faces common problems as she grows up. She learns to ride a two-wheeler bike. She copes with being sick. She even runs away when her family is too busy to notice her excellent first-grade report card.

1. When Vera Was Sick ◆ 1998
2. Vera's First Day of School ◆ 1999
3. Vera Runs Away ◆ 2000
4. Vera Goes to the Dentist ◆ 2002
5. Vera Rides a Bike ◆ 2004

VERNON BRIGHT

Barlow, Steve, and Steve Skidmore

PUFFIN ◆ GRADES 4–6

HUMOR

In England, Vernon Bright is interested in anything that relates to science. Like his name, he is "bright." In the first book, Vernon finds a way to transfer magnetic energy to nonmagnetic items—including himself. In *Vernon Bright and the Faster Than Light Show,* Vernon causes problems when he is in charge of lighting for the school play. Fans of Einstein Anderson should enjoy these books.

1. Vernon Bright and the Magnetic Banana ◆ 2000
2. Vernon Bright and Frankenstein's Hamster ◆ 2000
3. Vernon Bright and the Faster Than Light Show ◆ 2004
4. Vernon Bright and the End of the World ◆ 2004

VERONICA

Robinson, Nancy K.

SCHOLASTIC ◆ GRADES 3–6 ◆ A/R

HUMOR

Readers will have great fun reading about Veronica's exploits. Though she doesn't quite lie, Veronica's exaggerations often get her into trouble. For instance, there's the time she meets an international chess champion and hints that she is an extremely gifted chess player. Or the Groundhog Salad she makes for her first luncheon party. These are entertaining reads for this age group.

1. Veronica the Show-Off ◆ 1984
2. Veronica Knows Best ◆ 1987
3. Veronica Meets Her Match ◆ 1990
4. Countess Veronica ◆ 1994

VERY WORST MONSTER

Hutchins, Pat

GREENWILLOW ◆ GRADES K–2 ◆ A/R

FANTASY | HUMOR

Hazel Monster must accept a new baby into her family. At first, she resents the way her parents dote on Billy, but she finds a way to gain their attention by being *The Very Worst Monster.* Subsequent adventures show Billy as a toddler, wreaking havoc on the house. He pesters Hazel and acts up in nursery school—earning stars for his bad behavior. The colorful illustrations capture the monstrous antics and add to the humor.

1. The Very Worst Monster ◆ 1985
2. Where's the Baby? ◆ 1988
3. Silly Billy ◆ 1992
4. Three-Star Billy ◆ 1994
5. It's MY Birthday! ◆ 1999

VESPER HOLLY

Alexander, Lloyd

DUTTON ◆ GRADES 5–7 ◆ A/R

ADVENTURE | HUMOR

Vesper is the teenage daughter of a deceased famous scholar and adventurer. Her father's best friend, Brinnie, and his wife, Mary, have become Vesper's guardians, and together they travel the world from one adventure to another. The evil Dr. Helvitius is their arch enemy, always coming up with some evil scheme against innocent people. In Central America, he is building a canal that will ruin the land of the Indian people. In Europe, he is planning for a small country to be annexed by its neighbors. Vesper and Brinnie are always one step ahead of him, with the help of various friends they collect along the way. Brinnie's pompous behavior supplies humor, while Vesper is an exciting heroine.

1. The Illyrian Adventure ◆ 1986
2. The El Dorado Adventure ◆ 1987
3. The Drackenberg Adventure ◆ 1988
4. The Jedera Adventure ◆ 1989
5. The Philadelphia Adventure ◆ 1990
6. The Xanadu Adventure ◆ 2005

VET VOLUNTEERS *see* Wild at Heart

VICKY AUSTIN

L'Engle, Madeleine

FARRAR, STRAUS & GIROUX; BANTAM DOUBLEDAY DELL ◆ GRADES 4–7 ◆ A/R

FAMILY LIFE | MYSTERY | REAL LIFE

In *Meet the Austins*, Vicky is 12 and her family is faced with taking in a spoiled orphan girl. The father, a country doctor, is offered a position in New York, where they become involved in an international plot. On a cross-country camping trip, they meet a spoiled rich boy who takes a liking to Vicky. The Austins spend summers in their grandfather's house on an island off the East Coast. Here Vicky befriends a boy who is doing research on dolphins and discovers that she has a real affinity for the animals. This series tackles issues of life and death, faith and cynicism, and shows a loving family dealing intelligently with problems. A simple Christmas story, *The Twenty-Four Days Before Christmas* (1964), is a prequel written on a much easier level than the rest of the series.

1. Meet the Austins ◆ 1960
2. The Moon by Night ◆ 1963
3. The Young Unicorns ◆ 1968
4. A Ring of Endless Light ◆ 1980
5. Troubling a Star ◆ 1994

VIKING MAGIC

Ciddor, Anna

ALLEN & UNWIN ◆ GRADES 4–6

FANTASY

Thora and Oddo were switched at birth and have come to realize that they do not belong. Thora is being trained as a spellmaker, but none of her spells work. Oddo has magical skills that he keeps hidden from the farm family that is raising him. The two children meet, become friends, and begin a series of adventures together. In *Stormriders,* Thora helps Dungal, an Irish boy who has been a prisoner of the Vikings. These books were originally published in Australia. There is an author Web site along with a site for viking-magic.com.

1. Runestone ◆ 2007
2. Wolfspell ◆ 2007
3. Stormriders ◆ 2007

VIKING QUEST

Johnson, Lois Walfrid

MOODY ◆ GRADES 5–8 ◆ A/R

HISTORICAL | VALUES

Set in Ireland and Norway in the 10th century, this series features Briana "Bree" O'Toole and her brother Devin. After being abducted by Vikings from their home in Ireland, the two are separated and face different challenges. Bree serves as a slave but manages to escape from her captors. The Viking leader, Mikkel, pursues her, believing she has also taken a bag of coins. Bree and Devin find courage and solace in their faith in God.

1. Raiders from the Sea ◆ 2003
2. Mystery of the Silver Coins ◆ 2003
3. The Invisible Friend ◆ 2004
4. Heart of Courage ◆ 2005
5. Raider's Promise ◆ 2006

VIRGINIA *see* My America: Virginia

VISITORS

Philbrick, Rodman, and Lynn Harnett
SCHOLASTIC ◆ GRADES 5–8 ◆ A/R
SCIENCE FICTION

When Nick and his twin sister Jessie investigate a strange glow above the hills, their lives are changed. Brain-stealing aliens have invaded Earth. With their friend Frasier, they try to destroy the aliens' energy source. When Jessie is captured by the aliens, Nick and Frasier must get help from another alien to save her.

1. Strange Invaders ◆ 1997
2. Things ◆ 1997
3. Brain Stealers ◆ 1997

VOYAGE OF THE BASSET

Various authors
RANDOM HOUSE ◆ GRADES 4–7 ◆ A/R
FANTASY

The Voyage of the Basset is a magical series for dreamers. In each book, children encounter opportunities to use their imaginations. In the first book, two children are transported from their home in Victorian England to a realm of fairies and beasts. There, Hope and Apollo are given tasks that involve centaurs and Pegasus. In another book, Thor's hammer has been stolen and the Basset is sent to find a human to help recover it. This series is based on an oversized, profusely illustrated fantasy *Voyage of the Basset* by James C. Christensen.

1. Islands in the Sky (Lee, Tanith) ◆ 1999
2. The Raven Queen (Windling, Terri, and Ellen Steiber) ◆ 1999
3. Journey to Otherwhere (Smith, Sherwood) ◆ 2000
4. Thor's Hammer (Shetterly, Will) ◆ 2000
5. Fire Bird (Zambreno, Mary Frances) ◆ 2001

VOYAGE TO THE BUNNY PLANET

Wells, Rosemary

DIAL ◆ GRADES K–2 ◆ A/R

ANIMAL FANTASY

Visiting the Bunny Planet provides a remedy for some very bad days. Robert has a terrible visit to his relative. Claire has a bad day at school. Nothing goes right for Felix. Each bunny receives warmth and love from the Bunny Queen Janet in these reassuring stories.

1. First Tomato: A Voyage to the Bunny Planet ◆ 1992
2. The Island Light: A Voyage to the Bunny Planet ◆ 1992
3. Moss Pillows: A Voyage to the Bunny Planet ◆ 1992

WALTER, THE FARTING DOG

Kotzwinkle, William, and Glenn Murray

DUTTON ◆ GRADES K–3

HUMOR

Yes, Walter has a problem. He is about to be returned to the pound when burglars break in and Walter's highly aromatic excesses prove very useful. He gets to stay. And his heroic exploits continue in more books that may well please young readers.

1. Walter the Farting Dog ◆ 2001
2. Walter the Farting Dog: Trouble at the Yard Sale ◆ 2004
3. Rough Weather Ahead for Walter the Farting Dog ◆ 2005
4. Walter the Farting Dog Goes on a Cruise ◆ 2006

WARRIORS

Hunter, Erin

HARPERCOLLINS ◆ GRADES 5–9 ◆ A/R

FANTASY

A house cat named Rusty has lived in comfort with Twolegs but leaves to enter the world of the wildcat clans. A world with four different clans— ThunderClan, ShadowClan, WindClan, and RiverClan. Rusty becomes an apprentice named Firepaw. After he proves himself, he beecomes a warrior cat in training named Fireheart. He begins a quest to be a true warrior.

1. Into the Wild ◆ 2003
2. Fire and Ice ◆ 2003
3. Forest of Secrets ◆ 2003

4. Rising Storm ◆ 2004
5. A Dangerous Path ◆ 2004
6. The Darkest Hour ◆ 2004

WARRIORS: POWER OF THREE

Hunter, Erin

HARPERCOLLINS ◆ GRADES 5–9 ◆ A/R

FANTASY

This series follows the events in Warriors: The New Prophecy. Three Thunderclan kits—Hollypaw, Jaypaw, and Lionpaw—are descendants of Firestar and each has a gift. There are dark days approaching and these three will be challenged to protect the future of the Clans. As they develop their talents they also confront their own demons and they go on a quest to the mountains, seeking to understand their destiny.

1. The Sight ◆ 2007
2. Dark River ◆ 2007
3. Outcast ◆ 2008
4. Eclipse ◆ 2008
5. Long Shadows ◆ 2008

WARRIORS: THE NEW PROPHECY

Hunter, Erin

HARPERCOLLINS ◆ GRADES 5–9 ◆ A/R

FANTASY

A new generation of feline warriors faces more challenges to the clans. Humans ("Twolegs") are destroying the habitats of the cats. Six cats, children of the original warriors, join together to save the clans, eventually realizing that salvation lies in finding a new home.

1. Midnight ◆ 2005
2. Moonrise ◆ 2005
3. Dawn ◆ 2006
4. Starlight ◆ 2006
5. Twilight ◆ 2006
6. Sunset ◆ 2007

WARTON AND MORTON

Erickson, Russell E.

LOTHROP, LEE & SHEPARD ◆ GRADES 2–4 ◆ A/R

ANIMAL FANTASY

Toad brothers Warton and Morton live happily together in a little hole under a stump. Morton loves to cook and is very good at it. Warton prefers to clean. On a beautiful day when Warton has just finished his spring cleaning, he persuades the less adventurous Morton to go on a camping trip. They are separated by a flash flood; and as Warton is looking for Morton he joins a group of muskrats. Meanwhile, Morton has joined the beavers, who are the muskrats' sworn enemies. When they meet, the toads clear up the misunderstandings between the two. Other adventures with the toads and their neighbors continue the series.

1. A Toad for Tuesday ◆ 1974
2. Warton and Morton ◆ 1976
3. Warton's Christmas Eve Adventure ◆ 1977
4. Warton and the King of the Skies ◆ 1978
5. Warton and the Traders ◆ 1979
6. Warton and the Castaways ◆ 1982
7. Warton and the Contest ◆ 1986

WATCHERS

Lerangis, Peter

SCHOLASTIC ◆ GRADES 5–8 ◆ A/R

FANTASY

Each book features a different character in a supernatural adventure. In *Last Stop,* David's father disappeared six months ago. While riding the subrail, David is surprised when the train makes an unexpected stop at an abandoned station. As David looks at the platform, he is convinced that he sees his father. In *Rewind,* Adam's video camera can rewind reality. The action is fast-paced and will hold the interest of reluctant readers.

1. Last Stop ◆ 1998
2. Rewind ◆ 1998
3. I. D. ◆ 1998
4. War ◆ 1999
5. Island ◆ 1999
6. Lab 6 ◆ 1999

WAYSIDE SCHOOL

Sachar, Louis

MORROW ◆ GRADES 3–6 ◆ A/R

FANTASY | HUMOR

When Wayside School was constructed, the builders made a mistake and built it 30 stories straight up instead of 30 rooms on one level. That's why the school is so strange, as the two- or three-page stories in each book attest. Mrs. Gorf is the meanest teacher in the school. She turns all the children into apples until they figure out the trick. Then they turn her into an apple. The children on the 30th floor get Mrs. Jewls for a teacher, and she is terribly nice. The rest of the Sideways Stories are about her funny, bizarre interactions with her class. The same format of very short stories is used throughout, except for the arithmetic books.

1. Sideways Stories from Wayside School ◆ 1985
2. Sideways Arithmetic from Wayside School ◆ 1989
3. Wayside School Is Falling Down ◆ 1990
4. More Sideways Arithmetic from Wayside School ◆ 1994
5. Wayside School Gets a Little Stranger ◆ 1995

WEATHER FAIRIES *see* Rainbow Magic: Weather Fairies

THE WEDDING PLANNER'S DAUGHTER

Paratore, Coleen Murtagh
SIMON & SCHUSTER ◆ GRADES 5–9 ◆ A/R
REAL LIFE | FAMILY LIFE

Willa Havisham's mother is a wedding planner and, for now, the two of them are living in Cape Cod with Willa's grandmother. In the first book, Willa is 12. She wants to stay in one place, make friends, and lead a normal tween/teen life. With her mom dating her English teacher, Willa may just get her wish. As the series progresses, Willa's mother remarries and becomes pregnant. Willa grows up, too—she is 14 in the third book. Her interests and issues change as she deals with her mother's miscarriage and her own disappointments and achievements. Willa loves to read and there are quotes and comments about books throughout the series.

1. The Wedding Planner's Daughter ◆ 2005
2. The Cupid Chronicles ◆ 2006
3. Willa by Heart ◆ 2008

THE WEEBIE ZONE

Spinner, Stephanie, and Ellen Weiss
HARPERCOLLINS ◆ GRADES 3–5 ◆ A/R
FANTASY | HUMOR

After being bitten by his gerbil Weebie, Garth finds that he can understand animals. Of course, Weebie has lots to tell him, and so do other pets. His aunt's dog, Elvis, wants to sing; a bunny is upset and runs away; a talking bird helps with a mean substitute teacher. In one book, Weebie is lost in Texas and must find his own way back to Garth. This is a fun series that will appeal to readers who like silly characters in incongruous situations.

1. Gerbilitis ◆ 1996
2. Sing, Elvis, Sing ◆ 1996
3. Born to Be Wild ◆ 1997
4. Bright Lights, Little Gerbil ◆ 1997
5. The Bird Is the Word ◆ 1997
6. We're Off to See the Lizard ◆ 1998

WEIRD PLANET

Greenburg, Dan

RANDOM HOUSE ◆ GRADES 2–4 ◆ A/R

SCIENCE FICTION | HUMOR

When Klatu and his siblings crash their spaceship in the Nevada desert, the slapstick adventures begin. Ploo (Klatu's sister) is captured by the army and it is up to Klatu and his brother Lek to rescue her. Eventually the aliens arrive in Hollywood where they appear as extras in a science fiction television show. The humor, short sentences, and fast pace will appeal to reluctant readers.

1. Dude, Where's My Spaceship? ◆ 2006
2. Lost in Las Vegas ◆ 2006
3. Chilling with the Great Ones ◆ 2006
4. Attack of the Evil Elvises ◆ 2007
5. Lights, Camera . . . Liftoff! ◆ 2007
6. Thrills, Spills, and Cosmic Chills ◆ 2008

THE WEIRD ZONE

Abbott, Tony

SCHOLASTIC ◆ GRADES 3–5

HUMOR

What makes Grover's Mill the Weird Zone? For one thing, there is a secret U.F.O. government test base there—not to mention a dinosaur graveyard and the Humongous Horror Movie Studios. These three elements make for some weird happenings. Liz Duffey, Mike Mazur, Jeff Ryan, Holly Vickers, and Sean Vickers attend W. Reid Elementary School, where they discover a beast beneath the cafeteria and conduct unusual science projects. They encounter alien mole invaders and commandos from Mars. Mixed in with the traditional horror elements are moments of humor as the kids also cope with strange adults like Principal

Bell and his assistant, Miss Lieberman. This is a fun series for upper elementary school readers.

1. Zombie Surf Commandos from Mars! ◆ 1996
2. The Incredible Shrinking Kid! ◆ 1996
3. The Beast from Beneath the Cafeteria! ◆ 1996
4. Attack of the Alien Mole Invaders! ◆ 1996
5. The Brain That Wouldn't Obey! ◆ 1997
6. Gigantopus from Planet X! ◆ 1997
7. Cosmic Boy Versus Mezmo Head ◆ 1997
8. Revenge of the Tiki Men! ◆ 1997

WEREWOLF CHRONICLES

Philbrick, W. Rodman, and Lynn Harnett
SCHOLASTIC ◆ GRADES 5–8

HORROR

Fox Hollow looks like an ordinary town, but there is something very frightening in the woods. Only the wolf-boy knows the secret, and only he can save the town. The wolf-boy, who is later called Gruff, was raised by wolves, who protected him and fed him after he was abandoned. Now a danger has entered the woods: the werewolves. They want Gruff to join them, and, even though he tries to resist, their powers are beginning to affect him. His efforts to keep Fox Hollow from the werewolves put him into even more danger. Gruff may be able to save the town only by becoming a werewolf himself.

1. Night Creature ◆ 1996
2. Children of the Wolf ◆ 1996
3. The Wereing ◆ 1996

WEREWOLF CLUB

Pinkwater, Daniel (Manus)
ATHENEUM ◆ GRADES 2–4 ◆ A/R

FANTASY | HUMOR

Norman Gnormal is not normal. He has strange urges to howl and his hair sprouts when the moon is full. Luckily, his principal recognizes his needs and signs him up for the Werewolf Club. The group has exciting and wacky adventures featuring plenty of play on words.

1. The Magic Pretzel ◆ 2000
2. The Lunchroom of Doom ◆ 2000
3. The Werewolf Club Meets Dorkula ◆ 2001
4. The Werewolf Club Meets the Hound of the Basketballs ◆ 2001
5. The Werewolf Club Meets Oliver Twit ◆ 2002

WEST CREEK MIDDLE SCHOOL *see* Losers, Inc.

WESTMARK

Alexander, Lloyd

BANTAM DOUBLEDAY DELL ◆ GRADES 5–7 ◆ A/R

ADVENTURE | FANTASY

This series is set in a world much like our own in the late Renaissance. Theo is a printer's helper who is embroiled in a revolt against a corrupt government. When his master is killed, he falls in with the scheming Count and with Mickle, a poor girl with an amazing talent for ventriloquism. They meet up with a group of revolutionaries led by the charismatic Florian, who wants to do away with the monarchy altogether. Mickle and Theo fall in love, and she is revealed to be the king's long-lost daughter. She and Theo plan to marry, and the next two books in this trilogy concern their struggles against enemies in and out of Westmark.

1. Westmark ◆ 1981
2. The Kestrel ◆ 1982
3. The Beggar Queen ◆ 1984

WICKED WITCH

Kraan, Hanna

FRONT STREET ◆ GRADES 2–5

FANTASY

The animals of the forest—including a hare, a hedgehog, and an owl—complain about their resident witch and the mischievous spells she casts, but at the same time they find that they do rely on her and would miss her if she left.

1. Tales of the Wicked Witch ◆ 1995
2. The Wicked Witch Is at it Again ◆ 1997
3. Flowers for the Wicked Witch ◆ 1998

WILD AT HEART

Anderson, Laurie Halse

PLEASANT COMPANY ◆ GRADES 4–7 ◆ A/R

REAL LIFE

Animal lovers will love this series. At the Wild at Heart Animal Clinic, animals are cared for and protected. Maggie, 13, lives with her grandmother who is a vet at the clinic. She resents having to train some new volunteers but she appreciates their help when animals are found in abusive situations. Issues such as animal testing and cruelty to pets are explored. In 2007 and 2008, this series was being re-released with new covers under the series title Vet Volunteers.

1. Fight for Life: Book 1: Maggie ◆ 2000
2. Homeless: Book 2: Sunita ◆ 2000
3. Trickster: Book 3: David ◆ 2000
4. Manatee Blues: Book 4: Brenna ◆ 2000
5. Say Good-Bye: Book 5: Zoe ◆ 2001
6. Storm Rescue: Book 6: Sunita ◆ 2001
7. Teacher's Pet: Book 7: Maggie ◆ 2001
8. Trapped: Book 8: Brenna ◆ 2001
9. Fear of Falling: Book 9: David ◆ 2001
10. Time to Fly: Book 10: Zoe ◆ 2002
11. Masks: Book 11: Sunita ◆ 2002
12. End of the Race: Book 12: Maggie ◆ 2003

THE WILD THORNBERRYS

Various authors

SIMON & SCHUSTER; NICKELODEON ◆ GRADES K–5 ◆ A/R

ADVENTURE

The Wild Thornberrys family experiences many adventures in nature. Nigel and Marianne are the parents and they work on a television show called *Nigel Thornberry's Animal World*. Their daughter Eliza is often featured in the stories because, thanks to a magic spell, she has the ability to talk to animals. Donnie is a child who was found in the Congo and taken in by the Thornberry family. Darwin is their chimpanzee. These are popular characters from television and from a movie.

WILD THORNBERRYS READERS (K–2)

1. The Bird Who Cried Wolf (Richards, Kitty) ◆ 2000
2. Drawing the Line (Cherrington, Janelle) ◆ 2000
3. Snowbound (Thorpe, Kiki) ◆ 2000
4. In Too Deep (Richards, Kitty) ◆ 2000
5. Follow the Lemming (Thorpe, Kiki) ◆ 2001
6. Darwin's Family Tree (Ostrow, Kim) ◆ 2001

WILD THORNBERRYS READERS (2–5)

1. Family Face-Off (Rosado, Maria) ◆ 2000
2. Two Promises too Many! (Beechen, Adam) ◆ 2000
3. A Time to Share (Otfinoski, Steven) ◆ 2000
4. Gift of Gab (Dubowski, Cathy East) ◆ 2000
5. Race to the Sea (Spirn, Michele) ◆ 2001
6. One of a Kind (Richards, Kitty) ◆ 2001
7. Gem of a Mom (Ostrow, Kim) ◆ 2002

WILD WILLIE MYSTERIES

Joosse, Barbara M.

CLARION ◆ GRADES 2–4 ◆ A/R

MYSTERY

Willie and his friend Kyle investigate mysteries in their neighborhood. In *Ghost Trap,* Kyle, who had moved away, is back. His house has secret passages and, maybe, a ghost. In addition to solving the mystery, Willie helps his friend Lucy adjust to Kyle's return. Fans of Cam Jansen and the A to Z Mysteries will enjoy these books.

1. Wild Willie and King Kyle, Detectives ◆ 1993
2. The Losers Fight Back ◆ 1994
3. Ghost Trap ◆ 1998
4. Alien Brain Fryout ◆ 2000
5. Dead Guys Talk ◆ 2006

WILDERKING TRILOGY

Rogers, Jonathan

B & H PUBLISHING ◆ GRADES 4–6 ◆ A/R

FANTASY

Prophecy declares that Aidan, 12, is to be the future Wilderking. Before the prophecy can be fulfilled, Aidan and the residents of Corenwald face destruction from the Pyrthen Empire. In the tradition of David and Goliath, Aidan defeats the giant and secures the freedom of Corenwald. There are elements of Christian theology in this series with references to the power of One God, which may appeal to readers of C. S. Lewis's Narnia books.

1. The Bark of the Bog Owl ◆ 2004
2. The Secret of the Swamp King ◆ 2005
3. The Way of the Wilderking ◆ 2006

WILEY AND GRAMPA'S CREATURE FEATURE

Scroggs, Kirk

LITTLE, BROWN ◆ GRADES 3–6 ◆ A/R

HUMOR

Zombies, aliens, attacking eggnog bubbles, robot sharks, and even a vampire truck—Wiley and Grampa face them all. Numerous cartoon-style illustrations by the author add to the fun of these zany books and will attract reluctant readers. Fans of Franny K. Stein and Captain Underpants will enjoy this series.

1. Dracula vs. Grampa at the Monster Truck Spectacular ◆ 2006
2. Grampa's Zombie BBQ ◆ 2006
3. Monster Fish Frenzy ◆ 2006
4. Super Soccer Freak Show ◆ 2007
5. Bigfoot Backpacking Bonanza ◆ 2007
6. Hairball from Outer Space ◆ 2007
7. Night of the Living Eggnog ◆ 2007
8. Phantom of the Waterpark ◆ 2008
9. Curse of the Kitty Litter ◆ 2008
10. Jurassic Grampa ◆ 2009

WILLIMENA RULES!

Wesley, Valerie Wilson

HYPERION/JUMP AT THE SUN ◆ GRADES 2–4 ◆ A/R

REAL LIFE

Earlier books about a young African American girl have been reissued and expanded into this series. In one book, Willimena ("Willie") is in third grade and has taken the class guinea pig home for the weekend. Unfortunately, she loses Lester and must face the consequences. These books provide a realistic portrayal of an African American girl.

1. How to Lose Your Class Pet ◆ 2003
2. How to Fish for Trouble ◆ 2004
3. How to Lose Your Cookie Money ◆ 2004
4. How to (Almost) Ruin Your School Play ◆ 2005
5. 23 Ways to Mess Up Valentine's Day ◆ 2005
6. How to Face Up to the Class Bully ◆ 2007

WILLY

Browne, Anthony

CANDLEWICK ◆ GRADES K–2 ◆ A/R

ANIMAL FANTASY

A quiet, mild-mannered chimp named Willy is featured in this series of picture books. Willy likes to read, daydream, and go to movies with his friend Milly. He is scorned and laughed at by the neighborhood chimps, until he knocks out the neighborhood bully by accident. He longs to play soccer but isn't any good until a wizard gives him some magic shoes. In another book, Willy daydreams about being a movie star and a rock singer. The minimal text and very large type of this series contrast with the sophisticated and detailed paintings on each page, providing appeal to all ages.

1. Willy the Wimp ◆ 1985
2. Willy the Champ ◆ 1986
3. Willy and Hugh ◆ 1991
4. Willy the Wizard ◆ 1996
5. Willy the Dreamer ◆ 1998
6. Willy's Pictures ◆ 2000

WILLY FREEMAN *see* The Arabus Family Saga

WIMPY KID *see* Diary of a Wimpy Kid

THE WIND OF FIRE

Nicholson, William

HYPERION ◆ GRADES 5–8 ◆ A/R

FANTASY

Twins Kestrel and Bowman, born into the regimented society of Amaranth, rebel against the focus on work and order and set off on a quest to find the voice of the Wind Singer, believing this will free their people, the Manth. In the third book, the siblings lead the Manth on a dangerous journey to a new homeland.

1. The Wind Singer: An Adventure ◆ 2001
2. Slaves of the Mastery ◆ 2001
3. Firesong ◆ 2002

WINNIE

Jacobson, Jennifer Richard

HOUGHTON MIFFLIN ◆ GRADES 2–5 ◆ A/R

REAL LIFE

Winnie is an appealing character who struggles to find her place. In the first book, her friends Zoe and Vanessa enjoy their ballet class, but Winnie is not successful there. In *Winnie at Her Best,* Winnie's friends are again happily involved in activities while Winnie feels insecure about her choices. When she begins to tutor a young boy, Winnie discovers what she does best.

1. Winnie Dancing on her Own ◆ 2001
2. Truly Winnie ◆ 2003
3. Winnie at Her Best ◆ 2006

WINNIE PERRY

Myracle, Lauren

DUTTON ◆ GRADES 4–7 ◆ A/R

REAL LIFE

As Winnie Perry celebrates her 11th birthday (in *Eleven*), she begins a month-by-month account of her life. She makes a new friend (Dinah) and becomes distant from her former best friend (Amanda). The book ends (and the second book begins) as she turns 12. As Winnie matures, so do the situations that she confronts, including getting her period, her first bra, entering junior high, and her first romance. The books are told in Winnie's voice and tween readers will relate to her everyday struggles and successes.

1. Eleven ◆ 2004
2. Twelve ◆ 2007
3. Thirteen ◆ 2008

WINNIE THE HORSE GENTLER

Mackall, Dandi Daley

TYNDALE KIDS ◆ GRADES 4–8 ◆ A/R

REAL LIFE | VALUES

Although Winnie, 12, can connect with horses, she struggles in her relationships with people. The death of her mother two years ago has left Winnie hurt and afraid. Her father can't seem to settle down and Winnie and her sister have moved five times. Now Winnie has the chance to buy a horse, but her father wants to move again. Winnie's work with horses allows her to open up to God's love and she begins to place her trust in Him.

1. Wild Thing ◆ 2002
2. Eager Star ◆ 2002
3. Bold Beauty ◆ 2002
4. Midnight Mystery ◆ 2002
5. Unhappy Appy ◆ 2003
6. Gift Horse ◆ 2003
7. Friendly Foal ◆ 2004
8. Buckskin Bandit ◆ 2004

WINNIE THE POOH FIRST READERS

Gaines, Isabel

DISNEY PRESS ◆ GRADES K–2 ◆ A/R

ANIMAL FANTASY | HUMOR

This series adapts some of the familiar stories (including when Pooh eats too much honey and gets stuck in Rabbit's door) and also creates new adventures in a format that is designed for beginning readers. The familiar characters—Winnie the Pooh, Christopher, Tigger, Eeyore, and others—will attract young children who are familiar with the Disney videos and could be an incentive for beginning readers.

1. Pooh Gets Stuck ◆ 1998
2. Pooh's Honey Tree ◆ 1998
3. Pooh's Pumpkin ◆ 1998
4. Rabbit Gets Lost ◆ 1998
5. Bounce, Tigger, Bounce ◆ 1998
6. Happy Birthday, Eeyore! ◆ 1998
7. Tiggers Hate to Lose ◆ 1998
8. Eeyore Finds a Friend ◆ 1998
9. Pooh's Best Friend ◆ 1998
10. Pooh's Halloween Parade ◆ 1999
11. Pooh's Christmas Gifts ◆ 1999
12. Pooh and the Storm That Sparkled ◆ 1999
13. Be Quiet, Pooh! ◆ 1999
14. The Giving Bear ◆ 1999
15. Pooh's Easter Egg Huntt ◆ 1999
16. Pooh's Hero Party ◆ 1999
17. Pooh's Leaf Pile ◆ 1999
18. Pooh's Scavenger Hunt ◆ 1999
19. Pooh's Surprise Basket ◆ 1999
20. Tigger's Family Tree ◆ 1999
21. World's Best Mama ◆ 2000
22. Pooh's Fall Harvest ◆ 2000
23. Pooh's Sled Ride ◆ 2000
24. Pooh's Graduation ◆ 2000
25. Happy Valentine's Day, Pooh ◆ 2000

WINNING SEASON

Wallace, Rich

VIKING ◆ GRADES 4–7 ◆ A/R

RECREATION

Sports fans, get ready. Here's a new series of books featuring popular sports. In the first book, Manny wants to play football but, because he is small, he spends a lot of time on the bench. Manny hopes to prove that he deserves to play. Basketball is featured in the second book. Jared is a great player with a bad temper. Later books in this quick-read series feature other middle-school boys facing a variety of sports challenges.

1. The Roar of the Crowd ◆ 2004
2. Technical Foul ◆ 2004
3. Fast Company ◆ 2005
4. Double Fake ◆ 2005
5. Emergency Quarterback ◆ 2005
6. Southpaw ◆ 2006
7. Dunk Under Pressure ◆ 2006
8. Takedown ◆ 2006
9. Curveball ◆ 2007
10. Second-String Center ◆ 2007

WISHBONE: THE EARLY YEARS

Various authors

BIG RED CHAIR BOOKS/LYRICK PUBLISHING ◆ GRADES K–3 ◆ A/R

ADVENTURE

Wishbone looks back fondly to his puppy years and imagines himself in fairy tales.

1. Jack and the Beanstalk (Strickland, Brad, and Thomas E. Fuller) ◆ 1999
2. The Sorceror's Apprentice (Jablonski, Carla) ◆ 1999
3. Hansel and Gretel (Sathre, Vivian) ◆ 1999
4. The Brave Little Tailor (San Souci, Robert D.) ◆ 1999
5. Aladdin (Strickland, Brad) ◆ 1999
6. The Slave and the Lion (Barkan, Joanne) ◆ 2000

WISHBONE'S TALES OF A PUP

1. Wishbone and the Glass Slipper (Francis, A. D.) ◆ 2000
2. Wishbone and the Forty Thieves (Francis, A. D.) ◆ 2001
3. Wishbone in Wonderland (Francis, A. D.) ◆ 2001
4. Wishbone and the Nutcracker (Francis, A. D.) ◆ 2001
5. Wishbone and the Dancing Princess (Francis, A. D.) ◆ 2001

WISHBONE ADVENTURES

Various authors

BIG RED CHAIR BOOKS/LYRICK PUBLISHING ◆ GRADES 3–4 ◆ A/R

ADVENTURE

Cleverly retold traditional stories are given a fresh look for elementary readers by using a very smart dog named Wishbone who has a nose for adventure. Wishbone and his human friends—Joe Talbot, Samantha Kepler, and David Barnes—lead readers through action-packed plots retaining basic elements of the original stories. All the books in the series have been renamed. *The Three Musketeers* becomes *Muttketeer!*; *A Tale of Two Cities* is reborn as *A Tale of Two Sitters*. These entertaining books are accessible for children who might not consider the classic titles until high school.

1. Be a Wolf! (Strickland, Brad) ◆ 1997
2. Salty Dog (Strickland, Brad) ◆ 1997
3. The Prince and the Pooch (Leavitt, Caroline) ◆ 1997
4. Robinhound Crusoe (Leavitt, Caroline) ◆ 1997
5. The Hunchdog of Notre Dame (Friedman, Michael J.) ◆ 1997
6. Digging Up the Past (Sathre, Vivian) ◆ 1997
7. The Mutt in the Iron Muzzle (Friedman, Michael J.) ◆ 1997
8. Muttketeer! (Crider, Bill) ◆ 1997
9. A Tale of Two Sitters (Barkan, Joanne) ◆ 1998
10. Moby Dog (Steele, Alexander) ◆ 1998
11. The Pawloined Paper (Litowinsky, Olga) ◆ 1998
12. Dog Overboard! (Sathre, Vivian) ◆ 1998
13. Homer Sweet Homer (Jablonski, Carla) ◆ 1998
14. Dr. Jekyll and Mr. Dog (Butcher, Nancy) ◆ 1998
15. A Pup in King Arthur's Court (Barkan, Joanne) ◆ 1998
16. Last of the Breed (Steele, Alexander) ◆ 1999
17. Digging to the Center of the Earth (Steele, Michael Anthony) ◆ 1999
18. Gullifur's Travels (Strickland, Brad, and Barbara Strickland) ◆ 1999
19. Terrier of the Lost Mines (Strickland, Brad, and Thomas E. Fuller) ◆ 1999
20. Ivanhound (Holder, Nancy) ◆ 1999
21. Huckleberry Dog (Steele, Alexander) ◆ 2000

SUPER ADVENTURES OF WISHBONE

1. Dog Days of the West (Sathre, Vivian) ◆ 1998
2. The Legend of Sleepy Hollow (Jablonski, Carla) ◆ 1998
3. Unleashed in Space (Steele, Alexander) ◆ 1999
4. Tails of Terror ◆ 1999
5. Twenty Thousand Wags Under the Sea (Jablonski, Carla) ◆ 2000

WISHBONE CLASSICS

Various authors
HARPERCOLLINS ◆ GRADES 3–5 ◆ A/R
ADVENTURE

The main narrator of these retold classics is a personable dog, Wishbone, who guides readers to better understand the characters and their actions. The stories range from *Don Quixote* to *Ivanhoe* to *The Red Badge of Courage*. Brief information is given about the author, main characters, era, and events so readers obtain a sense of each classic tale. The character of Wishbone, made popular by the TV programs (and other books), does play the role of a fictional character but is the reader's guide to understanding these well-known stories.

1. Don Quixote (Burgan, Michael) ◆ 1996
2. The Odyssey (Mattern, Joanne) ◆ 1996
3. Romeo and Juliet (Aronson, Billy) ◆ 1996
4. Joan of Arc (Selene, Patrice) ◆ 1996
5. Oliver Twist (Mattern, Joanne) ◆ 1996
6. The Adventures of Robin Hood (Mattern, Joanne) ◆ 1996
7. Frankenstein (Burgan, Michael) ◆ 1996
8. The Strange Case of Dr. Jekyll and Mr. Hyde (Mattern, Joanne) ◆ 1996
9. A Journey to the Center of the Earth (Aronson, Billy) ◆ 1996
10. The Red Badge of Courage (Burgan, Michael) ◆ 1996
11. The Adventures of Tom Sawyer (Munell, Melanie) ◆ 1996
12. Ivanhoe (Mattern, Joanne) ◆ 1997

WISHBONE MYSTERIES

Various authors

BIG RED CHAIR BOOKS/LYRICK PUBLISHING ◆ GRADES 4–5 ◆ A/R MYSTERY

The characters from the popular books and TV programs are back in this series of mysteries. Wishbone's friends are now older and are involved in explaining hauntings, finding missing mascots, and recovering stolen goods. The friends—Joe, Samantha, and David—are all successful sleuths, with the expert assistance of Wishbone the dog, who has a great nose for mystery and adventure.

1. The Treasure of Skeleton Reef (Strickland, Brad, and Thomas E. Fuller) ◆ 1997
2. The Haunted Clubhouse (Leavitt, Caroline) ◆ 1997
3. The Riddle of the Wayward Books (Strickland, Brad, and Thomas E. Fuller) ◆ 1997
4. Tale of the Missing Mascot (Steele, Alexander) ◆ 1998
5. The Stolen Trophy (Friedman, Michael J.) ◆ 1998
6. The Maltese Dog (Capeci, Anne) ◆ 1998
7. Drive-In of Doom (Strickland, Brad, and Thomas E. Fuller) ◆ 1998
8. The Key to the Golden Dog (Capeci, Anne) ◆ 1998
9. Case of the On-Line Alien (Steele, Alexander) ◆ 1998
10. The Disappearing Dinosaurs (Strickland, Brad, and Thomas E. Fuller) ◆ 1998
11. Lights! Camera! Action Dog! (Butcher, Nancy) ◆ 1998
12. Forgotten Heroes (Steele, Alexander) ◆ 1998
13. Case of the Unsolved Case (Steele, Alexander) ◆ 1998
14. Disoriented Express (Strickland, Brad) ◆ 1998

15. Stage Invader (Sathre, Vivian) ◆ 1999
16. The Sirian Conspiracy (Friedman, Michael J.) ◆ 2000
17. The Case of the Impounded Hounds (Steele, Michael Anthony) ◆ 2000
18. The Phantom of the Video Store (Gantt, Leticia) ◆ 2000
19. Case of the Cyber-Hacker (Capeci, Anne) ◆ 2000
20. Case of the Breaking Story (Steele, Alexander) ◆ 2000

WISHBONE SUPER MYSTERIES

1. The Halloween Joker (Capeci, Anne) ◆ 1998
2. The Ghost of Camp Ka Nowato (Steele, Michael Anthony) ◆ 1999
3. The Haunting of Hathaway House (Steele, Alexander) ◆ 1999
4. Riddle of the Lost Lake (Barkan, Joanne) ◆ 1999

WITCH

Bridwell, Norman
SCHOLASTIC ◆ GRADES K–3 ◆ A/R
FANTASY | HUMOR

This series will be fun for beginning readers. Two children live next door to a nice, helpful witch. She takes them to school when they are late, finds Santa Claus when he is missing, and has other adventures with the children as she tries to help them out. Many humorous moments make for pleasant reading.

1. The Witch Next Door ◆ 1965
2. The Wtch's Christmas ◆ 1972
3. The Witch's Vacation ◆ 1975
4. The Witch Grows Up ◆ 1979
5. The Witch Goes to School ◆ 1992

WITCH

Naylor, Phyllis Reynolds
DELACORTE ◆ GRADES 5–7 ◆ A/R
HORROR

Lynn is convinced that her neighbor, Mrs. Tuggle, is a witch; but when she and her best friend Mouse try to convince people, no one will listen. Readers will want to keep turning the pages in this suspenseful series as Mrs. Tuggle is overcome, only to return in another form and another way.

1. Witch's Sister ◆ 1975
2. Witch Water ◆ 1977
3. The Witch Herself ◆ 1978

4. The Witch's Eye ◆ 1990
5. Witch Weed ◆ 1992
6. The Witch Returns ◆ 1992

W.I.T.C.H.—ADVENTURES

Kaaberbol, Lene, adapter
HYPERION ◆ GRADES 5–8
FANTASY

Each of these books features one of the W.I.T.C.H. girls and their elemental talents. Irma represents water; Taranee, fire; Cornelia, earth; Hay Lin, air; and Will holds an amulet that allows all the elements to meet and work together. In *The Cruel Empress,* Hay Lin finds a lantern that serves as a portal to a city imprisoned by the Cruel Empress.

1. When Lightning Strikes ◆ 2004
2. Heartbreak Island ◆ 2005
3. Stolen Spring ◆ 2005
4. The Cruel Empress ◆ 2005

W.I.T.C.H.—CHAPTER BOOKS

Various adapters
HYPERION/VOLO ◆ GRADES 5–8 ◆ A/R
FANTASY

Will, Irma, Taranee, Cornelia, and Hay Lin have secret magical powers. They join together to fight the evil of Prince Phobos. Meanwhile, they go to middle school, do homework, and have ups and downs with their friends.

1. The Power of Five (Lenhard, Elizabeth) ◆ 2004
2. The Disappearance (Lenhard, Elizabeth) ◆ 2004
3. Finding Meridian (Lenhard, Elizabeth) ◆ 2004
4. The Fire of Friendship (Lenhard, Elizabeth) ◆ 2004
5. The Last Tear (Lenhard, Elizabeth) ◆ 2004
6. Illusions and Lies (Lenhard, Elizabeth) ◆ 2004
7. The Light of Meridian (Komorn, Julie) ◆ 2004
8. Out of the Dark (Komorn, Julie) ◆ 2004
9. The Four Dragons (Lenhard, Elizabeth) ◆ 2004
10. A Bridge Between Worlds (Lenhard, Elizabeth) ◆ 2004
11. The Crown of Light (Lenhard, Elizabeth) ◆ 2004
12. The Return of a Queen (Lenhard, Elizabeth) ◆ 2005
13. A Different Path (Lenhard, Elizabeth) ◆ 2005
14. Worlds Apart (Egan, Kate) ◆ 2005
15. The Courage to Choose (Egan, Kate) ◆ 2005

16. Path of Revenge (Egan, Kate) ◆ 2005
17. The Darkest Dream (Egan, Kate) ◆ 2005
18. Keeping Hope (Egan, Kate) ◆ 2005
19. The Other Truth (Alfonsi, Alice) ◆ 2006
20. Whispers of Doubt (Alfonsi, Alice) ◆ 2006
21. A Weakened Heart (Alfonsi, Alice) ◆ 2006
22. A Choice Is Made (Alfonsi, Alice) ◆ 2006
23. Farewell to Move (Alfonsi, Alice) ◆ 2006
24. Trust Your Heart (Alfonsi, Alice) ◆ 2006
25. Enchanted Waters (Alfonsi, Alice) ◆ 2006
26. Friends Forever (Alfonsi, Alice) ◆ 2006

W.I.T.C.H.—Graphic Novels

Author Not Available

Hyperion ◆ Grades 5–8

Fantasy

The five girls from the W.I.T.C.H. books are featured in these graphic novels. Will, Irma, Taranee, Cornelia, and Hay Lin work as a team to fight evil and protect the Veil—the boundary between good and evil. Full-color art will attract many readers.

1. The Power of Friendship ◆ 2005
2. Meridian Magic ◆ 2005
3. The Revealing ◆ 2005
4. Between Light and Dark ◆ 2006
5. Legends Revealed ◆ 2006
6. Forces of Change ◆ 2006
7. Under Pressure ◆ 2007
8. An Unexpected Return ◆ 2007

Witch, Goblin and Ghost

Alexander, Sue

Pantheon Books ◆ Grades K–2

Fantasy

Here are heartwarming stories for beginning readers about a young witch, goblin, and ghost who are friends. They tell tall tales, get scared, and play games together. In *Witch, Goblin, and Ghost's Book of Things to Do* (1982), the three show how to write a rebus, play a game, use secret codes, and perform tricks.

1. Witch, Goblin and Sometimes Ghost ◆ 1976
2. More Witch Goblin and Ghost Stories ◆ 1978

3. Witch, Goblin and Ghost in the Haunted Woods ◆ 1981
4. Witch, Goblin and Ghost Are Back ◆ 1985

WITCH TWINS

Griffin, Adele

HYPERION ◆ **GRADES 3–5** ◆ **A/R**

FANTASY | HUMOR

Identical twins Claire and Luna, ordinary-looking 10-year-olds with quite different personalities, are actually witches. Adding to the humor of their bumbling efforts to affect situations in their lives is the fact that the only person aware of their special status is their accomplished witch grandmother.

1. Witch Twins ◆ 2001
2. Witch Twins at Camp Bliss ◆ 2002
3. Witch Twins and Melody Malady ◆ 2003
4. Witch Twins and the Ghost of Glenn Bly ◆ 2004

WIZARD AND WART

Smith, Janice Lee

HARPERCOLLINS ◆ **GRADES K–2** ◆ **A/R**

FANTASY | HUMOR

These I Can Read books follow a blundering Wizard and his wisecracking dog, Wart. Everywhere they go, they try to solve their problems with magic and only end up making things worse.

1. Wizard and Wart ◆ 1994
2. Wizard and Wart at Sea ◆ 1995
3. Wizard and Wart in Trouble ◆ 1998

WIZARD OF OZ *see* Oz

WIZARD TRILOGY

Ure, Jean

CANDLEWICK ◆ **GRADES 3–5**

FANTASY

Aspiring wizard Ben-Muzzy casts a bad spell and finds himself far from home in the world of Three Penny Wood. There he meets twins Joel and Gemma and the three have some exciting but nonviolent adventures full of witches, ogres, and giants as Ben-Muzzy tries to find his way home. The three continue their friendship and exploits in the sequels.

1. The Wizard in the Woods ◆ 1992
2. Wizard in Wonderland ◆ 1993
3. Wizard and the Witch ◆ 1995

WIZARD, TUBBY, SKINNY, & SNITCH *see*
Case of the . . .

WIZARDRY

Duane, Diane

HARCOURT ◆ GRADES 5–8 ◆ A/R

ADVENTURE | FANTASY

Nita is a 13-year-old girl tormented by bullies because she chooses not to fight back. While hiding in the local library, she discovers a book of instructions in the ancient art of wizardry. She meets Kit, a boy who is also a beginning wizard, and together they go on their first quest: to find the book that holds the key to preserving the universe. In the companion books, Nita and Kit go on other adventures: becoming whales to conquer the evil Lone Power in the deepest part of the Atlantic Ocean, cloning a computer and helping Nita's sister travel through several worlds in outer space, and becoming entangled in a magic battle in Ireland. With the popularity of fantasy books, this series has been reissued and expanded.

1. So You Want to Be a Wizard ◆ 1983
2. Deep Wizardry ◆ 1985
3. High Wizardry ◆ 1989
4. A Wizard Abroad ◆ 1993
5. The Wizard's Dilemma ◆ 2001
6. A Wizard Alone ◆ 2002
7. Wizard's Holiday ◆ 2003
8. Wizards at War ◆ 2005

WOLFBAY WINGS

Brooks, Bruce

HARPERCOLLINS ◆ GRADES 4–8 ◆ A/R

REAL LIFE | RECREATION

The Wolfbay Wings are a Squirt A ice hockey team that has become very successful. Unfortunately, a new coach and new players make the future uncertain. Each book in this series features a different player. Dixon "Woodsie" Woods is 11 years old and is worried about the team's prospects. William Fowler, "Billy," is only 10, and he is bothered by his teammates, Coach Cooper, and his overbearing father. There are statistics about the featured player on the back of each book and a tear-out sports card in the front. With lots of details about hockey and ample action, this should be a good choice for sports fans.

1. Woodsie ◆ 1997
2. Zip ◆ 1997
3. Cody ◆ 1997
4. Boot ◆ 1998
5. Prince ◆ 1998
6. Shark ◆ 1998
7. Billy ◆ 1998
8. Dooby ◆ 1998
9. Reed ◆ 1998
10. Subtle ◆ 1999
11. Barry ◆ 1999
12. Woodsie, Again ◆ 1999

WOLVES CHRONICLES

Aiken, Joan

DELACORTE; BANTAM ◆ GRADES 4–8 ◆ A/R

ADVENTURE | FANTASY

High melodrama and an "unhistorical" setting mark this loosely connected series. In the England of this alternate world, King James III rules, Hanoverians are constantly plotting to put Prince George on the throne, and packs of vicious wolves menace the countryside. The Wolves Chronicles begin with the story of two little girls who are left in the care of an evil woman who schemes to take their inheritance. The girls are rescued by the mysterious orphan boy Simon, who later in the series is revealed to be a duke. Simon befriends a Cockney girl, Dido, whose parents are evil Hanoverians, and the rest of the series is about their adventures, by themselves and with other friends, as they defend the true king.

1. The Wolves of Willoughby Chase ◆ 1963
2. Black Hearts in Battersea ◆ 1964
3. Nightbirds on Nantucket ◆ 1966
4. The Whispering Mountain ◆ 1968
5. The Cuckoo Tree ◆ 1971
6. The Stolen Lake ◆ 1981
7. Dido and Pa ◆ 1986
8. Is Underground ◆ 1993
9. Cold Shoulder Road ◆ 1996
10. Dangerous Games ◆ 2000
11. Midwinter Nightingale ◆ 2003
12. Witch of Clatteringshaws ◆ 2005

THE WORLD ACCORDING TO HUMPHREY
see Humphrey

WORLD OF ADVENTURE

Paulsen, Gary

BANTAM DOUBLEDAY DELL ◆ GRADES 3–6 ◆ A/R

ADVENTURE | FANTASY

This series features a variety of characters in locations around the world and in different time periods. *Time Benders* features two boys, Zack Griffin and Jeff Brown, who sneak into the laboratory of an eccentric scientist and end up in ancient Egypt. In *The Creature of Black Water Lake*, Ryan Swanner, 13, meets up with an ancient monster. The characters have exciting adventures and often find themselves in unusual or implausible situations. Warren Trumbull, 11, works for an agency that rescues people from monsters (*The Gorgon Slayer*); and Jess Rodriguez, 13, works at a skydiving school in Seattle (*Skydive!*). Short chapters and action-filled plots will interest reluctant readers.

1. The Legend of the Red Horse Cavern ◆ 1994
2. Rodomonte's Revenge ◆ 1994
3. Escape from Fire Mountain ◆ 1995
4. The Rock Jockeys ◆ 1995
5. Hook 'Em Snotty! ◆ 1995
6. Danger on Midnight River ◆ 1995
7. The Gorgon Slayer ◆ 1995
8. Captive! ◆ 1995
9. Project: A Perfect World ◆ 1996
10. The Treasure of *El Patrón* ◆ 1996
11. Skydive! ◆ 1996
12. The Seventh Crystal ◆ 1996
13. The Creature of Black Water Lake ◆ 1997
14. Time Benders ◆ 1997
15. Grizzly ◆ 1997
16. Thunder Valley ◆ 1998
17. Curse of the Ruins ◆ 1998
18. Flight of the Hawk ◆ 1998

WORMLING

Jenkins, Jerry B., and Chris Fabry

TYNDALE HOUSE ◆ GRADES 5–8 ◆ A/R

FANTASY

Owen Reeder has always seemed ordinary. Then he enters another world—the Lowlands—and joins with Watcher in the search for the

King's son. Facing many threats, including the evil Dragon, Owen accepts his role as the Wormling. Christian imagery and beliefs permeate this series for middle school readers.

1. The Book of the King ◆ 2007
2. The Sword of the Wormling ◆ 2007
3. The Changeling ◆ 2007
4. The Minions of Time ◆ 2008
5. The Author's Blood ◆ 2008

WORST PERSON

Stevenson, James

GREENWILLOW ◆ GRADES K–3

HUMOR

"The worst person in the world" lives in a dirty house surrounded by poison ivy and signs saying "Keep Out." Then he meets the kind and cheerful Ugly, who decides to have a party at the Worst's house. Ugly cleans everything up, buys food, and sends out invitations. The Worst angrily orders them all away, but later changes his mind. The series continues with the further encounters of the Worst with various funny, nice people who bring him out of his shell. When he goes on vacation, he meets an accordion-playing duo who, it turns out, are his neighbors at home. They all end up eating dry crackers and drinking prune juice on the Worst's front porch. Stevenson's expressive, cartoonish illustrations carry the fun along.

1. The Worst Person in the World ◆ 1978
2. The Worst Person in the World at Crab Beach ◆ 1988
3. The Worst Person's Christmas ◆ 1991
4. Worse Than the Worst ◆ 1994
5. The Worst Goes South ◆ 1995

WREN

Smith, Sherwood

HARCOURT ◆ GRADES 4–7 ◆ A/R

ADVENTURE | FANTASY

While living in an orphanage, Wren's friend Tess finds out that she is really Princess Teressa. This discovery changes the lives of both girls permanently. Along with their friends Tyron and Prince Connor, they battle the evil forces of King Andreus. The four friends learn to master the power of magic and use it only for the greater good.

1. Wren to the Rescue ◆ 1990
2. Wren's Quest ◆ 1993
3. Wren's War ◆ 1995

WRIGHT AND WONG MYSTERIES

Burns, Laura J., and Melinda Metz

SLEUTH/RAZORBILL ♦ GRADES 5–8 ♦ A/R

MYSTERY

Because of his unusual behavior, Orville Wright has been bullied and Agatha Wong has protected him since they met in second grade. She understands the impact of Orville's Asperger's syndrome. Now they are in middle school and they solve mysteries. In *The Case of the Slippery Soap Star,* Orville's mother is accused of theft and the kids find the real thief.

1. The Case of the Prank that Stank ♦ 2005
2. The Case of the Nana-Napper ♦ 2005
3. The Case of the Trail Mix-Up ♦ 2005
4. The Case of the Slippery Soap Star ♦ 2005

X FILES

Various authors

HARPERCOLLINS ♦ GRADES 5–8 ♦ A/R

FANTASY | HORROR

Terror in the forest, dying teenagers, a serial killer, a dead alligator man at the circus, and extraterrestrial entities—these are just a few of the problems investigated by Agents Mulder and Scully. Fans of the television program will flock to this series, which is based on teleplays of specific episodes. Like the show, these books are gritty and grim, with enough twists in the plot to leave you wondering what is really true. There are many different X Files books, including ones for young adult and adult readers.

X FILES (GRADES 5–8)

1. X Marks the Spot (Martin, Les) ♦ 1995
2. Darkness Falls (Martin, Les) ♦ 1995
3. Tiger, Tiger (Martin, Les) ♦ 1995
4. Squeeze (Steiber, Ellen) ♦ 1996
5. Humbug (Martin, Les) ♦ 1996
6. Shapes (Steiber, Ellen) ♦ 1996
7. Fear (Martin, Les) ♦ 1996
8. Voltage (Royce, Easton) ♦ 1996
9. E.B.E. (Martin, Les) ♦ 1996

10. Die Bug Die (Martin, Les) ◆ 1997
11. Ghost in the Machine (Martin, Les) ◆ 1997

X GAMES XTREME MYSTERIES

Hill, Laban C.

HYPERION ◆ GRADES 4–8

MYSTERY | RECREATION

Fans of the X Games (on ESPN) will enjoy these fast-paced mysteries with in-line skating, snowboarding, wakeboarding, snow mountain biking and other extreme sports. In one mystery, Jamil and his friends are at a mystery party and they investigate the theft of plans for a new wakeboard. In another book, Kevin is almost lost in a man-made avalanche. Other books feature Nat and Wall, who are also part of the Xtreme detectives. Merging sports action with mysteries could attract reluctant readers.

1. Crossed Tracks ◆ 1998
2. Deep Powder, Deep Trouble ◆ 1998
3. Rocked Out: A Summer X Games Special ◆ 1998
4. Half Pipe Rip-Off ◆ 1998
5. Lost Wake ◆ 1998
6. Out of Line ◆ 1998
7. Spiked Snow: A Winter X Games Special ◆ 1999
8. Totally Snowed ◆ 1999

XANTHE AND XAVIER *see* "Hour" books

YANG

Namioka, Lensey

LITTLE, BROWN ◆ GRADES 4–6 ◆ A/R

FAMILY LIFE | REAL LIFE

In the first book, Yingtao, 9, is the youngest in his musically talented family. Having been born and raised in China, living in Seattle is an adjustment for him. He wants to make friends and play baseball, but his family has other ideas. Other books focus on Yingtao's siblings.

1. Yang the Youngest and His Terrible Ear ◆ 1992
2. Yang the Third and Her Impossible Family ◆ 1995
3. Yang the Second and Her Secret Admirer ◆ 1998
4. Yang the Eldest and His Odd Jobs ◆ 2000

YOKO AND FRIENDS

Wells, Rosemary

HYPERION ◆ GRADES K–2 ◆ A/R

ANIMAL FANTASY

This series features popular animal characters from other books by Rosemary Wells. Yoko, Nora, and Timothy are in Mrs. Jenkins's class. Their stories focus on problems like chewing gum in class and feeling left out. On Nora's birthday, she can only include five of her classmates at her party. The rest of the class finds out and is angry with her. Nora solves the problem by organizing a special birthday party that the class delivers to the children's hospital. The easy-reading format of these books make them a good selection for primary-grade children.

1. Mama, Don't Go! ◆ 2001
2. The School Play ◆ 2001
3. Halloween Parade ◆ 2002
4. Doris's Dinosaur ◆ 2001
5. Be My Valentine ◆ 2001
6. The Germ Busters ◆ 2002
7. The Secret Birthday ◆ 2002
8. Read Me a Story ◆ 2002
9. Bubble-Gum Radar ◆ 2002
10. Practice Makes Perfect ◆ 2003
11. Make New Friends ◆ 2002
12. When I Grow Up ◆ 2003

YOUNG AMERICAN VOICES

Moss, Marissa

HARCOURT ◆ GRADES 3–5 ◆ A/R

HISTORICAL

Historical events are depicted through the eyes and experiences of young girls. Hannah's family, who are Jewish, leaves Lithuania to seek religious freedom in America. Hannah, 10, describes the difficulties the family faces and their experiences at Ellis Island. These books have been designed to look like handwritten journals.

1. Emma's Journal: The Story of a Colonial Girl ◆ 1999
2. Rachel's Journal: The Story of a Pioneer Girl ◆ 1999
3. Hannah's Journal: The Story of an Immigrant Girl ◆ 2000
4. Rose's Journal: The Story of a Girl in the Great Depression ◆ 2001

YOUNG AMERICANS: COLONIAL WILLIAMSBURG

Nixon, Joan Lowery

DELACORTE ◆ GRADES 4–6 ◆ A/R

HISTORICAL

As the series title indicates, these books focus on children in Colonial Williamsburg. The experiences are varied. From Caesar, a slave who is forced to leave his family's residence to live in the big house and be a personal servant, to Ann, 9, who knows she must start to act like a proper young lady. This series provides historical information from the perspective of children.

1. Ann's Story: 1747 ◆ 2000
2. Caesar's Story: 1759 ◆ 2000
3. Nancy's Story: 1765 ◆ 2000
4. John's Story: 1775 ◆ 2001
5. Maria's Story: 1773 ◆ 2001
6. Will's Story: 1771 ◆ 2001

YOUNG BOND

Higson, Charlie

MIRAMAX ◆ GRADES 5–9 ◆ A/R

MYSTERY | ADVENTURE

Before he was 007, he was James Bond, a student at Eton who seemed to attract mysteries and intrigue. In *Blood Fever*, James, 13, is on summer vacation visiting his cousin Victor on the island of Sardinia. There is a theft, a conspiracy, a kidnapping, and a mysterious millionaire. Can James rescue the kidnapped girl and stop the villain? This is an exciting series with many twists and turns.

1. Silverfin ◆ 2005
2. Blood Fever ◆ 2006
3. Double or Die ◆ 2008
4. Hurricane Gold ◆ 2009

YOUNG CAM JANSEN *see* Cam Jansen: Young Cam Jansen

YOUNG HEROES

Yolen, Jane, and Robert J. Harris
HARPERCOLLINS ◆ GRADES 4–7 ◆ A/R
FANTASY

Tales from mythology are brought to life in spirited renditions that look at heroes' younger years. In the first book, a 13-year-old Odysseus is captured by pirates and joins young prisoners Penelope and Helen in exciting adventures. Twelve-year-old Atalanta and her best friend, a bear, join in the hunt for the creature that killed her father in the third book.

1. Odysseus in the Serpent Maze ◆ 2001
2. Hippolyta and the Curse of the Amazons ◆ 2002
3. Atalanta and the Arcadian Beast ◆ 2003
4. Jason and the Gorgon's Blood ◆ 2004

YOUNG INDIANA JONES

Various authors
RANDOM HOUSE ◆ GRADES 4–6 ◆ A/R
ADVENTURE | FANTASY

The popularity of the Indiana Jones movies has led to several spin-offs, including a television program and paperback books. Two series of books are listed here. The books are very similar in that they follow Indiana's adventures as a youngster, including time travel and encounters with fantastic creatures. These early experiences helped develop his spirit of adventure and willingness to take risks. Ghosts, dragons, mummies, and pirates should appeal to readers who like books with monsters; while trips to the *Titanic,* the underworld, Stonehenge, and gold mines will attract those who like exotic locations. The two series of books differ in that one group parallels the episodes of the television series.

1. Young Indiana Jones and the Plantation Treasure (McCay, William) ◆ 1990
2. Young Indiana Jones and the Tomb of Terror (Martin, Les) ◆ 1990
3. Young Indiana Jones and the Circle of Death (McCay, William) ◆ 1990
4. Young Indiana Jones and the Secret City (Martin, Les) ◆ 1990
5. Young Indiana Jones and the Princess of Peril (Martin, Les) ◆ 1991
6. Young Indiana Jones and the Gypsy Revenge (Martin, Les) ◆ 1991
7. Young Indiana Jones and the Ghostly Riders (McCay, William) ◆ 1991
8. Young Indiana Jones and the Curse of the Ruby Cross (McCay, William) ◆ 1991

9. Young Indiana Jones and the Titanic Adventure (Martin, Les) ◆ 1993
10. Young Indiana Jones and the Lost Gold of Durango (Stine, Megan, and H. William Stine) ◆ 1993
11. Young Indiana Jones and the Face of the Dragon (McCay, William) ◆ 1994
12. Young Indiana Jones and the Journey to the Underworld (Stine, Megan, and H. William Stine) ◆ 1994
13. Young Indiana Jones and the Mountain of Fire (McCay, William) ◆ 1994
14. Young Indiana Jones and the Pirates' Loot (Fox, J. N.) ◆ 1994
15. Young Indiana Jones and the Eye of the Tiger (McCay, William) ◆ 1994

TV TIE-INS

1. The Mummy's Curse (Stine, Megan, and H. William Stine) ◆ 1992
2. Field of Death (Martin, Les) ◆ 1992
3. Safari Sleuth (Singer, A. L.) ◆ 1992
4. The Secret Peace (McCay, William) ◆ 1992
5. Trek of Doom (Martin, Les) ◆ 1992
6. Revolution! (Scott, Gavin) ◆ 1992
7. Race to Danger (Calmenson, Stephanie) ◆ 1993
8. Prisoner of War (Martin, Les) ◆ 1993

YOUNG INDIANA JONES CHRONICLES: CHOOSE YOUR OWN ADVENTURE

Brightfield, Richard
BANTAM ◆ GRADES 5–8
ADVENTURE | FANTASY

The series uses the popular Choose Your Own Adventure format in which readers turn to different pages based on what they want to happen. For example, if you decide to go to the party, turn to page 45; if you want to stay in the dorm, turn to page 51. These books feature the popular character of Indiana Jones when he is a young man and place him at the center of events around the world. The popularity of the character and the format should attract reluctant readers.

1. The Valley of the Kings ◆ 1992
2. South of the Border ◆ 1992
3. Revolution in Russia ◆ 1992
4. Masters of the Louvre ◆ 1993
5. African Safari ◆ 1993
6. Behind the Great Wall ◆ 1993
7. The Roaring Twenties ◆ 1993
8. The Irish Rebellion ◆ 1993

YOUNG JEDI KNIGHTS *see* Star Wars Young Jedi Knights

YOUNG MERLIN TRILOGY

Yolen, Jane

HARCOURT ◆ GRADES 4–6 ◆ A/R

FANTASY | HISTORICAL

When he was 8 years old, a boy was abandoned in the woods. Surviving as a wild thing, he was taken in by Master Robin, who tamed him and found his name, Merlin. This trilogy follows the adventures of Young Merlin (who uses the names of Hawk and Hobby), including his time with traveling performers and coming to understand and accept the importance of his dreams. In the third book, Merlin befriends a boy, Cub, who is later named Artus and will become King Arthur.

1. Passager ◆ 1996
2. Hobby ◆ 1996
3. Merlin ◆ 1997

THE YOUNG UNDERGROUND

Elmer, Robert

BETHANY HOUSE ◆ GRADES 5–8 ◆ A/R

HISTORICAL

Peter and Elise Andersen are 11-year-old twins involved in the Resistance in Denmark during World War II. They help their Jewish friend, Henrik, escape to Sweden and then help an injured RAF pilot. By the end of the series, the twins are 14 and try to stop a plot against a group of Jews traveling to Israel.

1. A Way Through the Sea ◆ 1994
2. Beyond the River ◆ 1994
3. Into the Flames ◆ 1995
4. Far From the Storm ◆ 1995
5. Chasing the Wind ◆ 1996
6. A Light in the Castle ◆ 1996
7. Follow the Star ◆ 1996
8. Touch the Sky ◆ 1997

YOUNG WOLF

Shefelman, Janice

RANDOM HOUSE ◆ GRADES 1–3 ◆ A/R

HISTORICAL

These books feature a Native American boy, Young Wolf, who chooses a mare to be his horse. Others tease him for his choice but Red Wind is a spirited horse that is just right for the warrior that Young Wolf hopes to be. In the third book, Red Wind runs away to join a wild stallion, Spirit Horse.

1. A Mare for Young Wolf ◆ 1993
2. Young Wolf's First Hunt ◆ 1994
3. Young Wolf and Spirit Horse ◆ 1997

THE ZACK FILES

Greenburg, Dan

GROSSET & DUNLAP ◆ GRADES 3–5 ◆ A/R

FANTASY | HUMOR

Zack is a 10-year-old boy who becomes involved in weird situations. In one book, a ghost named Wanda bothers him and his dad. Wanda haunts their apartment because she is lonely. When another ghost named Cecil appears, Zack helps them communicate and arranges for them to haunt the Haunted House at the Adventureland Amusement Park. Another book features Zack looking in on a parallel universe, where he meets his double, Zeke. Zack also can read minds and do body-traveling. With clones, ghosts, reincarnated grandpa, and Dr. Jekyll the Orthodontist, these are fast, funny books. Zack has a smart-aleck attitude that will appeal to many middle-grade readers.

1. Great-Grandpa's in the Litter Box ◆ 1996
2. Through the Medicine Cabinet ◆ 1996
3. A Ghost Named Wanda ◆ 1996
4. Zap! I'm a Mind Reader ◆ 1996
5. Dr. Jekyll, Orthodontist ◆ 1997
6. I'm Out of My Body . . . Please Leave a Message ◆ 1997
7. Never Trust a Cat Who Wears Earrings ◆ 1997
8. My Son, the Time Traveler ◆ 1997
9. The Volcano Goddess Will See You Now ◆ 1997
10. Bozo the Clone ◆ 1997
11. How to Speak Dolphin in Three Easy Lessons ◆ 1997

12. Now You See Me . . . Now You Don't ◆ 1998
13. The Misfortune Cookie ◆ 1998
14. Elvis, the Turnip . . . And Me ◆ 1998
15. Hang a Left at Venus ◆ 1999
16. Evil Queen Tut and the Great Ant Pyramids ◆ 1999
17. Yikes! Grandma's a Teenager ◆ 1999
18. How I Fixed the Year 1000 Problem ◆ 1999
19. The Boy Who Cried Bigfoot ◆ 2000
20. How I Went from Bad to Verse ◆ 2000
21. Don't Count on Dracula ◆ 2000
22. This Body's Not Big Enough for Both of Us ◆ 2000
23. Greenish Eggs and Dinosaurs ◆ 2001
24. My Grandma, Major League Slugger ◆ 2001
25. Trapped in the Museum of Unnatural History ◆ 2002
26. Me and My Mummy ◆ 2002
27. My Teacher Ate My Homework ◆ 2002
28. Tell a Lie and Your Butt Will Grow ◆ 2002
29. Just Add Water and Scream ◆ 2003
30. It's Itchcraft! ◆ 2003

ZACK FREEMAN *see* Butt Wars

ZACK PROTON

Anderson, Brian
ALADDIN ◆ GRADES 2–4 ◆ A/R
HUMOR | FANTASY

Commander Zack Proton has accidentally become separated from his space ship. How? He needed to go to the bathroom and went out the wrong door. Zack is rescued by Omega Chimp and they begin the search for the lost ship, encountering a space giant, space mice, and millions of pigs. Readers who enjoy the Weird Planet series will also like this series.

1. The Adventures of Commander Zack Proton and the Red Giant ◆ 2006
2. The Adventures of Commander Zack Proton and the Warlords of Nibblecheese ◆ 2006
3. The Adventures of Commander Zack Proton and the Wrong Planet ◆ 2007

ZELDA AND IVY

Kvasnosky, Laura Mcgee
CANDLEWICK ◆ GRADES K–2 ◆ A/R
FAMILY LIFE | ANIMAL FANTASY

Zelda and Ivy are sisters. Zelda is older and she is usually bossing Ivy around. There are three vignettes in the first book. In one, Zelda is the ringmaster of their pretend circus. Another shows the girls making their fox tails very fancy. Then, in the third vignettte, Zelda gives Ivy her baton. *Zelda and Ivy: The Runaways* received the 2007 Theodor Seuss Geisel Award.

1. Zelda and Ivy ◆ 1998
2. Zelda and Ivy and the Boy Next Door ◆ 1999
3. Zelda and Ivy: One Christmas ◆ 2000
4. Zelda and Ivy: The Runaways ◆ 2006

ZENDA

Petti, Ken, and John Amodeo

GROSSET & DUNLAP ◆ GRADES 4–7 ◆ A/R

FANTASY

On Azureblue, gazing balls reveal 13 messages that tell the destiny of each child. Unfortunately for Zenda, the balls are not used until a child is 12 ½ years old. But Zenda can't wait. When she takes her gazing ball too soon, it breaks. Now she must recover the 13 pieces.

1. Zenda and the Gazing Ball ◆ 2004
2. A New Dimension ◆ 2004
3. The Crystal Planet ◆ 2004
4. Lost on Aquaria ◆ 2004
5. The Impossible Butterfly ◆ 2004
6. A Test of Mirrors ◆ 2004
7. The Astral Summer ◆ 2005
8. A Light from Within ◆ 2005
9. Trapped in Time ◆ 2008

ZENON, GIRL OF THE 21ST CENTURY

Sadler, Marilyn

RANDOM HOUSE ◆ GRADES 2–4 ◆ A/R

FANTASY

Zenon Kar is in fifth grade and lives on a space station in the year 2049. In the first book, Zenon wants one of the new robotic Tobo dogs. It does everything—even your homework. Her dad buys her a less expensive robotic dog, Bobo. Zenon feels bad about this until all the Tobo dogs attack their owners. In the second book, Zenon finally makes the space-ball team. The Weird Planet books would be a good choice for Zenon fans.

1. Bobo Crazy ◆ 2001

2. Zenon Kar, Spaceball Star ◆ 2001
3. The Trouble with Fun ◆ 2001
4. Stuck on Earth ◆ 2002

ZIBBY PAYNE

Bell, Alison

LOBSTER PRESS ◆ GRADES 4–6 ◆ A/R

REAL LIFE

Zibby has been best friends with Sarah since the second grade. Now that they are both in sixth grade they are drifting apart. Zibby is a tomboy who loves to hang out with the boys and play sports. Sarah is more interested in being with other girls and discussing fashion and boys. Zibby is critical of Sarah and her friends only to realize that she misses her best friend. They agree to be different and be friends. In *Zibby Payne and the Trio Trouble,* Zibby has a new best friend, Gertrude, and Sarah does not like her. Zibby finds a way to bring the two girls together, but then she is on the outside.

1. Zibby Payne and the Wonderful, Terrible Tomboy Experiment ◆ 2006
2. Zibby Payne and the Drama Trauma ◆ 2007
3. Zibby Payne and the Party Problem ◆ 2008
4. Zibby Payne and the Trio Trouble ◆ 2008
5. Zibby Payne and the Red Carpet Revolt ◆ 2008

ZIGGY AND THE BLACK DINOSAURS

Draper, Sharon

JUST US BOOKS; ALADDIN ◆ GRADES 3–6 ◆ A/R

REAL LIFE | MYSTERY

Ziggy and three friends (all African Americans) are upset when their basketball court is vandalized. They form "the Black Dinosaurs" and work together to find the culprit. Along the way, they interact with Mr. Greene, an elderly man who, as the series progresses, gives them information about black history. In fact, African American history and heritage are important elements in these books. In *Lost in the Tunnel of Time,* the group explores an Underground Railroad site and in *The Space Mission Adventure,* they learn about African Americans' contributions to the space program. The information is woven into entertaining stories featuring friends in everyday experiences.

1. The Buried Bones Mystery ◆ 1994
2. Lost in the Tunnel of Time ◆ 1996
3. Shadows of Caesar's Creek ◆ 1997

4. The Space Mission Adventure ◆ 2006
5. The Backyard Animal Show ◆ 2006
6. Stars and Sparks on Stage ◆ 2007

ZOEY 101

Various authors

SCHOLASTIC ◆ GRADES 5–7 ◆ A/R

REAL LIFE

Zoey 101 was a television series on Nickelodeon. This series parallels some of the episodes in the program. In *Girls Got Game!*, Zoey arrives at Pacific Coast Academy, a boarding school that is accepting girls for the first time. Zoey is in Room 101 and she meets her new roommate, finds a new group of friends, and tries out for the basketball team. Many books feature opportunities for the girls to socialize with boys—a beach party, spring break, and the election for class president. This should be popular with tween readers.

1. Girls Got Game! (Mason, Jane B., and Sarah Hines Stephens) ◆ 2005
2. Dramarama (Mason, Jane B., and Sarah Hines Stephens) ◆ 2005
3. Pranks for Nothing! (Reisfeld, Randi) ◆ 2006
4. Beach Party (Mason, Jane B.) ◆ 2006
5. Back to Normal (Mason, Jane B.) ◆ 2006
6. Spring Break-Up (Mason, Jane B.) ◆ 2006
7. Lights Out! (Simpson, Fiona) ◆ 2006
8. Girls vs. Boys (Mason, Jane B., and Sarah Hines Stephens) ◆ 2007
9. A Quinn in Need (Mason, Jane B.) ◆ 2007
10. The Curse of PCA (Mason, Jane B., and Sarah Hines Stephens) ◆ 2007

Appendixes
and
Indexes

Books for Boys

These series were selected for their appeal to boys.

Adam Joshua Capers
Adam Sharp
Adirondack Kids
Adventures of a Young Sailor
Alden All Stars
Aldo Sossi
Ali Baba Bernstein
Alien Adventures
Al's World
Andrew Lost
Andy Russell
Angel Park All-Stars
Angel Park Hoop Stars
Angel Park Soccer Stars
Animorphs
Animorphs: Alternamorphs
Animorphs: Animorph Chronicles
Animorphs: Megamorphs
Anthony Monday
Barnstormers
Baseball Card Adventures
Bingo Brown
Black Stallion
Brian Robeson
Butt Wars
Cabin Creek Mysteries
Captain Underpants
Case of the . . .
Casebusters
Chip Hilton Sports Series
Cody
Comeback Kids
Culpepper Adventures
Danny Dunn
Dear Dragon
The Diamond Brothers
Diary of a Wimpy Kid
Don't Touch That Remote!
Dork in Disguise
Eddie Dickens Trilogy

Einstein Anderson
Eric Sterling, Secret Agent
Extreme Team
Fear Street: Ghosts of Fear Street
Fireball
Fraser Brothers
The Freaky Joe Club
Fred and Anthony
Funny Boy
Goners
Goosebumps
Goosebumps: Give Yourself
Goosebumps
Goosebumps Series 2000
Gordy Smith
Graveyard School
The Great Brain
The Great Brain Extreme Team
The Great McGoniggle
Hank the Cowdog
Hank Zipzer
Hardy Boys
Hardy Boys: Frank and Joe Hardy:
    The Clues Brothers
Hardy Boys, Undercover Brothers
Hardy Boys, Undercover Brothers:
    Graphic Novels
Harry
Help! I'm Trapped
Henry and Mudge
Henry Huggins
Henry Reed
Henry the Explorer
Herbie Jones
Hey, L'il D!
Hobie Hanson
Horrible Harry
Hot Dog and Bob
Ike and Mama
Jack Henry
Jack Jameson and Danny One

Jack Sparrow
Jake Drake
Jeffrey's Ghost
The Jersey
Jiggy McCue
Jigsaw Jones Mystery
Joey Pigza
Johnny Dixon
Johnny Mutton
Joshua T. Bates
Journey of Allen Strange
Judge and Jury
Lenny and Mel
Lewis Barnavelt
McGrowl
Mars Year One
Martin Bridge
Marvin Redpost
Matt Christopher Sports Stories
Matthew Martin
Max Malone
Maximum Boy
Mike and Harry
Million Dollar Series
Mind over Matter
Misfits, Inc.
Mr. Yowder
Mummy Chronicles
My America: Cody
My America: Joshua
My Name Is America
My Side of the Mountain
Mystic Knights of Tir Na Nog
NASCAR Pole Position
    Adventures
NASCAR Racers
Nate the Great
NFL Monday Night Football Club
Norby
Otto
Outcast

Owen Foote
Patrick's Pals
Peach Street Mudders
Pendragon
Ready, Freddy!
Ricky Ricotta
Riot Brothers
Riverside Kids: Russell
Robert
Ronald Morgan
Scrappers
Secrets of Dripping Fang
Shiloh

Slapshots
Slimeballs
Soup
Soup: Little Soup
Spencer's Adventures
Stanley
Super Hoops
Sword of the Spirits
Table Two
Tales from the Sandlot
Three Investigators
Time Surfers
Time Warp Trio Graphic Novels

Transformers Armada (Readers)
Trick Books
Tripods
The Tucket Adventures
Tyco Bass
Wiley and Grampa's Creature
    Feature
Winning Season
Wizard and Wart
Wolfbay Wings
World of Adventure
X Games Xtreme Mysteries
The Zack Files

BOOKS FOR GIRLS

These series were selected for their appeal to girls.

Abby Hayes: The Amazing Days of
  Abby Hayes
Abby's South Seas Adventures
Addie
The Adventures of Beatrice Bailey
Agnes Parker
Al (Alexandra)
Alice
Always Friends
Amelia
Amelia Rules!
American Diaries
American Girls
American Girls: Addy
American Girls: American Girl
  Mysteries
American Girls: Felicity
American Girls: Girl of the Year
American Girls: Girls of Many
  Lands
American Girls: History Mysteries
American Girls: Josefina
American Girls: Julie
American Girls: Kaya
American Girls: Kirsten
American Girls: Kit
American Girls: Molly
American Girls: Samantha
American Gold Gymnasts
American Gold Swimmers
Amy Hodgepodge
Anastasia Krupnik
Angel
Angela Anaconda Chapter Books
Angelina Ballerina
Angelina Ballerina: Angelina's
  Diary
Angels Unlimited
Annabel the Actress
Annie and Snowball
Annie Bananie

Avalon 1: Web of Magic
Avalon 2: Quest For Magic
Avonlea
Babes
Baby-Sitters Club
Baby-Sitters Club Friends Forever
Baby-Sitters Club Graphic Novels
Baby-Sitters Club Mysteries
Baby-Sitters Club Portrait
  Collection
Baby-Sitters Club Super Specials
Baby-Sitters Little Sister
Baby-Sitters Little Sister Super
  Specials
Ballerina Dreams
Ballet Friends
Ballet Slippers
Barbie Mystery Files
Barbie (Step into Reading)
Beany
Belinda
Bella Baxter
Beryl E. Bean
Best Enemies
Betsy-Tacy
Beware
Big Apple Barn
Bratz
Bratz: Clued In!
Bratz: Lil' Bratz
Brigid Thrush Books
B.Y. Times
B.Y. Times Kid Sisters
Camp Confidential
Camp Sunnyside
Candy Apple
Cardcaptor Sakura
¡Chana!
Chestnut Hill
Christy
Clarice Bean

Clementine
Cobble Street Cousins
The Complicated Life of Claudia
  Cristina Cortez
Danitra Brown
Daughters of Liberty
Dear America
Dear Dumb Diary
Dish
Disney Fairies
Disney Fairies (Chapter Books)
Disney Girls
Disney Princess
Disney Princess Secrets
Disney Princesses: My Side of the
  Story
Doll Hospital
The Double Dutch Club
Emma (Warner)
Emma Dilemma
The English Roses (Chapter
  Books)
Ernestine and Amanda
Fairy Houses
The Fairy Lair
Fairy Realm
Fairy School
Flower Girls
Friends for a Season
Frightmares
Full House: Club Stephanie
Full House: Dear Michelle
Full House: Michelle
Full House: Sisters
Full House: Stephanie
Get Ready for Gabi
Get Real
Girlhood Journeys: Juliet
Girlhood Journeys: Kai
Girlhood Journeys: Marie
Girlhood Journeys: Shannon

The Girls of Lighthouse Lane
Girls Only (Go!)
Go Girl
Gooney Bird Greene
Grace
Gymnasts
Hannah Montana
Hannah Montana (TokyoPop)
Here Come the Brownies
High School Musical Stories from East High
Hitty's Travels
Holiday Five
Hollywood Sisters
Hoofbeats
Horseshoe Trilogies
Horseshoes
How I Survived Middle School
Indie Kidd
Isabelle
Ivy and Bean
Jackson Friends
Jenna V.
Jenny Archer
Jewel Kingdom
Judy Moody
Julep O'Toole
Julia Redfern
Junior Gymnasts
Just Grace
Katie Kazoo, Switcheroo
Katie Lynn Cookie Company
Kyla May Miss. Behaves
Lili
Lily
Lily B.
Little Genie
Little House
Little House: My First Little House Books
Little House: The Caroline Years
Little House: The Charlotte Years
Little House: The Martha Years
Little House: The Rose Years
Little House Chapter Books: Caroline
Little House Chapter Books: Laura
Little House Chapter Books: Rose
Little Women Journals
Lizzie Logan

Lizzie McGuire
Lizzie McGuire Mysteries
Lizzie McGuire (Tokyopop)
Lucy Rose
Ludell
M and M
Magic Attic Club
Main Street
Mallory
Mary-Kate and Ashley: Adventures of Mary-Kate and Ashley
Mary-Kate and Ashley: Graduation Summer
Mary-Kate and Ashley: So Little Time
Mary-Kate and Ashley: Two of a Kind
Mary-Kate and Ashley in Action
Mary-Kate and Ashley Starring In . . .
Mary-Kate and Ashley Sweet 16
Mermaid S. O. S.
Molly Moon
Mustang Mountain
My America: Elizabeth
My America: Hope
My America: Meg
My America: Sofia
My America: Virginia
Nancy Drew
Nancy Drew: Girl Detective
Nancy Drew and the Clue Crew
Nancy Drew Graphic Novels
Nancy Drew Notebooks
Nora
Peanut Butter and Jelly
Pee Wee Scouts
Phantom Stallion
Pioneer Daughters
Pony-Crazed Princess
Pony Pals
Pony Tails
Portraits of Little Women
Princess Power
The Princess School
The Princess Tales
Rachel Yoder—Always Trouble Somewhere
Rainbow Magic: Fun Day Fairies
Rainbow Magic: Jewel Fairies

Rainbow Magic: Pet Fairies
Rainbow Magic: Rainbow Fairies
Rainbow Magic: Weather Fairies
The Rhianna Chronicles
Riding Academy
Riverside Kids: Elisa
Rosy Cole
Royal Ballet School Diaries
Sabrina the Teenage Witch
The Saddle Club
Saddles, Stars, and Stripes
Sandy Lane Stables
Sarah, Plain and Tall
Short Stirrup Club
Silver Blades
Silver Blades Figure Eights
Simply Sarah
Sister Sister
Skating Dreams
Sleepover Friends
Sleepover Squad
Sneaky Pony
Soccer Stars
Song Lee
Sweet Valley: Unicorn Club
Sweet Valley Kids
Thoroughbred
Thoroughbred: Ashleigh
Thoroughbred: Ashleigh's Collection
Tiara Club
Tiara Club: The Tiara Club at Pearl Palace
Tiara Club: The Tiara Club at Ruby Mansion
Tiara Club: The Tiara Club at Silver Towers
The Wedding Planner's Daughter
Wild at Heart
Willimena Rules!
Winnie
Winnie Perry
W.I.T.C.H.—Adventures
W.I.T.C.H.—Chapter Books
W.I.T.C.H.—Graphic Novels
Young American Voices
Zibby Payne
Zoey 101

Books for Reluctant Readers/ESL Students

These series were selected as those that would have the most appeal to reluctant readers. Series that are suitable for use with students of English as a second language are indicated with an asterisk.

A to Z Mysteries
Accidental Monsters
Adam Joshua Capers
Addie
Addie*
Adventures of Daniel Boom AKA Loud Boy
The Adventures of Uncle Stinky
Akiko
Aldo Sossi*
Alien Adventures
Aliens
Amber Brown
Amber Brown: A Is for Amber
American Girls
American Girls: Addy
American Girls: Felicity
American Girls: Girls of Many Lands
American Girls: History Mysteries
American Girls: Josefina
American Girls: Kaya
American Girls: Kirsten
American Girls: Kit
American Girls: Molly
American Girls: Samantha
Andrew Lost
Andy Shane*
Angela Anaconda Chapter Books
Angels Unlimited
Animorphs
Animorphs: Alternamorphs
Animorphs: Animorph Chronicles
Animorphs: Megamorphs
Annie and Snowball*
Annie Bananie*
Are You Afraid of the Dark?

Arthur*
Arthur Chapter Books*
Arthur Chapter Books: Good Sports*
Astrosaurs
Baby-Sitters Club
Baby-Sitters Club Friends Forever
Baby-Sitters Club Mysteries
Baby-Sitters Club Portrait Collection
Baby-Sitters Club Super Specials
Baby-Sitters Little Sister
Baby-Sitters Little Sister Super Specials
Babymouse
Bailey City Monsters
Bailey School: The Adventures of the Bailey School Kids
Ballet Slippers
Barbie
Barkham Street
Barkley's School for Dogs
Batman
Batman (Scholastic Reader)
Beany*
Bear*
Beezy*
Berenstain Bears*
Berenstain Bears: Bear Scouts*
Berenstain Bears: Big Chapter Books*
Beware*
Bionicle Adventures
Bionicle Chronicles
Biscuit*
Biscuit Readers
Black Belt Club
Black Cat Club
Black Lagoon

Bloodwater Mysteries
Bone Chillers
Boxcar Children
Boxcar Children: Adventures of Benny and Watch
Brady Brady
Bratz
Brian Robeson
Bunnicula
Bunnicula: Tales from the House of Bunnicula
Bunnicula and Friends
Butt Wars
Butt-Ugly Martians Chapter Books
Buzz Beaker Brainstorm
Cabin Creek Mysteries
Calico Cat*
Cam Jansen
Cam Jansen: Young Cam Jansen
Camp Zombie
Captain Underpants
Captain Underpants: Super Diaper Baby
Cardcaptor Sakura
Cascade Mountain Railroad Mysteries
Casebusters
CatDog (Chapter Books)
Choose Your Own Adventure
Choose Your Own Nightmare
Choose Your Own Star Wars Adventures
Clifford
Clue Jr.
Cody
Comeback Kids
Commander Toad

The Complicated Life of Claudia
    Cristina Cortez
Cowgirl Kate and Cocoa*
Culpepper Adventures
Cyber.kdz
D.W.*
Danger Guys
Danitra Brown*
Dear Dragon*
Dear Dumb Diary
Dexter's Laboratory Chapter Books
Diary of a Wimpy Kid
Digimon Digital Monsters
Disney Girls
Don't Touch That Remote!
Doug Chronicles
Doug (Disney Chapter Books)
Dragon*
Dragon Slayers' Academy
Duel Masters
Edison-Armstrong School*
Eerie Indiana
Einstein Anderson
Elephant and Piggie*
Encyclopedia Brown
Eoin Colfer's Legend . . .
Everybody Hates Chris
Extraordinary Adventures of
    Ordinary Boy
Extreme Team
Fairly OddParents
Fairly OddParents (TokyoPop)
Fear Street: Ghosts of Fear Street
Fiendly Corners
First Graders from Mars
Fitch and Chip*
Five Little Monkeys
Fly Guy*
Fourth Floor Twins
Fox
Franklin
Franny K. Stein, Mad Scientist
The Freaky Joe Club
Fred and Anthony
Friends and Amigos*
Frightmares
Frog and Toad*
Fudge
Funny Boy
Genghis Khan
George and Martha*
Geronimo Stilton
Ghost Stories
Ghosts of Fear Street

Ghostville Elementary
The Golden Hamster Saga
Golly Sisters
Goners
Goosebumps
Goosebumps: Give Yourself
Goosebumps Graphix
Goosebumps Horrorland
Goosebumps Presents Goosebumps
    Series 2000
Graveyard School
The Grosse Adventures
Gym Shorts*
Gymnasts
Hank Zipzer
Hannah Montana
Hannah Montana (TokyoPop)
Hardy Boys: Frank and Joe
Hardy: The Clues Brothers
Hardy Boys, Undercover Brothers
Hardy Boys, Undercover Brothers:
    Graphic Novels
Harry*
Harry and Emily*
Help! I'm Trapped
Henry and Mudge*
Henry and Mudge: Puppy
Mudge*
Herbie Jones
Here Come the Brownies
Hey Arnold!
Hey L'il D!
High-Rise Private Eyes*
High School Musical Stories from
    East High
Holiday Five
Holiday Friends
Hopscotch Hill School*
Horace Splattly: The Cupcaked
    Crusader
Hot Dog and Bob
Horrible Harry
Horrid Henry
Houdini Club Magic Mystery
Houndsley and Catina*
"Hour" books
House of Horrors
Humphrey*
I Was a Sixth Grade Alien
Internet Detectives
Invisible Inc.
Jack Jameson and Danny One
Jackie Chan Adventures
Jake Drake

The Jersey
Jewel Kingdom
Jigsaw Jones
Jimmy Sniffles
Joe Sherlock, Kid Detective
Joey Pigza
Johnny Mutton
Journal of a Cardboard Genius
Journey of Allen Strange
Judy Moody
Julian and Huey
Junie B. Jones*
Junior Gymnasts
Jurassic Park Adventures
Just . . .
Katie*
Katie Kazoo, Switcheroo
Kenan and Kel
Kids in Ms. Coleman's Class*
Kim Possible (Chapter Books)
Kim Possible (TokyoPop)
Kipper*
Kipper: Little Kippers*
Klooz
A Knight's Story
Lab Coat Girl
Lenny and Mel
Lilo and Stitch: The Series
Lily Quench
Lincoln Lions Band
Lionel*
Little Bear*
Little Bill*
Little Bill (Nickelodeon)*
Little House Chapter Books:
    Caroline
Little House Chapter Books: Laura
Little House Chapter Books: Rose
Little Wolf
The Littles
Liza, Bill and Jed
Lizzie Logan
Lizzie McGuire
Lizzie McGuire Mysteries
Lizzie McGuire (TokyoPop)
Lost in Space, The New Journeys
Lu and Clancy*
Lucky
Lunchroom
The Mack Family
Mad Science
Magic Matt*
Magic Shop
Magic Tree House

Main Street*
Malcolm in the Middle
Mallory
Mars Year One
Martin Bridge*
Marvin Redpost
Matt Christopher Sports
Max and Ruby
Maximum Boy
Meg Mackintosh: A Solve-It-Yourself Mystery
Melvin Beederman, Superhero
Mercer Mayer's Critters of the Night
Messy Bessey*
Miami
The Midnight Library
Mijos
Mind over Matter
Miss Nelson
Mittens*
Monster Manor
Moonbear*
Moongobble
Mostly Ghostly
Mouse and Mole (Yee)*
Mr. and Mrs. Green*
Mr. Putter and Tabby*
Mummy Chronicles
My Babysitter
My Dog
My Pony Jack*
My Teacher Is an Alien
My Weird School
My Weird School Daze
Mysteries in Our National Parks
Mystery Files of Shelby Woo
Nancy Drew
Nancy Drew: Girl Detective
Nancy Drew Notebooks
Nancy Drew Graphic Novels
NASCAR Pole Position Adventures
NASCAR Racers
Nate the Great
Never Sink Nine
NFL Monday Night Football Club
Nightmare Room
Nightmare Room Thrillogy
Nightmares! How Will Yours End?
Nose Pickers from Outer Space
Oliver and Amanda Pig*
P.J. Funnybunny
Park Pals Adventure

Patrick's Pals
Peach Street Mudders*
Peanut Butter and Jelly
Peanuts
Pee Wee Scouts*
Peter's Neighborhood*
Pigeon*
Pinky and Rex
The Plant That Ate Dirty Socks
Polk Street: New Kids at the Polk Street School*
Polk Street School: Kids of the Polk Street School*
Pony Pals
Pony Tails
Poppleton*
Power Rangers: Ninja Storm
Powerpuff Girls Chapter Books
Pretty Freekin Scary
Pup and Hound*
Puppy Friends
Puppy Patrol
Ralph S. Mouse
Ramona Quimby
Ready Freddy!*
Rex and Lilly*
Ricky Ricotta
Riding Academy
Riot Brothers
Riverside Kids: Elisa*
Riverside Kids: Nora and Teddy*
Riverside Kids: Russell*
Robin Hill School*
Rocket Power
Ronald Morgan*
Roscoe Riley Rules
Rosy Cole
Rugrats (Chapter Books)
Rugrats Files
Sabrina the Teenage Witch
The Saddle Club
Saddles, Stars, and Stripes
Scaredy Cats
Scooby Doo Mysteries
Scooby Doo Readers
Scream Shop
Secret World of Alex Mack
Secrets of Dripping Fang
Secrets of Droon
Shanna First Readers*
Short Stirrup Club
Silver Blades
Silver Blades Figure Eights
Sister Sister

Skating Dreams
Slapshots
Sleepover Friends
Slimeballs
Soccer 'Cats
Soccer Stars
Something Queer
Soup
Space Brat
Space Dog
Spencer's Adventures
SpongeBob SquarePants Chapter Books
SpongeBob SquarePants (TokyoPop)
Spooksville
Star Trek: Deep Space Nine
Star Trek: Starfleet Academy
Star Trek: The Next Generation: Starfleet Academy
Star Trek: Voyager: Starfleet Academy
Star Wars: A New Hope—Manga
Star Wars: Boba Fett
Star Wars: Episode I The Phantom Menace—Manga
Star Wars: The Empire Strikes Back—Manga
Star Wars: The Last of the Jedi
Star Wars: The Return of the Jedi—Manga
Star Wars (DK Readers)
Star Wars Episode 1: Journals
Star Wars Galaxy of Fear
Star Wars Junior Jedi Knights
Star Wars Young Jedi Knights
Static Shock
Stink*
The Stupids
Super Goofballs
Super Hoops
Survival!
Table Two
Tales of Terror
Third-Grade Detectives
Thoroughbred
Thoroughbred: Ashleigh
Thoroughbred: Ashleigh's Collection
Tiara Club
Tiara Club: The Tiara Club at Pearl Palace
Tiara Club: The Tiara Club at Ruby Mansion
Tiara Club: The Tiara Club at Silver Towers

Tiger Moth

Time Surfers

Time Warp Trio

Time Warp Trio Graphic Novels

Tiny*

Titch*

Totally Spies!

Transformers Armada (Readers)

Treasure Planet

Trick Books

The Tucket Adventures

Turtle and Snake*

26 Fairmount Avenue

Twisted Journeys

Watchers

Wayside School

Weird Planet

The Weird Zone

Werewolf Club

Wild at Heart

The Wild Thornberrys

Wild Willie Mysteries*

Wiley and Grampa's Creature
   Feature

Willimena Rules!

Winnie the Pooh First Readers*

Winning Season

Wishbone: The Early Years

Wishbone Adventures

Wishbone Classics

Wishbone Mysteries

Wolfbay Wings

World of Adventure

X Files

X Games Xtreme Mysteries

Young Indiana Jones Chronicles:
   Choose Your Own Adventure

The Zack Files

Zack Proton

Ziggy and the Black Dinosaurs

Author Index

Authors are listed with the series to which they contributed. Series are listed in alphabetical order in the main section of this book.

A

Abbott, Donald
  Oz
Abbott, Tony
  Danger Guys
  Don't Touch That Remote!
  Secrets of Droon
  Time Surfers
  The Weird Zone
Abela, Deborah
  Spy Force
Aber, Linda Williams
  Barbie Mystery Files
Abrashkin, Raymond
  Danny Dunn
Adler, David A.
  Andy Russell
  Bones
  Cam Jansen
  Cam Jansen: Young Cam Jansen
  Fourth Floor Twins
  Houdini Club Magic Mystery
  Jeffrey's Ghost
  My Dog
Ahlberg, Allan
  Funnybones
  The Gaskitts
Aiken, Joan
  Arabel and Mortimer
  Wolves Chronicles
Alberto, Daisy
  Barbie (Step Into Reading)
Alexander, Brandon
  Full House: Club Stephanie
Alexander, Heather
  Hannah Montana
  Mary-Kate and Ashley:
    Adventures of Mary-Kate and
    Ashley
Alexander, Lloyd
  Prydain Chronicles
  Vesper Holly
  Westmark
Alexander, Martha
  Blackboard Bear

Alexander, Nina
  Full House: Michelle
  Full House: Sisters
  Magic Attic Club
  Mary-Kate and Ashley:
    Adventures of Mary-Kate and
    Ashley
Alexander, Sue
  Witch, Goblin and Ghost
Alexander, Wilma E.
  On Time's Wing
Alfonsi, Alice
  Hannah Montana
  High School Musical Stories
    from East High
  Lizzie McGuire
  W.I.T.C.H.—Chapter Books
Allard, Harry
  The Stupids
Amato, Mary
  Riot Brothers
Amodeo, John
  Zenda
Anastasio, Dina
  Ghostwriter
  Space Above and Beyond
Anasti, Tedd
  Spider Riders
Anderson, Brian
  Zack Proton
Anderson, C. W.
  Blaze
Anderson, Jodi Lynn
  May Bird
Anderson, Kevin J.
  Crystal Doors
  Star Wars Young Jedi Knights
Anderson, Laurie Halse
  Wild at Heart
Anderson, M. T.
  M. T. Anderson's Thrilling
    Tales
Anderson, Margaret J.
  Time Trilogy
Angell, Judie
  Adventures of Shirley Holmes

Angelou, Maya
  Maya's World
Anholt, Laurence
  Seriously Silly Stories
Anthony, David
  Heroes A2Z
Antilles, Kem
  Star Trek: Deep Space Nine
Antle, Nancy
  Once Upon America
Appelt, Kathi
  Bubba and Beau
Applegate, K. A.
  Animorphs
  Animorphs: Alternamorphs
  Animorphs: Animorph
    Chronicles
  Animorphs: Megamorphs
  Remnants
Applegate, Katherine
  Roscoe Riley Rules
Appleton, Victor
  Tom Swift Young Inventor
Archer, Chris
  Pyrates
Ardagh, Philip
  Eddie Dickens Trilogy
  Unlikely Exploits
Arden, William
  Three Investigators
Armstrong, Jennifer
  Children of America
  Dear Mr. President
  Pets, Inc.
Armstrong, Robb
  Patrick's Pals
Arnold, Tedd
  Fly Guy
  Monster Under the Bed
  Parts
Aronson, Billy
  Wishbone Classics
Arthur, Robert
  Three Investigators
Asch, Frank
  Bear

Class Pets
Journal of a Cardboard Genius
Moonbear

Ashby, R. S.
Jackie Chan Adventures

Asim, Jabari
Jamestown's American Portraits

Asimov, Isaac
Norby

Asimov, Janet
Norby

Asprin, Robert
Myth Adventures

Atkinson, Chryssa
American Girls: Girl of the Year

Auch, Mary Jane
Third Grade

Auerbach, Annie
CatDog (Chapter Books)
The Grosse Adventures
Horseland
SpongeBob SquarePants
Chapter Books

Augustyn, Brian
Batman (Scholastic Reader)

Averill, Esther
Jenny and the Cat Club

Avi
Dimwood Forest

Ayres, Katherine
American Girls: History
Mysteries

B

Baccalario, Pierdomenico
Ulysses Moore

Bader, Bonnie
Carmen Sandiego Mysteries
Mary-Kate and Ashley:
Adventures of Mary-Kate and
Ashley

Badger, Meredith
Go Girl

Baglio, Ben M.
Animal Ark
Animal Ark Hauntings
Animal Ark Pets
Choose Your Own Adventure
Dolphin Diaries

Bailey, Gerry
Butt-Ugly Martians Chapter
Books

Bailey, Helen
Topaz

Bailey, Linda
Stevie Diamond Mysteries

Baker, Barbara
Digby and Kate

Baker, Cari Greenberg
Ghostwriter

Baker, E. D.
Tales of the Frog Princess

Baker, Keith
Mr. and Mrs. Green

Balaban, Bob
McGrowl

Balan, Bruce
Cyber.kdz

Baldry, Cherith
Eaglesmount Trilogy

Bale, Karen A.
Survival!

Balian, Lorna
Humbug

Ball, Duncan
Emily Eyefinger

Balliet, Blue
Petra and Calder

Balmes, Kathy
Adventures in America

Banerjee, Anjali
Dungeons and Dragons:
Knights of the Silver Dragon
Star Sisterz

Banim, Lisa
Lizzie McGuire Mysteries
Mary-Kate and Ashley: Two of a
Kind

Banks, Jacqueline Turner
Judge and Jury

Banks, Lynne Reid
The Indian in the Cupboard

Banks, Steven
CatDog (Chapter Books)
Fairly OddParents
Rocket Power
Rugrats Files
SpongeBob SquarePants
Chapter Books
SpongeBob SquarePants
Chapter Books

Banscherus, J.
Klooz

Barad, Alexis
Disney Princess Secrets

Barba, Rick
Spy Gear

Barkan, Joanne
Wishbone: The Early Years
Wishbone Adventures
Wishbone Mysteries

Barklem, Jill
Brambly Hedge

Barlow, Steve
Tales of the Dark Forest
Vernon Bright

Barnes, Dawn
Black Belt Club

Barnes, Johnny Ray, Jr
Strange Matter

Barnes-Svarney, Patricia
Secret World of Alex Mack
Star Trek: The Next
Generation: Starfleet
Academy
Star Trek: Voyager: Starfleet
Academy

Barrows, Annie
Ivy and Bean

Barry, Dave
Never Land
Peter and the Starcatchers

Barry, Miranda
Ghostwriter

Bartlett, Craig
Hey Arnold!

Bartoletti, Susan Campbell
Dear America
My Name Is America

Bates, Michelle
Sandy Lane Stables

Batrae, Margot
Sabrina the Teenage Witch

Bauer, Marion Dane
Dear America

Baum, Lyman Frank
Oz

Baum, Roger S.
Oz

Becker, Eve
Abracadabra

Beckett, Jim
Choose Your Own Adventure

Bee, Coach Clair
Chip Hilton Sports Series

Beechen, Adam
Fairly OddParents
Rocket Power
The Wild Thornberrys

Beechwood, Beth
Hannah Montana
High School Musical Stories
from East High
Suite Life of Zack and Cody

Beecroft, Simon
Star Wars (DK Readers)

Bell, Alison
Zibby Payne

Bell, Cece
Sock Monkey

Bellairs, John
Anthony Monday
Johnny Dixon
Lewis Barnavelt

Belton, Sandra
Ernestine and Amanda

Belviso, Meg
Malcolm in the Middle

Mary-Kate and Ashley:
Graduation Summer
Mary-Kate and Ashley: Two of a
Kind
Wishbone Adventures
Wishbone Mysteries

Byars, Betsy
Bingo Brown
The Blossom Family
Golly Sisters
Herculeah Jones

Byers, Richard Lee
Are You Afraid of the Dark?

Byng, Georgia
Molly Moon

Byrd, Sandra
Friends for a Season

C

Calamari, Barbara
Angela Anaconda Chapter
Books

Calhoun, B. B.
The Pink Parrots

Calhoun, Mary
Henry the Cat
Katie John

Calhoun, T. B.
NASCAR Pole Position
Adventures

Calmenson, Stephanie
Gator Girls
Young Indiana Jones

Cameron, Ann
Julian and Huey

Cameron, Eleanor
Julia Redfern
Tyco Bass

Cameron-Anasti, Patsy
Spider Riders

Campbell, Bill
Oz

Campbell, Danny
Doug Chronicles

Campbell, Gaetz Dayle
On Time's Wing

Campbell, Joanna
Thoroughbred
Thoroughbred: Ashleigh
Thoroughbred: Ashleigh's
Collection

Campbell, Joanna, creator
Thoroughbred

Canning, Shelagh
Sabrina the Teenage Witch

Cannon, A. E.
Pirate Pete and Pirate Joe

Capeci, Anne
Cascade Mountain Railroad
Mysteries
Mad Science
Magic School Bus
Magic School Bus Science
Chapter Books
Wishbone Mysteries

Capozzi, Suzy
Barbie (Step Into Reading)

Capucilli, Alyssa Satin
Biscuit Readers

Carey, Diane
Star Trek: Enterprise
Star Trek: Starfleet Academy

Carey, Elizabeth Doyle
The Callahan Cousins

Carey, M. V.
Three Investigators

Carlson, Karyl
Oz

Carlson, Melody
FaithGirlz: Girls of 622 Harbor
View

Carlson, Nancy L.
Arnie
Harriet
Henry
Louanne Pig
Loudmouth George

Carlson, Natalie Savage
Orphelines
Spooky the Cat

Carlstrom, Nancy White
Jesse Bear

Carman, Patrick
Elliot's Park
Land of Elyon

Carmi, Rebecca
Magic School Bus Science
Chapter Books

Carmody, Isobelle
Little Fur

Carrick, Carol
Christopher
Patrick's Dinosaurs

Carroll, Jacqueline
Full House: Michelle
Full House: Stephanie
Jackie Chan Adventures

Carse, Jodi
Stinky Boys Club

Casanova, Mary
American Girls: Girl of the Year
American Girls: Girls of Many
Lands
Dog Watch

Cascone, A. G.
Deadtime Stories

Caseley, Judith
Kane Family

Caszatt-Allen, Wendy
PaleoJoe's Dinosaur Detective
Club

Catalanotto, Peter
2nd-Grade Friends

Catanese, P. W.
Further Tales

Cates, Emily
Haunting with Louisa

Cazet, Denys
Grandpa Spanielson's Chicken
Pox Stories
Minnie and Moo

Cerasini, Marc
Kim Possible (Chapter Books)
7th Heaven
Totally Spies!

Chaconas, Dori
Cork and Fuzz

Chaikin, Miriam
Molly

Champion, Joyce
Emily and Alice

Charbonnet, Gabrielle
American Gold Gymnasts
Disney Girls

Charles, Donald
Calico Cat

Chatterton, Martin
Bad Dog

Cherrington, Janelle
The Wild Thornberrys

Chesterfield, Sadie
Horseland

Chevat, Richie
Ghostwriter

Child, Lauren
Charlie and Lola
Clarice Bean

Chipponeri, Kelli
Fairly OddParents

Choi, Sook Nyul
Sookan Bak

Christelow, Eileen
Five Little Monkeys

Christian, Mary Blount
Penrod
Sebastian (Super Sleuth)

Christie, Amanda
7th Heaven

Christopher, John
Fireball
Sword of the Spirits
Tripods

Christopher, Matt
Extreme Team
Matt Christopher Sports Stories
Mike and Harry
Peach Street Mudders
Soccer 'Cats

D'Amico, Carmela
  Ella, the Elegant Elephant
D'Amico, Steven
  Ella, the Elegant Elephant
Daniels, Lucy
  Horseshoe Trilogies
Danko, Dan
  Avatar: The Last Airbender
  Malcolm in the Middle
  Sidekicks
Danticat, Edwidge
  Royal Diaries
Danziger, Paula
  Amber Brown
  Amber Brown: A Is for Amber
  Matthew Martin
Daugherty, George
  Sagwa, The Chinese Siamese
    Cat (Readers)
David, Charles
  Heroes A2Z
David, Lawrence
  Horace Splattly: The Cupcaked
    Crusader
David, Peter
  Star Trek: The Next
    Generation: Starfleet
    Academy
Davis, Gibbs
  Full House: Michelle
  Never Sink Nine
Davoll, Barbara, adapt.
  Story Girl
Day, Alexandra
  Carl
  Frank and Ernest
Deary, Terry
  The Fire Thief Trilogy
de Beer, Hans
  Little Polar Bear
de Brunhoff, Jean
  Babar
de Brunhoff, Laurent
  Babar
DeCandido, Keith R. A.
  Star Trek: I. K. S. Gorkon
  Star Trek: S. C. E.
DeClements, Barthe
  Elsie Edwards
  Once Upon America
Decter, Ed
  Outriders
DeFelice, Cynthia
  Ghost
DeGroat, Diane
  Annie Pitts
  Gilbert
DeLage, Ida
  Old Witch

Delaney, Joseph
  Last Apprentice
Delaney, Mark
  Misfits, Inc.
Delton, Judy
  Angel
  Kitty
  Lottery Luck
  My Mom
  Pee Wee Scouts
Denenberg, Barry
  Dear America
  The Life and Times
  My Name Is America
  Royal Diaries
Denton, P. J.
  Sleepover Squad
dePaola, Tomie
  The Barkers
  Bill and Pete
  Strega Nona and Big Anthony
  26 Fairmount Avenue
Depken, Kristen L.
  Barbie (Step Into Reading)
Derby, Kathleen
  Are You Afraid of the Dark?
Deutsch, Stacy
  Blast to the Past
Devlin, Harry
  Cranberryport
Devlin, Wende
  Cranberryport
Dewin, Howard
  Dexter's Laboratory Chapter
    Books
  Powerpuff Girls Chapter Books
Dhami, Narinder
  Babes
DiCamillo, Kate
  Mercy Watson
Dicks, Terrance
  Baker Street Irregulars
  David and Goliath
Dickson, Louise
  Lu and Clancy
Dillard, J. M.
  Star Trek: Enterprise
Dilmore, Kevin
  Star Trek: S. C. E.
DiMartino, Michael Dante
  Avatar Graphic Novels
DiMeo, Crystal
  The Pink Parrots
DiTerlizzi, Tony
  Spiderwick: Beyond the
    Spiderwick Chronicles
  The Spiderwick Chronicles
Divakaruni, Chitra Banerjee
  American Girls: Girls of Many
    Lands

Dixon, Franklin W.
  Hardy Boys
  Hardy Boys: Frank and Joe
    Hardy: The Clues Brothers
  Hardy Boys, Undercover
    Brothers
  Hardy Boys, Undercover
    Brothers Murder House
    Trilogy
Doder, Joshua
  Grk
Dokey, Cameron
  Full House: Stephanie
  Mary-Kate and Ashley:
    Graduation Summer
Donkin, Andrew
  Transformers Armada (Readers)
Donnelly, Liza
  Dinosaurs
Donovan, Dale and Johns
  Dungeons and Dragons:
    Knights of the Silver Dragon
Doolittle, June
  Mary-Kate and Ashley:
    Adventures of Mary-Kate and
    Ashley
Dorman, Helen
  Okomi
Dowell, Frances O'Roark
  Phineas L. MacGuire
Dower, Laura
  Candy Apple
Downie, Mary Alice
  On Time's Wing
Dowswell, Paul
  Adventures of a Young Sailor
Doyle, Bill
  Crime Through Time
Doyle, Debra
  Circle of Magic
Doyle, Patrick
  Edgar Font's Hunt for a House
    to Haunt
Doyle, Roddy
  The Mack Family
Draper, Sharon
  Ziggy and the Black Dinosaurs
Driscoll, Laura
  Disney Fairies (Chapter Books)
Duane, Diane
  Wizardry
Dubanevich, Arlene
  Pigs
Dubowski, Cathy East
  Full House: Michelle
  Journey of Allen Strange
  Mary-Kate and Ashley:
    Adventures of Mary-Kate and
    Ashley
  Mary-Kate and Ashley: Two of a
    Kind

Fraustino, Lisa Rowe
  Dear America

Frazier, Kermit
  Ghostwriter

Frederick, Heather Vogel
  Spy Mice

Fredericks, Mariah
  In the Cards

Freedman, Jeff
  Oz

Freeman, Don
  Corduroy

Freeman, Martha
  Trouble With

Freeman, Steve
  Kenan and Kel

Fremont, Eleanor
  Little Bill (Nickelodeon)

French, Vivian
  Tiara Club
  Tiara Club: The Tiara Club at
    Pearl Palace
  Tiara Club: The Tiara Club at
    Ruby Mansion
  Tiara Club: The Tiara Club at
    Silver Towers

Friedman, Laurie
  Mallory

Friedman, Mel
  Carmen Sandiego Mysteries

Friedman, Michael J.
  Star Trek: The Next
    Generation: Starfleet
    Academy
  Wishbone Adventures
  Wishbone Mysteries

Frith, Margaret
  The Barkers

Fulani, K. T.
  Totally Spies!

Fuller, Thomas E.
  Mars Year One
  Pirate Hunter
  Wishbone: The Early Years
  Wishbone Adventures
  Wishbone Mysteries

Funke, Cornelia
  Ghosthunters
  Inkheart

Furrow, Robert
  Sly the Sleuth

G

Gaban, Jesús
  Harry the Hippo

Gackenbach, Dick
  Hattie Rabbit

Gage, Wilson
  Mrs. Gaddy

Gaines, Isabel
  Winnie the Pooh First Readers

Galbraith, Kathryn O.
  Roommates

Gallagher, Diana G.
  Are You Afraid of the Dark?
  Full House: Sisters
  Journey of Allen Strange
  Mary-Kate and Ashley: Two of a
    Kind
  Mystery Files of Shelby Woo
  Sabrina the Teenage Witch
  Secret World of Alex Mack
  Star Trek: Deep Space Nine
  Star Trek: Voyager: Starfleet
    Academy

Gallagher, Maria
  Stinky Boys Club

Gallagher , Diana G.
  The Complicated Life of
    Claudia Cristina Cortez

Gannett, Ruth Stiles
  Dragon

Gantos, Jack
  Jack Henry
  Joey Pigza
  Rotten Ralph
  Rotten Ralph Rotten Readers

Gantt, Leticia
  Wishbone Mysteries

Gardner, J. J.
  Lost in Space, The New
    Journeys

Garfunkel, Debby
  Baker's Dozen

Garland, Sherry
  Dear America

Garner, Alan
  Stone Book Quartet

Garton, Ray
  Sabrina the Teenage Witch
  Secret World of Alex Mack

Garvey, Dennis
  Doug Chronicles

Garvey, Linda K.
  Doug Chronicles

Gauch, Patricia Lee
  Christina Katerina
  Tanya

Gauthier, Bertrand
  Just Me and My Dad

Gayle, Sharon Shavers
  Girlhood Journeys: Kai

Geisert, Arthur
  Pigs

Gelsey, James
  Scooby Doo Mysteries

George, Jean Craighead
  Julie of the Wolves

My Side of the Mountain
  The Thirteen Moons

George, Lindsay Barrett
  Long Pond

George, William T.
  Long Pond

Gerstein, Sherry
  Avatar (Ready to Read)

Gerver, Jane E.
  LazyTown (Ready to Read)

Giff, Patricia Reilly
  Ballet Slippers
  Casey, Tracey and Company
  Friends and Amigos
  Lincoln Lions Band
  Nory Ryan
  Polk Street: New Kids at the
    Polk Street School
  Polk Street School: Kids of the
    Polk Street School
  Polka Dot Private Eye
  Ronald Morgan

Gikow, Louise
  Mary-Kate and Ashley: Two of a
    Kind

Gilden, Mel
  NASCAR Racers
  Star Trek: Deep Space Nine

Gilligan, Alison
  Choose Your Own Adventure

Gilligan, Shannon
  Choose Your Own Adventure

Gilman, Laura Anne
  Grail Quest

Gilmour, H. B.
  Candy Apple

Gilson, Jamie
  Hobie Hanson
  Table Two

Givner, Joan
  Ellen Fremedon

Gjovaag, Eric
  Oz

Glaze, Lynn
  Adventures in America

Gleitzman, Morris
  Toad Rage

Gliori, Debi
  Pure Dead Magic

Godwin, Laura
  Happy and Honey

Gold, Maya
  Harriet M. Welsch

Goldberg, Barry
  Fairly OddParents
  SpongeBob SquarePants
    Chapter Books

Goldberg, Mary, adapter
  Curious George

Harper, Charise Mericle
  Just Grace
Harris, Christine
  Undercover Girl
Harris, Robert J.
  Young Heroes
Harrison, Emma
  Mary-Kate and Ashley:
    Graduation Summer
Hart, Alison
  American Girls: American Girl
    Mysteries
  American Girls: History
    Mysteries
  Racing to Freedom Trilogy
  Riding Academy
Hartman, Butch
  Fairly OddParents (TokyoPop)
Hass, E. A.
  Incognito Mosquito
Hautman, Pete
  Bloodwater Mysteries
Hautzig, Deborah
  Little Witch
Havill, Juanita
  Jamaica
Haworth-Attard, Barbara
  On Time's Wing
Hayes, Sarah
  Fred Bear
Haynes, Betsy
  Bone Chillers
  Taffy Sinclair
Haywood, Carolyn
  Betsy
  Eddie Wilson
Hedderwick, Mairi
  Katie Morag
Heide, Florence Parry
  Treehorn
Hemphill, Kris
  Adventures in America
Henderson, Sara
  Howie
Hendry, Diana
  Harvey Angell Trilogy
Henkes, Kevin
  Lilly
Hennessy, Barbara G.
  Corduroy
Hennesy, Carolyn
  Mythic Misadventures
Henry, Marguerite
  Chincoteague
Herman, Charlotte
  Max Malone
Herman, Gail
  The Barkers
  Disney Fairies (Chapter Books)
  Everybody Hates Chris

Fairy School
Full House: Stephanie
Magic School Bus Science
  Chapter Books
Sabrina the Teenage Witch
Scooby Doo Readers
Herman, Hank
  Super Hoops
Hermes, Patricia
  Emma Dilemma
  Holiday Friends
  My America: Elizabeth
  My America: Joshua
  My Side of the Story
Hernandez-Rosenblatt, Jason
  Batman (Scholastic Reader)
Herndon, Ernest
  Eric Sterling, Secret Agent
Hess, Robin
  Oz
Hesse, Karen
  Dear America
Hest, Amy
  Baby Duck
  Casey, Jenny, and Kate
  Sam
Heyes, Eileen
  O'Dwyer and Grady
Hicks, Betty
  Gym Shorts
Higginson, Hadley
  Sneaky Pony
Higson, Charlie
  Young Bond
Hildick, E. W.
  Ghost Squad
  McGurk
Hill, Eric
  Spot
Hill, Janet Muirhead
  Starlight
Hill, Kirkpatrick
  American Girls: Girls of Many
    Lands
Hill, Laban C.
  Choose Your Own Adventure
  Choose Your Own Nightmare
  Ghostwriter
  X Games Xtreme Mysteries
Hill, Susan
  Ruby
Hillenburg, Stephen
  SpongeBob SquarePants
    (TokyoPop)
Hillert, Margaret
  Dear Dragon
Hinman, Bonnie
  The American Adventure
Hirsch, Danny
  Secret Agent MJJ

Hirsch, Odo
  Hazel Green
Hirschfeld, Robert
  Choose Your Own Nightmare
  Matt Christopher Sports Stories
Hissey, Jane
  Old Bear Stories
Hite, Sid
  My Name Is America
Hoban, Julia
  Amy
Hoban, Lillian
  Arthur the Chimpanzee
  Silly Tilly
Hoban, Russell
  Frances
Hobbie, Holly
  Toot and Puddle
Hodgman, Ann
  Choose Your Own Adventure
  Lunchroom
  My Babysitter
Hoehne, Marcia
  Jenna V.
Hoeye, Michael
  Hermux Tantamoq Adventures
Hoff, Syd
  Danny and the Dinosaur
  Henrietta
Hoffman, Mary
  Grace
Hogg, Gary
  Spencer's Adventures
Holabird, Katharine
  Angelina Ballerina
  Angelina Ballerina: Angelina's
    Diary
Holder, Nancy
  Sabrina the Teenage Witch
  Wishbone Adventures
Holl, Kristi
  FaithGirlz: Boarding School
    Mysteries
Holland, Steve
  Kenan and Kel
Holm, Jennifer
  Babymouse
  The Stink Files
Holm, Matthew
  Babymouse
Holman, Sheri
  Royal Diaries
Holohan, Maureen
  The Broadway Ballplayers
Holub, Joan
  Doll Hospital
Homzie, H. B.
  Alien Clones from Outer Space
Hood, Susan
  Pup and Hound

Jones, Rebecca C.
  Germy
Jones, Veda Boyd
  The American Adventure
Joosse, Barbara M.
  Wild Willie Mysteries
Jordan, Apple
  Barbie (Step Into Reading)

K

Kaaberbol, Lene, adapter
  W.I.T.C.H.—Adventures
Kalkipsakis, Thalia
  Go Girl
Kalman, Maria
  Max the Dog
Kane, Tracy I.
  Fairy Houses
Karbo, Karen
  Minerva Clark
Karr, Kathleen
  Dear Mr. President
  Petticoat Party
Kassirer, Sue
  Doug (Disney Chapter Books)
Katschke, Judy
  Full House: Dear Michelle
  Full House: Michelle
  Jackie Chan Adventures
  Mary-Kate and Ashley:
    Adventures of Mary-Kate and
    Ashley
  Mary-Kate and Ashley: Two of a
    Kind
Kay, Elizabeth
  The Divide Trilogy
Kaye, Marilyn
  Camp Sunnyside
Kchodl, Joseph J.
  PaleoJoe's Dinosaur Detective
    Club
Keane, Dave
  Joe Sherlock, Kid Detective
Keats, Ezra Jack
  Louie
  Peter
Keene, Carolyn
  Dana Girls
  Nancy Drew
  Nancy Drew: Girl Detective
  Nancy Drew and the Clue Crew
  Nancy Drew Notebooks
Keep, Linda Lowery
  Hannah and the Angels
Kehret, Peg
  Frightmares
  Pete the Cat

Keller, Beverly
  Desdemona
Keller, Holly
  Geraldine
Kellogg, Steven
  Pinkerton
Kelly, Katy
  Lucy Rose
Kennedy, Kim
  Pirate Pete
Kent, Deborah
  Saddles, Stars, and Stripes
Kerr, Judith
  Anna
Kerr, P. B.
  Children of the Lamp
Kerrin, Jessica Scott
  Martin Bridge
Kessler, Leonard
  Old Turtle
Kessler, Liz
  Emily Windsnap
Keyishian, Amy
  Ghostwriter
Kidd, Rob
  Jack Sparrow
Kimball, Katie
  Full House: Stephanie
Kimmel, Elizabeth Cody
  Lily B.
  Suddenly Supernatural
Kimpton, Diana
  Pony-Crazed Princess
Kindig, Tess Eileen
  Slam Dunk
King, M. C.
  Hannah Montana
  Suite Life of Zack and Cody
King-Smith, Dick
  Sophie
Kinkade, Thomas
  The Girls of Lighthouse Lane
Kinney, Jeff
  Diary of a Wimpy Kid
Kirby, Susan E.
  American Quilts
Kirk, David
  Miss Spider
Kirwan, Anna
  Girlhood Journeys: Juliet
  Royal Diaries
Kjelgaard, Jim
  Red
Klein, Abby
  Ready, Freddy!
Klein, Leah
  B.Y. Times
  B.Y. Times Kid Sisters

Kleinbaum, N. H.
  Ghostwriter
Kleven, Elisa
  Paper Princess
Kline, Suzy
  Herbie Jones
  Horrible Harry
  Mary Marony
  Orp
  Song Lee
Klise, Kate
  Regarding the . . .
Knotts, Kevin
  Amy Hodgepodge
Koller, Jackie French
  Dragonling
  The Keepers
  Mole and Shrew
Koltz, Tony
  Choose Your Own Adventure
Komaiko, Leah
  Annie Bananie
Komorn, Julie
  W.I.T.C.H.—Chapter Books
Koontz, Robin Michal
  Chicago and the Cat
Korman, Gordon
  Kidnapped
  NFL Monday Night Football
    Club
  Nose Pickers from Outer Space
  On the Run
  Slapshots
Korman, Justine
  Grumpy Bunny
Korman, Susan
  Ghostwriter
  Magic Attic Club
Kositsky, Lynne
  On Time's Wing
Koss, Amy Goldman
  American Girls: Girl of the Year
Kotzwinkle, William
  Walter, the Farting Dog
Kraan, Hanna
  Wicked Witch
Kraft, Erik P.
  Lenny and Mel
Krailing, Tessa
  Petsitters Club
Kraus, Robert
  Little Mouse
  Spider
Krensky, Stephen
  Arthur Chapter Books
  Arthur Chapter Books: Good
    Sports
  Lionel
  Louise
Krensky, Stephen, adapter
  Curious George

Liebold, Jay
  Choose Your Own Adventure
Limke, Jeff
  Twisted Journeys
Lindgren, Astrid
  Pippi Longstocking
Lipman, Ken
  Secret World of Alex Mack
Lisle, Janet Taylor
  Investigators of the Unknown
Litowinsky, Olga
  Wishbone Adventures
Little, Jean
  Emma
Lloyd, Alan
  House of Horrors
Lloyd, Ann
  Hannah Montana
Lobdell, Scott
  Hardy Boys, Undercover
    Brothers: Graphic Novels
Lobel, Arnold
  Frog and Toad
Locke, Joseph
  Sabrina the Teenage Witch
  Secret World of Alex Mack
Lofting, Hugh
  Doctor Dolittle
Logue, Mary
  Bloodwater Mysteries
London, Jonathan
  Froggy
Long, Loren
  Barnstormers
Lough, Loree
  The American Adventure
Lovelace, Maud Hart
  Betsy-Tacy
Lowell, Melissa
  Silver Blades
Lowry, Lois
  Anastasia Krupnik
  Gooney Bird Greene
  Sam Krupnik
Lubar, David
  Accidental Monsters
Lucas, George
  Star Wars: A New Hope—
    Manga
  Star Wars: Episode I The
    Phantom Menace—Manga
  Star Wars: The Empire Strikes
    Back—Manga
  Star Wars: The Return of the
    Jedi—Manga
Luckett, Dave
  The Rhianna Chronicles
Lukas, Catherine
  Little Bill (Nickelodeon)

Luke, David
  Rugrats (Chapter Books)
Lundell, Margo
  Sabrina the Teenage Witch
Lupica, Mike
  Comeback Kids
Lutz, Norma Jean
  The American Adventure

M

McAllister, Margaret I.
  Mistmantle Chronicles
McArthur, Nancy
  The Plant That Ate Dirty Socks
McAuley, Rowan
  Go Girl
MacBride, Roger Lea
  Little House: The Rose Years
  Little House Chapter Books:
    Rose
McCall Smith, Alexander
  Akimbo
  Harriet Bean
McCann, Jesse Leon
  Batman (Scholastic Reader)
Maccarone, Grace
  First-Grade Friends
  Magic Matt
McCay, William
  Three Investigators
  Young Indiana Jones
McCombie, Karen
  Indie Kidd
McCorkle, Mark
  Kim Possible: Pick a Villain
  Kim Possible (TokyoPop)
McCoy, Mimi
  Candy Apple
McCreary, Laura
  Angela Anaconda Chapter
    Books
McCully, Emily Arnold
  Grandmas
  Mirette
McDaniel, Becky Bring
  Katie
MacDonald, Alan
  Troll Trouble
MacDonald, Betty
  Mrs. Piggle-Wiggle
Macdonald, James D.
  Circle of Magic
McDonald, Megan
  American Girls: History
    Mysteries
  American Girls: Julie
  Beezy
  Dear America

Judy Moody
Stink
McElroy, Laurie
  Hannah Montana
McGahan, Mary
  Adventures in America
McGowen, Tom
  Age of Magic Trilogy
  Magician Trilogy
McGraw, Eloise Jervis
  Oz
MacGregor, Ellen
  Miss Pickerell
MacGregor, Roy
  Screech Owls
MacHale, D. J.
  Are You Afraid of the Dark?
  Pendragon
McInerney, Judith Whitelock
  Judge Benjamin
Mack, David
  Star Trek: S. C. E.
Mackall, Dandi Daley
  Winnie the Horse Gentler
McKay, Hilary
  Exiles
McKee, David
  Elmer
McKenna, Colleen O'Shaughnessy
  Murphy Family
  Third Grade
McKissack, Fredrick
  Jamestown's American Portraits
  Messy Bessey
  Miami
McKissack, Patricia C.
  Dear America
  Messy Bessey
  Miami
  Royal Diaries
  Scraps of Time
MacLachlan, Patricia
  Sarah, Plain and Tall
MacLean, Christine Kole
  Mary Margaret
McMahon, Maggie
  Full House: Michelle
McMahon, P. J.
  The Freaky Joe Club
McMullan, Kate
  Dragon Slayers' Academy
  Fluffy
  My America: Meg
  Myth-O-Mania
McMurtry, Ken
  Choose Your Own Nightmare
McNamara, Margaret
  Robin Hill School
McNaughton, Colin
  Preston

Minsky, Terri
Lizzie McGuire (TokyoPop)
Mitchell, Mark
Are You Afraid of the Dark?
Mitchell, V. E.
Are You Afraid of the Dark?
Secret World of Alex Mack
Star Trek: The Next
Generation: Starfleet
Academy
Moesta, Rebecca
Crystal Doors
Star Wars Junior Jedi Knights
Star Wars Young Jedi Knights
Monsell, Mary Elise
Mr. Pin
Montes, Marisa
Get Ready for Gabi
Montgomery, Anson
Choose Your Own Adventure
Montgomery, L. M.
Story Girl
Montgomery, Lucy Maud
Avonlea
Montgomery, R. A.
Choose Your Own Adventure
Choose Your Own Nightmare
Montgomery, Ramsey
Choose Your Own Adventure
Montgomery, Raymond
Choose Your Own Adventure
Montgomery, Richard
Choose Your Own Adventure
Mooney, E. S.
Powerpuff Girls Chapter Books
Moore, Eva
Magic School Bus
Magic School Bus Science
Chapter Books
Moore, Leslie
House of Horrors
Moore, Lilian
Cucumbers Trilogy
Moore, Stephanie Perry
Carmen Browne
Morgan, Melissa
Camp Confidential
Morganstern, Steve
Clue Jr.
Morris, Gilbert
Bonnets and Bugles
Time Navigators
Morris, Kimberly
Disney Fairies (Chapter Books)
Morse, Scott
Magic Pickle Graphic Novels
Mortenson, R. K.
Landon Snow
Morton, Hopi
Little Bill (Nickelodeon)

Moscovich, Rotem, adapter
Curious George
Moss, Alexandra
Royal Ballet School Diaries
Moss, Marissa
Amelia
Young American Voices
Mountain, Robert
Choose Your Own Adventure
Mueller, Kate
Choose Your Own Adventure
Muldrow, Diane
Dish
Mull, Brandon
Fablehaven
Munell, Melanie
Wishbone Classics
Muntz, Percival
Batman (Scholastic Reader)
Murphy, Elspeth Campbell
Ten Commandments Mysteries
Three Cousins Detective Club
Murphy, Jim
Dear America
My Name Is America
Murray, Glenn
Walter, the Farting Dog
Myers, Bill
Bloodhounds, Inc.
McGee and Me!
Secret Agent Dingledorf and His
Trusty Dog Splat
Myers, Walter Dean
My Name Is America
Myracle, Lauren
Winnie Perry

N

Namioka, Lensey
Yang
Napoli, Donna Jo
Angelwings
Prince of the Pond Trilogy
Sly the Sleuth
Soccer Shock
Nash, Mary
Mrs. Coverlet
Naylor, Phyllis Reynolds
Alice
Bessledorf Hotel
Club of Mysteries
Hatford Boys
Shiloh
Simply Sarah
Witch
Neill, John R.
Oz

Nerz, Ryan
Digimon Digital Monsters
Newman, Marc
Choose Your Own Adventure
Nicholson, William
The Wind of Fire
Nickel, Scott
Buzz Beaker Brainstorm
Jimmy Sniffles
Nimmo, Jenny
Children of the Red King
Gwyn Griffiths Trilogy
Nix, Garth
Keys to the Kingdom
Nixon, Joan Lowery
Casebusters
The Nic-Nacs and the Nic-Nac
News
Orphan Train Adventures
Orphan Train Children
Young Americans: Colonial
Williamsburg
Noble, Trinka Hakes
Jimmy's Boa
Nodelman, Jeffrey
Doug Chronicles
Noll, Katherine
Full House: Dear Michelle
Roller Coaster Tycoon
Norton, Mary
Borrowers
Numeroff, Laura
If You Give a . . .

O

O'Brien, Robert C.
Rats of NIMH
O'Connor, Charles
Bratz
O'Hara, Mary
Flicka
Oatman, Eric
I Am American
O'Connor, Jane
Fancy Nancy
Fancy Nancy Readers
Here Come the Brownies
O'Dell, Kathleen
Agnes Parker
Odgers, Darrel
Jack Russell: Dog Detective
Odgers, Sally
Jack Russell: Dog Detective
Odom, Mel
Journey of Allen Strange
Sabrina the Teenage Witch
Secret World of Alex Mack

Pielichaty, Helena
  Girls of Avenue Z
Pierce, Tamora
  Protector of the Small
Pike, Christopher
  Spooksville
Pilkey, Dav
  Captain Underpants
  Captain Underpants: Super
    Diaper Baby
  Dragon
  Ricky Ricotta
Pinkney, Andrea Davis
  Dear Mr. President
Pinkwater, Daniel (Manus)
  Big Bob
  Irving and Muktuk
  Larry the Polar Bear
  Werewolf Club
Plummer, Rachel
  Dungeons and Dragons:
    Knights of the Silver Dragon
Pollack, Pam
  Dexter's Laboratory Chapter
    Books
  Digimon Digital Monsters
  Malcolm in the Middle
  So Weird
Ponti, James
  Journey of Allen Strange
  Mystery Files of Shelby Woo
Poploff, Michelle
  The Barkers
Porte, Barbara Ann
  Harry
Porter, Connie
  American Girls: Addy
Posner-Sanchez, Andrea
  Disney Princess Secrets
Potter, Ellen
  Olivia Kidney
Poulsen, David A.
  Salt and Pepper Chronicles
Pratchett, Terry
  Johnny Maxwell
Preiss, Pauline
  Full House: Michelle
  Mary-Kate and Ashley:
    Adventures of Mary-Kate and
    Ashley
Preller, James
  Jigsaw Jones Mystery
Prenzlau, Sheryl
  B.Y. Times Kid Sisters
Pride, Felicia
  Everybody Hates Chris
Primavera, Elise
  Fred and Anthony
Prior, Natalie Jane
  Lily Quench

Probosz, Kathilyn Solomon
  The Pink Parrots
Proimos, James
  Johnny Mutton
Proysen, Alf
  Mrs. Pepperpot
Pryor, Bonnie
  American Adventures
Pugliano-Martin, Carol
  Barbie (Step Into Reading)
Pulver, Robin
  Mrs. Toggle

Q

Quackenbush, Robert
  Detective Mole
  Miss Mallard
Quattlebaum, Mary
  Jackson Jones
Quin-Harkin, Janet
  Full House: Club Stephanie
  Sister Sister
Quinn, Zoe
  The Caped 6th Grader

R

Raffa, Edwina
  Adventures in America
Ramirez, Michael Rose
  ¡Chana!
Rand, Gloria
  Salty
Rand, Johnathan
  American Chillers
Ransom, Candice F.
  Dungeons and Dragons:
    Knights of the Silver Dragon
  Kobie Roberts
  Time Spies
Rayner, Mary
  Mr. and Mrs. Pig
Redbank, Tennant
  Barbie (Step Into Reading)
Redeker, Kent
  Angela Anaconda Chapter
    Books
Reece, Colleen L.
  The American Adventure
  Juli Scott Super Sleuth
Reed, Teresa
  Magic Attic Club
Rees, Elizabeth M.
  The Jersey
  So Weird

Regan, Dian Curtis
  Monster of the Month Club
Reiche, Dietlof
  The Golden Hamster Saga
Reid, Robin
  Little Bill (Nickelodeon)
Reisfeld, Randi
  Candy Apple
  Sabrina the Teenage Witch
  Zoey 101
Reisner, Molly
  Avatar (Ready to Read)
Reiss, Kathryn
  American Girls: American Girl
    Mysteries
  American Girls: History
    Mysteries
  Time Travel Mysteries
Rey, Hans Augusto
  Curious George
Rey, Margret
  Curious George
Reymes, Ellen
  Full House: Michelle
Reynolds, Aaron
  Tiger Moth
Richards, Barbara
  Barbie (Step Into Reading)
Richards, Justin
  Invisible Detectives
Richards, Kitty
  Disney Fairies (Chapter Books)
  Hannah Montana
  Rugrats (Chapter Books)
  Rugrats Files
  SpongeBob SquarePants
    Chapter Books
  Suite Life of Zack and Cody
  The Wild Thornberrys
Richardson, Arleta
  Grandma's Attic
Richardson, Nancy
  Star Wars Junior Jedi Knights
Riddell, Chris
  Edge Chronicles
  Far-Flung Adventures
  A Knight's Story
Rinaldi, Ann
  Dear America
  My Name Is America
Riordan, James
  My Side of the Story
Riordan, Rick
  Percy Jackson and the
    Olympians
Rispin, Karen
  Anika Scott
Robberecht, Thierry
  Sam
Roberts, Bethany
  Holiday Mice

Roberts, Christine N.
  Bratz: Clued In!

Roberts, Jeremy
  Eerie Indiana

Roberts, Kerry Daniel
  Dungeons and Dragons:
    Knights of the Silver Dragon

Roberts, Rachel
  Avalon 1: Web of Magic
  Avalon 1: Web of Magic
  Avalon 2: Quest for Magic

Roberts, Shelly
  Avalon 1: Web of Magic

Robertson, Keith
  Henry Reed

Robertson, M. P.
  George and His Dragon

Robins, Joan
  Addie

Robinson, Barbara
  The Herdman Kids

Robinson, Nancy K.
  Angela
  Veronica

Rock, Gail
  Addie

Rodda, Emily
  Deltora: Deltora Quest
  Deltora: Deltora Shadowlands
  Deltora: Dragons of Deltora
  Fairy Realm
  Rowan of Rin

Roddy, Lee
  American Adventure
  D.J. Dillon Adventures
  Ladd Family

Rodriguez, K. S.
  Are You Afraid of the Dark?

Rogers, Amy Keating
  Powerpuff Girls Chapter Books

Rogers, Jonathan
  Wilderking Trilogy

Rogers, Mary
  Annabel Andrews

Roop, Peter
  Jamestown's American Portraits

Rosado, Maria
  Rugrats (Chapter Books)
  Rugrats Files
  The Wild Thornberrys

Rose, Miriam
  Baker's Dozen

Rosenberry, Vera
  Vera

Ross, Pat
  M and M
  Once Upon America

Rounds, Glen
  Mr. Yowder

Rovetch, L. Bob
  Hot Dog and Bob

Rowland, Della
  Clue Jr.

Rowling, J. K.
  Harry Potter

Roy, Ron
  A to Z Mysteries
  Capital Mysteries

Royce, Easton
  Space Above and Beyond
  X Files

Rubin, Jim
  Doug Chronicles

Ruby, Lois
  My Side of the Story

Ruditis, Paul
  Sabrina the Teenage Witch
  Star Trek: Enterprise

Rue, Nancy N.
  FaithGirlz: Sophie

Ruelle, Karen Gray
  Harry and Emily

Rumble, Chris
  The Adventures of Uncle Stinky

Runton, Andy
  Owly Graphic Novels

Rusch, Kristine K.
  Star Trek: Enterprise

Ryan, Margaret
  Airy Fairy

Ryan, Pam Munoz
  Doug Chronicles

Rylant, Cynthia
  Annie and Snowball
  Cobble Street Cousins
  Henry and Mudge
  Henry and Mudge: Puppy
    Mudge
  High-Rise Private Eyes
  Lighthouse Family
  Little Whistle
  Mr. Putter and Tabby
  Poppleton

S

Sachar, Louis
  Marvin Redpost
  Wayside School

Sachs, Marilyn
  Amy and Laura

Sadler, Marilyn
  Alistair
  P.J. Funnybunny
  Zenon, Girl of the 21st Century

Sage, Angie
  Araminta Spookie
  Septimus Heap

St. Antoine, Sara
  Ghostwriter

Sakai, Stan
  Usagi Yojimbo

Salat, Cristina
  Ghostwriter

Salmon, Michael
  Piganeers

Sampson, Fay
  Pangur Ban

Samuel, Catherine
  Fairly OddParents

Samuels, Barbara
  Duncan and Dolores

Sander, Heather
  Robbie Packford

Sansevere, J. R.
  Mercer Mayer's Critters of the
    Night

San Souci, Daniel
  Clubhouse

Sanvoisin, Eric
  The Ink Drinker

Sathre, Vivian
  Wishbone: The Early Years
  Wishbone Adventures
  Wishbone Mysteries

Saunders, Susan
  All-American Puppies
  Black Cat Club
  Neptune Adventures
  Sleepover Friends

Schachner, Judy
  Skippyjon Jones

Schade, Susan
  Cat
  Danger Joe Show
  Fog Mound

Schaefer, Lola M.
  Mittens

Scheffler, Ursel
  Rinaldo

Schembri, Pamela
  2nd-Grade Friends

Scheving, Magnus
  LazyTown (8 x 8 Books)

Schooley, Bob
  Kim Possible: Pick a Villain
  Kim Possible (TokyoPop)

Schreiber, Anne
  Magic School Bus Science
    Chapter Books

Schulte, Elaine L.
  Twelve Candles Club

Schulz, Charles M.
  Peanuts

Schwabacher, Martin
  Magic School Bus
  Magic School Bus Science
    Chapter Books

Schwartz, Ellen
 Starshine!
Schwartz, Roslyn
 Mole Sisters
Scieszka, Jon
 Time Warp Trio
 Time Warp Trio Graphic
  Novels
 Time Warp Trio (novelizations)
Scollon, E. W.
 Goners
Scott, Gavin
 Young Indiana Jones
Scotton, Rob
 Russell the Sheep
Scroggs, Kirk
 Wiley and Grampa's Creature
  Feature
Scull, Robert
 Little Bill (Nickelodeon)
Sedita, Francesco
 Candy Apple
Seidman, David L.
 Are You Afraid of the Dark?
Seldon, George
 Chester Cricket
Selene, Patrice
 Wishbone Classics
Selman, Matty
 The Jersey
Seuling, Barbara
 Robert
Sfar, Joan
 Sardine in Outer Space
Shahan, Sherry
 Eerie Indiana
Shannon, David
 David
Shanower, Eric
 Oz
Sharmat, Marjorie Weinman
 Genghis Khan
 Maggie Marmelstein
 Nate the Great
 Olivia Sharp, Agent for Secrets
Sharmat, Mitchell
 Olivia Sharp, Agent for Secrets
Sharp, Margery
 The Rescuers
Shaw, Janet B.
 American Girls: Kaya
 American Girls: Kirsten
Shaw, Janet Beeler
 American Girls: American Girl
  Mysteries
Shaw, Mary
 Brady Brady
Shaw, Nancy
 Sheep

Shealy, Dennis R.
 Treasure Planet
Sheely, Robert,
 Adventures in America
Shefelman, Janice
 Young Wolf
Sheldon, Dyan
 Harry and Chicken
Shetterly, Will
 Voyage of the Basset
Shields, Gillian
 Mermaid S. O. S.
Shreve, Susan Richards
 Joshua T. Bates
Siamon, Sharon
 Mustang Mountain
 Saddle Island
Siefken, Paul
 Powerpuff Girls Chapter Books
 Samurai Jack Chapter Books
Siegel, Malky
 Baker's Dozen
Siegman, Meryl
 Choose Your Own Adventure
Silverman, Erica
 Cowgirl Kate and Cocoa
Simon, Barbara Brooks
 I Am American
Simon, Francesca
 Horrid Henry
Simon, Lisa
 Full House: Stephanie
Simon, Seymour
 Einstein Anderson
Simons, Jamie
 Goners
Simpson, Fiona
 Zoey 101
Simpson, Robert
 Mystic Knights of Tir Na Nog
Sims, Blanche
 Polka Dot Private Eye
Sinclair, Jay
 The Jersey
Singer, A. L.
 Young Indiana Jones
Singletary, Mabel Elizabeth
 The Double Dutch Club
Singleton, Linda Joy
 My Sister, the Ghost
Sinykin, Sheri Cooper
 Magic Attic Club
Skidmore, Steve
 Tales of the Dark Forest
 Vernon Bright
Skinner, Daphne
 Disney Princesses: My Side of
  the Story
 Disney Villains: My Side of the
  Story

Skurzynski, Gloria
 Mysteries in Our National Parks
Skye, Obert
 Leven Thumps
Slack, David
 Jackie Chan Adventures
Slade, Arthur G.
 Northern Frights
Slate, Joseph
 Miss Bindergarten
Slater, Teddy
 Junior Gymnasts
Slobodkin, Louis
 Space Ship Under the Apple
  Tree
Slote, Alfred
 Jack Jameson and Danny One
Small, Charlie
 Charlie Small
Smith, Dean Wesley and Rusch
 Star Trek: Enterprise
Smith, Dona
 Clue
Smith, Elizabeth
 Magic School Bus
Smith, Janice Lee
 Adam Joshua Capers
 Wizard and Wart
Smith, Patricia Clark
 Royal Diaries
Smith, Sherwood
 Voyage of the Basset
 Wren
Smith, Susan
 Best Friends
Snelling, Lauraine
 High Hurdles
Snicket, Lemony
 A Series of Unfortunate Events
Sniegoski, Tom
 Billy Hooten, Owlboy
 Outcast
Snow, Jack
 Oz
Snyder, Carol
 Ike and Mama
Snyder, Zilpha Keatley
 Castle Court Kids
Sobol, Donald J.
 Encyclopedia Brown
Soesbee, Ree
 Dungeons and Dragons:
  Knights of the Silver Dragon
Soto, Gary
 American Girls: Girl of the Year
Spalding, Andrea
 The Summer of Magic Quartet
Spelvin, Justin
 LazyTown (8 x 8 Books)

T

Takeuchi, Naoko
Sailor Moon Novels

Talbot, Hudson, reteller
King Arthur

Tate, Eleanora E.
American Girls: History
Mysteries

Taylor, Julie, editor
Hannah Montana (TokyoPop)

Taylor, Mark
Henry the Explorer

Taylor, Mildred D.
Logan Family

Taylor, Sydney
All-of-a-Kind Family

Taylor, Theodore
Outer Banks Trilogy

Teague, Mark
LaRue

Teitelbaum, Michael
Avatar: The Earth Kingdom
Chronicles
Avatar: The Last Airbender
Avatar (Ready to Read)
Clue Jr.
LazyTown (8 x 8 Books)
Mystic Knights of Tir Na Nog
NASCAR Racers
Sonic the Hedgehog

Telep, Peter
Space Above and Beyond

Temple, Bob
Jimmy Sniffles

Terman, Douglas
Choose Your Own Adventure

Terry, Irwin
Oz

Teske, Robert T.
McGee and Me!

Thacker, Nola
Skating Dreams

Thaler, Mike
Black Lagoon
Funny Firsts

Thiesing, Lisa
Silly Thrillers with Peggy the Pig

Thomas, Dawn C. Gill
Girlhood Journeys: Kai

Thomas, Jim
Mary-Kate and Ashley:
Adventures of Mary-Kate and
Ashley
7th Heaven

Thomas, Lucinda
Full House: Stephanie

Thomas, Shelley Moore
Good Knight

Thompson, Carol
Mary-Kate and Ashley:
Adventures of Mary-Kate and
Ashley

Thompson, Colin
The Floods

Thompson, Gare
I Am American

Thompson, Jill
Scary Godmother

Thompson, Kay
Eloise

Thompson, Lisa
SWAT (Secret World Adventure
Team)

Thompson, Ruth Plumly
Oz

Thornhill, Samantha
Everybody Hates Chris

Thorpe, Kiki
Disney Fairies (Chapter Books)
Disney Princesses: My Side of
the Story
Disney Villains: My Side of the
Story
Kim Possible (Chapter Books)
Lizzie McGuire
Oswald (Ready-to-Read)
Treasure Planet
The Wild Thornberrys

Titus, Eve
Anatole
Basil of Baker Street

Tolan, Stephanie S.
The Great Skinner

Tolkien, J. R. R.
Lord of the Rings

Topek, Susan Remick
Noah

Torrey, Michelle
Science Detectives

Townley, Roderick
Sylvie Cycle

Travers, P. L.
Mary Poppins

Trine, Greg
Melvin Beederman, Superhero

Tripp, Valerie
American Girls: Felicity
American Girls: Josefina
American Girls: Kit
American Girls: Molly
American Girls: Samantha
Hopscotch Hill School

Trout, Richard
MacGregor Family Adventure

Trueit, Trudi
Julep O'Toole

Trumbauer, Lisa Trutkoff
Dungeons and Dragons:
Knights of the Silver Dragon

Tryon, Leslie
Albert (the Duck)

Turkle, Brinton
Obadiah Starbuck

Turner, Ann Warren
Dear America

Turner, Megan Whelan
Attolia

U

Uchida, Yoshiko
Rinko

Umansky, Diane
Full House: Stephanie

Ure, Jean
Wizard Trilogy

Ursu, Anne
The Cronus Chronicles

V

Vail, Rachel
Mama Rex and T

Vail, Virginia
Animal Inn

Valentine, E. J.
The Pink Parrots

Valentine, James
TimeJumpers

Van Draanen, Wendelin
Sammy Keyes
Shredderman

Van Leeuwen, Jean
Marvin the Magnificent
Oliver and Amanda Pig
Pioneer Daughters

Van Nutt, Julia
Cobtown

VanRiper, Gary
Adirondack Kids

VanRiper, Justin
Adirondack Kids

Velthuijs, Max
Frog

Verney, Sarah
Full House: Michelle
Full House: Stephanie

Vincent, Gabrielle
Ernest and Celestine

Vinge, Joan Dennison
Oz

Viorst, Judith
Alexander

Vitamina, Eduardo
Treasure Planet

Voigt, Cynthia
Tillerman Cycle
Von Moschzisker, Felix
Choose Your Own Adventure
Vornholt, John
Are You Afraid of the Dark?
Journey of Allen Strange
Sabrina the Teenage Witch
Secret World of Alex Mack
Star Trek: Starfleet Academy
Star Trek: The Next
Generation: Starfleet
Academy
Troll King

W

Waber, Bernard
Lyle
Waddell, Martin
Little Bear
Wallace, Bill
Upchuck and the Rotten Willy
Wallace, Jim
Choose Your Own Adventure
Wallace, Rich
Winning Season
Walls, Pamela
Abby's South Seas Adventures
Walsh, Ellen Stoll
Dot and Jabber
Ward, Dayton
Star Trek: S. C. E.
Wargin, Kathy-jo
Mitt and Minn
Waricha, Jean
Full House: Dear Michelle
Full House: Michelle
Mary-Kate and Ashley:
Adventures of Mary-Kate and
Ashley
Warner, Gertrude Chandler
Boxcar Children
Boxcar Children: Adventures of
Benny and Watch
Warner, Sally
Emma
Lily
Warriner, Holly
Spell Casters
Warriner, Mercer
Sabrina the Teenage Witch
Wasserman, Robin
Candy Apple
Watson, Jude
Star Wars: Jedi Quest
Star Wars: The Last of the Jedi
Star Wars Episode 1: Journals

Watson, Kim
Little Bill (Nickelodeon)
Watt, Melanie
Scaredy Squirrel
Waugh, Sylvia
Mennyms
Ormingat
Wax, Wendy
Adventures in America
Fairly OddParents
LazyTown (Ready to Read)
Rocket Power
Totally Spies!
Wayans, Kim
Amy Hodgepodge
Weaver, Lydia
Once Upon America
Webster, Christy
Barbie (Step Into Reading)
Weeks, Sarah
Boyds Will Be Boyds
Guy Strang
Weiner, Eric
Clue
Ghostwriter
Weiss, Bobbi J. G.
Are You Afraid of the Dark?
Are You Afraid of the Dark?
Dexter's Laboratory Chapter
Books
Journey of Allen Strange
Roller Coaster Tycoon
Sabrina the Teenage Witch
Secret World of Alex Mack
Star Trek: The Next
Generation: Starfleet
Academy
Star Trek: Voyager: Starfleet
Academy
Weiss, Dan
Super Hoops
Weiss, David Cody
Are You Afraid of the Dark?
Are You Afraid of the Dark?
Journey of Allen Strange
Sabrina the Teenage Witch
Secret World of Alex Mack
Star Trek: The Next
Generation: Starfleet
Academy
Star Trek: Voyager: Starfleet
Academy
Weiss, David M.
Roller Coaster Tycoon
Weiss, Ellen
Carmen Sandiego Mysteries
Hitty's Travels
The Weebie Zone
Welch, Leona Nicholas
Girlhood Journeys: Kai
Wells, Rosemary
Edward the Unready

McDuff
Max and Ruby
Voyage to the Bunny Planet
Yoko and Friends
Weninger, Brigitte
Davy
Wesley, Valerie Wilson
Willimena Rules!
West, Cathy
Full House: Michelle
Jackie Chan Adventures
West, Eliza
Full House: Stephanie
West, Nick
Three Investigators
West, Robert
McGee and Me!
West, Tracey
Atomic Betty
Carmen Sandiego Mysteries
Pixie Tricks
Roller Coaster Tycoon
Samurai Jack Chapter Books
Scream Shop
Totally Spies!
Weston, Carol
Melanie Martin
Weyn, Suzanne
Forever Angels
Full House: Michelle
Full House: Sisters
Full House: Stephanie
House of Horrors
Wheeler, Chase
Speed Racer
Wheeler, Lisa
Fitch and Chip
Whelan, Gloria
Starvation Lake
White, Ellen Emerson
Dear America
My Name Is America
Royal Diaries
White, John
The Archives of Anthropos
White, Nancy
Magic School Bus Science
Chapter Books
Whitman, John
Adventures of Shirley Holmes
Digimon Digital Monsters
Mystic Knights of Tir Na Nog
NASCAR Racers
Star Wars Galaxy of Fear
Whittemore, Jo
Silverskin Legacy
Whybrow, Ian
Little Wolf
Wiebe, Trina
Max-a-Million

TITLE INDEX

The series in which the title appears is shown in parentheses following the title. Series are listed in alphabetical order in the main section of this book.

A

Aang's School Days (Avatar (Ready to Read))

Abandoned! (Puppy Patrol)

Abandoned on the Wild Frontier (Trailblazers)

Abandoned Puppy (Animal Emergency)

Abby and the Best Kid Ever (Baby-Sitters Club)

Abby and the Mystery Baby (Baby-Sitters Club Mysteries)

Abby and the Notorious Neighbor (Baby-Sitters Club Mysteries)

Abby and the Secret Society (Baby-Sitters Club Mysteries)

Abby in Wonderland (Baby-Sitters Club)

Abby Takes a Stand (Scraps of Time)

Abby the Bad Sport (Baby-Sitters Club)

Abby's Book (Baby-Sitters Club Portrait Collection)

Abby's Lucky Thirteen (Baby-Sitters Club)

Abby's Twin (Baby-Sitters Club)

Abby's Un-Valentine (Baby-Sitters Club)

Abduction (Kidnapped)

Abigail the Breeze Fairy (Rainbow Magic: Weather Fairies)

Abner and Me (Baseball Card Adventures)

The Abominable Snow Monster (Graveyard School)

Abominable Snowman (Choose Your Own Adventure)

The Abominable Snowman Doesn't Roast Marshmallows (Bailey School: The Adventures of the Bailey School Kids)

The Abominable Snowman of Pasadena (Goosebumps)

About-Face Space Race (AstroKids)

Above the Rim (Super Hoops)

The Abracadabra Case (Hardy Boys: Frank and Joe Hardy: The Clues Brothers)

Abracadabra! (Mouse and Mole)

Abracadanger (Scream Shop)

Abracadeath (Hardy Boys, Undercover Brothers: Graphic Novels)

Abraham Lincoln (Dear Mr. President)

The Absent Author (A to Z Mysteries)

The Absolute (Animorphs)

Absolute Zero (Bagthorpe Saga)

Absolutely Positively Alexander (Alexander)

Accessory to the Crime (Bratz: Clued In!)

The Accident (Christopher)

The Accidental Cheerleader (Candy Apple)

Accidental Lily (Lily)

Accidentally Fabulous (Candy Apple)

Achingly Alice (Alice)

Acrobat Cats (Sagwa, The Chinese Siamese Cat (Readers))

Across the Puddingstone Dam (Little House: The Charlotte Years)

Across the Rolling River (Little House: The Caroline Years)

Across the Steel River (Across the Steel River)

Across the Wide and Lonesome Prairie (Dear America)

Action! (Nancy Drew: Girl Detective)

Adam Mouse's Book of Poems (Cucumbers Trilogy)

Adam Sharp (Adam Sharp)

Adam Sharp: The Spy Who Barked (Adam Sharp)

Addie Across the Prairie (Addie)

Addie and the King of Hearts (Addie)

Addie Meets Max (Addie)

Addie Runs Away (Addie)

Addie's Bad Day (Addie)

Addie's Dakota Winter (Addie)

Addie's Forever Friend (Addie)

Addie's Long Summer (Addie)

Addy Learns a Lesson (American Girls: Addy)

Addy Saves the Day (American Girls: Addy)

Addy's Surprise (American Girls: Addy)

Adios, Anna (Friends and Amigos)

The Adirondack Kids (Adirondack Kids)

Adopt-a-Pet (Animal Inn)

Adventure (Beryl E. Bean)

Adventure at Walt Disney World (Disney Girls)

Adventure in Gold Town (Klondike Kid)

Adventure in the Wilderness (The American Adventure)

Adventure on the Wilderness Road, 1775 (American Sisters)

An Adventure with Captain Brainstorm! (Little Bill (Nickelodeon))

The Adventures of Ali Baba Bernstein (Ali Baba Bernstein)

The Adventures of Captain Underpants (Captain Underpants)

The Adventures of Commander Zack Proton and the Red Giant (Zack Proton)

The Adventures of Commander Zack Proton and the Warlords of Nibblecheese (Zack Proton)

The Adventures of Commander Zack Proton and the Wrong Planet (Zack Proton)

The Adventures of Jack Ninepins (Jenny and the Cat Club)

The Adventures of Johnny May (Johnny May)

The Adventures of Laura and Jack (Little House Chapter Books: Laura)

The Adventures of Mole and Troll (Mole and Troll)

Adventures of Obadiah (Obadiah Starbuck)

The Adventures of Paddy Pork (Paddy Pork)

The Adventures of Robin Hood (Wishbone Classics)

The Adventures of Rose and Swiney (Little House Chapter Books: Rose)

The Adventures of Super Diaper Baby (Captain Underpants: Super Diaper Baby)

The Adventures of Tom Sawyer (Wishbone Classics)

Adventures on File Island (Digimon Digital Monsters)

African Safari (Young Indiana Jones Chronicles: Choose Your Own Adventure)

After School Ghost Hunter (Klooz)

After the Dinosaurs (Berenstain Bears)

After the Rain (My America: Virginia)

After the Storm (Heartland)

Aftermath (Remnants)

Aftermath (Star Trek: S. C. E.)

Afternoon on the Amazon (Magic Tree House)

Aftershock (Star Trek: Starfleet Academy)

The Against Taffy Sinclair Club (Taffy Sinclair)

Against the Empire (Star Wars: The Last of the Jedi)

Against the Rules (Soccer Stars)

Agapanthus Hum and Major Bark (Agapanthus Hum)

Agapanthus Hum and the Angel Hoot (Agapanthus Hum)

Agapanthus Hum and the Eyeglasses (Agapanthus Hum)

The Age of Aquariums (Sabrina the Teenage Witch)

The Age of Bronze (Jack Sparrow)

Aggie's Home (Orphan Train Children)

Agnes May Gleason, Walsenburg, Colorado, 1932 (American Diaries)

Agnes Parker . . . Girl in Progress (Agnes Parker)

Agnes Parker . . . Happy Camper? (Agnes Parker)

Agnes Parker . . . Keeping Cool in Middle School (Agnes Parker)

The Agony of Alice (Alice)

Ah-Choo! (Oswald (Ready-to-Read))

Ahoy, Ghost Ship Ahead! (Pirate School)

Ahoy There, Little Polar Bear (Little Polar Bear)

Aimer Gate (Stone Book Quartet)

The Akhenaten Adventure (Children of the Lamp)

Akiko (Akiko)

Akiko: The Training Master (Akiko)

Akiko and the Alpha Centauri 5000 (Akiko)

Akiko and the Great Wall of Trudd (Akiko)

Akiko and the Intergalactic Zoo (Akiko)

Akiko and the Journey to Toog (Akiko)

Akiko and the Missing Misp (Akiko)

Akiko in the Castle of Alia Rellapor (Akiko)

Akiko in the Sprubly Islands (Akiko)

Akiko on the Planet Smoo (Akiko)

Akimbo and the Crocodile Man (Akimbo)

Akimbo and the Elephants (Akimbo)

Akimbo and the Lions (Akimbo)

Akimbo and the Snakes (Akimbo)

Aladdin (Wishbone: The Early Years)

The Alaskan Adventure (Hardy Boys)

Albert's Alphabet (Albert (the Duck))

Albert's Ballgame (Albert (the Duck))

Albert's Birthday (Albert (the Duck))

Albert's Christmas (Albert (the Duck))

Albert's Field Trip (Albert (the Duck))

Albert's Halloween (Albert (the Duck))

Albert's Play (Albert (the Duck))

Albert's Thanksgiving (Albert (the Duck))

The Alchemist's Cat (Deptford Histories)

Alcott Library Is Falling Down (Peanut Butter and Jelly)

Aldo Applesauce (Aldo Sossi)

Aldo Ice Cream (Aldo Sossi)

Aldo Peanut Butter (Aldo Sossi)

Alex Ryan, Stop That (Losers, Inc.)

Alex, You're Glowing! (Secret World of Alex Mack)

Alexander and the Terrible, Horrible, No Good, Very Bad Day (Alexander)

Alexander, Who Used to be Rich Last Sunday (Alexander)

Alexander, Who's Not (Do You Hear Me? I Mean It!) Going to Move (Alexander)

Alexandra the Great (Al (Alexandra))

Alexia Ellery Finsdale, San Francisco, 1905 (American Diaries)

Alex's Challenge (Camp Confidential)

Alex's Triple Treat (Alex)

Alfie and the Birthday Surprise (Alfie Rose)

Alfie Gets in First (Alfie Rose)

Alfie Gives a Hand (Alfie Rose)

Alfie's ABC (Alfie Rose)

Alfie's Feet (Alfie Rose)

Alfie's 1 2 3 (Alfie Rose)

Ali Baba Bernstein, Lost and Found (Ali Baba Bernstein)

Alias Diamond Jones (Ghostwriter)

Alice Alone (Alice)

Alice in April (Alice)

Alice In-Between (Alice)

Alice in Blunderland (Alice)

Alice in Lace (Alice)

Alice in Rapture, Sort of (Alice)

Alice in the Know (Alice)

Alice on Her Way (Alice)

Alice on the Outside (Alice)

Alice the Brave (Alice)

The Alien (Animorphs)

Alien Alert (Ghostwriter)

Alien Androids Assault Arizona (American Chillers)

Amber and Alfie (Best Friends)

Amber Brown Goes Fourth (Amber Brown)

Amber Brown Is Feeling Blue (Amber Brown)

Amber Brown Is Green with Envy (Amber Brown)

Amber Brown Is Not a Crayon (Amber Brown)

Amber Brown Sees Red (Amber Brown)

Amber Brown Wants Extra Credit (Amber Brown)

Amber the Orange Fairy (Rainbow Magic: Rainbow Fairies)

Amber's First Task (Mermaid S. O. S.)

Ambush at Amboseli (Anika Scott)

Ambush in the Wilderness (Adventures in America)

Ambushed in Jaguar Swamp (Trailblazers)

Amelia Bedelia (Amelia Bedelia)

Amelia Bedelia and the Baby (Amelia Bedelia)

Amelia Bedelia and the Cat (Amelia Bedelia)

Amelia Bedelia and the Surprise Shower (Amelia Bedelia)

Amelia Bedelia, Bookworm (Amelia Bedelia)

Amelia Bedelia 4 Mayor (Amelia Bedelia)

Amelia Bedelia Goes Camping (Amelia Bedelia)

Amelia Bedelia Helps Out (Amelia Bedelia)

Amelia Bedelia, Rocket Scientist? (Amelia Bedelia)

Amelia Bedelia Talks Turkey (Amelia Bedelia)

Amelia Bedelia Under Construction (Amelia Bedelia)

Amelia Bedelia's Family Album (Amelia Bedelia)

Amelia Bedelia's Masterpiece (Amelia Bedelia)

Amelia Hits the Road (Amelia)

Amelia Lends a Hand (Amelia)

Amelia Takes Command (Amelia)

Amelia Works it Out (Amelia)

Amelia Writes Again (Amelia)

Amelia's 5th-Grade Notebook (Amelia)

Amelia's Are-We-There-Yet Longest Ever Car Trip (Amelia)

Amelia's Best Year Ever (Amelia)

Amelia's Book of Notes and Note Passing (Amelia)

Amelia's Bully Survival Guide (Amelia)

Amelia's Easy-As-Pie Drawing Guide (Amelia)

Amelia's Family Ties (Amelia)

Amelia's Itchy-Twitchy, Lovey-Dovey Summer at Camp Mosquito (Amelia)

Amelia's Longest, Biggest, Most-Fights-Ever Family Reunion (Amelia)

Amelia's Most Unforgettable Embarrassing Moments (Amelia)

Amelia's Notebook (Amelia)

Amelia's 7th-Grade Notebook (Amelia)

Amelia's 6th-Grade Notebook (Amelia)

Amelina Carrett, Bayou Grand Coeur, Louisiana, 1863 (American Diaries)

The American Revolution (The American Adventure)

An American Spring (My America: Sofia)

The American Victory (The American Adventure)

Among the Barons (Shadow Children)

Among the Betrayed (Shadow Children)

Among the Brave (Shadow Children)

Among the Enemy (Shadow Children)

Among the Free (Shadow Children)

Among the Hidden (Shadow Children)

Among the Imposters (Shadow Children)

Amos and the Alien (Culpepper Adventures)

Amos and the Chameleon Caper (Culpepper Adventures)

Amos and the Vampire (Culpepper Adventures)

Amos Binder, Secret Agent (Culpepper Adventures)

Amos Gets Famous (Culpepper Adventures)

Amos Gets Married (Culpepper Adventures)

Amos Goes Bananas (Culpepper Adventures)

Amos's Killer Concert Caper (Culpepper Adventures)

Amos's Last Stand (Culpepper Adventures)

The Amulet of Samarkand (The Bartimaeus Trilogy)

The Amusement Park Mystery (Boxcar Children)

Amy and Laura (Amy and Laura)

Amy Loves the Rain (Amy)

Amy Loves the Snow (Amy)

Amy Loves the Sun (Amy)

Amy Loves the Wind (Amy)

Amy Makes a Friend (Portraits of Little Women)

Amy Moves In (Amy and Laura)

Amy Onstage (Always Friends)

Amy the Amethyst Fairy (Rainbow Magic: Jewel Fairies)

Amy's Haunted House (Always Friends)

Amy's (Not So) Great Camp-Out (Here Come the Brownies)

Amy's Story (Portraits of Little Women)

Amy's True Prize (Little Women Journals)

Anacaona, Golden Flower (Royal Diaries)

Anakin Skywalker (Star Wars Episode 1: Journals)

Anakin's Quest (Star Wars Junior Jedi Knights)

Anastasia (Royal Diaries)

Anastasia, Absolutely (Anastasia Krupnik)

Anastasia Again! (Anastasia Krupnik)

Anastasia, Ask Your Analyst (Anastasia Krupnik)

Anastasia at This Address (Anastasia Krupnik)

Anastasia at Your Service (Anastasia Krupnik)

Anastasia Has the Answers (Anastasia Krupnik)

Anastasia Krupnik (Anastasia Krupnik)

Anastasia on Her Own (Anastasia Krupnik)

Anastasia's Chosen Career (Anastasia Krupnik)

Anatole (Anatole)

Anatole and the Cat (Anatole)

Anatole and the Piano (Anatole)

Anatole and the Pied Piper (Anatole)

Anatole and the Poodle (Anatole)

Anatole and the Robot (Anatole)

The Angry Intruder (Christy)

Anika's Mountain (Anika Scott)

Animal Adventures (Little House Chapter Books: Laura)

Animal Attraction and All the News (Kim Possible (TokyoPop))

Animal Riddles (Shanna First Readers)

The Animal Shelter Mystery (Boxcar Children)

Anisett Lundberg, California, 1851 (American Diaries)

Annabel the Actress Starring in Camping It Up (Annabel the Actress)

Annabel the Actress Starring in Gorilla My Dreams (Annabel the Actress)

Annabel the Actress Starring in Just a Little Extra (Annabel the Actress)

Annabel the Actress Starring in the Hound of the Barkervilles (Annabel the Actress)

Anne of Avonlea (Avonlea)

Anne of Green Gables (Avonlea)

Anne of Ingleside (Avonlea)

Anne of the Island (Avonlea)

Anne of Windy Poplars (Avonlea)

Anne's House of Dreams (Avonlea)

Annie and Snowball and the Dress-Up Birthday (Annie and Snowball)

Annie and Snowball and the Pink Surprise (Annie and Snowball)

Annie and Snowball and the Prettiest House (Annie and Snowball)

Annie and Snowball and the Teacup Club (Annie and Snowball)

Annie Bananie (Annie Bananie)

Annie Bananie: Best Friends to the End (Annie Bananie)

Annie Bananie and the Pain Sisters (Annie Bananie)

Annie Bananie and the People's Court (Annie Bananie)

Annie Bananie Moves to Barry Avenue (Annie Bananie)

Annie Pat and Eddie (Eddie Wilson)

Annie Pitts, Artichoke (Annie Pitts)

Annie Pitts, Burger Kid (Annie Pitts)

Annie Pitts, Swamp Monster (Annie Pitts)

Ann's Story (Young Americans: Colonial Williamsburg)

Another Day, Another Sand Dollar (SpongeBob SquarePants (TokyoPop))

Another Fine Myth (Myth Adventures)

The Answer (Animorphs)

Anthony Ant's Creepy Crawly Party (Anthony Ant)

Anthony Ant's Treasure Hunt (Anthony Ant)

Antimatter Formula (Choose Your Own Adventure)

The Antimatter Universe (Choose Your Own Adventure)

Any Way You Slice It (Katie Kazoo, Switcheroo)

The Anybodies (The Anybodies)

Anyone but Me (Katie Kazoo, Switcheroo)

Anyone Can Eat Squid! (Simply Sarah)

The Apeman's Secret (Hardy Boys)

The Apple Bandit (Nancy Drew Notebooks)

Apple Turnover Treasure (Alex)

Apple-y Ever After (The Princess School)

April Flowers (Angelwings)

April Fool (Harry and Emily)

April Fool! Watch Out at School! (Gilbert)

April Fools! (Full House: Michelle)

April Fools! (Little Bear: Maurice Sendak's Little Bear)

The April Fool's Day Mystery (Dixon Twins)

April Fools' Rules (Mary-Kate and Ashley: Two of a Kind)

April Ghoul's Day (Graveyard School)

Arabel and Mortimer (Arabel and Mortimer)

Arabel's Raven (Arabel and Mortimer)

Arabian Challenge (Thoroughbred)

Arcade (Star Trek: Deep Space Nine)

The Arctic Incident (Artemis Fowl)

The Arctic Patrol Mystery (Hardy Boys)

Are There Bears in Starvation Lake? (Starvation Lake)

Are We Having Fun Yet (Hmmm?) (Indie Kidd)

Are You Ready to Play Outside? (Elephant and Piggie)

Are You Terrified Yet? (Goosebumps Series 2000)

Ariel's Secret (Disney Princess Secrets)

The Ark (Lechow Family)

Army of Terror (Star Wars Galaxy of Fear)

Arnie and the New Kid (Arnie)

Arnie and the Skateboard Gang (Arnie)

Arnie and the Stolen Markers (Arnie)

Arnie Goes to Camp (Arnie)

Arnold (Kipper: Little Kippers)

Arnold for President (Hey Arnold!)

Arnold's Christmas (Hey Arnold!)

Arnold's E-Files (Hey Arnold!)

Arnold's Valentine (Hey Arnold!)

Around the Clock with Harriet (Harriet)

Around the World with the Lil' Bratz (Bratz: Lil' Bratz)

The Arrival (Animorphs)

The Arrival (Journey of Allen Strange)

The Art of Keeping Secrets (Full House: Stephanie)

The Art Teacher from the Black Lagoon (Black Lagoon)

The Art Teacher's Vanishing Masterpiece (Joe Sherlock, Kid Detective)

Artemis Fowl (Artemis Fowl)

Arthur (Time Soldiers)

Arthur Accused! (Arthur Chapter Books)

Arthur and the Bad-Luck Brain (Arthur Chapter Books)

Arthur and the Bellybutton Diamond (Arthur the Kid)

Arthur and the Best Coach Ever (Arthur Chapter Books: Good Sports)

Arthur and the Big Blow-Up (Arthur Chapter Books)

Arthur and the Big Snow (Arthur)

Arthur and the Comet Crisis (Arthur Chapter Books)

Arthur and the Cootie-Catcher (Arthur Chapter Books)

Arthur and the Crunch Cereal Contest (Arthur Chapter Books)

Arthur and the Dog Show (Arthur)

Arthur and the Double Dare (Arthur Chapter Books)

Arthur and the Goalie Ghost (Arthur Chapter Books: Good Sports)

Attaboy, Sam! (Sam Krupnik)

The Attack (Animorphs)

Attack in the Rye Grass (Trailblazers)

Attack of the Alien Mole Invaders! (The Weird Zone)

The Attack of the Aqua Apes (Fear Street: Ghosts of Fear Street)

Attack of the Bandit Cats (Geronimo Stilton)

Attack of the Beast (Disney Girls)

Attack of the Beastly Baby-Sitter (Goosebumps: Give Yourself Goosebumps)

Attack of the Evil Elvises (Weird Planet)

Attack of the Fiend (Last Apprentice)

Attack of the 50-Foot Alien Creep-oids (Super Goofballs)

Attack of the 50-Foot Cupid (Franny K. Stein, Mad Scientist)

Attack of the Giant Octopus (Secrets of Dripping Fang)

Attack of the Graveyard Ghouls (Goosebumps Series 2000)

Attack of the Jack-O'-Lanterns (Goosebumps)

Attack of the Jack-O'-Lanterns (Goosebumps Presents)

Attack of the Killer Ants (Bone Chillers)

Attack of the Killer Bebes (Kim Possible (Chapter Books))

Attack of the Killer Crabs (Spooksville)

Attack of the Living Mask (Choose Your Own Nightmare)

Attack of the Mole Master (Sidekicks)

Attack of the Mutant (Goosebumps)

Attack of the Mutant (Goosebumps Presents)

Attack of the Mutant Bugs (Shadow Zone)

Attack of the Mutant Lunch Lady (Buzz Beaker Brainstorm)

Attack of the Slime Monster (Ghostwriter)

The Attack of the Soggy Underwater People (Maximum Boy)

Attack of the Tagger (Shredderman)

The Attack of the Two-Inch Teacher (I Was a Sixth Grade Alien)

Attack of the Two-Ton Tomatoes (Eerie Indiana)

Attack of the Valley Girls (Melvin Beederman, Superhero)

Attack of the Vampire Worms (Fear Street: Ghosts of Fear Street)

Attack of the Video Villains (Hardy Boys)

Attack on the High Seas! (Pirate School)

Attack on the Tower of London (Screech Owls)

Atticus of Rome, 30 B.C. (The Life and Times)

Aunt Eater Loves a Mystery (Aunt Eater)

Aunt Eater's Mystery Christmas (Aunt Eater)

Aunt Eater's Mystery Halloween (Aunt Eater)

Aunt Eater's Mystery Vacation (Aunt Eater)

Aunt Nina and Her Nephews and Nieces (Aunt Nina)

Aunt Nina, Good Night! (Aunt Nina)

Aunt Nina's Visit (Aunt Nina)

Aunt Weird (House of Horrors)

The Austere Academy (A Series of Unfortunate Events)

Author Day (Kids in Ms. Coleman's Class)

The Author's Blood (Wormling)

Autocrats of Oz (Oz)

Autumn Story (Brambly Hedge)

Autumn Trail (The Saddle Club)

Avalanche Trail (Rocket Power)

Aw, Here It Goes! (Kenan and Kel)

The Awakening (Transformers Armada (Readers))

Awards and Rewards (Hannah Montana (TokyoPop))

Away West (Scraps of Time)

The Awful Pawful (Jack Russell: Dog Detective)

The Awfully Angry Ogre (Princess Power)

B

B-Bop's Brainwave (Butt-Ugly Martians Chapter Books)

B-e-s-t Friends (Polk Street: New Kids at the Polk Street School)

B Is for Betsy (Betsy)

Babar and Father Christmas (Babar)

Babar and His Children (Babar)

Babar and the Ghost (Babar)

Babar and the Professor (Babar)

Babar and the Succotash Bird (Babar)

Babar and the Wully-Wully (Babar)

Babar and Zephir (Babar)

Babar Comes to America (Babar)

Babar Learns to Cook (Babar)

Babar Loses His Crown (Babar)

Babar Saves the Day (Babar)

Babar the King (Babar)

Babar's ABC (Babar)

Babar's Battle (Babar)

Babar's Birthday Surprise (Babar)

Babar's Book of Color (Babar)

Babar's Castle (Babar)

Babar's Counting Book (Babar)

Babar's Cousin, That Rascal Arthur (Babar)

Babar's Fair Will Be Opened Next Sunday (Babar)

Babar's French Lessons (Babar)

Babar's Little Circus Star (Babar)

Babar's Little Girl (Babar)

Babar's Museum of Art (Babar)

Babar's Mystery (Babar)

Babar's Picnic (Babar)

Babar's Spanish Lessons (Babar)

Babar's World Tour (Babar)

Babe and Me (Baseball Card Adventures)

The Baby Angel (Forever Angels)

Baby Animal Zoo (Kids in Ms. Coleman's Class)

Baby Blues (Adam Joshua Capers)

The Baby Blues (Adam Joshua Capers)

Baby Duck and the Bad Eyeglasses (Baby Duck)

Baby Duck and the Cozy Blanket (Baby Duck)

The Baby Pony (Pony Pals)

A Baby Sister for Frances (Frances)

The Baby-Sitter Burglaries (Nancy Drew)

Baby-Sitters & Company (Full House: Sisters)

Baby-Sitters at Shadow Lake (Baby-Sitters Club Super Specials)

Baby-Sitters Beware (Baby-Sitters Club Mysteries)

Barbie in the Twelve Dancing Princesses (Barbie (Step Into Reading))

Barby and the Diamond Castle (Barbie (Step Into Reading))

Barfing in the Backseat (Hank Zipzer)

A Bargain for Frances (Frances)

The Bark of the Bog Owl (Wilderking Trilogy)

The Barking Ghost (Goosebumps)

Barnstormer in Oz (Oz)

Barred from Ballet (Ballet Friends)

Barry (Wolfbay Wings)

The Baseball Card Conspiracy (Hardy Boys)

Baseball Flyhawk (Matt Christopher Sports Stories)

Baseball Pals (Matt Christopher Sports Stories)

The Baseball Trick (Trick Books)

Baseball Turnaround (Matt Christopher Sports Stories)

Bases Loaded (Scrappers)

Basil and the Lost Colony (Basil of Baker Street)

Basil and the Pygmy Cats (Basil of Baker Street)

Basil in Mexico (Basil of Baker Street)

Basil in the Wild West (Basil of Baker Street)

Basil of Baker Street (Basil of Baker Street)

The Basket Counts (Matt Christopher Sports Stories)

A Basket of Roses (Cassie Perkins)

Basketball Bats (Gym Shorts)

Basketball Blues (Go Girl)

The Basketball Mystery (Boxcar Children)

Basketball Sparkplug (Matt Christopher Sports Stories)

Bathtime for Biscuit (Biscuit Readers)

Battle Fleet (Adventures of a Young Sailor)

The Battle for Skandia (Ranger's Apprentice)

Battle in a Bottle (Class Pets)

The Battle of Boach's Keep (Akiko Graphic Novels)

The Battle of Lookout Mountain (Bonnets and Bugles)

The Battle of the Bakers (Katie Lynn Cookie Company)

Battle of the Bands (High School Musical Stories from East High)

Battle of the Brain-Sucking Robots (Super Goofballs)

Battle of the Dum Diddys (Rotten School)

The Battle of the Labyrinth (Percy Jackson and the Olympians)

Battlecry Forever! (Thoroughbred: Ashleigh's Collection)

Battling the Klan (The American Adventure)

Batya's Search (B.Y. Times)

Bayport Buccaneers (Hardy Boys, Undercover Brothers)

Be a Wolf! (Wishbone Adventures)

Be Afraid—Be Very Afraid! (Goosebumps Series 2000)

Be Careful What You Wish For (Goosebumps)

Be Careful What You Wish For (Goosebumps Presents)

Be My Valentine (Yoko and Friends)

Be Nice, Nanette? (Angela Anaconda Chapter Books)

Be Nice to Mice! (Katie Kazoo, Switcheroo)

Be Quiet, Pooh! (Winnie the Pooh First Readers)

Be Well, Beware (Beware)

Beach Blues (The Complicated Life of Claudia Cristina Cortez)

Beach Party (Zoey 101)

Beach Ride (The Saddle Club)

Beagle in a Backpack (Animal Ark)

Beany and the Dreaded Wedding (Beany)

Beany and the Meany (Beany)

Beany Goes to Camp (Beany)

Beany (Not Beanhead) and the Magic Crystal (Beany)

Bear and Mrs. Duck (Bear)

Bear and Roly-Poly (Bear)

A Bear Called Paddington (Paddington)

The Bear Detectives (Berenstain Bears)

Bear Feels Scared (Bear)

Bear Feels Sick (Bear)

Bear Hunt (Shanna First Readers)

The Bear Scouts (Berenstain Bears)

Bear Shadow (Moonbear)

Bear Snores On (Bear)

Bear Stays Up for Christmas (Bear)

Bear Wants More (Bear)

Bear's Bargain (Moonbear)

The Bears' Christmas (Berenstain Bears)

Bear's Christmas Surprise (Bear)

Bears in the Barn (Animal Ark)

Bears in the Night (Berenstain Bears)

Bear's New Friend (Bear)

Bears on Wheels (Berenstain Bears)

The Bears' Picnic (Berenstain Bears)

The Bears' Vacation (Berenstain Bears)

Beast and the Halloween Horror (Polk Street School: Kids of the Polk Street School)

The Beast from Beneath the Cafeteria! (The Weird Zone)

The Beast from the East (Goosebumps)

The Beast in Ms. Rooney's Room (Polk Street School: Kids of the Polk Street School)

The Beast of Baskerville (Deadtime Stories)

The Beast under the Wizard's Bridge (Lewis Barnavelt)

Beastly Tales (Fear Street: Ghosts of Fear Street)

Beatrice's Spells (Monster Manor)

Beautiful Brittany (Always Friends)

Beautiful Land (Once Upon America)

Beauty in the Least (McGee and Me!)

Beauty Is a Beast (The Princess School)

Beauty Sleepover Bash! (Bratz: Lil' Bratz)

Beauty's Revenge (Disney Girls)

Beaver at Long Pond (Long Pond)

Beck and the Great Berry Battle (Disney Fairies (Chapter Books))

Beck Beyond the Sea (Disney Fairies (Chapter Books))

Becky's Brainstorm (Twelve Candles Club)

Becky's Secret Surprise (Twelve Candles Club)

Becoming a Witch (Sabrina the Teenage Witch)

Bedtime for Frances (Frances)

Bedtime for Laura (Little House: My First Little House Books)

Bedtime Story (Seven Little Monsters)

"Bee My Valentine" (First Grade)

Been There, Crossed Over (Pretty Freekin Scary)

Beezus and Ramona (Ramona Quimby)

The Berenstain Bears and the Female Fullback (Berenstain Bears: Big Chapter Books)

The Berenstain Bears and the G-Rex Bones (Berenstain Bears: Big Chapter Books)

The Berenstain Bears and the Galloping Ghost (Berenstain Bears: Big Chapter Books)

The Berenstain Bears and the Ghost of the Auto Graveyard (Berenstain Bears: Big Chapter Books)

The Berenstain Bears and the Ghost of the Forest (Berenstain Bears)

The Berenstain Bears and the Giddy Grandma (Berenstain Bears: Big Chapter Books)

The Berenstain Bears and the Great Ant Attack (Berenstain Bears: Big Chapter Books)

The Berenstain Bears and the Green-Eyed Monster (Berenstain Bears)

The Berenstain Bears and the Haunted Hayride (Berenstain Bears: Big Chapter Books)

The Berenstain Bears and the Homework Hassle (Berenstain Bears)

The Berenstain Bears and the In-Crowd (Berenstain Bears)

The Berenstain Bears and the Love Match (Berenstain Bears: Big Chapter Books)

The Berenstain Bears and the Mama's Day Surprise (Berenstain Bears)

The Berenstain Bears and the Messy Room (Berenstain Bears)

The Berenstain Bears and the Missing Dinosaur Bones (Berenstain Bears)

The Berenstain Bears and the Missing Honey (Berenstain Bears)

The Berenstain Bears and the Missing Watermelon (Berenstain Bears)

The Berenstain Bears and the Nerdy Nephew (Berenstain Bears: Big Chapter Books)

The Berenstain Bears and the New Girl in Town (Berenstain Bears: Big Chapter Books)

The Berenstain Bears and the No Guns Allowed (Berenstain Bears: Big Chapter Books)

The Berenstain Bears and the Papa's Day Surprise (Berenstain Bears)

The Berenstain Bears and the Perfect Crime (Almost) (Berenstain Bears: Big Chapter Books)

The Berenstain Bears and the Prize Pumpkin (Berenstain Bears)

The Berenstain Bears and the Real Easter Eggs (Berenstain Bears)

The Berenstain Bears and the Red-Handed Thief (Berenstain Bears: Big Chapter Books)

The Berenstain Bears and the School Scandal Sheet (Berenstain Bears: Big Chapter Books)

The Berenstain Bears and the Showdown at Chainsaw Gap (Berenstain Bears: Big Chapter Books)

The Berenstain Bears and the Sitter (Berenstain Bears)

The Berenstain Bears and the Slumber Party (Berenstain Bears)

The Berenstain Bears and the Spooky Old Tree (Berenstain Bears)

The Berenstain Bears and the Tic-Tac-Toe Mystery (Berenstain Bears)

The Berenstain Bears and the Trouble with Chores (Berenstain Bears)

The Berenstain Bears and the Trouble with Commercials (Berenstain Bears)

The Berenstain Bears and the Trouble with Friends (Berenstain Bears)

The Berenstain Bears and the Trouble with Grownups (Berenstain Bears)

The Berenstain Bears and the Truth (Berenstain Bears)

The Berenstain Bears and the Week at Grandma's (Berenstain Bears)

The Berenstain Bears and the Wheelchair Commando (Berenstain Bears: Big Chapter Books)

The Berenstain Bears and the Wishing Star (Berenstain Bears)

The Berenstain Bears and the Wishing Star (Berenstain Bears)

The Berenstain Bears and Too Much Birthday (Berenstain Bears)

The Berenstain Bears and Too Much Car Trip (Berenstain Bears)

The Berenstain Bears and Too Much Junk Food (Berenstain Bears)

The Berenstain Bears and Too Much Teasing (Berenstain Bears)

The Berenstain Bears and Too Much TV (Berenstain Bears)

The Berenstain Bears and Too Much Vacation (Berenstain Bears)

The Berenstain Bears at Camp Crush (Berenstain Bears: Big Chapter Books)

The Berenstain Bears at the Teen Rock Café (Berenstain Bears: Big Chapter Books)

The Berenstain Bears' Baby Easter Bunny (Berenstain Bears)

The Berenstain Bears' Bedtime Battle (Berenstain Bears)

The Berenstain Bears' Big Bear, Small Bear (Berenstain Bears)

The Berenstain Bears Blaze a Trail (Berenstain Bears)

The Berenstain Bears by the Sea (Berenstain Bears)

The Berenstain Bears Catch the Bus (Berenstain Bears)

The Berenstain Bears Clean House (Berenstain Bears)

The Berenstain Bears' Comic Valentine (Berenstain Bears)

The Berenstain Bears Count Their Blessings (Berenstain Bears)

The Berenstain Bears' Dollars and Sense (Berenstain Bears)

The Berenstain Bears Don't Pollute (Anymore) (Berenstain Bears)

The Berenstain Bears Down on the Farm (Berenstain Bears)

The Berenstain Bears Easter Surprise (Berenstain Bears)

The Berenstain Bears Fly It (Berenstain Bears)

The Berenstain Bears Forget Their Manners (Berenstain Bears)

The Berenstain Bears' Funny Valentine (Berenstain Bears)

The Berenstain Bears Get in a Fight (Berenstain Bears)

The Berenstain Bears Get Stage Fright (Berenstain Bears)

The Berenstain Bears Get the Don't Haftas (Berenstain Bears)

The Berenstain Bears Get the Gimmies (Berenstain Bears)

Best Friends Forever (Mary-Kate and Ashley: So Little Time)

The Best Halloween Ever (The Herdman Kids)

The Best Ice Show Ever! (Silver Blades Figure Eights)

Best in Show for Rotten Ralph (Rotten Ralph Rotten Readers)

The Best Is Yet to Come (Abby Hayes: The Amazing Days of Abby Hayes)

Best of Friends (Puppy Patrol)

The Best School Year Ever (The Herdman Kids)

The Best Sleepover Ever! (Angelina Ballerina: Angelina's Diary)

Best Thanksgiving Ever (Sweet Valley Kids)

The Best Way to Play (Little Bill)

Bet You Can't! (Secret World of Alex Mack)

Beth Makes a Friend (Portraits of Little Women)

Beth's Snow Dancer (Little Women Journals)

Beth's Story (Portraits of Little Women)

Betrayal (2099)

Betrayal at Cross Creek (American Girls: History Mysteries)

Betrayed! (Crime Through Time)

The Betrayer's Fortune (Trailblazers)

Betsy and Billy (Betsy)

Betsy and Joe (Betsy-Tacy)

Betsy and Mr. Kilpatrick (Betsy)

Betsy and Tacy Go Down Town (Betsy-Tacy)

Betsy and Tacy Go Over the Big Hill (Betsy-Tacy)

Betsy and the Boys (Betsy)

Betsy and the Circus (Betsy)

Betsy and the Great World (Betsy-Tacy)

Betsy in Spite of Herself (Betsy-Tacy)

Betsy Ross's Star (Blast to the Past)

Betsy-Tacy (Betsy-Tacy)

Betsy-Tacy and Tib (Betsy-Tacy)

Betsy Was a Junior (Betsy-Tacy)

Betsy's Busy Summer (Betsy)

Betsy's Little Star (Betsy)

Betsy's Play School (Betsy)

Betsy's Wedding (Betsy-Tacy)

Betsy's Winterhouse (Betsy)

A Better Bicycle (The American Adventure)

Better Not Get Wet, Jesse Bear (Jesse Bear)

Better Than Best (Girls Only (GO!))

Between Light and Dark (W.I.T.C.H.—Graphic Novels)

Beverly Billingsly Borrows a Book (Beverly Billingsly)

Beverly Billingsly Can't Catch (Beverly Billingsly)

Beverly Billingsly Takes a Bow (Beverly Billingsly)

Beverly Billingsly Takes the Cake (Beverly Billingsly)

Beware and Stogie (Beware)

Beware! Beware! A Witch Won't Share (Old Witch)

Beware Dawn! (Baby-Sitters Club Mysteries)

Beware! It's Friday The 13th! (Dragon Slayers' Academy)

Beware of Dog (McGrowl)

Beware of Mad Dog! (Boyds Will Be Boyds)

Beware of the Blabbermouth (Ghostville Elementary)

Beware of the Haunted Eye (Black Belt Club)

Beware of the Purple Peanut Butter (Goosebumps: Give Yourself Goosebumps)

Beware the Babysitter (Fairly OddParents (TokyoPop))

Beware the Bohrok (Bionicle Chronicles)

Beware the Dark Side (Star Wars (DK Readers))

Beware the Mare (Beware)

Beware the Pirate Ghost (Casebusters)

Beware the Shopping Mall! (Bone Chillers)

Beware the Snake's Venom (Choose Your Own Nightmare)

Beware, the Snowman (Goosebumps)

Beyond Escape! (Choose Your Own Adventure)

Beyond the Burning Lands (Sword of the Spirits)

Beyond the Deepwoods (Edge Chronicles)

Beyond the Great Wall (Choose Your Own Adventure)

Beyond the Heather Hills (Little House: The Martha Years)

Beyond the Horizon (Heartland)

Beyond the River (The Young Underground)

Beyond the Sunrise (Dolphin Diaries)

Beyond the Valley of Thorns (Land of Elyon)

Bhangra Babes (Babes)

Bicycle Mystery (Boxcar Children)

Bicycle to Treachery (Miss Mallard)

The Bidding War (Angela Anaconda Chapter Books)

Big Anthony (Strega Nona and Big Anthony)

Big Anthony and the Magic Ring (Strega Nona and Big Anthony)

The Big Audition (Silver Blades)

Big Bad Beans (Cul-de-Sac Kids)

Big Bad Bugs (Fear Street: Ghosts of Fear Street)

The Big Bang Theory (Butt-Ugly Martians Chapter Books)

Big Base Hit (Angel Park All-Stars)

Big Ben (Puppy Patrol)

The Big Blueberry Barf-Off! (Rotten School)

Big Boar's Mom Comes to Stay (Piganeers)

Big Bob and the Halloween Potatoes (Big Bob)

Big Bob and the Magic Valentine's Day Potato (Big Bob)

Big Bob and the Thanksgiving Potatoes (Big Bob)

Big Bob and the Winter Holiday Potato (Big Bob)

A Big Box of Memories (Pee Wee Scouts)

Big Break (Chosen Girls)

The Big Concrete Lorry (Tales of Trotter Street)

The Big Day at School (Little Bill (Nickelodeon))

A Big Decision (Girlhood Journeys: Kai)

The Big Fix-up Mix-up (Full House: Stephanie)

Big Foot, Big Trouble (Strange Matter)

The Big Honey Hunt (Berenstain Bears)

The Big Itch (Clifford)

The Big Leaf Pile (Clifford)

The Big Lie (McGee and Me!)

Big Match (David and Goliath)

The Big Nap (Chet Gecko Mysteries)

The Big Pig Puzzle (Bobbsey Twins: The New Bobbsey Twins)

Big Race (Sweet Valley Kids)

The Blackwing Puzzle (Hardy Boys)

Blast from the Past (Fairly OddParents)

A Blast with the Past (Ghostwriter)

Blaze and the Forest Fire (Blaze)

Blaze and the Gray Spotted Pony (Blaze)

Blaze and the Gypsies (Blaze)

Blaze and the Indian Cave (Blaze)

Blaze and the Lost Quarry (Blaze)

Blaze and the Mountain Lion (Blaze)

Blaze and Thunderbolt (Blaze)

Blaze Finds Forgotten Roads (Blaze)

Blaze Finds the Trail (Blaze)

Blaze Shows the Way (Blaze)

The Blind Pony (Pony Pals)

Blind Spot (RPM)

Blinded by the Shining Path (Trailblazers)

Blindside Blitz (Alden All Stars)

Blizzard (Survival!)

The Blizzard of Blue Mountain (Cabin Creek Mysteries)

Blizzard of the Blue Moon (Magic Tree House)

The Blob That Ate Everyone (Goosebumps)

Blockade Runner (Bonnets and Bugles)

Blood and Sand (The Midnight Library)

The Blood Bay Colt (retitled The Black Stallion's Blood Bay Colt) (Black Stallion)

Blood Fever (Young Bond)

Blood on the Handle (Choose Your Own Adventure)

Blood Tide (Never Land)

Blork's Evil Twin (Space Brat)

Blossom and Beany (Best Friends)

The Blossom Angel (Forever Angels)

Blossom Culp and the Sleep of Death (Blossom Culp)

A Blossom Promise (The Blossom Family)

Blossoming Out (Powerpuff Girls Chapter Books)

The Blossoms and the Green Phantom (The Blossom Family)

The Blossoms Meet the Vulture Lady (The Blossom Family)

Blown Away (Hardy Boys, Undercover Brothers)

blowtorch@psycho.com (Bone Chillers)

Blue Bay Mystery (Boxcar Children)

The Blue Djinn of Babylon (Children of the Lamp)

A Blue for Beware (Beware)

Blue-Ribbon Blues (Barkley's School for Dogs)

Blue Ribbon Christmas (Full House: Stephanie)

Blue Ribbon Friends (Short Stirrup Club)

Blue-Ribbon Henry (Henry the Cat)

Blue Skies, French Fries (Pee Wee Scouts)

Blue Wings (Phantom Stallion)

The Blue Witch of Oz (Oz)

The Bluebeard Room (Nancy Drew)

The Blunder Years (McGee and Me!)

Board Games (Rocket Power)

Board to Death (Hardy Boys, Undercover Brothers: Graphic Novels)

Boardwalk Bust (Hardy Boys, Undercover Brothers)

Bob the Bouncy Kitten (Kitten Friends)

Bobbsey Twins (Bobbsey Twins)

Bobbsey Twins and Baby May (Bobbsey Twins)

Bobbsey Twins and Doctor Funnybone's Secret (Bobbsey Twins)

Bobbsey Twins and Double Trouble (Bobbsey Twins)

Bobbsey Twins and the Big River Mystery (Bobbsey Twins)

Bobbsey Twins and the Blue Mystery (Bobbsey Twins)

Bobbsey Twins and the Blue Poodle Mystery (Bobbsey Twins)

Bobbsey Twins and the Camp Fire Mystery (Bobbsey Twins)

Bobbsey Twins and the Coral Turtle Mystery (Bobbsey Twins)

Bobbsey Twins and the Doodlebug Mystery (Bobbsey Twins)

Bobbsey Twins and the Dune Buggy Mystery (Bobbsey Twins)

Bobbsey Twins and the Flying Clown (Bobbsey Twins)

Bobbsey Twins and the Freedom Bell Mystery (Bobbsey Twins)

Bobbsey Twins and the Ghost in the Computer (Bobbsey Twins)

Bobbsey Twins and the Goldfish Mystery (Bobbsey Twins)

Bobbsey Twins and the Greek Hat Mystery (Bobbsey Twins)

Bobbsey Twins and the Grinning Gargoyle Mystery (Bobbsey Twins)

Bobbsey Twins and the Haunted House Mystery (Bobbsey Twins)

Bobbsey Twins and the Horseshoe Riddle (Bobbsey Twins)

Bobbsey Twins and the Missing Pony Mystery (Bobbsey Twins)

Bobbsey Twins and the Music Box Mystery (Bobbsey Twins)

Bobbsey Twins and the Mystery of the Hindu Temple (Bobbsey Twins)

Bobbsey Twins and the Mystery of the King's Puppet (Bobbsey Twins)

Bobbsey Twins and the Mystery of the Laughing Dinosaur (Bobbsey Twins)

Bobbsey Twins and the Rose Parade Mystery (Bobbsey Twins)

Bobbsey Twins and the Scarecrow Mystery (Bobbsey Twins)

Bobbsey Twins and the Secret in the Pirate's Cave (Bobbsey Twins)

Bobbsey Twins and the Secret of Candy Castle (Bobbsey Twins)

Bobbsey Twins and the Smoky Mountain Mystery (Bobbsey Twins)

Bobbsey Twins and the Sun-Moon Cruise (Bobbsey Twins)

Bobbsey Twins and the Tagalong Giraffe (Bobbsey Twins)

Bobbsey Twins and the Talking Fox Mystery (Bobbsey Twins)

Bobbsey Twins and Their Camel Adventure (Bobbsey Twins)

Bobbsey Twins and Their Schoolmates (Bobbsey Twins)

Bobbsey Twins at Big Bear Pond (Bobbsey Twins)

Bobbsey Twins at Cedar Camp (Bobbsey Twins)

Bobbsey Twins at Cherry Corners (Bobbsey Twins)

Bobbsey Twins at Cloverbank (Bobbsey Twins)

Bobbsey Twins at Home (Bobbsey Twins)

Bobbsey Twins at Indian Hollow (Bobbsey Twins)

Bobbsey Twins at Lighthouse Point (Bobbsey Twins)

The Borrowers Afield (Borrowers)

The Borrowers Afloat (Borrowers)

The Borrowers Aloft (Borrowers)

The Borrowers Avenged (Borrowers)

Boss for a Day (The Barkers)

Bossy Anna (Silver Blades Figure Eights)

Bossy Steven (Sweet Valley Kids)

The Boston Massacre (The American Adventure)

Boston Revolts! (The American Adventure)

Bounce, Tigger, Bounce (Winnie the Pooh First Readers)

Boundless Grace (Grace)

Bowling Over Halloween (Heroes A2Z)

The Box and the Bone (Castle Court Kids)

The Box That Watch Found (Boxcar Children)

Box Turtle at Long Pond (Long Pond)

The Boxcar Children (Boxcar Children)

A Boy, a Dog, a Frog, and a Friend (Frog)

A Boy, a Dog, and a Frog (Frog)

Boy Crazy (Mary-Kate and Ashley: So Little Time)

Boy-Crazy Stacey (Baby-Sitters Club)

A Boy in the Doghouse (Lucky)

The Boy Next Door (Candy Apple)

The Boy-Oh-Boy Next Door (Full House: Stephanie)

The Boy Who Ate Fear Street (Fear Street: Ghosts of Fear Street)

The Boy Who Cried Bigfoot (The Zack Files)

Boyfriends for Everyone (Sweet Valley: Unicorn Club)

Boys Against Girls (Hatford Boys)

Boys and Beauty Blunders (Hannah Montana (TokyoPop))

Boys in Control (Hatford Boys)

Boys in the Gym (Gymnasts)

Boys or Ballet? (Royal Ballet School Diaries)

The Boys Return (Hatford Boys)

Boys Rock! (Hatford Boys)

The Boys Start the War (Hatford Boys)

Bozo the Clone (The Zack Files)

Brady Brady and the B Team (Brady Brady)

Brady Brady and the Big Mistake (Brady Brady)

Brady Brady and the Great Exchange (Brady Brady)

Brady Brady and the Great Rink (Brady Brady)

Brady Brady and the Most Important Game (Brady Brady)

Brady Brady and the MVP (Brady Brady)

Brady Brady and the Runaway Goalie (Brady Brady)

Brady Brady and the Singing Tree (Brady Brady)

Brady Brady and the Twirlin' Torpedo (Brady Brady)

Brain Juice (Goosebumps Series 2000)

The Brain Spiders (Star Wars Galaxy of Fear)

Brain Stealers (Visitors)

The Brain That Wouldn't Obey! (The Weird Zone)

Bramble and Berry (Best Friends)

A Brand-New Day with Mouse and Mole (Mouse and Mole)

Brand-New Pencils, Brand-New Books (Gilbert)

The Brave Apprentice (Further Tales)

Brave Horse (Mustang Mountain)

The Brave Little Tailor (Wishbone: The Early Years)

Brave Norman (Pets to the Rescue)

Bravo, Amelia Bedelia! (Amelia Bedelia)

Bravo, Ernest and Celestine! (Ernest and Celestine)

Bravo, Grace! (Grace)

Bravo, Max! (Max)

Bravo, Mia! (American Girls: Girl of the Year)

Bravo, Tanya! (Tanya)

Bread and Honey (Bear)

Bread and Jam for Frances (Frances)

Break for the Basket (Matt Christopher Sports Stories)

Breakaway (Star Trek: The Next Generation: Starfleet Academy)

Breakdown (Remnants)

Breakdown (Star Trek: S. C. E.)

Breakdown in Axeblade (Hardy Boys)

Breakfast Time, Ernest and Celestine (Ernest and Celestine)

Breaking Free (Heartland)

Breaking Loose (Alden All Stars)

Breaking News (Bratz: Clued In!)

Breaking the Fall (Thoroughbred)

Breaking the Ice (Silver Blades)

Brianna, Jamaica, and the Dance of Spring (Jamaica)

Brian's Hunt (Brian Robeson)

Brian's Return (Brian Robeson)

Brian's Winter (Brian Robeson)

Bridal Bedlam (Sabrina the Teenage Witch)

Bridal Dreams (Thoroughbred)

The Bride of Frankenstein Doesn't Bake Cookies (Bailey School: The Adventures of the Bailey School Kids)

Bride of the Living Dummy (Goosebumps Series 2000)

The Bridesmaid Ballet (Angelina Ballerina: Angelina's Diary)

Bridesmaid Blues for Becky (Twelve Candles Club)

A Bridge Between Worlds (W.I.T.C.H.—Chapter Books)

The Bridge in the Clouds (Magician's House Quartet)

The Bridge to Cutter Gap (Christy)

Bridle Path (The Saddle Club)

Bright Lights for Bella (Star Sisterz)

Bright Lights, Little Gerbil (The Weebie Zone)

Bright, Shiny Skylar (Hopscotch Hill School)

Brigid Beware (Brigid Thrush Books)

Brigid Bewitched (Brigid Thrush Books)

Brigid the Bad (Brigid Thrush Books)

Brilliant Doctor Wogan (Choose Your Own Adventure)

Bring Me a Dream (Eerie Indiana)

Bring the Boys Home (Bonnets and Bugles)

The Brink of Life and Death (Usagi Yojimbo)

Brisingr (Inheritance)

Brittany's New Friend (Always Friends)

Broadway Dreams (High School Musical Stories from East High)

The Broken Anchor (Nancy Drew)

Broken Bow (Star Trek: Enterprise)

Broken Hearts (Lizzie McGuire)

Broken Horse (The Saddle Club)

Brookfield Days (Little House Chapter Books: Caroline)

Brookfield Friends (Little House Chapter Books: Caroline)

A Brother for the Orphelines (Orphelines)

The Brotherhood of Rotten Babysitters (Sidekicks)

The Brotherhood of the Traveling Underpants (Melvin Beederman, Superhero)

Brotherly Love (Christy)

Brothers of the Falls (Adventures in America)

The Brothers' War (My Side of the Story)

Brrr! (Grandpa)

Bryce and Zion (Adventures with the Parkers)

BSC in the USA (Baby-Sitters Club Super Specials)

Bubba and Beau, Best Friends (Bubba and Beau)

Bubba and Beau Go Night-Night (Bubba and Beau)

Bubba and Beau Meet the Relatives (Bubba and Beau)

Bubble-Gum Radar (Yoko and Friends)

Buckskin Bandit (Winnie the Horse Gentler)

Bud Barkin, Private Eye (Bunnicula: Tales from the House of Bunnicula)

Budding Star (Angels Unlimited)

Buddy (The Puppy Place)

Budgie and the Blizzard (Budgie)

Budgie at Bendick's Point (Budgie)

Budgie Goes to Sea (Budgie)

Budgie the Little Helicopter (Budgie)

Bueno Nacho (Kim Possible (Chapter Books))

Bueno Nacho and Tick Tick Tick (Kim Possible (TokyoPop))

Buffalo Arthur (Arthur the Kid)

Buffalo Before Breakfast (Magic Tree House)

The Buffalo Soldiers (Reflections of a Black Cowboy)

Bug in a Rug (Table Two)

Bugged Out! (Choose Your Own Nightmare)

The Bugman Lives! (Fear Street: Ghosts of Fear Street)

Bugs for Breakfast (Scaredy Cats)

The Bully Coach (American Gold Gymnasts)

The Bully from the Black Lagoon (Black Lagoon)

The Bully of Barkham Street (Barkham Street)

Bumps in the Night (Funnybones)

Bunches of Fun (Penelope Fritter, Super-Sitter)

The Bungalow Mystery (Nancy Drew)

Bungee Baboon Rescue (Danger Joe Show)

Bunk 3, Teddy and Me (Full House: Michelle)

Bunnicula (Bunnicula)

Bunnicula Meets Edgar Allan Crow (Bunnicula)

Bunnicula Strikes Again (Bunnicula)

Bunnies in the Bathroom (Animal Ark)

Bunny Bonanza (Animal Ark Pets)

Bunny Cakes (Max and Ruby)

The Bunny-Hop Hoax (Nancy Drew Notebooks)

Bunny in a Basket (Animal Ark)

Bunny Mail (Max and Ruby)

Bunny Money (Max and Ruby)

Bunny Party (Max and Ruby)

Bunny Trouble (Bunny Trouble)

Bureau of Lost (Eerie Indiana)

Buried Alive (Mysteries in Our National Parks)

The Buried Biscuits (Jack Russell: Dog Detective)

The Buried Bones Mystery (Ziggy and the Black Dinosaurs)

Buried Treasure (Barkley's School for Dogs)

Burned (Hardy Boys, Undercover Brothers)

The Burning (Guardians of Ga'Hoole)

The Burning Bridge (Ranger's Apprentice)

The Burning Pendulum (Fortune Tellers Club)

The Burning Questions of Bingo Brown (Bingo Brown)

The Bus Station Mystery (Boxcar Children)

Buster and the Dance Contest (Postcards from Buster)

Buster and the Giant Pumpkin (Postcards from Buster)

Buster and the Great Swamp (Postcards from Buster)

Buster Baxter, Cat Saver (Arthur Chapter Books)

Buster Catches a Wave (Postcards from Buster)

Buster Changes His Luck (Postcards from Buster)

Buster Climbs the Walls (Postcards from Buster)

Buster Hits the Trail (Postcards from Buster)

Buster Hunts for Dinosaurs (Postcards from Buster)

Buster Makes the Grade (Arthur Chapter Books)

Buster on the Farm (Postcards from Buster)

Buster on the Town (Postcards from Buster)

Buster Plays Along (Postcards from Buster)

Buster's Dino Dilemma (Arthur Chapter Books)

Buster's New Friend (Arthur Chapter Books)

Buster's Sugartime (Postcards from Buster)

Busybody Nora (Riverside Kids: Nora and Teddy)

But, Excuse Me, That Is My Book (Charlie and Lola)

But I Am an Alligator (Charlie and Lola)

Butt Wars! (Butt Wars)

Butterfly (Kipper: Little Kippers)

Butterfly Battle (Magic School Bus Science Chapter Books)

The Butterfly Garden (Little Bear: Maurice Sendak's Little Bear)

Buzzer Basket (Chip Hilton Sports Series)

By Balloon to the Sahara (Choose Your Own Adventure)

By Fire, By Moonlight (Unicorns of Balinor)

By The Book (Star Trek: Enterprise)

By the Light of the Study Lamp (Dana Girls)

By the Shores of Silver Lake (Little House)

Bye-Bye-Boy Friend (Mary-Kate and Ashley: Two of a Kind)

C

Cabin Fever (The Caped 6th Grader)

Cabin Six Plays Cupid (Camp Sunnyside)

Cabin Surprise (Lottery Luck)

Cable Car to Catastrophe (Miss Mallard)

Caboose Mystery (Boxcar Children)

Cadet Kirk (Star Trek: Starfleet Academy)

Caesar's Story (Young Americans: Colonial Williamsburg)

The Cafeteria Lady from the Black Lagoon (Black Lagoon)

Calamity Jinx (Thoroughbred)

The Calder Game (Petra and Calder)

Caleb's Story (Sarah, Plain and Tall)

Calico Cat at School (Calico Cat)

Calico Cat at the Zoo (Calico Cat)

Calico Cat Looks Around (Calico Cat)

Calico Cat Meets Bookworm (Calico Cat)

Calico Cat's Exercise Book (Calico Cat)

Calico Cat's Rainbow (Calico Cat)

Calico Cat's Sunny Smile (Calico Cat)

Calico Cat's Year (Calico Cat)

California Dreams (Mary-Kate and Ashley Sweet 16)

California Girls! (Baby-Sitters Club Super Specials)

California Gold (Abby's South Seas Adventures)

Call Me Francis Tucket (The Tucket Adventures)

Callie for President (Candy Apple)

Calling All Birdbrains (Rotten School)

Calling All Boys (Mary-Kate and Ashley: Two of a Kind)

Calling All Creeps! (Goosebumps)

Calling All Creeps (Goosebumps Presents)

Calling All Planets (Full House: Michelle)

Calling Dr. Amelia Bedelia (Amelia Bedelia)

Calling on Dragons (Enchanted Forest Chronicles)

Calling the Shots (Angels Unlimited)

Calling the Shots (Soccer Stars)

Cam Jansen and the Barking Treasure Mystery (Cam Jansen)

Cam Jansen and the Birthday Mystery (Cam Jansen)

Cam Jansen and the Catnapping Mystery (Cam Jansen)

Cam Jansen and the Chocolate Fudge Mystery (Cam Jansen)

Cam Jansen and the First Day of School Mystery (Cam Jansen)

Cam Jansen and the Ghostly Mystery (Cam Jansen)

Cam Jansen and the Green School Mystery (Cam Jansen)

Cam Jansen and the Mystery at the Haunted House (Cam Jansen)

Cam Jansen and the Mystery at the Monkey House (Cam Jansen)

Cam Jansen and the Mystery of Flight 54 (Cam Jansen)

Cam Jansen and the Mystery of the Babe Ruth Baseball (Cam Jansen)

Cam Jansen and the Mystery of the Carnival Prize (Cam Jansen)

Cam Jansen and the Mystery of the Circus Clown (Cam Jansen)

Cam Jansen and the Mystery of the Dinosaur Bones (Cam Jansen)

Cam Jansen and the Mystery of the Gold Coins (Cam Jansen)

Cam Jansen and the Mystery of the Monster Movie (Cam Jansen)

Cam Jansen and the Mystery of the Stolen Corn Popper (Cam Jansen)

Cam Jansen and the Mystery of the Stolen Diamonds (Cam Jansen)

Cam Jansen and the Mystery of the Television Dog (Cam Jansen)

Cam Jansen and the Mystery of the UFO (Cam Jansen)

Cam Jansen and the Mystery Writer Mystery (Cam Jansen)

Cam Jansen and the Scary Snake Mystery (Cam Jansen)

Cam Jansen and the School Play Mystery (Cam Jansen)

Cam Jansen and the Secret Service Mystery (Cam Jansen)

Cam Jansen and the Snowy Day Mystery (Cam Jansen)

Cam Jansen and the Tennis Trophy Mystery (Cam Jansen)

Cam Jansen and the Triceratops Pops Mystery (Cam Jansen)

Cam Jansen and the Valentine Baby Mystery (Cam Jansen)

The Camelot

Spell (Grail Quest)

Camp Babymouse (Babymouse)

Camp Barkalot (All-American Puppies)

Camp Bee-a-Champ (Slam Dunk)

Camp Buccaneer (Pirate School)

Camp Camden (7th Heaven)

Camp Can't (The Complicated Life of Claudia Cristina Cortez)

Camp Chaos (Go Girl)

Camp Dracula (Graveyard School)

Camp Fear Ghouls (Fear Street: Ghosts of Fear Street)

Camp Ghost-Away (Pee Wee Scouts)

Camp Hide-a-Pet (Full House: Michelle)

Camp Murphy (Murphy Family)

Camp Nowhere (Nightmare Room)

The Camp-Out Mystery (Boxcar Children)

Camp Rock 'n' Roll (Mary-Kate and Ashley: Two of a Kind)

Camp Rotten Time (Funny Firsts)

Camp Rules! (Katie Kazoo, Switcheroo)

Camp Saddlebrook (Thoroughbred)

Camp Spaghetti (Camp Sunnyside)

Camp Zombie (Camp Zombie)

Camp Zombie: The Lake's Revenge (Camp Zombie)

Camp Zombie: The Second Summer (Camp Zombie)

The Campfire Ghosts (Eagle-Eye Ernie)

Campfire Mallory (Mallory)

A-Campin' We Will Go (Kenan and Kel)

Camping Catastrophe! (Ready, Freddy!)

Camping Out (Sleepover Squad)

Can Adults Become Human? (Dear Dumb Diary)

Can Do, Jenny Archer (Jenny Archer)

Can You Get an F in Lunch? (How I Survived Middle School)

The Canary Caper (A to Z Mysteries)

Candles (On Time's Wing)

Candles, Cake, Celebrate! (Mary-Kate and Ashley: Two of a Kind)

The Candy Corn Contest (Polk Street School: Kids of the Polk Street School)

The Case of the Booby-Trapped Pickup (Hank the Cowdog)

The Case of the Blob (Totally Spies!)

Case of the Breaking Story (Wishbone Mysteries)

The Case of the Buried Treasure (Jigsaw Jones Mystery)

The Case of the Burning Building and the Case of the Ruby Ring (Adventures of Shirley Holmes)

The Case of the Burrowing Robot (Hank the Cowdog)

The Case of the Candy Cane Clue (Mary-Kate and Ashley: Adventures of Mary-Kate and Ashley)

The Case of the Captured Queen (Nancy Drew)

The Case of the Car-Barkaholic Dog (Hank the Cowdog)

The Case of the Cat's Meow (Case of the . . .)

The Case of the Cheerleading Camp Mystery (Mary-Kate and Ashley: Adventures of Mary-Kate and Ashley)

The Case of the Cheerleading Tattletale (Mary-Kate and Ashley: Adventures of Mary-Kate and Ashley)

The Case of the Chewable Worms (Secret Agent Dingledorf and His Trusty Dog Splat)

The Case of the Chocolate Fingerprints (Clue Jr.)

The Case of the Choosey Cheater (Darcy J. Doyle, Daring Detective)

The Case of the Christmas Caper (Mary-Kate and Ashley: Adventures of Mary-Kate and Ashley)

The Case of the Christmas Snowman (Jigsaw Jones Mystery)

The Case of the Christmas Thief (Sweet Valley Kids)

The Case of the Cinema Swindle (Baker Street Irregulars)

The Case of the Class Clown (Jigsaw Jones Mystery)

The Case of the Climbing Cat (High-Rise Private Eyes)

The Case of the Close Encounter (Bobbsey Twins: The New Bobbsey Twins)

The Case of the Clubhouse Thief (Clue Jr.)

The Case of the Clue at the Zoo (Mary-Kate and Ashley:

Adventures of Mary-Kate and Ashley)

The Case of the Comic Crooks (Baker Street Irregulars)

The Case of the Condemned Cat (McGurk)

The Case of the Cool-Itch Kid (Polka Dot Private Eye)

The Case of the Cop Catchers (Baker Street Irregulars)

The Case of the Cosmic Kidnapping (Hardy Boys)

The Case of the Counterfeit Cash (Nicki Holland)

The Case of the Counterfeit Criminals (Hardy Boys)

The Case of the Crazy Collections (Bobbsey Twins: The New Bobbsey Twins)

The Case of the Creative Crime (Nancy Drew)

The Case of the Creepy Campout (Darcy J. Doyle, Daring Detective)

The Case of the Creepy Castle (Mary-Kate and Ashley: Adventures of Mary-Kate and Ashley)

The Case of the Criminal Computer (Baker Street Irregulars)

The Case of the Crooked Contest (Bobbsey Twins: The New Bobbsey Twins)

The Case of the Crying Clown (Bobbsey Twins: The New Bobbsey Twins)

Case of the Cyber-Hacker (Wishbone Mysteries)

Case of the Dangerous Cruise (Ladd Family)

The Case of the Dangerous Solution (Nancy Drew)

The Case of the Deadly Ha-Ha Game (Hank the Cowdog)

The Case of the Desperate Drummer (McGurk)

The Case of the Desperate Duck (High-Rise Private Eyes)

The Case of the Detective in Disguise (Jigsaw Jones Mystery)

The Case of the Dirty Bird (Culpepper Adventures)

The Case of the Dirty Clue (Third-Grade Detectives)

The Case of the Disappearing Deejay (Nancy Drew)

The Case of the Disappearing Diamonds (Nancy Drew)

The Case of the Disappearing Dinosaur (Jigsaw Jones Mystery)

The Case of the Disappearing Diplomat (Baker Street Irregulars)

The Case of the Disappearing Princess (Mary-Kate and Ashley: Adventures of Mary-Kate and Ashley)

The Case of the Dog Camp Mystery (Mary-Kate and Ashley: Adventures of Mary-Kate and Ashley)

The Case of the Dog Show Mystery (Mary-Kate and Ashley: Adventures of Mary-Kate and Ashley)

The Case of the Double Bumblebee Sting (Hank the Cowdog)

The Case of the Double Cross (Case of the . . .)

The Case of the Double Trouble Detectives (Jigsaw Jones Mystery)

The Case of the Dragon in Distress (McGurk)

The Case of the Drooling Dinosaurs (Secret Agent Dingledorf and His Trusty Dog Splat)

The Case of the Dumb Bells (Case of the . . .)

The Case of the Easter Egg Race (Mary-Kate and Ashley: Adventures of Mary-Kate and Ashley)

The Case of the Eyeball Surprise (Black Cat Club)

The Case of the Fagin File (Baker Street Irregulars)

The Case of the Falling Sky (Hank the Cowdog)

The Case of the Fantastic Footprints (McGurk)

The Case of the Felon's Fiddle (McGurk)

The Case of the Fiddle-Playing Fox (Hank the Cowdog)

The Case of the Fidgety Fox (High-Rise Private Eyes)

The Case of the Firecrackers (Chinatown Mystery)

The Case of the Flapper 'Napper (Mary-Kate and Ashley: Adventures of Mary-Kate and Ashley)

The Case of the Floating Crime (Nancy Drew)

The Case of the Flying Phantom (Mary-Kate and Ashley:

The Case of the Missing Minds
(Bloodhounds, Inc.)

The Case of the Missing Monkey
(High-Rise Private Eyes)

The Case of the Missing Movie
(Clue Jr.)

The Case of the Missing Mummy
(Mary-Kate and Ashley:
Adventures of Mary-Kate and
Ashley)

Case of the Missing She-Geek
(Lizzie McGuire Mysteries)

The Case of the Mixed-Up
Monster (Darcy J. Doyle, Daring
Detective)

The Case of the Monkey Burglar
(Hank the Cowdog)

The Case of the Mossy Lake
Monster (Science Detectives)

The Case of the Most Ancient
Bone (Hank the Cowdog)

The Case of the Mummy Mystery
(Jigsaw Jones Mystery)

The Case of the Muttering
Mummy (McGurk)

The Case of the Mystery Cruise
(Mary-Kate and Ashley:
Adventures of Mary-Kate and
Ashley)

The Case of the Mystery Ghost
(Clue Jr.)

The Case of the Mystery Mark
(Nicki Holland)

The Case of the Nana-napper
(Wright and Wong)

The Case of the Near-Sighted
Neighbor (Darcy J. Doyle,
Daring Detective)

The Case of the Nervous Newsboy
(McGurk)

The Case of the Night-Stalking
Bone Monster (Hank the
Cowdog)

The Case of the Nutcracker Ballet
(Mary-Kate and Ashley:
Adventures of Mary-Kate and
Ashley)

Case of the On-Line Alien
(Wishbone Mysteries)

The Case of the One-Eyed Killer
Stud Horse (Hank the Cowdog)

The Case of the Pampered Poodle
(Darcy J. Doyle, Daring
Detective)

The Case of the Peculiar Pink Fan
(Enola Holmes)

The Case of the Perfect Prank
(Jigsaw Jones Mystery)

The Case of the Phantom Friend
(Nicki Holland)

The Case of the Phantom Frog
(McGurk)

The Case of the Photo Finish
(Nancy Drew)

The Case of the Prank That Stank
(Wright and Wong)

The Case of the Psychic Hamster
(The Freaky Joe Club)

The Case of the Psychic's Vision
(Hardy Boys)

The Case of the Purloined Parrot
(McGurk)

The Case of the Puzzling Possum
(High-Rise Private Eyes)

The Case of the Race Against Time
(Jigsaw Jones Mystery)

The Case of the Raging Rottweiler
(Hank the Cowdog)

The Case of the Rainy Day
Mystery (Jigsaw Jones Mystery)

The Case of the Rising Stars
(Nancy Drew)

The Case of the Rock and Roll
Mystery (Mary-Kate and Ashley:
Adventures of Mary-Kate and
Ashley)

The Case of the Rock Star's Secret
(Mary-Kate and Ashley:
Adventures of Mary-Kate and
Ashley)

The Case of the Runaway Dog
(Jigsaw Jones Mystery)

The Case of the Runaway Money
(Bobbsey Twins: The New
Bobbsey Twins)

The Case of the Runaway Turtle
(Clue Jr.)

The Case of the Saddle House
Robbery (Hank the Cowdog)

The Case of the Safecracker's
Secret (Nancy Drew)

The Case of the Santa Claus
Mystery (Jigsaw Jones Mystery)

The Case of the Savage Statue
(Three Investigators)

The Case of the Scaredy Cats (Case
of the . . .)

The Case of the Screaming
Scarecrow (Mary-Kate and
Ashley: Adventures of Mary-Kate
and Ashley)

The Case of the Sea World
Adventure (Mary-Kate and
Ashley: Adventures of Mary-Kate
and Ashley)

The Case of the Secret Message
(Clue Jr.)

The Case of the Secret Password
(Clue Jr.)

The Case of the Secret Santa
(Sweet Valley Kids)

The Case of the Secret Scribbler
(McGurk)

The Case of the Secret Valentine
(Jigsaw Jones Mystery)

The Case of the Shark Encounter
(Mary-Kate and Ashley:
Adventures of Mary-Kate and
Ashley)

The Case of the Shipwrecked Tree
(Hank the Cowdog)

The Case of the Silk King (Choose
Your Own Adventure)

The Case of the Singing
SeaDragons (The Freaky Joe
Club)

The Case of the Slam Dunk
Mystery (Mary-Kate and Ashley:
Adventures of Mary-Kate and
Ashley)

The Case of the Sleepy Sloth
(High-Rise Private Eyes)

The Case of the Slingshot Sniper
(McGurk)

The Case of the Slippery Soap Star
(Wright and Wong)

The Case of the Smiling Shark
(The Freaky Joe Club)

The Case of the Sneaker Sneak
(Jigsaw Jones Mystery)

The Case of the Sneaky Snowman
(Nancy Drew and the Clue
Crew)

The Case of the Snowboarding
Superstar (Jigsaw Jones Mystery)

The Case of the Soccer Camp
Mystery (Clue Jr.)

The Case of the Spoiled Rotten
Spy (Jigsaw Jones Mystery)

The Case of the Spooky Sleepover
(Jigsaw Jones Mystery)

The Case of the Stinky Science
Project (Jigsaw Jones Mystery)

The Case of the Stolen Baseball
Cards (Jigsaw Jones Mystery)

The Case of the Stolen Jewel (Clue
Jr.)

The Case of the Summer Camp
Caper (Mary-Kate and Ashley:
Adventures of Mary-Kate and
Ashley)

The Case of the Sundae Surprise
(Mary-Kate and Ashley:
Adventures of Mary-Kate and
Ashley)

The Case of the Surfing Secret
(Mary-Kate and Ashley:
Adventures of Mary-Kate and
Ashley)

Caught in the Rebel Camp (Trailblazers)

Caught on Tape (Hollywood Sisters)

Caution (Fear Street: Ghosts of Fear Street)

Cave-In! (Hardy Boys)

Cave-in (Survival!)

Cave of Fear (Nightmares! How Will Yours End?)

Cave of the Dark Wind (Never Land)

The Cave of Time (Choose Your Own Adventure)

Cavern of the Fear (Deltora: Deltora Shadowlands)

Cayman Gold (MacGregor Family Adventure)

Cecile (American Girls: Girls of Many Lands)

Cel Mates (Sailor Moon Novels)

The Celery Stalks at Midnight (Bunnicula)

Celeste Sails to Spain (Australian Children)

Celou Sudden Shout, Idaho, 1826 (American Diaries)

Centennial Celebration (The American Adventure)

Center Court Sting (Matt Christopher Sports Stories)

Center Ice (Silver Blades)

Centerfield Ballhawk (Matt Christopher Sports Stories)

Centerfield Ballhawk (Peach Street Mudders)

The Cereal Box Mystery (Boxcar Children)

Chain Reaction (NASCAR Racers)

A Chair for My Mother (Rosa Trilogy)

The Challenge (Mary-Kate and Ashley Starring In . . .)

Challenge at Second Base (Matt Christopher Sports Stories)

Challenge of the Masked Racer (Speed Racer)

The Challenger (Phantom Stallion)

The Chameleon Wore Chartreuse (Chet Gecko Mysteries)

Champion Rose (Magic Attic Club)

Champion's Luck (Skating Dreams)

Champion's Spirit (Thoroughbred)

Championship Ball (Chip Hilton Sports Series)

Championship Game (Angel Park All-Stars)

Championship Summer (Alden All Stars)

The Chance Factor (Star Trek: Voyager: Starfleet Academy)

The Chance of a Lifetime (Cassie Perkins)

Chance of a Lifetime (Saddles, Stars, and Stripes)

Chance of a Lifetime (Silver Blades)

The Change (Animorphs)

Change-Up (The Pink Parrots)

The Changeling (Wormling)

Changeling Diapers (Journey of Allen Strange)

Changes for Addy (American Girls: Addy)

Changes for Felicity (American Girls: Felicity)

Changes for Josefina (American Girls: Josefina)

Changes for Julie (American Girls: Julie)

Changes for Kaya (American Girls: Kaya)

Changes for Kirsten (American Girls: Kirsten)

Changes for Kit (American Girls: Kit)

Changes for Molly (American Girls: Molly)

Changes for Samantha (American Girls: Samantha)

The Changing of the Guard (Star Wars: Jedi Quest)

Changing Places (B.Y. Times Kid Sisters)

Changing Times (The American Adventure)

Changing Times (B.Y. Times)

The Chariot of Queen Zara (Secrets of Droon)

The Charioteer of Delphi (Roman Mysteries)

Charity at Home (Horseshoe Trilogies)

Charity's Gift (Horseshoe Trilogies)

Charlie Bone and the Beast (Children of the Red King)

Charlie Bone and the Castle of Mirrors (Children of the Red King)

Charlie Bone and the Hidden King (Children of the Red King)

Charlie Bone and the Invisible Boy (Children of the Red King)

Charlie Bone and the Shadow (Children of the Red King)

Charlie Bone and the Time Twister (Children of the Red King)

Charlotte's Choice (Doll Hospital)

The Charm Bracelet (Fairy Realm)

The Charmed Bracelet (Nancy Drew Graphic Novels)

Charmed Forces (Camp Confidential)

Charming Opal (Toot and Puddle)

The Charmingly Clever Cousin (Princess Power)

The Chase for the Mystery Twister (Hardy Boys)

Chasing Dad (Rocket Power)

Chasing the Dream (Dolphin Diaries)

Chasing the Falconers (On the Run)

Chasing the Wind (The Young Underground)

Chasing Vermeer (Petra and Calder)

Cheat Sheet (How I Survived Middle School)

Check in to Danger (Casebusters)

Check It Out (Suite Life of Zack and Cody)

Checkered Flag (RPM)

Checkout Time at the Dead-End Hotel (Goosebumps: Give Yourself Goosebumps)

A Cheese-Colored Camper (Geronimo Stilton)

Chelsea and the Alien Invasion (Best Friends)

Chelsea and the Outrageous Phone Bill (Best Friends)

Chelsea's Special Touch (Best Friends)

Cherry Bomb Squad (Heroes A2Z)

Cherry Cola Champions (Alex)

Chess! I Love It! I Love It! I Love It! (Table Two)

The Chessmen of Doom (Johnny Dixon)

Chester Cricket's New Home (Chester Cricket)

Chester Cricket's Pigeon Ride (Chester Cricket)

Chester's Way (Lilly)

The Chestnut Soldier (Gwyn Griffiths Trilogy)

Cheyenne Rose (Magic Attic Club)

Chicago and the Cat (Chicago and the Cat)

A Coal Miner's Bride (Dear America)

Cobra Connection (Choose Your Own Adventure)

The Cobra King of Kathmandu (Children of the Lamp)

A Cobtown Christmas (Cobtown)

The Cobweb Confession (Third-Grade Detectives)

Coco Grimes (Thomas and Grandfather)

The Cocoa Commotion (Carmen Sandiego Mysteries)

The Code (Spy X)

The Code Caper (Totally Spies!)

Code Word Kangaroo (Adam Sharp)

Cody (Wolfbay Wings)

Cody Unplugged (Cody)

Cody's Secret Admirer (Cody)

Cody's Varsity Rush (Spirit of the Game)

The Coiled Viper (Secrets of Droon)

C.O.L.A.R. (Jack Jameson and Danny One)

The Cold and Hot Winter (Seasonal Adventures)

The Cold Cash Caper (Hardy Boys)

The Cold People (Spooksville)

Cold Shoulder Road (Wolves Chronicles)

Collie with a Card (Animal Ark)

Color Day Relay (Magic School Bus Science Chapter Books)

Color Me Criminal (Carmen Sandiego Mysteries)

Color Me Dark (Dear America)

Color War! (Camp Sunnyside)

The Colossus of Rhodes (Roman Mysteries)

Colt in the Cave (Animal Ark Hauntings)

Colt on Christmas Eve (Animal Ark)

Come a Stranger (Tillerman Cycle)

Come Away with Me (Heartland)

Come Back, Amelia Bedelia (Amelia Bedelia)

Come Out and Play, Little Mouse (Little Mouse)

Come to School, Dear Dragon (Dear Dragon)

Come What May (Heartland)

Comeback Cagers (Chip Hilton Sports Series)

The Comeback Challenge (Matt Christopher Sports Stories)

Comeback of the Home Run Kid (Matt Christopher Sports Stories)

Comedy of Errors (China Tate)

Comet Crash (Choose Your Own Adventure)

Comet in Moominland (Moomintroll)

Comic Book Criminal (Mystery Files of Shelby Woo)

The Comic Book Mystery (Boxcar Children)

Comic Con Artist (Hardy Boys, Undercover Brothers)

Coming Home (The American Adventure)

Coming Home (Heartland)

The Coming of Dragons (The Darkest Age)

The Coming of Hoole (Guardians of Ga'Hoole)

The Coming Storm (Jack Sparrow)

Commander Toad and the Big Black Hole (Commander Toad)

Commander Toad and the Dis-asteroid (Commander Toad)

Commander Toad and the Intergalactic Spy (Commander Toad)

Commander Toad and the Planet of the Grapes (Commander Toad)

Commander Toad and the Space Pirates (Commander Toad)

Commander Toad and the Voyage Home (Commander Toad)

Commander Toad in Space (Commander Toad)

The Competition (Silver Blades)

Competition Fever (American Gold Gymnasts)

Computer Clues (Pee Wee Scouts)

Computer Crunch! (Secret World of Alex Mack)

The Computer Takeover (Choose Your Own Adventure)

Confessions of a Bitter Secret Santa (Candy Apple)

The Conspiracy (Animorphs)

The Constellation of Sylvie (Sylvie Cycle)

Contents Under Pressure (Lilo and Stitch: The Series)

The Cookie Caper (Lunchroom)

Cookie Crazy! (Clifford)

Cookies and Crutches (Pee Wee Scouts)

Cookin' With CatDog (CatDog (Chapter Books))

Cool as Ice (Matt Christopher Sports Stories)

The Cool Club (Mary-Kate and Ashley: Two of a Kind)

The Cool Ghoul Mystery (Fletcher Mysteries)

Cool in School (Sister Sister)

Cool Zone with the Pain and the Great One (The Pain and the Great One)

The Copycat Crime (Batman (Scholastic Reader))

The Copycat Mystery (Boxcar Children)

Cora Frear (Brave Kids)

Corby Flood (Far-Flung Adventures)

Corduroy (Corduroy)

Corduroy Lost and Found (Corduroy)

Corduroy Makes a Cake (Corduroy)

Corduroy Writes a Letter (Corduroy)

Corduroy's Birthday (Corduroy)

Corduroy's Christmas (Corduroy)

Corduroy's Garden (Corduroy)

Corduroy's Halloween (Corduroy)

Corduroy's Hike (Corduroy)

Corey and the Spooky Pony (Pony Tails)

Corey in the Saddle (Pony Tails)

Corey's Christmas Wish (Pony Tails)

Corey's Pony Is Missing (Pony Tails)

Corey's Secret Friend (Pony Tails)

Cork and Fuzz (Cork and Fuzz)

Cork and Fuzz: Finders Keepers (Cork and Fuzz)

Cork and Fuzz: Good Sports (Cork and Fuzz)

Cork and Fuzz: Short and Tall (Cork and Fuzz)

Cork and Fuzz: The Collectors (Cork and Fuzz)

Corn Raid (Jamestown's American Portraits)

Corrie's Secret Pal (Here Come the Brownies)

Cosmic Boy Versus Mezmo Head (The Weird Zone)

The Cosmic Camp Caper (AstroKids)

The Cost of Cool (Rocket Power)

A Costume for Noah (Noah)

Crossing the Colorado Rockies, 1864 (American Sisters)

The Crow and Mrs. Gaddy (Mrs. Gaddy)

The Crown of Light (W.I.T.C.H.—Chapter Books)

The Cruel Empress (W.I.T.C.H.—Adventures)

Crunch Time (High School Musical Stories from East High)

The Crunchy, Munchy Christmas Tree (Harry and Emily)

Crusade of the Flaming Sword (Hardy Boys)

Crush on the Coach (Gymnasts)

Crush-Tastic! (Hannah Montana)

Crushes and Camping (Hannah Montana (TokyoPop))

Cry of the Cat (Goosebumps Series 2000)

Cry of the Wolf (Avalon 1: Web of Magic)

Crybaby Lois (Sweet Valley Kids)

Crystal Doors (Crystal Doors)

Crystal Doors: Ocean Realm (Crystal Doors)

Crystal Doors: Sky Realm (Crystal Doors)

The Crystal Planet (Zenda)

The Crystal Prison (Deptford Mice)

Crystal the Snow Fairy (Rainbow Magic: Weather Fairies)

Cub in the Cupboard (Animal Ark)

The Cuckoo Clock of Doom (Goosebumps)

The Cuckoo Clock of Doom (Goosebumps Presents)

Cuckoo Feathers (Simply Sarah)

The Cuckoo Tree (Wolves Chronicles)

Culpepper's Cannon (Culpepper Adventures)

Cup Crazy (Slapshots)

Cupid Cakes (Lulu Baker)

The Cupid Chronicles (The Wedding Planner's Daughter)

Cupid Doesn't Flip Hamburgers (Bailey School: The Adventures of the Bailey School Kids)

The Curious Coronation (Dana Girls)

Curious George (Curious George)

Curious George: The Dog Show (Curious George)

Curious George: The Donut Delivery (Curious George)

Curious George: The Kite (Curious George)

Curious George: The Surprise Gift (Curious George)

Curious George and the Birthday Surprise (Curious George)

Curious George and the Dinosaur (Curious George)

Curious George and the Dump Truck (Curious George)

Curious George and the Dump Truck (Curious George)

Curious George and the Firefighters (Curious George)

Curious George and the Hot Air Balloon (Curious George)

Curious George and the Pizza (Curious George)

Curious George and the Puppies (Curious George)

Curious George at the Airport (Curious George)

Curious George at the Aquarium (Curious George)

Curious George at the Ballet (Curious George)

Curious George at the Baseball Game (Curious George)

Curious George at the Beach (Curious George)

Curious George at the Laundromat (Curious George)

Curious George at the Parade (Curious George)

Curious George at the Railroad Station (Curious George)

Curious George Bakes a Cake (Curious George)

Curious George Builds a House (Curious George)

Curious George Cleans Up (Curious George)

Curious George Feeds the Animals (Curious George)

Curious George Flies a Kite (Curious George)

Curious George Gets a Medal (Curious George)

Curious George Goes Camping (Curious George)

Curious George Goes Camping (Curious George)

Curious George Goes Fishing (Curious George)

Curious George Goes Fishing (Curious George)

Curious George Goes Hiking (Curious George)

Curious George Goes Sledding (Curious George)

Curious George Goes to a Costume Party (Curious George)

Curious George Goes to a Costume Party (Curious George)

Curious George Goes to a Movie (Curious George)

Curious George Goes to a Restaurant (Curious George)

Curious George Goes to a Toy Store (Curious George)

Curious George Goes to an Air Show (Curious George)

Curious George Goes to an Ice Cream Shop (Curious George)

Curious George Goes to School (Curious George)

Curious George Goes to the Aquarium (Curious George)

Curious George Goes to the Beach (Curious George)

Curious George Goes to the Chocolate Factory (Curious George)

Curious George Goes to the Circus (Curious George)

Curious George Goes to the Dentist (Curious George)

Curious George Goes to the Hospital (Curious George)

Curious George in the Big City (Curious George)

Curious George in the Snow (Curious George)

Curious George Learns the Alphabet (Curious George)

Curious George Lost and Found (Curious George)

Curious George Makes Pancakes (Curious George)

Curious George Plants a Seed (Curious George)

Curious George Plays Baseball (Curious George)

Curious George Plays Mini Golf (Curious George)

Curious George Rides a Bike (Curious George)

Curious George Roller Coaster (Curious George)

Curious George Snowy Day (Curious George)

Curious George Tadpole Trouble (Curious George)

Curious George Takes a Job (Curious George)

Curious George Takes a Train (Curious George)

Danger Guys and the Golden Lizard (Danger Guys)

Danger Guys Blast Off (Danger Guys)

Danger Guys Hit the Beach (Danger Guys)

Danger Guys on Ice (Danger Guys)

Danger in Dinosaur Valley (Screech Owls)

Danger in Disguise (On Time's Wing)

Danger in the Extreme (Hardy Boys)

Danger in the Fourth Dimension (Hardy Boys)

Danger in the Harbor (The American Adventure)

Danger in the Palace (Circle of Magic)

Danger in Tibet (Miss Mallard)

Danger on Crab Island (Neptune Adventures)

Danger on Midnight River (World of Adventure)

Danger on the Air (Hardy Boys)

Danger on the Diamond (Hardy Boys)

Danger on the Flying Trapeze (Trailblazers)

Danger on the Great Lakes (Nancy Drew)

Danger on the Railroad (The American Adventure)

Danger on Thunder Mountain (American Adventure)

Danger on Vampire Trail (Hardy Boys)

Danger Time (Goosebumps: Give Yourself Goosebumps)

Danger! Wizard at Work (Dragon Slayers' Academy)

The Danger Zone (Reel Kids Adventures)

The Dangerous Canoe Race (Ladd Family)

The Dangerous Diamond (Clue)

Dangerous Dolls of Delaware (American Chillers)

The Dangerous Games (Star Wars: Jedi Quest)

Dangerous Games (Wolves Chronicles)

A Dangerous Path (Warriors)

Dangerous Plays (Nancy Drew: Girl Detective)

A Dangerous Promise (Orphan Train Adventures)

The Dangerous Quest (Spooksville)

A Dangerous Ride (Thoroughbred: Ashleigh)

The Dangerous Snake and Reptile Club (Clubhouse)

The Dangerous Transmission (Hardy Boys)

The Dangerous Voyage (Reel Kids Adventures)

The Dangerous Voyage (Time Navigators)

Dangerous Waters (Strange Matter)

Dangerously Alice (Alice)

Danielle's Dollhouse Wish (Doll Hospital)

Daniel's Story (American Quilts)

Danitra Brown, Class Clown (Danitra Brown)

Danitra Brown Leaves Town (Danitra Brown)

Danny and the Dinosaur (Danny and the Dinosaur)

Danny and the Dinosaur Go to Camp (Danny and the Dinosaur)

Danny Dunn and the Anti-Gravity Paint (Danny Dunn)

Danny Dunn and the Automatic House (Danny Dunn)

Danny Dunn and the Fossil Cave (Danny Dunn)

Danny Dunn and the Heat Ray (Danny Dunn)

Danny Dunn and the Homework Machine (Danny Dunn)

Danny Dunn and the Smallifying Machine (Danny Dunn)

Danny Dunn and the Swamp Monster (Danny Dunn)

Danny Dunn and the Universal Glue (Danny Dunn)

Danny Dunn and the Voice from Space (Danny Dunn)

Danny Dunn and the Weather Machine (Danny Dunn)

Danny Dunn, Invisible Boy (Danny Dunn)

Danny Dunn on a Desert Island (Danny Dunn)

Danny Dunn on the Ocean Floor (Danny Dunn)

Danny Dunn, Scientific Detective (Danny Dunn)

Danny Dunn, Time Traveller (Danny Dunn)

Dare at the Fair (Nancy Drew Notebooks)

Dare to Scare (Mary-Kate and Ashley: Two of a Kind)

Daredevil (NASCAR Racers)

Daredevil Park (Choose Your Own Adventure)

Daredevils (Cascade Mountain Railroad Mysteries)

Daredevils (Hardy Boys)

Dark and Full of Secrets (Christopher)

A Dark and Noisy Night (Silly Thrillers with Peggy the Pig)

The Dark Corner (Spooksville)

Dark Day in the Deep Sea (Magic Tree House)

Dark Destiny (Bionicle Legends)

The Dark Hand (Jackie Chan Adventures)

The Dark Hills Divide (Land of Elyon)

Dark Horse (Mustang Mountain)

The Dark Is Rising (Dark Is Rising)

The Dark Lord's Demise (The Archives of Anthropos)

The Dark Mage (Avalon 2: Quest for Magic)

Dark of the Moon (On Time's Wing)

The Dark Portal (Deptford Mice)

Dark River (Warriors: Power of Three)

The Dark Secret of Weatherend (Anthony Monday)

Dark Side of the Sun (Space Above and Beyond)

Dark Sky Overhead (Power Rangers: Ninja Storm)

The Dark Stairs (Herculeah Jones)

Dark Sunshine (Phantom Stallion)

Dark Warning (Star Wars: The Last of the Jedi)

Dark Whispers (Unicorn Chronicles)

The Darkest Dream (W.I.T.C.H.—Chapter Books)

Darkest Hour (Heartland)

The Darkest Hour (Warriors)

Darkest Knight (Star Wars Young Jedi Knights)

Darkness Below (Bionicle Adventures)

Darkness Falls (X Files)

Darth Maul (Star Wars Episode 1: Journals)

Darwin's Family Tree (The Wild Thornberrys)

The Decision (Animorphs)

The Declaration of Independence (Abby Hayes: The Amazing Days of Abby Hayes)

Deep Freeze (Dish)

Deep in the Jungle of Doom (Goosebumps: Give Yourself Goosebumps)

Deep Powder, Deep Trouble (X Games Xtreme Mysteries)

Deep Trouble (Goosebumps)

Deep Trouble II (Goosebumps)

Deep Wizardry (Wizardry)

Deer in the Darkness (Animal Ark Hauntings)

The Deer in the Wood (Little House: My First Little House Books)

Defeat of the Ghost Riders (Trailblazers)

Defense! (Angel Park Soccer Stars)

Delusions of Grandeur (Star Wars Young Jedi Knights)

The Demolition Mission (Hardy Boys)

Demolition Winter (Space Above and Beyond)

Demon Mask (Usagi Yojimbo)

The Demon of River Heights (Nancy Drew Graphic Novels)

The Demon's Den (Hardy Boys)

The Dentist from the Black Lagoon (Black Lagoon)

The Departure (Animorphs)

Depend on Katie John (Katie John)

Deprivation House (Hardy Boys, Undercover Brothers Murder House Trilogy)

Depth Charge (Journey of Allen Strange)

Derby Day (Thoroughbred: Ashleigh)

Derby Dreams (Thoroughbred: Ashleigh)

Derby Fever (Thoroughbred)

Desdemona (Desdemona)

Desdemona Moves On (Desdemona)

Desert Danger (Frightmares)

Desert Danger (Phantom Stallion)

The Desert Thieves (Hardy Boys)

The Deserted Library Mystery (Boxcar Children)

The Desperate Mission (Star Wars: The Last of the Jedi)

The Desperate Search (American Adventure)

Destination Unknown (Remnants)

Detective Camp (A to Z Mysteries)

Detective LaRue (LaRue)

Detective Mole (Detective Mole)

Detective Mole and the Circus Mystery (Detective Mole)

Detective Mole and the Halloween Mystery (Detective Mole)

Detective Mole and the Haunted Castle Mystery (Detective Mole)

Detective Mole and the Seashore Mystery (Detective Mole)

Detective Mole and the Secret Clues (Detective Mole)

Detective Mole and the Tip-Top Mystery (Detective Mole)

Detective Pony (Pony Pals)

Detective's Duel (Klooz)

Devil's Breath Volcano (MacGregor Family Adventure)

Dew Drop Dead (Sebastian Barth)

The Dex-Terminator (Dexter's Laboratory Chapter Books)

Dexter's Big Switch (Dexter's Laboratory Chapter Books)

Dexter's Ink (Dexter's Laboratory Chapter Books)

The Diamond Champs (Matt Christopher Sports Stories)

The Diamond in the Window (The Hall Family)

Diamond Park Dinosaur (Never Sink Nine)

The Diamond Princess and the Magic Ball (Jewel Kingdom)

The Diamond Princess Saves the Day (Jewel Kingdom)

The Diamond Princess Steps Through the Mirror (Jewel Kingdom)

The Diamond War (Castle Court Kids)

Diamonds Not Forever (Sailor Moon Novels)

Diary of a Mad Mummy (Goosebumps: Give Yourself Goosebumps)

Diary of a Wimpy Kid (Diary of a Wimpy Kid)

Diary of a Wimpy Kid: Rodrick Rules (Diary of a Wimpy Kid)

Diary of a Wimpy Kid: The Last Straw (Diary of a Wimpy Kid)

The Diary of Melanie Martin (Melanie Martin)

Dicey's Song (Tillerman Cycle)

Dido and Pa (Wolves Chronicles)

Die Bug Die (X Files)

A Different Path (W.I.T.C.H.—Chapter Books)

Dig to Disaster (Miss Mallard)

Digby and Kate (Digby and Kate)

Digby and Kate Again (Digby and Kate)

Digby and Kate and the Beautiful Day (Digby and Kate)

Digby and Kate, 1, 2, 3 (Digby and Kate)

Digging for Clues (Ghostwriter)

Digging for Dinos (Heroes A2Z)

Digging to the Center of the Earth (Wishbone Adventures)

Digging Up the Past (Wishbone Adventures)

Digging Up Trouble (Amy Hodgepodge)

DigiArmor Energize! (Digimon Digital Monsters)

Dil in a Pickle (Rugrats (Chapter Books))

Dinah for President (Dinah)

Dinah Forever (Dinah)

Dinah in Love (Dinah)

Dingoes at Dinnertime (Magic Tree House)

Dinosaur Alert! (Nancy Drew Notebooks)

Dinosaur Beach (Dinosaurs)

Dinosaur Day (Dinosaurs)

Dinosaur Detectives (Magic School Bus Science Chapter Books)

Dinosaur Disaster (Hardy Boys: Frank and Joe Hardy: The Clues Brothers)

Dinosaur Dreams (Funnybones)

Dinosaur Garden (Dinosaurs)

Dinosaur Island (Choose Your Own Adventure)

The Dinosaur Mystery (Boxcar Children)

Dinosaur Valentine (Dinosaurs)

Dinosaurs Before Dark (Magic Tree House)

Dinosaurs' Christmas (Dinosaurs)

Dinosaurs' Halloween (Dinosaurs)

Dinosaurs' Thanksgiving (Dinosaurs)

Dirt Bike Racer (Matt Christopher Sports Stories)

Dirt Bike Runaway (Matt Christopher Sports Stories)

A Dirty Deed (Across the Steel River)

Dirty Tricks (Genghis Khan)

The Disappearance (W.I.T.C.H.—Chapter Books)

Don't Sit On My Lunch! (Ready, Freddy!)

Don't Stop, by Angel (The Broadway Ballplayers)

Don't Swap Your Sweater for a Dog (Roscoe Riley Rules)

Don't Tap Dance on Your Teacher (Roscoe Riley Rules)

Don't Tell Mummy (Graveyard School)

Don't Wake Up Mama! (Five Little Monkeys)

Don't You Feel Well, Sam? (Sam)

Don't You Know There's a War On? (James Stevenson's Autobiographical Stories)

Dooby (Wolfbay Wings)

Dooby Dooby Moo (Duck)

Dooger, the Grasshopper Hound (D.J. Dillon Adventures)

The Doom of the Haunted Opera (Lewis Barnavelt)

Doom Star (Time Surfers)

Doomed in Dreamland (Super Goofballs)

Doomsday (2099)

The Doomsday Dust (Spy Gear)

The Doomsday Ship (Star Wars Galaxy of Fear)

Doomwyte (Redwall)

The Door in the Dragon's Throat (Cooper Kids)

The Door in the Tree (Magician's House Quartet)

The Door-to-Door Deception (Nancy Drew)

The Door to Time (Ulysses Moore)

Doorway to Doom (Strange Matter)

Doppelganger (Bloodwater Mysteries)

Doris's Dinosaur (Yoko and Friends)

Dork in Disguise (Dork in Disguise)

Dork on the Run (Dork in Disguise)

Dorothy and the Magic Belt (Oz)

Dorothy and the Wizard of Oz (Oz)

Dorothy of Oz (Oz)

Dorothy's Darkest Days (Kane Family)

Dorrie and the Amazing Magic Elixir (Dorrie)

Dorrie and the Birthday Eggs (Dorrie)

Dorrie and the Blue Witch (Dorrie)

Dorrie and the Dreamyard Monsters (Dorrie)

Dorrie and the Fortune Teller (Dorrie)

Dorrie and the Goblin (Dorrie)

Dorrie and the Hallowe'en Plot (Dorrie)

Dorrie and the Haunted House (Dorrie)

Dorrie and the Haunted Schoolhouse (Dorrie)

Dorrie and the Museum Case (Dorrie)

Dorrie and the Pin Witch (Dorrie)

Dorrie and the Screebit Ghost (Dorrie)

Dorrie and the Weather Box (Dorrie)

Dorrie and the Witch Doctor (Dorrie)

Dorrie and the Witch's Camp (Dorrie)

Dorrie and the Witch's Imp (Dorrie)

Dorrie and the Witchville Fair (Dorrie)

Dorrie and the Wizard's Spell (Dorrie)

Dorrie's Magic (Dorrie)

Dorrie's Play (Dorrie)

Dossier 001 (The Stink Files)

Dossier 003 (The Stink Files)

Dossier 002 (The Stink Files)

Dot and Jabber and the Big Bug Mystery (Dot and Jabber)

Dot and Jabber and the Great Acorn Mystery (Dot and Jabber)

Dot and Jabber and the Mystery of the Missing Steam (Dot and Jabber)

Double-Booked (Chosen Girls)

Double-Crossed in Gator Country (Eric Sterling, Secret Agent)

The Double Dabble Surprise (Cul-de-Sac Kids)

Double Dare (Silver Blades)

Double Disaster! (The Magical States of America)

Double Dog Dare (Hobie Hanson)

Double Dragon Trouble (Dragon Slayers' Academy)

Double Fake (Winning Season)

Double Fault (Red Rock Mysteries)

Double Fudge (Fudge)

The Double Horror of Fenley Place (Nancy Drew)

Double Jeopardy (Hardy Boys)

The Double Jinx Mystery (Nancy Drew)

Double Life (Invisible Detectives)

Double or Die (Young Bond)

Double Play at Short (Matt Christopher Sports Stories)

Double Trouble (Goners)

Double Trouble (Jimmy Sniffles)

Double Trouble (Little Genie)

Double Trouble (Puppy Patrol)

Double Trouble (Rocket Power)

Double Trouble (Suite Life of Zack and Cody)

Double Trouble Dwarf (Pixie Tricks)

Double Trouble for Jess McColl! (Twelve Candles Club)

Double Trouble Monsters (Bailey City Monsters)

Double Trouble Squared (Starbucks Twins Mysteries)

Double Whammy! (Slam Dunk)

Doubles or Nothing (Full House: Stephanie)

Doug and the End of the World (Doug Chronicles)

Doug Cheats (Doug Chronicles)

Doug Rules (Doug Chronicles)

Doug's Big Comeback (Doug (Disney Chapter Books))

Doug's Hoop Nightmare (Doug (Disney Chapter Books))

Doug's Vampire Caper (Doug (Disney Chapter Books))

Down and Out Down Under (Geronimo Stilton)

The Down and Up Fall (Seasonal Adventures)

Down the Rio Grande, 1829 (American Sisters)

Down to the Bonny Glen (Little House: The Martha Years)

Down to the Wire (Thoroughbred)

Downfall (Bionicle Legends)

Downhill (Kim Possible (Chapter Books))

Downhill Megan (Magic Attic Club)

Dr. Amelia's Boredom Survival Guide (Amelia)

Dr. Carbles Is Losing His Marbles! (My Weird School)

Dr. Dee Dee and Dexter Hyde (Dexter's Laboratory Chapter Books)

Dulcie's Taste of Magic (Disney Fairies (Chapter Books))

Dumb Clucks (Rotten School)

Dunc and Amos and the Red Tattoos (Culpepper Adventures)

Dunc and Amos Go to the Dogs (Culpepper Adventures)

Dunc and Amos Hit the Big Top (Culpepper Adventures)

Dunc and Amos Meet the Slasher (Culpepper Adventures)

Dunc and Amos on Thin Ice (Culpepper Adventures)

Dunc and the Flaming Ghost (Culpepper Adventures)

Dunc and the Greased Sticks of Doom (Culpepper Adventures)

Dunc and the Haunted Castle (Culpepper Adventures)

Dunc Breaks the Record (Culpepper Adventures)

Dunc Gets Tweaked (Culpepper Adventures)

Duncan and Dolores (Duncan and Dolores)

Dunc's Doll (Culpepper Adventures)

Dunc's Dump (Culpepper Adventures)

Dunc's Halloween (Culpepper Adventures)

Dunc's Undercover Christmas (Culpepper Adventures)

The Dung Beetle Bandits (Tiger Moth)

The Dungeon of Doom (Hank the Cowdog)

Dungeon of Doom (Hardy Boys)

Dunk Under Pressure (Winning Season)

Dustland (Justice Trilogy)

D.W. All Wet (D.W.)

D.W., Go to Your Room (D.W.)

D.W. Rides Again (D.W.)

D.W. the Picky Eater (D.W.)

D.W. Thinks Big (D.W.)

Dwight D. Eisenhower (Dear Mr. President)

D.W.'s Guide to Perfect Manners (D.W.)

D.W.'s Guide to Preschool (D.W.)

D.W.'s Library Card (D.W.)

D.W.'s Lost Blankie (D.W.)

D.W.'s Perfect Present (D.W.)

D.W.'s the Big Boss (D.W.)

Dylan's Choice (Thoroughbred)

Dynamite Dawn vs. Terrific Terri (Best Friends)

Dynamite Dinah (Dinah)

E

The E-Mail Murders (P.C. Hawke Mysteries)

The E-Mail Mystery (Nancy Drew)

"E" Is for Elisa (Riverside Kids: Elisa)

Eager Star (Winnie the Horse Gentler)

The Eagle (Lighthouse Family)

Eagle-Eye Ernie Comes to Town (Eagle-Eye Ernie)

An Ear for Danger (Three Investigators)

Early Sunday Morning (Dear America)

The Ears of Corn (Ike and Mem)

Earth Geeks Must Go! (Goosebumps Series 2000)

Earth Hounds, As Explained by Professor Xargle (Professor Xargle)

Earth Mobiles, As Explained by Professor Xargle (Professor Xargle)

Earth Tigerlets, As Explained by Professor Xargle (Professor Xargle)

Earth to Matthew (Matthew Martin)

Earth Weather, As Explained by Professor Xargle (Professor Xargle)

Earthborn (Ormingat)

Earthlets, As Explained by Professor Xargle (Professor Xargle)

Earthquake! (Choose Your Own Adventure)

Earthquake (Survival!)

Earthquake! (Once Upon America)

Earthquake in Cincinnati (The American Adventure)

Earthquake in the Early Morning (Magic Tree House)

The East-West Contest (7th Heaven)

Easter Bunny Battle (Sweet Valley Kids)

Easter Egg Disaster (Harry and Emily)

The Easter Egg Haunt (Graveyard School)

Easter Egg Haunt (Heroes A2Z)

Easter Mice! (Holiday Mice)

Easy as Apple Pie (Harry and Emily)

Eat Your Poison, Dear (Sebastian Barth)

Eaten Alive (Star Wars Galaxy of Fear)

Eating Enchiladas (Simply Sarah)

E.B.E. (X Files)

Echoes of the White Giraffe (Sookan Bak)

Eclipse (Warriors: Power of Three)

Eco-Wolf and the Three Pigs (Seriously Silly Stories)

Eddie and Gardenia (Eddie Wilson)

Eddie and His Big Deals (Eddie Wilson)

Eddie and Louella (Eddie Wilson)

Eddie and the Fire Engine (Eddie Wilson)

Eddie Makes Music (Eddie Wilson)

Eddie the Dog Holder (Eddie Wilson)

Eddie's Friend Boodles (Eddie Wilson)

Eddie's Green Thumb (Eddie Wilson)

Eddie's Happenings (Eddie Wilson)

Eddie's Menagerie (Eddie Wilson)

Eddie's Pay Dirt (Eddie Wilson)

Eddie's Valuable Property (Eddie Wilson)

Edith and Little Bear Lend a Hand (The Lonely Doll)

Edith and Midnight (The Lonely Doll)

Edith and Mr. Bear (The Lonely Doll)

Edith and the Duckling (The Lonely Doll)

Edward in Deep Water (Edward the Unready)

Edward Unready for School (Edward the Unready)

Edward's Overwhelming Overnight (Edward the Unready)

Eenie, Meenie, Murphy, No! (Murphy Family)

Eerie in the Mirror (Eerie Indiana)

The Eerie Triangle (Eerie Indiana)

Eeyore Finds a Friend (Winnie the Pooh First Readers)

The Egg (George and His Dragon)

Egg-Drop Blues (Judge and Jury)

Egg-Drop Day (Mr. Rose's Class)

Emily Eyefinger and the Lost Treasure (Emily Eyefinger)

Emily Eyefinger, Secret Agent (Emily Eyefinger)

Emily Mouse Saves the Day (George and Matilda Mouse)

Emily Mouse's Beach House (George and Matilda Mouse)

Emily Mouse's First Adventure (George and Matilda Mouse)

Emily Mouse's Garden (George and Matilda Mouse)

Emily the Emerald Fairy (Rainbow Magic: Jewel Fairies)

Emily Windsnap and the Castle in the Mist (Emily Windsnap)

Emily Windsnap and the Monster from the Deep (Emily Windsnap)

Emily's Birthday (Little Bear: Maurice Sendak's Little Bear)

Emma (Emma)

Emma at the Beach (Emma)

Emma Dilemma and the New Nanny (Emma Dilemma)

Emma Dilemma and the Soccer Nanny (Emma Dilemma)

Emma Dilemma and the Two Nannies (Emma Dilemma)

Emma Eileen Grove, Mississippi, 1865 (American Diaries)

Emma's Journal (Young American Voices)

Emma's Magic Winter (Emma)

Emma's Pet (Emma)

Emma's Strange Pet (Emma)

Emma's Vacation (Emma)

Emma's Yucky Brother (Emma)

The Emperor's Plague (Star Wars Young Jedi Knights)

Empire Dreams (Adventures in America)

The Empty Envelope (A to Z Mysteries)

En Garde (Nancy Drew: Girl Detective)

The Enchanted Apples of Oz (Oz)

Enchanted Island of Oz (Oz)

Enchanted Kingdom (Choose Your Own Adventure)

Enchanted Waters (W.I.T.C.H.— Chapter Books)

Encore, Grace (Grace)

The Encounter (Animorphs)

Encounter at Cold Harbor (Bonnets and Bugles)

Encyclopedia Brown and the Case of Pablo's Nose (Encyclopedia Brown)

Encyclopedia Brown and the Case of the Dead Eagles (Encyclopedia Brown)

Encyclopedia Brown and the Case of the Disgusting Sneakers (Encyclopedia Brown)

Encyclopedia Brown and the Case of the Jumping Frogs (Encyclopedia Brown)

Encyclopedia Brown and the Case of the Midnight Visitor (Encyclopedia Brown)

Encyclopedia Brown and the Case of the Mysterious Handprints (Encyclopedia Brown)

Encyclopedia Brown and the Case of the Secret Pitch (Encyclopedia Brown)

Encyclopedia Brown and the Case of the Sleeping Dog (Encyclopedia Brown)

Encyclopedia Brown and the Case of the Slippery Salamander (Encyclopedia Brown)

Encyclopedia Brown and the Case of the Treasure Hunt (Encyclopedia Brown)

Encyclopedia Brown and the Case of the Two Spies (Encyclopedia Brown)

Encyclopedia Brown, Boy Detective (Encyclopedia Brown)

Encyclopedia Brown Carries On (Encyclopedia Brown)

Encyclopedia Brown Finds the Clues (Encyclopedia Brown)

Encyclopedia Brown Gets His Man (Encyclopedia Brown)

Encyclopedia Brown Keeps Peace (Encyclopedia Brown)

Encyclopedia Brown Lends a Hand (Encyclopedia Brown)

Encyclopedia Brown Saves the Day (Encyclopedia Brown)

Encyclopedia Brown Sets the Pace (Encyclopedia Brown)

Encyclopedia Brown Shows the Way (Encyclopedia Brown)

Encyclopedia Brown Solves Them All (Encyclopedia Brown)

Encyclopedia Brown Takes the Cake! (Encyclopedia Brown)

Encyclopedia Brown Takes the Case (Encyclopedia Brown)

Encyclopedia Brown Tracks Them Down (Encyclopedia Brown)

The End—Too Dreadful to Picture (A Series of Unfortunate Events)

End Game (The Midnight Library)

End of the Race (Wild at Heart)

The End of the Trail (Hardy Boys)

Endurance Ride (The Saddle Club)

The Enemies of Jupiter (Roman Mysteries)

The Enemy (Space Above and Beyond)

An Enemy at Green Knowe (Green Knowe)

Enemy in the Fort (American Girls: History Mysteries)

Enemy Match (Nancy Drew)

Enemy or Friend (The American Adventure)

Enemy Territory (Star Trek: I. K. S. Gorkon)

English Horse (The Saddle Club)

English Rider (The Saddle Club)

Enough is Enough! (Stinky Boys Club)

Enter . . . the Viper (Jackie Chan Adventures)

Enter the Dark Hand (Jackie Chan Adventures)

Eoin Colfer's Legend of Captain Crow's Teeth (Eoin Colfer's Legend of . . .)

Eoin Colfer's Legend of Spud Murphy (Eoin Colfer's Legend of . . .)

Eoin Colfer's Legend of the Worst Boy in the World (Eoin Colfer's Legend of . . .)

Epic Battles (Star Wars (DK Readers))

Epos the Winged Flame (Beast Quest)

Eragon (Inheritance)

Ereth's Birthday (Dimwood Forest)

Erin and the Movie Star (Camp Sunnyside)

Ernest and Celestine (Ernest and Celestine)

Ernest and Celestine at the Circus (Ernest and Celestine)

Ernest and Celestine's Patchwork Quilt (Ernest and Celestine)

Ernest and Celestine's Picnic (Ernest and Celestine)

Ernestine and Amanda (Ernestine and Amanda)

Ernestine and Amanda: Summer Camp, Ready or Not! (Ernestine and Amanda)

Expedition Sleepaway Camp (Beryl E. Bean)

Expedition to Blue Cave (Outriders)

Expedition to Pine Hollow (Outriders)

Expedition to Willow Key (Outriders)

The Experiment (Animorphs)

The Explorer of Barkham Street (Barkham Street)

Exploring the Chicago World's Fair, 1893 (American Sisters)

The Exposed (Animorphs)

Express Train to Trouble (Miss Mallard)

The Extreme (Animorphs)

Extreme (Kim Possible: Pick a Villain)

Extreme Danger (Hardy Boys, Undercover Brothers)

Extreme Stunt Dogs (Dog Watch)

Eye for an Eye (Jamestown's American Portraits)

Eye of Eternity (Pyrates)

Eye of Fortune (Dungeons and Dragons: Knights of the Silver Dragon)

The Eye of the Fortuneteller (Fear Street: Ghosts of Fear Street)

The Eye of the Hurricane (Ladd Family)

The Eye of the Warlock (Further Tales)

Eye on Crime (Hardy Boys)

Eye Spy Aliens (Scream Shop)

The Eyes of the Killer Robot (Johnny Dixon)

F

Fablehaven (Fablehaven)

The Fabulous Style Swap (Bratz: Lil' Bratz)

A Fabumouse Vacation for Geronimo (Geronimo Stilton)

The Face in the Bessledorf Funeral Parlor (Bessledorf Hotel)

Face-Off (Hannah Montana)

Face-Off (Matt Christopher Sports Stories)

The Face-Off Phony (Slapshots)

Face the Music (Hannah Montana)

Facing West (Once Upon America)

The Facts About Flirting (Mary-Kate and Ashley: Two of a Kind)

Faded Love (Hank the Cowdog)

Fading Tracks (FaithGirlz: Boarding School Mysteries)

Faerie Tale (Deadtime Stories)

The Fair-Share Pair (Hopscotch Hill School)

A Fair to Remember (Camp Confidential)

The Fairfield Triangle (Strange Matter)

Fairway Phenom (Matt Christopher Sports Stories)

Fairy Boat (Fairy Houses)

Fairy Cloud Parade (Fairy School)

Fairy Dust and the Quest for the Egg (Disney Fairies)

Fairy Flight (Fairy Houses)

Fairy Haven and the Quest for the Wand (Disney Fairies)

Fairy Houses (Fairy Houses)

The Fairy Killer (Clemency Pogue)

A Fairy Merry Christmas (Fairy School)

The Fairy-Tale Detectives (The Sisters Grimm)

The Fairy-Tale Friend (Jenna V.)

The Fairy's Mistake (The Princess Tales)

The Fairy's Return (The Princess Tales)

Faith in a Long Shot (Thoroughbred)

The Fake Cape Caper (Melvin Beederman, Superhero)

The Fake Heir (Nancy Drew Graphic Novels)

The Fake Teacher (Don't Touch That Remote!)

The Fakersville Power Station (Edgar Font's Hunt for a House to Haunt)

Falcon and the Carousel of Time (Falcon)

Falcon and the Charles Street Witch (Falcon)

Falcon of Abydos (MacGregor Family Adventure)

Falcon's Egg (Falcon)

The Falcon's Feathers (A to Z Mysteries)

The Falcon's Malteser (The Diamond Brothers)

Fall Leaf Project (Robin Hill School)

The Fall of Fergal (Unlikely Exploits)

Fall of the House of Mandible (Secrets of Dripping Fang)

The Fall of the Templar (Grey Griffins)

Fallen Star (Thoroughbred)

Falling In Like (Camp Confidential)

False Notes (Nancy Drew: Girl Detective)

The False Peace (Star Wars: Jedi Quest)

Fame (In the Cards)

The Familiar (Animorphs)

Family and Food and Orange Soda (Kenan and Kel)

A Family Apart (Orphan Train Adventures)

Family Face-Off (The Wild Thornberrys)

Family Reunion (So Weird)

Family Secrets (Christy)

Fancy Feet (Polk Street: New Kids at the Polk Street School)

Fancy Nancy (Fancy Nancy)

Fancy Nancy and the Boy from Paris (Fancy Nancy Readers)

Fancy Nancy and the Posh Puppy (Fancy Nancy)

Fancy Nancy at the Museum (Fancy Nancy Readers)

Fancy Nancy Bonjour Butterfly (Fancy Nancy)

Fancy Nancy Sees Stars (Fancy Nancy Readers)

Fancy Nancy's Collection of Fancy Words (Fancy Nancy)

Fang the Dentist (Funny Firsts)

Fangs for the Memories (Bloodhounds, Inc.)

Fangtastic! (My Sister the Vampire)

Far From the Storm (The Young Underground)

The Far Side of the Loch (Little House: The Martha Years)

Faradawn (Fog Mound)

Farewell, Dawn (Baby-Sitters Club)

Farewell, My Lunchbag! (Chet Gecko Mysteries)

Farewell to Earth (I Was a Sixth Grade Alien)

Farewell to Move (W.I.T.C.H.— Chapter Books)

The Farmer and the Witch (Old Witch)

Farmer Boy (Little House)

A Farmer Boy Birthday (Little House: My First Little House Books)

Firebird Rocket (Hardy Boys)

Firefly (Phantom Stallion)

Firefly and the Quest of the Black Squirrel (Fairy Chronicles)

The Firehouse Mystery (Boxcar Children)

Fireproof (Mystery Files of Shelby Woo)

Firesong (The Wind of Fire)

Firestorm (2099)

Firewing (Silverwing)

Fireworks and Flamingoes (Full House: Club Stephanie)

Fireworks at the FBI (Capital Mysteries)

First Brat (Totally Spies!)

The First Collier (Guardians of Ga'Hoole)

First Date (Gymnasts)

The First Day of School (Robin Hill School)

First Day, Worst Day (Hardy Boys: Frank and Joe Hardy: The Clues Brothers)

The First Four Years (Little House)

First-Grade Bunny (Robin Hill School)

First Grade, Here I Come! (Henry)

First Grade Takes a Test (First Grade)

First Heroes for Freedom (Adventures in America)

The First Journey (Animorphs: Alternamorphs)

First Meet (Gymnasts)

First Olympics (Choose Your Own Adventure)

First Test (Protector of the Small)

First Tomato (Voyage to the Bunny Planet)

Fish Face (Polk Street School: Kids of the Polk Street School)

The Fish-Faced Mask of Mystery (Hardy Boys: Frank and Joe Hardy: The Clues Brothers)

A Fish Named Yum (Mr. Pin)

A Fish Out of Water (Disney Girls)

Fishing at Long Pond (Long Pond)

Fishing for Clues (Nancy Drew: Girl Detective)

The Fishy Field Trip (CatKid)

The Fishy Field Trip (Magic School Bus Science Chapter Books)

Fishy Wishes (Pee Wee Scouts)

Five Alien Elves (Hamlet Chronicles)

The Five Cat Club (Eco Kids)

Five Flamingo Summer (Full House: Club Stephanie)

Five Girls and a Baby (Sweet Valley: Unicorn Club)

Five Little Monkeys Jumping on the Bed (Five Little Monkeys)

Five Little Monkeys Play Hide-and-Seek (Five Little Monkeys)

Five Little Monkeys Sitting in a Tree (Five Little Monkeys)

Five Little Monkeys Wash the Car (Five Little Monkeys)

Five Little Monkeys with Nothing to Do (Five Little Monkeys)

The Five Lost Aunts of Harriet Bean (Harriet Bean)

Five Smooth Stones (My America: Hope)

Fix It! (Emma)

Flamenco to Mischief (Miss Mallard)

Flames in the City (Time Spies)

The Flaming Trap (American Adventure)

Flamingo Revenge (Full House: Club Stephanie)

Flamingoes Forever? (Full House: Club Stephanie)

Flamingoes Overboard! (Full House: Club Stephanie)

Flash (The Puppy Place)

Flat Stanley (Stanley)

Flatfoot Fox and the Case of the Bashful Beaver (Flatfoot Fox)

Flatfoot Fox and the Case of the Missing Eye (Flatfoot Fox)

Flatfoot Fox and the Case of the Missing Schoolhouse (Flatfoot Fox)

Flatfoot Fox and the Case of the Missing Whooo (Flatfoot Fox)

Flatfoot Fox and the Case of the Nosy Otter (Flatfoot Fox)

The Fledgling (The Hall Family)

The Flickering Torch Mystery (Hardy Boys)

Flight of the Blue Serpent (Secrets of Droon)

Flight of the Fire Thief (The Fire Thief Trilogy)

Flight of the Fugitives (Trailblazers)

Flight of the Genie (Secrets of Droon)

Flight of the Hawk (World of Adventure)

Flight of the Phoenix (Mummy Chronicles)

The Fling (Hank the Cowdog)

The Flint Island Treehouse (Edgar Font's Hunt for a House to Haunt)

The Flock of Fury (Billy Hooten, Owlboy)

Flood (Survival!)

Florida Fog Phantoms (American Chillers)

The Flower Fairies (Fairy Realm)

Flower Power (Katie Kazoo, Switcheroo)

Flower Power (Nancy Drew Notebooks)

Flowers for the Wicked Witch (Wicked Witch)

The Flu Epidemic (The American Adventure)

Fluffy and the Firefighters (Fluffy)

Fluffy and the Snow Pig (Fluffy)

Fluffy Goes Apple Picking (Fluffy)

Fluffy Goes to School (Fluffy)

Fluffy Goes to Washington (Fluffy)

Fluffy Grows a Garden (Fluffy)

Fluffy Learns to Swim (Fluffy)

Fluffy Meets the Dinosaurs (Fluffy)

Fluffy Meets the Groundhog (Fluffy)

Fluffy Meets the Tooth Fairy (Fluffy)

Fluffy Plants a Jelly Bean (Fluffy)

Fluffy Saves Christmas (Fluffy)

Fluffy, the Secret Santa (Fluffy)

Fluffy's Funny Field Trip (Fluffy)

Fluffy's Happy Halloween (Fluffy)

Fluffy's Lucky Day (Fluffy)

Fluffy's 100th Day at School (Fluffy)

Fluffy's School Bus Adventure (Fluffy)

Fluffy's Silly Summer (Fluffy)

Fluffy's Spring Vacation (Fluffy)

Fluffy's Thanksgiving (Fluffy)

Fluffy's Trick-or-Treat (Fluffy)

Fluffy's Valentine's Day (Fluffy)

The Flunking of Joshua T. Bates (Joshua T. Bates)

Fly High, Fly Guy! (Fly Guy)

Fly the Unfriendly Skies (Strange Matter)

Flyboy of Underwhere (Underwhere)

Flyers (Jurassic Park Adventures)

Flying Blind (Cooper Kids)

Fowl Play, Desdemona (Desdemona)

Fox All Week (Fox)

Fox and His Friends (Fox)

Fox at School (Fox)

Fox Be Nimble (Fox)

Fox Hunt (The Saddle Club)

The Fox Hunt Mystery (Nancy Drew)

Fox in Love (Fox)

Fox in the Frost (Animal Ark)

Fox on Stage (Fox)

Fox on the Job (Fox)

Fox on Wheels (Fox)

Fox Outfoxed (Fox)

The Fox Steals Home (Matt Christopher Sports Stories)

Foxhunt (Riding Academy)

The Fragile Flag (The Hall Family)

Frame-Up (Mystery Files of Shelby Woo)

Framed (Nancy Drew: Girl Detective)

The Fran that Time Forgot (Franny K. Stein, Mad Scientist)

The Fran with Four Brains (Franny K. Stein, Mad Scientist)

Frances and Friends (Frances in the Fourth Grade)

Frances Dances (Frances in the Fourth Grade)

Frances Four-Eyes (Frances in the Fourth Grade)

Frances Takes a Chance (Frances in the Fourth Grade)

Francesca Vigilucci, Washington, D.C., 1913 (American Diaries)

Francine, Believe It or Not (Arthur Chapter Books)

Francine the Superstar (Arthur Chapter Books)

The Frandidate (Franny K. Stein, Mad Scientist)

Frank and Ernest (Frank and Ernest)

Frank and Ernest on the Road (Frank and Ernest)

Frank and Ernest Play Ball (Frank and Ernest)

FranKELstein (Kenan and Kel)

Frankenstein (Wishbone Classics)

Frankenstein Doesn't Plant Petunias (Bailey School: The Adventures of the Bailey School Kids)

Frankenstein Doesn't Slam Hockey Pucks (Bailey School: The

Adventures of the Bailey School Kids)

Frankenstein Doesn't Start Food Fights (Bailey School: The Adventures of the Bailey School Kids)

Frankenstein Moved In on the Fourth Floor (Sam and Robert)

Frankenturkey (Bone Chillers)

Frankie Rocks the House (Monster Manor)

Franklin and Harriet (Franklin)

Franklin and His Friend (Franklin)

Franklin and Me (Franklin)

Franklin and Otter's Visit (Franklin)

Franklin and the Baby (Franklin)

Franklin and the Babysitter (Franklin)

Franklin and the Big Kid (Franklin)

Franklin and the Bubble Gum (Franklin)

Franklin and the Computer (Franklin)

Franklin and the Contest (Franklin)

Franklin and the Cookies (Franklin)

Franklin and the Hero (Franklin)

Franklin and the Magic Show (Franklin)

Franklin and the New Teacher (Franklin)

Franklin and the Scooter (Franklin)

Franklin and the Thunderstorm (Franklin)

Franklin and the Tin Flute (Franklin)

Franklin and the Tooth Fairy (Franklin)

Franklin Celebrates (Franklin)

Franklin Delano Roosevelt (Dear Mr. President)

Franklin Fibs (Franklin)

Franklin Forgets (Franklin)

Franklin Forgives (Franklin)

Franklin Goes to Day Camp (Franklin)

Franklin Goes to School (Franklin)

Franklin Goes to the Hospital (Franklin)

Franklin Has a Sleepover (Franklin)

Franklin Helps Out (Franklin)

Franklin in the Dark (Franklin)

Franklin Is Bossy (Franklin)

Franklin Is Lost (Franklin)

Franklin Is Messy (Franklin)

Franklin Makes a Deal (Franklin)

Franklin Plants a Tree (Franklin)

Franklin Plays Hockey (Franklin)

Franklin Plays the Game (Franklin)

Franklin Rides a Bike (Franklin)

Franklin Runs Away (Franklin)

Franklin Says I Love You (Franklin)

Franklin Says Sorry (Franklin)

Franklin Snoops (Franklin)

Franklin Stays Up (Franklin)

Franklin the Detective (Franklin)

Franklin Wants a Badge (Franklin)

Franklin Wants a Pet (Franklin)

Franklin's Baby Sister (Franklin)

Franklin's Bad Day (Franklin)

Franklin's Bicycle Helmet (Franklin)

Franklin's Birthday Party (Franklin)

Franklin's Blanket (Franklin)

Franklin's Canoe Trip (Franklin)

Franklin's Christmas Gift (Franklin)

Franklin's Class Trip (Franklin)

Franklin's Halloween (Franklin)

Franklin's Library Book (Franklin)

Franklin's Music Lessons (Franklin)

Franklin's Neighborhood (Franklin)

Franklin's New Friend (Franklin)

Franklin's Nickname (Franklin)

Franklin's Pond Phantom (Franklin)

Franklin's Pumpkin (Franklin)

Franklin's Reading Club (Franklin)

Franklin's School Play (Franklin)

Franklin's Secret Club (Franklin)

Franklin's Soapbox Derby (Franklin)

Franklin's Surprise (Franklin)

Franklin's Thanksgiving (Franklin)

Franklin's Trading Cards (Franklin)

Franklin's Valentines (Franklin)

Frantastic Voyage (Franny K. Stein, Mad Scientist)

Freak Week (Don't Touch That Remote!)

Freaked Out (Lizzie McGuire)

Freaky Friday (Annabel Andrews)

Freaky Tuesday (Camp Confidential)

From the Horse's Mouth (Sabrina the Teenage Witch)

From This Day On (Heartland)

Front Court Hex (Matt Christopher Sports Stories)

Frontier Family (Little House Chapter Books: Caroline)

Frost Bites (Edgar and Ellen)

Frozen Dinners (Strange Matter)

Frozen Stiff! (Secret World of Alex Mack)

Fubble Bubble Trouble (Mary-Kate and Ashley in Action)

Fudge-a-mania (Fudge)

Fugitive (Choose Your Own Adventure)

Fugitive (Undercover Girl)

The Fugitive Factor (On the Run)

The Fugitive from Corinth (Roman Mysteries)

Full-Court Press (Spirit of the Game)

Full Moon Fever (Goosebumps Series 2000)

Full Moon Halloween (Nightmare Room)

Full Moon Magic (Spell Casters)

Fun Gus and Polly Pus (Slimeballs)

Fun Gus Slimes the Bus (Slimeballs)

Fun/No Fun (James Stevenson's Autobiographical Stories)

Fun, Sun, and Flamingoes (Full House: Club Stephanie)

Fun with the Molesons (Molesons)

Funhouse of Dr. Freek (Fear Street: Ghosts of Fear Street)

Funkhouse Adventure (Bratz: Lil' Bratz)

Funnie Family Vacation (Doug Chronicles)

The Funnie Haunted House (Doug Chronicles)

Funny Boy Meets the Airsick Alien from Andromeda (Funny Boy)

Funny Boy Takes On the Chit-Chatting Cheeses from Chattanooga (Funny Boy)

Funny Boy Versus the Bubble-Brained Barbers from the Big Bang (Funny Boy)

Funny Business (Three Investigators)

The Funny Face Fight (Nancy Drew Notebooks)

Funny, Funny Lyle (Lyle)

Funnybones (Funnybones)

Further Adventures of Hank the Cowdog (Hank the Cowdog)

Further Chronicles of Avonlea (Avonlea)

The Future Is Unknown (TimeJumpers)

The Fuzzy Lumpkins Show (Powerpuff Girls Chapter Books)

G

Gaal the Conqueror (The Archives of Anthropos)

Gabriel's Horses (Racing to Freedom Trilogy)

Gabriel's Journey (Racing to Freedom Trilogy)

Gabriel's Triumph (Racing to Freedom Trilogy)

Galactic Crisis (Star Wars (DK Readers))

Galilee Man (CyberQuest)

The Gallant Boys of Gettysburg (Bonnets and Bugles)

Gallop to the Sea (Saddle Island)

A Game Called Chaos (Hardy Boys)

Game 4 (Barnstormers)

Game of Hearts (Hannah Montana)

The Game of Silence (Omakayas)

Game On! (Adventures of Daniel Boom AKA Loud Boy)

Game On! (Kim Possible: Pick a Villain)

Game 1 (Barnstormers)

Game Plan for Disaster (Hardy Boys)

The Game Store Mystery (Boxcar Children)

Game 3 (Barnstormers)

Game 2 (Barnstormers)

Gangsters at the Grand Atlantic (American Girls: History Mysteries)

Garbage Juice for Breakfast (Polka Dot Private Eye)

The Garbage Monster from Outer Space (Hank the Cowdog)

Garbage Snooper Surprise (Spencer's Adventures)

Garden of the Purple Dragon (Dragon Keeper Trilogy)

Gargoyles Don't Drive School Buses (Bailey School: The Adventures of the Bailey School Kids)

Garth Pig and the Ice Cream Lady (Mr. and Mrs. Pig)

Garth Pig Steals the Show (Mr. and Mrs. Pig)

The Gathering (Justice Trilogy)

Gathering of Pearls (Sookan Bak)

'Gator Aid (Fraser Brothers)

The Gator Ate Her (Graveyard School)

The Gator Girls (Gator Girls)

Gator Halloween (Gator Girls)

Gem of a Mom (The Wild Thornberrys)

Genghis Khan (Genghis Khan)

Genghis Khan: A Dog Star Is Born (Genghis Khan)

Genies Don't Ride Bicycles (Bailey School: The Adventures of the Bailey School Kids)

Gen's Story (Usagi Yojimbo)

Gentle's Holler (Maggie Valley)

George and Martha (George and Martha)

George and Martha (George and Martha)

George and Martha: The Best of Friends (George and Martha)

George and Martha: Two Great Friends (George and Martha)

George and Martha Back in Town (George and Martha)

George and Martha Encore (George and Martha)

George and Martha One Fine Day (George and Martha)

George and Martha Rise and Shine (George and Martha)

George and Martha Round and Round (George and Martha)

George and Martha, Tons of Fun (George and Martha)

George and Matilda Mouse and the Doll's House (George and Matilda Mouse)

George and Matilda Mouse and the Floating School (George and Matilda Mouse)

George and Matilda Mouse and the Moon Rocket (George and Matilda Mouse)

George Mouse Learns to Fly (George and Matilda Mouse)

George Mouse's Covered Wagon (George and Matilda Mouse)

George Mouse's First Summer (George and Matilda Mouse)

George Mouse's Riverboat Band (George and Matilda Mouse)

The Ghost of Spirit Lake (Black Cat Club)

The Ghost of the Chattering Bones (Boxcar Children)

Ghost of the Jedi (Star Wars Galaxy of Fear)

The Ghost of the Lantern Lady (Nancy Drew)

Ghost of the Moaning Mansion (D.J. Dillon Adventures)

The Ghost of the Stanley Cup (Screech Owls)

Ghost of Thistle Ridge (Short Stirrup Club)

The Ghost Pony (Pony Pals)

Ghost Rider (The Saddle Club)

Ghost Ship (Sunken Kingdom)

The Ghost Ship Mystery (Boxcar Children)

Ghost Soldiers (Invisible Detectives)

The Ghost Squad and the Ghoul of Grunberg (Ghost Squad)

The Ghost Squad and the Halloween Conspiracy (Ghost Squad)

The Ghost Squad and the Menace of the Malevs (Ghost Squad)

The Ghost Squad and the Prowling Hermits (Ghost Squad)

The Ghost Squad Breaks Through (Ghost Squad)

The Ghost Squad Flies Concorde (Ghost Squad)

Ghost Story (Ghostwriter)

Ghost Town at Sundown (Magic Tree House)

The Ghost Town Mystery (Boxcar Children)

Ghost Train (Cascade Mountain Railroad Mysteries)

Ghost Train (Choose Your Own Adventure)

Ghost Train (Funnybones)

Ghost Trap (Wild Willie Mysteries)

The Ghost Who Ate Chocolate (Black Cat Club)

Ghost Wolf (Avalon 2: Quest for Magic)

The Ghost Wore Gray (Ghost Stories)

Ghostfire (Outcast)

Ghosthunters! (Baker's Dozen)

Ghosthunters and the Gruesome Invincible Lightning Ghost! (Ghosthunters)

Ghosthunters and the Incredibly Revolting Ghost! (Ghosthunters)

Ghosthunters and the Muddy Monster of Doom! (Ghosthunters)

Ghosthunters and the Totally Moldy Baroness! (Ghosthunters)

Ghostly Tales (Portraits of Little Women)

Ghosts Be Gone (Ghostville Elementary)

Ghosts Don't Eat Potato Chips (Bailey School: The Adventures of the Bailey School Kids)

Ghosts Don't Ride Wild Horses (Bailey School: The Adventures of the Bailey School Kids)

Ghosts I Have Been (Blossom Culp)

The Ghosts of Cougar Island (Liza, Bill and Jed)

Ghostsitters (Araminta Spookie)

Ghostyshocks and the Three Scares (Seriously Silly Stories)

Ghoul Friends (Fear Street: Ghosts of Fear Street)

Ghouls Don't Scoop Ice Cream (Bailey School: The Adventures of the Bailey School Kids)

Ghoul's Out for Summer (Scary Godmother)

The Giant Garden of Oz (Oz)

The Giant Germ (Magic School Bus Science Chapter Books)

The Giant Horse of Oz (Oz)

Giant in the Garden (Time Spies)

Giant Otto (Otto)

A Giant Problem (Spiderwick: Beyond the Spiderwick Chronicles)

The Giant Rat of Sumatra (Hardy Boys)

Giant Steps (B.Y. Times Kid Sisters)

The Giant Yo-Yo Mystery (Boxcar Children)

Giants Don't Go Snowboarding (Bailey School: The Adventures of the Bailey School Kids)

Gideon the Cutpurse (Gideon the Cutpurse)

A Gift for Amy (Portraits of Little Women)

A Gift for Beth (Portraits of Little Women)

A Gift for Jo (Portraits of Little Women)

A Gift for Meg (Portraits of Little Women)

A Gift from the Lonely Doll (The Lonely Doll)

Gift Horse (Animal Inn)

Gift Horse (Phantom Stallion)

Gift Horse (The Saddle Club)

Gift Horse (Winnie the Horse Gentler)

Gift of Gab (The Wild Thornberrys)

The Gigantic Ants and Other Cases (Einstein Anderson)

The Gigantic Genuine Genie (Princess Power)

Gigantopus from Planet X! (The Weird Zone)

Giggle, Giggle, Quack (Duck)

The Giggler Treatment (The Mack Family)

Gilbert, the Surfer Dude (Gilbert)

Gimme an "A" (Slam Dunk)

Gingerbread Sleepover (¡Chana!)

A Girl Called Al (Al (Alexandra))

Girl Power! (Full House: Stephanie)

Girl Reporter Blows Lid Off Town! (Get Real)

Girl Reporter Bytes Back (Get Real)

Girl Reporter Digs Up Zombies! (Get Real)

Girl Reporter Gets the Skinny! (Get Real)

Girl Reporter Rocks Polls! (Get Real)

Girl Reporter Sinks School! (Get Real)

Girl Reporter Snags Crush! (Get Real)

Girl Reporter Stuck in Jam! (Get Real)

Girl Talk (Mary-Kate and Ashley: So Little Time)

The Girl, the Apprentice, and the Dogs of Iron (The Rhianna Chronicles)

The Girl, the Dragon, and the Wild Magic (The Rhianna Chronicles)

The Girl, the Queen, and the Castle (The Rhianna Chronicles)

Girl Who Chased Away Sorrow (Dear America)

The Girl Who Couldn't Remember (Nancy Drew)

The Girl Who Cried Monster (Goosebumps)

The Girl Who Cried Monster (Goosebumps Presents)

Goliath's Easter Parade (David and Goliath)

The Golly Sisters Go West (Golly Sisters)

The Golly Sisters Ride Again (Golly Sisters)

Gondola to Danger (Miss Mallard)

Gone Jellyfishin' (SpongeBob SquarePants (TokyoPop))

Gone Nutty (SpongeBob SquarePants (TokyoPop))

Good-bye, Eva? (Sweet Valley Kids)

Good-Bye Grace? (The English Roses (Chapter Books))

Good-bye, Jasmine? (Disney Girls)

Good-Bye, Mrs. Otis (Sweet Valley Kids)

Good-bye Pony (Pony Pals)

Good-bye Stacey, Good-bye (Baby-Sitters Club)

Good Charlotte (Miss Know It All)

The Good Day Mice (Miss Know It All)

A Good Day to Die (Star Trek: I. K. S. Gorkon)

Good Dog! (McGrowl)

Good Dog, Bonita (Friends and Amigos)

Good Dog, Carl (Carl)

Good Driving, Amelia Bedelia (Amelia Bedelia)

The Good Fortunes Gang (Cousins Quartet)

Good Job, Little Bear (Little Bear)

Good Luck, Ronald Morgan (Ronald Morgan)

Good Morning, Gorillas (Magic Tree House)

Good Morning, Little Brown Bear! (Little Brown Bear)

Good Neighbors (The Floods)

Good Night, D.W. (D.W.)

Good Night, Good Knight (Good Knight)

Good Night, Mummy! (Shadow Zone)

Good Night, Sleep Tight, Don't Let the Bedbugs Bite! (Gilbert)

Good Sport, Gwen (Hopscotch Hill School)

Good Switch, Bad Switch (Sabrina the Teenage Witch)

The Good That Men Do (Star Trek: Enterprise)

The Good, the Bad & the Gassy (The Grosse Adventures)

The Good, the Bad and the Goofy (Time Warp Trio)

The Good, the Bad, and the Smelly (The Adventures of Uncle Stinky)

The Good, the Bad and the Very Slimy (Rotten School)

Good Things Come in Small Packages (Abby Hayes: The Amazing Days of Abby Hayes)

Good Times with the Molesons (Molesons)

Good Work, Amelia Bedelia (Amelia Bedelia)

Goodbye House (Moonbear)

Goodbye, Midnight Wanderer (Thoroughbred: Ashleigh)

Goodbye, Sweet Prince (Christy)

Goodknyght (Tales of the Dark Forest)

Goof-Off Goalie (Gym Shorts)

Goofballs in Paradise (Super Goofballs)

The Goofy, Goony Guy (Berenstain Bears)

Gooney Bird and the Room Mother (Gooney Bird Greene)

Gooney Bird Greene (Gooney Bird Greene)

Gooney, the Fabulous (Gooney Bird Greene)

Goose on the Loose (Animal Ark)

The Goose's Gold (A to Z Mysteries)

Gordo and the Girl and You're a Good Man Lizzie McGuire (Lizzie McGuire (TokyoPop))

The Gorgon Slayer (World of Adventure)

The Gorgon's Gaze (The Companions Quartet)

Gorgonzola Zombies in the Park (Sam and Robert)

Gorilla City (Charlie Small)

The Gosh Awful Gold Rush Mystery (Carole Marsh Mysteries: Real Kids, Real Places)

Got Cake? (Rotten School)

Got Game? (Patrick's Pals)

Gotcha! (Table Two)

Gotcha! Gotcha Back! (Katie Kazoo, Switcheroo)

Gotta Have It! (Stinky Boys Club)

The Gourmet Zombie (P.C. Hawke Mysteries)

Grace's Show of Strength (Royal Ballet School Diaries)

Grace's Twist (Camp Confidential)

Gracie, the Pixie of the Puddle (Prince of the Pond Trilogy)

Graduation Day (Baby-Sitters Club Friends Forever)

Graduation Day Is Here (First-Grade Friends)

Grampa in Oz (Oz)

Grampa's Zombie BBQ (Wiley and Grampa's Creature Feature)

Grand Canyon (Adventures with the Parkers)

Grand Canyon Odyssey (Choose Your Own Adventure)

Grand Designs (Star Trek: S. C. E.)

The Grand Escape (Club of Mysteries)

Grand Slam (Scrappers)

Grandaddy and Janetta (Grandaddy)

Grandaddy's Place (Grandaddy)

Grandaddy's Stars (Grandaddy)

Grandfather's Dance (Sarah, Plain and Tall)

The Grandma Mix-Up (Grandmas)

Grandmas at Bat (Grandmas)

Grandmas at the Lake (Grandmas)

Grandmas Trick or Treat (Grandmas)

A Grandmother for the Orphelines (Orphelines)

Grandpa's Great City Tour (Grandpa)

Grandpa's Monster Movies (Deadtime Stories)

Grandpa's Too-Good Garden (Grandpa)

The Granny Game (Cul-de-Sac Kids)

Granny Reardun (Stone Book Quartet)

Grapefruit Basket Upset (Alex)

Grasscutter (Usagi Yojimbo)

Grasscutter II: Journey to Atsuta Shrine (Usagi Yojimbo)

The Grateful Fred (Melvin Beederman, Superhero)

A Grateful Harvest (Prairie River)

Grave Robbers (Choose Your Own Adventure)

Grave Secrets (Deadtime Stories)

Grave Shadows (Red Rock Mysteries)

Gravity Buster (Journal of a Cardboard Genius)

The Gray-Eyed Goddess (Tales from the Odyssey)

Great Airport Mystery (Hardy Boys)

The Great Bicycle Race Mystery (Boxcar Children)

The Great Big Especially Beautiful Easter Egg (Grandpa)

The Great Brain (The Great Brain)

The Great Brain at the Academy (The Great Brain)

The Great Brain Does It Again (The Great Brain)

The Great Brain Is Back (The Great Brain)

The Great Brain Reforms (The Great Brain)

The Great Cheese Conspiracy (Marvin the Magnificent)

The Great Christmas Kidnapping Caper (Marvin the Magnificent)

The Great Coaster Contest (Roller Coaster Tycoon)

The Great Custard Pie Panic (Dr. Merlin)

The Great Depression (The American Adventure)

The Great Detective Race (Boxcar Children)

The Great Dragon Rescue (George and His Dragon)

The Great Escape (Puppy Patrol)

The Great Escape (Upchuck and the Rotten Willy)

Great Expectations (Thoroughbred)

The Great Galaxy Goof (AstroKids)

The Great Genghis Khan Look-Alike Contest (Genghis Khan)

The Great Good Thing (Sylvie Cycle)

The Great Googlestein Museum Mystery (Marvin the Magnificent)

Great-Grandpa's in the Litter Box (The Zack Files)

Great Groundhogs! (Harry and Emily)

The Great Gymkhana Gamble (Short Stirrup Club)

The Great Ice Battle (Secrets of Droon)

The Great Kate (Sleepover Friends)

The Great McGoniggle Rides Shotgun (The Great McGoniggle)

The Great McGoniggle Switches Pitches (The Great McGoniggle)

The Great McGoniggle's Gray Ghost (The Great McGoniggle)

The Great McGoniggle's Key Play (The Great McGoniggle)

The Great Mill Explosion (The American Adventure)

The Great NASA Flu (Cyber.kdz)

The Great Pet Project (Full House: Michelle)

The Great Plan (Speed Racer)

The Great Powers Outage (The Extraordinary Adventures of Ordinary Boy)

The Great Quarterback Switch (Matt Christopher Sports Stories)

The Great Rabbit Robbery (McGurk)

The Great Railroad Race (Dear America)

The Great Rescue Operation (Marvin the Magnificent)

The Great Shamrock Disaster (Lincoln Lions Band)

The Great Shark Escape (Magic School Bus Science Chapter Books)

The Great Shark Mystery (Boxcar Children)

The Great Skate Mystery (Bobbsey Twins: The New Bobbsey Twins)

The Great Skinner Enterprise (The Great Skinner)

The Great Skinner Getaway (The Great Skinner)

The Great Skinner Homestead (The Great Skinner)

The Great Skinner Strike (The Great Skinner)

The Great Smelling Bee (Rotten School)

The Great Smoky Mountains (Adventures with the Parkers)

The Great Snake Swindle (Klooz)

The Great Summer Camp Catastrophe (Marvin the Magnificent)

The Great Toilet Paper Caper (Spencer's Adventures)

The Great Train Robbery (Adirondack Kids)

The Great TV Turn-Off (Cul-de-Sac Kids)

The Great War (The American Adventure)

Greed, Guns, and Gold (Choose Your Own Adventure)

The Greedy Gremlin (Pixie Tricks)

Greedy Groundhogs (Pee Wee Scouts)

The Greek Symbol Mystery (Nancy Drew)

The Greek Who Stole Christmas (The Diamond Brothers)

Green Grass of Wyoming (Flicka)

Green Gravy (Cul-de-Sac Kids)

The Green Magician Puzzle (Eagle-Eye Ernie)

The Green Monster (Mystery Files of Shelby Woo)

The Green Monster in Left Field (Tales from the Sandlot)

The Green Team (Eco Kids)

Green Thumbs, Everyone (Polk Street School: Kids of the Polk Street School)

The Green Toenails Gang (Olivia Sharp, Agent for Secrets)

Green with Envy (Angela Anaconda Chapter Books)

Greenish Eggs and Dinosaurs (The Zack Files)

Greenwitch (Dark Is Rising)

Gregor and the Code of Claw (The Underland Chronicles)

Gregor and the Curse of the Warmbloods (The Underland Chronicles)

Gregor and the Marks of Secret (The Underland Chronicles)

Gregor and the Prophecy of Bane (The Underland Chronicles)

Gregor the Overlander (The Underland Chronicles)

Gremlins Don't Chew Bubble Gum (Bailey School: The Adventures of the Bailey School Kids)

The Grey King (Dark Is Rising)

Grey Shadows (Usagi Yojimbo)

The Grim Grotto (A Series of Unfortunate Events)

Grim Tuesday (Keys to the Kingdom)

Grip of the Shadow Plague (Fablehaven)

Grizzly (World of Adventure)

Grk (Grk)

Grk and the Hot Dog Trail (Grk)

Grk and the Pelotti Gang (Grk)

Grk Smells a Rat (Grk)

The Grooming of Alice (Alice)

The Gross Ghost Mystery (Hardy Boys: Frank and Joe Hardy: The Clues Brothers)

Groundhog Day (Robin Hill School)

Grover (Ellen Grae)

Growing Up (B.Y. Times Kid Sisters)

The Growing-Up Feet (Jimmy and Janet)

Growler's Horn (Misfits, Inc.)

The Growling Bear Mystery (Boxcar Children)

Growling Grizzly (Danger Joe Show)

Grudge Match (Kim Possible: Pick a Villain)

The Grumpy Bunny Goes to School (Grumpy Bunny)

The Grumpy Bunny Goes West (Grumpy Bunny)

The Grumpy Bunny Joins the Team (Grumpy Bunny)

The Grumpy Bunny's Field Trip (Grumpy Bunny)

The Grumpy Bunny's Snowy Day (Grumpy Bunny)

The Grumpy Bunny's Spooky Night (Grumpy Bunny)

The Grumpy Bunny's Too Many Bunnybabies (Grumpy Bunny)

The Grumpy Easter Bunny (Grumpy Bunny)

Grumpy Pumkins (Pee Wee Scouts)

Guess Who, Baby Duck! (Baby Duck)

Guess Who's Coming, Jesse Bear (Jesse Bear)

Guess Who's Dating a Werewolf? (Shadow Zone)

The Guide Dog Mystery (Boxcar Children)

Guilty! (The Complicated Life of Claudia Cristina Cortez)

Guinea Pig Gang (Animal Ark Pets)

Guinea Pig in the Garage (Animal Ark)

Gullifur's Travels (Wishbone Adventures)

The Gum Race (Disney Girls)

The Gumdrop Ghost (Nancy Drew Notebooks)

Gunfire at Gettysburg (Choose Your Own Adventure)

The Guns of Tortuga (Pirate Hunter)

Gus and Grandpa (Gus and Grandpa)

Gus and Grandpa and Show-and-Tell (Gus and Grandpa)

Gus and Grandpa and the Christmas Cookies (Gus and Grandpa)

Gus and Grandpa and the Halloween Costume (Gus and Grandpa)

Gus and Grandpa and the Piano Lesson (Gus and Grandpa)

Gus and Grandpa and the Two-Wheeled Bike (Gus and Grandpa)

Gus and Grandpa at Basketball (Gus and Grandpa)

Gus and Grandpa at the Hospital (Gus and Grandpa)

Gus and Grandpa Go Fishing (Gus and Grandpa)

Gus and Grandpa Ride the Train (Gus and Grandpa)

Gus the Greedy Puppy (Puppy Friends)

Guy Time (Guy Strang)

Guy Wire (Guy Strang)

The Gym Day Winner (First-Grade Friends)

The Gym Teacher from the Black Lagoon (Black Lagoon)

Gymnast Commandoes (Gymnasts)

The Gymnastics Mystery (Boxcar Children)

The Gymnasts' Gift (Gymnasts)

Gypsy Gold (Phantom Stallion)

Gypsy World (Star Trek: Deep Space Nine)

The Gypsy's Warning (Mind over Matter)

H

Hail! Hail! Camp Dragononka! (Dragon Slayers' Academy)

Hair in the Air (Spencer's Adventures)

The Hair-Pulling Bear Dog (D.J. Dillon Adventures)

Hairball from Outer Space (Wiley and Grampa's Creature Feature)

The Hairy Horror Trick (Trick Books)

Haley Danelle's Top Eight (Hardy Boys, Undercover Brothers: Graphic Novels)

Half Pipe Rip-Off (X Games Xtreme Mysteries)

Halfback Attack (Matt Christopher Sports Stories)

Hall Monitor (SpongeBob SquarePants Chapter Books)

Hallie's Horrible Handwriting (Hopscotch Hill School)

Halloween Bugs Me! (Fear Street: Ghosts of Fear Street)

The Halloween Candy Mystery (Dixon Twins)

The Halloween Costume Hunt (Little Bill (Nickelodeon))

Halloween Fraidy-Cat (Ready, Freddy!)

Halloween Fun (Robin Hill School)

The Halloween Goblin (Pixie Tricks)

Halloween Havoc (Sabrina the Teenage Witch)

Halloween Helpers (Pee Wee Scouts)

The Halloween Hoax (Nancy Drew and the Clue Crew)

The Halloween Horror and Other Cases (Einstein Anderson)

Halloween Invaders! (Secret World of Alex Mack)

Halloween Invasion (Atomic Betty)

The Halloween Joker (Wishbone Mysteries)

Halloween Knight (Mama Rex and T)

Halloween Mice! (Holiday Mice)

The Halloween Monster (Adam Joshua Capers)

Halloween Parade (Kids in Ms. Coleman's Class)

Halloween Parade (Yoko and Friends)

The Halloween Party (Choose Your Own Nightmare)

The Halloween Party from the Black Lagoon (Black Lagoon)

The Halloween War (Sweet Valley Kids)

Halloween with Morris and Boris (Morris and Boris)

Halloweird (Eerie Indiana)

Hammer Down (NASCAR Pole Position Adventures)

Hammer of the Gods (MythQuest)

Hamster Chase (Peter's Neighborhood)

Hamster Hotel (Animal Ark Pets)

Hamster in a Handbasket (Animal Ark)

Hamster in the Holly (Animal Ark)

The Hamster of the Baskervilles (Chet Gecko Mysteries)

Hand of Fate (Fortune Tellers Club)

The Hand of the Necromancer (Johnny Dixon)

Harold and Chester in Hot Fudge (Bunnicula)

Harold and Chester in Rabbit-Cadabra (Bunnicula)

Harold and Chester in Scared Silly (Bunnicula)

Harold and Chester in the Fright Before Christmas (Bunnicula)

Harold and the Purple Crayon (Harold and the Purple Crayon)

Harold at the North Pole (Harold and the Purple Crayon)

Harold's ABC (Harold and the Purple Crayon)

Harold's Circus (Harold and the Purple Crayon)

Harold's Fairy Tale (Harold and the Purple Crayon)

Harold's Trip to the Sky (Harold and the Purple Crayon)

Harriet and George's Christmas Treat (Harriet)

Harriet and the Garden (Harriet)

Harriet and the Roller Coaster (Harriet)

Harriet and Walt (Harriet)

Harriet at Home (Harriet)

Harriet at Play (Harriet)

Harriet at School (Harriet)

Harriet at Work (Harriet)

Harriet Bean and the League of Cheats (Harriet Bean)

Harriet Goes to the Circus (Harriet)

Harriet Reads Signs and More Signs (Harriet)

Harriet Spies Again (Harriet M. Welsch)

Harriet, the Hamster Fairy (Rainbow Magic: Pet Fairies)

Harriet the Spy (Harriet M. Welsch)

Harriet the Spy, Double Agent (Harriet M. Welsch)

Harriet's Halloween Candy (Harriet)

Harriet's Recital (Harriet)

Harry and Arney (Kane Family)

Harry and Chicken (Harry and Chicken)

Harry and the Lady Next Door (Harry the Dirty Dog)

Harry by the Sea (Harry the Dirty Dog)

Harry Cat's Pet Puppy (Chester Cricket)

Harry Dresses Himself (Harry the Hippo)

Harry Gets an Uncle (Harry)

Harry Gets Ready for School (Harry the Hippo)

Harry Goes to Day Camp (Harry the Hippo)

Harry Goes to Fun Land (Harry the Hippo)

Harry in Trouble (Harry)

Harry Kitten and Tucker Mouse (Chester Cricket)

Harry on Vacation (Harry and Chicken)

Harry Potter and the Chamber of Secrets (Harry Potter)

Harry Potter and the Deathly Hallows (Harry Potter)

Harry Potter and the Goblet of Fire (Harry Potter)

Harry Potter and the Half-Blood Prince (Harry Potter)

Harry Potter and the Order of the Phoenix (Harry Potter)

Harry Potter and the Prisoner of Azkaban (Harry Potter)

Harry Potter and the Sorcerer's Stone (Harry Potter)

Harry Takes a Bath (Harry the Hippo)

Harry the Dirty Dog (Harry the Dirty Dog)

Harry the Explorer (Harry and Chicken)

Harry the Hippo (Harry the Hippo)

Harry's Birthday (Harry)

Harry's Dog (Harry)

Harry's Mealtime Mess (Harry the Hippo)

Harry's Mom (Harry)

Harry's Pony (Harry)

Harry's Sandbox Surprise (Harry the Hippo)

Harry's Visit (Harry)

Harvest Moon (Sabrina the Teenage Witch)

Harvey Angell (Harvey Angell Trilogy)

Harvey Angell and the Ghost Child (Harvey Angell Trilogy)

Harvey Angell Beats Time (Harvey Angell Trilogy)

Harvey's Horrible Snake Disaster (Harvey)

Harvey's Marvelous Monkey Mystery (Harvey)

Harvey's Mystifying Raccoon Mix-Up (Harvey)

Harvey's Wacky Parrot Adventure (Harvey)

Hasta la Vista, Blarney (Carmen Sandiego Mysteries)

A Hat for Minerva Louise (Minerva Louise)

Hat Trick (Soccer 'Cats)

Hatchet (Brian Robeson)

The Hatching Horror (Astrosaurs)

The Hatchling (Guardians of Ga'Hoole)

The Hateful Plateful Trick (Trick Books)

Hattie Be Quiet, Hattie Be Good (Hattie Rabbit)

Hattie Rabbit (Hattie Rabbit)

Hattie, Tom, and the Chicken Witch (Hattie Rabbit)

Hattie's Story (American Quilts)

Haunted (Hardy Boys, Undercover Brothers)

The Haunted Baby (Choose Your Own Nightmare)

The Haunted Bridge (Nancy Drew)

The Haunted Cabin Mystery (Boxcar Children)

The Haunted Car (Goosebumps Series 2000)

The Haunted Carousel (Nancy Drew)

Haunted Castle on Hallow's Eve (Magic Tree House)

The Haunted Cave (Spooksville)

The Haunted Clocktower Mystery (Boxcar Children)

The Haunted Clubhouse (Wishbone Mysteries)

The Haunted Dollhouse (Nancy Drew Graphic Novels)

The Haunted Fort (Hardy Boys)

The Haunted Gargoyle (Clue)

Haunted Hike (Elliot's Park)

Haunted Hill (Sam and Stephanie)

The Haunted Hotel (A to Z Mysteries)

Haunted House (Liza, Bill and Jed)

Haunted House Hijinks! (Secret World of Alex Mack)

A Haunted House in Starvation Lake (Starvation Lake)

The Haunted House on Honeycutt Street (The Nic-Nacs and the Nic-Nac News)

The Haunted Lagoon (Dana Girls)

The Haunted Mansion Mystery (Barbie Mystery Files)

The Haunted Mask (Goosebumps)

Help! I'm Trapped in My Teacher's Body (Help! I'm Trapped)

Help! I'm Trapped in Obedience School (Help! I'm Trapped)

Help! I'm Trapped in Obedience School Again (Help! I'm Trapped)

Help! I'm Trapped in Santa's Body (Help! I'm Trapped)

Help! I'm Trapped in the First Day of School (Help! I'm Trapped)

Help! I'm Trapped in the First Day of Summer Camp (Help! I'm Trapped)

Help! I'm Trapped in the President's Body (Help! I'm Trapped)

Help! It's Parents Day at DSA (Dragon Slayers' Academy)

Help! Somebody Get Me Out of Fourth Grade (Hank Zipzer)

Help! There's a Ghost in My Room! (Full House: Dear Michelle)

Henrietta, Circus Star (Henrietta)

Henrietta Goes to the Fair (Henrietta)

Henrietta Lays Some Eggs (Henrietta)

Henrietta, the Early Bird (Henrietta)

Henrietta's Fourth of July (Henrietta)

Henrietta's Halloween (Henrietta)

Henry and Beezus (Henry Huggins)

Henry and Mudge (Henry and Mudge)

Henry and Mudge and a Very Merry Christmas (Henry and Mudge)

Henry and Mudge and Annie's Good Move (Henry and Mudge)

Henry and Mudge and Annie's Perfect Pet (Henry and Mudge)

Henry and Mudge and Mrs. Hopper's House (Henry and Mudge)

Henry and Mudge and the Bedtime Thumps (Henry and Mudge)

Henry and Mudge and the Best Day of All (Henry and Mudge)

Henry and Mudge and the Big Sleepover (Henry and Mudge)

Henry and Mudge and the Careful Cousin (Henry and Mudge)

Henry and Mudge and the Forever Sea (Henry and Mudge)

Henry and Mudge and the Funny Lunch (Henry and Mudge)

Henry and Mudge and the Great Grandpas (Henry and Mudge)

Henry and Mudge and the Happy Cat (Henry and Mudge)

Henry and Mudge and the Long Weekend (Henry and Mudge)

Henry and Mudge and the Sneaky Crackers (Henry and Mudge)

Henry and Mudge and the Snowman Plan (Henry and Mudge)

Henry and Mudge and the Starry Night (Henry and Mudge)

Henry and Mudge and the Tall Tree House (Henry and Mudge)

Henry and Mudge and the Tumbling Trip (Henry and Mudge)

Henry and Mudge and the Wild Goose Chase (Henry and Mudge)

Henry and Mudge and the Wild Wind (Henry and Mudge)

Henry and Mudge Get the Cold Shivers (Henry and Mudge)

Henry and Mudge in Puddle Trouble (Henry and Mudge)

Henry and Mudge in the Family Trees (Henry and Mudge)

Henry and Mudge in the Green Time (Henry and Mudge)

Henry and Mudge in the Sparkle Days (Henry and Mudge)

Henry and Mudge Take the Big Test (Henry and Mudge)

Henry and Mudge Under the Yellow Moon (Henry and Mudge)

Henry and Ribsy (Henry Huggins)

Henry and the Clubhouse (Henry Huggins)

Henry and the Paper Route (Henry Huggins)

Henry and the Valentine Surprise (Henry)

Henry Explores the Jungle (Henry the Explorer)

Henry Explores the Mountains (Henry the Explorer)

Henry Huggins (Henry Huggins)

Henry Reed, Inc. (Henry Reed)

Henry Reed's Baby-Sitting Service (Henry Reed)

Henry Reed's Big Show (Henry Reed)

Henry Reed's Journey (Henry Reed)

Henry Reed's Think Tank (Henry Reed)

Henry the Castaway (Henry the Explorer)

Henry the Christmas Cat (Henry the Cat)

Henry the Explorer (Henry the Explorer)

Henry the Sailor Cat (Henry the Cat)

Henry's Amazing Imagination (Henry)

Henry's 100 Days of Kindergarten (Henry)

Henry's Show and Tell (Henry)

Herbie Jones (Herbie Jones)

Herbie Jones and Hamburger Head (Herbie Jones)

Herbie Jones and the Birthday Showdown (Herbie Jones)

Herbie Jones and the Class Gift (Herbie Jones)

Herbie Jones and the Dark Attic (Herbie Jones)

Herbie Jones and the Monster Ball (Herbie Jones)

Herbie Jones and the Second Grade Slippers (Herbie Jones)

Herbie Jones Moves On (Herbie Jones)

Herbie Jones Sails into Second Grade (Herbie Jones)

Hercules Doesn't Pull Teeth (Bailey School: The Adventures of the Bailey School Kids)

Here Come McBroom (McBroom)

Here Come the Bridesmaids (Baby-Sitters Club Super Specials)

Here Comes Santa Claws (Graveyard School)

Here Comes the Brand-New Me (Full House: Stephanie)

Here We All Are (26 Fairmount Avenue)

Here We Go Again (B.Y. Times)

Here's Hermione (Rosy Cole)

Here's Spot (Spot)

Hermit Dan (Liza, Bill and Jed)

The Hermit of Mad River (D.J. Dillon Adventures)

Hero Over Here (Once Upon America)

The Hero Revealed (The Extraordinary Adventures of Ordinary Boy)

Heroes and Monsters (Fairly OddParents (TokyoPop))

He's All That (Sister Sister)

Homecoming (Tillerman Cycle)

Homegirl on the Range (Sister Sister)

Homeless (Wild at Heart)

Homer Sweet Homer (Wishbone Adventures)

The Homerun King (Scraps of Time)

Homework Hassles (Ready, Freddy!)

Homework Trouble (Mama Rex and T)

Honestly, Katie John! (Katie John)

Honestly, Mallory! (Mallory)

Honey Bunny Funnybunny (P.J. Funnybunny)

Honey Helps (Happy and Honey)

The Honeybee Mystery (Boxcar Children)

The Honeycutt Street Celebrities (The Nic-Nacs and the Nic-Nac News)

Honk! (Kipper: Little Kippers)

Honor Bound (Star Trek: I. K. S. Gorkon)

Honus and Me (Baseball Card Adventures)

The Hooded Hawk Mystery (Hardy Boys)

Hoof Beat (The Saddle Club)

Hoofbeats of Danger (American Girls: History Mysteries)

Hoofprints in the Snow (Thoroughbred)

Hook 'Em Snotty! (World of Adventure)

Hoop Crazy (Chip Hilton Sports Series)

Hooray for Fall! (Oswald (Ready-to-Read))

Hooray for Fly Guy! (Fly Guy)

Hooray for Mother's Day (Little Bill (Nickelodeon))

Hooray for Reading (Raggedy Ann and Andy)

Hooray for the Dandelion Warriors (Little Bill)

Hooray for the Golly Sisters! (Golly Sisters)

Hooray for the Holidays (The English Roses (Chapter Books))

Hope in My Heart (My America: Sofia)

Hope Springs Eternal (Prairie River)

Hoping for Rain (I Am American)

Hopper (Hopper)

Hopper Hunts for Spring (Hopper)

Hopper's Easter Surprise (Hopper)

Hopper's Treetop Adventure (Hopper)

Hoppin' Halloween (¡Chana!)

Hoppy Easter (Holiday Friends)

Horace Splattly (Horace Splattly: The Cupcaked Crusader)

The Hork-Bajir Chronicles (Animorphs: Animorph Chronicles)

Horrible Harry and the Ant Invasion (Horrible Harry)

Horrible Harry and the Christmas Surprise (Horrible Harry)

Horrible Harry and the Dead Letters (Horrible Harry)

Horrible Harry and the Dragon War (Horrible Harry)

Horrible Harry and the Drop of Doom (Horrible Harry)

Horrible Harry and the Dungeon (Horrible Harry)

Horrible Harry and the Goog (Horrible Harry)

Horrible Harry and the Green Slime (Horrible Harry)

Horrible Harry and the Holidaze (Horrible Harry)

Horrible Harry and the Kickball Wedding (Horrible Harry)

Horrible Harry and the Locked Closet (Horrible Harry)

Horrible Harry and the Mud Gremlins (Horrible Harry)

Horrible Harry and the Purple People (Horrible Harry)

Horrible Harry and the Triple Revenge (Horrible Harry)

Horrible Harry at Halloween (Horrible Harry)

Horrible Harry Bugs the Three Bears (Horrible Harry)

Horrible Harry Cracks the Code (Horrible Harry)

Horrible Harry Goes to Sea (Horrible Harry)

Horrible Harry Goes to the Moon (Horrible Harry)

Horrible Harry in Room 2B (Horrible Harry)

Horrible Harry Moves Up to Third Grade (Horrible Harry)

Horrible Harry Takes the Cake (Horrible Harry)

Horrible Harry's Secret (Horrible Harry)

The Horrible Play Date (Mama Rex and T)

Horrid Henry (Horrid Henry)

Horrid Henry Strikes It Rich (Horrid Henry)

Horrid Henry's Head Lice (Horrid Henry)

The Horror (House on Cherry Street)

The Horror at Camp Jellyjam (Goosebumps)

Horror Gets Slimed (Monster Manor)

Horror Hotel (Fear Street: Ghosts of Fear Street)

Horror Hotel: The Vampire Checks In (Fear Street: Ghosts of Fear Street)

Horror House (Choose Your Own Adventure)

Horror of High Ridge (Choose Your Own Adventure)

Horror on River Road (Screech Owls)

Horrors of the Black Ring (Goosebumps Series 2000)

The Horse and His Boy (Chronicles of Narnia)

Horse Blues (The Saddle Club)

A Horse Called Raven (Black Stallion: Young Black Stallion)

A Horse Called Wonder (Thoroughbred)

Horse Capades (The Saddle Club)

Horse Care (The Saddle Club)

Horse Crazy (The Saddle Club)

Horse Feathers (The Saddle Club)

Horse Fever (The Saddle Club)

Horse Fever (The Saddle Club)

A Horse for Christmas (Thoroughbred: Ashleigh)

A Horse for Mary Beth (Riding Academy)

A Horse for the Summer (Sandy Lane Stables)

Horse Games (The Saddle Club)

Horse Guest (The Saddle Club)

Horse in Danger (Sandy Lane Stables)

Horse in the House (Animal Ark)

Horse Love (The Saddle Club)

Horse Magic (The Saddle Club)

A Horse Named Dragon (Boxcar Children)

The Horse of Her Dreams (Thoroughbred)

Horse Play (The Saddle Club)

Horse Power (The Saddle Club)

How to (Almost) Ruin Your School Play (Willimena Rules!)

How to be a Girly Girl In Just Ten Days (Candy Apple)

How to Be a Pirate (Heroic Misadventures of Hiccup Horrendous Haddock III)

How to Be a Vampire (Fear Street: Ghosts of Fear Street)

How to Be Cool (Full House: Michelle)

How to Be Good (ish) (Indie Kidd)

How to Cheat a Dragon's Curse (Heroic Misadventures of Hiccup Horrendous Haddock III)

How to Face Up to the Class Bully (Willimena Rules!)

How to Fish for Trouble (Willimena Rules!)

How to Flunk Your First Date (Mary-Kate and Ashley: Two of a Kind)

How to Hide a Horse (Full House: Sisters)

How to Kill a Monster (Goosebumps)

How to Lose Your Class Pet (Willimena Rules!)

How to Lose Your Cookie Money (Willimena Rules!)

How to Meet a Superstar (Full House: Michelle)

How to Speak Dolphin in Three Easy Lessons (The Zack Files)

How to Speak Dragonese (Heroic Misadventures of Hiccup Horrendous Haddock III)

How to Train a Boy (Mary-Kate and Ashley: So Little Time)

How to Train Your Dragon (Heroic Misadventures of Hiccup Horrendous Haddock III)

How to Twist a Dragon's Tale (Heroic Misadventures of Hiccup Horrendous Haddock III)

How Will Santa Find Me? (Full House: Dear Michelle)

Howie Finds a Hug (Howie)

Howie Goes Shopping (Howie)

Howie Monroe and the Doghouse of Doom (Bunnicula: Tales from the House of Bunnicula)

Howie Wants to Play (Howie)

Howie's Tea Party (Howie)

The Howler (Nightmare Room)

Howliday Inn (Bunnicula)

Howling at the Hauntlys' (Bailey City Monsters)

The Howling Dog and Other Cases (Einstein Anderson)

The Howling Ghost (Spooksville)

Huckleberry Dog (Wishbone Adventures)

Huggly and the Toy Monster (Monster Under the Bed)

Huggly Gets Dressed (Monster Under the Bed)

Huggly Goes to School (Monster Under the Bed)

Huggly Takes a Bath (Monster Under the Bed)

Huggly's Christmas (Monster Under the Bed)

Huggly's Pizza (Monster Under the Bed)

Hugo Pepper (Far-Flung Adventures)

The Human Shark (American Gold Swimmers)

Humbug (X Files)

Humbug Potion (Humbug)

Humbug Rabbit (Humbug)

Humbug Witch (Humbug)

The Hunchdog of Notre Dame (Wishbone Adventures)

The Hundred-Year Mystery (Dana Girls)

The Hunger (Star Wars Galaxy of Fear)

Hungry Hurler (Chip Hilton Sports Series)

The Hungry Tiger in Oz (Oz)

The Hunk Machine (Salt and Pepper Chronicles)

The Hunt for the Four Brothers (Hardy Boys)

The Hunt Is On (Goners)

Hunted (Star Wars: Boba Fett)

The Hunted (Mysteries in Our National Parks)

Hunted in the Alaskan Wilderness (Ladd Family)

Hunting for Hidden Gold (Hardy Boys)

Hunting the Hunter (On the Run)

Hurray for Ali Baba Bernstein (Ali Baba Bernstein)

Hurray for Hattie Rabbit (Hattie Rabbit)

Hurricane! (Choose Your Own Adventure)

Hurricane (Survival!)

Hurricane Gold (Young Bond)

Hurricane Harry (Kane Family)

Hurricane Joe (Hardy Boys, Undercover Brothers)

The Hurricane Mystery (Boxcar Children)

Hurricane Rescue (Neptune Adventures)

Hurry Up, Franklin (Franklin)

Husky in a Hut (Animal Ark)

Husky with a Heart (Animal Ark)

Hyde and Shriek (Hardy Boys, Undercover Brothers: Graphic Novels)

The Hypersonic Secret (Hardy Boys)

Hyperspace (Choose Your Own Adventure)

I

I Am Invited to a Party! (Elephant and Piggie)

I Am Not Joey Pigza (Joey Pigza)

I Am Not Sleepy and I Will Not Go to Bed (Charlie and Lola)

I Am Really, Really Concentrating (Charlie and Lola)

I Am Too Absolutely Small for School (Charlie and Lola)

I Am Your Evil Twin (Goosebumps Series 2000)

I Amber Brown (Amber Brown)

I Can Do Anything That's Everything All on My Own (Charlie and Lola)

I Can See You (The Midnight Library)

The I-Can't-Cope Club (B.Y. Times Kid Sisters)

I Completely Know About Guinea Pigs (Charlie and Lola)

I. D. (Watchers)

I Do, I Don't and Come Fly with Me (Lizzie McGuire (TokyoPop))

I Don't Like to Read! (Henry)

I Dream of Dexter (Dexter's Laboratory Chapter Books)

I, Freddy (The Golden Hamster Saga)

I Got a "D" in Salami (Hank Zipzer)

I Had a Lot of Wishes (James Stevenson's Autobiographical Stories)

I Hate Rules (Katie Kazoo, Switcheroo)

I Hate the 80s (Totally Spies!)

I Heard a Rumor (How I Survived Middle School)

In Search of Scum (Cyber.kdz)

In Search of the Black Rose (Nancy Drew)

In the Circle of Time (Time Trilogy)

In the Dinosaur's Paw (Polk Street School: Kids of the Polk Street School)

In the Doghouse (Lizzie McGuire Mysteries)

In the Face of Danger (Orphan Train Adventures)

In the Groove (NASCAR Pole Position Adventures)

In the Hands of the Enemy (Adventures in America)

In the Ice Caves of Krog (Secrets of Droon)

In the Keep of Time (Time Trilogy)

In the Land of the Big Red Apple (Little House: The Rose Years)

In the Nick of Time (McGee and Me!)

In the Rain with Baby Duck (Baby Duck)

In the Shadow of Goll (Secrets of Droon)

In the Shadow of the Tower (Dana Girls)

In the Spotlight (High School Musical Stories from East High)

In the Spotlight (Silver Blades)

In the Time of Dinosaurs (Animorphs: Megamorphs)

In the Zone (Super Hoops)

In Too Deep (The Wild Thornberrys)

In Your Face! (Patrick's Pals)

In Your Face! (Super Hoops)

Inca Gold (Choose Your Own Adventure)

Including Alice (Alice)

Incognito Mosquito Flies Again (Incognito Mosquito)

Incognito Mosquito Makes History (Incognito Mosquito)

Incognito Mosquito, Private Insective (Incognito Mosquito)

Incognito Mosquito Takes to the Air (Incognito Mosquito)

Incredible India (SWAT (Secret World Adventure Team))

The Incredible Shrinking Dexter (Dexter's Laboratory Chapter Books)

The Incredible Shrinking Kid! (The Weird Zone)

The Incredible Shrinking Stanley (Eerie Indiana)

India the Moonstone Fairy (Rainbow Magic: Jewel Fairies)

The Indian in the Cupboard (The Indian in the Cupboard)

Inferno (Bionicle Legends)

The Infinity Clue (Hardy Boys)

The Ink Drinker (The Ink Drinker)

Inkdeath (Inkheart)

Inkheart (Inkheart)

Inkspell (Inkheart)

Inky the Indigo Fairy (Rainbow Magic: Rainbow Fairies)

Inline Skater (Matt Christopher Sports Stories)

Inner Beauty and Best Dressed for Less (Lizzie McGuire (TokyoPop))

Insect Invaders (Magic School Bus Science Chapter Books)

Inside Outside Upside Down (Berenstain Bears)

The Inside Story (Baker's Dozen)

Inside UFO 54-40 (Choose Your Own Adventure)

Instant Boyfriend (Mary-Kate and Ashley: So Little Time)

Instant Menace (Red Rock Mysteries)

The Internet Escapade (Casebusters)

Into the Abyss (Tom Swift Young Inventor)

Into the Blue (Dolphin Diaries)

Into the Danger Zone (Extreme Team)

Into the Dragon's Den (Abby's South Seas Adventures)

Into the Flames (The Young Underground)

Into the Jaws of Doom (Goosebumps: Give Yourself Goosebumps)

Into the Labyrinth (Sylvie Cycle)

Into the Land of the Lost (Secrets of Droon)

Into the Land of the Unicorns (Unicorn Chronicles)

Into the Mist (Land of Elyon)

Into the Mix (Dish)

Into the Twister of Terror (Goosebumps: Give Yourself Goosebumps)

Into the Wild (Warriors)

Into the Zonk Zone! (Time Surfers)

Intrigue at the Grand Opera (Nancy Drew)

Introducing Kyla May Miss. Behaves (Kyla May Miss. Behaves)

Intruder (Nancy Drew: Girl Detective)

Invaders from the Big Screen (Goosebumps: Give Yourself Goosebumps)

Invaders from Within (Choose Your Own Adventure)

Invaders of Planet Earth (Choose Your Own Adventure)

The Invasion (Animorphs)

Invasion (Journey of Allen Strange)

The Invasion from the Planet of the Cows (Maximum Boy)

Invasion of the Appleheads (Deadtime Stories)

The Invasion of the Black Gears (Digimon Digital Monsters)

Invasion of the Body Squeezers, Part 1 (Goosebumps Series 2000)

Invasion of the Body Squeezers, Part 2 (Goosebumps Series 2000)

Invasion of the Evil Teachers from Planet Buttface (Sidekicks)

Invasion of the Fast Food (Lunchroom)

Invasion of the Mind Sweepers from Asteroid 6! (Bunnicula: Tales from the House of Bunnicula)

Invasion of the No-Ones (Spooksville)

Invasion of the Nose Pickers (Nose Pickers from Outer Space)

Invasion of the Pig Sisters (Fitch and Chip)

The Invasion of the Shag Carpet Creature (Horace Splattly: The Cupcaked Crusader)

Invasion of the UFOs (Bloodhounds, Inc.)

The Invisible Day (Invisible)

The Invisible Day (The Invisible Trilogy)

The Invisible Enemy (Invisible)

The Invisible Enemy (The Invisible Trilogy)

The Invisible Fran (Franny K. Stein, Mad Scientist)

The Invisible Friend (Viking Quest)

The Invisible Harry (Invisible)

The Invisible Harry (The Invisible Trilogy)

I've Already Forgotten Your Name, Philip Hall (Philip Hall)

I've Got a Secret (Candy Apple)

I've Got a Secret (Full House: Michelle)

I've Got Bunny Business (Full House: Dear Michelle)

I've Won, No I've Won, No I've Won (Charlie and Lola)

Ivy and Bean (Ivy and Bean)

Ivy and Bean and the Ghost That Had to Go (Ivy and Bean)

Ivy and Bean Break the Fossil Record (Ivy and Bean)

Ivy and Bean Take Care of the Babysitter (Ivy and Bean)

Izak of Lapland (Maya's World)

J

Jack Adrift (Jack Henry)

Jack and the Beanstalk (Wishbone: The Early Years)

Jack and the Beanstalker (Graveyard School)

Jack and the Wanderers (Samurai Jack Chapter Books)

Jack on the Tracks (Jack Henry)

Jack Pumpkinhead of Oz (Oz)

Jackie and Jade Save the Day (Jackie Chan Adventures)

Jackie and Me (Baseball Card Adventures)

Jackrabbit Goalie (Matt Christopher Sports Stories)

Jack's Black Book (Jack Henry)

Jack's Knife (Sirius Mysteries)

Jack's New Power (Jack Henry)

Jackson Jones and Mission Greentop (Jackson Jones)

Jackson Jones and the Curse of the Outlaw Rose (Jackson Jones)

Jackson Jones and the Puddle of Thorns (Jackson Jones)

The Jade Monkey (Jackie Chan Adventures)

Jade's Secret Power (Jackie Chan Adventures)

Jafta (Jafta)

Jafta: The Homecoming (Jafta)

Jafta: The Journey (Jafta)

Jafta: The Town (Jafta)

Jafta and the Wedding (Jafta)

Jafta's Father (Jafta)

Jafta's Mother (Jafta)

The Jaguar's Jewel (A to Z Mysteries)

Jahanara (Royal Diaries)

Jake Drake, Bully Buster (Jake Drake)

Jake Drake, Class Clown (Jake Drake)

Jake Drake, Know-It-All (Jake Drake)

Jake Drake, Teacher's Pet (Jake Drake)

Jamaica and Brianna (Jamaica)

Jamaica and the Substitute Teacher (Jamaica)

Jamaica Tag-Along (Jamaica)

Jamaica's Blue Marker (Jamaica)

Jamaica's Find (Jamaica)

Jamela's Dress (Jamela)

Jane on Her Own (Catwings)

Janet's Thingamajigs (Jimmy and Janet)

Janey G. Blue, Pearl Harbor, 1941 (American Diaries)

A Jar of Dreams (Rinko)

Jasmine and the Jumping Pony (Pony Tails)

Jasmine Helps a Foal (Pony Tails)

Jasmine Trots Ahead (Pony Tails)

Jasmine's Christmas Ride (Pony Tails)

Jasmine's First Horse Show (Pony Tails)

Jasmine's Lucky Star (Ballerina Dreams)

Jason and the Gorgon's Blood (Young Heroes)

Jasper Dash and the Flame-Pits of Delaware (M. T. Anderson's Thrilling Tales)

The Jedera Adventure (Vesper Holly)

Jedi Bounty (Star Wars Young Jedi Knights)

Jedi Under Siege (Star Wars Young Jedi Knights)

Jeepers Creepers (House of Horrors)

Jeffrey's Ghost and the Fifth-Grade Dragon (Jeffrey's Ghost)

Jeffrey's Ghost and the Leftover Baseball Team (Jeffrey's Ghost)

Jeffrey's Ghost and the Ziffel Fair Mystery (Jeffrey's Ghost)

Jekyll and Heidi (Goosebumps Series 2000)

Jen Starts Over (B.Y. Times)

Jenna's Dilemma (Camp Confidential)

Jennifer Murdley's Toad (Magic Shop)

Jenny and the Cat Club (Jenny and the Cat Club)

Jenny Archer, Author (Jenny Archer)

Jenny Archer to the Rescue (Jenny Archer)

Jenny Goes to Sea (Jenny and the Cat Club)

Jenny's Adopted Brothers (Jenny and the Cat Club)

Jenny's Bedside Book (Jenny and the Cat Club)

Jenny's Birthday Book (Jenny and the Cat Club)

Jenny's First Party (Jenny and the Cat Club)

Jenny's Moonlight Adventure (Jenny and the Cat Club)

Jeremy Thatcher, Dragon Hatcher (Magic Shop)

Jess (American Girls: Girl of the Year)

Jess and the Fireplug Caper (Twelve Candles Club)

Jesse Bear, What Will You Wear? (Jesse Bear)

Jessi and the Awful Secret (Baby-Sitters Club)

Jessi and the Bad Baby-Sitter (Baby-Sitters Club)

Jessi and the Dance School Phantom (Baby-Sitters Club)

Jessi and the Jewel Thieves (Baby-Sitters Club Mysteries)

Jessi and the Superbrat (Baby-Sitters Club)

Jessi and the Troublemaker (Baby-Sitters Club)

Jessi Ramsey, Pet-Sitter (Baby-Sitters Club)

The Jessica and Elizabeth Show (Sweet Valley Kids)

Jessica and the Jumbo Fish (Sweet Valley Kids)

Jessica and the Spelling-Bee Surprise (Sweet Valley Kids)

Jessica Gets Spooked (Sweet Valley Kids)

Jessica Plays Cupid (Sweet Valley Kids)

Jessica Plus Jessica Equals Trouble (Sweet Valley Kids)

Jessica the Baby-Sitter (Sweet Valley Kids)

Jessica the TV Star (Sweet Valley Kids)

Journey to the End of the Earth (Trailblazers)

Journey to the Impossible Islands (Samurai Jack Chapter Books)

A Journey to the New World (Dear America)

Journey to the Planet of the Blawps (Lost in Space, The New Journeys)

Journey to the Volcano Palace (Secrets of Droon)

Journey Under the Sea (Choose Your Own Adventure)

Joust of Honor (A Knight's Story)

Joyride (Journey of Allen Strange)

Judge Benjamin (Judge Benjamin)

Judge Benjamin: The Superdog Gift (Judge Benjamin)

Judge Benjamin: The Superdog Rescue (Judge Benjamin)

Judge Benjamin: The Superdog Secret (Judge Benjamin)

Judge Benjamin: The Superdog Surprise (Judge Benjamin)

The Judgment (Feather and Bone: The Crow Chronicles)

Judy Moody (Judy Moody)

Judy Moody: Around the World in 8 ½ Days (Judy Moody)

Judy Moody and Stink (Judy Moody)

Judy Moody Declares Independence (Judy Moody)

Judy Moody Gets Famous! (Judy Moody)

Judy Moody Goes to College (Judy Moody)

Judy Moody, M.D. (Judy Moody)

Judy Moody Predicts the Future (Judy Moody)

Judy Moody Saves the World! (Judy Moody)

Julep O'Toole (Julep O'Toole)

Julep O'Toole: Miss Independent (Julep O'Toole)

Julep O'Toole: What I Really Want To Do Is Direct (Julep O'Toole)

Julia and the Hand of God (Julia Redfern)

Julian, Dream Doctor (Julian and Huey)

Julian, Secret Agent (Julian and Huey)

Julian's Glorious Summer (Julian and Huey)

Julian's Jinx (Spell Casters)

Julia's Magic (Julia Redfern)

Julie (Julie of the Wolves)

Julie and the Eagles (American Girls: Julie)

Julie of the Wolves (Julie of the Wolves)

Julie Tells Her Story (American Girls: Julie)

Julie the Karate Kid (Sweet Valley Kids)

Julie's Journey (American Girls: Julie)

Julie's Wolf Pack (Julie of the Wolves)

Juliet Dove, Queen of Love (Magic Shop)

Julius, the Baby of the World (Lilly)

July (James Stevenson's Autobiographical Stories)

Jump Ship to Freedom (Arabus Family Saga)

Jump Shot Detectives (Hardy Boys: Frank and Joe Hardy: The Clues Brothers)

Jumping Lessons (Horseshoes)

Junebug (Junebug)

Junebug and the Reverend (Junebug)

Junebug in Trouble (Junebug)

The Jungle Pyramid (Hardy Boys)

Junie B., Boo . . . and I Mean It! (Junie B. Jones)

Junie B., First Grader (Junie B. Jones)

Junie B., First Grader: Boss of Lunch (Junie B. Jones)

Junie B., First Grader: Cheater Pants (Junie B. Jones)

Junie B., First Grader: Dumb Bunny (Junie B. Jones)

Junie B., First Grader: Jingle Bells, Batman Smells! (P.S. So Does May) (Junie B. Jones)

Junie B., First Grader: One-Man Band (Junie B. Jones)

Junie B., First Grader: Shipwrecked (Junie B. Jones)

Junie B., First Grader: Toothless Wonder (Junie B. Jones)

Junie B., First Grader (at last!) (Junie B. Jones)

Junie B. Jones and a Little Monkey Business (Junie B. Jones)

Junie B. Jones and Her Big Fat Mouth (Junie B. Jones)

Junie B. Jones and Some Sneaky Peeky Spying (Junie B. Jones)

Junie B. Jones and That Meanie Jim's Birthday (Junie B. Jones)

Junie B. Jones and the Mushy Gushy Valentine (Junie B. Jones)

Junie B. Jones and the Stupid Smelly Bus (Junie B. Jones)

Junie B. Jones and the Yucky Blucky Fruitcake (Junie B. Jones)

Junie B. Jones Has a Monster Under Her Bus (Junie B. Jones)

Junie B. Jones Has a Peep in Her Pocket (Junie B. Jones)

Junie B. Jones Is a Beauty Shop Guy (Junie B. Jones)

Junie B. Jones Is a Graduation Girl (Junie B. Jones)

Junie B. Jones Is a Party Animal (Junie B. Jones)

Junie B. Jones Is (Almost) a Flower Girl (Junie B. Jones)

Junie B. Jones Is Captain Field Day (Junie B. Jones)

Junie B. Jones Is Not a Crook (Junie B. Jones)

Junie B. Jones Loves Handsome Warren (Junie B. Jones)

Junie B. Jones Smells Something Fishy (Junie B. Jones)

Junkyard Jitters! (Secret World of Alex Mack)

Jurassic Grampa (Wiley and Grampa's Creature Feature)

Just a Little Blue (Owly Graphic Novels)

Just Add Water and Scream (The Zack Files)

Just Annoying! (Just . . .)

Just Between Us (Mary-Kate and Ashley: So Little Time)

Just Disgusting! (Just . . .)

Just Grace (Just Grace)

Just Grace Walks the Dog (Just Grace)

Just in Time (Ghostwriter)

Just in Time for New Year's (Harry and Emily)

Just Joking! (Just . . .)

Just Jump! (The Double Dutch Club)

Just Like Dad (Little Bill (Nickelodeon))

Just like Lizzie (Lizzie McGuire)

Just Plain Al (Al (Alexandra))

Just Shocking! (Just . . .)

Just Stupid! (Just . . .)

Just Tell Me When We're Dead (Mary Rose)

Just Wacky! (Just . . .)

Just Wanna Have Fun (Rugrats (Chapter Books))

Karen's New Year (Baby-Sitters Little Sister)

Karen's Newspaper (Baby-Sitters Little Sister)

Karen's Paper Route (Baby-Sitters Little Sister)

Karen's Pen Pal (Baby-Sitters Little Sister)

Karen's Pilgrim (Baby-Sitters Little Sister)

Karen's Pizza Party (Baby-Sitters Little Sister)

Karen's Plane Trip (Baby-Sitters Little Sister Super Specials)

Karen's Pony (Baby-Sitters Little Sister)

Karen's Pony Camp (Baby-Sitters Little Sister)

Karen's President (Baby-Sitters Little Sister)

Karen's Prize (Baby-Sitters Little Sister)

Karen's Promise (Baby-Sitters Little Sister)

Karen's Pumpkin Patch (Baby-Sitters Little Sister)

Karen's Puppet Show (Baby-Sitters Little Sister)

Karen's Reindeer (Baby-Sitters Little Sister)

Karen's Roller Skates (Baby-Sitters Little Sister)

Karen's Runaway Turkey (Baby-Sitters Little Sister)

Karen's School (Baby-Sitters Little Sister)

Karen's School Bus (Baby-Sitters Little Sister)

Karen's School Mystery (Baby-Sitters Little Sister)

Karen's School Picture (Baby-Sitters Little Sister)

Karen's School Surprise (Baby-Sitters Little Sister)

Karen's School Trip (Baby-Sitters Little Sister)

Karen's Secret (Baby-Sitters Little Sister)

Karen's Secret Valentine (Baby-Sitters Little Sister)

Karen's Show and Share (Baby-Sitters Little Sister)

Karen's Ski Trip (Baby-Sitters Little Sister)

Karen's Sleepover (Baby-Sitters Little Sister)

Karen's Sleigh Ride (Baby-Sitters Little Sister)

Karen's Snow Day (Baby-Sitters Little Sister)

Karen's Snow Princess (Baby-Sitters Little Sister)

Karen's Softball Mystery (Baby-Sitters Little Sister)

Karen's Spy Mystery (Baby-Sitters Little Sister)

Karen's Stepmother (Baby-Sitters Little Sister)

Karen's Surprise (Baby-Sitters Little Sister)

Karen's Swim Meet (Baby-Sitters Little Sister)

Karen's Tattletale (Baby-Sitters Little Sister)

Karen's Tea Party (Baby-Sitters Little Sister)

Karen's Telephone Trouble (Baby-Sitters Little Sister)

Karen's Toothache (Baby-Sitters Little Sister)

Karen's Toys (Baby-Sitters Little Sister)

Karen's Treasure (Baby-Sitters Little Sister)

Karen's Tuba (Baby-Sitters Little Sister)

Karen's Turkey Day (Baby-Sitters Little Sister)

Karen's Twin (Baby-Sitters Little Sister)

Karen's Two Families (Baby-Sitters Little Sister)

Karen's Unicorn (Baby-Sitters Little Sister)

Karen's Wedding (Baby-Sitters Little Sister)

Karen's Wish (Baby-Sitters Little Sister Super Specials)

Karen's Witch (Baby-Sitters Little Sister)

Karen's Worst Day (Baby-Sitters Little Sister)

Karen's Yo-Yo (Baby-Sitters Little Sister)

Kate Be Late (Miss Know It All)

Kate Heads West (Kate)

Kate on the Coast (Kate)

Kate the Boss (Sleepover Friends)

Kate the Winner! (Sleepover Friends)

Kate's Camp-Out (Sleepover Friends)

Kate's Crush (Sleepover Friends)

Kate's Sleepover Disaster (Sleepover Friends)

Kate's Special Secret (Royal Ballet School Diaries)

Kate's Surprise (Sleepover Friends)

Kate's Surprise Visitor (Sleepover Friends)

Katherine's Story (The Girls of Lighthouse Lane)

Kathleen (American Girls: Girls of Many Lands)

Kathy and the Babysitting Hassle (Best Friends)

Kathy's New Brother (Best Friends)

Katie and the Mustang (Hoofbeats)

Katie and the Mustang: Book 1 (Hoofbeats)

Katie and the Mustang: Book 3 (Hoofbeats)

Katie and the Mustang: Book 2 (Hoofbeats)

Katie and the Snow Babies (Mermaid S. O. S.)

Katie Can (Katie)

Katie Couldn't (Katie)

Katie Did It (Katie)

Katie John (Katie John)

Katie John and Heathcliff (Katie John)

A Katie Kazoo Christmas (Katie Kazoo, Switcheroo)

Katie Kicks Off (Never Sink Nine)

Katie Morag and the Big Boy Cousins (Katie Morag)

Katie Morag and the Grand Concert (Katie Morag)

Katie Morag and the New Pier (Katie Morag)

Katie Morag and the Tiresome Ted (Katie Morag)

Katie Morag and the Two Grandmothers (Katie Morag)

Katie Morag and the Wedding (Katie Morag)

Katie Morag Delivers the Mail (Katie Morag)

Katie Steals the Show (Camp Sunnyside)

Katie, the Kitten Fairy (Rainbow Magic: Pet Fairies)

Katie's Angel (Forever Angels)

Katie's Big Move (Junior Gymnasts)

Katie's Gold Medal (Junior Gymnasts)

Kaya and Lone Dog (American Girls: Kaya)

Kaya Shows the Way (American Girls: Kaya)

The Knight at Dawn (Magic Tree House)

Knight for a Day (Dragon Slayers' Academy)

The Knight in Screaming Armor (Goosebumps: Give Yourself Goosebumps)

Knightmare (Strange Matter)

Knights Don't Teach Piano (Bailey School: The Adventures of the Bailey School Kids)

Knight's Honor (CyberQuest)

The Knights of Silversnow (Secrets of Droon)

Knights of the Kitchen Table (Time Warp Trio)

Knights of the Round Table (Choose Your Own Adventure)

Knock, Knock . . . You're Dead (House of Horrors)

Knock on Wood (Sabrina the Teenage Witch)

Know-It-All (Angelwings)

Know-It-All (Sabrina the Teenage Witch)

Knowledge Is Power (Abby Hayes: The Amazing Days of Abby Hayes)

Knyghtmare (Tales of the Dark Forest)

Kobayashi Maru (Star Trek: Enterprise)

The Krelboyne Parrot (Malcolm in the Middle)

Krissy and the Big Show (Here Come the Brownies)

Kristina (Royal Diaries)

Kristy + Bart = ? (Baby-Sitters Club)

Kristy and Mr. Mom (Baby-Sitters Club)

Kristy and the Baby Parade (Baby-Sitters Club)

Kristy and the Cat Burglar (Baby-Sitters Club Mysteries)

Kristy and the Copycat (Baby-Sitters Club)

Kristy and the Dirty Diapers (Baby-Sitters Club)

Kristy and the Haunted Mansion (Baby-Sitters Club Mysteries)

Kristy and the Kidnapper (Baby-Sitters Club Friends Forever)

Kristy and the Middle School Vandal (Baby-Sitters Club Mysteries)

Kristy and the Missing Child (Baby-Sitters Club Mysteries)

Kristy and the Missing Fortune (Baby-Sitters Club Mysteries)

Kristy and the Mother's Day Surprise (Baby-Sitters Club)

Kristy and the Mystery Train (Baby-Sitters Club Mysteries)

Kristy and the Secret of Susan (Baby-Sitters Club)

Kristy and the Sister War (Baby-Sitters Club)

Kristy and the Snobs (Baby-Sitters Club)

Kristy and the Vampires (Baby-Sitters Club Mysteries)

Kristy and the Walking Disaster (Baby-Sitters Club)

Kristy and the Worst Kid Ever (Baby-Sitters Club)

Kristy at Bat (Baby-Sitters Club)

Kristy for President (Baby-Sitters Club)

Kristy in Charge (Baby-Sitters Club)

Kristy Power! (Baby-Sitters Club Friends Forever)

Kristy Thomas, Dog Trainer (Baby-Sitters Club)

Kristy's Big Day (Baby-Sitters Club)

Kristy's Big News (Baby-Sitters Club Friends Forever)

Kristy's Book (Baby-Sitters Club Portrait Collection)

Kristy's Great Idea (Baby-Sitters Club)

Kristy's Great Idea (Baby-Sitters Club Graphic Novels)

Kristy's Mystery Admirer (Baby-Sitters Club)

Kristy's Worst Idea (Baby-Sitters Club)

Krusty Krab Adventures (SpongeBob SquarePants (TokyoPop))

Kung Pow Chicken (Tiger Moth)

Kyla May Miss. Behaves Around the World (Kyla May Miss. Behaves)

Kyla May Miss. Behaves as an International Superspy (Kyla May Miss. Behaves)

Kyla May Miss. Behaves Live on Stage (Kyla May Miss. Behaves)

L

Lab Coat Girl and the Amazing Benjamin Bone (Lab Coat Girl)

Lab Coat Girl in Cool Fuel (Lab Coat Girl)

Lab Coat Girl in My Triple-Decker Hero (Lab Coat Girl)

Lab 6 (Watchers)

Labrador on the Lawn (Animal Ark)

Lacrosse Firestorm (Matt Christopher Sports Stories)

Lady Ellen Grae (Ellen Grae)

Lady Friday (Keys to the Kingdom)

Lady Knight (Protector of the Small)

Lady of Ch'iao Kuo (Royal Diaries)

Lady of Palenque (Royal Diaries)

The Lake of Darkness (Eaglesmount Trilogy)

Lake of Skulls (A Knight's Story)

The Lake of Tears (Deltora: Deltora Quest)

Lamb in the Laundry (Animal Ark)

Lamb Lessons (Animal Ark Pets)

The Lamp from the Warlock's Tomb (Anthony Monday)

Lancelot (King Arthur)

The Land (Logan Family)

Land of the Buffalo Bones (Dear America)

The Land of the Dead (Tales from the Odyssey)

Landon Snow and the Auctor's Kingdom (Landon Snow)

Landon Snow and the Auctor's Riddle (Landon Snow)

Landon Snow and the Island of Arcanum (Landon Snow)

Landon Snow and the Shadows of Malus Quidam (Landon Snow)

Landon Snow and the Volucer Dragon (Landon Snow)

Lara and the Gray Mare (Hoofbeats)

Lara and the Moon-Colored Filly (Hoofbeats)

Lara and the Silent Place (Hoofbeats)

Lara at Athenry Castle (Hoofbeats)

Large and in Charge! (Patrick's Pals)

LaRue for Mayor (LaRue)

The Last Battle (Chronicles of Narnia)

Last Chance in France (Hannah and the Angels)

Last Chance Quarterback (Alden All Stars)

Last Clue (Pyrates)

Let's Get Invisible (Goosebumps Presents)

Let's Go, Dear Dragon (Dear Dragon)

Let's Go Fishing, Gus! (Gus the Hedgehog)

Let's Go, Froggy! (Froggy)

Let's Go Home, Little Bear (Little Bear)

Let's Go, Philadelphia! (Polk Street School: Kids of the Polk Street School)

Let's Party (Mary-Kate and Ashley: Two of a Kind)

Let's Pretend This Never Happened (Dear Dumb Diary)

Let's Put on a Show (Full House: Sisters)

Let's Scare the Teacher to Death (Graveyard School)

The Letter, the Witch, and the Ring (Lewis Barnavelt)

A Letter to Amy (Peter)

Letters from Calico Cat (Calico Cat)

Letting Go (High Hurdles)

Leven Thumps and the Eyes of the Want (Leven Thumps)

Leven Thumps and the Gateway to Foo (Leven Thumps)

Leven Thumps and the Whispered Secret (Leven Thumps)

Leven Thumps and the Wrath of Ezra (Leven Thumps)

Lewis and Clark...and Jodie, Freddi, and Samantha (Time Warp Trio (novelizations))

Lexi's Tale (Park Pals Adventure)

Leyla (American Girls: Girls of Many Lands)

Liar (The Midnight Library)

Liar, Liar (Nightmare Room)

Liar, Liar, Pants on Fire! (First Grade)

Liar, Liar, Pants on Fire (Gilbert)

The Librarian from the Black Lagoon (Black Lagoon)

Lies and Lemons (Angelwings)

Life (In the Cards)

Life Is Unfair (Malcolm in the Middle)

The Life of Me (Hank Zipzer)

Lifeline (Star Trek: Voyager: Starfleet Academy)

Lights, Camera . . . Cats! (Nancy Drew and the Clue Crew)

A Light from Within (Zenda)

A Light in the Castle (The Young Underground)

The Light in the Cellar (American Girls: American Girl Mysteries)

A Light in the Storm (Dear America)

The Light of Meridian (W.I.T.C.H.—Chapter Books)

The Lighthouse Mystery (Boxcar Children)

The Lighthouse Mystery (Nancy Drew Notebooks)

The Lightning Bugs (Ike and Mem)

Lightning Strike (Power Rangers: Ninja Storm)

Lightning Strikes! (The Caped 6th Grader)

The Lightning Thief (Percy Jackson and the Olympians)

Lightning's Last Hope (Thoroughbred: Ashleigh)

Lights, Action, Land-ho! (Pee Wee Scouts)

Lights, Camera . . . (Nancy Drew: Girl Detective)

Lights Camera Action (Secret World of Alex Mack)

Lights! Camera! Action Dog! (Wishbone Mysteries)

Lights! Camera! Clues! (Nancy Drew Notebooks)

Lights, Camera, Cook (Dish)

Lights, Camera... Liftoff! (Weird Planet)

Lights, Camera, Star! (Bratz: Lil' Bratz)

Lights for Minneapolis (The American Adventure)

Lights Out! (Zoey 101)

Lights Out, Sarah! (Here Come the Brownies)

Lightsabers (Star Wars Young Jedi Knights)

Likes Me, Likes Me Not (Mary-Kate and Ashley: Two of a Kind)

Lila on the Loose (Sweet Valley: Unicorn Club)

Lila's April Fool (Sweet Valley Kids)

Lila's Birthday Bash (Sweet Valley Kids)

Lila's Christmas Angel (Sweet Valley Kids)

Lila's Haunted House Party (Sweet Valley Kids)

Lila's Little Sister (Sweet Valley: Unicorn Club)

Lila's Secret (Sweet Valley Kids)

Lili at Ballet (Lili)

Lili Backstage (Lili)

Lili on Stage (Lili)

Lili the Brave (Children of America)

Lilly's Big Day (Lilly)

Lilly's Purple Plastic Purse (Lilly)

Lily B. on the Brink of Cool (Lily B.)

Lily B. on the Brink of Love (Lily B.)

Lily B. on the Brink of Paris (Lily B.)

Lily Quench and the Black Mountains (Lily Quench)

Lily Quench and the Dragon of Ashby (Lily Quench)

Lily Quench and the Hand of Manuelo (Lily Quench)

Lily Quench and the Lighthouse of Skellig Mor (Lily Quench)

Lily Quench and the Magician's Pyramid (Lily Quench)

Lily Quench and the Search for King Dragon (Lily Quench)

Lily Quench and the Treasure of Mote Ely (Lily Quench)

Lily the Lost Puppy (Puppy Friends)

Lily Vanessa and the Pet Panic (Twelve Candles Club)

Lily's Pesky Plant (Disney Fairies (Chapter Books))

The Limerick Trick (Trick Books)

Lincoln's Legacy (Blast to the Past)

Linda and the Little White Lies (Best Friends)

Lindsey (American Girls: Girl of the Year)

Lindy's Happy Ending (Hopscotch Hill School)

Line Drive (Angel Park All-Stars)

Line Drive to Shore (Matt Christopher Sports Stories)

A Line in the Sand (Dear America)

Line of Fire (Star Trek: The Next Generation: Starfleet Academy)

The Lion, the Witch, and the Wardrobe (Chronicles of Narnia)

Lionboy (Lionboy Trilogy)

Lionboy: The Chase (Lionboy Trilogy)

Lionboy: The Truth (Lionboy Trilogy)

Lionel and His Friends (Lionel)

Lionel and Louise (Lionel)

Lionel at Large (Lionel)

Lionel at School (Lionel)

Little Old Mrs. Pepperpot, and Other Stories (Mrs. Pepperpot)

The Little People (Spooksville)

Little People of the Lost Coast (Eric Sterling, Secret Agent)

Little Pet Shop of Horrors (Bone Chillers)

Little Pet Werewolf (Graveyard School)

Little Polar Bear (Little Polar Bear)

Little Polar Bear and the Big Balloon (Little Polar Bear)

Little Polar Bear and the Brave Little Hare (Little Polar Bear)

Little Polar Bear and the Husky Pup (Little Polar Bear)

Little Polar Bear Finds a Friend (Little Polar Bear)

Little Polar Bear, Take Me Home! (Little Polar Bear)

A Little Prairie House (Little House: My First Little House Books)

Little Red Ink Drinker (The Ink Drinker)

Little Red Riding Wolf (Seriously Silly Stories)

Little School of Horrors (Graveyard School)

A Little Shopping (Cobble Street Cousins)

Little Soup's Birthday (Soup: Little Soup)

Little Soup's Bunny (Soup: Little Soup)

Little Soup's Hayride (Soup: Little Soup)

Little Soup's Turkey (Soup: Little Soup)

Little Star (Fairy School)

Little Toot (Little Toot)

Little Toot and the Loch Ness Monster (Little Toot)

Little Toot on the Grand Canal (Little Toot)

Little Toot on the Mississippi (Little Toot)

Little Toot on the Thames (Little Toot)

Little Toot Through the Golden Gate (Little Toot)

Little Town at the Crossroads (Little House: The Caroline Years)

Little Town in the Ozarks (Little House: The Rose Years)

Little Town on the Prairie (Little House)

Little Whistle (Little Whistle)

Little Whistle's Christmas (Little Whistle)

Little Whistle's Dinner Party (Little Whistle)

Little Whistle's Medicine (Little Whistle)

Little White Lies (Mary-Kate and Ashley Sweet 16)

Little Witch Goes to School (Little Witch)

Little Witch Learns to Read (Little Witch)

Little Witch Loves to Write (Little Witch)

Little Witch's Bad Dream (Little Witch)

Little Witch's Big Night (Little Witch)

Little Wolf, Forest Detective (Little Wolf)

Little Wolf, Pack Leader (Little Wolf)

Little Wolf, Terror of the Silvery Sea (Little Wolf)

Little Wolf's Book of Badness (Little Wolf)

Little Wolf's Diary of Daring Deeds (Little Wolf)

Little Wolf's Handy Book of Poems (Little Wolf)

Little Wolf's Haunted Hall for Small Horrors (Little Wolf)

The Littles (The Littles)

The Littles and the Big Blizzard (The Littles)

The Littles and the Big Storm (The Littles)

The Littles and the Lost Children (The Littles)

The Littles and the Scary Halloween (The Littles)

The Littles and the Secret Letter (The Littles)

The Littles and the Summer Storm (The Littles)

The Littles and the Terrible Tiny Kid (The Littles)

The Littles and the Trash Tinies (The Littles)

The Littles and Their Amazing New Friend (The Littles)

The Littles and Their Friends (The Littles)

The Littles Do Their Homework (The Littles)

The Littles Get Trapped! (The Littles)

The Littles Give a Party (The Littles)

The Littles Go Around the World (The Littles)

The Littles Go Exploring (The Littles)

The Littles Go on a Hike (The Littles)

The Littles Go to School (The Littles)

The Littles Have a Happy Valentine's Day (The Littles)

The Littles Have a Merry Christmas (The Littles)

The Littles Have a Wedding (The Littles)

The Littles Make a Friend (The Littles)

The Littles Take a Trip (The Littles)

The Littles to the Rescue (The Littles)

Live Free, Die Hardy! (Hardy Boys, Undercover Brothers: Graphic Novels)

Live from Cedar Hills! (¡Chana!)

The Living Dead (Spooksville)

Living Freight (On Time's Wing)

Living Legend (Thoroughbred)

Lizabeth's Story (The Girls of Lighthouse Lane)

Lizzie at Last (Losers, Inc.)

Lizzie for President (Lizzie McGuire)

Lizzie Goes Wild (Lizzie McGuire)

Lizzie Logan Gets Married (Lizzie Logan)

Lizzie Logan, Second Banana (Lizzie Logan)

Lizzie Logan Wears Purple Sunglasses (Lizzie Logan)

Lizzie Loves Ethan (Lizzie McGuire)

Lizzie's Nightmare and Sibling Bonding (Lizzie McGuire (TokyoPop))

Loamhedge (Redwall)

Locked in the Library (Arthur Chapter Books)

Locker 13 (Nightmare Room)

The Log Cabin Christmas (Log Cabin)

The Log Cabin Church (Log Cabin)

The Log Cabin Quilt (Log Cabin)

The Log Cabin Wedding (Log Cabin)

Logan Likes Mary Anne! (Baby-Sitters Club)

Louise Takes Charge (Louise)

Louisiana's Song (Maggie Valley)

Lovable Lyle (Lyle)

Love (In the Cards)

Love and Kisses (Mary-Kate and Ashley Sweet 16)

Love Burning Bright (Cassie Perkins)

The Love Factor (Mary-Kate and Ashley: So Little Time)

Love, from the Fifth-Grade Celebrity (Casey, Tracey and Company)

Love Is a Gift (Heartland)

Love Is in the Air (Barbie (Step Into Reading))

Love Is in the Air (Mary-Kate and Ashley: So Little Time)

Love-Lies-Bleeding (On Time's Wing)

The Love Potion (Abracadabra)

Love Potion #8 (Avatar (Ready to Read))

Love-Set-Match (Mary-Kate and Ashley: Two of a Kind)

Love Stinks (Funny Firsts)

Love Stinks! (Katie Kazoo, Switcheroo)

Love Thy Neighbor (Dear America)

Lovestruck! (Fairly OddParents)

Lovingly Alice (Alice)

Lower! Higher! You're a Liar! (Molly)

Loyalties (Star Trek: The Next Generation: Starfleet Academy)

Lucinda's Secret (The Spiderwick Chronicles)

Luck Follows Me (Heartland)

The Luck of the Irish (Robin Hill School)

Luckiest Day of Your Life (Choose Your Own Adventure)

The Lucky Baseball Bat (Matt Christopher Sports Stories)

Lucky Bucky in Oz (Oz)

Lucky Christmas (Lucky)

Lucky Days with Mr. and Mrs. Green (Mr. and Mrs. Green)

Lucky Dog Days (Pee Wee Scouts)

Lucky Horse (The Saddle Club)

The Lucky Horseshoes (Nancy Drew Notebooks)

Lucky in Left Field (Lucky)

Lucky Little Bear (Little Bear: Maurice Sendak's Little Bear)

The Lucky Lottery (A to Z Mysteries)

Lucky, Lucky Day (Full House: Michelle)

Lucky on the Loose (Lucky)

Lucky Stars (Houdini Club Magic Mystery)

Lucy and the Magic Crystal (Mermaid S. O. S.)

Lucy Rose (Lucy Rose)

Lucy Rose: Busy Like You Can't Believe (Lucy Rose)

Lucy Rose: The Beginning (Lucy Rose)

Lucy Rose: Working Myself to Pieces & Bits (Lucy Rose)

Lucy the Diamond Fairy (Rainbow Magic: Jewel Fairies)

Lucy the Lonely Kitten (Kitten Friends)

Lucy's Advice (Peanuts)

Lucy's Angel (7th Heaven)

Lucy's Wish (Orphan Train Children)

Ludell (Ludell)

Ludell and Willie (Ludell)

Ludell's New York Time (Ludell)

Luke (American Adventures)

Luke on the High Seas (American Adventures)

Luna and the Well of Secrets (Fairy Chronicles)

The Lunch Box Surprise (First-Grade Friends)

Lunch Walks Among Us (Franny K. Stein, Mad Scientist)

The Lunchroom of Doom (Werewolf Club)

Lunchtime Rules (Go Girl)

The Lure of the Italian Treasure (Hardy Boys)

Luv, Amelia Luv, Nadia (Amelia)

The Lying Postman (Jack Russell: Dog Detective)

Lyle and the Birthday Party (Lyle)

Lyle at Christmas (Lyle)

Lyle at the Office (Lyle)

Lyle Finds His Mother (Lyle)

Lyle, Lyle, Crocodile (Lyle)

Lyric's World (Star Wars Junior Jedi Knights)

M

M and M and the Bad News Babies (M and M)

M and M and the Big Bag (M and M)

M and M and the Halloween Monster (M and M)

M and M and the Haunted House Game (M and M)

M and M and the Mummy Mess (M and M)

M and M and the Santa Secrets (M and M)

M and M and the Superchild Afternoon (M and M)

Mabel Makes the Grade (Sister Magic)

Mac Attack! (Adventures of Daniel Boom AKA Loud Boy)

Mc Flora McFlimsey's Birthday (Miss Flora McFlimsey)

The Macaroni Mess (Sweet Valley Kids)

McBroom and the Beanstalk (McBroom)

McBroom and the Big Wind (McBroom)

McBroom and the Great Race (McBroom)

McBroom Tells a Lie (McBroom)

McBroom Tells the Truth (McBroom)

McBroom the Rainmaker (McBroom)

McBroom's Almanac (McBroom)

McBroom's Ear (McBroom)

McBroom's Ghost (McBroom)

McBroom's Wonderful One-Acre Farm (McBroom)

McBroom's Zoo (McBroom)

McDuff and the Baby (McDuff)

McDuff Comes Home (McDuff)

McDuff Goes to School (McDuff)

McDuff Moves In (McDuff)

McDuff Saves the Day (McDuff)

McDuff's New Friend (McDuff)

McDuff's Wild Romp (McDuff)

McGurk Gets Good and Mad (McGurk)

Mad Dog of Lobo Mountain (D.J. Dillon Adventures)

The Mad Gasser of Bessledorf Street (Bessledorf Hotel)

The Mad Hatter (Batman (Scholastic Reader))

Mad House (Hardy Boys, Undercover Brothers: Graphic Novels)

Madame Amelia Tells All (Amelia)

Madame President (How I Survived Middle School)

The Magic School Bus Sleeps for the Winter (Magic School Bus)

The Magic School Bus Spins a Web (Magic School Bus)

The Magic School Bus Takes a Dive (Magic School Bus)

The Magic School Bus Takes a Moonwalk (Magic School Bus)

The Magic School Bus Takes a Moonwalk (Magic School Bus)

The Magic School Bus Takes Flight (Magic School Bus)

The Magic School Bus Ups and Downs (Magic School Bus)

The Magic School Bus Wet All Over (Magic School Bus)

The Magic Shades (Fortune Tellers Club)

The Magic Show Mystery (Boxcar Children: Adventures of Benny and Watch)

Magic Train and Grubby Longjohn's Olde Tyme Revue (Lizzie McGuire (TokyoPop))

The Magical Fellowship (Age of Magic Trilogy)

The Magical Mimics in Oz (Oz)

Magician in the Trunk (Time Spies)

The Magician's Apprentice (Magician Trilogy)

The Magician's Challenge (Magician Trilogy)

The Magician's Company (Magician Trilogy)

The Magician's Nephew (Chronicles of Narnia)

Magyk (Septimus Heap)

Maia of Thebes, 1463 B.C. (The Life and Times)

Maid Mary Anne (Baby-Sitters Club)

Mail-Order Brother (Full House: Stephanie)

Mailbox Mania (Cul-de-Sac Kids)

The Mailbox Trick (Trick Books)

Maisy at the Fair (Maisy the Mouse)

Maisy at the Farm (Maisy the Mouse)

Maisy Cleans Up (Maisy the Mouse)

Maisy Dresses Up (Maisy the Mouse)

Maisy Goes Camping (Maisy the Mouse)

Maisy Goes Shopping (Maisy the Mouse)

Maisy Goes Swimming (Maisy the Mouse)

Maisy Goes to Bed (Maisy the Mouse)

Maisy Goes to School (Maisy the Mouse)

Maisy Goes to the Playground (Maisy the Mouse)

Maisy Goes to Work (Maisy the Mouse)

Maisy Makes Gingerbread (Maisy the Mouse)

Maisy Makes Lemonade (Maisy the Mouse)

Maisy Takes a Bath (Maisy the Mouse)

Maisy's ABC (Maisy the Mouse)

Maisy's Bedtime (Maisy the Mouse)

Maisy's Morning on the Farm (Maisy the Mouse)

Maisy's Pirate Treasure Hunt (Maisy the Mouse)

Maisy's Snowy Christmas Eve (Maisy the Mouse)

Major-League Melissa (Never Sink Nine)

Major League Mess-up (Katie Kazoo, Switcheroo)

Major League Trouble (Full House: Michelle)

Make a New Friend, Gus! (Gus the Hedgehog)

Make a Trade, Charlie Brown! (Peanuts)

Make a Wish (Little Genie)

The Make-Believe Mystery (Nancy Drew Notebooks)

Make Like a Tree and Leave (Matthew Martin)

Make Mine with Everything (Robbie Packford)

Make New Friends (Yoko and Friends)

Make Room for Elisa (Riverside Kids: Elisa)

Make the Team, Baby Duck! (Baby Duck)

Make Up Your Mind, Marsha! (Here Come the Brownies)

The Makeover Experiment (Mary-Kate and Ashley: So Little Time)

Makeovers by Marcia (Losers, Inc.)

Makeup Mayhem (Totally Spies!)

Makeup Shake-Up (Mary-Kate and Ashley in Action)

Makin' It Up! (Bratz: Lil' Bratz)

Making a Splash (Mary-Kate and Ashley: Two of a Kind)

Making Strides (Chestnut Hill)

Making the Save (Soccer 'Cats)

Making the Team (Angel Park All-Stars)

Making Tracks (Adventures in America)

Making Waves (Angels Unlimited)

Making Waves (Candy Apple)

Makuta's Revenge (Bionicle Chronicles)

Malcolm for President (Malcolm in the Middle)

Mall Madness (Nancy Drew and the Clue Crew)

Mall of the Universe (Spy Kids Adventures)

Malled (Hardy Boys, Undercover Brothers: Graphic Novels)

Mallory and the Dream Horse (Baby-Sitters Club)

Mallory and the Ghost Cat (Baby-Sitters Club Mysteries)

Mallory and the Secret Diary (Baby-Sitters Club)

Mallory and the Trouble with the Twins (Baby-Sitters Club)

Mallory Hates Boys (and Gym) (Baby-Sitters Club)

Mallory on Board (Mallory)

Mallory on Strike (Baby-Sitters Club)

Mallory on the Move (Mallory)

Mallory Pike, #1 Fan (Baby-Sitters Club)

Mallory vs. Max (Mallory)

Mallory's Christmas Wish (Baby-Sitters Club)

The Malted Falcoln (Chet Gecko Mysteries)

The Maltese Dog (Wishbone Mysteries)

Mama, Don't Go! (Yoko and Friends)

Mama Elizabeti (Elizabeti)

Man Out at First (Peach Street Mudders)

Man Overboard! (Mystery Files of Shelby Woo)

The Man Who Vanished (Ghostwriter)

The Man Who Wore All His Clothes (The Gaskitts)

Manatee Blues (Wild at Heart)

Mandie and the Invisible Troublemaker (Mandie)

Martin Bridge: Out of Orbit! (Martin Bridge)

Martin Bridge: Ready for Takeoff! (Martin Bridge)

Martin Bridge: Sound the Alarm! (Martin Bridge)

Martin Bridge: The Sky's the Limit (Martin Bridge)

Martin Luther King Jr. Day (Robin Hill School)

Martin the Warrior (Redwall)

The Marvelous Land of Oz (Oz)

Marvin Redpost (Marvin Redpost)

Marvin Redpost: A Magic Crystal? (Marvin Redpost)

Marvin Redpost: Alone in His Teacher's House (Marvin Redpost)

Marvin Redpost: Class President (Marvin Redpost)

Marvin Redpost: Is He a Girl? (Marvin Redpost)

Marvin Redpost: Kidnapped at Birth? (Marvin Redpost)

Marvin Redpost: Super Fast, Out of Control! (Marvin Redpost)

Marvin Redpost: Why Pick on Me? (Marvin Redpost)

Mary (Royal Diaries)

Mary Alice Peale, Philadelphia, 1777 (American Diaries)

Mary Anne + 2 Many Babies (Baby-Sitters Club)

Mary Anne and Camp BSC (Baby-Sitters Club)

Mary Anne and Miss Priss (Baby-Sitters Club)

Mary Anne and the Great Romance (Baby-Sitters Club)

Mary Anne and the Haunted Bookstore (Baby-Sitters Club Mysteries)

Mary Anne and the Library Mystery (Baby-Sitters Club Mysteries)

Mary Anne and the Little Princess (Baby-Sitters Club)

Mary Anne and the Memory Garden (Baby-Sitters Club)

Mary Anne and the Music Box Secret (Baby-Sitters Club Mysteries)

Mary Anne and the Playground Fight (Baby-Sitters Club)

Mary Anne and the Search for Tigger (Baby-Sitters Club)

Mary Anne and the Secret in the Attic (Baby-Sitters Club Mysteries)

Mary Anne and the Silent Witness (Baby-Sitters Club Mysteries)

Mary Anne and the Zoo Mystery (Baby-Sitters Club Mysteries)

Mary Anne and Too Many Boys (Baby-Sitters Club)

Mary Anne Breaks the Rules (Baby-Sitters Club)

Mary Anne in the Middle (Baby-Sitters Club)

Mary Anne Misses Logan (Baby-Sitters Club)

Mary Anne Saves the Day (Baby-Sitters Club)

Mary Anne Saves the Day (Baby-Sitters Club Graphic Novels)

Mary Anne to the Rescue (Baby-Sitters Club)

Mary Anne vs. Logan (Baby-Sitters Club)

Mary Anne's Bad Luck Mystery (Baby-Sitters Club)

Mary Anne's Big Breakup (Baby-Sitters Club Friends Forever)

Mary Anne's Book (Baby-Sitters Club Portrait Collection)

Mary Anne's Makeover (Baby-Sitters Club)

Mary Anne's Revenge (Baby-Sitters Club Friends Forever)

Mary Beth's Haunted Ride (Riding Academy)

Mary Margaret and the Perfect Pet Plan (Mary Margaret)

Mary Margaret, Center Stage (Mary Margaret)

Mary Margaret Mary Christmas (Mary Margaret)

Mary Margaret Meets Her Match (Mary Margaret)

Mary Marony and the Chocolate Surprise (Mary Marony)

Mary Marony and the Snake (Mary Marony)

Mary Marony Hides Out (Mary Marony)

Mary Marony, Mummy Girl (Mary Marony)

Mary Poppins (Mary Poppins)

Mary Poppins and the House Next Door (Mary Poppins)

Mary Poppins Comes Back (Mary Poppins)

Mary Poppins from A to Z (Mary Poppins)

Mary Poppins in Cherry Tree Lane (Mary Poppins)

Mary Poppins in the Kitchen (Mary Poppins)

Mary Poppins in the Park (Mary Poppins)

Mary Poppins Opens the Door (Mary Poppins)

Mary's Rescue (7th Heaven)

Mary's Story (7th Heaven)

The Mask of Maliban (Secrets of Droon)

Mask of the Wolf Boy (Trailblazers)

The Masked Monkey (Hardy Boys)

Masks (Wild at Heart)

Masquerade in Oz (Oz)

The Massively Multiplayer Mystery (Spy Gear)

Master of Aikido (Choose Your Own Adventure)

Master of Deception (Star Wars: The Last of the Jedi)

Master of Disaster (Soccer 'Cats)

The Master of Disguise (Star Wars: Jedi Quest)

Master of Judo (Choose Your Own Adventure)

Master of Karate (Choose Your Own Adventure)

Master of Kendo (Choose Your Own Adventure)

Master of Kung Fu (Choose Your Own Adventure)

Master of Martial Arts (Choose Your Own Adventure)

Master of Tae Kwon Do (Choose Your Own Adventure)

A Masterpiece for Bess (Disney Fairies (Chapter Books))

Masters of Mayhem (Kim Possible: Pick a Villain)

Masters of the Louvre (Young Indiana Jones Chronicles: Choose Your Own Adventure)

A Match of Wills (Ghostwriter)

Matchmakers (Full House: Sisters)

Matilda Mouse's Garden (George and Matilda Mouse)

Mattimeo (Redwall)

Matt's Story (7th Heaven)

Maui Mystery (Abby's South Seas Adventures)

Max and Maggie (The Puppy Place)

Max and Mo Build a Snowman (Max and Mo)

Max and Mo Go Apple Picking (Max and Mo)

Max and Mo's First Day at School (Max and Mo)

Meg's Dearest Wish (Little Women Journals)

Meg's Story (Portraits of Little Women)

Melanie and the Cruise Caper (Twelve Candles Club)

Melanie and the Modeling Mess (Twelve Candles Club)

Melanie Martin Goes Dutch (Melanie Martin)

Melanie's Double Jinx (Thoroughbred)

Melanie's Last Ride (Thoroughbred)

Melanie's Treasure (Thoroughbred)

Meltdown (2099)

The Melted Coins (Hardy Boys)

Menace of Alia Rellapor, Part 1 (Akiko Graphic Novels)

Menace of Alia Rellapor, Part 3 (Akiko Graphic Novels)

Menace of Alia Rellapor, Part 2 (Akiko Graphic Novels)

The Mennyms (Mennyms)

Mennyms Alive (Mennyms)

Mennyms Alone (Mennyms)

Mennyms in the Wilderness (Mennyms)

Mennyms Under Siege (Mennyms)

Meow! (Kipper: Little Kippers)

Meow . . . Like a Snail?! (SpongeBob SquarePants (TokyoPop))

The Merchant of Death (Pendragon)

Mercury Rising (Sailor Moon Novels)

Mercy Watson (Mercy Watson)

Mercy Watson Fights Crime (Mercy Watson)

Mercy Watson Goes for a Ride (Mercy Watson)

Mercy Watson Thinks Like a Pig (Mercy Watson)

Mercy Watson to the Rescue (Mercy Watson)

Meridian Magic (W.I.T.C.H.—Graphic Novels)

Merlin (Young Merlin Trilogy)

Mermaids Don't Run Track (Bailey School: The Adventures of the Bailey School Kids)

Merry Christmas, Amelia Bedelia (Amelia Bedelia)

Merry Christmas, Curious George (Curious George)

Merry Christmas, Davy! (Davy)

Merry Christmas, Dear Dragon (Dear Dragon)

Merry Christmas, Ernest and Celestine! (Ernest and Celestine)

Merry Christmas from Betsy (Betsy)

Merry Christmas from Eddie (Eddie Wilson)

Merry Christmas, Geraldine (Geraldine)

Merry Christmas, Geronimo! (Geronimo Stilton)

Merry Christmas, Grumpy Bunny (Grumpy Bunny)

Merry Christmas, Gus! (Gus the Hedgehog)

Merry Christmas, Henrietta (Henrietta)

Merry Christmas, Strega Nona (Strega Nona and Big Anthony)

Merry Christmas, World! (Full House: Michelle)

Merry Go Round in Oz (Oz)

The Message (Animorphs)

A Message from the Match Girl (Investigators of the Unknown)

The Message in the Haunted Mansion (Nancy Drew)

The Message in the Hollow Oak (Nancy Drew)

Message in the Mountain (Time Spies)

Message in the Sky (My America: Corey)

Messy Bessey (Messy Bessey)

Messy Bessey and the Birthday Overnight (Messy Bessey)

Messy Bessey's Closet (Messy Bessey)

Messy Bessey's Family Reunion (Messy Bessey)

Messy Bessey's Garden (Messy Bessey)

Messy Bessey's Holidays (Messy Bessey)

Messy Bessey's School Desk (Messy Bessey)

Mexican Treasure Hunt (Hannah and the Angels)

Mia (American Girls: Girl of the Year)

Miami Gets It Straight (Miami)

Miami Makes the Play (Miami)

Miami Sees It Through (Miami)

The Michigan Mega-Monsters (American Chillers)

Mickey and Me (Baseball Card Adventures)

Mid-Air Zillionaire (AstroKids)

The Middle Moffat (The Moffats)

Middle Sister (7th Heaven)

Midnight (Warriors: The New Prophecy)

Midnight at Lonesome Hollow (American Girls: American Girl Mysteries)

Midnight for Charlie Bone (Children of the Red King)

The Midnight Game (Strange Matter)

The Midnight Horse (Sandy Lane Stables)

Midnight Madness and Mayhem (Story Girl)

The Midnight Mystery (Boxcar Children)

The Midnight Mystery (Cul-de-Sac Kids)

Midnight Mystery (Winnie the Horse Gentler)

Midnight on the Moon (Magic Tree House)

Midnight Over Sanctaphrax (Edge Chronicles)

Midnight Phone Calls (Clue)

Midnight Rescue (Christy)

Midnight Snack (Mercer Mayer's Critters of the Night)

Midsummer at Greenchapel (Girlhood Journeys: Juliet)

A Midsummer Night's Dork (Dork in Disguise)

Midwinter Nightingale (Wolves Chronicles)

Mighty Adventurer of the Planet (Beryl E. Bean)

A Mighty Big Wish (Fairly OddParents)

The Mighty Pigeon Club (Clubhouse)

Mikale of Hawaii (Maya's World)

Mike's Mystery (Boxcar Children)

Miko's Muzzy Mess (AstroKids)

Milady Alex! (Secret World of Alex Mack)

Milady's Dragon (Sabrina the Teenage Witch)

Milk and Cookies (Bear)

Millennium Madness (Sabrina the Teenage Witch)

The Million Dollar Goal (Million Dollar Series)

Million-Dollar Horse (The Saddle Club)

The Million Dollar Kick (Million Dollar Series)

Miss Know It All and the Three-Ring Circus (Miss Know It All)

Miss Know It All and the Wishing Lamp (Miss Know It All)

Miss Know It All Returns (Miss Know It All)

Miss Lazar Is Bizarre! (My Weird School)

Miss Malarkey Doesn't Live in Room 10 (Miss Malarkey)

Miss Malarkey Leaves No Reader Behind (Miss Malarkey)

Miss Malarkey Won't Be In Today (Miss Malarkey)

Miss Malarkey's Field Trip (Miss Malarkey)

Miss Mallard's Case Book (Miss Mallard)

Miss Nelson Has a Field Day (Miss Nelson)

Miss Nelson Is Back (Miss Nelson)

Miss Nelson Is Missing! (Miss Nelson)

Miss Pickerell and the Blue Whales (Miss Pickerell)

Miss Pickerell and the Geiger Counter (Miss Pickerell)

Miss Pickerell and the Lost World (Miss Pickerell)

Miss Pickerell and the Supertanker (Miss Pickerell)

Miss Pickerell and the War of the Computers (Miss Pickerell)

Miss Pickerell and the Weather Satellite (Miss Pickerell)

Miss Pickerell Goes on a Dig (Miss Pickerell)

Miss Pickerell Goes to Mars (Miss Pickerell)

Miss Pickerell Goes to the Arctic (Miss Pickerell)

Miss Pickerell Goes Undersea (Miss Pickerell)

Miss Pickerell Harvests the Sea (Miss Pickerell)

Miss Pickerell Meets Mr. H. U. M. (Miss Pickerell)

Miss Pickerell on the Moon (Miss Pickerell)

Miss Pickerell on the Trail (Miss Pickerell)

Miss Pickerell Tackles the Energy Crisis (Miss Pickerell)

Miss Pickerell Takes the Bull By the Horns (Miss Pickerell)

Miss Pickerell to the Earthquake Rescue (Miss Pickerell)

Miss Popularity (Candy Apple)

Miss Small Is Off the Wall! (My Weird School)

Miss Spider's ABC (Miss Spider)

Miss Spider's New Car (Miss Spider)

Miss Spider's Sunny Patch Kids (Miss Spider)

Miss Spider's Tea Party (Miss Spider)

Miss Spider's Wedding (Miss Spider)

Miss Suki Is Kooky! (My Weird School)

Missing! (B.Y. Times Kid Sisters)

Missing! (Cascade Mountain Railroad Mysteries)

Missing! (Mars Year One)

The Missing Beach Ball (Clifford)

The Missing Chums (Hardy Boys)

The Missing Horse Mystery (Nancy Drew)

The Missing Mummy (A to Z Mysteries)

Missing Piece in Greece (Hannah and the Angels)

Missing Pieces (Red Rock Mysteries)

The Missing Pony Pal (Pony Pals)

The Missing Princess (Secret Agent MJJ)

Missing Tea Set (Sweet Valley Kids)

The Missing Video (Reel Kids Adventures)

Mission (Spy Force)

Mission: Impossible Friendship (Beryl E. Bean)

Mission: in Search of the Time and Space Machine (Spy Force)

Mission: Spy Force Revealed (Spy Force)

Mission: The Nightmare Vortex (Spy Force)

Mission Down Under (Hannah and the Angels)

A Mission for Her Village, Africa, 1440 (Girlhood Journeys: Kai)

Missouri Bound (Little House Chapter Books: Rose)

Missouri Madhouse (American Chillers)

Missouri School Days (Little House Chapter Books: Rose)

Mistaken Identity! (Secret World of Alex Mack)

Mistaken Identity (SpongeBob SquarePants (TokyoPop))

Mister Monday (Keys to the Kingdom)

Mister Tinker of Oz (Oz)

The Mistletoe Mystery (Nancy Drew)

The Mists of Time (Time Trilogy)

Misty of Chincoteague (Chincoteague)

Misty to the Rescue (Mermaid S. O. S.)

Misty's Twilight (Chincoteague)

Mitt and Minn at the Wisconsin Cheese Jamboree (Mitt and Minn)

Mitt and Minn's Illinois Adventure (Mitt and Minn)

Mitt, the Michigan Mouse (Mitt and Minn)

Mittens (Mittens)

Mixed Signals (The Pink Parrots)

Mixed-Up Magic (Fairy School)

The Mixed-Up Mask Mystery (Fletcher Mysteries)

Moans and Groans and Dinosaur Bones (Pee Wee Scouts)

The Mob (Feather and Bone: The Crow Chronicles)

Moby Dog (Wishbone Adventures)

Moby Stink (The Adventures of Uncle Stinky)

Model Friendship (Bratz)

The Moffat Museum (The Moffats)

The Moffats (The Moffats)

Mojo and Mini-Mo (Powerpuff Girls Chapter Books)

Mojo Mayhem (Powerpuff Girls Chapter Books)

Mole and Shrew All Year Through (Mole and Shrew)

Mole and Shrew Are Two (Mole and Shrew)

Mole and Shrew Find a Clue (Mole and Shrew)

Mole and Shrew Have Jobs to Do (Mole and Shrew)

Mole and Shrew Step Out (Mole and Shrew)

Mole and Troll Trim the Tree (Mole and Troll)

The Mole Sisters and the Blue Egg (Mole Sisters)

The Mole Sisters and the Busy Bees (Mole Sisters)

The Mole Sisters and the Cool Breeze (Mole Sisters)

The Mole Sisters and the Fairy Ring (Mole Sisters)

More Adventures of the Great Brain (The Great Brain)

More Adventures of the Plant That Ate Dirty Socks (The Plant That Ate Dirty Socks)

More All-of-a-Kind Family (All-of-a-Kind Family)

More Bunny Trouble (Bunny Trouble)

More from the Molesons (Molesons)

More Mr. and Mrs. Green (Mr. and Mrs. Green)

More Parts (Parts)

More Perfect than the Moon (Sarah, Plain and Tall)

More Sideways Arithmetic from Wayside School (Wayside School)

More Stories from Grandma's Attic (Grandma's Attic)

More Stories Huey Tells (Julian and Huey)

More Stories Julian Tells (Julian and Huey)

More Tales of Amanda Pig (Oliver and Amanda Pig)

More Tales of Oliver Pig (Oliver and Amanda Pig)

More Than Friends (Silver Blades)

The More, the Merrier (Abby Hayes: The Amazing Days of Abby Hayes)

More To and Again (later renamed Freddy Goes to the North Pole) (Freddy)

More Witch Goblin and Ghost Stories (Witch, Goblin and Ghost)

Morgain's Revenge (Grail Quest)

Morgie's Surprise (The Barkers)

Morris and Boris (Morris and Boris)

Morris and Boris at the Circus (Morris and Boris)

Morris Goes to School (Morris and Boris)

Morris Has a Birthday Party (Morris and Boris)

Morris Has a Cold (Morris and Boris)

Morris Is a Cowboy, a Policeman, and a Baby Sitter (Morris and Boris)

Morris Tells Boris Mother Goose Stories and Rhymes (Morris and Boris)

Morris the Moose (Morris and Boris)

Mortimer Says Nothing, and Other Stories (Arabel and Mortimer)

Mortimer's Cross (Arabel and Mortimer)

Moses Goes to a Concert (Moses)

Moses Goes to School (Moses)

Moses Goes to the Circus (Moses)

Moses Sees a Play (Moses)

Moss Pillows (Voyage to the Bunny Planet)

Mossflower (Redwall)

The Most Beautiful Girl in the World (Sweet Valley: Unicorn Club)

The Most Dangerous Race (Speed Racer)

The Most Evil, Friendly Villain Ever (Horace Splattly: The Cupcaked Crusader)

The Most World Records (CatDog (Chapter Books))

Mother Bear's Picnic (Little Bear: Maurice Sendak's Little Bear)

Mother Knows Best (SpongeBob SquarePants Chapter Books)

Mother, May I? (Remnants)

Mother Murphy (Murphy Family)

The Mother of Mountains (Usagi Yojimbo)

Mother Rabbit's Son Tom (Hattie Rabbit)

Mother, You're the Best! (But Sister, You're a Pest!) (Gilbert)

Mother's Day Mess (Harry and Emily)

Motocross Madness (Hardy Boys)

Motocross Mania (Choose Your Own Adventure)

Mountain Bike Mania (Matt Christopher Sports Stories)

Mountain Biker (Choose Your Own Adventure)

Mountain Madness (Christy)

Mountain Mare (Phantom Stallion)

Mountain Men (Reflections of a Black Cowboy)

Mountain of Mayhem (Samurai Jack Chapter Books)

The Mountain-Peak Mystery (Dana Girls)

Mountain Survival (Choose Your Own Adventure)

Mountain Top Mystery (Boxcar Children)

The Mountains of the Moon (The Unicorn's Secret)

Mouse and Mole and the All-Weather Train Ride (Mouse and Mole)

Mouse and Mole and the Christmas Walk (Mouse and Mole)

Mouse and Mole and the Year-Round Garden (Mouse and Mole)

The Mouse and the Motorcycle (Ralph S. Mouse)

The Mouse Island Marathon (Geronimo Stilton)

Mouse Magic (Animal Ark Pets)

Mousekin Finds a Friend (Mousekin)

Mousekin Takes a Trip (Mousekin)

Mousekin's ABC (Mousekin)

Mousekin's Christmas Eve (Mousekin)

Mousekin's Close Call (Mousekin)

Mousekin's Easter Basket (Mousekin)

Mousekin's Fables (Mousekin)

Mousekin's Family (Mousekin)

Mousekin's Frosty Friend (Mousekin)

Mousekin's Golden House (Mousekin)

Mousekin's Lost Woodland (Mousekin)

Mousekin's Mystery (Mousekin)

Mousekin's Thanksgiving (Mousekin)

Mousekin's Woodland Birthday (Mousekin)

Mousekin's Woodland Sleepers (Mousekin)

The Movie Star Angel (Forever Angels)

The Movie Star Mystery (Boxcar Children)

Movie Star Pony (Pony Pals)

Moving Pony (Pony Pals)

Moving to Mars (Funny Firsts)

Moving Up (High Hurdles)

Moving Up (Lottery Luck)

Mr. and Mrs. Pig's Evening Out (Mr. and Mrs. Pig)

Mr. Bass's Planetoid (Tyco Bass)

Mr. Cheeters Is Missing (Nancy Drew Graphic Novels)

Mr. Docker Is Off His Rocker! (My Weird School)

Mr. Granite Is from Another Planet! (My Weird School Daze)

Mummies in the Morning (Magic Tree House)

Mummy (Time Soldiers)

The Mummy Case (Hardy Boys)

Mummy Dearest (Sabrina the Teenage Witch)

The Mummy Lives! (Sam, Dog Detective)

The Mummy, the Will, and the Crypt (Johnny Dixon)

The Mummy Walks (Goosebumps Series 2000)

The Mummy Who Wouldn't Die (Choose Your Own Nightmare)

The Mummy with No Name (Geronimo Stilton)

The Mummy's Curse (Hardy Boys, Undercover Brothers)

The Mummy's Curse (Young Indiana Jones)

The Mummy's Footsteps (Mind over Matter)

Murder at Hockey Camp (Screech Owls)

Murder at the Mall (Hardy Boys, Undercover Brothers)

Murder at the Winter Games (Screech Owls)

Murder House (Hardy Boys, Undercover Brothers Murder House Trilogy)

Murder in the Middle Pasture (Hank the Cowdog)

Murder, My Tweet (Chet Gecko Mysteries)

Murder on the Ridge (Across the Steel River)

Murder on the Set (Nancy Drew: Girl Detective)

Murder to Go (Three Investigators)

Murphy's Island (Murphy Family)

The Music Festival Mystery (Nancy Drew)

The Music Meltdown (Mary-Kate and Ashley in Action)

Music, Music for Everyone (Rosa Trilogy)

The Music Teacher from the Black Lagoon (Black Lagoon)

Mustang in the Mist (Animal Ark)

Mustang Moon (Phantom Stallion)

Mutant Garbage (Lunchroom)

Mutant Mammoths of Montana (American Chillers)

The Mutation (Animorphs)

Mutation (Remnants)

Mutiny! (Pirate Hunter)

Mutiny (Space Above and Beyond)

Mutiny in Space (Choose Your Own Adventure)

The Mutt in the Iron Muzzle (Wishbone Adventures)

Muttketeer! (Wishbone Adventures)

Mutton Soup (Johnny Mutton)

My Almost Perfect Plan (Full House: Michelle)

My Aunt, the Monster (Magical Mystery)

My Babysitter Bites Again (My Babysitter)

My Babysitter Flies by Night (My Babysitter)

My Babysitter Goes Bats (My Babysitter)

My Babysitter Has Fangs (My Babysitter)

My Babysitter Is a Movie Monster (My Babysitter)

My Babysitter Is a Vampire (My Babysitter)

My Best Friend Is a Movie Star! (Full House: Michelle)

My Best Friend Is Ariel (Disney Princess)

My Best Friend Is Belle (Disney Princess)

My Best Friend Is Cinderella (Disney Princess)

My Best Friend Is Invisible (Goosebumps)

My Best Friend Is Jasmine (Disney Princess)

My Best Friend's Boyfriend (Mary-Kate and Ashley Sweet 16)

My Big Lie (Little Bill)

My Brother, the Ghost (House of Horrors)

My Brother's Keeper (My America: Virginia)

My Cat Is Going to the Dogs (Funny Firsts)

My Dog and the Birthday Mystery (My Dog)

My Dog and the Green Sock Mystery (My Dog)

My Dog and the Key Mystery (My Dog)

My Dog and the Knock Knock Mystery (My Dog)

My Dog's a Scaredy-Cat (Hank Zipzer)

My Dog's Brain (Sally)

My Face to the Wind (Dear America)

My Father's Dragon (Dragon)

My Fourth-Grade Mess (Full House: Michelle)

My Friend Flicka (Flicka)

My Friend Is Sad (Elephant and Piggie)

My Friends Call Me Monster (Goosebumps Horrorland)

My Grandma, Major League Slugger (The Zack Files)

My Guy (Guy Strang)

My Hairiest Adventure (Goosebumps)

My Hairiest Adventure (Goosebumps Presents)

My Haunted House (Araminta Spookie)

My Heart Is on the Ground (Dear America)

My Ho-Ho Horrible Christmas (Full House: Michelle)

My Life Is a Three-Ring Circus (Full House: Michelle)

My Little House ABC (Little House: My First Little House Books)

My Little House Book of Animals (Little House: My First Little House Books)

My Little House Book of Family (Little House: My First Little House Books)

My Little House 123 (Little House: My First Little House Books)

My Mom Hates Me in January (My Mom)

My Mom Made Me Go to Camp (My Mom)

My Mom Made Me Go to School (My Mom)

My Mom Made Me Take Piano Lessons (My Mom)

My Name Is Evil (Nightmare Room)

My Name is Stilton, Geronimo Stilton (Geronimo Stilton)

My Pants Are Haunted (Dear Dumb Diary)

My Pony Jack (My Pony Jack)

My Pony Jack at Riding Lessons (My Pony Jack)

My Pony Jack at the Horse Show (My Pony Jack)

My Pops Is Tops! (Katie Kazoo, Switcheroo)

My Robot Buddy (Jack Jameson and Danny One)

The Mystery in New York City (Carole Marsh Mysteries: Real Kids, Real Places)

The Mystery in San Francisco (Boxcar Children)

The Mystery in the Amazon Rainforest (Carole Marsh Mysteries: Around the World in 80 Mysteries)

The Mystery in the Cave (Boxcar Children)

The Mystery in the Computer Game (Boxcar Children)

The Mystery in the Fortune Cookie (Boxcar Children)

The Mystery in the Mall (Boxcar Children)

Mystery in the Moonlight (Clue)

The Mystery in the Old Attic (Boxcar Children)

The Mystery in the Old Mine (Hardy Boys)

The Mystery in the Rocky Mountains (Carole Marsh Mysteries: Real Kids, Real Places)

Mystery in the Sand (Boxcar Children)

The Mystery in the Snow (Boxcar Children)

The Mystery in Tornado Alley (Nancy Drew)

The Mystery in Washington, D.C. (Boxcar Children)

Mystery Messages (Totally Spies!)

Mystery Mutt (Cul-de-Sac Kids)

The Mystery of Alligator Swamp (Boxcar Children)

The Mystery of Big Ben (Carole Marsh Mysteries: Around the World in 80 Mysteries)

The Mystery of Biltmore House (Carole Marsh Mysteries: Real Kids, Real Places)

The Mystery of Blackbeard The Pirate (Carole Marsh Mysteries: Real Kids, Real Places)

Mystery of Cabin Island (Hardy Boys)

The Mystery of Case D. Luc (Cul-de-Sac Kids)

Mystery of Chimney Rock (Choose Your Own Adventure)

Mystery of Crocodile Island (Nancy Drew)

The Mystery of Dead Man's Curve (Mystic Lighthouse Mysteries)

The Mystery of Death Trap Mine (Three Investigators)

Mystery of Echo Lodge (Choose Your Own Adventure)

Mystery of Metru Nui (Bionicle Adventures)

The Mystery of Mineral Gorge (Cobtown)

The Mystery of Misty Canyon (Nancy Drew)

The Mystery of Misty Island Inn (Haunting with Louisa)

The Mystery of Monster Mountain (Three Investigators)

The Mystery of Mr. Nice (Chet Gecko Mysteries)

Mystery of Smuggler's Cove (Hardy Boys)

The Mystery of the African Gray (Three Cousins Detective Club)

The Mystery of the Alamo Ghost (Carole Marsh Mysteries: Real Kids, Real Places)

The Mystery of the Attic Lion (Three Cousins Detective Club)

Mystery of the Aztec Warrior (Hardy Boys)

The Mystery of the Backdoor Bundle (Three Cousins Detective Club)

The Mystery of the Bad Luck Curse (Mystic Lighthouse Mysteries)

The Mystery of the Bamboo Bird (Dana Girls)

The Mystery of the Bermuda Triangle (Hey Arnold!)

The Mystery of the Birthday Party (Three Cousins Detective Club)

The Mystery of the Black Hole Mine (D.J. Dillon Adventures)

The Mystery of the Black Raven (Boxcar Children)

The Mystery of the Black Rhino (Hardy Boys)

The Mystery of the Blazing Cliffs (Three Investigators)

The Mystery of the Blue Ring (Polka Dot Private Eye)

The Mystery of the Book Fair (Three Cousins Detective Club)

The Mystery of the Brass-Bound Trunk (Nancy Drew)

The Mystery of the Butterfly Garden (Three Cousins Detective Club)

The Mystery of the California Mission Trail (Carole Marsh Mysteries: Real Kids, Real Places)

The Mystery of the Campus Crook (The Home School Detectives)

The Mystery of the Carousel Horse (Ten Commandments Mysteries)

Mystery of the Chinese Junk (Hardy Boys)

The Mystery of the Coon Cat (Three Cousins Detective Club)

The Mystery of the Copycat Clown (Three Cousins Detective Club)

The Mystery of the Coughing Dragon (Three Investigators)

The Mystery of the Cranky Collector (Three Investigators)

The Mystery of the Creep-Show Crooks (Three Investigators)

The Mystery of the Cupboard (The Indian in the Cupboard)

The Mystery of the Dancing Angels (Three Cousins Detective Club)

The Mystery of the Dancing Devil (Three Investigators)

The Mystery of the Dark Lighthouse (Mystic Lighthouse Mysteries)

Mystery of the Dark Tower (American Girls: History Mysteries)

The Mystery of the Dead Man's Riddle (Three Investigators)

The Mystery of the Deadly Double (Three Investigators)

Mystery of the Desert Giant (Hardy Boys)

The Mystery of the Disappearing Dinosaurs (The Freaky Joe Club)

The Mystery of the Dolphin Detective (Three Cousins Detective Club)

The Mystery of the Double Trouble (Ten Commandments Mysteries)

The Mystery of the Eagle Feather (Three Cousins Detective Club)

The Mystery of the Empty Safe (Boxcar Children)

The Mystery of the Fiery Eye (Three Investigators)

The Mystery of the Fire Dragon (Nancy Drew)

The Mystery of the Flaming Footprints (Three Investigators)

Mystery of the Flying Express (Hardy Boys)

The Mystery of the Gingerbread House (Three Cousins Detective Club)

The Mystery of the Glowing Eye (Nancy Drew)

The Mystery of the Sand Castle (Three Cousins Detective Club)

The Mystery of the Scar-Faced Beggar (Three Investigators)

The Mystery of the Screaming Clock (Three Investigators)

The Mystery of the Screech Owl (Boxcar Children)

The Mystery of the Second Map (Ten Commandments Mysteries)

The Mystery of the Secret Message (Boxcar Children)

Mystery of the Secret Room (Choose Your Own Adventure)

The Mystery of the Shrinking House (Three Investigators)

The Mystery of the Silent Idol (Ten Commandments Mysteries)

The Mystery of the Silent Nightingale (Three Cousins Detective Club)

The Mystery of the Silly Goose (Three Cousins Detective Club)

Mystery of the Silver Coins (Viking Quest)

The Mystery of the Silver Dolphin (Ten Commandments Mysteries)

The Mystery of the Silver Spider (Three Investigators)

The Mystery of the Silver Star (Hardy Boys)

The Mystery of the Singing Ghost (Boxcar Children)

The Mystery of the Singing Serpent (Three Investigators)

The Mystery of the Sinister Scarecrow (Three Investigators)

The Mystery of the Smashing Glass (Three Investigators)

The Mystery of the Sock Monkeys (Three Cousins Detective Club)

The Mystery of the Spider's Clue (Boxcar Children)

Mystery of the Spiral Bridge (Hardy Boys)

The Mystery of the Star Ruby (Boxcar Children)

The Mystery of the Stolen Bike (Arthur Chapter Books)

The Mystery of the Stolen Boxcar (Boxcar Children)

The Mystery of the Stolen Music (Boxcar Children)

The Mystery of the Stolen Statue (Third-Grade Detectives)

The Mystery of the Stolen Sword (Boxcar Children)

The Mystery of the Stone Tiger (Dana Girls)

The Mystery of the Stuttering Parrot (Three Investigators)

The Mystery of the Swimming Gorilla (The Freaky Joe Club)

The Mystery of the Talking Skull (Three Investigators)

The Mystery of the Tattletale Parrot (Ten Commandments Mysteries)

The Mystery of the Tiger's Eye (Boxcar Children)

The Mystery of the Tolling Bell (Nancy Drew)

The Mystery of the Too Many Elvises (Fletcher Mysteries)

The Mystery of the Trail of Terror (Three Investigators)

The Mystery of the Traveling Button (Three Cousins Detective Club)

The Mystery of the Traveling Tomatoes (Boxcar Children)

The Mystery of the Two-Toed Pigeon (Three Investigators)

The Mystery of the Vanishing Cave (The Home School Detectives)

The Mystery of the Vanishing Present (Ten Commandments Mysteries)

The Mystery of the Vanishing Treasure (Three Investigators)

The Mystery of the Wandering Caveman (Three Investigators)

The Mystery of the Wax Queen (Dana Girls)

The Mystery of the Wedding Cake (Three Cousins Detective Club)

Mystery of the Whale Tattoo (Hardy Boys)

The Mystery of the Whispering Mummy (Three Investigators)

The Mystery of the White Elephant (Three Cousins Detective Club)

The Mystery of the Widow's Watch (The Home School Detectives)

The Mystery of the Wild Ponies (Boxcar Children)

The Mystery of the Wild Surfer (Ladd Family)

Mystery of the Winged Lion (Nancy Drew)

Mystery of the Wizard's Tomb (Dungeons and Dragons: Knights of the Silver Dragon)

The Mystery of the Wrong Dog (Three Cousins Detective Club)

The Mystery of the Zoo Camp (Three Cousins Detective Club)

Mystery of Ura Senke (Choose Your Own Adventure)

The Mystery of Wrecker's Rock (Three Investigators)

The Mystery on Blizzard Mountain (Boxcar Children)

Mystery on Makatunk Island (Hardy Boys)

Mystery on Maui (Nancy Drew)

Mystery on Skull Island (American Girls: History Mysteries)

The Mystery on Stage (Boxcar Children)

The Mystery on the Freedom Trail (Carole Marsh Mysteries: Real Kids, Real Places)

The Mystery on the Great Barrier Reef (Carole Marsh Mysteries: Around the World in 80 Mysteries)

The Mystery on the Great Wall of China (Carole Marsh Mysteries: Around the World in 80 Mysteries)

The Mystery on the Ice (Boxcar Children)

Mystery on the Menu (Nancy Drew)

The Mystery on the Mighty Mississippi (Carole Marsh Mysteries: Real Kids, Real Places)

Mystery on the Mississippi (Bobbsey Twins: The New Bobbsey Twins)

The Mystery on the Train (Boxcar Children)

The Mystery on the Underground Railroad (Carole Marsh Mysteries: Real Kids, Real Places)

Mystery Ranch (Boxcar Children)

Mystery Ride (The Saddle Club)

Mystery Tour (Funnybones)

Mystery Unplugged (Barbie Mystery Files)

Mystery with a Dangerous Beat (Hardy Boys)

Myth Alliances (Myth Adventures)

Myth Conceptions (Myth Adventures)

Myth Directions (Myth Adventures)

M.Y.T.H. Inc. in Action (Myth Adventures)

M.Y.T.H. Inc. Link (Myth Adventures)

Myth-ing Persons (Myth Adventures)

The New Kid at School (Dragon Slayers' Academy)

The New Kid from the Black Lagoon (Black Lagoon)

New Kid in School (Lizzie McGuire)

The New Kid in School Is a Vampire Bat (Scaredy Cats)

New Kid in Town (The Hit and Run Gang)

The New Kids (B.Y. Times)

A New Kind of Super Spy (Spy Kids Adventures)

A New Little Cabin (Little House Chapter Books: Caroline)

The New Me (7th Heaven)

A New Move (Silver Blades)

New Neighbors for Nora (Riverside Kids: Nora and Teddy)

The New One (Judge and Jury)

New Pig in Town (Fitch and Chip)

New Pup on the Block (All-American Puppies)

New Rider (The Saddle Club)

The New Ron (Kim Possible (Chapter Books))

The New Ron and Mind Games (Kim Possible (TokyoPop))

The New Stephanie (Sleepover Friends)

New Student Starfish (SpongeBob SquarePants Chapter Books)

The New Teacher (First Grade)

A New Threat (Star Wars: Boba Fett)

New Voices (Angelwings)

The New Wizard of Oz (Oz)

New Year's Clean-Up (Sagwa, The Chinese Siamese Cat (Readers))

New Year's Revolution! (Secret World of Alex Mack)

New York City (SWAT (Secret World Adventure Team))

New York, New York! (Baby-Sitters Club Super Specials)

New York Nightmare! (Secret World of Alex Mack)

New York Ninjas (American Chillers)

The Newborn Pony (Pony Pals)

Next Door Witch (Magical Mystery)

The Next Passage (Animorphs: Alternamorphs)

Next Stop, New York City! (Polk Street School: Kids of the Polk Street School)

Next Stop, The White House (Lottery Luck)

The Niagara Falls Mystery (Boxcar Children)

Niagara Falls or Does It? (Hank Zipzer)

Nibble, Nibble, Jenny Archer (Jenny Archer)

Nice Shot, Cupid (Myth-O-Mania)

Nicki (American Girls: Girl of the Year)

Nick's a Chick (The Jersey)

The Night Before Easter (The Night Before . . .)

The Night Before First Grade (The Night Before . . .)

The Night Before Halloween (The Night Before . . .)

The Night Before Kindergarten (The Night Before . . .)

The Night Before Summer Camp (The Night Before . . .)

The Night Before Summer Vacation (The Night Before . . .)

The Night Before Thanksgiving (The Night Before . . .)

The Night Before the New Baby (The Night Before . . .)

The Night Before the Night Before Christmas (The Night Before . . .)

The Night Before the 100th Day of School (The Night Before . . .)

The Night Before the Tooth Fairy (The Night Before . . .)

The Night Before Valentine's Day (The Night Before . . .)

Night Bird (Once Upon America)

Night Creature (Werewolf Chronicles)

The Night Fliers (American Girls: History Mysteries)

Night Horse (Mustang Mountain)

The Night I Flunked My Field Trip (Hank Zipzer)

A Night in Terror Tower (Goosebumps)

Night in Werewolf Woods (Goosebumps: Give Yourself Goosebumps)

Night Journey to Vicksburg (Adventures in America)

Night Noises (Mole and Troll)

Night of a Thousand Claws (Goosebumps: Give Yourself Goosebumps)

Night of a Thousand Pizzas (Lunchroom)

Night of the Black Bear (Mysteries in Our National Parks)

The Night of the Blue Heads (Klooz)

Night of the Creepy Things (Rotten School)

Night of the Gargoyle (House of Horrors)

Night of the Jungle Cat (Eric Sterling, Secret Agent)

Night of the Living Cavemen (Ghostwriter)

Night of the Living Clay (Bone Chillers)

Night of the Living Dummy (Goosebumps)

Night of the Living Dummy II (Goosebumps)

Night of the Living Dummy II (Goosebumps Presents)

Night of the Living Dummy III (Goosebumps)

Night of the Living Eggnog (Wiley and Grampa's Creature Feature)

Night of the Living Gerbil (Sam and Robert)

Night of the New Magicians (Magic Tree House)

Night of the Ninjas (Magic Tree House)

Night of the Pet Zombies (Deadtime Stories)

Night of the Shifter's Moon (Unicorns of Balinor)

Night of the Soul Stealer (Last Apprentice)

Night of the Vampire (Spooksville)

The Night of the Vanishing Lights (Ladd Family)

Night of the Walking Dead, Part 1 (Mercer Mayer's Critters of the Night)

Night of the Walking Dead, Part 2 (Mercer Mayer's Critters of the Night)

Night of the Werecat (Fear Street: Ghosts of Fear Street)

Night of the Werewolf (Choose Your Own Nightmare)

Night of the Werewolf (Hardy Boys)

Night on the Mountain of Fear (Black Belt Club)

The Night Squawker (Bone Chillers)

The Night They Stole the Stanley Cup (Screech Owls)

Nightbirds on Nantucket (Wolves Chronicles)

Nothing but Net (Angel Park Hoop Stars)

Nothing's Fair in Fifth Grade (Elsie Edwards)

Nova and the Charmed Three (Star Sisterz)

Nova Command (Star Trek: The Next Generation: Starfleet Academy)

Nova Rocks! (Star Sisterz)

Now and Again (Sabrina the Teenage Witch)

Now or Never (Silver Blades)

Now We're Talking (Scrappers)

Now You See Her, Now You Don't (Sabrina the Teenage Witch)

Now You See Him, Now You Don't (Mary-Kate and Ashley: Two of a Kind)

Now You See It, Now You Don't (Abby Hayes: The Amazing Days of Abby Hayes)

Now You See It! (Mad Science)

Now You See Me . . . Now You Don't (The Zack Files)

Now You See Me, Now You Don't! (Scream Shop)

Now You See Them, Now You Don't (On the Run)

Nowhere Land (Remnants)

Nowhere to Turn (Ballet Friends)

Nuclear Jellyfish of New Jersey (American Chillers)

Nudie Dudie (Jiggy McCue)

The Nutcracker Ballet Mystery (Nancy Drew)

Nutcracker on Ice (Silver Blades)

Nutty and the Case of the Mastermind Thief (Nutty Nutsell)

Nutty and the Case of the Ski-Slope Spy (Nutty Nutsell)

Nutty Can't Miss (Nutty Nutsell)

Nutty for President (Nutty Nutsell)

Nutty Knows All (Nutty Nutsell)

Nutty, the Movie Star (Nutty Nutsell)

Nutty's Ghost (Nutty Nutsell)

Nzingha (Royal Diaries)

O

The Oaken Throne (Deptford Histories)

Oathbreaker (Chronicles of Ancient Darkness)

Obadiah the Bold (Obadiah Starbuck)

The Ocean of Osyria (Hardy Boys, Undercover Brothers: Graphic Novels)

The Octonauts and the Frown Fish (Octonauts)

The Octonauts and the Only Lonely Monster (Octonauts)

The Octonauts and the Sea of Shade (Octonauts)

The Octopus (Grandpa Spanielson's Chicken Pox Stories)

O'Dwyer and Grady Starring in Acting Innocent (O'Dwyer and Grady)

O'Dwyer and Grady Starring in the Missing Reel (O'Dwyer and Grady)

O'Dwyer and Grady Starring in Tough Act to Follow (O'Dwyer and Grady)

Odysseus in the Serpent Maze (Young Heroes)

The Odyssey (Wishbone Classics)

The Odyssey of Ben O'Neal (Outer Banks Trilogy)

Of Heroes and Villains (Misfits, Inc.)

Off Sides (Spy Kids Adventures)

Off to School, Baby Duck! (Baby Duck)

Off to See the Wizard (Sabrina the Teenage Witch)

Off-Worlder (Strange Matter)

Officer Spence Makes No Sense! (My Weird School Daze)

Ogres Don't Hunt Easter Eggs (Bailey School: The Adventures of the Bailey School Kids)

Ogres of Ohio (American Chillers)

Oh, Baby! (Katie Kazoo, Switcheroo)

Oh Boy, Amelia (Amelia)

Oh Boy, Boston! (Polk Street School: Kids of the Polk Street School)

Oh, Brother! (Lizzie McGuire)

Oh, Deer! (Animal Inn)

Oh Honestly, Angela! (Angela)

Oh No, It's Robert (Robert)

Oh Say, I Can't See (Time Warp Trio)

Oink (Pigs)

Oink Oink (Pigs)

Ojo in Oz (Oz)

Okomi and the Tickling Game (Okomi)

Okomi Climbs a Tree (Okomi)

Okomi Enjoys His Outings (Okomi)

Okomi Goes "Fishing" (Okomi)

Okomi Plays in the Leaves (Okomi)

Okomi the New Baby (Okomi)

Okomi Wakes Up Early (Okomi)

Okomi Wanders Too Far (Okomi)

Old Bear (Old Bear Stories)

Old Bear Tales (Old Bear Stories)

The Old-Fashioned Mystery (Nancy Drew Notebooks)

Old Friends, New Friends (Raggedy Ann and Andy)

Old Hat, New Hat (Berenstain Bears)

The Old Meadow (Chester Cricket)

The Old Motel Mystery (Boxcar Children)

Old Turtle's Baseball Stories (Old Turtle)

Old Turtle's Soccer Team (Old Turtle)

Old Turtle's Winter Games (Old Turtle)

The Old Witch and Her Magic Basket (Old Witch)

The Old Witch and the Crows (Old Witch)

The Old Witch and the Dragon (Old Witch)

The Old Witch and the Ghost Parade (Old Witch)

The Old Witch and the Snores (Old Witch)

The Old Witch and the Wizard (Old Witch)

The Old Witch Finds a New House (Old Witch)

The Old Witch Gets a Surprise (Old Witch)

The Old Witch Goes to the Ball (Old Witch)

The Old Witch's Party (Old Witch)

Olga Carries On (Olga da Polga)

Olga Meets Her Match (Olga da Polga)

Olga Takes Charge (Olga da Polga)

Oliver, Amanda, and Grandmother Pig (Oliver and Amanda Pig)

Oliver and Albert, Friends Forever (Oliver and Amanda Pig)

Operation (Hardy Boys, Undercover Brothers)

Operation Baby-Sitter (Soccer 'Cats)

Operation Evaporation (Mary-Kate and Ashley in Action)

Operation Sherlock (The A.I. Gang)

Operation Spy School (Adam Sharp)

Operation Squish! (Sidekicks)

The Opposite Numbers . . . (Hardy Boys, Undercover Brothers: Graphic Novels)

Orange Knight of Oz (Oz)

The Orange Outlaw (A to Z Mysteries)

Orange You Glad It's Halloween, Amber Brown? (Amber Brown: A Is for Amber)

Orbit Wipeout! (Time Surfers)

Orchard of the Crescent Moon (Gwyn Griffiths Trilogy)

The Orchid Thief (Nancy Drew: Girl Detective)

Ordinary Jack (Bagthorpe Saga)

Oregon, Sweet Oregon (Petticoat Party)

Orp (Orp)

Orp and the Chop Suey Burgers (Orp)

Orp and the FBI (Orp)

Orp Goes to the Hoop (Orp)

The Orphelines in the Enchanted Castle (Orphelines)

The Oscar J. Noodleman Television Network (Oscar J. Noodleman)

Oscar the Fancy Rat (Petsitters Club)

OSS Wilderness (Spy Kids Adventures)

Oswald's Garden (Oswald (Ready-to-Read))

The Other (Animorphs)

The Other Truth (W.I.T.C.H.— Chapter Books)

The Other Way Round (Anna)

Otto and the Bird Charmers (The Karmidee)

Otto and the Flying Twins (The Karmidee)

Otto and the Magic Potatoes (Otto)

Otto at Sea (Otto)

Otto in Africa (Otto)

Otto in Texas (Otto)

Otto in the Time of the Warrior (The Karmidee)

Our Journey West (I Am American)

Our Lips Are Sealed (Mary-Kate and Ashley Starring In . . .)

Our Strange New Land (My America: Elizabeth)

Our Veronica Goes to Petunia's Farm (Petunia)

Out and About with Anthony Ant (Anthony Ant)

Out of Bounds (Hey L'il D!)

Out of Bounds! (Super Hoops)

Out of Control (Gymnasts)

Out of Control (Rachel Yoder— Always Trouble Somewhere)

Out of Line (X Games Xtreme Mysteries)

Out of Sight, Out of Mind (Abby Hayes: The Amazing Days of Abby Hayes)

Out of the Blue (High Hurdles)

Out of the Dark (W.I.T.C.H.— Chapter Books)

Out of the Darkness (Heartland)

Out of the Deep (Mysteries in Our National Parks)

Out of This World! (Mad Science)

Out to Lunch (Katie Kazoo, Switcheroo)

Outcast (Chronicles of Ancient Darkness)

The Outcast (Guardians of Ga'Hoole)

Outcast (Warriors: Power of Three)

Outcast of Redwall (Redwall)

The Outer Space Mystery (Boxcar Children)

Outlaw Gulch (Choose Your Own Adventure)

Outlaw Red, Son of Big Red (Red)

Outlaw's Gold (CyberQuest)

Outlaws of Sherwood Forest (Choose Your Own Adventure)

The Outlaw's Silver (Hardy Boys)

Outrageously Alice (Alice)

Over & Out (Camp Confidential)

Over Sea, Under Stone (Dark Is Rising)

Over the Edge (Mysteries in Our National Parks)

Over the Hill and Just Friends (Lizzie McGuire (TokyoPop))

Over the Wall (RPM)

Overdrive (RPM)

The Overland Escape (American Adventure)

Overload (Chosen Girls)

Owen Foote, Frontiersman (Owen Foote)

Owen Foote, Mighty Scientist (Owen Foote)

Owen Foote, Money Man (Owen Foote)

Owen Foote, Second Grade Strongman (Owen Foote)

Owen Foote, Soccer Star (Owen Foote)

Owen Foote, Super Spy (Owen Foote)

Owl in the Office (Animal Ark)

Own the Zone (Duel Masters)

Ozma of Oz (Oz)

Ozoplaning with the Wizard of Oz (Oz)

P

Pa Lia's First Day (Jackson Friends)

Pacific Odyssey to California, 1905 (American Sisters)

Pack Trip (The Saddle Club)

Paddington Abroad (Paddington)

Paddington at Large (Paddington)

Paddington at Work (Paddington)

Paddington Goes to Town (Paddington)

Paddington Helps Out (Paddington)

Paddington Marches On (Paddington)

Paddington on Stage (Paddington)

Paddington on Top (Paddington)

Paddington Takes the Air (Paddington)

Paddington Takes the Test (Paddington)

Paddy Goes Traveling (Paddy Pork)

Paddy Pork, Odd Jobs (Paddy Pork)

Paddy Pork's Holiday (Paddy Pork)

Paddy to the Rescue (Paddy Pork)

Paddy Under Water (Paddy Pork)

Paddy's Evening Out (Paddy Pork)

Paddy's New Hat (Paddy Pork)

Page (Protector of the Small)

Pageant Perfect Crime (Nancy Drew: Girl Detective)

The Perfect Bone (CatDog (Chapter Books))

Perfect Challenge (Thoroughbred)

Perfect Cover (Nancy Drew: Girl Detective)

Perfect Escape (Nancy Drew: Girl Detective)

The Perfect Formula (Rugrats (Chapter Books))

The Perfect Gift (Mary-Kate and Ashley: Two of a Kind)

The Perfect Horse (Horseshoes)

Perfect Image (Thoroughbred)

Perfect Joy (Carmen Browne)

A Perfect Match (Girls Only (GO!))

A Perfect Pair (The English Roses (Chapter Books))

The Perfect Pair (Silver Blades)

A Perfect Place (My America: Joshua)

The Perfect Plan (7th Heaven)

Perfect Planet (Choose Your Own Adventure)

The Perfect Pony (Sandy Lane Stables)

Perfect Puppy (Puppy Patrol)

The Perfect Summer (Mary-Kate and Ashley Sweet 16)

Perfectly Martha (Martha)

The Perfectly Proper Prince (Princess Power)

The Perfumed Pirates of Perfidy (Charlie Small)

Peril at King's Creek (American Girls: American Girl Mysteries)

Peril at Pirate's Point (Ladd Family)

Peril at the Grand Prix (Secret Agent Jack Stalwart)

Peril in the Bessledorf Parachute Factory (Bessledorf Hotel)

Perils of Quadrant X (Lost in Space, The New Journeys)

Periwinkle and the Cave of Courage (Fairy Chronicles)

The Peskie Spell (Fairy Realm)

The Pet (Star Trek: Deep Space Nine)

Pet Day (Mr. Rose's Class)

A Pet for the Orphelines (Orphelines)

The Pet Makeover (Animal Inn)

Pet Parade (Polk Street School: Kids of the Polk Street School)

The Pet Shop (Funnybones)

The Pet Shop Mystery (Boxcar Children)

Pet Show (Peter)

The Pet-Store Sprite (Pixie Tricks)

Pete the Magnificent (Never Sink Nine)

Peter and the Secret of Rundoon (Peter and the Starcatchers)

Peter and the Shadow Thieves (Peter and the Starcatchers)

Peter and the Starcatchers (Peter and the Starcatchers)

Peter Pan/Captain Hook (Disney Villains: My Side of the Story)

Peter's Chair (Peter)

Petnapped! (Animal Inn)

The Petrified Parrot (P.C. Hawke Mysteries)

Pets Are for Keeps (Animal Inn)

Pets' Party (Animal Ark Pets)

Pet's Revenge (Edgar and Ellen)

Petunia (Petunia)

Petunia and the Song (Petunia)

Petunia, Beware! (Petunia)

Petunia, I Love You (Petunia)

Petunia Takes a Trip (Petunia)

Petunia's Christmas (Petunia)

Petunia's Treasure (Petunia)

The Phantom Freighter (Hardy Boys)

Phantom Horse (The Saddle Club)

The Phantom in the Mirror (Hank the Cowdog)

The Phantom Mudder (Jack Russell: Dog Detective)

The Phantom of 86th Street (P.C. Hawke Mysteries)

The Phantom of Pine Hill (Nancy Drew)

Phantom of the Auditorium (Goosebumps)

Phantom of the Haunted Church (Bloodhounds, Inc.)

The Phantom of the Roxy (Mind over Matter)

The Phantom of the Subway (Geronimo Stilton)

The Phantom of the Video Store (Wishbone Mysteries)

Phantom of the Waterpark (Wiley and Grampa's Creature Feature)

The Phantom of Venice (Nancy Drew)

The Phantom Pen Pal (Black Cat Club)

Phantom Submarine (Choose Your Own Adventure)

The Phantom Surfer (Dana Girls)

Phantom Writer (Red Rock Mysteries)

Phantoms Don't Drive Sports Cars (Bailey School: The Adventures of the Bailey School Kids)

Pharaoh's Tomb (CyberQuest)

The Philadelphia Adventure (Vesper Holly)

Philip Hall Likes Me, I Reckon Maybe (Philip Hall)

Phineas L. MacGuire . . . Blasts Off! (Phineas L. MacGuire)

Phineas L. MacGuire . . . Erupts! (Phineas L. MacGuire)

Phineas L. MacGuire . . . Gets Slimed! (Phineas L. MacGuire)

Phoebe's Folly (Petticoat Party)

Phoebe's Fortune (Spell Casters)

Phone Call from a Flamingo (Full House: Stephanie)

Phone Fear (Spooksville)

Phone Home, Persephone! (Myth-O-Mania)

Photo Finish (The Saddle Club)

Photo Perfect (Girls Only (GO!))

Physik (Septimus Heap)

Piano Lessons Can Be Murder (Goosebumps)

Pick a Pet, Gus! (Gus the Hedgehog)

Pick Your Poison (FaithGirlz: Boarding School Mysteries)

Pickle Pizza (Cul-de-Sac Kids)

Pickle Puss (Polk Street School: Kids of the Polk Street School)

Picnic (Kipper: Little Kippers)

Picnic Day (LazyTown (Ready to Read))

Picnic with Piggins (Piggins)

The Pictish Child (Tartan Magic Trilogy)

A Picture for Harold's Room (Harold and the Purple Crayon)

A Picture for Patti (Doug Chronicles)

Picture Me Famous (Full House: Stephanie)

A Picture of Freedom (Dear America)

The Picture-Perfect Crime (Clue)

The Picture-Perfect Mystery (Nancy Drew)

Picture This (Lizzie McGuire)

A Picture's Worth (Cyber.kdz)

Pig Latin—Not Just for Pigs! (Dragon Slayers' Academy)

Pig Pickin' (Moose and Hildy)

The Plant That Ate Dirty Socks Goes Hollywood (The Plant That Ate Dirty Socks)

The Plant That Ate Dirty Socks Goes Up in Space (The Plant That Ate Dirty Socks)

Play Ball! (Scrappers)

Play Ball, Amelia Bedelia (Amelia Bedelia)

Play-Off (Angel Park All-Stars)

Playground Bully (Barkley's School for Dogs)

The Playground Problem (Robin Hill School)

Playing Favorites (The Hit and Run Gang)

Playing for Keeps (Chestnut Hill)

Playing for Keeps (Short Stirrup Club)

Playing Games (Amy Hodgepodge)

Playing Games (Angelwings)

Playing Games (Mary-Kate and Ashley Sweet 16)

Playing with Fire (Fortune Tellers Club)

Playoff Champion (Choose Your Own Adventure)

Please Don't Eat the Children (Secrets of Dripping Fang)

Please Don't Feed the Vampire! (Goosebumps: Give Yourself Goosebumps)

Please Don't Go! (Get Ready for Gabi)

Pleasure Horse (The Saddle Club)

Plymouth Pioneers (The American Adventure)

A Pocket for Corduroy (Corduroy)

A Pocket in My Heart (Jenna V.)

Poetry in Motion (High School Musical Stories from East High)

Pogo and Pip (Best Friends)

Point Guard (Angel Park Hoop Stars)

The Poison Frog Mystery (Boxcar Children)

Poison in Paradise! (Secret World of Alex Mack)

Poisonous Pythons Paralyze Pennsylvania (American Chillers)

Polar Bear Patrol (Magic School Bus Science Chapter Books)

Polar Bears on the Path (Animal Ark)

Polar Bears Past Bedtime (Magic Tree House)

Polka Dot Pox (Pinky Dinky Doo)

Polo's Mother (Club of Mysteries)

The Poltergoose (Jiggy McCue)

Ponies at the Point (Animal Ark)

Ponies from the Past (Pony Pals)

Ponies on Parade (Pony Pals)

The Pony and the Bear (Pony Pals)

The Pony and the Haunted Barn (Pony Pals)

The Pony and the Lost Swan (Pony Pals)

The Pony and the Missing Dog (Pony Pals)

Pony Club Rider (Horseshoes)

Pony Crazy (Pony Tails)

Pony Express (Short Stirrup Club)

Pony Express (Time Soldiers)

A Pony for Keeps (Pony Pals)

Pony-4-Sale (Pony Pals)

Pony in a Package (Animal Ark)

Pony in Trouble (Animal Emergency)

A Pony in Trouble (Pony Pals)

Pony on the Porch (Animal Ark)

Pony Parade (Animal Ark Pets)

Pony Party! (Sleepover Squad)

Pony Problem (Pony Pals)

Pony Problems (Nancy Drew and the Clue Crew)

Pony-Sitters (Pony Pals)

Pony to the Rescue (Pony Pals)

Pony Trouble (Petsitters Club)

Pooh and the Storm That Sparkled (Winnie the Pooh First Readers)

Pooh Gets Stuck (Winnie the Pooh First Readers)

Pooh's Best Friend (Winnie the Pooh First Readers)

Pooh's Christmas Gifts (Winnie the Pooh First Readers)

Pooh's Easter Egg Huntt (Winnie the Pooh First Readers)

Pooh's Fall Harvest (Winnie the Pooh First Readers)

Pooh's Graduation (Winnie the Pooh First Readers)

Pooh's Halloween Parade (Winnie the Pooh First Readers)

Pooh's Hero Party (Winnie the Pooh First Readers)

Pooh's Honey Tree (Winnie the Pooh First Readers)

Pooh's Leaf Pile (Winnie the Pooh First Readers)

Pooh's Pumpkin (Winnie the Pooh First Readers)

Pooh's Scavenger Hunt (Winnie the Pooh First Readers)

Pooh's Sled Ride (Winnie the Pooh First Readers)

Pooh's Surprise Basket (Winnie the Pooh First Readers)

The Pool of Fire (Tripods)

Pool Party and Picture Day (Lizzie McGuire (TokyoPop))

Pool Party Panic! (Secret World of Alex Mack)

The Pooped Troop (Pee Wee Scouts)

Poopsie Pomerantz, Pick Up Your Feet (Casey, Tracey and Company)

Poor Mallory! (Baby-Sitters Club)

Poor Roger (Doug Chronicles)

Poor Stainless (Borrowers)

Popcorn (Bear)

Poppleton (Poppleton)

Poppleton and Friends (Poppleton)

Poppleton Everyday (Poppleton)

Poppleton Forever (Poppleton)

Poppleton Has Fun (Poppleton)

Poppleton in Fall (Poppleton)

Poppleton in Spring (Poppleton)

Poppleton in Winter (Poppleton)

Poppy (Dimwood Forest)

Poppy and Rye (Dimwood Forest)

Poppy's Babies (Brambly Hedge)

Poppy's Return (Dimwood Forest)

Poppy's Secret Wish (Ballerina Dreams)

The Popularity Potion (Abracadabra)

The Porcupine Year (Omakayas)

Porkchop to the Rescue (Doug Chronicles)

Port of Spies (Pirate School)

The Portrait in the Sand (Dana Girls)

Poseidon's Peak (Jack Sparrow)

Posh Pup (Puppy Patrol)

Possessed! (Choose Your Own Adventure)

The Possum Always Rings Twice (Chet Gecko Mysteries)

The Postcard Pest (Polk Street School: Kids of the Polk Street School)

Powder Monkey (Adventures of a Young Sailor)

The Powder Puff Puzzle (Polka Dot Private Eye)

The Power Dome (Choose Your Own Adventure)

The Power of Five (W.I.T.C.H.— Chapter Books)

Princess Sheegwa (Sagwa, The Chinese Siamese Cat (Readers))

Princess Sonora and the Long Sleep (The Princess Tales)

Princess Sophia and the Prince's Party (Tiara Club: The Tiara Club at Silver Towers)

Princess Sophia and the Sparkling Surprise (Tiara Club)

The Princess Test (The Princess Tales)

The Principal from the Black Lagoon (Black Lagoon)

The Principal's on the Roof (Fletcher Mysteries)

Prison Ship (Adventures of a Young Sailor)

Prisoner of Cabin 13 (Sabrina the Teenage Witch)

Prisoner of the Ant People (Choose Your Own Adventure)

Prisoner of War (Young Indiana Jones)

The Prisoners and the Paintings (Salt and Pepper Chronicles)

Prisoners of Peace (Star Trek: Deep Space Nine)

Prisoners of the Pit (Bionicle Legends)

Private Lily (Lily)

The Private Worlds of Julia Redfern (Julia Redfern)

The Prize (Thoroughbred: Ashleigh)

Prize-Winning Private Eyes (Lottery Luck)

Probe (Strange Matter)

The Problem Child (The Sisters Grimm)

The Problem with Here Is That It's Where I'm From (Dear Dumb Diary)

The Problem with Parents (Camp Sunnyside)

The Problem with Pelly (First Graders from Mars)

The Problem with Pen Pals (Full House: Michelle)

Problems in Paradise (Full House: Sisters)

Professor Popkin's Prodigious Polish (Coven Tree)

Program for Destruction (Hardy Boys)

Project (World of Adventure)

Project: Girl Power (FaithGirlz: Girls of 622 Harbor View)

Project: Mystery Bus (FaithGirlz: Girls of 622 Harbor View)

Project: Raising Faith (FaithGirlz: Girls of 622 Harbor View)

Project: Rescue Chelsea (FaithGirlz: Girls of 622 Harbor View)

Project: Runaway (FaithGirlz: Girls of 622 Harbor View)

Project: Secret Admirer (FaithGirlz: Girls of 622 Harbor View)

Project: Ski Trip (FaithGirlz: Girls of 622 Harbor View)

Project: Take Charge (FaithGirlz: Girls of 622 Harbor View)

Project Black Bear (China Tate)

Project UFO (Choose Your Own Adventure)

Project Wheels (Judge and Jury)

Prom Princess (Mary-Kate and Ashley: Two of a Kind)

Prom Time (Sabrina the Teenage Witch)

The Promethian Flame (The Cronus Chronicles)

The Promise (Black Stallion: Young Black Stallion)

A Promise and a Rainbow (The Double Dutch Club)

Promises (Star Wars Junior Jedi Knights)

Proof Positive (Spy X)

The Prophecy (Animorphs)

The Proposal (Animorphs)

The Proposal (Christy)

The Protester's Song (Misfits, Inc.)

P.S. Friends Forever (Full House: Stephanie)

P.S. I Really Like You (How I Survived Middle School)

P.S. Wish You Were Here (Mary-Kate and Ashley: Two of a Kind)

Psych Out (Duel Masters)

Psyched! (Angel Park Soccer Stars)

Ptolemy's Gate (The Bartimaeus Trilogy)

Public Enemies (On the Run)

Public Enemy, Number Two (The Diamond Brothers)

Puddle's ABC (Toot and Puddle)

A Puff of Pink (Little Genie)

Pugsley (The Puppy Place)

The Pumped Up Pizza Problem (Hardy Boys: Frank and Joe Hardy: The Clues Brothers)

The Pumpkin Elf Mystery (Ready, Freddy!)

The Pumpkin Patch (Robin Hill School)

Pumpkins from the Sky (Cobtown)

Punk'd and Skunked (Rotten School)

Pup and Hound (Pup and Hound)

Pup and Hound at Sea (Pup and Hound)

Pup and Hound Catch a Thief (Pup and Hound)

Pup and Hound Hatch an Egg (Pup and Hound)

Pup and Hound in Trouble (Pup and Hound)

Pup and Hound Lost and Found (Pup and Hound)

Pup and Hound Move In (Pup and Hound)

Pup and Hound Play Copycats (Pup and Hound)

Pup and Hound Scare a Ghost (Pup and Hound)

Pup and Hound Stay Up Late (Pup and Hound)

Pup at the Palace (Animal Ark)

A Pup in King Arthur's Court (Wishbone Adventures)

The Pup Tent (Ike and Mem)

The Puppet Master (Charlie Small)

Puppies in the Pantry (Animal Ark)

Puppies on Parade (Barkley's School for Dogs)

Puppy in a Puddle (Animal Ark)

Puppy Love (Barkley's School for Dogs)

Puppy Love (Puppy Patrol)

Puppy Mudge Finds a Friend (Henry and Mudge: Puppy Mudge)

Puppy Mudge Has a Snack (Henry and Mudge: Puppy Mudge)

Puppy Mudge Loves His Blanket (Henry and Mudge: Puppy Mudge)

Puppy Mudge Takes a Bath (Henry and Mudge: Puppy Mudge)

Puppy Mudge Wants to Play (Henry and Mudge: Puppy Mudge)

The Puppy Problem (Nancy Drew Notebooks)

Puppy Project (Pets, Inc.)

Puppy Puzzle (Animal Ark Pets)

Puppy School (Puppy Patrol)

Puppy Trouble (Barkley's School for Dogs)

Puppysaurus (All-American Puppies)

Raiders from the Sea (Viking Quest)

Raider's Promise (Viking Quest)

Railroad Arthur (Arthur the Kid)

Rain Dance (Phantom Stallion)

The Rainbow Fish (Rainbow Fish)

Rainbow Fish: The Dangerous Deep (Rainbow Fish)

Rainbow Fish A,B,C (Rainbow Fish)

Rainbow Fish and the Big Blue Whale (Rainbow Fish)

Rainbow Fish and the Sea Monsters' Cave (Rainbow Fish)

Rainbow Fish Finds His Way (Rainbow Fish)

Rainbow Fish 1,2,3 (Rainbow Fish)

Rainbow Fish to the Rescue! (Rainbow Fish)

Rainbow Valley (Avonlea)

The Rainbow Wand (Fairy Realm)

Raising the Bar (High Hurdles)

Rakkety Tam (Redwall)

Ralph S. Mouse (Ralph S. Mouse)

Ramona and Her Father (Ramona Quimby)

Ramona and Her Mother (Ramona Quimby)

Ramona, Forever (Ramona Quimby)

Ramona Quimby, Age 8 (Ramona Quimby)

Ramona the Brave (Ramona Quimby)

Ramona the Pest (Ramona Quimby)

Ramona's World (Ramona Quimby)

Ranch Hands (The Saddle Club)

A Rancid Little Christmas (CatDog (Chapter Books))

Randi's Missing Skates (Silver Blades Figure Eights)

Randi's Pet Surprise (Silver Blades Figure Eights)

Rani and the Fashion Divas (Star Sisterz)

Rani and the Wedding Ghost (Star Sisterz)

Rani in the Mermaid Lagoon (Disney Fairies (Chapter Books))

Raptors Revenge (PaleoJoe's Dinosaur Detective Club)

Rare Beasts (Edgar and Ellen)

Rascal (The Puppy Place)

Rat Teeth (Casey, Tracey and Company)

The Ratastrophe Catastrophe (The Illmoor Chronicles)

Rats! (Fraser Brothers)

The Raven Queen (Voyage of the Basset)

Raven Rise (Pendragon)

Raven's Gate (The Gatekeepers)

Ray and Me (Baseball Card Adventures)

Re-elect Nutty! (Nutty Nutsell)

Re-Vamped! (My Sister the Vampire)

Reach for the Stars (Abby Hayes: The Amazing Days of Abby Hayes)

Reach for the Stars (Girls Only (GO!))

The Reaction (Animorphs)

Read Me a Story (Yoko and Friends)

The Reading Champion (Mama Rex and T)

Ready, Set, Podrace! (Star Wars (DK Readers))

Real Fake (Nancy Drew: Girl Detective)

The Real Hole (Jimmy and Janet)

The Real-Skin Rubber Monster Mask (First Grade)

The Real Thing (Full House: Club Stephanie)

Reality Bites (Camp Confidential)

The Reality Bug (Pendragon)

Reality Check (Sabrina the Teenage Witch)

The Reality Machine (Choose Your Own Adventure)

Realty Tour (Chosen Girls)

Rebecca's Flame (On Time's Wing)

The Rebel Spy (The American Adventure)

Rebound! (Super Hoops)

Recess Mess (First-Grade Friends)

A Recipe for Trouble (Dish)

Recipe for Trouble (Nancy Drew Notebooks)

Reckoning (Star Wars: The Last of the Jedi)

Red Alert (Puppy Patrol)

The Red Badge of Courage (Wishbone Classics)

Red Feather Filly (Phantom Stallion)

Red Flag (NASCAR Racers)

Red-Hot Hightops (Matt Christopher Sports Stories)

Red Means Good Fortune (Goldin, Barbara Diamond) (Once Upon America)

Red Pizzas for a Blue Count (Geronimo Stilton)

Red Tide Alert (Neptune Adventures)

Red Velvet (Friends for a Season)

The Red, White, and Blue Valentine (Lincoln Lions Band)

Red Wolf's Daughter (MythQuest)

Redwall (Redwall)

Reed (Wolfbay Wings)

Reel Thrills (Hardy Boys)

Reel Trouble (Three Investigators)

Regarding the Bathrooms (Regarding the . . .)

Regarding the Bee (Regarding the . . .)

Regarding the Fountain (Regarding the . . .)

Regarding the Sink (Regarding the . . .)

Regarding the Trees (Regarding the . . .)

Reggie's Secret Admirer (Rocket Power)

Regular Guy (Guy Strang)

Reign of the Soul Eater (Spider Riders)

Rein or Shine (Horseland)

Relativity, As Explained by Professor Xargle (Professor Xargle)

Relax Max (Max)

The Reluctant Pitcher (Matt Christopher Sports Stories)

Reluctantly Alice (Alice)

Renée Marie of France (Maya's World)

The Renegade (Phantom Stallion)

The 'Rents (Lizzie McGuire)

The Reptile Room (A Series of Unfortunate Events)

The Rescue (Guardians of Ga'Hoole)

Rescue (Kidnapped)

Rescue at Marlehead Manor (Girlhood Journeys: Juliet)

The Rescue of Babar (Babar)

Rescue on Bald Mountain (Adirondack Kids)

The Rescuers (The Rescuers)

The Resistance (Animorphs)

Rest in Pieces (House of Horrors)

The Return (Animorphs)

Riddle of the Raptors (Astrosaurs)

The Riddle of the Red Purse (Polka Dot Private Eye)

The Riddle of the Ruby Gazelle (Nancy Drew)

The Riddle of the Stolen Sand (Third-Grade Detectives)

The Riddle of the Wayward Books (Wishbone Mysteries)

The Riddle of Zorfendorf Castle (Secrets of Droon)

Ride by Moonlight (Sandy Lane Stables)

Ride like the Wind (Berenstain Bears)

Ride Otto Ride (Otto)

Rider in the Night (Time Spies)

Riding Camp (The Saddle Club)

Riding Class (The Saddle Club)

The Riding Club Crime (Nancy Drew)

Riding Lesson (The Saddle Club)

Riding the Pony Express (Saddles, Stars, and Stripes)

Riding the Storm (Dolphin Diaries)

Rilla of Ingleside (Avonlea)

Rilo Buro's Summer Vacation (Strange Matter)

Rinaldo on the Run (Rinaldo)

Rinaldo, the Sly Fox (Rinaldo)

A Ring of Endless Light (Vicky Austin)

Ringin' It In (High School Musical Stories from East High)

The Ringmaster's Secret (Nancy Drew)

Ringo Saves the Day! (Pets to the Rescue)

Rinkside Romance (Silver Blades)

Rinktink in Oz (Oz)

Riot in the Night (The American Adventure)

Rip-Roaring Russell (Riverside Kids: Russell)

The Rise and Fall of the Kate Empire (Lizzie McGuire)

The Rise of the Black Wolf (Grey Griffins)

Rise of the Evening Star (Fablehaven)

The Rise of the House of McNally (Unlikely Exploits)

Rising Star (Thoroughbred)

Rising Storm (Warriors)

Risk Your Life Arcade (Choose Your Own Nightmare)

Risking the Forbidden Game (Trailblazers)

Rival Roomates (Silver Blades)

Rivals (7th Heaven)

Rivals in the Ring (Riding Academy)

The River (Brian Robeson)

The River at Green Knowe (Green Knowe)

River of No Return (Choose Your Own Adventure)

The River of Wind (Guardians of Ga'Hoole)

Riverboat Ruse (Nancy Drew: Girl Detective)

The Rivers of Zadaa (Pendragon)

Rivky's Great Idea (B.Y. Times Kid Sisters)

The Road from Roxbury (Little House: The Charlotte Years)

The Road to Balinor (Unicorns of Balinor)

The Road to Freedom (Jamestown's American Portraits)

The Road to Memphis (Logan Family)

The Road to Oz (Oz)

The Roar of the Crowd (Winning Season)

The Roaring River Mystery (Hardy Boys)

The Roaring Twenties (Young Indiana Jones Chronicles: Choose Your Own Adventure)

Roast and Toast (Mercer Mayer's Critters of the Night)

Robbie Packford—Alien Monster (Robbie Packford)

Robert and the Back-to-School Special (Robert)

Robert and the Great Escape (Robert)

Robert and the Great Pepperoni (Robert)

Robert and the Happy Endings (Robert)

Robert and the Lemming Problem (Robert)

Robert and the Practical Jokes (Robert)

Robert and the Weird and Wacky Facts (Robert)

Robert Finds a Way (Robert)

Robert Goes to Camp (Robert)

Robert Henry Hendershot (Brave Kids)

Robert Takes a Stand (Robert)

Robin in the Middle (Sweet Valley Kids)

Robinhound Crusoe (Wishbone Adventures)

The Robot Olympics (Tom Swift Young Inventor)

Robot Rampage (Buzz Beaker Brainstorm)

Robot Trouble (The A.I. Gang)

Robots Don't Catch Chicken Pox (Bailey School: The Adventures of the Bailey School Kids)

The Robot's Revenge (Hardy Boys)

Robotworld (Lost in Space, The New Journeys)

Rock and Roll Mystery (Choose Your Own Adventure)

The Rock Jockeys (World of Adventure)

The Rock 'n' Roll Mystery (Boxcar Children)

Rock 'n' Roll Renegades (Hardy Boys)

Rock 'n' Roll Robbery (Mystery Files of Shelby Woo)

Rock On (Extreme Team)

Rocked Out (X Games Xtreme Mysteries)

Rocket (Kipper: Little Kippers)

Rocket Racers (Tom Swift Young Inventor)

Rockin' Reptiles (Gator Girls)

Rocking Horse (The Saddle Club)

Rocky Road (Hardy Boys, Undercover Brothers)

The Rocky Road to Revenge (Hardy Boys)

Rocky Road Trip (Magic School Bus Science Chapter Books)

Rodeo Horse (Mustang Mountain)

Rodeo Rider (The Saddle Club)

Rodomonte's Revenge (World of Adventure)

Roll of Thunder, Hear My Cry (Logan Family)

The Roller Coaster for the Twins! (Sweet Valley Kids)

Roller Hockey Radicals (Matt Christopher Sports Stories)

Roller Hockey Rumble (Extreme Team)

Roller Star (Choose Your Own Adventure)

Rolling Thunder (NASCAR Pole Position Adventures)

Romancing the Shriek (CatDog (Chapter Books))

Rumble the Dragon's Cave (Rumble's Cave Hotel)

Rumble's Famous Granny (Rumble's Cave Hotel)

Rumblings of War (The American Adventure)

Rumor Has It (Full House: Club Stephanie)

Rumors and I've Got Rhythmic (Lizzie McGuire (TokyoPop))

Rumors at the Rink (Silver Blades)

Rumply Crumply Stinky Pin (Seriously Silly Stories)

Run Away Home (Phantom Stallion)

Run, Billy, Run (Matt Christopher Sports Stories)

Run for It (Matt Christopher Sports Stories)

Run for Your Life (On Time's Wing)

The Runamuck Dog Show (Berenstain Bears)

Runaway (The Sixth Sense: Secrets from Beyond)

The Runaway Dolls (The Doll People)

The Runaway Friend (American Girls: American Girl Mysteries)

Runaway Hamster (Sweet Valley Kids)

The Runaway in Oz (Oz)

Runaway Pony (Pony Pals)

The Runaway Pony (Sandy Lane Stables)

The Runaway Rabbit (Clifford)

The Runaway Racehorse (A to Z Mysteries)

Runaway Ralph (Ralph S. Mouse)

Runaway Wolf Pups (Animal Emergency)

Runaway Zombie (Monster Manor)

The Runaway's Revenge (Trailblazers)

Runestone (Viking Magic)

The Runner (Tillerman Cycle)

Runnin' with the Big Dawgs (Patrick's Pals)

Running Away (Angelwings)

Running Away (B.Y. Times Kid Sisters)

Running Back Conversion (NFL Monday Night Football Club)

Running on Fumes (Hardy Boys, Undercover Brothers)

Running Scared (Mysteries in Our National Parks)

Running Wild (Upchuck and the Rotten Willy)

Russell and Elisa (Riverside Kids: Elisa)

Russell and Elisa (Riverside Kids: Russell)

Russell and the Lost Treasure (Russell the Sheep)

Russell Rides Again (Riverside Kids: Russell)

Russell Sprouts (Riverside Kids: Russell)

Russell the Sheep (Russell the Sheep)

Russell's Christmas Magic (Russell the Sheep)

Ryan's Brain (Jiggy McCue)

S

Saba (American Girls: Girls of Many Lands)

The Saber-Toothed Poodnoobie (Space Brat)

Sabotage (Choose Your Own Adventure)

Sabotage! (Roller Coaster Tycoon)

Sabotage at Sports City (Hardy Boys)

Sabotage on the Set (Casebusters)

Sabrina the Schemer (Anika Scott)

Sabrina, the Teenage Boy (Sabrina the Teenage Witch)

Sabrina, the Teenage Witch (Sabrina the Teenage Witch)

Sacagawea's Strength (Blast to the Past)

The Sacrifice (Animorphs)

The Saddest Pony (Pony Pals)

Saddle Sore (The Saddle Club)

Saddle Up, Happy! (Big Apple Barn)

Saddlebags (The Saddle Club)

Safari Sleuth (Young Indiana Jones)

Safe at First (Angel Park All-Stars)

Safe at Home (Comeback Kids)

Sailing for Gold (Klondike Kid)

The St. Patrick's Day Shamrock Mystery (Dixon Twins)

Salamandastron (Redwall)

The Salamander Spell (Tales of the Frog Princess)

Salem on Trial (Sabrina the Teenage Witch)

Salem Witch (My Side of the Story)

Sally Gets a Job (Sally)

Sally Gets Silly (Monster Manor)

Sally Goes to the Beach (Sally)

Sally Goes to the Farm (Sally)

Sally Goes to the Mountains (Sally)

Sally Goes to the Vet (Sally)

Sally's Snow Adventure (Sally)

Salty Dog (Salty)

Salty Dog (Wishbone Adventures)

Salty Sails North (Salty)

The Salty Scarecrow Solution (Alex)

Salty Takes Off (Salty)

Sam and Delilah (Puppy Patrol)

Sam at the Seaside (Sam (the dog))

Sam Finds a Monster (Sam (the dog))

Sam Gets Lost (Sam (the dog))

Sam Goes Next Door (Sam (the dog))

Sam Goes to School (Sam (the dog))

Sam Is Never Scared (Sam)

Sam Is Not a Loser (Sam)

Sam Makes Trouble (Boxcar Children: Adventures of Benny and Watch)

Sam Samurai (Time Warp Trio)

Sam Tells Stories (Sam)

Samantha Learns a Lesson (American Girls: Samantha)

Samantha Saves the Day (American Girls: Samantha)

Samantha's Irish Luck (Thoroughbred)

Samantha's Journey (Thoroughbred)

Samantha's Pride (Thoroughbred)

Samantha's Surprise (American Girls: Samantha)

Sammy Keyes and the Art of Deception (Sammy Keyes)

Sammy Keyes and the Cold Hard Cash (Sammy Keyes)

Sammy Keyes and the Curse of Moustache Mary (Sammy Keyes)

Sammy Keyes and the Dead Giveaway (Sammy Keyes)

Sammy Keyes and the Hollywood Mummy (Sammy Keyes)

Sammy Keyes and the Hotel Thief (Sammy Keyes)

Sammy Keyes and the Psycho Kitty Queen (Sammy Keyes)

Sammy Keyes and the Runaway Elf (Sammy Keyes)

The School for Cats (Jenny and the Cat Club)

The School Nurse from the Black Lagoon (Black Lagoon)

The School of Fear (Star Wars: Jedi Quest)

The School of Mandy (Totally Spies!)

School of Wizardry (Circle of Magic)

The School Play (Iris and Walter)

The School Play (Yoko and Friends)

School Plot (The Floods)

The School Secretary from the Black Lagoon (Black Lagoon)

The School Skeleton (A to Z Mysteries)

School Spirit (Edison-Armstrong School)

School Spirit (Suddenly Supernatural)

School Time Style (Bratz: Lil' Bratz)

School Trouble for Andy Russell (Andy Russell)

Schoolhouse Mystery (Boxcar Children)

Schoolin' (Patrick's Pals)

Schooling Horse (The Saddle Club)

The Schoolmarm Mysteries (Girlhood Journeys: Shannon)

School's Out (Edison-Armstrong School)

School's Out! (Rachel Yoder—Always Trouble Somewhere)

The Schoolyard Mystery (Invisible Inc.)

Science Fair (Kids in Ms. Coleman's Class)

The Science Fair from the Black Lagoon (Black Lagoon)

Scooby-Doo! and the Apple Thief (Scooby Doo Readers)

Scooby-Doo! and the Big Bad Blizzard (Scooby Doo Readers)

Scooby-Doo! and the Bowling Boogeyman (Scooby Doo Mysteries)

Scooby-Doo! and the Cactus Creature (Scooby Doo Mysteries)

Scooby-Doo! and the Camping Caper (Scooby Doo Readers)

Scooby-Doo! and the Carnival Creeper (Scooby Doo Mysteries)

Scooby-Doo! and the Caveman Caper (Scooby Doo Mysteries)

Scooby-Doo! and the Deep Sea Diver (Scooby Doo Mysteries)

Scooby-Doo! and the Disappearing Donuts (Scooby Doo Readers)

Scooby-Doo! and the Fairground Phantom (Scooby Doo Mysteries)

Scooby-Doo! and the Farmyard Fright (Scooby Doo Mysteries)

Scooby-Doo! and the Football Fright (Scooby Doo Readers)

Scooby-Doo! and the Frankenstein Monster (Scooby Doo Mysteries)

Scooby-Doo! and the Ghost in the Garden (Scooby Doo Readers)

Scooby-Doo! and the Ghostly Gorilla (Scooby Doo Mysteries)

Scooby-Doo! and the Groovy Ghost (Scooby Doo Mysteries)

Scooby-Doo! and the Gruesome Goblin (Scooby Doo Mysteries)

Scooby-Doo! and the Haunted Castle (Scooby Doo Mysteries)

Scooby-Doo! and the Haunted Halloween Party (Scooby Doo Readers)

Scooby-Doo! and the Haunted Road Trip (Scooby Doo Readers)

Scooby-Doo! and the Haunted Ski Lodge (Scooby Doo Readers)

Scooby-Doo! and the Headless Horseman (Scooby Doo Mysteries)

Scooby-Doo! and the Hoopster Horror (Scooby Doo Mysteries)

Scooby-Doo! and the Howling on the Playground (Scooby Doo Readers)

Scooby-Doo! and the Howling Wolfman (Scooby Doo Mysteries)

Scooby-Doo! and the Karate Caper (Scooby Doo Mysteries)

Scooby-Doo! and the Map in the Mystery Machine (Scooby Doo Readers)

Scooby-Doo! and the Masked Magician (Scooby Doo Mysteries)

Scooby-Doo! and the Mixed-Up Museum (Scooby Doo Readers)

Scooby-Doo! and the Mummies at the Mall (Scooby Doo Readers)

Scooby-Doo! and the Mummy's Curse (Scooby Doo Mysteries)

Scooby-Doo! and the Phony Fortune-Teller (Scooby Doo Mysteries)

Scooby-Doo! and the Race Car Monster (Scooby Doo Readers)

Scooby-Doo! and the Rowdy Rodeo (Scooby Doo Mysteries)

Scooby-Doo! and the Runaway Robot (Scooby Doo Mysteries)

Scooby-Doo! and the Scary Skateboarder (Scooby Doo Mysteries)

Scooby-Doo! and the School Play Surprise (Scooby Doo Readers)

Scooby-Doo! and the Sea Monster Scare (Scooby Doo Readers)

Scooby-Doo! and the Seashore Slimer (Scooby Doo Mysteries)

Scooby-Doo! and the Secret Santa Mystery (Scooby Doo Readers)

Scooby-Doo! and the Shiny Spooky Knights (Scooby Doo Readers)

Scooby-Doo! and the Sinister Sorcerer (Scooby Doo Mysteries)

Scooby-Doo! and the Snack Snatcher (Scooby Doo Readers)

Scooby-Doo! and the Snow Monster (Scooby Doo Mysteries)

Scooby-Doo! and the Spooky Strikeout (Scooby Doo Mysteries)

Scooby-Doo! and the Sunken Ship (Scooby Doo Mysteries)

Scooby-Doo! and the Thanksgiving Mystery (Scooby Doo Readers)

Scooby-Doo! and the Toy Store Terror (Scooby Doo Mysteries)

Scooby-Doo! and the Valentine's Day Dognapping (Scooby Doo Readers)

Scooby-Doo! and the Vampire's Revenge (Scooby Doo Mysteries)

Scooby-Doo! and the Vicious Viking (Scooby Doo Mysteries)

Scooby-Doo! and the Virtual Villain (Scooby Doo Mysteries)

Scooby-Doo! and the Witch Doctor (Scooby Doo Mysteries)

Scooby-Doo! and the Zombie's Treasure (Scooby Doo Mysteries)

Scout (The Puppy Place)

A Scout Is Born (Sailor Moon Novels)

Scouts on Film (Sailor Moon Novels)

Scrambled (Sam and Stephanie)

Scrambled Brains! (Totally Spies!)

Scream Around the Campfire (Graveyard School)

Scream Around the Campfire (Shadow Zone)

Scream for Ice Cream (Nancy Drew and the Clue Crew)

The Secret at Solitaire (Nancy Drew)

The Secret at the Gatehouse (Dana Girls)

The Secret at the Hermitage (Dana Girls)

The Secret at the Polk Street School (Polka Dot Private Eye)

The Secret Birthday (Yoko and Friends)

The Secret Book Club (Main Street)

Secret City (Pyrates)

The Secret Club (Go Girl)

Secret Crush (Mary-Kate and Ashley: So Little Time)

The Secret Engine (Speed Racer)

Secret Horse (The Saddle Club)

Secret Identity (Nancy Drew: Girl Detective)

Secret Identity (Shredderman)

The Secret in the Dark (Nancy Drew)

The Secret in the Kitchen (China Tate)

The Secret in the Old Attic (Nancy Drew)

The Secret in the Old Lace (Nancy Drew)

The Secret in the Old Well (Dana Girls)

The Secret in the Spooky Woods (Nancy Drew Notebooks)

The Secret in the Stars (Nancy Drew)

Secret in the Tower (Time Spies)

The Secret in Time (Nancy Drew)

The Secret Ingredient (Katie Lynn Cookie Company)

The Secret Laundry Monster Files (Hank the Cowdog)

The Secret Life of Mary Anne Spier (Baby-Sitters Club)

The Secret Lost at Sea (Nancy Drew)

The Secret Lunch Special (2nd-Grade Friends)

The Secret of Cacklefur Castle (Geronimo Stilton)

The Secret of Candlelight Inn (Nancy Drew)

The Secret of Cravenhill Castle (Nicki Holland)

The Secret of Fantasy Forest (Sweet Valley Kids)

The Secret of Jungle Park (Bobbsey Twins: The New Bobbsey Twins)

The Secret of Lizard Island (Eric Sterling, Secret Agent)

Secret of Lost Arrow (Fortune Tellers Club)

The Secret of Lost Lake (Dana Girls)

The Secret of Mirror Bay (Nancy Drew)

The Secret of Mystery Hill (Choose Your Own Adventure)

The Secret of Phantom Lake (Three Investigators)

The Secret of Pirates' Hill (Hardy Boys)

The Secret of Red Gate Farm (Nancy Drew)

The Secret of Richmond Manor (Bonnets and Bugles)

The Secret of Robber's Cave (Cabin Creek Mysteries)

The Secret of Sagawa Lake (Sam, Dog Detective)

The Secret of Shadow Ranch (Nancy Drew)

The Secret of Shady Glen (Nancy Drew)

The Secret of Shark Reef (Three Investigators)

The Secret of Sigma Seven (Hardy Boys)

The Secret of Skeleton Island (Three Investigators)

The Secret of Skeleton Reef (Hardy Boys)

The Secret of Skull Mountain (Hardy Boys)

The Secret of Stoneship Woods (Spy Gear)

The Secret of Terror Castle (Three Investigators)

The Secret of the Attic (Magic Attic Club)

Secret of the Caves (Hardy Boys)

The Secret of the Crooked Cat (Three Investigators)

The Secret of the Deep Woods (Screech Owls)

The Secret of the Desert Stone (Cooper Kids)

The Secret of the Digimon Emperor (Digimon Digital Monsters)

Secret of the Dolphins (Choose Your Own Adventure)

The Secret of the Fiery Chamber (Nancy Drew)

The Secret of the Flying Cows (Klooz)

The Secret of the Forgotten Cave (Nancy Drew)

The Secret of the Forgotten City (Nancy Drew)

The Secret of the Ghostly Hot Rod (Bloodhounds, Inc.)

The Secret of the Golden Pavilion (Nancy Drew)

The Secret of the Green Skin (Third-Grade Detectives)

The Secret of the Haunted Mirror (Three Investigators)

The Secret of the Howling Cave (American Adventure)

The Secret of the Indian (The Indian in the Cupboard)

The Secret of the Island Treasure (Hardy Boys)

The Secret of the Jade Ring (Dana Girls)

Secret of the Lizard People (Star Trek: The Next Generation: Starfleet Academy)

The Secret of the Lost Tunnel (Hardy Boys)

The Secret of the Mask (Boxcar Children)

The Secret of the Minstrel's Guitar (Dana Girls)

Secret of the Ninja (Choose Your Own Adventure)

The Secret of the Old Clock (Nancy Drew)

The Secret of the Old Mill (Hardy Boys)

The Secret of the Plant That Ate Dirty Socks (The Plant That Ate Dirty Socks)

Secret of the Pyramids (Choose Your Own Adventure)

The Secret of the Sacred Temple (Secret Agent Jack Stalwart)

The Secret of the Sand Castle (Bobbsey Twins: The New Bobbsey Twins)

The Secret of the Scarlet Hand (Nancy Drew)

The Secret of the Shark Pit (Ladd Family)

The Secret of the Silver Dolphin (Dana Girls)

Secret of the Sirens (The Companions Quartet)

The Secret of the Soldier's Gold (Hardy Boys)

Secret of the Spa (Nancy Drew: Girl Detective)

The Shaggy Man of Oz (Oz)

Shake, Rattle, and Hurl! (Rotten School)

Shake Up (Angel Park Soccer Stars)

The Shakespeare Stealer (The Shakespeare Stealer)

Shakespeare's Scribe (The Shakespeare Stealer)

Shakespeare's Spy (The Shakespeare Stealer)

Shampoozel (Seriously Silly Stories)

Shamrock Shenanigans (Sabrina the Teenage Witch)

Shanghaied to China (Trailblazers)

Shani's Scoop (B.Y. Times)

Shanna's Lost Shoe (Shanna First Readers)

Shanna's Party Surprise (Shanna First Readers)

Shanna's Pizza Party (Shanna First Readers)

Shape-Shifter (Pangur Ban)

Shapes (X Files)

Shards of Alderaan (Star Wars Young Jedi Knights)

Shards of the Oracle (Spider Riders)

Sharing Time Troubles (First-Grade Friends)

Shark (Wolfbay Wings)

Shark Shock (Soccer Shock)

Shark Tooth Tale (Ready, Freddy!)

The Shattered Helmet (Hardy Boys)

The Shattering (Guardians of Ga'Hoole)

Sheep in a Jeep (Sheep)

Sheep in a Shop (Sheep)

Sheep on a Ship (Sheep)

Sheep Out to Eat (Sheep)

Sheep Take a Hike (Sheep)

Sheep Trick or Treat (Sheep)

Sheepdog in the Snow (Animal Ark)

Shelley Shock (Soccer Shock)

Shelter (So Weird)

Sheltie and the Runaway (Sheltie!)

Sheltie Finds a Friend (Sheltie!)

Sheltie in Danger (Sheltie!)

Sheltie Rides to Win (Sheltie!)

Sheltie Saves the Day! (Sheltie!)

Sheltie the Shetland Pony (Sheltie!)

Sheltie to the Rescue (Sheltie!)

Shendu Escapes! (Jackie Chan Adventures)

Shetland in the Shed (Animal Ark)

Shhhhh! (Hardy Boys, Undercover Brothers: Graphic Novels)

Shield of Fear (Hardy Boys)

The Shifting Sands (Deltora: Deltora Quest)

Shiloh (Shiloh)

Shiloh Season (Shiloh)

Shining's Orphan (Thoroughbred)

Ship Ahoy (Lottery Luck)

Ship of Ghouls (Goosebumps: Give Yourself Goosebumps)

Shipwreck on the Pirate Islands (Geronimo Stilton)

Shipwreck Saturday (Little Bill)

Shiver Me, Shipwreck! (Pirate School)

The Shluffmuffin Boy Is History (Secrets of Dripping Fang)

Shock Wave (Time Surfers)

A Shocker on Shock Street (Goosebumps)

Shockwave (Star Trek: Enterprise)

Shoelaces and Brussels Sprouts (Alex)

Shoeless Joe and Me (Baseball Card Adventures)

Shoo, Fly Guy! (Fly Guy)

Shoot for the Hoop (Matt Christopher Sports Stories)

Shoot the Works (Three Investigators)

Shop 'Til You Drop . . . Dead (Goosebumps: Give Yourself Goosebumps)

The Shore Road Mystery (Hardy Boys)

Shore Thing (Mary-Kate and Ashley: Two of a Kind)

Short-Wave Mystery (Hardy Boys)

Shortstop from Tokyo (Matt Christopher Sports Stories)

The Shortstop Who Knew Too Much (Tales from the Sandlot)

Shot from Midfield (Alden All Stars)

Show and Tell Mystery (Bobbsey Twins: The New Bobbsey Twins)

Show-and-Tell Surprise (Clifford)

The Show-and-Tell War (Adam Joshua Capers)

The Show-and-Tell War, and Other Stories About Adam Joshua (Adam Joshua Capers)

Show Horse (The Saddle Club)

Show Judge (The Saddle Club)

Show Jumper (The Saddle Club)

Show Jumper Wanted (Horseshoes)

The Show-Off (Moose and Hildy)

Show Time! (Super Hoops)

Showdown (Choose Your Own Adventure)

Showdown at Camp Wannaweep (Kim Possible (Chapter Books))

Showdown at the Mall (Sabrina the Teenage Witch)

Shredderman (Shredderman)

The Shrieking Shadow (Spy Gear)

The Shrinking of Treehorn (Treehorn)

Shrinky Jinx (Powerpuff Girls Chapter Books)

Shrinky Pinky! (Pinky Dinky Doo)

The Shrouded Moon (Usagi Yojimbo)

The Shrunken Head (Grandpa Spanielson's Chicken Pox Stories)

Shut Your Mouth (The Midnight Library)

Siamese in the Sun (Animal Ark)

The Sickness (Animorphs)

Sidekicks (Sidekicks)

Sideline Blues, by Wil (The Broadway Ballplayers)

Sidesaddle (The Saddle Club)

Sidetracked to Danger (Hardy Boys)

Sideways Arithmetic from Wayside School (Wayside School)

Sideways Stories from Wayside School (Wayside School)

The Siege (Guardians of Ga'Hoole)

Sienna the Saturday Fairy (Rainbow Magic: Fun Day Fairies)

Sierra (Spirit of the Cimarron)

The Sierra Gold Mystery (Dana Girls)

Sierra's Steeplechase (Thoroughbred)

The Sight (Warriors: Power of Three)

The Sign of the Crooked Arrow (Hardy Boys)

Sign of the Dragon (MacGregor Family Adventure)

The Sign of the Falcon (Nancy Drew)

Sign of the Ox (Jackie Chan Adventures)

Sign of the Shapeshifter (Dungeons and Dragons: Knights of the Silver Dragon)

The Slave and the Lion (Wishbone: The Early Years)

Slaves of the Mastery (The Wind of Fire)

Sleep Out (Christopher)

The Sleep Over (First-Grade Friends)

Sleeping Beauty/Maleficent (Disney Princesses: My Side of the Story)

The Sleeping Giant of Goll (Secrets of Droon)

Sleeping Over (Sleepover Squad)

Sleepless in LazyTown (LazyTown (8 x 8 Books))

Sleepover (Go Girl)

The Sleepover (Iris and Walter)

Sleepover and Over (Fairly OddParents)

Sleepover Larry (Larry the Polar Bear)

The Sleepover Secret (Mary-Kate and Ashley: Two of a Kind)

Sleepover Sleuths (Nancy Drew and the Clue Crew)

Sleight of Dan (Nancy Drew Graphic Novels)

Sliced Heather on Toast (China Tate)

Slide, Danny, Slide (Matt Christopher Sports Stories)

Slime Lake (Graveyard School)

Slime Time (Bone Chillers)

Slim's Goodbye (Hank the Cowdog)

Slip, Slide, and Slap Shot (Hardy Boys: Frank and Joe Hardy: The Clues Brothers)

Slippers at Home (Slippers)

Slippers at School (Slippers)

Slippers Loves to Run (Slippers)

The Slippery Slope (A Series of Unfortunate Events)

The Slithers Buy a Boa (Slimeballs)

Slugger Mike (Never Sink Nine)

The Slumber Party Secret (Nancy Drew Notebooks)

The Slump (The Hit and Run Gang)

The Sly Spy (Olivia Sharp, Agent for Secrets)

Sly the Sleuth and the Food Mysteries (Sly the Sleuth)

Sly the Sleuth and the Pet Mysteries (Sly the Sleuth)

Sly the Sleuth and the Sports Mysteries (Sly the Sleuth)

A Small Person Far Away (Anna)

Smallpox Strikes! (The American Adventure)

Smashing Lumpkins (Powerpuff Girls Chapter Books)

Smile and Say "Woof!" (Full House: Michelle)

Smile, Ernest and Celestine (Ernest and Celestine)

Smoke Jumper (Choose Your Own Adventure)

Smoke Screen (FaithGirlz: Boarding School Mysteries)

The Smoke Screen Mystery (Hardy Boys)

Smugglers on Grizzly Mountain (Eric Sterling, Secret Agent)

The Smuggler's Treasure (American Girls: History Mysteries)

The Snack Attack Mystery (Invisible Inc.)

Snaggle Doodles (Polk Street School: Kids of the Polk Street School)

Snake Alarm! (Petsitters Club)

Snarf Attack, Underfoodle, and the Secret of Life (Riot Brothers)

The Snarling Suspect (Klooz)

Snatched (Bloodwater Mysteries)

Snatched from Earth (I Was a Sixth Grade Alien)

The Sneezing Spell (Abracadabra)

Snoopy, Flying Ace to the Rescue (Peanuts)

The Snottle (Jiggy McCue)

A Snout for Chocolate (Grandpa Spanielson's Chicken Pox Stories)

The Snow Angel (Forever Angels)

Snow Bunnies (Sweet Valley: Unicorn Club)

Snow Day (Barkley's School for Dogs)

Snow Day (Robin Hill School)

The Snow Dog (Clifford)

Snow Fun (Powerpuff Girls Chapter Books)

Snow Is My Favorite and My Best (Charlie and Lola)

The Snow Lady (Tales of Trotter Street)

Snow Monster Mystery (Bailey City Monsters)

The Snow Queen's Surprise (Nancy Drew Notebooks)

Snow Ride (The Saddle Club)

The Snow Spider (Gwyn Griffiths Trilogy)

Snow Valentines (Harry and Emily)

Snow War (Kids in Ms. Coleman's Class)

Snow White and the Seven Aliens (Seriously Silly Stories)

Snow White/The Queen (Disney Princesses: My Side of the Story)

Snow White's Secret (Disney Princess Secrets)

Snowball (The Puppy Place)

The Snowball Fight (Little Bear: Maurice Sendak's Little Bear)

Snowboard Champ (Matt Christopher Sports Stories)

Snowboard Maverick (Matt Christopher Sports Stories)

Snowboard Racer (Choose Your Own Adventure)

Snowboard Showdown (Matt Christopher Sports Stories)

Snowbound (Baby-Sitters Club Super Specials)

Snowbound (The Wild Thornberrys)

Snowbound Mystery (Boxcar Children)

Snowbound with Betsy (Betsy)

Snowflake and Sparkle (Best Friends)

The Snowman Surprise (Nancy Drew Notebooks)

The Snowy Day (Peter)

So Far from Home (Dear America)

So Not the Drama! (Kim Possible: Pick a Villain)

So What? (First Grade)

So You Want to Be a Wizard (Wizardry)

Soccer Circus (Hobie Hanson)

Soccer Duel (Matt Christopher Sports Stories)

The Soccer Game (LazyTown (Ready to Read))

Soccer Halfback (Matt Christopher Sports Stories)

Soccer Hero (Matt Christopher Sports Stories)

The Soccer Mystery (Boxcar Children)

Soccer Scoop (Matt Christopher Sports Stories)

Soccer Shock (Soccer Shock)

The Soccer Shoe Clue (Nancy Drew Notebooks)

Soccer Star (Choose Your Own Adventure)

South of the Border (Young Indiana Jones Chronicles: Choose Your Own Adventure)

South Pole or Bust (an Egg) (Time Warp Trio)

South Pole Sabotage (Choose Your Own Adventure)

Southpaw (Winning Season)

Space and Beyond (Choose Your Own Adventure)

Space Bingo (Time Surfers)

Space Brat (Space Brat)

Space Camp (Star Trek: Deep Space Nine)

Space Case (Nancy Drew Notebooks)

Space Case (Totally Spies!)

Space Case (Treasure Planet)

Space Dog and Roy (Space Dog)

Space Dog and the Pet Show (Space Dog)

Space Dog in Trouble (Space Dog)

Space Dog, the Hero (Space Dog)

Space Explorers (Magic School Bus Science Chapter Books)

Space Food (Lunchroom)

The Space Hotel (Tom Swift Young Inventor)

The Space Mission Adventure (Ziggy and the Black Dinosaurs)

Space Patrol (Choose Your Own Adventure)

Space Race (Goners)

Space Race (Ormingat)

The Space Ship in the Park (Space Ship Under the Apple Tree)

The Space Ship Returns to the Apple Tree (Space Ship Under the Apple Tree)

The Space Ship Under the Apple Tree (Space Ship Under the Apple Tree)

Space Station Mars (Clubhouse)

Space Vampire (Choose Your Own Adventure)

Spaced Out! (Roller Coaster Tycoon)

Spaniel in a Stocking (Animal Ark)

Spark of Suspicion (Hardy Boys)

Sparring and Charring (Lilo and Stitch: The Series)

Special Delivery Mess (Silver Blades Figure Eights)

Special Gifts (Cobble Street Cousins)

A Special Place (The Fairy Lair)

The Speckled Rose of Oz (Oz)

Spectacular Spain (SWAT (Secret World Adventure Team))

Spectacular Stone Soup (Polk Street: New Kids at the Polk Street School)

The Specter from the Magician's Museum (Lewis Barnavelt)

Speed Demon (NASCAR Pole Position Adventures)

Speed Surf (Internet Detectives)

Speed Times Five (Hardy Boys)

Speedy in Oz (Oz)

Spell Bound (Goners)

Spell of the Screaming Jokers (Fear Street: Ghosts of Fear Street)

The Spell of the Sorcerer's Skull (Johnny Dixon)

Spelling Bee (Kids in Ms. Coleman's Class)

Spellsinger (Avalon 1: Web of Magic)

The Spider Beside Her (Graveyard School)

Spider McGhee and the Hoopla (Slam Dunk)

The Spider Sapphire Mystery (Nancy Drew)

Spider's Baby-Sitting Job (Spider)

Spider's First Day at School (Spider)

Spiderweb for Two (Melendy Family)

Spiderwort and the Princess of Haiku (Fairy Chronicles)

Spies in Disguise (Totally Spies!)

Spies in Space (Totally Spies!)

Spies vs. Spy (Totally Spies!)

Spike It! (Matt Christopher Sports Stories)

Spike the Special Puppy (Puppy Friends)

Spiked Snow (X Games Xtreme Mysteries)

Spinout (NASCAR Pole Position Adventures)

Spirit (Spirit of the Cimarron)

Spirit Walker (Chronicles of Ancient Darkness)

Spitting Image (Goners)

Splash Crash! (Time Surfers)

Splash Party (American Gold Swimmers)

The Splintering of Time (Gideon the Cutpurse)

Split Decision (American Gold Gymnasts)

Split Decision (Spirit of the Game)

Split Ends (Edgar and Ellen)

Split Image (Journey of Allen Strange)

Splitting Image (Strange Matter)

Splosh! (Kipper: Little Kippers)

SpongeBob Airpants (SpongeBob SquarePants Chapter Books)

SpongeBob NaturePants (SpongeBob SquarePants Chapter Books)

SpongeBob Saves the Day (SpongeBob SquarePants (TokyoPop))

The SpongeBob SquarePants Movie (SpongeBob SquarePants (TokyoPop))

SpongeBob Superstar (SpongeBob SquarePants Chapter Books)

Spookier Than a Ghost (Harry and Emily)

Spooktacular Stories (Scary Godmother)

Spooky and the Bad Luck Raven (Spooky the Cat)

Spooky and the Ghost Cat (Spooky the Cat)

Spooky and the Witch's Goat (Spooky the Cat)

Spooky and the Wizard's Bats (Spooky the Cat)

Spooky Night (Spooky the Cat)

The Spooky Sleepover (Eagle-Eye Ernie)

Spooky Spells (Bailey City Monsters)

Spooky's Nightmare (Mijos)

Spore (Star Wars Galaxy of Fear)

Sport (Harriet M. Welsch)

Sporty Sprite (Pixie Tricks)

Spot and Friends Dress Up (Spot)

Spot and Friends Play (Spot)

Spot at Home (Spot)

Spot at Play (Spot)

Spot at the Fair (Spot)

Spot Bakes a Cake (Spot)

Spot Counts from One to Ten (Spot)

Spot Goes Splash! (Spot)

Spot Goes to a Party (Spot)

Spot Goes to School (Spot)

Spot Goes to the Beach (Spot)

Spot Goes to the Circus (Spot)

Spot Goes to the Farm (Spot)

Spot Goes to the Park (Spot)

Spot in the Garden (Spot)

Spot Joins the Parade (Spot)

Spot Learns to Count (Spot)

Spot Looks at Colors (Spot)

Stanley and the Magic Lamp (Stanley)

Stanley, Flat Again (Stanley)

Stanley in Space (Stanley)

Stanley's Christmas Adventure (Stanley)

The Star Cloak (Fairy Realm)

Star for a Day (Silver Blades Figure Eights)

The Star Ghost (Star Trek: Deep Space Nine)

Star in Danger (Thoroughbred)

A Star in the Breaking (McGee and Me!)

Star Jumper (Journal of a Cardboard Genius)

Star Light, Star Bright (Cassie Perkins)

Star of Shadowbrook Farm (Thoroughbred: Ashleigh's Collection)

Star of the Parade (Sweet Valley Kids)

The Star of the Show (Clifford)

Star Paws (Puppy Patrol)

Star Pilot (Star Wars (DK Readers))

Star Quality (Hollywood Sisters)

Star Quality (Sister Sister)

The Star Queen (Sunken Kingdom)

Star Rider (The Saddle Club)

Star-Spangled Babies (Rugrats (Chapter Books))

Star Spangled Summer (Holiday Five)

Star Status (Girls Only (GO!))

Star the Snowy Kitten (Kitten Friends)

Star Wars (Choose Your Own Star Wars Adventures)

Star Wars: Return of the Jedi (Choose Your Own Star Wars Adventures)

Star Wars: The Empire Strikes Back (Choose Your Own Star Wars Adventures)

Stardust's Foal (Thoroughbred: Ashleigh)

Starfall (Star Trek: The Next Generation: Starfleet Academy)

Stargazer (Land of Elyon)

Starlight (Warriors: The New Prophecy)

Starlight Christmas (The Saddle Club)

Starlight Comes Home (Starlight)

Starlight Shines for Miranda (Starlight)

Starlight, Star Bright (Starlight)

Starlight's Courage (Starlight)

Starlight's Shooting Star (Starlight)

Starring Alex (Girls of Avenue Z)

Starring Brody (Girls of Avenue Z)

Starring Dorothy Kane (Kane Family)

Starring First Grade (First Grade)

Starring Grace (Grace)

Starring Jolene (Girls of Avenue Z)

Starring Mirette and Bellini (Mirette)

Starring Rosie (Ballet Slippers)

Starring Sammie (Girls of Avenue Z)

Starring Stephanie (Sleepover Friends)

Starring the Baby-Sitters Club (Baby-Sitters Club Super Specials)

Starring Winston Egbert (Sweet Valley Kids)

Starring You and Me (Mary-Kate and Ashley Sweet 16)

Stars and Sparks on Stage (Ziggy and the Black Dinosaurs)

Star's Chance (Thoroughbred)

The Stars from Mars (Slapshots)

Stars in Their Eyes (Baker's Dozen)

Star's Inspiration (Thoroughbred)

Starshine! (Starshine!)

Starshine and the Fanged Vampire Spider (Starshine!)

Starshine at Camp Crescent Moon (Starshine!)

Starshine on TV (Starshine!)

Starstruck (Thoroughbred)

Starstruck Stephanie (Sleepover Friends)

Starting Gate (The Saddle Club)

Starting Over (The American Adventure)

Starting School (Edison-Armstrong School)

Starting with Alice (Alice)

The Starving Time (My America: Elizabeth)

Statue of Liberty Adventure (Choose Your Own Adventure)

The Statue Walks at Night (Casebusters)

Stay Away from the Treehouse (Fear Street: Ghosts of Fear Street)

Stay in Bed, Davy! (Davy)

Stay Out of the Basement (Goosebumps)

Stay Up Late (Mama Rex and T)

Staying Balanced (Skating Dreams)

Stealing Home (Matt Christopher Sports Stories)

Stealing Home (Spirit of the Game)

Stealing Home (Thomas and Grandfather)

Steer Clear of Haunted Hill (Ghostwriter)

Step Fourth, Mallory! (Mallory)

Stephanie and the Magician (Sleepover Friends)

Stephanie and the Wedding (Sleepover Friends)

Stephanie Strikes Back (Sleepover Friends)

Stephanie's Big Story (Sleepover Friends)

Stephanie's Family Secret (Sleepover Friends)

Stepping on the Cracks (Gordy Smith)

The Steps Up the Chimney (Magician's House Quartet)

Sterling's Second Chance (Thoroughbred)

Steven's Big Crush (Sweet Valley Kids)

Steven's Twin (Sweet Valley Kids)

Stevie (The Saddle Club)

Sticks and Stones and Doggie Bones (Barkley's School for Dogs)

Sticks and Stones and Skeleton Bones (Hobie Hanson)

Still Just Grace (Just Grace)

Still More Stories from Grandma's Attic (Grandma's Attic)

The Sting of the Scorpion (Hardy Boys)

Stink (Stink)

Stink and the Great Guinea Pig Express (Stink)

Stink and the Incredible Super-Galactic Jawbreaker (Stink)

Stink and the World's Worst Super-Stinky Sneakers (Stink)

Stink Trek (The Adventures of Uncle Stinky)

Stinky & Stan Blast Off! (The Grosse Adventures)

Stinky and Successful (Riot Brothers)

Stinky Business (Don't Touch That Remote!)

Sudden Turn (Roller Coaster Tycoon)

Suddenly! (Preston)

Suddenly Last Summer (Camp Confidential)

Suddenly Twins! (The Magical States of America)

Sugar and Spice Advice (Full House: Stephanie)

Sugar Snow (Little House: My First Little House Books)

Sugarcane Island (Choose Your Own Adventure)

Summer Begins (The Callahan Cousins)

The Summer Camp Mysteries (Cam Jansen)

The Summer Camp Mystery (Boxcar Children)

Summer Daze (B.Y. Times)

Summer Daze (Sister Sister)

Summer Horse (The Saddle Club)

Summer in the Country (Girlhood Journeys: Marie)

Summer Jobs (Baker's Dozen)

Summer Love (Hey Arnold!)

Summer MacCleary, Virginia, 1749 (American Diaries)

Summer of the Sea Serpent (Magic Tree House)

Summer Party (Cobble Street Cousins)

Summer Reading Is Killing Me (Time Warp Trio)

Summer Rider (The Saddle Club)

Summer School (Kids in Ms. Coleman's Class)

Summer School! What Genius Thought Up That? (Hank Zipzer)

Summer Shenanigans (Story Girl)

Summer Story (Brambly Hedge)

Summer Switch (Annabel Andrews)

A Summer to Remember (Heartland)

Summer Vacation (Kenan and Kel)

Summer with Elisa (Riverside Kids: Elisa)

A Summer Without Horses (The Saddle Club)

Summertime in the Big Woods (Little House: My First Little House Books)

Summertime Secrets (Full House: Club Stephanie)

The Sun King (Secret Agent MJJ)

Sunchaser's Quest (Unicorns of Balinor)

Sunflower Diary (On Time's Wing)

Sunflower Girl (Jenna V.)

Sunny-Side Up (Polk Street School: Kids of the Polk Street School)

Sunny the Yellow Fairy (Rainbow Magic: Rainbow Fairies)

Sunset (Warriors: The New Prophecy)

The Sunset Gates (The Unicorn's Secret)

Sunset of the Sabertooth (Magic Tree House)

Sunwing (Silverwing)

Super Amos (Culpepper Adventures)

Super Beach Myster (Sleepover Friends)

Super Brown Switch (NFL Monday Night Football Club)

Super Detective Little Bill (Little Bill (Nickelodeon))

Super Diaper Baby 2 (Captain Underpants: Super Diaper Baby)

The Super-Duper Blooper (AstroKids)

The Super-Duper Cookie Caper (Bobbsey Twins: The New Bobbsey Twins)

Super Duper Pee Wee! (Pee Wee Scouts)

The Super-Duper Sleepover Party (Full House: Michelle)

Super Emma (Emma)

Super-Fine Valentine (Little Bill)

Super Fly Guy (Fly Guy)

The Super-Powered Sneeze (Jimmy Sniffles)

Super-Secret Valentine (Ready, Freddy!)

Super Sneak (Hannah Montana)

Super Soccer Freak Show (Wiley and Grampa's Creature Feature)

Super Underwear . . . and Beyond (Super Goofballs)

Superbike (Choose Your Own Adventure)

Supercharged Infield (Matt Christopher Sports Stories)

Supercomputer (Choose Your Own Adventure)

Superduper Teddy (Riverside Kids: Nora and Teddy)

Superfudge (Fudge)

Superhero . . . or Super Thief? (Maximum Boy)

Superheroes (Amelia Rules!)

Superior Saturday (Keys to the Kingdom)

Superkid! (Adam Joshua Capers)

Superstar Babes (Babes)

Superstar Spies (Spy Kids Adventures)

Superstar Team (Angel Park All-Stars)

Supertwins and the Sneaky, Slimy Book Worms (Supertwins)

Supertwins and Tooth Trouble (Supertwins)

Supertwins Meet Bad Dogs from Space (Supertwins)

Supertwins Meet the Dangerous Dino-Robots (Supertwins)

Supreme Overlord Penelope (Atomic Betty)

Surak's Soul (Star Trek: Enterprise)

Surf Holiday (Mary-Kate and Ashley: So Little Time)

Surf Monkeys (Choose Your Own Adventure)

Surf, Sand, and Secrets (Mary-Kate and Ashley: Two of a Kind)

Surfboard to Peril (Miss Mallard)

The Surfing Corpse (P.C. Hawke Mysteries)

Surf's Up! (Go Girl)

Surf's Up (Rocket Power)

Surf's Up, Geronimo! (Geronimo Stilton)

A Surprise for Princess Ellie (Pony-Crazed Princess)

Surprise Island (Boxcar Children)

Surprise, Surprise! (Mary-Kate and Ashley: Two of a Kind)

Surprise! Surprise! (Sweet Valley Kids)

A Surprise Twist (Silver Blades)

Surprises According to Humphrey (Humphrey)

Survival (Remnants)

Survival (Star Trek: The Next Generation: Starfleet Academy)

Survival at Sea (Choose Your Own Adventure)

Survival in the Storm (Dear America)

Survival School (Class Pets)

Survivor (Jurassic Park Adventures)

Survivor (The Sixth Sense: Secrets from Beyond)

The Suspect in the Smoke (Nancy Drew)

The Tale of the Secret Mirror (Are You Afraid of the Dark?)

The Tale of the Shimmering Shell (Are You Afraid of the Dark?)

The Tale of the Sinister Statues (Are You Afraid of the Dark?)

The Tale of the Souvenir Shop (Are You Afraid of the Dark?)

The Tale of the Stalking Shadow (Are You Afraid of the Dark?)

The Tale of the Terrible Toys (Are You Afraid of the Dark?)

The Tale of the Three Wishes (Are You Afraid of the Dark?)

Tale of the Toa (Bionicle Chronicles)

Tale of the Unfinished Masterpiece (Rugrats Files)

The Tale of the Virtual Nightmare (Are You Afraid of the Dark?)

The Tale of the Zero Hour (Are You Afraid of the Dark?)

The Tale of Toph (Avatar: The Earth Kingdom Chronicles)

A Tale of Two Alisons (Magic Attic Club)

A Tale of Two Sitters (Wishbone Adventures)

The Tale of Zuko (Avatar: The Earth Kingdom Chronicles)

Talent Night Aboard the Hogwash (Piganeers)

The Talent Show (Jackson Friends)

The Talent Show from the Black Lagoon (Black Lagoon)

Talent Show Scaredy-Pants (Ready, Freddy!)

The Talented Clementine (Clementine)

Tales from Bikini Bottom (SpongeBob SquarePants (TokyoPop))

Tales from Bikini Bottom (SpongeBob SquarePants (TokyoPop))

Tales from Moominvalley (Moomintroll)

Tales from the Hood (The Sisters Grimm)

Tales of a Fourth Grade Nothing (Fudge)

Tales of Amanda Pig (Oliver and Amanda Pig)

The Tales of Olga da Polga (Olga da Polga)

Tales of Oliver Pig (Oliver and Amanda Pig)

Tales of the Masks (Bionicle Chronicles)

Tales of the Wicked Witch (Wicked Witch)

Tales Too Scary to Tell at Camp (Graveyard School)

Talking It Over (B.Y. Times)

The Talking T. Rex (A to Z Mysteries)

Talking to Dragons (Enchanted Forest Chronicles)

Tall Man in the Pivot (Matt Christopher Sports Stories)

Tallulah the Tuesday Fairy (Rainbow Magic: Fun Day Fairies)

Tallyho, Pinkerton (Pinkerton)

The Taming of the Pyre (Mystic Knights of Tir Na Nog)

Tangled Fortunes (Cousins Quartet)

Tangled Web (Star Wars: The Last of the Jedi)

The Tangled Web (American Girls: American Girl Mysteries)

Tanya and Emily in a Dance for Two (Tanya)

Tanya and the Magic Wardrobe (Tanya)

Tanya and the Red Shoes (Tanya)

Tanya Steps Out (Tanya)

The Tap Dance Mystery (Eagle-Eye Ernie)

Tap Dance Trouble (Full House: Michelle)

Tara and Tiree, Fearless Friends! (Pets to the Rescue)

Taran Wanderer (Prydain Chronicles)

Tarantula Toes (Cul-de-Sac Kids)

Tarot Says Beware (Herculeah Jones)

Tartok the Ice Beast (Beast Quest)

A Taste for Noah (Noah)

A Taste of Danger (Nancy Drew)

Taste of Thailand (SWAT (Secret World Adventure Team))

Tatiana Comes to America (Doll Hospital)

Tattle Tails (Barkley's School for Dogs)

The Tattletale Mystery (Boxcar Children)

Tattoo of Death (Choose Your Own Adventure)

Taxi to Intrigue (Miss Mallard)

Tea at the Treedome (SpongeBob SquarePants Chapter Books)

Teach Us, Amelia Bedelia (Amelia Bedelia)

Teacher Creature (Bone Chillers)

The Teacher from Heck (Rotten School)

The Teacher from the Black Lagoon (Black Lagoon)

Teacher Trouble (LazyTown (8 x 8 Books))

Teacher Trouble (My Sister, the Ghost)

Teacher's Pest (Powerpuff Girls Chapter Books)

Teacher's Pet (B.Y. Times Kid Sisters)

Teacher's Pet (David and Goliath)

Teacher's Pet (Edison-Armstrong School)

Teacher's Pet (Kids in Ms. Coleman's Class)

Teacher's Pet (Puppy Patrol)

Teacher's Pet: Book 7: Maggie (Wild at Heart)

Teacher's Pets (Clifford)

Team Play (The Saddle Club)

Team Player (The Jersey)

Team Player (Scrappers)

Team Player (Thoroughbred)

The Team That Couldn't Lose (Matt Christopher Sports Stories)

The Team That Stopped Moving (Matt Christopher Sports Stories)

Team Trouble (Gymnasts)

Teaming Up (Soccer Stars)

Teamwork at Camp Tioga (Keystone Stables)

Teasing Trouble (Hopscotch Hill School)

Technical Foul (Winning Season)

Teddy Bears ABC (Teddy Bears)

Teddy Bears at the Seaside (Teddy Bears)

Teddy Bears Cure a Cold (Teddy Bears)

Teddy Bears Go Shopping (Teddy Bears)

Teddy Bears' Moving Day (Teddy Bears)

Teddy Bears 1 to 10 (Teddy Bears)

Teddy Bears Stay Indoors (Teddy Bears)

Teddy Bears Take the Train (Teddy Bears)

The Teen Model Mystery (Nancy Drew)

Teenage Spaceland (Butt-Ugly Martians Chapter Books)

Teeny Weeny Zucchinis (Pee Wee Scouts)

Teetoncey (Outer Banks Trilogy)

Think, Corrie, Think! (Here Come the Brownies)

Think Pink! (Pinky Dinky Doo)

Third Grade Ghouls! (Third Grade)

Third-Grade Reporter (Nancy Drew Notebooks)

Third Grade Stinks! (Third Grade)

Third Grade Wedding Bells? (Third Grade)

Third Planet from Altair (Choose Your Own Adventure)

The Third Wish (Fairy Realm)

Thirteen (Kobie Roberts)

Thirteen (Winnie Perry)

Thirteen Means Magic (Abracadabra)

Thirteen Ways to Sink a Sub (Hobie Hanson)

The Thirteenth Pearl (Nancy Drew)

This Body's Not Big Enough for Both of Us (The Zack Files)

This Generation of Americans (Jamestown's American Portraits)

This Gum for Hire (Chet Gecko Mysteries)

This Is Actually My Party (Charlie and Lola)

This Is the Bear (Fred Bear)

This Is the Bear and the Bad Little Girl (Fred Bear)

This Is the Bear and the Picnic Lunch (Fred Bear)

This Is the Bear and the Scary Night (Fred Bear)

This Rocks! (The Jersey)

Thistle and the Shell of Laughter (Fairy Chronicles)

Thomas (Deptford Histories)

Thomas: 1778, Patriots on the Run (American Adventures)

Thomas in Danger (American Adventures)

Thomas Jefferson (Dear Mr. President)

Thorn in Her Side (The Princess School)

Thor's Hammer (Voyage of the Basset)

The Threat (Animorphs)

Three Cheers for Keisha (Magic Attic Club)

Three Cheers for Tacky (Tacky the Penguin)

A Three-Cornered Mystery (Dana Girls)

Three Evil Wishes (Fear Street: Ghosts of Fear Street)

Three of Diamonds (The Diamond Brothers)

Three-Point Play (Spirit of the Game)

Three-Ring Terror (Hardy Boys)

Three Rotten Eggs (Hamlet Chronicles)

The Three-Seated Space Ship (Space Ship Under the Apple Tree)

Three-Star Billy (Very Worst Monster)

Three Strikes and You're a Monster! (Scream Shop)

Three's a Crowd (Full House: Club Stephanie)

Three's a Crowd (CatKid)

Thrill on the Hill (Nancy Drew Notebooks)

Thrill Ride (Hardy Boys, Undercover Brothers)

Thriller Diller (Three Investigators)

Thrills, Spills, and Cosmic Chills (Weird Planet)

Throne of Zeus (Choose Your Own Adventure)

Through the Black Hole (Choose Your Own Adventure)

Through the Medicine Cabinet (The Zack Files)

Through the Year with Harriet (Harriet)

Through Thick and Thin (Baker's Dozen)

Thump, Quack, Moo (Duck)

Thunder on the Sierra (Adventures in America)

Thunder Strangers (Power Rangers: Ninja Storm)

Thunder Valley (World of Adventure)

Thunderhead (Flicka)

Thursday Trials (Juli Scott Super Sleuth)

Thy Friend, Obadiah (Obadiah Starbuck)

Tianna the Terrible (Anika Scott)

Tic-Tac Terror (Hardy Boys)

Tick Tock, You're Dead! (Goosebumps: Give Yourself Goosebumps)

Ticket Trouble (Nancy Drew and the Clue Crew)

Tide Stealers (Sunken Kingdom)

Tidy Titch (Titch)

Tie Breaker (Matt Christopher Sports Stories)

Tiger Counter (Nancy Drew Graphic Novels)

Tiger Moth and the Dragon Kite Contest (Tiger Moth)

Tiger Moth, Insect Ninja (Tiger Moth)

Tiger Tale (Sabrina the Teenage Witch)

Tiger, Tiger (X Files)

Tigers at Twilight (Magic Tree House)

Tigger's Family Tree (Winnie the Pooh First Readers)

Tiggers Hate to Lose (Winnie the Pooh First Readers)

Tight End (Matt Christopher Sports Stories)

Tight Rein (The Saddle Club)

Tik-Tok of Oz (Oz)

Tiki Doll of Doom (Bone Chillers)

Tilly the Tidy Puppy (Puppy Friends)

Time and Mr. Bass (Tyco Bass)

Time Benders (World of Adventure)

The Time Bike (The Hall Family)

Time for Battle (The American Adventure)

A Time for Courage (Dear America)

The Time Machine and Other Cases (Einstein Anderson)

The Time Paradox (Artemis Fowl)

Time Spies When You're Having Fun (Totally Spies!)

Time Stops for No Mouse (Hermux Tantamoq Adventures)

Time Terror (Spooksville)

Time Thaw (Batman (Scholastic Reader))

The Time Thief (Gideon the Cutpurse)

A Time to Be Brave (Owly Graphic Novels)

A Time to Climb (Rocket Power)

A Time to Dance (My America: Virginia)

Time to Fly (Wild at Heart)

Time to Rhyme with Calico Cat (Calico Cat)

A Time to Share (The Wild Thornberrys)

The Time Travel Trap (Twisted Journeys)

Time Twister (Journal of a Cardboard Genius)

Totally Snowed (X Games Xtreme Mysteries)

Totally Toxic (The Caped 6th Grader)

Touch the Sky (The Young Underground)

Touchdown for Tommy (Matt Christopher Sports Stories)

Touchdown Pass (Chip Hilton Sports Series)

Touching the Waves (Dolphin Diaries)

Tough at the Top (Gymnasts)

Tough Choices (Once Upon America)

Tough Choices for Roxie (Best Friends)

Tough Jim (First Grade)

Tough to Tackle (Matt Christopher Sports Stories)

Tourist Trap (Edgar and Ellen)

Tournament Crisis (Chip Hilton Sports Series)

Tournament Trouble (Soccer Stars)

Tow-Away Stowaway (AstroKids)

The Tower at the End of the World (Lewis Barnavelt)

The Tower of Geburah (The Archives of Anthropos)

Tower of the Elf King (Secrets of Droon)

The Tower Treasure (Hardy Boys)

The Toy Shop of Terror (Choose Your Own Nightmare)

Toy Terror (Goosebumps: Give Yourself Goosebumps)

Toy Trouble (Strange Matter)

The Toys' Wedding (Little Bear: Maurice Sendak's Little Bear)

Track of the Bear (Choose Your Own Adventure)

The Track of the Zombie (Hardy Boys)

Tracked by the Wolf Pack (Ladd Family)

Trade Wind Danger (Nancy Drew: Girl Detective)

The Tragic School Bus (Graveyard School)

Trail Mates (The Saddle Club)

The Trail of the Jedi (Star Wars: Jedi Quest)

The Trail of the Screaming Teenager (Polka Dot Private Eye)

Trail Ride (The Saddle Club)

Trail Ride Terror (Horseland)

Trails of Treachery (Nancy Drew: Girl Detective)

Train Wreck (Survival!)

Training for Trouble (Hardy Boys)

Traitor (2099)

A Traitor Among the Boys (Hatford Boys)

Traitor in the Tower (Trailblazers)

Traitor in Williamsburg (American Girls: American Girl Mysteries)

Trapped! (Baker's Dozen)

Trapped! (Pete the Cat)

Trapped (Wild at Heart)

Trapped at Sea (Hardy Boys)

Trapped at the Bottom of the Sea (Cooper Kids)

Trapped Beyond the Magic Attic (Magic Attic Club)

Trapped in Bat Wing Hall (Goosebumps: Give Yourself Goosebumps)

Trapped in the Mall (Sweet Valley: Unicorn Club)

Trapped in the Museum of Unnatural History (The Zack Files)

Trapped in Time (Star Trek: Deep Space Nine)

Trapped in Time (Zenda)

Trapped in Tiny Town (Deadtime Stories)

Trapped in Toyland (Sweet Valley Kids)

Trapped! (Crime Through Time)

Trash Bash (Pee Wee Scouts)

Trash or Treasure? (Nancy Drew Notebooks)

Trash Talk (Super Hoops)

Trashmaster (Patrick's Pals)

The Travels of Babar (Babar)

Travels of Thelonious (Fog Mound)

Travels with Jotaro (Usagi Yojimbo)

Treachery and Betrayal at Jolly Days (Secrets of Dripping Fang)

The Treasure at Dolphin Bay (Hardy Boys)

Treasure at Eagle Mountain (Lassie)

Treasure Diver (Choose Your Own Adventure)

The Treasure Haunt (Ghostville Elementary)

The Treasure Hunt (Little Bill)

The Treasure in the Royal Tower (Nancy Drew)

The Treasure of El Patrón (World of Adventure)

The Treasure of Alpheus Winterborn (Anthony Monday)

The Treasure of Bessledorf Hill (Bessledorf Hotel)

The Treasure of Green Knowe (Green Knowe)

The Treasure of Mount Fate (Twisted Journeys)

The Treasure of Skeleton Reef (Wishbone Mysteries)

Treasure of the Onyx Dragon (Choose Your Own Adventure)

Treasure of the Orkins (Secrets of Droon)

Treasure Planet (Treasure Planet)

Treasure Trouble (Pirate School)

Treasures from Grandma (Grandma's Attic)

Tree House Mystery (Boxcar Children)

Tree House Trouble (Cul-de-Sac Kids)

Treehorn Times Three (Treehorn)

Treehorn's Treasure (Treehorn)

Treehorn's Wish (Treehorn)

The Treehouse Kids (B.Y. Times Kid Sisters)

Trek of Doom (Young Indiana Jones)

Tremble at the Terror of Zis-Boom-Bah (Billy Hooten, Owlboy)

Trial and Terror (Hardy Boys)

Trial by Fire (Avalon 1: Web of Magic)

Trial by Fire (Bionicle Adventures)

Trial by Poison (Trailblazers)

The Trial of Magic (Age of Magic Trilogy)

Tricia and the Money Mystery (Twelve Candles Club)

Tricia's Got T-R-O-U-B-L-E! (Twelve Candles Club)

Trick or . . . Trapped (Goosebumps: Give Yourself Goosebumps)

Trick or Treat, Smell My Feet (Gilbert)

Trick-or-Trouble (Hardy Boys)

Trick or Trouble? (Holiday Five)

Tricks and Treats (Pee Wee Scouts)

Tricks of the Trade (Hardy Boys)

Trickster (Wild at Heart)

Tricky Business (Hardy Boys)

The Trip (Louie)

Tucket's Gold (The Tucket Adventures)

Tucket's Home (The Tucket Adventures)

Tucket's Ride (The Tucket Adventures)

Tuff's Luck (Puppy Patrol)

Tug of Love (Puppy Patrol)

Tumbling Ghosts (Gymnasts)

Tummy Trouble (Clifford)

Tundra 2000 (NASCAR Racers)

Tune into Terror (Strange Matter)

The Tunnel Behind the Waterfall (Magician's House Quartet)

Tunnel Vision (Spy X)

Turkey Trouble (Holiday Friends)

Turkey Trouble (Nancy Drew Notebooks)

Turkey Trouble (Polk Street School: Kids of the Polk Street School)

Turkey Trouble: Adam Joshua's Thanksgiving (Adam Joshua Capers)

The Turkey's Side of It (Adam Joshua Capers)

A Turn for Noah (Noah)

Turn Off the TV (Mama Rex and T)

Turn Up the Heat (High School Musical Stories from East High)

The Turnabout Trick (Trick Books)

The Turning Point (Skating Dreams)

Turning Up the Heat (Dish)

Turns on a Dime (Goldstone Trilogy)

The Turret (The Rescuers)

The Turtle (Lighthouse Family)

Turtle and Snake and the Christmas Tree (Turtle and Snake)

Turtle and Snake at Work (Turtle and Snake)

Turtle and Snake Fix It (Turtle and Snake)

Turtle and Snake Go Camping (Turtle and Snake)

Turtle and Snake's Day at the Beach (Turtle and Snake)

Turtle and Snake's Spooky Halloween (Turtle and Snake)

Turtle and Snake's Valentine's Day (Turtle and Snake)

The Turtle-Hatching Mystery (Dog Watch)

Tut Tut (Time Warp Trio)

'Twas the Fight Before Christmas (McGee and Me!)

Tweeb Trouble (Kim Possible: Pick a Villain)

Twelve (Winnie Perry)

The Twelve Tasks of Flavia Gemina (Roman Mysteries)

26 Fairmount Avenue (26 Fairmount Avenue)

Twenty Thousand Wags Under the Sea (Wishbone Adventures)

23 Ways to Mess Up Valentine's Day (Willimena Rules!)

Twice the Trouble! (The Magical States of America)

Twilight (Warriors: The New Prophecy)

Twin Again (My Sister, the Ghost)

The Twin Dilemma (Nancy Drew)

Twin Trouble (Kids in Ms. Coleman's Class)

Twin Troubles (Full House: Stephanie)

Twins and the Wild West (Sweet Valley Kids)

Twin's Big Pow-Wow (Sweet Valley Kids)

Twins Go to the Hospital (Sweet Valley Kids)

Twins in Trouble (B.Y. Times)

Twins' Mystery Teacher (Sweet Valley Kids)

Twist and Shout (Mary-Kate and Ashley: Two of a Kind)

Twisted (Undercover Girl)

The Twisted Claw (Hardy Boys)

The Twisted Tale of Tiki Island (Goosebumps: Give Yourself Goosebumps)

Twister and Shout (McGee and Me!)

Twister on Tuesday (Magic Tree House)

Twister Trouble (Magic School Bus Science Chapter Books)

Twister's Big Break (Rocket Power)

Two Dog Biscuits (Jimmy and Janet)

Two-For-One Christmas Fun (Full House: Stephanie)

Two for the Road (Mary-Kate and Ashley: Two of a Kind)

Two Friends Too Many (Peanut Butter and Jelly)

Two Heads Are Better Than One (Abby Hayes: The Amazing Days of Abby Hayes)

Two Heads Are Better Than One (Alien Clones from Outer Space)

Two-Minute Drill (Comeback Kids)

Two on the Town (Full House: Sisters)

Two Princesses (Barbie (Step Into Reading))

Two Promises too Many! (The Wild Thornberrys)

Two Strikes on Johnny (Matt Christopher Sports Stories)

2095 (Time Warp Trio)

The Two Towers (Lord of the Rings)

2-T's Spoof Video (Butt-Ugly Martians Chapter Books)

Two's a Crowd (Mary-Kate and Ashley: Two of a Kind)

Typhoon! (Choose Your Own Adventure)

Typhoon Island (Hardy Boys)

U

The Ultimate (Animorphs)

Ultimate Challenge (Spirit of the Game)

The Ultimate Challenge (Goosebumps: Give Yourself Goosebumps)

Ultimate Risk (Thoroughbred)

Ultimate Scoring Machine (NFL Monday Night Football Club)

U.N. Adventure (Choose Your Own Adventure)

Un-happy New Year, Emma! (Emma)

The Un-Magician (Outcast)

Unbridled Fury (Thoroughbred)

Uncivil Acts (Nancy Drew: Girl Detective)

Uncle's Big Surprise (Jackie Chan Adventures)

The Undead Express (Shadow Zone)

Under Copp's Hill (American Girls: History Mysteries)

Under Loch and Key (Goners)

Under Pressure (W.I.T.C.H.— Graphic Novels)

Under the Big Top (Lassie)

Under the Magician's Spell (Goosebumps: Give Yourself Goosebumps)

Under the Radar (Tom Swift Young Inventor)

A Very Lizzie Christmas (Lizzie McGuire)

A Very Merry Christmas (Geronimo Stilton)

A Very Special Secret (Angelina Ballerina: Angelina's Diary)

The Very Worst Monster (Very Worst Monster)

The Veteran's Day Visitor (2nd-Grade Friends)

Victoria (Royal Diaries)

Victory Goal (Angel Park Soccer Stars)

Victory Ride (Short Stirrup Club)

Vidia and the Fairy Crown (Disney Fairies (Chapter Books))

Viking It and Liking It (Time Warp Trio)

Viking Raiders (Choose Your Own Adventure)

Viking Ships at Sunrise (Magic Tree House)

The Viking Symbol Mystery (Hardy Boys)

Vikings Don't Wear Wrestling Belts (Bailey School: The Adventures of the Bailey School Kids)

The Vile Village (A Series of Unfortunate Events)

Violet (Flower Girls)

Violet Makes a Splash (Sister Magic)

Violet Strikes a Chord (Sister Magic)

Violet Takes the Cake (Sister Magic)

The Viper (Silly Thrillers with Peggy the Pig)

Virtual Cody (Cody)

Virtual Vampires of Vermont (American Chillers)

Virtual Zone (On Time's Wing)

The Virus (Lost in Space, The New Journeys)

A Visit to the Dentist (Little Bill (Nickelodeon))

A Visit to the Farm (Little Bill (Nickelodeon))

The Visitor (Animorphs)

Visitors (Nightmare Room)

Visser (Animorphs: Animorph Chronicles)

Viva Heather! (Magic Attic Club)

A Voice in the Wind (Starbucks Twins Mysteries)

Voices (The Midnight Library)

Voices at Whisper Bend (American Girls: History Mysteries)

Volcano! (Choose Your Own Adventure)

The Volcano (Secret Agent MJJ)

The Volcano Goddess Will See You Now (The Zack Files)

Voltage (X Files)

Von Skalpel's Experiment (Monster Manor)

Voodoo Child (Tales of Terror)

The Voodoo Plot (Hardy Boys)

Vote! (The Complicated Life of Claudia Cristina Cortez)

Vote for Katie Suzanne (Katie Kazoo, Switcheroo)

Vote 4 Amelia (Amelia)

Voting Rights Days (Hitty's Travels)

Vox (Edge Chronicles)

Voyage of Fear (Bionicle Adventures)

Voyage of Slaves (Castaways of the Flying Dutchman)

The Voyage of the Dawn Treader (Chronicles of Narnia)

Voyage of the Jaffa Wind (Secrets of Droon)

Voyage on the Great Titanic (Dear America)

Voyage to a Free Land, 1630 (American Sisters)

Voyage to the Volcano (Magic School Bus Science Chapter Books)

Voyagers of the Silver Sand (Secrets of Droon)

The Voyages of Doctor Dolittle (Doctor Dolittle and the Pirates) (Doctor Dolittle)

W

Wacky Jacks (Houdini Club Magic Mystery)

Wagon Trail (The Saddle Club)

The Wailing Siren Mystery (Hardy Boys)

Waiting for Stardust (Thoroughbred: Ashleigh)

Waiting in the Wings (Ballet Friends)

Wake-Up Call (Sabrina the Teenage Witch)

Wake Up, Emily, It's Mother's Day (Polk Street School: Kids of the Polk Street School)

The Walkie-Talkie Mystery (Nancy Drew Notebooks)

The Walking Snowman (Hardy Boys: Frank and Joe Hardy: The Clues Brothers)

The Walnut Cup (Elliot's Park)

Walter the Farting Dog (Walter, the Farting Dog)

Walter the Farting Dog: Trouble at the Yard Sale (Walter, the Farting Dog)

Walter the Farting Dog Goes on a Cruise (Walter, the Farting Dog)

Walter's Lucky Socks (Never Sink Nine)

The Wanderer's Road (Usagi Yojimbo)

Wanted (Hardy Boys, Undercover Brothers)

Wanted: One Perfect Boy (Silver Blades)

Wanted—Mud Blossom (The Blossom Family)

War! (B.Y. Times)

War (Watchers)

War Comes to Willy Freeman (Arabus Family Saga)

The War of the Ember (Guardians of Ga'Hoole)

War of the Trolls (Scream Shop)

War of the Wardrobes (Mary-Kate and Ashley: Two of a Kind)

War Strikes (The American Adventure)

War with the Evil Power Master (Choose Your Own Adventure)

War with the Mutant Spider Ants (Choose Your Own Adventure)

Warehouse Rumble (Hardy Boys)

The Warning (Animorphs)

Warriors (Lost in Space, The New Journeys)

The Warrior's Challenge (Trailblazers)

War's End (The American Adventure)

Warton and Morton (Warton and Morton)

Warton and the Castaways (Warton and Morton)

Warton and the Contest (Warton and Morton)

Warton and the King of the Skies (Warton and Morton)

Warton and the Traders (Warton and Morton)

Warton's Christmas Eve Adventure (Warton and Morton)

The Werewolf of Fever Swamp (Goosebumps)

The Werewolf of Twisted Tree Lodge (Goosebumps: Give Yourself Goosebumps)

Werewolf Skin (Goosebumps)

Werewolves Don't Go to Summer Camp (Bailey School: The Adventures of the Bailey School Kids)

Werewolves Don't Run for President (Bailey School: The Adventures of the Bailey School Kids)

Werewolves for Lunch (Mercer Mayer's Critters of the Night)

West Along the Wagon Road, 1852 (American Sisters)

The West Coast Murders (Screech Owls)

West to a Land of Plenty (Dear America)

Western Pony (Pony Pals)

Western Riding Winner (Horseland)

Western Star (The Saddle Club)

Westmark (Westmark)

Westward to Home (My America: Joshua)

Westward, Whoa! (Kenan and Kel)

The Whale (Lighthouse Family)

Whales on Stilts (M. T. Anderson's Thrilling Tales)

What a Blast (Mad Science)

What a Catch! (Angel Park All-Stars)

What a Doll! (Sabrina the Teenage Witch)

What a Scare, Jesse Bear! (Jesse Bear)

What a Trip, Amber Brown (Amber Brown: A Is for Amber)

What a Year (26 Fairmount Avenue)

What Can You Grow on a Family Tree? (Full House: Stephanie)

What Does a Witch Need? (Old Witch)

What Eric Knew (Sebastian Barth)

What Goes Up . . . (Nancy Drew Graphic Novels)

What Goes Up Must Come Down (Abby Hayes: The Amazing Days of Abby Hayes)

What Happened at Midnight? (Hardy Boys)

What Happened to Patrick's Dinosaurs? (Patrick's Dinosaurs)

What Have You Done, Davy? (Davy)

What Is a Wookiee? (Star Wars (DK Readers))

What Makes You Happy (Amelia Rules!)

What Planet Are You From, Clarice Bean? (Clarice Bean)

What Price Honor (Star Trek: Enterprise)

What Scares You the Most? (Nightmare Room Thrillogy)

What Time Is It? (Seven Little Monsters)

What Would Joey Do? (Joey Pigza)

Whatever! (The Complicated Life of Claudia Cristina Cortez)

Whatever Happened to My Dog Cuddles? (Robbie Packford)

What's a Daring Detective Like Me Doing in the Doghouse? (Stevie Diamond Mysteries)

What's a Serious Detective Like Me Doing in Such a Silly Movie? (Stevie Diamond Mysteries)

What's Cooking, Jamela? (Jamela)

What's Cooking, Jenny Archer? (Jenny Archer)

What's That, Mittens? (Mittens)

What's the Matter, Davy? (Davy)

What's the Matter with Herbie Jones? (Herbie Jones)

What's Under My Bed? (Grandpa)

What's Wrong with My Pony? (Pony Pals)

Wheel of Misfortune (Dragon Slayers' Academy)

Wheel Wizards (Matt Christopher Sports Stories)

Wheels (Tales of Trotter Street)

When Bad Snakes Attack Good Children (Secrets of Dripping Fang)

When Christmas Comes Again (Dear America)

When Frank Was Four (Australian Children)

When Freedom Comes (My America: Hope)

When Hitler Stole Pink Rabbit (Anna)

When I Dream of Heaven (Jamestown's American Portraits)

When I Grow Up (Yoko and Friends)

When I Was Nine (James Stevenson's Autobiographical Stories)

When in Rome (Mary-Kate and Ashley Starring In . . .)

When Jenny Lost Her Scarf (Jenny and the Cat Club)

When Lightning Strikes (W.I.T.C.H.—Adventures)

When Moms Attack! (Lizzie McGuire)

When Moms Attack and Misadventures in Babysitting (Lizzie McGuire (TokyoPop))

When Pigs Fly (Fitch and Chip)

When Second Graders Attack (Horace Splattly: The Cupcaked Crusader)

When the Chips Are Down (Cyber.kdz)

When the Mission Padre Came to the Rancho (I Am American)

When the Past Is a Present (Amelia Rules!)

When the Tripods Came (Tripods)

When Tiny Was Tiny (Tiny)

When Vera Was Sick (Vera)

When Will I Read? (First Grade)

When Will This Cruel War Be Over? (Dear America)

When Wishes Come True (Fairy School)

Where Are My Shoes? (Pinky Dinky Doo)

Where Are You, Ernest and Celestine? (Ernest and Celestine)

Where Are You Going, Little Mouse? (Little Mouse)

Where Have All the Flowers Gone? (Dear America)

Where Have You Gone, Davy? (Davy)

Where in the World Is Sabrina Spellman? (Sabrina the Teenage Witch)

Where Is Christmas, Jesse Bear? (Jesse Bear)

Where There's Hope (Horseshoe Trilogies)

Where There's Hope (Horseshoe Trilogies)

Where's Gary? (SpongeBob SquarePants Chapter Books)

Where's Iggy? (Petsitters Club)

Where's Jamela? (Jamela)

Where's Nancy (Nancy Drew: Girl Detective)

Where's Patti (Sleepover Friends)

Where's Spot (Spot)

Where's the Baby? (Very Worst Monster)

Will You Mind the Baby, Davy? (Davy)

Will You Please Feed Our Cat? (Grandpa)

Willa by Heart (The Wedding Planner's Daughter)

Willie's Birthday (Peter's Neighborhood)

Willow Chase, Kansas Territory,1847 (American Diaries)

Willow the Wednesday Fairy (Rainbow Magic: Fun Day Fairies)

Will's Choice (Orphan Train Children)

Will's Story (Young Americans: Colonial Williamsburg)

Willy and Hugh (Willy)

Willy the Champ (Willy)

Willy the Dreamer (Willy)

Willy the Wimp (Willy)

Willy the Wizard (Willy)

Willy's Pictures (Willy)

Win or Lose (Hannah Montana)

Wind Chill (Red Rock Mysteries)

A Wind in the Door (Time Fantasy Series)

Wind on the River (Jamestown's American Portraits)

Wind Power Whiz Kid (Buzz Beaker Brainstorm)

The Wind Singer (The Wind of Fire)

Windmill Windup (Matt Christopher Sports Stories)

Winds of Change (Story Girl)

Windy City Danger (Red Rock Mysteries)

The Windy City Mystery (Boxcar Children)

Winging It (Angels Unlimited)

Wingman on Ice (Matt Christopher Sports Stories)

Wings of Darkness and Other Cases (Einstein Anderson)

The Winking Ruby Mystery (Dana Girls)

Winner (Gymnasts)

Winner Take All (Mary-Kate and Ashley: Two of a Kind)

Winner Takes All! (Stinky Boys Club)

Winner Takes the Cake (Dish)

Winner's Circle (Short Stirrup Club)

Winnie at her Best (Winnie)

Winnie Dancing on her Own (Winnie)

The Winning Edge (Skating Dreams)

Winning Is Everything (Full House: Stephanie)

Winning London (Mary-Kate and Ashley Starring In . . .)

The Winning Pony (Pony Pals)

The Winning Spirit (Silver Blades)

Winning Streak (Angel Park All-Stars)

Winning Streak (Duel Masters)

Winning Stroke (American Gold Swimmers)

The Winning Stroke (Matt Christopher Sports Stories)

The Winning Summer (Keystone Stables)

Winning Ticket! (Lottery Luck)

Winter Ball (7th Heaven)

Winter Days in the Big Woods (Little House: My First Little House Books)

Winter Games (Camp Confidential)

Winter Games (Doug Chronicles)

The Winter Knights (Edge Chronicles)

The Winter of Red Snow (Dear America)

Winter of the Ice Wizard (Magic Tree House)

Winter on the Farm (Little House: My First Little House Books)

Winter on the Island (Story Girl)

Winter Race Camp (Thoroughbred: Ashleigh)

Winter Story (Brambly Hedge)

Winter Tidings (Prairie River)

The Winter Worm Business (Casey, Tracey and Company)

A Winter's Gift (Heartland)

A Winter's Tale (Puppy Patrol)

Wipeout (Hardy Boys)

Wired Wonder Woof (AstroKids)

Wisconsin Werewolves (American Chillers)

The Wish Giver (Coven Tree)

The Wish I Wish I Never Wished (Full House: Michelle)

Wish on a Star (Mary-Kate and Ashley: Two of a Kind)

Wish upon a Mom (Fairly OddParents)

Wish Upon a VCR (Full House: Stephanie)

Wish You Were Here (Toot and Puddle)

Wish You Weren't Here (Camp Confidential)

Wishbone and the Dancing Princess (Wishbone: The Early Years)

Wishbone and the Forty Thieves (Wishbone: The Early Years)

Wishbone and the Glass Slipper (Wishbone: The Early Years)

Wishbone and the Nutcracker (Wishbone: The Early Years)

Wishbone in Wonderland (Wishbone: The Early Years)

Wishes and Dreams (Mary-Kate and Ashley Sweet 16)

Wishful Thinking (Hannah Montana)

Wishing for Gold (Skating Dreams)

Wishing Horse of Oz (Oz)

The Wishing Stone (Spooksville)

Wishing Upon a Star (China Tate)

Witch at the Door (Spell Casters)

Witch Friend (The Floods)

Witch Glitch (Sabrina the Teenage Witch)

Witch, Goblin and Ghost are Back (Witch, Goblin and Ghost)

Witch, Goblin and Ghost in the Haunted Woods (Witch, Goblin and Ghost)

Witch, Goblin and Sometimes Ghost (Witch, Goblin and Ghost)

The Witch Goes to School (Witch)

The Witch Grows Up (Witch)

The Witch Herself (Witch)

Witch Hunt! (Secret World of Alex Mack)

A Witch in Cabin Six (Camp Sunnyside)

Witch in the Pumpkin Patch (Sweet Valley Kids)

The Witch Next Door (Witch)

Witch of Clatteringshaws (Wolves Chronicles)

The Witch Returns (Witch)

Witch Switch (Katie Kazoo, Switcheroo)

The Witch That Launched a Thousand Ships (Sabrina the Teenage Witch)

The Witch Tree Symbol (Nancy Drew)

Witch Twins (Witch Twins)

Wren's War (Wren)

The Wright 3 (Petra and Calder)

A Wrinkle in Time (Time Fantasy Series)

Writ in Stone (Nancy Drew Graphic Novels)

Write On! (Katie Kazoo, Switcheroo)

Write On, Rosy! (Rosy Cole)

Write Up a Storm with the Polk Street School (Polk Street School: Kids of the Polk Street School)

The Wrong Crowd (Berenstain Bears)

The Wrong Way (B.Y. Times Kid Sisters)

The Wtch's Christmas (Witch)

Wurm War (Outcast)

Wushu Were Here (Time Warp Trio (novelizations))

X

The X-ed-Out X-Ray (A to Z Mysteries)

X Marks the Spot (X Files)

The Xanadu Adventure (Vesper Holly)

Y

Yang the Eldest and His Odd Jobs (Yang)

Yang the Second and Her Secret Admirer (Yang)

Yang the Third and Her Impossible Family (Yang)

Yang the Youngest and His Terrible Ear (Yang)

Yankee Belles in Dixie (Bonnets and Bugles)

Yankee Blue or Rebel Grey? (I Am American)

Yankee Doodle Drumsticks (Lincoln Lions Band)

Yankee in Oz (Oz)

Yankee Swap (The Saddle Club)

Yard Sale (Mud Flat)

The Year Mom Won the Pennant (Matt Christopher Sports Stories)

Year of Impossible Goodbyes (Sookan Bak)

The Yearling (Black Stallion: Young Black Stallion)

The Yellow Feather Mystery (Hardy Boys)

The Yellow House Mystery (Boxcar Children)

The Yellow Knight of Oz (Oz)

The Yellow Yacht (A to Z Mysteries)

Yellowstone (Adventures with the Parkers)

Yikes! Bikes! (Ready, Freddy!)

Yikes! Grandma's a Teenager (The Zack Files)

Yo-Ho-Ho! (Pirate School)

Yo Ho Ho and a Bottle of Milk (Rugrats Files)

Yosemite (Adventures with the Parkers)

You and Me, Little Bear (Little Bear)

You Are a Genius (Choose Your Own Adventure)

You Are a Millionaire (Choose Your Own Adventure)

You Are a Monster (Choose Your Own Adventure)

You Are a Shark (Choose Your Own Adventure)

You Are a Superstar (Choose Your Own Adventure)

You Are an Alien (Choose Your Own Adventure)

You Are Microscopic (Choose Your Own Adventure)

You Are My Sunshine (Toot and Puddle)

You Can Be My Friend (Charlie and Lola)

You Can Do It, Sam (Sam)

You Can Swim, Baby Duck (Baby Duck)

You Can't, but Genghis Khan (Time Warp Trio (novelizations))

You Can't Eat Your Chicken Pox, Amber Brown (Amber Brown)

You Can't Scare Me! (Goosebumps)

You Can't Scare Me! (Goosebumps Presents)

You Lucky Dog (Soccer 'Cats)

You Read My Mind (Sister Sister)

You Smell Dead (Pretty Freekin Scary)

You'll Soon Grow into Them, Titch (Titch)

The Young Black Stallion (Black Stallion)

Young Cam Jansen and the Baseball Mystery (Cam Jansen: Young Cam Jansen)

Young Cam Jansen and the Dinosaur Game (Cam Jansen: Young Cam Jansen)

Young Cam Jansen and the Double Beach Mystery (Cam Jansen: Young Cam Jansen)

Young Cam Jansen and the Ice Skate Mystery (Cam Jansen: Young Cam Jansen)

Young Cam Jansen and the Library Mystery (Cam Jansen: Young Cam Jansen)

Young Cam Jansen and the Lions' Lunch Mystery (Cam Jansen: Young Cam Jansen)

Young Cam Jansen and the Lost Tooth (Cam Jansen: Young Cam Jansen)

Young Cam Jansen and the Missing Cookie (Cam Jansen: Young Cam Jansen)

Young Cam Jansen and the Molly Shoe Mystery (Cam Jansen: Young Cam Jansen)

Young Cam Jansen and the New Girl Mystery (Cam Jansen: Young Cam Jansen)

Young Cam Jansen and the Pizza Shop Mystery (Cam Jansen: Young Cam Jansen)

Young Cam Jansen and the Spotted Cat Mystery (Cam Jansen: Young Cam Jansen)

Young Cam Jansen and the Substitute Mystery (Cam Jansen: Young Cam Jansen)

Young Cam Jansen and the Zoo Note Mystery (Cam Jansen: Young Cam Jansen)

Young Indiana Jones and the Circle of Death (Young Indiana Jones)

Young Indiana Jones and the Curse of the Ruby Cross (Young Indiana Jones)

Young Indiana Jones and the Eye of the Tiger (Young Indiana Jones)

Young Indiana Jones and the Face of the Dragon (Young Indiana Jones)

Young Indiana Jones and the Ghostly Riders (Young Indiana Jones)

Young Indiana Jones and the Gypsy Revenge (Young Indiana Jones)

Young Indiana Jones and the Journey to the Underworld (Young Indiana Jones)

Genre/Subject Index

This index gives access by genre (in bold capital letters) and by subject, enabling you to find series by genre and to identify books that deal with specific topcis, such as horses or U.S. history.

Aardvarks
Arthur (K–3)
Arthur Chapter Books (3–6)
Arthur Chapter Books: Good
   Sports (3–6)
D.W. (K–2)

Acting
Annabel the Actress (2–4)
Annie Pitts (2–4)
Topaz (3–5)

ADVENTURE
Abby's South Seas Adventures
   (5–8)
Adirondack Kids (3–6)
Adventures of a Young Sailor (5–8)
Adventures with the Parkers (5–8)
The A.I. Gang (4–6)
Akimbo (2–4)
The American Adventure (3–6)
American Adventures (4–6)
Anika Scott (5–8)
Animorphs (4–8)
Animorphs: Alternamorphs (4–8)
Animorphs: Animorph Chronicles
   (4–8)
Animorphs: Megamorphs (5–8)
Anthony Monday (5–7)
Black Stallion (5–8)
Brian Robeson (4–8)
Cardcaptor Sakura (4–6)
Cascade Mountain Railroad
   Mysteries (4–6)
Choose Your Own Adventure
   (4–8)
Choose Your Own Nightmare
   (4–8)
Choose Your Own Star Wars
   Adventures (4–8)

Chronicles of Ancient Darkness
   (5–9)
Clubhouse (1–4)
Cooper Kids (5–7)
Cucumbers Trilogy (2–4)
Culpepper Adventures (3–5)
Cyber.kdz (4–6)
Danger Guys (3–5)
Danny Dunn (3–6)
Dark Is Rising (4–8)
D.J. Dillon Adventures (4–6)
Dog Watch (3–5)
Dragon (1–3)
Dragonling (2–4)
Emily Eyefinger (2–4)
Eric Sterling, Secret Agent (4–6)
Fablehaven (5–8)
Far-Flung Adventure (3–5)
Frightmares (2–6)
The Gatekeepers (5–9)
Goners (4–6)
Goosebumps: Give Yourself
   Goosebumps (4–8)
The Great McGoniggle (2–3)
Grk (5–7)
Hannah and the Angels (3–5)
Henry the Cat (K–2)
Henry the Explorer (K–3)
The Indian in the Cupboard (4–6)
Inkheart (5–12)
Internet Detectives (4–6)
Island Stallion (4–6)
Jack Jameson and Danny One
   (2–4)
Jackie Chan Adventures (4–8)
Julie of the Wolves (5–8)
Kidnapped (5–8)
A Knight's Story (4–8)
Ladd Family (4–6)
The Life and Times (4–7)
Lilo and Stitch: The Series (2–4)

Little Toot (K–1)
Liza, Bill and Jed (2–5)
MacGregor Family Adventure
   (5–8)
Magic Attic Club (2–4)
Magic School Bus (1–4)
Magic School Bus: Ms. Frizzle's
   Adventures (1–4)
Magic School Bus Science Chapter
   Books (2–5)
Mandie (4–6)
Mind over Matter (4–8)
Mirette (K–2)
Miss Pickerell (4–5)
Mustang Mountain (5–8)
My Teacher Is an Alien (4–6)
Mysteries in Our National Parks
   (5–8)
Neptune Adventures (4–7)
Never Land (4–7)
Nora (1–3)
Norby (5–7)
On the Run (5–8)
Outer Banks Trilogy (5–8)
Outriders (5–7)
Paperboy (4–6)
Peter and the Starcatchers (4–8)
Pirate Hunter (5–8)
Pirate Pete (K–2)
Pirate Pete and Pirate Joe (K–2)
Pirate School (1–3)
Red (4–6)
Redwall (4–8)
Reel Kids Adventures (5–7)
The Rescuers (4–6)
Roller Coaster Tycoon (4–7)
Salty (K–2)
Secret Agent Jack Stalwart (1–4)
Secret Agent MJJ (4–7)
Secret World of Alex Mack (5–8)
Sirius Mysteries (5–9)

ADVENTURE (cont.)

Soup (3–5)
Speed Racer (4–8)
Spy Force (4–7)
Spy Gear (4–6)
Star Trek: Deep Space Nine (4–8)
Star Trek: Enterprise (5–10)
Star Trek: I. K. S. Gorkon (5–10)
Star Trek: S. C. E. (5–10)
Star Trek: Starfleet Academy (4–8)
Star Trek: The Next Generation: Starfleet Academy (4–8)
Star Trek: Voyager: Starfleet Academy (4–8)
Star Wars Episode 1: Journals (4–8)
Star Wars Galaxy of Fear (4–8)
Star Wars Junior Jedi Knights (4–8)
Star Wars Young Jedi Knights (4–8)
Survival! (5–8)
SWAT (Secret World Adventure Team) (2–4)
Sword of the Spirits (5–8)
Three Investigators (5–7)
Time Fantasy Series (4–8)
Time Spies (2–4)
Time Surfers (4–6)
Tom Swift Young Inventor (5–9)
Totally Spies! (3–5)
Treasure Planet (K–2)
The Tucket Adventures (5–8)
Twisted Journeys (4–8)
Ulysses Moore (4–6)
Vesper Holly (5–7)
Westmark (5–7)
The Wild Thornberrys (K–5)
Wishbone: The Early Years (K–3)
Wishbone Adventures (3–4)
Wishbone Classics (3–5)
Wizardry (5–8)
Wolves Chronicles (4–8)
World of Adventure (3–6)
Wren (4–7)
Young Bond (5–9)
Young Indiana Jones (4–6)
Young Indiana Jones Chronicles: Choose Your Own Adventure (5–8)

Africa

Akimbo (2–4)
Elizabeti (K–2)
Jafta (K–3)
Jamela (K–2)

African Americans

American Girls: Addy (2–5)
Arabus Family Saga (5–8)
Carmen Browne (4–6)
Ernestine and Amanda (4–5)
Ethan (K–1)
Everett Anderson (K–2)
Everybody Hates Chris (4–6)
Grace (1–4)
Hey L'il D! (2–4)
Jackson Jones (3–6)
Jamaica (K–2)
Journey of Allen Strange (4–7)
Julian and Huey (2–4)
Junebug (4–7)
Justice Trilogy (5–8)
Kenan and Kel (4–6)
Little Bill (K–2)
Little Bill (Nickelodeon) (K–2)
Logan Family (4–7)
Ludell (5–8)
Messy Bessey (K–1)
Miami (2–4)
Patrick's Pals (3–6)
Peter (K–2)
Peter's Neighborhood (K–2)
Philip Hall (4–7)
Racing to Freedom Trilogy (5–8)
Reflections of a Black Cowboy (4–6)
Scraps of Time (3–6)
Secret Agent MJJ (4–7)
Shanna First Readers (K–1)
Sister Sister (4–6)
Thomas and Grandfather (3–6)
Willimena Rules! (2–4)
Ziggy and the Black Dinosaurs (3–6)

Aliens

Alien Adventures (4–7)
Alien Clones from Outer Space (2–4)
Aliens (2–4)
Harry and Chicken (3–5)
I Was a Sixth Grade Alien (3–6)
Journey of Allen Strange (4–7)
My Teacher Is an Alien (4–6)
Ormingat (5–8)
Professor Xargle (K–3)
Robbie Packford (4–6)
Space Above and Beyond (5–8)
Space Ship Under the Apple Tree (3–5)
Tripods (5–8)
Visitors (5–8)
Weird Planet (2–4)

Alligators and crocodiles

Bill and Pete (K–2)
Gator Girls (1–3)
Lyle (K–3)
Mr. and Mrs. Green (K–2)

Amish

Rachel Yoder—Always Trouble Somewhere (4–6)

Angels

Angels Unlimited (4–7)
Angelwings (3–5)
Forever Angels (4–7)
Hannah and the Angels (3–5)

ANIMAL FANTASY

Albert (the Duck) (K–2)
Anatole (K–2)
Angelina Ballerina (K–2)
Angelina Ballerina: Angelina's Diary (1–3)
Anthony Ant (K–2)
Arnie (K–2)
Arthur (K–3)
Arthur Chapter Books (3–6)
Arthur Chapter Books: Good Sports (3–6)
Arthur the Chimpanzee (K–2)
Aunt Eater (K–2)
Babar (K–3)
Baby Duck (K–1)
Babymouse (3–6)
Bad Dog (3–5)
The Barkers (K–2)
Barkley's School for Dogs (2–4)
Basil of Baker Street (2–5)
Bear (K–2)
Berenstain Bears (K–2)
Berenstain Bears: Bear Scouts (1–3)
Berenstain Bears: Big Chapter Books (1–3)
Best Friends (1–3)
Bill and Pete (K–2)
Bizzy Bones (K–2)
Blackboard Bear (K–1)
Brambly Hedge (3–5)
Bunnicula (3–5)

ANIMAL FANTASY
(cont.)
Sam (K–2)
Sam, Dog Detective (3–5)
Scaredy Squirrel (K–1)
Sebastian (Super Sleuth) (3–5)
Sheep (K–3)
Silly Thrillers with Peggy the Pig (K–2)
Silly Tilly (K–2)
Silverwing (5–8)
Spider (K–2)
Spooky the Cat (K–2)
Spot (K–1)
Tacky the Penguin (K–2)
Tiny (K–2)
Toby (K–2)
Toot and Puddle (K–1)
Turtle and Snake (K–2)
Upchuck and the Rotten Willy (3–6)
Voyage to the Bunny Planet (K–2)
Warton and Morton (2–4)
Willy (K–2)
Winnie the Pooh First Readers (K–2)
Yoko and Friends (K–2)
Zelda and Ivy (K–2)

Animals *see also* specific kinds of animals (e.g., Cats) that may be real or anthropomorphic
Animal Ark (3–5)
Animal Ark Hauntings (3–5)
Animal Ark Pets (3–5)
Animal Emergency (2–4)
Animal Inn (3–6)
Bill and Pete (K–2)
Bunnicula (3–5)
Chester Cricket (3–6)
Doctor Dolittle (4–6)
Long Pond (K–2)
Mud Flat (K–2)
Pets, Inc. (3–5)
Pets to the Rescue (K–2)
Rainbow Magic: Pet Fairies (1–3)
Sophie (3–5)
The Thirteen Moons (3–6)
Wild at Heart (4–7)

Anteaters
Aunt Eater (K–2)

Ants
Anthony Ant (K–2)

Art
Petra and Calder (5–8)

Arthurian legends
Grail Quest (5–8)
King Arthur (3–5)
Young Merlin Trilogy (4–6)

Asian Americans
Mystery Files of Shelby Woo (4–6)
Rinko (4–6)
Song Lee (2–4)
Yang (4–6)

Asperger's syndrome
Wright and Wong (5–8)

Autobiography
James Stevenson's Autobiographical Stories (1–3)
26 Fairmount Avenue (1–3)

Automobile racing
NASCAR Pole Position Adventures (5–8)
NASCAR Racers (3–5)
RPM (5–8)
Speed Racer (4–8)

Baby-sitting
Angel (3–5)
Baby-Sitters Club (4–7)
Baby-Sitters Club Friends Forever (4–7)
Baby-Sitters Club Mysteries (4–7)
Baby-Sitters Club Super Specials (4–7)
Baby-Sitters Little Sister (2–3)
Baby-Sitters Little Sister Super Specials (2–4)
Mary Poppins (4–6)
My Babysitter (4–6)
Penelope Fritter, Super-Sitter (2–4)

Badgers
Frances (K–3)

Ballet *see* Dancing

Baseball
Angel Park All-Stars (4–6)
Barnstormers (3–6)
Baseball Card Adventures (4–8)
The Hit and Run Gang (2–4)
Never Sink Nine (3–4)
Peach Street Mudders (2–4)
The Pink Parrots (3–5)
Scrappers (4–6)
Tales from the Sandlot (4–6)

Basketball
Angel Park Hoop Stars (4–6)
Hey L'il D! (2–4)
Patrick's Pals (3–6)
Slam Dunk (4–6)
Super Hoops (4–6)

Bats
Silverwing (5–8)

Bears *see also* Polar bears, Toys—Bears
Bear (K–2)
Berenstain Bears (K–2)
Berenstain Bears: Bear Scouts (1–3)
Berenstain Bears: Big Chapter Books (1–3)
Blackboard Bear (K–1)
Edward the Unready (K–1)
Emma (K–3)
Ernest and Celestine (K–3)
Frank and Ernest (2–5)
Jesse Bear (K–1)
Little Bear (K–2)
Little Bear: Maurice Sendak's Little Bear (K–2)
Little Brown Bear (K–1)
Moonbear (K–2)
Morris and Boris (K–2)
Paddington (2–5)
Penrod (K–2)
Sam (K)
Winnie the Pooh First Readers (K–2)

Birds—crows
Feather and Bone: The Crow Chronicles (5–8)

Boats and ships
Little Toot (K–1)

Books and reading
The Ink Drinker (4–7)
Inkheart (5–12)
The Wedding Planner's Daughter (5–9)

Dancing

Angelina Ballerina (K–2)
Ballerina Dreams (2–5)
Ballet Friends (4–7)
Ballet Slippers (2–4)
Belinda (K–3)
Lili (K–2)
Royal Ballet School Diaries (4–7)
Tanya (K–3)

Diaries

Abby Hayes: The Amazing Days of
Abby Hayes (4–6)
Amelia (4–8)
American Diaries (4–6)
Angelina Ballerina: Angelina's
Diary (1–3)
Charlie Small (3–5)
Dear America (4–6)
Dear Dumb Diary (5–8)
Diary of a Wimpy Kid (5–8)
Lily B. (5–8)
Lucy Rose (3–5)
Melanie Martin (4–6)
My America: Corey (2–5)
My America: Elizabeth (2–5)
My America: Hope (2–5)
My America: Joshua (2–5)
My America: Meg (2–5)
My America: Sofia (2–5)
My America: Virginia (2–5)
My Name Is America (4–6)
Royal Diaries (3–7)
Young American Voices (3–5)

Dinosaurs

Danny and the Dinosaur (K–3)
Dinosaurs (K–2)
How Do Dinosaurs . . . (K–2)
Jurassic Park Adventures (4–7)
Mama Rex and T (1–3)
PaleoJoe's Dinosaur Detective
Club (3–5)
Patrick's Dinosaurs (K–2)
Rex and Lilly (K–2)

Disabilities

Deaf Child Crossing (4–6)
Hank Zipzer (3–5)
Joey Pigza (5–9)
Mary Marony (2–4)
Moses (K–2)

Dogs

All-American Puppies (2–4)
Bad Dog (3–5)
Barkley's School for Dogs (2–4)
Biscuit Readers (K–1)
Boxcar Children: Adventures of
Benny and Watch (1–3)
Carl (K–1)
Christopher (K–2)
Clifford (K–2)
David and Goliath (1–3)
Digby and Kate (1–2)
Dog Watch (3–5)
Fletcher Mysteries (2–5)
Genghis Khan (2–3)
Grk (5–7)
Hank the Cowdog (4–6)
Happy and Honey (K–1)
Harriet (K–2)
Harry the Dirty Dog (K–3)
Henry and Mudge (K–3)
Henry and Mudge: Puppy Mudge
(K–2)
Jack Russell: Dog Detective (3–5)
Judge Benjamin (4–6)
Kipper (K–2)
Kipper: Little Kippers (K–2)
LaRue (K–2)
Lassie (4–8)
Lucky (2–4)
McDuff (K–1)
McGrowl (3–6)
Martha (K–2)
Max the Dog (K–2)
Mike and Harry (1–3)
Mishmash (3–4)
My Dog (1–2)
Otto (1–3)
Pinkerton (K–2)
Pup and Hound (K–1)
Puppy Friends (1–3)
The Puppy Place (3–5)
Red (4–6)
Sally (K–2)
Salty (K–2)
Sam (K–2)
Sam, Dog Detective (3–5)
Sam (the dog) (K–2)
Santa Paws (3–5)
Shiloh (3–6)
Sirius Mysteries (5–9)
Skippyjon Jones (K–3)
Slippers (K–2)
Space Dog (1–3)

Spot (K–1)
Tiny (K–2)
Upchuck and the Rotten Willy
(3–6)
Walter, the Farting Dog (K–3)
Wishbone Adventures (3–4)
Wishbone Classics (3–5)
Wishbone Mysteries (4–5)
Wizard and Wart (K–2)

Dolphins

Dolphin Diaries (3–6)

Dragons

Beast Quest (3–5)
Dear Dragon (K–3)
Deltora: Deltora Quest (4–7)
Deltora: Deltora Shadowlands
(4–7)
Deltora: Dragons of Deltora (4–7)
Dragon (1–3)
Dragon Keeper Trilogy (5–8)
Dragon Slayers' Academy (3–5)
Dragonling (2–4)
Enchanted Forest Chronicles (4–7)
Falcon (4–7)
George and His Dragon (K–2)
Heroic Misadventures of Hiccup
Horrendous Haddock III (3–5)
Inheritance (5–12)
Lily Quench (4–7)
Rumble's Cave Hotel (K–2)
Shimmer and Thorn (5–8)
Wormling (5–8)

Ducks

Albert (the Duck) (K–2)
Baby Duck (K–1)
Duck (K–2)
Miss Mallard (2–4)

Ecology and environment

Adirondack Kids (3–6)
Dolphin Diaries (3–6)
Eco Kids (3–5)
Neptune Adventures (4–7)

Elephants

Babar (K–3)
Elephant and Piggie (K–2)
Elmer (K–2)
Frank and Ernest (2–5)
Harriet (K–1)

FAMILY LIFE (cont.)

Lyle (K–3)
McGee and Me! (4–6)
Maggie Valley (5–8)
Malcolm in the Middle (4–6)
Marsha (1–3)
Marvin Redpost (1–3)
Mary-Kate and Ashley: Adventures of Mary-Kate and Ashley (4–7)
Mary-Kate and Ashley: So Little Time (4–7)
Mary-Kate and Ashley: Two of a Kind (4–7)
Mary-Kate and Ashley in Action (4–7)
Mary-Kate and Ashley Starring In . . . (4–7)
Mary-Kate and Ashley Sweet 16 (4–7)
Matthew Martin (4–5)
Melanie Martin (4–6)
Melendy Family (4–6)
Mennyms (5–8)
Mishmash (3–4)
The Moffats (3–6)
Molesons (K–2)
Molly (4–7)
Moonbear (K–2)
Mr. and Mrs. Pig (K–3)
Mrs. Coverlet (3–5)
Murphy Family (4–6)
My Mom (1–3)
Noah (K–1)
Obadiah Starbuck (K–3)
Oliver and Amanda Pig (K–2)
Orphan Train Adventures (5–8)
Orphelines (3–4)
The Pain and the Great One (1–3)
Peter (K–2)
Pigs (K–2)
Pinkerton (K–2)
Portraits of Little Women (4–6)
The Quigleys (2–4)
Ramona Quimby (2–4)
Rex and Lilly (K–2)
Rinko (4–6)
Riverside Kids: Elisa (1–3)
Riverside Kids: Nora and Teddy (3–4)
Riverside Kids: Russell (1–3)
Roommates (1–3)
Rosa Trilogy (K–3)
Rosy Cole (3–5)
Sam Krupnik (3–5)
7th Heaven (4–7)

Sister Sister (4–6)
Sookan Bak (5–8)
Sophie (3–5)
Starshine! (4–6)
Stone Book Quartet (3–5)
The Stupids (K–2)
Tales of Trotter Street (K–2)
Thomas and Grandfather (3–6)
Tillerman Cycle (5–8)
Titch (K–2)
Tom and Pippo (K–1)
Trouble With (3–5)
26 Fairmount Avenue (1–3)
Vicky Austin (4–7)
The Wedding Planner's Daughter (5–9)
Yang (4–6)
Zelda and Ivy (K–2)

FANTASY

Abracadabra (5–7)
Accidental Monsters (4–6)
The Adventures of Beatrice Bailey (5–8)
Age of Magic Trilogy (5–9)
Airy Fairy (2–4)
Akiko (4–7)
Akiko Graphic Novels (4–7)
Alien Clones from Outer Space (2–4)
Alistair (K–2)
Andrew Lost (2–4)
Angels Unlimited (4–7)
Angelwings (3–5)
Annabel Andrews (5–7)
The Anybodies (5–8)
Araminta Spookie (2–4)
The Archives of Anthropos (4–8)
Artemis Fowl (5–8)
Astrosaurs (3–5)
Attolia (5–10)
Avalon 1: Web of Magic (4–7)
Avalon 2: Quest for Magic (4–7)
Avatar: The Earth Kingdom Chronicles (4–7)
Avatar: The Last Airbender (4–7)
Avatar Graphic Novels (4–7)
Avatar (Ready to Read) (2–4)
Bailey City Monsters (2–4)
Bailey School: The Adventures of the Bailey School Kids (2–4)
Barbie (Step Into Reading) (K–3)
Barnstormers (3–6)
The Bartimaeus Trilogy (5–9)

Baseball Card Adventures (4–8)
Batman (Scholastic Reader) (1–4)
Beast Quest (3–5)
Billy Hooten, Owlboy (3–6)
Bionicle Adventures (4–7)
Bionicle Chronicles (4–7)
Bionicle Legends (4–7)
Black Belt Club (3–6)
Blast to the Past (2–4)
Blossom Culp (5–7)
Borrowers (3–6)
Brigid Thrush Books (2–3)
Budgie (K–1)
Butt-Ugly Martians Chapter Books (2–5)
The Caped 6th Grader (4–6)
Cardcaptor Sakura (4–6)
Castaways of the Flying Dutchman (5–8)
CatDog (Chapter Books) (2–5)
Cat's Eye Corner (4–7)
Children of the Lamp (5–8)
Children of the Red King (4–7)
Chronicles of Ancient Darkness (5–9)
Chronicles of Narnia (4–8)
Circle of Magic (4–6)
CLAMP School Detectives (4–8)
Clemency Pogue (4–6)
The Companions Quartet (5–8)
Corduroy (K–1)
Coven Tree (3–6)
The Cronus Chronicles (5–9)
Crystal Doors (5–8)
CyberQuest (5–8)
Dark Is Rising (4–8)
Dark Reflections Trilogy (5–8)
The Darkest Age (5–8)
Dear Dragon (K–3)
Deltora: Deltora Quest (4–7)
Deltora: Deltora Shadowlands (4–7)
Deltora: Dragons of Deltora (4–7)
Dexter's Laboratory Chapter Books (2–5)
Digimon Digital Monsters (2–5)
Disney Fairies (1–3)
Disney Fairies (Chapter Books) (1–4)
Disney Princess (1–3)
Disney Princess Secrets (1–3)
Disney Princesses: My Side of the Story (1–3)
Disney Villains: My Side of the Story (1–3)

FANTASY (cont.)

MythQuest (4–8)

Never Land (4–7)

NFL Monday Night Football Club (4–7)

Nora (1–3)

Northern Frights (5–8)

Nose Pickers from Outer Space (3–5)

Octonauts (K–1)

Old Bear Stories (K–2)

Old Witch (K–2)

Olivia Kidney (3–6)

Ormingat (5–8)

Oswald (Ready-to-Read) (K–1)

Otto (1–3)

Outcast (4–7)

Oz (4–8)

Pangur Ban (5–8)

Paper Princess (K–2)

Pendragon (5–8)

Penelope Fritter, Super-Sitter (2–4)

Percy Jackson and the Olympians (5–9)

Peter and the Starcatchers (4–8)

Pixie Tricks (2–4)

Power Rangers: Ninja Storm (4–6)

Powerpuff Girls Chapter Books (2–5)

Prince of the Pond Trilogy (3–6)

Princess Power (3–5)

The Princess Tales (3–6)

Protector of the Small (5–8)

Prydain Chronicles (5–8)

Pure Dead Magic (5–8)

Pyrates (5–7)

Raggedy Ann and Andy (1–3)

Rainbow Magic: Fun Day Fairies (1–3)

Rainbow Magic: Jewel Fairies (K–3)

Rainbow Magic: Pet Fairies (1–3)

Rainbow Magic: Rainbow Fairies (1–3)

Rainbow Magic: Weather Fairies (1–3)

Ranger's Apprentice (5–9)

The Rhianna Chronicles (4–7)

Rowan of Rin (4–6)

Rugrats Files (2–5)

Rumble's Cave Hotel (K–2)

Sabrina the Teenage Witch (4–6)

Sailor Moon Novels (4–7)

Salt and Pepper Chronicles (3–6)

Samurai Jack Chapter Books (3–6)

Scary Godmother (3–5)

Scream Shop (3–5)

Secret World of Alex Mack (5–8)

Secrets of Droon (2–5)

Septimus Heap (5–8)

A Series of Unfortunate Events (3–7)

Seven Little Monsters (K–1)

Shadow Children (5–8)

Shadow Zone (4–6)

Shimmer and Thorn (5–8)

Silver Sequence (5–9)

Silverskin Legacy (5–8)

Sindbad (2–5)

Sirius Mysteries (5–9)

Sister Magic (2–4)

The Sisters Grimm (4–6)

The Sixth Sense: Secrets from Beyond (5–7)

So Weird (4–7)

Soccer Shock (4–6)

Spell Casters (5–8)

Spider Riders (4–6)

Spiderwick: Beyond the Spiderwick Chronicles (4–6)

The Spiderwick Chronicles (4–6)

SpongeBob SquarePants Chapter Books (2–5)

SpongeBob SquarePants (TokyoPop) (3–5)

Spy Kids Adventures (4–6)

Spy Mice (4–6)

Stanley (K–3)

The Stoneheart Trilogy (5–9)

Strega Nona and Big Anthony (K–3)

Suddenly Supernatural (5–8)

The Summer of Magic Quartet (4–7)

Sunken Kingdom (3–5)

Supertwins (K–3)

Sylvie Cycle (5–9)

Tales from the Odyssey (4–8)

Tales from the Sandlot (4–6)

Tales of the Dark Forest (4–6)

Tales of the Frog Princess (4–7)

Tartan Magic Trilogy (4–7)

Teddy Bears (K–3)

Third Grade (2–4)

Tiara Club (1–4)

Tiara Club: The Tiara Club at Pearl Palace (1–4)

Tiara Club: The Tiara Club at Ruby Mansion (1–4)

Tiara Club: The Tiara Club at Silver Towers (1–4)

Tiger Moth (2–5)

Time Fantasy Series (4–8)

Time Navigators (4–6)

Time Soldiers (3–5)

Time Spies (2–4)

Time Surfers (4–6)

Time Trilogy (5–8)

TimeJumpers (5–8)

Tom Swift Young Inventor (5–9)

Transformers Armada (Readers) (1–3)

Treasure Planet (K–2)

Treehorn (3–6)

Troll King (4–7)

Troll Trilogy (5–8)

The Underland Chronicles (4–8)

Unicorn Chronicles (5–8)

Unicorns of Balinor (4–6)

The Unicorn's Secret (2–4)

Unlikely Exploits (4–6)

Usagi Yojimbo (5–8)

Very Worst Monster (K–2)

Viking Magic (4–6)

Voyage of the Basset (4–7)

Warriors (5–9)

Warriors: Power of Three (5–9)

Warriors: The New Prophecy (5–9)

Watchers (5–8)

Wayside School (3–6)

The Weebie Zone (3–5)

Werewolf Club (2–4)

Westmark (5–7)

Wicked Witch (2–5)

Wilderking Trilogy (4–6)

The Wind of Fire (5–8)

Witch (K–3)

W.I.T.C.H.—Adventures (5–8)

W.I.T.C.H.—Chapter Books (5–8)

W.I.T.C.H.—Graphic Novels (5–8)

Witch, Goblin and Ghost (K–2)

Witch Twins (3–5)

Wizard and Wart (K–2)

Wizard Trilogy (3–5)

Wizardry (5–8)

Wolves Chronicles (4–8)

World of Adventure (3–6)

Wormling (5–8)

Wren (4–7)

X Files (5–10)

Friendship (cont.)

Kids from Kennedy Middle School (5–7)

Kids in Ms. Coleman's Class (1–3)

Kids on Bus 5 (1–3)

Kitty (3–6)

Leo and Emily (K–3)

Little Bill (K–2)

Lizzie Logan (2–4)

Lottery Luck (4–6)

Louise (2–4)

Magic Attic Club (2–4)

Mallory (2–4)

Mandie (4–6)

Martin Bridge (2–4)

Miami (2–4)

Mole and Troll (K–3)

Molly (4–7)

Mouse and Mole (K–2)

Never Sink Nine (3–4)

Nutty Nutsell (4–6)

Orp (4–6)

Owly Graphic Novels (1–4)

Peanut Butter and Jelly (2–4)

Pee Wee Scouts (2–4)

Peter (K–2)

Peter's Neighborhood (K–2)

Petsitters Club (2–4)

Pinky and Rex (1–3)

Pippi Longstocking (3–5)

Polk Street: New Kids at the Polk Street School (1–3)

Poppleton (K–3)

Princess Power (3–5)

Reel Kids Adventures (5–7)

Riding Academy (4–6)

Ruby (K–2)

Secret World of Alex Mack (5–8)

Silver Blades (4–7)

Silver Blades Figure Eights (2–4)

Sleepover Friends (3–5)

Sleepover Squad (1–3)

Sly the Sleuth (2–4)

Soccer 'Cats (2–4)

Soccer Stars (3–6)

Soup (3–5)

Soup: Little Soup (2–3)

Space Ship Under the Apple Tree (3–5)

Starshine! (4–6)

Sweet Valley: Unicorn Club (4–6)

Sweet Valley Kids (3–5)

Thoroughbred (4–7)

Toot and Puddle (K–1)

Twelve Candles Club (4–6)

Winnie (2–5)

Witch, Goblin and Ghost (K–2)

Wolfbay Wings (4–8)

Zibby Payne (4–6)

Ziggy and the Black Dinosaurs (3–6)

Frogs and toads

Commander Toad (K–3)

Frog (K–1)

Frog and Toad (K–3)

Froggy (K–3)

Warton and Morton (2–4)

Frontier and pioneer life

Addie (4–6)

American Girls: Kirsten (2–5)

Golly Sisters (K–2)

Little House (3–6)

Little House: My First Little House Books (K–2)

Little House: The Caroline Years (3–6)

Little House: The Charlotte Years (3–6)

Little House: The Martha Years (3–6)

Little House: The Rose Years (3–6)

Little House Chapter Books: Caroline (K–2)

Little House Chapter Books: Laura (K–2)

Little House Chapter Books: Rose (K–2)

Log Cabin (K–3)

The Tucket Adventures (5–8)

Gardens and gardening

Jackson Jones (3–6)

Geese

Petunia (K–2)

Geography

Carmen Sandiego Mysteries (4–6)

Gerbils

The Weebie Zone (3–5)

Germany

Lechow Family (5–8)

Ghosts

Araminta Spookie (2–4)

Blossom Culp (5–7)

Edgar Font's Hunt for a House to Haunt (4–7)

Fred and Anthony (3–4)

Georgie (1–3)

Ghost (4–6)

Ghost Squad (5–8)

Ghost Stories (5–6)

Ghosthunters (3–5)

Ghostwriter (4–6)

Green Knowe (4–8)

Haunting with Louisa (5–8)

Jeffrey's Ghost (4–6)

May Bird (5–7)

Mostly Ghostly (3–5)

My Sister, the Ghost (4–6)

Graphic novels/manga

Adventures of Daniel Boom AKA Loud Boy (4–7)

Akiko (4–7)

Akiko Graphic Novels (4–7)

Amelia Rules! (3–5)

Avatar Graphic Novels (4–7)

Baby-Sitters Club Graphic Novels (4–7)

Babymouse (3–6)

Captain Underpants: Super Diaper Baby (3–6)

Cardcaptor Sakura (4–6)

CLAMP School Detectives (4–8)

Fairly OddParents (TokyoPop) (3–6)

Goosebumps Graphix (4–8)

The Grosse Adventures (4–7)

Hannah Montana (TokyoPop) (3–6)

Hardy Boys, Undercover Brothers: Graphic Novels (5–9)

Jimmy Sniffles (2–5)

Johnny Mutton (3–5)

Kim Possible (Chapter Books) (4–7)

Kim Possible (TokyoPop) (4–7)

Lilo and Stitch: The Series (2–4)

Lizzie McGuire (TokyoPop) (4–7)

Magic Pickle Graphic Novels (5–8)

Nancy Drew Graphic Novels (4–8)

Owly Graphic Novels (1–4)

Paperboy (4–6)

Power Rangers: Ninja Storm (4–6)

Sailor Moon Novels (4–7)

Sardine in Outer Space (4–7)

Scary Godmother (3–5)

SpongeBob SquarePants (TokyoPop) (3–5)

HISTORICAL (cont.)

Racing to Freedom Trilogy (5–8)
Reflections of a Black Cowboy (4–6)
Rinko (4–6)
Roman Mysteries (5–8)
Rosie (4–6)
Royal Diaries (3–7)
Saddles, Stars, and Stripes (4–7)
Sarah, Plain and Tall (3–5)
Scraps of Time (3–6)
The Shakespeare Stealer (5–8)
Sookan Bak (5–8)
Stone Book Quartet (3–5)
Story Girl (5–7)
Survival! (5–8)
Trailblazers (4–7)
The Tucket Adventures (5–8)
Viking Quest (5–8)
Young American Voices (3–5)
Young Americans: Colonial Williamsburg (4–6)
Young Merlin Trilogy (4–6)
The Young Underground (5–8)
Young Wolf (1–3)

Holidays

Addie (3–5)
Cranberryport (1–3)
Dear Dragon (K–3)
Emma (K–3)
Gilbert (K–2)
Grumpy Bunny (K–1)
Harry and Emily (K–2)
Henrietta (K–2)
Holiday Five (3–5)
Holiday Friends (3–5)
Holiday Mice (K–2)
Humbug (K–1)
Lincoln Lions Band (2–4)
Miss Flora McFlimsey (K–2)
The Night Before . . . (K–2)
Noah (K–1)
Rotten Ralph (K–1)
Rotten Ralph Rotten Readers (1–3)
Silly Tilly (K–2)
Spider (K–2)

HORROR

American Chillers (4–6)
Are You Afraid of the Dark? (5–8)
Bone Chillers (5–8)
Camp Zombie (5–7)

Choose Your Own Nightmare (4–8)
Deadtime Stories (4–7)
Eerie Indiana (5–8)
Fear Street: Ghosts of Fear Street (4–8)
Fiendly Corners (5–8)
Fred and Anthony (3–4)
Goosebumps (4–8)
Goosebumps: Give Yourself Goosebumps (4–8)
Goosebumps Graphix (4–8)
Goosebumps Horrorland (4–8)
Goosebumps Presents (3–6)
Goosebumps Series 2000 (4–8)
Graveyard School (4–7)
House of Horrors (5–7)
Last Apprentice (5–8)
The Midnight Library (5–8)
My Babysitter (4–6)
Nightmare Room (4–7)
Nightmare Room Thrillogy (4–7)
Nightmares! How Will Yours End? (4–7)
Secrets of Dripping Fang (4–6)
Spooksville (5–8)
Strange Matter (4–6)
Tales of Terror (4–7)
Twisted Journeys (4–8)
Werewolf Chronicles (5–8)
Witch (5–7)
X Files (5–10)

Horseback riding

My Pony Jack (K–2)
Pony Pals (3–5)
Pony Tails (3–5)
The Saddle Club (4–6)
Short Stirrup Club (4–6)

Horses

Beware (3–5)
Big Apple Barn (3–5)
Black Stallion (5–8)
Black Stallion: Young Black Stallion (5–8)
Blaze (K–2)
Chestnut Hill (4–7)
Chincoteague (3–6)
Cowgirl Kate and Cocoa (K–2)
Heartland (4–7)
High Hurdles (4–7)
Hoofbeats (3–5)
Horseland (3–6)
Horseshoe Trilogies (4–6)

Horseshoes (5–7)
Island Stallion (4–6)
Keystone Stables (5–8)
Mustang Mountain (5–8)
Phantom Stallion (4–6)
Pony-Crazed Princess (2–4)
Pony Pals (3–5)
Pony Tails (3–5)
Racing to Freedom Trilogy (5–8)
Riding Academy (4–6)
The Saddle Club (4–6)
Saddle Island (5–8)
Saddles, Stars, and Stripes (4–7)
Sandy Lane Stables (5–8)
Sheltie! (2–4)
Short Stirrup Club (4–6)
Sneaky Pony (1–3)
Spirit of the Cimarron (4–6)
Starlight (4–6)
Thoroughbred (4–7)
Thoroughbred: Ashleigh (4–7)
Thoroughbred: Ashleigh's Collection (4–7)
Winnie the Horse Gentler (4–8)
Young Wolf (1–3)

Hotels

Suite Life of Zack and Cody (3–6)

HUMOR

Abby Hayes: The Amazing Days of Abby Hayes (4–6)
Addie (K–3)
Adventures of Daniel Boom AKA Loud Boy (4–7)
The Adventures of Uncle Stinky (4–7)
Airy Fairy (2–4)
Aldo Sossi (3–5)
Alexander (K–3)
Ali Baba Bernstein (2–4)
Alice (5–8)
Alien Adventures (4–7)
Alien Clones from Outer Space (2–4)
Aliens (2–4)
Alistair (K–2)
All-American Puppies (2–4)
Al's World (4–8)
Amber Brown (2–4)
Amber Brown: A Is for Amber (K–2)
Amelia Bedelia (K–2)
Anastasia Krupnik (4–6)

HUMOR (cont.)

Judge Benjamin (4–6)
Julia Redfern (4–6)
Junie B. Jones (1–2)
Just . . . (5–8)
Kyla May Miss. Behaves (4–7)
Lab Coat Girl (3–5)
Larry the Polar Bear (K–3)
LaRue (K–2)
LazyTown (8 x 8 Books) (K–1)
LazyTown (Ready to Read) (K–1)
Lenny and Mel (2–5)
Leo and Emily (K–3)
Lilly (K–2)
Lincoln Lions Band (2–4)
Little Wolf (3–5)
Loudmouth George (K–1)
Lucky (2–4)
Lunchroom (4–6)
M and M (1–3)
M. T. Anderson's Thrilling Tales (4–7)
McBroom (3–5)
McGurk (2–5)
The Mack Family (2–5)
Mad Science (3–5)
Madeline (K–2)
Maggie Marmelstein (4–6)
Magic Pickle Graphic Novels (5–8)
Magic School Bus (1–4)
Magic School Bus: Ms. Frizzle's Adventures (1–4)
Magic School Bus Science Chapter Books (2–5)
Malcolm in the Middle (4–6)
Martha (K–2)
Marvin Redpost (1–3)
Mary Rose (3–5)
Matthew Martin (4–5)
Max-a-Million (3–5)
Max and Mo (K–1)
Max and Ruby (K–2)
Max Malone (2–5)
Maximum Boy (3–5)
Melvin Beederman, Superhero (2–4)
Mercer Mayer's Critters of the Night (K–4)
Mercy Watson (K–2)
Messy Bessey (K–1)
Mike and Harry (1–3)
Minerva Louise (K–3)
Minnie and Moo (1–3)
Mishmash (3–4)

Miss Bindergarten (K–2)
Miss Malarkey (K–3)
Miss Mallard (2–4)
Miss Nelson (K–3)
Monster Manor (3–5)
Monster Under the Bed (K–2)
Moongobble (3–5)
Moose and Hildy (K–2)
Morris and Boris (K–2)
Mr. and Mrs. Pig (K–3)
Mr. Pin (2–4)
Mr. Putter and Tabby (K–3)
Mr. Yowder (3–5)
Mrs. Coverlet (3–5)
Mrs. Gaddy (K–3)
Mrs. Pepperpot (2–5)
Mrs. Piggle-Wiggle (3–6)
Mrs. Toggle (K–3)
Mud Flat (K–2)
Murphy Family (4–6)
My Weird School (2–5)
My Weird School Daze (2–5)
Myth-O-Mania (4–7)
Nate the Great (1–3)
The Night Before . . . (K–2)
Nose Pickers from Outer Space (3–5)
Nutty Nutsell (4–6)
Old Turtle (K–3)
Old Witch (K–2)
Olga da Polga (3–5)
Orp (4–6)
Oscar J. Noodleman (3–5)
Paddington (2–5)
Parts (K–2)
Patrick's Dinosaurs (K–2)
Peanuts (1–3)
Petunia (K–2)
Pig Pig (K–2)
Piganeers (K–2)
Pigeon (K–2)
Pigs (K–2)
Pinkerton (K–2)
Pinky Dinky Doo (1–3)
Pippi Longstocking (3–5)
Pirate Pete (K–2)
P.J. Funnybunny (K–1)
The Plant That Ate Dirty Socks (4–6)
Polk Street School: Kids of the Polk Street School (1–3)
Poppleton (K–3)
Preston (K–1)
Pretty Freekin Scary (5–8)

Prince of the Pond Trilogy (3–6)
The Princess School (4–7)
Professor Xargle (K–3)
The Quigleys (2–4)
Ralph S. Mouse (2–4)
Ramona Quimby (2–4)
Regarding the . . . (4–6)
Rinaldo (2–4)
Riot Brothers (4–7)
Riverside Kids: Elisa (1–3)
Riverside Kids: Russell (1–3)
Ronald Morgan (K–3)
Roscoe Riley Rules (1–2)
Rosy Cole (3–5)
Rotten Ralph (K–1)
Rotten Ralph Rotten Readers (1–3)
Rotten School (4–6)
Rugrats (Chapter Books) (2–4)
Sabrina the Teenage Witch (4–6)
Sam and Robert (2–4)
Sam Krupnik (3–5)
Scaredy Cats (1–3)
Scooby Doo Readers (1–3)
Seasonal Adventures (4–6)
Secret Agent Dingledorf and His Trusty Dog Splat (2–4)
Secrets of Dripping Fang (4–6)
Seriously Silly Stories (2–4)
Sheep (K–3)
Sidekicks (5–8)
Silly Thrillers with Peggy the Pig (K–2)
Skippyjon Jones (K–3)
Slimeballs (5–7)
Sock Monkey (K–2)
Song Lee (2–4)
Sophie (3–5)
Soup (3–5)
Soup: Little Soup (2–3)
Space Brat (3–5)
Space Dog (1–3)
Spencer's Adventures (1–3)
Stanley (K–3)
Stink (2–4)
Stinky Boys Club (3–6)
The Stupids (K–2)
Suite Life of Zack and Cody (3–6)
Super Goofballs (4–8)
Tales from the Sandlot (4–6)
Tales of the Frog Princess (4–7)
Time Warp Trio (3–6)
Time Warp Trio Graphic Novels (3–6)

Media tie-in (cont.)

Bratz: Lil' Bratz (4–7)

Butt-Ugly Martians Chapter Books (2–5)

Carmen Sandiego Mysteries (4–6)

CatDog (Chapter Books) (2–5)

Charlie and Lola (K–2)

Choose Your Own Star Wars Adventures (4–8)

Christy (5–8)

Dexter's Laboratory Chapter Books (2–5)

Digimon Digital Monsters (2–5)

Disney Girls (3–5)

Doug Chronicles (2–4)

Doug (Disney Chapter Books) (2–4)

Duel Masters (3–5)

Eerie Indiana (5–8)

Everybody Hates Chris (4–6)

Fairly OddParents (1–5)

Fairly OddParents (TokyoPop) (3–6)

Full House: Club Stephanie (4–6)

Full House: Dear Michelle (2–5)

Full House: Michelle (2–4)

Full House: Sisters (3–5)

Full House: Stephanie (4–6)

Goosebumps Presents (3–6)

Hannah Montana (3–6)

Hannah Montana (TokyoPop) (3–6)

Harry Potter (3–9)

Hey Arnold! (3–6)

High School Musical Stories from East High (4–8)

Horseland (3–6)

I Was a Sixth Grade Alien (3–6)

Inheritance (5–12)

Jackie Chan Adventures (4–8)

Jurassic Park Adventures (4–7)

Kenan and Kel (4–6)

Kim Possible (Chapter Books) (4–7)

Kim Possible (TokyoPop) (4–7)

Kipper (K–2)

Kipper: Little Kippers (K–2)

LazyTown (8 x 8 Books) (K–1)

LazyTown (Ready to Read) (K–1)

Lilo and Stitch: The Series (2–4)

Little Bear: Maurice Sendak's Little Bear (K–2)

Little Bill (K–2)

Little Bill (Nickelodeon) (K–2)

Lizzie McGuire (4–7)

Lizzie McGuire Mysteries (4–7)

Lizzie McGuire (TokyoPop) (4–7)

Lord of the Rings (5–12)

Malcolm in the Middle (4–6)

Mary-Kate and Ashley: Adventures of Mary-Kate and Ashley (4–7)

Mary-Kate and Ashley: So Little Time (4–7)

Mary-Kate and Ashley: Two of a Kind (4–7)

Mary-Kate and Ashley in Action (4–7)

Mary-Kate and Ashley Starring In . . . (4–7)

Mary-Kate and Ashley Sweet 16 (4–7)

Mystery Files of Shelby Woo (4–6)

Mystic Knights of Tir Na Nog (5–8)

MythQuest (4–8)

Pinky Dinky Doo (1–3)

Postcards from Buster (K–3)

Powerpuff Girls Chapter Books (2–5)

Rugrats (Chapter Books) (2–4)

Rugrats Files (2–5)

Sabrina the Teenage Witch (4–6)

Samurai Jack Chapter Books (3–6)

Scary Godmother (3–5)

Scooby Doo Mysteries (3–5)

Scooby Doo Readers (1–3)

Secret World of Alex Mack (5–8)

7th Heaven (4–7)

Sister Sister (4–6)

The Sixth Sense: Secrets from Beyond (5–7)

Speed Racer (4–8)

Spirit of the Cimarron (4–6)

SpongeBob SquarePants Chapter Books (2–5)

SpongeBob SquarePants (TokyoPop) (3–5)

Spy Kids Adventures (4–6)

Star Trek: Deep Space Nine (4–8)

Star Trek: Enterprise (5–10)

Star Trek: I. K. S. Gorkon (5–10)

Star Trek: S. C. E. (5–10)

Star Trek: Starfleet Academy (4–8)

Star Trek: The Next Generation: Starfleet Academy (4–8)

Star Trek: Voyager: Starfleet Academy (4–8)

Star Wars: A New Hope—Manga (5–10)

Star Wars: Episode I The Phantom Menace—Manga (5–10)

Star Wars: The Empire Strikes Back—Manga (5–10)

Star Wars: The Return of the Jedi—Manga (5–10)

Star Wars Episode 1: Journals (4–8)

Star Wars Galaxy of Fear (4–8)

Star Wars Junior Jedi Knights (4–8)

Star Wars Young Jedi Knights (4–8)

Suite Life of Zack and Cody (3–6)

Time Warp Trio Graphic Novels (3–6)

Time Warp Trio (novelizations) (3–6)

Totally Spies! (3–5)

Treasure Planet (K–2)

The Wild Thornberrys (K–5)

Winnie the Pooh First Readers (K–2)

Wishbone Adventures (3–4)

Wishbone Classics (3–5)

Wishbone Mysteries (4–5)

X Files (5–10)

Zoey 101 (5–7)

Mermaids and mermen

Emily Windsnap (4–7)

Mice

Anatole (K–2)

Angelina Ballerina (K–2)

Angelina Ballerina: Angelina's Diary (1–3)

Babymouse (3–6)

Basil of Baker Street (2–5)

Bizzy Bones (K–2)

Brambly Hedge (3–5)

Class Pets (2–4)

Cucumbers Trilogy (2–4)

Deptford Histories (5–8)

Deptford Mice (5–8)

Dimwood Forest (4–6)

Dot and Jabber (K–2)

Ernest and Celestine (K–3)

The Fourteen Forest Mice (K–3)

George and Matilda Mouse (K–3)

Geronimo Stilton (3–5)

Holiday Mice (K–2)

Lilly (K–2)

Little Mouse (K–1)

Maisy the Mouse (K–2)

Marvin the Magnificent (3–5)

Mitt and Minn (2–4)

MYSTERY (cont.)

Encyclopedia Brown (2–6)

Enola Holmes (5–8)

FaithGirlz: Boarding School Mysteries (4–6)

Flatfoot Fox (2–4)

Fletcher Mysteries (2–5)

Fourth Floor Twins (1–4)

Frightmares (2–6)

Ghost Squad (5–8)

Ghost Stories (5–6)

Ghostwriter (4–6)

Graveyard School (4–7)

The Great McGoniggle (2–3)

Hannah West (4–6)

Hardy Boys (5–7)

Hardy Boys: Frank and Joe Hardy: The Clues Brothers (2–3)

Hardy Boys, Undercover Brothers (5–9)

Hardy Boys, Undercover Brothers: Graphic Novels (5–9)

Harvey (3–5)

Harvey Angell Trilogy (4–7)

Haunting with Louisa (5–8)

Herculeah Jones (5–7)

Hermux Tantamoq Adventures (5–8)

High-Rise Private Eyes (K–2)

Hollywood Sisters (5–8)

The Home School Detectives (4–6)

Houdini Club Magic Mystery (1–3)

Incognito Mosquito (4–6)

Internet Detectives (4–6)

Invisible Detectives (5–9)

Invisible Inc. (1–3)

Jack Russell: Dog Detective (3–5)

Jeffrey's Ghost (4–6)

Jigsaw Jones Mystery (K–2)

Joe Sherlock, Kid Detective (3–6)

Johnny Dixon (5–8)

Johnny May (4–6)

Juli Scott Super Sleuth (5–8)

Klooz (4–7)

Liza, Bill and Jed (2–5)

Lizzie McGuire Mysteries (4–7)

Lu and Clancy (K–2)

M and M (1–3)

M. T. Anderson's Thrilling Tales (4–7)

McGurk (2–5)

Magic Tree House (2–4)

Magical Mystery (4–6)

Mandie (4–6)

Mary-Kate and Ashley: Adventures of Mary-Kate and Ashley (4–7)

Mary-Kate and Ashley in Action (4–7)

Meg Mackintosh: A Solve-It-Yourself Mystery (1–3)

Mind over Matter (4–8)

Minerva Clark (5–8)

Misfits, Inc. (5–9)

Miss Mallard (2–4)

Mr. Pin (2–4)

My Dog (1–2)

Mysteries in Our National Parks (5–8)

Mystery Files of Shelby Woo (4–6)

Mystic Lighthouse Mysteries (2–4)

Nancy Drew (4–7)

Nancy Drew: Girl Detective (4–7)

Nancy Drew and the Clue Crew (2–4)

Nancy Drew Graphic Novels (4–8)

Nancy Drew Notebooks (2–4)

Nate the Great (1–3)

The Nic-Nacs and the Nic-Nac News (2–4)

Nicki Holland (5–6)

O'Dwyer and Grady (4–6)

PaleoJoe's Dinosaur Detective Club (3–5)

P.C. Hawke Mysteries (5–8)

Pete the Cat (4–7)

Petra and Calder (5–8)

Piggins (K–3)

Polka Dot Private Eye (1–3)

Red Rock Mysteries (5–8)

Roman Mysteries (5–8)

Salt and Pepper Chronicles (3–6)

Sam and Robert (2–4)

Sam and Stephanie (4–7)

Sam, Dog Detective (3–5)

Sammy Keyes (5–8)

Science Detectives (3–5)

Scooby Doo Mysteries (3–5)

Scooby Doo Readers (1–3)

Screech Owls (4–7)

Sebastian Barth (5–7)

Sebastian (Super Sleuth) (3–5)

Secret Agent Dingledorf and His Trusty Dog Splat (2–4)

Sirius Mysteries (5–9)

Sly the Sleuth (2–4)

Something Queer (3–5)

Starbucks Twins Mysteries (4–6)

Stevie Diamond Mysteries (4–6)

The Stink Files (3–5)

Ten Commandments Mysteries (3–5)

Third-Grade Detectives (2–4)

Three Cousins Detective Club (2–4)

Three Investigators (5–7)

Tiger Moth (2–5)

Time Travel Mysteries (5–9)

Ulysses Moore (4–6)

Undercover Girl (5–7)

Vicky Austin (4–7)

Wild Willie Mysteries (2–4)

Wishbone Mysteries (4–5)

Wright and Wong (5–8)

X Games Xtreme Mysteries (4–8)

Young Bond (5–9)

Ziggy and the Black Dinosaurs (3–6)

Mythology

The Companions Quartet (5–8)

The Cronus Chronicles (5–9)

The Fire Thief Trilogy (4–6)

Myth-O-Mania (4–7)

Mythic Misadventures (5–8)

MythQuest (4–8)

Northern Frights (5–8)

Percy Jackson and the Olympians (5–9)

Tales from the Odyssey (4–8)

Young Heroes (4–7)

Native Americans

American Girls: Kaya (2–5)

The Indian in the Cupboard (4–6)

Omakayas (5–8)

Young Wolf (1–3)

Nature

Long Pond (K–2)

Neptune Adventures (4–7)

Nigeria

Girlhood Journeys: Kai (4–6)

Opossums

Gilbert (K–2)

Orphans

Boxcar Children (2–5)

Dana Girls (3–5)

Miss Know It All (2–4)

Orphan Train Adventures (5–8)

Orphan Train Children (3–5)

Orphelines (3–4)

Owls

Guardians of Ga'Hoole (4–8)
Owly Graphic Novels (1–4)

Paranormal

Fortune Tellers Club (4–6)

Penguins

Mr. Pin (2–4)
Penguin Pete (K–2)
Tacky the Penguin (K–2)

Pigeons

Pigeon (K–2)

Pigs

Elephant and Piggie (K–2)
Freddy (3–5)
Geraldine (K–2)
Louanne Pig (K–2)
Mercy Watson (K–2)
Moose and Hildy (K–2)
Mr. and Mrs. Pig (K–3)
Oliver and Amanda Pig (K–2)
Olivia (K–2)
Paddy Pork (K–3)
Pig Pig (K–2)
Piganeers (K–2)
Piggins (K–3)
Pigs (K–1)
Poppleton (K–3)
Preston (K–1)
Silly Thrillers with Peggy the Pig (K–2)
Toot and Puddle (K–1)

Pirates

Edge Chronicles (5–9)
Jack Sparrow (4–6)
Never Land (4–7)
Peter and the Starcatchers (4–8)
Piganeers (K–2)
Pirate Hunter (5–8)
Pirate Pete (K–2)
Pirate Pete and Pirate Joe (K–2)
Pirate School (1–3)

Polar bears

Irving and Muktuk (K–3)
Larry the Polar Bear (K–3)
Little Polar Bear (K–3)

Porcupines

Penrod (K–2)

Prehistoric peoples

Chronicles of Ancient Darkness (5–9)

Princesses

Disney Princess (1–3)
Disney Princess Secrets (1–3)

Rabbits

Annie and Snowball (K–2)
Bunny Trouble (K–2)
Chicago and the Cat (K–2)
Davy (K–2)
Grumpy Bunny (K–1)
Hattie Rabbit (K–2)
Hopper (K–2)
Loudmouth George (K–1)
Max and Ruby (K–2)
P.J. Funnybunny (K–1)
Voyage to the Bunny Planet (K–2)

Raccoons

Ruby (K–2)

Rats

Rats of NIMH (3–6)

Ravens

Arabel and Mortimer (4–6)

REAL LIFE

Abby Hayes: The Amazing Days of Abby Hayes (4–6)
Adam Joshua Capers (1–4)
Addie (4–6)
Agapanthus Hum (1–3)
Agnes Parker (4–6)
Akimbo (2–4)
Al (Alexandra) (5–8)
Alden All Stars (4–8)
Aldo Sossi (3–5)
Alex (2–4)
Alfie Rose (K–2)
Ali Baba Bernstein (2–4)
Always Friends (2–4)
Amber Brown: A Is for Amber (K–2)
Amelia (4–8)
Amelia Rules! (3–5)
American Adventures (4–6)
American Diaries (4–6)
American Girls (2–5)
American Girls: Addy (2–5)
American Girls: Felicity (2–5)

American Girls: Girl of the Year (3–6)
American Girls: Girls of Many Lands (4–8)
American Girls: Josefina (2–5)
American Girls: Julie (2–5)
American Girls: Kaya (2–5)
American Girls: Kirsten (2–5)
American Girls: Kit (2–5)
American Girls: Molly (2–5)
American Girls: Samantha (2–5)
American Sisters (4–6)
Amy (K–2)
Amy and Laura (4–6)
Amy Hodgepodge (4–6)
Andy Russell (2–5)
Andy Shane (1–3)
Angel Park All-Stars (4–6)
Angel Park Hoop Stars (4–6)
Angel Park Soccer Stars (4–6)
Angela Anaconda Chapter Books (2–4)
Anika Scott (5–8)
Animal Ark (3–5)
Animal Ark Hauntings (3–5)
Animal Ark Pets (3–5)
Animal Emergency (2–4)
Animal Inn (3–6)
Annabel the Actress (2–4)
Annie and Snowball (K–2)
Annie Bananie (2–4)
Annie Pitts (2–4)
Australian Children (K–2)
Avonlea (5–8)
Babes (5–7)
Baby-Sitters Club (4–7)
Baby-Sitters Club Friends Forever (4–7)
Baby-Sitters Club Graphic Novels (4–7)
Baby-Sitters Club Mysteries (4–7)
Baby-Sitters Club Portrait Collection (4–7)
Baby-Sitters Club Super Specials (4–7)
Baby-Sitters Little Sister (2–3)
Baby-Sitters Little Sister Super Specials (2–4)
Baker's Dozen (4–6)
Ballerina Dreams (2–5)
Ballet Friends (4–7)
Ballet Slippers (2–4)
Barkham Street (4–6)
Beany (2–5)
Belinda (K–3)

REAL LIFE (cont.)

Bella Baxter (2–4)
Beryl E. Bean (3–6)
Best Enemies (2–3)
Best Friends (4–6)
Betsy-Tacy (2–5)
Beware (3–5)
Big Apple Barn (3–5)
Bingo Brown (4–7)
Biscuit Readers (K–1)
Black Stallion: Young Black
  Stallion (5–8)
Blaze (K–2)
Bratz (4–7)
Bratz: Clued In! (4–7)
Bratz: Lil' Bratz (4–7)
Brian Robeson (4–8)
Bubba and Beau (K–2)
B.Y. Times (4–8)
B.Y. Times Kid Sisters (2–6)
Camp Confidential (4–7)
Camp Sunnyside (4–7)
Candy Apple (4–6)
Carmen Browne (4–6)
Casey, Jenny, and Kate (2–4)
Casey, Tracey and Company (3–6)
Cassie Perkins (4–7)
Castle Court Kids (3–5)
¡Chana! (3–5)
Chestnut Hill (4–7)
China Tate (5–8)
Chincoteague (3–6)
Christina Katerina (K–3)
Christopher (K–2)
Christy (5–8)
Clarice Bean (2–5)
Clementine (2–5)
Cobble Street Cousins (1–4)
Cody (2–4)
Comeback Kids (4–6)
The Complicated Life of Claudia
  Cristina Cortez (5–7)
Cowgirl Kate and Cocoa (K–2)
Cul-de-Sac Kids (3–6)
Danitra Brown (2–5)
David and Goliath (1–3)
Deaf Child Crossing (4–6)
Dear America (4–6)
Dear Dumb Diary (5–8)
Diary of a Wimpy Kid (5–8)
Dish (4–7)
Disney Girls (3–5)
Dog Watch (3–5)
Dolphin Diaries (3–6)

Don't Touch That Remote! (5–7)
Dork in Disguise (4–6)
Dot and Jabber (K–2)
The Double Dutch Club (5–7)
Eco Kids (3–5)
Eddie Wilson (1–3)
Edison-Armstrong School (3–5)
Elizabeti (K–2)
Ellen Fremedon (5–7)
Ellen Grae (3–6)
Elsie Edwards (4–8)
Emily and Alice (K–2)
Emma (1–3)
Encyclopedia Brown (2–6)
The English Roses (Chapter
  Books) (2–4)
Ernestine and Amanda (4–5)
Ethan (K–1)
Everett Anderson (K–2)
Everybody Hates Chris (4–6)
FaithGirlz: Girls of 622 Harbor
  View (5–7)
FaithGirlz: Sophie (4–6)
Fat Glenda (4–8)
First Grade (K–2)
First-Grade Friends (1–3)
Flicka (5–8)
Flower Girls (2–4)
Frances in the Fourth Grade (3–5)
Fraser Brothers (3–5)
Friends and Amigos (2–4)
Friends for a Season (5–8)
Fudge (3–5)
Full House: Club Stephanie (4–6)
Full House: Dear Michelle (2–5)
Full House: Michelle (2–4)
Full House: Sisters (3–5)
Full House: Stephanie (4–6)
Germy (3–6)
Get Real (4–6)
Girls of Avenue Z (5–7)
The Girls of Lighthouse Lane
  (4–6)
Go Girl (3–5)
Goldstone Trilogy (5–7)
Gooney Bird Greene (1–3)
Grace (1–4)
Grandaddy (2–4)
The Great Brain (5–7)
Gus and Grandpa (K–2)
Guy Strang (5–8)
Gymnasts (4–6)
Hank Zipzer (3–5)
Hannah Montana (3–6)

Hannah Montana (TokyoPop)
  (3–6)
Happy and Honey (K–1)
Harriet (K–2)
Harriet M. Welsch (4–6)
Harry (1–3)
Hatford Boys (3–5)
Hazel Green (3–5)
Heartland (4–7)
Henry and Mudge (K–3)
Henry and Mudge: Puppy Mudge
  (K–2)
Henry Huggins (1–4)
Henry Reed (4–6)
Herbie Jones (1–4)
Here Come the Brownies (1–3)
Hey Arnold! (3–6)
High Hurdles (4–7)
High School Musical Stories from
  East High (4–8)
The Hit and Run Gang (2–4)
Hobie Hanson (4–6)
Holiday Five (3–5)
Holiday Friends (3–5)
Hollywood Sisters (5–8)
Hoofbeats (3–5)
Hopscotch Hill School (1–2)
Horrible Harry (2–4)
Horseland (3–6)
Horseshoe Trilogies (4–6)
Horseshoes (5–7)
How I Survived Middle School
  (4–7)
In the Cards (5–8)
Indie Kidd (3–5)
Iris and Walter (K–2)
Isabelle (3–6)
Ivy and Bean (1–4)
Jackson Friends (2–4)
Jackson Jones (3–6)
Jake Drake (2–5)
Jamaica (K–2)
Jamela (K–2)
James Stevenson's
  Autobiographical Stories (1–3)
Jenny Archer (2–4)
Joey Pigza (5–9)
Joshua T. Bates (3–6)
Judge and Jury (4–6)
Judy Moody (3–5)
Julia Redfern (4–6)
Junebug (4–7)
Junie B. Jones (1–2)
Junior Gymnasts (3–5)

REAL LIFE (cont.)

Super Hoops (4–6)
Sweet Valley: Unicorn Club (4–6)
Sweet Valley Kids (3–5)
Table Two (2–3)
Taffy Sinclair (4–6)
Tanya (K–3)
Third Grade (2–4)
The Thirteen Moons (3–6)
Thoroughbred (4–7)
Thoroughbred: Ashleigh (4–7)
Thoroughbred: Ashleigh's Collection (4–7)
TJ Barnes (3–4)
Topaz (3–5)
Triplet Trouble (K–3)
Trouble With (3–5)
Twelve Candles Club (4–6)
26 Fairmount Avenue (1–3)
Vera (K–2)
Vicky Austin (4–7)
The Wedding Planner's Daughter (5–9)
Wild at Heart (4–7)
Willimena Rules! (2–4)
Winnie (2–5)
Winnie Perry (4–7)
Winnie the Horse Gentler (4–8)
Wolfbay Wings (4–8)
Yang (4–6)
Zibby Payne (4–6)
Ziggy and the Black Dinosaurs (3–6)
Zoey 101 (5–7)

RECREATION

Alden All Stars (4–8)
American Gold Gymnasts (4–7)
American Gold Swimmers (4–7)
Angel Park All-Stars (4–6)
Angel Park Hoop Stars (4–6)
Angel Park Soccer Stars (4–6)
Arthur Chapter Books: Good Sports (3–6)
Barnstormers (3–6)
Baseball Card Adventures (4–8)
Brady Brady (1–3)
The Broadway Ballplayers (4–7)
Bunny Trouble (K–2)
Cat (K–2)
Chip Hilton Sports Series (5–8)
Comeback Kids (4–6)
Extreme Team (4–7)

Girls Only (GO!) (4–6)
Gym Shorts (2–5)
Gymnasts (4–6)
Hey L'il D! (2–4)
The Hit and Run Gang (2–4)
Horseshoes (5–7)
Junior Gymnasts (3–5)
Lili (K–2)
Matt Christopher Sports Stories (3–7)
Million Dollar Series (4–6)
NASCAR Pole Position Adventures (5–8)
NASCAR Racers (3–5)
Never Sink Nine (3–4)
NFL Monday Night Football Club (4–7)
Patrick's Pals (3–6)
Peach Street Mudders (2–4)
The Pink Parrots (3–5)
Pony Pals (3–5)
Pony Tails (3–5)
Riding Academy (4–6)
Rocket Power (K–2)
The Saddle Club (4–6)
Scrappers (4–6)
Short Stirrup Club (4–6)
Silver Blades (4–7)
Silver Blades Figure Eights (2–4)
Skating Dreams (3–6)
Slam Dunk (4–6)
Slapshots (5–8)
Soccer 'Cats (2–4)
Soccer Stars (3–6)
Spirit of the Game (5–8)
Super Hoops (4–6)
Tales from the Sandlot (4–6)
Thoroughbred (4–7)
Thoroughbred: Ashleigh (4–7)
Thoroughbred: Ashleigh's Collection (4–7)
Winning Season (4–7)
Wolfbay Wings (4–8)
X Games Xtreme Mysteries (4–8)

Robots

Jack Jameson and Danny One (2–4)
Norby (5–7)
Sonic the Hedgehog (2–3)

Romance

Christy (5–8)

Royalty

Disney Princesses: My Side of the Story (1–3)
Jewel Kingdom (3–4)
Princess Power (3–5)
Tiara Club (1–4)
Tiara Club: The Tiara Club at Pearl Palace (1–4)
Tiara Club: The Tiara Club at Ruby Mansion (1–4)
Tiara Club: The Tiara Club at Silver Towers (1–4)

Sailing *see also* Boats and ships

Salty (K–2)

Scary stories

Black Cat Club (2–4)
Deadtime Stories (4–7)
Frightmares (2–6)
Mercer Mayer's Critters of the Night (K–4)
Scaredy Cats (1–3)
The Weird Zone (3–5)
Werewolf Chronicles (5–8)

School stories

Adam Joshua Capers (1–4)
Alistair (K–2)
Andy Russell (2–5)
Andy Shane (1–3)
Arthur (K–3)
Arthur Chapter Books (3–6)
Bailey School: The Adventures of the Bailey School Kids (2–4)
The Barkers (K–2)
Best Enemies (2–3)
Best Friends (4–7)
Bingo Brown (4–7)
Black Lagoon (K–4)
B.Y. Times (4–8)
B.Y. Times Kid Sisters (2–6)
Christie & Company (5–7)
Christy (5–8)
Cody (2–4)
The Complicated Life of Claudia Cristina Cortez (5–7)
Dana Girls (3–5)
Dear Dumb Diary (5–8)
Diary of a Wimpy Kid (5–8)
Dinah (3–6)
Don't Touch That Remote! (5–7)
Dork in Disguise (4–6)
Eagle-Eye Ernie (1–3)

Science

SCIENCE FICTION

SCIENCE FICTION
(cont.)

Star Wars: Jedi Quest (5–9)

Star Wars: The Empire Strikes Back—Manga (5–10)

Star Wars: The Last of the Jedi (5–9)

Star Wars: The Return of the Jedi—Manga (5–10)

Star Wars (DK Readers) (1–4)

Star Wars Episode 1: Journals (4–8)

Star Wars Galaxy of Fear (4–8)

Star Wars Junior Jedi Knights (4–8)

Star Wars Young Jedi Knights (4–8)

Sword of the Spirits (5–8)

Time Warp Trio (3–6)

Time Warp Trio Graphic Novels (3–6)

Time Warp Trio (novelizations) (3–6)

Treasure Planet (K–2)

Tripods (5–8)

2099 (5–8)

Tyco Bass (4–6)

Visitors (5–8)

Weird Planet (2–4)

Scotland

Horseshoes (5–7)

Katie Morag (1–2)

Sophie (3–5)

Tartan Magic Trilogy (4–7)

Sea stories *see also* Boats and ships

Adventures of a Young Sailor (5–8)

Seasons

Amy (K–2)

Brambly Hedge (3–5)

The Fourteen Forest Mice (K–3)

Lionel (1–2)

Long Pond (K–2)

Seasonal Adventures (4–6)

Sheep

Russell the Sheep (K–2)

Sheep (K–3)

Sign language

Moses (K–2)

Slavery

American Girls: Addy (2–5)

Arabus Family Saga (5–8)

Racing to Freedom Trilogy (5–8)

Snakes

Jimmy's Boa (K–2)

Soccer

Angel Park Soccer Stars (4–6)

Bunny Trouble (K–2)

Soccer 'Cats (2–4)

Soccer Stars (3–6)

Space and space ships *see also* Aliens

Astrosaurs (3–5)

Choose Your Own Star Wars Adventures (4–8)

Commander Toad (K–3)

Goners (4–6)

Jack Jameson and Danny One (2–4)

Journal of a Cardboard Genius (3–5)

Norby (5–7)

Star Trek: Deep Space Nine (4–8)

Star Trek: Starfleet Academy (4–8)

Star Trek: The Next Generation: Starfleet Academy (4–8)

Star Trek: Voyager: Starfleet Academy (4–8)

Star Wars: A New Hope—Manga (5–10)

Star Wars: Episode I The Phantom Menace—Manga (5–10)

Star Wars: The Empire Strikes Back—Manga (5–10)

Star Wars: The Return of the Jedi—Manga (5–10)

Star Wars Episode 1: Journals (4–8)

Star Wars Galaxy of Fear (4–8)

Star Wars Junior Jedi Knights (4–8)

Star Wars Young Jedi Knights (4–8)

Tyco Bass (4–6)

Zack Proton (2–4)

Zenon, Girl of the 21st Century (2–4)

Spiders

Miss Spider (K–2)

Spider (K–2)

Spider Riders (4–6)

Spies and spying

Adam Sharp (2–4)

Secret Agent Jack Stalwart (1–4)

Secret Agent MJJ (4–7)

Spy Force (4–7)

Spy Kids Adventures (4–6)

Spy Mice (4–6)

Spy X (4–6)

Undercover Girl (5–7)

Sports *see also* specific sports (e.g., Baseball, Basketball)

Alden All Stars (4–8)

Arthur Chapter Books: Good Sports (3–6)

Black Belt Club (3–6)

Brady Brady (1–3)

The Broadway Ballplayers (4–7)

Cat (K–2)

Chip Hilton Sports Series (5–8)

Comeback Kids (4–6)

Extreme Team (4–7)

Girls Only (GO!) (4–6)

Gym Shorts (2–5)

The Jersey (4–7)

Matt Christopher Sports Stories (3–7)

Million Dollar Series (4–6)

Mud Flat (K–2)

Rocket Power (K–2)

Screech Owls (4–7)

Spirit of the Game (5–8)

Winning Season (4–7)

X Games Xtreme Mysteries (4–8)

Squirrels

Elliot's Park (3–5)

Park Pals Adventure (2–4)

Scaredy Squirrel (K–1)

Supernatural *see also* Ghosts, Monsters and creatures

Accidental Monsters (4–6)

Animal Ark Hauntings (3–5)

Bloodhounds, Inc. (4–6)

Blossom Culp (5–7)

Bunnicula (3–5)

CLAMP School Detectives (4–8)

Dark Is Rising (4–8)

Ghostville Elementary (3–5)

Goldstone Trilogy (5–7)

Goosebumps Horrorland (4–8)

VALUES (cont.)
Jenna V. (4–6)
Juli Scott Super Sleuth (5–8)
Ladd Family (4–6)
Landon Snow (5–8)
Lassie (4–8)
Little Bear (K–1)
Little Bill (K–2)
Little Bill (Nickelodeon) (K–2)
Little Toot (K–1)
McGee and Me! (4–6)
Reel Kids Adventures (5–7)
RPM (5–8)
Secret Agent Dingledorf and His Trusty Dog Splat (2–4)
7th Heaven (4–7)
Slam Dunk (4–6)
Spirit of the Game (5–8)
Story Girl (5–7)
Ten Commandments Mysteries (3–5)
Three Cousins Detective Club (2–4)
Time Navigators (4–6)
Trailblazers (4–7)
Twelve Candles Club (4–6)

Viking Quest (5–8)
Winnie the Horse Gentler (4–8)

Weather
Amy (K–2)

Weddings
Flower Girls (2–4)

Weight control
Fat Glenda (4–8)

Witches and wizards *see also* **Magic**
Age of Magic Trilogy (5–9)
Dorrie (K–3)
Dungeons and Dragons: Knights of the Silver Dragon (5–8)
Emma (K–3)
Enchanted Forest Chronicles (4–7)
The Floods (5–7)
Harry Potter (3–9)
Last Apprentice (5–8)
Lewis Barnavelt (5–8)
Little Witch (K–2)
Magical Mystery (4–6)
Old Witch (K–2)

Sabrina the Teenage Witch (4–6)
Septimus Heap (5–8)
Spell Casters (5–8)
Spooky the Cat (K–2)
Wicked Witch (2–5)
Witch (K–3)
W.I.T.C.H.—Adventures (5–8)
W.I.T.C.H.—Graphic Novels (5–8)
Witch, Goblin and Ghost (K–2)
Witch Twins (3–5)
Wizard Trilogy (3–5)
Wizardry (5–8)
Young Merlin Trilogy (4–6)

Wolves
Chronicles of Ancient Darkness (5–9)
Julie of the Wolves (5–8)
Little Wolf (3–5)

World War II
American Girls: Molly (2–5)
Anna (4–8)
Gordy Smith (5–7)
The Young Underground (5–8)

About the Authors

REBECCA L. THOMAS is an elementary school librarian, Shaker Heights City Schools, Ohio. She is the author of numerous reference books, including *Across Cultures* (Libraries Unlimited, 2007) and the recent supplement to the 7th edition of *A to Zoo* (Libraries Unlimited, 2008).

CATHERINE BARR is editor of the Libraries Unlimited Children's and Young Adult Literature Reference series and author or coauthor of other Libraries Unlimited titles including *High/Low Handbook* and the Best Books series (*Best Books for Children, Best Books for Middle School and Junior High Readers, Best Books for High School Readers*, and *Best New Media*).